CHINA

Dawn of a Golden Age, 200–750 AD

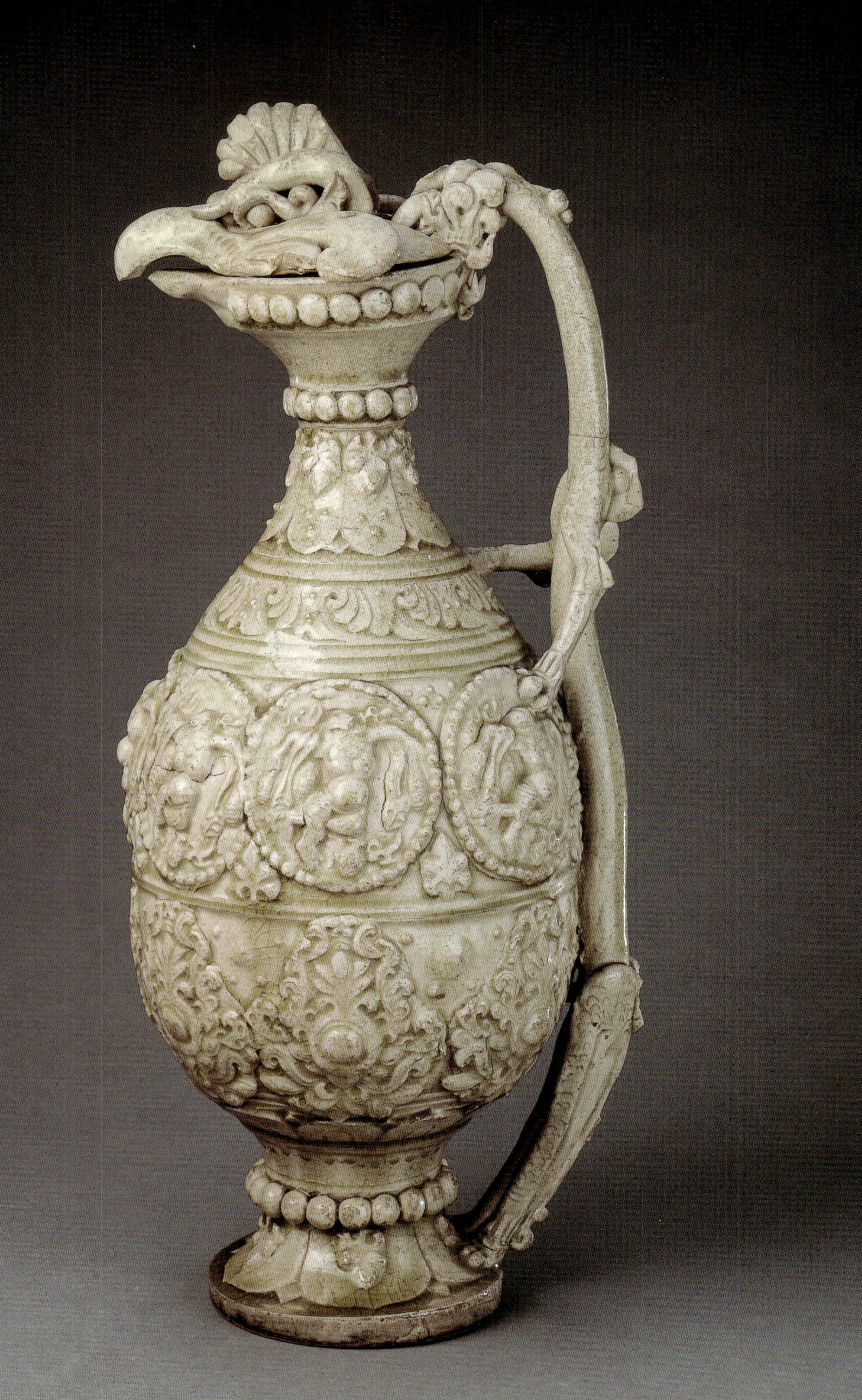

CHINA

Dawn of a Golden Age, 200–750 AD

James C. Y. Watt

An Jiayao, Angela F. Howard, Boris I. Marshak, Su Bai, Zhao Feng

with contributions by
Prudence O. Harper, Maxwell K. Hearn, Denise Patry Leidy,
Chao-Hui Jenny Liu, Valentina Raspopova, Zhixin Sun

The Metropolitan Museum of Art, New York
Yale University Press, New Haven and London

This publication is issued in conjunction with the exhibition "China: Dawn of a Golden Age, 200–750 AD," held at The Metropolitan Museum of Art, New York, October 12, 2004–January 23, 2005.

The exhibition and its accompanying catalogue are made possible by The Starr Foundation.

Additional support for education programs has been provided by The Freeman Foundation.

Support for the catalogue has also been provided by The Andrew W. Mellon Foundation.

An indemnity has been granted by the Federal Council on the Arts and the Humanities.

Photography of Chinese exhibition objects by Hu Chui, Chief Photographer, The Palace Museum, Beijing. China site photography by Oi-Cheong Lee, The Photograph Studio, The Metropolitan Museum of Art.

Maps by Anandaroop Roy

Translations from the Chinese by Ching-Jung Chen, Shiyee Liu, and Min Mao.

Published by The Metropolitan Museum of Art, New York

John P. O'Neill, Editor in Chief
Gwen Roginsky, Associate General Manager of Publications
Emily Walter, Editor
Joan Holt, Coordinator
Bruce Campbell, Designer
Jill Pratzon, Production
Robert Weisberg, Desktop Publishing
Jean Wagner, Bibliographic Editor, with Chao-Hui Jenny Liu

Separations by Nissha Printing Co., Ltd., Kyoto, Japan
Printed and bound by Nissha Printing Co., Ltd., Kyoto, Japan

Cover and jacket: Cat. no 181. Female figure (detail), Tang dynasty (618–907). Xinjiang Uygur Autonomous Region Museum

Frontispiece: Cat. no. 218. Bird-headed ewer with molded decoration, Tang dynasty (618–907). The Palace Museum, Beijing

Library of Congress Cataloging-in-Publication Data

China : dawn of a golden age, 200–750 AD / James C.Y. Watt, An Jiayao, Angela F. Howard . . . [et al.].
p. cm.

Catalog of an exhibition held at the Metropolitan Museum of Art, New York, Oct. 12, 2004–Jan. 23, 2005.
Includes bibliographical references and index.
ISBN 1-58839-126-4 (hardcover)—ISBN 1-58839-127-2 (pbk.)—ISBN 0-300-10487-1 (Yale University Press)
1. Art, Chinese—Qin-Han dynasties, 221 B.C.–220 A.D.—Exhibitions. 2. Art, Chinese—Three kingdoms-Sui dynasty, 220–618—Exhibitions. 3. Art, Chinese—Tang-Five dynasties, 618–960—Exhibitions. 4. China—Civilization—221 B.C.–960 A.D.—Exhibitions. I. Watt, James C. Y. II. An Jiayao. III. Metropolitan Museum of Art (New York, N.Y.)
N7343.23.C55 2004
709'.51'0747471—dc22 2004015286

Contents

Director's Foreword

For the past several decades, astonishing archaeological finds have been made in China with remarkable regularity. In 1980, as part of the exhibition "The Great Bronze Age of China," The Metropolitan Museum of Art showed some of the most significant discoveries at Bronze Age sites, which greatly enhanced our knowledge of early Chinese history. The exhibition also presented, for the first time outside China, the sequence of the development of the striking art of archaic Chinese bronzes from its very beginning to its maturity during the Shang and Zhou periods.

Important archaeological discoveries since the 1980s have made it possible for the Museum to mount another major exhibition: "China: Dawn of a Golden Age, 200–750 AD." The project traces the growth of a brilliant civilization that absorbed and transformed ideas and art styles from all over Asia during a period of exceptional openness. Because of the long time span and extensive geographic coverage of the exhibition, we have drawn objects from forty-six institutions throughout China. This would not have been possible without the full support of the State Administration for Cultural Heritage in Beijing and the cooperation of many colleagues in museums and archaeological institutes in fourteen provinces and municipalities. The years of preparation have also engendered a close working relationship between the professional staff of the Metropolitan Museum and their Chinese counterparts, with a free exchange of information and practical knowledge.

Field archaeology provides physical objects with associated scientific data, but the deeper understanding of cultures of past ages can only be achieved through the appreciation and interpretation of the objects as works of art. We hope this exhibition helps to fulfill these expectations of the works on view.

I am most grateful to James C. Y. Watt, Brooke Russell Astor Chairman, Department of Asian Art, for the conception and realization of this exhibition and to his collaborators on this major initiative.

The Starr Foundation made an extraordinary commitment to this project in its earliest stages. We are deeply indebted to their vision and their generous support of both the exhibition and its accompanying catalogue. The Metropolitan also thanks The Freeman Foundation for its gift toward the exhibition's education programs. Likewise, we remain grateful to The Andrew W. Mellon Foundation for the funding its publications endowment has provided for this catalogue. Finally, the Museum thanks the Federal Council on the Arts and the Humanities for its critical assistance toward the realization of this exhibition.

Philippe de Montebello
Director
The Metropolitan Museum of Art

Foreword

On the occasion of the opening of "China: Dawn of a Golden Age, 200–750 AD," I should like to express my warmest greetings and best wishes to American museum visitors as well as my heartfelt gratitude to my American colleagues who have worked with great dedication for this exhibition.

Twenty-four years ago, The Metropolitan Museum of Art held the exhibition "The Great Bronze Age of China." The exhibition, regarded as a classic example of its kind, made a lasting impression on many who saw it. Now the Metropolitan, in cooperation with its Chinese colleagues, has organized another exhibition that covers the historical period from the late Han to the height of the Tang dynasty, with a focus on the Three Kingdoms, the Western and Eastern Jin, and the Southern and Northern Dynasties. The more than three hundred spectacular works of art, assembled from forty-six Chinese museums and cultural institutions in fourteen provinces and cities, illustrate the philosophical ideas, religious beliefs, social practices, and artistic accomplishment of third-to-eighth-century China and the rise of new social ideals and artistic expression that resulted from the integration of ethnic groups of the Southern and Northern Dynasties, as well as cultural exchanges between China and the West. The exhibition aims to establish historical truth through the presentation and examination of historical artifacts. "China: Dawn of a Golden Age" attests to the fact that the vigorous development during this critical period in Chinese civilization laid a solid foundation for the glorious Tang dynasty.

I wish the exhibition every success and expect another lasting experience for museum visitors.

Shan Jixiang
Director General, State Administration of Cultural Heritage
The People's Republic of China

献 辞

值此<<走向盛唐>>展隆重开幕之际，我谨向美国观众表示诚挚问候和美好祝愿，并向为展览付出辛勤劳动的美国博物馆同仁致以诚挚的谢意！

二十四年前，颇具盛名的纽约大都会艺术博物馆举办了<<伟大的青铜时代>>展，获得巨大成功。至今许多亲历者仍对这个被称作"经典之作"的展览留有深刻印象。今天，该馆再次与中国同仁合作，将新的筹展视角锁定在三国两晋南北朝时段。此次展览始于汉末，止于盛唐。展览的主办者集十四省市四十六家文博单位的三百余件文物珍品于一堂，力求在哲学思想、宗教信仰、社会习俗和艺术创作上反映公元三至六世纪的中国，在南北朝民族融合、中西方文化交流上创造的精湛艺术和新的社会理念，以历史的文物来还原历史的真实。<<走向盛唐>>展以充足的理由证明中华文明在这一时期获得蓬勃发展，奠定并促进了璀灿辉煌的大唐盛世的到来。

预祝展览成功，期待着又一个"经典之作"问世。

中国国家文物局局长
单霁翔

Sponsor's Statement

The Starr Foundation is proud to collaborate with The Metropolitan Museum of Art in sponsoring "China: Dawn of a Golden Age, 200–750 AD." The treasures in the exhibition, many of which were excavated only in recent decades, mark a period of extensive trade and migration, a glorious mixing of cultures.

Cornelius Vander Starr's fortune began in China in 1919 with the establishment of what is now know as American International Group, one of the largest financial services and insurance companies in the world. From China, the company grew to include businesses in more than 130 countries and jurisdictions. Mr. Starr understood the importance of global trade and international relations in a way that echoes the transforming commerce that flowed through China many centuries ago.

This extraordinary exhibition furthers our mission at the Foundation of linking East and West, celebrating the connections that great art makes possible. We hope everyone comes away with a deeper sense of the history and beauty of Chinese culture from a fascinating era.

Maurice R. Greenberg
Chairman

Florence A. Davis
President

Acknowledgments

Acknowledgments are frequently the last part of an exhibition catalogue to be written and usually approached with a sense of relief, the rest of the catalogue having, irretrievably, gone to the printer. In the present case, they are also approached with eagerness, as they offer the opportunity to thank publicly the numerous individuals and institutions who have contributed to this large and complex project.

The idea of an archaeological exhibition from China was generated some years ago by Philippe de Montebello, Director of the Metropolitan Museum, and Wen C. Fong, then Consultative Chairman of the Department of Asian Art. Wen Fong also directed the initial stages of planning.

From the beginning, we were met with a cordial reception and the full support of the State Administration of Cultural Heritage (SACH) in Beijing, under the former Director, Zhang Wenbin, and the present Director, Shan Jixiang. Wang Limei, former Head of the External Affairs Office of SACH, guided the project on the Chinese side to the final approval by the State Council of the Chinese Government. After Ms. Wang's retirement, Zhang Jianxin, under the direction of Dong Baohua, Deputy Director of SACH, and Wang Jun, Chief Executive Officer of SACH, worked out the remaining details of the exhibition agreement between the Cultural Property Promotion Association of the People's Republic of China and The Metropolitan Museum of Art.

Coordinating and liaising with forty-six lending institutions and the logistics of gathering hundreds of objects in Beijing for packing and shipment fell to Art Exhibitions China, a branch of SACH, under the direction of Luo Bojian. To Yang Yang, Deputy Director of Art Exhibitions China, and his team we owe the flawless accomplishment of this complex task. Besides Mr. Yang, we wish, in particular, to thank Yin Jia, Qian Wei, Chen Lie, Mu Xiangqian, Zhao Gushan, and Chen Xiaocheng.

The early plans for the exhibition were reviewed by a panel of senior scholars in China: Professors Su Bai, Xu Pingfang, Sun Ji, Yang Hong, and Zhu Fenghan, who offered many helpful suggestions. Valuable advice was also received from Meng Xianmin, Director of the Department of Museums, and Song Xinchao, Deputy Director of the Department of Monuments and Sites Protection, of SACH.

At the various museums and research institutes visited, we were received with warmth and professional courtesy. It is not possible to list the names of all the colleagues who provided hospitality, advice, and information. Nevertheless, we would like to give special thanks to the following: at the National Museum of China, Director Pan Zhenzhou and Deputy Director Wang Xiaotian; at The Palace Museum, Director Zheng Xinmiao and Deputy Director Li Ji; at the Hebei Province Administration of Cultural Heritage, Director Zhang Lizhu and Chief of the Department of Museums Li Xia; at the Hebei Provincial Museum, Director Gu Tongwei and Deputy Directors Li Jishu and Li Jianli; at the Henan Province Administration of Cultural Heritage, Director Chang Jianchuan, Deputy Director Chen Ailan, Chief of the Department of Museums Li Yunli, and Deputy Head of the Department of Overseas Exhibitions You Zhiyuan; at the Henan Museum, Director Zhang Wenjun and Deputy Director Tian Kai; at the Henan Institute of Archaeology, Director Sun Weimin; at the Luoyang Museum, Director Wang Xiu; at the Longmen Caves Research Institute, Director Li Zhen'gang; at the Shandong Provincial Museum, Director Lu Wensheng and Deputy Director Zhang Yan; at the Qingzhou City Museum, Director Sun Xinsheng; at the Shanxi Province Administration of Cultural Heritage, Director Shi Lianxiu and Chief of the Department of Museums Hao Xiaowei; at the Shanxi Museum, Director Xia Lu and Deputy Director Zhang Shaokun; at the Shanxi Institute of Archaeology, Director Shi Jingmin and former Director Zhang Qingjie; at the Datong City Museum, former Director Wang Yintian; at the Datong Institute of Archaeology, Director Liu Junxi; at the Shaanxi Province Administration of Cultural Heritage, Director Zhang Tinghao and Deputy Director Liu Yunhui; at the Shaanxi Museum of History, Director Zhou Tianyou, Deputy Director Ma Zhenzhi, and Chief of the Department of Collections Shen Qinyan; at the Shaanxi Institute of Archaeology, Director Jiao Nanfeng, Deputy Director Cao Wei, and former Director Han Wei; at the Xi'an City Institute of Archaeology, former Director Wang Changqi; at the Xi'an Museum of the Forest of Steles, Executive Officer Li Jugang and Deputy Director of the Department of Collections

Pei Jianping; at the Gansu Province Administration of Cultural Heritage, former Director Ma Wenzhi and Chief of the Department of Museums Dong Yanwen; at the Gansu Provincial Museum, Director E Jun and former Director Chu Shibin; at the Guyuan Museum, Director Chen Kun; at the Ningxia Institute of Archaeology, Director Luo Feng; at the Xinjiang Uygur Autonomous Region Administration of Cultural Heritage, Director Sheng Chunshou and Deputy Director Erkin Mijit; at the Xinjiang Uygur Autonomous Region Museum, Deputy Director Yisilafeier Yusufu; at the Xinjiang Institute of Archaeology, Deputy Director Zhang Yuzhong and Archaeologist Li Wenying; at the Nanjing Museum, Director Xu Huping and Curator Qiang Mingzhong; at the Nanjing City Administration of Cultural Heritage, Director Wei Zhengjin; at the Nanjing City Museum, Director Bai Ning; at the Inner Mongolia Autonomous Region Administration of Cultural Affairs, former Director Zhao Fangzhi and Director of the Department of Cultural Properties Su Jun; at the Inner Mongolia Museum, Director Shao Qinglong, Deputy Director Huang Xueyin, and Senior Photographer Kong Qun; at the Inner Mongolia Institute of Archaeology, Deputy Directors Wei Jian and Liu Laixue; at the Jerim League Museum, Inner Mongolia, Director Ximude; at the Liaoning Provincial Museum, Director Tian Likun and former Director Xu Bingkun; at the Liaoning Institute of Archaeology, Director Wang Jingchen; at the Sichuan Province Administration of Cultural Affairs, Director Zhang Zhongyan, former Chief of the Department of Cultural Properties Liang Xuzhong, and Chief of the Museums Office Zhao Chuanrong; at the Chengdu City Institute of Archaeology, Director Wang Yi and Deputy Director Jiang Cheng; at the Qinghai Province Administration of Cultural Heritage, Deputy Director Su Shengxiu (Kesangben); and at the Qinghai Institute of Archaeology, Director Xu Xinguo. In addition to the many loans from China, we were fortunate to secure one loan each from the Museum of Fine Arts, Boston, and The Cleveland Museum of Art essential to the completion of the narrative of the exhibition. We are grateful to Wu Tung and Chou Ju-hsi for their cooperation.

A very special note of thanks is owed to Hu Chui, Chief Photographer, The Palace Museum, Beijing, who photographed the objects from China. He traveled with his equipment to all the lending institutions, some of them in remote areas, and often worked under trying conditions. In the end, he achieved remarkable results.

As is usual with large exhibitions, many members of the Museum staff contributed to the organization and realization of the exhibition and the catalogue. Director Philippe de Montebello, who made two trips to China and inspected many of the sites where exhibition objects were found, secured the most difficult loans. Mahrukh Tarapor, Associate Director for Exhibitions, negotiated the agreement with SACH and made two trips to China to oversee practical arrangements. Martha Deese, of the Director's Office, coordinated various aspects of the administration.

Emily Rafferty, Senior Vice President for External Affairs, was a most effective advocate, and with Nina Diefenbach and Christine Scornavacca of the Development Office, secured major financial support.

The immense task of organizing the packing and shipment of hundreds of exhibits was handled by Aileen Chuk, Registrar, in her customary efficient manner. The many fragile articles put an inordinately heavy demand on our conservators. Nobuko Kajitani, former Conservator in Charge in Textile Conservation, visited various institutions in China to inspect textiles that we proposed to borrow; at the Museum, Florica Zaharia and Midori Sato prepared the delicate ancient textiles for display. In Objects Conservation, Lawrence Becker, Richard Stone, and Ellen Howe ensured the safe packing, transportation, and installation of the objects.

The installation of the exhibition was ably coordinated by Linda Sylling, Manager for Special Exhibitions and Gallery Installations. The creative work of exhibition and graphic design was in the hands of Michael Batista and Sophia Geronimus, of the Department of Design, who were a joy to work with.

In ensuring the accurate translation of texts by Chinese colleagues on highly specialized topics, we benefited from the advice of Lisa Pilosi of the Department of Objects Conservation, who corrected translations of technical terms in An Jiayao's essay and entries on glass. Joyce Denney of the Department of Asian Art worked indefatigably at long distance with Zhao Feng to clarify his texts on textiles.

The contributors to this catalogue did more than write essays and entries. They also gave valuable suggestions on the organization of the catalogue and the selection of material for the exhibition. Professor Su Bai gave valuable advice on overall planning. The choice of Buddhist sculptures was made almost entirely by Angela Howard. An Jiayao and Zhao Feng proposed the selections in their respective areas. Prudence Harper and Boris Marshak have over the years taught me the little I know about the arts of ancient Iran and Central Asia. They read what I wrote for the catalogue and made valuable suggestions. Needless to say, any remaining errors are entirely my own.

The daunting task of editing an exhibition catalogue with many unfamiliar names and endlessly confusing chronology was accepted unflinchingly by Emily Walter. As usual, her editing has been carried out with care, diligence, and sympathy for the authors. Joan Holt coordinated the final stages of the editing process. The production was expertly supervised by Gwen Roginsky, assisted by Jill Pratzon. John O'Neill presided over the entire procedure with understanding and patience, displaying the wisdom gained from years of experience.

Two colleagues in the Department of Asian Art made major contributions to the making of the exhibition. Zhixin Sun was our chief liaison with officials in Beijing and with colleagues at all the lending institutions, and through his tireless efforts ensured the integrity of the selection of objects. Within the department, Judith Smith managed to keep all of us on track at various stages of the project, particularly in giving order to the many aspects of work on the catalogue and helpful suggestions on the editing.

Maxwell Hearn and Denise Leidy both participated in the planning sessions and the final shaping of the exhibition.

Other members of the department have contributed in various capacities. Jenny Liu, with a contingent of interns, assembled research files for the objects and developed the Bibliography and the Index. Some of her work was initiated by Yangming Chu a few years back. Hwai-ling Yeh-Lewis and her team in Collections Management—Kendal Parker, Jillian Schultz, and Jacqueline Taeschler—prepared many illustrated lists, in every possible permutation, during the research and the planning. Linda Shulsky, a volunteer in the department, helped to assemble photographic materials. Anne Boberski gave needed support in administrative matters, and Sarah Buchwald provided order for my own work. In the age of computers, it is most unusual to acknowledge colleagues who type one's manuscript. This acknowledgment I have to make to Nina Sweet, who typed, and sometimes retyped, every word I wrote.

James C. Y. Watt
Brooke Russell Astor Chairman
Department of Asian Art

Lenders to the Exhibition

Beijing
Institute of Archaeology, Chinese Academy of Social Sciences 129, 130, 135, 136, 160
National Museum of China 58, 66, 100, 119, 121b, 145, 149, 172, 186, 187, 199, 200, 201, 202, 203, 207, 216, 230
The Palace Museum 105, 218

Gansu Province
Dunhuang Research Institute, Dunhuang 79, 232
Gansu Institute of Archaeology, Lanzhou 85, 86, 88
Gansu Provincial Museum, Lanzhou 2, 17, 18, 80, 81, 82, 83, 87, 89, 90, 150, 191, 215

Hebei Province
Cixian Office of Cultural Properties Preservation, Cixian 132, 133, 134
Dingzhou City Museum, Dingzhou 7, 11, 12
Hebei Institute of Archaeology, Shijiazhuang 3, 67, 68
Hebei Provincial Museum, Shijiazhuang 6, 15, 16, 45, 74, 75, 137, 215, 228
Zhengding Office of Cultural Properties Preservation, Zhengding 152, 153, 168

Henan Province
Henan Museum, Zhengzhou 121a, c–f, 151, 190
Longmen Caves Research Institute, Longmen 192
Luoyang Museum, Luoyang 1, 13, 14, 205, 220, 224, 225, 226
Yanshi City Museum, Yanshi 131, 233

Inner Mongolia Autonomous Region
Inner Mongolia Autonomous Region Museum, Hohhot 26, 27, 28, 29, 32, 33, 43, 48, 49, 50, 76, 208, 209
Jerim League Museum, Tongliao 30, 31, 35

Jiangsu Province
Nanjing City Museum, Nanjing 104, 106, 110, 115, 118
Nanjing Museum, Nanjing 4, 5, 8, 9, 10, 107, 108, 109, 111, 112, 113, 114, 116
Nantong Textile Museum, Nantong 173
Jurong Museum, Jurong 117

Liaoning Province
Liaoning Institute of Archaeology, Shenyang 23, 24, 25
Liaoning Provincial Museum, Shenyang 34, 36, 37, 38, 39, 40, 41, 42

Ningxia Autonomous Region
Guyuan Museum, Yinchuan 73, 154, 155, 156, 157, 158, 221, 222, 223

Qinghai Province
Qinghai Institute of Archaeology, Xining 243, 244, 245, 246, 247

Shaanxi Province
Museum of the Forest of Steles, Xi'an 22, 78
Shaanxi History Museum, Xi'an 84, 120, 183, 184, 189, 194, 197, 198, 204, 210, 211, 212, 213, 214, 219, 230
Shaanxi Institute of Archaeology, Xi'an 46, 47, 161, 159, 188, 195, 196
Xi'an City Institute of Cultural Properties Protection and Archaeology, Xi'an 44, 169, 170, 171, 206, 231
Zhaoling Museum, Liquan County 185

Shandong Province
Linqu City Museum, Linqu 166
Qingzhou City Museum, Qingzhou 162, 163, 165, 164, 227

Shanxi Province
Datong City Institute of Archaeology, Datong 51, 52, 53, 54, 55, 56, 57
Datong City Museum, Datong 60, 61, 62, 63, 64, 65
Jinyuan Bureau of Cultural Properties and Tourism, Taiyuan 175, 176
Shanxi Institute of Archaeology, Taiyuan 139, 140, 141, 142, 143, 144, 146, 147
Shanxi Provincial Museum, Taiyuan 59, 69, 70, 71, 72, 148
Taiyuan City Institute of Archaeology, Taiyuan 138

Sichuan Province
Chengdu City Institute of Archaeology, Chengdu 127, 128
Pengzhou City Museum, Pengzhou 229
Sichuan Provincial Museum, Chengdu 21, 122, 123, 124, 125, 126

Xinjiang Uygur Autonomous Region
Bayingolin Mongolian Autonomous Prefecture Museum, Korla 91, 92, 93
Ili Kasak Autonomous Prefecture Museum, Yining 94, 95
Kashi City Museum, Kashi 97
Xinjiang Institute of Archaeology, Urumqi 19, 20
Xinjiang Uygur Autonomous Region Museum, Urumqi 96, 98, 99, 101, 102, 103, 174, 177, 178, 179, 180, 181, 182, 234, 235, 236, 237, 238, 239, 240, 241, 242

Museum of Fine Arts, Boston 193
The Cleveland Museum of Art 217

Chronology

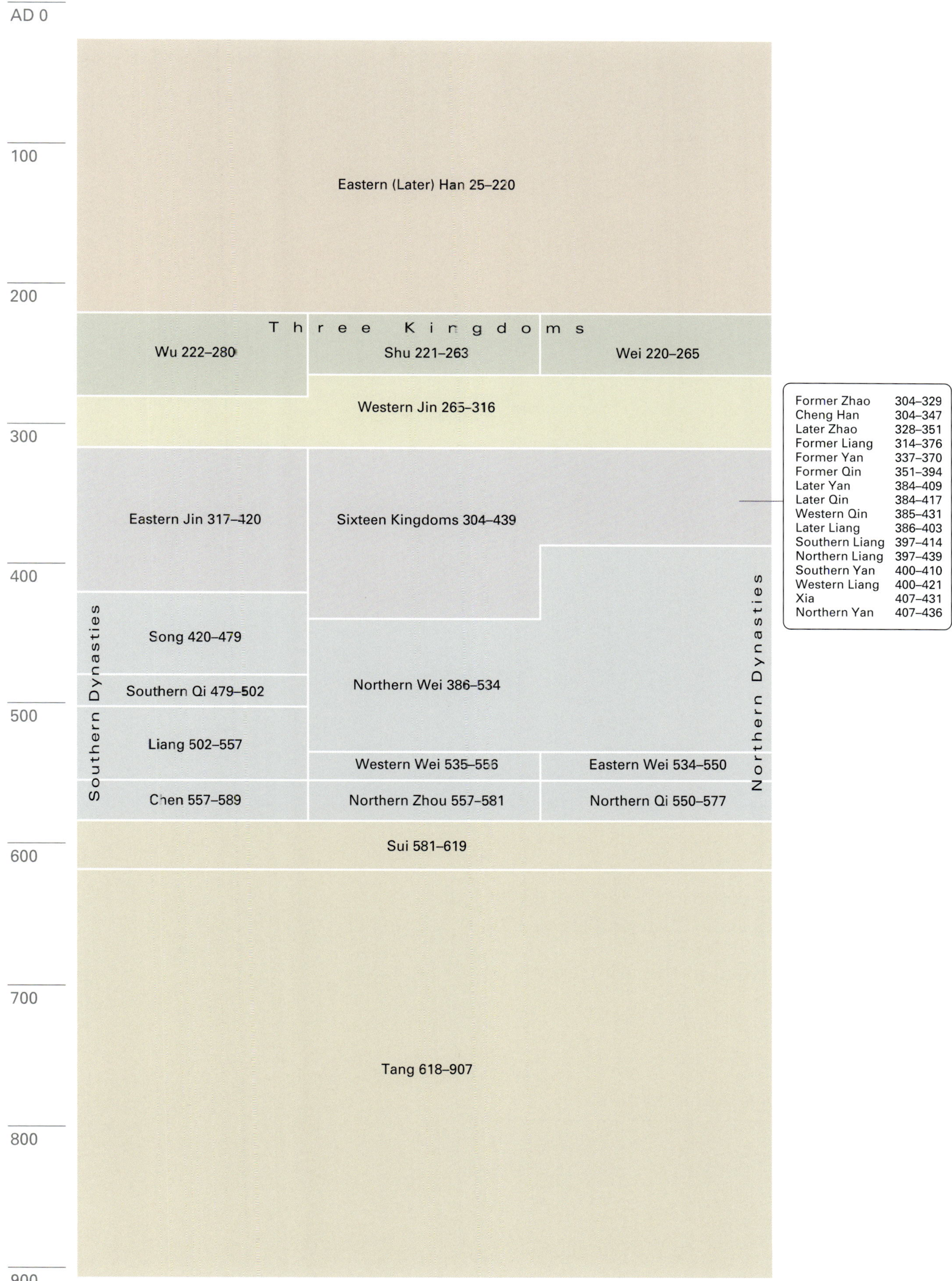

AD 0
100
200
300
400
500
600
700
800
900
Eastern (Later) Han 25–220
Three Kingdoms
Wu 222–280
Shu 221–263
Wei 220–265
Western Jin 265–316
Eastern Jin 317–420
Sixteen Kingdoms 304–439
Former Zhao 304–329
Cheng Han 304–347
Later Zhao 328–351
Former Liang 314–376
Former Yan 337–370
Former Qin 351–394
Later Yan 384–409
Later Qin 384–417
Western Qin 385–431
Later Liang 386–403
Southern Liang 397–414
Northern Liang 397–439
Southern Yan 400–410
Western Liang 400–421
Xia 407–431
Northern Yan 407–436
Southern Dynasties
Song 420–479
Southern Qi 479–502
Liang 502–557
Chen 557–589
Northern Dynasties
Northern Wei 386–534
Western Wei 535–556
Eastern Wei 534–550
Northern Zhou 557–581
Northern Qi 550–577
Sui 581–619
Tang 618–907

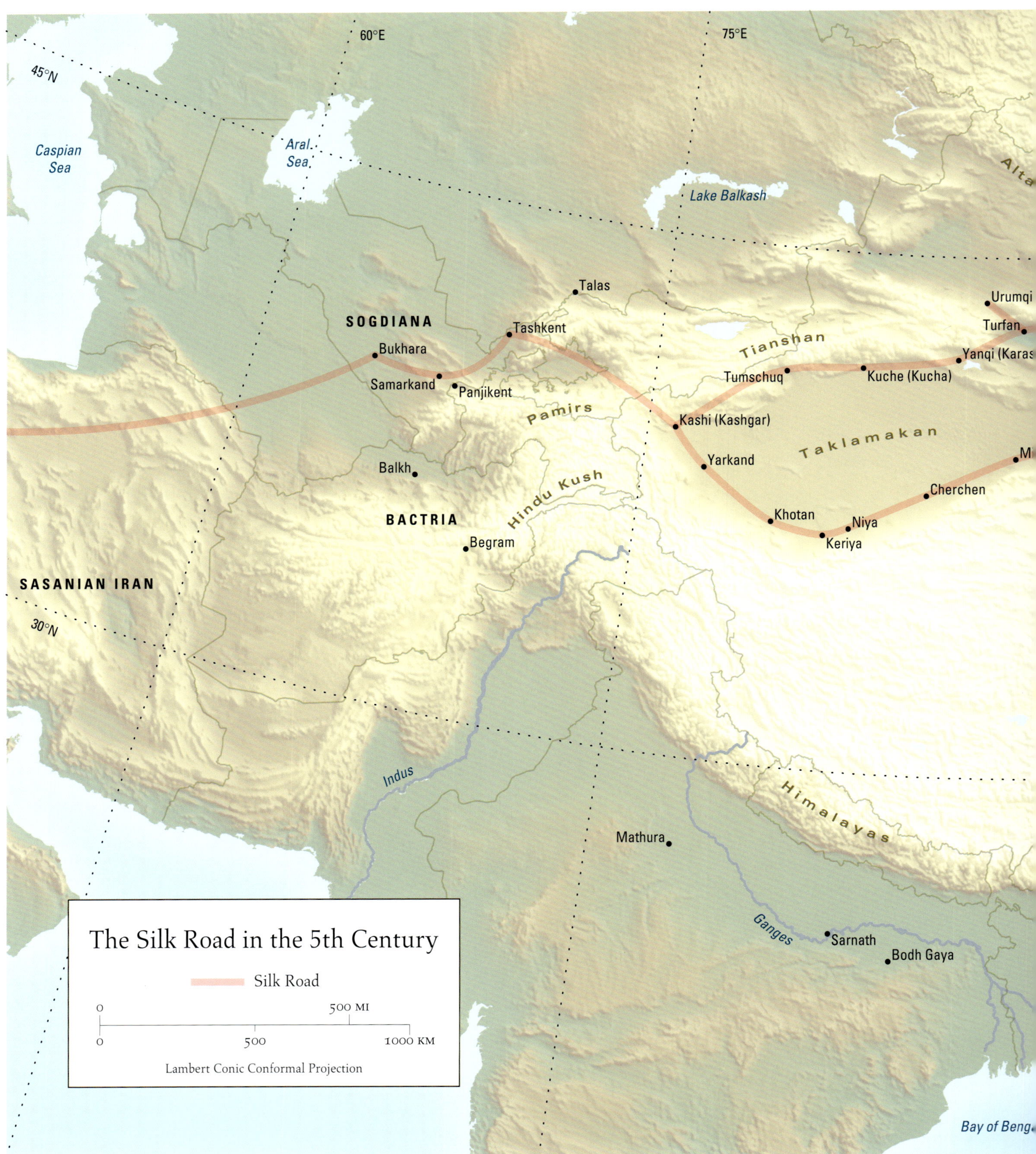
60°E
75°E
45°N
30°N
Caspian Sea
Aral Sea
Lake Balkash
Talas
Urumqi
SOGDIANA
Tashkent
Turfan
Bukhara
Tianshan
Yanqi (Karas
Tumschuq
Kuche (Kucha)
Samarkand
Panjikent
Pamirs
Kashi (Kashgar)
Taklamakan
Yarkand
Balkh
Hindu Kush
Cherchen
Khotan
Niya
BACTRIA
Keriya
Begram
SASANIAN IRAN
Indus
Himalayas
Mathura
Ganges
Sarnath
Bodh Gaya
Bay of Beng
The Silk Road in the 5th Century
Silk Road
0
500 MI
0
500
1000 KM
Lambert Conic Conformal Projection

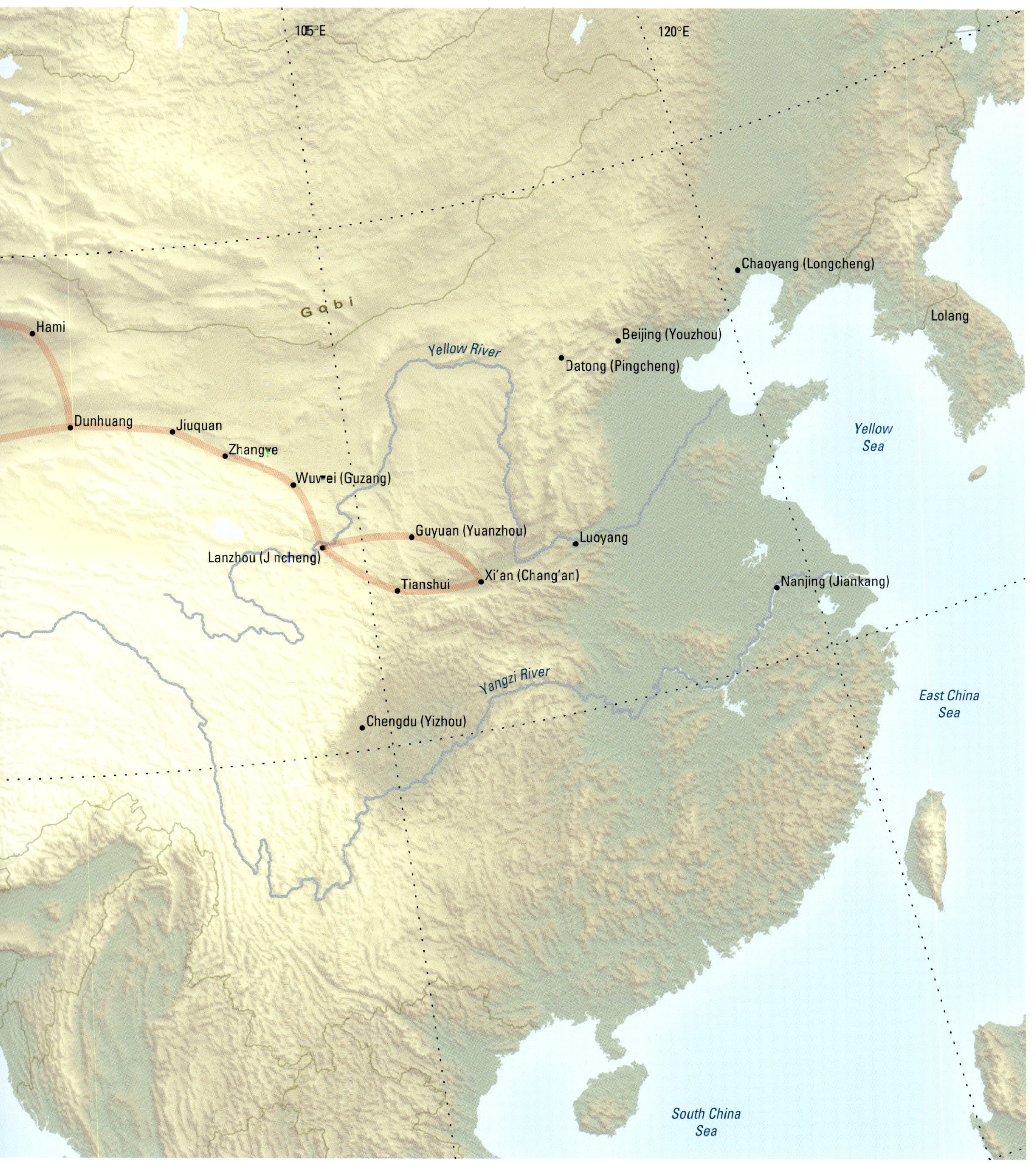
105°E
120°E
Gobi
Hami
Chaoyang (Longcheng)
Lolang
Beijing (Youzhou)
Datong (Pingcheng)
Yellow River
Dunhuang
Jiuquan
Zhangye
Wuwei (Guzang)
Yellow Sea
Guyuan (Yuanzhou)
Luoyang
Lanzhou (Jincheng)
Xi'an (Chang'an)
Tianshui
Nanjing (Jiankang)
Yangzi River
East China Sea
Chengdu (Yizhou)
South China Sea

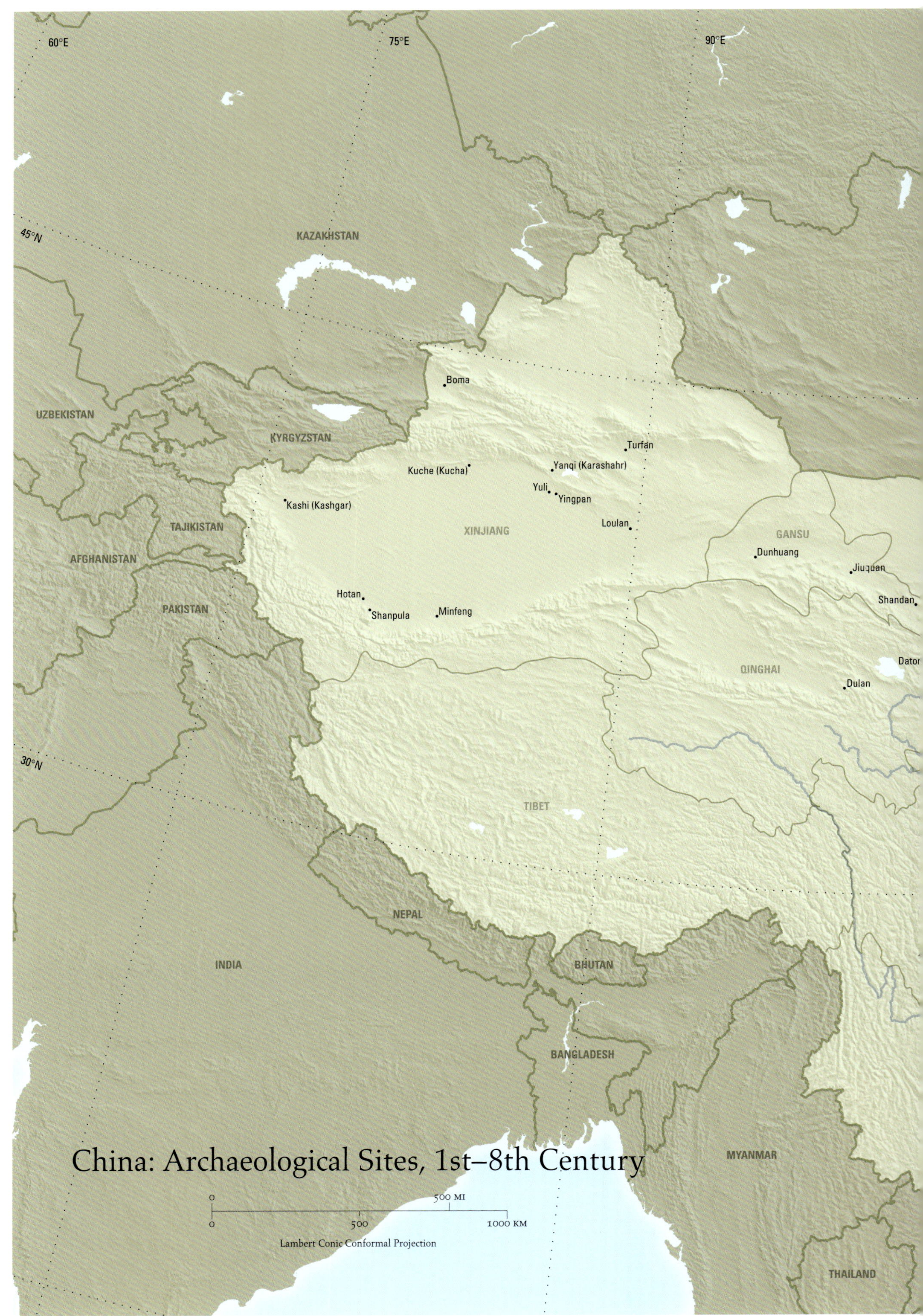

China: Archaeological Sites, 1st–8th Century

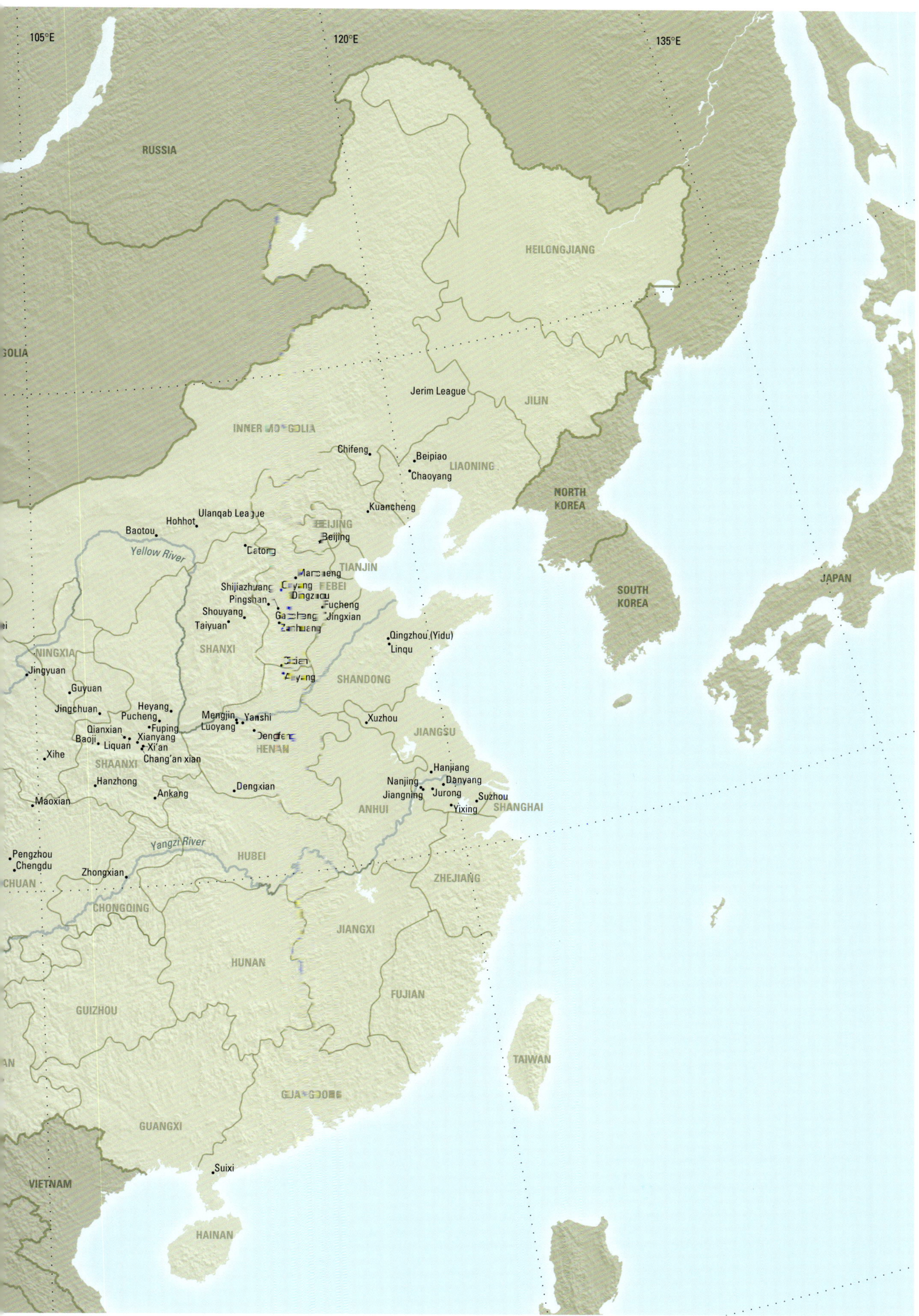

105°E
120°E
135°E
RUSSIA
HEILONGJIANG
Jerim League
JILIN
Chifeng
Beipiao
Chaoyang
LIAONING
NORTH KOREA
Kuancheng
Hohhot
Baotou
Beijing
TIANJIN
Yellow River
Shijiazhuang
Pingshan
Shouyang
Taiyuan
Fucheng
Jingxian
Qingzhou (Yidu)
Linqu
SOUTH KOREA
JAPAN
NINGXIA
Jingyuan
SHANXI
SHANDONG
Guyuan
Jingchuan
Heyang
Pucheng
Mengjin
Yanshi
Luoyang
Qianxian
Fuping
Xianyang
Baoji
Liquan
Xi'an
Chang'an xian
Xuzhou
JIANGSU
Xihe
SHAANXI
HENAN
Hanzhong
Ankang
Dengxian
Hanjiang
Danyang
Nanjing
Jiangning
Jurong
Suzhou
Yixing
SHANGHAI
ANHUI
Maoxian
Yangzi River
HUBEI
Pengzhou
Chengdu
Zhongxian
ZHEJIANG
CHONGQING
JIANGXI
HUNAN
FUJIAN
GUIZHOU
TAIWAN
GUANGXI
Suixi
VIETNAM
HAINAN

About This Exhibition

This exhibition presents some of the odds and ends left behind on the long trail of Chinese history between the fall of the Han dynasty in the early third century to the glory days of the Tang empire, which ruled over a unified China from the second quarter of the seventh century to the mid-eighth century.

Odds and ends they may be, but these objects tell a story more vividly—if not more completely—than can any written history. Whether or not one lends credence to the hypothesis that objects fashioned in any given period in history somehow reveal the spirit of the age, one can in any case be fascinated by what they are and by the part they played in the daily life of people active at the time. At the very least, viewing these objects is an experience that comes as close to time travel as can be achieved at the moment. But of course they can simply be enjoyed and studied as works of art.

The period covered by the exhibition has been chosen for two reasons. First, it is a time that began and ended with cataclysmic events which can be said to have changed the course of the country's history and that can be treated on its own, without constant reference to antecedents and later developments. Second, this period saw the coming together of cultural influences from all over Asia, with faint reflections from the Mediterranean world, into a unified whole that found its greatest expression in the arts and letters of the High Tang—in art history, roughly the first half of the eighth century. The exhibition is thus an attempt to follow the genesis of a unique civilization that emerged as a result of the gradual amalgamation of many cultural strains under the general rubric of established Chinese political, social, and cultural order.

Organization of the Exhibition

The exhibition is divided into seven sections. Each is centered on a particular geographic area that would eventually constitute part of the greater Tang empire at its height in the seventh and early eighth centuries. And each deals with a time period during which the area in question played a significant role in the political and cultural affairs of the country. In addition, owing to the requirements of conservation, there is a special room devoted to textiles.

1. Late Han, Late 2nd–Early 3rd Century

The first section shows three aspects of late Han culture. A set of mounted guards and chariots in bronze gives an idea of the ceremonial pomp accorded high officials in the empire (cat. no. 2). Then there is a selection of luxury articles used by people who could afford them, including objects of gold (cat. nos. 8–12), jade (cat. nos. 6, 7, 14–16), and imported Roman glass (cat. no. 13). There are also models of a watchtower (cat. no. 3) and farm buildings (not in the catalogue) that represent typical structures on large estates, the owners of which would take center stage in the political and military affairs of the state during and after the fall of the Han dynasty.

2. The Coming of the Xianbei

In the third century B.C., a confederation of nomadic tribes, led by the Xiongnu, built a powerful empire on the steppe north of the Great Wall of China. For centuries, there was political and military equilibrium between the Han empire and that of the Xiongnu. The latter began to break up about the middle of the first century. Some of the Xiongnu tribes migrated west into Central Asia, while others moved into China proper and settled in the Ordos (northern Shaanxi Province) and in northern Shanxi Province (then known as Bingzhou). The vacuum left by the departure of Xiongnu was gradually filled by another confederation led by tribes known collectively as the Xianbei. By the third century, various Xianbei tribes had amassed along the entire northern border of China. The group known as the Tuoba Xianbei began to penetrate into Bingzhou from their base in Shengle (southwest of Hohhot in Inner Mongolia). To the east, the Murong Xianbei extended into northern Hebei Province (including present-day Beijing). The Xianbei confederations vied for power in North China from the late third century until the early fifth century, when the Tuoba vanquished the Murong and all other peoples of steppe origin who had established themselves in North China during a period known as the Sixteen Kingdoms (304–439).

This section of the exhibition includes archaeological finds from sites in North China associated with the Xianbei and dating from the late third to the early fifth century. They are mostly metal objects, as artifacts made of organic material have perished. They demonstrate, inter alia, survival of the earlier tradition of the art of the nomads from the Siberian and Mongolian steppes (cat. nos. 26, 29–32); contacts with ancient Bactria in Central Asia (roughly northern Afghanistan; gold ornaments, cat. nos. 33–37); trade with the Roman Near East (cat. no. 42) and areas along the Silk Road (jade from Khotan, cat. no. 38); and contact with India, as shown by early Buddhist images (cat. nos. 44, 45) and jewelry (cat. no. 43).

There is a group of bronze and gilt-bronze objects, all from the area of present-day Chaoyang and Beipiao in western Liaoning Province, that can be identified as specific to the Murong Xianbei (cat. nos. 23–25). The typical design on Murong Xianbei artifacts (cat. no. 25) would later be seen in the arts of the Northern Wei in China and the Silla kingdom in Korea.

Perhaps the object that best represents this period is the gold hat ornament (cat. no. 37). The basic form is that of the cicada ornament worn by senior officials beginning in the Han period but with additions of disk pendants (as seen in gold ornaments from Bactria) and a Buddha image on the back.

3. Early Northern Wei Dynasty, 398–493

In the year 398, Tuoba Gui (r. 386–409), founder of the Northern Wei dynasty (386–534), led his people across the then Great Wall into northern Shanxi and established his capital at Pingcheng (present-day Datong). By 439, the Northern Wei ruled all of North China, extending into present-day Gansu Province in the northwest, thus opening direct access to Central Asia along the Silk Road. For fifty years the city of Pingcheng was the center of power, culture, and riches in North China. This section of the exhibition shows some of the objects found in the Pingcheng area and several other important sites within the realm of the Northern Wei up to the year 493, when the capital was moved to Luoyang.

There are three main groups of objects in this section. The first consists of pottery funerary figures of camels, horses and grooms, entertainers, and tomb guardians (cat. nos. 46–57). The use of pottery funerary figures is indicative of the adaptation of burial customs that had been practiced in China for centuries. Stylistically, they owe very little to earlier Chinese antecedents. The pottery figures of the Xianbei exhibit a new vitality that perhaps reflects the steppe origin of the people. This distinctive style would persist through the Pingcheng period and survive into the Northern Zhou state (557–581) in Shaanxi Province and Ningxia.

The second group consists of imported objects of metal and glass (cat. nos. 58–66). These are luxury articles that came from or through Central Asia during the years of greatest power and prosperity of the Northern Wei dynasty—the last fifty years of the Pingcheng period. The glass bowls are of Roman or Sasanian Persian origin; and the metalware, displaying Hellenistic, Persian, and Indian forms and motifs, was presumably made somewhere in Central Asia—the exact locations remain to be determined. (For a full discussion of imported metal objects in the exhibition, see the essay by Boris Marshak in this catalogue.)

Some locally manufactured objects also show signs of western (Central Asian) influence (cat. nos. 71, 72). But perhaps the clearest evidence of Western influence on Chinese material culture at this time is a group of locally made glass vessels found in a stone coffer, with an inscription dated 481, in the crypt of a pagoda in Dingxian, Hebei. These bottles and bowl (cat. nos. 67, 68) are the earliest known blown glass in China, made by a technique transmitted all the way from the Roman world. (See the essay by An Jiayao for the history of glass in China during the period covered by this exhibition.)

In the third group are several early Buddhist sculptures of stone and bronze dating from the late fifth century (cat. nos. 74–77). These were found outside the capital of Pingcheng, but from important administrative centers within the Northern Wei state.

During the time that Central Asian influence was strong, there were nevertheless some Northern Wei objects that display vestiges of motifs from the days when the Tuoba were based in Inner Mongolia. One example is the ring handle held by a mask (cat. no. 73). In the center of the upper portion of the mask is the image of a god or human straddling two dragons, and on the ring handle is a human figure astride two quadrupeds with dragonlike heads. These are derived from motifs such as that on a gold ornament associated with the Xianbei of the late third to fourth century (cat. no. 35).

One object in this section, a lacquer screen (cat. no. 69), has aroused great interest among academic historians of Chinese art. Apart from its importance as a key document in the study of early Chinese painting, it is also of interest for the subject matter—texts and illustrations on such subjects as filial piety, female virtues, general admonitions for good social behavior, and guidelines for ways of staying out of trouble. Such themes are a throwback to an earlier tradition of pictorial art in the Han period dominated by Confucian principles.

4. The Western Regions and the Way Thither, 200–700

This section of the exhibition encompasses two regions and two periods. The two regions are the Hexi Corridor (present-day Gansu Province) and that part of the vast area spanned by the Western Regions, which is present-day Xinjiang Uygur Autonomous Region (Chinese Central Asia; see the map on pp. xvi–xvii). The first period, covering the third and fourth centuries, concerns mainly Gansu in northwestern China. At that time, Gansu (then known as Liangzhou) was the region where Han culture and classical learning were preserved to a greater degree than in any other area in North China, as it was not affected by the destructive nomad-style warfare that took place elsewhere. The writing brush and inscribed wooden boards (cat. nos. 85, 86) serve as reminders of the importance accorded the written word in Gansu, although their survival owes as much to the climate of the region as to the sheer quantity of such material produced at the time.

Wood was one of the few natural resources available in Gansu and was often used for funerary furniture, substituting for bronze and pottery. The prevalent use of wood gave rise to a class of highly skilled craftsmen who, besides producing realistic objects like the chariot (cat. no. 80), also made sculptures of striking effect (cat. nos. 17, 18, 81). The sense of spontaneity is enhanced (and the mastery evident) in leaving unpolished the surface of the sculpture so that the mark made by each stroke of the axe or chisel remains clearly visible—in this respect paralleling calligraphy, where no retouching is possible.

From early historical times there was a large indigenous population in Gansu consisting of peoples known as the Qiang and the Di. Following the practice of the Han dynasty, the Wei (220–265) and the Western Jin (265–316) conferred honorific titles on tribal chiefs who had authority over their own people but owed allegiance to the Chinese emperor. These titles came in the form of gold seals, which served as insignia of office (cat. no. 83).

The second period begins in the fifth century, when traffic along the Silk Road rapidly increased, taking over from the northern route over the steppe north of the Tianshan. Gold and silver objects have been found in Gansu and Xinjiang dating from the fifth to the early eighth century (cat. nos. 90–95). All presumably of Central Asian origin, some of them bear inscriptions in Bactrian, Sogdian, or Middle Persian. Some were trade goods; others, like the pottery vessels (cat. nos. 97, 98), were for local use.

Gansu in the fifth century was a major conduit for the transmission of Buddhism into China. It was not possible to transport the murals and fragile sculptures from the cave temples in Gansu for the exhibition, but the aftereffects of the transmission can be seen in later sections.

Textiles

A special section is devoted to textiles found in Xinjiang and Gansu (Dunhuang), covering the entire period of the exhibition. There are two groups. In the first group are several fabrics woven in western Central Asia with strong Roman, nomadic, or Indian influence (cat. nos. 101–103). The second group consists of Chinese textiles that represent major types of weaving and design from the third to the eighth century (all other textiles in the exhibition). They have been selected to illustrate the successive steps in the adoption of western weaving techniques and motifs in China. (For a detailed discussion, see the essay by Zhao Feng.)

5. South China, 3rd–6th Century

In this exhibition South China refers to all areas of present-day China south of the Yangzi River that were at most times under the control of "native" dynasties from the third to near the end of the sixth century. This is only a cultural demarcation, as the political boundaries to the north often extended to the Hwai River valley and at times included the Shandong Peninsula. The political and cultural center of South China from the fourth century on was in Jiankang (present-day Nanjing). In the third century, it was the capital (then called Jianye) of the state of Wu, one of the Three Kingdoms.

The cultural development of South China in this period took a different direction from that of North China. Literature and philosophy flourished, taking off from the revolutionary changes at the end of the Han dynasty, while in the north classical learning in the Han tradition persisted. There are parallel courses in the propagation of Buddhism in the north and in the south. Broadly speaking, the quest in the north was for salvation and earthly blessing through faith and worship, while in the south the emphasis was on theological questioning. There are generally many more Buddhist images and monuments that are extant from this period in the north. The only area in the south where a relatively large number of Buddhist sculptures have survived is in Sichuan Province in the southwest, particularly in the vicinity of Chengdu—at some distance from the capital, Jiankang, but accessible by land routes from India. A selection of some of these sculptures is included in this exhibition, showing direct Indian influence (cat. nos. 122–123). They date mostly from the second quarter of the sixth century. Earlier contacts with India along the so-called Southern Silk Road are attested by the appearance of Buddhist images on the pottery bases of money trees (see fig. 96) found in Sichuan and on pottery vessels of the third to fourth century near Jiankang (cat. no. 104).

The majority of archaeological finds in the Jiankang area are high-fired green-glazed pottery (these were not of interest to grave robbers in earlier times). They draw our attention for several reasons. First, this type of porcelaneous ware represents the initial step toward the development of the famed celadon porcelain of the twelfth to thirteenth century. Second, the vessels (cat. nos. 107–109) are a delightful expression of natural playfulness, which would not have been possible in the earlier Han period when conventions were more strictly applied to social activities, including the making of burial furniture. Third, and most noteworthy, they reveal the presence of foreigners and foreign influences. The bearded figure sitting on a fabulous animal (cat. no. 105) wears a dress with a Parthian pattern—as also seen on murals in the cave temples in Kizil, Xinjiang. The jar with a bird-head decoration (cat. no. 106) intimates the first signs of distant Iranian influence. Such objects make up for the lack of information on foreigners in South China in the official histories of this period.

Of the greatest significance in the history of Chinese pictorial art are the finds of brick walls in burial chambers of the late fourth to fifth century that bear impressed images of famous personages from the period prior to the Western Jin (cat. no. 113). They represent the refinement of a style of figure drawing that began in the early Han period—as seen in wall paintings in Western Han tombs in Luoyang—and they established a standard for centuries to come. The elegance of the raised lines in these impressed pictures echoes the elegant demeanor of the subjects portrayed.

As in North China, luxury articles used by the aristocracy were mainly imported items, such as the glass vessels (cat. nos. 116, 117) and the nautilus cup (cat. no. 118; the nautilus shell would have come from the islands of Southeast Asia). For people who used these articles, the oxcart (cat. no. 115) was the usual vehicle for travel.

As a result of incessant wars and general social unrest, a large number of peasants became retainers and menial servants on large estates. They chose this course to seek protection from banditry and to avoid heavy taxes and corvée labor. Their activities are well represented on a set of impressed bricks from a tomb at Dengxian, Henan. Some of these bricks are in the exhibition (cat. no. 121) and includes illustrations of filial piety and Daoist immortals.

6. Luoyang and After, 6th Century in the North

Politically, the sixth century in North China was a most complicated period. It was also a time of violence, both for the ruling classes and for the peasantry. Artistically, the first half of the sixth century emerged as one of the most brilliant eras in Chinese history. Luoyang, in the center of China, became the capital of the Northern Wei in 394 during the reign of Emperor Xiaowendi (r. 471–99). The greatest achievement in art and architecture in Luoyang in the early sixth century was the imperial temple, Yongningsi (Temple of Eternal Peace), built in 516–17 by order of the Dowager Empress Ning (née Hu). Sadly, the only surviving artifacts from this temple are some terracotta figures that were attached to the walls of the pagoda (cat. no. 129). Technically they are in high relief, but they can be viewed as sculptures in the round—a departure from sculptural styles in previous times. The heads were modeled separately and attached to the bodies (cat. no. 130). Pottery tomb figures from the same period made with heads attached are in the same style, realistically representing people of various ethnic origins and their mode of dress (cat. no. 131a–j).

The great pagoda of Yongningsi burned down during a storm in 534, the year that saw the end of the Northern Wei dynasty. The empire split in two, with Luoyang more or less on the border between the two states known as the Eastern Wei and the Western Wei—which soon became the Northern Qi (550–577) and the Northern Zhou (557–581), respectively.

The Eastern Wei–Northern Qi inherited the culture of Luoyang, while the Western Wei–Northern Zhou retained many traits of early Xianbei traditions of the Northern Wei before the move of the capital south to Luoyang. The difference in artistic expression can be plainly seen by comparing the pottery tomb sculptures from the Eastern Wei to the Northern Qi (cat. nos. 132, 133, 135–138, 142, 144) with those from the Northern Zhou (cat. nos. 154–156).

By far the most striking aspect of the art of Northern Qi is the overwhelming influence from the west, that is, Central Asia. Many of the pottery vessels recovered from Northern Qi tombs display distinct forms and motifs from this region, which, in turn, were the offspring of the union of Hellenistic, Persian, and Indian art. Typical Northern Qi vessels are represented by catalogue numbers 139–141, 145, 146, 148, and 149. The absorption of Western styles began already in Luoyang in the late Northern Wei, as demonstrated by a glazed pottery bowl (cat. no. 160). Many more such objects would have been found in Luoyang if the great city had not been so utterly destroyed by successive sieges. Most of the western forms and motifs came from metalwork, of which hardly any, whether imported or locally made, have remained. An exception is a silver cup (cat. no. 152) found in the same tomb as a number of Byzantine gold coins (cat. no. 153). It is of local manufacture after a Sogdian form.

By contrast few, if any, locally produced vessels or pottery figures in the Northern Zhou show signs of western influence. This is because the Central Asian craftsmen, musicians, and dancers all followed the Northern Wei court on its move to Luoyang. Nevertheless, the Northern Zhou aristocracy also used imported luxury articles such as the gilt-silver ewer (cat. no. 157) and the glass bowl (cat. no. 158) from the tomb of Li Xian, a military lord who enjoyed a close association with the ruling house of Northern Zhou.

Western motifs can also be found on Buddhist images. The distinctly Iranian symbols of the orb and the crescent, for example, can be seen as components in the complex decoration on the crown of the Northern Zhou or Sui bodhisattva found in the vicinity of Xi'an (cat. no. 171). A recently discovered group of Buddhist sculptures in Shandong Province in the east reveals a hitherto unknown school of Buddhist art in sixth-century China that owed its origin to contact by sea with Southeast Asia with further links to India. Several examples are in the exhibition (cat. nos. 163–166; for a more detailed account, see the essay by Angela Howard.)

Toward the Seventh Century

In 577, the economically weaker and militarily tougher Northern Zhou conquered the Northern Qi and in 581 was, in turn, taken over by one of its military lords, Yang Jian, who, as Emperor Wendi (r. 581–604), established the Sui dynasty (581–619) and went on to unify all of China. In government and military institutions the Sui dynasty followed in the main the Northern Zhou model, but in material culture the Northern Qi provided the major component. The typical Northern Zhou pottery figure, such as catalogue numbers 154 and 155, practically vanished with the demise of the dynasty.

One object of note, dating from the end of the Northern Qi period, is a pottery bottle (cat. no. 151) with dark green splashes over a light green glaze (not unlike color-field painting of the twentieth century). It marks the beginning of a style of splash glaze decoration that became one of the favorite techniques of ceramic decoration throughout the Tang period.

Of all the archaeological finds from the late sixth century, those which have attracted the most attention are the stone "sarcophagi" in the form of houses or couches with relief and painted decoration on the walls that depict western themes and motifs. One of the best-known examples is in the exhibition (cat. no. 175). It is from the tomb of Yu Hong (interred 592) and his wife (d. 597). Yu Hong came from one of those Central Asian families that had settled in the northwestern region of China at the end of the Silk Road, had acculturated to local conditions, and was fluent in all the common languages spoken in the region. He was thus amply qualified to serve as an emissary for all the states on the northern border of China and across Central Asia. This was exactly what he did, and he ended up in the service of the Sui dynasty. The carved and painted decoration on the walls of the stone house in his tomb is essentially Central Asian in theme and subject matter, with a strong Iranian component. It is generally assumed that people like Yu Hong were Sogdians who had brought their religion and way of life into China. Nevertheless, even if the imagery and the allusions they used in their carvings and paintings were Sogdian in origin, the pictorial style had been radically modified in the course of transmission to China. In particular, there is a dynamism in the depiction of hunting and animal combat scenes that is more exaggerated than in the murals of buildings in Sogdian cities such as Panjikent (in Tajikistan). Years of moving about and living on the borders between China and nomadic communities to the north had generated, among expatriate Central Asians, a pictorial art that combined elements from areas over the entire continent of Asia.

The bas-relief on the walls of the marble house is also a reflection of cultural integration. By this time in China, ethnic differences counted for less than cultural differences, which were fast diminishing. By the beginning of the seventh century, Chinese civilization had reached a stage almost unrecognizable from that of the late second century—where our exhibition began.

7. Arts of the Sui and Early Tang Dynasties, 581–755

In 618, Li Yuan (r. 618–26) took over the rule of the empire from the Sui and founded the Tang dynasty. Culturally, the two dynasties formed a continuum. The Tang reigned over a unified country and extended its administration far into Central Asia. The mutual influence of China and Central Asia is the main theme of the final section of the exhibition.

It opens with a group of archaeological finds from Turfan in eastern Central Asia, which for most of the first half of the Tang dynasty was an integral part of the empire. These spectacular tomb guardians are based on Chinese prototypes, but artists in Turfan gave them animation and vivid colors (cat. nos. 178–180). The use of vibrant colors, particularly red and green, was soon transmitted to Chang'an (Xi'an), the capital, as seen in a pair of pottery figures from a tomb dated 664 (cat. no. 184). It was the same with fashion. The dress of the pottery figure of a court lady from the 664 tomb in Xi'an (cat. no. 185) follows the lead from Turfan—as seen on the clothed doll (cat. no. 181)—although the fashion may have originated in one of the rich oasis towns farther to the west. Fashion statements also extended to horses. Both female riders, from Turfan (cat. no. 182) and Chang'an (cat. no. 183), are mounted on a piebald horse, first introduced into China during the reign of Emperor Taizong (r. 627–49). Pottery figures of mounted hunters from tombs of the imperial family illustrate the importance of the hunt for the aristocracy. The hunting leopardlike feline (the cheetah, cat. no. 198) came as tribute from somewhere in the Western Regions—Sogdiana, India, Persia, and the Caliphate. A decorative pattern that was introduced from the west at this time is marbled clay, as seen on the horse with the mounted archer (cat. no. 197).

Other funerary figures of stone (cat. no. 203) and pottery (cat. nos. 183–185, 199–202) are all from tombs of important personages at the early Tang court: eunuchs, generals, and senior officials who were often related to the imperial family. Those in service to the emperor were from diverse ethnic backgrounds, but there is little to differentiate the contents of their tombs. The pottery figures also represent people from all parts of Asia, and some came from as far as Africa (cat. no. 204).

Imported silverware in the seventh century can be firmly identified as Sogdian (cat. nos. 208, 209), as Sogdian merchants began to dominate trade along the Silk Road. A number of locally made silver vessels illustrate the gradual incorporation of Sogdian motifs and techniques (cat. nos. 209–213) and fully developed Tang style (cat. nos. 214–215).

In the early seventh century, there was also imported jewelry (cat. no. 187). The combination of gold and jade in Tang jewelry and decorative plaques was a throwback to a tradition initiated on the Mongolian steppes by the Xiongnu of the Han period, but with decorative elements introduced from the west.

A Sasanian glass bottle (cat. no. 220) found in an early Tang tomb in Guanlin, Luoyang, tells more than a glass story. It is the kind of glass bottle used to transport perfumes in international Asian trade, and it reminds us that the Silk Road was by no means mainly for the trading of silk, but that aromatics and spices were equally important commodities.

The one object that represents the ultimate Chinese tribute to the Western Regions is the porcelain ewer (cat. no. 218). The material and workmanship are quintessentially Chinese, but the design comfortably employs all the various motifs that had been seeping into China for the past two centuries—particularly those on metalwork.

A special section is devoted to Wu Zetian (r. 690–705), the only female monarch in Chinese history who ruled in her own right. (The title she gave herself was the gender neutral *huangdi*, or emperor.) Her ascendancy began early in the reign of her husband, Gaozong (r. 650–83), and she assumed absolute power after his death. The Empress Wu had grand visions for herself and for the empire, then at the peak of its power and prestige. In 690, she changed the name of the dynasty to Zhou until she was forced to abdicate in 705 in favor of her son, Zhongzong (r. 705–12).

In 1982, a shepherd found a gold tablet on one of the peaks of Songshan in Henan, one of the sacred mountains where Chinese emperors communicated with Heaven. The tablet, dated 700, is inscribed with a supplication by the empress to the gods in the Daoist heaven to absolve her of her sins (cat.

no. 190). Wu Zetian was also a strong patron of Buddhism, and she established in every prefecture a temple named Dayunsi (Great Cloud Temple). The reliquary in this exhibition (cat. no. 191) is from the Dayunsi of Jingzhou, Gansu. Also closely associated with the empress are two sculptures (cat. nos. 192, 193).

By the eighth century, there was a merging of Buddhist and secular art. The pair of gilt-bronze guardians (cat. no. 230) could have been made for a Buddhist temple or could have served as tomb guardians—pottery versions are commonly found in Tang tombs. The two stone guardians (cat. no. 231) would have been made for a temple but wear similar armor. The bodhisattva from Quyang, Hebei (cat. no. 228), has lost the iconic aspects of earlier Buddhist images and can be appreciated as a sculpture of a human body.

Calligraphy of the Tang period has survived in two forms: writing on paper stored or buried at sites in the desert areas of northwestern China and inscriptions carved on stones. One example of the former is an incomplete copy of an essay by a third-century writer in the finest calligraphic style of the early Tang (cat. no. 232), while the epitaph inscribed on a stone slab (cat. no. 233) is by the hand of the calligrapher Zhang Xu, who was known in particular for his cursive script—not the standard script seen on the stone epitaph.

Hardly any painting of the early Tang period has survived in the original. This makes the paintings on silk from a screen found in a tomb in Astana, Turfan, extremely precious (cat. no. 177). Otherwise, pictorial styles of the early eighth century can be gauged only from murals in imperial tombs (cat. nos. 194–196).

In 755–56, a major part of the country, including the two capitals (Chang'an and Luoyang) and what is today Hebei Province, was devastated by a rebellion led by An Lushan (703–757), the military governor from the northeastern frontier prefecture, with the center of command in Fanyang (now Beijing). The rebellion put an end to the reign of the aging Minghuang (the Bright Emperor, also Xuanzong, r. 712–56) and to a particularly brilliant period in Chinese cultural history. Of the cultural riches of the hundred years or so that ended in 755, only the literature has come down to us more or less intact. The music and dance inevitably are lost. Of the plastic arts, what survives are a number of Buddhist sculptures in bronze and stone and what was interred in the tombs of the nobility and left behind by robbers. Nevertheless, these odds and ends that have somehow remained may suffice to reveal to us some essential aspects of a wondrous world born of an ancient civilization and transformed by the willing acceptance of the many cultures that came into its orbit.

James C. Y. Watt

CHINA

Dawn of a Golden Age

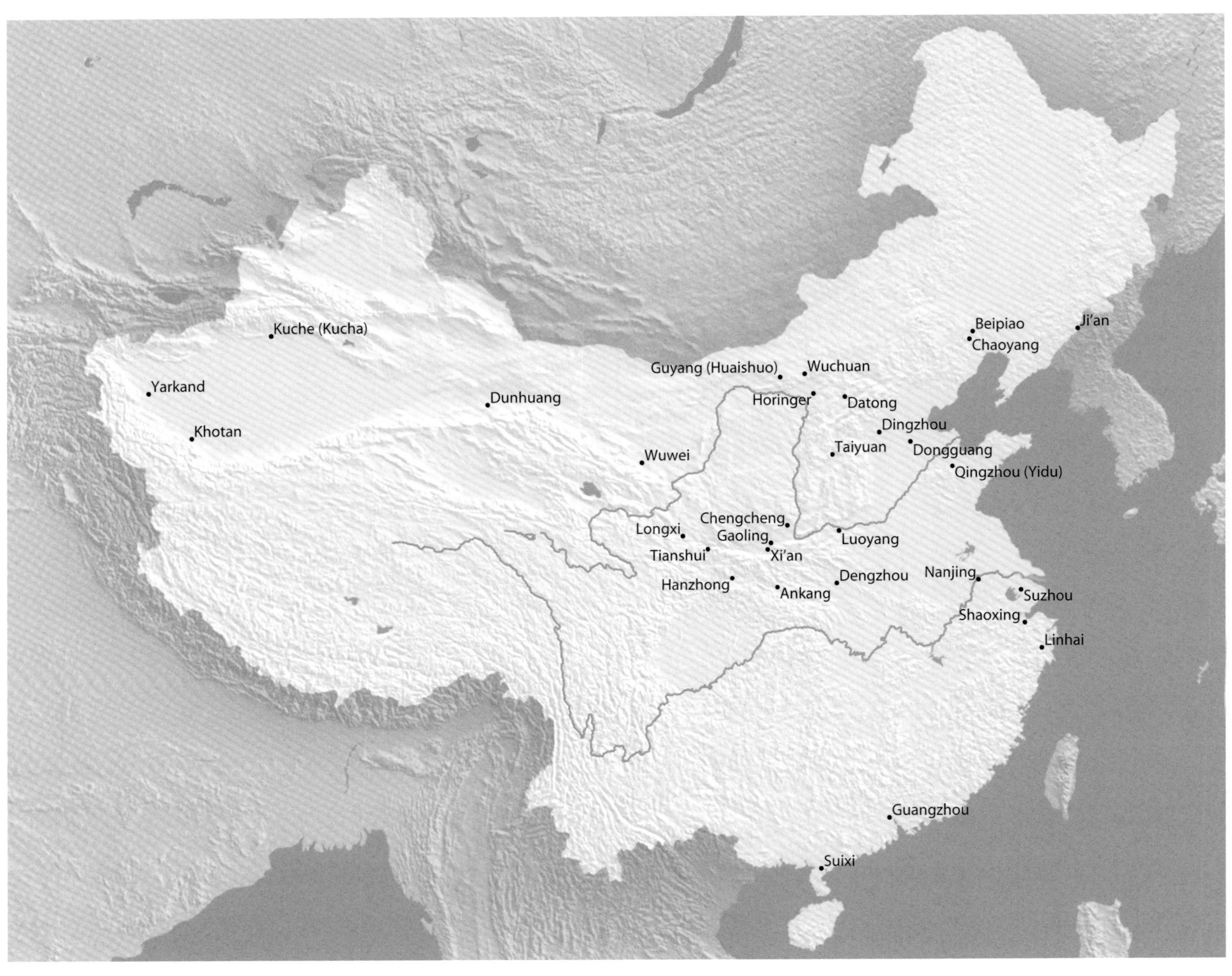
Kuche (Kucha)
Yarkand
Khotan
Dunhuang
Wuwei
Guyang (Huaishuo)
Wuchuan
Horinger
Datong
Beipiao
Chaoyang
Ji'an
Dingzhou
Taiyuan
Dongguang
Qingzhou (Yidu)
Chengcheng
Longxi
Gaoling
Tianshui
Xi'an
Luoyang
Hanzhong
Ankang
Dengzhou
Nanjing
Suzhou
Shaoxing
Linhai
Guangzhou
Suixi

Art and History in China from the Third to the Eighth Century

JAMES C.Y. WATT

The Han dynasty (206 B.C.–A.D. 220), having lasted for four centuries, officially ended in the year 220 with the abdication of the last (nominal) emperor, Xiandi (r. 189–220), but the collapse of law and order in the realm began some time before he ascended the throne in 189.

There are many events and underlying causes that can be adduced to account for the decline and fall of the Han empire, and there are interesting parallels that can be drawn with the Roman empire.[1] For the art historian, the most important events took place in the capital city of Luoyang in 189/190, which ended with the sacking of the city by the troops of Dong Zuo (d. 192). These events were the culmination of continuing intrigues and power struggles between two parties: the families of successive empresses—with the occasional support of the scholar-officials—and the palace eunuchs.[2]

Dong Zuo, a Han Chinese, was raised in Longxi commandery in the northwest (south of Lanzhou, Gansu), where there was a large Qiang population (ethnically related to Tibetans). He was raised among the Qiang people and made friends with their leaders, impressing them with his physical prowess.[3] The army he led into Luoyang consisted mainly of three thousand cavalry, including many Qiang and *hu* (usually translated as "barbarians," a general description for people originally from the steppe, but referring at this time to the Xiongnu in particular). This army was assembled in Bingzhou (Shanxi Province), where he was governor. Upon arrival in the wealthy city of Luoyang, his men were allowed to loot, rape, and kill. The following year, Dong Zuo was forced out of Luoyang by other armies converging on the city. He retreated to Chang'an (Xi'an), nearer his home base, but not before he devastated the city of Luoyang, destroying all palace buildings and the riches of the city. He also sent his troops to plunder the imperial tombs and take the treasures therein. And he ordered the people of the demolished city to move with him to Chang'an. Many fled or died along the way. This was the first instance of nomadic warfare brought into the very heart of China, and it would be repeated all over North China for the next two centuries.

The wanton destruction of Luoyang, capital of the Eastern (or Later) Han (25–220), marked the end of many traditional crafts, for even if they escaped the massacre and survived the move to Chang'an, the craftsmen would have lost their patrons. Two types of luxury articles, patterned silk and lacquer, which had production centers in Sichuan, in southwestern China, continued to be made. Their subsequent history, however, was very different. Colorful patterned silks, woven or embroidered, continued to be produced and traded. This exhibition includes examples of patterned silks that illustrate all major stages in the development of silk weaving in China from about the third to the eighth century (see the essay by Zhao Feng in this catalogue). The history of silk weaving in this period also perfectly parallels exchanges between East and West that took place in other areas of cultural and artistic activities—and the study of the evolution of weaves and patterns is particularly illuminating in this regard. Lacquer, on the other hand, was not an important trade commodity, and the finest articles with lacquer decoration were too expensive to produce except under imperial patronage. Its use as an artistic medium declined rapidly after the third century, and by the eighth century its main artistic use was to serve as background for inlaid decoration (cat. no. 217).

The craft that suffered an almost irreversible setback after the sack of Luoyang was jade carving. Jade (nephrite) has had an exalted position in Chinese material culture since the

Neolithic period, and by the second century the working of jade had already a continuous tradition of several thousand years. Jade carvings in the first two centuries of our era (the Eastern Han period) were not as intricate as those from the preceding centuries, but the level of technical skill remained very high, as can be seen in the examples in this exhibition (cat. nos. 6, 15, 16). After the cataclysmic events at the end of the second century, the tradition of jade working was interrupted. There are several reasons for this. The first is that jade carving is an elaborate and time-consuming business and requires stable and peaceful working conditions, no longer available in the third century. The second is that the potential patrons had fled the capital city. Third, traffic between central China and the Western Regions (Khotan and Yarkand in present-day Xinjiang), where the material (nephrite) came from, was temporarily halted. The result was the loss of a long tradition that would not be reestablished for about a thousand years, although in Gansu Province in the northwest, corridor to Central Asia, there may be the occasional find of a jade carving at a fourth-century site such as cat. no. 89, but the carving could date from an earlier period. It should be noted that carvings in the round of animals, real or imaginary, began relatively late, not before the third century B.C. Archaeologically, they are usually found at Han-period sites in the metropolitan area around Xi'an, in Shaanxi. Such carvings represent a tradition distinct from that of ceremonial and ornamental jades, which had deep roots going back to the Neolithic period.

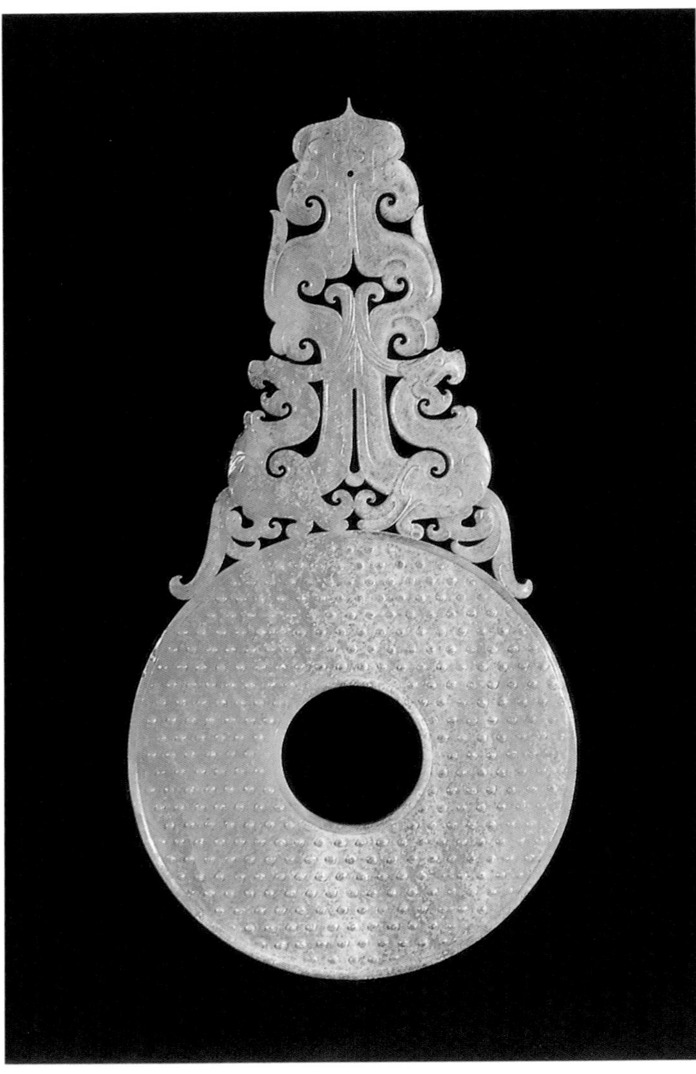

Figure 1. *Bi* disk. Western Han dynasty (206 B.C.–A.D. 9). White jade, height 10¼ in. (25.9 cm). Excavated from the tomb of Liu Sheng (d. 113 B.C.), Mancheng, Hebei Province. Hebei Provincial Museum

We may also take jade carving as an example to illustrate the general development of the plastic arts in the later years of the Han dynasty. There are, broadly speaking, two aspects to the art of jade carving at this time. The first is exemplified by the *bi* disk (cat. no. 6) from the tomb of Liu Yan, Prince Jian of Zhongshan, who died in A.D. 90. In terms of the general form and motifs, it follows established models from early in the dynasty such as the *bi* disk from the tomb of Liu Sheng (d. 113 B.C., also prince of Zhongshan but not related to Liu Yan; fig. 1), but it lacks the vitality and fluidity of line that one sees in the earlier version. The lively "comma" pattern on the earlier disk is reduced to static round knobs—which also required less work. This is a general tendency in all the plastic arts of the Eastern Han period. Near the end of the Han dynasty one sees the screen from the tomb of Liu Chang, Prince Mu of Zhongshan, a descendant of Liu Yan, who died in 174 (see cat. no. 7). The openwork carving on the two horizontal plaques follows a style similar to that of Liu Yan's *bi* disk but with a different subject matter. Instead of dragons with foliated extensions, the gods of Xiwangmu and Dongwanggong are portrayed. The workmanship is also greatly simplified. The two openwork plaques are flat pieces with roughly incised lines. There was thus already a steady decline in the craft before the final interruption at the end of the second century.

The other development in jade carving in the Eastern Han is toward greater abstraction, as seen in the cicada (cat. no. 15) and the pig (cat. no. 16), also from the tomb of Liu Yan. With such pieces the lack of detail in the carving is likely to be deliberate, as the effect is striking and the polished surfaces show off the luminous quality of the stone. The jade cup from a tomb in Luoyang dated 247 (cat. no. 14), similarly plain, can be regarded in the same light. Outside the metropolitan areas, the abstract style is also seen in wooden sculptures of the late

Han period found at Wuwei, Gansu, in the northwest (cat. nos. 17, 18). All these sculptures reflect a sensibility in many ways similar to that of the modernist movement in the twentieth century. In the case of jade, it seems fitting that the highly abbreviated carvings brought to a close a millennia-long tradition that began with simple, undecorated forms, now polished to a high gloss. The form of such cups as cat. no. 14 most likely derived from imported Roman glass cups such as those found at ancient market towns like Begram.[4] While there are as yet no archaeological finds of glass cups of similar shape in interior China, there are quite a number of Roman glass vessels, such as the marbled bottle in the present exhibition (cat. no. 13), found in late Han burials.

Throughout the two Han dynasties, there was constant contact with West and Central Asia by land and sea. It would appear that by the middle of the second century, there was a great increase of foreign populations in China, bringing to the metropolitan areas not only trade goods but music, dance, costumes, and furniture. This began in the time of Huandi (r. 147–67) and reached a peak during the reign of Lingdi (r. 168–89). The latter was said to be fond of "foreign dress, foreign hangings, foreign beds, foreign chairs, foreign food, foreign harps, foreign flutes, foreign dance," and this fashion was widespread among the nobility in the capital city.[5] The foreigners (*hu*) came from oasis towns like Qiuci (Kucha) on the Silk Road in Central Asia, from the Kushan empire beyond the Pamirs, and from as far as the Parthian or Iranian world. They would have brought with them exotic articles such as the Roman glass bottle. However, a greater influence on the material culture of the Han period came from the nomadic confederations on the Eurasian steppes north of the Silk Road. This is evident in the gilt-bronze case for an inkstone in the form of a crouching chimera, with inlays of semi-precious stones (cat. no. 5). Even more indicative of direct influence from the steppes are the openwork gold plaques and ornaments, cold-worked with decoration in granulation and stone inlays, that are found in Eastern Han tombs (cat. nos. 8, 9, 11, 12). The two chimeras and the ornamental plaque (cat. nos. 11, 12) are from the tomb of the aforementioned Liu Chang in Dingzhou, Hebei, an area where there had been a major nomadic presence even before the Han period. On the other hand, the ornamental plaque with a dragon and the ring in the shape of a crown (cat. nos. 8, 9) were found in a tomb dated to about A.D. 70 in Jiangsu Province in the southeast with no direct contact with North or Central Asia. This would suggest that such gold ornaments had found universal currency in China by, at the latest, the middle of the first century.

One particularly interesting piece is the image of a winged figure (known in China as a "feathered person," an immortal) riding a dragonlike creature (cat. no. 10). This motif can be traced in Chinese art to the first century B.C.[6] A close parallel is also seen on an openwork gold diadem with stone inlay from Kargali Valley, Kazakhstan, in Central Asia (fig. 2), and given the general date of second century B.C. to first century A.D.[7] The affinity between the images of the riders on the two gold pieces is unmistakable. The winged figure is from an Eastern Jin tomb (317–420), but the style and workmanship are exactly like the Eastern Han pieces. One of the benefits of recent archaeology is in drawing our attention to the influence from the steppes on the material culture of Han China.

During the late Han period, Central Asians and Indians brought into China more than foreign goods and customs. They also introduced Buddhism. Among the earliest and best-known translators of Buddhist scriptures in China was the Parthian An Shigao (An Qing), who arrived in Luoyang in the time of Huandi (r. 147–67). After more than twenty years of teaching and translating, when "towards the end of Lingdi's reign [168–89] there was unrest and chaos in [the metropolitan areas of] Guanzhong and Luoyang, he traveled to south of the [Yangzi] River."[8] Other Parthians and entire foreign communities must have moved south at the same time. The presence of foreigners in Jiangnan (south of the lower reaches of the Yangzi) in the third century is attested by porcelain figures such as cat. no. 105. The rider on the mythical animal, with foreign features and a beard, wears a

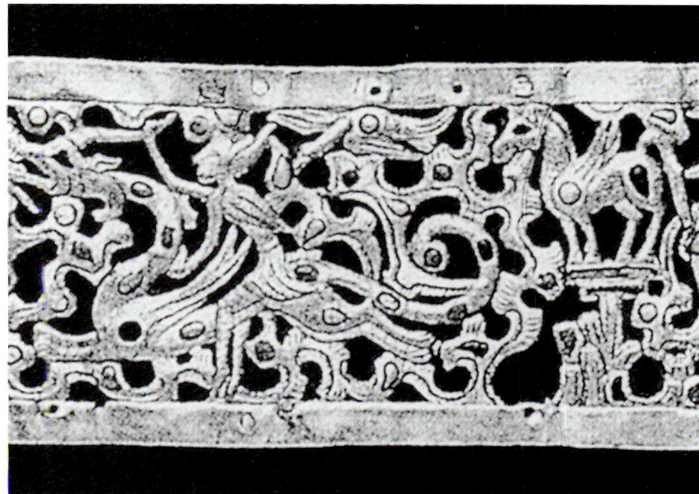

Figure 2. Section of an openwork diadem with image of feathered man. 2nd century B.C.–1st century A.D. Gold. Excavated at Kargali Valley, Almaty region, Kazakhstan

coat with a typically Parthian pattern of a rosette (here indicated by a circle) within each square of a lattice ground.

Writers on the early history of Buddhism in China often dwell on the lack of distinction between Buddhism and Daoism (itself a conglomeration of native beliefs). A graphic illustration can be seen on a third-century pottery jar (cat. no. 104) on which Buddhist and Daoist images freely mix (see also the essay by Angela Howard). There are other instances of indiscriminate association of Buddhist and Daoist images, the best known being the decoration on the "money trees" found in southwestern China.[9] That the southwest was one of the areas in China where the earliest Buddha image showed up can be attributed to overland commerce between India and China along the so-called southwestern Silk Road.[10] This early exchange provides a clue as to the origin of a form of headdress seen on a number of southwestern pottery figures of the late Han period (cat. no. 21). The style may have been slowly transmitted from India (fig. 3).

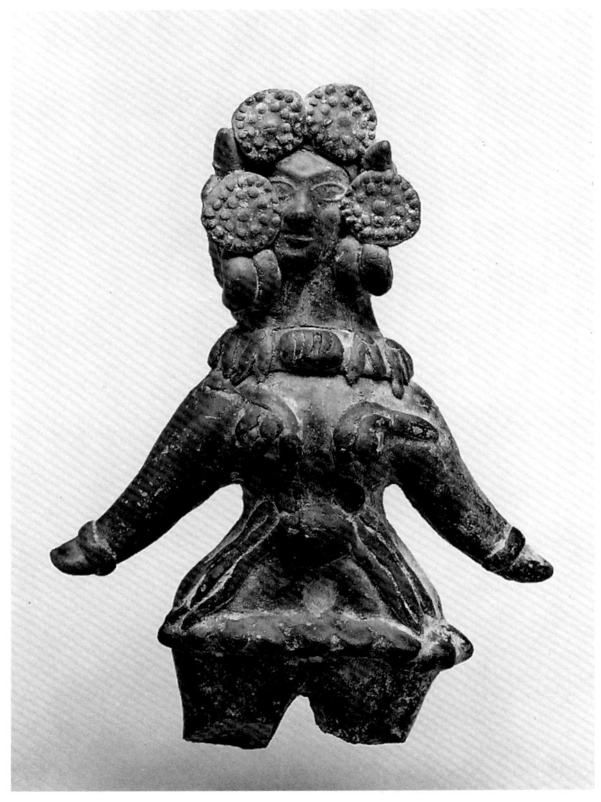

Figure 3. Female deity. India, 3rd–2nd century B.C. Terracotta, height 6¼ in. (15.9 cm). The Metropolitan Museum of Art. Anonymous Gift, 1978 (1978.539)

In the late Han period, calligraphy began to be consciously practiced as an independent art form. Certain leading scholars were also accomplished calligraphers. Cai Yong (133–192) was one such practitioner, and his copy of the standard texts of the classics was carved on stone tablets at the Imperial Academy in Luoyang in 175. Surviving Han inscriptions cut in stone have in recent centuries become standard models for calligraphy in the "clerical script," the style current in the Han period. An inscription on a stone stele dated 185 is one of the most celebrated examples of Han calligraphy (cat. no. 22). Known as the Stele for Cao Quan, it records the exploits of Cao Quan, including his participation in a military expedition to Sule (Kashgar) in Central Asia in the year 170. Until recently, the historical significance of the inscription has drawn little attention, as its fame rests on the elegance of the calligraphy. Nevertheless, the historical event it records is itself important in the study of the Han empire in Central Asia.[11] The Sule expedition—undertaken to quell unrest in the area—may well have been one of the last, if not the last, such military action of the Han dynasty before its demise.

The Third Century

The third century witnessed the collapse of social and political order in China. This caused immense suffering and untold loss of life, not to mention the destruction of buildings and monuments and the devastation of the countryside. However, in the wake of this upheaval, the yoke of orthodox Confucianism, imposed on the population by the Eastern Han government, was shattered, ushering in a period of free questioning and the unleashing of human imagination.

Unfortunately, it is only in literature that a substantial body of the creative works of this period has been preserved. The music is understandably lost—to be hinted at only in literary essays on the subject, of which the best known is that by Ji Kang (223–262).[12] His image, as conceived by a late fourth- to fifth-century artist, is depicted on the brick walls in tombs near Nanjing (fig. 4; cat. no. 113). In the visual arts, we have only what was painted on the walls of tomb chambers and objects interred with the deceased, most of them made expressly to provide for the afterlife. The tomb murals of the third century continued very much in the style of those of the Eastern Han, but pottery vessels from the Nanjing area and to the south (Wu state in the period of the Three Kingdoms) began to manifest delightful signs of breaking away from conventional forms, seen for example in the animal-shaped vessels (cat. nos. 107, 108).

The state of Wu (222–280), with its political and cultural centers in present-day Jiangsu Province, in the lower reaches of the Yangzi River, occupied one of the richest agricultural areas of China, its alluvial plains irrigated by many rivers and lakes. Fish and rice were the staples of the people and were plentiful when there was no war. The artistic and cultural traditions in this region go back to Neolithic times, when jade objects of exquisite design and workmanship were already being produced at several centers. Two of the great writers of the third century came from Wujun (Suzhou): Lu Ji (261–303) and his younger brother Lu Yun. Their grandfather Lu Xun was chancellor of Wu, and their father, Lu Kang, was grand marshal, both famous generals and statesmen. After the fall of the Wu state in 280, the two brothers were in Luoyang, capital of the Western Jin dynasty (265–316), which ruled over a briefly unified country. There Lu Ji wrote his immortal composition, the "Wen fu," a prose poem on the art of letters.[13] In it he deals with questions of form and content, originality, and the importance of feeling and imagination. He describes the creative process with remarkable reflective insight, in a diction that is both fanciful and precise. The poem is a clear manifestation of the awakening of artistic self-consciousness at this time in China, revered for centuries in Chinese literary circles as a composition that itself perfectly demonstrates what it advocates. It found a distant response in the twentieth century in the English critic and man of letters Herbert Read, who commented: "I do not think that Western psychology has added anything of value to the explanation it gives of the artistic process."[14]

In Luoyang, Lu Ji became enmeshed in the never-ending internecine wars between eight imperial princes. The princes succeeded in destroying some of the finest writers and scholars of the day, the government, and, ultimately, themselves, thus preparing the country for the most chaotic and miserable period in Chinese history, which occurred in the fourth century. Lu Ji, although descended from an illustrious lineage of military leaders, was not much of a soldier. Placed in command, against his own wishes, of a large army in one of the decisive battles of the civil wars, he met with ignominious defeat, as the professional officers, while they accused him of failing to lead them, refused to follow his orders. His patron Sima Ying, prince of Chengdu, listening to slander, put Lu Ji to death, at the age of forty-two. On the day he died, the heavens protested his innocence, "dark clouds gathered, trees were felled by strong winds, and the snow was a foot high. Officers and men wept."[15]

In the meantime, the prefecture of Bingzhou (present-day Shanxi Province) was being taken over by the Xiongnu, nomadic tribes who had settled in the Ordos (enclosed by the great loop of the Yellow River in northern Shaanxi) and Bingzhou. The Xiongnu confederation had earlier on, in the late third century B.C., established a mighty nomadic empire on the Mongolian steppe, but that had weakened considerably by the first century. Large groups of its population began to move west into Central Asia and south into North China. The power vacuum left behind by the Xiongnu in Mongolia was filled by a new confederation, known as the Xianbei, of which there were several branches. In the late third century, the branch called the Tuoba Xianbei made their headquarters in Shengle, north of Bingzhou. Led by the brothers Yituo and Yilu, the Tuoba Xianbei would make regular incursions into northern Bingzhou. However, when in 304 the Xiongnu of Bingzhou declared independence and began their uprising, the Tuoba Xianbei came to the aid of the Jin government forces and repeatedly defeated the Xiongnu. One of the most

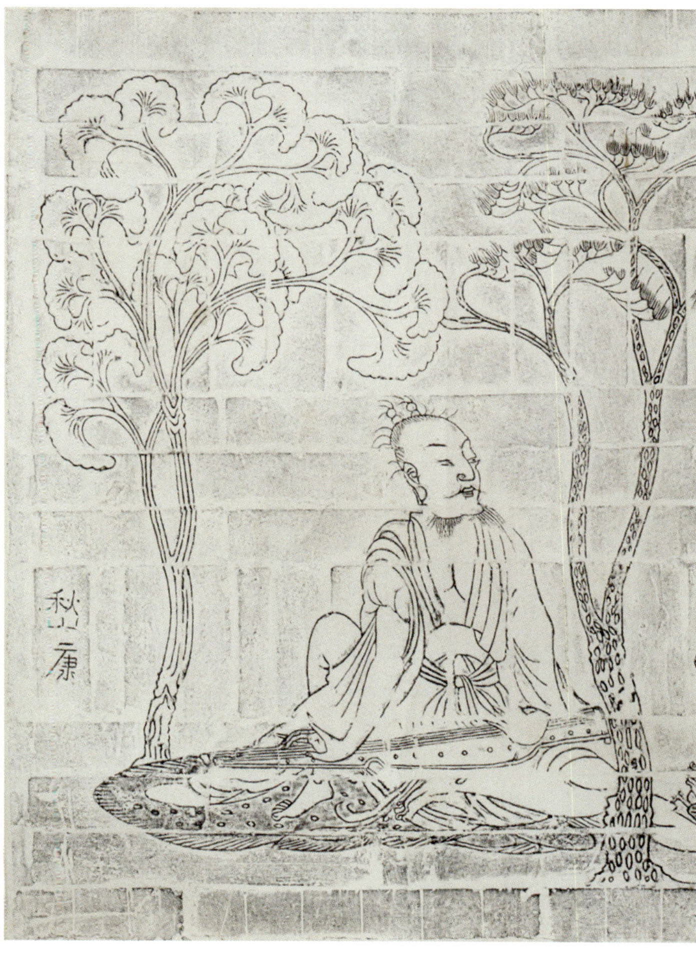

Figure 4. Ji Kang, one of the Seven Sages of the Bamboo Grove. Southern Dynasties (317–589). Rubbing from stamped brick. (See also cat. no. 113.)

important archaeological finds in Inner Mongolia in the last fifty years is the openwork gold ornament inscribed with Yituo's name (cat. no. 32). This object was found together with two gold seals granting honorific titles to Xianbei chiefs, one of which may have been given to Yituo as reward for his services to the Jin dynasty. (See cat. no. 83a for similar seals.)

The last Jin governor of Bingzhou was Liu Kun (271–318), who arrived in Jinyang, the capital of Bingzhou, in 307. By this time, all of Bingzhou was in the hands of the Xiongnu except Jinyang itself. In 311, the capital of the Jin dynasty, Luoyang, fell to the Xiongnu forces and the emperor was taken captive. Nevertheless, Liu Kun waged a desperate last-ditch defense of the isolated Jinyang—until 316, when his ally Yilu was murdered by his own son. In 317, the Jin court reestablished itself in Jiankang (Nanjing) in the south, and in 318 Liu Kun was killed by his erstwhile friend and "sworn brother," the Xianbei chief Duan Pidi.[16] With the death of Liu Kun, traditional Chinese rule in North China would be discontinued for about two centuries.

Liu Kun, like Lu Ji, was more of a poet than a soldier. He was a descendant of Liu Sheng, prince of Zhongshan (whose jade *bi* is illustrated in fig. 1). As a young man in Luoyang, he was a member of the beau monde, known as the "twenty-four friends," who gathered in the mansion of the fabulously rich Shi Chong. Li was proficient in all the fashionable pursuits, such as discoursing on Daoist philosophy and a kind of whistling, *xiao*, practiced by a group of socially and intellectually exalted people with Daoist tendencies. This whistle, which was supposed to produce a long piercing sound, may have been related to Daoist breathing exercises. Ruan Ji (210–263), one of the Seven Sages of the Bamboo Grove, was famous for his *xiao* and is portrayed in the Southern Dynasties tomb reliefs as engaged in this activity (fig. 5; cat. no. 113a). It was said that on one occasion, when Jinyang was under siege by an army of Xiongnu cavalry, "Liu Kun ascended a tall building by moonlight and emitted a clear *xiao*. When the Xiongnu soldiers heard it, they sighed sadly. In the middle of the night he played the *hujia* [a kind of oboe originating on the steppes, perhaps the predecessor of the *sona*]; the Xiongnu became homesick on hearing it. He played again at dawn and the Xiongnu lifted the siege and left."[17] This story was, of course, an apocryphal one, not without a quixotic element, but it is worth telling. For the life of Liu Kun, scion of one of the grand families of the old regime, brings into sharp focus the clash of two incompatible cultures, the one refined and tired, the other fresh and vigorous.

As mentioned above, from the middle of the first century, the nomadic tribes that replaced the Xiongnu in Mongolia were collectively called the Xianbei. Some or most of them may have come originally from the northeast—the extreme northeastern tip of Inner Mongolia. By the third century, there were a number of Xianbei confederations lined up on the northern border of China. Of these confederations, the most important were the Tuoba Xianbei, who were located north of Bingzhou and helped to defend Bingzhou against the rebellious Xiongnu, and the Murong Xianbei in the northeast, who occupied areas in modern Liaoning Province and expanded in the fourth century into Hebei, Shandong, and the western part of Henan. It should be pointed out that the names of the various peoples, or subdivisions of peoples, who came into China at this time do not indicate distinct ethnicities. Take the simplest and best-known example. When the Xianbei (not necessarily an ethnically or culturally homogeneous group) became the dominant power in Mongolia after the migration of the Xiongnu to the west and south, "the Xiongnu tribes who remained, estimated to be over one hundred households [extended families], all called themselves Xianbei. From this time on, the Xianbei grew strong."[18]

There are many examples of single families or individuals who became totally acculturated, or "naturalized," into another ethnic group—the Feng family, for example, who became rulers of the Northern Yan (409–436), a small state in the northeast founded on the ruins of the Murong Xianbei state of Later Yan (384–409). There were also people who moved between two cultures, such as the founder of the Northern Qi dynasty, Gao Huan (495–547). The Gao family claimed to have come originally from Bohai (in present-day Hebei), but "having lived for generations in the border areas in the north, they adopted the customs [of the northern peoples] and became identified with the Xianbei."[19] The situation with regard to the ethnic groups in China in the third to the early sixth century is not unlike that in Europe in the early Middle Ages, and many approaches employed in recent scholarship relating to ethnicity in early medieval Europe can be applied to China.[20]

When the Tuoba Xianbei began to participate in military and, to some extent, political activities in North China at the beginning of the fourth century, their social structure and way of life remained as those of traditional tribal societies on the steppes. This can be inferred from historical records and from their material culture—or what is left of it. In understanding

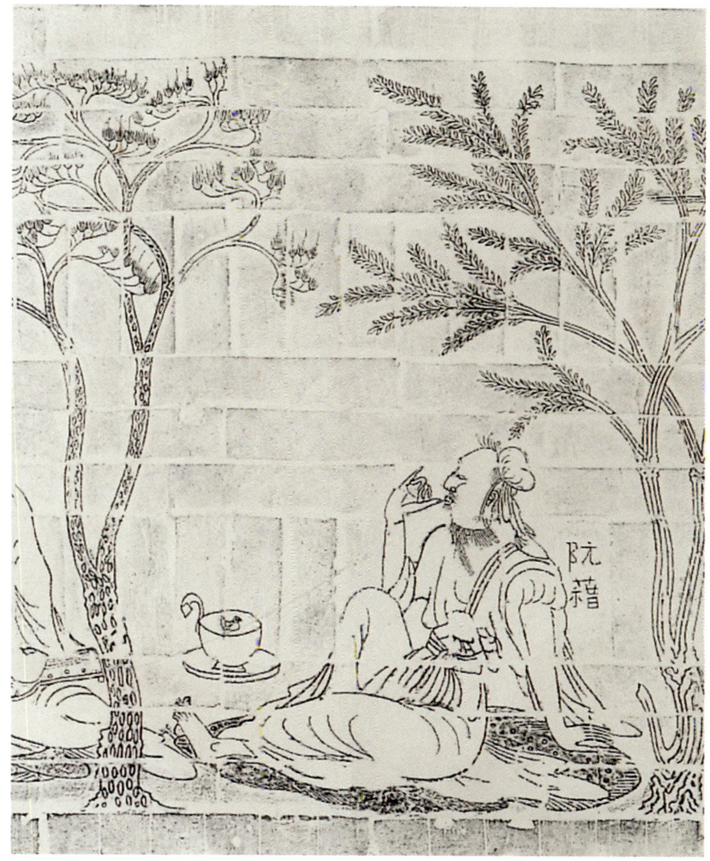

Figure 5. Ruan Ji, one of the Seven Sages of the Bamboo Grove. Southern Dynasties (317–589). Rubbing from stamped brick. (See also cat. nos. 113, 114.)

the latter, the archaeological find of the openwork gold plaque in this exhibition (cat. no. 32) is of great importance. The inscription of "Yituo gold" gives a terminus ante quem for the piece, as the aforementioned Xianbei prince Yituo died in 305.[21] What it indicates is that in the time of Yituo the vocabulary of the earlier Xiongnu culture was still seen on decorative plaques of the Xianbei. This can be illustrated if we compare Yituo's plaque with a Xiongnu example dating from the third to the second century B.C. (fig. 6). Not only is the treatment of the animals (wolves?) very similar, but the bodies are marked by drop-shaped raised bands, perhaps a decorative idiom that derived from beds for stone inlays. The continuation of certain cultural modes of the Xiongnu into the Xianbei period in Mongolia lends credence to the near-contemporary record that a large number of Xiongnu became Xianbei in the first century. The place where the plaque was found, Horinger (ancient Shengle), Inner Mongolia, also confirms that this area was one of the centers of Xianbei rule.

However, Xianbei decorative arts are not a simple continuation of Xiongnu tradition. One obvious trait in Xianbei gold plaques found in Inner Mongolia is the tendency toward abstraction or geometrization. The plaque (cat. no. 29), for instance, is an example of one of the most common gold objects found at Xianbei sites. It can be regarded as a composition in geometric forms suggesting three standing deer glancing backward. The tendency toward abstraction is not entirely a Xianbei innovation. As pointed out by the Russian archaeologist Sergei Minyaev, it had already started in the later Xiongnu period.[22]

One of the most intriguing aspects of Xianbei art is the possible influence from Bactria and other areas in Central Asia. The image on the openwork plaque (cat. no. 35) is that of a female figure held in the middle by two animals. The idea, if not the style and iconographic detail, is reminiscent of a gold ornament from Tillya-Tepe in northern Afghanistan (ancient Bactria) dating to about the first century B.C. (fig. 7). This motif has been identified by some scholars as "mistress of animals," with early antecedents farther west.[23] The Bactrian connection can also be discerned in finds of a later period, in Liaoning in northeastern China, and will be discussed in a later section.

Another object found in central Inner Mongolia also suggests long-distance connections: the gold loop-in-loop chain necklace with pendants in the form of weapons and shields (cat. no. 43). It has been the subject of a detailed study by Sun Ji.[24] For comparison, he points to a necklace carved on the North Gate of the Great Stupa at Sanchi in India, dating to about the first century (fig. 8). The Indian necklace, of long and short beads, also has pendants of weapons and shields together with Buddhist symbols, such as the double fish.

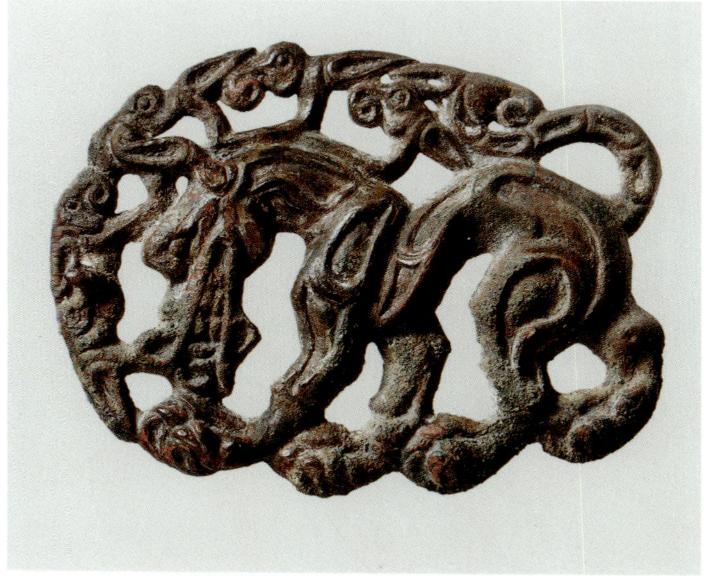

Figure 6. Belt buckle. Southern or eastern Siberia, 3rd–2nd century B.C. Bronze, height 3¼ in. (8.3 cm). The Metropolitan Museum of Art. Gift of Mr. and Mrs. Eugene V. Thaw, 2002 (2002.201.130)

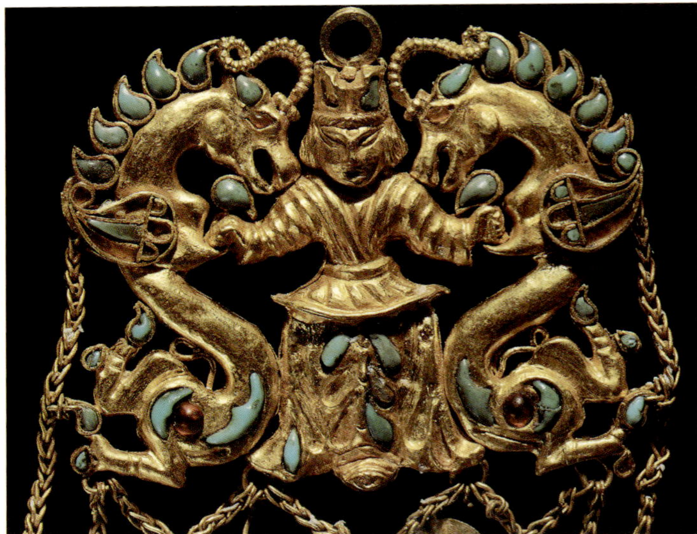

Figure 7. Pendant with female figure flanked by dragons (detail), ca. 1st century B.C. Gold, inlaid with garnet, lapis lazuli, and turquoise, length 4¾ in. (12.5 cm). Excavated at Tillya-Tepe, northern Afghanistan. National Museum of Afghanistan, Kabul

What is interesting is that in the Chinese version, the shields and some of the weapons have been sinicized. Compare, for example, the shields on the necklace with the shield held by the fourth-century tomb guardian from Nanjing (cat. no. 111). The halberd and comb ornaments are also Chinese. Sun Ji quotes from a record in the *Songshu* (History of the Song) that states: "In the Yuankang reign [291–99] of Emperor Huidi of the Western Jin dynasty, women wore 'five-weapon ornaments' and hairpins of gold, silver and tortoise-shell in the shape of axes and halberds." The *Songshu* was compiled in the late fifth century, but the origin of this account dates from at least the previous century.[25] And indeed, ax-shaped gold hairpins have been found in fourth-century burials in Nanjing in the south.[26] Then, as now, fashion traveled fast.

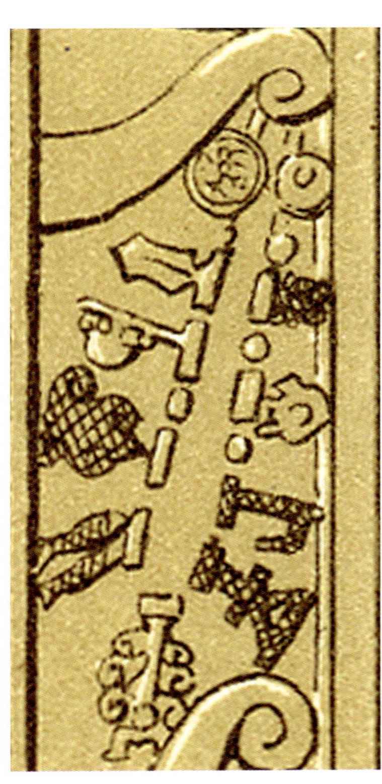

Figure 8. Drawing of necklace carved on the North Gate of the Great Stupa at Sanchi, India, ca. 1st century A.D.

The Migration Period in China, 4th–Early 5th Century

There were numerous movements of people within China that began at the turn of the third century, reached massive proportions in the fourth century, and ended only with the unification of the empire under the Sui. The movements were occasioned by different circumstances, and the end results were the redistribution and mixing of ethnic groups.

Early instances of ethnic mixing were the consequence of the recruitment of horse-riding nomadic tribes to serve in the cavalry of the contending factions in the civil wars that erupted at the end of the Han dynasty. This began with the aforementioned army of Dong Zuo, who came from Bingzhou to devastate Luoyang. Particularly famous were the horsemen of Wuhuan (an ethnic group related to the Xianbei), who formed a major component of the army of Cao Cao (155–220), founder of the Wei state (200–265) in the Three Kingdoms period. It should perhaps be noted that already in the Eastern Han, there were *hu* cavalry in the imperial army, albeit in relatively small numbers. In the year 59, when Liu Yan, prince of Zhongshan (whose jade *bi* and burial jades are in this exhibition, cat. nos. 6–8), set off to his fief from the capital, Luoyang, he was accompanied by a guard of one hundred *hu* cavalry.[27] It was during the Three Kingdoms period that nomadic tribes began to play a major role in internal warfare in China.

Another major cause of relocation of people in the fourth to early fifth centuries was nomadic-style warfare. Entire populations of conquered areas were moved to serve their new masters at their home base. Yet another cause of mass migration was famine that resulted from wars or weather.

The Wubao and Buqu

With the exception of the Former Liang (314–376), the states in the fourth century were formed when nomadic confederacies claimed lordship over territories they overran, in the process subduing minor warlords and capturing fortified estates (*wubao* or *wubi*). The *wubao* were set up by powerful local clans with a large number of retainers and dependents in various types and degrees of servitude, known collectively as *buqu*. The *buqu* in large *wubao* could number in the thousands, as peasants in surrounding areas sought protection and offered their services in times of unrest. Up to the middle of the fourth century, the size and importance of the territory under the rule of a warlord or the leader of a confederacy could be measured by the number of *wubao* within the territory. The *wubao* was not an entirely new phenomenon in the third century. Already in the Eastern Han, particularly toward the end of the dynasty, major landowners would fortify their estates with armed guards, in effect, private armies. Some of the most powerful landowners turned warlords at the fall of the Han, along with some provincial governors.

Among the most common objects found in late Han tombs are pottery figures of peasants and models of farm structures including watchtowers with armed guards. One of the most spectacular is the example excavated at Sangzhuang, Hebei (cat. no. 3). These models provide a glimpse of life within the large estates. Unfortunately, there are no such finds at fourth-century sites, which are few in number and sparse in content, valuable objects having been looted long ago. Nevertheless, we may assume that the architecture would not have changed significantly from the second to fourth century. For the representation of the *buqu* and their activities, we have to refer to objects from the fifth century.

The most informative objects in this regard are the set of impressed bricks from Dengxian, Henan (cat. no. 121). Dengxian was in the border area between the Northern (386–581) and Southern (420–589) Dynasties. It was inhabited by minority groups more or less indigenous to the region known collectively as the Man (to be discussed below). The archaeological finds from this area, officially ruled by the Southern Dynasties, are different from what one sees from tombs near Nanjing. On the Dengxian bricks, one sees the *buqu* engaged in various activities, such as bearing ceremonial objects (cat. no. 121d), playing music in a procession (cat. no. 121b), leading a caparisoned horse (cat. no. 121c), and parading with arms (cat. no. 121a). Music played on drums and horns was introduced into China from the steppe zone in the north sometime early in the Han dynasty, as military music but also to accompany official processions. In later developments, the "drum and horn" music also included wind and other percussion instruments.[28] The chief functions of the *buqu* were farming and fighting, as we know from contemporary texts, but they also served in other capacities, as demonstrated by the Dengxian bricks.

The Sixteen Kingdoms

The history of the Sixteen Kingdoms period (304–439) is complex in its details, but can be roughly summarized. For most of the fourth century, Gansu in the west was ruled by the Zhang family of the Former Liang dynasty. The northeast (Liaoning Province) was the stronghold of the Murong Xianbei of the various Yan states. The area between was early on dominated by a confederacy built by Shi Le (274–333), who founded the Later Zhao state (328–351), and subsequently by Fu Jian (338–385), of the Former Qin dynasty (351–394), who briefly unified all of North China by conquering the Yan in the east and the Liang in the west. Finally, all of North China came under the rule of the Northern Wei in 439.

Shi Le is one of the most interesting characters in Chinese history. He was a heroic warrior, a wily politician, and an able ruler. He was a Jie, a people of mixed origins mostly from Central Asia with possible connections to Sogdiana.[29] His life story includes many of the typical events in Chinese history and society at that time—but on an epic scale. Born in Bingzhou, he did odd jobs in his youth, including work as a farmhand. In his twenties, during a time of famine, he was sold with a group of people, "two barbarians [*hu*] to a cangue," from Bingzhou to east of the Taihangshan (i.e., Hebei) by Sima Teng, Liu Kun's predecessor as governor of Bingzhou. He was soon freed by his new master and, starting with a group of eight horsemen that grew to eighteen, he formed an army that, in a few years, swelled to more than a hundred thousand men. This follows a classic mode of the explosive formation of nomadic confederations in the steppes, carried into China. (It is also seen in the formation of the Huns in Europe.)[30] In 311, Shi Le vanquished the main body of the military force of the Jin, sounding the death knell of the Jin dynasty in North China, subsequently known as the Western Jin (265–316). By 329, he had overthrown the state of Former Zhao (304–329), ruled by the Xiongnu to whom he owed nominal allegiance when he started his campaign, and claimed sovereignty over all of China, except the northeast. After entering Chang'an, Shi Le moved one hundred and fifty thousand Di and Qiang (peoples native to the area surrounding Chang'an) to his power base in Hebei and an equal number (mostly Di) to Fangtou, south of Ye, the eventual capital of the state of Later Zhao, which he founded.

Of all the capital cities of the Sixteen Kingdoms that found a brief existence in the fourth century, it is only the city of Ye of which we have a contemporary description, albeit one that has survived in fragments. This is the *Ye zhong ji*, by the Eastern Jin writer Lu Xiang. The version in use today has been reassembled from various sources by eighteenth-century scholars. It consists of anecdotes on the court of Shi Hu (295–349), successor to Shi Le as ruler of Later Zhao, who moved the capital to Ye and transformed the palace grounds into a veritable "pleasure dome." Shi Hu was typical of another type of ruler in the fourth to sixth centuries in both North and South China. He abused every privilege of the sovereign to the fullest. He never stopped large-scale construction work; took over vast tracts of agricultural land for his hunting ground; and inflicted cruel punishments on his subjects for his sadistic pleasure. The *Ye zhong ji* is filled with descriptions of Shi Hu's extravagances. These provide valuable information for historians and art historians, especially as hardly any remains of the material culture of this period have so far been found archaeologically.[31] For example, there are names of luxury silk textiles manufactured locally—like all nomadic, as in all early, empires the finest craftsmen were concentrated in the capital—that probably refer to several types of silk fabrics found in the desert ruins of Xinjiang (see the essay by Zhao Feng). The description of the use of mica with gold foil decoration for fans, windows, and screens provides a clue as to the original use of the bits of mica found in the several burial sites of the Sixteen Kingdoms—all looted clean of whole objects long ago. On his dining table, Shi Hu used a double-deck turntable (the earliest lazy Susan?) decorated with inlay and holding one hundred and twenty dishes. The patterns are so fine they can be seen only on close inspection.[32]

When the Later Zhao collapsed in 351, communities previously moved from their native places were allowed or forced to return to their homeland. It was said that millions were on the move. "Their paths crossed, they robbed and killed each other, many died of starvation and disease, and only two or three out of ten would eventually arrive at their destination. All of [North] China was in chaos, and there was no more farming."[33]

Some of the communities being relocated organized themselves into armies and fought their way home. Of these, the most spectacularly successful was that of the Di people from Fangtou (referred to above), who, after they arrived back in Guanzhong (the area surrounding Chang'an) established the Former Qin state (351–394) which eventually overran all of North China. They vanquished the remnants of the Jie and the Murong Xianbei in the northwest, drove back the Tuoba Xianbei in Bingzhou to Mongolia, and annexed the Former Liang state in Liangzhou. These feats of conquest were accomplished in the years 370 to 376 under the brilliant leadership of Fu Jian (338–385), who was elected chief by the Di people during their exodus from Fangtou back to Guanzhong.

In Chang'an, Fu Jian (r. 357–85) declared himself emperor of Former Qin. For the first decade of his rule, there was peace in Guanzhong—the first time for one and a half centuries—and the land was reclaimed. By 382, he was impatient to unify all of China. He sent an expeditionary force to Central Asia under the command of Lü Guang (338–399) that reached as far as Qiuci (Kucha), and he himself prepared to invade the Eastern Jin in the south. In 383, he assembled an ethnically mixed army said to be a million strong, composed of both cavalry and infantry. He had advanced nearly four hundred miles toward the front before the troops from Liangzhou (Gansu) had reached Chang'an, where he had started out. Before the entire army could be deployed, he suffered a crushing defeat on the banks of the Fei River near where it flows into the Huai (to the west of Huainan). This was the famous battle of Feishui, which ensured that South China would be independent for another two hundred years, and resulted in the immediate fragmentation of the north.

Fu Jian's timing was unfortunate. Had he delayed his action for a few years the result might have been quite different. As it was, his ramshackle troops met the resistance of a well-disciplined army of some eight thousand led by seasoned military officers and members of the Xie family under the general command of Xie Shi (327–388), younger brother of the chief minister of Eastern Jin, Xie An (320–385). Among the field commanders was Xie Xuan (343–388), a nephew, who directed the battle at Feishui. The Xie family was at that time perhaps the most prominent of the grand families of the Eastern Jin, with Xie An at the head. The aristocratic chief minister remained unflinchingly calm from the time the news of Fu Jian's advance reached Jiankang, the capital, to the moment of victory. He played *weiqi* (chess, known in the West generally by the Japanese name of *go*) with Xie Xuan before sending him off to battle and gave few instructions. He was playing *weiqi* when news of the great victory reached him. He read the dispatch without changing his expression and put it away. When his friend asked what the news was, he replied, "The children drove the bandits away."[34] Xie An was fond of music. When not managing the affairs of state, he could have been quite at home in the company of people such as those portrayed in the brick reliefs of Nanjing (cat. no. 113a, b).

In 383, Lü Guang was in Qiuci (Kucha) and ignorant of Fu Jian's defeat. He had every intention of staying in this cosmopolitan oasis town, but at the urging of his officers and the Kuchean Indian Buddhist monk Kumārajiva (350–410) he began his return with "twenty thousand camels carrying treasures from foreign lands," as well as entertainers, exotic birds and animals, and more than ten thousand fine horses.[35] Whether or not this is an accurate record, it does indicate the tremendous wealth and cultural richness that accumulated in oasis towns on the Silk Road in Central Asia at this time. Qiuci was also a center of learning—at least Buddhist learning. Kumārajiva accompanied Lü Guang back to Guzang (Wuwei, Gansu), where Lü stopped. Kumārajiva made his way in 401 to Chang'an, then under the rule of Yao Xing (r. 394–416) of the Later Qin dynasty (384–417), which had been founded by his father Yao Chang (r. 384–94), leader of the Qiang. Kumārajiva, whose fame as a Buddhist scholar preceded him in China, translated many sutras in Chang'an, and by 405, he had been made state preceptor. There were constantly a thousand monks studying with him. With the ruler, Yao Xing, and his court as models, "nine out of ten families became Buddhists" in the Chang'an area, and spread to the provinces (of the state of Later Qin).[36]

If there is no extant object that can be positively identified as having been brought to interior China by Lü Guang, it is still an intriguing thought that some of the fourth-century objects of Central Asian origin (such as cat. nos. 63, 64) found in the vicinity of Pingcheng (present-day Datong), the capital of the Northern Wei (386–534), which annexed Liangzhou in 439, could have been part of the original loot plundered by Lü Guang's army. In any case, the fourth and fifth centuries saw unprecedented activity along the Silk Road in Xinjiang, north and south of the Tarim Basin.

Gansu

During the fourth century, what is today Gansu Province, known as Liangzhou at the time, had a rather distinctive cultural history. It began in the year 301, when the Western Jin ruling house was in the thick of internecine strife and the dynasty was coming to an end. A court official, Zhang Gui (254–314), asked for and was granted the governorship of Liangzhou—where his family came from, although he himself grew up in Luoyang. His father served at the Jin court where he also began his own career. It was said that he sought the post to secure the safety of himself and his family. Liangzhou under Zhang Gui's rule enjoyed relative peace and prosperity, although initially Zhang had to placate powerful local families and quell uprisings from "minorities," such as the Qiang and the Xianbei. In the meantime, central China was descending into chaos. It is well known that the Gansu Corridor occupied the final stretch of the Silk Road, which led to Chang'an—or to Pingcheng in the latter part of the fifth century. And certainly there are archaeological finds of objects of Central Asian origin in Gansu Province, especially in the vicinity of Guzang (Wuwei), the capital of Liangzhou (e.g., cat. no. 90).

What is less generally known is that Liangzhou was the place at which much of traditional Chinese culture was preserved when the rest of China was devastated by war, first between factions of the Jin imperial family and then between the various states established by peoples of nomadic origin.[37] This was the result of the steady migration of peoples from central China to the region throughout the Han period and, more important still, the large number of scholar gentry who took refuge there at the final breakup of the Jin empire. The new immigrants reinforced a tradition of learning that had been established in Liangzhou during the Han period. In the area around Wuwei, a large quantity of Han texts of Confucian classics written on wooden strips and bamboo were found in the last century.[38] The art of calligraphy, which was associated with learning, also flourished in Liangzhou, particularly at Dunhuang. Among the most famous calligraphers in the late Han and Wei–Jin periods were the Dunhuang scholars Zhang Zhi (d. 192) and Suo Jing (239–303). Although the best-known scholar-calligraphers were educated in the capital, Luoyang, and served at the imperial court, there is also evidence of fine calligraphy by unknown scribes in Dunhuang itself. Buddhist texts (of the fourth century) on paper found at Dunhuang are often written in an elegant hand in the standard script of the time (see cat. no. 87). The prominence of Dunhuang in learning and in the art of calligraphy attests indirectly to the prosperity of the city as the chief gateway to the Chinese world. It was the combination of traditional learning and openness to the West that made the reincorporation of Liangzhou into North China in the year 439 such an important event in Chinese political and cultural history. This development will be discussed in a later section.

One aspect of the art of Gansu may be unique to the region. This is the abstract style of the wooden sculpture that is usually found in the vicinity of Wuwei, such as the "unicorn" in this exhibition (cat. no. 81). However, as mentioned earlier in connection with jade carving in the late Han period (cat. nos. 15, 16), there was also a tendency toward abstraction in the sculptural arts of central China at the same time. There may yet be other sources of the Gansu abstract style that remain to be discovered.

The Northeast, Late 4th–Early 5th Century

In the fourth century, as a consequence of political divisions, traffic between Liangzhou and interior China was necessarily curtailed. But the steppe route leading from Central Asia to the Mongolian plain and ultimately to Korea continued to flourish, and activity seemed to reach a peak in the late fourth century. In this connection, the finds from the tomb of Feng Sufu in Beipiao, Liaoning, are of particular interest.

Feng Sufu (d. 415) was the brother of Feng Ba (r. 409–30), ruler of the state of Northern Yan (407–436). The Northern Yan had been established from the remnants of the Later Yan (384–409) of the Murong Xianbei, which for a brief time took over most of eastern central China after Fu Jian's Former Qin empire broke up in 383. The Northern Yan suffered heavy defeats at the hands of the Tuoba Xianbei who came south to reoccupy Bingzhou in 396 and made Pingcheng (Datong) the capital of their state of (Northern) Wei in 398. In 397, the Murong Xianbei retreated to their home base in Longcheng, present-day Chaoyang in the western part of Liaoning Province. After the inevitable power struggle and assassinations, the house of Murong was finished. The first non-Xianbei ruler of the state after the assassination of the last Murong ruler was Gao Yun, whose family was from Koguryŏ,[39] the kingdom in the northern part of the Korea Peninsula. After the assassination of Gao Yun by the captains of his own guard in 409, Feng Ba, a Han Chinese who served the Murong Xianbei together with Gao Yun, declared himself the ruler.

By this time, ethnic labeling is essentially arbitrary and almost pointless. Gao Yun was the adopted son of Murong Bao (the second ruler of the Later Yan who led the retreat to Longcheng; r. 396–98) and was known as Murong Yun for most of his life. Feng Ba's family was originally from Hebei and was technically Han, but he grew up among the Murong Xianbei and was a thoroughly acculturated Xianbei. The Murong Xianbei tribes, in turn, after living with Han Chinese for two centuries, had picked up many Han Chinese ways. In fact, the term "Murong" as a name for an ethnic group was soon to disappear.

The contents of Feng Sufu's tomb, or what remained when the tomb was excavated in 1965, demonstrates well the rich, if undigested, cultural mix that was available to the Murong Xianbei at the end of their political run. Feng had himself buried with seals bearing all the Chinese-style titles conferred on him during his life, including one that he received before his brother usurped the throne. His tomb furniture includes an inkstone and a piece of ink, commonly found in tombs of Chinese scholar-officials beginning in the Eastern Han. The storage jars and cooking utensils are mostly Chinese in style, except the bronze cauldron with cutout ring foot and iron lid and handle (cat. no. 40). This cauldron is based on an archetypal steppe vessel, modified by the addition of a handle. The animal-shaped vessel (cat. no. 39, perhaps a chamber pot) is similar to many vessels that are found in burials in South China dating from the third to the fifth century—except that the southern versions are all pottery. The pair of stirrups (cat. no. 41) are among the earliest that have been found in China. They are similar to those found in Korea dating from about the same period and may well be among the earliest stirrups known.[40] The luxury articles are imports from the West, such as the jade bowl (cat. no. 38) and the glass bowl (cat. no. 42), although the former could possibly be of local manufacture.

Also in Feng Sufu's tomb are three gold hat ornaments. Two of them are more or less the same shape and may have been attached to a gold frame also found in the tomb (fig. 9). This type of hat ornament, known as the *dang*, originated in the Han period and was worn by senior court officials.[41] The usual image on the *dang* is a cicada. It is interesting that one of the ornaments (cat. no. 37) has, instead of the cicada, a Buddha image in repoussé with attached circular gold disks. This image demonstrates that Buddhism had spread to Yan territory in the northeast by the early fifth century, a fact that we have so far known only from literature.[42] The disks demonstrate unmistakable contact with Bactria, as can be seen by comparison with the gold crown from Tillya-Tepe, in northern Afghanistan, dating from the first century (fig. 11).[43]

Another ornament from a contemporary tomb near Feng Sufu's, north of Longcheng, is entirely in the style of Tillya-Tepe, combining Nomadic and Bactrian elements (cat. no. 36).

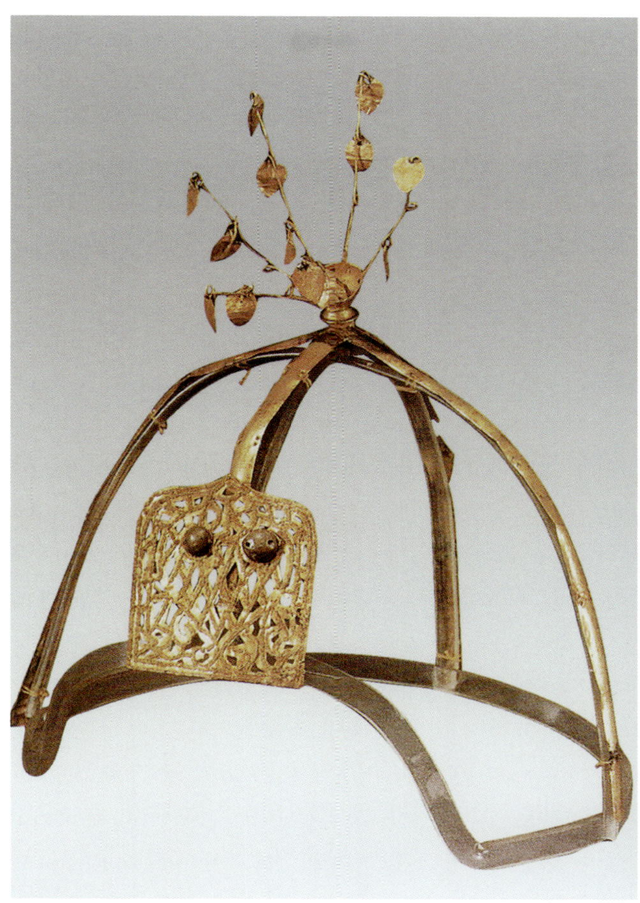

Figure 9. Hat frame, reconstructed with *dang* ornament. Northern Yan dynasty (407–436). Gold, height 2¾ in. (7.1 cm). Hat frame excavated at Beipiao, Liaoning Province

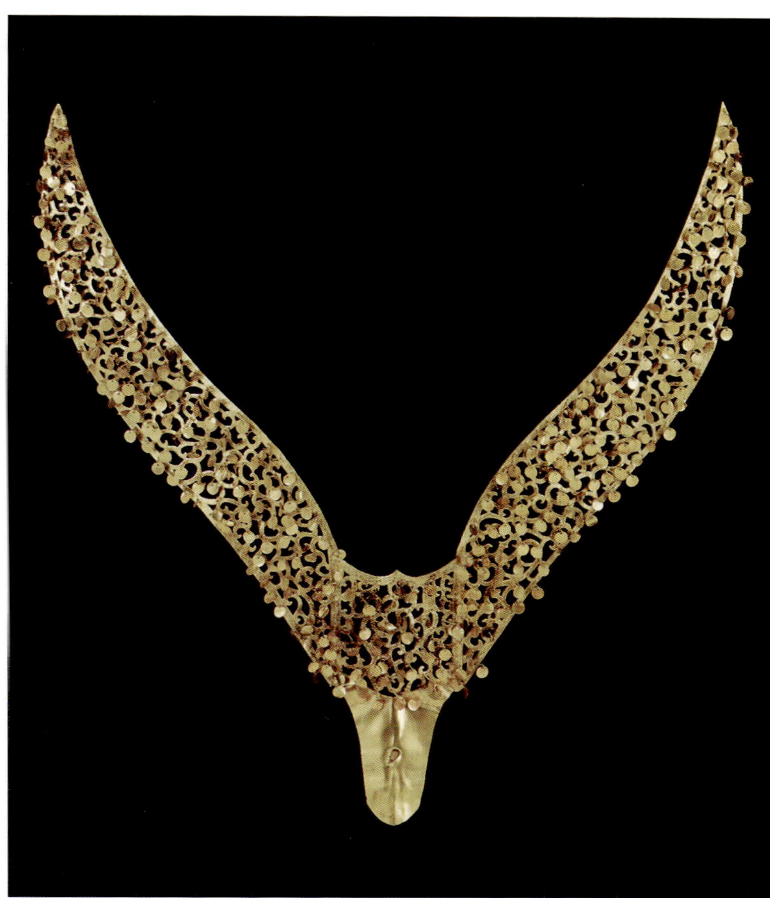

Figure 10. Crown ornament. Silla, second half of the 5th century. Gold, height 17¾ in. (45 cm). Excavated at Ch'ŏnmach'ong, Kyŏngju, North Kyŏngsang Province, South Korea. Kyŏngju National Museum

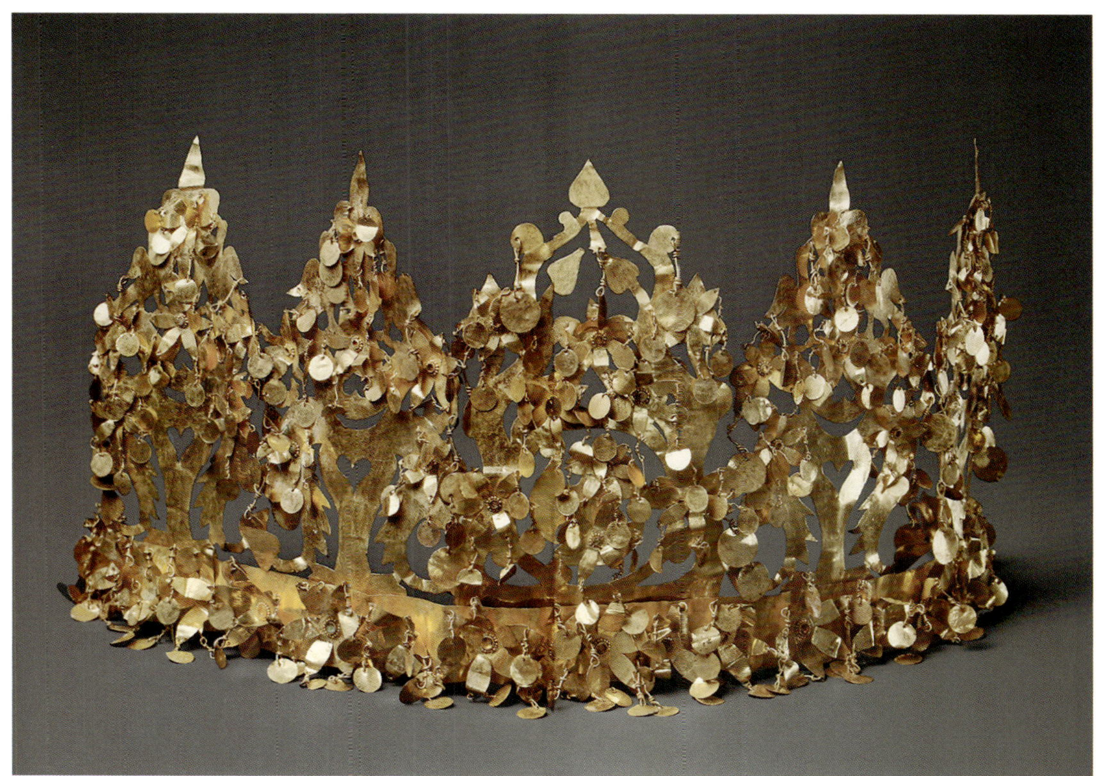

Figure 11. Crown. 1st century A.D. Gold, height 5¼ in. (13 cm). Excavated at Tillya-Tepe, northern Afghanistan. National Museum of Afghanistan, Kabul

Metalwork of this type in gold and silver has been found in Kyŏngju, South Korea, in Silla tombs dating from the fifth to the sixth century. One example is the crown ornament from the Ch'ŏngmach'ong, the Tomb of the Heavenly Horse (fig. 10; note that the central part of the ornament is framed like that of the *dang* of the Northern Yan). There are also southern versions of the gold cicada ornament. An example is the *dang* found in 1998 in the fourth-century Gao family cemetery in Nanjing.[44] The workmanship is very similar to the gold ornament with a design of a winged figure in the exhibition (cat. no. 35).

The Fifth Century

The early fifth century saw the gradual consolidation of political power in both North and South China, leading to the period known as Northern and Southern Dynasties (420–589). In the north, the Tuoba Xianbei of the Northern Wei dynasty, having established their capital in Pingcheng in 398, began to take over the small states that emerged after the collapse of Fu Jian's Qin empire in 383—with the exception of the Southern Yan (400–410) in the Shandong Peninsula. Particularly important was the conquest of the Northern Yan in 436 and the Northern Liang in Gansu in 439. In the south, the military commander Liu Yü (363–422), after quelling revolts in all parts of the Eastern Jin and having recovered large areas north of the Huai River and in Sichuan, former territories of the Qin, assumed power and declared himself emperor in the year 420, establishing the Song dynasty (420–479).

The leader of the Tuoba Xianbei who moved the capital of the Northern Wei to Pingcheng in 398 was Tuoba Gui (371–409). In 399, he declared himself emperor of Wei, built palaces and temples to his ancesters, practiced Confucianist rites, and generally behaved like a Chinese emperor. He also began the process of creating an administration based on Han-style bureaucracy superimposed on a tribal system. In all this he was advised by Han Chinese officials.[45] It would take another hundred years before the tribal element in the Wei administration was officially suppressed. In the meantime, nomadic-style warfare continued, with the riches of the conquered states and a large number of their people, especially craftsmen, taken back to the capital in Pingcheng. The one important difference from previous practice on the steppes is that an administration would be set up in the newly conquered lands, answerable to the government in Pingcheng. This process continued until 439, when the Northern Wei army, under the command of Tuoba Tao (r. 424–52), a grandson of Tuoba Gui, overran Liangzhou.

Tuoba Gui was the grandson of Shiyijian (320–after 376), a ruler who had established the Dai state in 338, ruling over southern central Mongolia and northern Shanxi, with his capital at Shengle (present-day Horinger, Inner Mongolia). Shiyijian was in turn the grandson of a younger brother of Yituo, whose name appears on the openwork gold plaque in this exhibition (cat. no. 32). Shiyijian was one of the victims of Fu Jian's campaign of conquest, and in 376 he was captured and taken to Chang'an, Fu Jian's capital, together with his grandson Gui.[46] The fifty-six-year-old former ruler of Dai was sent to the Imperial Academy "to learn etiquette,"[47] and his five-year-old grandson presumably also received a Chinese education. Certainly, Tuoba Gui displayed tendencies and habits that indicate strong Chinese influence. He was fond of Daoist thought and would give lectures on Daoism to an audience composed of members of the imperial family and senior officials.[48] He also took drugs—the *hanshisan* (swallow-cold powder),[49] a mineral preparation that was taken as a stimulant—a common practice of upper-class Chinese in the south. This habit may have contributed to his death at the relatively early age of thirty-eight.

From about 440 to 493, before the Northern Wei capital was transferred to Luoyang, Pingcheng was the political, economic, and cultural center of North China. Section 3 of the exhibition provides a glimpse of the material culture of this period in Pingcheng. The two pottery guardian figures (cat. no. 48) can be regarded as the northern versions of the type of armored guards that are found in Western Jin burials in Luoyang dating from the late third century, just as the guardian warrior (cat. no. 111) is a southern derivative of the same. The pair of Northern Wei figures indicate an early adaptation of Chinese burial customs, but the sculptural style and facial features of the figures betray a different culture. The menacing expressions are obviously meant to serve an apotropaic purpose, perhaps reflecting the northerners' greater awareness of the dark world of spirits. The fearful aspect is absent in the southern version, which is probably no more than a representation of a guard in real life. Moreover, the southern figure wears an amused expression and has an air of nonchalance, perhaps a reflection of the craftsman's indulging in a little creative liberty.

Another type of Northern Wei tomb guardian is the pair of mystical beasts, one with an animal head and the other a human head (cat. nos. 54, 55—not found together but contemporaneous and from the same area). Again, they derive from a Western Jin prototype (fig. 12), except that by the fifth century in the north, such creatures had evolved into a pair of fantastic beasts with human and animal heads. These types of guardian beasts went through several stages of metamorphosis and, by the early Tang, in the seventh century, had taken spectacular forms (cat. nos. 178, 179). During this same period, the warrior guardian would transmogrify, under Buddhist influence (see cat. no. 231), into a fully armored warrior trampling on a demon of mixed human and beastly form (cat. no. 180; see also cat. no. 230). Meanwhile, both types of tomb guardian all but disappeared in the south after the Eastern Jin (317–420). The divergent development of tomb guardians in the north and in the south is also a reflection of cultural differences in the two regions. Northerners, being more mindful of demons and spirits—perhaps a carryover from shamanistic beliefs from the steppes—were more inclined to making serious efforts to protect the dead from undesirable influences. Southerners simply continued the age-old practice of providing for the daily life of the deceased in the afterlife.

Another major category of pottery figure found in Northern Wei tombs in Datong was foreign entertainers—musicians, dancers, and acrobats (cat. nos. 51–53). Central Asian entertainers would all have come in through Gansu—under the control of the Northern Wei after 439. The presence of Central Asian entertainers in China was not new. Already by the end of the Han dynasty, Emperor Lingdi was said to be "fond of foreign [*hu*] dress, foreign hangings, foreign beds, foreign chairs, foreign food, foreign harps, foreign flutes, foreign dance," so that "the nobles in the capital [Luoyang] all competed to emulate [him]."[50] The Northern Wei figures are the first representations of such Central Asian entertainers in China.

The love of western culture and fashion provides the background for another group of objects found in fifth-century tombs at Datong. These are the silver and gilt-bronze vessels, all of foreign (Central Asian) manufacture (cat. nos. 58–64). These are discussed in the essay by Boris Marshak. It is sufficient to note here that they are of Central Asian origin and predate the year 493, when the capital was moved to Luoyang. It is at present possible to make only a reasonable

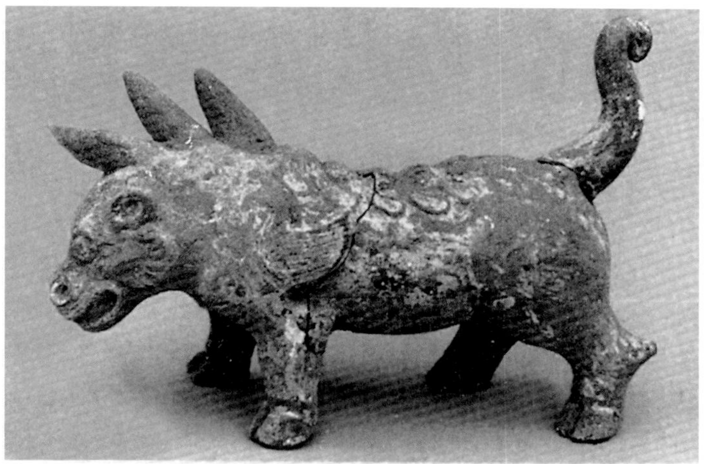

Figure 12. Tomb guardian. Western Jin dynasty (265–316). Earthenware, length 13⅝ in. (34.5 cm). Excavated at Yanshi, Henan Province

guess at the origin of these pieces from internal evidence—i.e., style, motifs, construction, and inscriptions. As to the mode and route of importation, there is as yet insufficient evidence from which to draw any conclusions.

Judging from the contents of the tomb of Feng Sufu and its relevance to archaeological finds at sites in Silla, in Korea, it can be seen that the steppe route was active until at least the early part of the fifth century. After the Northern Wei conquest of Gansu in 439, the Silk Road in Central Asia was wide open and must have been the main conduit for articles traded into China. There is also the possibility that some of what we are now finding in Datong are the remnants of Lü Guang's massive loot (having been preserved in Guzang [Wuwei] in the meantime), especially since some of the metal and the glass articles (cat. nos. 65, 66) can be dated to the fourth century or even earlier, again from internal evidence. One interesting observation we can make about the finds of Central Asian metalwork in Datong is that the major group of five pieces (cat. nos. 58–61, 63) was found at a habitation site south of the old city of Pingcheng rather than in tombs.[51] By analogy with the future capital at Luoyang where the quarters for foreigners were situated in the southern suburbs,[52] one may conjecture that the arrangements for foreigners at Pingcheng were the same.

Among the objects found at late fifth-century sites in Datong are some of local manufacture that show distinct western (i.e., Central Asian) influence. Examples are the "inkstone" (cat. no. 72), found at the same location as the five metal objects referred to in the last paragraph, and the pole base (cat. no. 71) from the tomb of Sima Jinlong (d. 484) and his first wife (d. 475), a burial of unusually large size. Like nearly all ancient tombs in North China, it was pillaged long ago. Nevertheless, what remained for archaeologists to find in 1965 was still quite substantial, at least in numbers. One can assume that the looters were interested only in objects of high value as the rest were left, but in great disorder. This tomb deserves special attention for various reasons, particularly because it reveals several important aspects of the art and culture of the Northern Wei at the height of its power and wealth and on the eve of the capital's relocation to the ancient city of Luoyang in the Central Plain.

Sima Jinlong was the son of Sima Chuzhi (309–464) and a princess of the Northern Wei imperial house. Chuzhi, a member of the extensive Jin imperial family, defected to Northern Wei in 419 at the collapse of the Eastern Jin dynasty. Jinlong's second wife was the daughter of Juqu Mujian, the second ruler of the Northern Liang (in Gansu) and the princess Wuwei, sister of Taiwudi. She was thus related by marriage to the Grand Empress Dowager Wenming (442–490), of whom she was a favorite. At the time of Sima Jinlong's death, Wenming was de facto ruler of the Northern Wei. The lavishness of Sima Jinlong's burial can be explained as a favor conferred on his widow by the empress dowager rather than on himself. In any case, we can assume that the contents of Sima Jinlong's tomb are fairly representative of those of the Xianbei aristocracy of the Northern Wei in the late Pingcheng era.

The majority of the finds in the tomb of Sima Jinlong and his wife are not different in kind from other Northern Wei tombs of the same time. Most of the hundreds of objects are pottery figures of servants, entertainers, animals, and tomb guardians. What is unusual is that most of the pottery figures are glazed (see, for example, cat. no. 70). They are the earliest known glazed pottery figures after the Han period. Another indication of the special status of Sima Jinlong is that the bricks of the tomb were made to order, as they bear a stamped inscription to that effect.[53]

The one object that has drawn most attention among academic art historians is the fragmentary wooden screen with painting on a red lacquer ground (cat. no. 69 is the best-preserved panel). This is because of certain striking similarities between the screen and a painting (originally a handscroll) in the British Museum entitled *Admonitions of the Instructress to the Court Ladies*, traditionally attributed to the legendary painter Gu Kaizhi (ca. 345–ca. 406), who was active in Later Eastern Jin in the second half of the fourth to the early years of the fifth century. The association of the name of Gu Kaizhi with the *Admonitions* scroll is no longer credible.[54] What the Sima Jinlong screen and the scroll painting together demonstrate is that in the fifth century there were "copybooks" for the representation of common themes in painting. (We shall see more examples in the sixth century.)

As to the subject matter of the lacquer screen, the scenes are all illustrations of Confucian virtues such as filial piety and loyalty, following the Eastern Han ideology that paintings should be instructive. The pictorial style is also somewhat old-fashioned for the late fifth century, at least when compared with contemporary pictorial style in the south (see cat. no. 113). Nevertheless, the painter of the screen did "modernize" at least one detail—the depiction of the palanquin bearers. Their attire of a short tunic and tied-up trouser legs is the standard form of dress for physical work and military action at this time.[55] No doubt originally introduced into China by nomadic peoples from the north, the style was also adopted in areas outside the domain of the Northern Dynasties (see, for example, the images of servants on the impressed bricks from Dengxian, Henan [cat. no. 121]).

Of greater interest are the decorative patterns on the objects from the tomb of Sima Jinlong, as they throw light on the migration of decorative motifs across Asia in the fifth century. The first pattern to notice is the palmette scroll, seen on the sides of the pole base (fig. 13; cat. no. 71) and also on the stone mortuary couch (fig. 14), the major item of furniture in the tomb of Sima Jinlong. This type of decorative pattern in different variations made its first appearance in China no earlier than 439, the year of conquest of Liangzhou by the Northern Wei. It derives ultimately from the Mediterranean world and was transmitted east by stages at different periods of history in different geographic areas, where modifications to the basic pattern may have occurred.[56] For North China in the late fifth century, the source would be Gandhara or the area of Bactria, where Indian motifs would have been incorporated. The mode of transmission and the carriers of the transmitted motifs are not known and may never be known. What is certain is that imported images and decorative motifs began to appear on works of art in different media and in architectural ornamentation in Pingcheng and other important administrative and commercial centers of Northern Wei by the eighties of the fifth century. One can point to the lacquer coffin from Guyuan (fig. 15), dated to the 480s,[57] and the silk embroidery found in

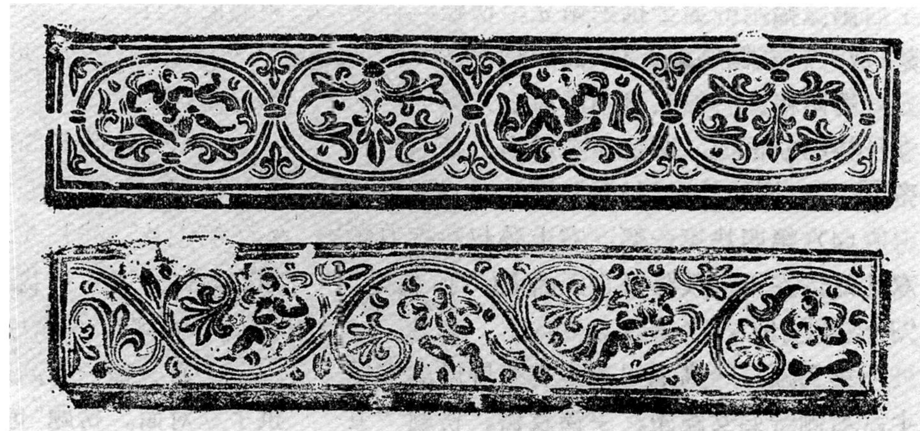

Figure 13. Rubbing of inhabited palmette scrolls on stone pole base. Northern Wei dynasty (386–534). Excavated from the tomb of Sima Jinlong (d. 484), Datong, Shanxi Province

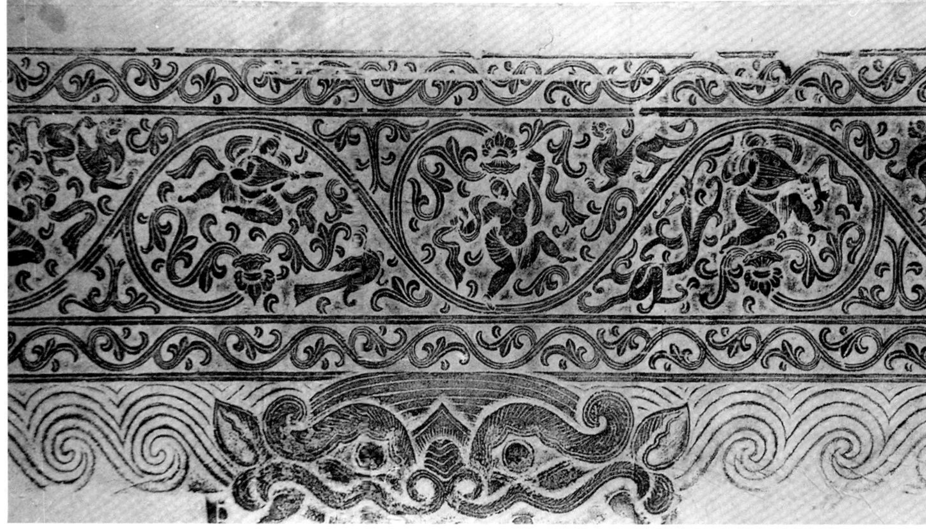

Figure 14. Rubbing of inhabited palmette scroll on stone mortuary couch. Northern Wei dynasty (386–534). Excavated from the tomb of Sima Jinlong (d. 484), Datong, Shanxi Province

Dunhuang, dated 487 (cat. no. 79, lower border; here the palmette takes a rather spindly shape). The same patterns are seen in the so-called second-phase caves (those constructed after 470) of the Buddhist cave temples at Yungang. A good example is the decorative frieze on the lintel of the entrance to Cave 10, which provides a lively version of the "inhabited" vegetal scroll (fig. 16), with figures enclosed in the foliage, as seen on Sima Jinlong's pole base (cat. no. 71). The inhabited scroll would eventually evolve into the "boys and lotus" motif on porcelain of the Chinese Song (960–1279) and Korean Koryŏ (918–1392) dynasties.

Another major decorative motif in the arts of the late fifth century in North China is the row of hexagons, often enclosing animals and mythical creatures, hereafter referred to as the hexagon pattern. It is sometimes superimposed on the palmette scroll, as is the case on a painted board that served as part of the frame for the lacquer screen from the tomb of Sima Jinlong (fig. 17). On the 487 embroidery (cat. no. 79), a series of circles are superimposed on the row of hexagons, creating cells that enframe the spindly palmettes. A similar pattern is seen on the lintel in Cave 10 at Yungang (fig. 16). The most complex pattern with the hexagon as a major element occurs on the right-side board of the painted coffin from Guyuan referred to above (fig. 18). Here, the intersection of the hexagon and the pearl roundels form cells inhabited by haloed figures with flowing scarves, mythical animals, and vegetal motifs. Both the roundels and the hexagons are composed of rows of "pearls" between circular or straight lines, indicating an Iranian influence. The figures, in the treatment of the naked bodies and postures, look Indian. In the interstices between the roundels are quatrefoil palmettes adopted from the "four-leaf" pattern of Han China.

The source, or at least the antecedent, of the hexagonal motif may be traced to the northeast. It can be seen on the saddle plates (cat. no. 25, detail) from Chaoyang, Liaoning, dating from the fourth century. A number of similarly designed horse trappings in openwork gilt bronze have been found in the area near Chaoyang, the ancient city of Longcheng, the

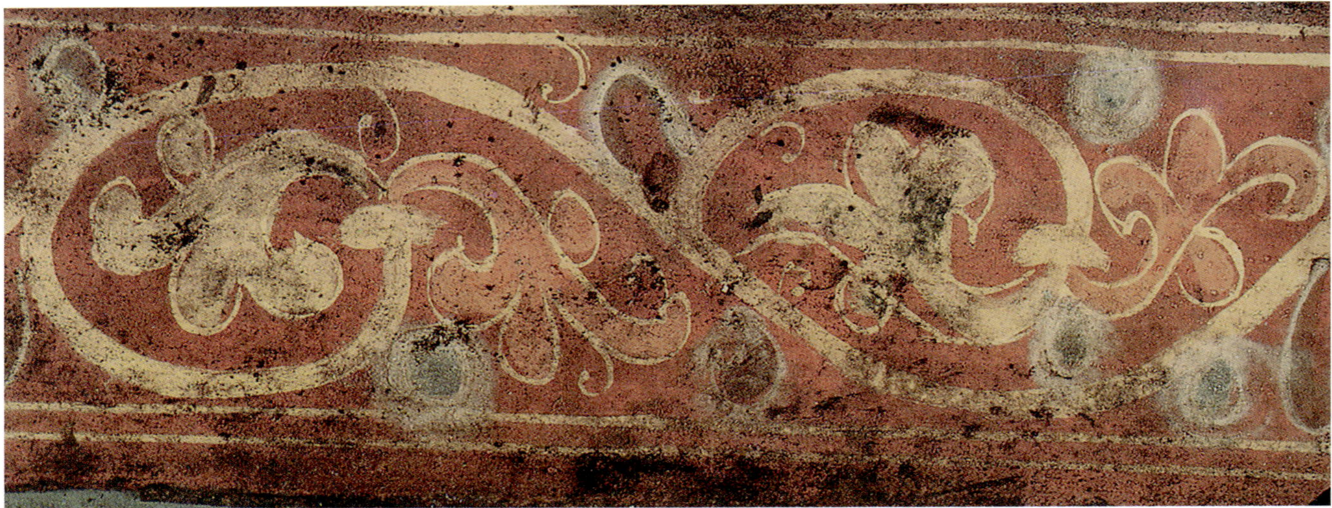

Figure 15. Border of lacquer coffin with palmette scroll. Northern Wei dynasty (386–534), 480s. Excavated at Guyuan, Ningxia Autonomous Region

home base from which the Murong Xianbei expanded into the Central Plains and established the state of Former Yan (337–370). We note, in particular, that the hexagons are formed by double lines and that there is a circle at every intersection of the sides. Within each hexagon are dragons, phoenixes, mythical animals, deer, and human-headed birds (early forms of the *kalavinkha*?). It can be said with a fair degree of certainty that the Murong Xianbei in northeastern China popularized this pattern—or perhaps invented it. In any case, the several types of decorative pattern one sees on objects from the late fifth century, as discussed above, all incorporate the hexagonal pattern to various degrees, with superimposed or additional motifs from other sources.

The hexagonal pattern was also transmitted to Korea. A number of metal objects from Silla tombs, dating from the late fifth to early sixth century, display this pattern in a fairly pure form. The best-known example is the silver cup from Tomb 98 (the Twin-tumulus Tomb) in Kyŏngju, South Korea (fig. 19). It is not clear why the transmission should have skipped Koguryŏ, which was not only adjacent to but had much to do with the various Yan states politically and militarily, particularly with the Northern Yan.[58] The connection to Silla by sea is, on the other hand, to be expected.

Farther afield, we find the same hexagon pattern in sixth-century Japan. It is seen, for example, on a bronze saddle plate of the Kofun period from Sukedo Ashikaga City, Tochiqi Prefecture, now in the Tokyo National Museum.[59] Like the patterns from northeastern China and Silla Korea, the hexagon pattern is formed by two or three straight lines connecting circles at the corners of the hexagon. So far, the most puzzling object with the hexagonal pattern is the gilt-bronze cup (fig. 20a, b) found at Suixi, in Guangdong Province in the south, together with a lobed and footed silver bowl of typical Sogdian shape and with a Sogdian inscription. In this hoard, there were also Sasanian coins dating from Shapur III (r. 383–88) to Peroz (r. 457/59–84). The hoard has been dated by the Suixi

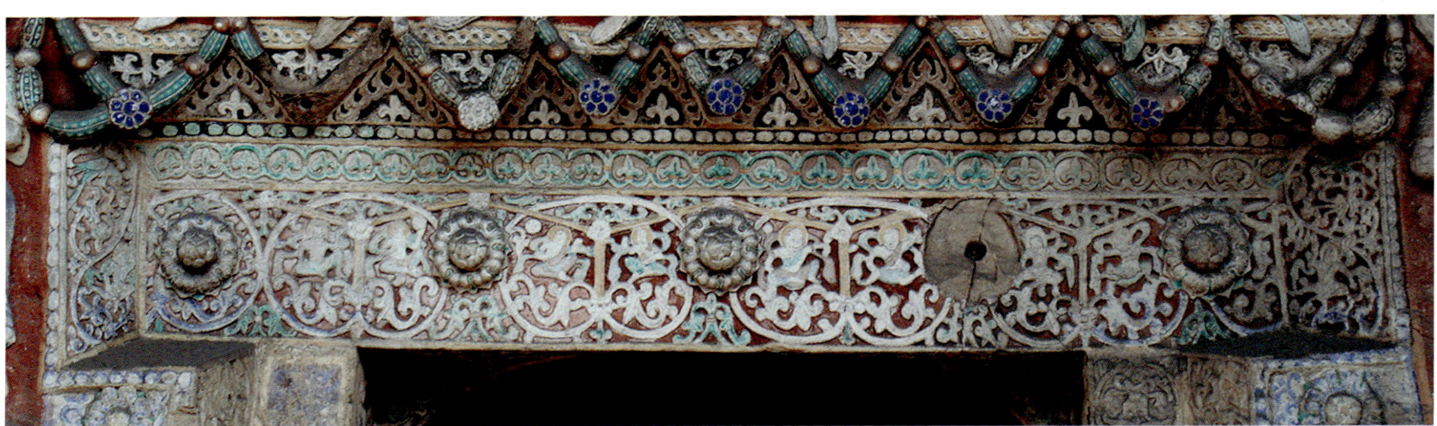

Figure 16. Frieze with carved floral scroll. 5th century. From lintel at entrance of Cave 10, Yungang, Datong, Shanxi Province

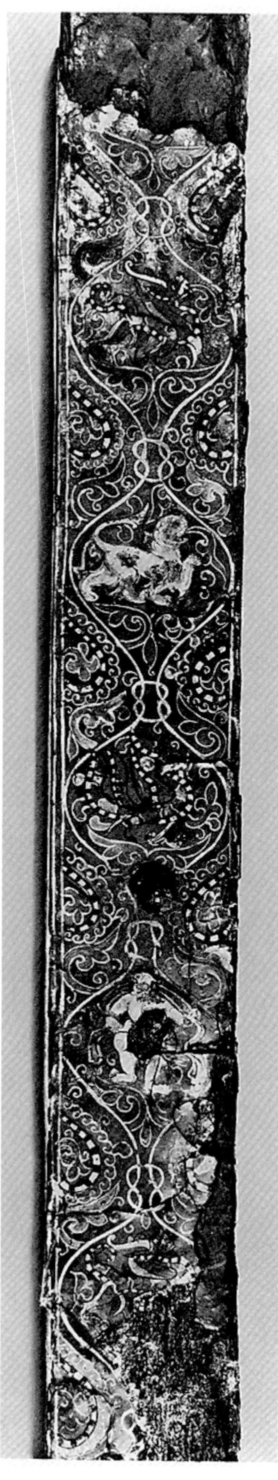

Figure 17. Painted wooden board with inhabited palmette scroll. Northern Wei dynasty (386–534). Excavated from the tomb of Sima Jinlong (d. 484), Datong, Shanxi Province

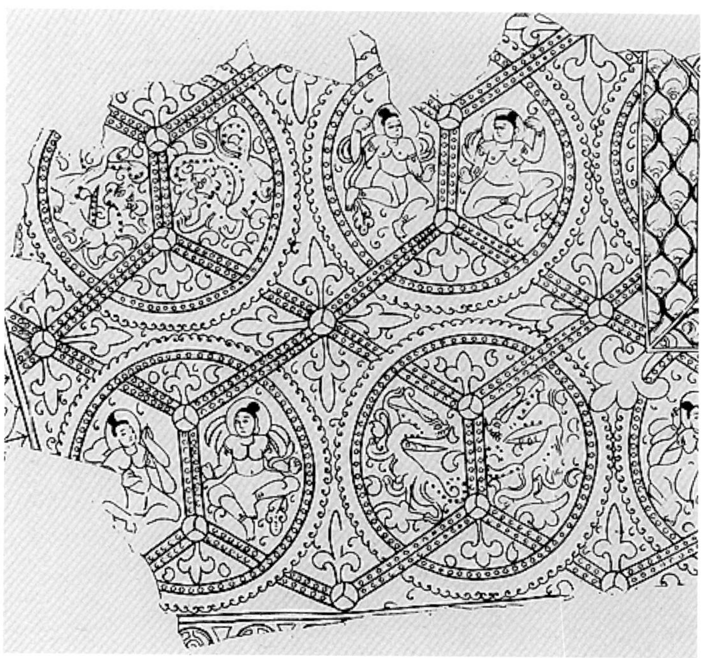

Figure 18. Side board of lacquer coffin (fig. 15) with hexagonal pattern. Northern Wei dynasty (386–534), 480s. Excavated at Guyuan, Ningxia Autonomous Region

Municipal Museum to the "late Southern Dynasties," i.e., sixth century.[60] The inscription on the lobed bowl, as translated by Yoshida Yutaka from "the published eye-copy," suggests that it came from Chach (Tashkent).[61] The puzzling feature is that a bowl with such typical northeastern Asian features should be found in South China together with objects from Iran and Central Asia. Perhaps this attests to the active sea trade along the coastal areas of continental Asia.

Given that most, if not all, of the reported finds of riding gear with the hexagonal pattern are from Chaoyang—ancient Longcheng, home base of the Murong Xianbei—and that Longcheng did not fall to the Northern Wei until 436, plus the fact that this pattern did not appear in major Northern Wei cities until late in the fifth century, it can be inferred that the introduction of the hexagonal element in the decorative arts of the Northern Wei had something to do with the capture of Longcheng and the subsequent transfer of craftsmen to Pingcheng, the Northern Wei capital.

By the same token, the Western elements in Northern Wei decoration, whatever their original sources, would have been introduced after the conquest of Liangzhou in 439. This year was indeed a turning point in the history of the Northern Wei. Politically, the Tuoba Xianbei dynasty was finally the ruler of all of North China. The removal of some thirty thousand households from Liangzhou to Pingcheng would have included craftsmen as well as scholars, Han Chinese as well as *hu* (in this case, Central Asians).[62] The transfer of craftsmen from both the east (Longcheng) and the west (Liangzhou) would account for the immense richness of the arts of Northern Wei at Pingcheng.

Before continuing with the narrative of the consequences of the 439 conquest, it would be useful to return to the beginning of the century when Lü Guang took over Liangzhou on his return from Central Asia and established the Later Liang

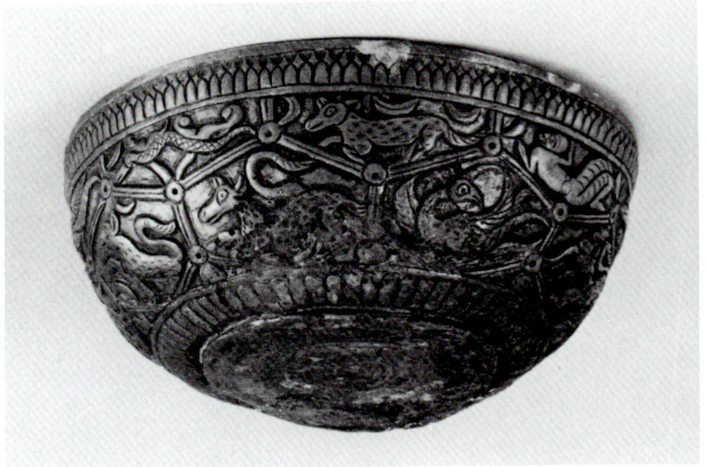

Figure 19. Cup with hexagon and animal designs. 5th–6th century. Silver, diameter 2¾ in. (7 cm). Excavated at Hwangnam daech'ong, Kyŏngju, North Kyŏngsang Province, South Korea. Kyŏngju National Museum

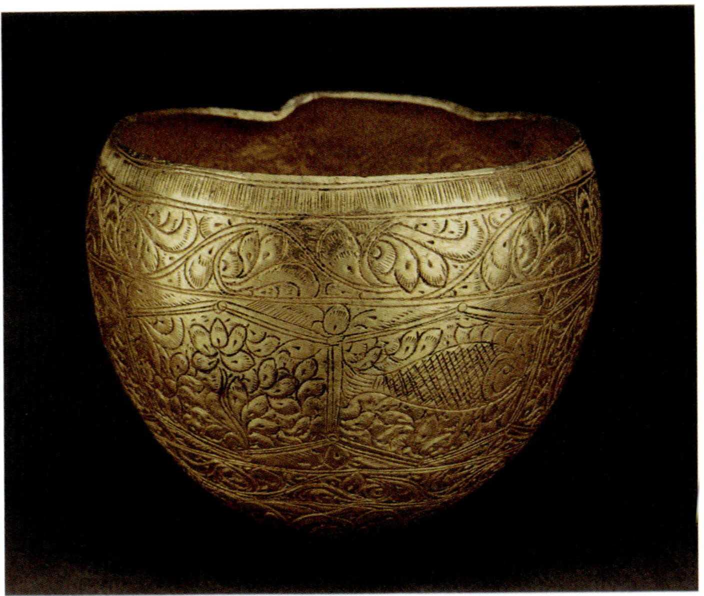

Figure 20a. Cup. 6th century. Gilt bronze, diameter 3¼ in. (8.3 cm). Excavated at Suixi, Guangdong Province. Suixi Municipal Museum

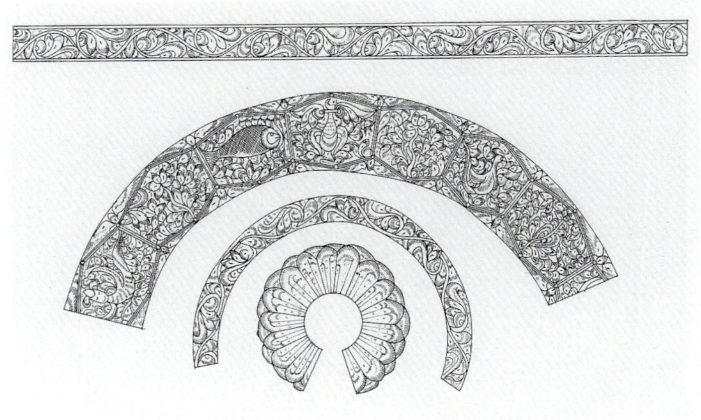

Figure 20b. Drawing of decoration on cup in fig. 20a

dynasty (386–403). Lü Guang's rule from the start was somewhat tenuous, and the state began to disintegrate almost as soon as he proclaimed himself governor of Liangzhou. The first separatist state established was the Northern Liang (397–460), which occupied the western half of Gansu and later the entire region. The rulers of Northern Liang, the house of Juqu, were traditionally said to be a branch of the Xiongnu, but, more recently, scholars tend to think they were a branch of the (Little) Yuezhi, with strong ties to Central Asia.[63] This identification would go some way toward explaining the flourishing of both commerce and Buddhism in Northern Liang. Monks came to the capital, Guzang (Wuwei), from India and Central Asia beginning about 412. Of these the best known is Dharmaksema (Ch: Tanwuchan, d. 433), who translated numerous sutras. These included the Nirvana (Mahāparinirvāna) Sutra, which provided the authority for one of the most important doctrines expounded by the monk Zhu Daosheng (355–434), who had studied with Kumārajiva in Chang'an.[64] (This doctrine, in some ways comparable to the Christian Pelagian heresy current at about the same time, was initially regarded as heretical, until the appearance of Dharmaksema's translation of the Nirvana Sutra.)

One of the most important consequences of the 439 conquest was thus the revival of Buddhism, which was persecuted during the Northern Wei in the later years of the reign of the emperor Taiwudi (r. 424–52). Among the people transplanted to Pingcheng after the conquest were a number of Buddhist monks, who would play a major role in establishing state-supported monasteries with grants of land, tenant farmers (the *sengqihu*, or *sānghika*, households), and servants (*fotuhu*, or *sihu*, monastery households).[65] The monk Tanyao, in the year 460, when he became Shamentong (head priest-in-charge of Shamen [*śramana*]), started the construction of the first five cave temples at Yungang, outside of Pingcheng.[66]

Buddhist art in the period covered by this exhibition is discussed by Angela Howard in her essay. It is here proposed to add a historical note on the patronage of Buddhist temples and monuments in late fifth-century Northern Wei. Beyond the imperial family, there are two names most often mentioned in academic writings on this topic: Wang Yu and Feng Xi. Both are connected with the Grand Empress Dowager Wenming, a powerful presence at the imperial Northern Wei court from 466 and absolute ruler from 471.

Wang Yu (d. after 500) began his career as a palace eunuch in his youth and achieved senior positions at court, ending his days with all the highest honorifics heaped upon him. Apparently, he was a conscientious and tireless official, working well into his old age. But the chief reason for his success was that he was a favorite of the Grand Empress Dowager Wenming.[67] She lavished gifts on him, and with his riches he became one of the great patrons of Buddhist activities of his time. Su Bai has attributed the construction of the twin cave 9–10 at Yungang (the most sumptuously decorated of all the cave temples at the site) to Wang Yu's patronage.[68] There is a stele in Chengcheng, Shaanxi, recording his donation of a large temple in that area in the year 488.[69] The present county town of Chengcheng, about a hundred miles northeast of Xi'an, was the ancient town of Lirun, where there was a great concentration of Qiang people. The fact that Wang Yu built a great temple there confirms the statement in his official biography in the *Weishu* (History of the Wei) that he was a Qiang from Lirun in Fengyi prefecture.[70] Ma Changshou has pointed out that the most likely cause of Wang Yu's entering the palace service of the Northern Wei was that he or his family took part in the Qiang rebellion which was quelled in 446. A common fate to befall the younger elite of rebellious tribes was to serve as eunuchs in the palace.[71] The case of Wang Yu provides confirmation of the historical record that during the Later Qin dynasty (384–417), ruled by the Yao family of Qiang origin, Chang'an (Xi'an, capital of Later Qin) had become the center for the dissemination of Buddhism in the vicinity of Guanzhong (Chang'an and surrounding areas).[72] In this connection, it may be noted that the names of donors inscribed on Buddhist statuary from Guanzhong in the fifth and sixth centuries are mostly Qiang.

It is perhaps no accident that both the Grand Empress Dowager Wenming and her elder brother Feng Xi were devout Buddhists, as they were both born in Chang'an. They were the children of Feng Lang, a son of the second and last ruler of the Northern Yan. (Feng Lang was the brother of Feng Sufu, whose burial furniture in this exhibition has been discussed above.) Feng Lang defected to Northern Wei in 433, before the final fall of Northern Yan in 436, and was made governor of the prefectures of Qinzhou and Yongzhou (roughly the southern part of present-day Shaanxi Province), with the prefectorial seat in Chang'an where Wenming was born in 442. Feng Lang was later executed (implicated in his brother's surrender to the Ruru during a battle), and the young girl, the future empress, was sent to Pingcheng to serve in the palace, while the brother, Xi, was taken by his nurse to hide among the Di and Qiang communities.[73] Feng Xi, granted great status and wealth by his sister after she took power, sponsored numerous Buddhist temples and monuments, had sixteen copies made of the complete Buddhist canon (known at the time), and held endless discourses with Buddhist monks. But his religiosity seems to have had little effect on his ethics—as an administrator or in his personal life. His callousness at the loss of human lives and livestock in the process of clearing ground for the construction of stupas reflects his blatant disregard for at least one important Buddhist precept.[74] Nevertheless, in this behavior he was by no means unique at this time in Chinese history. Shi Hu (r. 335–49), of the Later Zhao, the most debauched, violent, and bloodthirsty of all rulers of the Sixteen Kingdoms, was also known to support Buddhist priests, but not to the same fanatical degree.

The Empress Wenming was one of the most remarkable personalities in Chinese political history. At the age of fourteen (eighteen in some accounts), she became empress to Wenchengdi (r. 452–65), empress dowager on the accession of Xianwendi (r. 466–71, poisoned by Wenming in 476), and grand empress dowager after 476, at which time the nine-year-old boy emperor Xiaowendi (r. 471–99) was supposed to be the sole ruler.[75] Xiaowendi was brought up by Wenming, who ordered the death of his mother, in accordance with the ancient custom of the Tuoba Xianbei whereby the mother of the heir apparent is put to death, a practice going back to nomadic times on the steppe.[76]

Her ruthlessness notwithstanding, Wenming was a wise and extremely able ruler. With the advice of her senior ministers, she initiated a series of major administrative changes in the Northern Wei government, including land and tax reforms, thereby removing previous practices carried over, in time and distance, from the steppe. Officials were put on a regular salary, and administrators in the provinces were no longer permitted to extract whatever they could from the people within their jurisdiction. These reforms were necessary for the stable government of an agrarian society. (Centuries later, the Mongols would make similar adjustments when Kubilai Khan became ruler of North China—and later emperor of Yuan China.)

In terms of the bureaucratic structure, it can be said that the Northern Wei was now moving toward a Han Chinese model. Culturally, the dynasty was a synthesis of many strains coming from different parts of the world. This synthesis is

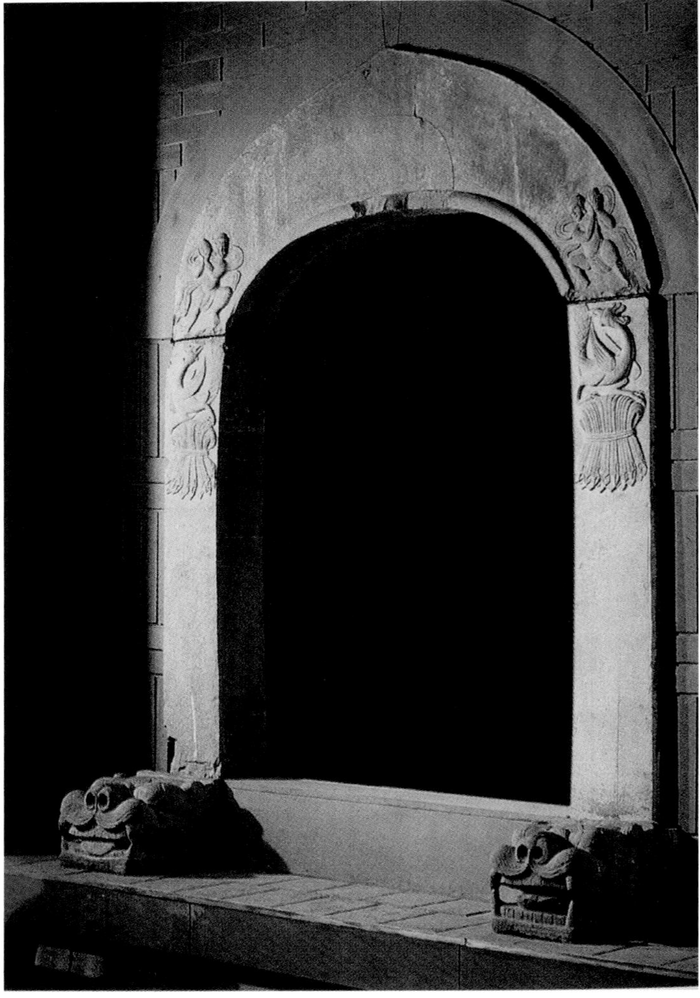

Figure 21. Entrance to the tomb of the Grand Empress Dowager Wenming (d. 490). Northern Wei dynasty (386–534). Stone, overall height 8 ft. 6 in. (2.54 m). Fangshan, near Datong, Shanxi Province. National Museum, Beijing

reflected in the plastic arts, of which the most glorious surviving works are the so-called Phase 2 cave temples at Yungang, particularly the twin caves of 9 and 10, attributed to the patronage of Wang Yu. The discussion of the ornamental motifs in the architecture and decorative arts of the 480s earlier in this essay provides a glimpse of the creative synthesis that took place in the metropolitan areas of the Northern Wei at this time.

When the grand empress dowager died in 490, she was not buried, like all other empresses before her, in her husband's tomb, which was in Yunzhong in Inner Mongolia, but on a mountain, Fangshan (now Liangshan), to the north of Pingcheng, overlooking the city. All that remains of her grave are the stone doors which are now in the National Museum in Beijing (fig. 21).

After the death of Wenming, Emperor Xiaowendi continued to pursue her policies and rigorously instituted further reforms.[77] Although he was devoted to his official grandmother and in total agreement with her in matters of state policy, he could not have had an easy time when the extraordinarily powerful Wenming was alive. He was married successively to two of her nieces (Feng Xi's daughters) and both made him very unhappy.[78] For political and perhaps personal reasons he moved his capital, against strenuous opposition from the Xianbei aristocracy, to Luoyang in 493. Xiaowendi took with him the officials and craftsmen who ran the administrative system and practiced the artistic skills developed during his early reign in Pingcheng. The Sogdians and other peoples from places along the Silk Road followed.

The South in the Fifth Century

Not much of the material culture from the fifth century in the south is extant. The most visible remains from the period of the Southern Dynasties (420–589) are the monumental stone sculptures that stand before the imperial tombs, such as the winged chimera standing at the tomb of Emperor Wendi of Song (r. 424–53, the Yuanjia era)[79] (fig. 22). These large sculptures, usually about nine feet high (2.75 m) and somewhat greater in overall length, represent a continuation of the monumental sculptures of the Eastern Han, such as the chimera in this exhibition (cat. no. 1). Such figures were made in pairs, standing on either side of the "spirit way" (the approach) to the tomb together with stone steles and columns (fig. 23). The columns are a curious feature of the monumental art of the Southern Dynasties. Unlike the steles and sculptures of mythical animals, which have a long history in China, the stone columns are unique to the Nanjing area in the time of the Southern Dynasties (fig. 24). It is reasonable to speculate that these columns, which are crowned by an animal on a lotus dais, were inspired by the description, or perhaps drawings of, the columns associated with King Ashoka (ca. 269–232 B.C.) of Mauryan India. One obvious source would be the monk Faxian, who returned to Jiankang (Nanjing), capital of the Eastern Jin, in 412, after traveling for fifteen years, six of them in India. The accounts of Faxian's travels include records of the Mauryan columns—also known as Ashoka columns.[80] (The name of Ashoka, the great patron of Buddhism, would have been familiar to Chinese Buddhists from the time of the introduction of Buddhism into China in the third century.[81] See also the discussion in cat. no. 128.) The Chinese columns that mark the spirit way to the tombs of members of the imperial families (mostly those of the Xiao family of the Liang dynasty) owe little in iconography to the Indian "originals."

The animals at the top are simply smaller versions of the large sculptures on the ground, and the column is fluted, whereas the Mauryan columns are plain. The fluting is indicative of western influence transmitted through Central Asia.

Wendi of Song is known as one of the more enlightened rulers of the Southern Dynasties. During his relatively long rule, there was peace more or less both within the borders of the empire and with foes to the north. His father, Emperor Wudi (Liu Yü, r. 420–22)—founder of the Song dynasty, which replaced the Eastern Jin—had left a reasonably stable and unified empire. (It was to escape Liu Yü's persecution of the imperial family of the Eastern Jin that the father of Sima Jinlong defected to the north.) After an unsuccessful expedition in 430, there was no military engagement with the Northern Wei for twenty years. In the meantime, Emperor Taiwudi of the Northern Wei was preoccupied with campaigns to unify North China and attempts to fend off threats from the Ruru to the north, another confederation of nomadic tribes that had formed on the other side of the Great Wall. During this period South China, under a less oppressive administration and reduced taxation for the farmers, enjoyed general prosperity. In the north, on the other hand, wealth was concentrated in

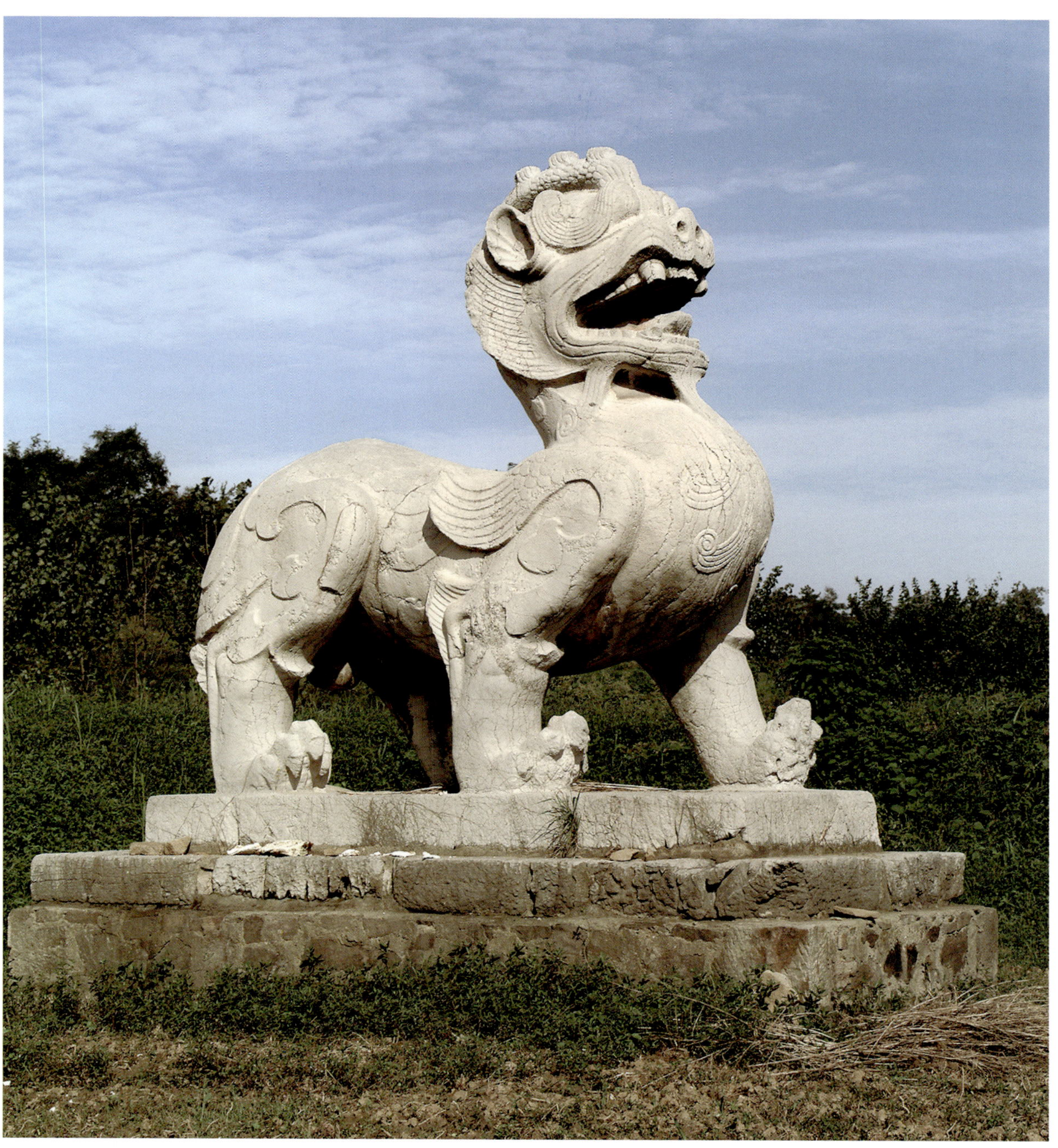

Figure 22. Winged chimera in front of the tomb of Emperor Wendi (d. 453). Song dynasty (420–479). Stone, height 9 feet (2.75 m). Nanjing, Jiansu Province

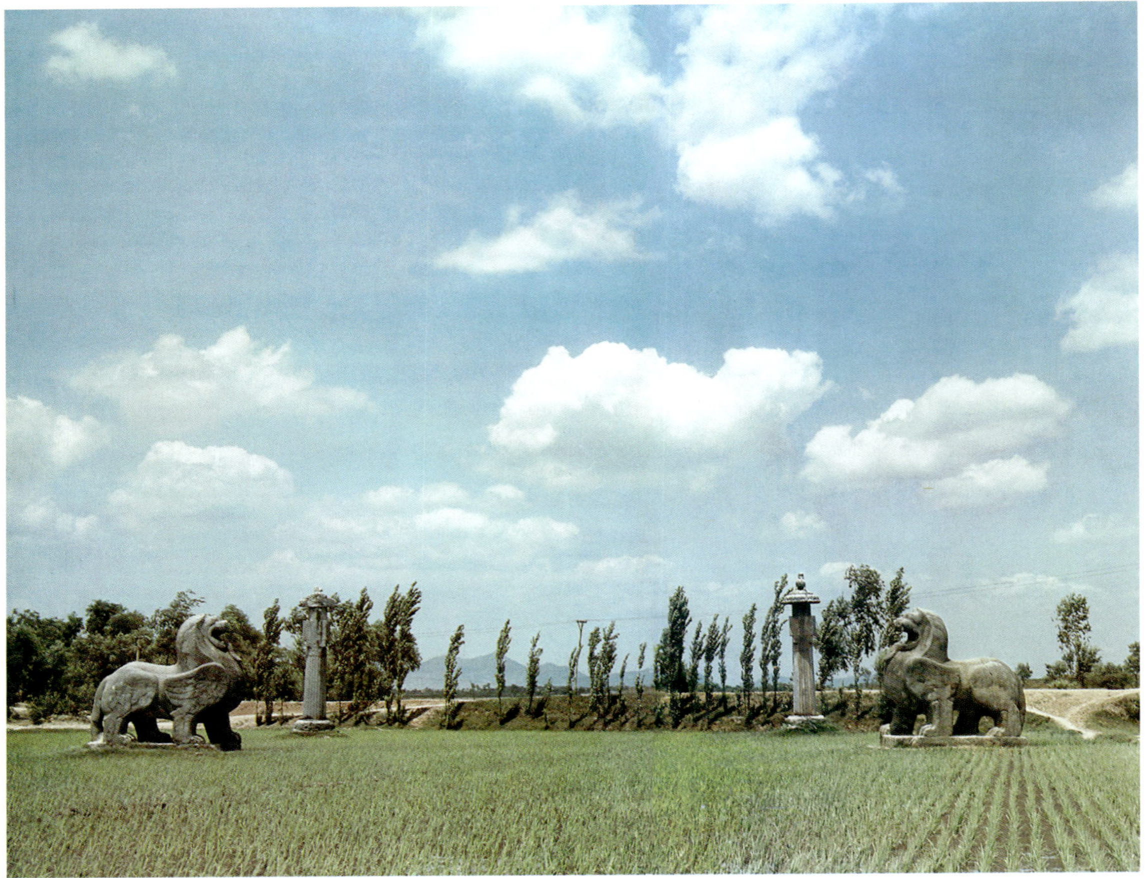

Figure 23. "Spirit way" to the tomb of Emperor Qi Wu (d.493). Qi dynasty (479–502), 483–93. Nanjing, Jiangsu Province

one city, Pingcheng, as a result of the conquests by the Northern Wei. It is useful to bear in mind these contrasting situations when contemplating the arts and letters of fifth-century China.

The Eastern Jin dynasty had depended on the aristocratic families—particularly those who came from the north—to establish its rule in South China and for defense of the land. The rulers of the Song and subsequent dynasties, all founded by military officers, had no need of this support. Members of the old aristocracy were still given positions of high rank in the government but no real power. One salient example is Xie Lingyun (385–433), a grandson of Xie Xuan, victor of the famous battle of Feishui in 383, which saved South China from being overrun by the "barbarian" army of Fu Jian. Coming from a family at the apex of Chinese society and being exceptionally gifted, Xie Lingyun was admitted to the court of the new dynasty to add luster to social and ceremonial occasions. But he was not consulted on policy matters. He responded by neglecting his official duties, both at court and as district governor, and was soon dismissed from office. He repaired to his vast estate at his ancestral home in Shining, eventually extending it to neighboring Kuaiji (both in Zhejiang Province). Xie went for hundred-mile hikes, attended by an

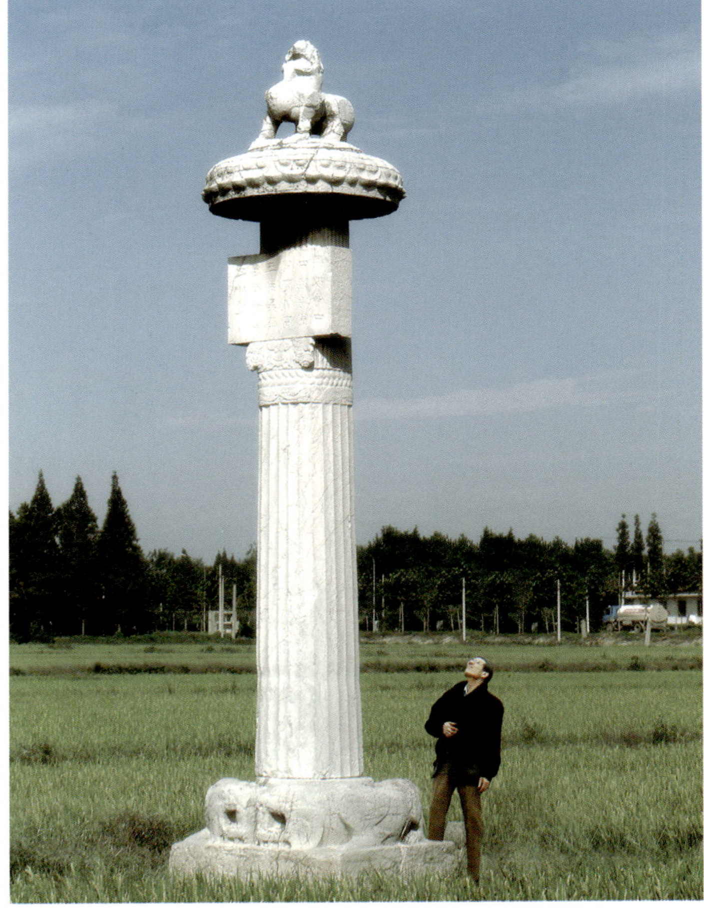

Figure 24. Column in front of the tomb of Xiao Jing (d. 523). Liang dynasty (502–557). Nanjing, Jiangsu Province

entourage of hundreds, hacking mountain trails from Shining south to Linhai and causing much alarm to local populations—his party often mistaken for a band of bandits. He wrote a long prose poem describing his estate, a remarkable composition in many ways. It is both a description of the landscape and its inhabitants—animals, fish, and fowl, and plants domestic and wild—and a record of his response to the scenery, all written in the complicated idiom of his time and replete with all manner of allusions and literary and historical references. All of this he annotated himself. Specific views evoked in his mind Buddhist scenes such as Deer Park and Vulture Peak (locations where the Buddha preached), while others aroused in him Daoist musings as he contemplated the abundance of life and the limits of time.[82]

Together with Tao Qian (better known as Tao Yuanming, 365–427), Xie Lingyun is regarded as one of the earliest "pastoral poets" in Chinese literature. Tao Yuanming was much the greater poet, but Xie was the cultural and literary hero of his time. Both opted out of officialdom, Tao in poverty to his small farm and Xie to grand living with aristocratic unconcern. Like the great literary figure Ji Kang before him (see fig. 4; cat. no. 113a), Xie was eventually executed for no greater crime than lack of cooperation with the new political power. There is good reason that Ji Kang and the group associated with him, known as the Seven Sages of the Bamboo Grove in popular lore, became celebrated in the fourth and fifth centuries in both literature and the pictorial arts. A contemporary of Xie, Yan Yanzhi (384–456), equally well known as a poet and as disgruntled, but not as grand, composed a cycle of poems on the Five Gentlemen (five of the Seven Sages), praising their character and incurring the displeasure of the authorities.[83] The qualities of the Seven Sages that he admired are independence of spirit, learning and other accomplishments ranging from music to love of wine, and general elegance of appearance and manners. Some of these qualities are expressed or implied in the pictorial representation that fortunately has survived in the form of impressions on bricks (cat. no. 121a, b). There are several sets of bricks with molded images of the Seven Sages, all found in the vicinity of Nanjing, capital of all the Southern Dynasties. The eighth figure on the set in the exhibition is the legendary Rong Qiqi (cat. no. 113), said to have been a contemporary of Confucius. The earliest set of the Seven Sages bricks is estimated to date from the late Eastern Jin to the early Song, that is, the early decades of the fifth century.[84] This date would fit in with that of the poems by Yan Yanzhi.

The Seven Sages bricks are the only guide we have to the pictorial style of the Southern Dynasties. Irrespective of whether the original drawings came from the hand of a lowly professional artist or the famous Gu Kaizhi (ca. 344–ca. 406), who moved only in politically powerful and socially exalted circles, the Seven Sages bricks can be seen as representing a new pictorial style to portray new themes embodying new attitudes to life and society. By contrast, the painting on the lacquer screen from Sima Jinlong's tomb (cat. no. 69) preserves a more archaic style and traditional subject matter—although a minor scene on a damaged part of the screen has been identified as representing three of the Sages.[85] The Seven Sages remained a popular theme in Chinese decorative arts for at least another century, during which it spread north to Shandong Province. They are seen on murals in two tombs dating from the mid-sixth century, each occupying a panel of a screen in the painting.[86] These later images show compositional and iconographic developments that had taken place since the beginning of the sixth century.[87] An intriguing possible pictorial reference to Ji Kang is seen as far north as Ji'an, Jilin, in a Koguryŏ tomb.[88] This is an image of a man hammering a piece of iron (?) on an anvil under a tree (fig. 25). Among Ji Kang's many talents was that of an ironsmith. It was said that on his property there was a large willow tree. He dug a channel around it, filled it with water, and in the summer months would forge iron underneath the tree. His friend Xiang Xiu (on the extreme right of cat. no. 113b) would work the bellows.[89]

Southern Natives

Much has been written about the different ethnic groups in North China from the third to the sixth century. The indigenous population in the south who were there before the arrival of waves of immigrants from North China beginning in the third century have received attention only recently, with the pioneering studies by the historians Zhou Yiliang and Chen Yinke.[90] In Zhou's extensive article, he draws attention, inter alia, to the prefecture of Yongzhou (which includes present-day northern Hubei and southwestern Henan, with the administrative center in today's city of Xiangfan) as an area "bordering on *hu* country, mostly populated by the Man people. Even if the territory was within the realm of the Southern Dynasties, the customs [of the people] were actually

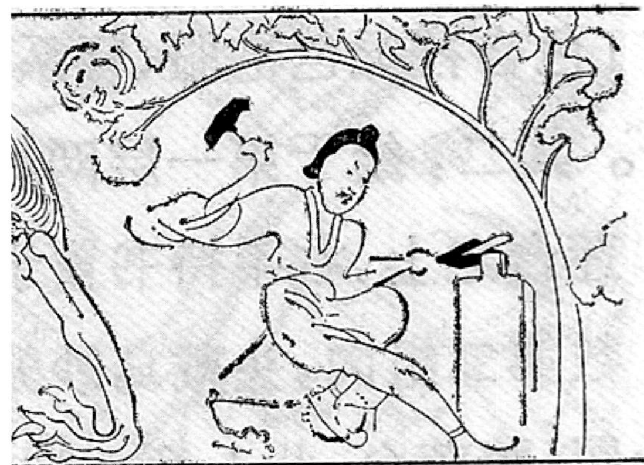

Figure 25. Scene of metalworking. Koguryŏ kingdom, after 6th century. Wall painting from a tomb, Ji'an, Jilin Province

While the two pottery figures discussed above may indicate distinctive local styles, which may be tentatively identified as those of the Man, the impressed bricks from Dengxian do not suggest a radical departure from mainstream Chinese culture. The brick with the story of Guo Ju (cat. no. 121e), a paragon of filial piety, comes straight out of the Eastern Han Confucian canon. The brick with the *sheng* (bamboo mouth organ) player calling the phoenix (cat. no. 121f) and other bricks with Daoist themes seem appropriate to this region, as Hanzhong was the stronghold of the Five-pecks-of-rice Daoist movement in its early days in the third century.

closer to those of the North."[91] The name Man was generally applied to all non-Han peoples in the south, but it was also the designation of a particular group of peoples. In the section on the Man in the *Nanqishu* (History of the Southern Qi), it is stated that "there are many kinds of Man and their languages are not the same. They live in valleys and are spread over the prefectures of Jing, Xiang, Yong, Ying and Si."[92] (In this account, Man territory covers most of Hubei and extends south into Hunan.)

The distinctiveness of Yongzhou and surrounding areas is underscored by recent archaeological finds from Dengxian (in the heart of Yongzhou) and from Ankang and Hanzhong in southern Shaanxi to the west, all connected by tributaries of the Han River. In Dengxian, where the impressed bricks (cat. no. 121) come from, are found pottery figures like the one from Ankang (cat. no. 120), wearing the duck-shaped hat not seen in areas outside the Han River drainage.[93] Farther up the Han River, in Hanzhong, one sees the type of pottery figure such as cat. no. 119, with the front of the head shaved, hair tied back in a pointed knot, and not obviously shod. This image accords well with the description of the Man in the *Nanqishu* as "going on barefoot and wearing their hair cut or tied up in a pointed knot."[94] We have thus a lead in the further study of non-Han Chinese in the Southern Dynasties territories. However, the geographical links may be more complicated. While Hanzhong and Ankang are connected to Dengxian by the Han River, the Hanzhong area is also accessible by riverways from Sichuan in the south, the Ba territory where the Chong people (another kind of Man) lived. Further archaeological finds from this extensive area remain to be studied.

Buddhism in the South and North

The impact of Buddhism in the south was very different from that in the north. There was nothing in the south in the fifth century like the massive cave temples at Yungang and Longmen or the large number of individual devotional images that were made in the north, although there are images carved on the stone cliff at Qixia Temple outside Nanjing, and freestanding images must have been produced and imported. Some translations of Buddhist texts were made in the south, and monks from the south also took part in the great translation project in Chang'an in the north over which Kumārajiva presided. Before the sixth century, the influence of Buddhism, and Indian thought in general, was most keenly felt among the intellectuals of the Southern Dynasties. Indian ideas affected many areas of Chinese culture in the fifth century, ranging from cosmology to philosophy, semantics, phonetics, and literary form.[95] Among intellectuals with a strong interest in Buddhism, Xie Lingyun is again the best example. There is little mention of his activities in connection with Buddhism in his official biography in the *Songshu* (History of the Song), by Shen Yue (441–513), who, in his strong advocacy of the tonal structure of poetic writing, was himself directly or indirectly influenced by Indian languages. Xie's Buddhist activities have been summarized by Tang Yongtong in his magisterial work on the early history of Buddhism in China.[96] However, it should be noted that Xie, like many of his generation, was interested in Buddhism primarily as a philosophical and spiritual quest rather than as a religion of magic, salvation, and wish granting, as it was in the north. He was equally at home with Daoist thought and literature and with traditional learning, as were not a few monks of his time, including his friend

Huiyuan (334–416). This focus goes to explain the relative absence of devotional images in the south in the fifth century, and, accordingly, none are included in the exhibition. All would change with the accession of Emperor Wudi (r. 502–49), founder of the Liang dynasty, in 502.

The Sixth Century

A New Beginning and the End of the Northern Wei, 493–534

The decision by Xiaowendi of the NorthernWei to move his capital south to Luoyang was to have major consequences in the political and cultural history of China. First, it allowed a new class of educated warriors who grew up in the garrison towns on the northern border of the empire to come into the interior and, with Chang'an as the base, eventually unify all of China. Second, it launched an artistic revolution in Luoyang.

To appreciate the change in artistic expression that took place in Luoyang in the early sixth century, one need only compare the pottery figures of the acrobats (cat. no. 53) from the late Pingcheng period (ca. 480) with the group of officials and attendants from a tomb in Yanshi, outside of Luoyang, dating from the first decade of the sixth century (cat. no. 131). The Yanshi figures are more accurately proportioned, with detailed depiction of individual features and dress, resulting in a greater degree of realism. This dramatic change can be accounted for by the introduction of a new artistic language and a new approach to representation. For the Pingcheng craftsmen, the preoccupation may well have been to portray living beings by capturing the moment of animation. In this way, they are closer to an earlier (Han) sculptural tradition, which is related to a particular concept of form—as the Daoists of the Han period put it: "It is *qi* [life force or breath] that fills out the form."[97] The Luoyang artists would seem to regard form in terms of a three-dimensional solid, taking a geometric rather than organic view of the physical world. One can postulate that this change resulted from the influence of the Hellenistic tradition, carried to Luoyang by Central Asian craftsmen. Already on imported Central Asian metalware found in Datong, such as the female figures on the stem cup (cat. no. 60), one can see the type of figural art that would be the inspiration for the pottery figures appearing for the first time in Luoyang (for example, cat. no. 131a).

There were indeed a large number of foreigners residing in Luoyang in the early sixth century. The *Luoyang Qielan ji* (Record of the Buddhist Monasteries in Luoyang, written in the mid-sixth century), for example, records the presence of more than ten thousand families from "west of the Pamirs to Daqin [Eastern Roman Empire]."[98] There was also a monastery in Luoyang built by a *hu* (presumably Indian) monk, Tanmoluo from Wuchang (somewhere in the Swat Valley), which was decorated entirely in *hu* (western) style.[99]

Perhaps the most striking sculptures from late Northern Wei Luoyang are the fragmentary terracotta figures of donors or worshippers found in the crypt of the fabled pagoda of Yongningsi (Temple of Eternal Peace), situated in the inner city to one side of the Imperial Way leading to the palace.[100] From this group, two headless figures (cat. no. 129) and six small heads (cat. no. 130) are included in the exhibition. (The heads and bodies of pottery figures in the late Northern Wei were sculpted independently and assembled after firing, and thus easily separated.) Found near the center of the ruins of the pagoda, the figures are flat on one side and are thought to have been attached to the interior walls, perhaps those of the central column. None of the heads found can now be matched with any of the bodies.[101] What distinguishes the Yongningsi figures is the perfect union of a "realistic" representation of the figures as three-dimensional objects—even if they are actually high-relief sculptures attached to the wall—and an expressive linearity. The former quality is new in this period but the latter recalls an ancient tradition in the native art of the Central Plain—seen also in the pictorial art of the Southern Dynasties (cat. nos. 113, 114). However, this very attractive style, which is again different from that of the funerary figures (cat. no. 131), did not survive the fall of the Northern Wei dynasty (in 534).

The building of the misnamed Yongningsi (the country was anything but peaceful during the period of its existence) was begun by order of Empress Hu in 516, when her four-year-old son ascended the throne and she assumed power and the title of Empress Dowager, and finished in 519 when she climbed to the pagoda, presumably to perform the topping-up ceremony.[102] The temple was the grandest of (by one count) 1,367 Buddhist institutions in Luoyang.[103] At the center was a nine-storied pagoda rising, according to one estimate, to about 400 feet.[104] In 534, the pagoda burned down during a thunderstorm, and thus ended the splendor, and folly, of the Northern Wei dynasty.

As mentioned in the last section, there was a vast concentration of wealth in Pingcheng, the old capital, in the late fifth century. This was achieved at great cost to outlying districts, which descended into increasing poverty and hardship that the administrative reforms in the Taihe era (the reigns of Wenming and Xiaowendi, 477–99) could not reverse. During the late Taihe period, beginning about the time of the move to the new capital, rebellions rose up over all of North China and reached a peak in the years 524–25 with the revolt of the men stationed at the six garrison towns on the northern borders of the empire. The garrisons had been established in the early Northern Wei, after the Xianbei had taken root in the interior of China, to prevent incursions by other nomadic tribes. They were strategically located to guard all the northern approaches to Pingcheng (see the map on pp. XIV–XV and fig. 26). After the move of the capital to Luoyang, the northern garrisons suffered increasing administrative neglect and lack of economic support.

As conditions deteriorated, the inhabitants of the garrison towns—soldiers (all officers and most of the fighting men were Xianbei), convicts (transferred from all over the country as punishment), and other workers—rebelled against local officials and took matters in to their own hands. In desperation, the Northern Wei government invited the Ruru to attack the garrison towns from the north as imperial troops advanced from the south. The Ruru, a people whom the garrisons were supposed to guard against, were only too happy to oblige. After their defeat, a large number of the rebel army, destitute and hungry, were sent together with people from the devastated Pingcheng area to Hebei, a normally rich agricultural area, where there was supposed to be more food. But there was famine in Hebei, and civil unrest spread—to Hebei and farther east to Shandong.

Independent of the six garrisons uprising, there were also revolts in other regions, half of them led by Buddhist monks who had swelled in number since the revival of Buddhism during the Northern Wei in the mid-fifth century.[105] The majority of Buddhist monks were by this time being drawn from the peasantry, as they sought protection from taxation and refuge from corvée labor—for the same reasons they had in an earlier period volunteered to serve in large estates.

There is only one Daoist sculpture in this exhibition (cat. no. 172). It serves as a standard-bearer for the religion that was practiced—albeit unevenly—over all of China among the populace and would occasionally offer a challenge to Buddhism for power and influence at court. Daoist art, however, was overshadowed by that of Buddhism—by the latter's sheer quantity and scale. Our sculpture carries a date of the eleventh month of the year of Longxu (527) and represents a miracle of survival—as the reign of Longxu lasted only a few months. The reign title was proclaimed by Xiao Baoyin (487–530) in Chang'an in the tenth month of that year, and it is doubtful whether it was observed much beyond the limits of the city. Xiao Baoyin was unusual among rebel leaders, as he was an aristocrat, the son of one of the short-lived emperors at the end of the Southern Qi (479–502). In 502, he sought refuge with the Northern Wei, after Xiao Yan (r. 502–49), founder of the Liang dynasty, put an end to the disorder in the land of the Southern Qi, changed the dynasty to Liang, and took over the slaughter of the scions of the previous dynasty—an activity they had already been carrying out most effectively among themselves.

Xiao Baoyin married a Northern Wei princess and served his new country loyally. He led some victorious battles against the Liang—partly inspired by his wish for revenge. In 524, when rebellions erupted all over North China, Xiao was sent to quell the uprisings in Guanzhong (the area surrounding Chang'an). There he fought for three years with some initial success. But his army became worn down by incessant action. In 527, he suffered a major defeat and retreated to Chang'an. In mortal fear of reprisal from the irrational imperial court in Luoyang, Xiao declared independence, with the reign title of Longxu. He was quickly defeated by imperial forces but managed to escape and joined another rebel, Moqi Chounu. In 530, Moqi and Xiao were captured by an army consisting of soldiers from the garrison town of Wuchuan (including a young officer named Yuwen Tai, of whom more later) and sent to Luoyang for execution.[106] By this time, the Northern Wei itself was about to come to a disorderly end. (The life of Xiao Baoyin is told here in some detail because it connects some of the major events in Chinese history in the first quarter of the sixth century.)

Against this background, the Xianbei aristocracy in Luoyang indulged in newly learnt luxurious living. Rich officials and palace eunuchs donated temples by the hundreds. A corrupt court was presided over, on and off, by the Empress Dowager Hu from 516 to 528. In personal appetite, Hu was the equal of the earlier Wenming, but she lacked the qualities that made Wenming a great ruler. She was bent on promoting both herself and Buddhism—her aunt was a famous nun who preached at court. In 528, when the entire country was in turmoil, Hu

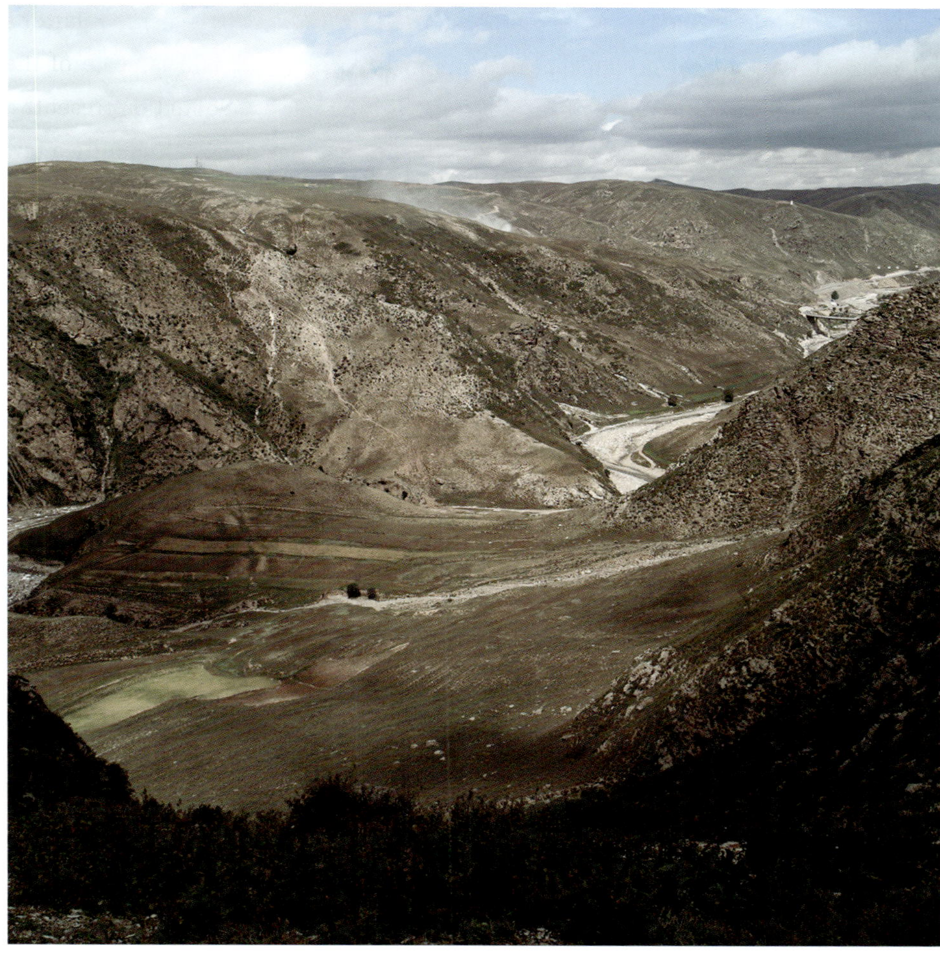

Figure 26. The road from Wuchuan (Inner Mongolia) to Pingcheng (Datong, Shanxi)

poisoned the emperor—her own son—and placed on the throne an infant not yet two years old and not a direct descendant of the imperial line. This provided the excuse for Erzhu Rong, a chieftain of a tribe of nomadic origin, and likely to have Central Asian connections, to march on the capital from Xiurong (in Shanxi, about fifty-six miles north of Taiyuan), where the Erzhu tribe had settled in the beginning of the Northern Wei. Outside the city of Luoyang, Erzhu Rong massacred more than two thousand nobles and officials, nearly the entire Northern Wei court, and threw the bodies of the empress dowager and the infant emperor into the river.[107] This was in effect the end of the Tuoba Wei dynasty. Thereafter, a series of puppet emperors were installed by various military warlords. In 534, there were two Wei emperors: one in the west, ruling from Chang'an under the protection of Yuwen Tai; and one in the east, ruling from Ye (in southern Hebei) under the protection of Gao Huan. The two halves of the empire were subsequently known as the Western and Eastern Wei. They would later become the states of Northern Zhou and Northern Qi, respectively. In the following decades, Luoyang, on the border between the two states, changed hands several times, each occasioning more damage by fierce fighting. This is why there is pitifully little that has survived of the fabulous material culture of Luoyang in the early sixth century—with the exception of a few Buddhist cave temples in the vicinity.

Northern Qi (550–577) and Northern Zhou (557–581)

Both Gao Huan (496–547) and Yuwen Tai (507–556), protectors and overlords of the emperors of Eastern Wei and Western Wei, respectively, came from northern garrison towns, Gao from Huaishuo (fig. 27) and Yuwen from Wuchuan (see fig. 26). They both served at one time or another in the armies of Erzhu Rong and, when the civil wars subsided somewhat and the Erzhu clan was virtually wiped out, Gao Huan ended up with his army in Jinyang (Taiyuan in Shanxi) and Yuwen in Chang'an. Gao's army was assembled in Hebei, where the soldiers from the northern garrisons were sent after their defeat; and Yuwen Tai was with the army dispatched to suppress rebellions in Guanzhong—capturing Xiao Baoyin in the process.

From Jinyang, Gao exercised complete control over the Northern Wei court in Luoyang. The emperor, unwilling to be a puppet ruler, left in 534 for Chang'an, where Yuwen Tai was the military lord. Gao installed another emperor for the

Northern Wei and moved the capital with its inhabitants to Ye (in southern Hebei). Thus culturally, Eastern Wei–Northern Qi was a continuation of late Northern Wei in Luoyang, dominated by Central Asian influences; while the Northern Zhou in Shaanxi, not affected by the artistic innovations in Luoyang, continued the earlier Northern Wei traditions when the capital was in Pingcheng.

Artistic Influences from Central Asia

The overwhelming influence of Central Asians on the plastic arts of Eastern Wei–Northern Qi is plainly evident (cat. nos. 139–141, 145, 146). Some of the forms of vessels and the decorative motifs came from as far as the Mediterranean world and were transmitted in stages across Central Asia. The form of the brown glazed bottle (cat. no. 149) is recognizably derived from the pilgrim's bottle of West Asia,[108] and it is possible to regard the ewer with a bird-head spout (cat. no. 140) as a recombination of various elements of Iranian vessel shapes, including the so-called wine birds.[109] As to the individual decorative motifs, it is not always possible to trace the exact origin and the mode and path of transmission. One of the most common motifs in the arts of the Northern Qi is the lotus-petal base (cat. no. 141), which often serves as a pedestal for Buddhist images (cat. no. 170). This design most likely arrived with Buddhist art from India, where early forms of the design appeared on third-century B.C. Mauryan columns.[110]

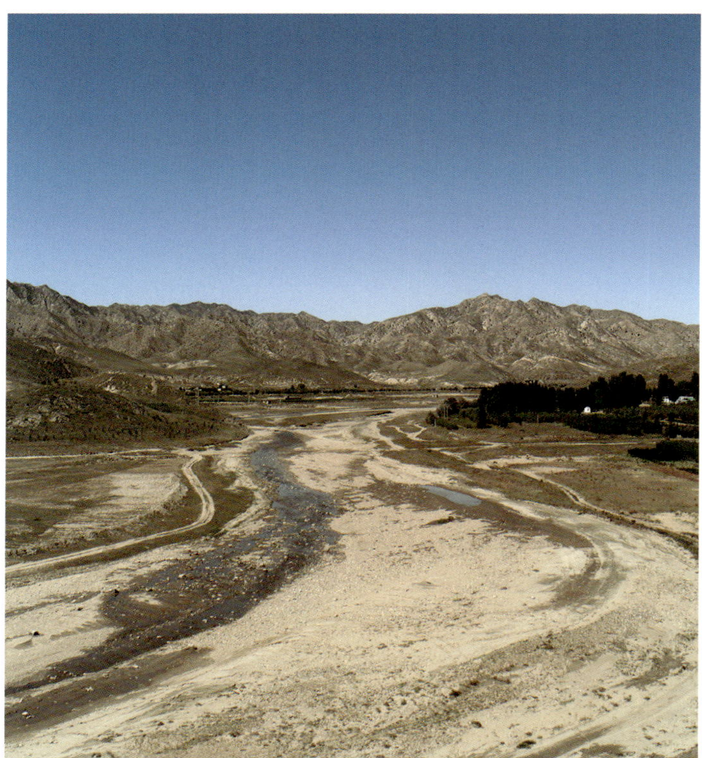

Figure 27. Site of the northern garrison town of Huaishuo, Inner Mongolia

An interesting instance of the newly adopted motifs is the monster mask holding a ring (cat. no. 139). The motif of an animal mask with a ring handle, in a loop extending below the mask, is seen on Chinese vessels from the sixth century B.C. onward, and remained popular in Han times. It may therefore be assumed that the motif of a mask holding a ring handle seen on Northern Qi vessels evolved from earlier Chinese versions. However, it has been fairly convincingly pointed out that the animal mask holding a ring handle *in its mouth* may well have traveled to China all the way from the Mediterranean world.[111] Thus, the somewhat familiar and somewhat strange motif (because the earlier Chinese mask is as placid as the new mask is forbidding) is another example of a new idea in the decorative arts of China in the sixth century.

There are also pictorial representations of western entertainers, such as the tamer of lions and elephants (cat. no. 148) and performers of the whirling dance (cat. no. 149), which became very popular in China in the sixth century. The aforementioned Erzhu Rong, who terrorized the Northern Wei court (or the remnants after the massacre), was fond of doing the whirling dance. At banquets, he would himself perform, and he made the court ladies and senior officials follow suit.[112] It is not clear whether he acquired the skill in Luoyang or whether it was part of his ethnic background—given the suspected Central Asian connections of the Erzhu tribe.

Material Culture of the Northern Qi

There is no discernible difference in the contents of the tombs of the Xianbei aristocracy and that of Han families. We find the same kind of heavily decorated wares in the tombs of the Feng family in Hebei (cat. no. 145) as those from the tomb of the Xianbei Lou Rui (cat. nos. 139–141) in Taiyuan. As to the general run of tomb figures and utensils, the contents of the near-contemporary tombs of Cui Ang (566), Fan Cui (576), and Li Xizong and his wife (575) are almost identical. (These tombs are represented in the exhibition by selected items of special interest and not by any of the hundreds of standardized tomb figures of attendants and guards.) For example, in the tomb of Fan Cui is a guardian figure that resembles in every respect the one from Cui Ang's tomb in the exhibition (cat. no. 137).

There are two tombs near the capital city of Ye that, because of their scale and the quantity and quality of grave furniture (after looting), deserve special attention. The first is that of the Ruru princess who was a five-year-old child bride in 542 when she married an eight-year-old son of Gao Huan. This was a political marriage, as the Ruru at the time were the greatest threat on China's northern borders. The princess died in 550 at the age of thirteen, as recorded in the epitaph, and was accorded a magnificent funeral—the Ruru still held sway. As is usual in tombs of this period, there were no precious articles to be found in this tomb by modern archaeologists. The one exception is an openwork gold ornament inlaid with pearls, amber, and stones (cat. no. 134). The pottery figures still display a sculptural style close to that of late Northern Wei Luoyang (cat. nos. 132, 133). But a mere decade later, the probable date of the tomb at Wanzhang, there was a notable change—a turning away from the three-dimensional treatment and a return to an emphasis on frontality with little attention to drapery (cat. nos. 135, 136). No epitaph has been found in the Wanzhang tomb, but the scale of the tomb, the magnificent wall paintings (fig. 28), and the large number of artifacts (over 2,000) all indicate that it was the burial of a person of the highest social order—possibly Gao Yang, the son of Gao Huan and first emperor of the Northern Qi (r. 550–59).

Problems of Ethnicity

Although the material culture and related lifestyles were homogeneous among the ruling classes of the Northern Qi—the Xianbei and Han Chinese—the country could not hold together. Immediately after the death of Gao Yang in 559, rivalry broke out between the Xianbei and Han factions. The first victims were the wife of Gao Yang, the Empress Li, and her son Gao Yin—who was dethroned as soon as he succeeded in 560. The Empress Li was the daughter of Li Xizong and his wife, Cui Yuji (see entries on cat. nos. 152, 153), both members of prominent Han families.[113] The person who was instrumental in this coup d'état was the Empress Dowager Lou, wife of Gao Huan and aunt of Lou Rui (see entries on cat. nos. 139–142), who normally stayed in the background. Fearful of a shift of power to the Han Chinese, she ordered the removal and death (by brutal means) of her daughter-in-law, her grandson, and various senior Han officials, one of whom was her son-in-law. With power firmly in the hands of the Xianbei, the Northern Qi met the same fate as the late Northern Wei.

Not that ethnic problems were not foreseen by Gao Huan. Early in his campaign, he practiced an ethnographical ideology not dissimilar to that of Theodoric the Ostrogoth in Italy in the late fifth century by maintaining a peaceful coexistence between soldiers (Goths, Xianbei) and taxpaying civilians (Romans, Han Chinese).[114] He would say to the Xianbei: "The Han people are your servants; the men farm for you, the women weave for you, giving you food and clothes, keeping you warm and fed. Why then do you bully them?" To the Han Chinese he would say: "The Xianbei are your retainers: they receive grain and cloth from you, protect you from bandits and give you peace. Why then do you hate them?"[115] (Gao Huan was perfectly bilingual.) He also married his children to noble Han families, as in the case of Gao Yang, who also befriended the Han Chinese.

The ethnic problem for the Yuwen family was simpler. The people in the Guanzhong area (southern Shaanxi) were already a highly heterogeneous ethnic mix when the northern garrison warriors arrived there. There were no prominent Han Chinese families to contend with. Yuwen Tai had no difficulty in uniting his people, irrespective of ethnic origin, into a powerful fighting force organized into artificially created "tribes," giving each member of a military division a Xianbei name. On the other hand, he organized the civil administration after what was believed to be a model of the ancient Zhou dynasty.

Artistic Differences between Northern Qi and Northern Zhou

In contrast to tomb figures of the Northern Qi, those of the Northern Zhou (cat. nos. 154–156) retain some of the characteristics of the early Northern Wei style (cat. nos. 48–50) and show little sign of the innovative vitality seen in Northern Qi art. Compare, for example, the camels of the Eastern Wei–Northern Qi (cat. no. 133) with those of the Northern Zhou (cat. no. 156)—although in the eyes of the modern critic, there is artistic merit in both.

Geographically, Northern Zhou was much more accessible from the Silk Road, and it is not surprising that the *Zhoushu* (History of the Northern Zhou) should include records of trade missions from the major oasis towns of Central Asia all the way to Sogdiana and farther west to Persia. There was probably no shortage of imported luxury goods. Representative examples of these imports are the glass bowl from a Northern Zhou tomb dated 583 (cat. no. 159), the spectacular silver-gilt ewer (cat. no. 157), and the glass bowl (cat. no. 158) from the (extensively looted) tomb of Li Xian. Li Xian (d. 569, aged sixty-seven) was one of the generals who brought the Gansu Corridor under Western Wei control in 546, before the formal

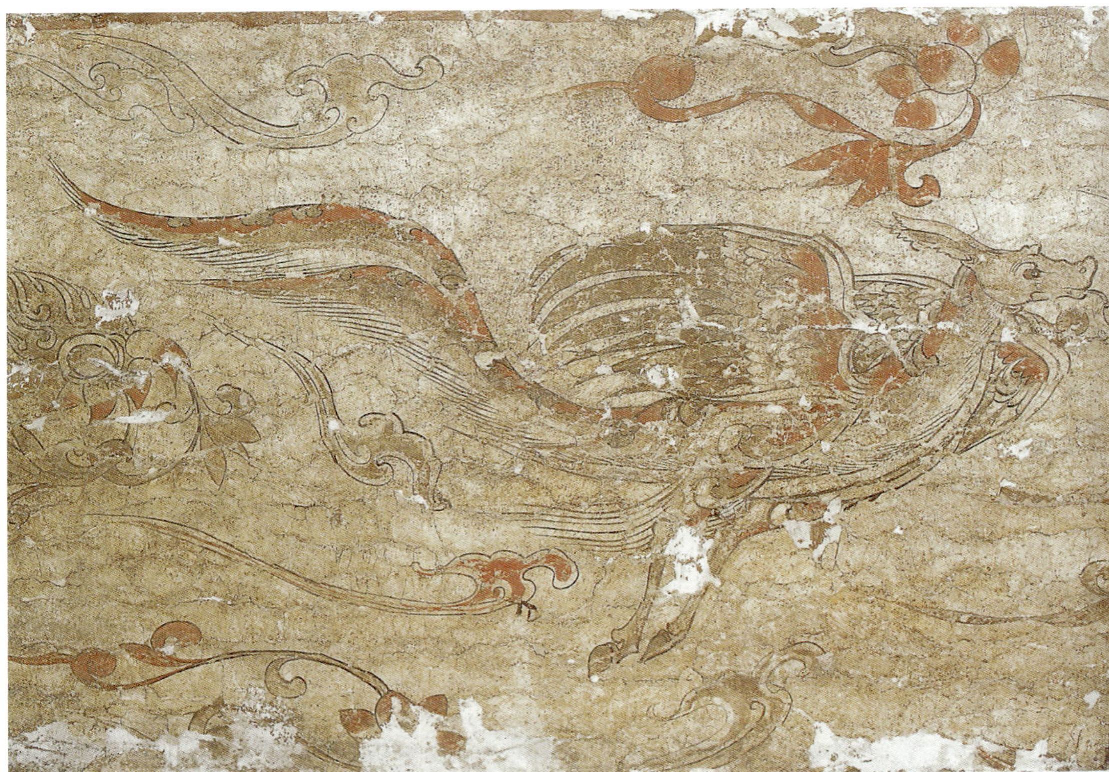

Figure 28. Mythical animal. Northern Qi dynasty (550–577). Wall painting from a tomb in Wanzhang, Hebei Province

establishment of the Northern Zhou dynasty. He was close to Yuwen Tai, the founder of the Northern Zhou, and was entrusted with the upbringing of two of Yuwen's young sons, who lived with the Li family for six years.[116] One of the sons was to become the emperor Wudi (r. 561–65), conqueror of the Northern Qi.

Buddhist Art in the Late Sixth Century

An archaeological discovery in 1996 of a large group of Buddhist stone sculptures in Qingzhou, Shandong (see the map on pp. XVI–XVII), has raised a number of questions and helped to clarify others in the history of Buddhist art in China.[117] The find was at the site of the ancient Longxing Temple, where some four hundred Buddhist images in stone were found smashed and buried in a large pit. The majority of the sculptures date from the late Northern Wei to Northern Qi periods (ca. 520–ca. 570). This particular group of sculptures has drawn the attention of scholars to a distinctive regional style of Buddhist art that developed in Shandong over a fifty-year span in the sixth century. Three main image types from the Longxingsi site are presented in this exhibition (cat. nos. 163, 165, 166) and one from nearby Linqu (cat. no. 164).

What is striking about the Qingzhou sculptures, in addition to their artistic qualities, is the stylistic affinity of some of the images with the earliest known Buddhist images in Southeast Asia, particularly the Mon type from Cambodia (fig. 29), both tracing their origins to Gupta India (ca. 300–ca. 500). Although the Southeast Asian sculptures are generally dated later than the Qingzhou group, there is no reason not to associate the stylistic similarity to the spread of the Gupta style of Buddhist art from India to China, and intermediate points in between, in the sixth century. The *Liangshu* (History of the Liang), compiled in the decades immediately following the fall of the dynasty in 557, with court records still available, includes a description of Middle Tianzhu (Gupta India) and a record of a trade mission from the Indian state in the early sixth century. There is also a telling account of a meeting, in the third century, of emissaries from the Wu state in China with a delegation from Middle Tianzhu at the court of the king of Funan (Cambodia).[118] Funan in the year 503 sent to the Liang court gifts of Buddhist images in coral and in 519 an "Indian sandalwood image."[119] These sketchy records of contacts between India, Funan, and Liang China are confirmed not so much by archaeological finds in southern China, but by the Buddhist sculptures of Shandong, farther up the coast from Liang territory. It should be remembered that for most of the duration of the Liang dynasty, the eastern coast of China all the way to just short of the Shandong peninsula was under the rule of the Liang from the south. That maritime trade went farther north up the Asian Pacific coast has been substantiated by the discovery at sixth-century sites in Korea of glass beads of Indian and Southeast Asian origin.[120]

Buddhist sculptures from Sichuan Province (cat. nos. 122–128) also display direct influence from India, except that the transmission was over land. The identification of the Shandong and the Sichuan schools of Buddhist art throw into sharp relief the images from the Central Plain (cat. nos. 167, 168) and the northwest (cat. nos. 169–171). The iconography of these images is more complex, as they reflect a transmission route along the Silk Road—through several important centers of Buddhist art—all the way to the terminal of Chang'an, where they further absorbed influences from the native art of China. To cite one aspect of one example, the bodhisattva from Xi'an (cat. no. 171) wears a richly decorated crown on which the originally Iranian motif of the orb and crescent is a chief component. More than a religious icon, it represents the creative combination of many elements of visual culture along the entire stretch of the Silk Road into a coherent and imposing work of art. This happened at the end of the sixth century, when China itself was about to undergo a grand political and cultural unification.

Toward the Seventh Century

The political complications that began with the sixth century were gradually resolved in the latter part of the century. In 577, the Northern Zhou finally subdued its rival in the east, the Northern Qi, and was set to unite all of China but for the untimely death of its able ruler, the emperor Wudi (r. 561–78), at the age of thirty-six. The tomb of Wudi and his wife (d. 582), the Empress Ašina, a Turkic princess, daughter of Mugan Khagan, has been found. It is located northeast of the city of Xianyang, near the new airport that serves Xi'an.[121] Apart from the stone epitaphs that enabled the archaeologists to identify the tomb, not much of its original content remains. Of relative interest are the gold seal of the empress and a set of bronze belt ornaments of Wudi, which is in the exhibition (cat. no. 161).

When he died, Wudi left a vastly expanded Northern Zhou to his mentally unstable and dissolute son, Xuandi (r. 579), who abdicated in favor of his six-year-old son and proceeded to die within the following year. All this time, power was in the hands of Yang Jian (541–604), chancellor and father-in-law of Xuandi. In 581, Yang Jian took over the government

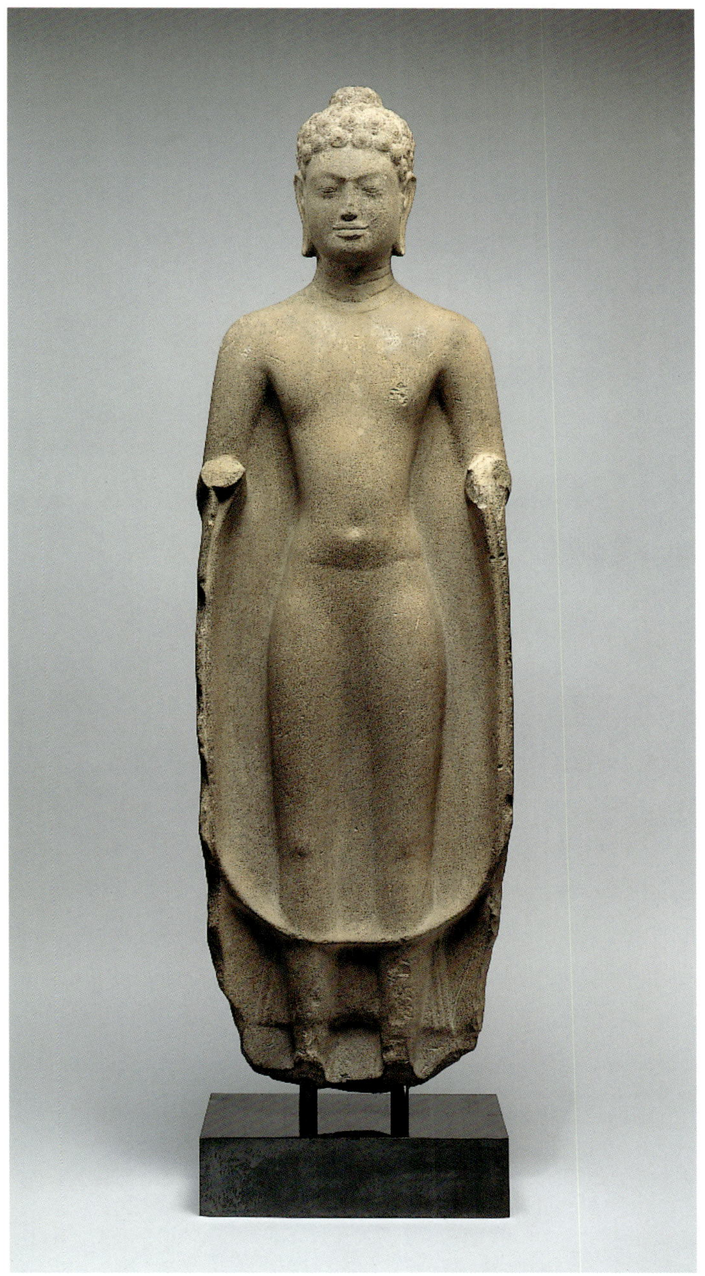

Figure 29. Standing Buddha. Cambodia, ca. first half of 7th century. Stone, height 39½ in. (100.3 cm). The Metropolitan Museum of Art. Gift of Florence and Herbert Irving, 1993 (1993.477.3)

and changed the dynasty to the Sui (581–619). In many ways, the Sui was a continuation of the Northern Zhou, but it now commanded the rich resources of the fertile plains of the former Northern Qi, in addition to the previously annexed western part of former Liang territory (not the Liang of Gansu) in the south. This was one of the major reasons for the rapid conquest of the straitened southern dynasty of Chen (557–589), accomplished within a few months in the year 589.

In the meantime, there were also major changes in the north. In the early sixth century, the Ruru had been the dominant power on China's northern borders. By the 550s, the Turks, who had been vassals of the Ruru, had become the new masters of the Eurasian steppes and posed the major threat along the entire length of the Great Wall of China. The change in the power structure of the north is reflected in two political marriages: that of Gao Huan's son to a Ruru princess in 542 (see cat. nos. 132–134), and that of Wudi of the Northern Zhou to a Turkic princess in 568 (mentioned above). As it turned out, the latter union was a happy one, while Gao Huan's own marriage to (another) Ruru princess (with the connivance of his wife, the Empress Dou, mentioned in the previous section) was singularly unsuccessful—the princess was stern and never spoke a word of Chinese.[122]

Sogdian Burials

As the Turks rose to power in the second half of the sixth century and built up a vast empire on the steppes, the Sogdians, who came under the sovereignty of the Turks, began to find a new role on the international stage. They became administrators for the Turkic empire.[123] It was also expedient for the Chinese government(s) to employ Sogdians and other Central Asians with linguistic and diplomatic skills to serve as intermediaries in dealing with the Turks and as *sabao*, administrators, of the large foreign settlements in the northern areas of the country, especially in northern Shanxi, the Ordos, and the Gansu Corridor.[124] Whereas Sogdians had formerly been traders, entertainers, and artisans in China, they were now not only rich but politically important—in the late Northern Dynasties through the Sui and into the beginning of the Tang (618–907). This may explain why some of the burials of Sogdians, and those of other Central Asians who held positions of *sabao* in the late sixth century (at the height of the first Turkic empire), display a greater degree of cultural assertiveness than those of any other period. Their confidence is manifested in the decorations on stone sarcophagi and couches, which depict Central Asian customs and religious practices. The three known tombs with this type of decoration excavated archaeologically all date from the late sixth century. Two are in Xi'an, one of a *sabao* by the name of Shi (dated 580) and that of An Jia (579), and another is in Taiyuan, that of Yu Hong (592), which is in this exhibition (cat. no. 175).[125]

Not all prominent Sogdians in this period were *sabao*. There is the interesting case of Shi Shewu, whose tomb (dated 610) in Guyuan shows little difference in structure, decoration, or contents from those of Sui burials of the same period at the Sui capital city of Daxing (Xi'an).[126] Shi Shewu's great-grandfather and grandfather were *sabao*, but his father held no office. Shi himself served in the Northern Zhou army under the successive commands of two sons of Li Xian (see cat. no. 157) and fought against the invading Turks. He later served in the army of the Sui official Yang Su in the victorious battle against the Turks in the year 599 and was promoted to the rank of general.[127]

By the eighth century, there would be little sign of Central Asian exceptionalism in Sogdian burials in China. For example, the contents of the tomb of the Sogdian An Pu in Luoyang (An Pu died and was buried in 664 in Chang'an but in 709 was reburied by his son alongside his recently deceased wife in Luoyang) is typical of the lavishly furnished tombs of the same period.[128] The only indication of a western custom in this burial is that a Byzantine gold coin (cat. no. 224) was held in the hand of one of the corpses, presumably that of An Pu's wife.[129] It would seem that this custom persisted among Central Asian communities in China irrespective of their religious belief. This Sogdian family was Buddhist.[130]

Much still remains to be studied on Central Asian elements in the funerary art of North China in the second half of the sixth century. Archaeological finds from tombs are all that we have to go by for knowledge of the arts of this period generally. Apart from overt Central Asian motifs, such as the Zoroastrian fire-altar, the ribbons on human (or divine) beings, and the horses on Yu Hong's sarcophagus, there are also elements shared with Chinese art of the period (see the entry on cat. no. 175). Compositions seen in decorations in the tombs of *sabao* also appear in Chinese burials. A striking example is that of the stone slabs with incised line decoration from a Northern Qi burial in Qingzhou, Shandong, dated 573. The pictorial composition and border patterns on one of the Qingzhou slabs (cat. no. 162a) are basically the same as those on one of Yu Hong's slabs (cat. no. 175h), except that the recipient of the offering is Chinese. Given that the Qingzhou burial is almost two decades earlier than that of Yu Hong, it has been postulated that the compositions, motifs, and pictorial style may have originated under Sogdian influence in Luoyang in the late Northern Wei and spread to Qingzhou in the Northern Qi and that the same copybook patterns were used in (or reverted to) a more Central Asian context in the *sabao* burials in areas where there were greater concentrations of Central Asians.[131] This would seem to be a reasonable approach to the study of what we may now call Sino-Sogdian art. The art-historical study of sixth-century North China seems increasingly to confirm the point repeatedly made by the historian Chen Yinke that Northern Qi was highly "westernized" (*huhua*).[132]

Arts of the Sui and Early Tang, 600–750

There is not enough information on which to gauge the effect of the conquest of Northern Qi on the arts of the Northern Zhou. The pottery figures in the tomb of Emperor Wudi (578) show little difference from those in the tomb of Li Xian (dated 569; see cat. nos. 154–156). The dynasty itself was to fall to the Sui soon after the death of Wudi.

The dramatic change in the arts—perhaps also in sartorial fashion—occurred around the turn of the seventh century under the unified empire. This is evident in the contents of the tomb (dated 608) of Li Jingxun, an aristocratic young girl. Two of the imported luxury items from the tomb are in the exhibition (cat. nos. 186, 187), but what interests us at this point are locally produced pottery figures (figs. 30a, b). Stylistically, they come close to the figures from the late Northern Wei tomb in Luoyang (cat. nos. 131a, 131c) and are very different from those of Northern Zhou in the same area. No longer are the figures press-molded on one side (leaving the back flat; see cat. no. 154) but modeled in three dimensions and with some attention to drapery. Whether this western naturalism was transmitted through the Northern Qi—especially from Taiyuan, the second capital of the dynasty—or was the result of a second wave of direct influence from the west in the Sui capital is not yet possible to determine. One can only note here that many of the social and government institutions of the Sui (and Tang) were inherited from the Northern Qi, as the historian Chen Yinke pointed out.[133]

Turfan

The second change in the arts of the seventh century came after the expansion of the Tang empire into Central Asia. Whereas in former times, the influence from Central Asia came into China with Sogdians and other Central Asians from rich oasis towns like Kucha, Tang China now reached into Central Asia. The emperor Taizong (r. 627–49), the second ruler of the Tang dynasty, took advantage of the temporary weakness of the Turkic empire and established garrisons at the major oasis towns around the Tarim Basin.[134] For art history, the most important aspect of Taizong's expansion into the Western Regions was that the former Gaochang kingdom (Karakhoja, now Turfan in Xinjiang) became a regular prefecture of the Tang empire in 640. For the next hundred years or so, there developed a cultural symbiosis between Turfan and the capital city of Chang'an, and that would have a far-reaching effect on the arts and fashion of Tang China until near the end of the dynasty. The initial impact, of course, was paramount. A few objects from the second half of the seventh century from these two places will illustrate the point.

The pair of tomb guardians (cat. nos. 178, 179; the two are not from the same tomb but they do in effect make a standard pair) and the guardian in armor (cat. no. 180) are all based on Chinese models. Early versions are exemplified in this exhibition by cat. nos. 54 and 55 for the pair of tomb guardians and by cat. no. 137 for the armored guard. However, the exuberance of form and color is entirely Central Asian. The roots of this style are found in the lively art of the Eurasian steppe in the early nomadic period. The expressionistic use of color is seen on the felt covers from the fourth- to third-century B.C. tombs in Pazyryk in the Altai, where the colors of the objects represented bear no relationship to their natural coloring.[135] The pair of tomb guardians represent the continuation of this tradition.

The influence from Turfan on the art of Chang'an is evident on tomb figures of the second half of the seventh century, such as those from the tomb of Zheng Rentai (dated 664; cat. nos. 183–185), all of which are very colorful. This is the more striking if one remembers that pottery figures before this time were mostly unglazed gray pottery; only occasionally are they depicted with naturalistic coloring and details such as facial features (as in cat. no. 154). The Zheng Rentai figures are painted over the glaze—a highly unusual method of decoration, as unfired pigments do not stay comfortably on glazed surfaces. The coloring of the Zheng Rentai figures is generally naturalistic, reflecting a more conventional usage.

Similarity in dress style can be seen between that of the exquisite doll from Astana, Turfan (cat. no. 181, possibly also a funerary figure) and that of the female figure from the tomb of Zheng Rentai (cat. no. 185, right)—with shawl and high-waisted vertically striped skirt. Fashion also applied to means of conveyance. Female riders in Turfan (cat. no. 182) and in the capital (cat. no. 183, again from the tomb of Zheng Rentai) are both mounted on piebald horses, a breed from northern Central Asia that was first recorded in Chinese history in the early Tang period and was likely to have been

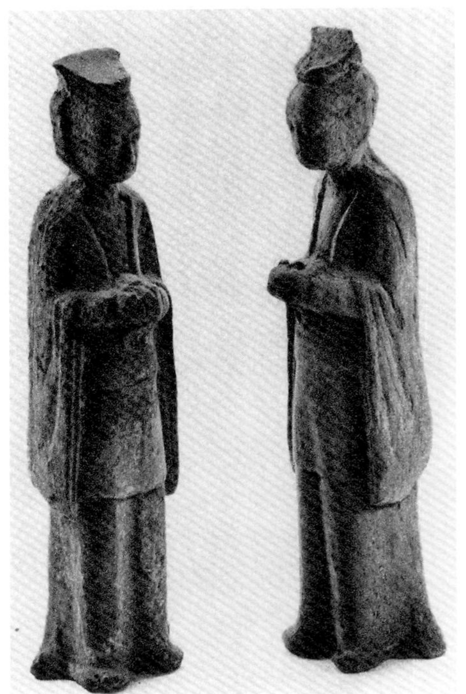

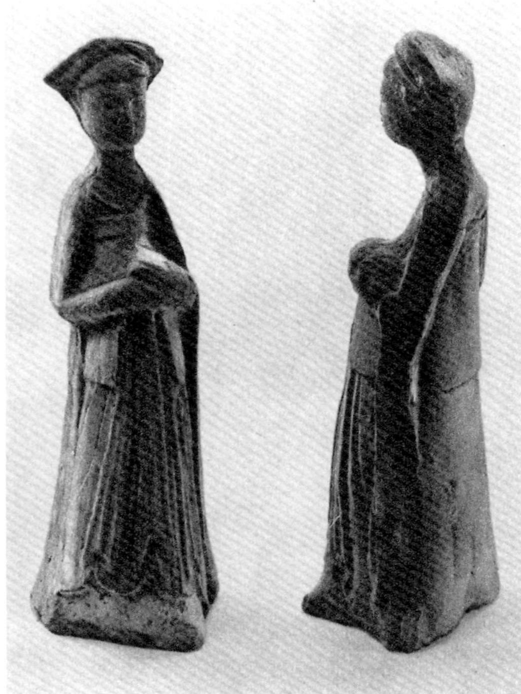

Figure 30a. Figures of officials. Sui dynasty (581–619). Earthenware, height 9 in. (23 cm). Excavated from the tomb (dated 608) of Li Jingxun, Xi'an, Shaanxi Province

Figure 30b. Female figures. Sui dynasty (581–619). Earthenware, height 10⅝ in. (27 cm). Excavated from the tomb (dated 608) of Li Jingxun, Xi'an, Shaanxi Province

highly prized at the time.[136] Perhaps also the result of nomadic influence, there was far less social segregation of women. They dressed in men's costumes if they felt like it (cat. no. 185, left), and they played polo, as seen in a number of Tang pottery figures.

The Elite

The objects from the Sui and Tang selected for this exhibition were excavated from the tombs of the ruling classes, many of them not pure Han Chinese. But by this time, after centuries of cultural integration and intermarriage, there were hardly any distinct ethnic groups remaining. Someone with the name of Li may not have been completely Han; nor was a Dugu necessarily wholly Xianbei. What is certain is that the ruling classes of the early Tang were all descended from the elite of the Northern Zhou and Sui.

One of the most important archaeological finds in recent decades is that of the undisturbed tomb, dated 608 in the Sui period, of a young girl, Li Jingxun. It is the only complete assemblage known to date of objects gathered together for an event that was of particular cultural significance at the time.[137] A thorough study of the structure and contents of the tomb and the stone house-shaped sarcophagus would tell us a great deal about a critical period in China's cultural history, when many elements were about to coalesce in the formation of a new civilization. This study has yet to be made, and for the purpose of this exhibition only two imported luxury objects from the tomb have been included (cat. nos. 186, 187). Li Jingxun was not quite nine years old when she died, in the year 608. Her ancestry is typical of the high aristocracy of the Sui and early Tang. She was the great-granddaughter, on her father's side, of Li Xian, whose ewer and several funerary figures are in this exhibition (cat. nos. 154–158). Her maternal grandparents were Emperor Xuandi of Northern Zhou (r. 579) and his wife, who was a daughter of Yang Jian—the first emperor of Sui—and a sister of Yangdi, the second emperor of the Sui (r. 605–18).

One of the most beautifully crafted objects from the early Tang period is the gold and jade belt (cat. no. 188) from the tomb of Dou Jiao (d. 646), a cousin of the wife of Li Yuan (r. 618–26), the founder of the Tang dynasty. It is a highly successful combination of jade and metalwork with stone inlay, rarely achieved in any other period.

Another prominent family in the Sui and early Tang periods was the Dugu. Both Yang Jian, Emperor Wendi of Sui, and Emperor Taizong of Tang married a Dugu. There are two horses in the exhibition from the tomb (dated 709) of a Dugu Sijing and his wife (née Yuan), a descendant of the imperial house of Northern Wei (cat. no. 199). This tomb was looted long ago, and only a few pottery funerary figures are left, including this pair of horses. Like other pottery sculptures of the early eighth century, the horses are beautifully observed in natural postures; they are among the better works of art to have survived from this period.

The Empress Wu

A special subsection in the exhibition is devoted to the Empress Wu (Wu Zetian), the only woman in Chinese history who ruled in her own right (r. 690–705). Even before she declared herself *huangdi* (emperor, a gender-neutral term in Chinese) in 690, she was, as it were, the power behind the throne of her husband, Emperor Gaozong (r. 650–83), who was in constant poor health. The Empress Wu presided over an empire at the height of its wealth and power, appointed able administrators, and fended off invasions from the north and west.[138] The subsection features two Buddhist sculptures, one from Chang'an (cat. no. 193) and the other from Luoyang (cat. no. 192), the two capitals of the Tang empire. (The dynastic name was changed to Zhou in 690–705, during Wu Zetian's reign.) Another object that is intimately related to her reign is the reliquary from the site of the Dayun Temple in Jingchuan, Gansu (cat. no. 191). In 690, the critical year in which the empress was to assume absolute power, a number of monks, including her monk-lover, Xue Huaiyi, produced the Dayun (*Mahāmegha*) Sutra, where it was foretold that Maitreya, the bodhisattva and future Buddha, would be incarnated as a female ruler to maintain peace and order in the world. Soon it was all agreed that Wu was that incarnation. This gave her the justification to declare herself emperor. As *huangdi,* she ordered every prefecture in the land to build a Dayun Temple, each of which would be provided with a copy of the all-important Dayun Sutra. The reliquary in this exhibition is from the Dayun Temple in Jingzhou prefecture (now Jingchuan County, Gansu).

The Empress Wu was a major patron of Buddhism even before the Buddhists confirmed her claim to the throne. She contributed royally to the carving of the great Buddha in the Fengxiansi at Luoyang (constructed from 672 to 676), the grandest Buddhist monument to have survived to this day (fig. 31).[139] But Buddhism did not provide the only support for her ambition. She also pursued other paths to legitimacy. In 665, she persuaded her husband, Gaozong, to perform the rites of *fengshan* at Taishan (the most important sacred mountain in China), in which she participated as an equal partner. The rites of *feng* and *shan* (homages to Heaven and Earth) had somehow since the Han period been regarded as the most solemn ritual in Confucian culture, in which the emperor, in addressing directly Heaven and Earth, affirmed his (or, in the present case, also her) mandate to rule. The rites performed in 665 must have been one of the most extravagant and spectacular events in Chinese history. The procession, which started from the eastern capital, Luoyang, was a hundred miles long, and the imperial party was accompanied by representatives from every country in Asia, from Persia to Korea.[140]

The gold tablet in this exhibition (cat. no. 190) provides yet more evidence of the Empress Wu's obsession with ritual, particularly ritual that related to the role of sovereign. In the case of the gold tablet, the association was with Daoism, with which the empress had close affinities, perhaps more than with Buddhism. On the tablet is inscribed a supplication to the gods by the sick and aging empress, with a plea for the forgiveness of her sins. It was delivered in the year 700, on top of the sacred mountain Songshan, Henan, on the empress's behalf by a Daoist who had gained favor with her by producing an elixir (at vast expense) that temporarily improved her condition and would, she hoped, give her longevity.[141] She did live until 705, after having returned power to her son Zhongzong (r. 684; 705–10) and having restored the Tang dynasty.

The High Tang

There are several objects in this exhibition from tombs dated 706, the year after the Empress Wu's death. These are from the tombs of Prince Zhanghuai (Li Xian, 654/5–684) and his wife; Princess Yongtai (684–701) and her husband (d. 701); and Yongtai's elder brother, Prince Yide (682–701). Zhanghuai was the Empress Wu's own son, Yide and Yongtai her grandchildren, and the latter's husband, also Wu, was a great-nephew. All were victims of the empress's merciless ascent to power. Li Xian, at one time heir apparent, was banished to Bazhou in Sichuan and either killed or, like Yide, ordered to commit suicide. Prince Yide, Princess Yongtai, and her husband died at the same time, most likely in Luoyang. All of them were returned in 706 to Chang'an to be interred in "attending tombs" near Qianling, the tomb of Gaozong and Wu Zetian. All three tombs are grand in scale and contain some of the finest wall paintings (cat. no. 194) and pottery figures (cat. nos. 197, 198). It is ironic that what has been left behind in these tombs after robbers long ago deprived them of valuable luxury articles (most likely similar to those from the tomb of Li Jingxun, cat. nos. 186, 187) is what, fourteen

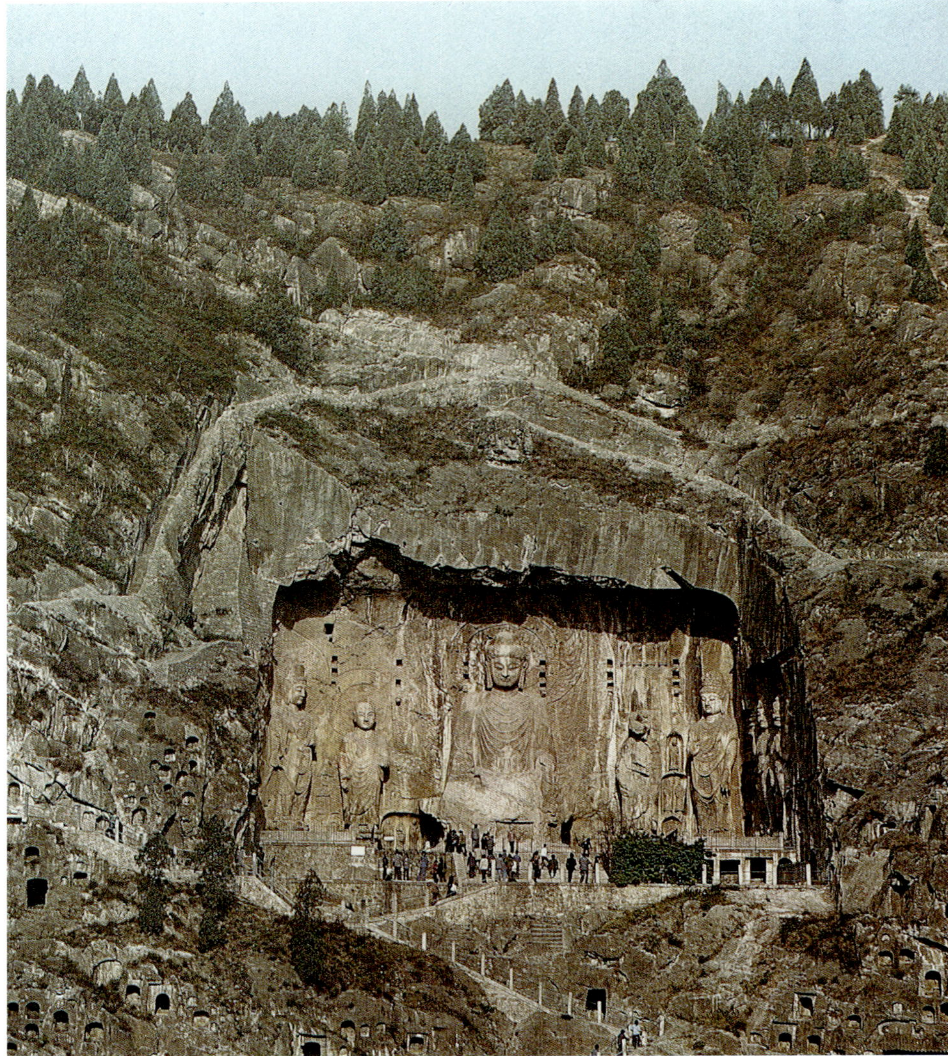

Figure 31. Fengxiansi, with the figure of the great Buddha. Tang dynasty (618–907). Longmen, Luoyang, Henan Province

centuries later, is regarded as the more highly valued works of art. The contents of these precisely dated tombs of Chang'an allow the unimaginative art historian, without too much embarrassment, to call the early eighth century a golden age in Chinese art.

Another brother of Yide and Yongtai, Prince Jiemin (Li Chongjun), also came to grief, in 709 after killing Wu Sansi, a nephew of the empress and the lover of Empress Wei (the wife of Zhongzong but not the mother of Jiemin) and Wu Sansi's son, who was married to Jiemin's half sister, Princess Anle. The wall painting from Prince Jiemin's tomb (of which cat. no. 195 is a small section) is one of the earliest surviving examples of landscape painting in China, while the painting in Zhanghuai's tomb (cat. no. 194), with a pair of figures, one turning back to face the other, continues an age-old tradition going back to at least the early Han period.[142] It is, of course, another manifestation of the principle of complementary opposites, a concept endemic in Chinese thinking. The same compositional device would continue for centuries to come, particularly in flower and bird paintings.

Emperor Zhongzong reascended the throne after the death of the Empress Wu. His wife, the Empress Wei, whose lover was killed by Prince Jiemin, became overly ambitious and was herself killed in a palace coup in 710 led by the imperial prince Li Longji (later Xuanzong, the Bright Emperor, r. 712–56). Several military officers who participated in this insurrection rose to senior positions at the court of Xuanzong. Funerary figures from the tombs of two of the officers are in this exhibition.

The pair of stone military officers (cat. no. 203) were found in the tomb of Yang Sixu (654–740). Yang is representative of a new elite class in the early Tang dynasty: the palace eunuchs. Unlike those of later periods, eunuchs in the early Tang did not necessarily volunteer their services at the palace. They generally began life as leaders of ethnic groups in border areas that eventually were incorporated into the empire. Yang Sixu followed this path. He was captured in an early pacification

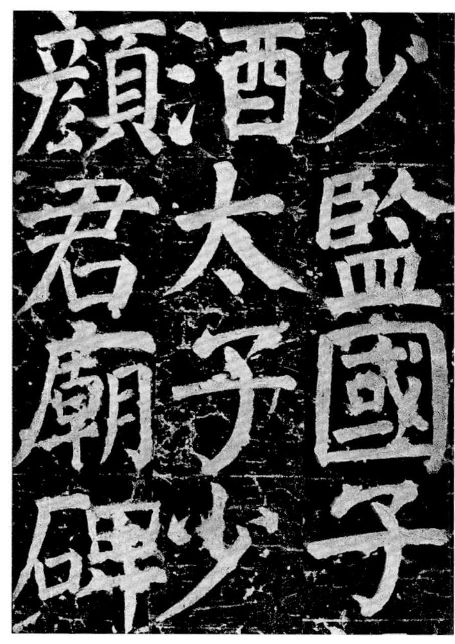

Figure 32. Rubbing of inscription on a stone stele. Calligraphy by Yan Zhenqing (708–784). Museum of the Forest of Steles, Xi'an, Shaanxi Province

campaign in South China (now Guangdong Province) and made a eunuch to serve in the palace. We have already seen an example of this type of eunuch official in Wang Yu, at the time of the Empress Dowager Wenming of the Northern Wei. Yang Sixu gained favor by taking part in the palace coup of 710 and was later promoted to the highest military rank. He was credited with the success of military operations in the south against his own people.[143] The pair of stone sculptures of officers in his tomb are among the best of their kind.

Another military officer who rose rapidly in rank after 710 was Xianyu Tinghui (660–723). Xianyu's family was from the northeast, and his ancestors served as military governors in border regions in the time of the Northern Dynasties.[144] At the time of his death in 723, the arts of the Tang had reached their full maturity and the pottery figures in his tomb, apart from being works of art themselves, provide excellent illustrations of the entertainment activities and fashions of the time. The camel (cat. no. 200) carries a band of Central Asian musicians, probably from Qiuci (Kucha), as Kuchean music was the most influential or popular of the imported music in Tang China.[145] The pair of actors (cat. no. 201) are considered to be the representation of an early form of theater usually performed by two actors and including dialogue, singing, and dancing.[146] The dialogue is usually comic, sometimes with a satirical edge.[147] The pair of figures in Xianyu's tomb can be regarded as court jesters.

Less than two decades after 706, the date of the several tombs discussed above, there was a considerable change in the concept of human beauty, at least in Chang'an, the capital and center of sophistication. This can be seen in both the male and female figures (cat. no. 202) from the tomb of Xianyu Tinghui, dated 723. Beginning at this time in the Tang dynasty, a certain degree of rotundity in the face and figure was preferred. It was also roughly from this time until the end of the Tianbao era in 755 that nearly all pottery figures from Tang tombs were covered with the three-color glaze that has become famous throughout the world.

There was something of a parallel change in the art of calligraphy in the eighth century, with slightly different timing. Catalogue no. 232 is a copy of an essay by a third-century author titled "Destiny and Fate" (a subject typical of the philosophical concerns of the time) that was written about the year of Li Jingxun's tomb or shortly after, that is, the early seventh century. The calligraphy marks the beginning of a new style in standard script. The brushwork is lean and structured, and there is a dynamic balance between the thinner and thicker strokes within each character. As abstraction, it is the purest expression of early Tang aesthetics. By the middle of the eighth century, the delicate structure of the brushwork has been modified and the strokes are more even in thickness (see cat. no. 233). By the late eighth century, the calligraphic stroke has taken on a certain quality of spreading. This style is seen in the late work of the highly regarded calligrapher Yan Zhenqing (708–784), exemplified in the rubbing of an inscription on a stele in Xi'an (fig. 32).

Yet another important development during the reign of Xuanzong was in Buddhist art. Sometime during his reign, sculptures of bodhisattvas assumed a sensuous human form, neither male nor female (cat. no. 228). From this point on, images of bodhisattvas (beings who are not yet Buddhas) would leave behind the hieratic form of an earlier period (cat. no. 227) and come to embody for each age what was conceived as a beautiful being, although they perhaps never achieved the artistic excellence seen in the High Tang. But this event did not engender a "crisis of the image," as has been attributed to a similar development in Christian art from the late Middle Ages to the Renaissance,[148] because the eighth century in China witnessed the rapid rise of a school of Buddhist thought, the Chan (Zen) sect, for which the worship of the Buddha and bodhisattvas—let alone the image—was irrelevant.

The Decorative Arts

The first half of the Tang dynasty was one of the rare periods in Chinese history when gold and silver objects were a major component of Chinese material culture, and Chinese workmanship in precious metals achieved a relatively high standard—at least in the metropolitan areas of Chang'an and Luoyang. Most important in the study of metalwork of this period is the discovery of a large hoard of precious objects of gold, silver, and jade at Hejiacun, southeast of Xi'an.[149] Five pieces from this hoard are in the exhibition, arranged in the order of their probable dates of manufacture, the latest being about the middle of the eighth century (cat. nos. 210–214). This sequence demonstrates the gradual adaptation of foreign forms (cat. nos. 212, 213) and motifs (cat. no. 210) until they achieved an unmistakable Chinese character (cat. no. 214). The strongest influence on early Tang metalware was Sogdian silver.[150] An early Tang silver dish comes close to Sogdian silver both in design and workmanship (cat. no. 209) but has an obvious look of an imitative work. It was found in Chifeng, Inner Mongolia, together with an authentic Sogdian silver ewer (cat. no. 208). Perhaps the dish was made locally for an immigrant Sogdian community, or, even more likely, for the Turks—as an unframed image of a beast in a large empty field is alien to Sogdian taste.[151] Sogdian silver is also found in other areas where Sogdians may be expected to have lived and worked. An example is the bowl with a stag (cat. no. 207), found in Xi'an.

Hardly any locally made glass of the Tang period has been found archaeologically. This is perhaps because of the fragility of the material. Nevertheless, although the technique of glass blowing was introduced into China by the fifth century (see cat. nos. 67, 68), there may not have been much incentive to manufacture glass utensils when there were burgeoning ceramic industries in both North and South China. The two glass vessels in this section of the exhibition are both imported (cat. nos. 219, 220), the perfume bottle being included to remind us that silk was by no means the only, or even the chief, commodity traded on the Silk Road.[152]

The ceramic art of the Tang period is so well known that it needs only to be summarized by pointing out that most of the pottery forms of North China, in particular the white wares of Hebei, derive from metal and glass objects. The green wares in the south, on the other hand, after a period of playful exploration of sculptural forms (cat. nos. 107–109), settled down to functional shapes that grew naturally on the potter's wheel, with occasional incised or carved decoration. The fifth-century covered jar (cat. no. 110) is the forerunner of the southern pottery style in the Tang period.

The only porcelain piece in this section is the early Tang ewer in the collection of The Palace Museum, Beijing (cat. no. 218). It is the apotheosis of Central Asian influence on art in China. The bird-shaped body is basically Iranian, but the handle of animal form is reminiscent of handles on metal vessels from Central Asia (see cat. no. 95), a tradition that can be traced back to the early nomadic period in the steppes. Within the pearl roundels are obese figures that may be based on the image of the Indic god Kubera, as seen on a silver dish in the British Museum, London, found in India and dated to the fifth century.[153] To do all this in porcelain—or what is nearly porcelain—is, of course, in the selection of the clay and in the modeling and firing, a considerable technical feat. But the melding of disparate elements into a coherent and complex whole is an artistic triumph.

At the same time, the silk textile industry had also matured. Three examples in this exhibition represent the classic types of Tang silk up to about the middle of the eighth century (cat. nos. 239–241). The reader is referred to the essay by Zhao Feng for a discussion of the technical and stylistic development in silk weaving from the late Han to the High Tang period.

Late in the year 755, music and dance at the court in Chang'an were shattered by war drums from Yuyang—to paraphrase the poet Bo (Bai) Juyi's (772–846) immortal "Song of Everlasting Regret," which tells of the tragic events in the last days of the reign of Xuanzong (r. 712–56) and his love for his consort, Lady Yang. The war drums were those of the army of An Lushan (d. 757), military governor of the northeastern province of Fanyang, with headquarters in Yuyang, near present-day Beijing. The complex causes of the rebellion have been a subject keenly studied by historians in the twentieth century. Whatever the cause, whether it was the ethnicity of the rebels (An Lushan was Turko-Sogdian and his soldiers were presumably, for the most part, non-Han Chinese), policy differences at court, or the incompetence of the imperial guards, the immediate result was the fall, in quick succession, of the two capitals, Luoyang and Chang'an. The emperor fled to take refuge in Sichuan after having been forced to put to death Lady Yang and her cousin Yang Guozhong, both of whom were believed to exert evil influences on him.

The civil war waged for eight years, during which time the armies stationed in Central Asia were gradually recalled to reinforce the loyalists. The final decisive battle took place in 762 outside the city of Luoyang. It put an end to the rebellion, but it also put an end to a very special period of Chinese art history. The victorious government troops, composed mainly of Uygurs who had come down from Mongolia in support of the Tang, systematically plundered the city, leaving it in ruins. The consequences of this event are not unlike the destruction of Luoyang by Dong Zuo in the third century, with which our narrative began.

In the meantime, the Tibetans, taking advantage of the withdrawal of Chinese troops from the Western Regions, had occupied the Gansu Corridor, cutting off Chang'an from Central Asia. Central Asians in the thousands were stranded in the Chinese capital, and gradually they were absorbed into the local population. Writers in later periods have left accounts of the popularity of western music and fashion in Chang'an well into the next century.[154] But this was more of an internal development within Chang'an than an active exchange between two living cultures.

After 757, Chang'an and Luoyang remained capital cities for another one and a half centuries but would never recover their central positions in the arts and culture of China. It would take another two centuries for the next major period in Chinese art to emerge.

Coda

In the history of China, the gestation period for the civilization that emerged in the early Tang dynasty was an exceptionally long one. The significance of the cultural changes that took place during the five centuries in question cannot be overstated. The changes gave a new life to a society governed by traditions that had roots going back millennia to the beginning of agrarian communities. The old social order came to a violent end together with the Han dynasty. But the same ancient traditions held through the centuries of disruptions and provided the basis of a new—or rather a renewed—civilization that was generated from the acceptance of many ideas and attitudes brought in by peoples from throughout the vast Asian continent. The telling of the long and complex story of this slow transformation will occupy historians for some time to come. The objects in our exhibition will continue to supply important material for the study of a particular stretch of history. As works of art they will stand on their own, for all time.

1. Twitchett 1979: 357–76.
2. Wang Zhongluo 1994, vol. 1: 20; Twitchett 1979: 341–57.
3. *HHS* "Biography of Dong Zhuo" 72: 2319ff.
4. Hackin et al. 1954: 574.
5. "Monograph on the Five Elements" chapter of the *Xu Hanshu* quoted in *HHS* "Record of the Five Elements" 11: 3272.
6. For an early image, see *Kaogu xuebao*, no. 2 (1964), pl. 8. For mention of the "feathered man" in literature, see Wang Chong (27–97), *Lun Heng*.
7. Arbore-Popescu, Antonini, and Baipakov 1998, pl. 468.
8. *GSZ*: 5.
9. Rhie 1999: 56–58.
10. Haraprasad 1995: 263–89; Jao Tsung-i 1993: 223–60.
11. Ma Yong 1990: 41–45.
12. Translated by Robert van Gulik as "Poetical Essay on the Lute." See van Gulik 1941.
13. For an excellent English translation and study by E. R. Hughes, see Lu Ji 1951.
14. Read 1965.
15. *JS* "Biography of Lu Ji" 54: 1467–81.
16. *JS* "Biography of Liu Kun" 62: 1687.
17. Ibid.: 1690.
18. *HHS* "The history of the Wuhuan and Xianbei" 90: 2986.
19. *BQS* "The biography of Emperor Shenwu" 1: 1.
20. See, for example, Pohl and Reimitz 1998: intro. and chaps. 1, 2.
21. *WS* "Preface" 1: 7.
22. Minyaev 2000: 293–303.
23. Davis-Kimball 2000: 223–39.
24. Sun Ji 1996b: 107–21.
25. The fourth-century writer Gan Bao was said to have commented on this type of jewelry as "extremely wicked"; quoted in Sun Ji 1996b.
26. Nanjing shi bowuguan 1972: 23–41.
27. *HHS* "The biographies of the ten princes of Guangwu" 42: 1423–56.
28. Yi Shui 1981: 85–89.
29. There are many conjectures as to the origin of the Qie. The most convincing seem to be that of Tang Zhangru 1978: 414–26.
30. Geary 2002: 93–96.
31. For a discussion of the material culture of Ye, see Zhou Yiliang 1991: 151–66.
32. Ibid.
33. Loosely translated from *JS* "The record of Ran Min"107: 2793ff.
34. *JS* "Biography of Xie An" 79: 2075.
35. *JS* "A record of Lü Guang" 122: 3053–64.
36. *ZZTJ* 114: 3579.
37. Chen Yinke 1974: 21–42.
38. Chen Mengjia 1964.
39. *JS* "Records of Murong Yun" 124: 3108–9.
40. For a discussion of the development of the stirrup in East Asia, see Xu Bingkun 1996: 148–53.
41. *HHS* "The biography of Zhu Mu" 6: 1472–73; *TPYL* "Insects" 944: 4192–93.
42. Tang Yongtong 1991: 488–89.
43. Sarianidi 1985, pl. 15.
44. Nanjing shi bowuguan 2001: 4–40, 91.
45. *WS* "Biography of Taizu" 2: 19–47.
46. *JS* "Record of Fujian" 113: 2899.
47. The official history, *Weishu*, glosses over the inglorious ten-year period, 376–386) and does not mention the capture of Shiyijian and Gui. For a summary of the reconstruction of this period by recent scholars, see Li Ping 2000: 16–36.
48. *WS* "The biographies of the Houses of Shenyuan and Pingwen" 14: 347; *WS* "The biographies of the House of Zhaocheng" 15: 383.

49. *WS* "The biography of Taizu" 2: 44. For an account of mineral elixirs in China, see Needham 1974: 282–304.
50. See note 5, above.
51. Sun Peiliang 1977.
52. Wang Yi-t'ung 1984: 148–51.
53. Shanxi sheng Datong shi bowuguan and Shanxi sheng wenwu gongzuo wei yuan hui 1972.
54. Murck 2003: 138–45.
55. Zhou Yiliang 1985: 226–28.
56. For a discussion of this transmission of decorative motifs from the west to China, see Rawson 1984: intro., chaps. 1, 2.
57. Luo Feng 1988: 14–15.
58. See note 39, above.
59. Miki 1964, pl. 62.
60. Suixi xian bowuguan 1986: 243–46.
61. Yoshida 1996: 69–78.
62. *ZZTJ* 123: 3874, 3877; *WS* "Biography of Shizu" 4: 90.
63. Tang Zhangru 1978: 403–14. For a ready reference for Yuezhi (Yueh-chih), see Narain 1994.
64. For the biography of Daosheng, see *GSZ*. For an exposition of the doctrine, see *GSZ*: 647–51.
65. Tang Yongtong 1991: 499, quoting "Shi lao zhi"; translated by Gernet 1995: 100, and discussed on pp. 100–105.
66. *WS* "Shi lao zhi," 114: 3037.
67. *WS* "Biographies of eunuch officials" 94: 2023; *BS* "Biography of Wang Yu" 92: 3035.
68. Su Bai 1996: 52–75, esp. p. 61.
69. Extensively discussed in Ma Changshou 1985, chap. 3.
70. Ibid.
71. Ma Changshou 1985: 43.
72. See note 36, above.
73. For events leading up to this episode, see *WS* "Record of distaff kin" 83: 1818–20, although the actual dates of the event are not recorded. There are also inconsistencies in the record of the age of Wenming at the time.
74. Ibid.
75. For the historical background and detailed account of Wenming's rise to power, see Li Ping 2000.
76. Tian Yuqing 1998: 359–405.
77. Wang Zhongluo 1994: 545–53.
78. *WS* "Biography of Emperor Shizu" 7: 135–89, and "Biographies of Empresses" 13: 332, 335.
79. For a discussion of the possible dates of this sculpture, see Luo Zongzhen 1994: 71–76.
80. For an account of the Ashokan columns (pillars) seen by Faxian, see Pandey 1982: 47–48.
81. Tang Yongtong 1991: 5–6.
82. *JS* "Biography of Xie Lingyun" 67: 1743ff.
83. *SS* "Biography of Yan Yanzhi" 73: 1893.
84. Luo Zongzhen 1994: 136.
85. Xie Zhenfa 2001: 1–50.
86. Shandong sheng wenwu kaogu yanjiusuo et al. 1989.
87. Yang Hong 1991.
88. Jiling sheng wenwu gongzuodui 1984.
89. *JS* "Biography of Ji Kang" 49: 1369–74; *JS* "Biography of Xiang Xiu" 49: 1374–75.
90. Zhou Yiliang 1997.
91. Ibid.: 75.
92. *NQS* "Biographies of the Man and Southeast Barbarians" 58: 1007.
93. Henan sheng wenhuaju wenwu gongzuodui 1958: 37.
94. *NQS* "Records of the Man and Southeast Barbarians" 58: 1009.
95. Jao Tsung-i 1993.
96. Tang Yongtong 1991: 436–41.
97. There are several passages that deal with form and spirit in the early Han work, the *Huainanzi*, particularly in chapter 7, "On the Spirit." The quote is from an Eastern Han annotation on the line, "What fills out the form is not form." *HNZ* 10: 105.
98. *LQJ*: 161. See also the English translation by Wang Yi-t'ung 1984.
99. *LQJ*: 201; for identification of Wuchang: 306.
100. Wang Yi-t'ung 1984: 13 and map on p. 14.
101. Zhongguo shehui kexueyuan kaogu yanjiusuo 1996.
102. *WS* "Biography of Cui Guang" 4: 1495.
103. Wang Yi-t'ung 1984: 246.
104. Zhong Xiaoqing 2000: 574, 559–77.
105. Wang Zhongluo 1994: 563–65.
106. *WS* "The biography of Xiao Baoyin" 59: 1313–24.
107. *LQJ* "Yongning temple" 1: 1–38.
108. As pointed out some time ago in Willetts 1958: 472–73.
109. Melikian-Chirvani 1995: 41–97.
110. Pandey 1982.
111. Gombrich 1984: 270–72, quoting Otto Kurz.
112. *BS* "Biography of Erzhu Rong" 48: 1762.
113. For Cui Yuji's family, see Ebrey 1978.
114. See Geary 2002: 110–11.
115. *ZZTJ* 157: 4882.
116. *ZS* "Biography of Li Xian" 25: 413–18.
117. For the initial report, see Shandong sheng Qingzhou shi bowuguan 1998.
118. *LS* "Zhuyi" 54: 797–99. For a general account of early maritime trade in Southeast Asia, see Wolters 1967, chaps. 2, 5.
119. *LS* "Zhuyi" 54: 789–90.
120. Lee In-sook 1993, 2001, and 2002.
121. Shaanxi kaogu yanjiusuo et al. 1997: 8–28.
122. *BS* "Empresses and consorts" 14: 517–18.
123. Marshak and Negmatov 1996: 1236.
124. Luo Feng 1998b: 215–49.
125. For references, see the entry on cat. no. 175.
126. Ningxia huizu zhiziqu guyuan bowuguan and Luo Feng 1996: 7–30.
127. Ibid.
128. Luoyang shi wenwu gongzuodui 1982: 21–26.
129. For a discussion of gold coins in burials of Central Asians in China, see Ningxia huizu zhiziqu guyuan bowuguan and Luo Feng 1996: 159–63.
130. For the very interesting history of this family, see Zhao Zhenhua and Zhu Liang 1982: 37–40.
131. Zheng Yan 2001: 73–109.
132. Wan Shengnan 1995: 327–36.
133. Chen Yinke 1974.
134. Twitchett 1979: 224–28, map on p. 227.
135. Griaznov 1969: 196. See also Watt 2002: 207.
136. *XTS* "Huigu" 217: 6146.
137. In 602, the death of Empress Xian (wife of Yang Jian, first emperor of Sui) occasioned a major discussion on funerary rites. See Chen Yinke 1974.
138. Denis Twitchett (1979, chaps. 5, 6) gives a detailed account of her reign.
139. *JSC* 73: 268–69.
140. *THY*, chap. 7.
141. Dong Li 2001.
142. See the Han bricks with painted scenes in the Museum of Fine Arts, Boston (1982: 98–99).

143. *JTS* "Eunuchs" 184: 4755–56; *XTS* 132: 5857; epitaph in Zhongguo shehui kexueyuan kaogu yanjiusuo 1980: 83–86.
144. According to the epitaph in Zhongguo shehui kexueyuan kaogu yanjiusuo 1980: 83–86.
145. Yang Yinliu 1985: 215.
146. Tian Jin (Xu Pingfang) 1959: 43–46.
147. Yang Yinliu 1985: 208–9.
148. Belting 1994: 458ff.
149. Shaanxi sheng bowuguan geiweihui xiezuo xiaozu 1972.
150. Melikian-Chirvani 1970; Marshak 1971: 47–59, 82 (English summary: 139–42, 152).
151. I owe this observation to Boris Marshak.
152. For commodities traded on the Silk Road, see Schafer 1963; for commodities of an earlier period, see Laufer 1919.
153. Dalton 1964: 204, pl. XXXIII, but see Marshak 1986 for dating.
154. Xiang Da 1933.

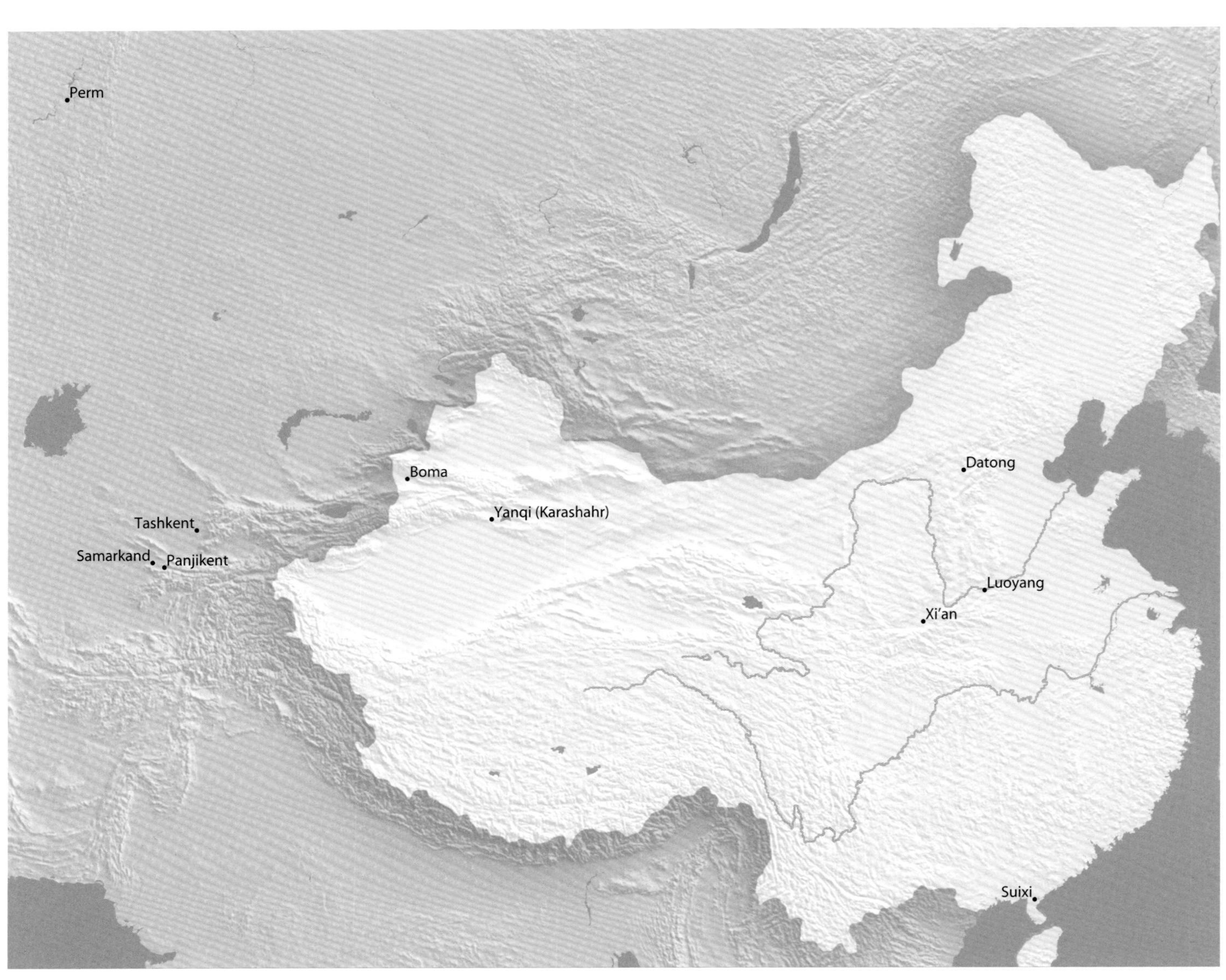

Perm
Boma
Yanqi (Karashahr)
Tashkent
Samarkand
Panjikent
Datong
Luoyang
Xi'an
Suixi

Central Asian Metalwork in China

BORIS I. MARSHAK

Luxury vessels from Central Asia dating from the third to the seventh century that have been found in China are made of silver and, occasionally, of gold.[1] In West and Central Asia, such objects were among the most important attributes of the lifestyle of the aristocracy. The vessels are decorated with symbolic imagery, in particular, scenes of hunting and feasting, making them a rich iconographic resource. In China, on the other hand, there is virtually no association of precious metals with the elite. Objects that reflect the domain's ancient cultural traditions as well as its wealth and prosperity are made of bronze and jade, although gold and silver were in use from the very beginning of Chinese history.

As a rule, the objects crafted of these two metals were banquet tableware and jewelry. They belonged to the nonofficial sphere of luxury and pleasure. Thus imported vessels, notwithstanding their foreign motifs, became fashionable, and many replicas of western models were produced in China, especially between the third and the mid-eighth century, when steppe cavalrymen together with Central Asian traders and craftsmen became an important element of society in North China.

The greater part of Central Asia was conquered by the Chinese from 630 to 660, during the Tang dynasty (618–907). But even the first Tang emperors wished to gain favor with their non-Chinese subjects, and despite the reproaches of the Confucians, they adopted certain practices of the steppe leaders. For example, Taizong (r. 627–49), who in 630 formally became the Heavenly Qaghan of the Turks who had been conquered by his army, was criticized by his advisers for his frequent participation in the royal hunts.[2] But Taizong knew very well that the Iranian and Turkic peoples considered such hunts obligatory for their rulers and military leaders. It is notable that about 660, when Sogdiana formally became a part of Tang China, a heroic scene of the Tang emperor hunting was depicted on a wall painting displayed in Samarkand, the Sogdian capital.[3]

Taizong compared himself with the ancient monarchs. He declared that his politics were better than theirs because in ancient times everybody liked the Chinese but despised the barbarians Rong and Di. But he loved them equally and supported their people like their father and mother.[4] The banquet was another activity in the steppes and in greater Iran that was enjoyed by royalty for both amusement and prestige. And banquets, too, were shared by Chinese rulers and generals with warriors from the steppes. An incidental result of their participation was their introduction to luxury tableware.

Any attempt to characterize cultural ties between China and Central Asia as reflected in their metalwork must take into account the crucial role of the nomads. Indeed, the relationship of the nomadic peoples of the steppes both with each other and with the sedentary civilizations was more important than the trade between China, the oases states of Central Asia, and the Greek colonies of the Black Sea.

The peripatetic nature of nomadic cultures helps to explain the wide geographic distribution of silver in Europe and Asia, far from the centers of production in Byzantium, Iran, and western Central Asia, and usually we can speak only about approximate dates and general regions of manufacture. Over the past thirty years, metalwork unearthed in Chinese tombs has provided important examples of vessels produced in Iran, Bactria (present-day northern Afghanistan, southern Uzbekistan, and southern Tajikistan), Sogdiana (present-day central Uzbekistan and central Tajikistan), and other regions in Central Asia. Many of these add different forms and designs to the repertory of material from these areas. In addition, dated Chinese tombs provide crucial information regarding the termini ante quem of these vessels. Much of the

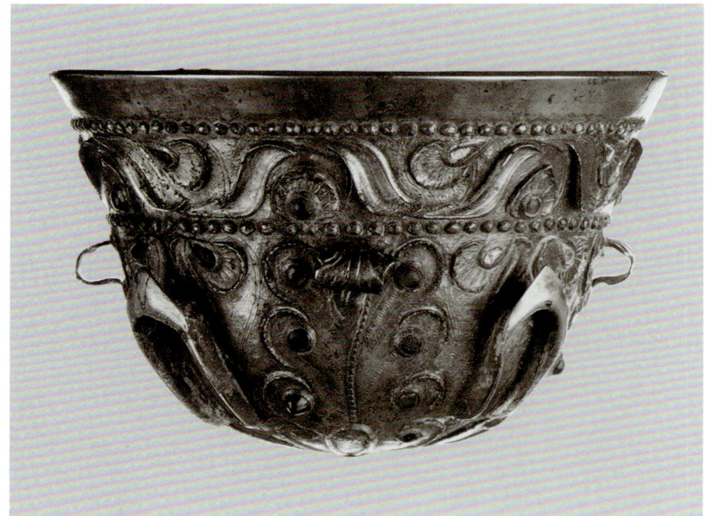

Figure 33. Drinking cup. Possibly Afghanistan, 1st century B.C. Gilt silver, inlaid with glass and semiprecious stones, height 3¼ in (8.3 cm). J. Paul Getty Museum, Villa Collection, Los Angeles (86.AM.754.4). © J. Paul Getty Museum

material found in China, however, was made centuries before it was buried and thus is not useful in dating the period of production. For example, a silver vessel of a nomadic shape decorated with slightly simplified Hellenistic ornaments (cat. no. 100) is datable not later than the first century B.C., but it was found in a Chinese cemetery of the third to fourth century A.D. A ring handle, added later, made this foreign vessel similar to the Chinese *hu* jars. Such hybrid objects do not reveal any direct Sino-Hellenistic contact. On the contrary, the vessel was made in accordance with the tastes of the nomadic milieu with ties to both the Hellenistic world and China.

Several intriguing vessels most likely produced in the Bactrian region that illustrate strong ties to Hellenistic traditions have been unearthed in Pingcheng (present-day Datong), the capital of the Northern Wei (386–534) until the late fifth century. These include two footed cups (cat. nos. 58, 60), a bowl for such a cup (cat. no. 63), and a bowl from Tomb 107, in a cemetery south of the city (cat. no. 64). The vessels share several features. They are all decorated with acanthus leaves shown with a deep furrow dividing each lobe and two lines marking the middle vein. This is a stylization of the motif well known in the decoration of Hellenistic metalwork.[5] The vessels may have been made at the same production center about the same time, although the styles and dates of their prototypes in Central Asia or the Greco-Roman world vary noticeably.

For example, the footed cup with glass and red stone inlays, which probably dates to the fifth century (cat. no. 58), is similar to a Hellenistic silver cup in the J. Paul Getty Museum, Los Angeles, dating to as early as the first century B.C. (fig. 33).[6] The latter has neither a foot nor the soldered figures seen on the vessel excavated in China. Such figures are rare in Hellenistic metalwork but are found on the stem cup from Pingcheng (cat. no. 60). A cylindrical cup from Pingcheng (cat. no. 59)

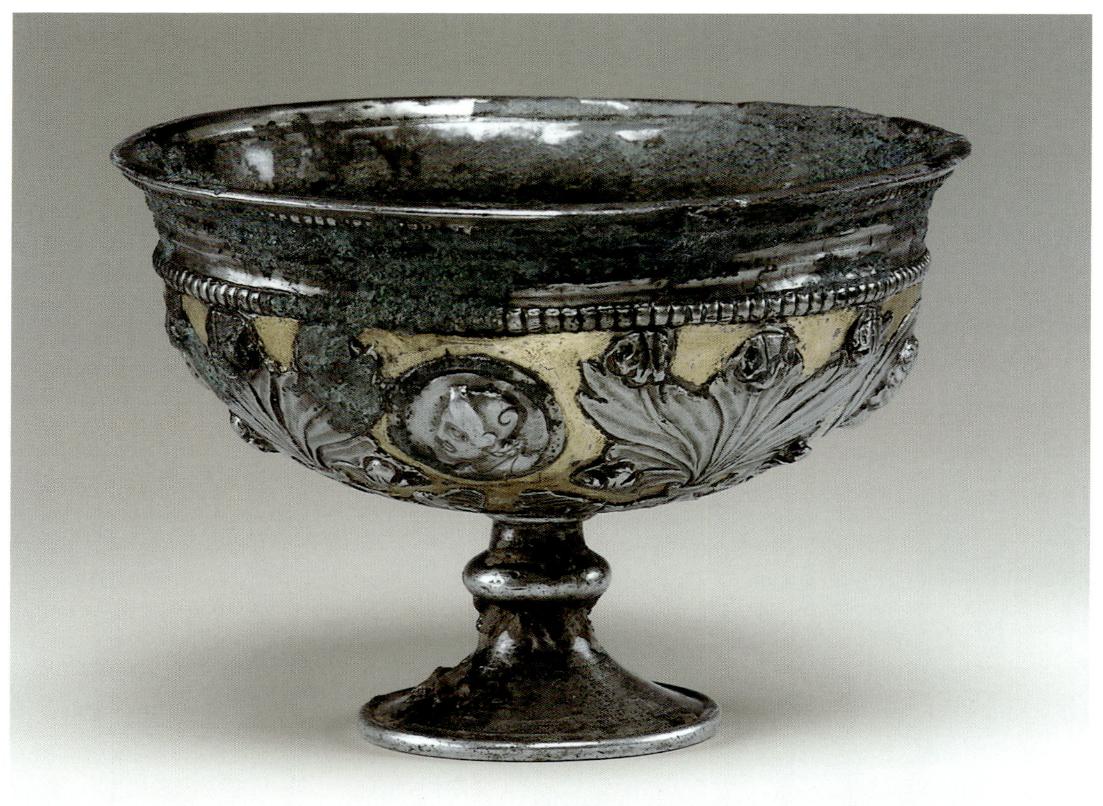

Figure 34. Stem bowl. Afghanistan or Central Asia, 3rd–4th century. Gilt silver, height 2¼ in. (5.8 cm). The Metropolitan Museum of Art, Louis V. Bell Fund, 2000 (2000.503)

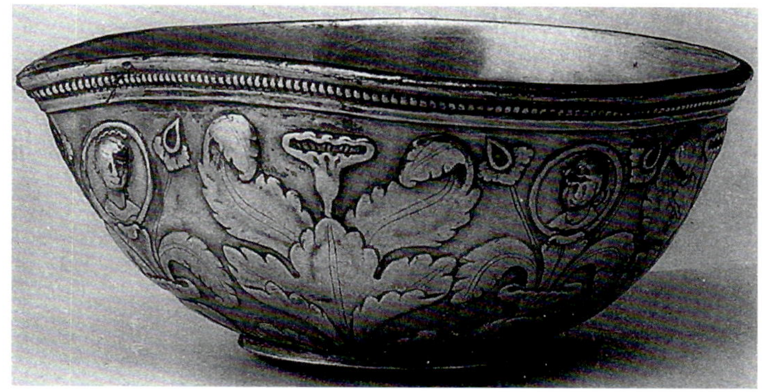

Figure 35. Bowl. Afghanistan or Central Asia, 3rd–4th century. Silver, diameter 5½ in. (14 cm). The State Historical Museum, Saint Petersburg (inv. no. 83746)

shows vintaging boys, a theme common in Late Roman art,[7] including metalwork. The foliate ornament on the lower part of the cup is similar to that on the bottom of the bowl found in Tomb 107 (cat. no. 64). On the stem cup with soldered figures (cat. no. 60), there is a row of similar leaves, while on the cylindrical cup (cat. no. 59) the boys-and-grapevine motif is enframed by two rows of similar leaves. The vessels seem to be cast of bronze or some other whitish alloy with a high content of copper, and gilded, but their western counterparts are of gilded silver. The shared stylistic features were popular in the Bactrian region about 400, when artisans imitated both earlier Hellenistic and more contemporary Roman shapes and decorative motifs.[8]

The two bowls excavated at Pingcheng (cat. nos. 63, 64) belong to a group of silver vessels adorned with roundels enframing portrait busts in relief. A stem bowl recently acquired by The Metropolitan Museum of Art (fig. 34) provides another example, as does a fourth bowl (fig. 35) found at Bartym (the Perm district in northern Russia).[9] The faces on the vessels found in China and on the bowl in the Metropolitan are shown in full profile; those on the Bartym bowl are in three-quarter profile. The style of the medallion bowls is quite different from the authentic Hellenistic manner. They belong to the group of so-called Bactrian vessels of the third to the sixth century, the period of the Bactrian Renaissance.[10]

The Bartym bowl, which is the earliest of the group, is one of numerous silver vessels found in the upper Kama River basin. None of the datable works from this area are earlier than the second half of the third century. To establish a relative chronology of the three remaining bowls, we might consider the stylistic evolution of the acanthus leaf. On the Metropolitan bowl (fig. 34), the upper parts are executed in high relief. These were made separately and then inlaid. On the silver bowl from Tomb 107 (cat. no. 64), the leaves are flat and carefully delineated, and high relief is used only for the portraits. Finally, on the fourth bowl (cat. no. 63), the flat foliate ornament becomes schematized and shows a lack of vitality.

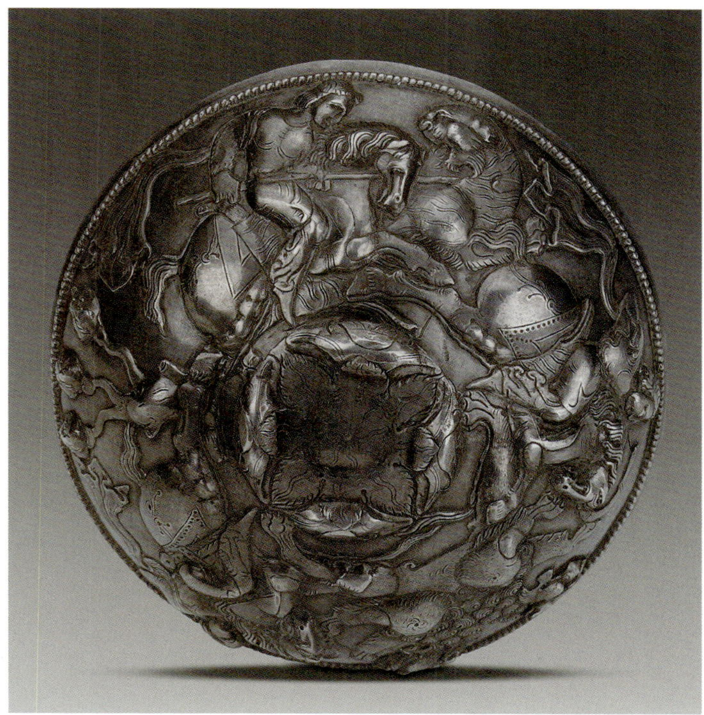

Figure 36. Bowl with hunting scene. Afghanistan or Central Asia, 4th century. Silver, diameter 5½ in. (13.9 cm). The State Hermitage Museum, Saint Petersburg (inv. no. s-8)

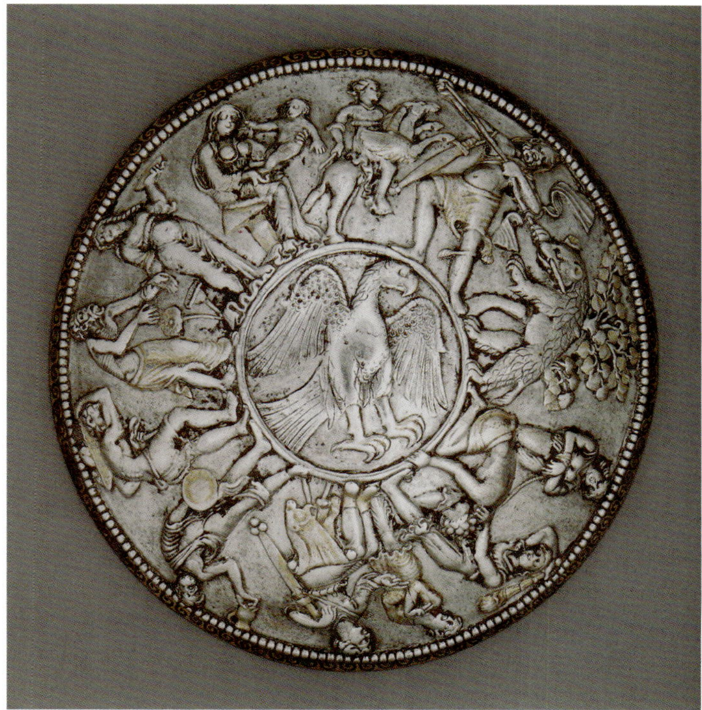

Figure 37. Bowl with Greek legends. Afghanistan or Central Asia, 4th–5th century. Gilt silver, diameter 7½ in. (19.1 cm). Freer Gallery of Art, Smithsonian Institution, Washington, D.C.: Purchase, F1945.33

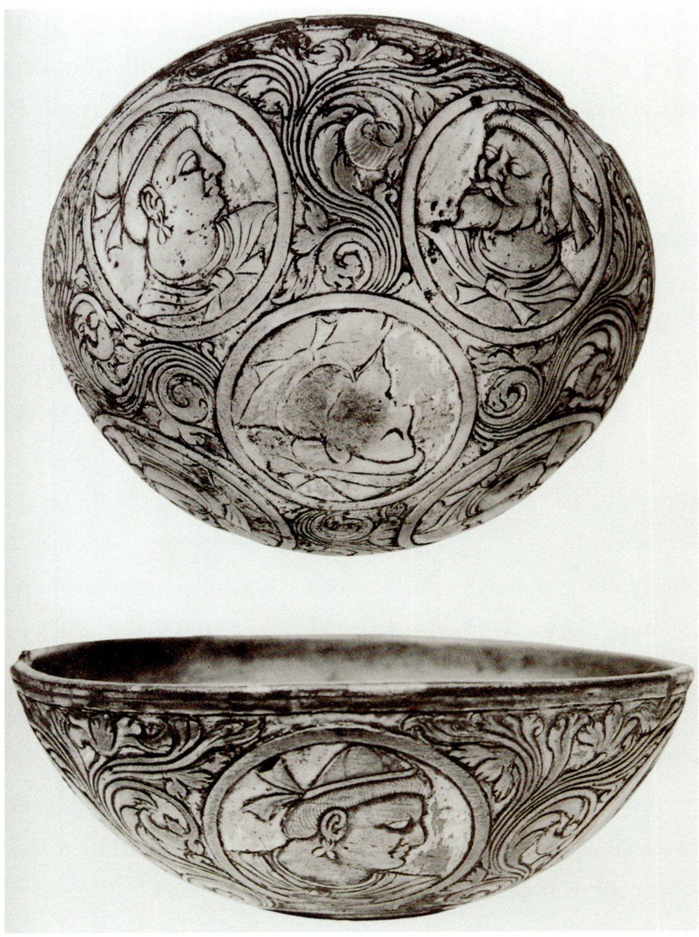

Figure 38. Bowl. Afghanistan or Central Asia, 5th century. Silver, diameter 5¼ in. (13.5 cm). British Museum, London

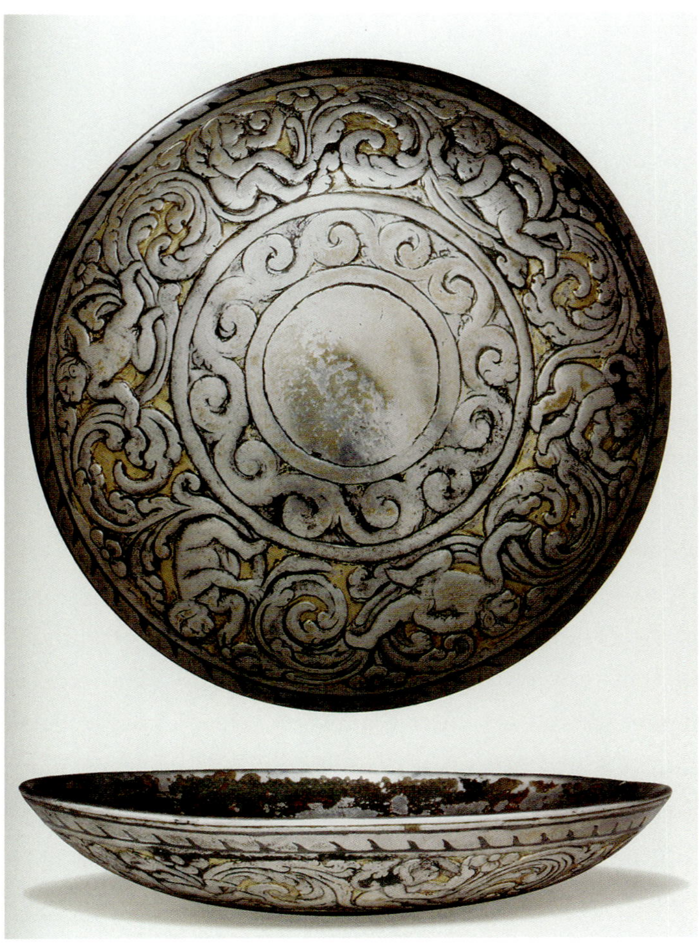

Figure 39. Bowl. Possibly Tibet, 4th–5th century. Gilt silver, diameter 6¾ in. (17.1 cm)

Stylistic changes in the representation of the faces on the four vessels also provide clues to their dating. Those on the earlier vessels are more or less classical. In particular, each of the four faces on the bowl from Tomb 107 is individualized. The rendering, however, is somewhat distorted, as the artist exaggerated the features of the classical model, which were alien to him. The combination of frontal head and shoulders turned in profile on the cup that may be missing a foot (cat. no. 63) is similar to those on fifth-century Kidarite or early Hephthalite seals,[11] and to the hunters' heads on a fourth-century silver bowl in the State Hermitage Museum, Saint Petersburg (fig. 36), especially the hairdo, with a narrow band, a small round top, and ample curls below.[12]

The silversmiths of Central Asia often reproduced prestigious models—in Bactria these were Hellenistic or, occasionally, Roman—but they did not copy them mechanically and would invariably add small, seemingly incidental ornamental details that they had memorized in their early training. One such detail is a large flower in the form of an inverted bell. This ornament is not present on the Hellenistic vessel in the Getty Museum (see fig. 33) but became typical in the later decoration of Bactrian vessels.[13] In Datong, it is attested on the foot of the stem cup with soldered figures (cat. no. 58). The same type of blossom is found on the Bartym bowl with portrait medallions (see fig. 35), a Bactrian bowl in the Freer Gallery of Art, Washington, D.C. (fig. 37), and a silver plate from the Bibliothèque Nationale, Paris, that has Indian and Sasanian imagery.[14] If the silver portrait bowls and stem cups are from one area of Bactria, the bronze (?) vessels found in China may also have been produced in Bactria, but at some center of production that remains unidentified. The white (or nearly white) relief details placed against the gold background on all the vessels unearthed in China appear to be similar.

The shape of another silver bowl excavated in Pingcheng (cat. no. 61), oblong with eight lobes, resembles several Sasanian bowls, although the décor derives from Gupta period India (ca. 300–ca. 500). It bears an inscription giving a name and the title Khingula, perhaps a reference to one of the fifth-century

Hephthalite rulers whose dominions were populated by both Indians and Bactrians.[15] Indo-Bactrian contacts are shown in the decoration of other fifth-century silver vessels. Among them is a bowl in the British Museum, London, executed in the Gupta style, with five busts of Northern "barbarians" in Bactrian attire (fig. 38). Another interesting example (fig. 39) is a shallow bowl with reliefs on the exterior, reportedly from Tibet. The shape is Bactrian and the motif of the scroll inhabited by putti is Hellenistic, while the leaves of the scroll are typically early Gupta.

Sometimes the interaction of styles was more complicated. The silver ewer that recounts a Greek legend (cat. no. 157) displays not only Sasanian elements but Bactrian and Gupta characteristics as well. The vessel was found in the tomb of the Northern Zhou general Li Xian, who died in 569. It is possible, however, that the ewer was made earlier, perhaps in the fifth century. A silver plate that depicts a hunt scene and is Sasanian in origin (cat. no. 62) reached China no later than about 500. To date, there is one comparable plate extant (fig. 40), which is said to have been sold in a Kabul bazaar. The dish was probably found in Afghanistan, a region that was Bactrian both linguistically and culturally.[16] It is thus likely that in the fifth century, Bactrians served as middlemen for trade between Iran and China.

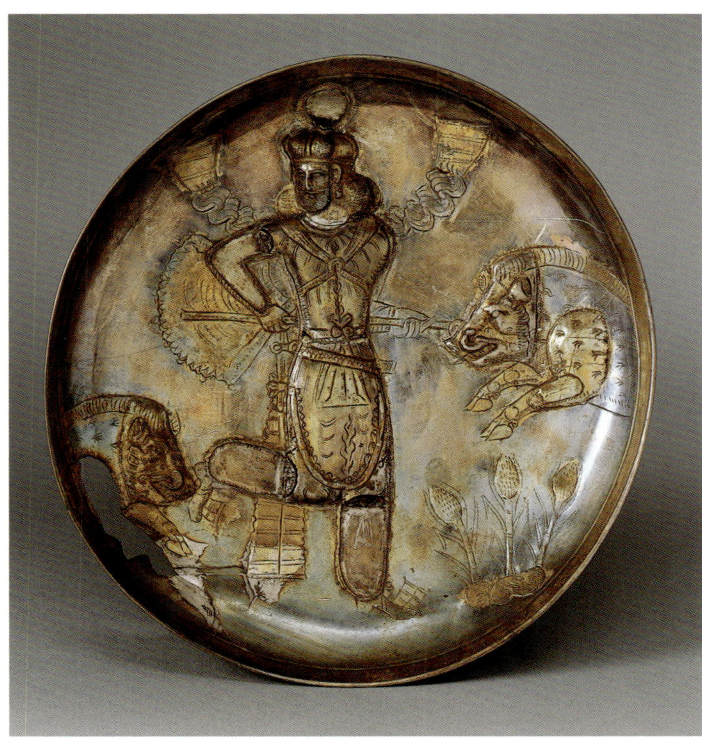

Figure 40. Plate. Possibly Afghanistan, late 4th–early 5th century. Gilt silver, diameter 9 1/4 (23.4 cm). Collection of Shelby White and Leon Levy

But cross-cultural and economic ties were more complex still. Among the upper Indus inscriptions dating from the fourth to the sixth century written on rocks along the route crossing the Karakoram Range, many are Sogdian but few are Bactrian, suggesting that in this region the Sogdians served as middlemen.[17] In China, on the other hand, Sogdian inscriptions on silver vessels, made in Sogdiana and elsewhere, cannot be dated earlier than the sixth century. This would suggest that the role of the Sogdians became gradually more important and that they reached primacy beginning at this time.

No Bactrian (or Indo-Bactrian) silver vessels have been found in Xinjiang, but two have surfaced in Tibet.[18] It is notable that Bactrian stylistic elements occur in the decoration of the metalwork made during the first kingdom of Tibet (7th–9th century), which encompassed parts of Central Asia and northwestern China. Among these elements are a grotesque man's head on the bottom of the Afanas̆evo cup in the Nizhni Novgorod Art Museum, in Russia,[19] and the Pan-like figures of drunkards on the great Jokong ewer,[20] which perhaps symbolize the people of the land of grapes and wine. In addition, the compositional scheme of the reliefs of the Afanas̆evo cup and a plate in the Shumei Culture Foundation, Shigaraki (fig. 41), are similar. In both, stylized plants alternate with human (in Bactria) and animal (in Tibet) figures on the sides. It is possible that some of the metalwork found in China traveled along a route linking the southern part of Afghanistan with Tibet.

Finds in the Xinjiang region, on the other hand, have yielded examples of metalwork produced in Central Asia during the Great Migrations period involving the various tribes of the steppe belt between areas as disparate as Europe and Korea. In 2001, Dang Tong acquired nine items from the Boma tumulus in the basin of the Ili River that had been looted in 1997.[21] We do not know who made these works, but we do know that they were made for the nomadic nobility. It is possible that many of them were imported from the Roman (later Byzantine) dominions in Crimea or from the Transcaucasian and western Central Asian sedentary states, while some could have been made by wandering artisans or by prisoners in nomadic camps. These objects, usually made of gold and inlaid with red precious stones or red glass, were fashionable at the courts of the nomadic chiefs, among them that of Attila the Hun (r. 434–53), who invaded Western Europe in the fifth century. The style is thus often referred to as Hunnish.[22]

The vessels from Boma are especially interesting. A tall gold cup from this group (cat. no. 95) has a handle in the form

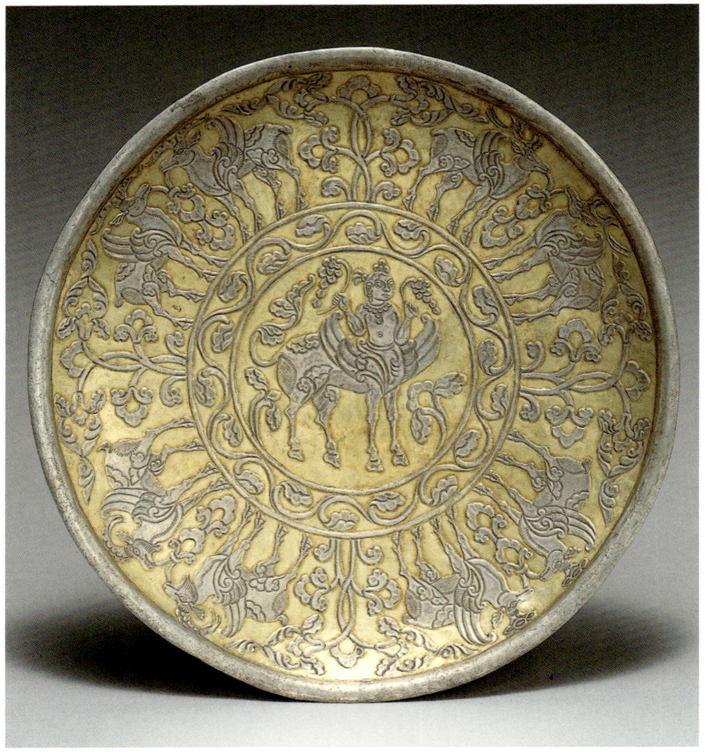

Figure 41. Plate. Tibet, 8th–9th century. Gilt silver, diameter 11 ½ in. (29.2 cm). Shumei Culture Foundation, Shigaraki

bowl decorated with images of seven ostriches (cat. no. 91), a Sasanian bowl with a Middle Persian inscription on the base (cat. no. 92), and a plate with a long Sogdian inscription below the rim (cat. no. 93). The design on the plate, despite the Sogdian inscription, is more Sasanian than Sogdian in style, although the details are not purely Sasanian. It is difficult to determine where it was made, but a Sogdian merchant certainly could have brought it (and probably the other two vessels as well) to Xinjiang from a center farther west.

Sogdian vessels are found in China beginning in the sixth century. One example of a silver vessel from Sogdiana is a plain sixth-century poly-lobed bowl (fig. 43) that, according to the Sogdian inscription below the rim, belonged to a dignitary of the kingdom of Chach (present-day Tashkent, Uzbekistan). In this period, Chach was already highly "Sogdianized" by colonists from adjacent Sogdiana proper in the Zarafshan valley. This bowl was found in northern Guandong Province together with a Korean (?) silver vessel and several late fifth-century Sasanian coins.[24]

of a tiger that is similar to the handle of a Sasanian silver mug in The Cleveland Museum of Art (fig. 42). Another Boma vessel resembles both Late Roman kantharis and seventh-century Sogdian silver cups with handles, thus confirming the hypothesis that one of the main sources of inspiration for the Sogdian silversmiths was Late Roman and Byzantine metalwork. Red stones enrich the ornaments both on this vessel and on those of a lidded golden jar (cat. no. 94); they are more precisely placed than similar ornaments executed in the Hunnish style.

It is difficult to say where the handled cup was produced. The lidded jar may be Sasanian. We do not know whether the lid was made specifically for this jar because details of the lid find no parallel in the decoration of the jar itself. The ornament on the lid, a rosette of stylized acanthus leaves, resembles a motif seen on Sasanian stuccos and on the base of the cylindrical cup excavated in Datong (cat. no. 59). However, other features of the cup indicate strong ties to Late Roman art. The Boma objects undoubtedly belonged to a nomadic aristocrat, probably of the Yueban state.[23] They reflect a taste similar to that of the aristocracy of the Middle East and Mediterranean world.

A small group of metal vessels was also found in a sixth-century hoard from Laocheng village in Yanqi (ancient Karashahr), Xinjiang. It comprises three silver vessels: a Sasanian

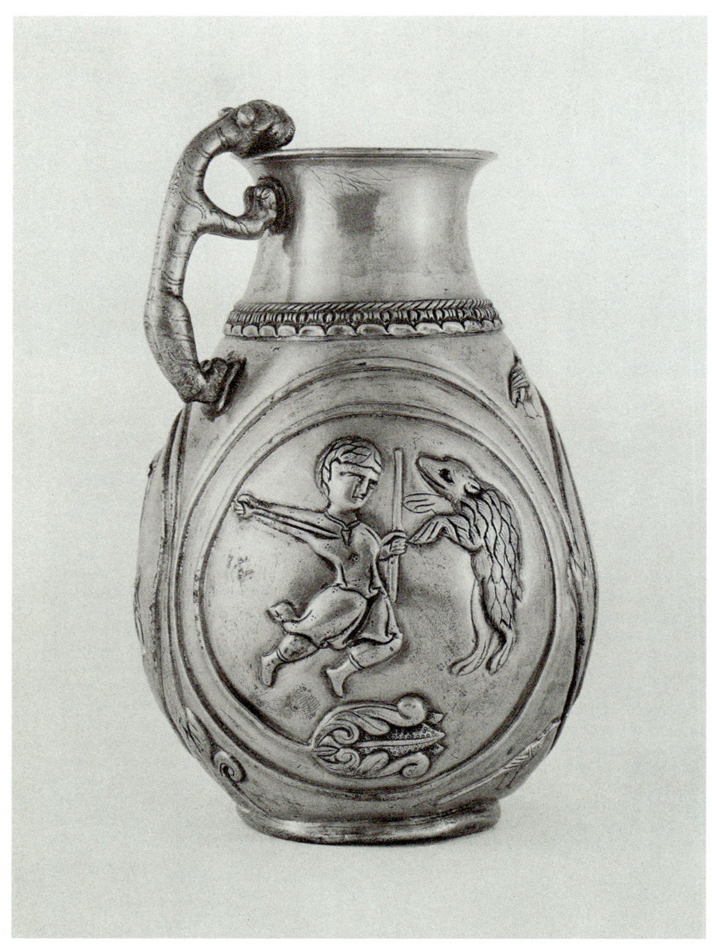

Figure 42. Ewer with handle in the form of a tiger. Eastern Iran, 5th–6th century. Silver, height 5¼ in. (13.4 cm). © The Cleveland Museum of Art, 2004. Purchase from the J. H. Wade Fund, 1961.200

A twelve-lobed silver bowl decorated with the image of a seated lion, now in the Freer Gallery was reportedly found in Luoyang (fig. 44). It bears two Sogdian inscriptions and most likely dates to the late sixth or early seventh century.[25] Another lobed bowl, showing a stag (cat. no. 207), has the Sogdian name of the owner inscribed below the rim. This vessel can also be dated to the sixth or seventh century. A silver bowl of the same shape was found in the western suburbs of Xi'an. The delicate incised and partly gilded decoration suggests a date in the seventh century.[26] The form is typical of the metalwork produced in central Sogdiana, but the decoration may derive from the eastern school, which probably flourished in Chach and adjacent regions. A characteristic design seen in this area consists of outlined floral scrolls incised against a background that is ring-matted—i.e., covered with small circles. In particular, a stem crowned with a tripartite symmetrical leaf is a feature of metalwork in the area of Chach.[27] The combination of central and eastern Sogdian traditions on the bowl from Xi'an illustrates the close ties between these schools.

One of the finest examples of Sogdian silver is a ewer excavated in Inner Mongolia in 1975 (cat. no. 208). The handle of the ewer is crowned by the head of a young man whose shaven temples and stripe of hair extending from the back to the forehead are identical to the hairdo of the Sogdians in the Panjikent murals of the first half of the eighth century. One cannot, however, exclude a seventh-century date, as a close analogue found in Kazakhstan has on the bottom a design that mimics five Byzantine cross-stamps. In Byzantium, such stamps disappeared about the mid-seventh century.[28] It is possible that artisans in Sogdiana were trying to imitate the more valued Byzantine production, presumably for commercial purposes.

As noted above, many Chinese replicas of West and Central Asian silverware were produced during the seventh and eighth centuries. A sixth-century example is provided by a small silver footed bowl found in the tomb of Li Xizhong (d. 569) and his wife at Nanxingguo village, Hebei (cat. no. 152). The Chinese bowl, which is part of a larger set of metal and pottery vessels, is smaller than its Central Asian prototypes. The form, proportions, embossed bottom, and circles of little "beads" are typical of Sogdian metalwork. The fluted side wall is also characteristically Central Asian, with Sogdian, Bactrian (Tokharistanian), Punjaban, and Khorazmian parallels. The wavy flutes occur in Punjab already in the fifth and sixth centuries, while in Sogdiana they are known only from the seventh and eighth centuries.[29] It is impossible to ascertain whether this motif perhaps reached Sogdiana much earlier, as so few examples of sixth-century Sogdian metalwork are at our disposal. The lotus on the bottom is not Central Asian; it was executed in the Chinese Buddhist style of the period.

The motif of a tiger also made its appearance in the Sui (581–619) or early Tang period. Generally, it was inscribed in the central medallion of a bowl made of silver or pottery. One silver bowl is in the Museum für Islamische Kunst, Berlin;[30] another is in the Uldry collection in Switzerland.[31] The prototype of the series was probably Sogdian, but the manner of depicting the tiger is Chinese.

Such hybrid vessels are frequent from the mid-seventh to the mid-eighth century, when Sogdian ewers, cups with handles, and three-legged trays were reproduced by Chinese metalworkers and potters (see cat. no. 215). Another example is the Sasanian lobed oblong bowl,[32] which was also reproduced in China and in northwestern India.

Ring-matting, which originated in Persia, is typical of Tang metalwork.[33] The technique reached China via Sogdiana. In Persian examples, it filled only small zones of the relief design.[34] In western and central Sogdiana, the reserved incised design was applied to the less important parts of the vessel, whereas the more important areas were done in low relief.[35] Farther to the east, in Chach as well as in China, the surface was almost completely covered with ring-matting.

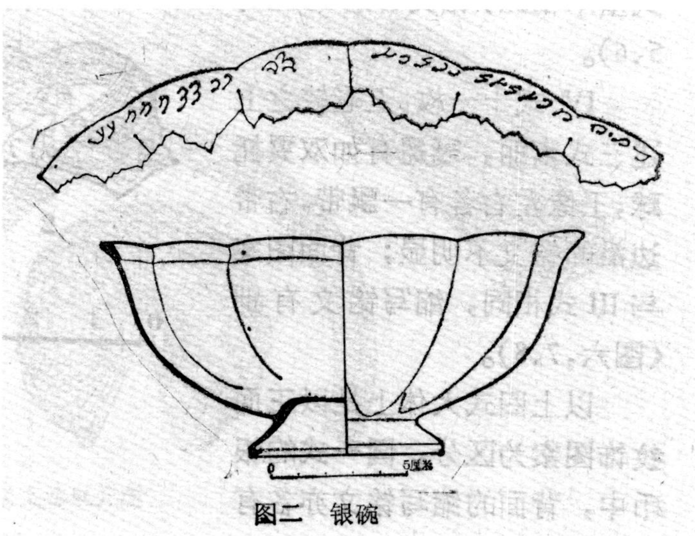

Figure 43. Bowl. Sogdiana, 6th century. Silver, height 3 ⅛ in. (8 cm). Excavated at Suixi, Guangdong Province

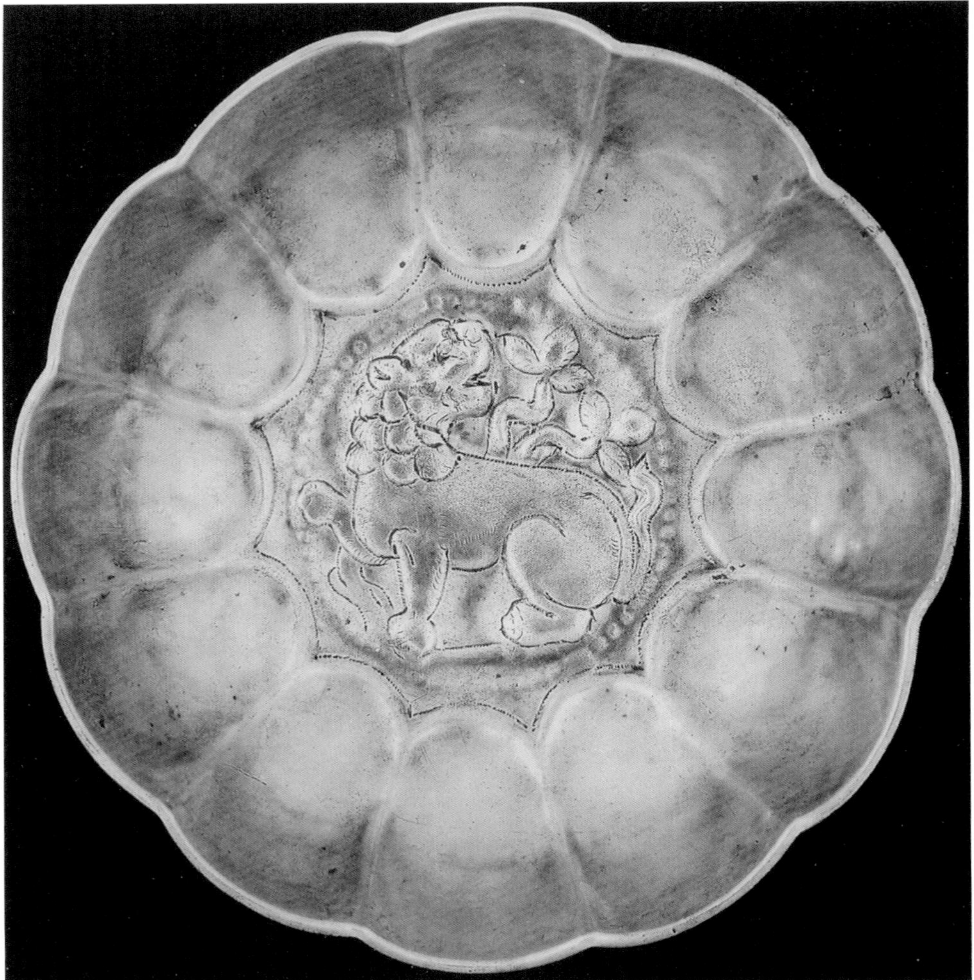

Figure 44. Lobed bowl. Sogdiana, 6th–7th century. Gilt silver, diameter 6 in. (15.3 cm). Freer Gallery of Art, Smithsonian Institution, Washington, D.C.: Purchase, F1997.13

In this case, the Sogdian silver served as a link between Iranian and Chinese art. Similarly, Tang motifs also occur in seventh- and eighth-century Sogdian art.[36] The decoration of Sogdian metalwork is, however, more vigorous, without the overrefinement of the deliberately complex composition of Chinese ornamentation.

This brief survey of luxury imported vessels and their Chinese replicas has illustrated that in the sphere of the secular applied arts, China's contacts with Central Asia were significantly more fruitful than those with Sasanian Iran and even India, notwithstanding the latter's decisive role in the quite different sphere of Buddhist art.

1. For examples of exchanges between the metalworking traditions of West Asia, Central Asia, and China prior to this period see Yunnan sheng bowuguan 1959, vol. 1: 69, fig. 21; Laing 1995: 11–16; Sun Ji 1996b: 138–45; and Harper 2002: 97–100. Further examples of Chinese motifs of Hellenized Central Asian silverware (2nd–1st century B.C.) include Smirnov 1909: 72–73, pls. IX, CCXXIV; Trever 1940: 103–4, nos. 3, 4, pls. 3–5, 31; Seipel 1996: 263, 411, no. 128; and Desroches 2000: 58, no. 21.
2. Popova 1999: 154, 172, 173.
3. Marshak 1994: 5–10.
4. Popova 1999: 206.
5. Pfrommer 1993: 118–19, no. 5; Trever 1940, pl. 31.
6. Pfrommer 1993: 180–81, no. 67.
7. For example, the sarcophagus of Constantina and the ceiling mosaic of her mausoleum in Rome, both ca. 354; Oakeshott 1968, pls. 28, 36, 38.
8. Marshak 1986: 35–39, 247–51.
9. Bader and Smirnov 1954, fig. 3; Fajans 1957, pls. 8, 9.
10. Marshak 1986: 35–39, 246–51; Marshak 1978: 258–68.
11. Callieri 1997: 36–30, no. 7, pl. 22.
12. Smirnov 1909, pl. XXXIX; Trever 1940: 87–90, no. 17; Marshak 1986: 34, 249; Seipel 1996: 266, 412, no. 132; Desroches 2000: 63, no. 29.
13. Weitzmann 1943: 307–19, figs. 13–16, 20–23; Marshak 1986, 38, pl. 19; Gunter and Jett 1992: 40, 148–56, no. 23.
14. Smirnov 1909, ill. 40: Marshak 1986: 270, pl. 187.
15. Callieri 2002: 121–41.
16. Ma Yong 1983: 8–12; Ma Yuji 1983: 1–4; Xia Nai 1983: 5–7; Harper 1990a: 51–59; Harper 1990b, no. 43.
17. Sims-Williams 1989.
18. One is now in the Ancient Orient Museum, Tokyo. See Denwood 1973: 121–27, and Carter 1995a: 229–38, fig. 10. The date of this bowl must be circa fourth century because two characters hold typical late Roman amphoras with the long neck above the handles like those in Conceštis. and the Sevso hoard; see Effenberger et al. 1978, pl. 44; for another vessel, see Mango 1990: 80–81, figs. 1, 13, and Elsner 1998, fig. 69.
19. Shumei Family Collection 1996: 80–82, no. 33; Darkevich 1976: 33–36, pl. 15.
20. Schroeder 2001: 792–94, no. 190, pls. 190–92; Heller 2003: 213, 219, figs. 1, 2, 10.
21. An Yingxin 1999: 4–15; *Wenwu* 1999.4: 4–19; Xinjiang Weiwuer zizhiqu wenwu shiye guanliju et al. 1999: 381–83; Tōkyō kokuritsu hakubutsukan 2002, nos. 9, 10; Wang Binghua 2003: 57–63.
22. Zasetskaia 1975; Ambroz 1981: 10–23, colorpls. between pp. 32 and 33, figs. 1–3, 5–7; Zasetskaia 1982: 14–20, 246–48. One of the arrowheads from Boma is typically Hunnish; An Yingxin 1999: 8, 11, figs. 10, 6.
23. Wang Binghua 2003: 62–63.
24. *Kaogu* 1986.3: 243–46; Rawson 1991: 144; Yoshida 1996: 73–74.
25. Marshak 1999: 101–10.
26. *Wenwu* 1982.1: 54–58; Qi Dongfang 1999b: 339–42; Li Jian 2003, no. 99.
27. Marshak 1986, 54, 55, 68–69, 86–91, 244, figs. 49, 54, 79–85, esp. fig. 110.
28. Ibid., fig. 71.
29. See Smirnov 1909, ill. 44, and Li Jian 2003, no. 204. See also Marshak 1986, fig. 80; *Sāsān-cho Perusiano koin* 2003, fig. 17 and cover ill. (inside the foot of the cup there is a Turkic runic inscription).
30. Schmidt 1932: 126, fig. 12 (inv. no. j.5357); Marshak 1986, fig. 109.
31. Uldry 1994, no. 128.
32. Marshak 1986: 60–71; Qi Dongfang 1999b: 321–25, 348–51, 356–62, 393–97, colorpls. 6, 12, 18, 19, figs. 10–22, 38, 42, 108, 109.
33. Gyllensvärd 1957: 34–36.
34. For example *Splendeur des Sassanides* 1993, nos. 90 (a bottle from the State Hermitage Museum, inv. no. S-37) and 93 (a bottle from the Museum für Islamische Kunst, Berlin, inv. no. i.4968); both are late Sasanian.
35. Marshak 1986, pls. 20, 21, 42, 49, 50, 56–59; Desroches 2000, nos. 38, 39, 44.
36. Marshak 1986: 69–71, figs. 42–47, 53, 54, 61–65, 81; Qi Dongfang 1999b: 365–77.

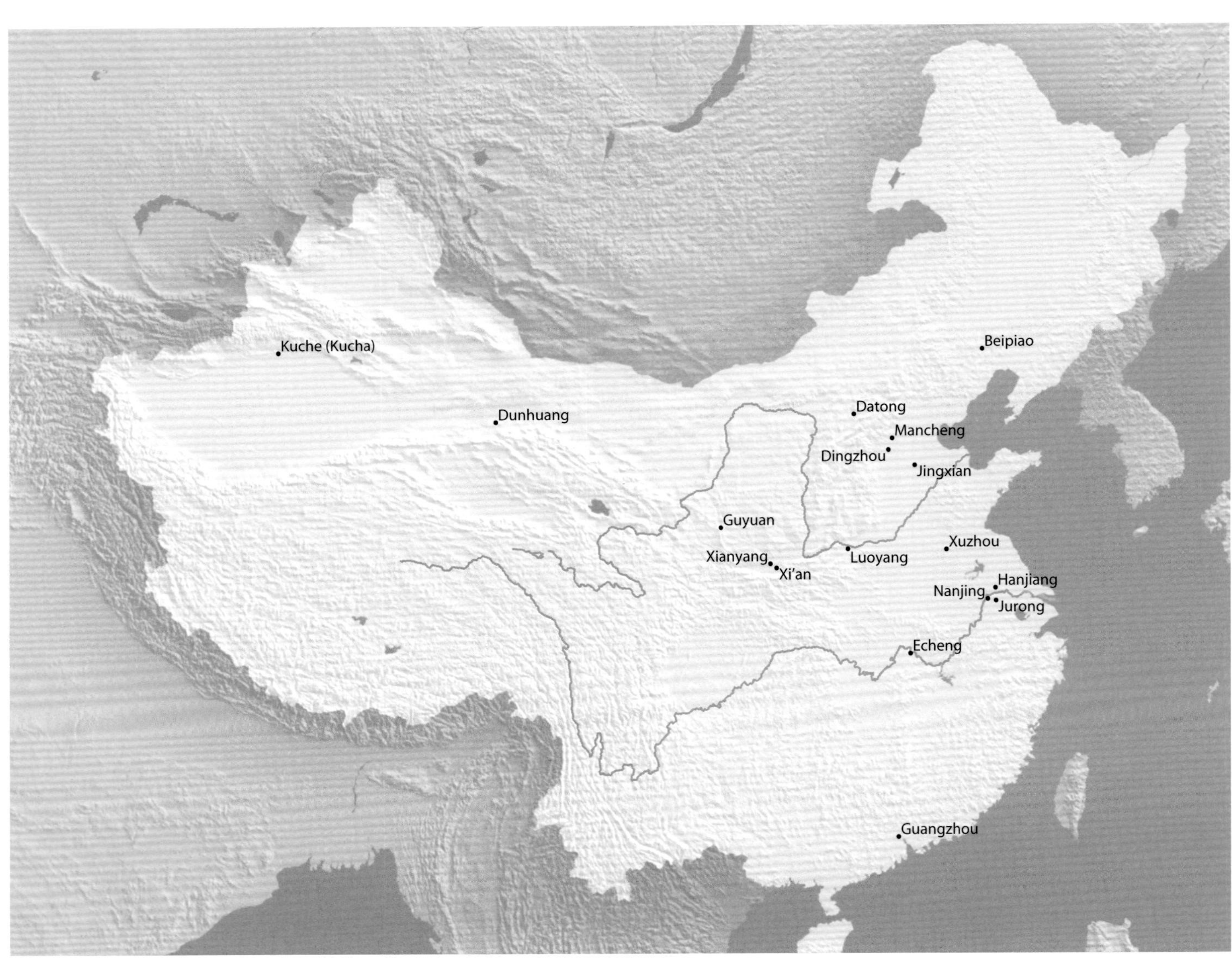

Kuche (Kucha)
Dunhuang
Beipiao
Datong
Mancheng
Dingzhou
Jingxian
Guyuan
Xianyang
Xi'an
Luoyang
Xuzhou
Hanjiang
Nanjing
Jurong
Echeng
Guangzhou

The Art of Glass Along the Silk Road

AN JIAYAO

The periods from the Qin (221–206 B.C.) to the Han (206 B.C.–A.D. 220) dynasty and from the Sui (581–619) to the Tang (618–907) marked two triumphant heights in the history of China. The cultural manifestations of the two are, however, quite different. How should we account for these differences? The attempt in this essay to trace the evolution of the art of glass in China may shed some light on one aspect of the distinctive culture of the later period.

The Impact of Roman Glass on the Jadelike Glass of the Han Dynasty

Toward the end of the Spring and Autumn period (770–481 B.C.) and the beginning of the Warring States (481–221 B.C.), accessories of glass beads made in West Asia were transported as commercial commodities by Central Asian nomads to the Central Plain of China.[1] By the middle and late Warring States, the Chinese themselves were producing glass beads that, in appearance, resembled those from West Asia, but they were made from very different materials. The Chinese glass industry, newly established under West Asian influence, soon merged with Chinese cultural traditions to produce a kind of glass that simulated jade. Glass made during the Han dynasty inherited the legacy of the Warring States period. It continued to simulate jade; it was produced in greater quantities; and the types of objects for which it was used proliferated.

The Chinese have always had a strong affinity for jade. The ancients believed that jade could prevent corpses from decaying. Consequently, some jades, so-called mortuary jades, were made specifically for this purpose (see cat. nos. 15, 16). Mortuary jades make up a large part of jades produced during the Han dynasty, but because the stone is so rare and so precious, glass was often substituted. Glass *bi* disks, glass suits, glass plugs for the openings of the human body, and glass pieces to be placed in the mouth and hands of the deceased were all eventually produced.

Glass vessels were being produced in China by the Western Han (206 B.C.–A.D. 9). A group of sixteen cups from this period was excavated in 1986 from the tomb (dated 128 B.C.) of the prince of Chu on Mount Beidong in Xuzhou, Jiangsu. Cast in molds, they are made of lustrous green opaque glass and have tiny air bubbles inside. In color and transparency they resemble natural jade, which would explain why they were mistakenly described as "jade cups" in the original excavation report.[2] In Mancheng, Hebei, three glass vessels—two ear-cups (fig. 45) and a plate—were excavated from the tombs of Liu Sheng, Prince Jing of Zhongshan, and his consort, Dou Wan. All three display a similar transparency, refinement, and lustrous green color.[3]

Glass production is clearly recorded in Han literature. In the chapter "Shuai xing" (On Spontaneity) of the *Lun heng* (The Balanced Inquiries), Wang Chong (27–ca. 100) of the

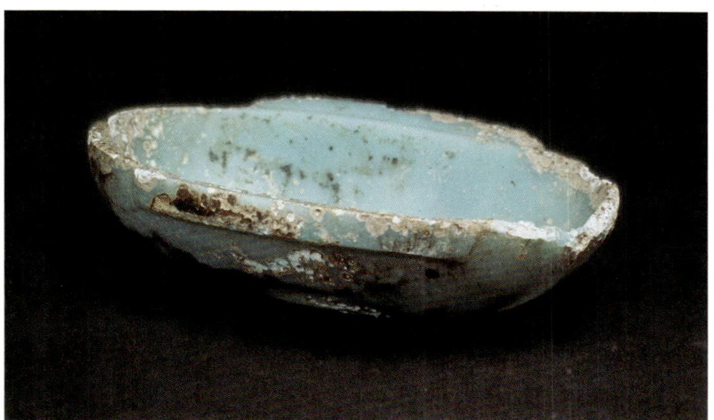

Figure 45. Ear-cup. Western Han dynasty (206 B.C.–A.D. 9). Glass. Excavated from the tomb of Liu Sheng (d. 113 B.C.), Prince Jing of Zhongshan, Mancheng, Hebei Province

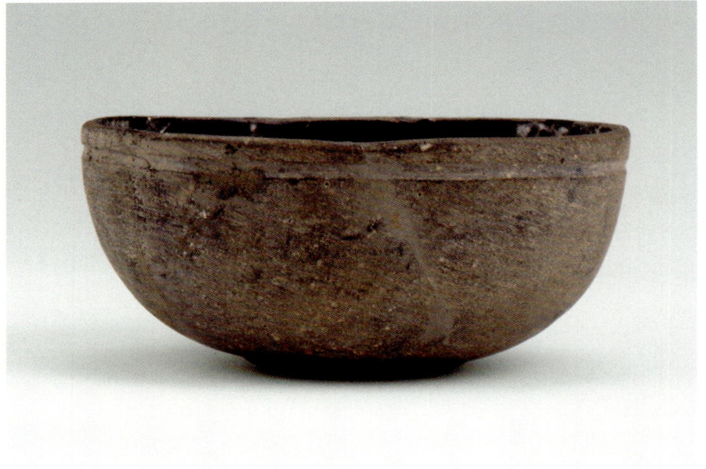

Figure 46. Bowl. Western Han dynasty (206 B.C.–A.D. 9). Glass. Excavated from a tomb in Hengzhigang, Guangzhou, Guangdong Province

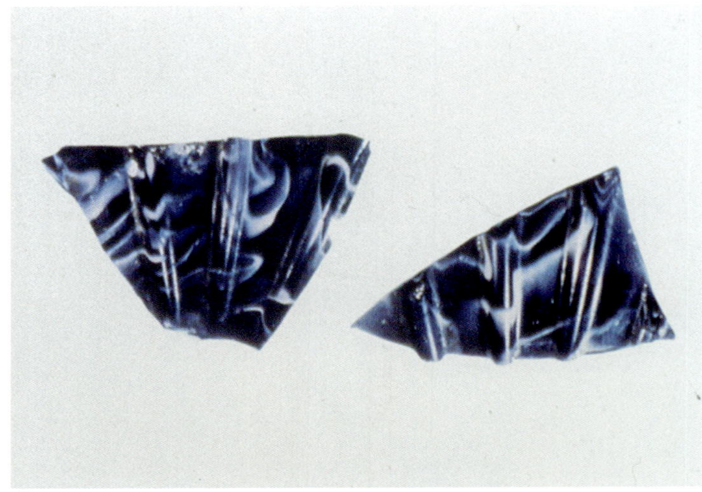

Figure 47. Shards of a mosaic vessel. Eastern Han dynasty (25–220). Glass. Excavated from Tomb 2 (dated 67), Ganquanshan, Hanjiang, Jiangsu Province

Eastern Han (25–220) wrote, "The Daoist smelts the five stones to make jade of five colors, whose luster shows no difference from the real jade."[4] The "jade of five colors" is a specific reference to the jadelike glass of the Han period. It was believed that because glass was merely a simulation of jade, its value could never compare with that of the real stone. This concept, however, came to be challenged by a new import to China from the west.

Roman glass refers to the glass produced during the time of the Roman Empire, the vast empire around the Mediterranean Sea at the end of the first century B.C. Glass manufacturing was one of its major industries, and the glassware made during the centuries of Roman rule occupies a pivotal position in the history of glass in both quality and typological variety.

Roman glass may have been imported to China as early as the Western Han, as indicated by three glass bowls excavated from a tomb of the middle Western Han period in Hengzhigang, Guangzhou, Guangdong (fig. 46).[5] The shape and color of the three bowls are identical. They are purplish blue and translucent, and all three have a flat bottom, straight mouth, and curved body. The outer wall is polished, with an incised line below the mouth rim, and the interior is perfectly smooth.

The Eastern Han witnessed a great increase in the quantity of Roman glass imported to China. In 1981, three shards of a glass vessel were found in Han Tomb 2 (dated 67) at Ganquanshan in Hanjiang, Jiangsu. Made of mosaic glass, in purplish red and cream colors, the outer surfaces of this fragment are decorated with radiating vertical ridges formed by a pressed mold (fig. 47). After restoration, the shards were found to have been parts of a bowl. This type of vertically ridged vessel was rarely seen in China, but it was common along the Mediterranean coast during the first century B.C. and the first century A.D.[6]

The glass bottle decorated with marbled veins in this exhibition (cat. no. 13) was excavated from an Eastern Han tomb in Luoyang, Henan. The form is distinct from that of traditional Chinese glassware, and it was manufactured by glassblowing, a process that first appeared on the eastern coast of the Mediterranean in the middle of the first century B.C.[7] Except for the making of glass itself, glassblowing is the most significant invention in the history of glass production. It is discussed in greater detail below.

Luoyang was the capital of the Eastern Han dynasty, and during that period many Central Asians made it their home. Among them were two renowned translators of Buddhist scriptures, Zhichan, from Yuezhi (Kushan) in Central Asia, and An Shigao, a native of Parthia on the Plateau of Iran. Further indication of Central Asian traffic to the east is seen in archaeological finds. In 1979, an excavation team from the Soviet Union discovered more than twenty thousand gold objects buried in an elite cemetery in the territory of ancient Bactria.[8] The cemetery is situated about three miles northeast of Shibarghan in northern Afghanistan. Also found were quantities of artifacts from ancient Rome, Parthia, India, Scythia, and Western Han China. Among them, two glass bottles resemble the Roman bottle excavated from the tomb in Luoyang. It would thus appear that the latter was most likely imported to China by land.

Roman glass is altogether different from the simulated-jade glass made in China. In lightness, thinness, transparency, and brilliance of color, there is no comparison, and its appearance in China dealt a fatal blow to the Chinese glass industry. Indeed, glass from foreign lands quickly became de rigueur for wealthy families of the aristocracy.

Western Glass as a Measure of Wealth

The Wei (220–265), Jin (265–420), and Southern (420–589) and Northern (386–581) Dynasties marked a very unusual period in Chinese history. On the one hand, Chinese society fell into chaos, with a succession of wars and territorial shifts. On the other, cultural exchange, the flowering of intellectual discourse, and the integration of different ethnic peoples laid the foundation for reunification under the Sui and the glorious achievements of the Tang. There was incessant warfare and a never-ending struggle for survival for millions of Chinese. But there was also high living among the wealthy, with prominent families indulging themselves in extravagance and vying for the status of being the richest in the land. In this competition, contenders would display their possessions to assert their material status. One of the special treasures was glassware imported from the west. In *Luoyang qielanji* (The Buddhist Temples of Luoyang), written during the Northern Wei (386–534), it is recorded that "[Yuan] Chen, prince of Hejian, surpassed everyone else in wealth. . . . Often [he would] gather his clansmen together and show off his various treasures. . . . Among the wine vessels were crystal bowls, agate glass bowls, and red jade cups. There were scores of them, all marvelously made. They were not native products, but came from the Western Regions."[9]

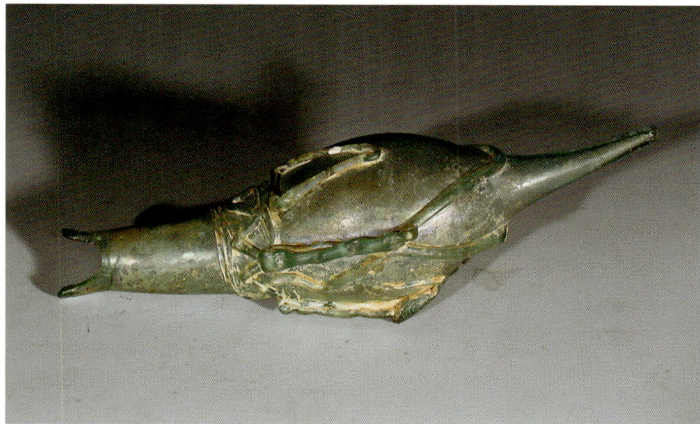

Figure 48. Duck-shaped vessel. Northern Yan dynasty (407–436). Glass. Excavated from the tomb of Feng Sufu, Beipiao (d. 415), Liaoning Province

By this time as well, people were attuned to the aesthetic qualities of western glass, its lustrous transparency in particular. Indeed, the beauty of glass was celebrated in many literary compositions. The most famous is the "Ode to a Glass Bowl," by the Western Jin (265–316) poet Pan Ni, which extolls the fine craftsmanship and transparent clarity of a glass vessel.[10] The book *Shishuo xinyu* (A New Account of Tales of the World) describes ". . . the prince [who] drank with his courtiers. Raising a glass bowl in his hand, he asked Zhou Boren, 'This bowl is empty inside. Why do people call it a treasure?' Zhou replied, 'This bowl shines in its sheer lucidity. That is why it is precious.'"[11]

The Western Jin historian Yu Huan wrote in his *Wei lue* (A Brief Account of the Wei Kingdom), "The Daqin Empire produced glass in ten colors: crimson, white, black, yellow, blue, green, light blue, reddish brown, red, and purple."[12] Daqin was the Chinese appellation for the Roman Empire used in literature of the time. The very precise description of the colors found in Roman glass is a reflection of the high esteem in which it was held. During the Wei, Jin, and Southern and Northern Dynasties, Roman glass imported to China increased in both variety and quantity. Many examples are found in and around the area of Nanjing, Jiangsu, the political, economic, and cultural center of the Southern Dynasties.

Two barrel-shaped glass cups with cut decoration were excavated from Tomb 7 at Xiangshan, Nanjing. One of them is shown in this exhibition (cat. no. 116); the other was crushed.[13] Tomb 7 is situated within the cemetery of the Wang family of Langye, Shandong, one of the most powerful clans of the Eastern Jin period (317–420). Archaeologists believe it is the tomb of Wang Yi. If it is, the two cups can be dated prior to 322. In addition, many glass shards found in an early Six Dynasties (220–589) tomb at Shimenkan, Nanjing,[14] in an Eastern Jin tomb in what is now the North Park of Nanjing University,[15] and in an Eastern Jin tomb in the northern suburb of Nanjing,[16] all have surface decoration produced using the grinding technique in which Roman artisans excelled.

Roman glass has also been excavated in North China. The largest find is from the tomb of Feng Sufu (d. 415) of the Northern Yan kingdom (407–436) in Beipiao, Liaoning.[17] Among five glass vessels, the most exquisite is the one in

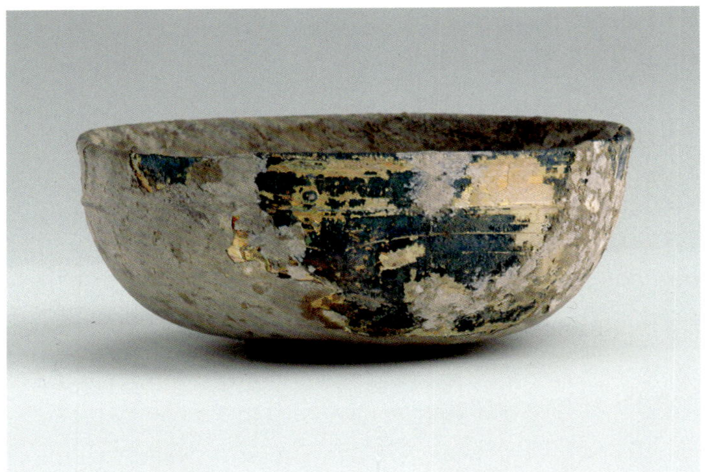

Figure 49. Bowl. Northern Wei dynasty (386–534). Glass. Excavated from the tomb of Feng Monu (d. 483/4), Jingxian, Hebei Province

the shape of an animal with a long neck, bulging body, and long slender tail. Its flat, open beak recalls that of a duck (fig. 48). It is basically in excellent condition, except for some damage on the tail. The glass is a transparent light green, and the surface is covered with a thin layer of whitish iridescent material. Certain areas show blue purple iridescence. In quality and color, it is comparable to the glass bowl in this exhibition (cat. no. 42), and it is possible that the two were manufactured in the same workshop.

Four imported glass bowls were excavated from the Feng family cemetery of the Northern Wei period in Jing county, Hebei. Only two survive. One is from the tomb of Feng Monu (d. 483/4), and the other, from the tomb of Madame Zu (early 6th century),[18] is a light green bowl with wavy appliqué decoration (cat. no. 66).

The glass bowl excavated from the tomb of Feng Monu was broken but has been restored (fig. 49). It is green and transparent. The weathered layer is bright yellow, and the surface of the flaked-off areas is uneven and appears iridescent. There are a relatively large number of air bubbles in the glass. The vessel has a straight mouth, rounded lip, and short foot ring. A thin raised line circles the body. There is a pontil mark on the bottom.

In addition to Roman glass from the east coast of the Mediterranean, a significant portion of the glassware imported to China during the Wei, the Jin, and the Southern and Northern Dynasties came from the Plateau of Iran. Glass manufacturing, which had a long history in this region, peaked between the third and the seventh century. The upscale glassware that was produced was made for export and to serve the elite. It has generally been known as Sasanian glass because this period was dominated primarily by the Sasanian Empire.[19] Sasanian glass can be recognized by the simplicity of its shapes. It is often decorated with series of circular forms akin to the decorative motif of a string of pearls prevalent in the Sasanian period. Sasanian glassmakers inherited the technology of Roman glass and developed the process of cutting applied to the cooled, still unfinished product. Artisans would grind facets on the surface of the vessel or on the surface of the relief ornaments, creating small concave lenses. Through the lenses on the front wall, one can often see the decorative circles on the back wall, which enhances the illuminative magic of the glass.

One such bowl, made from Sasanian glass from the Plateau of Iran, was excavated in Beijing from the tomb of Hua Fang, who lived during the Western Jin period (fig. 50).[20] Hua Fang was the wife of Wang Jun, army commander of Youzhou. She was buried in the year 307, the first year of the Yongjia reign era (307–12). The army commander was in charge of northern Hebei and Liaoning, and Hua Fang, as his wife, was thus privileged to have access to glassware from the plateau region. The bowl from her tomb has a curved bottom, spherical body, constricted neck, and flaring mouth. The body is decorated

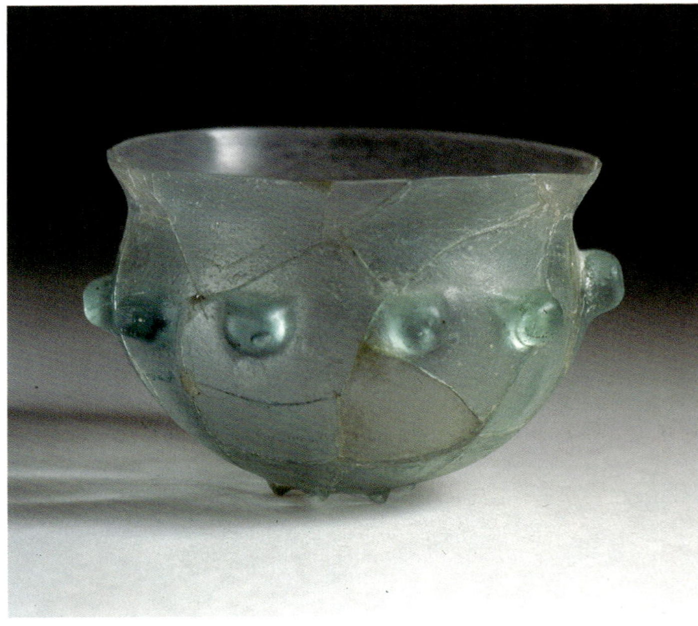

Figure 50. Bowl. Western Jin dynasty (265–316). Glass. Excavated from the tomb of Hua Fang, Beijing

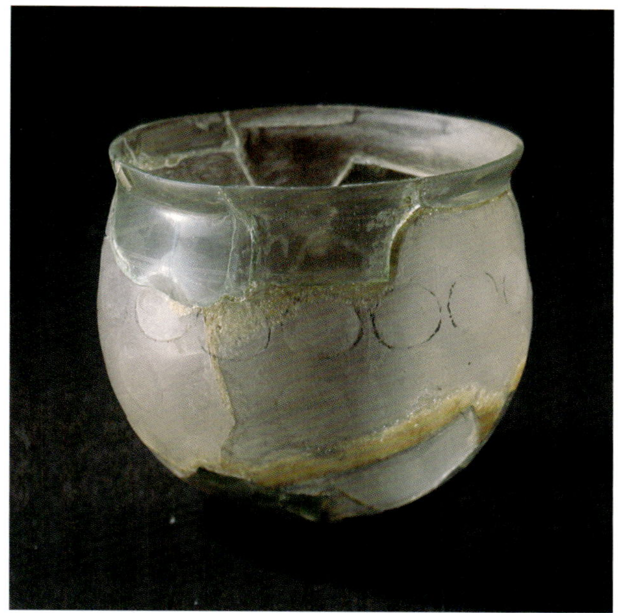

Figure 51. Bowl. Six Dynasties (220–589). Excavated from Tomb 121, Wulidun, Echeng, Hubei Province

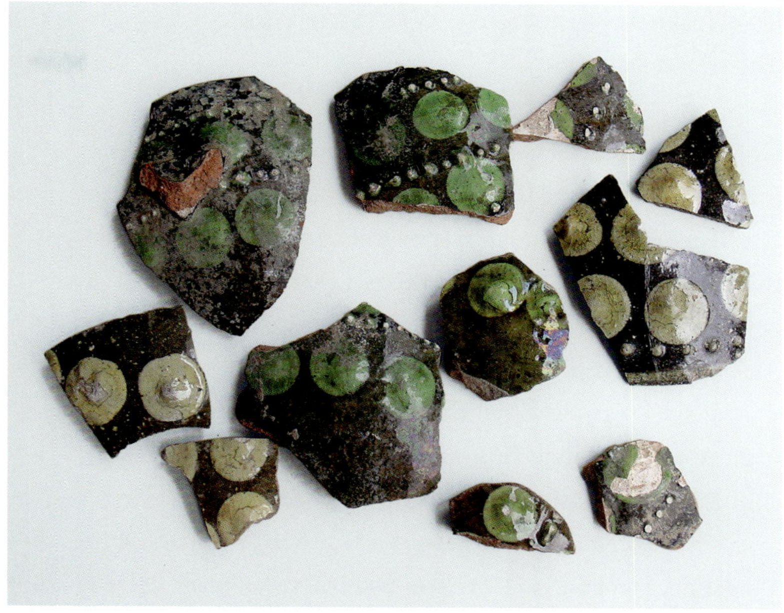

Figure 52. Shards of bowls. Northern Wei dynasty (386–534). Glazed earthenware. Excavated at Luoyang, Henan Province

with a circle of ten oval bosses. At the bottom, arranged in an oval, are seven pairs of small spurs, which serve both as ornament and as the foot. A bowl with similar bosses, also from the Plateau of Iran, was excavated by an archaeological team of Tokyo University.[21] This type of glass bowl, with ornamental bosses, was widespread in the region over a long period of time. It has been excavated from tombs dating from the first to the fifth century. Its popularity culminated during the late Parthian Empire (250 B.C.–A.D. 225).

A different type of vessel was excavated from Tomb 121 at Wulidun in Echeng, Hubei (fig. 51).[22] It has a curved bottom and four rows of small oval concavities ground on the body for decoration. A circular concavity is also ground on the bottom. Tomb 121 in Echeng is Western Jin, which indicates that its date cannot be later than the early fourth century. The bowl is therefore among the earliest imports of Sasanian glass to the east.

One of the prettiest glass bowls with cut faceting, which is included in the exhibition (cat. no. 117), was excavated from a tomb dating to the Song dynasty (420–479) at Chuncheng, Jurong, Jiangsu. The occupant of the tomb, Liu Zong, was buried in 439, the sixteenth year of the Yuanjia reign era (424–53).[23] Another glass bowl of comparable quality, also in the exhibition (cat. no. 65), was excavated from Tomb 107 in the Northern Wei cemetery in the southern suburb of Datong, Shanxi.[24] This bowl was found together with silver jars, gilded silver bowls with incised design, gold ear-cups, and glass beads, all of which show distinctly foreign characteristics.

The Tuoba clan of the Xianbei people established the Northern Wei dynasty in 386 and proceeded to unify the small states in the north. The Northern Wei was the first political regime founded by a minority ethnic group that could rival the Han kingdom in the south. Pingcheng, present-day Datong, was the capital of the early Northern Wei. For nearly a hundred years, the ruling class in Pingcheng strove to assimilate Han culture. It also overran the region of Hexi, Gansu, so that the Silk Road would extend eastward to the capital.

Among the best of Sasanian glass is a type with high-relief ornaments; it has also been found in China. A bowl with this characteristic in this exhibition (cat. no. 158) was excavated in Guyuan county, Ningxia, from the tomb of Li Xian and his wife, of the Northern Zhou. It is dated to 569, the fourth year of the Tianhe reign era.[25] This type of bowl was greatly treasured by the elite, and simulations were made in a kind of glazed earthenware to emulate the original. A number of shards of glazed earthen bowls were excavated from the site of the "big market" of Luoyang, which, according to contemporary literature such as the *Luoyang qielanji*, was the largest market for trade in the Northern Wei period (fig. 52). The glazed earthen bowl in this exhibition (cat. no. 160) was restored from some of these shards.

The Introduction of Western Glass Technology

Unlike imported Roman glass and Sasanian glass, glassware made in China during the Wei, Jin, and Southern and Northern Dynasties is seldom found in archaeological excavations. This is most plausibly explained by the fact that production of the jadelike glass of the Han, cast in molds, was drastically cut back during this period of social and political turmoil. Then, during the Northern Wei, the first batch of Chinese blown glass vessels appeared. This is another aspect of the East–West cultural exchange that took place at this time.

A stone coffer from the base of a Northern Wei pagoda in Dingzhou, Hebei, is the site from which seven glass vessels were excavated in 1964.[26] Judging from the quality of the glass and the manufacturing technique, they may have come from the same source. Two glass bottles and one glass bowl from this group are in the exhibition (cat. nos. 67, 68). They are representative of the technical level attained by this time. Three small gourd-shaped glass bottles, also from the coffer, are light blue and transparent. They have a spherical belly and long neck. The top of the neck is twisted into a short hook.

These seven vessels differ from Han glassware in the manufacturing technique. Instead of being cast in molds, which is the process used in metal manufacturing, they were blown into shape. Glassblowing takes full advantage of the unique inflatability of glass in its liquid state; as the temperature drops, the glass hardens into a solid form. The method cannot be applied to any other material and is thus a unique creation of the glass industry. Apart from the invention of glass itself, that of glassblowing is the most important event in the history of glassmaking, as the formerly rare and expensive commodity became common throughout the Mediterranean region. The adoption of the blown-glass technique in Northern Wei is the result of the eastward transmission of Roman glass technology.

There is an interesting passage in the section on the Western Regions in the *Beishu* (History of the Northern Dynasties). It reads, "During the reign of Emperor Taiwudi [of the Northern Wei; r. 424–52], a merchant from that country [Yuezhi] came to the capital, saying he could refine stones into glass of five colors. He then gathered stones from the mountains and smelted them in the capital. When he was finished, the luster [of his creations] surpassed that of western imports. The merchant was summoned to [decorate a room in the] palace, which could accommodate more than a hundred people. The brilliant transparency [of his creations] amazed those who saw them, as if they had been created by the gods. From that day forward, glass in China lost its value. It was no longer cherished."[27] It is likely that the glass of "brilliant transparency" made by the Yuezhi merchant referred to the kind of highly transparent glassware found in the Northern Wei pagoda.

Although glassblowing emerged on the Mediterranean coast as early as the mid-first century B.C. and blown-glass vessels had been imported to China by the second century A.D., the transmission of technology was at that time much slower

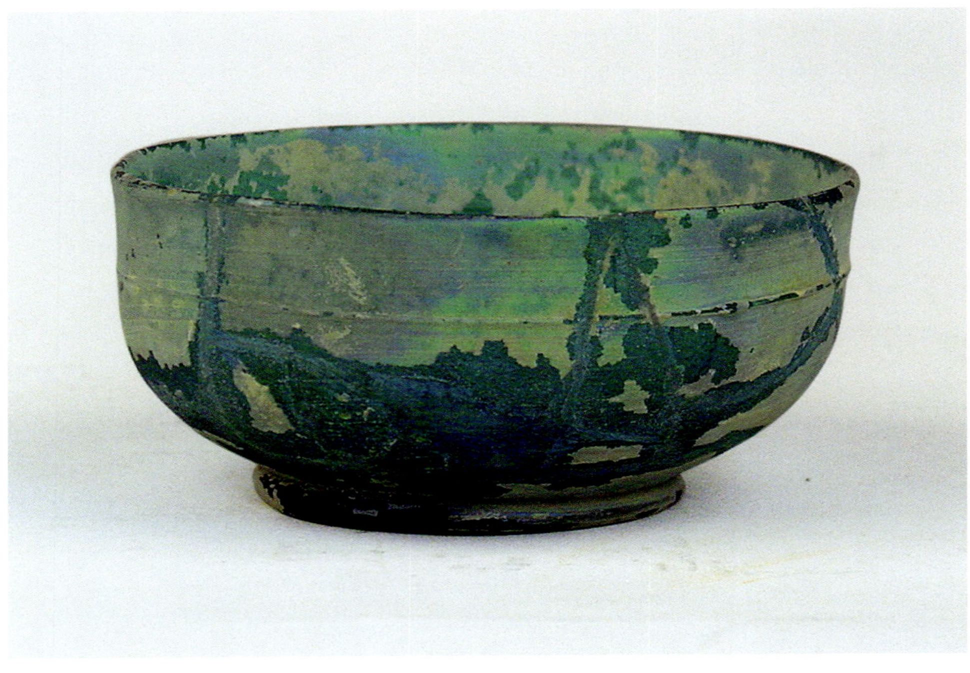

Figure 53. Bowl. Northern Wei dynasty (386–534). Glass. Excavated from a tomb in Datong, Shanxi Province

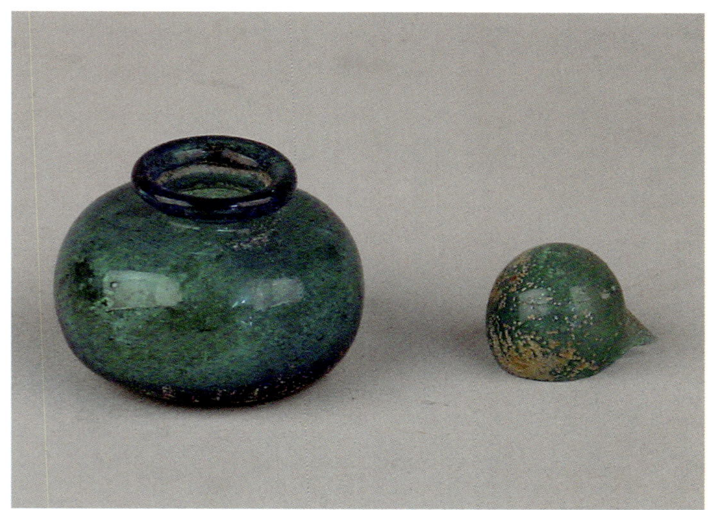

Figure 54. Bottle. Northern Wei dynasty (386–534). Glass. Excavated from a tomb in Datong, Shanxi Province

than that of the commodity itself. The latter was often associated with the migration of artisans, and the Chinese adoption of the glassblowing technique was most likely initiated by the arrival of foreign workers. If there is, in fact, a connection between the story of the Yuezhi merchant and the glass vessels excavated from the Northern Wei pagoda, we may conclude that Central Asian artisans transmitted the technique of glassblowing to China in the fifth century. This was an important turning point in the history of Chinese glass. After the Northern Wei, the majority of Chinese glass was produced by this method. In recent years, archaeologists have excavated many glass vessels in the Northern Wei tombs near Datong (figs. 53, 54), and it is very likely that they were made in Pingcheng by artisans from the greater Yuezhi area.

Glass Production During the Sui–Tang Period

The Sui, which reigned from 581 to 619, put an end to the three-hundred-year division of China into North and South, and in spite of its short duration of only thirty-odd years, it laid a solid foundation for the prosperity of the ensuing Tang dynasty. The Sui opened its doors to the outside world and maintained active commercial and cultural exchange with its neighbors. The Tang not only continued this policy, it also expanded its practice to an even greater extent.

Several glass objects included in the exhibition were made during this period. The cut glass bowl (cat. no. 159) was excavated in 1988 from the tomb of Wang Shiliang (dated 583), a high-ranking general of the Sui dynasty, in Xianyang, Shaanxi. The bottle with high-relief decoration (cat. no. 219) was excavated from a Sui *sarira* (relics of the Buddha) tomb in the eastern suburb of Xi'an (dated 589). Also found in the tomb were ten colorful glass beads (fig. 55) and a group of twenty-six gaming counters. Thirteen of the twenty-six are made of green transparent glass and are conical in shape (fig. 56). Of the thirteen, twelve are of the same size; one is shorter. The other thirteen counters are made of agate. In this case as well, one is shorter than the others. The pieces are different from those in the Chinese game of *weiqi* (generally known in the West by the Japanese name *go*), popular during the Sui–Tang period, and were perhaps used in a game imported from West or Central Asia.

The glass goblet with applied decoration excavated in 1989 from the Senmusaimu (Simsim) Grottoes in Kucha county, Xinjiang (cat. no. 96), was made in the sixth or seventh

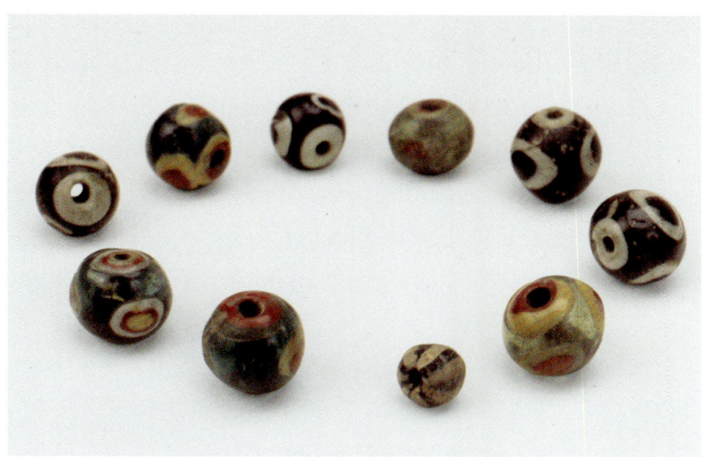

Figure 55. Beads. Sui dynasty (581–619). Glass. Excavated from a *sarira* tomb, Xi'an, Shaanxi Province

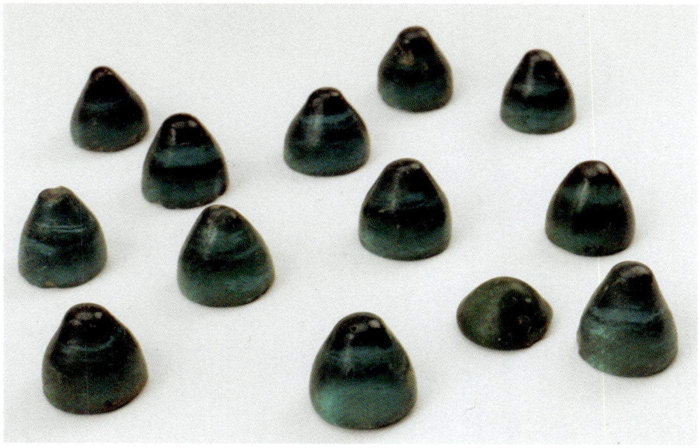

Figure 56. Game pieces. Sui dynasty (581–619). Glass. Excavated from a *sarira* tomb, Xi'an, Shaanxi Province

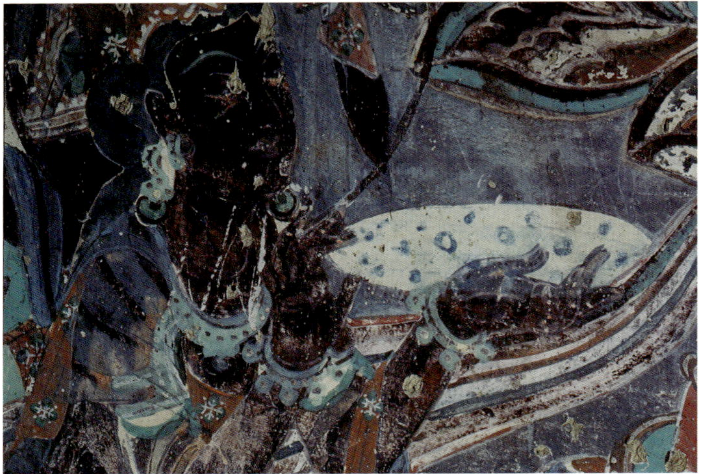

Figure 57. Bodhisattva with an offering dish. Tang dynasty (618–907), early 8th century. Wall painting. Cave 217, Dunhuang, Gansu Province

century, roughly contemporaneous with the Sui period, in the Central Plain of China. Kucha, situated between the southern slope of Tianshan and the northern border of the Taklamakan Desert, was on the Silk Road. The goblet, which is Iranian in origin, is another example that testifies to the trade between east and west current at this time. Evidence of the importation of western glass to China along the Silk Road can also be found in the wall paintings of the Sui–Tang period, specifically those in the Thousand Buddha Grottoes in Dunhuang. On the south wall of Cave 217, a bodhisattva is shown holding a glass dish for offerings (fig. 57). The dish is so transparent that the bodhisattva's fingers are distinctly visible through the glass. It is decorated with blue circles and dots, most likely representing the ground facets often seen in Sasanian examples. One could say that the dish in the painting is a pictorial rendering of the kind of cut glass vessel that was excavated from the tomb of the Sui general Wang Shiliang.

Glass bottles used as perfume containers were also imported to the Central Plain region, in direct response to the demand for western perfume among the Sui and Tang elite. The glass bottle excavated from Tomb 118 at Guanlin in Luoyang (cat. no. 220) is a type of perfume container commonly seen on the Syrian coast during the Late Roman and early Islamic periods (6th–7th century). After the middle Tang (late 8th century), high-quality Islamic glass was imported to China in quantity.

The glass industry within China also thrived during the Sui–Tang and, notably, its production was closely related to the influx of Central Asian immigrants. Many foreigners traveled to China during this time, and quite a few of them settled there. According to historical documents, it was He Chou (540–620), the descendant of a Sogdian family that specialized in West Asian technology, who revived glass production in the Sui dynasty.[28] The eight exquisite glass vessels made in China that were excavated in Xi'an from the tomb of Li Jingxun (599–608) of the Sui dynasty may be related in

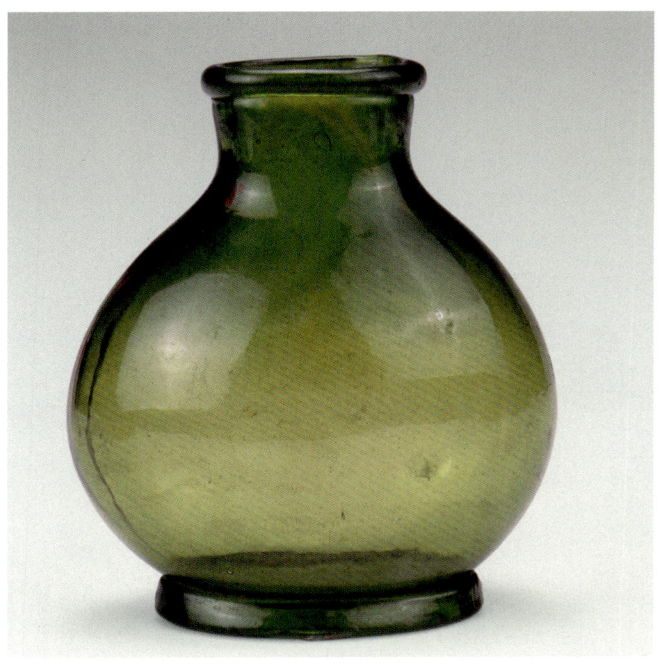

Figure 58. Flat bottle. Sui dynasty (581–619). Glass. Excavated from the tomb (dated 608) of Li Jingxun, Xi'an, Shaanxi Province

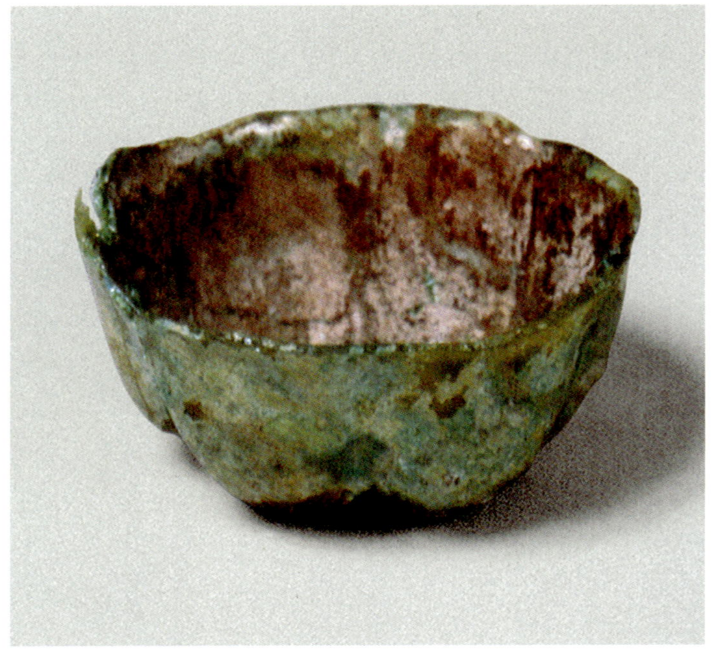

Figure 59. Six-lobed cup. Sui–Tang period (581–907). Glass. Excavated from the tomb (dated 669) of Shi Hedan, Guyuan, Ningxia Autonomous Region

some way to He Chou's revival (fig. 58).[29] In recent years, the excavation of another Sogdian cemetery, that of the Shi family in the southern suburb of Guyuan, Ningxia, has revealed further evidence of cross-cultural influence. Among the many vessels unearthed was a six-lobed glass cup which clearly displays certain characteristics of silverware from Persia (fig. 59).[30]

The pioneering of the Silk Road during the Han dynasty led to direct contact between East and West and interaction between two great civilizations. Glass vessels and accessories were among the major western commodities imported to China, and western glass technology gradually reached China about the same time. In this sense, the Silk Road can also be regarded as the Glass Road. The evolution of Chinese glass from the Qin–Han period to the Sui–Tang reflects this commercial and cultural exchange; it also indicates that such interaction was a powerful impetus behind social change.

1. An Jiayao 1996: 351–68.
2. Xuzhou bowuguan et al. 1988: 2–18.
3. Zhongguo shehui kexueyuan kaogu yanjiusuo, Hebei sheng wenwu guanlichu 1980: 212.
4. *LH*: 26.
5. Guangzhou wenwu weiyuanhui 1955: 40–45.
6. Grose 1984: 25–34.
7. Grose 1977: 24.
8. See Sarianidi 1985.
9. *LQJ*, chap. 4.
10. Pan Ni, "Liuli wan fu," *YWLJ*, chap. 73: 1259.
11. *SSXY*: 473.
12. *HS*, chap. 96a: 3885.
13. Nanjing shi bowuguan 1972: 23.
14. Li Jianzhao and Tu Sihua 1958: 69.
15. Nanjing daxue lishixi kaoguzu 1973: 44.
16. Nanjing shi bowuguan 1983: 315.
17. Li Yaobo 1973: 6.
18. Zhang Ji 1957: 33.
19. Zerwick 1990: 32.
20. An Jiayao 1986a: 173–81.
21. Fukai 1973: 148–50, pl. 15, fig. 11.
22. *Echeng Liuchao mu* n.d.
23. An Jiayao 1986c: 28–29.
24. Wang Yintian et al. 2000: 143–62.
25. Ningxia Huizu zizhiqu bowuguan and Ningxia Guyuan bowuguan 1985: 1–20.
26. Hebei sheng wenhuaju wenwu gongzuodui 1966: 252–59.
27. *BS*, chap. 97: 3226.
28. *SuS*, chap. 68: 1596.
29. Zhongguo shehui kexueyuan kaogu yanjiusuo 1980: 22–23.
30. Yuanzhou lianhe kaogudui 1999: 166, pl. 28.

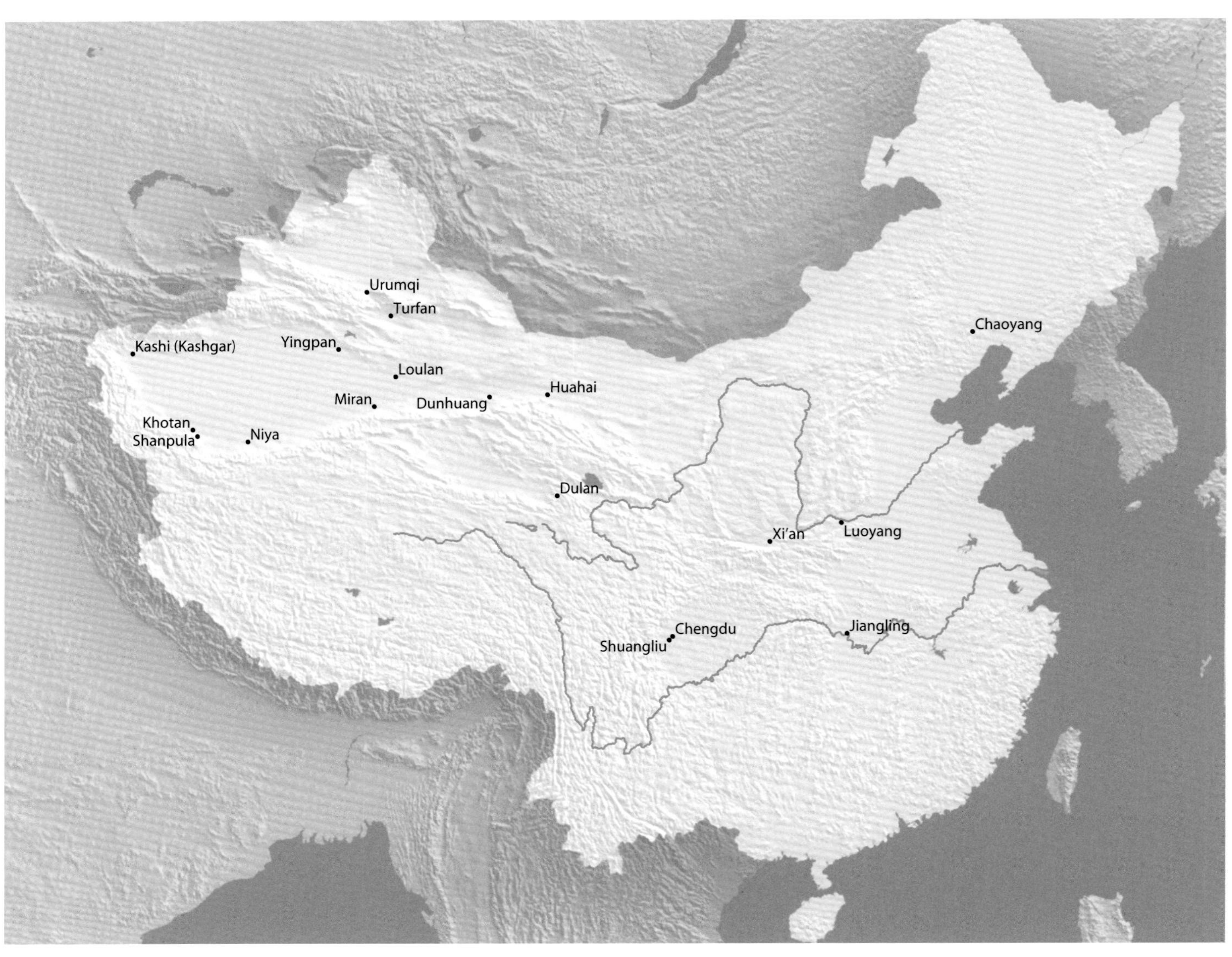

Urumqi
Turfan
Kashi (Kashgar)
Yingpan
Loulan
Miran
Dunhuang
Huahai
Khotan
Shanpula
Niya
Chaoyang
Dulan
Xi'an
Luoyang
Chengdu
Shuangliu
Jiangling

The Evolution of Textiles Along the Silk Road

ZHAO FENG

The exchange of commodities along the Silk Road from the Han to the Tang dynasty had a major impact in China. Of the goods that were bartered or sold, textiles were among the most essential. From China, silks were transported to the west, and, from the west, wool and cotton textiles were imported to China. During the process of this exchange, silk production underwent a complex but very fruitful evolution, the result of the cross-cultural fertilization of techniques and styles. In this essay we shall discuss the three major groups of silk textiles found along the Silk Road—*jin*, taquete, and samite—each one representing a different stage in the development of textile technique during this crucial time of cultural exchange.

Jin: The Chinese Tradition of Silk Weaving

Jin is the Chinese term for polychrome woven silk. Technically, during the Han dynasty it refers to a special weave structure, warp-faced compound tabby, which had been used since the Western Zhou dynasty (1046–771 B.C.). Among the textiles excavated from a tomb at Jiefangyingzhi, Chaoyang, Liaoning, was a fragment of warp-faced compound tabby carbon dating to the Western Zhou.[1] *Jin* is also mentioned in the collection of poems *Shi jing*, which was written mostly in the Western Zhou. During the Warring States period (475–221 B.C.) *jin* was widespread and archaeological finds are reported not only in central China, primarily in the Chu area (present-day Hunan and Hubei), but also at sites far from central China, such as Aragou near Urumqi, Xinjiang,[2] and Pazyryk, Russia.[3] The most important group of *jin* silks was found in a tomb at Mashan, Jiangling, Hubei. One of these, woven in three colors, shows dragons, phoenixes, dancers, and other motifs (fig. 60).[4]

The production of *jin* reached its apogee during the Han dynasty with three silk centers. The first center was in the capital of Chang'an (present-day Xi'an), where the silks of the highest quality were made at the East and West Weaving Workshops. The second center was the coastal area of Shandong Province, where *jin* production had a long history and the *san fu guan* (Office for Dresses of the Three Seasons) was established to produce textiles exclusively for the imperial court. The third center was in Chengdu, Sichuan, the site of a special office for textiles, the *jin guan* (Office for *jin* Weaving).[5] *Jin* was one of the two representative types of textiles; the other was *xiu*, meaning embroidery. These two words have ever since been combined to denote the best things, such as *jin xiu he shan* (a landscape as beautiful as woven and embroidered silk) or *jin xiu qian cheng* (a future as wonderful as woven and embroidered silk).

Early Han tombs yield various types, such as *jin* with loops (*rong quan jin*), and advanced techniques, but the designs are largely traditional—small geometric motifs and animals. Finds from the late Han represent the classical style of *jin* silks, with patterns of clouds and animals, motifs that are more or less related to Daoism and the concept of immortality. Clouds are associated with the heavenly realm, in which the immortals dwell. It is a realm inhabited by snakes and tigers, monkeys, lions, birds, and various other creatures. These appear most often on ceramics, incense burners, bronzes with gold and silver inlay, lacquerware, and stone carvings. Textual records from the late Han also refer to "*jin* with continuous mists" and "*jin* with a cloud pattern in five colors."[6]

Weaving workshops continued to produce textiles with the pattern of clouds and animals until as late as the reign of Shi

Figure 60. Textile with dragons, phoenixes, and dancers (detail). Warring States period (485–221 B.C.), ca. 3rd century B.C. *Jin* silk, width 19 7/8 in. (50.5 cm). Excavated from Tomb 1, Mashan, Jiangling, Hubei Province, 1982. Jingzhou Museum, Jiangling

Hu (335–49) of the Later Zhao (328–351), with names such as *deng gao, ming guang, bo shan, zhu yu, jiao long, pu tao, ban wen, feng huang,* and *zhu que.*[7] Many of these names are substantiated by finds in Xinjiang. Comparisons between names and finds indicate that some names are inscriptions woven into the textiles, while others are the motifs appearing on the textiles. For example, *deng* and *gao* (ascending or climbing) are the first two characters of the inscription *deng gao ming wang si hai shou wei guo qing* (climbing while watching the seas and celebrating longevity), *ming* and *guang* are the last two characters of *chang shou ming guang* (longevity and brightness; see cat. no. 19), and *chang le ming guang* (happiness and brightness), but *zhu yu* is the name of the dogwood motif (cat. no. 20). *Jiao long* refers to a pattern with interlaced dragons; *feng huang* is a phoenix, and *zhu que* is a kind of spiritual bird representing the south. These motifs and inscriptions were usually woven in five colors, blue, green, white, red and yellow, sometimes in 1:3 warp-faced compound tabby and sometimes in 1:4 warp-faced compound tabby. The most beautiful and complicated piece, found at the site of Niya, Xinjiang (fig. 61), and representing the finest quality Han-style *jin*, has the characters *wu xing chu dong fang li zhong guo* (the five planets all appear in the east—a highly auspicious sign).[8]

The key element of this group of *jin* silks with cloud and animal patterns is the clouds. There were two major types of cloud. The first is variously described as fork-shaped or shaped like ears of grain: the clouds are discontinuous, the head resembling an ear of wheat. The second type is hill-shaped: the clouds are continuous, with hill-like undulations. These textiles can also be classified into two types according to the arrangement of the clouds and animals. One consists of small separated units, and the other of a continuous design spreading across the width of the fabric, which sometimes appears repetitious, either in one direction or symmetrically.[9] Tiny differences between the horizontal repeats can easily be

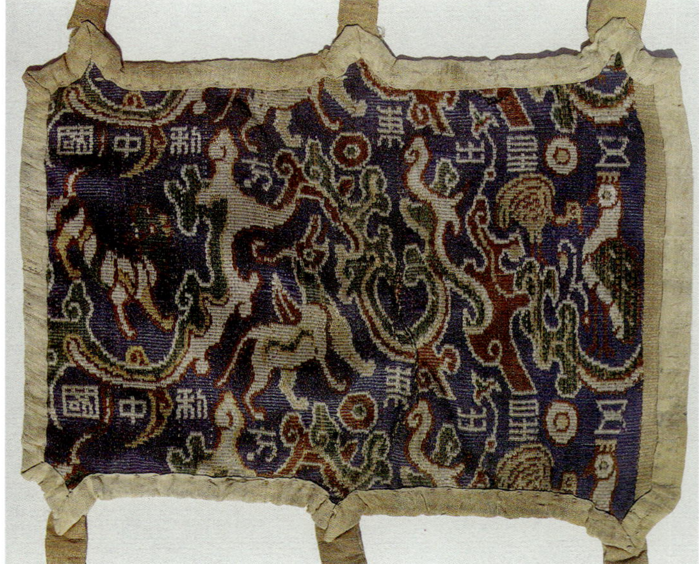

Figure 61. Arm protector with animals and clouds. 1st–3rd century. *Jin* silk, 7 1/4 x 4 7/8 in. (18.5 x 12.5 cm). Excavated from Tomb 8, Niya, Xinjiang Uygur Autonomous Region, 1995. Xinjiang Institute of Archaeology, Urumqi

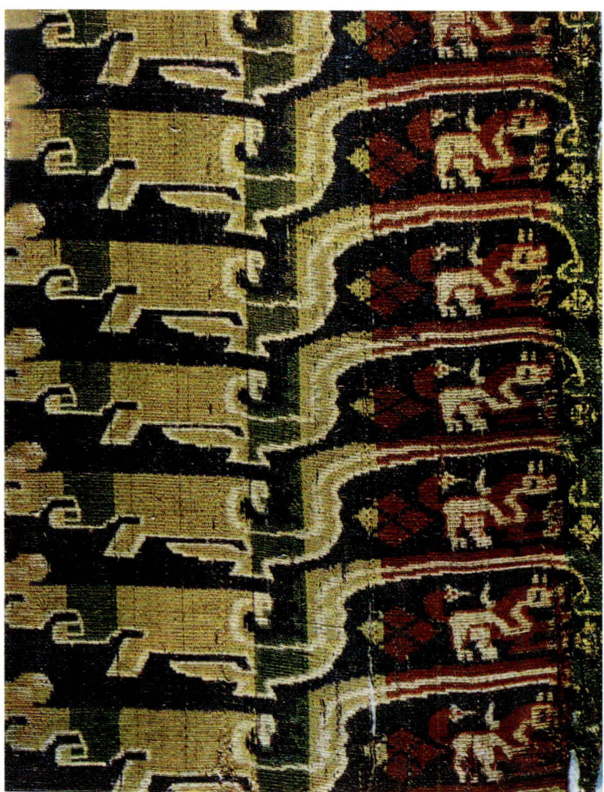

Figure 62. Textile with clouds and small *kui* dragons (detail). Northern Dynasties (386–581). *Jin* silk, 11¾ x 6½ in. (30 x 16.5 cm). Excavated at Astana, Turfan, Xinjiang Uygur Autonomous Region, 1967. Xinjiang Uygur Autonomous Region Museum

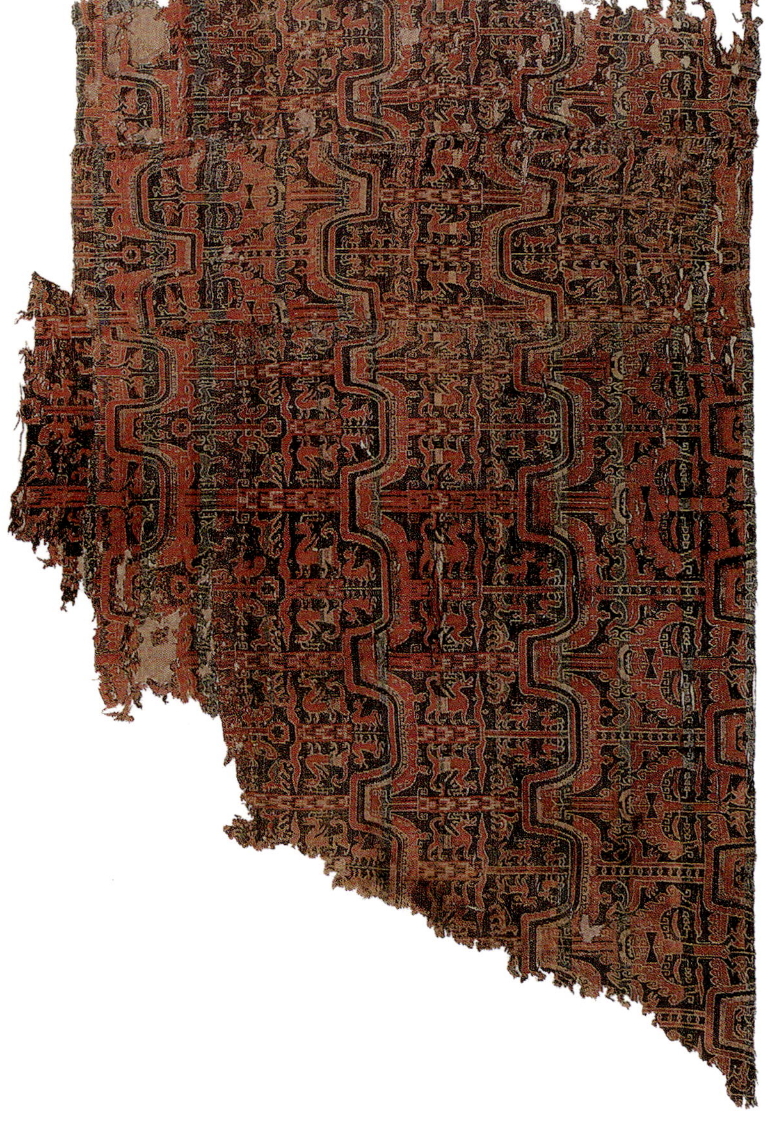

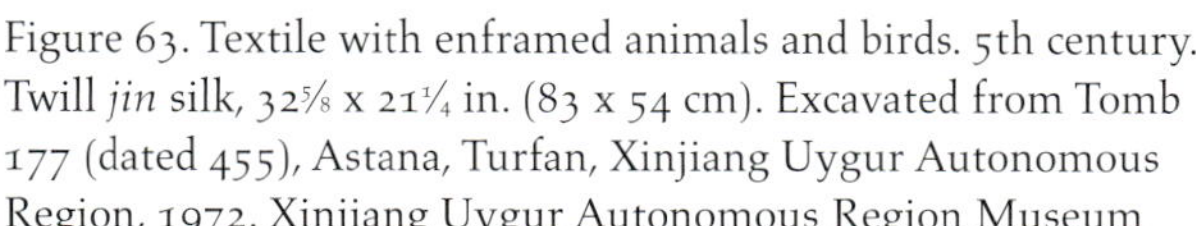

Figure 63. Textile with enframed animals and birds. 5th century. Twill *jin* silk, 32⅝ x 21¼ in. (83 x 54 cm). Excavated from Tomb 177 (dated 455), Astana, Turfan, Xinjiang Uygur Autonomous Region, 1972. Xinjiang Uygur Autonomous Region Museum

found, for example, in the textile with the woven inscription *chang shou ming guang* (see cat. no. 19). This feature of the weaving occurred on many other woven silk textiles from the period, and it suggests that the loom for pattern weaving during the Han dynasty was equipped with devices to control repeats in the warp direction, but not in the weft direction.

Clouds on Han-period *jin* became further stylized and simplified, as in the pattern with clouds and small *kui* dragons (fig. 62) found at Astana near Turfan, Xinjiang.[10] Some designs were influenced by the western style and became whorl-shaped arched structures enframing various kinds of auspicious creatures. These motifs are seen in a fragment with animals and birds also from Astana and datable to 455 (fig. 63)[11] and on a textile with a dragon, phoenix, and tiger found in the Dunhuang Library Cave.[12] Toward the end of the Northern and Southern Dynasties, the cloud framework fell out of favor. Instead, creatures were enclosed in complete geometric forms such as roundels, rings, or frames, and sometimes independent of such a structure. In this exhibition, textiles such as the one with Helios (cat. no. 174), with drinkers (cat. no. 173), and with a barbarian king (cat. no. 234) are examples of patterns in roundels. All these designs show strong influences from the west, mainly in such motifs as the lion, the camel, and the elephant.

Taquete: Imitations of *Jin* Silk

Jin silk had been transported along the Silk Road to the west since the Warring States period. Finds at Pazyryk, Russia, and Aragou, Xinjiang, demonstrate that both *jin* and embroidered

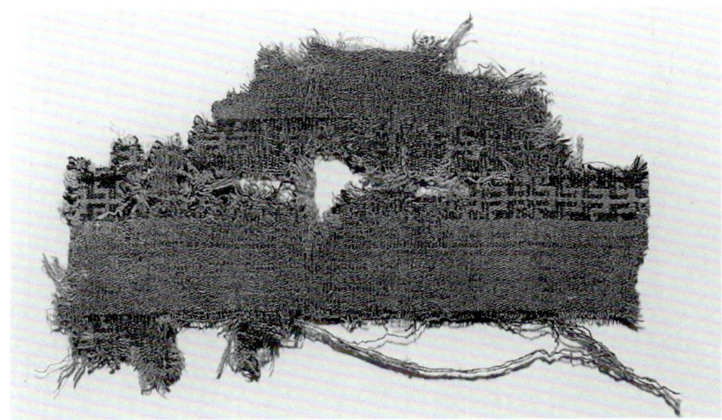

Figure 64. Textile with geometric pattern. First half of 3rd century. Silk taquete, 3⅛ x 6⅝ in. (8 x 16.8 cm). Yale University Art Gallery, New Haven, Yale-French Excavations at Dura-Europos, 1933.486

silk reached these sites around the fifth century B.C. Silks with Han-style designs have frequently been found along the Silk Road, from Mongolia west even as far as the Mediterranean Sea, such as an example from Dura-Europos, Syria (fig. 64).[13] Undoubtedly, *jin* was greatly admired in the west, where previously only tapestry and embroidery had been available, and weavers on the Silk Road, quick to discern a ready market, began to imitate it. Three groups of silk textiles can be considered imitations, probably produced in different cultural regions, including West Asia, Central Asia, and especially northwestern China.

The first group of imitations comprises very narrow silk textiles, almost like ribbons, made in warp-faced compound tabby, which is the same structure as *jin*. Many such ribbons dating from the third to the fourth century were found in a Yingpan site in Xinjiang.[14] They are usually between 1.5 and 2.5 cm (⅝ and 1 in.) in width and include three pattern repeats in the weft, normally animal or simplified animal motifs or geometric designs. The most typical motif is a running dragon with horned head, elongated body, and four legs. Notably, however, those units do not really repeat in the warp direction. The absence of a repeat in the warp direction occurs in one textile that shows two rows of dragons, only some of which have wings (fig. 65). The pattern on *jin*, on the other hand, is always repeated in the warp direction but not in the weft direction. Technically, the ribbons display another distinctive feature: the threads of both warp and weft are z-twisted silk.[15] The former characteristic—that is, the warp-faced compound tabby weave structure and the dragon pattern—relate to the Chinese tradition, but the z-direction twist of the silk and the lack of a pattern repeat in the warp direction suggest that the ribbons are reproductions of Chinese silks from a comparatively western region. And the fact that the fiber is silk, which has been produced in the Xinjiang area since the second to the third century, tells us that ribbons of this type were probably made in northwestern China. It is likely, then, that this type of textile was the first step by weavers on the Silk Road in making copies of Chinese *jin*.

Compared to ribbons in the same structure as *jin*, the taquete weave structure played a more important role in the development of textile cultural exchange on the Silk Road. Taquete is a special term indicating textiles woven in weft-faced compound tabby weave. Early taquete textiles include either wool or silk materials, but more frequently are wool. There are several wool taquete pieces found in the sites of

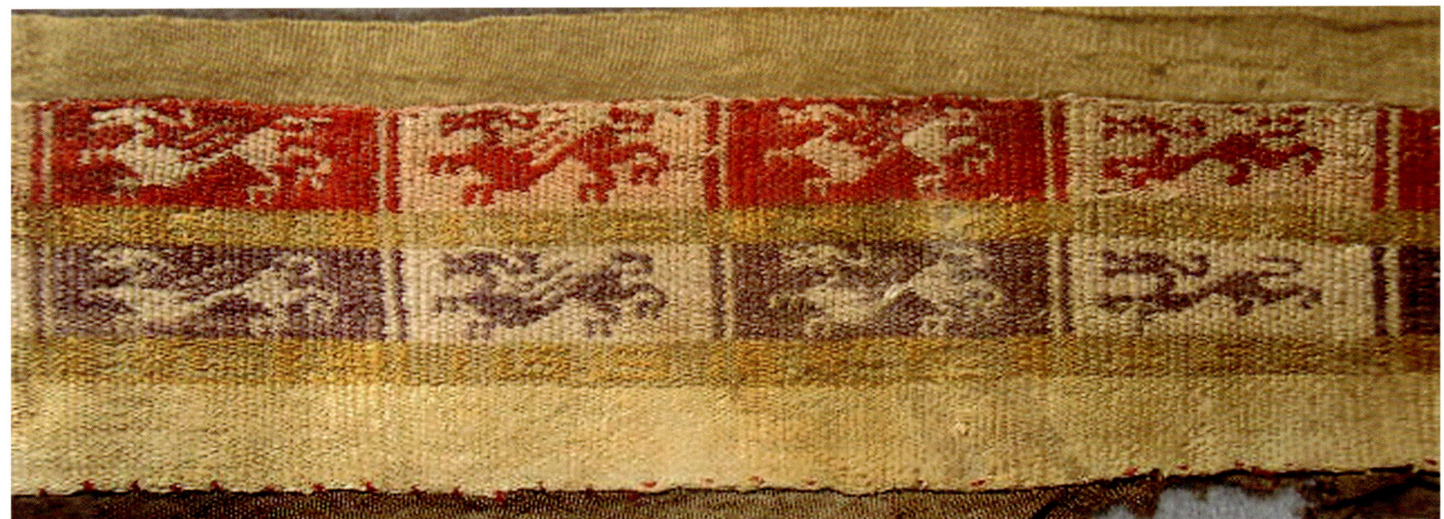

Figure 65. Textile with pattern of animals (detail). 3rd–4th century. Silk textile in warp-faced compound tabby, 21¼ x 1¼ in. (54 x 3.2 cm); 21¼ x 1⅞ in. (54 x 4.7 cm) including added silks. Private collection

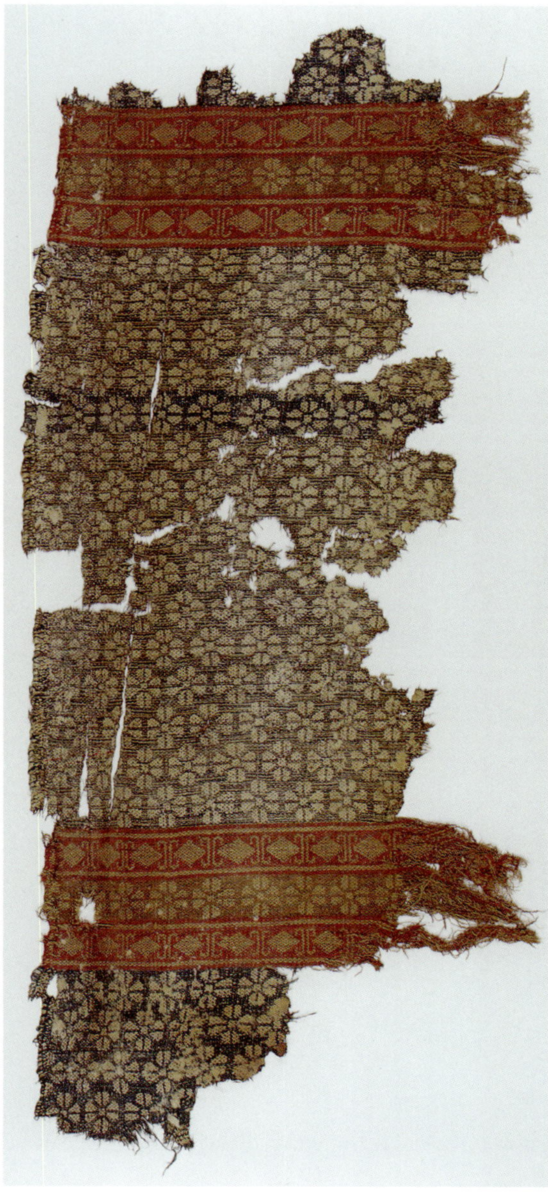

Figure 66. Textile fragment with pattern of rosettes and bands. 3rd–4th century. Wool taquete, 28⅜ x 12⅝ in. (72 x 32 cm). Excavated at Yingpan, Xinjiang Uygur Autonomous Region, 1989–99. Xinjiang Institute of Archaeology, Urumqi

Niya and Yingpan, in Xinjiang. Finds from Niya include two examples. One with rosettes in a lozenge grid was excavated in 1959,[16] and the other with a geometric design was found in 1994.[17] More examples of wool taquete were excavated from the Yingpan site. The first example is a fragment with rosette and geometric designs, which has a selvage preserved (fig. 66).[18] The second, sewn together in the famous caftan with Roman-style figures, trees, and goats in red and yellow colors, was woven in a design of rosettes and waves with a brocaded spot in the center of the rosettes.[19] The third example also has a remarkable design with figures, snakes, eagles and grapevines.[20] This type of wool textile was also found at Shanpula, Xinjiang, for example, a fragment with a design of an ear of wheat.[21] The wool taquete textiles all were woven with clearly western-style patterns and were likely made in the Western Regions along the Silk Road, most probably in Hellenistic areas of Central Asia, such as Bactria or Gandhara.[22] Other wool taquete textiles have patterns with a stronger eastern style, such as the wool taquete with hunting and animal motifs in the collections of the Abbeg Foundation, Riggisberg, and the Philadelphia Museum of Art (fig. 67).[23] All these textiles have patterns similar to those of *jin*, and a technical structure turned 90 degrees from *jin* silk weave, so that the pattern repeats only in the weft direction, not in the warp direction. In this respect, these taquete textiles can be considered imitations of *jin* silk.

Not long after wool taquete made its appearance, silk taquete also occurred in the western world. The earliest known piece of silk taquete is the example with a geometric pattern

Figure 67. Textile with hunting scene (detail). Syria, 3rd century. Wool and linen taquete, 8 x 26½ in. (20.3 x 67.3 cm). Philadelphia Museum of Art: Purchased with the Bloomfield Moore Fund, 1933.50.1

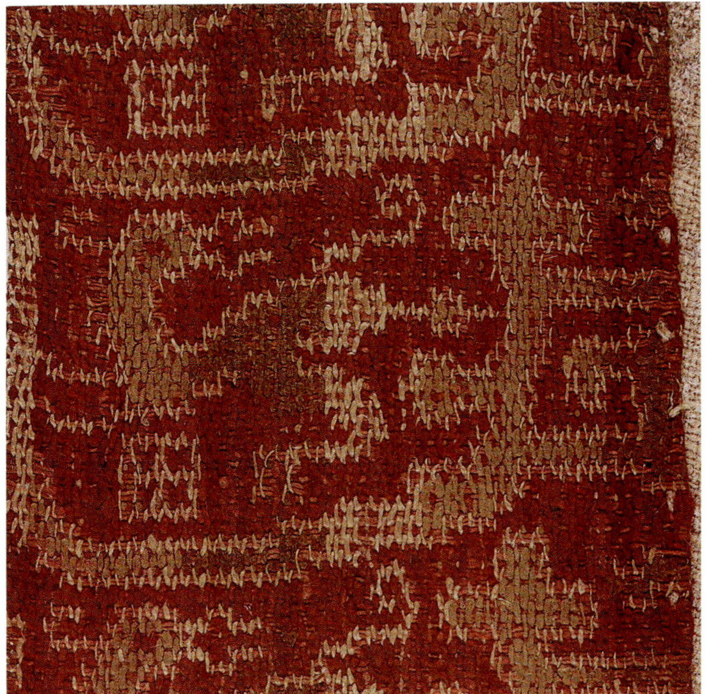

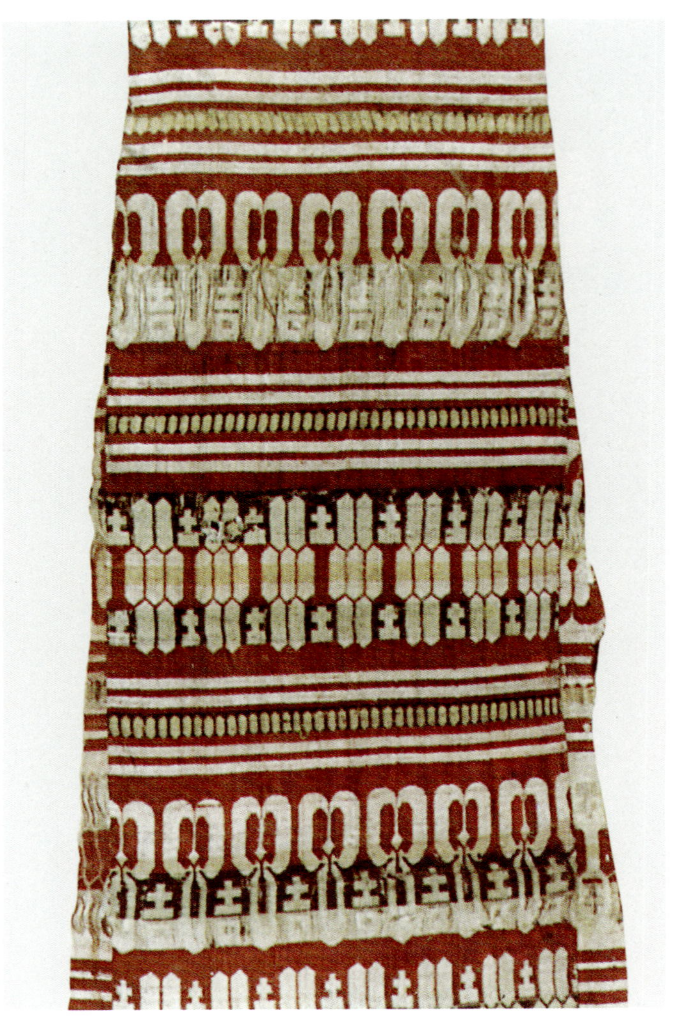

Figure 68. Dragon pattern (detail) on caftan band. 3rd–4th century. Spun silk taquete, width 1⅝–1¾ in. (4–4.5 cm). Excavated at Yingpan, Xinjiang Uygur Autonomous Region, 1989–99. Xinjiang Institute of Archaeology, Urumqi

Figure 69. Texile with the character *ji* (detail). 6th century. Silk taquete. Excavated from Tomb 169 (dated 558), Astana, Turfan, Xinjiang Uygur Autonomous Region, 1972–73. Yinjiang Uygur Autonomous Region Museum

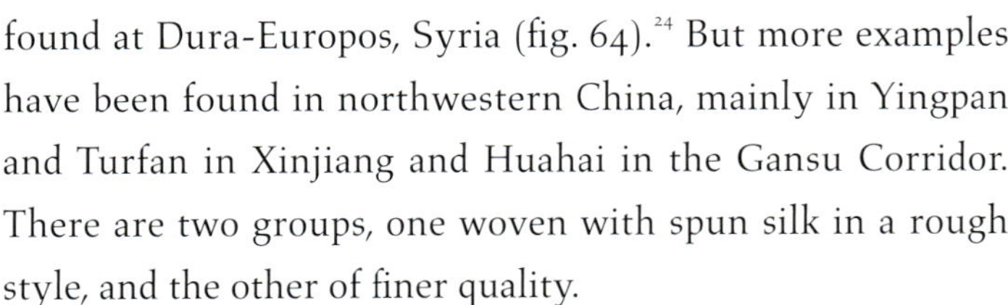

found at Dura-Europos, Syria (fig. 64).[24] But more examples have been found in northwestern China, mainly in Yingpan and Turfan in Xinjiang and Huahai in the Gansu Corridor. There are two groups, one woven with spun silk in a rough style, and the other of finer quality.

Many examples of taquete with spun silk were excavated from Turfan, Yingpan, and Huahai, mostly in a simplified style of animal and cloud design. All are very similar. Some are dated pieces, including one found in Turfan, excavated together with a document dated 548,[25] and another found in a series of tombs dated 364 to 403, in Huahai.[26] More examples were found at Yingpan, including those on a cotton caftan (fig. 68) and silk jacket.[27] All the examples of taquete in spun silk have a very similar style, occurring basically in red, yellow, and white, usually with animal patterns, in a treatment very close to the running animals on *jin* ribbons, the animals on *jin* found at Turfan, and the four-petaled rosette closely resembling the Chinese character *tian* (field). In all the known examples of spun silk taquete, the pattern is repeated only in the weft direction but not in the warp direction. These can be considered imitations of Chinese *jin*.

Regarding the source of spun silk taquete, the story of the silk princess in Khotan, Xinjiang, might lead us to the place of origin.[28] The story relates that a princess of the "eastern country" (China) married the king of Khotan. At the king's request, the princess hid silkworm eggs in her crown, and by deceiving the guards at the frontier pass brought them surreptitiously into the kingdom. From that time on, the kingdom was able to establish its own sericulture and silk industry, and the princess later came to be worshipped in the Xinjiang region as the Goddess of Silkworms. To promote sericulture, and also probably as a result of Buddhist teachings, the local people did not kill the pupae within the silk cocoons. Instead, they let the moths break out of the cocoons to mate and lay eggs. Broken cocoons yield short lengths of silk that must be spun to form the long threads required for weaving. This would explain why spun silk was used for this group of taquete textiles.

The other group of taquete textiles, from a somewhat later period, was made of very fine reeled silk instead of spun silk. Examples were found mostly in Turfan, and they include silks that incorporate the characters *ji* (auspicious; fig. 69) and *wang* (king or prince; see cat. no. 236) and designs with animals, such as confronted goats.[29] All these fine silk taquetes date to the Northern Dynasties, mostly the sixth and early seventh centuries. According to a document found at Turfan,[30] polychrome silk textiles produced in local areas were called Qiuci *jin* (Kizil silk) and Sule *jin* (Kashgar silk). The former, a patterned silk on yellow ground woven with spun silk, in Gaochang (Turfan), most likely referred to taquete with spun silk, the latter to taquete with reeled silk. The taquete weave was probably employed because the technique had been handed down from one generation to the next. Furthermore, there were many residents of Han ethnicity who had immigrated from inner China, so the local weavers, after long contact with Han people, may have understood enough of the Han language to use Chinese characters. Based on this evidence, silk taquete was probably also produced in the Xinjiang area, but starting in a slightly later period.

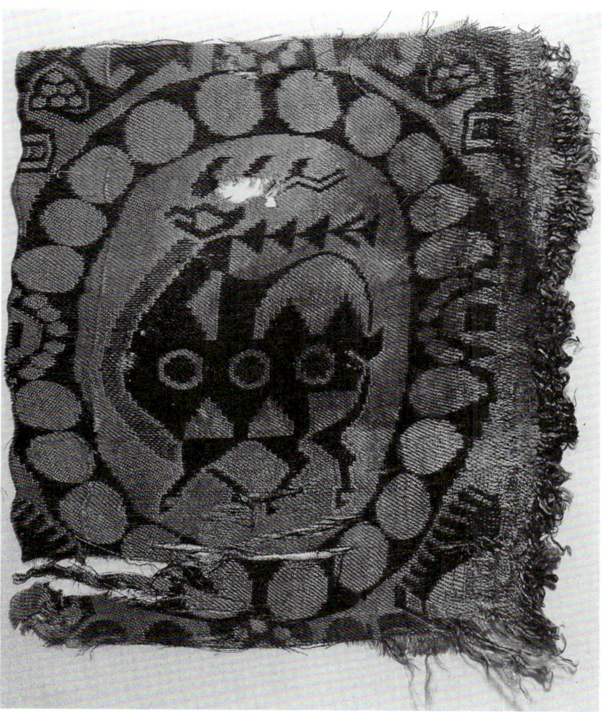

Figure 70. Textile with stag in pearl roundel. 7th century. Silk samite, 8½ x 7 ⅞ in. (21.5 x 20 cm). Excavated at Astana, Turfan, Xinjiang Uygur Autonomous Region, 1959. Xinjiang Uygur Autonomous Region Museum

Samite: Forming a New System

Samite, or weft-faced compound twill, is the final stage in the development of textile techniques on the Silk Road during the Han and Tang dynasties. Technically, it can be considered a development either from taquete (weft-faced compound tabby), by changing the foundation weave from tabby to 2.1 twill, or from twill *jin* (warp-faced compound twill), by turning the warp and weft directions 90 degrees. Samite weave seems to have appeared somewhat later than taquete on the Silk Road in China. None of the samite silks from excavations can be dated earlier than the Tang dynasty, although it is certain that some samite silks must have been produced before the Tang dynasty.

The major types of samite made in the Tang dynasty can be divided into four groups or subgroups based on style or two groups based on technique. The first group is in western style and belongs to the Turfan period (7th century). Samite silks excavated from Astana, near Turfan, Xinjiang, are the best examples. On them large pearl roundels enclose animals or birds as the major motif. Mostly they appear independently, but sometimes as confronted images. Examples of the single images include the textiles with a boar's head (cat. no. 237), with a stag (fig. 70), with a hunter, and with a bird that is standing and holding a ribbon; confronted images are represented by textiles with paired cocks (cat. no. 238), paired ducks, and paired stags. All of them utilize the same technique: paired z-twisted inner warps, flatness of the weft threads on the front, and sometimes the use of threads with mixed colors as one weft. Beyond the pearl roundel and central motif, the secondary motif outside the roundel is comparatively simple, probably a tree or flower form. The pattern has real repeats only in the weft direction but not in the warp direction. Similarly, the secondary motif is usually symmetrical in the weft but not in the warp direction. The earliest example

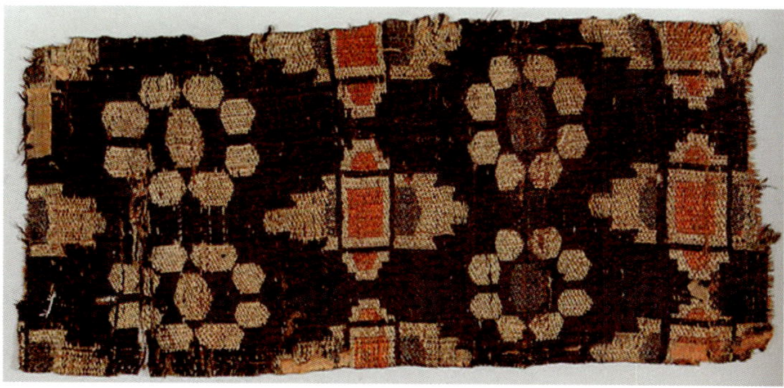

Figure 71. Textile with rosettes. 7th century. Silk samite, 7⅝ x 3⅜ in. (19.3 x 8.6 cm). Excavated at Astana, Turfan, Xinjiang Uygur Autonomous Region, 1973. Xinjiang Uygur Autonomous Region Museum

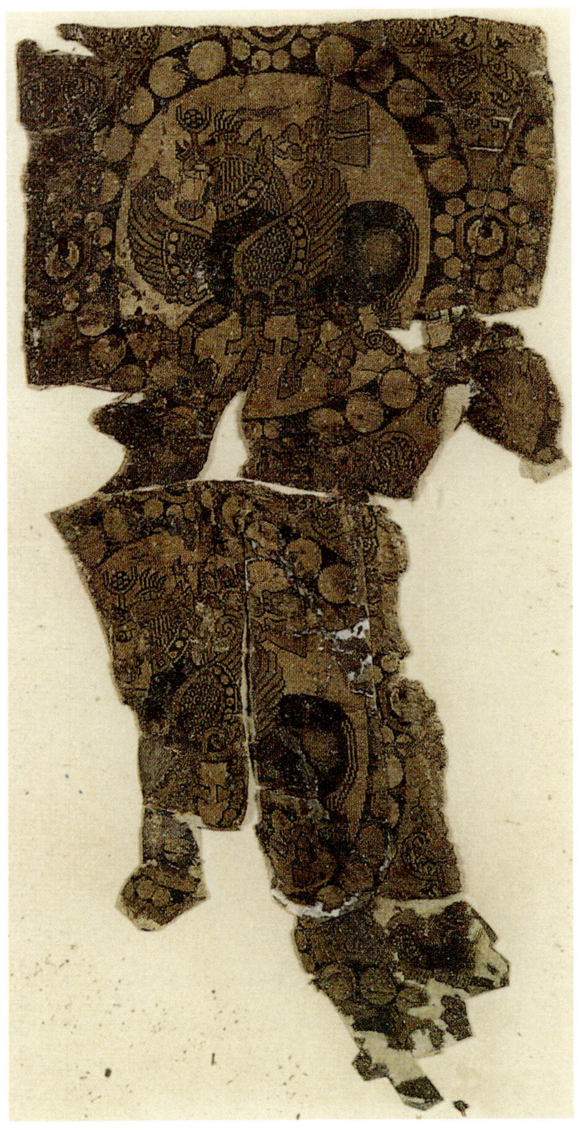

Figure 72. Textile with winged horse in pearl roundel. 7th century. Silk samite, 12¼ x 6½ in. (31 x 16.5 cm). Excavated at Antinoe, Egypt, 1897. Musée historique des tissus, Lyon

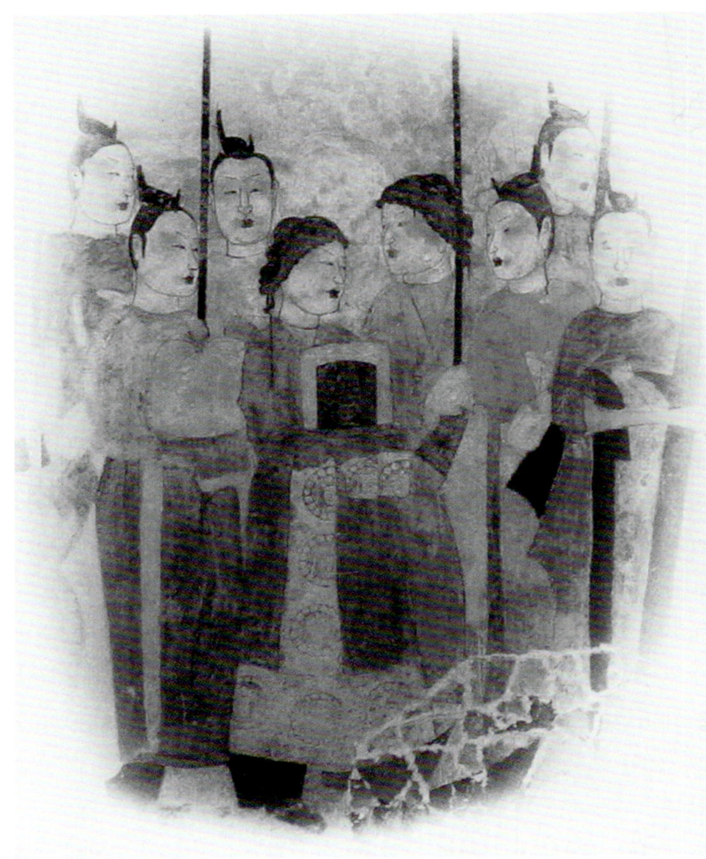

Figure 73. Tomb mural showing pearl roundel with face. Northern Qi dynasty (550–577). Taiyuan, Shanxi Province

of samite known from Turfan finds has a small rosette motif on a dark blue ground (fig. 71) and was excavated together with a document dated 619.[31] However, most of the examples of samite with pearl roundels were found in Turfan tombs of the 630s to the 650s. Some samite silks in the collections of Western museums can also be put into this group. Famous examples include the horse roundel found at Antinoe, Egypt (fig. 72).[32]

The second stylistic group of samite textiles appeared in daily life starting in the early Tang dynasty. Examples have been found at Turfan in early Tang tombs and in Dulan, Qinghai, but also in the Shōsō-in and Hōryūji in Nara, Japan. They combine western and eastern styles to make a new group. As in the previous western group, the designs are large, with pearl roundels enclosing major motifs, but in this

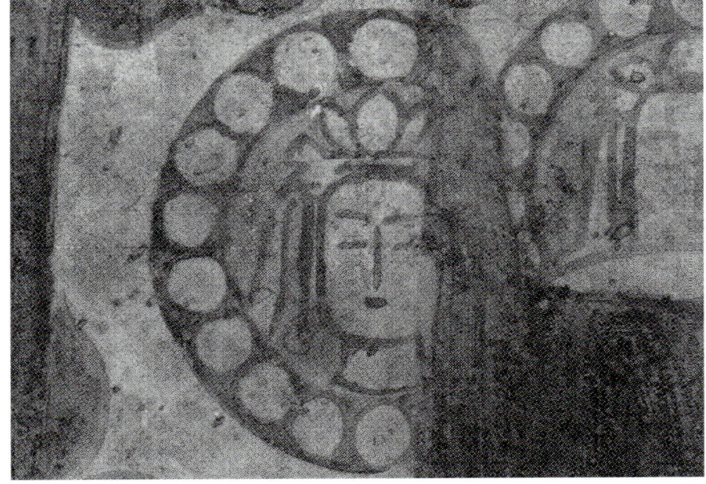

Figure 73, detail

group the major motif is more Chinese in style. One example is the silk roundel found by Kozui Otani,[33] where the confronted stags are more realistic and colorful than the stag from the first group; the Chinese inscription woven between the stags, *hua shu dui lu* (floral tree and confronted stags), also strongly reflects Chinese culture. Another textile, woven with four horsemen hunting lions, was collected at Hōryūji.[34] Each horse is marked with the Chinese characters *shan* (mountain) and *ji* (auspicious), which also suggests the textile's eastern provenance. This style is also characterized by the secondary motif of quatrefoils in the interstices. The quatrefoils are symmetrical in both the warp and weft directions. Technically, this group of samites has some distinguishing characteristics. The warps, for example, exhibit an s-twist and are doubled or tripled, and the pattern is truly repeated in both the warp and weft directions. Similar fragments from the same group were found in Turfan, and the earliest one was excavated from a tomb dating from the third year of the reign of Wude (620).[35]

However, the use of large pearl roundels on textiles, whether the first, western, group or the second, in the Chinese style, must have occurred earlier than the dates of the excavated textiles. A mural from a Northern Qi tomb shows many costumes with designs of pearl roundels, one with a large human head (fig. 73), and another with confronted stags.[36] A similar pattern with pearl roundel and hunting motif was also found on a mud sculpture from Dunhuang, dating from the Sui dynasty.[37] These examples certainly depict samite textiles, but judging from the secondary motif, they seem more likely to represent the western style. This may suggest that the western-style pearl roundel is earlier than the Chinese pearl roundel.

Both the eastern and western samite groups had subgroups during the High or middle Tang dynasty. The technique used in the eastern-style silk samites was adopted for Tang medallion design by the Lingyang school,[38] probably for floral roundels enclosing animal and bird motifs, which played a dominant role in Tang-dynasty silk. Of the many extant examples in this group, two were excavated at Dulan, Qinghai. One shows a floral roundel framing a standing phoenix (fig. 74);[39] the other shows a floral roundel enclosing paired birds.[40] The same technique was still used in a later samite textile with a more flexible design, which dates from 778 (cat. no. 242).

The subgroup of samite silk in the western manner was mainly found in Dulan. Most of its technical features are nearly the same as those of the first, or western, group. These

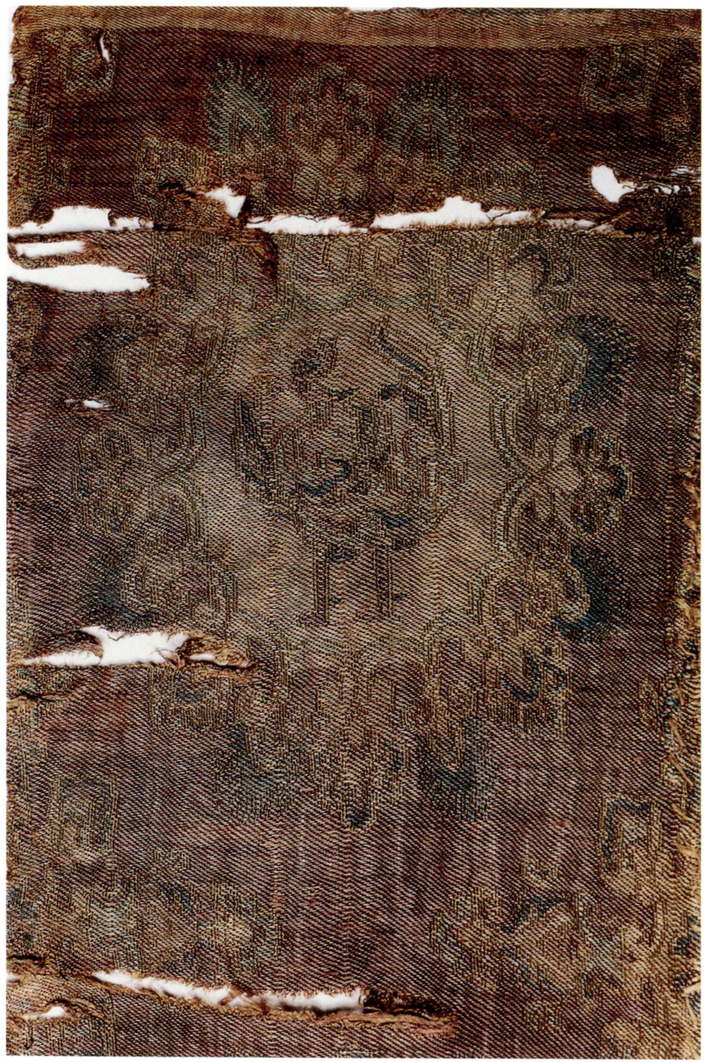

Figure 74. Textile with phoenix in floral roundel (detail). 8th–9th century. Silk samite, 11⅜ x 4⅞ in. (29 x 12.5 cm). Excavated at Reshui, Dulan, Qinghai Province, 1983–85. Qinghai Institute of Archaeology

include z-twisted warps in pairs or threes, the flat surface of the weft, and a true repeat in the weft direction but not in the warp direction. Sometimes this subgroup exhibits a wide loom width and weft floats on the back. However, the roundel designs tend to be more floral and decorative. Not only pearl shapes but also laurel wreaths, heart chains, and petals were chosen for the roundel borders, which were frequently found in sites in West and Central Asia, such as Taq-i Bostan, Iran,[41] and Panjikent, Uzbekistan.[42] The chief motifs for this group are lions, ibexes, and birds holding ribbons, instead of the horses, boars' heads, and stags of group one, but the secondary motif is usually quatrefoils symmetrical in four directions, instead of only two. The textiles in this group are often called Zandaniji silks[43] and are usually attributed to Sogdian weavers. According to Dorothy Shepherd and Anna Ierusalimskaia, the Zandaniji textiles could also be divided into

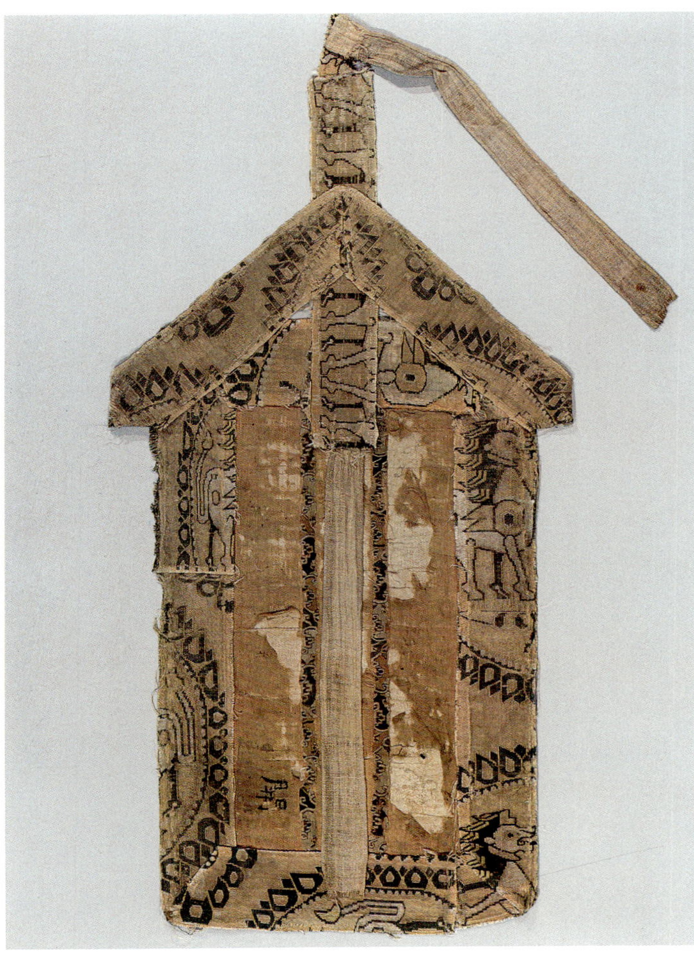

Figure 75. Sutra wrapper with pattern of lions. Late 8th–9th century. Silk samite, 31 x 12 in. (78.6 x 30.6 cm). Excavated at the Library Cave, Dunhuang, Gansu Province, 1907. British Museum, London

several groups based on color and motif.[44] Examples are found in museum collections all over the world, including the textiles with lions from the Library Cave at Dunhuang (fig. 75)[45] and the textile with duck at The Cleveland Museum of Art.[46] One piece (cat. no. 244) features a woven Middle Persian inscription, so that some scholars attribute this group of textiles to Sasanian Persia.[47] However, it is not known who wove this group of samites—Persian weavers in western areas, Sogdian weavers in Central Asia, or even Chinese weavers in northwestern China. They are mostly dated from the second half of the eighth to the first half of the ninth century.

By the High Tang, samite had become the major type of woven silk, but it is hard to find the source of the weave structure. There are two basic elements in samite weave, the weft-faced patterning method and the 2.1 twill weave. Weft-faced patterning obviously derived from taquete. The source of the 2.1 twill is more difficult to identify. There are three possibilities—twill *jin*, Tang samite, or western samite—but it is not known which used twill first, because both twill *jin* and samite occurred at the same time, and the 2.1 twill weave is not found in China or in western areas before the fifth century.

Samite is a very important type of weave. After the mid-Tang, samite, which combines the weft-faced patterning principle and a twill foundation, became the dominant type of patterning method. In the late Tang, Liao, and Song dynasties (mid-eighth century–1273), samite was still used, though in a new version, the so-called Liao samite.[48]

Conclusion

Jin, taquete, and samite were three major types of woven silks found along the Silk Road during the Han and Tang dynasties. They also represent three stages in the development of silk weaving. From the preliminary discussion above, a basic progression can be delineated. During the Han, *jin* (warp-faced compound tabby) was the traditional silk-weaving technique in central China. When introduced to regions northwest of China or even farther west, *jin* was copied or imitated by the local people, with either wool or silk, and took the form of *jin* ribbons (silk ribbons woven in warp-faced compound tabby), wool taquete, and silk taquete (weft-faced compound tabby); made in the area of Xinjiang. Based on the combination of the weft-faced patterning method and a 2.1 twill foundation weave, samite (weft-faced compound twill) came into existence and became the dominant technique for weaving patterns after the early Tang. Samite then evolved into Liao-style samite in the late Tang, Liao, and Song dynasties.

1. Zhao Chengze et al. 1979.
2. Xinjiang Weiwuer zizhiqu wenwu shiye guanliju et al. 1999: 165.
3. Lu Kinko 1957: 37, fig. 1 opp. p. 48.
4. Hubei sheng Jingzhou diqu bowuguan 1985, colorpls. XIV–XVII, black-and-white pl. XXV.
5. Zhu Xinyu 1992: 47–54.
6. Zhao Feng 1999a: 1–2.
7. *YZJ*: 8.
8. Zhao Feng and Yu Zhiyong 2000: 62–63.
9. From a technical point of view, however, any pattern unit or repeat in the weft direction is not a real repeat.
10. Xinjiang bowuguan chutu wenwu zhanlan xiaozu 1972, pl. 24.
11. Zhao Feng 2003: 25–31.
12. Whitfield 1982, vol. 3, not paginated.
13. Pfister and Bellinger 1945, pl. 263. See also Pfister 1934, pl. XVI, and Schmidt-Colinet 1995: 113.
14. Li Wenying and Zhou Jinling 1998: 63–74.
15. Zhao Feng 2002a: 62, 65.
16. Xinjiang bowuguan chutu wenwu zhanlan xiaozu 1972, pl. 15.
17. Zhao Feng and Yu Zihyong 2000: 78–79.
18. Zhao Feng 2002a: 50–51.
19. Xinjiang wenwu kaogu yanjiusuo 1999: 4–16.
20. Qian Boquan 1995: 33, figs. 3, 4.
21. Xinjiang Weiwuer zizhiqu bowuguan and Xinjiang wenwu kaogu yanjiusuo 2001: 232.
22. Lin Meicun 2003: 2–35.
23. Blum 1997: 109.
24. Pfister and Bellinger 1945, pl. 263.
25. Zhao Feng 1999c: 88–89.
26. Huahai tombs are located in Gansu Province and are not yet published.
27. Zhao Feng 2002a: 58–61.
28. *DTX*: 1021.
29. Zhongguo Xinjiang Weiwuer zizhiqu bowuguan and Riben Nailiang sichou zhi lu xue yanjiu zhongxin 2000, pls. 77, 83.
30. Wu Zhen 2000: 84–103.
31. Shiruku rodo-gaku kenkyu senta 2000, pl. 88.
32. Martiniani-Reber 1986: 27.
33. Tatsumura 1993, no. 16; Hayashi 1975: 120, fig. 131.
34. Matsumoto 1984, no. 38.
35. Wu Min 1984: 70–80.
36. Chang Yimin 2003: 1–5.
37. K420, Mogao Grottoes, Dunhuang, Sui dynasty; see Wang Jingyu 2001: 215.
38. According to the records of Zhang Yanyuan, Duke Lingyang, under his formal name Dou Shilun, was director of the imperial workshop in Sichuan at the beginning of the Tang. His innovative designs became known as Duke Lingyang silks.
39. Zhao Feng 1999c: 142–43.
40. Zhao Feng 2002a: 96.
41. Otavsky 1998: 133–49.
42. Azarpay 1980: 118–20.
43. Shepherd and Henning 1959: 15–40.
44. Ierusalimskaia 1972: 5–46.
45. Whitfield 1982, vol. 3, not paginated.
46. *Woven Treasures* 1959: 19, 20, no. 1.
47. Xu Xinguo 1996: 3–25.
48. Zhao Feng 1999b: 46–63.

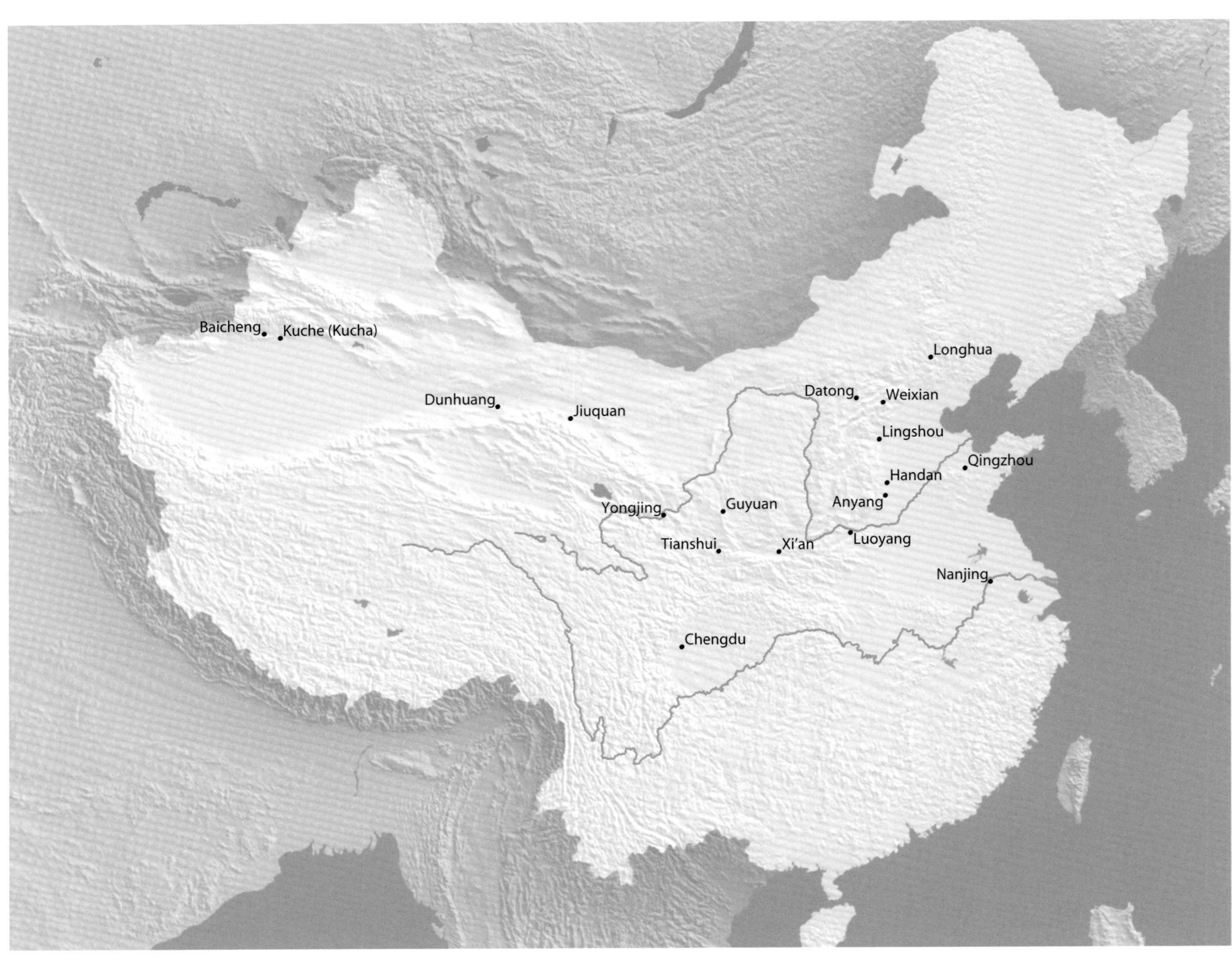

Baicheng
Kuche (Kucha)
Longhua
Datong
Weixian
Dunhuang
Jiuquan
Lingshou
Qingzhou
Handan
Anyang
Yongjing
Guyuan
Luoyang
Tianshui
Xi'an
Nanjing
Chengdu

Buddha Images of the Northern Plain, 4th–6th Century

SU BAI

Buddhism was introduced to China's Central Plain, according to the more reliable sources, around the first century A.D. The earliest dated image of the Buddha, a gilt-bronze Shakyamuni (fig. 76), is inscribed Later Zhao, Jianwu fourth year (i.e., Later Zhao, fourth year of the Jianwu reign era; 338), during the Sixteen Kingdoms period (304–439).[1] The Buddha is seated in yogic posture wearing a long, close-fitting outer robe. The robe, which does not represent an eastern fashion, and the face, marked by distinctively non-eastern features, indicate a Central Asian origin.

In 1975, a small bronze image (fig. 77), inscribed Northern Wei, Taichang fifth year (420), was discovered in Longhua, Hebei.[2] In terms of facial features and clothing, it is quite close to the 338 gilt-bronze Buddha. However, they are separated in time by more than eighty years. Moreover, images similar to the 420 Buddha have recently been found in North China, stretching from Gansu to Shaanxi, Henan, Hebei, and Liaoning provinces. Some of the gilt bronzes are dated as late as the end of the fifth century.

Even more significant are two small bronze Buddhas inscribed Liu Song, Yuanjia fourteenth year (437; fig. 78), and Yuanjia twenty-eighth year (451; fig. 79), that have survived from the Song dynasty (420–479).[3] With the same costume and posture as the two mentioned above, these two works suggest that the Taichang–Yuanjia type spread over a broad geographic area during a long period of time. Very likely, this

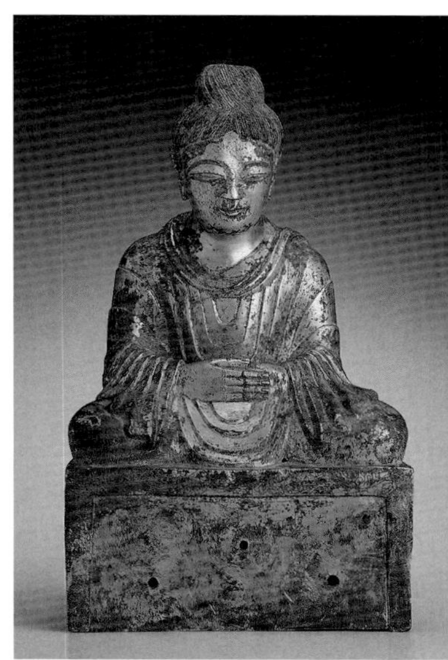

Figure 76. Seated Buddha. Later Zhao dynasty (328–351), 338. Gilt bronze, height 15½ in. (39.4 cm). The Avery Brundage Collection, B60 B1034. © Asian Art Museum of San Francisco. Used by permission

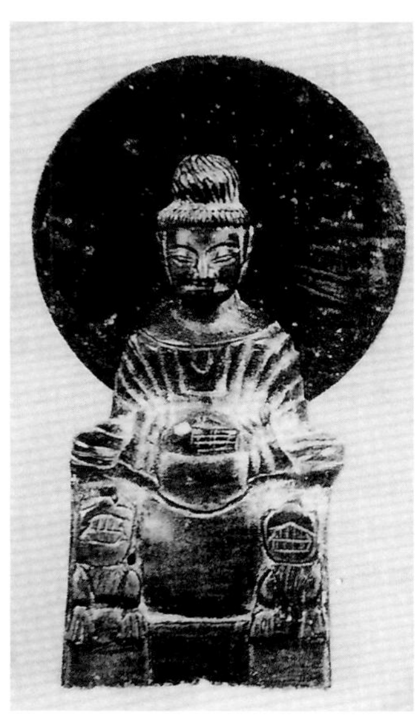

Figure 77. Seated Buddha. Northern Wei dynasty (386–534), 420. Bronze

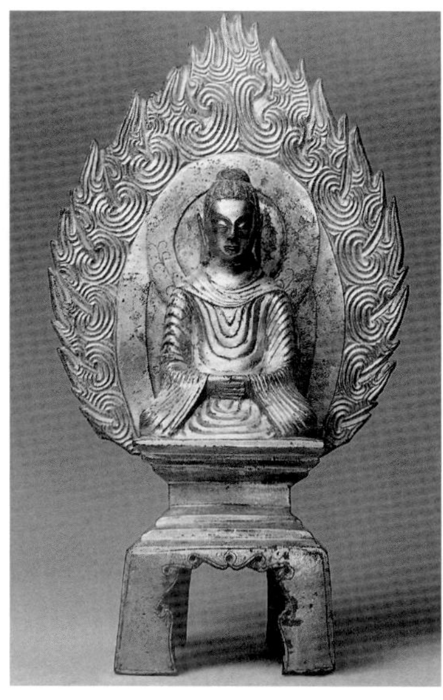

Figure 78. Seated Buddha. Song dynasty (420–479), 437. Bronze

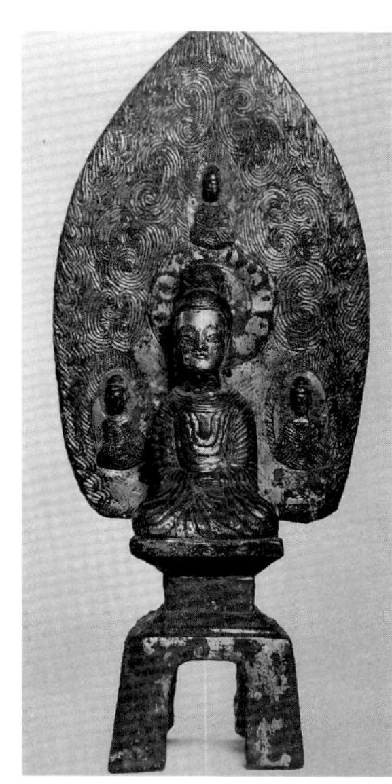

Figure 79. Seated Buddha. Song dynasty (420–479), 451. Bronze

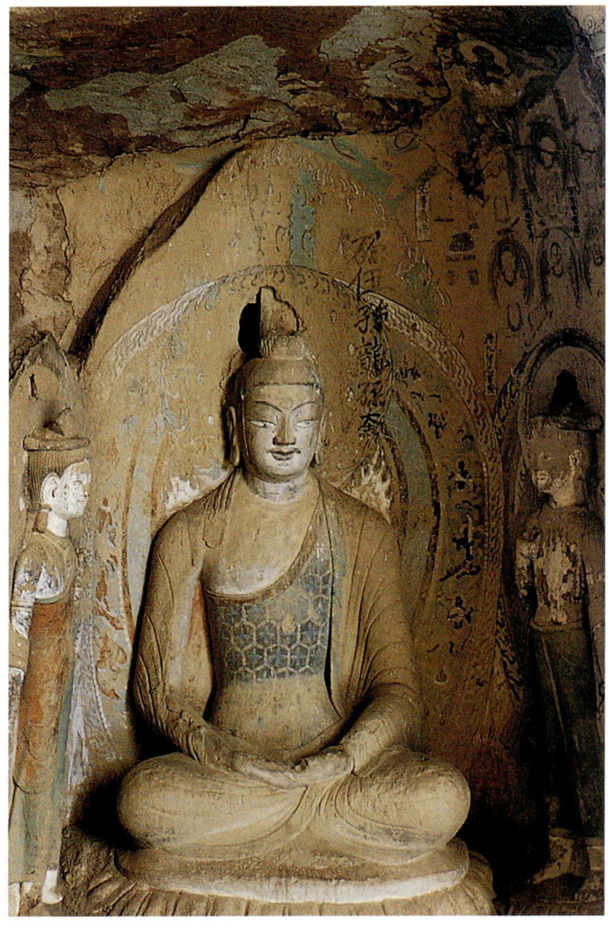

Figure 80. Seated Buddha. Western Qin dynasty (385–431), 420. Cave 169, Binglingsi, Yongjing, Gansu Province

Figure 81. Drawing of the front and side views of a seated Buddha. Northern Wei dynasty (386–534), 444. Stone. Weixian, Hebei Province

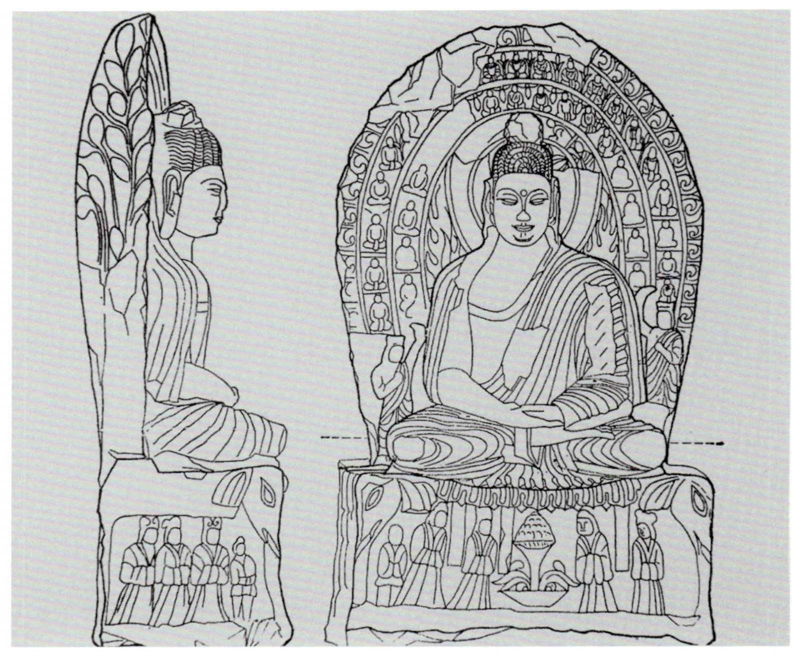

is the prototype in China's Central Plain prior to the Eastern Jin (317–420) and Sixteen Kingdoms periods. This Buddha image evolved gradually and assumed fair, delicate facial features, narrow shoulders, and a slender body. Surviving works from the South displayed this tendency before those from the North, as exemplified by the bronze Buddha dated 451.

In the early fifth century, in western as well as eastern Gansu, Buddhas in *abhaya,* the "fear not" mudra, begin to appear. They wear the robe in western style, with the right shoulder exposed. A variant of this type of garment—which differs from the long, close-fitting outer robe—leaves the right shoulder only partially exposed. Later, the fashion of covering both shoulders became popular. These Buddha images, characterized by square faces and broad, sloping shoulders, are quite distinct from the seated Buddhas wearing the long, close-fitting robe of the earlier Jianwu–Taichang period.

Examples from western Gansu occur on small votive stupas made in the vicinity of Dunhuang and Jiuquan during the Northern Liang dynasty (397–460). Carved on these stupas are preaching Buddhas seated in yogic posture with the right shoulder exposed. The earliest dated Ma Dehui stupa (Ma Dehui refers to the donor), from Jiuquan (with preaching Buddhas shown with the right shoulder exposed), is inscribed Northern Liang, Chengyang second year (426). Among the latest in date are the Bai Shuangju stupa from Jiuquan—with seated Buddhas in meditation, some with the right shoulder partially exposed, others with both shoulders covered—inscribed Northern Liang, Yuanhe third year (434); and the Cheng Duan'er stupa, also from Jiuquan—with Buddhas seated in yogic posture and with both shoulders covered—inscribed Northern Liang, Taiyuan second year (436).[4]

In eastern Gansu, similar Buddha images are found on the rear north wall of Cave 169 at Binglingsi, Yongjing, such as the central standing Buddha with the right shoulder exposed in niche 9 and the three painted Buddhas of niche 11—all seated in yogic posture with the right shoulder partially exposed—and the central seated Buddha of niche 6 (fig. 80). The last forms a triad with two bodhisattvas. He is shown with the right shoulder partially exposed and performing the *dhyana,* or "meditation," mudra. All these images are dated Western Qin, Jianhong first year (420). The date is inscribed at the upper left of the triad in niche 6.

Appearing in the first half of the fifth century, slightly later than in Gansu, Buddha images with the right shoulder partially exposed prevailed east of Gansu. The earliest example was discovered at Weixian, Hebei, a stone sculpture of a seated *dhyana* Buddha inscribed Northern Wei, Taiping Zhenjun fifth year (444; fig. 81).[5] This type of image became quite popular at Yungang in the Five Imperial Caves. The imperial site of Yungang was carved out of Xiwuzhoushan, near present-day Datong, Shanxi. The site was located west of Pingcheng, the capital of the Northern Wei dynasty from 386 to 494. The earliest sculptures at Yungang date to Northern Wei, Heping first year (460). The main Buddha in Cave 20, a seated *dhyana* Buddha (fig. 82), and the main Buddha in Cave 19, shown seated in *dharmachakra*, or "preaching the Law," exemplify Buddha images portrayed with the right shoulder partially exposed.

The Buddha image with both shoulders covered developed slightly later at Yungang. The Shakyamuni and Duobao Buddhas seated and facing each other in niche 14 on the cliff, to the east of Cave 11, are the earliest dated examples. They are inscribed Northern Wei, Taihe thirteenth year (489). The best-preserved images are probably the standing and seated Buddhas in Caves 5 and 6, all portrayed in the *dharmachakra* mudra (fig. 83), with the exception of the main Buddha in Cave 5, who is a seated Buddha in meditation. The monastic robe worn by these Buddhas probably evolved from the silky, loose-fitting robe with wide sash popular at the southern court, which the Northern Wei adopted during Taihe tenth year (486).[6] When represented on seated images, the robe overhang forms a cascade over the throne.

From the early years of Heping to the mid- and late-Taihe era (ca. 461–99), Yungang Buddha images are characterized by round faces and wide shoulders; the early standing figures even feature disproportionately large heads and short bodies (fig. 84). Generally speaking, they look more robust and powerful than those from Gansu. It has been speculated that the

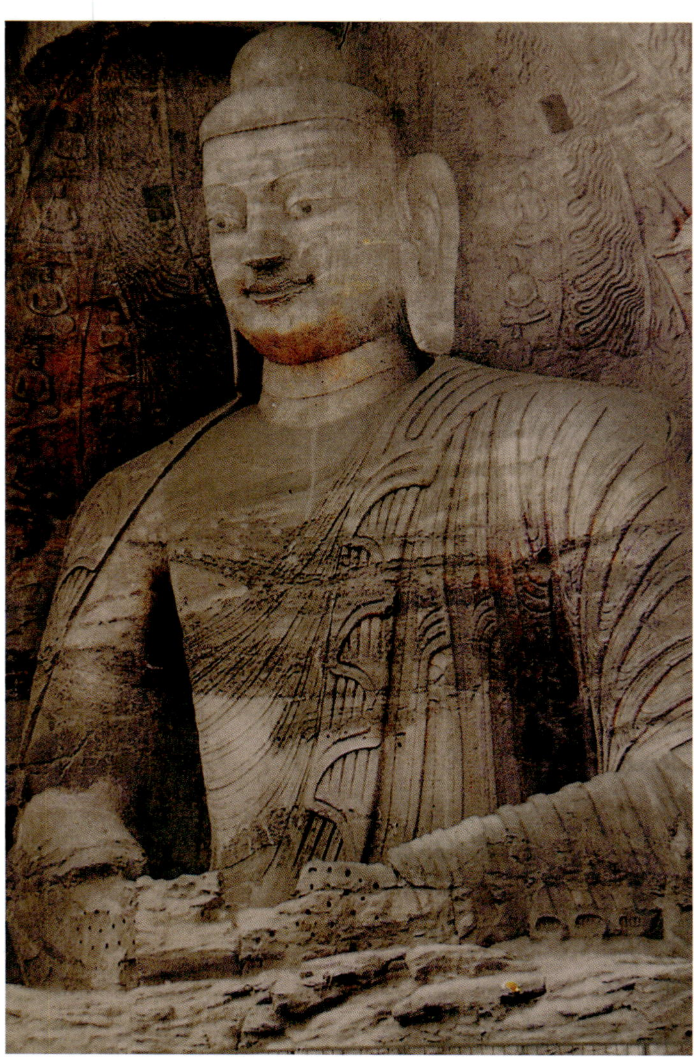

Figure 82. Seated Buddha. Northern Wei dynasty (386–534), 460–70. Cave 20, Yungang, Datong, Shanxi Province

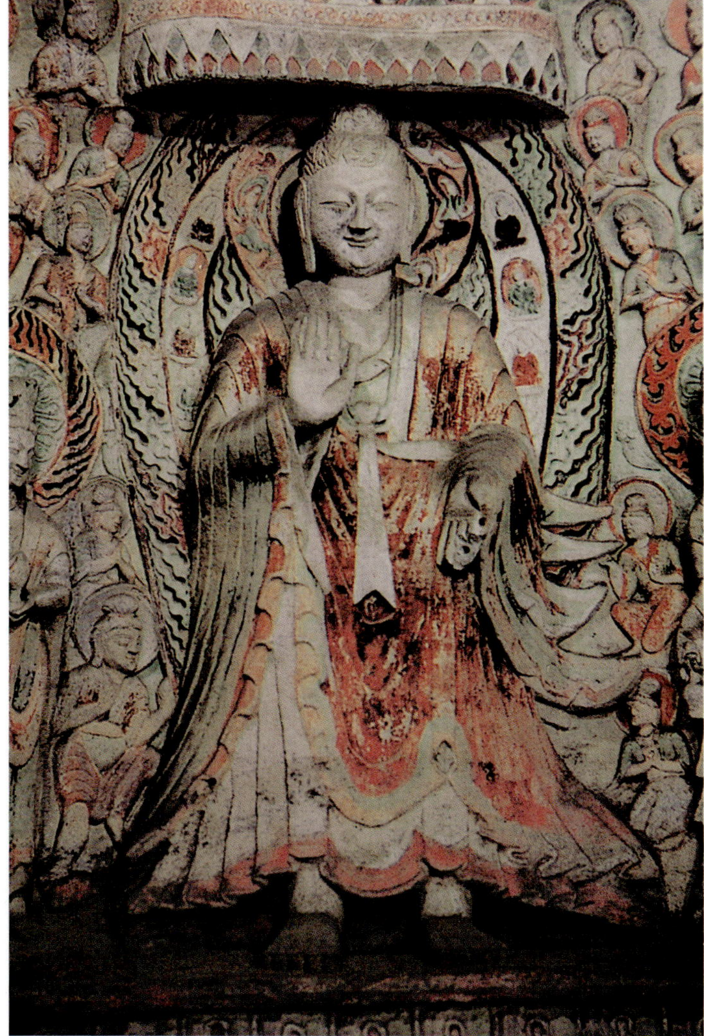

Figure 83. Standing Buddha. Northern Wei dynasty (386–534), 480s. Cave 6, Yungang, Datong, Shanxi Province

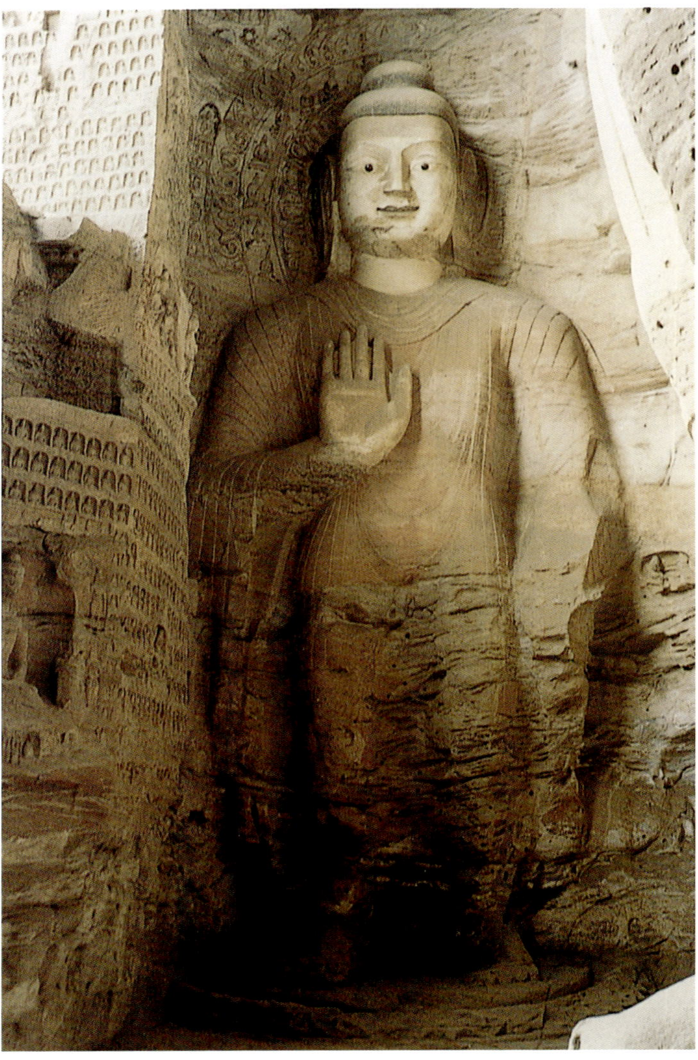

Figure 84. Standing Buddha. Northern Wei dynasty (386–534), 460–70. Cave 18, Yungang, Datong, Shanxi Province

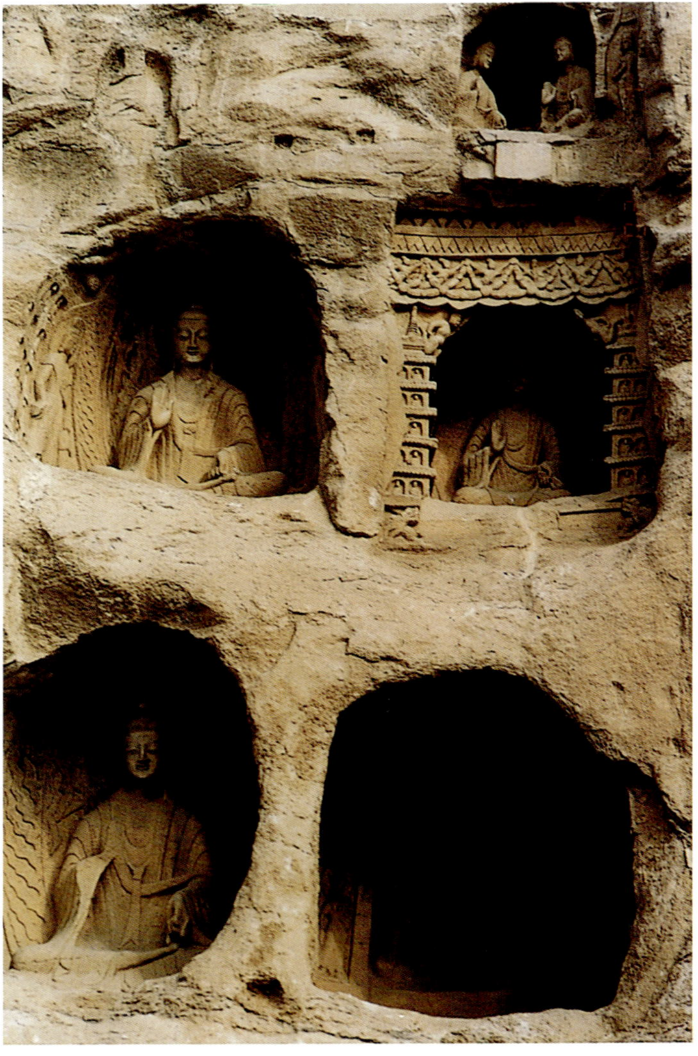

Figure 85. Shakyamuni and Duobao. Northern Wei dynasty (386–534), 489. Cave 11, Yungang, Datong, Shanxi Province

prototype for these Buddhas probably came from the nomadic tribes in North China, and it is distinctly different from the images found in Central and West Asia, Xinjiang, and Gansu. Buddha sculptures executed during the Sixteen Kingdoms and Northern Wei periods, for example, reflect the physique of the Xianbei Tuoba, who were at that time moving south from their territories in the northeast.[7]

The process of sinicization within the Northern Wei accelerated toward the end of the fifth century. Reflecting the court's admiration for Han culture, not only were Buddhist images attired in the southern costume of loose-fitting robe with wide sash, but their bodies became slender and delicate, as was the fashion among the southern elite. The Shakyamuni and Duoba Buddhas both on the interior and outside of Cave 11 (fig. 85), dated Northern Wei, Taihe thirteenth to twentieth year (489–96), are representative of this new style, which first appeared at Yungang before the capital moved to Luoyang in 493. This type of image became widespread in the early sixth century, as we see in the niche outside of Cave 28, dated Northern Wei, Zhenshi fourth year (507), and in the small niche, inscribed Yanchang fourth year (515), at the entrance of Cave 30 (fig. 86). This type developed somewhat later at Luoyang, reaching the height of popularity during Yanchang and Shanggui (roughly 512–20), after the capital had moved there in Taihe eighteenth year (494). The sculptures in the Cixiang Cave of Longmen (fig. 87), carved in Shengui third year (520), exemplify this style. Although the head of the principal statue was stolen and severely damaged, its sloping shoulders clearly indicate a slim, elegant body.

Around the late 520s, sculptures of Buddha in North China again evolved to connote strong, rotund images. Beginning at the Gongxian Caves, carved in Dalishan near Luoyang,[8] this process continued to the east at Baoshan, near Anyang, Henan, within the boundary of Eastern Wei and Northern Qi, and at the cave site of Xiangtangshan in Handan, Hebei. To the west, the trend toward full figures was carried out at the site of Maijishan in Tianshui, Gansu (fig. 88), and at the Northern Wei cave site of Xumishan in Guyuan, Ningxia. Among the surviving works, a group of white marble sculptures (fig. 89) commissioned by Gao Rui, Prince Zhaojun of Northern Qi, Tianbao seventh year (556), expresses most clearly this trend.[9] These Buddha images display a rotund, heroic figure with a round face, called "full moon," fashionable in the south during the Liang dynasty.[10] At the same time, the complex and elaborate draperies of these images became more simplified.

In recent years, numerous Eastern Wei and Northern Qi stone Buddha images that were buried underground have been retrieved. They were executed in eastern China in the former territory of Eastern Wei and Northern Qi, by the time the aforementioned evolution was reaching maturity. The 1996 discovery in the city of Qingzhou, Shandong, in the location of the former Longxingsi, is the most important find.[11] Among these sculptures, several stone standing Buddhas display many novel characteristics, the most relevant being that of wearing a diaphanous robe, an innovation of Northern Qi style. There are basically two approaches to the rendering of the robe: one features regular, U-shaped, close-fitting draperies (fig. 90); the other simply outlines the shape of the body, with no indication of drapery at all. Sculptures of both types were originally gilded. In the case of the Cosmological Buddha images, the monastic robe was divided into patches within which were painted scenes of the Dharmadhatu, the Buddhist universe, placed on the axis of the sculpture—top, center, and bottom. In some examples, the scenes were first incised on the surface, gilding and painting being applied afterward. Buddha figures whose bodies were modeled without draperies looked as if naked once the gilt peeled off (fig. 91).

The type with regular, U-shaped draperies was quite popular in the northern Central Plain. Sculptures of the Buddha

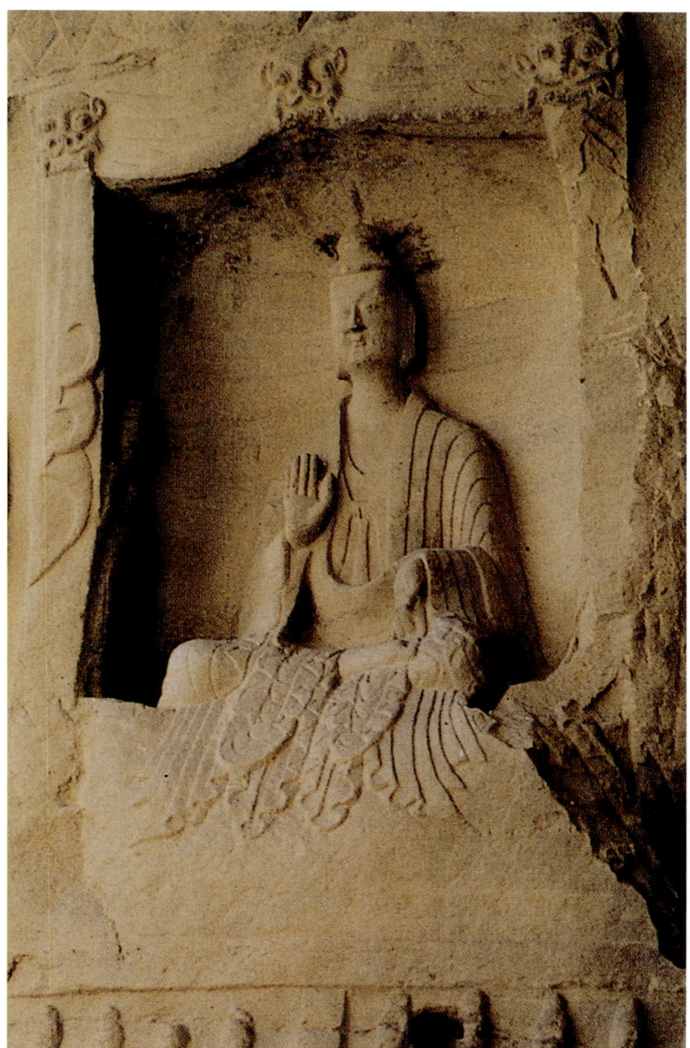

Figure 86. Seated Buddha. Northern Wei dynasty (386–534), 515. Cave 30, Yungang, Datong, Shanxi Province

Figure 87. Seated Buddha. Northern Wei dynasty (386–534), 520. Cixiang Cave, Longmen, Luoyang, Henan Province

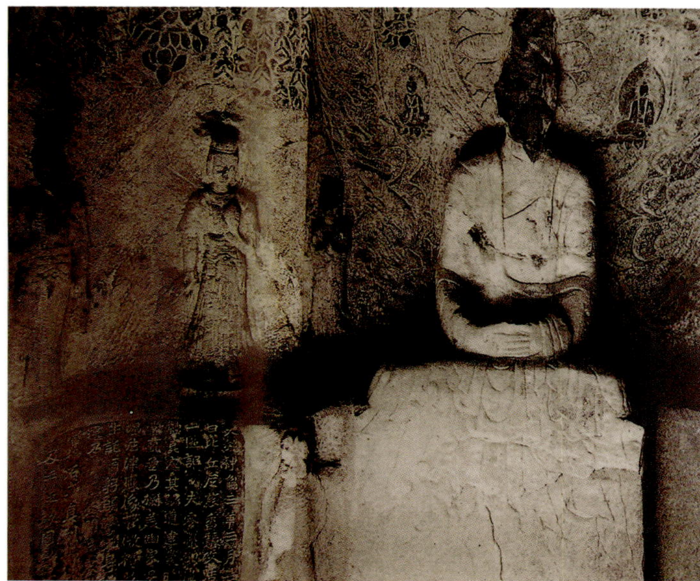

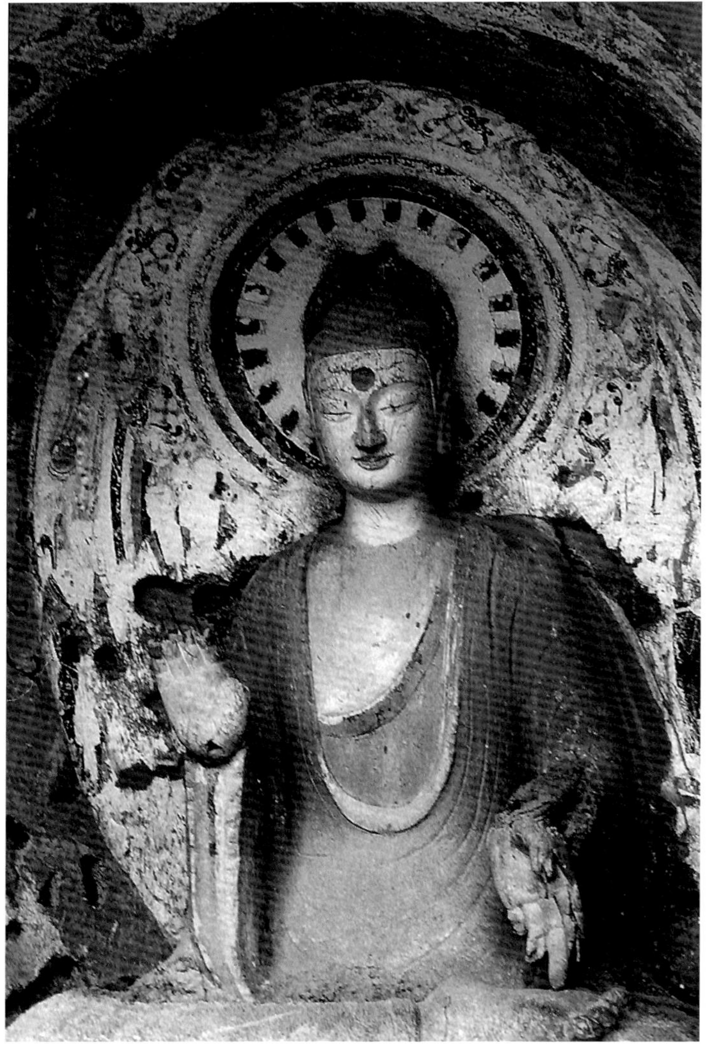

Figure 88. Seated Buddha. Northern Wei dynasty (386–534), 520s. Cave 22, Maijishan, Tianshui, Gansu Province

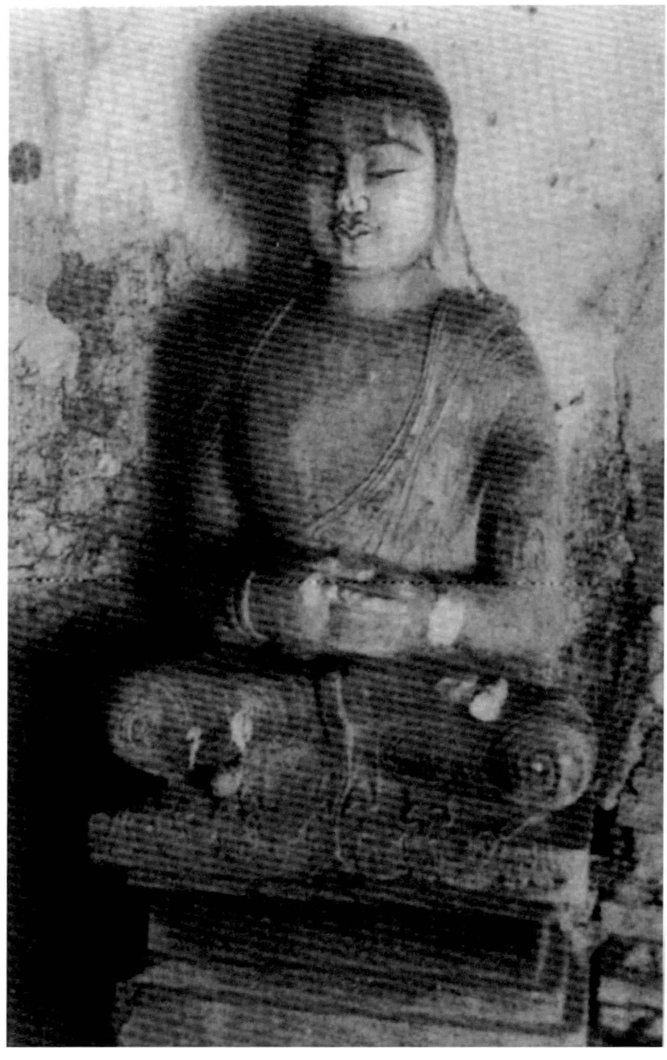

Figure 89. Seated Buddha. Northern Qi dynasty (550–577), 556. Marble. Youjusi, Lingshou, Hebei Province

with similar drapery patterns have also been found in Chengdu, Sichuan. Among them is a rather early sculpture identified in the inscription as an Ashoka-type Buddha (fig. 92) and dated to Southern Liang, Taiqing fifth year (551). Because Chengdu Buddhist art was transmitted from Jiankang (present-day Nanjing) along the lower Yangzi River, Northern Qi sculptures that bear a similar style also likely originated in the south.[12]

Sculptures with a smooth body and no indication of draperies—found neither in Chengdu, Sichuan, nor along the lower reaches of the Yangzi—were quite popular in Xinjiang in the fifth and sixth centuries. Numerous examples have turned up among the cave paintings and sculptures in the area from Kucha to Baicheng (figs. 93, 94). To the west of Kucha was the region of Sogdiana, an area dominated geographically by the Pamirs plateau and the Amu-Daria and Syr-Daria (the ancient Oxus and Jaxartes rivers). From Sogdiana, the road leads southeast to Mathura and Sarnath, where sculptures depicting figures attired in diaphanous, close-fitting robes originated. Both Kucha and Sogdiana, two connecting points along the route from the east to India, were important Buddhist centers.

During the fifth and sixth centuries, citizens of Kucha and Sogdiana moved to the east in large numbers. Especially during the Northern Qi period, they were favored and trusted at court. In addition, monks came from many regions, including India, to congregate in Northern Qi, facilitating the exchange of ideas between the Northern Qi and India. It is very likely that figures with seemingly naked bodies clad in diaphanous robes, which became popular in the late Northern Qi period, originated in Central Asia.

Two eminent monks of the early Tang, Daoxuan and Yanzong, active in the seventh century, praised the Indian-style Buddha

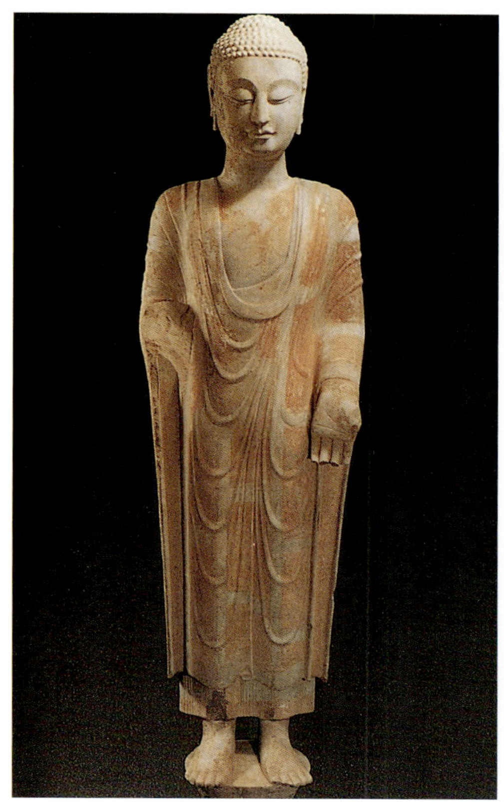

Figure 90. Standing Buddha. Northern Qi dynasty (550–577). Stone. Qingzhou, Shandong Province

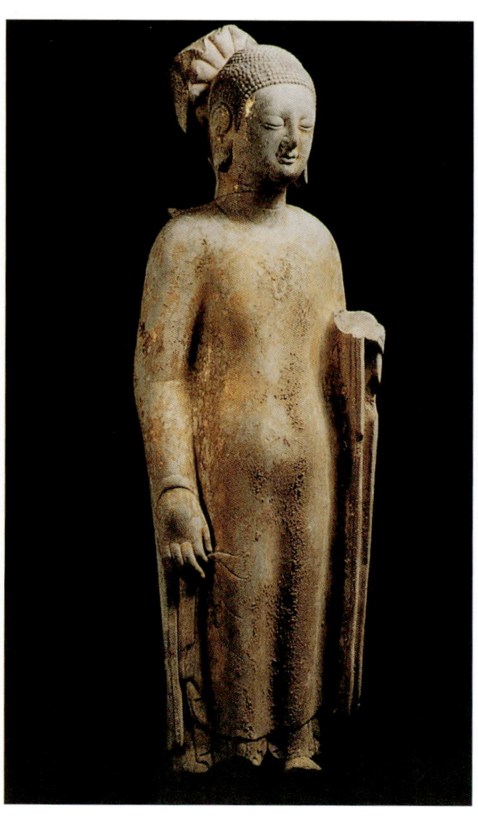

Figure 91. Standing Buddha. Northern Qi dynasty (550–577). Qingzhou, Shandong Province. Qingzhou City Museum (See also cat. no. 166)

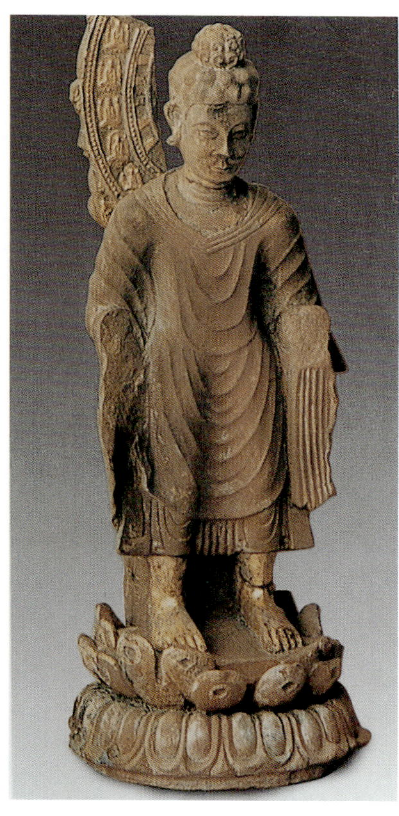

Figure 92. Standing Ashoka-type Buddha. Liang dynasty (502–557), dated 551. Stone. Chengdu City Institute of Archaeology (See also cat. no. 128)

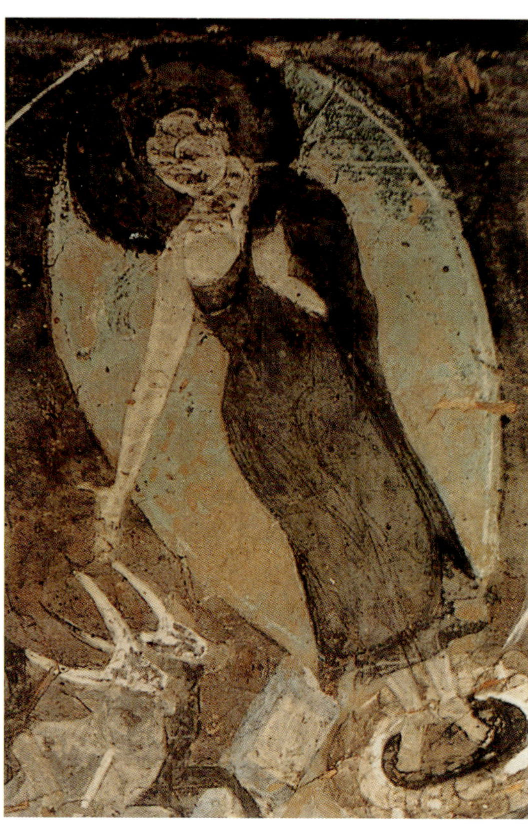

Figure 93. Standing Buddha. 5th–6th century. Wall painting. Cave 175, Kizil, Xinjiang Uygur Autonomous Region

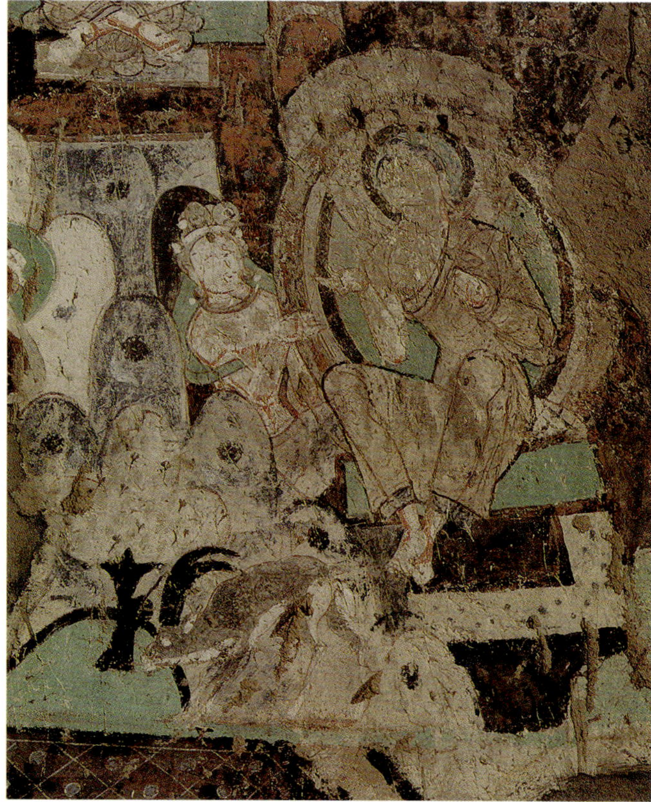

Figure 94. Seated Buddha. 5th–6th century. Wall painting. Cave 196, Kizil, Xinjiang Uygur Automous Region

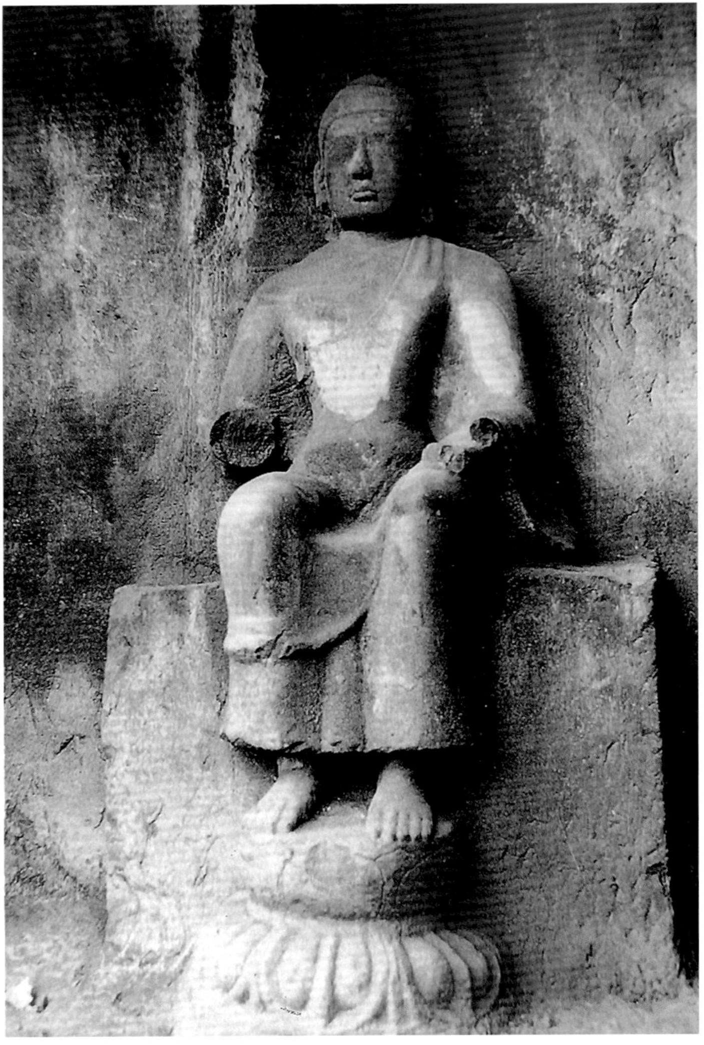

Figure 95. Seated Buddha. Tang dynasty (618–907), 655–63. Jingshansi, Longmen, Luoyang, Henan Province

images by the Northern Qi Sogdian painter Cao Zhongda as "wondrous painted Buddhas," "auspicious [images] whose model was transmitted from the west,"[13] and "foreign Buddha images, of which [Cao Zhongda] is the finest interpreter."[14] Zhang Yanyuan, a leading ninth-century connoisseur, commented enthusiastically on Cao's work: "Cao Zhongda, a native of Sogdiana, the most accomplished Northern Qi painter, is famous for his paintings of Indian-looking Buddhas . . . which impart a supernatural feeling." Zhang Yanyuan further credited Cao as the founder of a new painterly style: "Cao made Buddha images distinguished by his own style."[15] The noted eleventh-century connoisseur Guo Ruoxu characterized the Cao style as "overlapping, tight, close-fitting draperies, popularly known as Cao draperies dripping water." In addition, Guo Ruoxu said, "[Cao] made sculptural, three-dimensional Buddhas" that were exact interpretations of his style.[16] It seems that statues with diaphanous, close-fitting clothing had been associated with Sogdiana as early as the Tang dynasty and throughout the Northern Song, roughly from the ninth to the eleventh century.

During the Northern Qi period, the relationship between the Han Chinese and the northern Xianbei rulers began to grow strained. At court, Han officials belittled the Xianbei as "chariot- and horse-riding guests."[17] Xianbei officials cursed Han Chinese as "bastard Han."[18] The policy of discriminating against Han Chinese presented a stark contrast to the earlier policy of sinicization initiated by the Northern Wei emperor Xiao Wendi (r. 471–99). Consequently, Xianbei enthusiasm for southern manners and institutions abated considerably and the Xianbei would not worship Buddhas dressed in the Han style. It is therefore understandable that they replaced Han clothing with the more congenial Western Regions–Indian-style attire.

Until the seventh century, in the early Tang, sculptures of figures clothed in fine, gossamer garments could still be seen in the temples of Chang'an, the Tang capital. The aforementioned quote by the eminent monk Daoxuan states that the paintings by Cao Zhongda, the "auspicious [images] whose model was transmitted from the west . . . presently grace the temple walls as his [Cao's] authentic creations."[19] These authentic works by Cao, which in the quotation are said to be in the temples of Chang'an, have long since been lost. However, a sculpture of a seated figure dressed in gauzy clothing (fig. 95), whose patron was Prince Youtian, located in the Jingshan cave temple of Longmen, Luoyang, and dated to the late Yongshui–Longshuo reign era (655–63), may represent the Cao style. Moreover, the date of execution coincides with the time of Daoxuan's activity, providing a further point of reference.

In the middle of the seventh century, the Chinese Buddhist pilgrims Xuanzang (602–664) and Wang Xuanci brought to North China Indian icons that further stimulated interest in foreign (Indian) images. However, the popularity of Buddha images clothed entirely in a non-eastern manner lasted only a short period; judging from extant works, the fashion never became widespread. Production of this type of image seems to have diminished at the end of the seventh century, around the reign of Wu Zetian (r. 690–705) and the early years of Emperor Zhongzhong (r. 705–10). This period was not far from the time of the great painter of the eighth century Wu Daoxuan (Daozi), whose images were known for their "billowing scarves in the Wu style,"[20] and that of the sculptor Yang Huizhi,[21] which ushered in the High Tang, a period renowned for its achievements in art and literature. The works of Yang Huizhi and Wu Daoxuan, as well as those of their followers, have not survived. With the exception of the extant High Tang sculptures now dispersed in collections the world over, the Mogao Caves in Dunhuang, built during the High Tang, are the most direct and systematic evidence of Yang's and Wu's creations.[22] Specifically, the painted and sculpted Buddhas in Cave 130 and Cave 148—spanning the period from Kaiyuan ninth year to Dali eleventh year (721–76)—enable us to understand the style of these two great masters who initiated a uniquely Chinese style of Buddhist art.

1. The provenance of this gilt bronze is not clear.
2. See Liu Jianhua 2002: 371–98.
3. The date and location of discovery of these two sculptures are not known. See Matsubara 1995: 87–88.
4. On Northern Liang small votive stupas, see Yin Guangming 2000.
5. See Weixian bowuguan 1989: 807–10.
6. See "Da Jin Xijing Wuzhoushan chongxiu Dashikusi bei de faxian yu yanjiu," in Su Bai 1996: 104–6. The manner of wearing a monastic robe with a cowl may have preceded that of wearing a robe with long sleeves. Chen Yuexin, a student at Beijing University, suggests that the cowled, or round-collar. robe probably originated from a long, close-fitting robe. It could also have been inspired by the merging of a costume used in southern and eastern China. The robe covering both shoulders that came later shows increasing influence from eastern China and merged gradually with the silky, close-fitting robe with wide sash popular in South China. Support for this theory comes from the simultaneous appearance of both types in the east. For an example, see the Shakyamuni and Duobao Buddhas, dated Taihe thirteenth year (489), outside Cave 11 at Yungang, where one Buddha is dressed with the cowled robe in contrast with the other Buddha, who is shown with both shoulders covered. Because Ms. Chen's article is unpublished, her view is noted here.
7. See Fan Wenlan 1994, vol. 2: 654.
8. The Buddha images carved in Dalishan, Gongxian, are not sufficiently characterized, but donors' images are already quite fleshy. For illustrations, see *Zhongguo shiku* 1989: 144–49.
9. See Liu Jianhua 1999: 66–77.
10. Numerous references can be found in *Yiwen leiju*, compiled in the third decade of the seventh century. For example, Liu Xiaoyi, who lived during the Liang dynasty (502–558), wrote in *Yongzhou jinxiangshi Wuliangshou Foxiangbei*, "Like a refulgent sun wheel, a face shaped like a moon, a demure demeanor" (chap. 76). Emperor Jianwen of the Liang dynasty, in *Shijiawen Fo xiangming*, hailed the Buddha image thus, "His face is like a full moon, his eyes like a young lotus" and in *Weiwei Fo xiangming*, "A shining golden face, a majestic full moon." Lastly "A shining urna, a half-moon face [?]" (*Jiaye Fo xiangming*, chap. 77).
11. See Su Bai 1999c: 44–59.
12. Ibid., n. 31 and app.
13. Daoxuan, *Ji shengzhou sanbao gantong ji*, middle chapter, as quoted in *LMJ*, chap. 8.
14. Yanzong, *Hua ping*, as quoted in *LMJ*, chap. 8.
15. *LMJ*, chap. 8.
16. *TJZ*, chap. 1.
17. *BQS* "Biography of *Du Bi*": 346ff.
18. *BQS* "Biography of Han Feng": 692–93.
19. See note 13 above.
20. *TJZ*, chap. 1.
21. Liu Daochun, who lived in the eleventh century, wrote about the accomplishments of Huizhi in *Wudai minghua buyi*.
22. I follow the convention for poetry established in the fourteenth century, during the Yuan and Ming dynasties, in defining the High Tang as the period from early Kaiyuan (713) of Emperor Xuanzong's reign to early Dali (766) of Emperor Daizong. A time lag in artistic development should be expected in Dunhuang since Dunhuang is far from the capital, Chang'an, the pacesetter of artistic conventions.

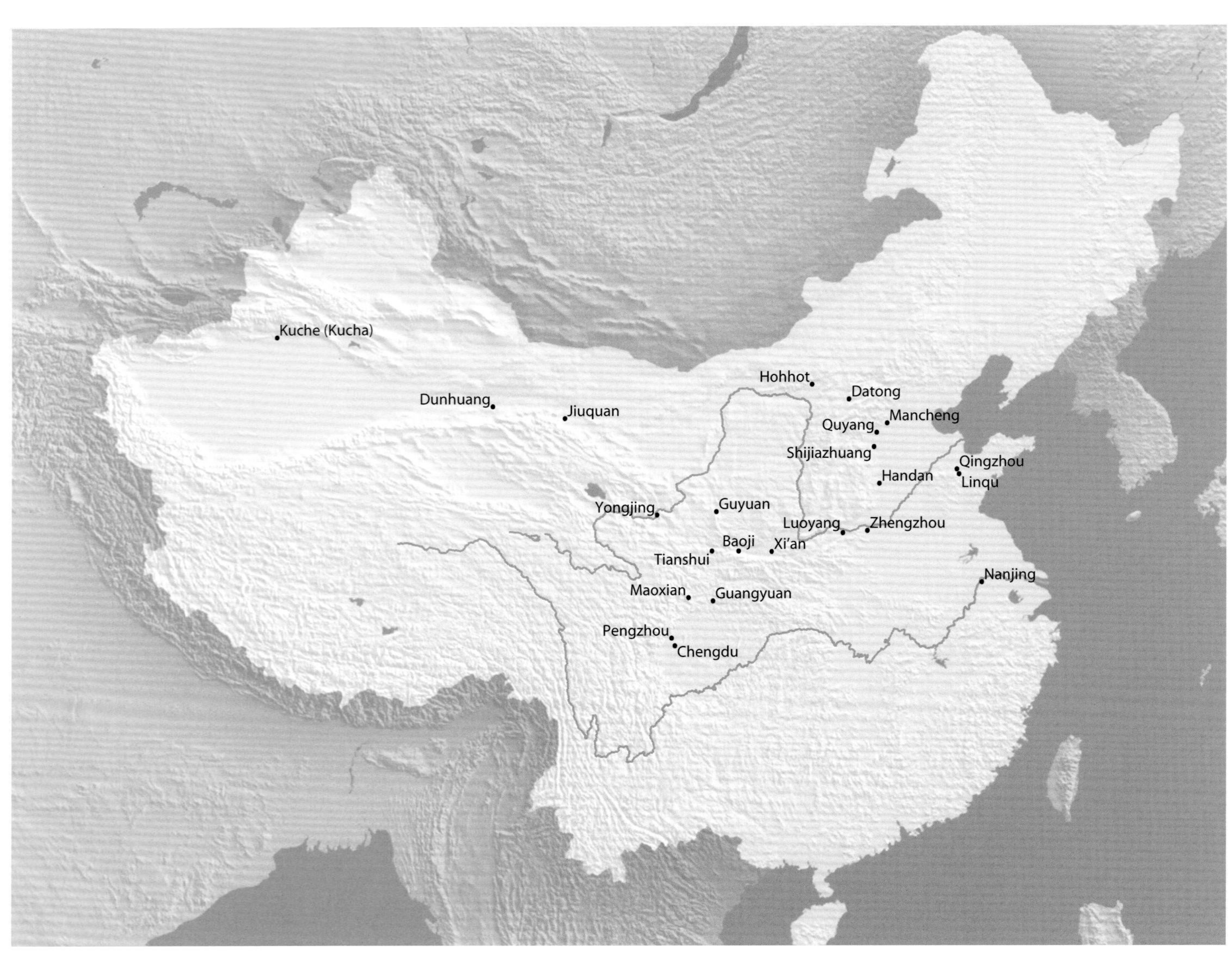
Kuche (Kucha)
Dunhuang
Jiuquan
Hohhot
Datong
Quyang
Mancheng
Shijiazhuang
Handan
Qingzhou
Linqu
Yongjing
Guyuan
Luoyang
Zhengzhou
Baoji
Xi'an
Tianshui
Nanjing
Maoxian
Guangyuan
Pengzhou
Chengdu

Buddhist Art in China

ANGELA F. HOWARD

As the Han Empire was inevitably drawing to its close, Buddhism was conquering China.[1] Western Han (206 B.C.–A.D. 9) expansion in Central Asia had opened the door to the incoming religion, while the political and socioeconomic crisis during the Eastern Han (25–220) undermined the confidence Chinese had placed in Confucianism, their ruling ideology, thus encouraging the acceptance of the foreign faith. Another potent factor in the surge of interest in Buddhism was the possibility it offered of life after death, a promise that was absent in both Confucianism and Daoism, the two most entrenched ideologies in China for centuries past. Buddhism, in short, benefited from the social and spiritual disquiet of the waning imperial age.

The acceptance and spread of Buddhism were crucial in creating a field for the development of figurative art—a totally new chapter in China's artistic tradition. With figurative art arose the necessity of adapting traditional skills, such as metallurgy, and acquiring new ones, which would facilitate the production of stone sculpture. In the centuries following the Han Empire, elite patronage, at times of the highest order, ensured the growth of Buddhist art and advanced the adaptation of alien modes and skills, transforming them into Chinese forms. The works in this exhibition eloquently illustrate this process, tracing a remarkable course of acculturation, from the earliest foreign-looking gilt-bronze seated Buddha in Meditation (cat. no. 44), ascribed to about A.D. 300, to the confidently indigenous sculptures of the mature Tang phase, such as the majestic Vairocana Buddha from Longmen (cat. no. 192), executed in stone and dating to about 700.

Buddhist Images of the Late Eastern Han Period

The adaptation of Buddhist images was a slow but steady process. In the earliest phase, Buddhism and its devotional art were not consonant with their Indian models because they rested on a still-misconstrued doctrine; they were promoted by a body of practitioners who were not yet organized; and they lacked the supervision of an established clergy. Hearsay and misinformation shaped the making of the first Buddhist icons. These initial images, which derived from foreign ideas grafted onto popularized Daoist beliefs, were fashioned in South China, in Sichuan, in the provinces along the Yangzi River, and along the coast. Sichuanese money trees, which usually displayed the Queen Mother of the West and her magical land, sometimes hosted Buddha images, revealing that the two deities were ambivalently linked. Similarly, money-tree pedestals showed a rudimentary Buddhist triad

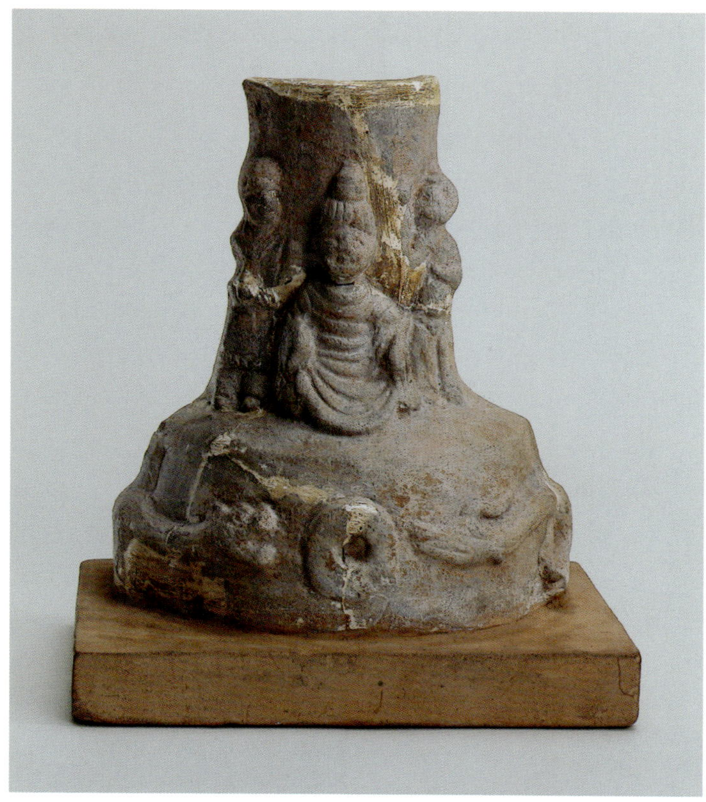

Figure 96. Pedestal of a money tree with Buddha image. Eastern Han dynasty (25–220), late 2nd century. Clay, height 8⅜ in. (21.4 cm). Excavated at Pengshan, Sichuan Province, 1942. Nanjing Museum

or the goddess's mysterious abode (fig. 96). An ample urn (cat. no. 104) from coastal Jiangsu Province displays a painted décor of sylphs belonging to Daoism but also attached decorations of Buddhas seated on a lion throne. These ambiguities indicate that in the late second century, Buddhist ideas and their accompanying icons merged with preexisting Daoist beliefs and Buddhist-like images became interchangeable with Daoist deities.[2]

Sichuan, in particular, acted as the fertile crossroads for these two diverse movements—earliest Buddhist and earliest Daoist ferment—which eventually became two distinct religions. Because they were evolving side by side, it is difficult at this early stage to make clear-cut distinctions between the two and to discern the respective contribution of each. It is, however, evident that these Buddhist-like icons, often referred to as "proto-Buddhist," were not self-contained images but an intrinsic part of Han burial custom. Proto-Buddha images and symbols—stupas, lotus flowers, elephants—regarded as *xiangrui*, or auspicious emblems, lingered on even after Buddhism took hold in China. Such symbols were used as decorations, as is the case with the Buddha chiseled in the hat ornament found in the Liaoning tomb of Feng Sufu (d. 415), an elite member of the northeastern state of Yan (cat. no. 37).

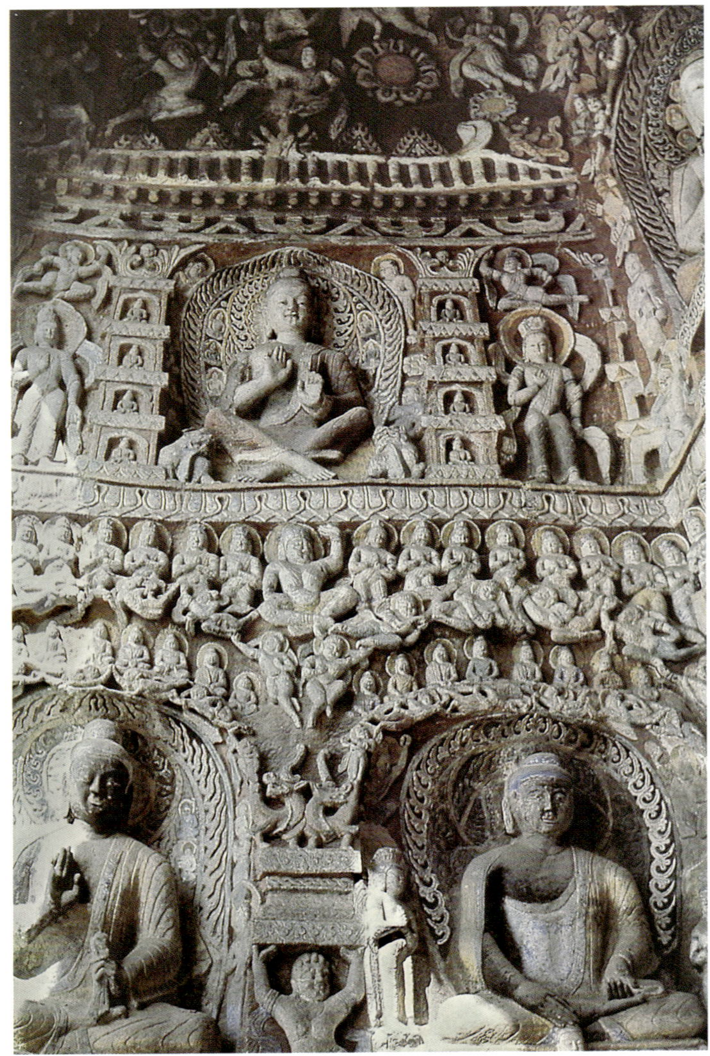

Figure 97. Buddhist images. Northern Wei dynasty (386–534), 470–94. Sandstone. Cave 9, Yungang, Datong, Shanxi Province

Buddhist Art in the Period of Division (317–589)

The roughly three centuries of partition into North China and South China, from 317 to 589, witnessed the gradual transformation of Buddhism into a Chinese religion, now fully comprehended and supported by a well-established monastic community and an assimilated textual tradition. Sections of the Sutra of Dharma Verses (Skt: *Dharmapada sutra;* cat. no. 87) in the exhibition are palpable proof of this transformative process: the Chinese translation of the Indian text was already circulating in the Gansu Corridor by the mid-fourth century. In contrast to the preceding phase, the art of this later period was thus based on the correct interpretation of Buddhism, which foreign and native clergy had spread effectively throughout the land.

During the Period of Division, the foundation was laid for the creative dynamism that erupted during the sixth century. Gilt-bronze images emerge as the most sophisticated artifacts, while stone steles betray the more modest skills of their makers. The greatest number of independent images are made of clay, and they are found in the numerous cave temple sites along the Gansu Corridor—notably, Dunhuang, Wenshushan, Jintasi, Binglingsi, and Maijishan. Similarly, of the thousands of images made of stone, the majority, while an integral part of cave sites, are also freestanding—in this case, in the fifth- and sixth-century imperially sponsored cave temples in the Central Plain of North China—Yungang, Longmen, Gongxian, and Xiangtangshan. The sandstone cross-legged bodhisattva Maitreya (cat. no. 74) is one of the few very early examples of a sculpted image not recovered from a cave temple. It is a miniature rendering of similar monumental sculptures in Yungang, the imperial site that the Northern Wei Tuoba (Datong, Shanxi) (386–534) opened near their first capital, Pingcheng (fig. 97). This sculpture, furthermore, is a striking example of how foreign, that is, non-Chinese, patrons projected their own ethnicity onto the images they sponsored.

The wide face of the deity and its general mien resemble those of the Tuoba female attendant (cat. no. 70) from the tomb of Sima Jinlong (d. 484) and his wife, Yichen.

Thus the earliest images, while they display traditional Indic conventions, also reflect the aesthetic preferences of the non-Chinese patrons who ruled the north, as seen in the example noted above (cat. no. 70). The patrons represented various ethnicities, an aspect James C. Y. Watt explores in his essay. Because there was such a variety of ethnic backgrounds in the population, three-dimensional images executed in different media initially bore a many-faceted character that only gradually gave way to a fully Chinese style, which emerged during the late fifth century and thrived during the sixth. Yet even then, the Chinese manner, as it was the outcome of numerous regional interpretations, never became monolithic, as discussed below.

Northern Gilt Bronzes

The artistic and doctrinal evolution manifest in gilt-bronze production from 300 to 525 eventually led to a completely Chinese style of artistic expression. Existing examples suggest that in China the earliest Buddhist images were made of bronze, an assumption further supported by the extraordinary metallurgical skills mastered by Chinese craftsmen over the course of two millennia.[3] Artisans were thoroughly familiar with making three-dimensional objects in metal and clay by adding parts to a base rather than by cutting away from the mass, an ability intrinsic to working in stone. The latter skill they increasingly mastered as the demand for Buddhist sculpture grew.

Among the group of gilt-bronze images in the exhibition, the striking Buddha in Meditation (cat. no. 44) is the most foreign-looking. It is an early fourth-century work and reflects the stylistic preferences of a Yuezhi patron who resided in Xi'an. The Yuezhi were a nomadic tribe that during the second century B.C. moved from northwestern China across Central Asia. Some tribesmen remained on the northeastern fringe of the Tibetan plateau, but the majority reached the Oxus region and settled in Bactria. Later on, as rulers of the northern and northwestern region of India, they became known as the Kushan.[4] The inscription on the sculpture, written in the Kharoshthi language, which is associated with the Yuezhi people, indicates possible links with a Yuezhi colony situated in the Shanshan kingdom, along the southern Silk Road. The rug on which the Buddha sits bears some resemblance to textile fragments from the same area.

The Buddha altarpiece with canopy (cat. no. 45) is very likely contemporaneous with the previous work, although it originated elsewhere and embodies the artistic preference of a patron of different ethnicity. This ingeniously constructed work hails from Zhao territory (Hebei), which was administered by the Shi clan. The Shi belonged to the Jie, an ethnic

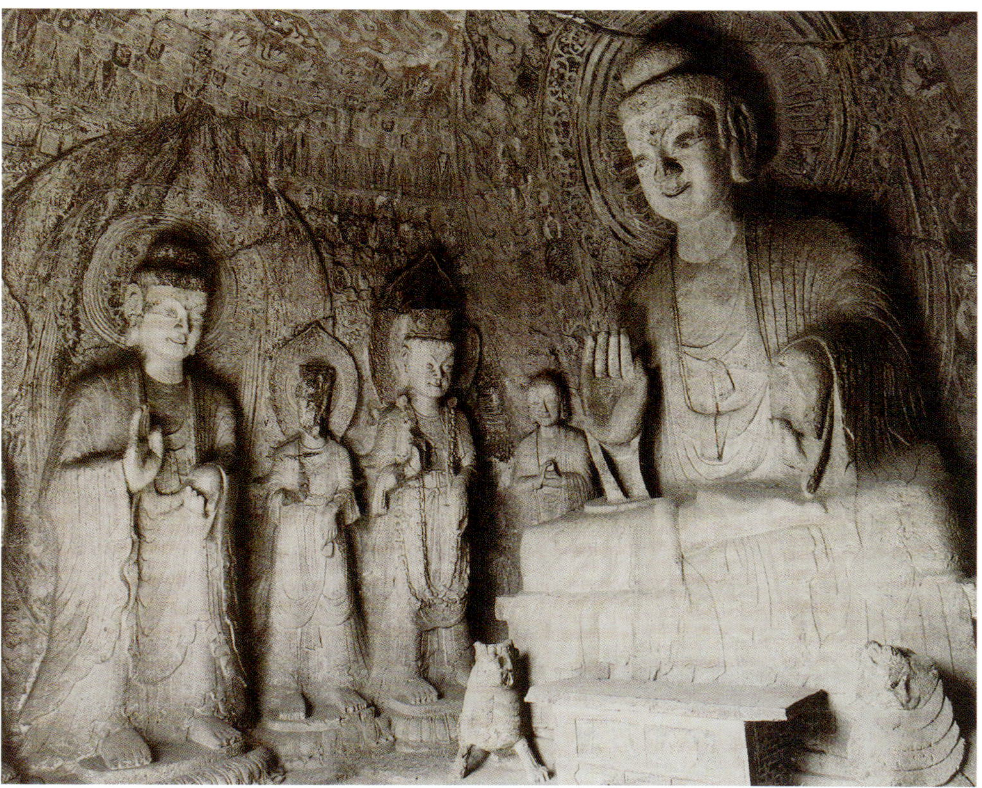

Figure 98. Buddhist images. Northern Wei dynasty (386–534), ca. 523. Limestone. Southwestern corner of central Binyang, Longmen, Luoyang, Henan Province

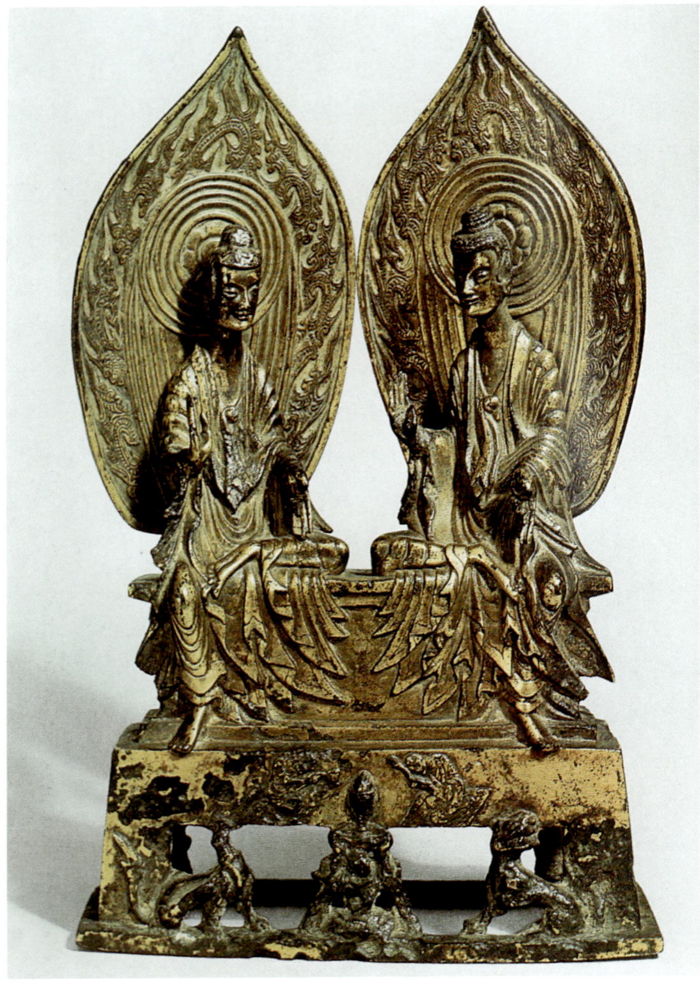

Figure 99. Shakyamuni and Prabutharatna. Northern Wei dynasty (386–534), dated 518. Gilt bronze, height 10¼ in. (26 cm). Musée Guimet, Paris

group that may in turn have originally been Indo-Scythian. The altarpiece introduces us to the prominent role Hebei played in the production of gilt bronzes. Here, the superior skills of metalworkers were placed at the service of the eminent monk Fotudeng (also Fotucheng; d. ca. 349), possibly a native of the Central Asian kingdom of Kucha, who arrived in Luoyang in 310 and resided thereafter at the court of Shi Le (r. 328–33), where he served as Shi Le's political and spiritual adviser. This collaboration of an energetic and highly influential clergyman with talented artisans generated an impressive and steady production of bronzes that continued well beyond the rule of the Shi family. We now regard such a production as forming a distinctive Hebei school.

The Maitreya altarpiece in the Metropolitan Museum, dated Northern Wei 524 (cat. no. 167), represents the artistic pinnacle of the Hebei school and a completely acculturated, or Chinese, work. This magnificent and uncommonly large masterpiece belongs to the time of Tuoba Xianbei rule over North China, when their capital—the second—was Luoyang (494–535). The bronze parallels chronologically the central Binyang cave at the dynastic site of Longmen, which was completed in 523 (fig. 98). The artistry of the altarpiece reveals how this alien dynasty, between about 400 and 500, metamorphosed into a Chinese cultural entity. Northern Wei style no longer reflected an imported tradition, but had become synonymous with the aesthetic taste of North China's Central Plain, the seat of dynastic capitals. The Tuoba Xianbei patrons of this style favored angular, elongated body forms swathed in layered garments whose pleats became an ingenious display of fluid linear patterns. Aureoles and haloes backing the image bear darting flame motifs and more sedate, stylized vegetal scrolls that combine to create an effect of energized harmony (fig. 99).

Southern Stone Sculpture of the Liang Dynasty (502–557)

As noted above, the production of northern gilt bronzes was permeated by regionalism. This characteristic may be applied as well to the artistic production of the south, which developed parallel to that of the northern Central Plain. In this context, regionalism takes on a very special dimension; one speaks of a "southern" style that is unmistakably distinct from its contemporaneous "northern" style. Su Bai in his essay suggests that southern sculptures served as models for northern production, an inference that favors the south over the north, since the south represented the "legitimate" Han culture as opposed to the culture surging in the Northern Plain under non-Chinese rulers.[5]

While the north, at the introduction of Buddhism, produced a large and remarkable body of gilt bronzes, the south, by contrast, concentrated on independent stone sculpture—freestanding images and steles. The earliest examples of the latter are ascribed to the mid-fifth century and postdate sculptures of gilt bronze. Produced within a Confucian and Daoist framework, the genre was adapted by the Buddhist community for its own devotional purposes. Between 450 and 600, a great number of Buddhist steles were carved all over China, both in the north and in the south, their styles differing according to geographic provenance (fig. 100).

Buddhist art originating in Jiankang (present-day Nanjing), the southern capital during the Period of Division, was meticulously recorded in the dynastic histories and in Buddhist literature, but material evidence originating in the capital is, regrettably, extremely scarce. Nevertheless, astonishing finds of Buddhist sculpture recovered from areas administered by or having close contact with the southern court clearly disclose that Sichuan gravitated toward a southern not a northern tradition. The new evidence, moreover, enables us to speculate about the style and content of this lost art.

These finds include the excavation, in 1953, of a large body of sculpture from Wanfosi, Chengdu, Sichuan, and more recently, in 1995, from a location in Xi'an Road, also in Chengdu. All these works are correctly labeled southern because Sichuan was an integral part of the South after being annexed in 347 by the Eastern Jin. By assuming that provincial Chengdu (the main city of Sichuan) followed Jiankang (the southern capital) as its aesthetic model and that the art of Sichuan reflected that of Jiankang, we can hypothesize on the style and doctrinal content of the latter. One acknowledges, however, the artistic independence of this southwestern province, which claims an outstanding tradition of figurative art reaching back to the Shu culture, contemporary with the Shang (ca. 1600–ca. 1046 B.C.).[6]

The art of the south developed differently from that of the north, in matters of both style and doctrine, as is evident in the sizable group of steles and freestanding images from the Chengdu excavations in this exhibition, the majority executed during the Liang dynasty (502–558). Southern style, in contrast to northern style, favors realism and volume in a humanized interpretation of the image, and it often includes exotic elements from India itself or from Indianized cultures of Southeast Asia. For example, the procession of devotees—likely inhabitants of Southeast Asia—that embellishes the pedestal from Wanfosi (cat. no. 125) forcefully illustrates the incorporation of distinctly foreign accretions into the art of the south.

A comparison of the previously discussed Northern Wei 524 altarpiece (cat. no. 167) with the stone twin Buddha steles dated Liang 545 (cat. no. 127) effectively exemplifies this

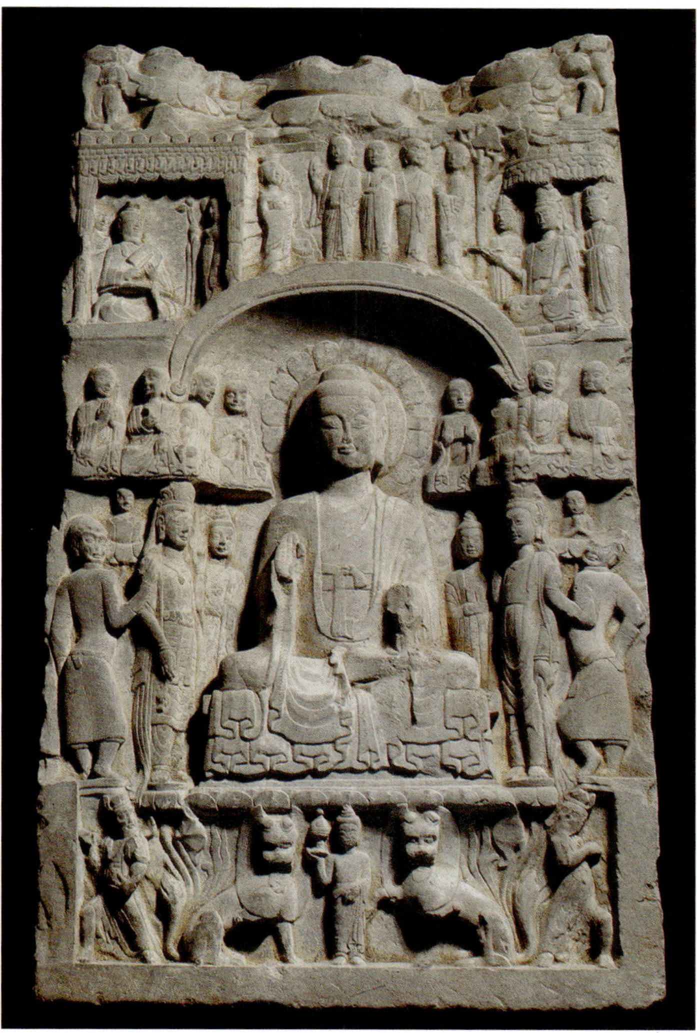

Figure 100. Buddhist stele. Northern Qi dynasty (550–577), dated 563. Sandstone, height 44½ in. (113 cm). Excavated at Haoxian, Anhui Province, 1965. Anhui Provincial Museum

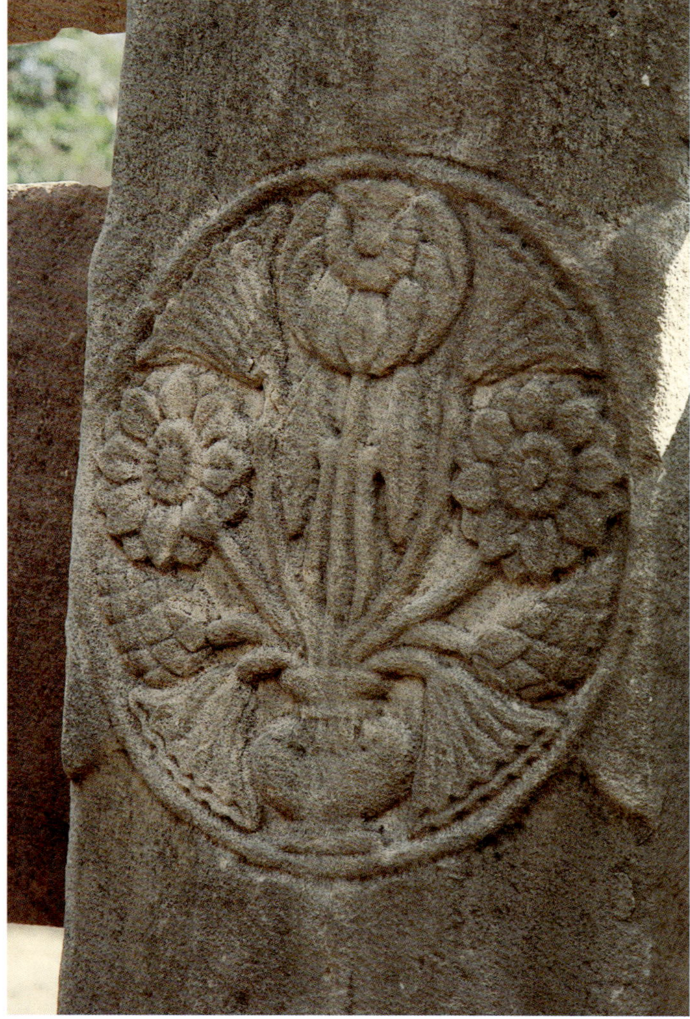

Figure 101. *Purnaghata* (urn of plenty). Sandstone roundel from the railing of Stupa 2, Sanchi, Bhopal, Madya Pradesh

contrast. The Northern Wei group displays ethereal forms hierarchically distinguished by size; deities and patrons are all projected against a stylized backdrop of glittering flames and vegetal motifs. The Liang stele, using a distinctly different formal language, portrays two weighty, friendly-looking Buddhas surrounded by smiling and likeable assistants. The twin Buddhas are seated on sturdy, fleshy lotuses that form two separate thrones; the flowers' robust stalks emerge from a large urn, or *purnaghata*, a motif lifted directly from Indian sculpture (fig. 101). On the back of the 545 stele, the male and female donors differ unequivocally in both costume and type from their Tuoba counterparts in the 524 altar.

Linkage to an Indian style and the portrayal of icons rooted in Indian lore were components intrinsic to Liang Buddhist art, but not to its northern counterpart. Thus, a standing Buddha dated Liang 529 from Wanfosi (cat. no. 123) and a standing Ashoka-type Buddha dated Liang 551 and excavated at Xi'an Road (cat. no. 128) are both modeled on Indian prototypes. The headless, life-size Buddha from Wanfosi wears the *kasaya*, or outer robe, which covers both shoulders in the manner of the Indian Gupta style of Mathura (ca. 450), an idiom possibly combined here with a southern Indian variation practiced at Amaravati (fig. 102). In fact, the carver used two distinctive pleat patterns for the light outer robe—horizontal U-shaped loops on the right side and more pronounced vertical drapes on the left. The high patronage of the sculpture reveals the favor that the ruling elite bestowed on Indian art. Two high-ranking members of the retinue of Xiao Fan, prince of Poyang, a nephew of the Liang emperor Wudi (r. 502–49) and governor of Yizhou (present-day Chengdu), commissioned this imposing sculpture during his term of office.

The Ashoka Buddha image privileged in Sichuan during the Liang is exemplified by the 551 sculpture (cat. no. 128); it, too, is Indian in origin. This miraculous icon was said to be a replica of the original commissioned by Ashoka, the Indian ruler of the Mauryan Empire (ca. 325–ca. 183 B.C.). According to literary records, many such images had by extraordinary circumstances traveled all the way to China, alighting in particular along the coast during the rule of Emperor Wudi. Indian monks residing in Jiangsu and Zhejiang recognized them as authentic Indian works. Even the Buddha's facial appearance shows a foreign dependence—the mustache, the headdress, and in particular the shape of the eyes.

On matters of doctrine, southern icons were a visual manifestation of beliefs that only later became accessible in the

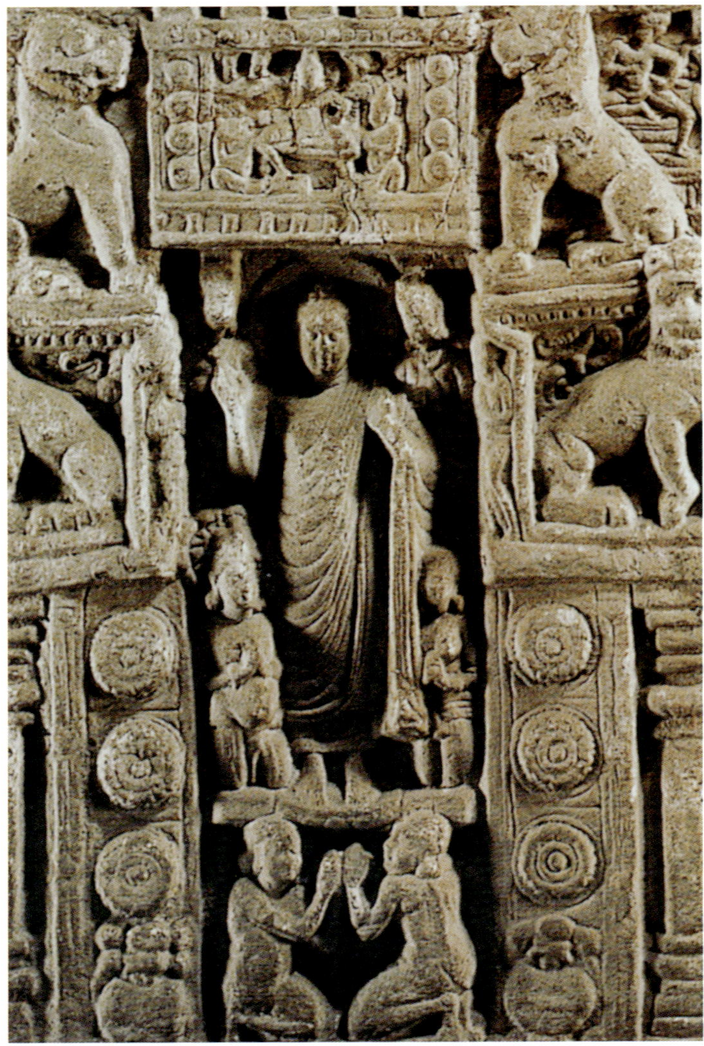

Figure 102. Standing Buddha. Ca. 200. Detail of the limestone relief, Amaravati Stupa, Andhra Pradesh. British Museum, London

north. In the south, Buddhists venerated, simultaneously, Maitreya (C: Mile), Amitayus (C: Wuliangshou; also called Amitabha, C: Omito), and the Buddha (another appellation of Amitabha) and their Pure Lands, or paradises. They were also fervently devoted to Avalokiteshvara (C: Guanyin), the most compassionate of the bodhisattvas. The stele dated Southern Qi 483 (cat. no. 122) combines a seated Maitreya in the front and a standing Amitayus (left incomplete) on the back. The fashion of Maitreya's attire—an ample, pleated robe gathered at the waist by a long sash—possibly derives from a similar costume worn at the southern court. While the two Buddhas are shown here as independent images, two steles in the exhibition instead focus on their heavenly abodes (cat. nos. 124, 126).

One of these is tall and fragmented (cat. no. 124), with an image of the Pure Land of Amitayus, Buddha of the West, carved on the back. The front displays the Buddha's canonical attendants, the bodhisattvas Avalokiteshvara and Mahasthama-

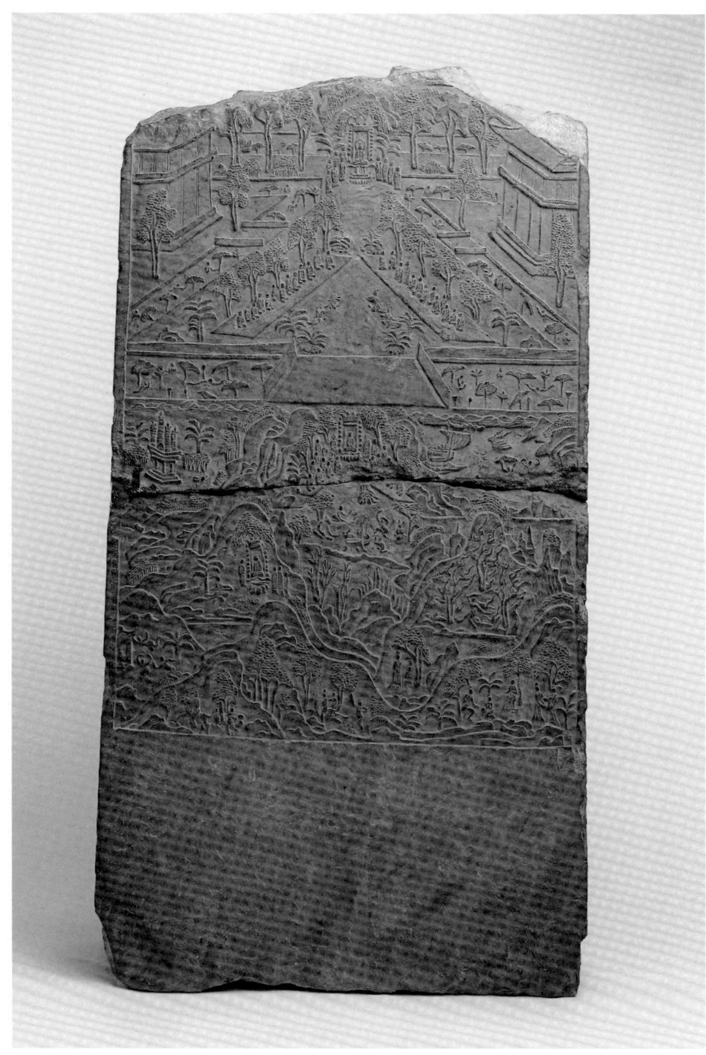

Figure 103. Stele showing the Pure Land of the West. Liang dynasty (502–557), first half of 6th century. Sandstone, height 47¼ in. (120 cm). Excavated at Wanfosi, Chengdu, Sichuan Province, 1953. Sichuan Provincial Museum, Chengdu (See also cat. no. 124)

prapta (C: Dashizhi), unfortunately damaged, surrounded on each side by joyful attendants in relaxed poses. The bodhisattvas stand on lotuses that grow upward from an ample *purnaghata*. Menacing guardians and playful lions are placed below the two central images and above a row of exotic, mirthful dancers and musicians. The southern (Sichuanese) ability to convey the sensuousness of both moving bodies and swaying plants is undiminished by the fragmentary condition of the work. Additional episodes of the Buddha's last life were originally carved around the stele frame, but the scenes on the back—the first known representation of the Pure Land of the West—were pathbreaking (fig. 103).

On the upper portion at the back is a schematic garden comprising ponds, allées, and pavilions. The use of spatial perspective, by which the landscape recedes in the distance to culminate in the image of the Buddha as lord of his Pure Land, is surprising, as this convention is ignored in Chinese secular painting. Buddhist painters, on the other hand, embraced this device to create a visual illusion and to facilitate meditation practices that centered on the Buddha. In the lower portion are additional episodes enclosed in spatial cells delimited by hills and trees. Images are again enveloped in a kind of landscape. There is no consensus as to the identification of these episodic representations, but they may refer to the miraculous power of the bodhisattva Avalokiteshvara, who saves people in need, as described in chapter 25 of the Lotus Sutra.

Northern Art of the Northern Qi (550–577) and Northern Zhou (557–581) Dynasties

After 550, two antithetical styles developed in the north, embodied in individual freestanding images of both Buddhas and bodhisattvas. The Northern Qi (550–577) and Northern Zhou (557–581) styles coexisted chronologically but not geographically, as the former spread in the northeast (chiefly Shanxi, Hebei, Henan, and Shandong) while the latter proliferated in the northwest (roughly Gansu, Ningxia, Shaanxi, and part of Shanxi). Undeniably, the Indian aesthetic so prominent in the earlier Liang art of the south formed and permeated these two northern styles. But the dynamics of this influence are far more complex than art historians have assumed.

The Northern Zhou style was rooted in the local aesthetic preferences of the northwest and was influenced by the encounter with Indianized elements that seeped north from Sichuan. In Buddha images the first factor prevails, while the second shapes the appearance of bodhisattvas. The standing Buddha (cat. no. 169) and the two Guanyins (cat. no. 170) retrieved from the vicinity of Xi'an, the seat of the Northern Zhou court, are excellent examples. Buddha's stocky physique is overlaid with a simple but heavy pleated robe painted with large red patches, and his squarish face with unnaturally wide cheeks is somber and severe. The body proportions and the shape and expression of the face are the same as those used to denote the contemporary burial clay figures from Ningxia (cat. no. 154). Should one go farther back in time, one realizes that these are the indigenous physical traits of the non-Chinese inhabitants of the region. Seated and standing Buddhas from major Northern Zhou cave temple sites (Xumishan in Ningxia, Lasaosi [fig. 104] and Maijishan in Gansu) adhere without exception to this Buddha type.

In Northern Zhou bodhisattvas, however, this typology is altered. Whereas a brooding solemnity characterizes the Buddhas, opulence is the foremost feature of the bodhisattvas.

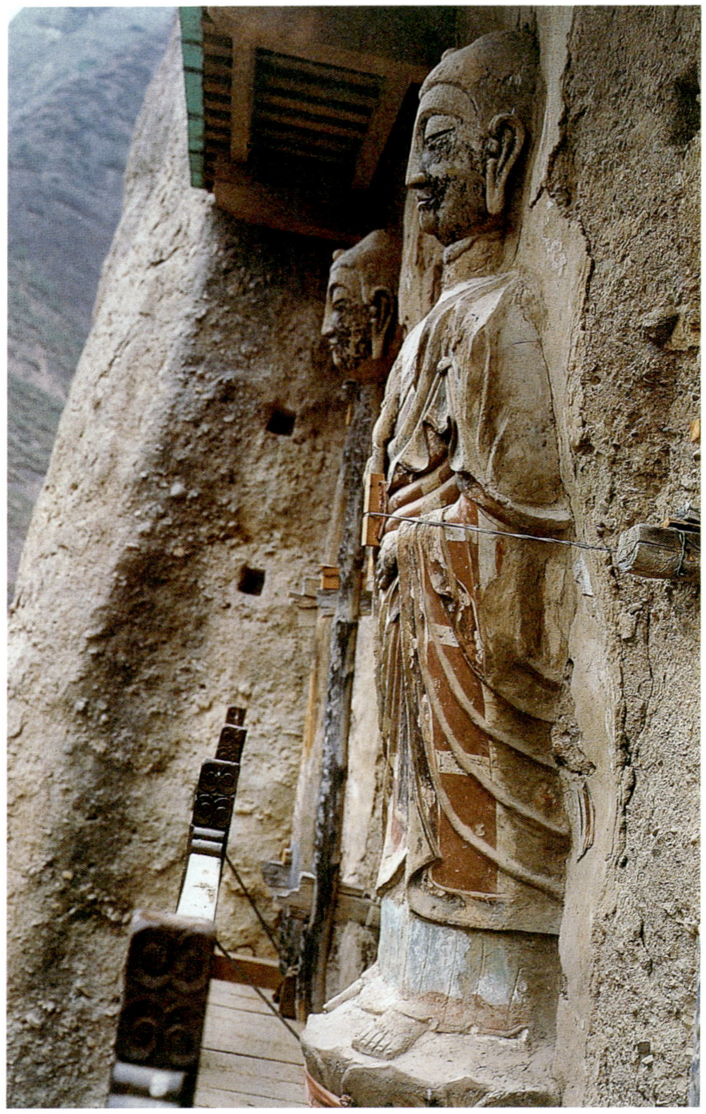

Figure 104. Standing Buddha. Northern Zhou dynasty (557–581). Sandstone. Lasaosi, Wushan, Gansu Province

The bodies of the two Guanyins are still thickset and minimally modeled, but they are adorned front and back with an exorbitant amount of three-dimensional jewelry. Such a flair for embellishment is a trait usually associated with Indian style. Why and how were these Northern Zhou sculptures drawn into this mode? The annexation in 553 of southern territories, inclusive of Sichuan, to the north (Western Wei dynasty) offers some explanation of the formation of this peculiar taste, which the south had long since adopted and the northwest was beginning to implement.

Northern Qi style stands in sharp contrast to that of Northern Zhou.[7] Responding to Guptan models, specifically the statuary executed in the Indian centers of Mathura and Sarnath during the fifth century (fig. 105), Hebei carvers shaped handsome, lightly clad bodies with spheroid heads distinguished by a serene and introverted expression. Northern Qi style, however, was an adaptation not an imitation of this Indian language. The fuller, rounder bodies and spheroid heads of Northern Qi Buddhas still respond to a geometric paradigm, as they resemble cylinders and spheres. They do not match the naturalism of the Indian Gupta style, its suppleness of forms and body articulation. This novel artistic approach was used for the sculpture of both northern and southern Xiangtangshan, the two imperial sites clustered on the Henan–Hebei border (fig. 106).

Most art historians believe that this Indian-like style came to the northern Central Plain by way of the Southern Dynasties, Liang in particular, where it had been introduced a half-

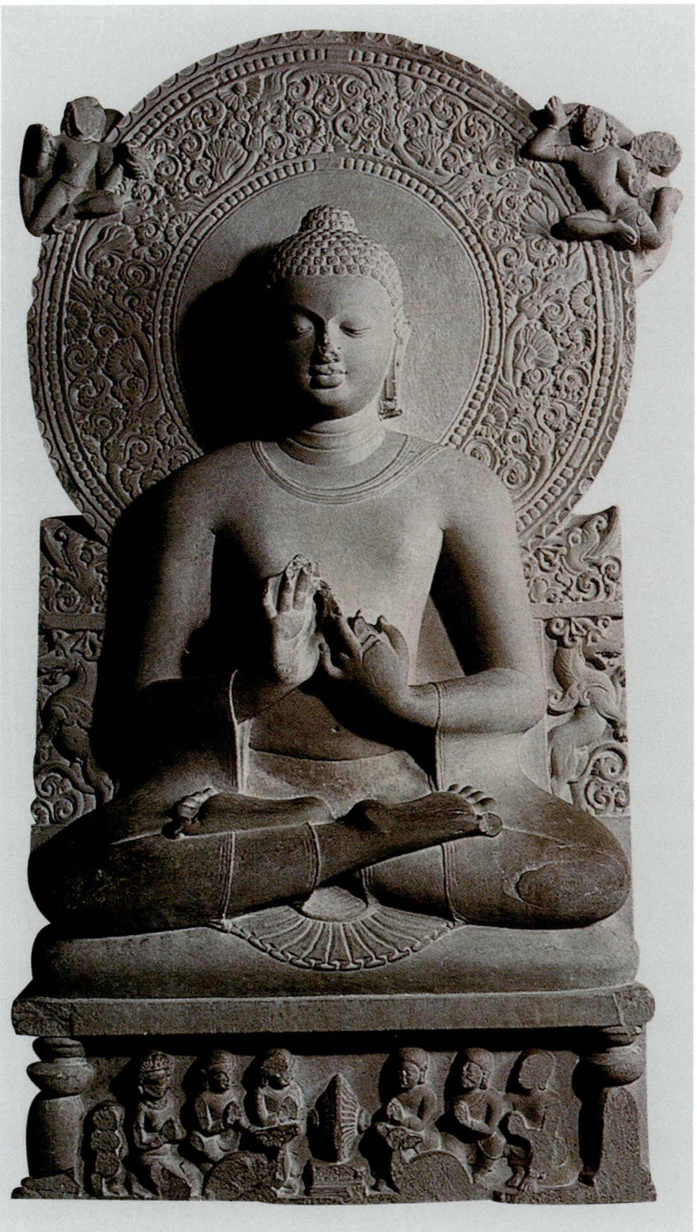

Figure 105. Buddha preaching the First Sermon. Gupta period, Sarnath, ca. 465. Sandstone, height 63 in. (160 cm). Archaeological Museum, Sarnath

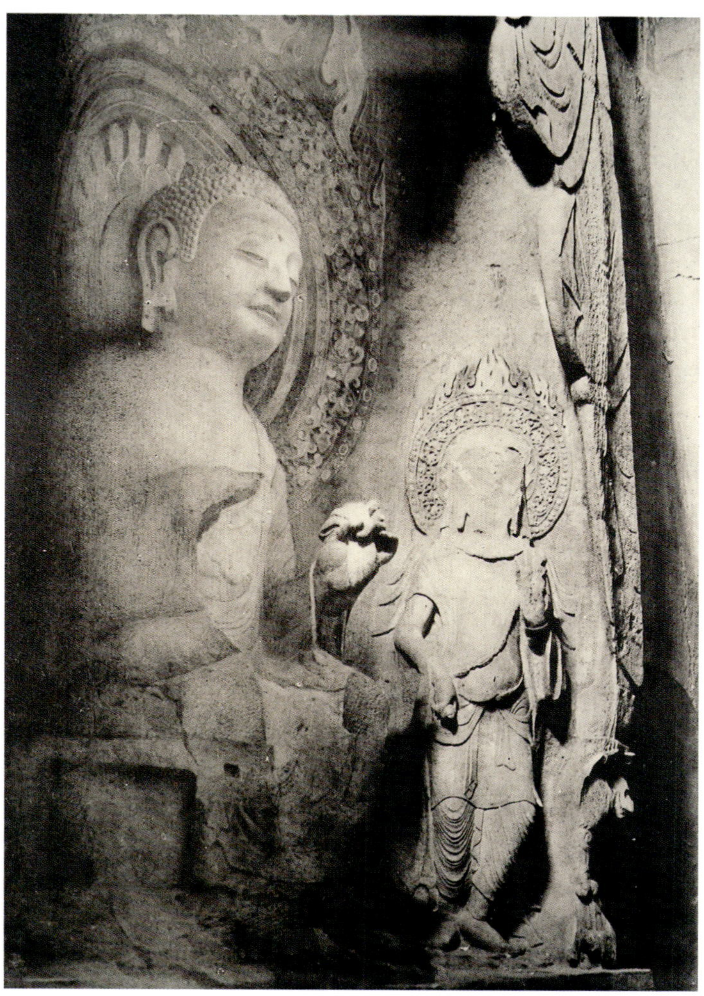

Figure 106. Seated Buddha. Northern Qi dynasty (550–577). South side of central shaft, Cave 7, Xiangtangshan, Handan, Hebei Province

century earlier. In his essay, Su Bai explores new elements of transmission. He notes that Sogdian minorities had held an influential position at the Northern Qi court as a result of their mercantile strength and patronage of the arts—which we can gauge from the sumptuous marble sarcophagus in the exhibition (cat. no. 175). Su Bai interprets the aesthetic shift as a response to Central Asian or Sogdian artistic trends. He specifically singles out the style of the Central Asian painter Cao Zhongda, who was active at the Northern Qi court. Cao's works no longer exist, but detailed descriptions survive in literary sources that postdate the Northern Qi. This Central Asian/Sogdian influence is certainly one possible explanation for the transmission of the Indian manner. Su Bai's interpretation, however, privileges painting over sculpture and diminishes the role of the Buddhist community, notably the eminent monks residing in Ye (present-day Handan, Hebei), who must also have played an important role in the choice and making of devotional images.

The numerous findings of the last twenty years in the province of Shandong, which peaked in 1995 with the discovery of a large cache of sculpture in the city of Qingzhou, at the location of the former Longxingsi, have added another intriguing dimension to this already complex artistic landscape.[8] The Northern Qi Shandong school also favored an Indianized style and produced masterpieces that resemble and share elements with the art of the Southern Liang during the first half of the sixth century. The style is similar, concurrently, to that of Hebei, though it differs in its pronounced naturalism, which brings it closer to Indian ideals. This is clear when looking at the sculpture of the standing Buddha (cat. no. 164)—a masterly interpretation of a Guptan–Sarnath model. The sensitively modeled, softly gilded body is completely visible beneath a clinging gossamer robe, so diaphanous that its presence is only hinted at by the undulating hem and by the ripples formed as it is grasped in the Buddha's hand. Shandong naturalism is absent in contemporary Hebei statuary, which is still defined by geometric reductionism. It also surpasses the earlier (Liang) Sichuanese interpretation.

These innovative traits inherent in the Buddhas and bodhisattvas of Shandong pose a challenge as to their provenance. Are they the outcome of contacts with Nanjing-based art? Or do they derive from Indian prototypes received via the maritime route directly from India or from the Indianized cultures of Southeast Asia? This question is fostered by the presence among Shandong statuary of many more interpretations of the Gupta style than have been found among southern works. It appears that Shandong carvers had a wider choice of models, which I would suggest arrived by sea. This exposure renders Shandong art different both from that of Hebei and from that of the Southern Liang. In conclusion, I would suggest that Shandong/Qingzhou art emerged from the northern stylistic polyphony of the second half of the sixth century. Paradoxically, although Shandong creativity belongs geographically to the north, its ideals are closer to those of the south.

The creation of Qingzhou bodhisattva images during the Northern Qi and the Sui (581–619) draws attention once more to the complexities of cross-cultural influences in North China toward the end of the sixth century. Moving beyond geographic boundaries, Shandong carvers reached out to the northwest—to the cultural sphere of the Northern Zhou—and adopted the sumptuous surface decoration characteristic of Northern Zhou bodhisattvas. The almost intact statue of a bodhisattva in this exhibition (cat. no. 227) is carved in the round and detailed with equal lavishness front and back. A pearl-studded openwork crown adorns the majestic head, and traces of red and gold pigments highlight the body, which is elaborately appareled and embellished with long strands of jewels. The profuse and inventive jewelry is the most emphatic and striking aspect of this sculpture.

The pluralism of aesthetic idioms and content together with the dynamics of style that surfaced during the sixth century in North and South China is far more complicated than previously thought. The adoption of a softer Indian-like or Indianized style remains the most influential factor in that it liberated the medieval Northern Wei style from its angularity and linearism, thus opening the way to images of incipient naturalism. These, in turn, became the foundations of the "new" style of the imperial Tang, the last phase of the artistic evolution under consideration.

Artistic Synthesis during the Tang Period (618–907)

The unobstructed expansion of the Tang dynasty on the Asian continent and the unprecedented commercial and cultural exchanges with many foreign cultures transformed the urban centers of China's Central Plain—especially Chang'an, the Tang capital—into a vast international metropolis. From the start of the dynasty, in 618, through 750, artistic achievements attained ever increasing standards of excellence in every possible field, secular and religious. Given its cosmopolitan flavor and the inquisitive openness that Tang China adopted in dealing with its neighbors, carvers moved toward a more natural and realistic style distinct from the abstract and linear formal language of earlier times. The Chinese aesthetic acquired a measure of expansiveness and grandeur that reflected the majesty of the imperial court itself and the self-assurance of the age in general. The robust pair of marble Heavenly Kings, of about 725, from Xi'an (cat. no. 231), projects the masculine assertiveness of this triumphant age. These guardians par excellence transcend their religious sphere and personify the imperial sway of China over Asia. The same concerns imbue their flamboyant counterparts executed in bronze, unearthed in Baoji, Shaanxi (cat. no. 230).

Imperial patronage was vital in the realization of this new style and to the growth of new Buddhist doctrines—the subject matter of much Tang art. Emperors augmented the ongoing artistic process not merely through their lavish donations but above all with their vision of transforming imported doctrines and images into genuine Chinese expressions.[9] No one better exemplifies this influential role than Wu Zetian (r. 690–705). Three major Buddhist schools emerged under her auspices: Huayan, which derived from the teachings of the homonymous Garland Sutra; incipient Esoteric teachings (which came into full blossom after the empress's rule); and Chan (Contemplative: fig. 107).

The new teachings spread from Chang'an through the northern Central Plain as Chinese monks journeyed to India and foreign monks reached China, where they settled. The eminent monk Xuanzang (602–664) returned to the Tang capital in 645, having spent sixteen years in India and Central Asia, while the monk Sikshananda (652–670) arrived in Chang'an from Khotan upon the invitation of the empress herself. The newly imported doctrines were of a higher speculative content than those transmitted earlier, during the Period of Division, and their translation into sculpture and painting posed a galvanizing challenge.

The monumental Vairocana Buddha (cat. no. 192), one of the earliest interpretations of this Esoteric deity, was originally carved for the South Cave of Leigutai, Longmen, about 700, upon the command of the Empress Wu. The Buddha is the fitting centerpiece and icon of this imperial age, equating the empress as ruler of the Tang empire with Buddha Vairocana as Lord of the Universe. (In Huayan Buddhism, Vairocana is the primordial principle behind all that exists, and presides over the entire Buddhist cosmos.) To express such majestic status, the carver broke with the earlier tradition, in which the Buddha is starkly unadorned, and presented him crowned with jewels and sumptuously attired. Rather than offering himself as compassionate and human, Vairocana is regal and dignified, expressing simultaneously his spiritual authority and the temporal power of his imperial patroness. Here, the mature artistry of a superb sculpture in the round successfully projects the interweaving of sophisticated doctrinal teachings and political concerns.

The far-reaching influence of Wu Zetian's patronage assumed another character in the architectural sculpture decorating the interior of the Seven Jewels Tower (Qibaotai), one of the buildings in the program of the Guangzhai complex in Chang'an, ascribed to 703–4.[10] This monument no longer exists, and its reliefs are dispersed in several world collections. The limestone reliefs are important in showing the Buddhist

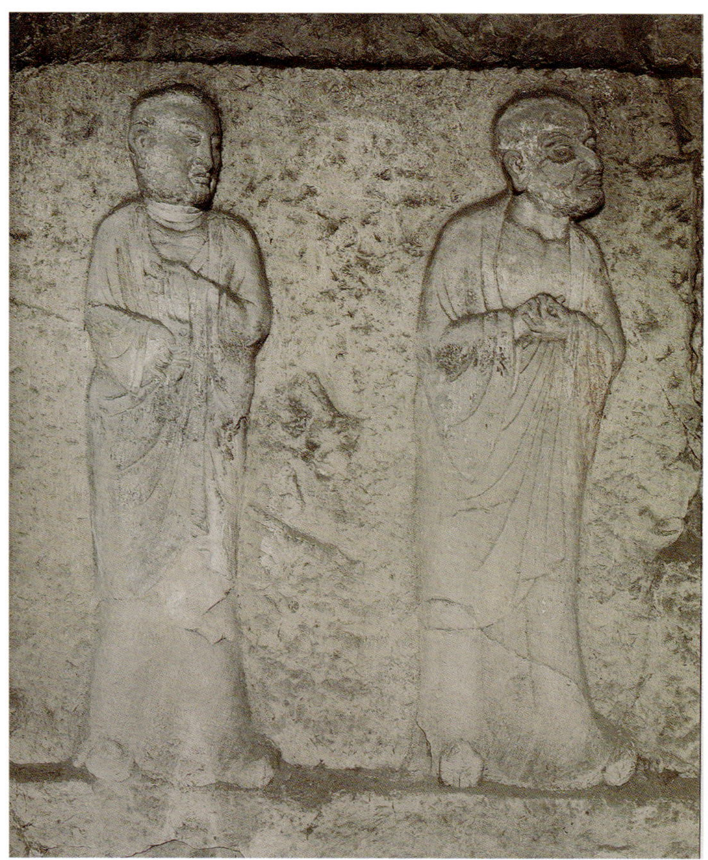

Figure 107. Two arhats, detail from a procession of arhats. Tang dynasty (618–907), ca. 700. Limestone. Kanjingsi, Longmen, Luoyang, Henan Province

teachings favored by the empress and the realistic style that pleased the court. Both aspects are exemplified in the slab relief of the Esoteric deity, Eleven-headed Guanyin (cat. no. 193). This relief is one of an original set of seven that asserts the leading role of the deity in the monument. The image carved on the panel displays a well-formed, supple body, naturalistically posed and enhanced by deftly executed robes and jewels. The varied expressions of the eleven faces, signifying different stages of attained spirituality, are but one more example of realism.

Within this prolific and creative age, by the early eighth century sculpture had also acquired a pronounced secularism—the inclusion of worldly concerns, an emphasis on material culture, and the opulent taste of the court. Furthermore, regional differences proposed various stylistic interpretations. The exhibition offers two splendid bodhisattvas, executed contemporaneously, about 725, in the south and in the north, respectively. These are the headless white marble bodhisattva from Quyang, Hebei (cat. no. 228), and the Avalokiteshvara with a rosary, once part of a set of divine images recovered at Longxing Pagoda in Pengzhou, Sichuan (cat. no. 229). The versatility of the carvers is obvious in the accomplished, realistic rendering of implements, costume, and jewelry that are fashioned on contemporary life. But as the Hebei carver emphasized the opulence of jewelry over the translucent surface of a sensuously modeled body, thereby expressing the taste of the court, the Sichuanese carver opted for a more humanized and demure interpretation, which brought the deity closer to the devotee.

One can summarize the story of this rich and intriguingly complex development of Chinese Buddhist art as the continuous adaptation and transformation into a Chinese aesthetic of foreign stimuli that reached China's heartland from different geographic regions and the maritime route. The success of this evolution derived from a sustained elite patronage that spanned many centuries, from 200 to 750. Patronage began during the Period of Division, with non-Chinese petty rulers who administered different areas of the north and pious emperors such as Liang Wudi in the south, and culminated during the Tang dynasty with the unstinting support of the Empress Wu. Wu Zeitan's personal involvement with foreign and domestic clergy led to the enrichment of Chinese Buddhism by new and novel doctrines, which, in turn, became fertile ground for the interpretation of devotional images.

1. Zürcher 1972. Additional bibliographical references are available in the catalogue entries.
2. For more on this subject, see Abe 2002.
3. For the most recent and extensive discussion of existing gilt bronzes, see Rhie 2002.
4. Rosenfield 1967: 10–11.
5. See essay by Su Bai in this publication. Alexander C. Soper also proposed this notion in his pioneering study "South Chinese Influence on the Buddhist Art of the Six Dynasties Period" (1960).
6. Bagley 2001.
7. Howard 1996: 6–25.
8. Nickel 2002b.
9. Gregory and Ebrey 1993: 1–44.
10. On the sculpture from the Tower of Seven Jewels, see Yen Chüan-ying 1986.

CATALOGUE

Contributors to the Catalogue

POH Prudence O. Harper, Curator Emeritus, Department of Ancient Near East Art check correct title of Dept.

MKH Maxwell K. Hearn, Curator, Department of Asian Art, The Metropolitan Museum of Art

AFH Angela F. Howard, Special Consultant in Chinese Buddhist Art, The Metropolitan Museum of Art; Professor of Asian Art, The State University of New Jersey at Rutgers

AJ An Jiayao, Director, Department of the Han-Tang Periods and Director, Xi'an Branch, Institute of Archaeology, Chinese Academy of Social Sciences

DPL Denise Patry Leidy, Associate Curator, Department of Asian Art, The Metropolitan Museum of Art

CJL Chao-Hui Jenny Liu, Research Associate, Department of Asian Art, The Metropolitan Museum of Art

BIM Boris I. Marshak, Chief Researcher and Head of Central Asian and Caucasian Section, State Hermitage Museum, St. Petersburg

VR Valentina Raspopova, Leading Researcher, Institute of the History of Material Culture, Academy of Sciences of the Russian Federation, St. Petersburg

ZS Zhixin Sun, Associate Curator, Department of Asian Art, The Metropolitan Museum of Art

JCYW James C. Y. Watt, Brooke Russell Astor Chairman, Department of Asian Art, The Metropolitan Museum of Art

ZF Zhao Feng, Vice Director, China National Silk Museum, Hangzhou, Zhejiang Province

I

Late Han, Late 2nd–Early 3rd Century

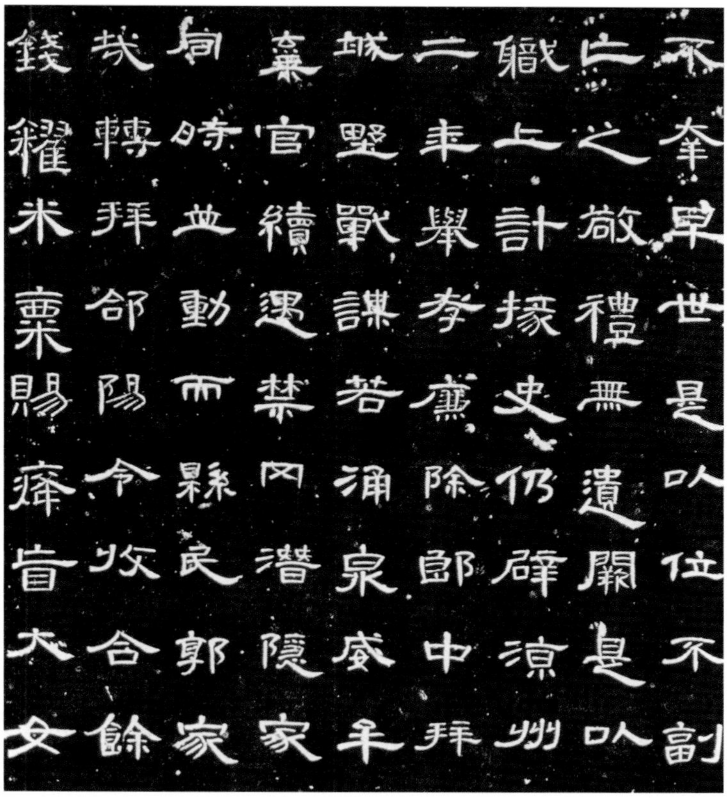

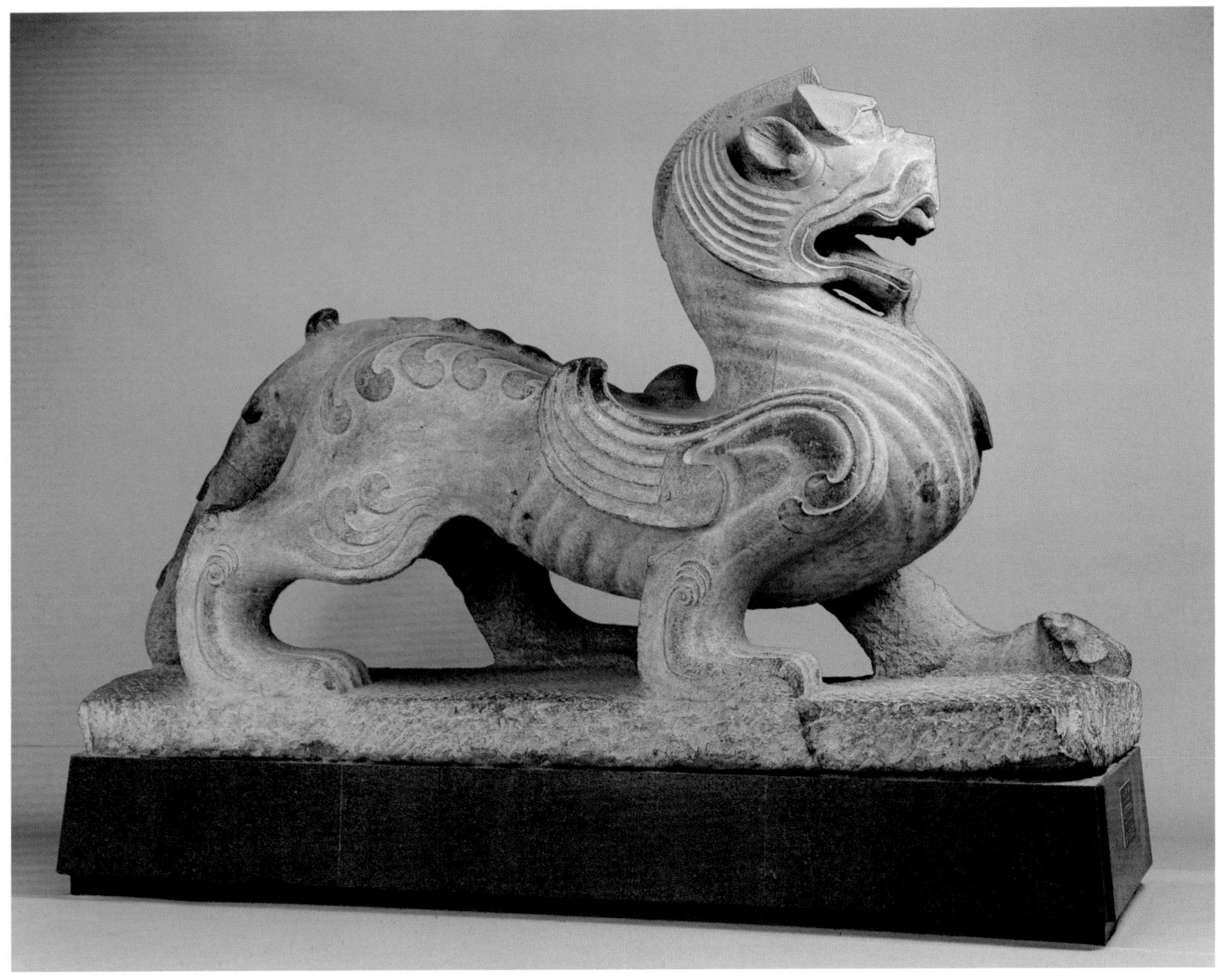

1

Chimera

Eastern Han dynasty (25–220)
Stone
Length 115 3/8 in. (293 cm)
Found in Mengjin, Henan Province, 1992
Luoyang Museum

REFERENCE: Su Jian 1995

Winged chimeras are known in traditional Chinese literature as *bixie,* meaning "to ward off evil spirits." A mythical hybrid, these fantastic creatures possess the attributes of a feline but also have wings and horns. Many were carved in stone and placed in pairs at the entryway of a tomb, for it was believed that these ferocious-looking animals not only enhanced the dignity of the tomb but also protected the dead from malevolent intrusions.

The image of the fabulous animal may have come into China from more than one source and at more than one time. Recent studies suggest that sources for the chimera are found in Mesopotamian art, starting from Babylon and traveling to Achaemenid Persia and Bactria and into China by way of Central Asia.[1] The winged creature with sinuous body first appeared in China on bronze vessels of the sixth and fifth centuries B.C. In the following centuries, it became more feline in character and developed clawed feet and pointed wings. Well-known examples of this type are the silver-inlaid bronze beasts found in the tomb of the king of the Zhongshan state in the late fourth century B.C.[2] The chimera appears to have acquired its standard form in the late Western and early Eastern Han period, as the empire asserted its military dominance into the Pamirs and contact with the West increased along the Silk Road. A common motif at this time, the chimera took its form in nearly all media, including gold, silver, bronze, ceramic, stone, and jade. The practice of placing large stone chimeras at the entrance to the tomb seems to have begun in the Eastern Han

(25–220) and continued over the following centuries until the more naturalistic lions replaced them in the Tang dynasty (618–907).

With a staggering height of six feet, the present example is the largest among all extant stone chimeras. It was found by accident at Mengjin, north of Luoyang, in 1992.[3] Also recovered at the site were fragments of stone gate towers. Despite the scarcity of contextual archaeological evidence, comparison with dated examples suggests that the sculpture is likely from the middle or even early Eastern Han period. Its arched back and taut legs convey a dynamic force and vigor, in stark contrast to the stylized chimeras of the late Han. This fabulous beast was found not too far from the tomb of Liu Xiu (r. 25–57), the first emperor of the Eastern Han dynasty. Nevertheless, it was reportedly moved from elsewhere on the site.[4] Considering its monumental size and extraordinarily accomplished craftsmanship, it was most likely at the entrance to the tomb.

ZS

1. For a comprehensive study on winged mythical animals, see Li Ling 2001: 62–134. See also Till 1980: 261–81.
2. Hebei sheng wenwu yanjiusuo 1995, pls. 94, 95.
3. Su Jian 1995: 66.
4. Ibid.

2

Chariots and mounted guards

Eastern Han dynasty (25–220)
Bronze
Chariots: max. height 22 7/8 in. (58 cm); figures: max. height 20 5/8 in. (52.5 cm)
Excavated at Leitai, Wuwei, Gansu Province, 1969
Gansu Provincial Museum

Excav. report in *Kaogu xuebao* 1974.2

This group of chariots and mounted guards is part of an unusually large set of bronze figures found in the front chamber of an early third-century tomb. Although the tomb was plundered twice in ancient times, these figures miraculously escaped the

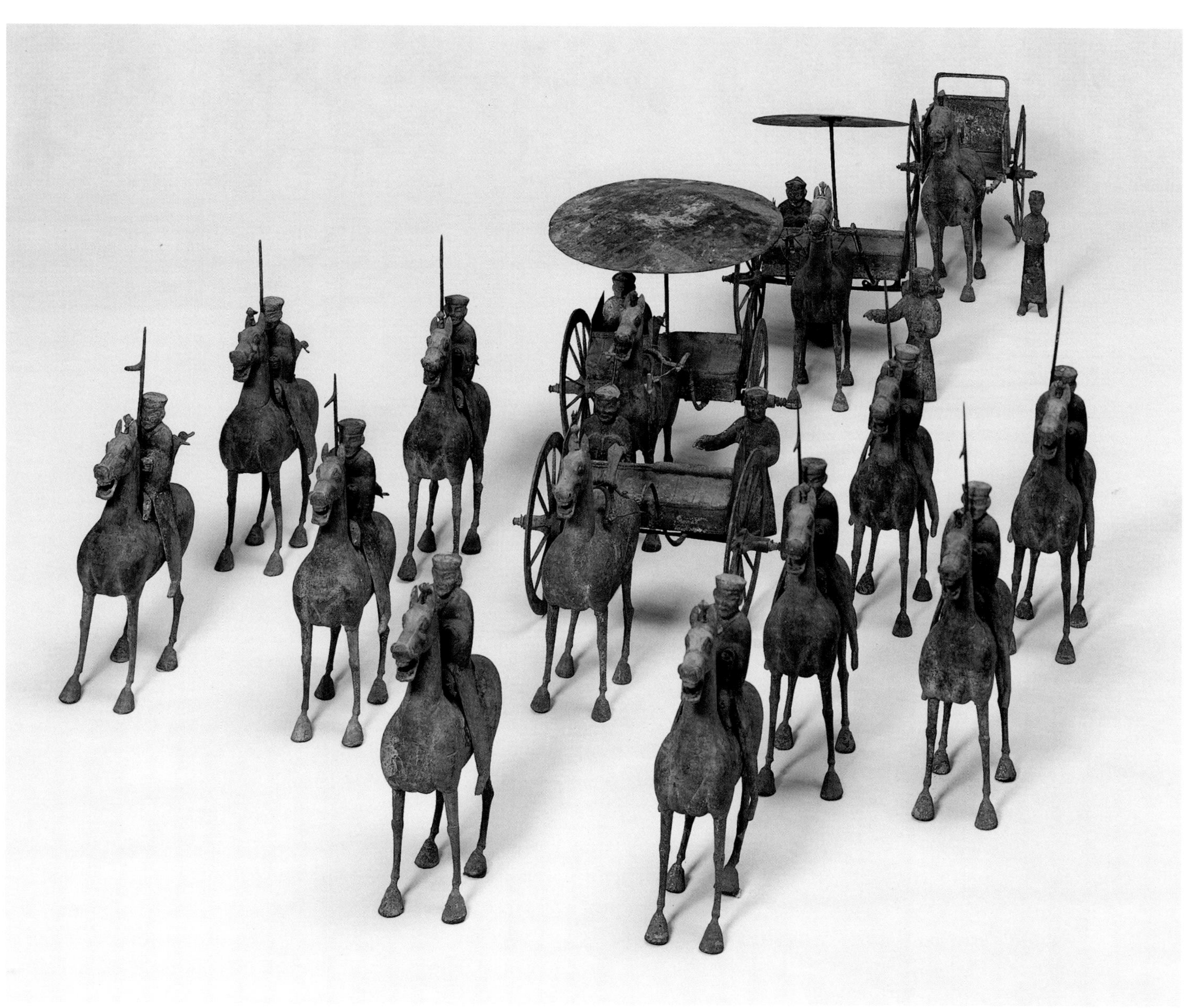

looting and remained nearly intact. An ostentatious procession of a high-ranking official in the Han dynasty, the complete set consists of 17 mounted guards and musicians, 28 escorts, 14 vehicles of various sorts, 39 horses, and an ox.

The present selection includes ten mounted warriors from the honor guard, a chariot with an umbrella for the deceased, a chariot with a large ax symbolizing his military authority, a light chariot, and a carriage with protective side panels for his family. A driver and an escort on foot accompany each chariot. With raised heads and staring eyes, the horses stand poised and alert. Each is equipped with an ornamental headpiece and a movable saddle that originally had painted decoration. The chariots are meticulous miniatures of the originals made precisely to scale, with every detail—harness, seat, umbrella, shafts, wheels, even the pins—painstakingly cast.

The city of Wuwei in Gansu Province, where the tomb is situated, was the capital of Wuwei Prefecture in the late Han dynasty, a garrison on the Silk Road that guarded the critical passage through the western corridor. As the seals recovered from the tomb suggest, the deceased was likely a commandery governor, a position among the highest ranks at the Han court.

ZS

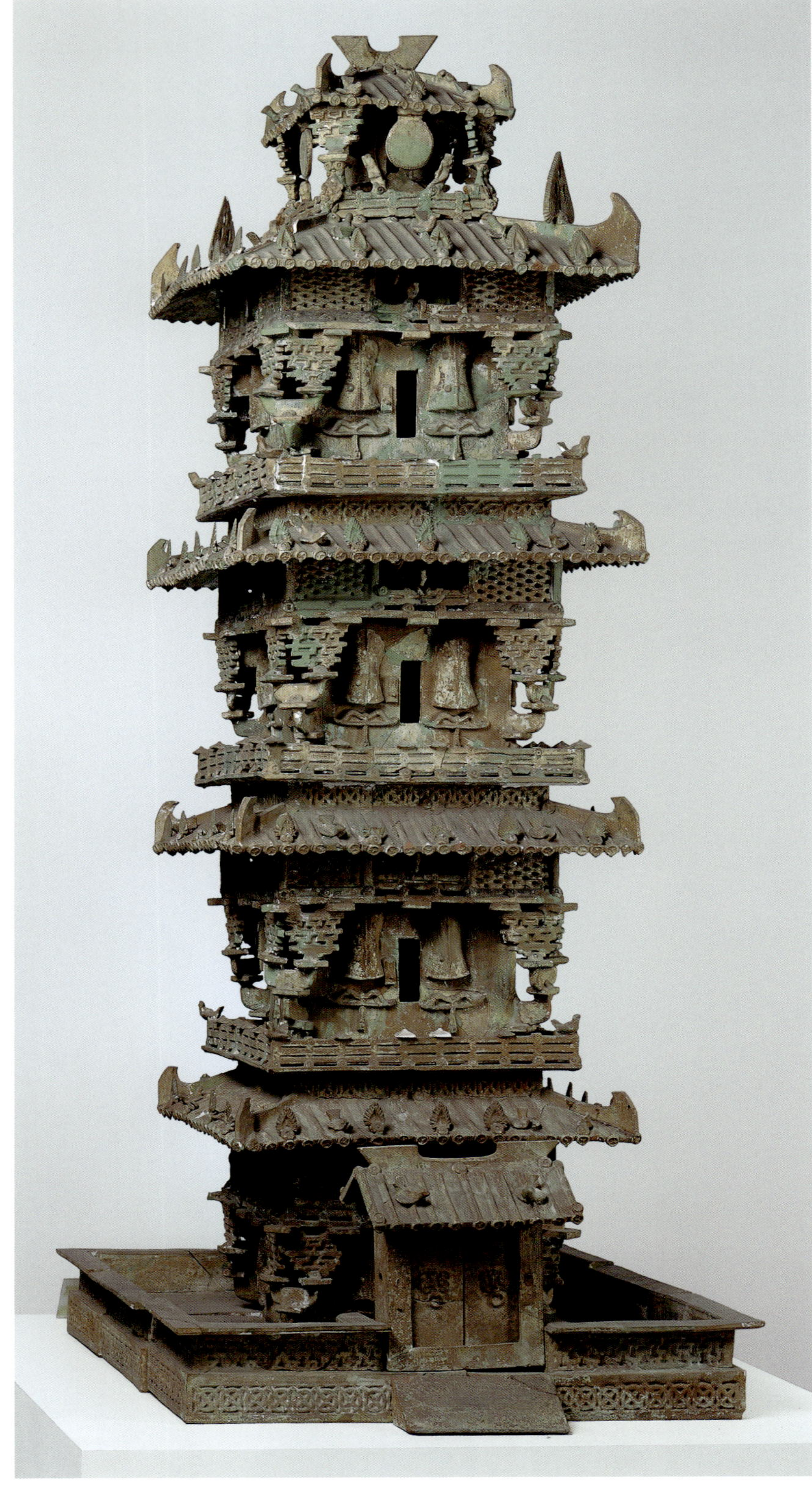

3
Model of a watchtower

Eastern Han dynasty (25–220)
Glazed earthenware
Height 85 in. (216 cm)
Excavated at Sangzhuang, Fucheng, Hebei Province, 1990
Hebei Institute of Archaeology

Excav. report in *Wenwu* 1990.1

This exceptionally complete architectural model, recently excavated from a multichambered tomb at Fucheng, Hebei, depicts a strongly fortified watchtower. It rises to a compelling height in a walled courtyard, whose front and only entrance is guarded by a tall gate with gabled roof and heavy doors. Two monster-faced door knockers convey a sense of awe and signify the importance of the edifice. The seemingly five-storied wooden structure has, in fact, nine floors, for under each of the five roofs is an overhung mezzanine supported by brackets. The mezzanine has latticed windows and a wide opening in the middle, behind which sits a guard, ever on the alert. The main floor underneath has solid walls and a narrow central opening flanked by a pair of shields and crossbows that declare the watchtower's military purpose. Above each roof is a railed porch where the archers could take their positions. Four large gongs hang beneath the top roof of the tower, one on each side. Men with hammers, ready to strike, are seated next to the gongs. Given the gigantic size of the gongs (see detail below), the sound would carry over long distances, reverberating through the fields in time of crisis.

The grave at the site of Sangzhuang at Fucheng, Hebei, was looted long before its recent discovery and was left with little of its furnishings except for pottery figures and models. Nevertheless, judging from the large scale of the tomb, the fragments of the elaborate wall paintings, and especially this magnificent watchtower, we can assume that the tomb owner was a powerful landlord, with unchallenged authority in the Fucheng area. Such local figures, many of them directly or indirectly related to the imperial family, played an increasingly important role in economic and political life during the late Han period. They possessed not only abundant wealth and vast landholdings but also great numbers of serfs, or *buqu*, who served as farmhands in times of peace and as soldiers in their armies during times of war. The historian Jacques Gernet describes Liang Ji, a high-ranking minister and a relative of the emperor in the late Eastern Han, as a typical example of this gentry class.[1] At his downfall, the sale of Liang's property is said to have provided the state exchequer with three billion coins, a sum sufficient to fund half the annual grain tax for the entire country. This watchtower, with its grand scale, complex structure, and formidable defense system, vividly illustrates the staggering power and wealth of a member of the gentry class.

ZS

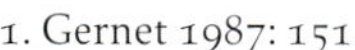

1. Gernet 1987: 151.

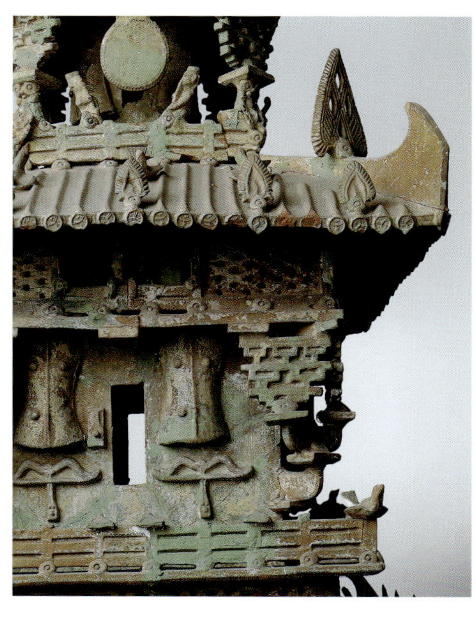

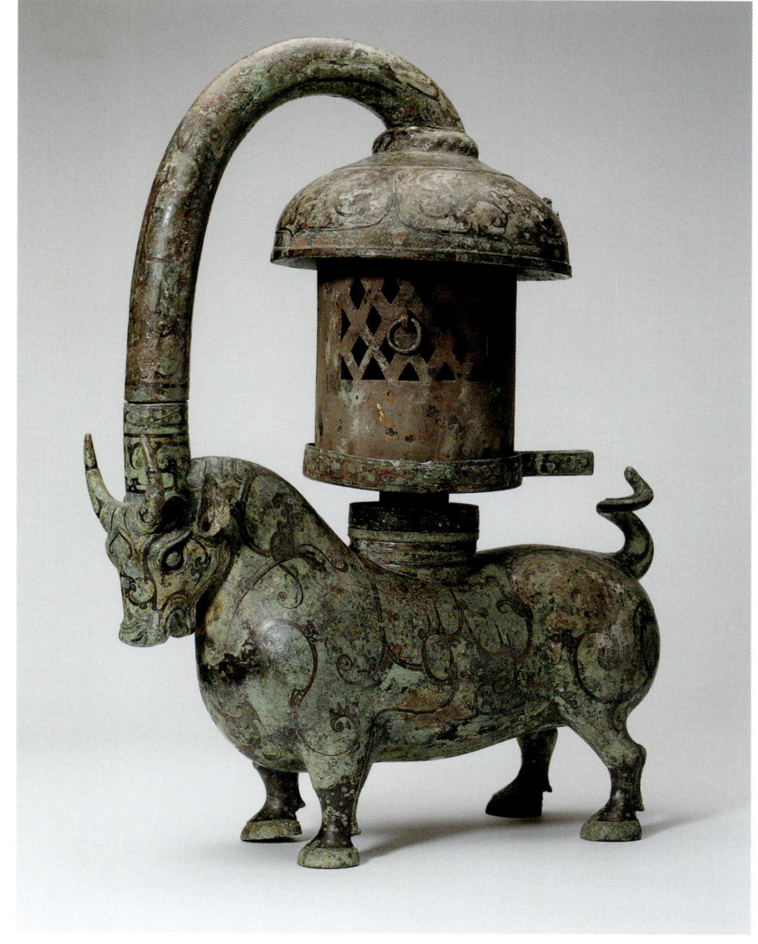

4

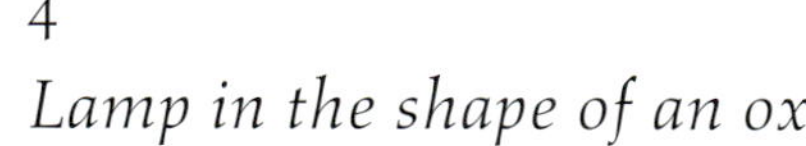

Lamp in the shape of an ox

Eastern Han dynasty (25–220)
Bronze inlaid with silver
Height 18⅛ in. (46 cm)
Excavated at Hanjiang, Jiangsu Province, 1980
Nanjing Museum

Excav. report in *Wenwu* 1981.11

Chinese burial practice underwent a significant change during the late Eastern Zhou period (4th–3rd century B.C.), when the preoccupation with rituals gave way to concern for mundane needs. As a result, exalted ritual bronzes were by and large replaced by such practical items as food and wine vessels, musical instruments, furniture, and luxury items. Among the new tomb furnishings were lamps, which soon became an indispensable category in the burials of the subsequent Han dynasty. Lamps were made in a variety of shapes and materials. Bronze examples found in the tombs of the elite seem to have been individually cast and are known for their ingenious designs and sumptuous decoration.

This lamp is cast in the form of a standing bull, whose broad neck, stout legs, and brawny haunches convey a sense of weight and power. On his back is the round base of the lamp, which in turn supports a movable tray with a handle. The shade is composed of two curved bronze sheets with latticework, which can slide to adjust the direction and intensity of light. A long tube extends downward from the domed top to join to the back of the bull's head. Serving to channel the smoke into the hollow body of the bull, the tube thus functions to keep the room clean from soot. The entire lamp is decorated with long, flowing scrolls executed in silver inlay, an embellishment that mimics the elegant patterns on contemporary lacquer and silk.

A fine example of the craftsman's inventiveness and technical sophistication, the lamp is composed of a number of movable parts; the base, the shade, and the domed top with tube can all be disassembled to allow easy access for cleaning. It was made by the lost-wax process, a technique relatively unexploited in early Chinese bronzes but which became increasingly popular during the Han period to meet the demand for more complex and plastic figures.

ZS

5

Inkstone case in the shape of a chimera

Eastern Han dynasty (25–220)
Gilt bronze inlaid with semiprecious stones
Length 9⅞ in. (25 cm)
Excavated at Tushan, Xuzhou, Jiangsu Province, 1970
Nanjing Museum

The chimera, a fantastic animal inspired by western Asian art, captured the imagination of Han dynasty China. It assumed many forms and was made in all manner of media. The entryways of Han tombs were dominated by monumental sculptures of stone. By contrast, small figures of gold, jade, bronze, and ceramic prevailed among the luxury items and practical utensils buried with the deceased. This inkstone case, cast in the shape of a chimera, is one of the innumerable implements that would have enabled the deceased to continue his daily activities in the afterlife.

The back of the present chimera forms the domed lid of the case, and the deep belly holds the inkstone. The craftsman gave the beast an unusually short body to accommodate the shape of the stone. He also elongated the ribbed horns to offset the oversize head. Colorful inlays of semiprecious stones—carnelian, turquoise, and lapis lazuli—embellish the lustrous gilt-bronze surface. Of particular significance is the lapis lazuli imported from Bactria, which reflects China's increasing contact with Central and West Asia.

The inkstone is one the four essential writing implements in China, the other three being the brush, ink, and paper. Except for paper, the invention of these tools dates back to pre-Han times. The earliest known inkstone was found in a third-century B.C. tomb in Yunmeng, Hubei.[1] Fairly crude in form, it largely retains the original shape of the stone and exhibits minimal carving. The use of inkstones seems to have become widespread during the Han dynasty, as the numerous examples recovered in the last few decades suggest. Many of them were found with small grinding stones, since, before the development of ink sticks, ink was made in the form of small blocks and had to be ground for use. This inkstone and case were also accompanied by a grinding stone when they were found in a second- to third-century tomb in Xuzhou, Jiangsu, in 1970.[2]

ZS

1. Zou Houben 2000: 233.
2. You Zhenyao 1989: 61.

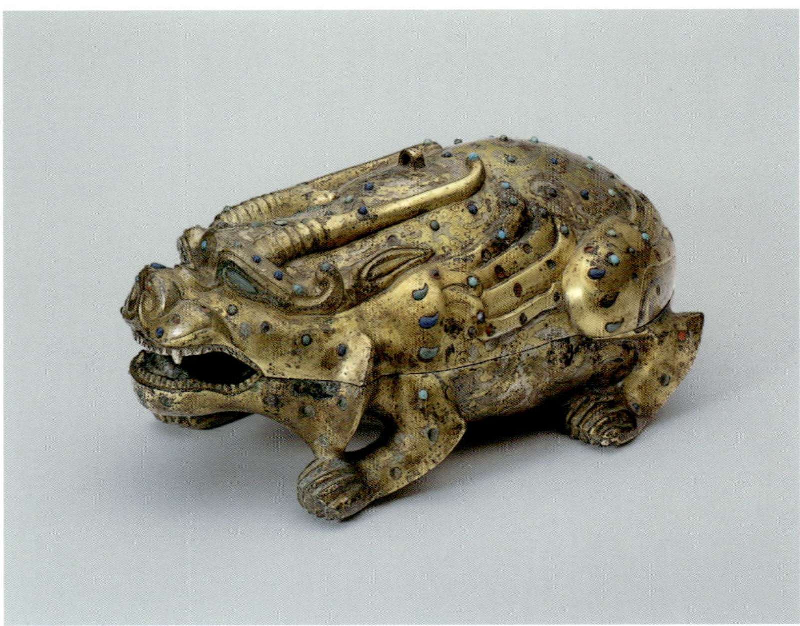

6

Disk with openwork design of dragons

Eastern Han dynasty (25–220)
Jade (nephrite)
Height 10 in. (25.5 cm)
Excavated from the tomb of Liu Yan (d. 90), Dingzhou, Hebei Province, 1959
Hebei Provincial Museum

Excav. report in *Kaogu xuebao* 1964.2

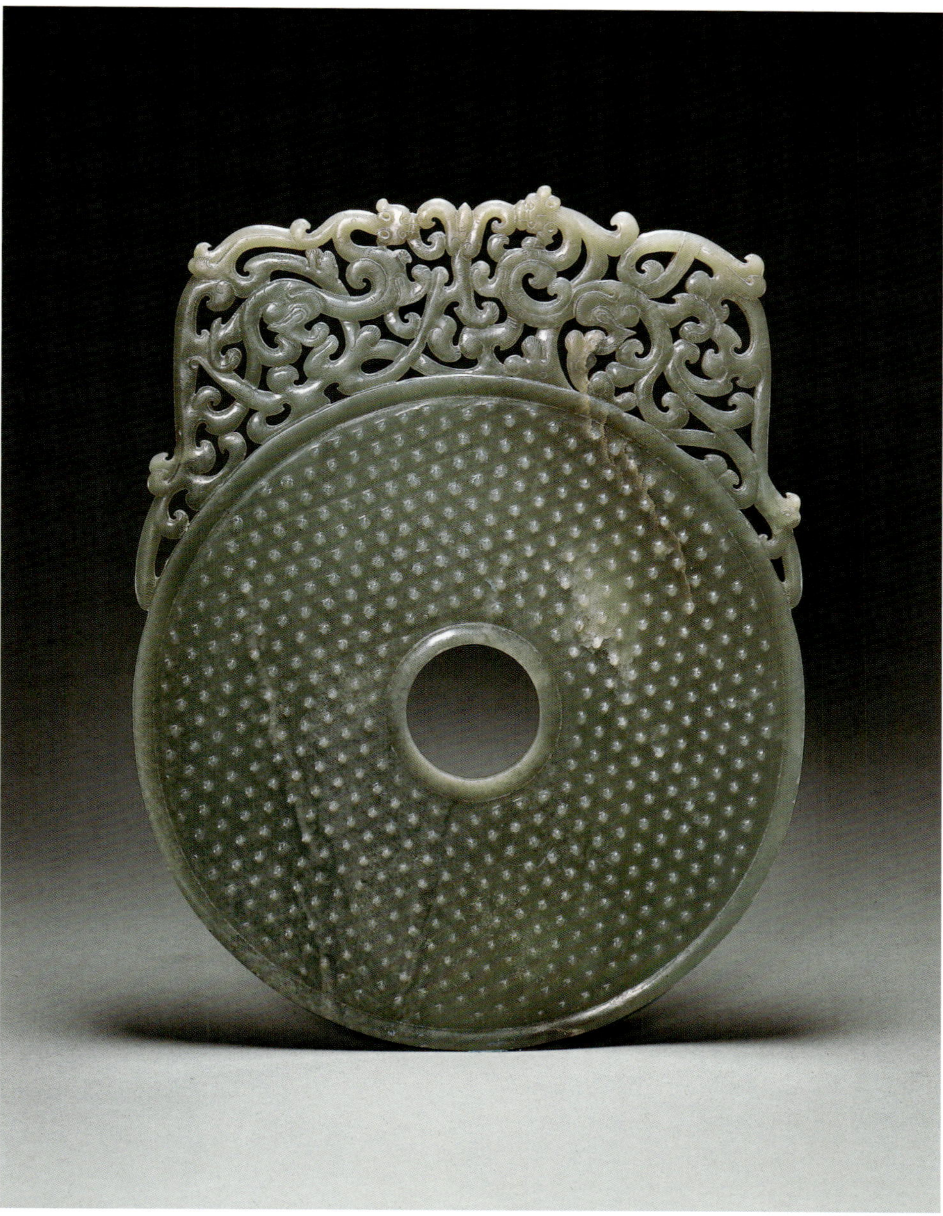

The surface decoration of this circular disk features small raised hemispheres in diagonal rows. Close inspection reveals that the tiny domes are actually organized on a hexagonal grid composed of three sets of parallel lines intersected at angles of 60 degrees. This concise decorative scheme, known in traditional Chinese literature as the "grain" pattern, is the final stage in the development of the raised spiral motif, which first appeared in the sixth century B.C. Inspired by decoration on works of gold, the pattern was painstakingly modified to maximize the light-catching quality of jade, so that the varied reflections from the raised spirals would produce a shimmering effect.

From the upper edge of the disk extend two dragons carved in openwork, whose long, sinuous bodies writhe through curled clouds to form an intricate design. Though lightly modeled, the dragons look rather flat, in contrast with those on the disks of the late Eastern Zhou and early Western Han periods, in the late fourth and early third centuries B.C. They bear a close affinity to slightly later examples recovered from an Eastern Han tomb, possibly that of the Prince of Guangling, in Yangzhou, Jiangsu,[1] by which time artistic focus had shifted from plastic form to complex interlaced pattern.

Disks surmounted by openwork dragons were first made in the Warring States period (481–222), when jade carvers combined the circular disks known as *bi* with openwork ornaments. By the middle of the Western Han they had become a popular form and were made on a grand scale. One of the most striking examples is a disk found in the late second-century B.C. tomb of Prince Liu Sheng, which displays two spirited dragons posing back to back and holding aloft a complex pattern of rolling clouds.[2] The function of these disks was evidently different from that of the purely circular disks and the openwork ornaments from which they evolved. They are too large and their shapes too complex to accommodate a pendant or another form of personal adornment. Some of them have auspicious sayings carved in openwork, suggesting that they were meant to be talismans or gifts for special occasions.[3]

ZS

1. Yangzhou bowuguan 1991: 62.
2. Zhongguo shehui kexueyuan kaogu yanjiusuo, Hebei sheng wenwu guanlichu 1980: 135.
3. Rawson 1995: 250–51.

7
Screen

Eastern Han dynasty (25–220)
Jade (nephrite)
Height 6½ in. (16.5 cm)
Excavated from the tomb of Liu Chang (d. 174), Dingzhou, Hebei Province, 1969
Dingzhou City Museum

Excav. report in *Wenwu* 1973.11

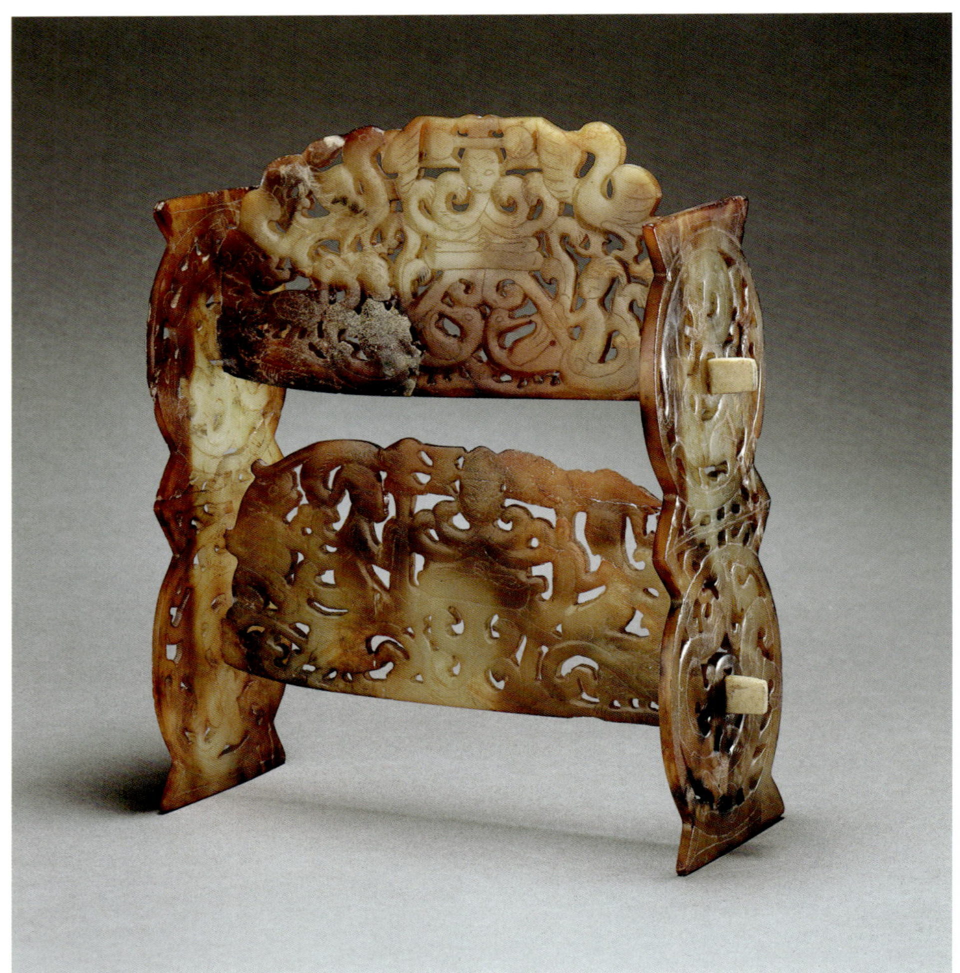

This extraordinary jade carving is composed of four separate parts that include a pair of semicircular plaques held on two flat side supports. The supports are in the shape of two connected roundels, each decorated with a coiled dragon. At the top center of the upper plaque is the King Father of the East (Dongwanggong), flanked by two birds with spread wings and two figures in long flowing robes. On the lower plaque, the Queen Mother of the West (Xiwangmu), seated between two kneeling figures, is identified by her special headdress known as a *sheng*. An animal stands behind each figure; one of them has been identified as a bear.[1] Pairs of turtles and snakes, symbols of the north, are placed below. The decoration is executed in openwork with fluent, engraved outlines.

The Queen Mother of the West, whose name first appeared in philosophical texts of the Eastern Zhou (770–256 B.C.), became the most powerful deity in Han China as the quest for immortality reached unprecedented heights and her cult permeated hundreds and thousands of households.[2] Representing the *yin* force of the universe, she was believed to dwell in Kunlunshan, the entrance to heaven, and with her elixir to confer eternal life. The King Father of the East, her counterpart, came into being during the Eastern Han, when he was created to serve as a symbol of the *yang* force to complement her in a perfectly balanced cosmos. Together they became omniscient icons in the art of the late Han, appearing on bronzes, ceramics, jades, stone engravings, and wall paintings. A rare example of this widespread cult, the present jade carving is generally referred to as a desk screen. Its exact function, however, remains unknown. Considering the imagery, it probably had some religious significance or protective power for the owner. ZS

1. Dingxian bowuguan 1973: 11.
2. For an extensive and detailed study of the Queen Mother of the West, see Wu Hung 1989: 110–41.

8
Ornament with a dragon

Eastern Han dynasty (25–220)
Gold
Height 1⅛ in. (3 cm)

9
Ornament in the shape of a crown

Eastern Han dynasty (25–220)
Gold inlaid with semiprecious stones
Diameter ⅝ in. (1.5 cm)

Cat. nos. 8 and 9 excavated in Hanjiang, Jiangsu Province, 1980
Nanjing Museum

Excav. report in *Wenwu* 1981.11

10

Ornament with winged figure on a chimera

Eastern Jin dynasty (317–420) or earlier
Gold
Height 1 in. (2.5 cm)
Excavated from the tomb of Zhang Zhen, Suzhou, Jiangsu Province, 1979
Nanjing Museum

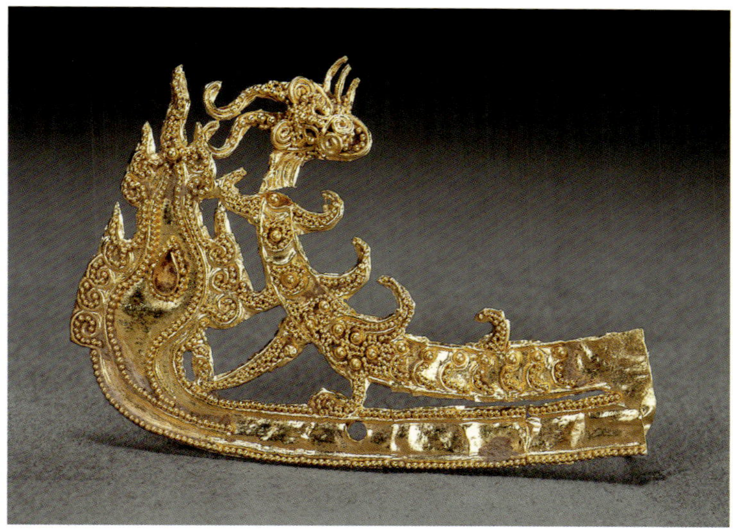

8

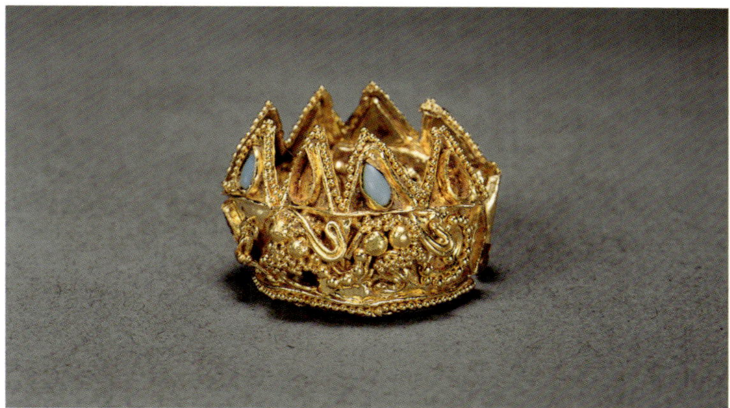

9

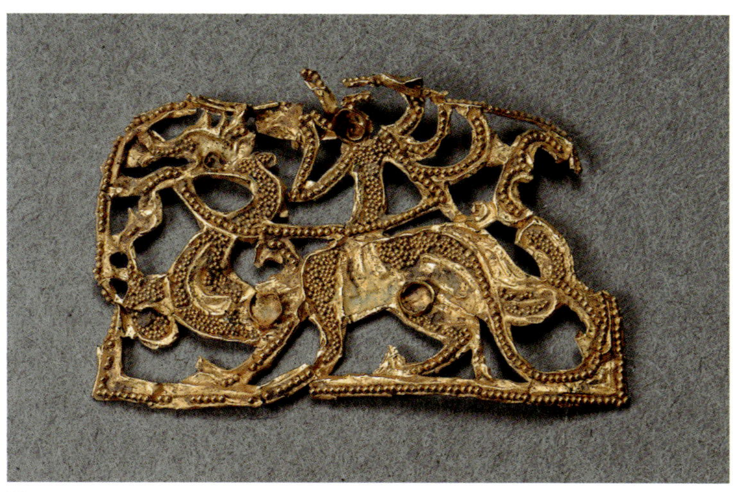

10

These three exquisite works of gold may have originally been attached on other objects. The ornament at the upper right depicts a spirited dragon sailing on a scrolled cloud. Less than two inches long, the plaque is executed in minute detail with filigree and fine granules. The circular ornament in the middle has eight tiny triangles arranged in the form of a crown. The textured surface is sumptuously enlivened by colorful inlays of semiprecious stones.

The ornament at the lower right is a plaque crafted in openwork, on which raised lines and fine granules portray a winged figure on a chimera. Comparison with a similar pair of plaques in the Musée Guimet, Paris, suggests that it was originally affixed to a sheet-metal base and inlaid with semiprecious stones.[1] Part of an ear pendant, it recalls the art of the steppes, indicated by its likeness to two small plaques, excavated from a first-century nomadic tomb in Inner Mongolia.[2] The chimera and winged figures were among the most popular images of the Eastern Han period and were made in various media, including gold, bronze, stone, jade, and ceramic. The sources of these fantastic creatures, as well as the technique of granulation, however, are found in the art of ancient West Asia and were brought to China over the Silk Road and across the steppes.

The crown-shaped ornament and the ornament with the dragon were excavated from the first-century tomb of Zhang Zhen, the ninth son of Liu Xiu (r. 25–57), the first emperor of the Eastern Han. The prince's identity is verified by the inscription on a bronze lamp and by his official seal recovered near the site.[3] The plaque with the winged figure was found in an early fourth-century tomb also in southern Jiangsu.[4] The stylistic and technical features of the plaque, however, suggest that it may have been an heirloom and, in fact, not much later in date from the other two ornaments.

ZS

1. Delacour 2001: 245–47.
2. Ibid.: 246; Tian Guangjin and Guo Suxin 1986: 379–81.
3. Nanjing bowuyuan 1981: 10.
4. Zou Houben 2000: 312.

11
Two chimeras

Eastern Han dynasty (25–220)
Gold inlaid with semiprecious stones
Max. height 1⅝ in. (4 cm)

12
Ornamental plaque

Eastern Han dynasty (25–220)
Gold
Height 2½ in. (6.4 cm)

Cat. nos. 11 and 12 excavated from the tomb of Liu Chang (d. 174), Dingzhou, Hebei Province, 1969
Dingzhou City Museum

Excav. report in *Wenwu* 1973.11

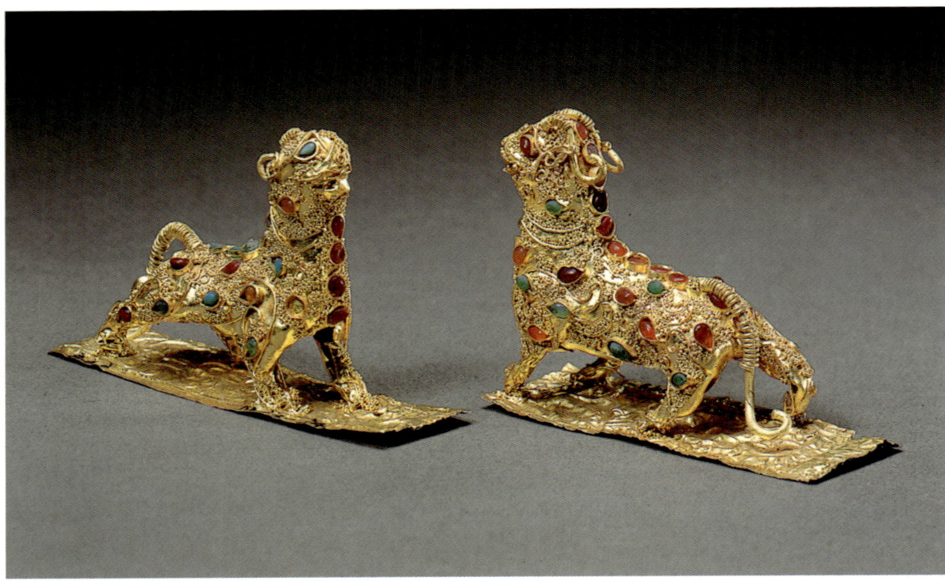

11

The Han dynasty was a seminal period in the development of Daoism. Central to this complex belief system was the concept of the land of the immortals, and depictions of this fantasy world inhabited by fabulous and exotic creatures are found in works of all media. These two chimeras and the openwork plaque, excavated from the tomb of Liu Chang (r. 141–74), prince of Zhongshan state, are typical representations of this imagery.

The hollow bodies of the two chimeras—apparently a pair—are made of sheet gold enlivened by tiny gold granules and colorful inlays of semiprecious stones. Fine gold filigree describes the eyes, horns, and wings and coils tightly around the long, curving tails. Standing tall, with proud, regal bearing, the tiny creatures impart a monumentality to match that of a great tomb guardian, an effect that belies their diminutive size.

The openwork plaque presents a microcosmos in gold sheet that is less than three inches high. A lively fabulous animal stands at the center. Around him are the animals of the cardinal directions: the blue dragon of the east at his left, the white tiger of the west at his right, the red bird of the south above, and the turtle and snake of the north below. Inside the three triangles that extend from the lower edge of the plaque are a bird, a scorpion, and a snake, symbols of the Chinese constellations.

The granulation on these delicate works—the minute spherical beads fused on the surface to highlight the design and create a rich and dazzling texture—is of particular interest. The technique was introduced to China around the third century B.C., and, as archaeological evidence suggests, its transmission over the land route probably coincided with its diffusion through maritime trade.[1] By the Eastern Han, when the chimeras and the plaque were made, Chinese goldsmiths had largely mastered the technique and put it to extensive use. ZS

1. Bunker 2002: 114.

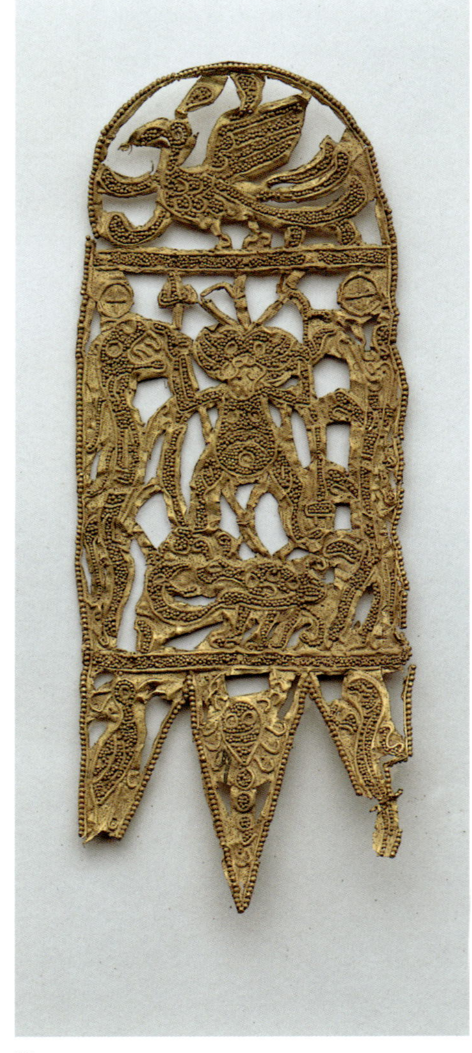

12

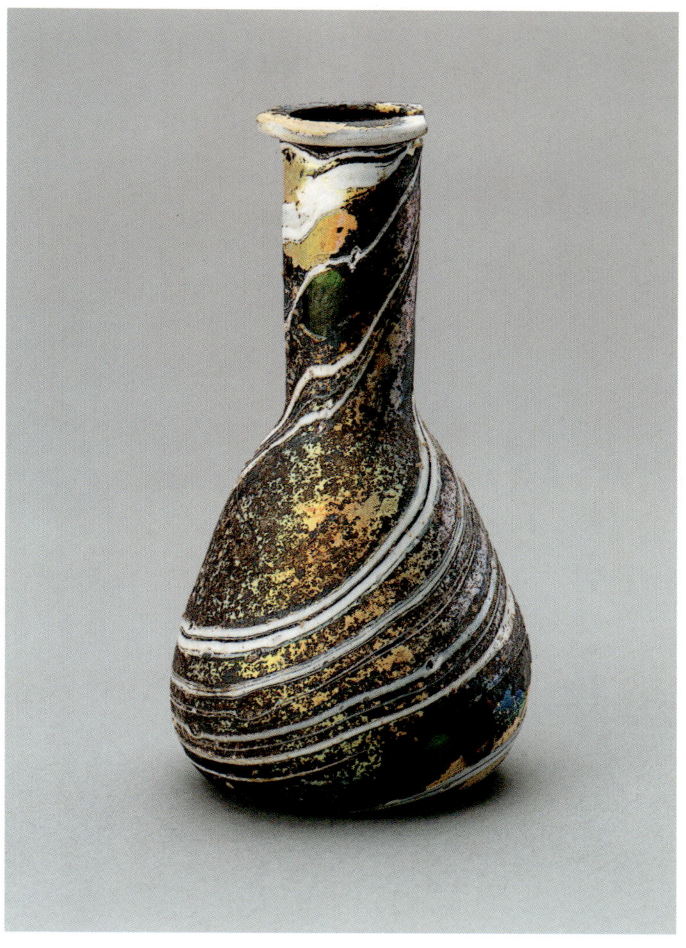

13
Bottle

Ca. 1st–3rd century
Glass
Height 5³⁄₈ in. (13.6 cm)
Excavated at Luoyang, Henan Province, 1987
Luoyang Museum

The shape of this glass bottle—with flat bottom, conical body, and long neck—resembles that of a flask in a modern chemical laboratory. The mouth flares out and folds back to form a flat lip. The glass is green and transparent, decorated with white marbled veins on the outside, and the surface is covered by a blackish weathered layer as a result of burial for nearly two thousand years. The shape of the bottle differs from that of any traditional Chinese vessel, as does the method of manufacture. Glassware in Han China was cast in molds. The present bottle was formed through a process of blowing into the glass in its hot, softened state.

The shape of the present bottle, excavated from an Eastern Han (25–220) tomb in Luoyang, is commonly seen in Roman glass along the Mediterranean coast. The type first appeared in the thirties of the first century A.D. and seems to have remained in production until the end of the first century or the beginning of the second century.[1] It is thus highly probable that the bottle is Roman, from the Mediterranean coast.

The fragility of glass makes it extremely difficult to transport over long distances. During the reign of Emperor Wudi (r. 140–87 B.C.) of the Western Han (206 B.C.–A.D. 9), Zhang Qian (d. 114), the emissary sent by Wudi into Central Asia, opened the way to the Western Regions, which made possible direct communication between the Roman Empire and China, the two great civilizations of the East and of the West. Central Asian peoples were resourceful traders, and as early as the Han dynasty they began to make their way to the Central Plain of China for commercial activities. This would explain the presence of a Roman glass bottle in a Chinese tomb in Luoyang, the capital of the Eastern Han.

AJ

1. Isings 1957: 34.

14
Cup

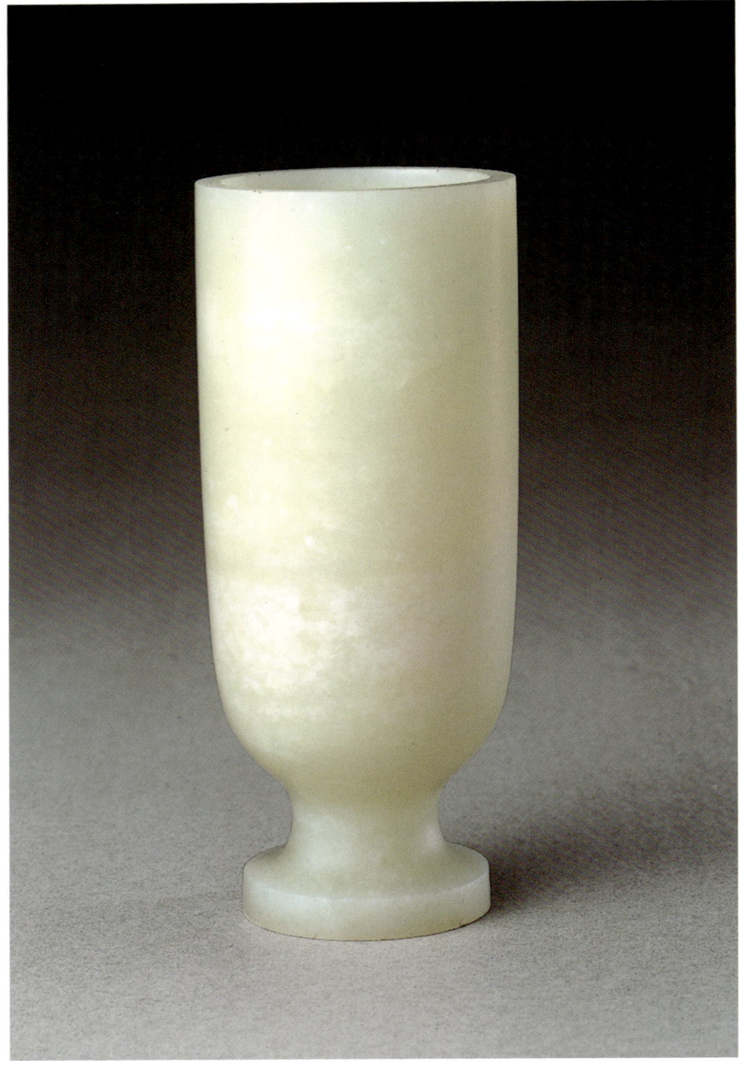

Three Kingdoms, Wei (220–265)
Jade (nephrite)
Height 5 1/8 in. (13 cm)
Excavated from a tomb (dated 247) in Luoyang, Henan Province, 1956
Luoyang Museum

EXCAV. REPORT in *Kaogu* 1989.4

Inspired by imports from West Asia, glass-making emerged in China around the fourth century B.C. The industry seems to have developed rapidly and large-scale manufacturing followed. Like jade, early glass was translucent and had a lustrous appearance, but its production was far less labor-intensive, making it a preferred material for affordable copies of the highly desired precious stone. Archaeological excavations in the last few decades have yielded numerous glass substitutes, particularly those for burial jades, such as *bi* disks, eye covers, orifice plugs, and "hand warmers," objects in the shape of pigs that were placed in the hands of the deceased.

The imported glass not only brought about the development of Chinese glass-making but also provided inspiration to Chinese jade carvers. The tall, elegantly contoured goblet was one of the favored models. Among the early examples is a jade cup found in a second-century B.C. tomb that has exactly the same shape as the glass original but is embellished with the small raised spirals typical of contemporary jades.[1] A more innovative example is a goblet cast in bronze whose exterior is inlaid with jade to simulate the effect of glass.[2]

As trade between China and the West continued to expand during the late Han dynasty, a new type of glass—made in the Roman Empire—began to enter the Chinese market. Roman glass, especially vessels, was prized for being thin, light, clear, and brightly colored, for which locally made glass was no match. An exotic and sought-after commodity, it caught the Chinese imagination and subsequently contributed to a dramatic change in the traditional art of jade carving. The present example, recovered from an early third-century tomb, as well as the jade cicada and pig in the exhibition (cat. nos. 15, 16), illustrate this stylistic trend. Free of surface decoration, as are the other two jades, the goblet exemplifies the contemporary aesthetic of pure form, which would best present the beauty of the stone. ZS

1. Guangzhou shi wenwu guanli weiyuanhui et al. 1991, pl. 119.
2. Ibid., pl. 118.

15
Cicada

Eastern Han dynasty (25–220)
Jade (nephrite)
Length 2 ½ in. (6.4 cm)
Excavated from the tomb of Liu Yan (d. 90), Dingzhou, Hebei Province, 1959
Hebei Provincial Museum

Excav. report in *Kaogu xuebao* 1964.2

The use of jades as tomb offerings dates back to the fifth millennium B.C., when small jade articles, such as rings, pendants, and earrings, were buried with the dead. By the Eastern Han dynasty (25–220), this had become standard practice among the elite. Members of the royal family, in particular, were encased in jade suits, and their orifices—ears, eyes, nostrils, mouth, anus, and genitals—were plugged with small pieces of jade, as jade was believed to have the power to preserve the corpse from decay. The cicada was one of the standard forms for small burial jades during this period and in following centuries. They were generally placed in the mouth of the deceased.

The present example is carved in a highly abstract style. A few sharp cuts represent the cicada's head, eyes, and pointed wings on the back and the mouth and ribbed belly on the underside. The craftsman who made this little sculpture minimized the carvings so as to best present the lustrous quality of the polished stone. This reductionist approach is typical of the decorative style of the time, which is seen also in the jade pig found in the same tomb (cat. no. 16).

ZS

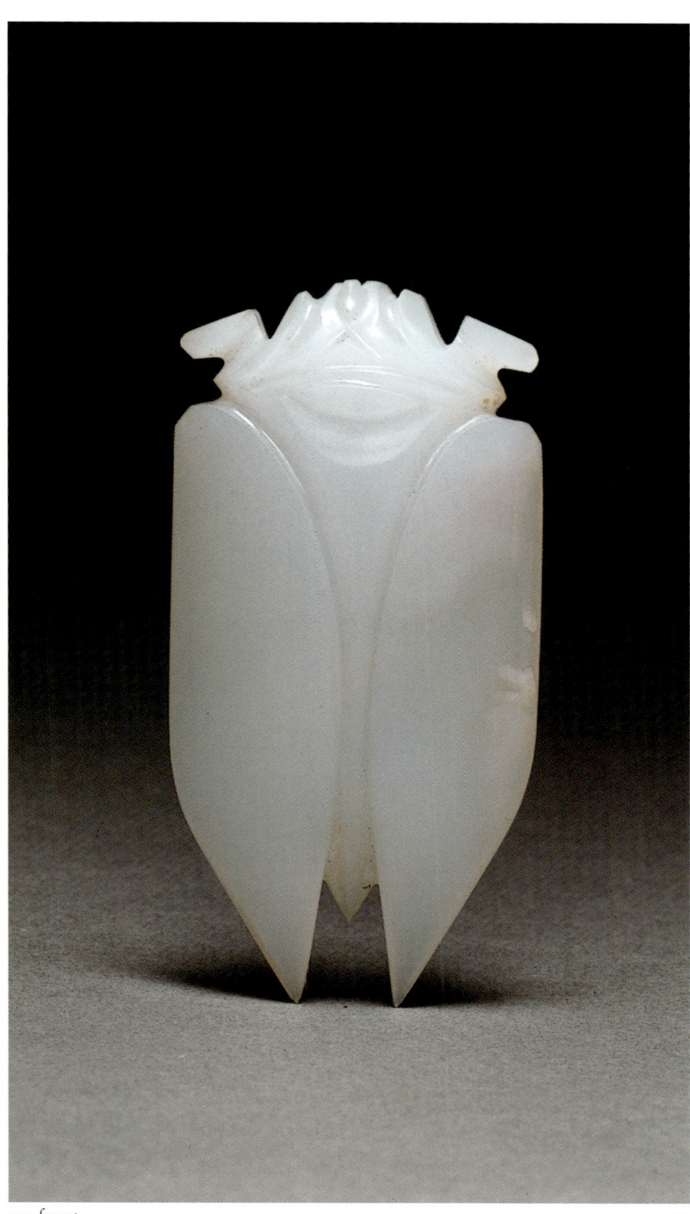

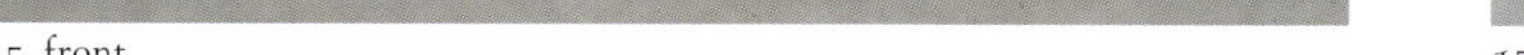
15, front

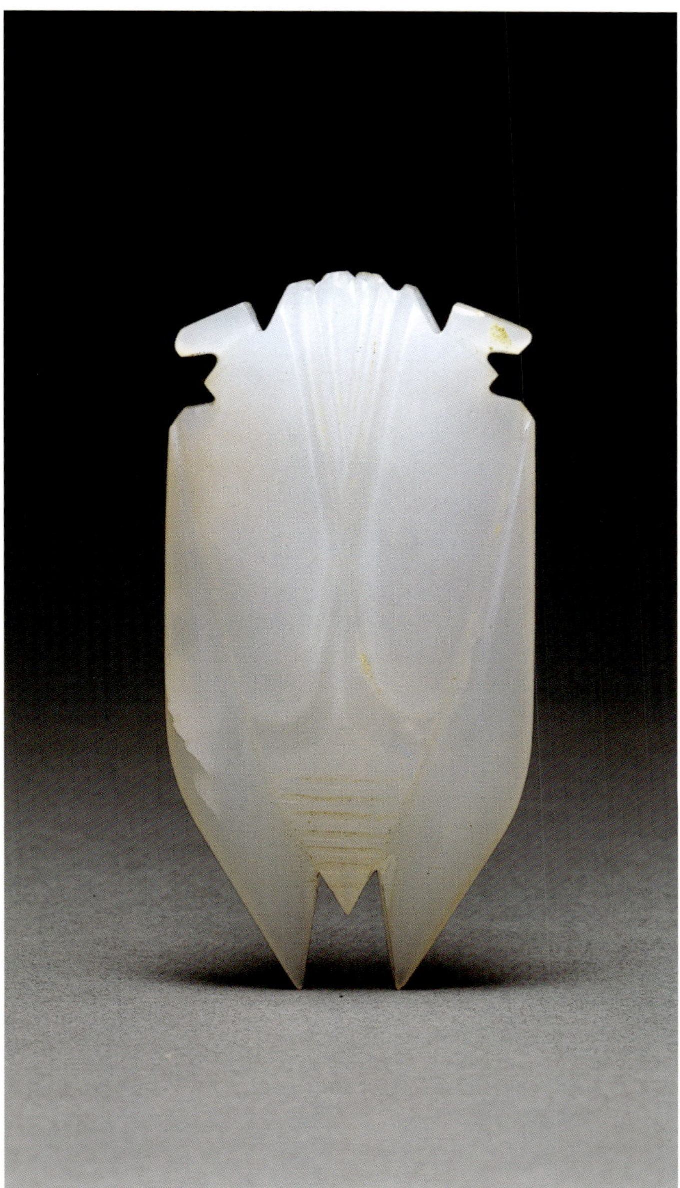
15, back

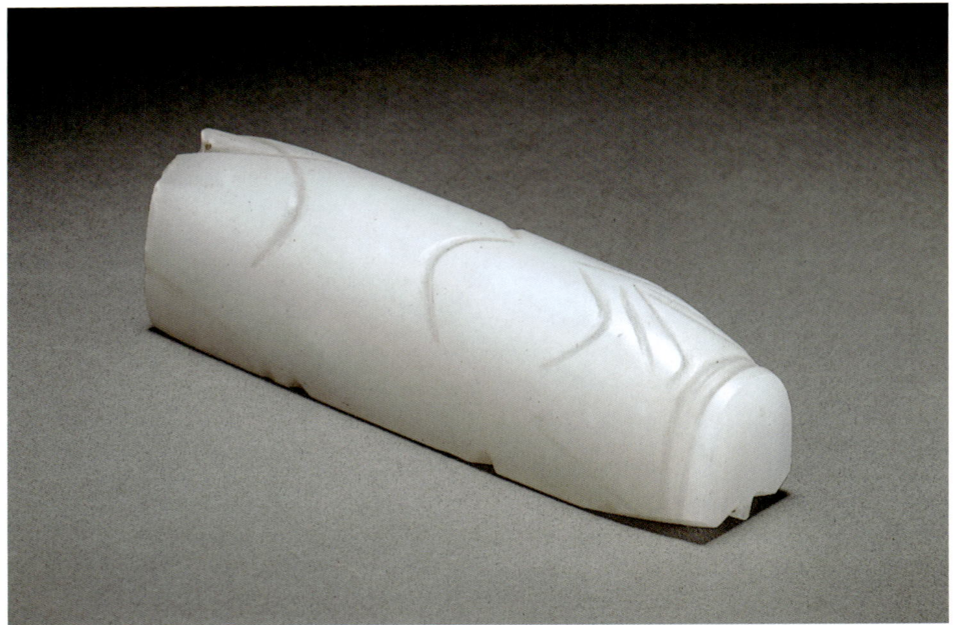

16

Recumbent Pig

Eastern Han dynasty (25–220)
Jade (nephrite)
Length 4 in. (10.3 cm)
Excavated from the tomb of Liu Yan (d. 90), Dingzhou, Hebei Province, 1959
Hebei Provincial Museum

EXCAV. REPORT in *Kaogu xuebao* 1964.2

This sculpture of a recumbent pig is carved out of a rectangular block of white jade. Deeply beveled cuts define the broad snout, ears, shoulders, haunches, and curled tail. Four small notches on the sides represent the feet. Two small holes, one under the tail and the other under the snout, were drilled for purposes of attachment. The surface of the pig is polished to a high gloss.

One of the most common tomb furnishings, jade pigs have been found in numerous burials that date from the Han (206 B.C.–A.D. 220) through the Six Dynasties (220–589), with their representation ranging from fairly realistic to completely stylized. The earliest examples, a pair, were found in the hands of the deceased in an early Western Han (206 B.C.–A.D. 9) tomb at Xuzhou, Jiangsu.[1] They are somewhat crudely fashioned, with one end tapered to a blunt point to represent the snout and the other end rounded to represent the haunch. Nearly all jade pigs found in slightly later tombs of the Western Han are carved in a more realistic style—the head, snout, and legs well modeled and their ears carefully dished to a low concave with raised rims. The present example illustrates a dramatic stylistic change that occurred in the Eastern Han (25–220), when the carving is reduced to a few sharp cuts, creating a severely abstract form. Also by this time, the placing of jade pigs in the hands of the deceased had become standard practice. The meaning of such a practice is not found in the historical records of the burial code, but because pigs were regarded as a symbol of wealth, it was probably desirable for the dead to hold them as they stepped into the afterlife.

ZS

1. Xuzhou bowuguan 1974: 121.

17

Monkey

Eastern Han dynasty (25–220)
Wood
Height 12¾ in. (32.5 cm)
Excavated at Wuwei, Gansu Province
Gansu Provincial Museum

18

Geese

Eastern Han dynasty (25–220)
Wood
Max. height 2 in. (5 cm)
Excavated at Wuwei, Gansu Province
Gansu Provincial Museum

REFERENCE: Zhang Pengchuan and Wu Yiru 1984

The district of Wuwei was the administrative seat of the prefecture of Liangzhou (present-day Gansu) in the Eastern Han period (25–220). It was also a center of learning. Both of these aspects of Wuwei history have been amply confirmed by recent archaeological finds of books (the classics and medicinal formulae) and documents (administrative and funerary) written on strips of wood or bamboo. Wooden boards were sometimes used for short documents (see cat. no. 86).

For art history, the most rewarding archaeological finds from Wuwei have been the wooden funerary sculptures from (mostly Eastern) Han tombs.[1] These sculptures are mostly of domestic animals and chariots (see cat. no. 80). Irrespective of size, Wuwei wooden sculptures display a remarkable sureness of touch in the craft of sculpting, resulting in lively forms with minimal "cuts" that were never retouched and were left unpolished; some pieces were subsequently decorated with pigments. The monkey (opposite, top) and the flock of geese (opposite, bottom) are representative examples.

The minimalist style seems to have been an innovation of the Eastern Han. Wooden funerary sculptures of the earlier (Western) Han period (206 B.C.–A.D. 9)

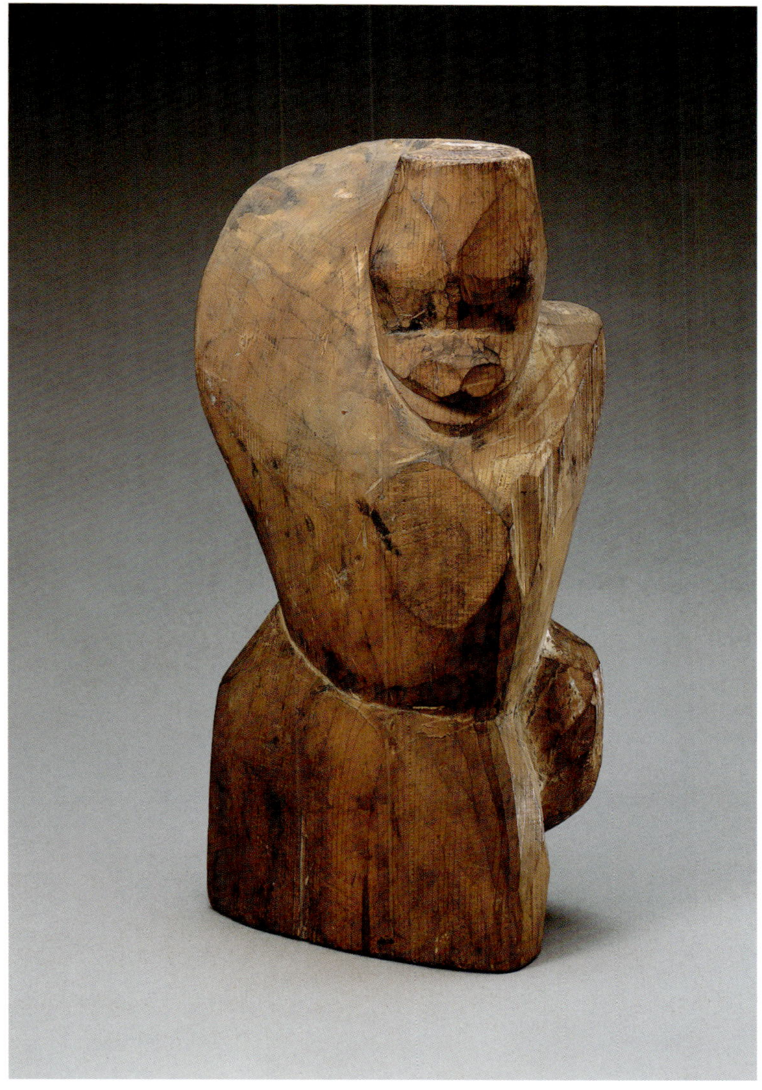

17

were polished and generally lacquered.[2] Eastern Han carvings of jade also show signs of minimalism (see cat. nos. 15, 16).

JCYW

1. Zhang Pengchuan and Wu Yiru 1984.
2. Nanjing bowuyuan 2003.

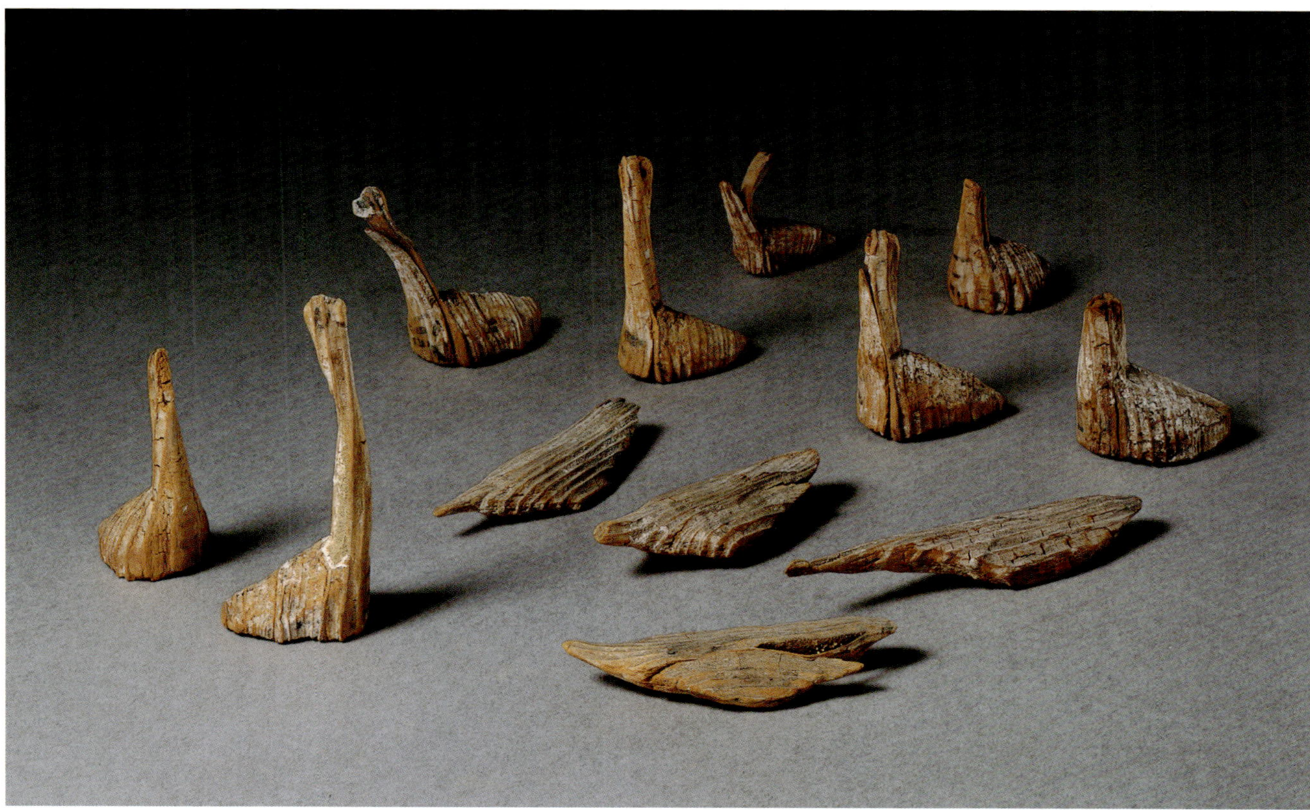

18

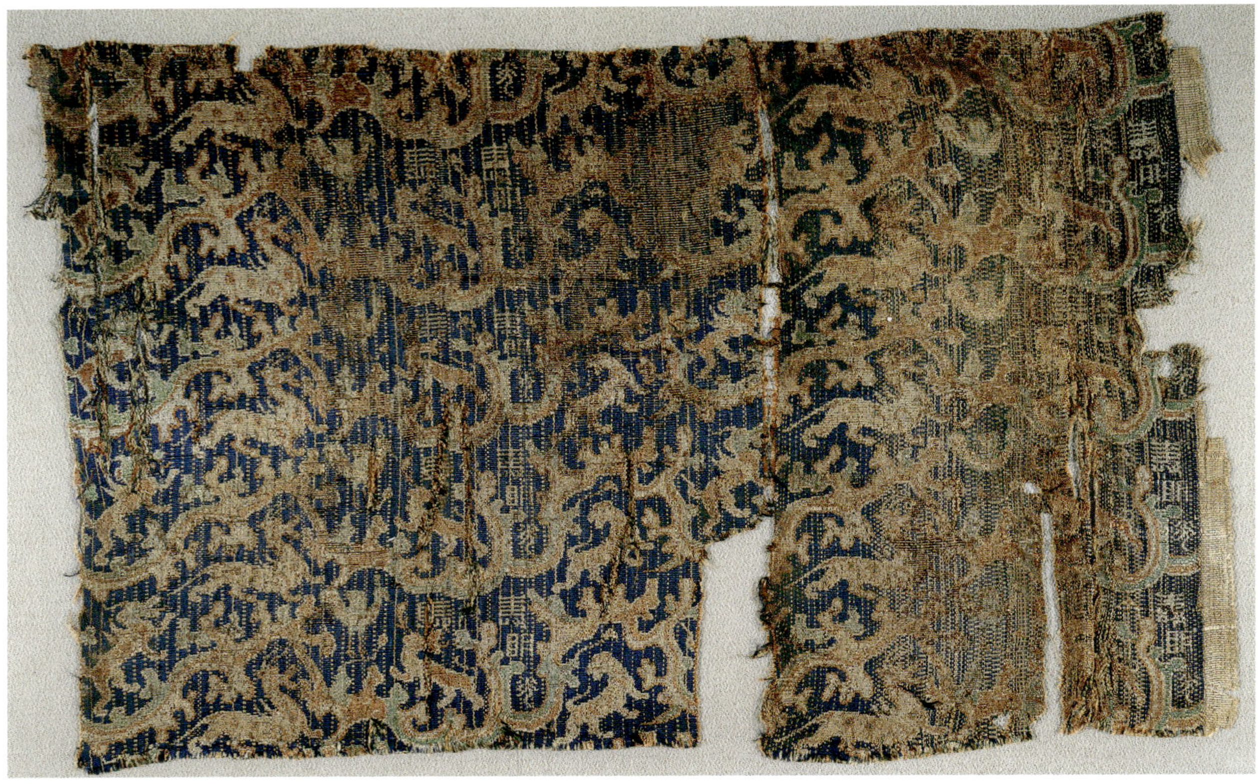

19

Textile with animals and woven inscription

1st–3rd century
Woven silk (1:4 warp-faced compound tabby)
Warp 8⅞ in. (22.5 cm); weft 14½ in. (37 cm)
Excavated at Loulan, Bayingolin, Xinjiang Uygur Autonomous Region, 1980
Xinjiang Institute of Archaeology

Excav. report in *Wenwu* 1988.7

From the Han to the Jin dynasty (ca. 1st–3rd century), the pattern of clouds and animals was a popular motif on Chinese *jin* silk—referred to as Han-style *jin* silk—along the Silk Road. Examples of this type of silk have been found archaeologically all over China, extending to the far western areas.

This textile fragment, from Tomb 2 at Gutai in Loulan, Xinjiang, is representative of the type. It is woven with the Chinese characters *chang shou ming guang* (longevity and brightness). The motif of mountain-shaped clouds, symbolizing the mists and clouds surrounding the immortal mountains, was adopted in other contemporary textiles. Two such examples are *jin* silks woven, respectively, with the characters *guang shan* (broad mountain)[1] and *deng gao ming wang si hai* (ascending to have a clear view of the four seas).[2] In addition to the inscriptions, which refer or allude to mountains, trees and tree leaves among clouds, seen also in the present textile, further indicate the presence of a mountain. Here, four animals and one bird are visible: from the right selvedge, a bear climbing a mountain, a tiger looking back, a small animal (probably a wolf), a vermilion bird, and a powerful, winged dragon. The four Chinese characters in seal script, woven between the tiger and the wolf, provide the title.[3]

This textile consists of two surviving fragments that have been joined. The selvedge on the right is preserved. Contemporary *jin* silks suggest that the original loom width would have been about 45 cm, with two pattern repeats—visually, not technically—in the weft direction. This piece is woven with five colors in the structure of 1:4 warp-faced compound tabby. Dark blue and intermittent brown warps in a sprinkled pattern are used for the ground; yellow and green for the body of the design; and brown (originally red) and cream (originally white) for the outlines. Five-colored silk textiles, quite popular during the Han dynasty, correspond to the theory of the Five Elements (metal, wood, water, fire, and earth), the Five Directions (west, north, east, south, and center), and the Five Planets (Venus, Jupiter, Mercury, Mars, and Saturn). Another piece with five colors, excavated at Niya, is a *jin* silk inscribed *wu xing chu dong fang li zhong quo* (the appearance of the Five Planets in the east is symbolic of China's prosperity).[4] Textiles such as the present one, in which five colors are used throughout the loom width, were extremely difficult to weave and were produced only in imperial workshops.

Jin silks with the characters *ming guang* are documented in contemporary sources. For example, Lu Hui (ca. 350) of the Jin dynasty notes in the *Ye zhong ji* (Notes on the City of Ye) that both *da* (large) *ming guang* and *xiao* (small) *ming guang* were produced in the imperial silk workshop established by the Later Zhao emperor Shi Hu (r. 335–49). Comparable excavated examples include a piece of poorly preserved *jin* silk with the characters *chang le ming guang* also from Tomb 2 at Gutai.[5] Except for the inscription and the vermilion bird, which is replaced by a horse and rider, the design is quite similar to that of the present example. Another similar textile is a pair of silk trousers with the inscription *chang le da ming guang* from Tomb 3 at Niya.[6] Its design corresponds closely to that of the *chang le ming guang jin* silk, although the characters *chang le da ming guang* are scattered among the pictorial elements. This piece, a 1:3 warp-faced compound tabby, also has a dark blue ground with intermittent yellow warps.

The *ming guang* in all three textiles refers to the Ming Guang Palace, built during the reign of the Han emperor Wudi (140–87 B.C.). All three inscriptions—*chang shou* (longevity) *ming guang*, *chang le* (eternal happiness) *ming guang*, and *chang le da* (immense eternal happiness) *ming guang*—are thus meant to celebrate the longevity and bliss of the Lord of the Ming Guang Palace. ZF

1. Huang Nengfu 1985: 34, 92, no. 80, pl. 80.
2. Ibid.: 36, 94, no. 82, pl. 82.
3. *Jin* silks are often referred to in contemporary documents solely by their woven inscriptions.
4. Zhao Feng and Yu Ziyong 2000: 62–63, no. 24, fig. 24f.
5. Huang Nengfu 1986: 37, 94–95, no. 83, pl. 83.
6. Zhao Feng and Yu Ziyong 2000: 58–59, no. 21, figs. 21a, d.

20

Face cover with dogwood

1st–3rd century
Woven silk (1:3 warp-faced compound tabby)
24½ x 22⅞ in. (62.1 x 58 cm)
Excavated at Niya, Minfeng, Xinjiang Uygur Autonomous Region, 1995
Xinjiang Institute of Archaeology

REFERENCE: Ruan Qiurong 1998

The motif of the dogwood is a notable exception to the prevalent pattern of animals and clouds among the designs of Han *jin* silk. The dogwood, a deciduous tree, blooms in March with red-purple flowers and bears pepper-shaped fruits in the summer. At maturity, the fruit breaks open to yield seeds with an intense fragrance. It was the custom to wear sprigs of dogwood to ward off evil spirits while climbing hills during the Zhongyang festival, held on the ninth day of the ninth lunar month of the Chinese calendar. The pattern of three-lobed leaves on Han textiles was considered to represent the dogwood and was probably adopted for its auspicious connotations.

This piece, a face cover excavated from Tomb 3 at Niya Cemetery 1, has red silk tabby sewn along three sides and a silk ribbon on each of two corners. Structurally a 1:3 warp-faced compound tabby, it is woven with white warps for the ground and red, blue, gray green, and light orange for the pattern. While five colors are employed, only four are present in any given area, as the gray green and light orange alternate in different sections.

The dogwood is represented with lobed leaves, curling tendrils and branches, and roots and trunks of geometric shapes. The loom width measures 45.3 cm, with 4 cm repeats in the warp direction. The pattern appears to repeat one and a half times in the weft direction, but in fact from selvedge to selvedge the pattern repeats visually but not technically.

Among the earliest textiles with recognizable dogwood patterns are three textiles—woven, embroidered, and printed—found in the Han tombs at Mawangdui.[1] The woven example, a dark red *jin*, shows a combination of dogwood fruit, seeds, and branches. The best-defined and most realistic depiction of the dogwood is to be found in the embroidered textile.[2] The third piece is a fine tabby with printed and painted floral scrolls. Dogwood-patterned *jin* silks were found in Loulan as well; the designs are similar but on a red ground. During the Sixteen Kingdoms period (304–439), *jin* silks with designs of dogwood were recorded among

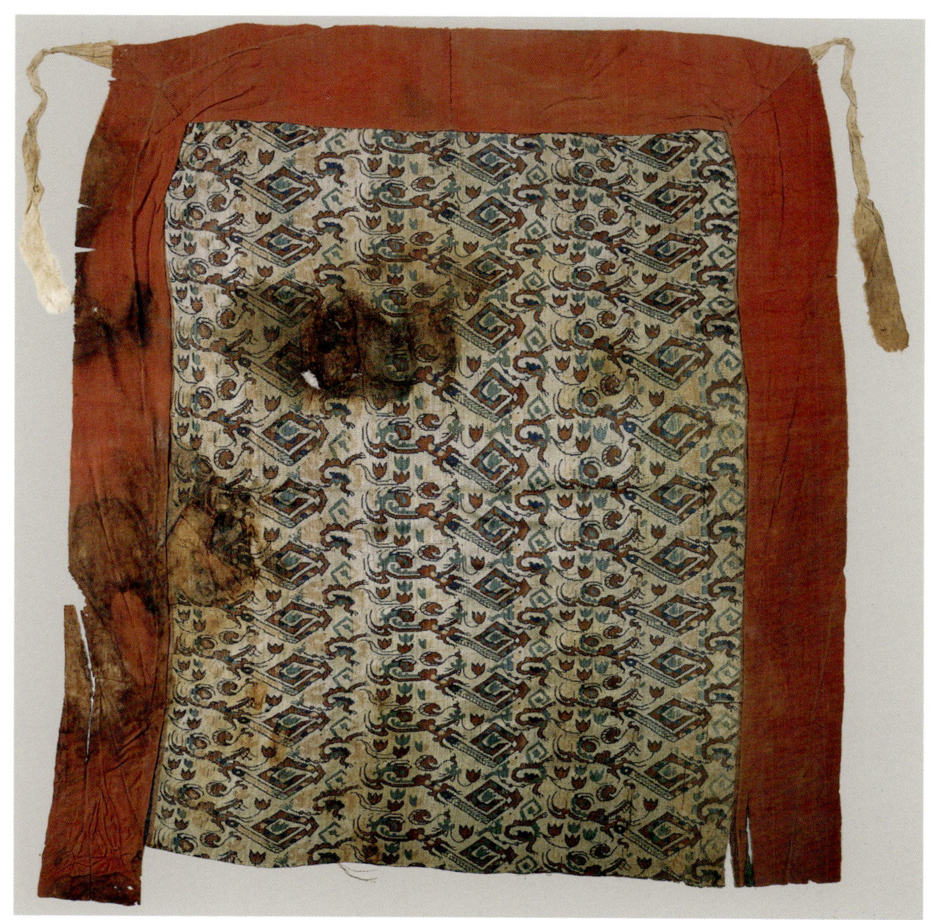

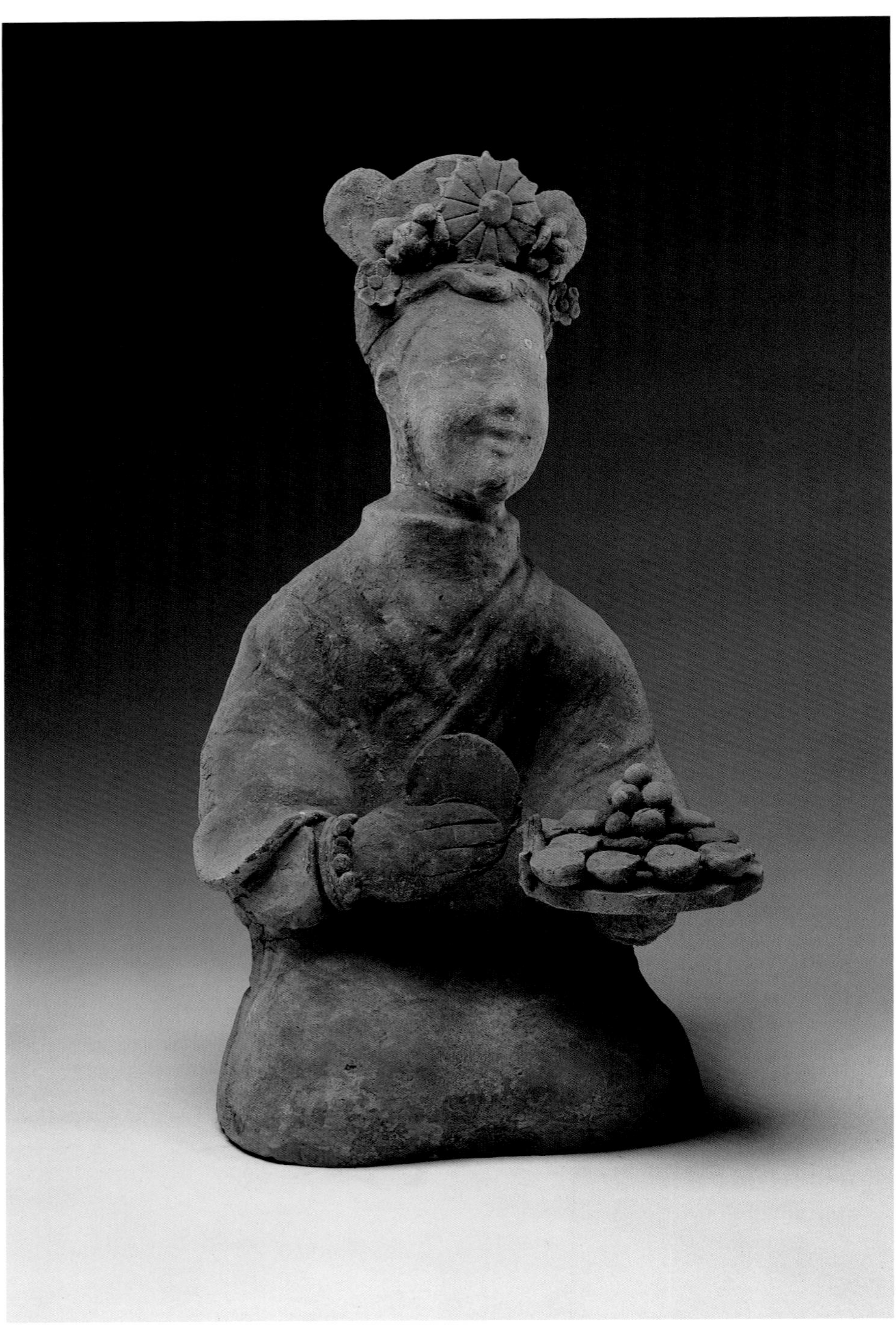

the production at the imperial weaving workshop of the Later Zhao emperor Shi Hu (r. 335–49), attesting to the pattern's enduring popularity.

ZF

1. Illustrated in Huang Nengfu 1985, vol. 6: 70, no. 60.
2. Shanghai shi fangzhi kexue yanjiuyuan et al. 1980.

21

Attendant holding a platter

Three Kingdoms, Shu (221–263)
Earthenware
Height 18⅛ in. (46 cm)
Excavated at Tujing, Zhongxian, Sichuan Province, 1981
Sichuan Provincial Museum

Excav. report in *Wenwu* 1985.7

This female attendant, holding a platter with cups and what looks like a dish of fruit in one hand and a disk (mirror?) in the other, is one of a large number of pottery figures found in chamber tombs that were cut into the cliff surface on the banks of a tributary of the Yangzi River in eastern Sichuan. Judging by the coins and types of objects found in the tombs, they can be attributed to the state of Shu (221–263) in the period of the Three Kingdoms.

The sculptural style of the figures, of which the present example is representative, is not unlike what is found in other parts of China at sites of the same period. What distinguishes the Sichuan sculptures is the unusual headgear of the female figures, which hints at early contact with India.

JCYW

22

Stele for Cao Quan

Eastern Han dynasty (25–220), dated 185
Rubbing, ink on paper
107⅛ x 37⅜ in. (272 x 95 cm)
Excavated at Heyang, Shaanxi Province, 16th century
Museum of the Forest of Steles

Reference: Shaanxi sheng bowuguan 1988

Inscribed stone monuments date back to at least the fifth century B.C. in China, but it was during the last century of the Eastern or Later Han dynasty (25–220), particularly during the reigns of Emperors Huandi (r. 147–67) and Lingdi (r. 168–89), that monumental stone steles (*libei*) became the preferred way in which to memorialize deceased members of one's family or to celebrate virtuous deeds.[1] In its standard form, the Han stele is a vertical rectangular slab whose polished face is engraved with a commemorative text. The slab is held upright by a base carved to resemble a tortoise, while an ornamental capstone—often depicting intertwined dragons—forms the crown.[2] Thus, the body of the stele, framed by the mythical creatures of the earthly and heavenly realms, became a suitable space on which to leave a permanent record of human affairs.

The study of steles by later calligraphers was usually not conducted through examination of the stone itself, however, but through ink rubbings. By this means, accurate reproductions of the original text were widely disseminated. In this modern example, the rubbing preserves the vertical format of the original stone. More often, such rubbings were cut up and reconfigured into the more convenient album format.[3]

The Stele for Cao Quan (dated 185) celebrates the life of the virtuous official Cao Quan.[4] The text, written in large-scale characters arrayed in twenty columns of forty-five characters each, begins by stating Cao's given name and place of birth near present-day Dunhuang, Gansu. It next recounts his illustrious ancestry and includes a brief description of his youth.

In the year 169, Cao was appointed sector commander in the Western Regions and sent to punish Hede, the king of Shule (a vassal state in the region of Kashgar, in present-day Xinjiang), who had stopped sending tribute. Cao responded with such force that "Hede's face turned white, he retreated, and died."[5] This account is particularly noteworthy because it reveals both Han domination deep in Central Asia and the great importance placed on trade along the Silk Road at this time.

In 184, after serving in various administrative posts and then enjoying a period in retirement, Cao was summoned to administer Heyang, in present-day Shaanxi, which is where the stele was commissioned. The bulk of the text praises Cao's compassionate administration of Heyang, as further attested by the more than fifty donors listed on the back of the stele.

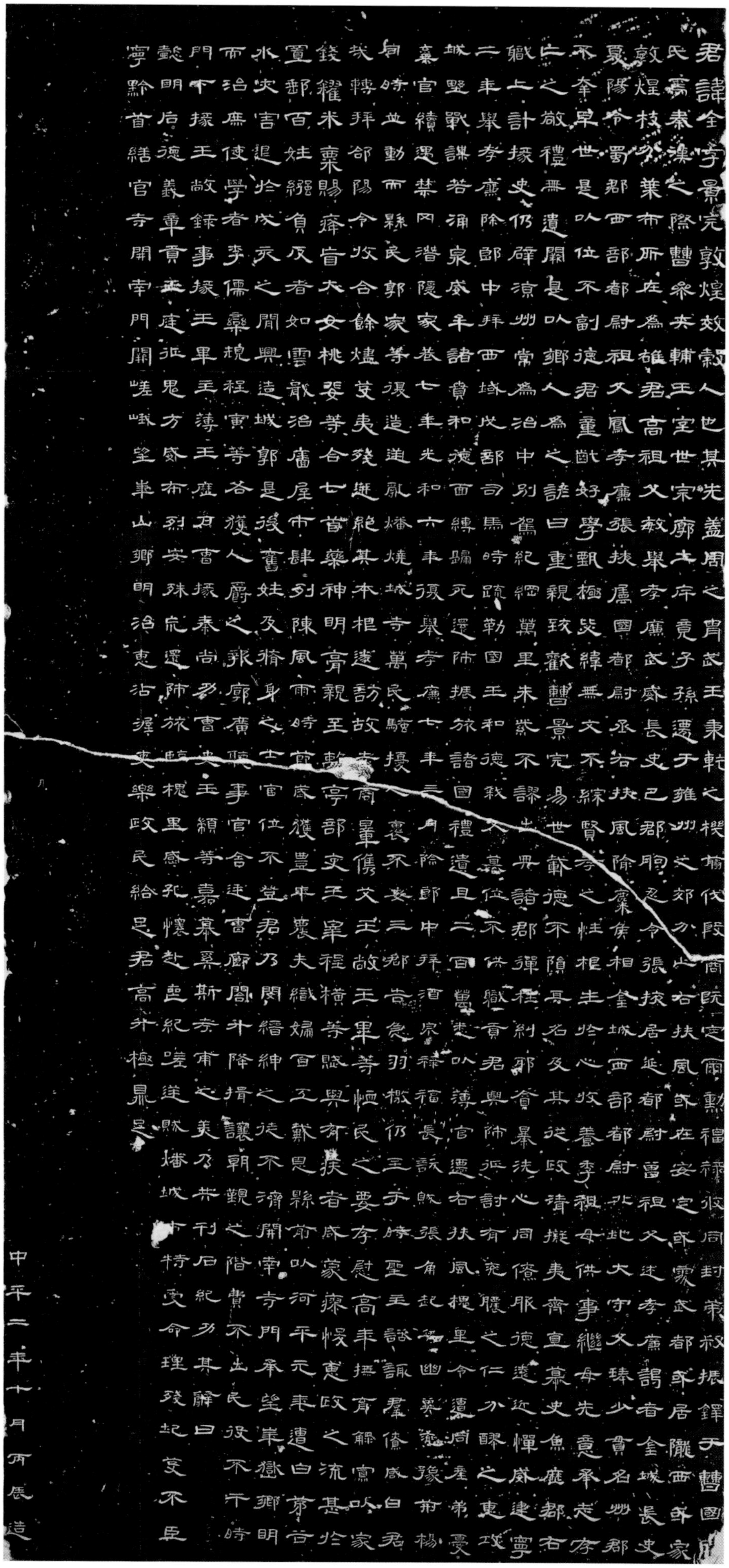

The unknown calligrapher was a master of the Han institutional style of writing known as clerical script. In contrast to standard script, which developed later, clerical script, using lines of uniform width, is balanced, rectilinear, symmetrical, and regularly proportioned to fit a uniform grid. Only the flared endings of some of the horizontal and diagonal strokes reveal the use of a flexible-tipped brush rather than a stylus. By the fifth century, standard script had replaced clerical script for the majority of stele inscriptions and clerical script was reserved for large-scale titles or other contexts in which a degree of formality was sought.

At some point in its history, the Stele for Cao Quan lost its capstone and base and was covered with soil. It was unearthed early in the Wanli reign era (1573–1619). The well-preserved text immediately became a standard source for the study of Han clerical script. In 1957, it was moved to the Forest of Steles, the former Confucian temple in Xi'an that holds the finest collection of ancient steles in China. MKH

1. The earliest extant Chinese inscribed stone monuments are the Ten Stone Drums, which date to the fifth century B.C. and bear poems commemorating hunting expeditions; see *Shodō zenshū* 1954–69, vol. 1 (1954), pls. 131–34.
2. For the origins of the stele form, see ibid., vol. 2 (1958): 30–36.
3. For rubbings as dated by the evolving state of the stele, see Wang Zhuanghong 1981: 123–26. For Ming-era rubbings of the stone, see Qi Gong 1987 and Zhongguo guojia tushuguan 2001, vol. 2: 5–67. For a discussion of the role of ink rubbings in the history of Chinese calligraphy, see McNair 1995. On the reconfiguration of stele texts into the album format, see Ledderose 2001: 228–30.
4. For a complete reproduction and transcription of this stele's text, see Matsui 1959. For a summary of Qing scholarly evaluations of the stele's artistic significance, see *Zhongguo shufa jianshang da cidian* 1989: 116; see also *Shodō zenshū* 1954–69, vol. 2 (1958): 197–98, pls. 118–19.
5. For an analysis of how the stele account differs from that recorded in the *Hou Hanshu* (History of the Later Han), see Ma Yong 1990.

II

The Coming of the Xianbei

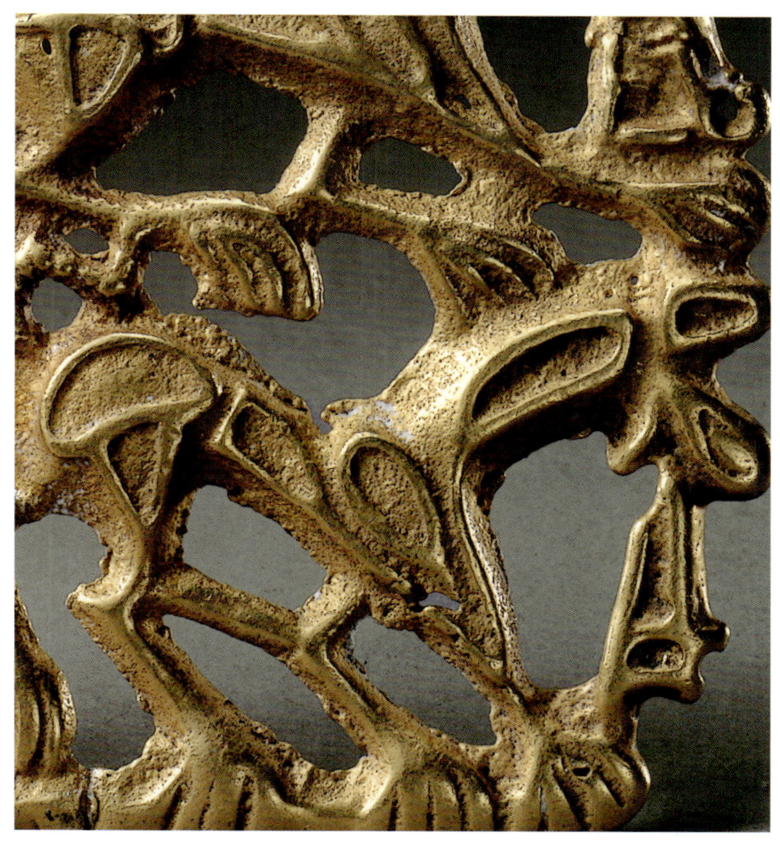

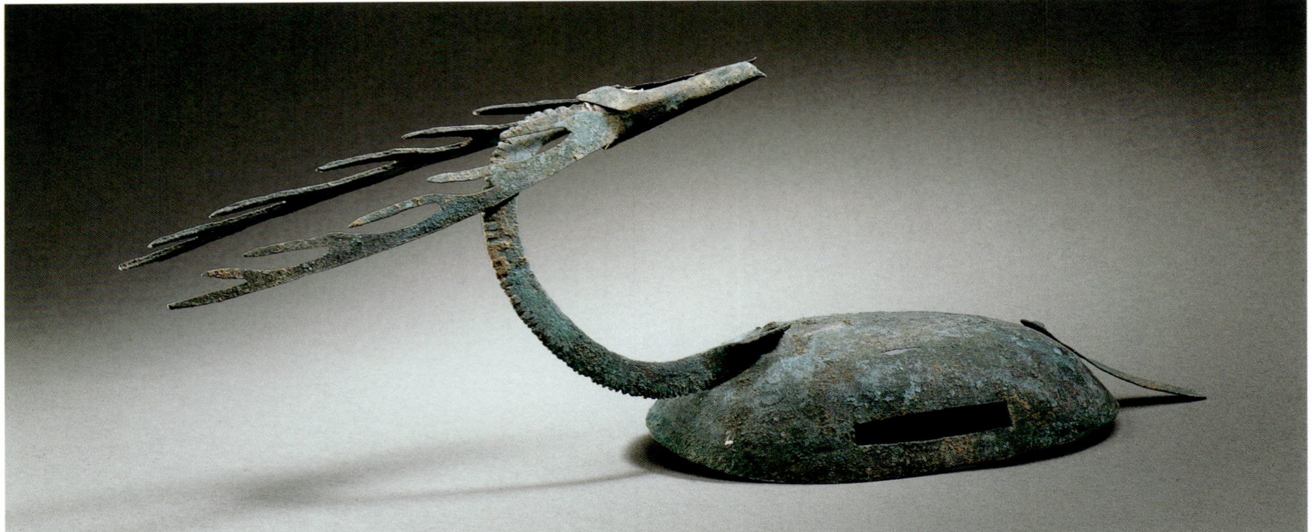

23

Deer-shaped object

Sixteen Kingdoms, Former Yan (337–370)
Bronze
Length 12¼ in. (31 cm)
Excavated at Lamadong, Beipiao, Liaoning Province, 1993–97
Liaoning Institute of Archaeology

REFERENCE: Liaoning sheng wenwu kaogu yanjiusuo 2002, no. 108

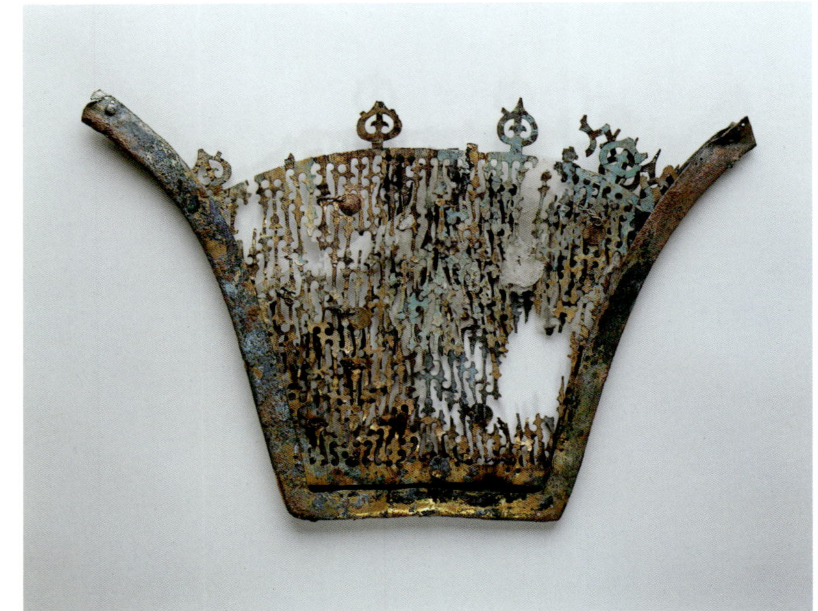

24

Horse ornament

Sixteen Kingdoms, Former Yan (337–370)
Gilt bronze
Max. width 11 in. (28 cm)
Found at Lamadong, Beipiao, Liaoning Province, 1993–98
Liaoning Institute of Archaeology

EXCAV. REPORT in *Wenwu* 2003.3

25

Saddle plates

Sixteen Kingdoms, Former Yan (337–370)
Gilt bronze
a. Front plate: max. width 17¾ in. (45 cm)
b. Back plate: max. width 23¼ in. (59 cm)
Excavated at Chaoyang, Liaoning Province, 1988
Liaoning Institute of Archaeology

EXCAV. REPORT in *Wenwu* 1997.11

These objects were all found in the vicinity of the city of Chaoyang, Liaoning, the area that the Murong Xianbei made their base after they came into western Liaoning from the north sometime in the third century. From this base, they expanded into central China as far as Henan Province during the mid-fourth century and to which they retreated at the end of the same century. The precise chronology of the numerous sites around Chaoyang has yet to be established, but these objects are generally held to be from the Former Yan (337–370) period.[1]

The striking object with an attachment of antlers, suggesting a deer looking backward, is of uncertain use. The deer is one of the oldest motifs in nomadic art.

The fan-shaped ornament, a crupper finial, is representative of early Murong Xianbei metalwork. The gilt-bronze object is in openwork, with attachments of

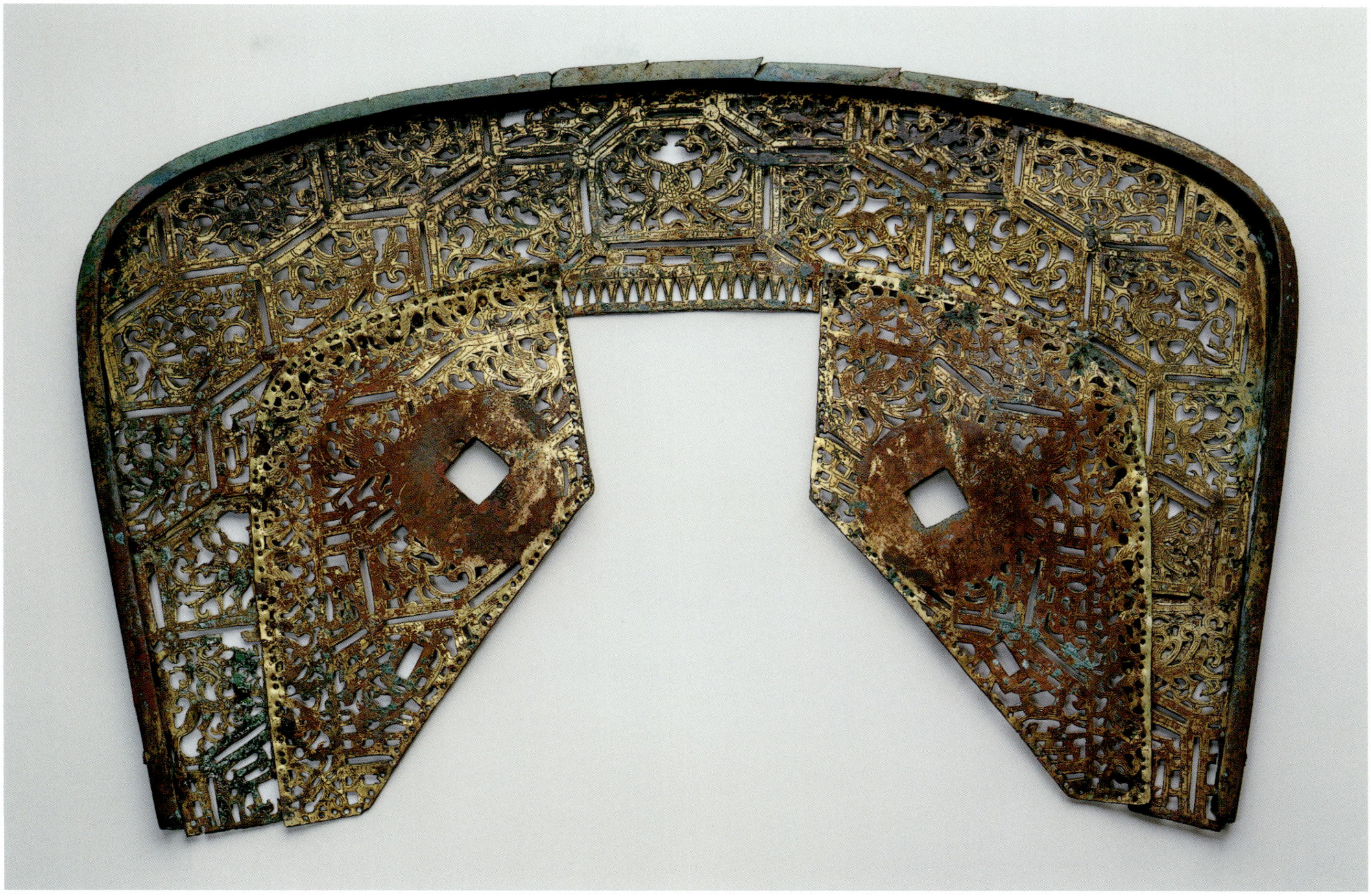

25 a

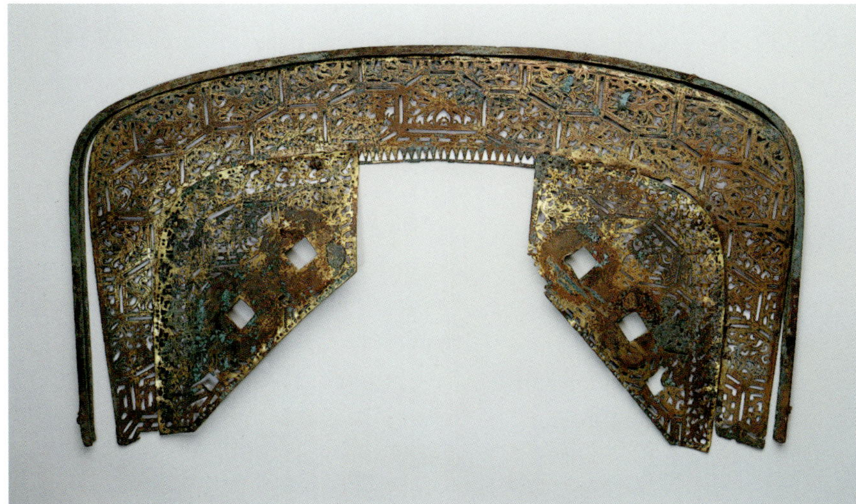

25 b

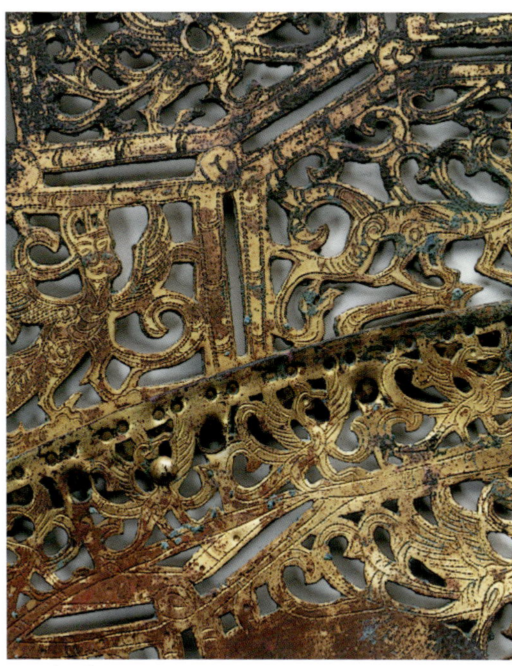

25 a, detail

circular disks. This style of ornamentation suggests contacts with Central Asia, as far as Bactria (see cat. no. 36).

Of greatest interest are the pair of saddle plates (above). The openwork pattern on these decorative plates, composed of hexagons enclosing fantastic animals and birds, appears to be unique to the Murong Xianbei at this time; it would later be transmitted to the Northern Wei, after the conquest of the last of the Yan dynasties in 436. At about the same time, the pattern was adopted by Koreans of the Silla kingdom, in the southeast quarter of the peninsula.

JCYW

1. Liaoning sheng wenwu kaogu yanjiusuo 2002.

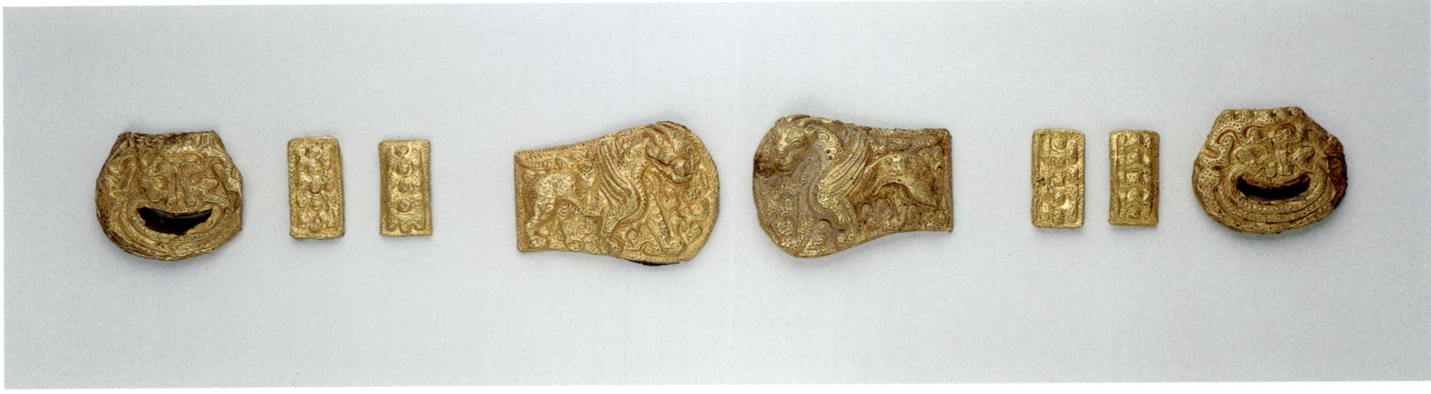

26

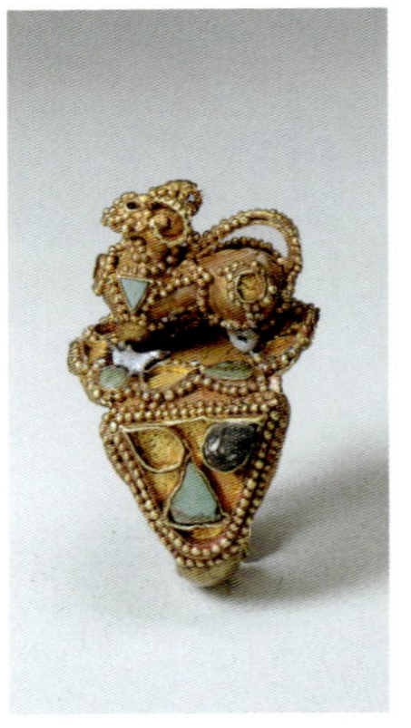

27

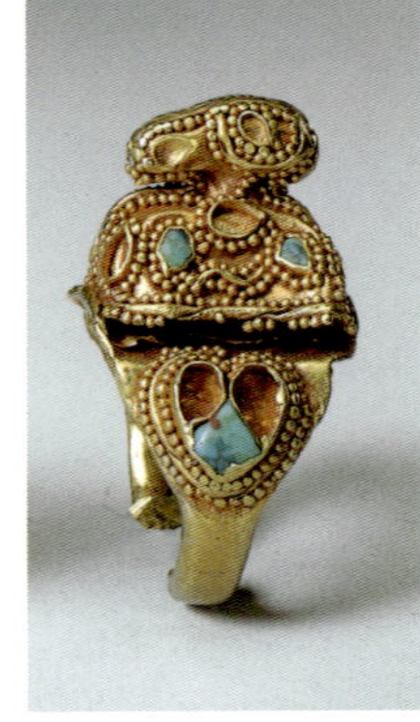

28

26

Belt buckle and plaques with mythical animals

4th–5th century
Gold with iron core
Buckle: length 1⅝ in. (4.2 cm)
Each plaque: length 1⅝ in. (4.2 cm)
Excavated at Tumd zuo Banner, Hohhot, Inner Mongolia Autonomous Region
Inner Mongolia Autonomous Region Museum

Reference: Neimenggu zizhiqu bowuguan 1987: 55

27

Ring with standing ram

4th–5th century
Gold inlaid with turquoise
Height 1¼ in. (3.2 cm)
Excavated at Tumd you Banner, Baotou, Inner Mongolia Autonomous Region
Inner Mongolia Autonomous Region Museum

Reference: Zhang Jingming et al. 1995

28

Ring with recumbent ram

4th–5th century
Gold inlaid with turquoise
Height 1⅝ in. (4.2 cm)
Excavated at Hohhot, Inner Mongolia Autonomous Region
Inner Mongolia Autonomous Region Museum

Reference: Zhang Jingming et al. 1995

The set of belt buckle and plaques and the two rings have been given a relatively late date—fourth to fifth century—because they were found in the general area of activity of the Tuoba Xianbei. However, the style and workmanship of the gold on both the buckle and the plaques are in a much earlier steppe tradition.

Similarly, the use of granulation and stone inlays on the two rings can be traced back to a much earlier period in Central Asia. Indeed, these decorative techniques were introduced into interior China long before the Xianbei appeared on the northern borders of the country.

JCYW

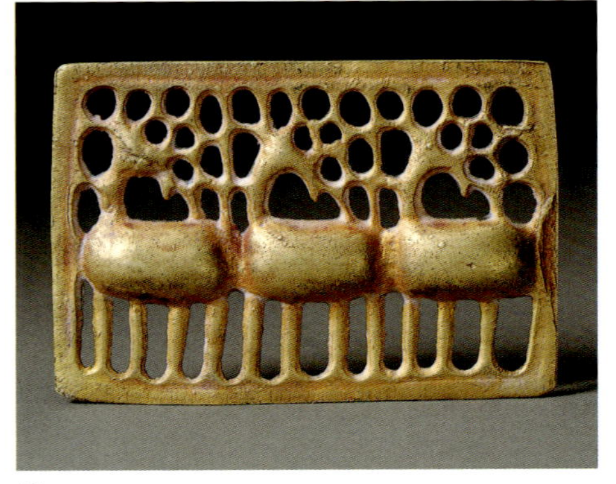

29

29

Plaque with three deer

1st–3rd century
Gold
1¾ x 2 in. (4.5 x 6.8 cm)
Excavated at Sandaowan cemetery, Qahar Youyihou Banner, Ulanqab League, Inner Mongolia Autonomous Region, 1983
Inner Mongolia Autonomous Region Museum

Reference: Zhang Jingming et al. 1995

This type of decorative plaque, with a geometricized image of three deer, has been found in all areas associated with the confederation of nomadic tribes known as the Xianbei and is one of the markers of early Xianbei culture.

The geometricization of animal motifs can be regarded as the final stage of the "animal style" art of the eastern Eurasian steppe. The "geometric" style seems to have begun in about the first century, toward the end of the period of Xiongnu dominance of the Mongolian steppe, and continued into the early Xianbei period.

JCYW

30

Pendant in the shape of a crouching horse

2nd–3rd century
Gold
Pendant: length 3⅛ in. (8 cm)
Excavated at Horqin Zuoyizhong Banner,

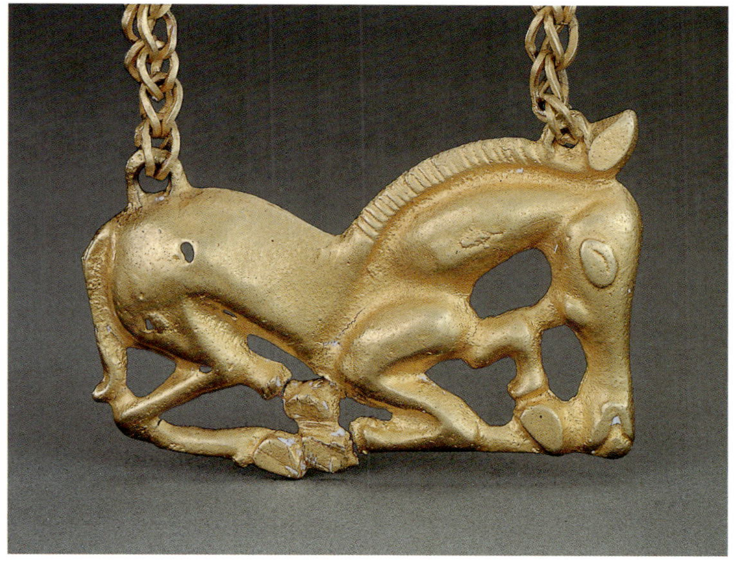

30

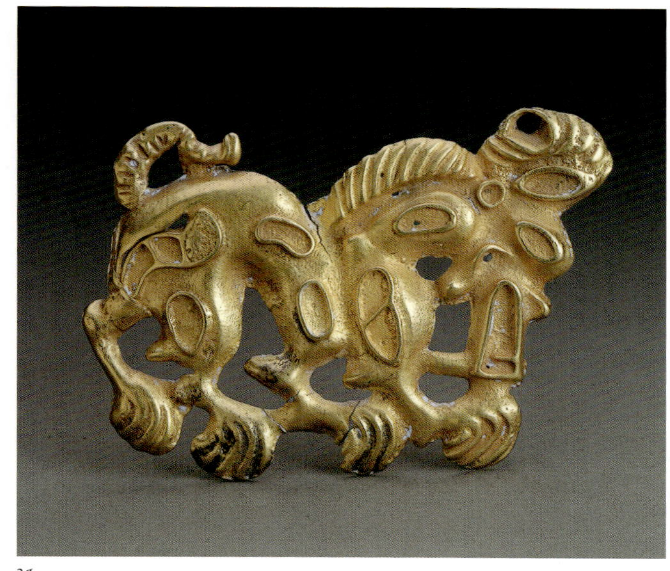

31

Jerim League, Inner Mongolia Autonomous Region, 1984
Jerim League Museum

Excav. report in *Kaogu* 1989.5

The wearing of animal plaques as a pendant on a chain, as opposed to attaching them to clothing or objects, appears to be a Xianbei initiative. JCYW

31

Plaque in the shape of an animal

2nd–3rd century
Gold
Length 3¾ in. (9.5 cm)
Excavated at Kezuozhong Banner, Jerim League, Inner Mongolia Autonomous Region, 1984
Jerim League Museum

Excav. report in *Kaogu* 1989.5

This highly stylized animal (its powerful claws suggesting a predator) is from the same site as the pendant in the shape of a crouching horse (cat. no. 30). Superficially, it is strongly related to the earlier art of the Xiongnu. However, there are features that can be attributed to later developments. The irregularly shaped raised enclosures on the body may be a survival of the cloisons for stone inlays on animal plaques of the Xiongnu period (before the first century A.D.) and were used on this piece as a decorative device with no other function. This aspect and the stylization of the animal form can be regarded as characteristics of Xianbei art.

JCYW

32

Plaque with four animals and inscription "Gold of Yituo" (Yituo jin)

Ca. 300
Gold
Length 4 in. (10 cm)
Found at Xiaobazitan, Ulanqab League, Inner Mongolia Autonomous Region, 1956
Inner Mongolia Autonomous Region Museum

Excav. report in *Wenwu* 2002.8

This is the most important Xianbei plaque that has been discovered to date. Not only is it inscribed with the name of Yituo (d. 305), a leader of the Tuoba Xianbei at the time of their ascendancy in central Mongolia and North China, but it also provides a standard example for dating Xianbei objects of the late third to early fourth century.

Stylistically, the animals of which this plaque is composed are exactly like the plaque in the shape of a crouching animal

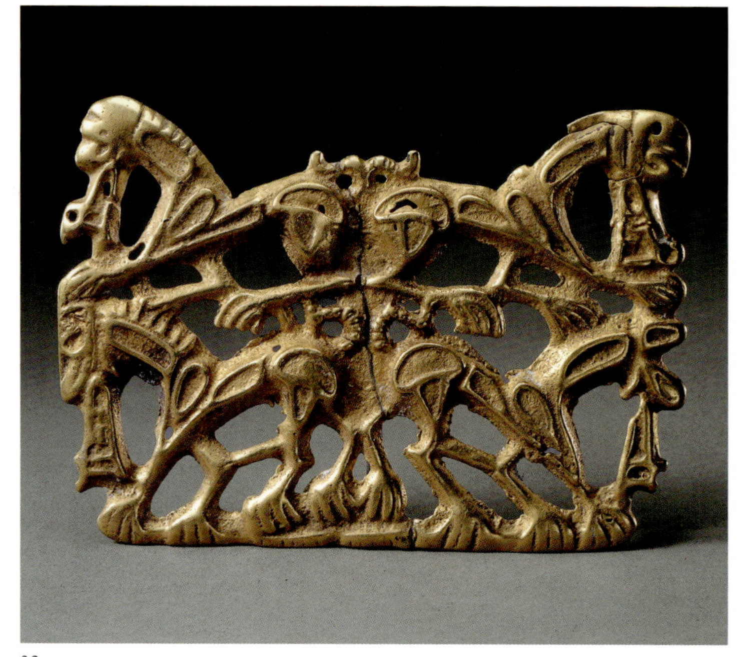

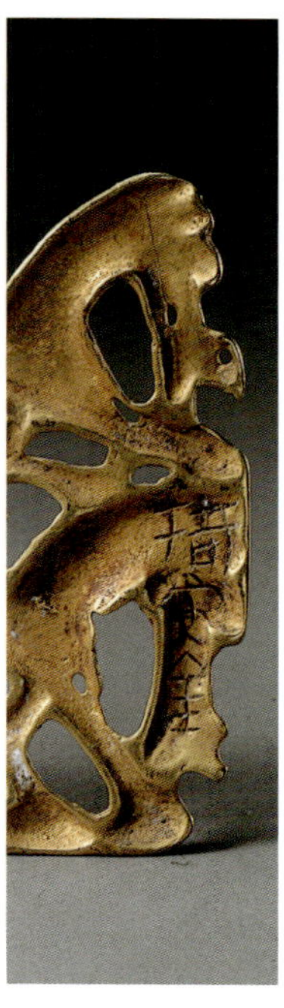

32

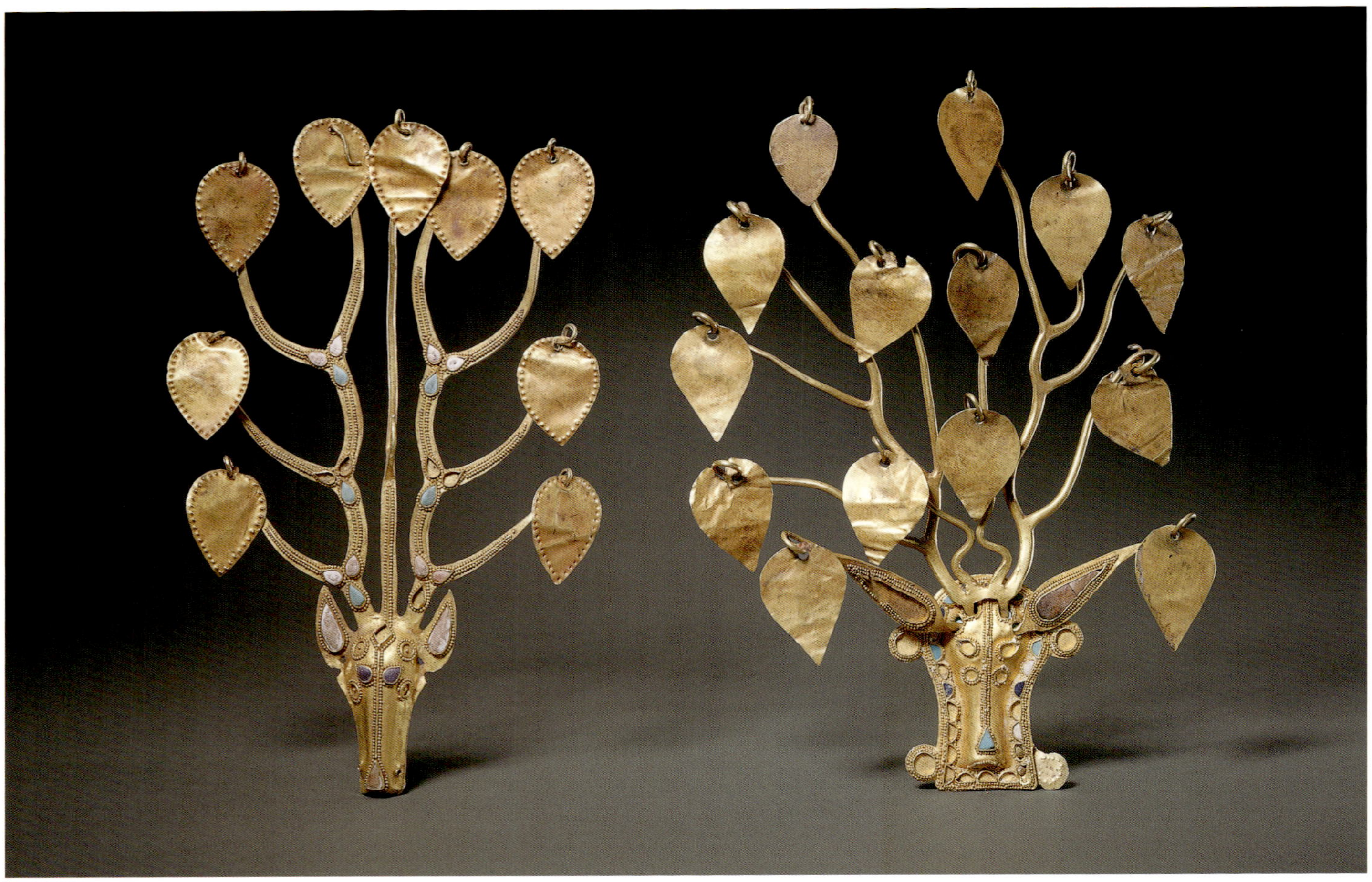

33

(cat. no. 31), which we can regard as typically Xianbei. The one unusual feature is the symmetrical pattern on either side of a vertical central axis. This aspect and the use of Chinese characters for the inscription—*Yituo jin* (Gold of Yituo)—suggest increasing Chinese influence on Xianbei culture by the beginning of the fourth century. JCYW

33
Pair of hat ornaments

3rd–5th century
Gold
Height 6⅜ in. (16.2 cm)
Excavated at Darhan Mumingan Banner, Ulanqab League, Inner Mongolia Autonomous Region, 1981
Inner Mongolia Autonomous Region Museum

Excav. report in *Wenwu* 1984.1

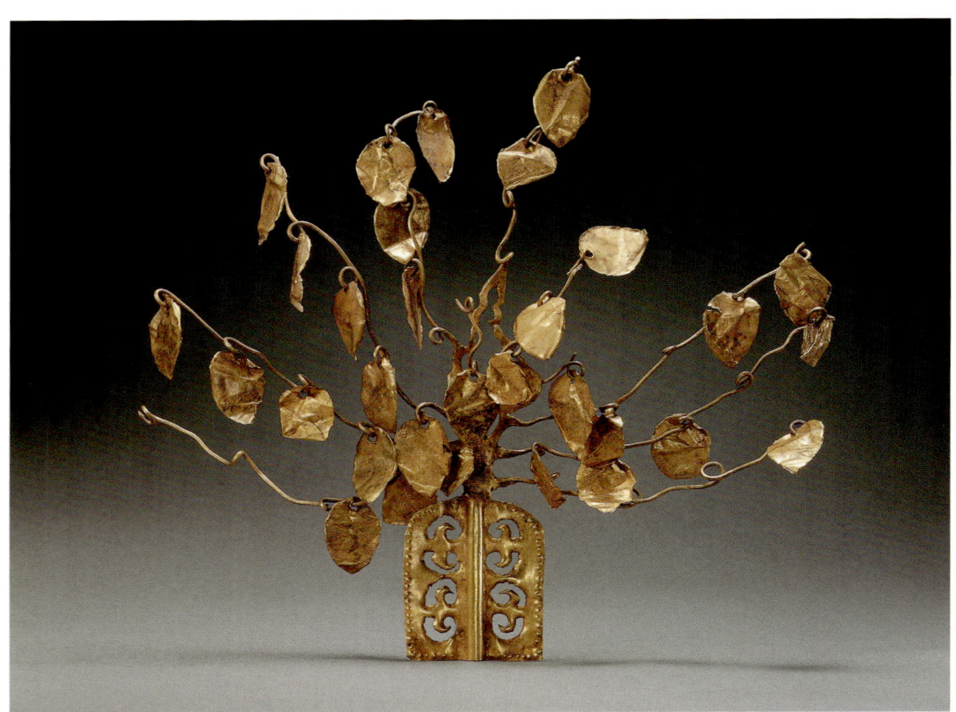

34

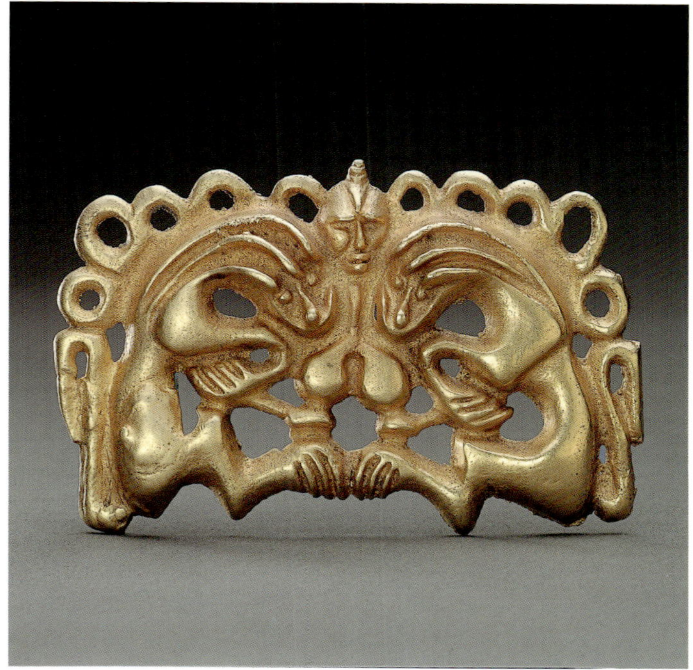

35

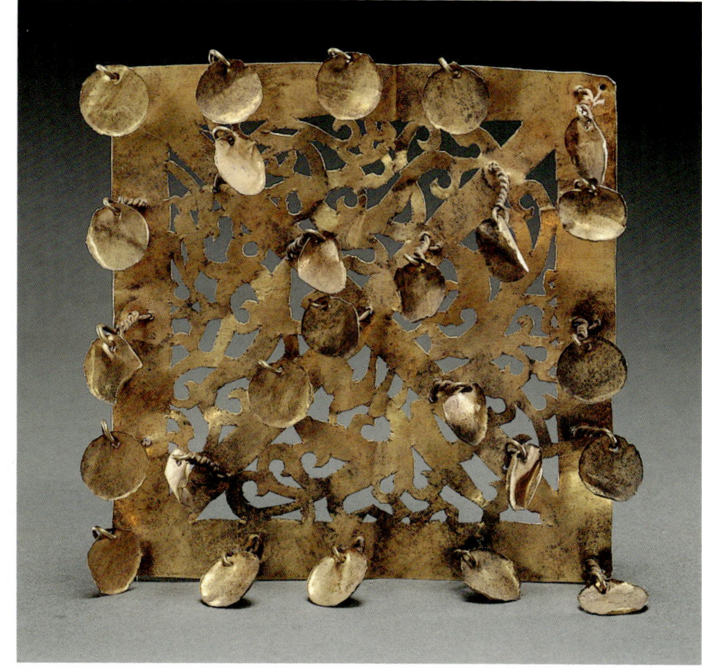

36

34
Hat ornament

Late 3rd–mid-4th century
Gold
Height 5¾ in. (14.5 cm)
Excavated at Fangshen, Beipiao, Liaoning Province, 1957
Liaoning Provincial Museum

EXCAV. REPORT in *Kaogu* 1960.1

These hat ornaments (cat. nos. 33, 34) are variations of a type of ornament common to all people in the Xianbei confederation. The basic elements are antlerlike forms and leaf-shaped pendants. The pair of ornaments with animal heads and antlers (opposite, top) comes from central Inner Mongolia, an area associated with Tuoba Xianbei activity. The ornament with a vegetal form (opposite, bottom) is from Beipiao, Liaoning, which can be identified as the location of one of the earliest settlements of the Murong Xianbei in the third to fourth century.

JCYW

35
Plaque with female figure and animals

3rd–4th century
Gold
2½ x 4 in. (5.8 x 10 cm)
Excavated at Horqin Zuoyizhong Banner, Jerim League, Inner Mongolia Autonomous Region, 1990
Jerim League Museum

REFERENCE: Shanghai bowuguan 2000

The image on this plaque, with two animals flanking a female figure, strongly suggests an iconographic link to the art of Bactria (see fig. 7), although the interpretation of the motif may be very different.

JCYW

36
Plaque with disk pendants

Sixteen Kingdoms, Former Yan (337–370)
Gold
3½ x 3½ in. (9 x 9 cm)
Excavated at Fangshen, Beipiao, Liaoning Province, 1957
Liaoning Provincial Museum

EXCAV. REPORT in *Kaogu* 1960.1

This openwork plaque with disk pendants comes very close in ornamental style to finds from the Bactrian site of Tillya Tepe in Afghanistan, dated to the first century (see fig. 7).

A find of this type of artifact in northeastern China raises two questions. The first concerns the transmission of art styles and techniques over long periods of time. The second relates to the fact that it is mainly in the eastern part of Inner Mongolia and western Liaoning that third- to fourth-century artifacts displaying strong stylistic influence from Bactria are found, whereas similar objects have generally been absent at archaeological sites in central Inner Mongolia, which lies on the steppe route connecting Central Asia to northeastern China. There is the further question of the transmission of this style of ornament to Korea in the fifth century (see fig. 11). The answers to these questions await further research.

JCYW

37, front

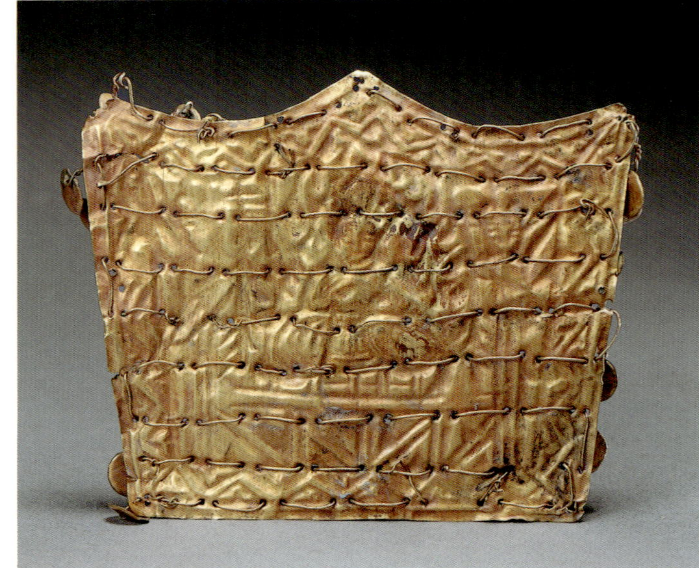

37, back

37
Hat ornament with Buddha image and disk pendants

Sixteen Kingdoms, Northern Yan (407–436)
Gold
2¾ x 3⅜ in. (6.8 x 8.4 cm)

38
Bowl

Sixteen Kingdoms, Northern Yan (407–436)
Jade (nephrite)
Diameter 3⅜ in. (8.6 cm)

39
Vessel in the shape of an animal

Sixteen Kingdoms, Northern Yan (407–436)
Bronze
Length 15 in. (38 cm)

40
Cauldron

Sixteen Kingdoms, Northern Yan (407–436)
Bronze and iron
Height 6½ in. (16.5 cm)

41
Pair of stirrups

Sixteen Kingdoms, Northern Yan (407–436)
Wood and gilt bronze
Each: height 9 in. (23 cm)

Cat. nos. 37–41 excavated from the tomb of Feng Sufu (d. 415), Beipiao, Liaoning Province, 1965
Liaoning Provincial Museum

Excav. report in *Wenwu* 1973.3

These five objects, along with the glass bowl (cat. no. 42), are from the tomb of Feng Sufu (d. 415), an official who helped his brother Feng Ba to gain the throne of the Later Yan in Longcheng (present-day Chaoyang) in 409. The dynasty thus founded by Feng Ba was later known as the Northern Yan (407–436). This short-lived dynasty, during which the Yan people (originally the Murong Xianbei) again occupied the relatively small area where they first settled in the third century, represents the last phase of the flourishing of a distinct culture associated with the Murong Xianbei.

The objects have been selected for this exhibition to represent different aspects of Northern Yan culture. The hat ornament with Buddha image (cat. no. 37) combines Central Asian and Buddhist elements in the decoration of the insignia, which traces its origin to the court of the Eastern Han (25–220). The jade bowl (cat. no. 38) indicates trade with Khotan in Central Asia. The glass bowl (cat. no. 42) comes from farther afield. The animal-shaped iron vessel (cat. no. 39) is of a form commonly found in South China at the time (although the southern versions were ceramic). The bronze cauldron with iron lid and handle (cat. no. 40) is a reminder of the nomadic

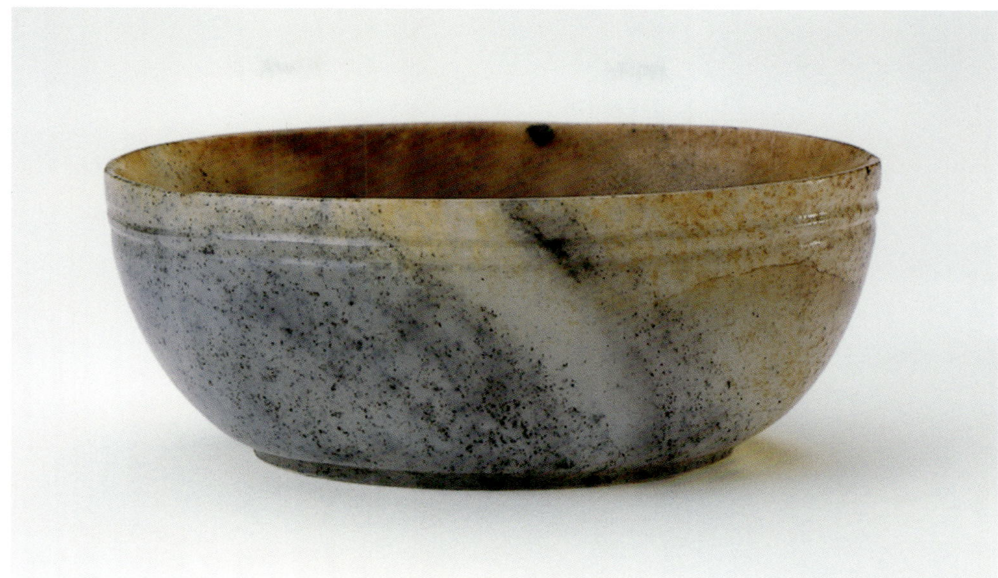

38

years on the steppes. Finally, the stirrups (cat. no. 41) are among the earliest found in China. Somewhat earlier stirrups have been found in other territories associated with the Murong Xianbei. One day the Murong Xianbei may be credited with the invention of this important device or its introduction into China.

For further discussion of these objects, excluding the glass bowl, see essay by James C. Y. Watt, under "The Northeast, Late 4th–Early 5th century." JCYW

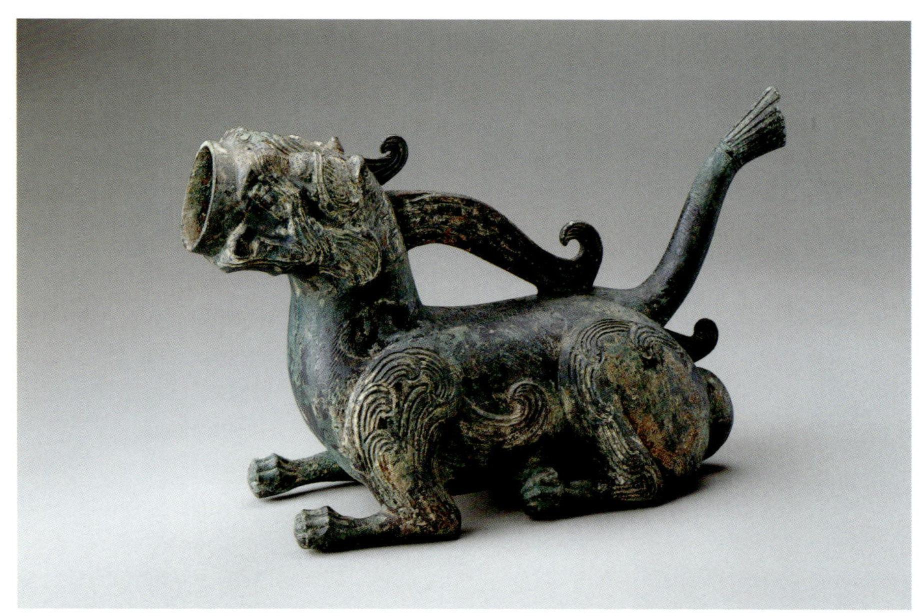

39

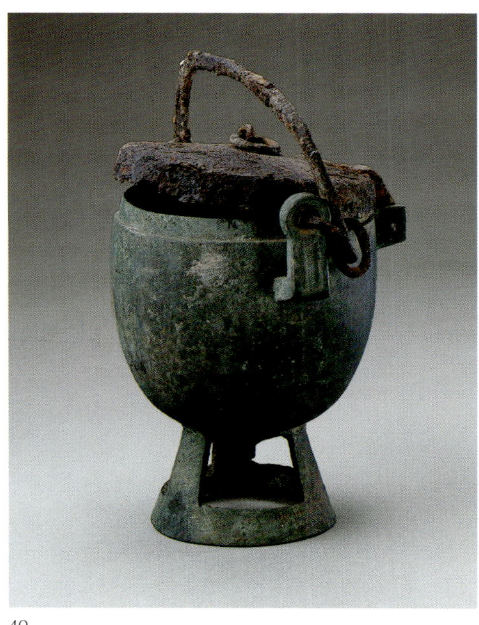

40

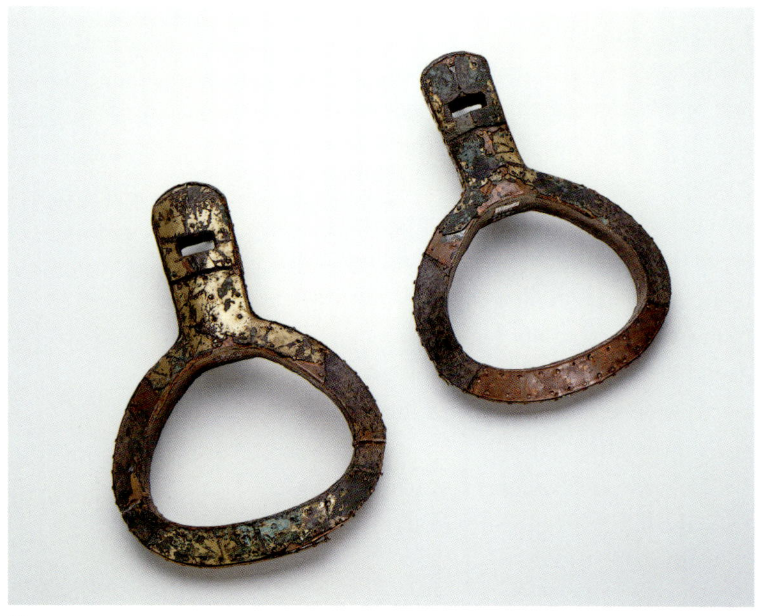

41

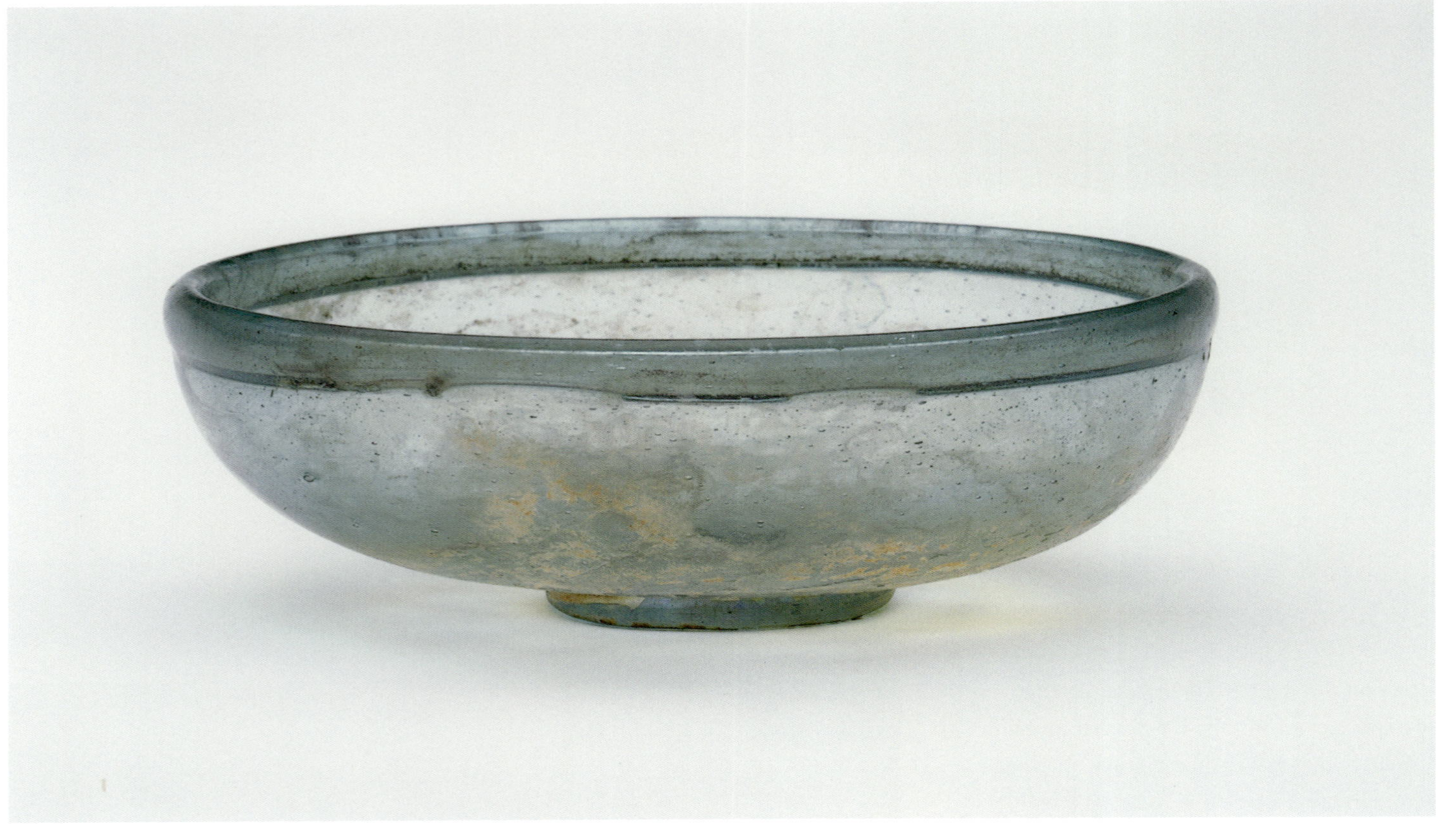

42
Bowl

Early 5th century
Glass
Diameter 5⅛ in. (13 cm)
Excavated from the tomb of Feng Sufu (d. 415), Beipiao, Liaoning Province, 1965
Liaoning Provincial Museum

Excav. report in *Wenwu* 1973.3

Complete and undamaged, this glass dish of slightly irregular shape is light green and highly transparent. The upper part of the inner and outer walls has traces of iridescence, and the lower body is partially covered with a whitish, lightly weathered layer. It has a straight mouth, bulging body, and ring foot. The rim folds inward to make a rounded lip. A glass ring foot was attached to the base. The joint is distinctly visible. At the center of the bottom is a pontil mark.

The dish is one of five excavated in 1965 from the tomb of Feng Sufu (d. 415). Feng Sufu was the younger brother of Feng Ba (r. 409–30), ruler of the Northern Yan of the Sixteen Kingdoms period (304–439), and second only to his brother in power. Of the glass vessels in his tomb, the duck-shaped vessel (see fig. 4) is the most unusual in shape and the most skillfully made. The quality and color of this bowl are comparable to those of the duck-shaped vessel. The two may have been manufactured in the same workshop.

All five vessels are made of regular soda-lime glass, which is the same as Roman glass. And all five were free blown, which was typical of Roman glass production. The glass was melted at a relatively high temperature, has few air bubbles and impurities, and is highly transparent. Quite a few examples of this bowl type can be found in Roman glass.

AJ

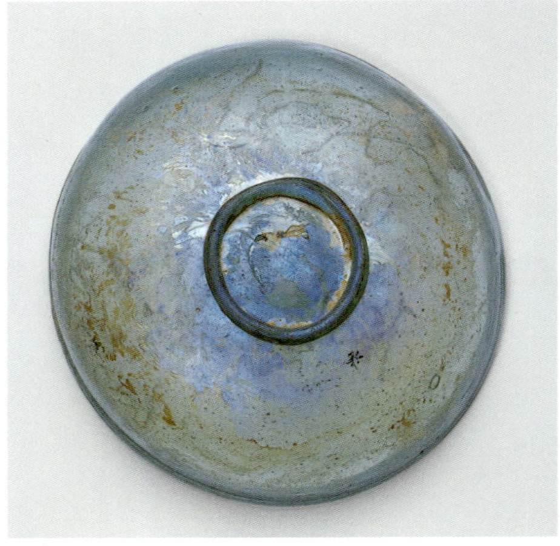

42, base

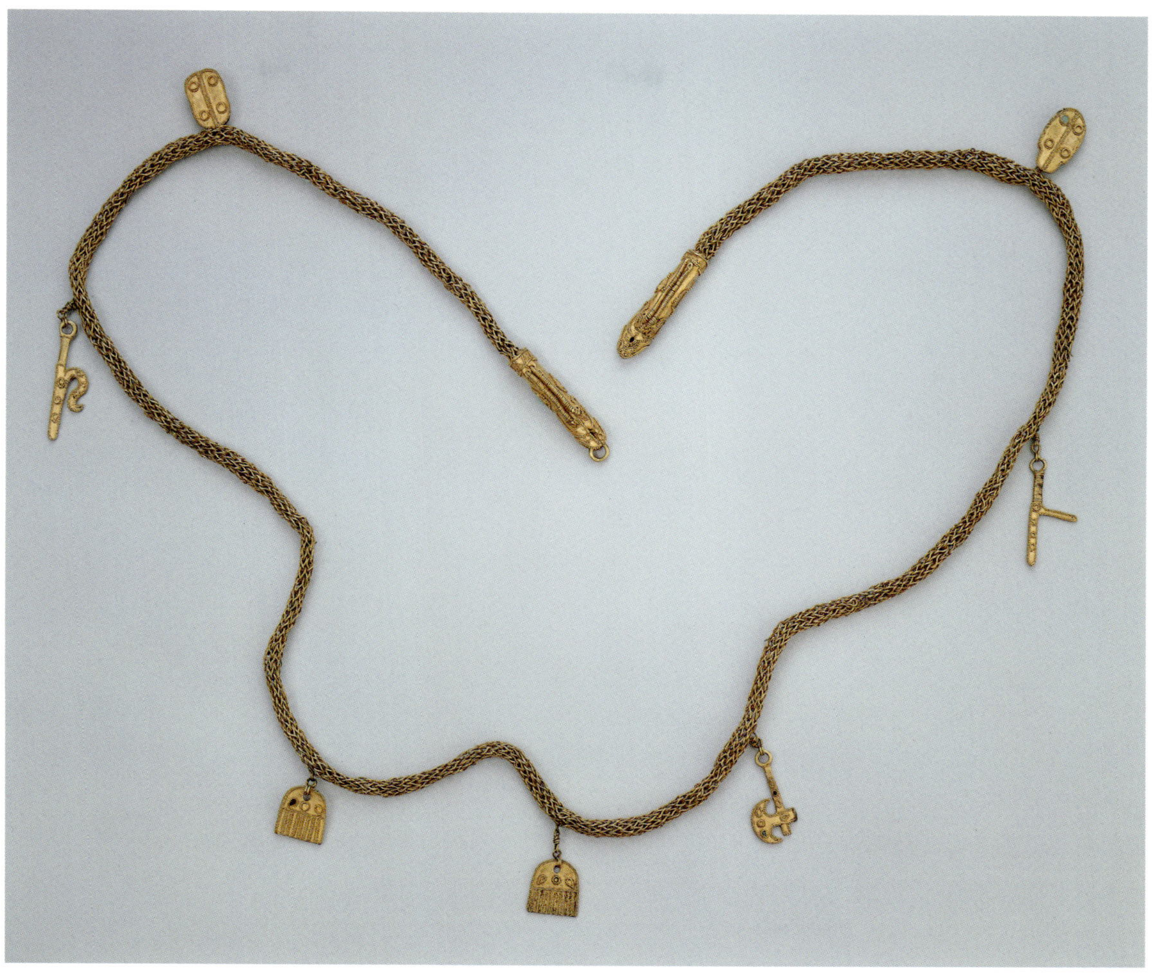

43
Chain with pendants in the shape of weapons and shields

3rd–4th century
Gold
Length 50³⁄₈ in. (128 cm)
Excavated at Darhan Mumingan Banner, Ulanqab League, Inner Mongolia Autonomous Region, 1981
Inner Mongolia Autonomous Region Museum

Excav. report in *Wenwu* 1984.1

This chain, found in central Inner Mongolia, is proof of the travel of fashion between India and China from the first to the third century. It is likely that the Indian-style necklace or bracelet with pendants shaped like weapons and shields first entered China in the north. By the late third century, this form of ornament was popular all over China.

JCYW

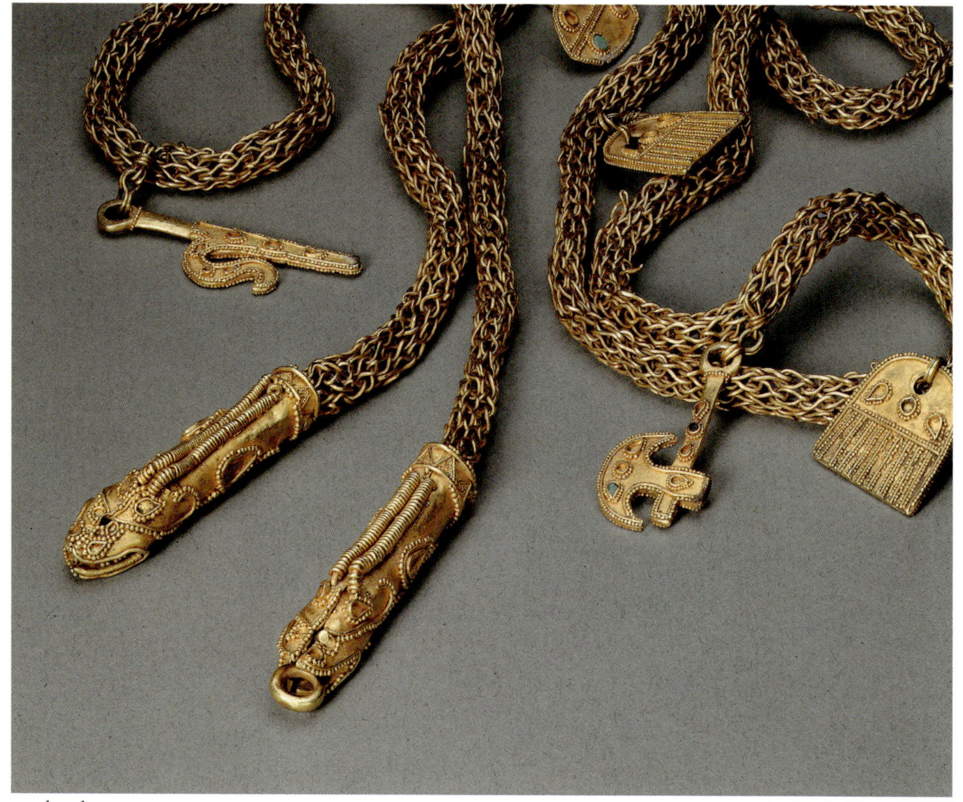

43, detail

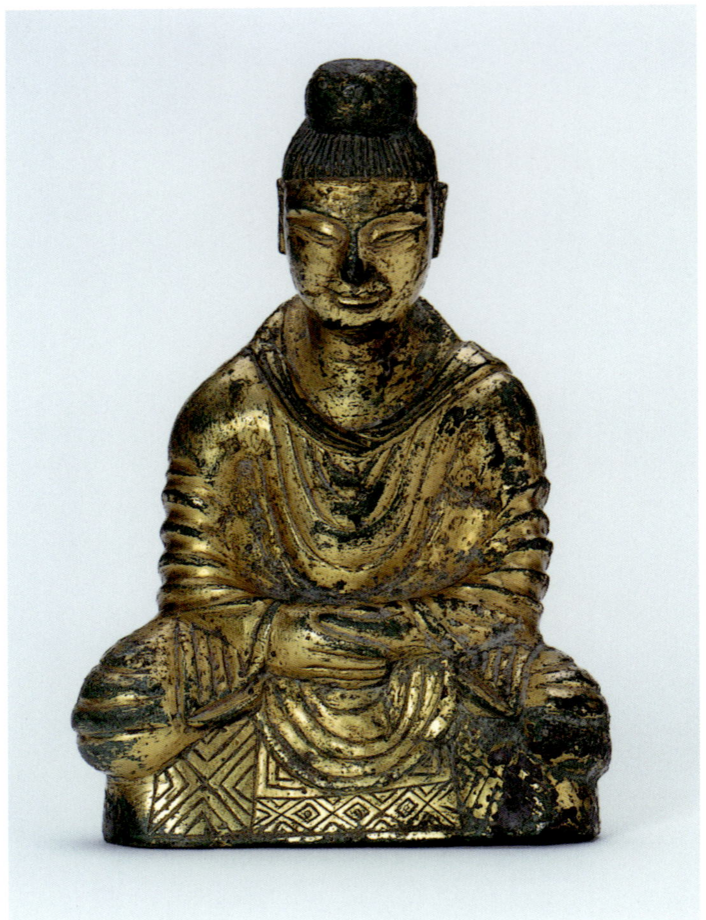

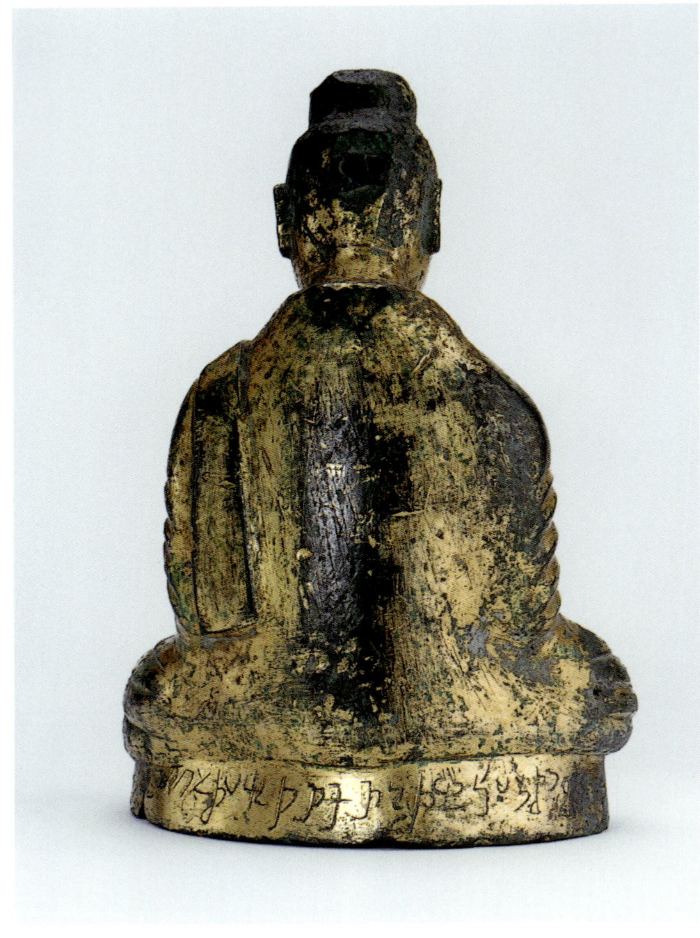

44
Seated Buddha in meditation

Sixteen Kingdoms (304–439), ca. 300
Gilt bronze
Height 5¼ in. (13.4 cm)
Xi'an City Institute of Cultural Properties Protection and Archaeology

Reference: Han Baoquan 1998

This magnificent and unique gilt-bronze Buddha in Meditation was purportedly found in 1979 in the vicinity of Xi'an. The inscription carved on the lower back of the bronze, in the Yuezhi *kharoshthi* language, is the most notable trait in that it links the work to the presence of the ethnic group in Chang'an (Xi'an, Shaanxi), the magnet for the trade coming from Central Asia. The translation of the text transcribed by the scholar Lin Meicun reads "Cittaka Sattva commissioned this Buddha [*buca*] to honor the descendant of the Marega clan, Pustaka Vidyarama."[1] Lin explains that some of the terms used, notably the family name, Marega, are also found in documents from Niya, a station on the southern Silk Road dating from the second to the fourth century. He concludes that both the donor and the beneficiary may also have hailed from the same region and settled as immigrants in Chang'an. The absence of works in metal in the city-states of the Silk Road (wood was the primary medium) suggests that this Buddha, while it retains some stylistic characteristics of Central Asia, was executed on Chinese soil in the early fourth century.

The hollow bronze was cast in one piece; a halo, now missing, was hooked to the head. Because the back is not modeled, the image was certainly intended to be seen frontally. The Buddha is shown in meditation, with hands aligned on top of one another and resting on his lap, a standard gesture of fourth-century bronzes. The broad, oval face and the proportions of the body are reminiscent of a typology favored at the site of Karadong in Khotan, along the southern Silk Road.[2] The slightly inclined head and half-closed eyes reinforce the mood of introspection, and the hint of a smile imparts a sense of peaceful tranquillity.

The broad, compact body is draped in a monastic robe, forming graceful curving patterns that contrast with the triangular striped lappets that hang from the sleeves and the diamond motifs on the rug on which the Buddha sits. The rug décor bears some resemblance to textile fragments from Shanshan, indicating a further link to Central Asia. In conclusion, this bronze Buddha is a fourth-century work executed in Chang'an in response to the eclectic Central Asian taste of a Yuezhi patron.

AFH

1. Lin Meicun 1991, vol. 1: 119–31.
2. See Debaine-Francfort and Idriss 2001.

45
Buddha altarpiece with canopy

Sixteen Kingdoms (304–439),
early 4th century
Gilt bronze
Height 8⅜ in. (21.4 cm)
Found at Shijiazhuang, Hebei Province,
1955
Hebei Provincial Museum

REFERENCE: Hebei sheng bowuguan 1999

The remarkably intact condition of this work testifies to the very early existence of a complex altarpiece type likely used for private devotion. It originated from the same area that became a prominent and influential Buddhist center in the north through the proselytizing efforts of the famous monk Fotudeng (died ca. 349) under the patronage of Shi Le (r. 328–33) and Shi Hu (r. 335–49), rulers of the short-lived Later Zhao dynasty (328–351).

The three-lobed mandorla frames a group comprising a central Buddha seated in meditation on a lion throne and two diminutive monks—or a nun and a monk—on either side. Two celestials and another Buddha, shown emerging from a lotus, hover above the trio below. All are gathered under an honorific umbrella or canopy. This elaborate construction rests on a pedestal, which, in turn, is supported by a rectangular four-footed stand. All the images are rendered with little definition, although the small attendants possess a naïve freshness and the floating celestials impart a sense of festivity. The central Buddha's posture, demeanor, and overall appearance are related to a type embodied by the Buddha dated 338 and also executed in Hebei now in the Museum of Asian Art, San Francisco. This stylistic affinity confirms the work's dating to the early fourth century.

The shape of the aerial canopy suggests lotus petals radiating from the center, which is composed of a smaller lotus. Originally, gold spangles were suspended from the rim. (When the bronze was found, three were still intact.) Such ornaments are also seen on the late third- and fourth-century gold headpieces unearthed in the burials of Yan elites, in present-day Liaoning Province. The two examples included in the exhibition (cat. nos. 33, 34) reveal the passage of the motif from the secular to the religious sphere. Canopies started to be used in the second century for both Buddhist and Daoist images. According to literary sources, "Emperor Huan [r. 147–67] planned the Palace of the Gleaming Dragon and equipped it with flowered canopies or honorific umbrellas for the worship of Buddha and Laozi." Members of the Eastern Han court and the imperial family practiced a form of Buddhism integrated with Daoist rituals called Huang Lao.[1] This would suggest that the canopy type antedates its use on the present altarpiece. Furthermore, during the Eastern Han (25–220) and Three Kingdoms period (221–265), bronze mirrors often display, on the upper axis, images of immortals similarly shaded by a large canopy. The sharing of this feature in both Buddhist and Daoist imagery was later abandoned in China as Buddhism progressed and consciously sought its own identity. After the Three Kingdoms, the use of the canopy itself was abandoned in Buddhist imagery altogether.

AFH

1. The reference is from the commentary appended to *HHS*, roll 7; it is quoted in Tsukamoto 1979: 67.

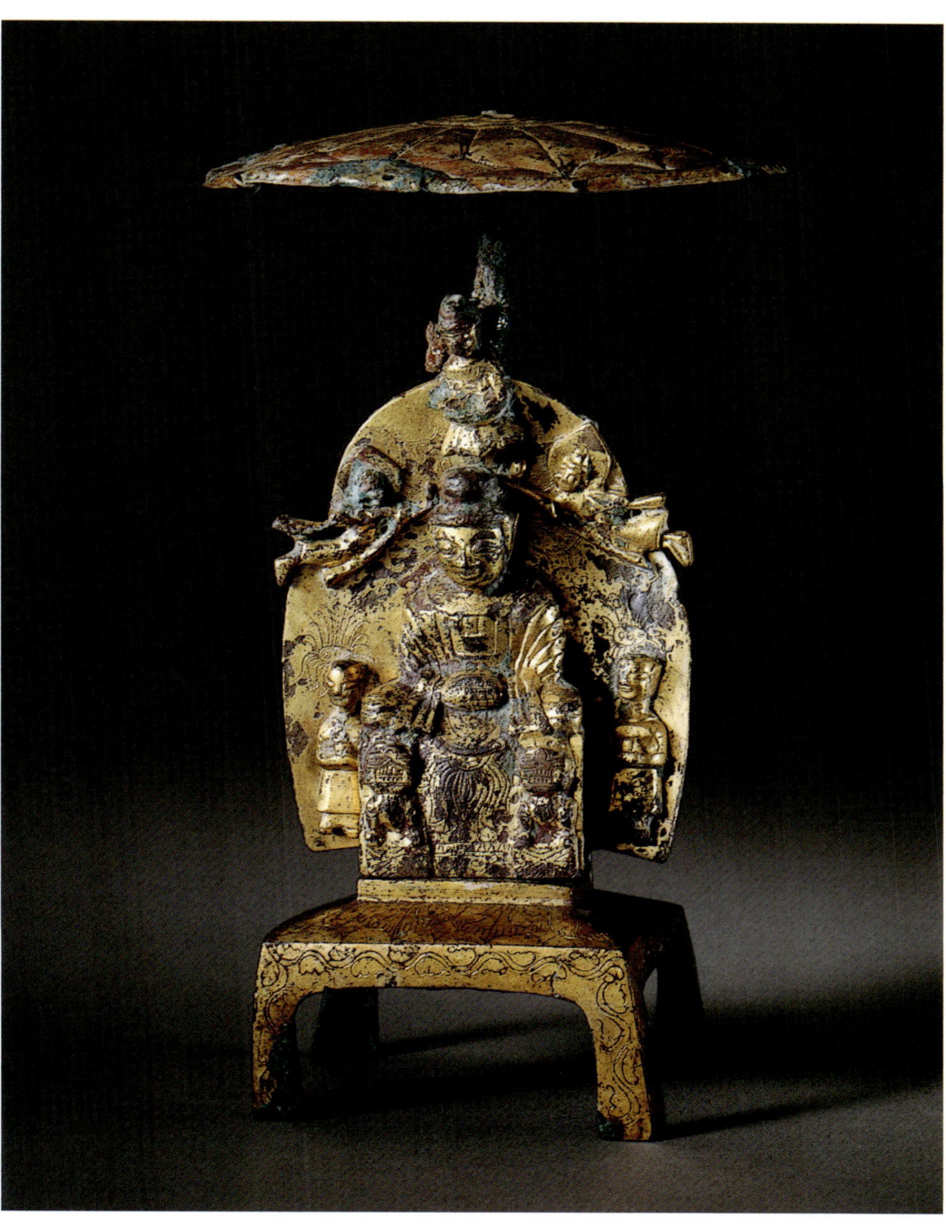

III

Early Northern Wei Dynasty

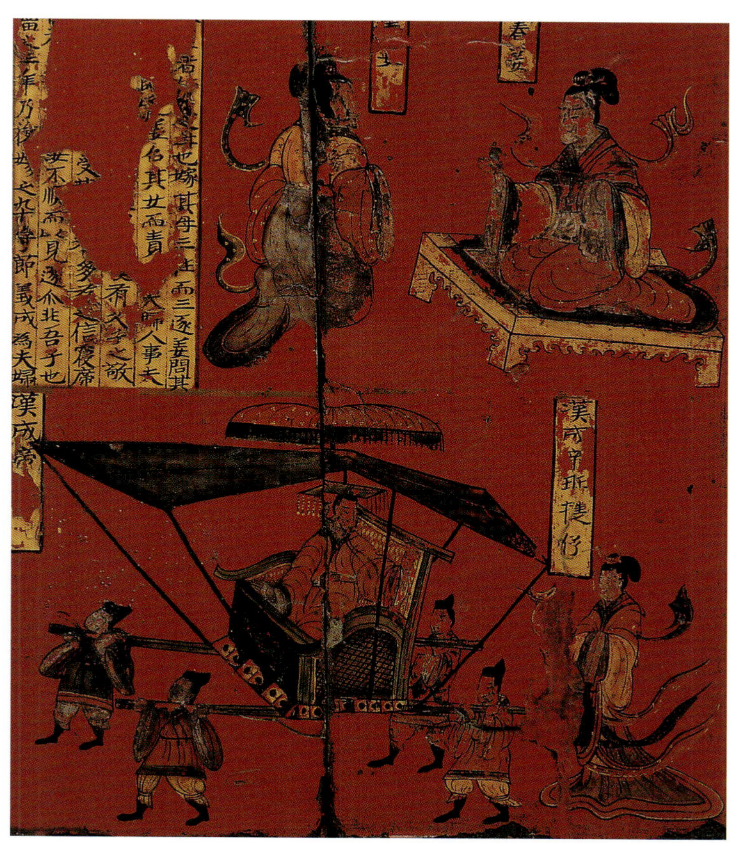

46
Two armored horses

Sixteen Kingdoms (304–439)
Earthenware
Height 14³⁄₈ in. (36.5 cm)

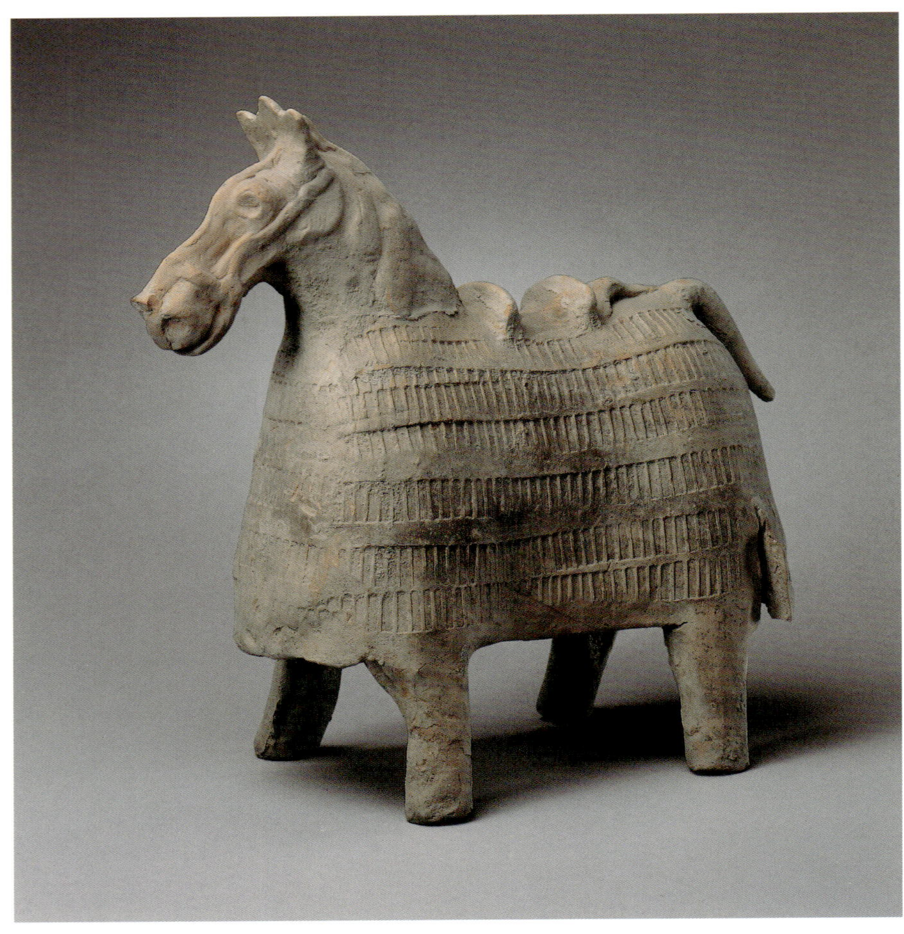

47
Two mounted musicians

Sixteen Kingdoms (304–439)
Earthenware
Height 13⁷⁄₈ in. (35.2 cm)

Cat. nos. 46 and 47 excavated at Dongjiacun, Xi'an, Shaanxi Province, 1996
Shaanxi Institute of Archaeology

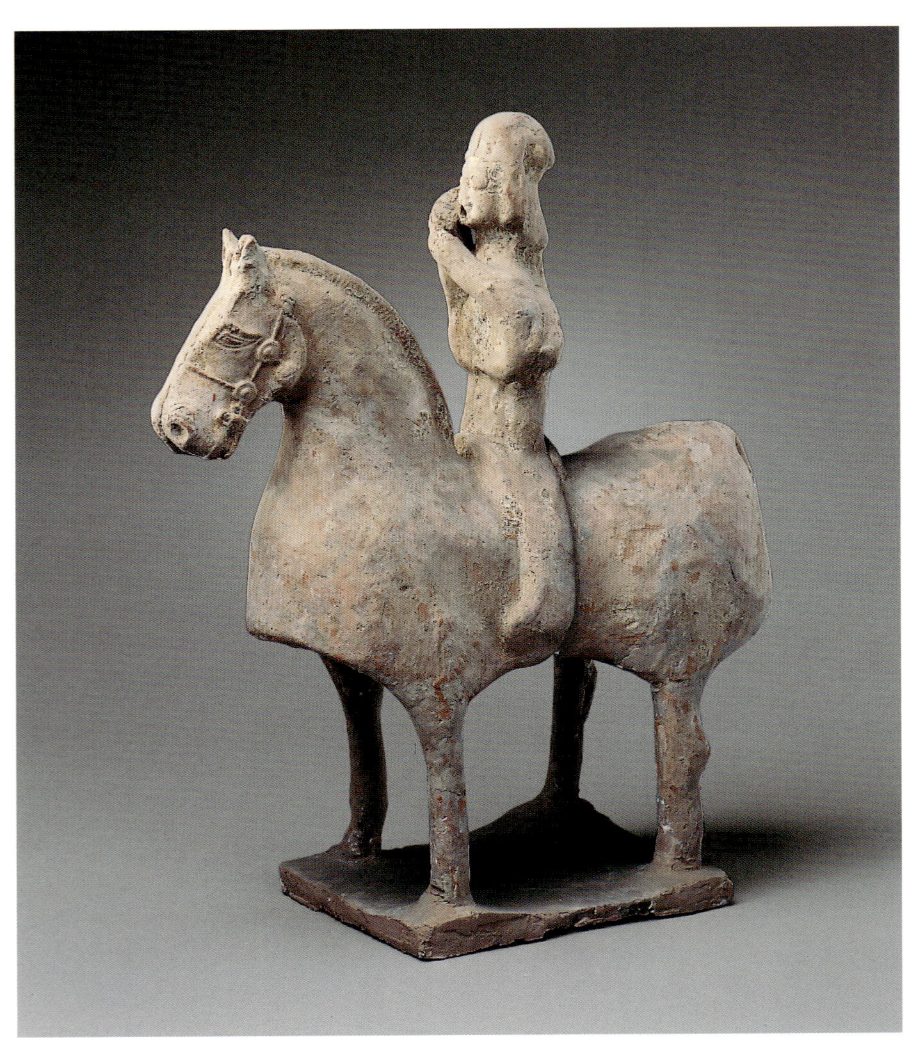

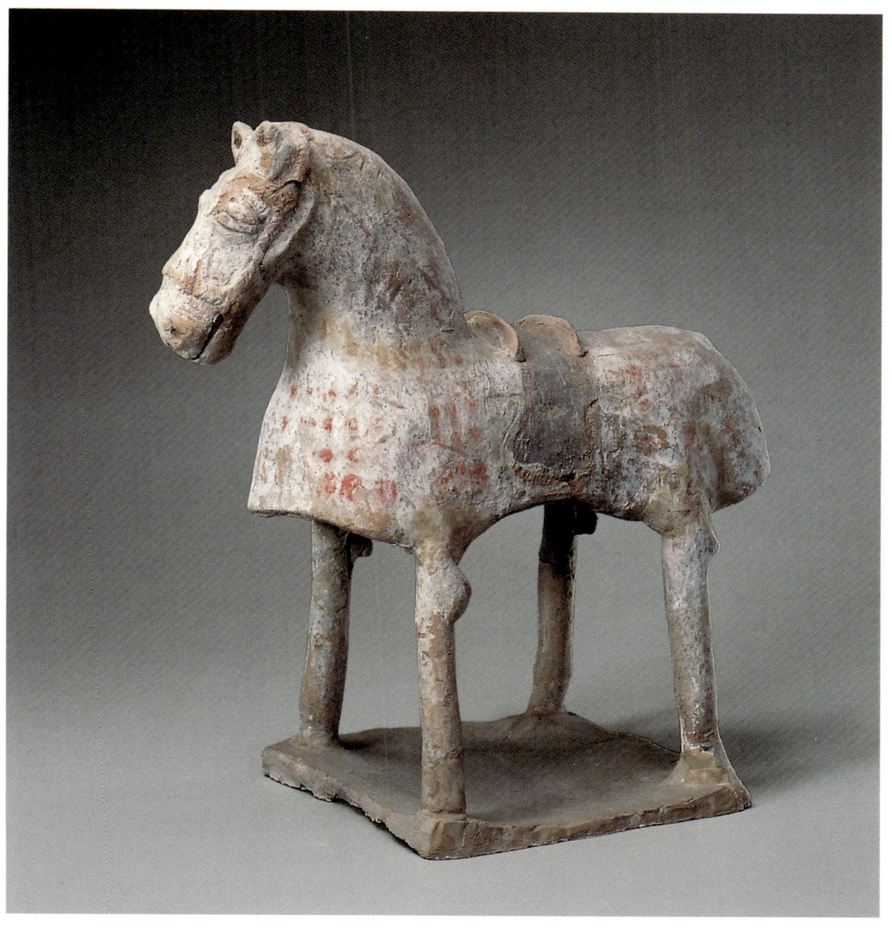

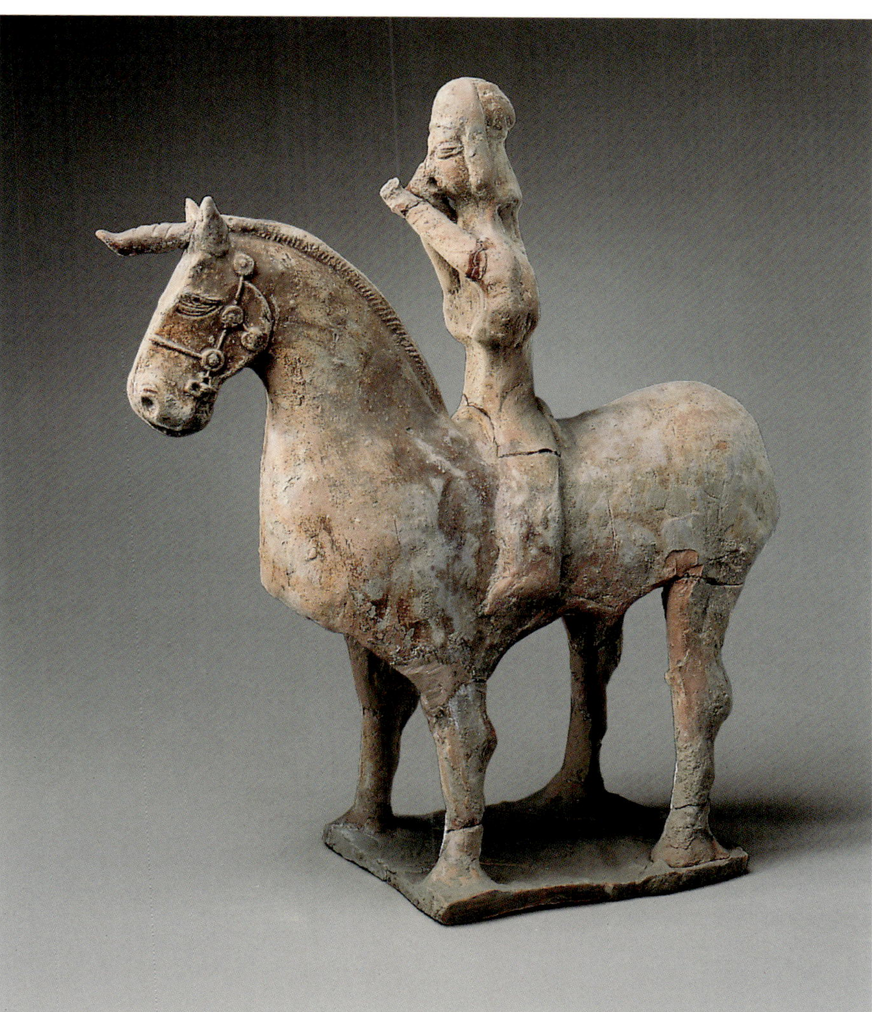

These pottery figures of armored horses and mounted musicians were found in tombs in a suburb of Xi'an, Shaanxi, and dated to the Sixteen Kingdoms period (304–439) by archaeologists at the Shaanxi Institute of Archaeology (report forthcoming). This means that the tombs are likely to be those of the Former Qin (351–394), ruled by the Di people, or those of the Later Qin (384–417), ruled by the Qiang people. Both states had their capital in Xi'an. In any case, they predate the annexation of the Xi'an area into the Northern Wei empire a little after 417.

Horse armor began to be used in China during the Eastern Han period (25–220).[1] The pottery figure opposite (top left) is one of the earliest representations of full-body horse armor discovered to date in North China.

Military music at this time was performed on drums and horns, which the mounted musicians seem to be playing.

JCYW

1. Yang Hong 1980: 40.

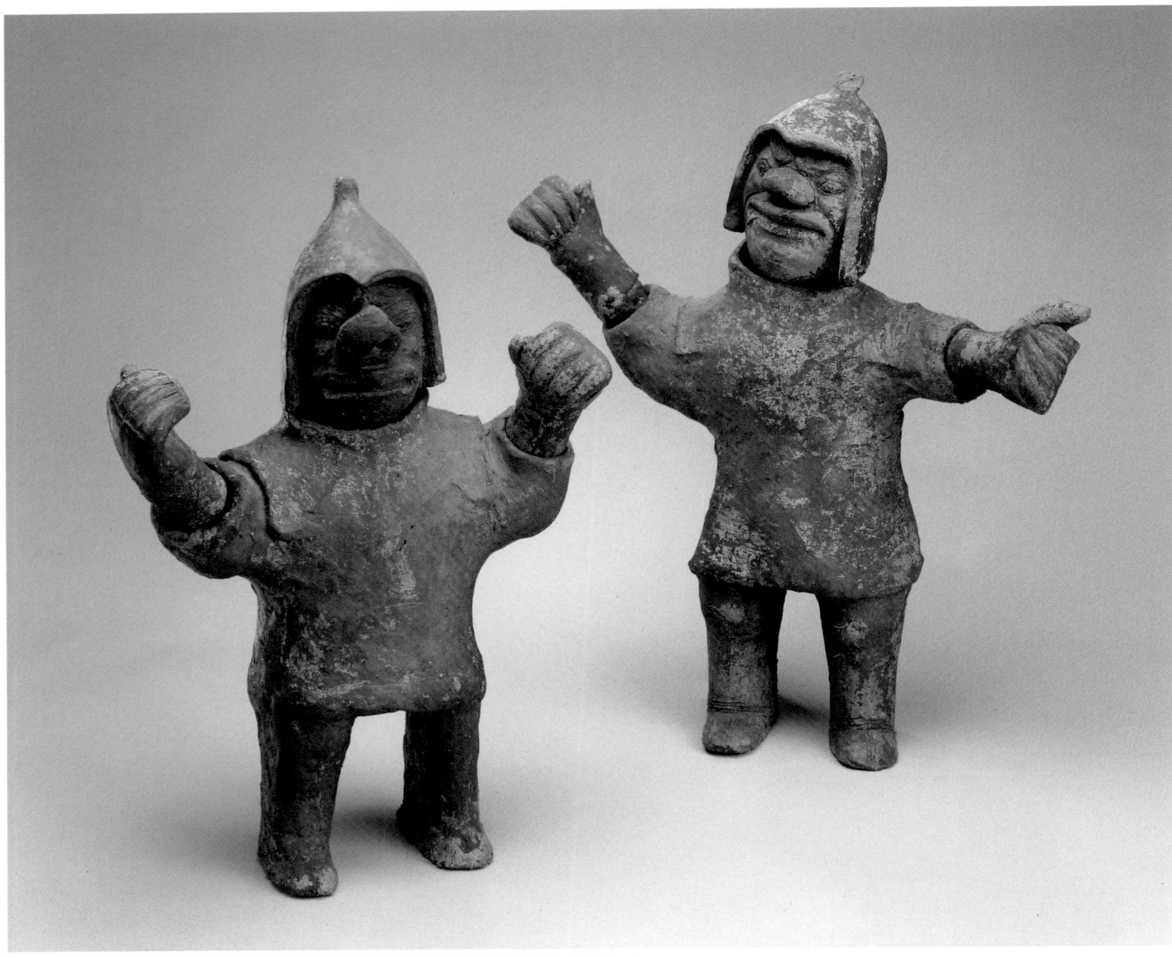

48

Pair of guardian warriors

Northern Wei dynasty (386–534), 5th century
Earthenware with pigments
Height: left 15½ in. (39.5 cm.); right 17⅛ in. (43.5 cm)
Excavated at Hohhot, Inner Mongolia Autonomous Region, 1975
Inner Mongolia Autonomous Region Museum

Reference: Neimenggu zizhiqu bowuguan 1987: 56–57

Distinguished by their bulging eyes, astonishing noses, and grimacing expressions, these two guardian warriors are the largest of the thirty-four handmade pottery figures found in a fifth-century tomb at Hohhot in Inner Mongolia in 1975 (see also cat. nos. 49, 50).[1] They stand with their legs apart and hands held partially open in a gesture which perhaps indicates that they once held weapons or shields. The heavy, tuniclike garments that cover the torsos appear to be made of a stiff, protective material. Like the thick, high boots, they show traces of red pigment. Traces of white are found on the pointed helmets.

The figures belong to a tradition of tomb guardian warriors, found singly or in pairs, that characterizes funerary culture, particularly from the sixth to the eighth century. The beginning of this tradition is found in tombs in North China that date to the Three Kingdoms (220–280) and Western Jin (265–316) periods. A prototype for the conception of the Hohhot guardians—with bulging eyes, high cheekbones, prominent nose, and grimacing mouth—is seen in an earthenware sculpture excavated from a Western Jin tomb at Xingyuancun, Yanshi, Henan.[2] Also comparable are the upper fangs on the Henan figure with the lower fangs on one of the Hohhot pair. On the other hand, the greater intensity in the face and posture of the present warriors may reflect contributions by the Xianbei to the art of the funerary cult. Some of the Western Jin figures were found with shields, and others were paired with tomb guardian beasts of a type that would also become widespread from the fifth to the eighth century (see cat. nos. 54, 55, 178, 179). Both humanoid and bestial protectors are often the largest sculptures in a tomb. They are generally placed at the entrance to the tomb chamber.

DPL

1. Guo Suxin 1977: 38–41, 77.
2. Zhongguo shehui kexueyuan kaogu yanjiusuo 1985, pl. 6.5.

49
Horse and groom

Northern Wei dynasty (386–534), 5th century
Earthenware with pigments
Groom: height 7⅝ in. (19.5 cm); horse: height 7⅝ in. (19.5 cm)
Excavated at Hohhot, Inner Mongolia Autonomous Region, 1975
Inner Mongolia Autonomous Region Museum

Reference: Neimenggu zizhiqu bowuguan 1987:59

Both the groom and horse are handmade, as opposed to molded, and painted in shades of white, red, and black. The tunic and the conical hat with long flaps worn by the groom are standard items of Xianbei clothing. Such garments are often found on funerary sculptures (see cat. nos. 51, 52, 70), as well as in representations of donors found at Buddhist sites such as Yungang, Shanxi,[1] and Dunhuang, Gansu (cat. no. 79).

The horse has stocky legs and an elongated and somewhat awkward body. He wears a decorated band around his head, most likely used to hold a bell or other adornment, a blanket and saddle, and an elaborate crupper. Tied to the saddle and passing under the tail, the crupper serves to prevent the saddle from slipping. Made with appliqués of clay, the crupper consists of bands of leather (or some comparable material) decorated with metal plaques and bells. Similar fittings are found on tomb sculptures dating to the early fourth century.[2] A contemporaneous example was excavated at Xiaomincun in Anyang, Hebei.[3]

Elaborate cruppers are often seen on sculptures of horses found in tombs dating from the fifth to the eighth century. Such fittings are often placed before a group of horses and riders, suggesting that they may have had some ceremonial function, possibly either as symbols of the social position of the interred or as illustrations of the activities accompanying the burial.

At least two examples of oxen wearing similar decorations are known. One was found in the late fifth-century tomb of Song Shaozu, a high-ranking official under the Northern Wei (see cat. nos. 56, 57),[4] and the other in that of another official, Lou Rui (cat. no. 142), who was buried in 570. Both animals are further distinguished by dramatically long and pointed horns. It seems likely that rather than functioning as farm animals or beasts of burden, caparisoned oxen also played some role in funerary practices.

DPL

1. *Unkō sekkutsu* 1989–90, vol. 1, pl. 104.
2. Nanjingshi bowuguan 1972, fig. 38.
3. Zhongguo shehui kexueyan kaogu yanjiusuo Anyang gongzuodui 1983: 501–11.
4. Shanxi sheng kaogu yanjiusuo and Datong shi kaogu yanjiusuo 2001: 37 and fig. 40/2.

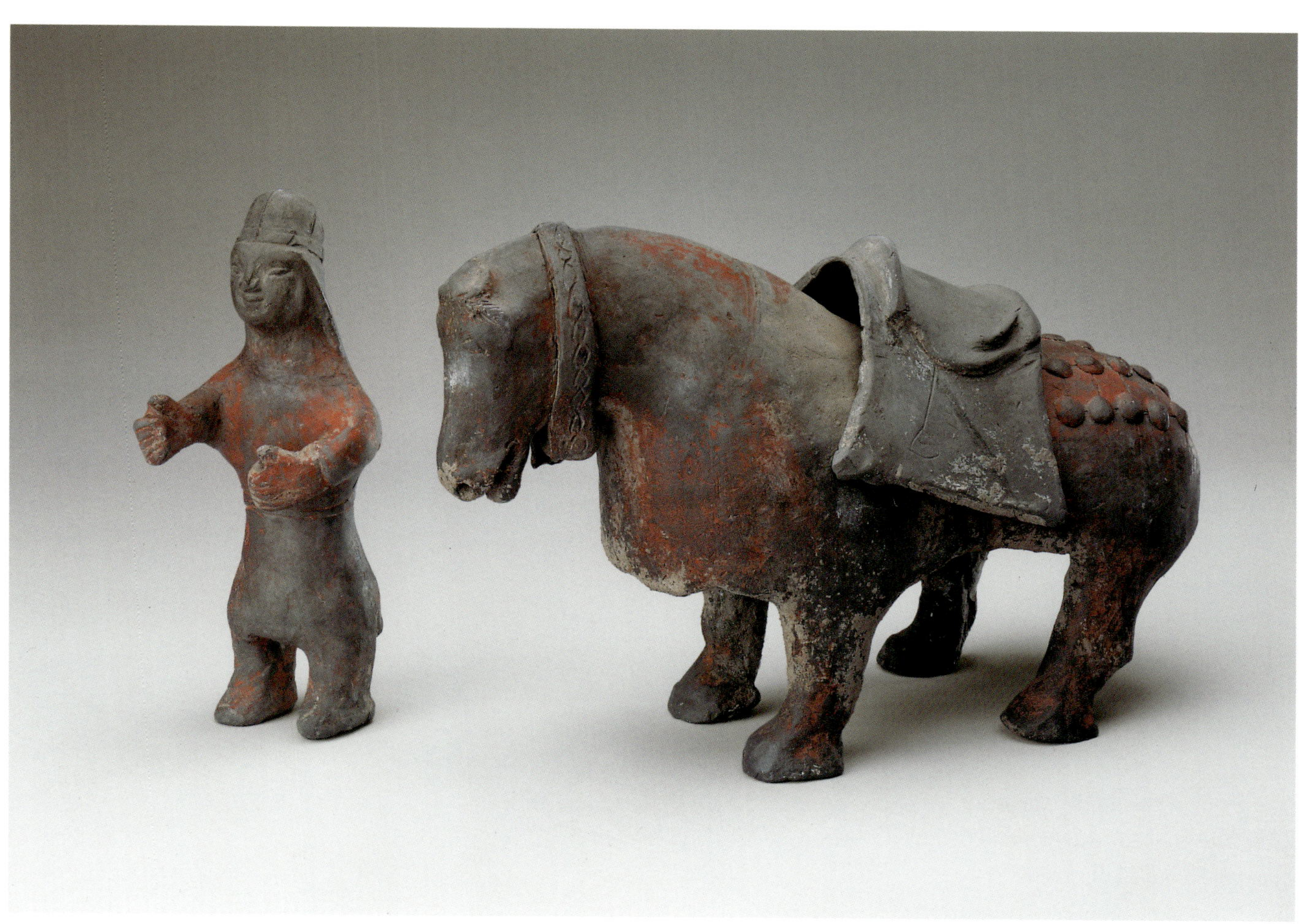

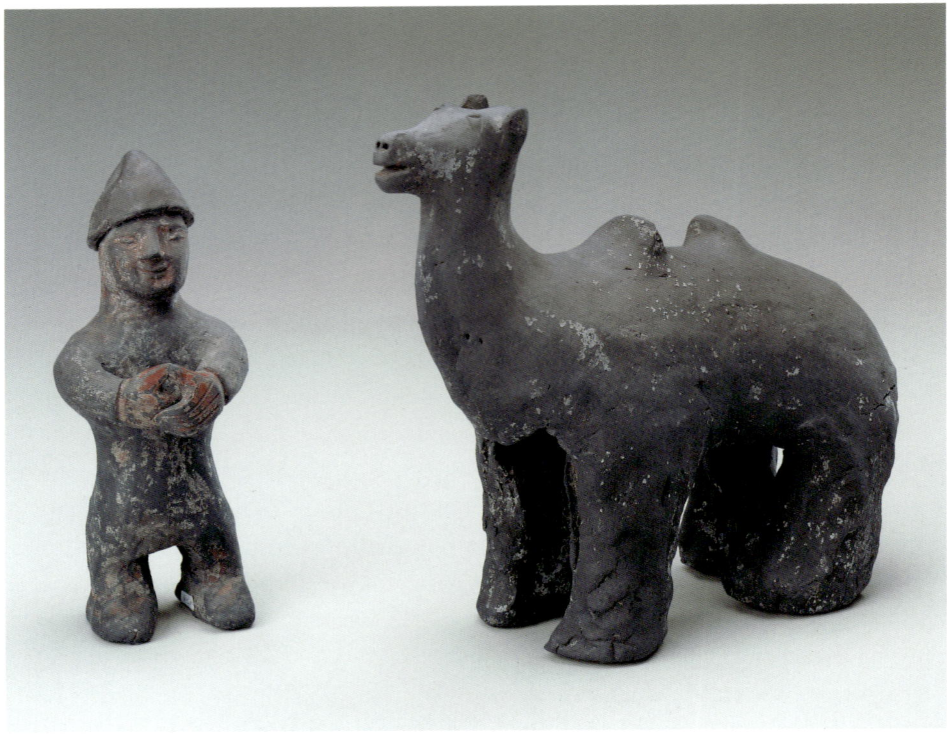

50

Groom and camel

Northern Wei dynasty (386–534), 5th century
Earthenware with pigments
Groom: height 6 7/8 in. (17.3 cm); camel: height 6 7/8 in. (17.5 cm)
Excavated at Hohhot, Inner Mongolia Autonomous Region, 1975
Inner Mongolia Autonomous Region Museum

Reference: Neimenggu bowuguan zizhiqu 1987:59

Changes in tomb construction and burial goods demonstrate the continuing interplay that marked the relationships between the sedentary Han Chinese and their northern neighbors such as the Xianbei, a nomadic people with roots in Manchuria. A tomb excavated at Daxue Road in Inner Mongolia illustrates the adoption by the Xianbei of Chinese burial practices after their conquest of much of North China in the mid-fourth century. Unlike earlier graves, which were dug into the ground, this tomb was made of brick and had an entryway, a small coffin chamber, and a burial platform.[1]

The inclusion of funerary sculptures depicting farm animals such as sheep and goats along with stoves and mills reflects the spread of agricultural practices among the nomadic Xianbei. Figures of women—some dancing—and men, as well as guardian warriors (cat. no. 48), were found in the tomb along with pottery vessels. The groom and camel seen here are handmade and painted in shades of gray, red, and white. The conical hat with flaps worn by the groom is typical of Xianbei clothing. The belted tunic, however, is shorter than the more caftanlike garments generally found on tomb sculptures. Despite the inaccurate proportions of the body, particularly the short, thick legs and minuscule humps, the camel has an irresistible liveliness and charm. His small head is lifted in an engaging manner reiterated by the perked ears and open mouth. Such deliberately awkward figures are also found in funerary sculptures produced in northwestern China during the Northern Zhou dynasty (557–581). Later examples may illustrate the taste of a military elite with strong ties to earlier nomadic traditions (cat. nos. 154–156), represented here in these rare fifth-century works.

DPL

1. Guo Suxin 1977: 38–41, 77.

51

Female dancer

Northern Wei dynasty (386–534), third quarter of the 5th century
Earthenware with pigments
Height, approx. 8 in. (20.3 cm)
Excavated at Datong, Shanxi Province, 2000
Datong City Institute of Archaeology

Reference: Liu Junxi 2001: 3

This charming dancer was found in a side chamber of Tomb M52, one of five tombs excavated at Yanbei Teachers College, Shanxi.[1] The figure, with arms outstretched, has apparently been captured in performance. Her youthful, round face, almond-shaped eyes, and slight smile are also found in Buddhist sculptures and tomb figures made in the Pingcheng (Datong) area from about 475 to 490. The conical cap with decorative crossed bands and back flaps is a more elegant version of the traditional Xianbei headdress. The figure also wears a long caftanlike garment that crosses from left to right and has an open neck. Comparison with the images of donors on a textile dated 487, excavated

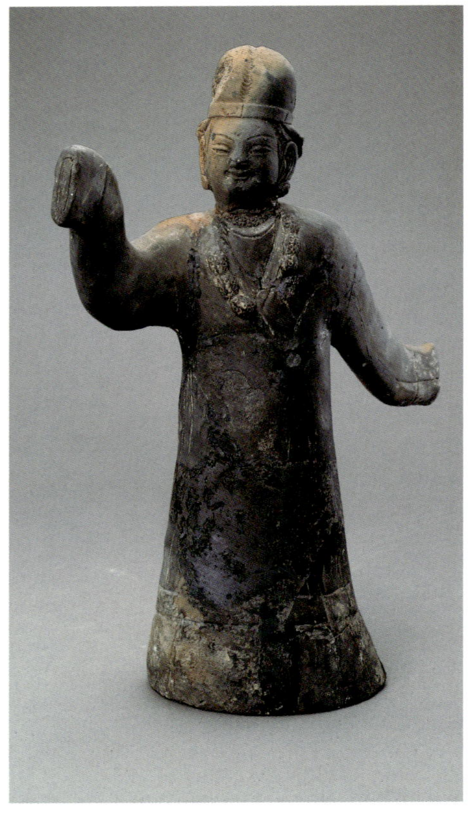

at Dunhuang, Gansu (cat. no. 79), suggests that the wide band at the bottom of the costume represents an inner garment worn beneath the outer robe.

Encircling the neck is a choker composed of two strands of pearls or beads. The impressive necklace that drapes across the chest consists of large oval beads inlaid with smaller, circular ones. A similar adornment made of gold beads inlaid with pearls was excavated in 1957 from the tomb of a young princess named Li Jingxun, who died in 608 (cat. no. 187). The sculpted version represents the only other known example of this type of jewelry, which was most likely produced somewhere in western or Central Asia.

DPL

1. Liu Junxi 2001, fig. 3.

52

Troupe of female musicians

Northern Wei dynasty (386–534), last quarter of the 5th century
Earthenware with pigments
Height, approx. 6 in. (15 cm)
Excavated at Datong, Shanxi Province, 2000
Datong City Institute of Archaeology

Sculptures of performers playing reed or stringed instruments, at times accompanied by dancers, are found in Chinese tombs as early as the Western Han period (206 B.C.–A.D. 9). Such troupes became increasingly important during the Sui (581–619) and Tang (618–907) periods. This rare example of eight musicians dating to the late fifth century was found in one of the five tombs excavated in 2000 at the site of what is now Yanbei Teachers College, Datong.[1]

The long caftanlike garments worn by the figures identify the musicians as female. They are similar to those worn by the standing dancer (cat. no. 51) and another musician (cat. no. 70) that are also from the Datong area and also dated to the end of the fifth century. The sculptures are made of gray earthenware. Traces of pigment on the sculptures further suggest that the colored robes were vibrantly patterned with designs in red, white, and blue.

The instruments originally held by the musicians have been lost, possibly as a result of the low-fired technology that was used in making them. In the sixth century, such figures were high-fired, and therefore less fragile, and have retained their instruments. Comparisons with similar musicians found, for example, as subsidiary figures in the cave temples at Yungang and in later tomb sculptures suggest that they played a range of instruments, including drums, cymbals, flutes and other wind instruments, and zitherlike instruments such as the *se* or the *qin*.

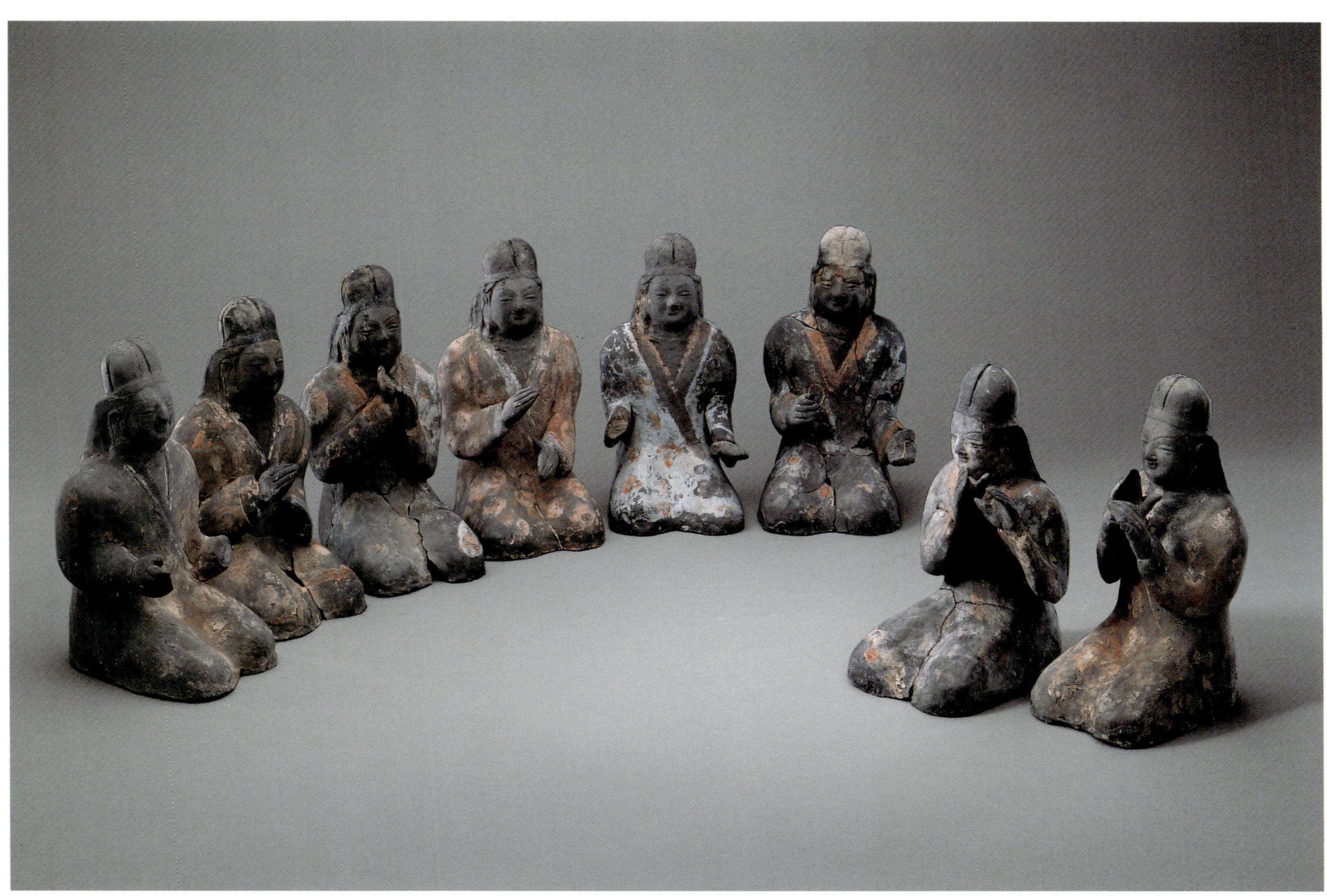

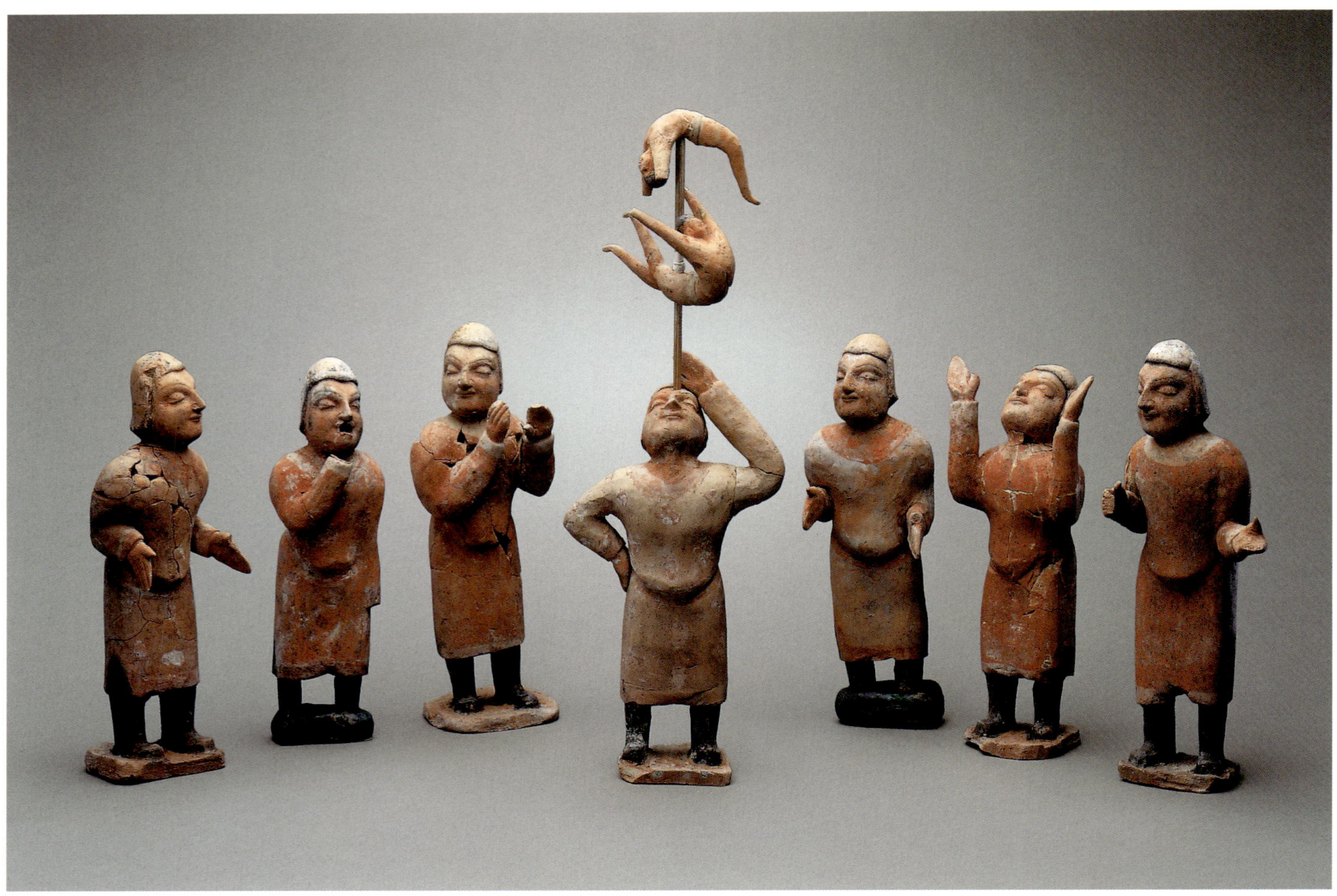

The position of the hands also suggests the type of instrument a figure once held. For example, the musician wearing a light blue robe, placed roughly in the center of the troupe, holds her left hand in a downward-turned pose that might be used for playing a zither. The two figures to the left, whose hands are held nearer to the mouth, most likely played wind instruments such as the *dizi*, or vertical flute; the *sheng*, which is similar to panpipes; or a conch shell.

DPL

1. Guojia wenwuju 2000: 91.

53
Acrobats

Northern Wei dynasty (386–534),
Late 5th century
Earthenware with pigments
Max. height 10¼ in. (26 cm)
Excavated at Datong, Shanxi Province, 2000
Datong City Institute of Archaeology

REFERENCE: Guojia wenwuju 2000

Both written records and visual materials indicate that acrobatics, often accompanied by musical performances, flourished during the Han dynasty (206 B.C.–A.D. 220). The famous *Xijingfu* (Rhyme Prose on the Western Capital), by Zhang Heng (78–139), describes troupers balancing poles on their heads.[1] A dramatic image of a portly figure supporting three children whirling on a cross-shaped bamboo pole is included among the representations of fifty-four performances on a stone, presumably part of a tomb, excavated in Yinan county, Shandong.[2] The latter has been identified as an act brought to China from Dulu, a small state along the Silk Road noted for the agility of its acrobats. Similar feats are also recorded in *Ye zhong ji* (Notes on the City of Ye), written during the Eastern Jin dynasty (317–420), and in poetry dating to the Tang (618–907), when the names of performers, such as the Amazonian Auntie Wang and Zhao Jiechou, are also preserved.

This rare late fifth-century group of seven acrobats, shown performing a pole-balancing act, was recently excavated from Tomb M2 at the site of Yanbei Teachers College in Datong, Shanxi.[3] Despite their somewhat damaged condition, the figures provide an appealing glimpse into the work of a performance troupe. Six men, shown clapping and playing instruments (now missing), accompany the seventh, who balances on his forehead a bamboo pole that supports two whirling children. The principal trouper is the largest of the seven figures. They wear long robes over black boots. Traces of pigment on the robes suggest that they were originally decorated with floral patterns similar to those on the garments of an ensemble of female musicians unearthed at the same site (cat. no. 52). Their heavyset physiques suggest that the acrobats are in middle age and, presumably, have the requisite strength for the feat, although they may lack the flexibility needed for other forms of their trade.

DPL

1. Wu Zhen 1987: 77.
2. Fu Qifeng 1985, fig. 23.
3. Guojia wenwuju 2000: 88–94.

54
Tomb guardian

Northern Wei dynasty (386–534), ca. 477
Earthenware with pigments
Height 13 in. (33 cm)
Excavated from the tomb (dated 477) of Song Shaozu, Datong, Shanxi Province, 2000
Datong City Institute of Archaeology

Excav. report in *Wenwu* 2001.7

This spirited guardian creature was found at the front of a procession placed near the house-shaped sarcophagus that dominated the coffin chamber in the tomb of Song Shaozu (see also cat. nos. 56, 57), who was buried in 477. Such protective figures are often found, in sets of four, in tombs in the Central Plain region from the late fifth to the early eighth century. Two of the figures are generally creature-like, as they are here, one with a human and the other with a leonine face, and two are humanoid and wear armor (see cat. no. 180). According to the excavation report, one human guardian figure was placed at either side of the entryway to the main chamber.[1] In addition to the present guardian creature, it is possible that a second creature—now lost—was included in the original burial.

Made of gray clay, the figure once had vertical strips painted on the back.[2] He has a lively, almost laughing expression, with an open mouth and even teeth, a retroussé nose, almond-shaped eyes, and exaggerated, curling eyebrows. Four openings at the top of the head may once have held material intended to represent a mane or possibly dorsal spikes. The use of such openings is common in guardian creatures produced in the late fifth century (see also cat. no. 55), as is the pneumatic modeling of the body.

In the early sixth century, the forms of the guardian creatures become elongated and stiff. By the late sixth century, they are sometimes enhanced with horns on the forehead and lances or other embellishment along the back. Dorsal spikes, wings, and other additions, as well as a change from lions' paws to cloven hoofs,

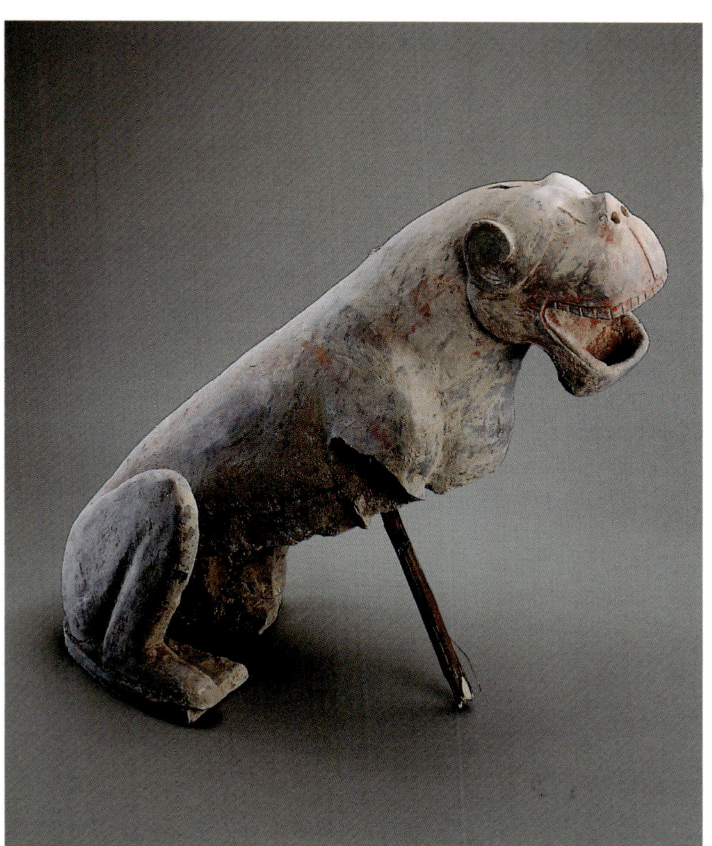
54

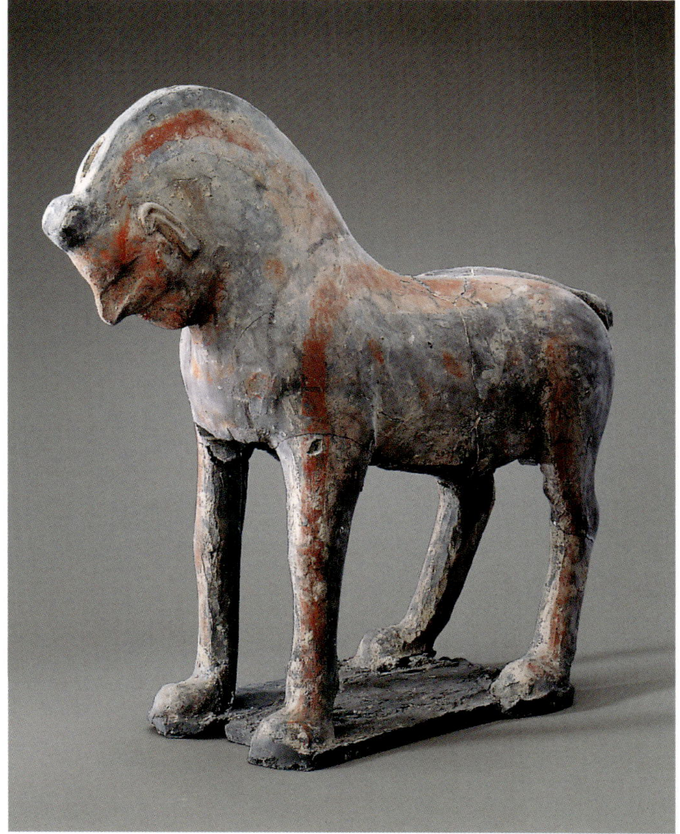
55

define the phantasmagorical renderings of the late seventh and eighth centuries (see cat. no. 179).[3]

DPL

1. Shanxi sheng kaogu yanjiusuo and Datong shi kaogu yanjiusuo 2001: 22. See the line drawing showing placement of tomb contents. The guardians are numbers 1 and 156 in the report.
2. Ibid.: 27, fig.14, no. 1.
3. Fong 1991a: 159–87.

55
Tomb guardian

Northern Wei dynasty (386–534), ca. 477
Earthenware with pigments
Height 13 in. (33 cm)
Excavated from the tomb (dated 477) of Song Shaozu, Datong, Shanxi Province, 2000
Datong City Institute of Archaeology

Excav. report in *Wenwu* 2001.7

Crouching animals with human faces are often paired with creatures that have lionlike features, as well as with standing warriors, in tombs dating from the late fifth through the eighth century. Standing squarely on all four legs, this guardian figure, found in one of the five tombs at Yanbei Teachers College in 2000, is looking downward, as is often the case in examples produced in the late fifth century.[1] The openings along the back of the head, which may have been used to secure a mane of some sort, and the subtle modeling of the broad forms of the body are also typical of that time (see cat. no. 54). Painted in shades of red, white, and black, the figure has claws rather than hooves and a vestigial horn at the top of the head.

Although the precise origin of such figures is unclear, they may derive from the many hybrid creatures listed in texts dating to the Western Han (206 B.C.–A.D. 9) period.[2] One such text, the *Shenyijing* (Classic of Spirit and Marvels), by Dongfang Shuo (154–93 B.C.), mentions the *taowu*, a tigerlike species with a human face, which may have provided a prototype.

The traces of the horn also link such beasts to the unicorn figures (see cat. nos. 81, 82) first found during the Eastern Han (25–220), as well as to rhinoceros-like sculptures, often with three dorsal spikes, that became common in tombs of the Western Jin (265–316).[3] At least one figure, a bronze sculpture excavated from an Eastern Han tomb in Zhucheng, Shandong, combines the frontal horn of the unicorn with the spikes of later examples.[4] In addition, a clay sculpture of a creature with a lowered head and two dorsal spikes excavated in Luoyang,[5] has patterning painted on the body similar to that found on earlier unicorns in bronze and wood. It was found standing before the coffin chamber facing inward and was paired with a standing guardian figure.

The earliest human-faced guardians are found in southern Chinese tombs of the Wu period (222–280). The contemporaneous *Wudu fu* (Rapsody on the Wu Capital), by Zuo Si (ca. 250–ca. 305), discusses a beast known as the *shanhui*, which among other features has a human face.[6] One of the earliest known pairings of the human-faced guardian with his more leonine counterpart is found on a stone relief decorating an early fifth-century tomb excavated at Wenggunliang, Wushan Banner, Inner Mongolia.[7] Despite the lack of comparable evidence from the Central Plain region, it seems likely that such pairings were in use also in Chinese funerary culture by that time.

DPL

1. A well-known example was excavated in 1966 from the tomb of Sima Jinlong, dated 484; see *Quest for Eternity* 1987: 124, fig. 52.
2. Fong 1991b: 87.
3. Ibid., figs. 13, 14.
4. Ren Rixin 1981: 14, fig. 2.
5. Luoyang shi di er wenwu gongzuodui 2000: 27, fig. 4 and frontis. no. 4.
6. Fong 1991b: 87.
7. *Neimenggu wenwu kaogu wenji* 1994, vol. 2: 480, fig. 4.3.

56
Two equestrians

Northern Wei dynasty (386–534)
Earthenware with pigments
Height, left 12 in. (30.4 cm); right 12¼ in. (31.2 cm)

57
Horse and donkey

Northern Wei dynasty (386–534)
Earthenware with pigments
Height, a. 13½ in. (34.2 cm); b. 9 in. (22.8 cm)

Cat. nos. 56 and 57 excavated from the tomb (dated 477) of Song Shaozu, Datong, Shanxi Province, 2000
Datong City Institute of Archaeology

Excav. report in *Wenwu* 2001.7

The tomb of Song Shaozu (d. 477) is the most elaborate and well-preserved of the eleven tombs excavated from the site of Yanbei Teachers College in 2000.[1] The brick structure, which consists of a long ramp leading to a domed chamber, was common from the late fifth through the early eighth century. Song Shaozu was a member of the Song clan of the Dunhuang region of Gansu Province. It seems likely that his family was relocated to Shanxi after the Northern Wei conquest of the northwest in 439. He later served the Northern Wei as magistrate for the Youzhou district. As was common practice, he was buried with his wife.

Placed around the sides and back of the sarcophagus were 117 pottery sculptures, including ninety representations of military figures, shown either standing or mounted. The latter were arranged in a cavalcade surrounding an ox-drawn cart at the side of the coffin. The cart most likely represented the vehicle containing the remains of the deceased, and the procession re-created his funerary rites.

Twelve horses without riders were also included in the cavalcade. A more complicated method of manufacture and the

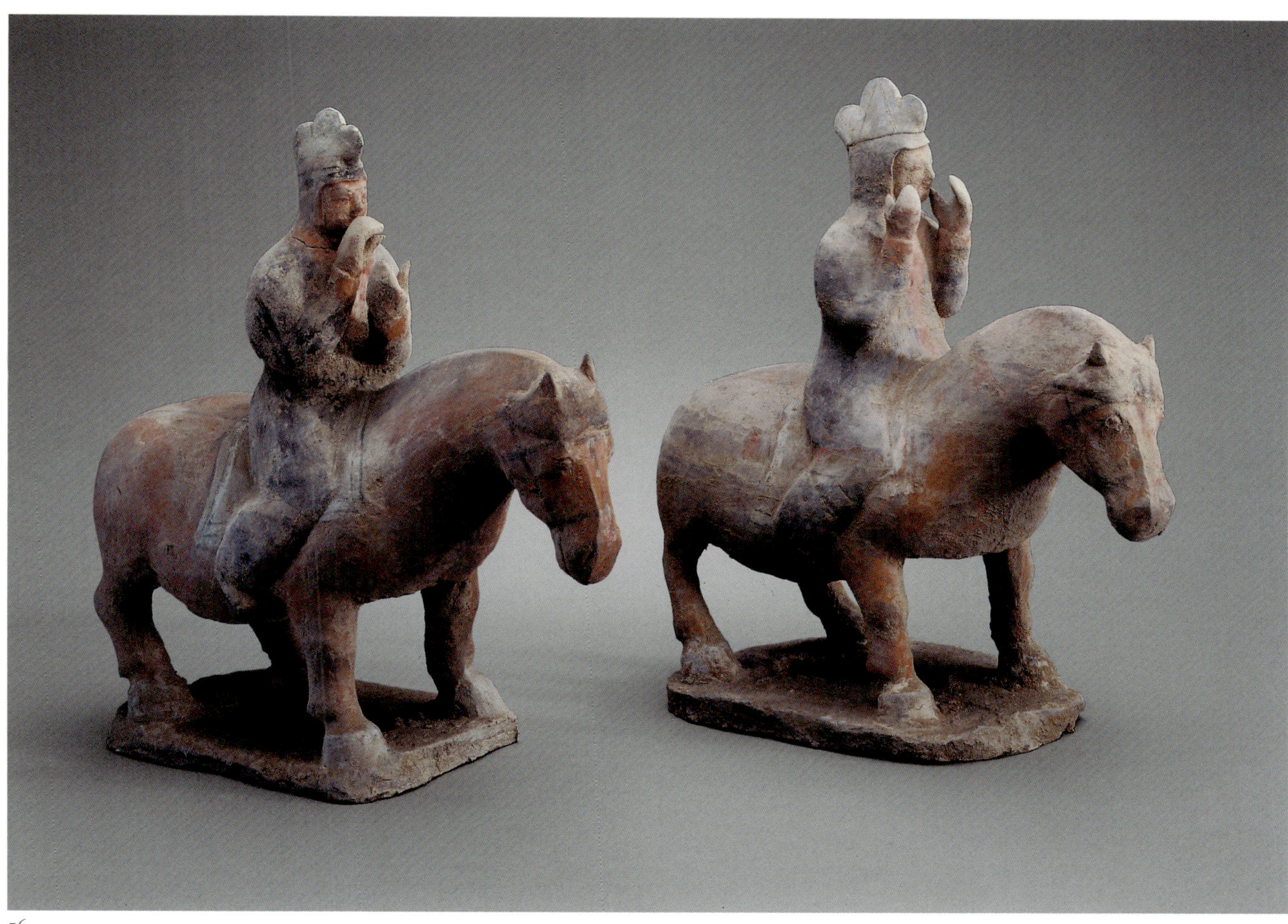

56

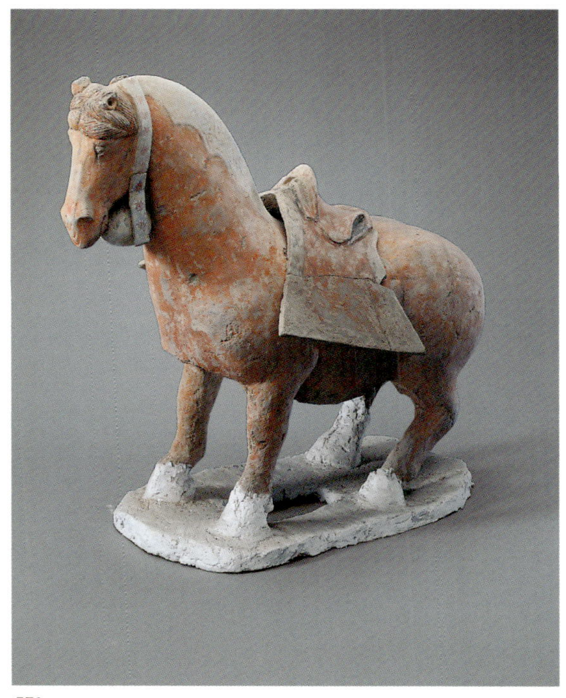

57a

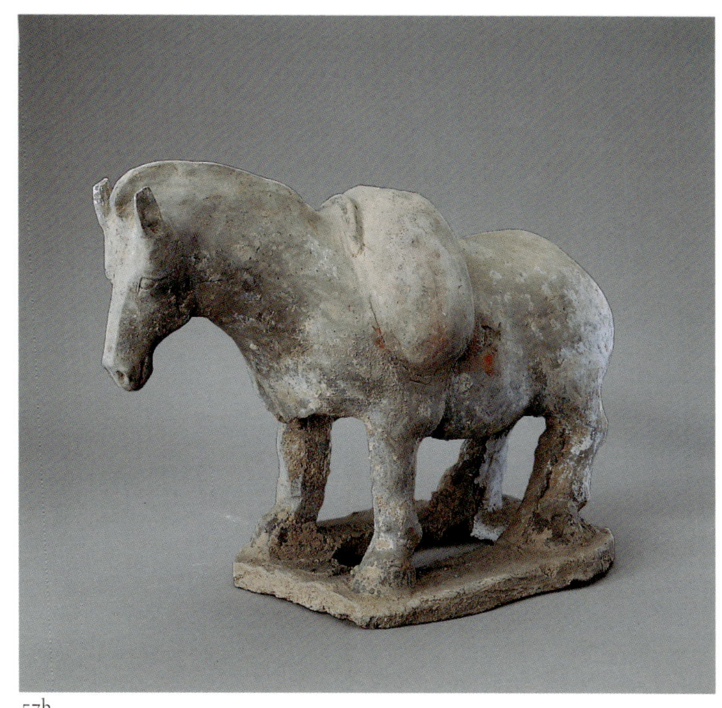

57b

detailing of the fittings distinguish the largest horse, which was placed at the front of the group (cat. no. 57a). A saddle was added to the molded figure of the horse, which also has a carefully groomed mane and a bell suspended from a thick strap around his neck. Traces of a black crupper are visible on the rump. Horses with such elaborate gear and long arched necks placed prominently in Northern Wei tombs are often thought to symbolize the presence of the deceased.

Thirty-two riders with cockscomb-shaped headgear and wearing long tunics over trousers (cat. no. 56) were placed toward the middle of the procession. Equestrians with cockscomb headdresses are a common feature in tomb assemblages of the early Northern Wei period at Datong and are often identified as military figures. Unlike other equestrians, however, neither they nor their horses wear armor. In addition, the position of their hands, which are often held near the mouth, suggests that they are holding instruments rather than weapons. It seems likely that such figures were part of a band, presumably participating in the funeral proceedings rather than a military formation.

Pack animals, including the donkey seen here (cat. no. 57b), were found at the end of the procession. Like the horses, the donkeys are missing their tails, which were molded separately and added later. Despite their clumsy forms, the animals have an immediacy and charm that are characteristic of tomb sculptures produced in the Pingcheng area in the late fifth century.

DPL

1. Shanxi sheng kaogu yanjiusuo and Datong shi kaogu yanjiusuo 2001: 19–39.

58
Stem cup

4th–5th century
Gilt bronze inlaid with stone and glass
Height 3⅞ in. (9.8 cm)
Excavated at Datong, Shanxi Province, 1970
National Museum of China

EXCAV. REPORT in *Wenwu* 1977.9

This footed cup was found at the same site as four other objects in the exhibition (cat. nos. 59, 60, 61, 63). It has been suggested by the art historian Martha Carter that the cup is Bactrian[1] and cannot be dated later than the second century A.D. as it is stylistically similar to a Hellenistic silver cup in the J. Paul Getty Museum, Malibu (see fig. 33). But one cannot say how far apart these two vessels are chronologically—three, five, or six centuries—since the region produced Hellenistic compositions, such as those on the ewer from the tomb of Li Xian (cat. no. 157), as late as the fifth and sixth centuries. The acanthus leaves on the present cup find better parallels with those on other metal vessels from Datong than with the Getty example.

The floral motifs on the foot, however, display similarities with those on a group of Bactrian silver bowls, including four vessels with portrait medallions: a stem cup in The Metropolitan Museum of Art. (see figs. 00, 00 on p. 00), the Bartym bowl in the State Historical Museum, Moscow, and the other two bowls from Datong (cat. nos. 63, 64). It is worth noting that the pointed sockets of the Getty and Bartym bowls are also similar to those of this stem cup. The Bartym bowl was found in the Perm district of Russia, as were a large number of imported silver vessels, none earlier than the second half of the third century A.D. Thus, the present cup cannot be much earlier than the Datong portrait bowls. While the typical "Bactrian flower" is placed between two narrow, curved acanthus leaves as on the Bartym bowl,[2] the shape of the leaves corresponds more to the motif on the silver bowls with portrait medallions. On the foot of this stem cup are plants shown upside down.

BIM

1. Carter 1995a: 232–36.
2. Gunter and Jett 1992, colorpl. on p. 40.

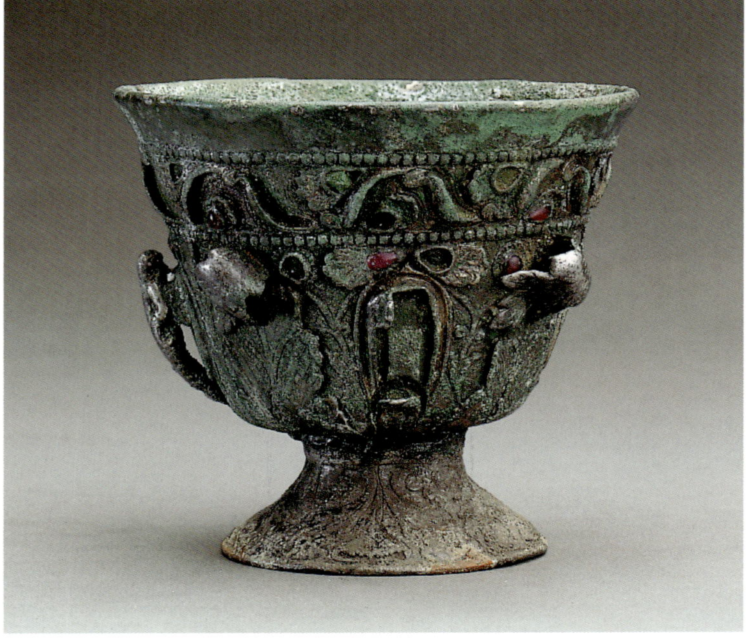

59
Stem cup with figures and grapevine

Ca. 4th century
Gilt bronze
Height 4½ in. (11.5 cm)
Excavated at Datong, Shanxi Province, 1970
Shanxi Provincial Museum

EXCAV. REPORT in *Wenwu* 1977.9

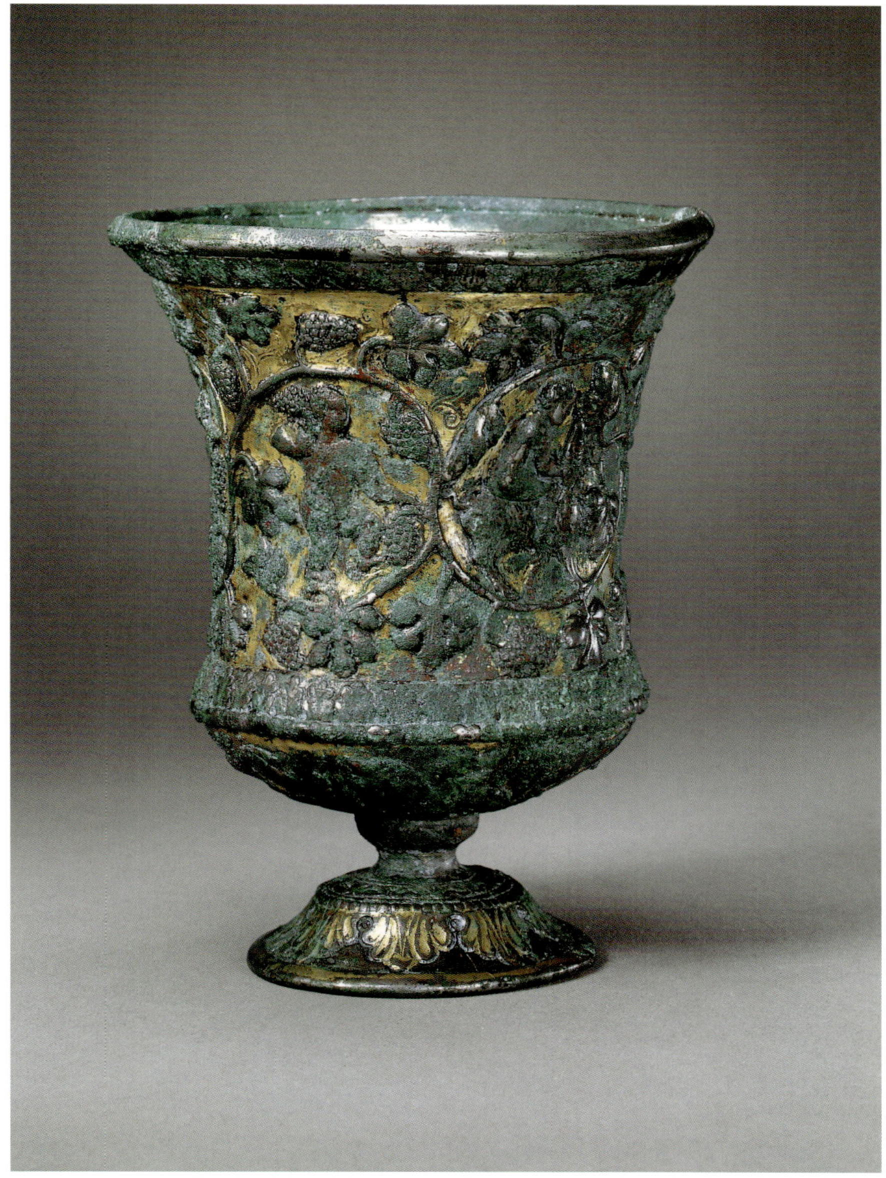

This cast (?) bronze cup was found at the same site as cat. nos. 58, 60, 61, and 63.[1] On the body, only the background is gilded; the relief figures remain untouched. The cup itself seems to be made of an alloy different from that of the foot. It is lighter in color and perhaps contains silver. There are spots of the green copper oxide on both the background and the figures. It is evident that the cup was fashioned by two master craftsmen, one for the body and one for the foot.

At first glance, the cup seems to be an imported Late Roman vessel. The figures of the young boys and birds that inhabit the vine scroll are similar to motifs found on many Roman works of art, especially those of the fourth century A.D., such as the famous porphyry sarcophagus of Constantina from Santa Costanza in Rome.[2] Five boys are depicted on the cup. One of them carries a lamb on his shoulders, an image that, in Early Christian art, symbolizes Christ as the Good Shepherd. The enframing rows of leaves are also typically Roman; stylistically, they resemble the leaves below the vine on the silver plate from Beitan, Gansu (cat. no. 90). It is not by chance that both the cup and the plate find analogues in art made in Alexandria, where both the porphyry sarcophagi and silver vessels with Dionysian motifs were produced.[3]

Several features, including the gilding, the color of the metal, the copper oxide, state of preservation, and weight, are shared with the two other vessels from Datong (cat. nos. 58, 60) despite the obvious diversity of their styles. It would seem that the three vessels were cast at a single center of production but that their prototypes were of different origins. The "genealogy" was perhaps even more complex, involving two stages of production. First, the metalworkers hammered and chiseled replicas of various Hellenistic, Roman or other models. In this process, they would add ornamental details absent on the model but learned and adopted over the years of their apprenticeship. The founders would then cast copies that were nearly identical to the original vessels.

Hammered and cast vessels produced at different centers could have the same details, suggesting shared prototypes. The foliate motifs on the present cup, on the other vessels from Datong, and on the gold lid of the jar from Boma, Xinjiang (cat. no. 94), for example, are very close stylistically. Narrow vertical leaves with dented edges alternating with folded acanthus leaves are also seen both here and on the silver bowl with portrait medallions (cat. no. 64). Motifs of this kind are diagnostic of the "Megara" bowls often imitated by Bactrian silversmiths, one of whom added this familiar ornament to his copy of the Roman prototype, possibly a fourth-century Bactrian silver replica of the approximately contemporary East Roman (perhaps Alexandrian) vessel.

BIM

1. Ma Yong 1983: 8–12; Ma Yuji 1983: 1–4; Xia Nai 1983: 5–7; Nara kōkuritsu hakubutsukan 1988: 126, 210, no. 89; Chutu wenwu zhanlan gongzuozu 1973: 15 (explanatory vol.), 150 (pictorial vol.); Sun Peiliang 1977: 73; Shih Hsio-Yen 1983: 64, fig. 3.
2. Delbrück 1932: 210 ff., pl. 104.
3. Parlasca 1980: 297–304, figs. 4, 5; Baratte 1996: 142–46, fig. 4.

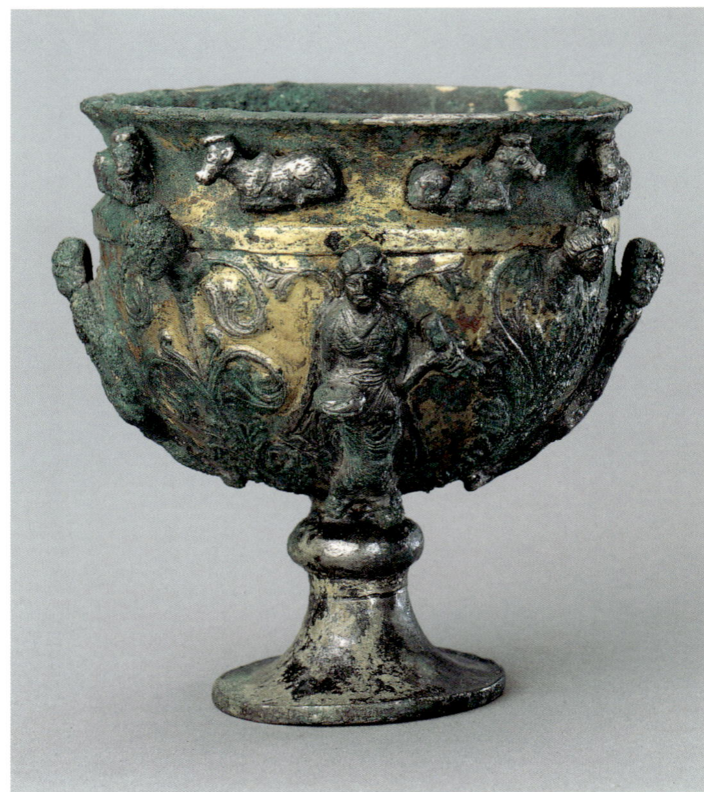

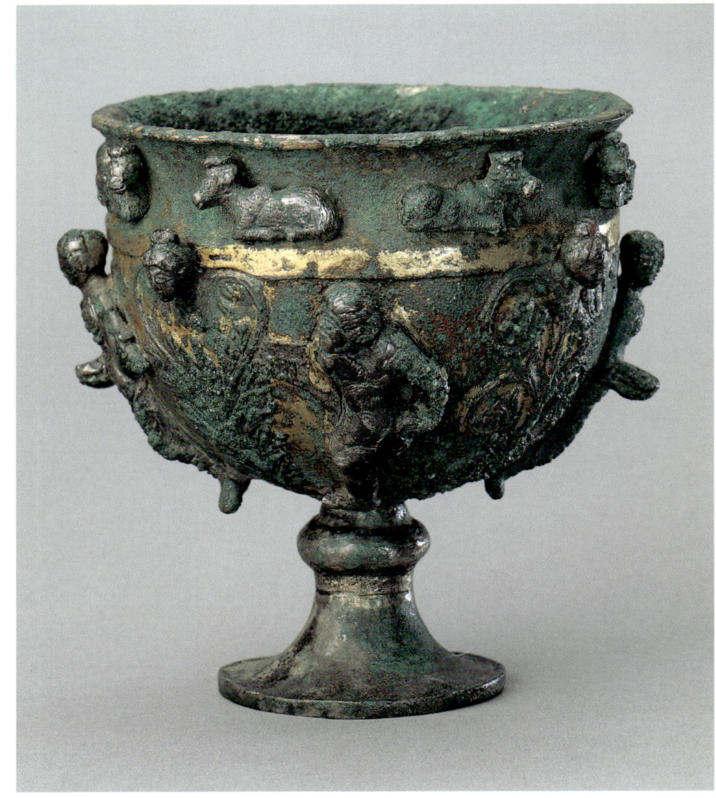

60

Stem cup with animal and human figures

4th–5th century
Bronze or silver alloy
Height 4 in. (10.3 cm)
Excavated at Datong, Shanxi Province, 1970
Datong City Museum

Excav. report in *Wenwu* 1977.9

This heavy cast stem cup was found together with cat. nos. 58, 59, 61, and 63. The cup is gilded; the figures remain unadorned. The stem has a gilded strip under the collar. Two female figures appear on opposite sides of the cup with two male figures equidistant between them. The women wear long, flowing attire that is more or less Greek in style. The men are almost naked. The human figures alternate with plants topped by female heads. Originally, there were eight recumbent deer along the border; one is now missing. Instead of horns, each deer has a low "crown," perhaps a prototype of the crownlike horns seen on the fantastic stags of the seventh and eighth centuries, during the Tang period (618–907).[1] However, it is possible that the deer are depicted as having lost their horns in the early spring, in which case the entire scene could be a symbolic representation of the season.

Each human figure has its own attributes. One woman holds a drinking vessel and a bowl filled with food. Leaves sprout above her shoulders. The bowl of the second woman is missing. Each man holds in his right hand the plant that spreads before him. One man also holds a *kantharus* in his left hand, the other a "waisted" drum. Below the figures is a row of small acanthus leaves. Also depicted are a tree reminiscent of the fantastic plants on middle- and late-Sasanian silver (4th–7th century) and an acanthus bush with a heart-shaped section at the top. A more geometricized variant of the latter motif appears on the silver bowl with portrait medallions (cat. no. 63), which is datable to the fifth century. The distribution of the figures is similar to that on the footed bowl with red stones.

BIM

1. For an example see Hayashi 1975, pl. 112.

61

Eight-lobed bowl

5th century
Silver
Diameter 9⅜ in. (23.8 cm)
Excavated at Datong, Shanxi Province, 1970
Datong City Museum

Excav. report in *Wenwu* 1977.9

This oblong bowl, while its refinement is reminiscent of Sasanian vessels of similar shape, accords also with the dynamic, organic forms of the fifth-century Gupta style.[1] The confluence of the Gupta and Sasanian styles was centered in Gandhara and the adjacent area of present-day Afghanistan. Typical of this Indian style is the fantastic image of the tiger attacking a sea monster from whose mouth and tail emerge rich, leafy sprays. The motif is seen also on an Indo-Bactrian bowl in the British Museum, London, also datable to the fifth century, on which are birds whose crests, wings, and tails are composed of the same foliate elements.[2]

The present bowl and its foot were produced from thick sheets of silver pressed between two molds. The richly decorated central medallion was made separately. On the exterior is a Bactrian inscription that reads: χιγγιλο ι χοιοχο.[3] (The inscription is incised on the exterior surface.) A drawing of this inscription has been published by Lin Meicun in which the last syllable is βο.[4] The syllables χο and βο are written separately. The last word could be χοβο—"one's own"—whereas in the text χιγγιλο ι χοιοχο βο an additional χο could mistakenly have been omitted. In other words, one could read χιγγιλο ι χοιοχο [χο]βο as "Khingila xoioxo's [bowl]." On the seal of one of the several kings whose name was Khingila, the name and title are written as *eškiggilo [ ](r)ōkano xoē*.[5] The owner of the seal is possibly a different Khingila, who lived not later than the sixth century.

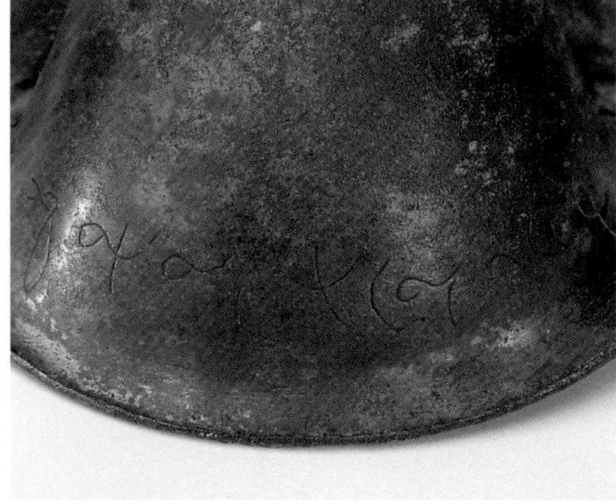

61, inscription

BIM

1. Anonymous 1972: 83–87; Chutu wenwu zhanlan gongzuozu 1973: 15, 151; Hsia Nai 1980: 156–58, pl. 1.2; Shih Hsio-Yen 1983: 64, fig. 6; Qi Dongfang 1999b: 384–85.
2. In Caves 2 and 17, in Ajanta, similar fighting monsters are shown on the ceilings; see Zin 1999: 15–16, 28–29, frontis.

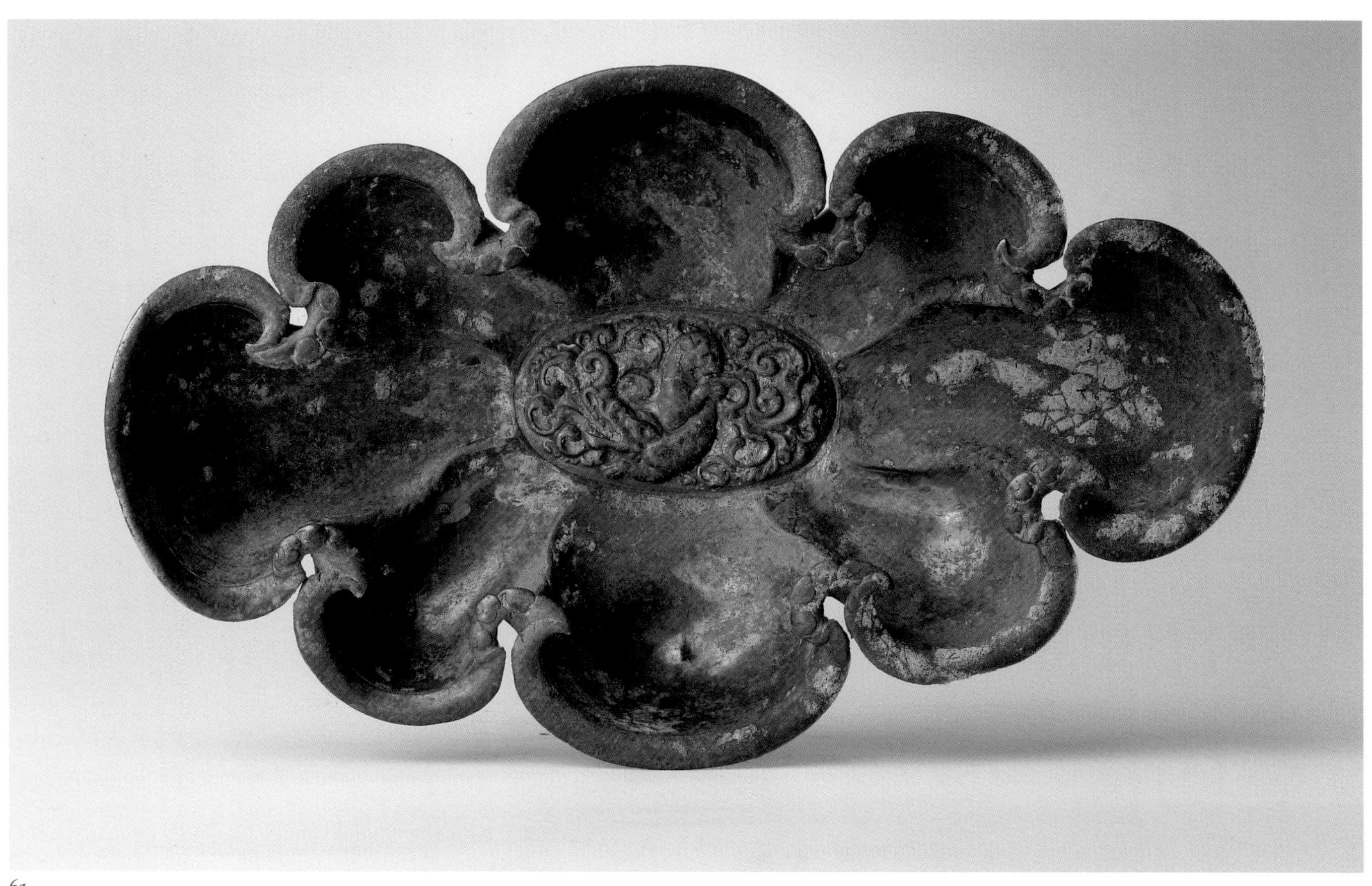

61

3. I wish to thank Nicholas Sims-Williams for his reading of this inscription. The last syllable was not visible in the photograph that he saw.
4. Lin Meicun 1998: 185.
5. Callieri 2002: 121–41; Sims-Williams 2002: 143–48; Callieri's date for the seal is the mid-fifth century. However, it is too narrow because the Dilberjin mural, his most important analogue, is datable from the mid-fifth to the mid-sixth century while his other analogue, the Stroganoff bowl, belongs to the following Turkic period as do the Balalyk and the latest Dilberjin murals; Marshak 2002b: 13–15, 210.

62
Plate with hunting scene

Gilt silver
Late 3rd or early 4th century
Diameter 7⅛ in. (18 cm)
Excavated from the tomb (dated 504) of Feng Hetu, Datong, Shanxi Province, 1981
Datong City Museum

Excav. report in *Wenwu* 1983.8

When this silver-gilt plate decorated with an unusual hunting scene was discovered, it was viewed with some excitement as a direct link between the courts of Iran and China during the Sasanian period (3rd–mid-7th century).[1] During these centuries in Iran there was a controlled production of prestigious and highly valued silver-gilt plates on which a Sasanian monarch, wearing a distinctive crown, was depicted hunting wild animals.[2] These precious luxury vessels of Sasanian Iran were donative objects made in court workshops and given to faithful courtiers and neighboring rulers. Many of the pieces were eventually transported and traded beyond the borders of the kingdom. The hunting scenes on the official Sasanian works were standardized in form and appearance from the end of the fourth century into the sixth century. The royal hunter, wearing a crown known from Sasanian coins, was generally depicted on horseback pursuing pairs of animals in a balanced and unrealistically static composition. Artistic canons dictated the representation of the royal dress and other details, and landscape elements formed only a minor part of the scene.

Obviously this plate, which was found in China, differs from the official Sasanian type. The hunter wears no known Sasanian royal crown; the action is dynamic, and the landscape of tall reeds is an overwhelming presence in the design. Though not seen on Sasanian coins, similar hunters wearing headdresses are represented in the art of Sasanian Iran on silver plates and in stone carvings dating from the end of the third century through the early fourth century, before the Sasanian royal hunt type was established. The persons who commissioned these early vessels are thought to have been princes of the royal family, who served as governors of provinces within the kingdom. It is probable that the hunter on this plate found in the tomb, dated A.D. 504, of Feng Hetu, in Datong, Shanxi, is such an early Sasanian prince-governor of a region on the eastern borders of Iran.[3]

The extraordinary pose of the hunter is an indication that the scene is a representation of some particular epic or heroic feat rather than a standard royal hunt. North and east of Iran, the conquests of Alexander the Great in the fourth century B.C. and the rule of his successor Seleucus (312–281 B.C.) brought Greek settlers and artisans to Bactria, and Greek literary works, among them the tales of Homer and the plays of Euripides, became known to the local populace. Among eastern Iranians there were also heroic tales of skillful hunters, tales that eventually entered the great story of the Iranian Empire later recorded by the Persian epic poet Ferdowsi (late 10th–early 11th century A.D.) in his *Shahnameh* (Book of Kings). The scene on the plate found in China probably illustrates an event from a familiar epic, but there is no evidence to suggest whether the actions of the bold hunter led, in the eyes of the viewer, to the association of the princely figure with Heracles, Odysseus, Bizhan, Gerschasp, or some other hero.

Because of formal, stylistic, and iconographic features, as well as the apparent reliance of the scene on a familiar heroic narrative, the most likely place of manufacture is in the lands newly conquered by the early Sasanian rulers in present-day northern Afghanistan or southern Turkmenistan. This hypothesis is supported by the appearance of another silver plate on the Kabul market at about the same time the plate from the tomb of Feng Hetu was found.[4] On the Kabul plate, the same scene is represented: a princely hunter, with a headdress unlike the crowns appearing on Sasanian coins, spears a boar and turns, raising his right leg awkwardly behind him, to ward off a second boar. The Kabul plate has both a Middle Persian and a Bactrian inscription giving the weight of the piece and the name of the owner, respectively. The inscriptions are incised within the foot ring on the reverse, a technique characteristic of inscriptions on silver vessels found in western Central Asia. In Sasanian Iran, inscriptions almost without exception are dotted onto the reverse surface of a silver vessel. The iconography and the style of the images on the Kabul plate, however, follow the Sasanian canon in the representation of a pair of animal quarry, in the paired-line stylization of the drapery worn by the hunter, and in the minor role of landscape elements. The probable date of the piece is the late fourth or early fifth century, almost a century later than the plate found in China, but the reliance on Sasanian modes suggests that this image is also a reference to some form of Sasanian authority in the region where it was made.

While it is probable that the plate found in China was made in a workshop outside the court centers of the new Sasanian kingdom in Iran, it nevertheless illustrates the extension of Sasanian power and authority, at least temporarily, in the region north and east of Iran, where roads of trade and conquest led ultimately to China. Other objects in the tomb of Feng Hetu also reflect a taste for forms and styles associated with Iran and western Central Asia. Four "candle holders" found in the tomb are not typically Chinese in form but resemble Iranian fire altars in the stepped base,

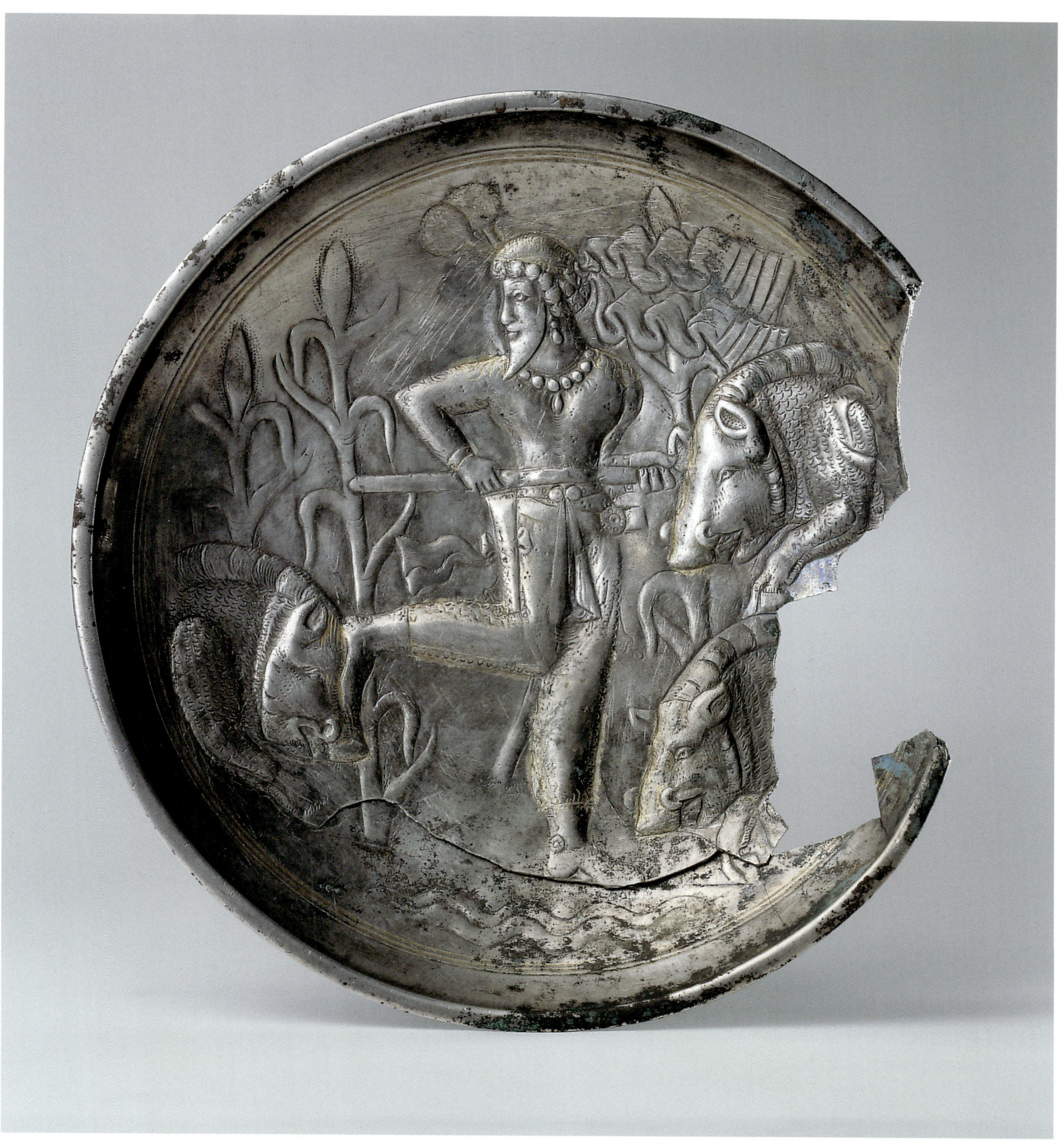

columnar support, and bowl at the top. An elliptical silver bowl differs from Chinese examples of this vessel shape in the diminutive "ear handles" with beaded borders.[5]

As commandant of garrison cavalry, Feng Hetu led a life that must have provided many contacts with western Central Asia, the source for the Chinese of the most-prized horses.[6] One piece of evidence for these contacts is this fragmentary silver vessel, an antique by the time it was placed in the tomb of Feng Hetu but nevertheless a princely Sasanian presence in the East. POH

1. Xia Nai 1983: 5–7.
2. Harper and Meyers 1981.
3. Harper 1990a: 51–59.
4. Ibid.: 58–59.
5. Ma Yuji 1983: 1–4.
6. Ma Yong 1983: 8–39.

63
Bowl with portrait medallions and plant motif

Ca. 5th century
Gilt silver
Diameter of mouth rim 3³/₈ in. (8.5 cm)
Excavated at Datong, Shanxi Province, 1970
Datong City Museum

Excav. report in *Wenwu* 1977.9

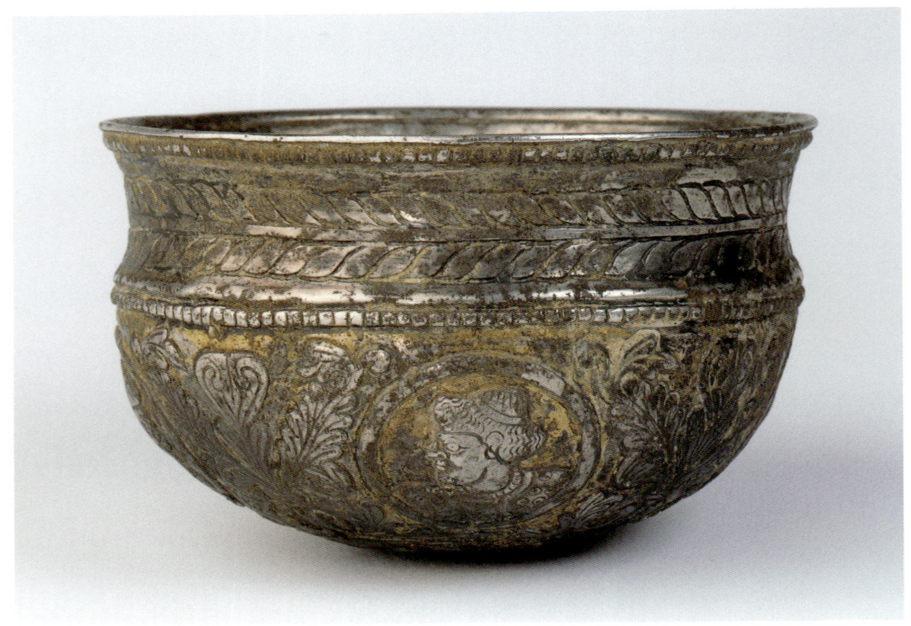

63

This silver bowl was excavated together with the four other imported metal vessels in this exhibition (cat. nos. 58–61) at a site in the southern part of the Northern Wei capital, Pingcheng (Datong).[1] It is probable that these western luxury goods reached the Northern Wei court after the defeat of the Ruru (Ruanruan) in the 450s, when delegations from Khotan, Kashmir, and Persia—actually, more merchants' caravans than diplomatic missions—traveled to the city.[2]

The bowl may have had a foot, and its shape and relief designs are similar to those of a Sasanian silver stem cup belonging to the Sasanian king Varahran II who reigned in the third quarter of the third century.[3] However, the gilded background and the flat relief decoration without inlaid details are typical of much later silver vessels: Byzantine, beginning in the sixth century, for example, and more or less contemporary late Sasanian and late Bactrian.[4] A shallow fifth-century silver bowl in the State Hermitage Museum, Saint Petersburg displaying a portrait medallion on the bottom and a scene with unmounted hunters is the earliest example of this kind of background in Central Asia. It is executed in the mixed Gupta–Bactrian style.[5] In Rome, the abstract gold background of the mosaics appears in the first half of the fifth century. The treatment of the laurel-leaf garland around the upper register of the present bowl is far removed stylistically from its classical prototype. In this case, each of the two rows of leaves seems an independent ornamental motif similar to the frieze of the Gupta–Bactrian vessel. In Rome, simplified laurel garlands with two rows of leaves frequently occur on fourth-century silver.[6] The portraits in the medallions are somewhat formalized, like those on fifth-century Bactrian seal gems or the heads of the mounted hunters on another Bactrian (but not Gupta) bowl from the Hermitage.

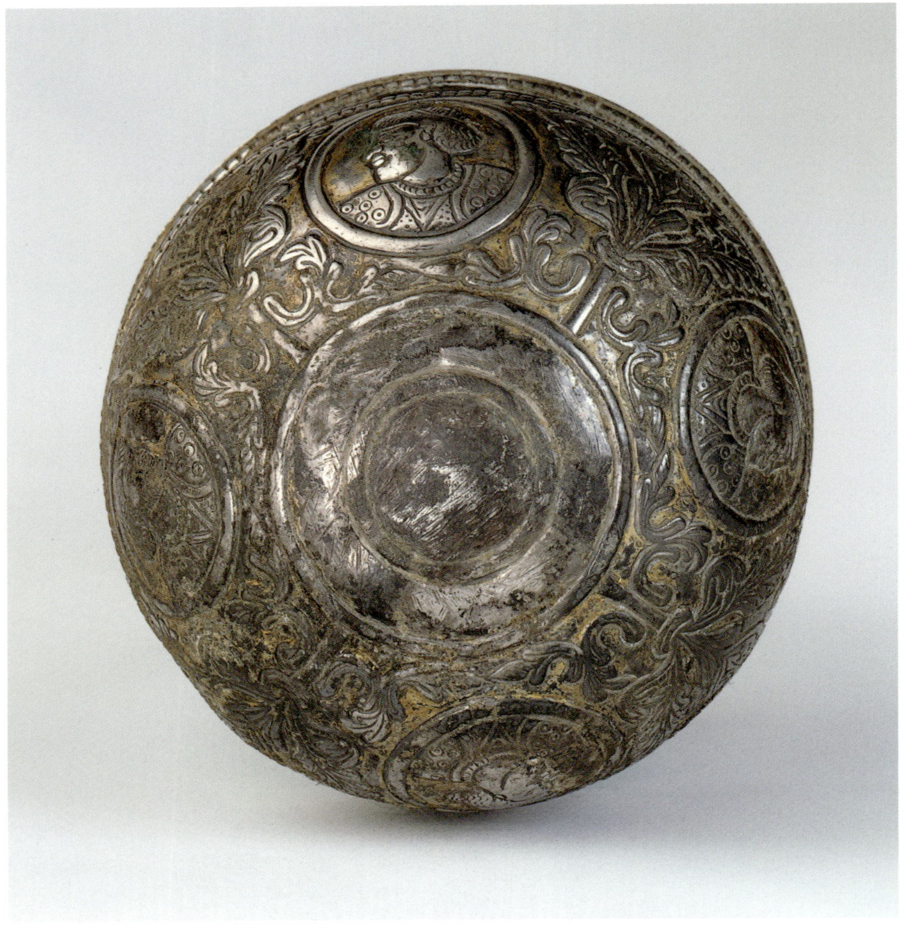

63, bottom

This bowl may date latest among the Pingcheng finds that can be described as Hellenized. The Hermitage bowl showing the equestrian hunters (see fig. 36) cannot be dated earlier than the fourth century, as the reliefs find two analogues that are datable to a later period. The rare and complex floral decoration on the bottom has a single parallel with the bottom of another bowl, also in the Hermitage, that displays the head of a goddess protecting a city repeated four times.[7] Such a group first made its appearance in the 290s, when the Roman Empire was divided into four parts, each with its own capital city. The second analogue is with a depiction of the royal hunt on a Bactrian silver bowl in the British Museum, London, datable to the mid-fifth century. The latter shows two Kidarite, one early Hephthalite, and one Bactrian rider.[8] The acanthus leaves on the present bowl, on the other hand, are highly schematized and must therefore be the latest variant of this motif present on silver bowls with portrait medallions dating from the third to the fifth century.

BM

1. Chutu wenwu zhanlan gongzuozu 1973: 15 (explanatory vol.), 150 (pictorial vol.); Sun Peiliang 1977: 63, 65–75; Rawson 1982: 2; Shih Hsio-Yen 1983: 64, fig. 5; Nara kokuritsu hakubutsukan 1988: 104, 105, 200, 201, no. 88; Sun Ji 1989: 38–44; Chu Shibin 1990: 1–9; Qi Dongfang 1999b: 257–58.
2. Müller 2002: 37–41.
3. Harper and Meyers 1981, pl. 2.
4. Effenberger et al. 1978: 13 (no. 14), fig. 88 (no. 18); Marshak 1986: 35–36, figs. 15, 16; Seipel 1996, no. 131; Desroches 2000: 64, no. 31.
5. Ivanov, Lukonin, and Smesova 1984: 37, no. 37, pls. 46–48.
6. See, for example, Projecta's casket and San Nazaro reliquary, 386 A.D.; Elsner 1998: 40, 42, 230–31, figs. 17, 155.
7. Compare Trever 1940, pls. 22–24 (the lion-and-tiger hunt bowl) and 27 (the four-Tyche bowl).
8. Dalton 1964, pls. 29–31; Harper and Meyers 1981: 129–31, fig. 44; Marshak 1986: 32–35, fig. 14.

64
Bowl with portrait medallions and plant motif

Probably 4th or early 5th century
Gilt silver
Diameter 4 in. (10.2 cm)
Excavated at Datong, Shanxi Province, 1988
Datong City Museum

EXCAV. REPORT in *Wenwu* 1992.8

This silver bowl, found together with a Sasanian glass bowl, is similar to cat. no. 63 but it displays several notable differences. The four portraits, enclosed in medallions, are more individualized;[1] possibly they represent childhood, youth, maturity, and old age. The last is depicted rather satirically. The floral motifs are rendered in a less stylized manner, exemplified in particular by the easily recognizable acanthus leaf with folded upper edge. The plain border and leaf calyx at the bottom are features inherited from the "Megara" bowls of the late Hellenistic period (second half of 3rd–2nd century B.C.).[2] The plain roundel in the center of the bottom, unlike that on cat. no. 63, is without any trace of a soldered foot. Two dense rows of beads—below the rim and below the plain border—are typical of Bactrian bowls of the third to the fifth century A.D. On bowls from Sogdiana, they are not as densely grouped. The gilded background of the relief composition is also a late feature.

Tomb 107 is dated slightly later than 493, the year the Northern Wei capital was moved from Pingcheng to Luoyang. It is possible that the dates of the present vessel and cat. no. 63 are not widely different, but it is evident that the master craftsman who made the latter included details that were in accordance with the style of his own day, whereas the maker of the present bowl followed more closely the ancient model. In any case, it is certainly much later than the Bartym bowl in the State Hermitage Museum, St. Petersburg, datable to about 300 (see fig. 35).[3]

BIM

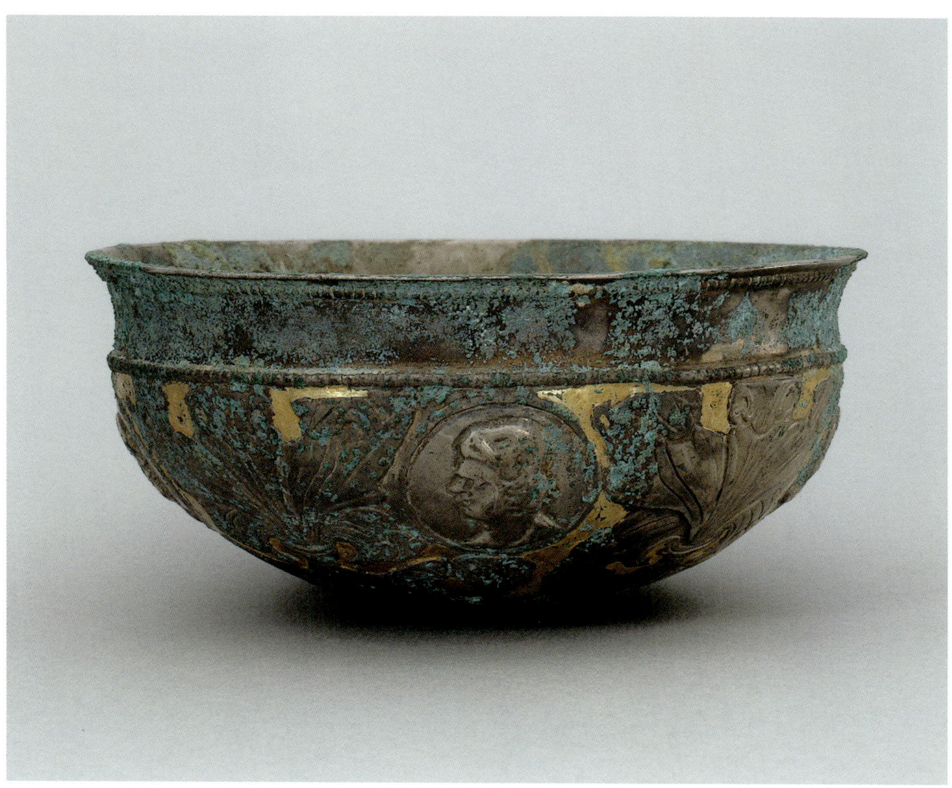

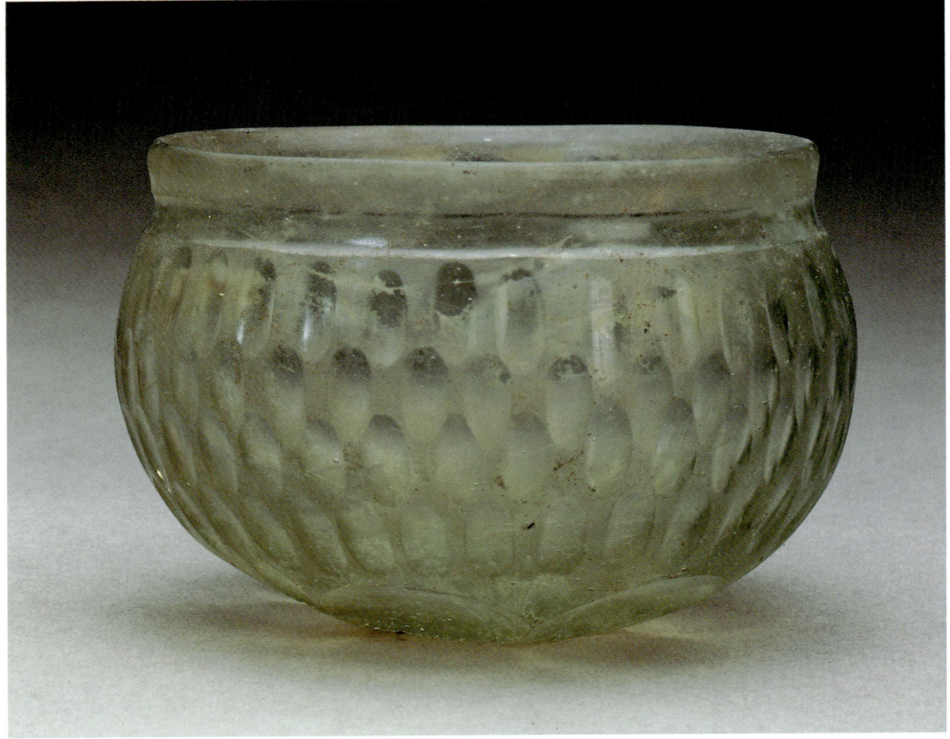

65

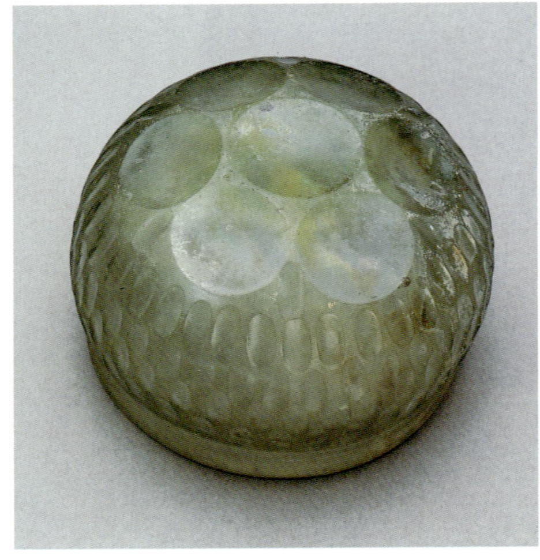

1. Shanxi sheng kaogu yanjiusuo 1992: 1–11; Qi Dongfang 1999b: 248–60.
2. *Antichnye gosudarstva Severnogo Prichernomor'ia* 1984, pls. 103, 104.
3. Bader and Smirnov 1954, fig. 3; Fajans 1957, pls. 8, 9.

65
Bowl

Ca. 4th–5th century
Glass
Diameter of mouth rim 4 in. (10.3 cm)
Excavated at Datong, Shanxi Province, 1988
Datong City Museum

Excav. report in *Wenwu* 1992.8

This glass bowl was excavated from Tomb 107 in a Northern Wei (386–534) cemetery in the southern suburb of Datong, Shanxi Province. It has a large mouth, short, compressed neck, spherical body, and curved bottom. The entire body is decorated with cut designs of subtly varying patterns. Three interlaced rows consisting of vertical oval facets embellish the surface. A fourth row comprises six horizontal oval facets. At the bottom is a circular facet. The transparent glass is almost colorless, with a slight tinge of yellow. The bowl is a high-quality Sasanian glass in very good condition, with few air bubbles, and except for a few speckles of weathering on the outer wall, it is lustrous and smooth as if new.

Also excavated from Tomb 107 were a number of objects with distinctly foreign characteristics (see cat. no. 64). Judging from the excavated earthenware and the structure of the tomb, Tomb 107 dates prior to the reign of Emperor Xiaowendi (r. 471–99), that is, no later than the mid-fifth century.

AJ

66
Bowl with applied decoration

Ca. 5th–6th century
Glass
Diameter of mouth rim 4 in (10.3 cm)
Found at the Feng family cemetery, Jingxian, Hebei Province, 1948
National Museum of China

Excav. report in *Kaogu tongxun* 1957.3

This light green glass bowl with wavy applied decoration was found in the tomb of Madame Zu at the Feng family cemetery in Jingxian, Hebei. Both the inner and outer walls are covered with a whitish weathered layer. Three undulating applied trails circle the body, each comprising ten waves and connected into a net pattern. The mouth rim curls inward and forms a rounded lip, and the bottom has an attached short ring foot. The pontil mark can be seen at the bottom. The techniques used to make the rim, foot, and ornamental trails are the same as those applied to the glass vessels from the tomb of Feng Sufu

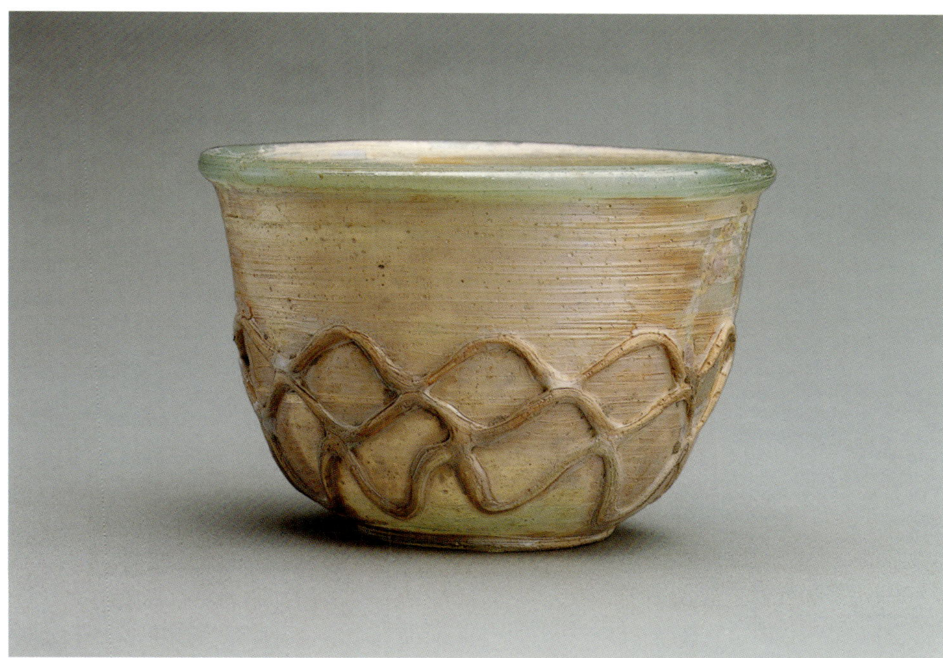

66

(cat. no. 42), although this bowl is more regular in shape. The wall is very thin, approximately .2 cm. The inner surface is smooth, while the outer surface has distinct horizontal texturing. The material is regular soda-lime glass.

Glass vessels decorated with similar wave or net patterns have also been found outside of China. Many glass shards with such decoration have been excavated from fifth-century Roman sites on the north coast of the Black Sea. The decoration and manufacturing techniques of a tall-stemmed goblet found in southern Russia compare closely with this bowl.[1] A tomb at Sop'ung[2] and Tomb 98 at Hwangnam, in Kyŏngju on the Korean Peninsula, contained similar glass cups, with wave patterns produced with similar methods.[3] All these vessels, excavated in both China and the Korean Peninsula, may have originated on the north coast of the Black Sea and were made in the Roman period.

AJ

1. Yoshimizu 1977: 63.
2. Koizumi 1927.
3. Kungnip Chungang pangmulgwan 1975.

67
Two jars

Ca. 5th century
Glass
Max. height 1¾ in. (4.3 cm)
Found in a stone coffer (dated 481) excavated at Dingzhou, Hebei Province, 1964
Hebei Institute of Archaeology

Excav. report in *Wenwu* 1966.5

In 1964, seven glass vessels were found in a stone coffer excavated from the crypt of a Northern Wei (386–534) pagoda in Dingzhou, Hebei. Among them were these two blown glass jars, which are sky blue in color and translucent. The walls are especially thin, about .1 centimeter, and covered with a whitish weathered layer. The two jars are nearly identical in shape. Both have a small mouth, rounded lip, short neck, spherical body, and curved bottom. One has a foot ring; the other does not. The glass foot ring is fused to the base. The shape is seen also in earthenware jars of the same period, but the jars of glass are much smaller in size. The glass-blowing technique was traditionally used for Roman and Sasanian glass but not applied to Chinese glassware before the Northern Wei period. It is evident that the artisans who made the present jars had not fully

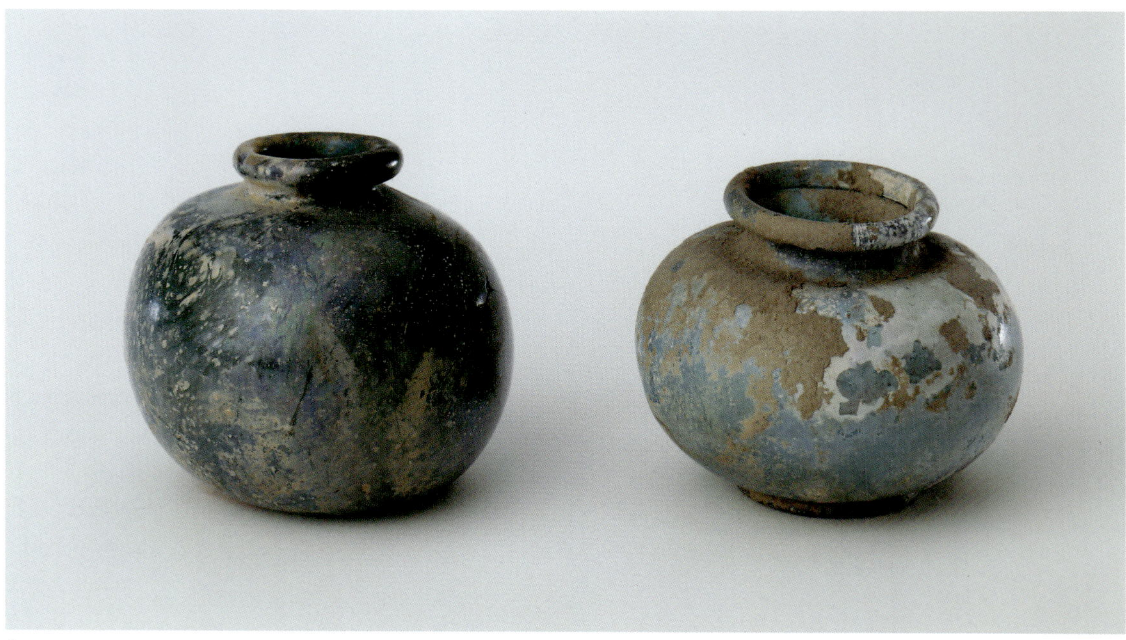

67

mastered the new method. The shape of the vessels is simple and not very regular, and the glass has dense clusters of air bubbles. Compared with West Asian glassware, they are noticeably inferior.

AJ

68
Bowl

Ca. 5th century
Glass
Diameter of mouth rim 5¼ in. (13.4 cm)
Found in a stone coffer (dated 481) excavated at Dingzhou, Hebei Province, 1964
Hebei Institute of Archaeology

EXCAV. REPORT in *Wenwu* 1966.5

Of the seven glass vessels excavated from a Northern Wei pagoda in Dingzhou (see cat. no. 67), this bowl is the largest and best made. Like the two jars, the glass is sky blue and transparent, but in this example there are more air bubbles. The surface is partially covered with a whitish weathered layer. The vessel is of blown glass, and the mouth was rounded by heating. Besides glassware, the finds from the pagoda include Roman gold coins, Sasanian silver coins, and objects of gold and silver, offerings made for the construction of the pagoda. Some of these precious artifacts were likely to have come from the Northern Wei imperial palace. It has been documented that some of the glass objects for the imperial family in Pingcheng (Datong) were made in Yuezhi in Central Asia. The glass vessels excavated from the pagoda in Dingzhou may thus have had some connection to the activities of Central Asian artisans in Datong.

AJ

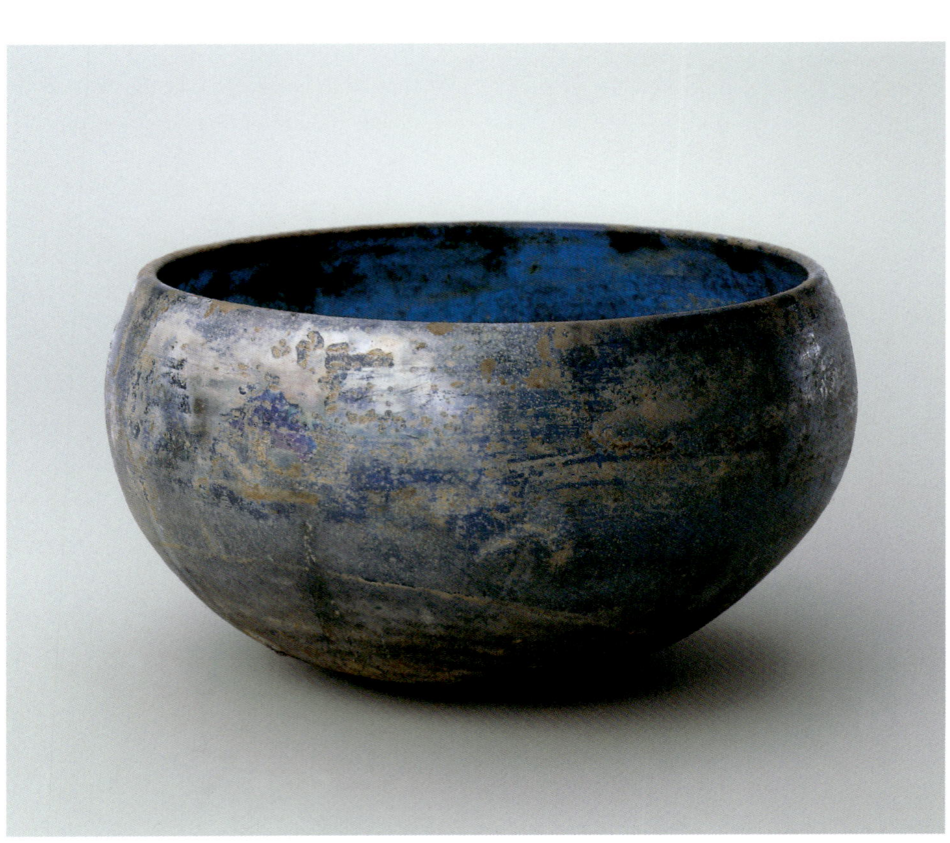

69
Section of a painted screen

Northern Wei dynasty (386–534), second half of the 5th century
Lacquer and pigments on wood
32½ x 16 in. (81.5 x 40.5 cm)
Excavated from the tomb of Sima Jinlong (d. 484) and his wife, Datong, Shanxi Province, 1965–66
Shanxi Provincial Museum

EXCAV. REPORT in *Wenwu* 1972.3

One of the most important discoveries from the Northern Wei period (386–534) is the remains of a low lacquer screen with paintings illustrating virtuous women, filial sons, and other moral exemplars. The screen belonged to Sima Jinlong (after 420–484), a descendant of the Jin royal house whose father, Sima Chuzhi (390–464), had fled from Eastern Jin court rivalries and pledged his allegiance to the Northern Wei in 419, and eventually was enfeoffed as king of Langye.[1] Sima Jinlong's mother was a Wei princess. The screen probably stood on a dais used by Sima Jinlong, where it would have served as a constant admonition, prompting him to conduct himself according to the dictates of Confucian ritual propriety and ethics.

The screen was constructed of lacquered wood panels with flanges that fit into adjacent panels of the frame.[2] Once the red lacquer ground was laid down, a grid of yellow lines was added. Next, text panels were inserted within the resulting compartments. Finally, the figures and other narrative details were drawn in, with details often abutting or even overlapping the text panels, as in the case of Lady Ban Refusing to Ride in the Palanquin (opposite, bottom right).

The vignettes depicted on the screen are all recorded in well-known texts, although variations in the wording of the text panels indicate that they were sometimes transcribed from other sources.[3] On the front side of the screen (opposite, right) the top register depicts scenes from the life of

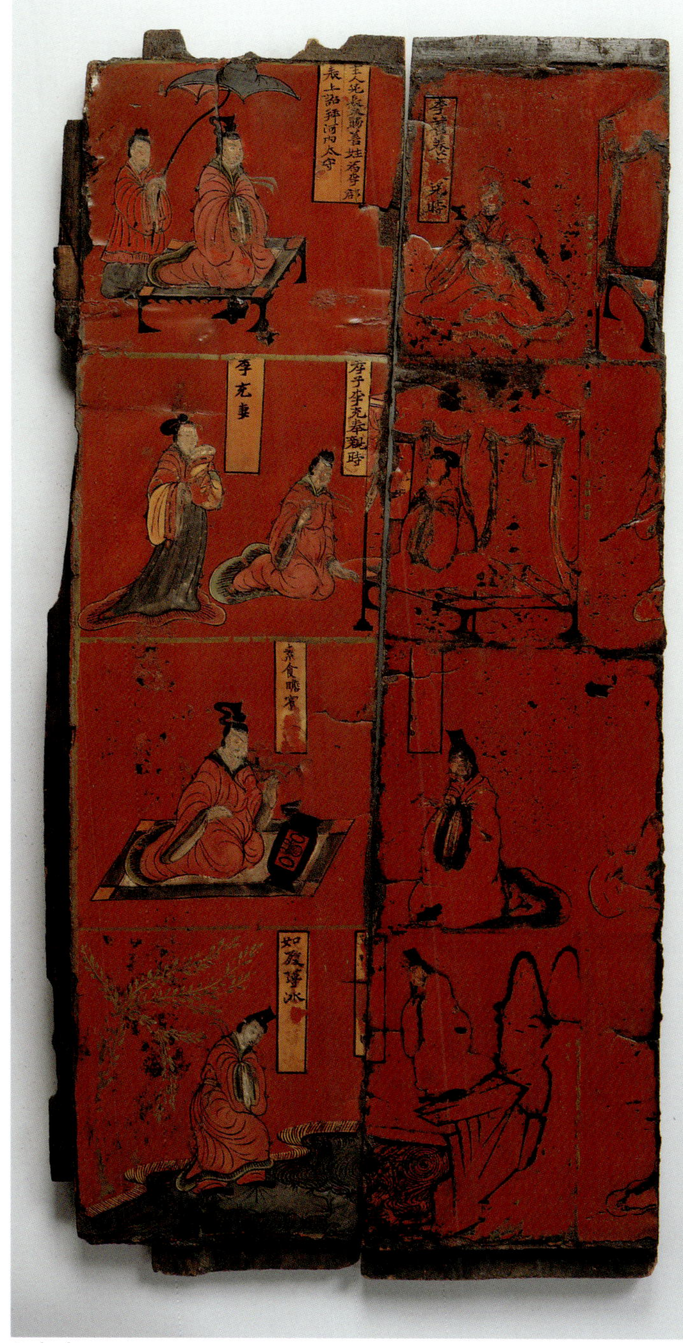

69, back

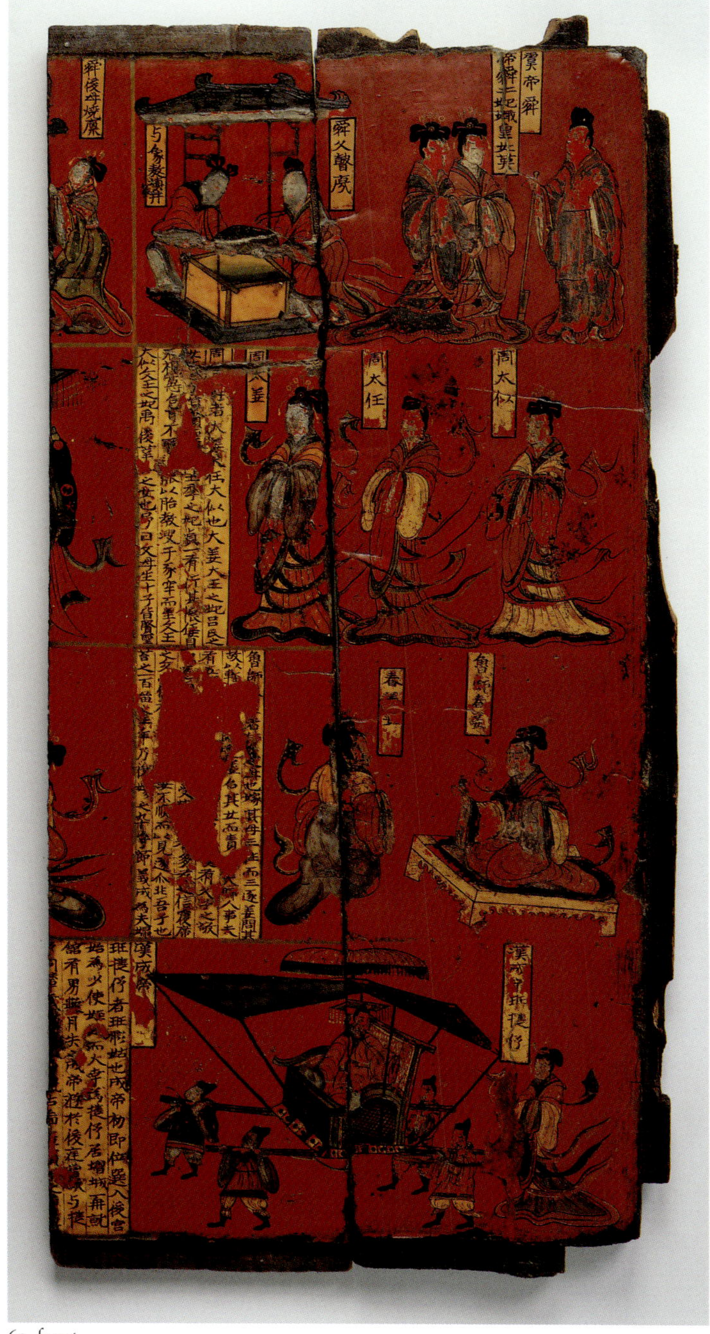

69, front

Shun, who remained filial to his family even after they attempted to kill him.[4] On the right, Shun is shown with his wives, Nüying and Ehuang, the virtuous daughters of the legendary Emperor Yao. He holds a shovel as he prepares to dig a well at his parents' request. To the left, Shun's father and younger brother prepare to drop a basket of soil down the well into which Shun has climbed in order to bury him. On the far left, Shun's mother attempts to kill him by burning down the granary that she has asked him to repair. In both cases, Shun manages to escape and is eventually made Yao's successor as emperor.

The second register depicts three virtuous mothers from the early years of the Zhou dynasty (ca. 1046–256 B.C.): Taijiang, the grandmother of King Wen, Tairen, the mother of King Wen, and Taisi, the mother of King Wu. The story of Lu Shi Chunjiang, a virtuous woman who instructed her daughter on how to be a proper wife, is illustrated in the third register.[5] The fourth register shows Lady Ban, a favorite of Han emperor Chengdi (r. 32–7 B.C.), refusing to ride with him in his palanquin. Instead, she admonishes him: "Your handmaid has heard that the wise rulers of the Three Dynasties of old were always accompanied by virtuous ministers, but never that they rode out with women by their side."[6]

The top register on the back (above left) depicts Li Shan, who fled with the infant son of a wealthy landholder when his family died of illness and the servants wanted to kill him in order to divide the

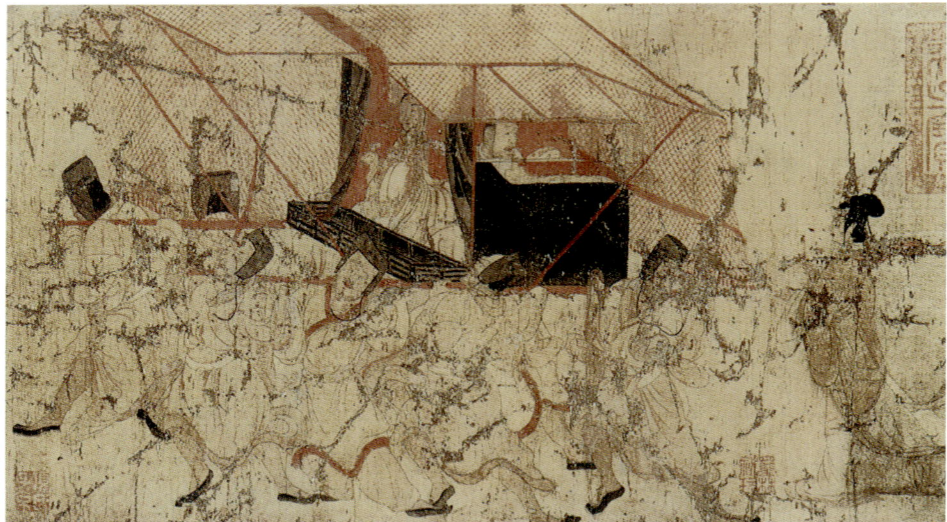

estate among themselves. When the boy was older, Shan exposed the servants' treachery and regained for him his rightful inheritance. As a result of his virtuous conduct, Emperor Guangwu (r. 25–57) made both Shan and the young man retainers in the household of the heir apparent. Subsequently, they both earned high official ranks. The screen depicts Li Shan seated on the right, possibly holding the infant in his arms. To the left, an official seated on a dais with a servant holding a parasol is, presumably, the son after having attained an official position.[7]

The second register illustrates the story of Li Chong (act. early 2nd century). Li was one of six sons born to a poor family. When his wife suggested that they take their share of the family property and leave, Li announced to his mother that his wife was unworthy and should be sent away.[8] In the illustration, Li's mother is seated on a canopied dais while Li kneels before her. The disgraced wife stands behind him.

The third register on the back illustrates the story of Mao Rong. When the distinguished scholar Guo Tai (127–169) visited his home, Mao prepared vegetables for Guo and himself but served his mother a more desirable dish with chicken, whereupon Guo declared Mao to be a man of true virtue. The screen depicts Guo Tai seated on a mat before a low table set with dishes. Mao Rong kneels before him.[9]

The bottom register is not about filial behavior, but is an admonition to exercise good judgment. The scene shows two forms of risky behavior: a man on an ice floe and a man standing at the edge of a rocky precipice. Other sections of the screen show similar scenes of virtuous women and filial sons as well as at least a partial representation of the Seven Sages of the Bamboo Grove (cat. no. 113).[10]

In its subject matter and style, the screen reflects the southern influence of Eastern Jin dynasty (317–420) prototypes such as the *Admonitions of the Instructress to the Court Ladies,* a handscroll in the British Museum, London, attributed to Gu Kaizhi (ca. 344–ca. 406).[11] Both works are characterized by tight-knit figural groups that are depicted in profile, set against a neutral background, and interspersed with text passages. The treatment of figures in the two works—coiffures, costumes, and accompanying furnishings—are virtually identical. Women are tall and slender and wear floor-length robes with fluttering scarves; men wear billowing garments and the ritual paraphernalia of rulers or officials. In both works, sensitively drawn faces contrast with exuberantly drawn draperies defined by rhythmic, fluid arcs that convey a sense of volume and buoyant movement.

But the differences are equally telling, as is apparent when one compares an episode the two works have in common, Lady Ban Refusing to Ride in the Palanquin. In the version on the screen (previous page), not only are the bearers dwarflike—reflecting the convention of depicting less important figures on a smaller scale—but they are also given nearly identical poses. The scroll, on the other hand (see illustration at left), shows a complex knot of figures grimacing and struggling under the weight of a litter that holds the emperor and his concubine—making explicit the impropriety of the emperor's action. The subtle portrait of the emperor, peering sheepishly out of the enclosed compartment, underscores the shamefulness of his behavior. The local artisans responsible for the screen clearly had knowledge of Eastern Jin pictorial conventions, but they lacked the skill necessary to evoke the psychological nuances conveyed by master artists such as Gu Kaizhi.

The screen demonstrates that artistic influences from the courts of South China had an impact on Northern Wei elite culture years before the Wei capital was relocated from Pingcheng to Luoyang in 494, when Emperor Xiaowen (r. 471–99) advocated the sinicizing of many Xianbei customs. As a descendant of the Jin royal house, it is perhaps not surprising that Sima Jinlong would have owned a painted screen influenced by Eastern Jin models. But the differences between this Northern Wei luxury object and the *Admonitions* handscroll also point to a significant time lag between artistic developments in the south and their appearance in the Wei capital in the north.

MKH

1. For a thorough analysis of the screen's style and function and a complete transcription of the inscribed texts, see Hsieh Cheng-fa 2001. On Sima Jinlong and his father, see *WS* 37: 854–57.
2. For sections of the frame, see Chutu wenwu zhanlan gongzuozu 1973: 145. For the other three surviving sections of the screen see *Zhongguo meishu quanji: Huihua bian, 1,* 1986, pl. 100.
3. See *Biographies of Virtuous Women (LNZ),* by Liu Xiang (77–6 B.C.), the *History of the Han Dynasty (HS),* by Ban Gu (died A.D. 92), and the *History of the Later Han Dynasty (HHS),* by Fan Ye (398–445).

4. See *LNZ* 1: 3–4. See also Giles 1898: 663–64, no. 1741, "Shun."
5. See *TPYL* 541: 2453.
6. See *HS* 97b: 3983–84. Translation from Giles 1898: 610, no. 1599, "Pan Chieh-yü." It is notable that a poem by Lady Ban, quoted in her *Hanshu* biography, mentions the virtuous daughters of Yao and the mothers of King Wen and King Wu, all of whom are depicted in registers above Lady Ban's portrayal. For a translation of Lady Ban's *Hanshu* biography, see Watson 1974, pp. 261–64.
7. *HHS* 81: 2679–80. The text on the screen differs somewhat from the *Hou Hanshu* account.
8. See ibid.: 2684–85.
9. For Mao Rong, see *HHS* 68: 2228; for Guo Tai, see ibid.: 2225–27, and Giles 1898: 410, no. 1073, "Kuo T'ai."
10. See *Zhongguo meishu quanji: Huihua bian, 1*, 1986: 160, 163, pl. 100.
11. See McCausland 2003. The scroll is probably a copy of the sixth or seventh century, but appears to faithfully reproduce an Eastern Jin model that has long been associated with Gu Kaizhi.

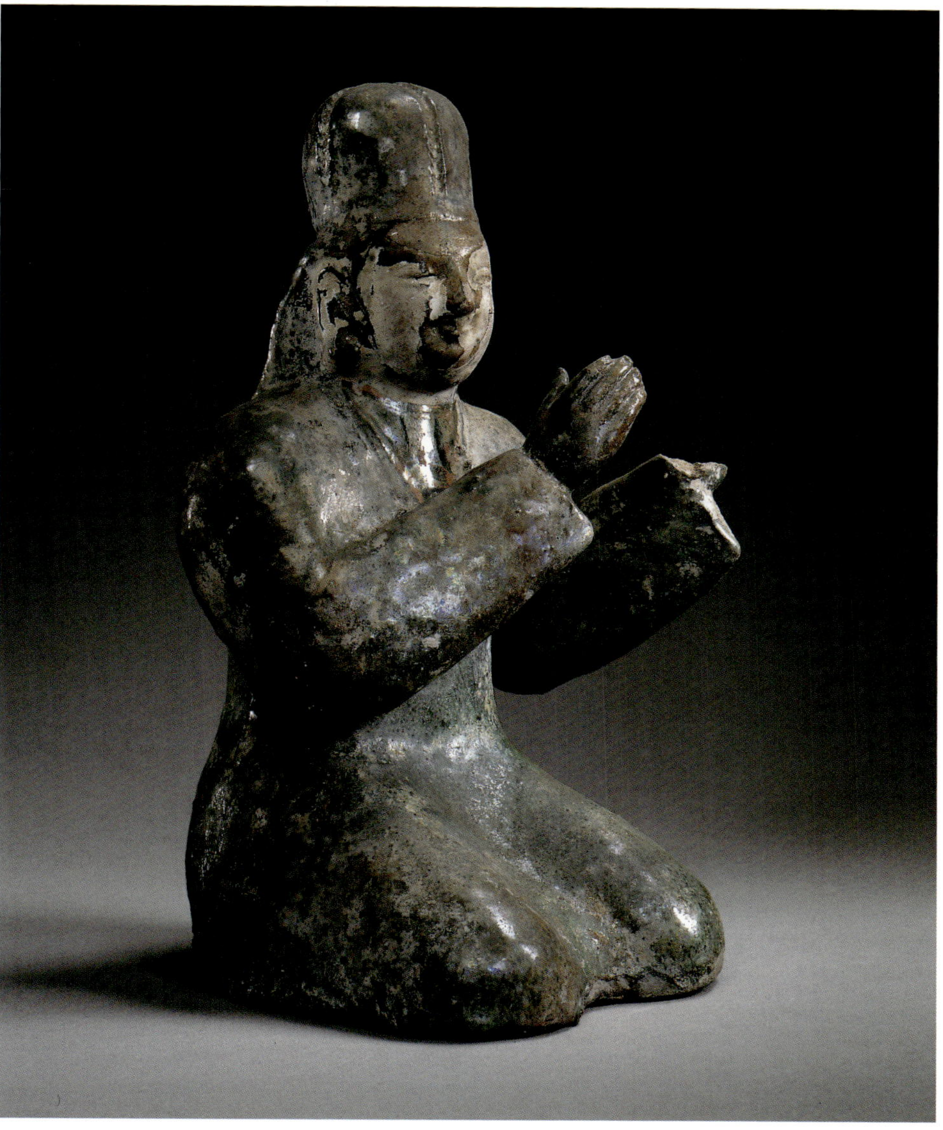

70
Female attendant

Northern Wei dynasty (386–534)
Glazed earthenware
Height 8 ¼ in. (21 cm)
Excavated from the tomb of Sima Jinlong (d. 484) and his wife, Datong, Shanxi Province, 1965–66
Shanxi Provincial Museum

Excav. report in *Wenwu* 1972.3

The tomb, dated 484, of Sima Jinlong and his wife (see cat. no. 69) measures close to forty-six and a half feet in length.[1] Although it had been opened prior to its official excavation in 1965, 484 grave goods remained, primarily in the antechamber. In addition, more than 400 ceramic funerary sculptures were found in the tomb. They are standard types in the assemblages of fifth-century tombs, including military personnel, servant figures, guardian creatures, and a host of animals—horses, Bactrian camels, sheep, oxen, chickens, and dogs.

Among these finds were several female figures, including twelve musicians. This kneeling performer was most likely part of an ensemble similar to that excavated from a Northern Wei tomb in Datong in 2000 (cat. no. 52). She wears the same type of clothing and headgear as those figures and is shown with her hands held up and slightly to the left, as if playing an instrument, possibly a transverse flute (*dizi*). The frequent use of molds to make tomb sculptures perhaps explains the similarity between the musicians in the two tombs.

Unlike the slightly earlier figures from the tomb of Song Shaozu, however, those found in Sima Jinlong's tomb were covered with glaze, a glassy coating fired onto the surface of a pottery vessel or sculpture. Glazes, which come in various colors (in this case, it is dark green), both enhance the surface and render it impermeable. In China, the use of glazing was known as early as the Shang dynasty (ca. 1600–ca. 1046 B.C.), and lead glazes were commonly used in funerary ceramics produced during the Han (206 B.C.–A.D. 220). The use of glazing for the sculptures in Sima Jinlong's tomb reflects the reemergence, in the late fifth century, of this technology in the north. The traces of red pigment seen on the neckline of the musician suggest that parts of the glazed surface were once painted, a rarefied practice that appears to have no parallels.

DPL

1. See Shanxi sheng Datong shi bowuguan and Shanxi sheng wenwu gongzuo wei yuan hui 1972: 20–33, 64. See also Quest for Eternity 1987, nos. 46–52.

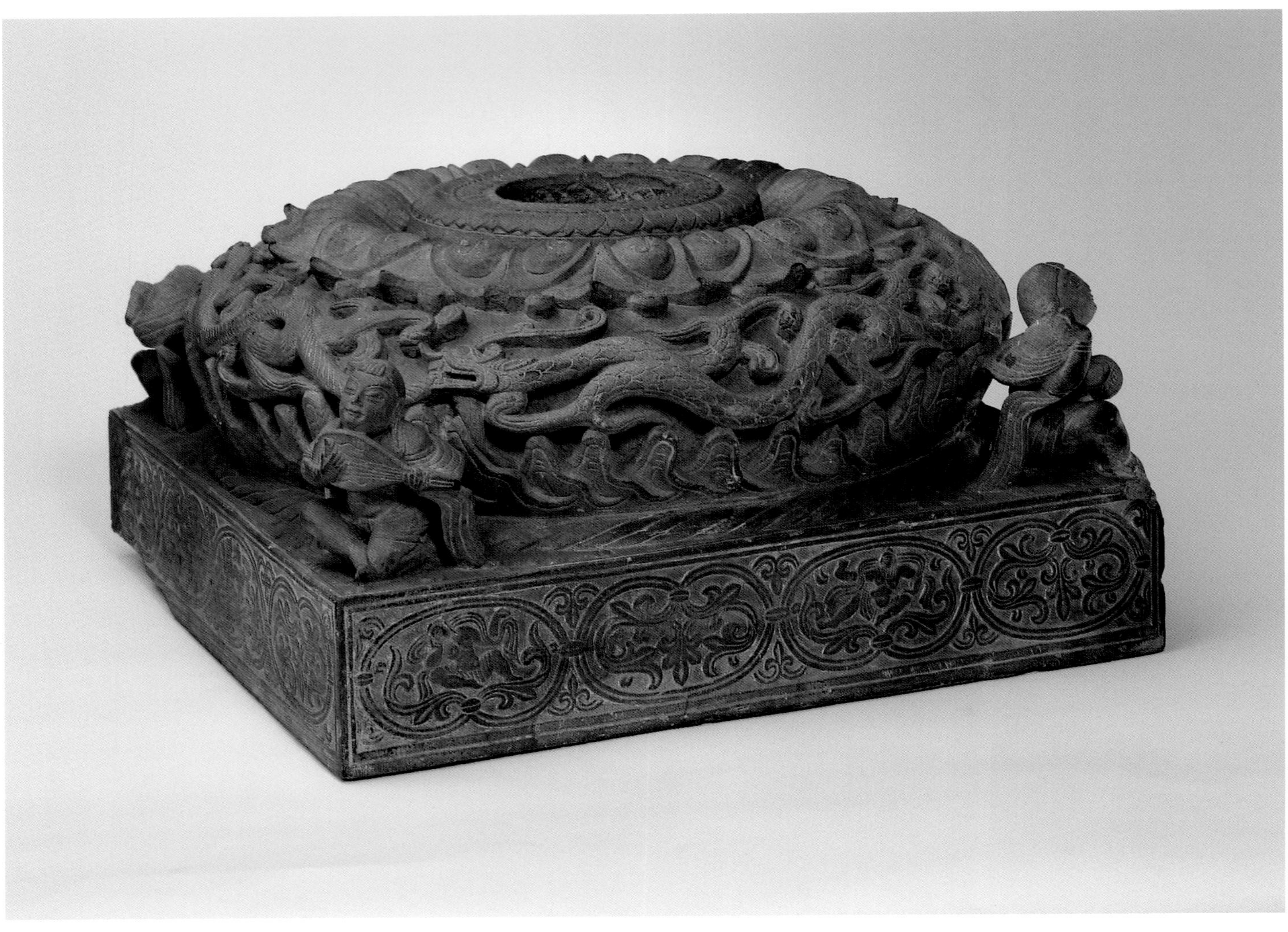

71
Pole base

Northern Wei dynasty (386–534), second half of the 5th century
Stone
Length and width, each 12⅝ in. (32 cm)
Excavated from the tomb of Sima Jinlong (d. 484) and his wife, Datong, Shanxi Province, 1965–66
Shanxi Provincial Museum

Excav. report in *Wenwu* 1972.3

This is one of four stone bases for poles from the tomb of Sima Jinlong (d. 484) and his wife (d. 474). In spite of the early removal of the more valuable objects by looters, the contents of this tomb are particularly important for studying the material culture of the Northern Wei at the height of its power and prosperity prior to the transfer of the capital south to Luoyang in 493.

The motifs and embellishment on the objects in this tomb represent a synthesis of the decorative arts in areas conquered by the Northern Wei between the years 436 and 439. This base exhibits influence from the western parts of the Northern Wei empire—the former territory of the Northern Liang (Gansu) leading to Central Asia. The palmette scroll on the sides of the base is of western origin and made its first appearance in China at about this time. This form of the scroll, with human figures, is seen also on the decorative friezes in the Buddhist cave temples at Yungang of the same period (fig. 16). The *pipa*, or four-string lute, played by the freestanding musicians at the corners, is an instrument introduced from the steppes. The high-relief carving on the upper part of the base is also an innovation in Chinese art; previously, the emphasis was on planes and lines.

Another important object from the tomb of Sima Jinlong is the painted lacquer screen (cat. no. 69), which is fully discussed in the entry.

JCYW

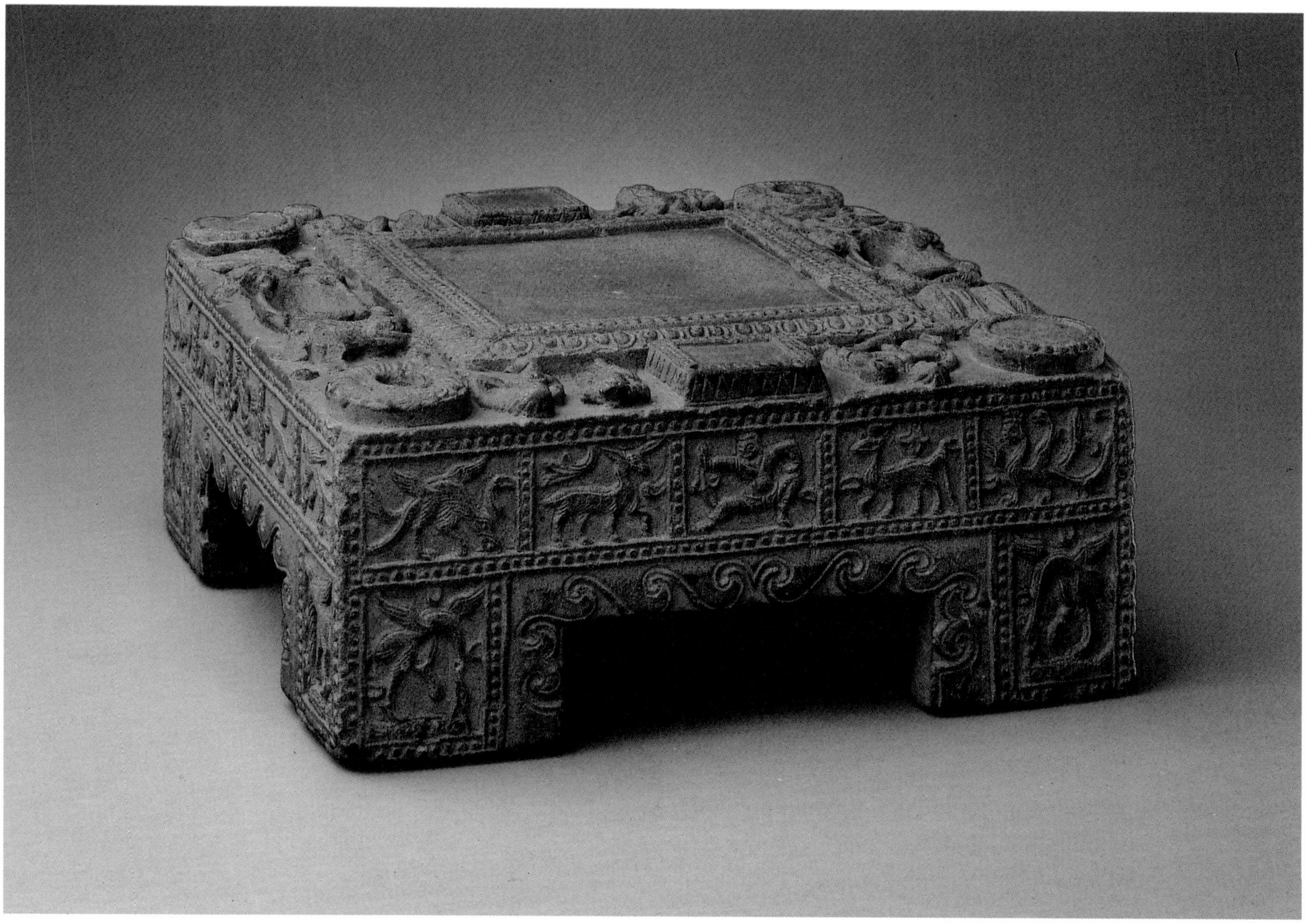

72

Stand

Northern Wei dynasty (386–534),
5th century
Stone
Height $3\frac{3}{8}$ in. (8.5 cm); length $8\frac{3}{8}$ in. (21.2 cm)
Excavated at Datong, Shanxi Province, 1970
Shanxi Provincial Museum

Excav. report in *Wenwu* 1977.9

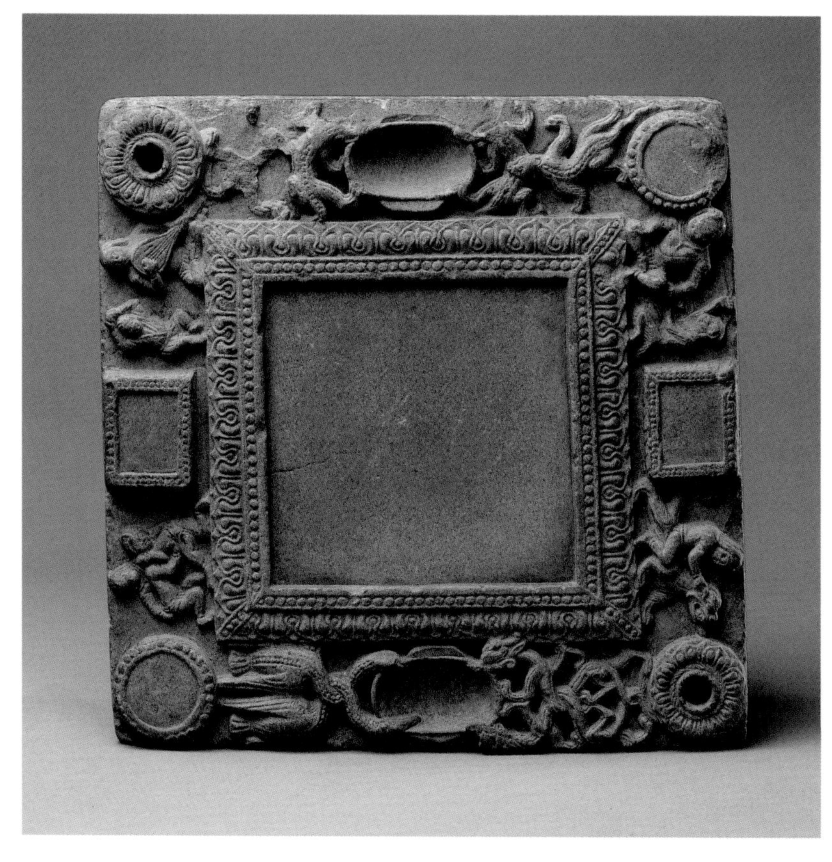

Profusely decorated on the sides and top, this small, square object was found in the southern part of the Northern Wei capital, Pingcheng (Datong), in the same vicinity that yielded many examples of foreign metalwork (see cat. nos. 58–61, 63). Pearl borders divide the sides into rectangular spaces. Long-necked birds—possibly geese—eating fish inhabit the lower cartouches, while other creatures, including a human-headed species, fill the upper register. Dancing figures are found in the central rectangle on two sides; partially seated figures fill the comparable spaces on the other sides.

Also carved in high relief, the imagery on the top is equally complex. A large square space bordered with pearls and lotus petals fills the center, and four circular platforms, two with central concavities, are placed at the corners. Figural scenes surround the smaller rectangular areas. These include, on one side, a man riding a lion or some other feline and, on the other, two wrestlers, a seated musician, and a dancer. Lizards with ear-cups and entwined geese and dragons complete the extraordinary décor. The figure riding a lion may have Indic roots. The wrestlers have prototypes in the earlier art of the steppes. The musician and dancer stem from Central Asia. And the ear-cups derive from Chinese traditions.

It seems unlikely that the piece is an inkstone, as has been suggested.[1] The square shape distinguishes it from known inkstones, which are rectangular, and the lavish decoration of the top surface would make such use difficult. It is worth noting that three small stone objects dating to the second or third century, with elaborate geometric patterning and floral imagery, were excavated at Taxila in Afghanistan.[2] They are identified as "stool querns," or mills used to grind grain or spices. As is true of the present piece, found in China, the extensive decoration on the surface of these objects would have made grinding impractical. Examples of the better-known saddle querns, or metates, have also been found in some number at Taxila.

It is possible that this object, excavated in China, and those found at Taxila once served a ritual function, perhaps as a stand for offerings in funerary or seasonal observances. Such use would help explain their extensive decoration, as well as the circular openings on the corners at the top of the Chinese example, which may have been used to hold an implement or some other object, perhaps an incense stick. As such, they may be related to the offering plaque (cat. no. 99), which may also have played a role in observances of some type.

DPL

1. Anonymous 1972, fig. 24; Chutu wenwu zhanlan gongzuozu 1973: 148.
2. Marshall 1951, pl. 140.

73
Mask with pendant ring handle

Northern Wei dynasty (386–534), 5th century
Bronze
Height 7³/₈ in. (18.7 cm)
Excavated at Leizumiao, Guyuan, Ningxia Autonomous Region, 1981
Guyuan Museum

Excav. report: Ningxia Guyuan bowuguan 1988: 1–8

This object from a fifth-century Northern Wei site is one of the few artifacts with a motif that survives from an earlier period of Xianbei culture on the steppes: the image of a human figure placed between animals. The motif is comparable to that on the gold ornament from Inner Mongolia dating to nearly two centuries earlier (cat. no. 35).

JCYW

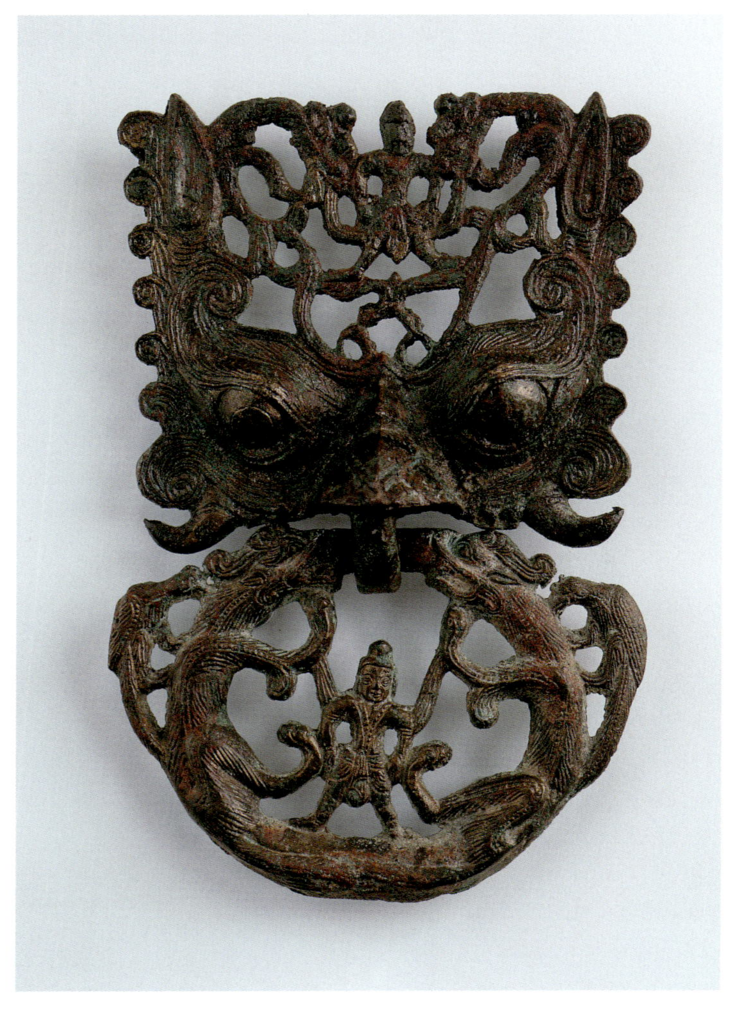

74
Seated Maitreya stele

Northern Wei dynasty (386–534), ca. 450
Sandstone
Height 17 3/8 in. (44 cm)
Found at Xiudesi, Quyang, Hebei Province, 1954
Hebei Provincial Museum

Excav. report in *Kaogu tongxun* 1955.3

The Chinese Buddhist stele was an adaptation of the earlier Confucian monument (see cat. no. 22). Remarkably, the production of stone steles postdates that of gilt bronzes. The earliest bronzes were cast at the beginning of the fourth century, if not earlier, while stone steles were not made until the early or mid-fifth century. This stele represents a seated Maitreya, Buddha of the Future. The crisscrossed legs indicate the deity's status as bodhisattva in his last incarnation, as does the presence of jewelry—the triple-disk crown and the beaded rope forming an X over the chest. The spiritual heir of Shakyamuni—the historical Buddha—sits on a lion throne, overwhelming his attendants on either side, who stand piously with hands joined. Behind them is a partially intact aureole with concentric bands of Buddha emanations, kneeling devotees, and darting flames. The four-footed stand on which Maitreya sits displays, on the horizontal register, a central incense burner attended by kneeling worshipers, six on each side. On the frontal legs are two donors clad in long tunics. A scroll runs along the rim.

The stele's style and content remind us of the political circumstances that enabled the Tuoba Wei to become so productive in the making of Buddhist images. Executed about 450 in Hebei this stele is modeled on the large Maitreya in Cave 275 in Dunhuang ascribed to Northern Liang patronage between 420 and 439, prior to the Tuoba Wei defeat of the Liang and their annexation of Gansu. The victory over northwestern China entailed the deportation of laborers, skilled workers, and clerics to Pingcheng (Datong), the capital of the Northern Wei until 494. The doctrinal and artistic riches of Dunhuang were reinterpreted in the late fifth century at the dynastic site of Yungang, Shanxi. While this small stele precedes—rather than postdates—the grand site by a decade, it, too, is the product of the conquest.

The appearance of the deity offers another insight. The large head and wide face were physical traits seen among the non-Chinese Tuoba. Such features are recognizable, for instance, in the burial figure of the dancer from Datong (cat. no. 51) and in the group of eight seated musicians from the same location (cat. no. 52). The affirmation of Tuoba ethnic roots is also associated with the early phase of Northern Wei art, which reflects the period before the court had initiated its program of sinicization. By the 480s, under the leadership of the empress dowager Wenming, the de facto ruler between 479 and 490, the court had, for all intents and purposes, suppressed its own origins and become completely acculturated. This development is reflected most vividly in the sculpture of Caves 5 and 6 at Yungang, which had been sponsored directly by the empress. The images unearthed in these caves no longer bear any connection to their Tuoba heritage.

AFH

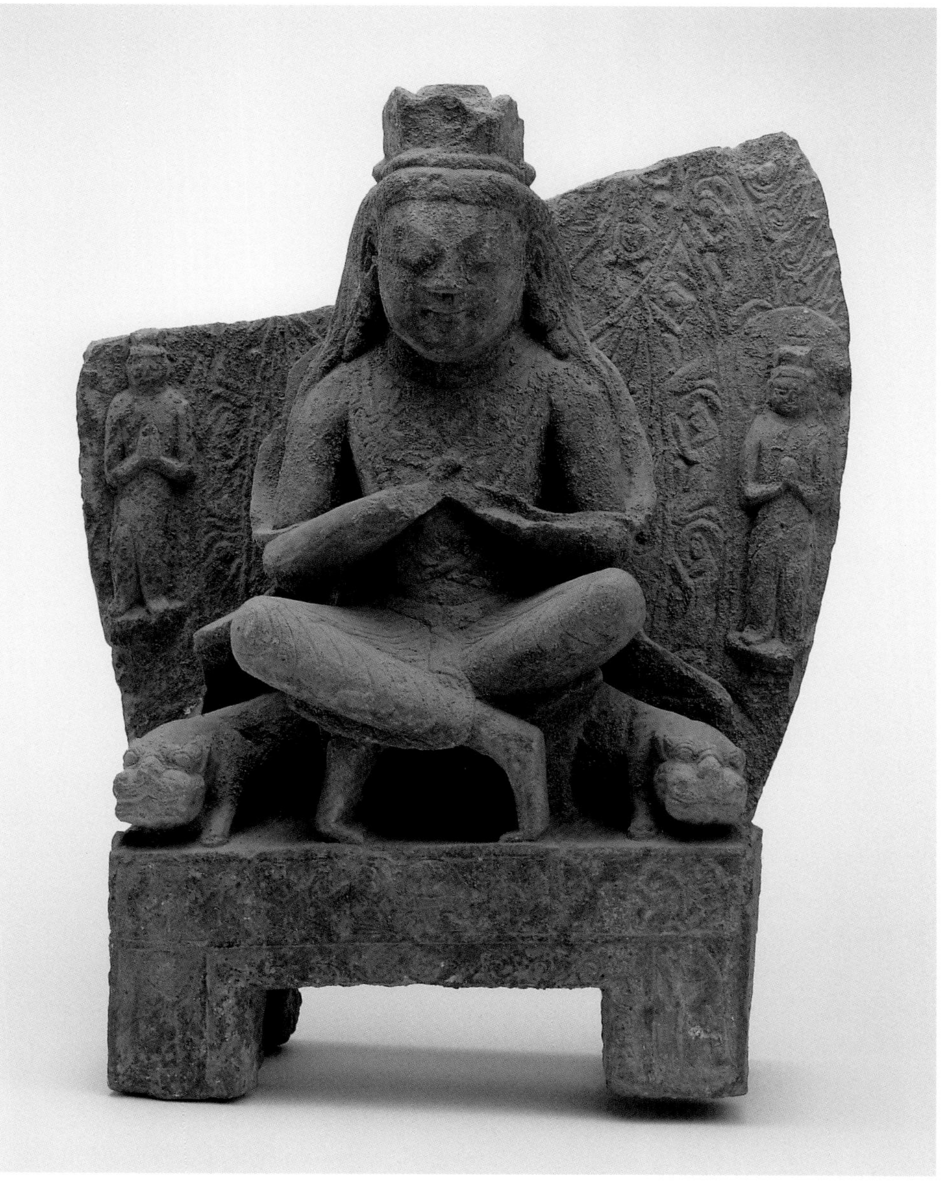

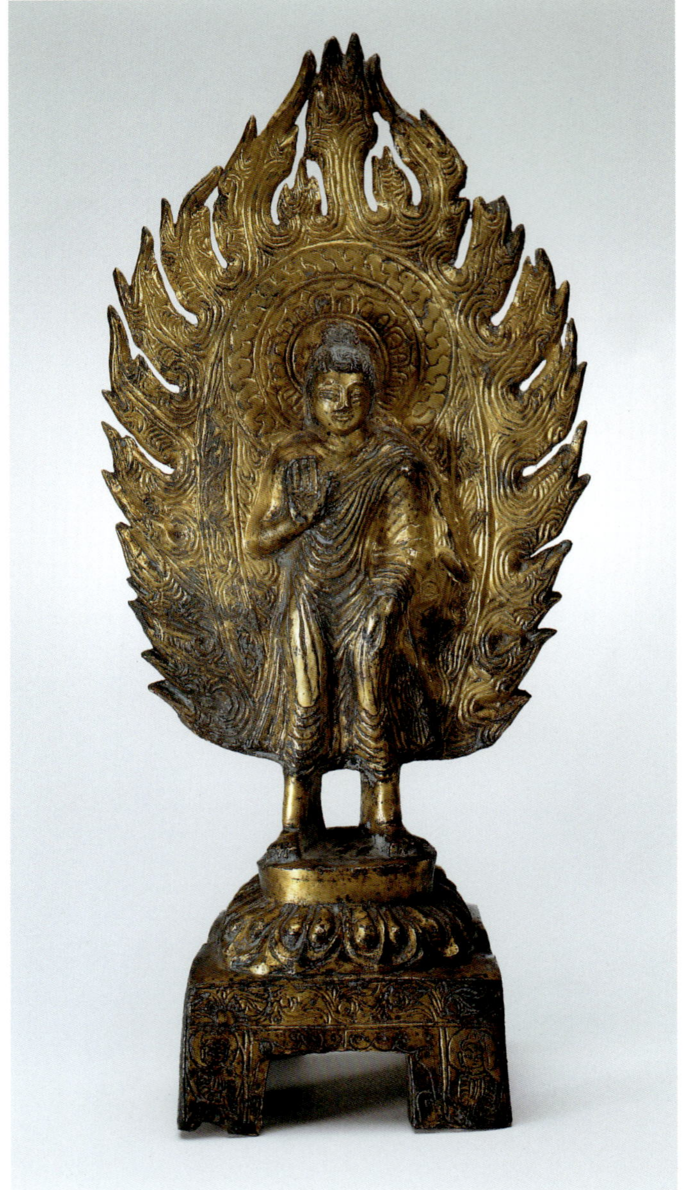

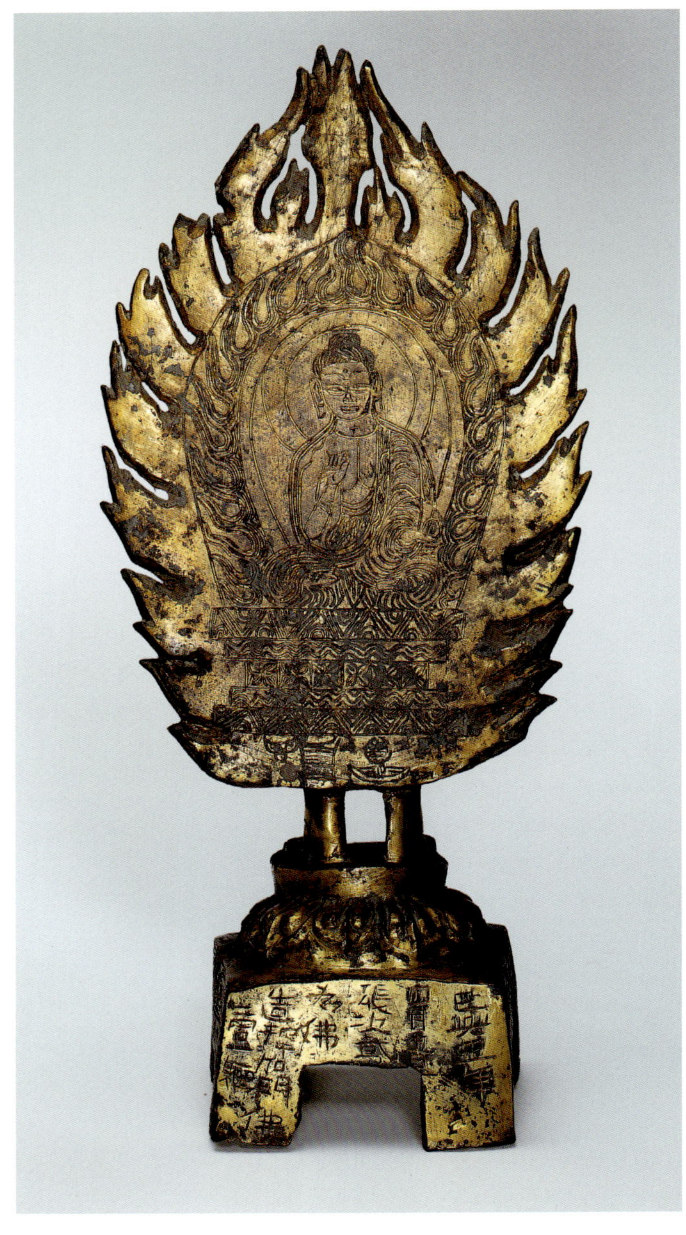

75
Standing Buddha Shakyamuni

Northern Wei dynasty (386–534), dated 475
Gilt bronze
Height 13⅞ in. (35.2 cm)
Found at Mancheng, Hebei Province, 1967
Hebei Provincial Museum

Reference: Hebei sheng bowuguan 1999

This impressive masterpiece, like the altarpiece of the Buddha under a canopy (cat. no. 45), is also representative of the Hebei school, which started casting gilt-bronze votive images in the early fourth century (if not earlier) and in the fifth took the lead over other production centers in North China. The richness of the imagery both front and back, the self-assured competence in the casting, and the advanced stylistic transformation of the image into a Northern Wei interpretation are all factors indicating the approach of a mature phase of gilt bronze-making.

On the front, the Buddha is shown garbed in the Indian Gandharan "open mode," namely, the monastic robe leaves the right shoulder bare. He performs the Fear Not gesture with the right hand, while in the left he holds the garment. In keeping with the western preference, the modeling of the body asserts itself under the draped robe, which is embellished with round linear patterns. The rendering of the imposing aureole, on the other hand, displays characteristics perfected in China, such as the inventive abstractions that fill the halo and the dynamic motif of perforated darting flames that shoot out from the aureole's rim.

On the back, the representation is less flamboyant. In contrast with the deeply carved grooves on the front, the technique relies on shallow incisions. Here, too, the Buddha performs the Fear Not mudra and a motif of bursting flames again contours the aureole. Dressed in a fashion still consonant with foreign models, he is seated on a Sumeru-type throne covered with bands of geometric patterns that can likely be traced to contemporary textiles. In front of the throne, an incense burner and offerings are crudely etched.

A short inscription is incised on the back of the pedestal: "In the fifth day of the fourth month, fifth year of Yanxing [475], to honor the Buddha, Zhang Cidai had this image of Shakyamuni cast."

AFH

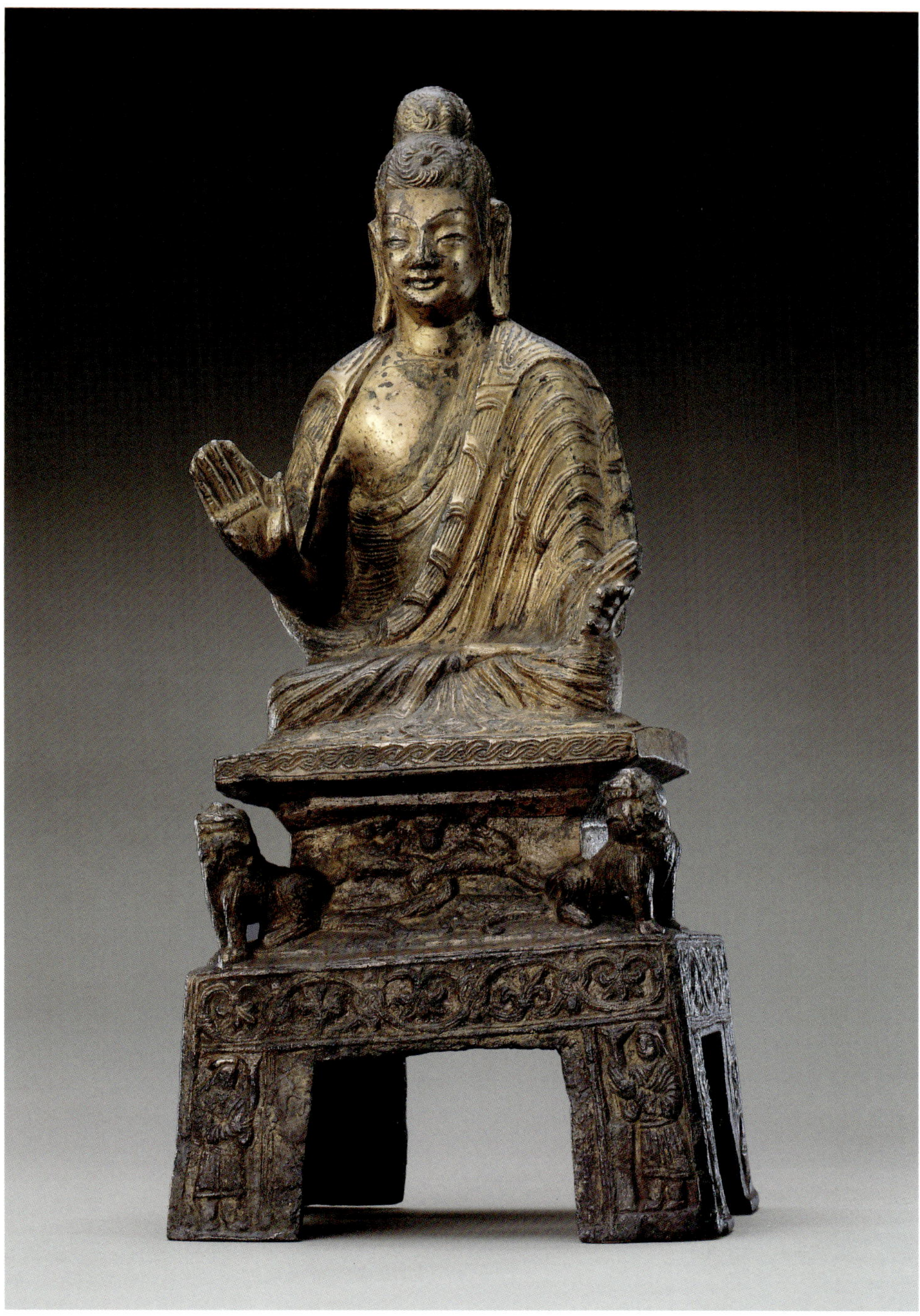

76
Seated Buddha on Sumeru throne

Northern Wei dynasty (386–534), dated 484
Gilt bronze
Height 11¼ in. (28.5 cm)
Found at Togeton, Hohhot, Inner Mongolia Autonomous Region, 1956
Inner Mongolia Autonomous Region Museum

Reference: Zhang Jingming et al. 1995

The Northern Wei dynasty's Taihe era, which spanned the last quarter of the fifth century (477–99), was marked by an impressive production of gilt bronzes, especially in the northeastern provinces of Shanxi and Hebei at the heart of Xianbei dominance. The last quarter of the fifth century coincides also with the last years during which Pingcheng (Datong) was the capital (in 493 the court moved south to Luoyang). Although found in Inner Mongolia, this seated Buddha, because of its high quality, was very likely executed in Hebei, the main center of bronze production. The fragmentary inscription carved on the back states the precise date at which it was made—the eighth year of Taihe (484). It identifies the donor as the monk Seng'an and the figure as Shakyamuni. And it expresses the hope that the offering may benefit the ruler, the immediate family of the donor, and all sentient beings.[1]

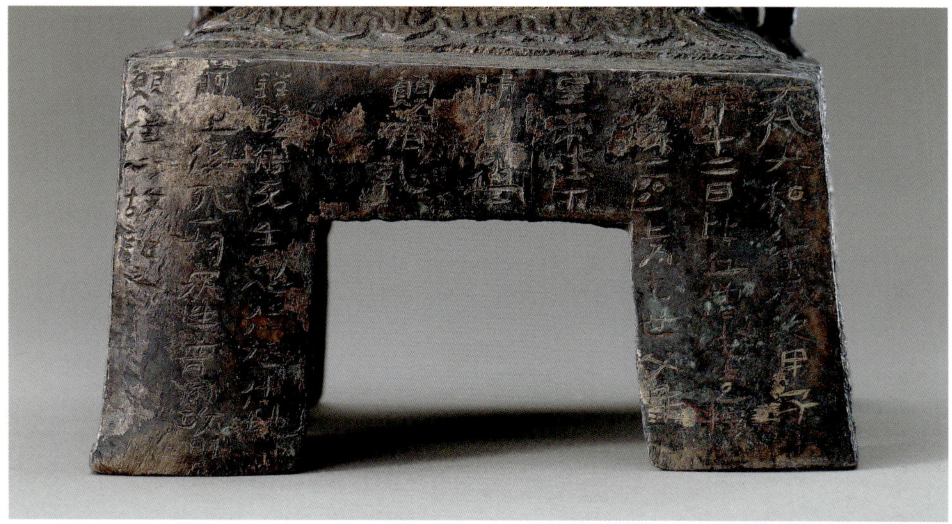

76, inscription

The development of Buddhist art in China may be viewed as a process parallel to that of the development of the religion itself. As Buddhism slowly penetrated China's heartland, foreign missionaries at first found it difficult to explain the recondite concepts of the alien faith, but over time the monks—most of them by now Chinese by birth—were able to bridge the gap between Indian and Chinese thought. Eventually, Buddhism became completely absorbed by the culture and was, in essence, Chinese. Similarly, Taihe bronzes, while they perhaps reflect a Xianbei aesthetic, are distinctly Chinese, having shed all vestiges of foreign influence.

This gilt-bronze Buddha is part of a typology (of the Taihe era) known as *Fo shuo fa*, or Buddha Preaches the Law, recognized by the right hand raised in front of the chest with the palm facing out. Shakyamuni is seated in full lotus pose on a tall Sumeru throne—a reference to the axial mountain that links the phenomenal to the spiritual world. (Such thrones are conventionally distinguished by two parts with a pronounced midsection.) Every part of the gilt bronze shows great artistry and inventiveness. The robe—worn in the open mode, leaving the right shoulder partially bare—displays intricate linear patterns with contrasting borders. The richly embellished *ushnisha*, or cranial protuberance, is embedded in an extravagant arrangement of hair whorls. The shape of the webbed hand is, notably, a concession to an earlier, typically Indian style used to connote Buddha's supernatural nature. A simple scroll adorns the edge of the platform, and a more elaborate scroll with vegetal motifs embellishes the wider borders of the lower pedestal. Two growling lions project from beneath the throne. The legs of the lower pedestal contain four Xianbei donors in their native nomadic costume. A sumptuously decorated aureole originally complemented the image.

AFH

1. Cheng Yongkui 1994: 67–69.

77
Buddha Maitreya

Northern Wei dynasty (386–534), dated 486
Gilt bronze
Height 55¼ in. (140.5 cm)
The Metropolitan Museum of Art, John Stewart Kennedy Fund 1926 (26.123)

Acquired in 1926, the nearly lifesize sculpture of the Buddha Maitreya in The Metropolitan Museum of Art is the largest extant gilt-bronze image known from China. An inscription incised on the back of the base, in the area between the feet, indicates that the sculpture was made in 486 in honor of Wenming (442–490), the dowager empress who controlled the Northern Wei dynasty (386–534) for much of the late fifth century.[1] Additional inscriptions, which are carved on the top and bottom layers of the base and in the spaces between the lotus petals, list the names of the donors, members of prominent families such as the Yan, Zui, and Wang.

The rendering of the Buddha's body and the folds of his drapery illustrates the astonishing range of prototypes used in Chinese Buddhist art in the late fifth century. The broad shoulders and the flatness of the figure derive from sculptures made in India in the late fourth and first half of the fifth century. This type of physique was known in China by the second decade of the fifth century;[2] the pronounced waistline and shorter legs, however, are characteristics found at late fifth-century sites such as the complex at Yungang, near the capital, Pingcheng (present-day Datong).[3]

The Buddha Maitreya wears three garments: a long, skirtlike undergarment, a middle layer, and an enveloping rectangular shawl that drapes across the body. The patterning of the folds into inverted crescents above the chest and the vertical pleats along the sides derive from Central Asian traditions. On the other hand, the raised, appliqué-like rendering of the folds and the joining of the pleats above the chest stem from artistic conventions found in Pakistan (known in the ancient world as Gandhara) during the third and fourth centuries. Also found in sites such as Kizil on the northern branch of the Silk Road, this style of drapery first appears in China in the mid-fifth century[4] and flourishes in the late fifth century. It appears on several of the colossi in the famous Tanyao caves at Yungang[5] and on high-quality stone and gilt-bronze sculptures (see cat. no. 76) produced between 470 and 490.[6]

Although this style of drapery is associated with the Buddha Shakyamuni in later traditions of East Asia,[7] the Buddhas Amitabha and Maitreya are also represented in late fifth-century examples. Devotion to Maitreya was widespread during the Northern Wei. He is worshipped as a bodhisattva in this world age and as a Buddha in the next. Maitreya maintains and governs two perfected worlds, the Tushita Heaven, which he currently inhabits, and Ketumati. The latter, in which Maitreya will serve as the teaching Buddha of the age, is an ideal realm conducive to the pursuit of enlightenment.

DPL

1. I am grateful to Richard Stone and Diana Harvey of the Museum's Sherman Fairchild Center for Objects Conservation for their help in studying this sculpture. Cleaning of the corrosion covering the inscription has revealed a date in the tenth year of the Taihe era. The inscription had previously been read as the first year, which explains the discrepancy between the date of 477, previously assigned to this image, and the 486 cited herein.
2. *Heireiji sekkutsu* 1986, fig. 34.
3. *Unkō sekkutsu* 1989–90, vol. 2, pl. 56.
4. Matsubara 1995, vol. 1, pl. 23.
5. *Unkō sekkutsu* 1989–90, vol. 2, pls. 147, 148, 184–185.
6. Matsubara 1995, vol. 1, pls. 42, 51, 60, 63, 64, 71.
7. Carter 1990. The most famous example is a Chinese sculpture preserved in the Seiryō-ji in Kyoto, Japan. See MacCallum 1996: 51–67.

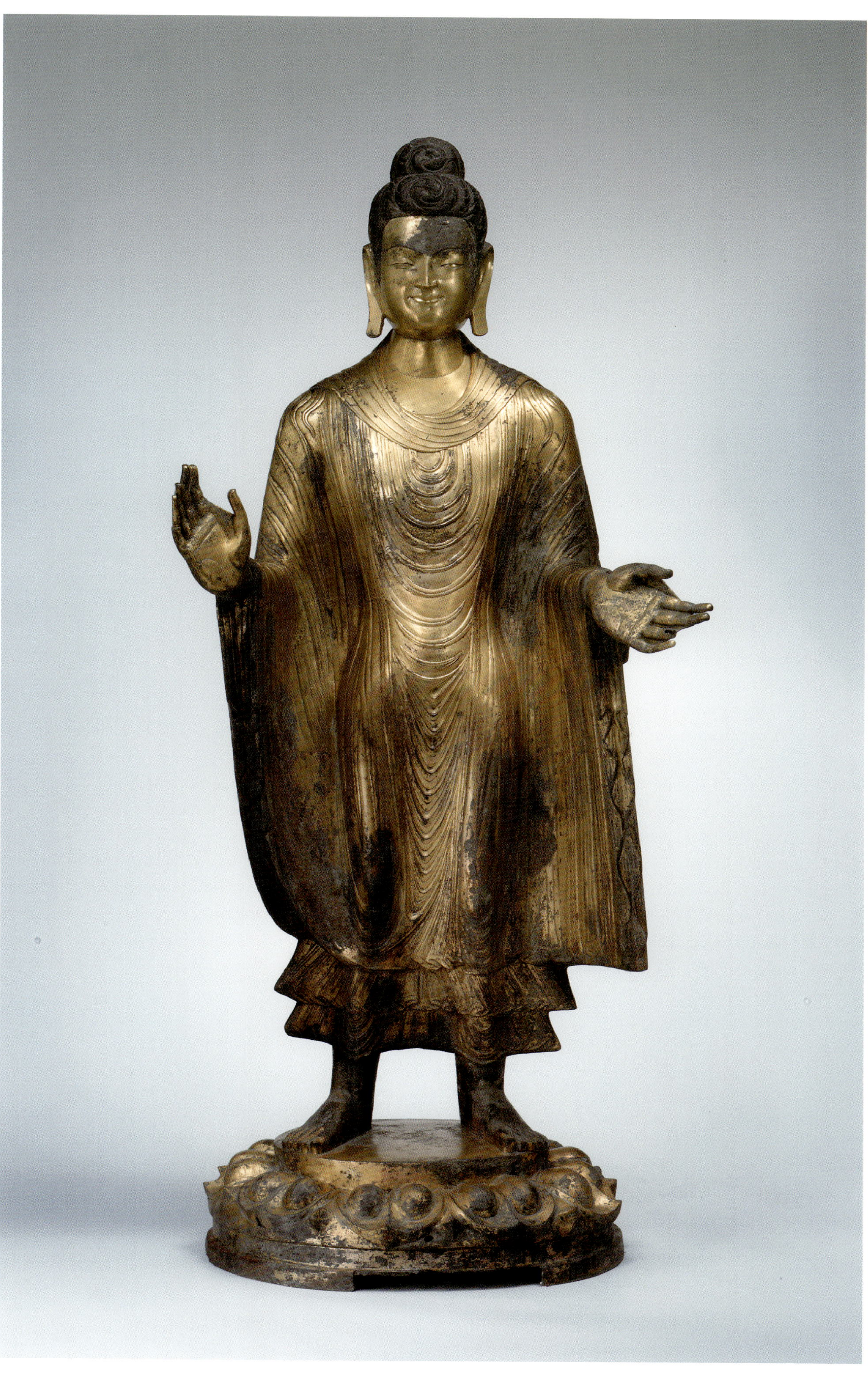

78
Four-sided stele

Northern Wei dynasty (386–534), dated 501
Stone
Height 23 5/8 in. (60 cm)
Excavated at Zhajiazhai, Chang'an Xian, Shaanxi Province, 1953
Museum of the Forest of Steles

REFERENCE: Li Jian 2003

This intriguing work is roughly shaped like a cube, with four niches in which are displayed four different stylistic and doctrinal representations of the Buddha. The doctrinal meaning still eludes us. The fragmentary inscription framed by two lions states that a "pure-hearted practitioner [*qingxin shi*]" (the name is illegible) donated the stele to acknowledge the heavenly rebirth of his wife who had recently died. This type of stele was popular in Shaanxi and also in neighboring southern Shanxi toward the end of the fifth and early sixth centuries.[1]

The side bearing the inscription is likely the back of the stele, as was common for inscriptions carved on contemporary stone and metal works. Here, a Buddha with elongated face and lean body sits in meditation on a low lion throne supported on the axis by an Atlantes-like image emerging from a lotus. He wears a monastic robe executed in pure Shaanxi style, its crisply serrated linear folds meandering over the body to form exquisite, controlled patterns. A halo and aureole serve as a backdrop. The tiny heads of ten disciples peer over the aureole to behold the master below, while two lanky, crowned bodhisattvas assist him on each side. Enframing the central group are pairs and trios of Buddhas seated in niches.

The front of the stele, on the opposite side, is a study in contrast with the arrangement on the back. Instead of using a compact organization, the carver chose a wider and architectonically more complex niche delimited by ornate pillars. The nimbed and aureoled Buddha sits on a much larger lion throne. He performs the Fear Not gesture, although the palm of his raised right hand is not fully exposed to the viewer. The body is sturdier, the face more filled out. The robe retains the Shaanxi serrated pleats, but with wider creases. Tucked under the body, the robe, in an artful tripartite display, spills over the throne. Proportions and attire suggest a more imposing interpretation of the deity. Outside the niche, in ascending order, are two guardians, possibly with *vajras* (thunderbolts), four Buddhas seated on lotuses, and a personage in a pensive pose. Here, too, the ten disciples look down at their master below. A row of donors fills the somewhat damaged lower band.

The arrangement and content of the front niche is the model for the two lateral niches, where similar Buddhas performing the same gesture are seated on slightly taller, narrower thrones. The robes, however, emphatically cascading over the dais, present new, inventive patterns, such as the series of axial loops deeply carved from the chest to the hem. To differentiate between the four presentations, the carver shows the attending bodhisattvas standing on lotuses borne by playful, chubby dwarfs. Filling the lower bands, in place of donors, are Spirit Kings, or Shen Wang, personifications of natural forces.

A patron of substantial means chose an excellent Chang'an workshop to execute this stele. The inventiveness of the carving, the crisp, linear embellishments, and the playfulness of the minor characters all point to the best available skills. The style is that of the northwest—Shaanxi and Gansu—which privileged round-faced and full-bodied Buddhas swathed in robes rendered by means of precise geometric linear patterns, a style that diverges from the formal language seen in the art of contemporary Northern Wei Shanxi and Henan.

AFH

1. Abe 2002: 266–69.

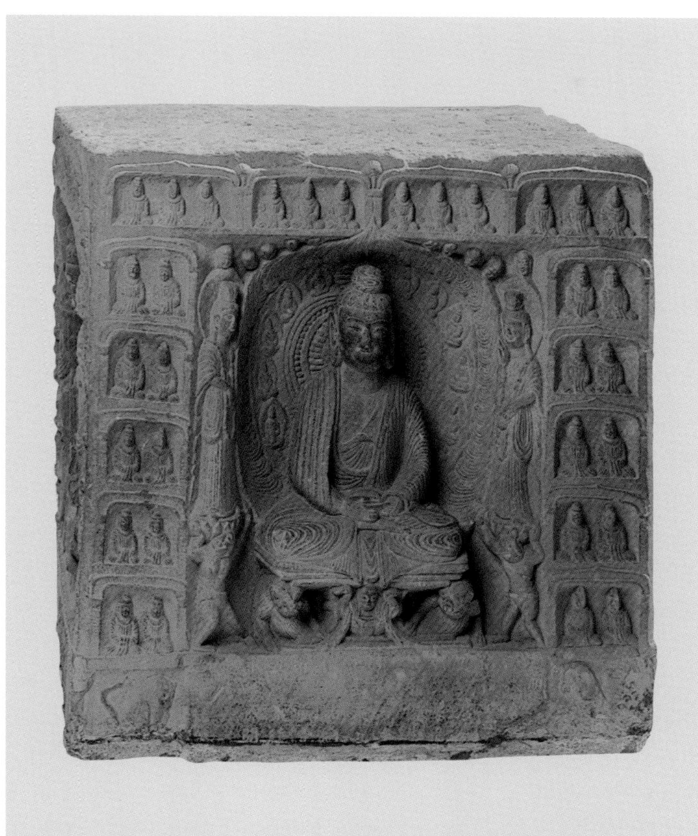

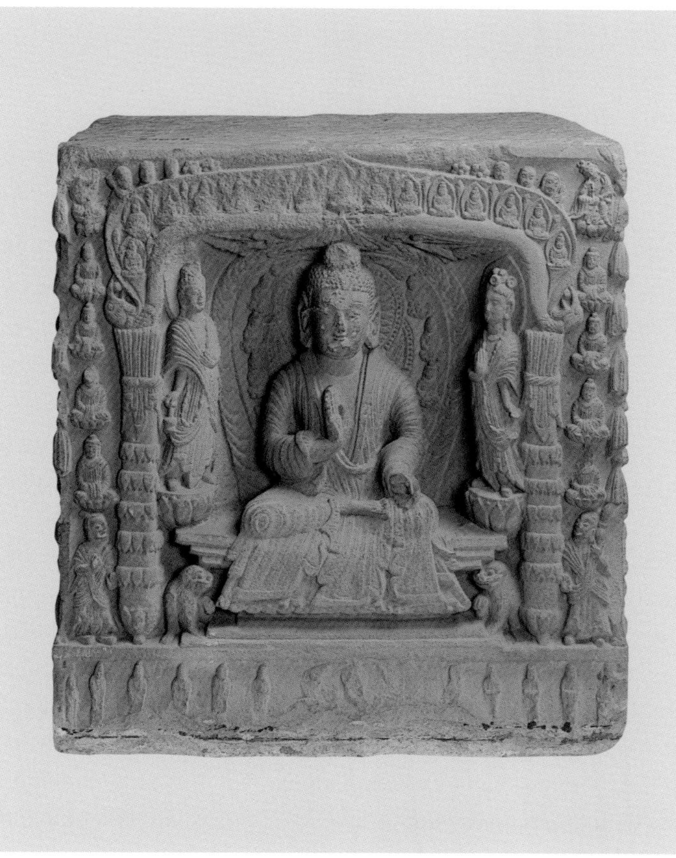

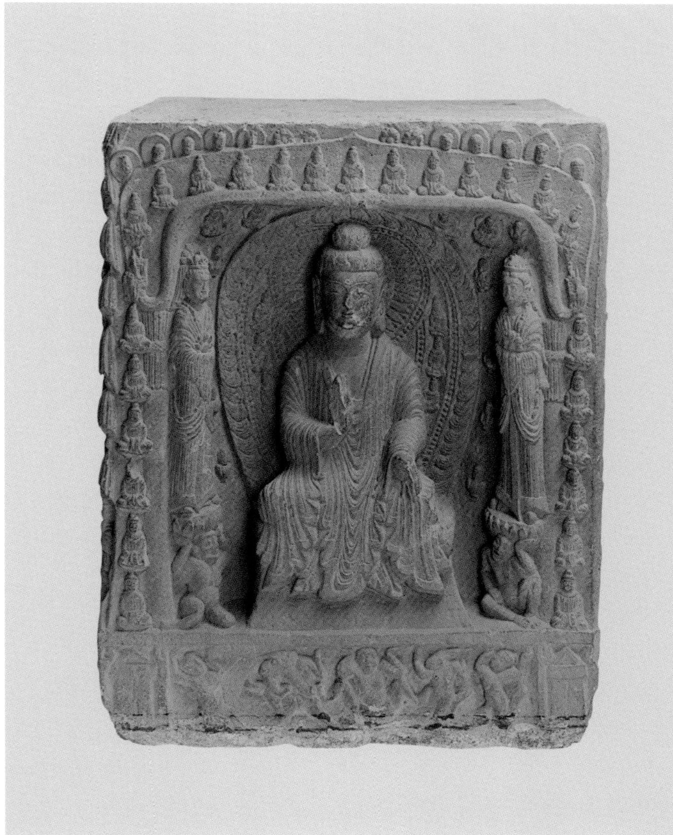

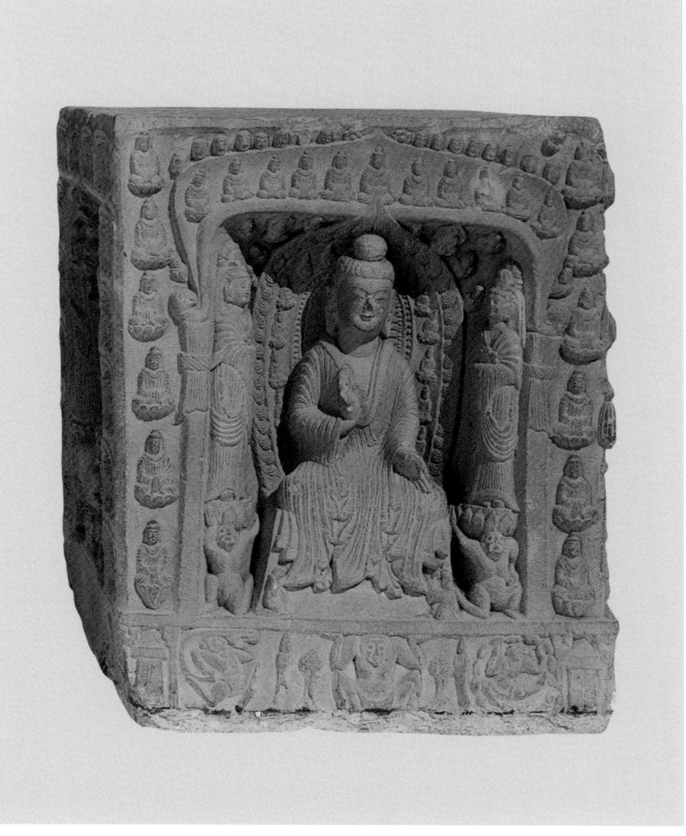

79
Textile with donors and partial Buddha

Northern Wei dynasty (386–534), dated 487
Embroidered silk (split stitch on tabby)
Fragment: 29½ x 20 ⅛ in. (75 x 51 cm)
Border: 5 ⅛ x 24½ in. (13 x 62 cm)
Found between Caves 125 and 126, Dunhuang, Gansu Province, 1965
Dunhuang Research Institute

EXCAV. REPORT in *Wenwu* 1972.2

Originally hanging in a temple as an offering to the Buddha, this embroidery was discovered in the front room of Caves 125 and 126 at the Mogao Grotto in Dunhuang, Gansu. The original design probably consisted of a preaching Buddha in the center framed by a border above and donors and inscription below.

Pearl hexagons, roundels, and floral scrolls are embroidered in split stitch on the yellow-brown silk tabby border, which measures 13 cm high and 62 cm wide in its present damaged condition. The pearl hexagons are patterned in white against a purple ground, while bright yellow, blue, and green are used for the roundels and decorative floral scrolls. The floral motif is reminiscent of those found in Caves 259 and 248 at Dunhuang, as well as in Cave 9 at Yungang, Datong, all dated to the Northern Wei (386–534).[1] Such borders, archaeologists suggest, are employed only above a preaching Buddha.

In the center a Buddha wearing a red shawl-like vestment, or *kasaya*, sits cross-legged on a lotus pedestal. The inverted lotus with compound petals is embroidered in layers of red and green. To the left of the Buddha stands a bodhisattva on a lotus, only the lower half and a hand remaining.[2] The bodhisattva wears a green skirt with a red sash hanging from the waist between the legs. Fluttering red drapery further adds to the figure's grace. Floral scrolls are scattered between the Buddha and the bodhisattva. The fragmentary Buddha with lotus pedestal measures 26 cm high. In the original state, the Buddha would probably have reached 80 to 90 cm high and the bodhisattva 35 cm high. Quite possibly other bodhisattvas or *apsaras* (celestials) were represented in the upper portion, as is the case with painted or sculpted preaching Buddhas executed during the Northern Wei.[3]

Beneath the Buddha are embroidered the inscription and images of the donors. The inscription, 11 cm high and 16 cm wide, is placed in the center with a purple frame and blue characters. With lotus flowers in their hands, the donors, each about 15 cm high, line up on both sides. Only two of the male donors on the right have survived. The first was probably an anonymous monk. The second, with only head and feet still visible, wears a tall black hat and a pair of black boots. He is identified by inscription, but only the last character, *wang* (prince), is now visible. The first of the female donors on the left is a nun in a red *kasaya*, identified as Shi Fazhi (Master Fazhi). The second female donor, identified as *Guangyang wang mu* (mother of Prince of Guangyang), wears a high, purple-brown hat, and, like the other female donors, a tight-sleeved gown with a pattern of red spade shapes and with scrolling patterns on the lapel and at the hem. Under the gown, she wears a long skirt of teal green. The third figure, in a similar pose, wears a green tunic with tight sleeves and long, light yellow skirt under her robe. She is identified as *qi Puxian* (the wife Puxian). The following two fragmentary figures, one in a red tunic and green skirt and the other in a green tunic and yellow skirt under their robes, are identified as *xinu Sengci* (the daughter Sengci) and *xinu Dengming* (the daughter Dengming). Except for the monk and the nun, the donors are all members of the same family. The male donor is Prince Guangyang, and the females his mother, wife, and two daughters.

According to the inscription, this embroidery was offered by Huian, Prince Guangyang, in the eleventh year of the Taihe reign of the Northern Wei dynasty (487). The title Prince Guangyang was documented in the *Beishi* (History of the Northern Dynasties), as well as in the *Weishu* (History of the Wei). There were altogether four generations bearing the title Prince Guangyang. The donor of this piece is Yuanjia, the second Prince Guangyang. Given the Buddhist name Huian, he was the most devout of the four princes. Because Yuanjia never visited Dunhuang himself, this embroidery was probably made in Luoyang and brought to Dunhuang by a high-ranking Buddhist cleric. This was a popular practice at the time, as was recorded in the *Luoyang qielanji* (Record of Buddhist Temples in Luoyang). When the monks Song Yun and Hui Sheng traveled to the west in the early sixth century, they saw "tens of thousands of colored hanging canopies, half of which came from the Northern Wei. . . . Embroidered images [canopies embroidered with Buddha's image] as well as statues of the Buddha are displayed whenever the Dharma is preached." An important element in Buddhist rites, hangings embroidered with images of the Buddha were usually given by lay donors.

ZF

1. Dunhuang wenwu yanjiusuo 1972: 54–60.
2. The hand may require further study.
3. For an example on the northern wall of Cave 249 at the Mogao site, see Dunhuang yanjiuyuan 1986: 13.

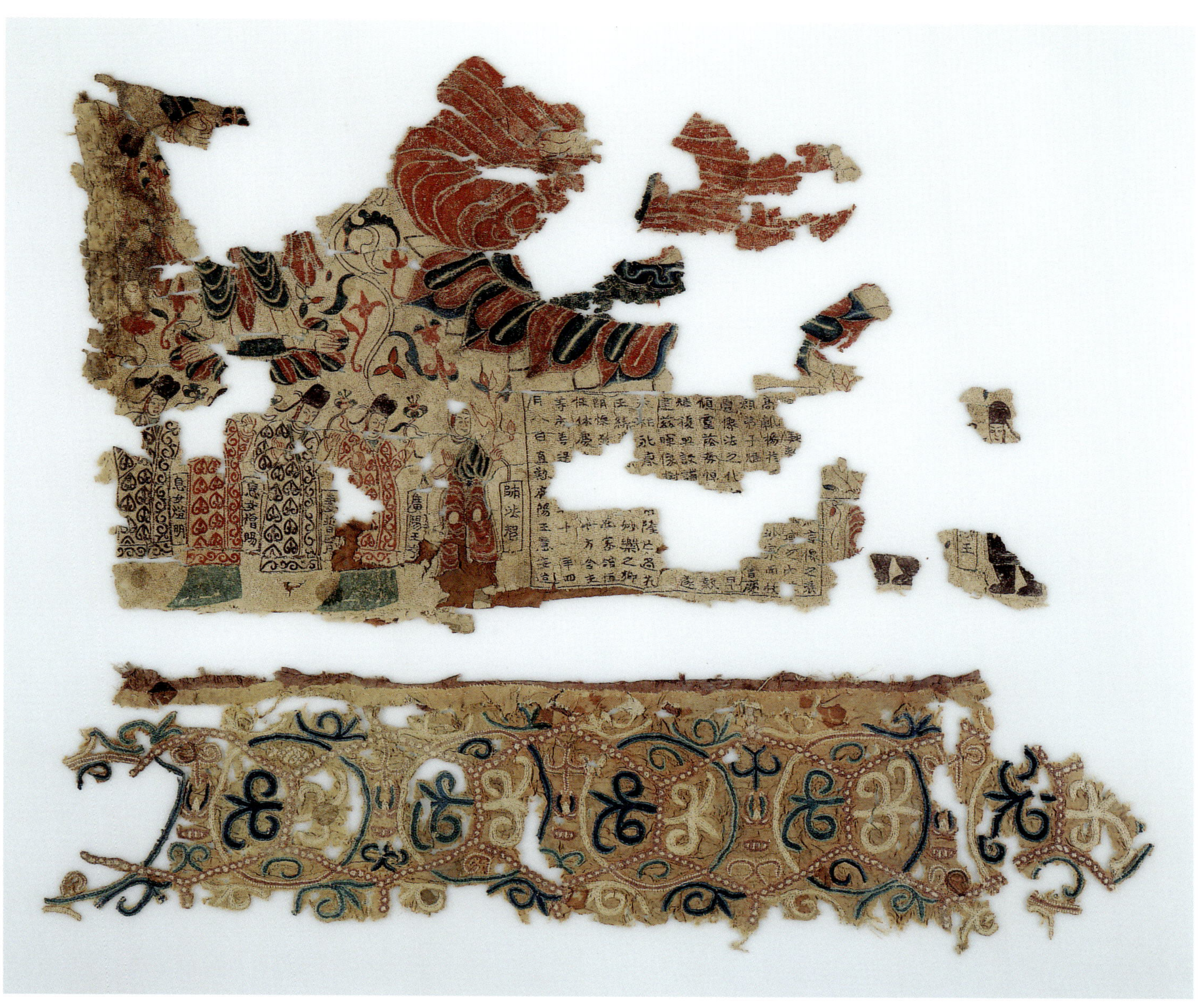

IV

The Western Regions and the Way Thither

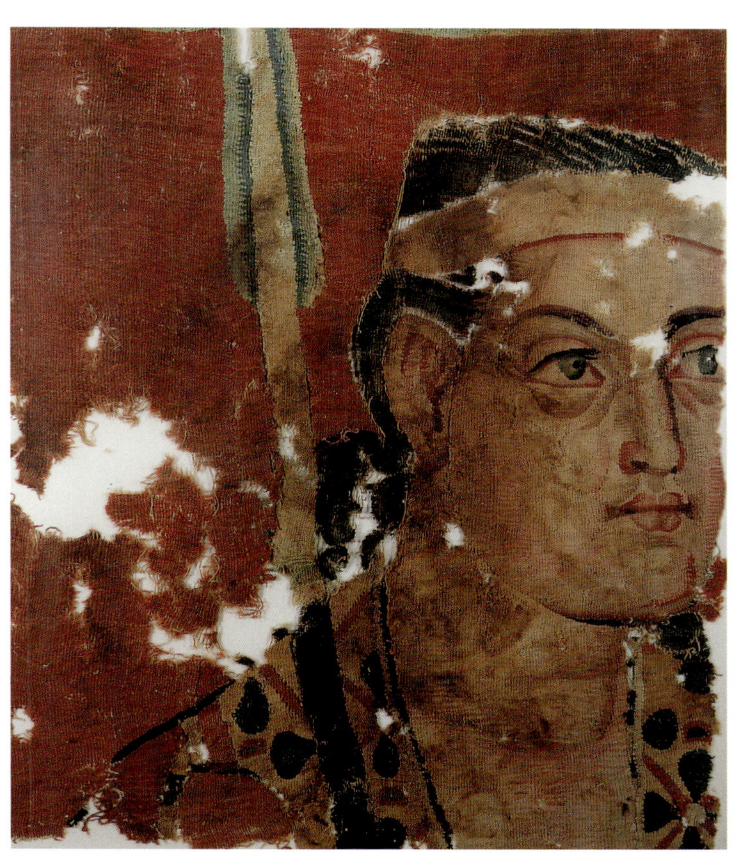

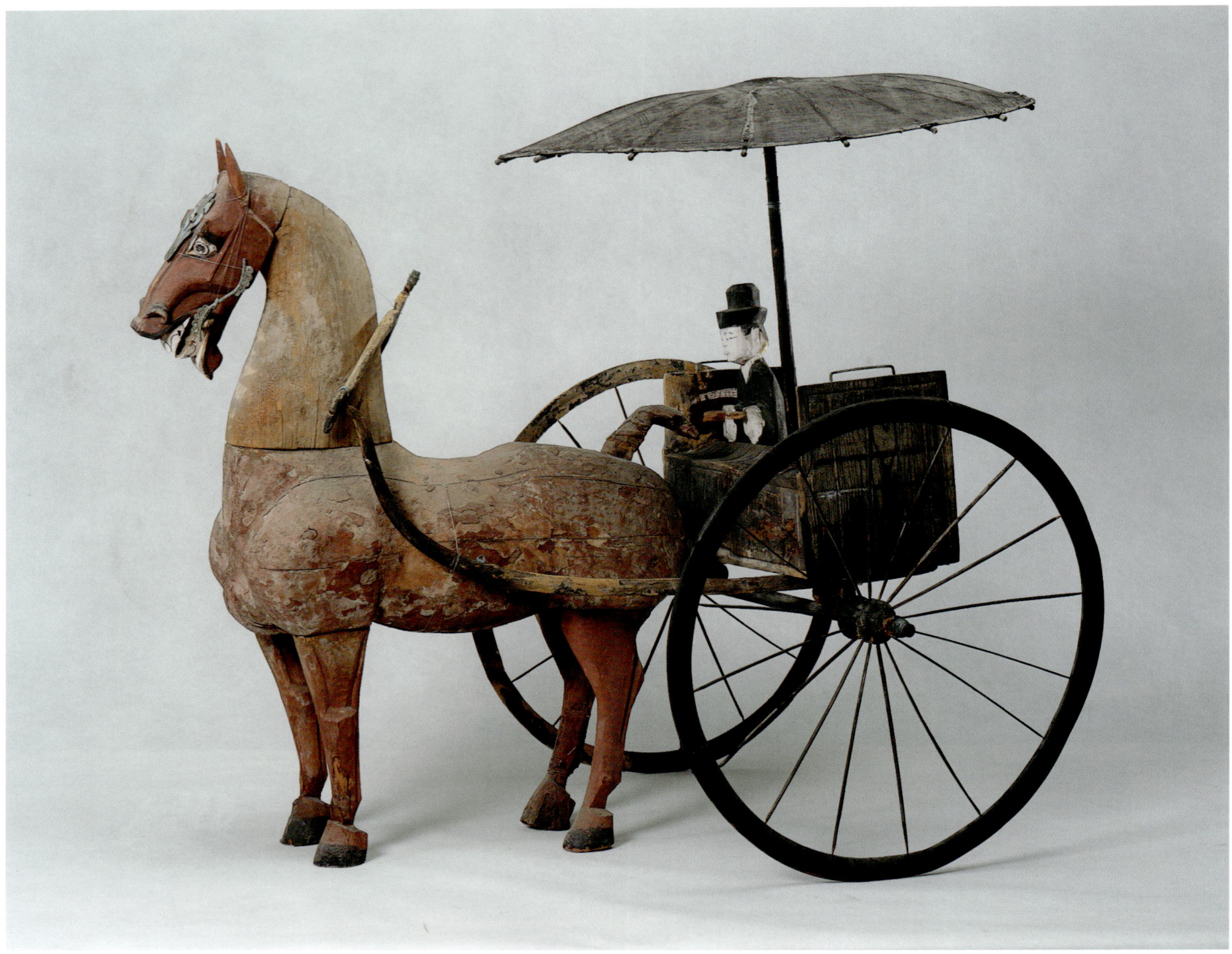

80

Chariot and horse

Eastern Han dynasty (25–220)
Wood with pigments
Chariot: height 38 3/16 in. (97 cm); horse: height 35 1/16 in. (89 cm)
Excavated at Mozuizi, Wuwei, Gansu Province, 1972
Gansu Provincial Museum

Excav. report in *Wenwu* 1972.12

Wood carving in China has a long history, though few works have survived because of their extremely perishable nature. The earliest example, a small figure of a fish from the neolithic Hemudu culture on China's eastern coast, dates from the fifth millennium B.C.[1] Patterned marks on the earth and on wood ashes found in a number of Shang dynasty tombs (ca. 16th–11th century) suggest that the craft was fairly widespread in the early Bronze Age. The art of wood carving appears to have flourished in the fifth and fourth centuries B.C., as demonstrated by the sophisticated works of the Chu state. The most representative piece is an exquisite screen with naturalistically depicted deer, birds, frogs, and interlaced snakes, all carved in the round and enhanced with colored lacquer.[2]

The present model of a horse and chariot, excavated from a first-century A.D. tomb in Wuwei, Gansu, illustrates a novel style in the Han dynasty that emphasizes abstraction over naturalism, a development that can also be seen in the wooden monkey (cat. no. 17) and the geese (cat. no. 18) found in the same general area.[3] The magnificent horse is assembled from separate parts—head, neck, body, and legs. A few simple, deep cuts create a robust beast with bulging chest and voluminous haunches. The exaggerated large hooves assure a firm stance. The chariot, with imposing wheels that complement the horse's great size, sports a high flat umbrella. Small parts made of bronze help to hold the components together and provide a modest trim. The driver, dwarfed by the immense horse, is also shaped by no more than a dozen angled cuts. Simplicity of form, represented by this model, was not limited to wood carving during this period but appeared also in other media, particularly jade.

ZS

1. Hemudu yizhi kaogudui 1980: 9.
2. Hubei sheng wenhuaju wenwu gongzuodui 1966: 37.
3. Zhang Pengchuan and Wu Yiru 1984: 32.

81

Unicorn

Eastern Han dynasty (25–220)
Wood with pigments
Height 15½ in. (39.5 cm)
Excavated at Mozuizi, Wuwei, Gansu Province, 1972
Gansu Provincial Museum

Excav. report in *Wenwu* 1972.12

82

Unicorn

Eastern Han dynasty (25–220)
Bronze
Height 7⅞ in. (20 cm)
Excavated at Xiaheqing, Jiuquan, Gansu Province, 1956
Gansu Provincial Museum

Excav. report in *Wenwu* 1959.10

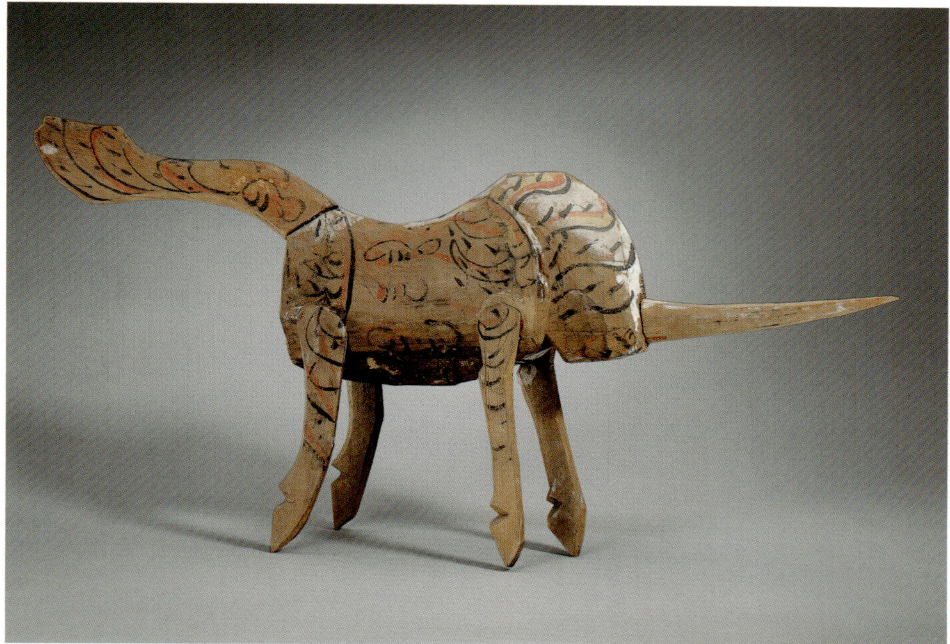

81

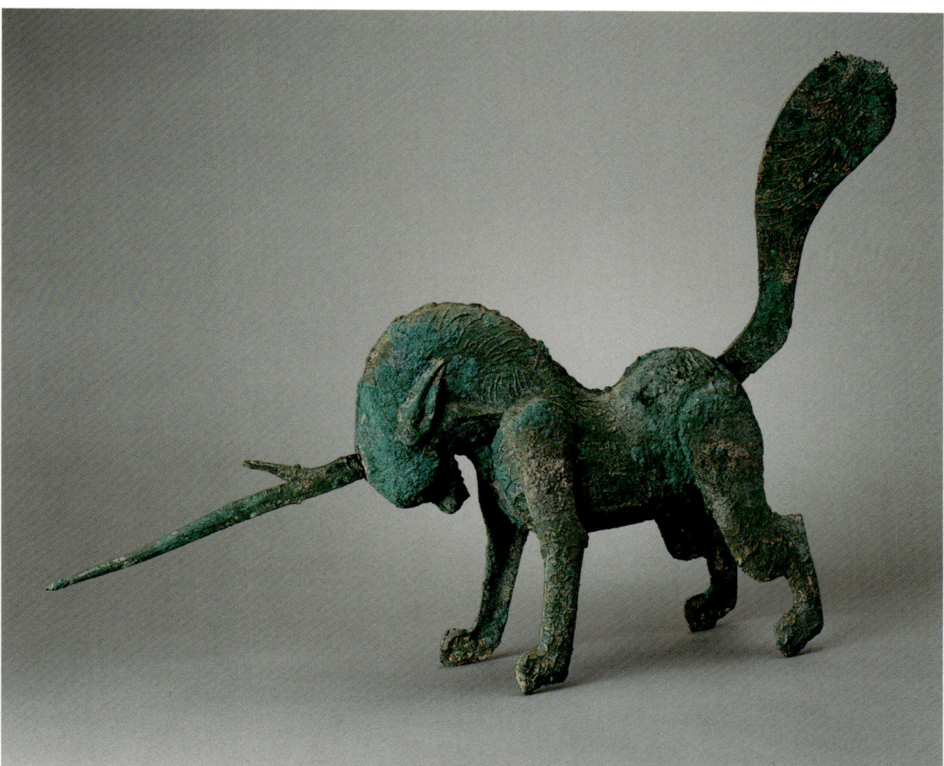

82

Made in both bronze and wood, beasts shown charging forward with lowered heads and pointing a dramatically long horn are among the most intriguing sculptures produced in the northwestern province of Gansu during the second and third centuries. The body, head, legs, tail, and horn of the bronze unicorn (cat. no. 82) were cast separately and then assembled.[1] The horn of this sculpture has a small secondary spike. The raised lines cast along the neck and tail are comparable to the decorations, painted in shades of red and black, on the wooden unicorn (cat. no. 81), which also appears to have been assembled from separate pieces. Such designs may be intended to represent fur or some type of adornment.

Unicorn-like animals first appear sporadically as embellishment on ritual vessels dating to the Warring States period (481–221 B.C.).[2] They are also found, generally in pairs, engraved on the doorways of tombs dating from the Warring States to the Han. Their prominence as both engraved images and freestanding sculptures in the Eastern Han reflects the widespread belief in magical practices and good omens *(xiangrui)* during this period. Unicorn-like creatures, often called *qilin*, play a continuing role in later Chinese art and literature.

The present creatures were intended to guard the tomb and its inhabitants. Unlike the other objects in the tomb, which were placed at the rear or in the coffin chamber, the bronze unicorn stood alone in the center of the front chamber. Its placement in the tomb and its aggressive stance indicate that its role was protective. The wooden figure was one of a pair; its mate was unpainted. It seems likely that the two wood sculptures were also placed in a prominent and defensive location in the tomb.

What remains unclear is the relationship such figures have to other guardian sculptures, particularly those with horns, found in tombs dating to later periods. For example, creatures with one horn or three horns or more are found in tombs in many parts of China dating from the first to the fourth century.[3] Remnants of a single horn on the forehead are seen on guardian beasts in tombs dating to the late fifth century (see cat. no. 54). And several variant horned creatures are found at sites dating from the sixth to the eighth century (see cat. no. 179).

The relationship, if any, between the Chinese unicorn and unicorns of other cultures is also ambiguous. The earliest reference to the unicorn in Western sources is roughly contemporaneous with their appearance on bronze vessels in China. The citation is found in the discredited writings of the Greek physician and historian Ctesias (born ca. 416 B.C.), who worked at the Achaemenid court (ca. 550–330 B.C.) of Persia for seventeen years before his return to Greece in 398.

The earliest known visual images of unicorns are found in the Harappan civilization (ca. 2600–1900 B.C.), in parts of what is today Pakistan and northern India. Freestanding examples in terracotta and images on pendants and seals are known from this period.[4] They are thought to be symbols of either a prominent clan or a merchant group of some importance. Although unicorns disappear from South Asian art after the Harappan era, the concept may have been preserved in western Asia, which perhaps accounts for its eventual appearance farther west in Greece and Rome.

DPL

1. Gansu sheng wenwu guanli weiyuanhui 1959: 74–77.
2. Juliano and Lerner 2001: 44–46. See also the electronic book on the mythic Chinese unicorn by Jeannie T. Parker available from the Web site of the Royal Ontario Museum at www.rom.on.ca.
3. Fong 1991b: 88–91.
4. Aruz et al. 2003, figs. 276, 295a,b.

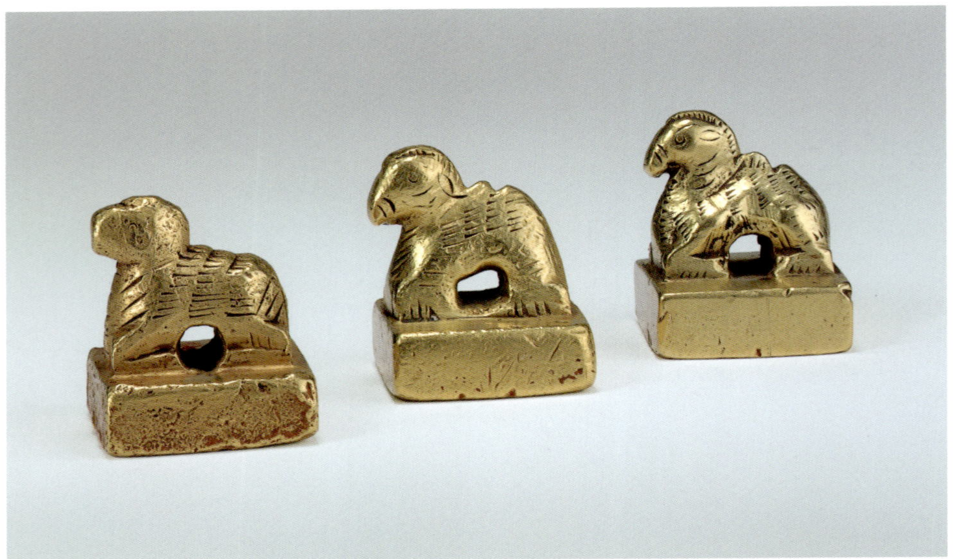

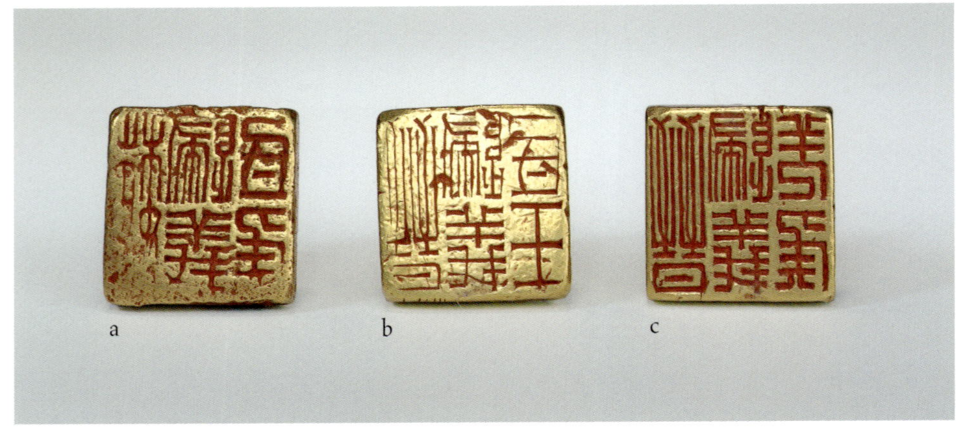

83
Three seals

Wei (220–65) and Western Jin (265–316) dynasties
Gold
Each: Height 1 in. (2.5 cm)
Excavated at Xihe, Gansu Province
Gansu Provincial Museum

Reference: Gansu sheng bowuguan 1994

In the time of the Han dynasty (206 B.C.–A.D. 220), the chiefs of ethnic groups native to certain areas of the empire were given titles such as *wang* (prince) or *hou* (marquis). This practice was continued by the governments of the subsequent dynasties of Wei (220–65) and Western Jin (265–316). When titles were conferred, the chiefs also received a seal of office in gold (or silver, depending on the rank), such as the three examples seen here.

The legends may be translated as:

a. Marquis of Di [people] loyal to the Wei
b. Prince of Di [people] loyal to the Jin
c. Marquis of Qiang [people] loyal to the Jin

All three seals were found together in Xihe in southern Gansu Province not far from Sichuan. The area was inhabited by both the Di and the Qiang.

The Xianbei princes in the third century who assisted the Jin dynasty in fighting the Xiongnu were awarded similar seals. Two seals not in this exhibition with comparable designs and cut with titles for Xianbei leaders were found in the same hoard as cat. no. 32.[1]

JCYW

1. Zhang Jingming 2002: 50–52, 69, and cover ills.

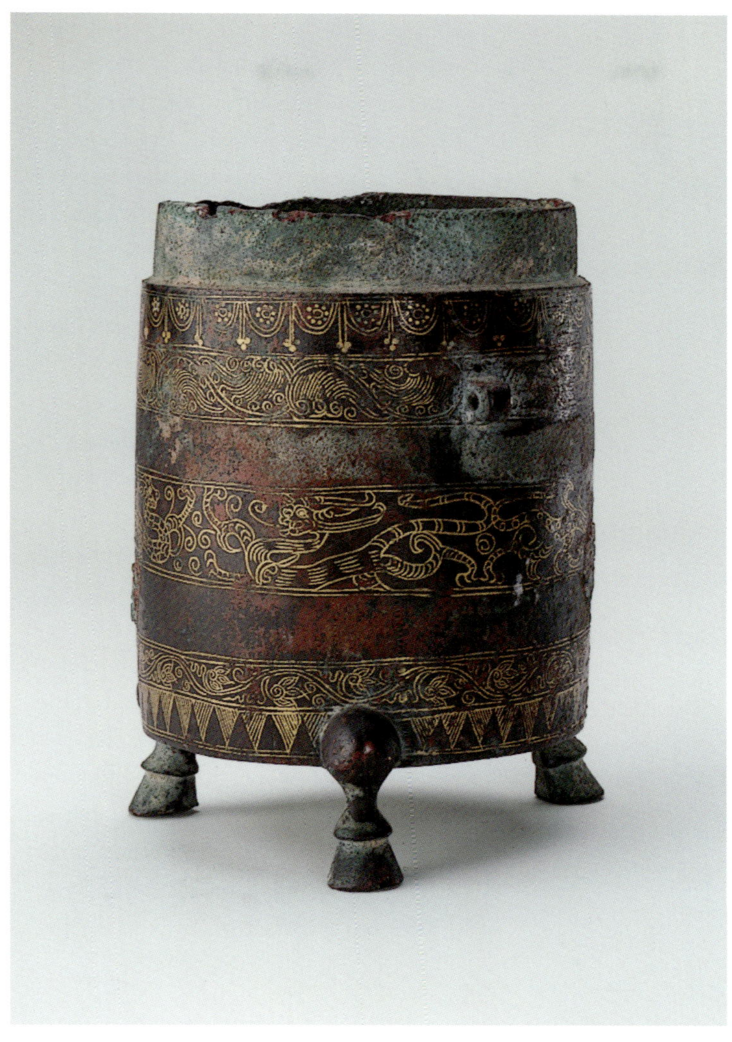

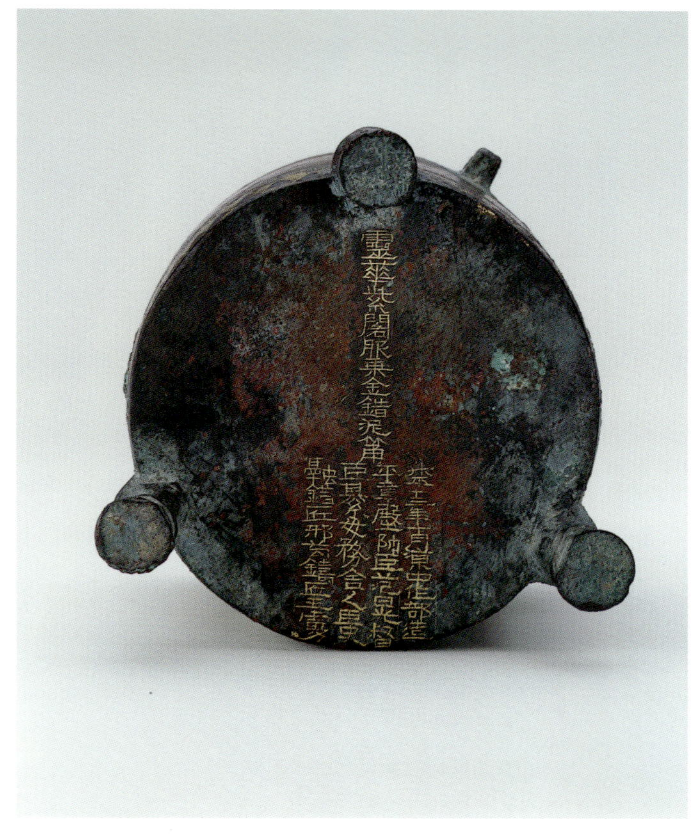

84
Seal-clay container

Sixteen Kingdoms, Former Liang dynasty (314–76), inscription dated 369
Bronze inlaid with gold
Height 4⅝ in. (11.7 cm)
Shaanxi History Museum

Excav. report in *Wenwu* 1972.6

The inscription on the base of this cylindrical vessel (now missing its lid) describes it as a container for clay. The clay was used for sealing documents written on bamboo or wooden strips or on wooden boards. It was applied to the knot of the string that tied together the strips or boards and stamped with a seal such as those in the previous entry (cat. no. 83).

This container provides evidence for the continuation of Han-style administration in the Former Liang state (314–76) up to the time of its demise. The inscription gives the name of the piece, the palace building for which it was made, the date of manufacture, the government department and the supervising officer, and the name of the craftsman who executed the gold inlay and of the one who cast the vessel itself. Such precision is very much in keeping with Han-dynasty bureaucratic practice—long forgotten or ignored elsewhere in former territories of the Han empire. The treatment of the dragon and tiger images in the inlay is more or less Han in style. On the other hand, the upper and lower decorative friezes, with foliated scrolls, suggest an early influence of Western art at Guzang (Wuwei, Gansu, capital of the Former Liang), where this piece was made.

The container was collected by the Shaanxi Provincial Museum (now the Shaanxi History Museum) in Xi'an and was presumed to have been found locally. As it was made only a few years before the conquest of the Former Liang by the Di state of Former Qin in 376 and the last Liang ruler, Zhang Tianxi (r. 363–76), was transferred to Chang'an, the container, which was obviously well cared for, was most likely taken there as part of Zhang Tianxi's personal effects.[1]

JCYW

1. Qin Liexin 1972: 36–37.

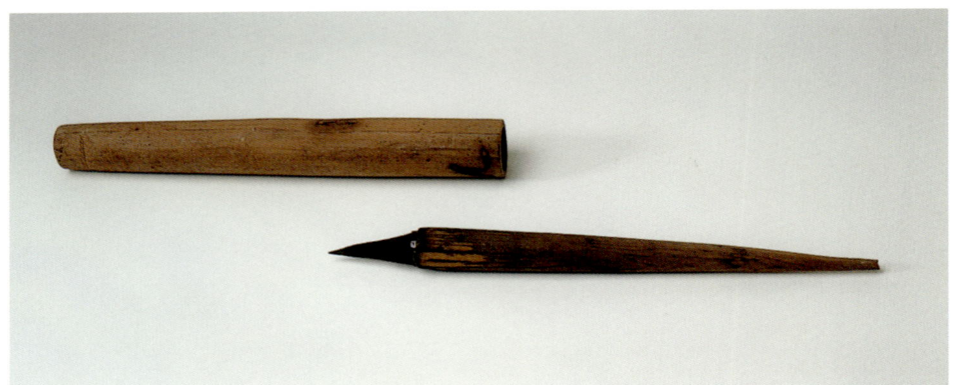

85

85
Writing brush and cap

Sixteen Kingdoms, Former Liang dynasty (314–76)
Wolf's fur and wood
Length: Brush 11¼ in. (29.9 cm); cap 9⅞ in. (25 cm)
Excavated at Songshuxiang, Wuwei, Gansu Province, 1985
Gansu Institute of Archaeology

Excav. report in *Wenbo* 1990.3

More writing instruments and written material from early historical periods have been found in the province of Gansu in the northwest than in any other area in China. These survivals are attributable to the dryness of the region. Beyond the use of writing for learning, letters, and administration, calligraphy was practiced as a fine art in Gansu in the late Han. Gansu calligraphers numbered among the most famous of the second and third centuries.

This brush is detachable from the wooden handle, which is tapered. The design would have made it possible for the brush to be carried by court officials (in the Secretariat, for example) as a hairpin, which was the custom at the time.[1]

1. *JS*: 773; also quoted and discussed in excavation report.

86
Three inscribed wooden tablets

Sixteen Kingdoms, Former Liang dynasty (314–76), dated 355–60
Ink on wood
Maximum height 11¼ in. (28.6 cm)
Excavated from the tomb of Ji Yu, Hantanpo, Wuwei, Gansu Province, 1985
Gansu Institute of Archaeology

Reference: Li Junming and He Shuangquan 1990

During most of the fourth century the city of Wuwei, situated along the Silk Road in northwestern China, served as the capital of the Former Liang dynasty (314–76), a small kingdom that had carved out its territories from a portion of the former Jin empire. Over the past thirty years, excavations of an ancient burial ground southwest of the city have uncovered numerous Han and Jin tombs. These have yielded, among other artifacts, a number of inscribed wooden slips, or tablets, which have survived because of the region's dry climate.[1]

These three wooden tablets were excavated from the tomb of Ji Yu, a high official under the Former Liang dynasty, and his wife. Inscribed with Ji's successive ranks and placed next to the head of the deceased, the slips, dated, respectively, 355, 356, and 360, presumably functioned as a kind of passport to announce Ji Yu's credentials on his journey to the afterlife.[2] A fourth tablet (not included in the exhibition) records the grave goods that

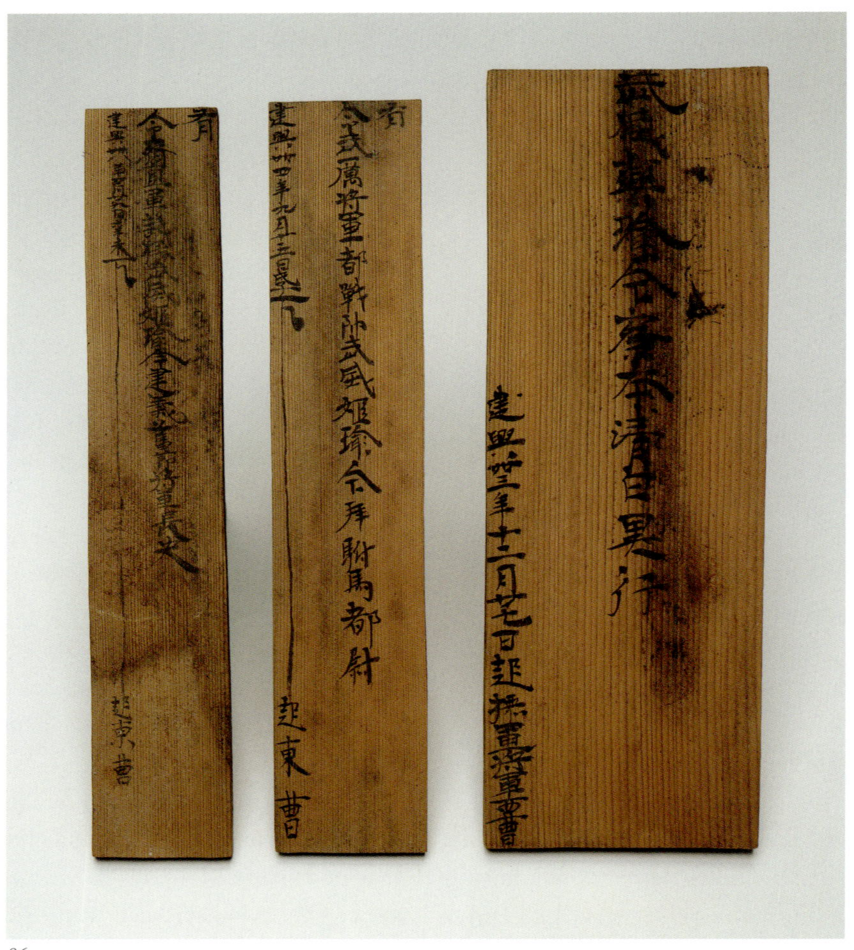

86

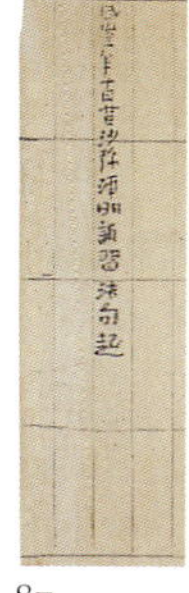

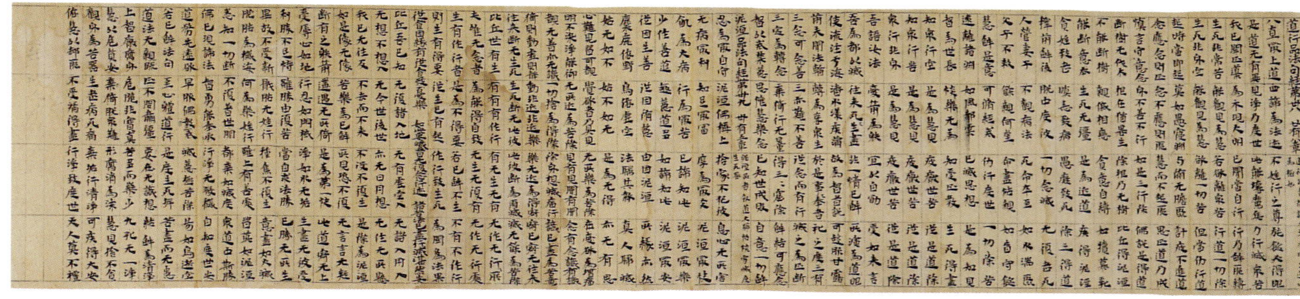

87

accompanied him. A similar list of grave articles is inscribed on a tablet buried next to his wife. It is notable that all three tablets are dated using the Jianxing-reign designation of the last Western Jin emperor, Mindi (r. 313–16), which continued to be used during the Former Liang dynasty.[3]

Written by an anonymous scribe, the calligraphy still possesses many features found in the clerical script of the Stele for Cao Quan of almost two hundred years earlier (cat. no. 22), specifically, the emphatic horizontal and diagonal strokes. But the characters seen here reveal a distinct advance over the earlier style and thus occupy an intermediate stage in the evolution from clerical to running and standard scripts. The balanced, rectilinear forms of the earlier script have been replaced by forms that are more dynamic and asymmetrical. Characters tilt toward the upper right, and there is a greater variety in the size and modulation of individual lines. Occasionally, two distinct components are linked by a single brushstroke.[4]

MKH

1. For an archaeological report on the excavation of Han dynasty documents from the Hantanpo site, see Gansu sheng bowuguan, Gansu sheng Wuwei Xian wenhuaguan 1973: 18–22.
2. A full transcription of the text on the wooden tablets from Ji Yu's tomb has been published in Li Junming and He Shuangquan 1990: 26–29. A summary of the earlier report appears in Xie Guihua 2001: 553.
3. See *Shodō zenshū* 1954–68, vol. 3 (1959), no. 18.
4. This more cursive form of clerical script (*zhangcao*) began to evolve in the late Han dynasty, as seen in inscribed wooden tablets of Han date also excavated in Wuwei. See Gansu sheng bowuguan, Gansu sheng Wuwei Xian wenhuaguan 1973, pls. 1–4.

87
Two chapters from the Sutra of Dharma Verses

Sixteen Kingdoms, Former Liang dynasty (314–76), datable to 368
Handscroll, ink on yellow hemp paper with ruled columns
9¾ x 53⅛ in. (24.9 x 135 cm)
Recovered from Cave 17, Dunhuang, Gansu Province, 1900
Gansu Provincial Museum

Reference: Xu Zufan, Qin Mingzhi, and Rong Siqi 1985

Following the introduction of Buddhism into China, the transcribing of Buddhist scriptures, or sutras, came to be regarded as an act of religious merit. By the fourth century, this practice was followed not only by Buddhist devotees but also by a group of professional scribes who would copy a specific sutra on behalf of a patron. The result was a distinctive "sutra style" that differed from the script used in contemporary official documents (see cat. no. 86).

This handscroll was preserved in a walled-up library at the Mogao Buddhist cave temples at Dunhuang, in western Gansu Province, which was reopened in the first years of the twentieth century. The manuscript is one of the earliest discovered at this site and one of the earliest handscrolls in existence, marking the adoption of paper as the principal medium for writing in place of bamboo or wooden tablets.[1] This transcription of chapters 38 and 39 of the Sutra of Dharma Verses (*Dharmapada sutra*) is an early collection of verses on the ethical life from the Hinayana Buddhist canon,

87, detail

which was first translated into Chinese in the early third century.[2] Chapter 38 is entitled "Practicing the Way."[3] Chapter 39, which continues on the same sheet, is entitled "Nirvana."[4] Two colophons record that the novice Jingming (Pure Brightness) recited the sutra at two different times, once in the year 368 and again in 373.[5] The calligraphy of both of these colophons is less accomplished than that of the sutra, indicating that the sutra was copied by a professional scribe, presumably not long before Jingming added his first colophon.

The calligraphy of the sutra represents a transitional stage in the evolution of written Chinese from the archaic clerical script (see cat. nos. 22, 86) to the classical standard script (cat. nos. 232, 233). Here, the balanced rectilinear forms of clerical script have given way to freer, more dynamically asymmetrical forms. The individual strokes are now composed of brush movements that register the changing direction and pressure applied to the brush tip as the calligrapher executes the beginning, middle, and end of a line.[6]

The two dates on the scroll suggest something of the unstable political fortunes of North China at this time. The first date (368) refers to the twelfth year of the Shengping reign era of the Former Liang dynasty. That reign period, however, actually ended in its sixth year (362). Five years later, when Jingming added his second colophon to the scroll, he dated it in accordance with an Eastern Jin reign era. Since the Former Liang dynasty generally did not adopt formal reign titles, the disparate dates on this scroll are a clear sign of the chaotic conditions that prevailed at the time of its creation. Given the unsettled political environment of North China, it is no wonder that many Chinese sought sanctuary in the Buddhist faith.

MKH

1. The Library Cave, walled up around the year 1035, was reopened by a Chinese Daoist monk in 1900; it was subsequently visited by a number of foreign explorers, including Sir Aurel Stein (1907) and Paul Pelliot (1908), so that today its contents have been dispersed to a number of museums and libraries; see Dunhuang Research Institute 2000: 180–87. On the manuscript's rarity as an early paper document in handscroll form, see Juliano and Lerner 2001: 148–49.
2. I am indebted to Dr. Chun-fang Yu for the English translation of this sutra's title (personal correspondence, December 14, 2003). Dr. Yu notes: "The Theravada canon was compiled in Pali during the second century before the Common Era. Since the Prakrit version is dated to the second century, it was later than the Pali version. But we do not know if the former was a translation from the latter. It could be a compilation from another oral source." A manuscript of the *Dharmapada* in the Gandharan Prakrit language that dates to the first or second century was found at Khotan in Xinjiang Province; see Juliano and Lerner 2001: 148–49.
3. I am using Dr. Chun-fang Yu's translation of this chapter's title "because the passages are all about how to behave as a good Buddhist" (personal correspondence, December 14, 2003).
4. According to Zhang Guangda, these chapters conform closely to chapters 28 and 36 of this sutra as preserved in the Taisho edition of the Buddhist canon (*Tripitaka*), vol. 4: 201; see Zhang's entry to this sutra in Juliano and Lerner 2001: 148–49, no. 46.
5. For translations of these colophons, see Dunhuang Research Institute 2000: 166–67; and Juliano and Lerner 2001: 148.
6. For a close comparison of individual characters from this text and those on Han-era wooden tablets from Wuwei, see the essay in Xu Zufan, Qin Mingzhi, and Rong Siqi 1985, sec. 4, unpaged.

88
Lamp

Sixteen Kingdoms, Former Liang dynasty (314–76)
Wood with pigments
Height 47¼ in. (120 cm)
Excavated at Baishuxiang, Wuwei, Gansu Province, 1985
Gansu Institute of Archaeology

Reference: Tian Jian 1990

The origin of Chinese oil lamps remains unknown. The earliest datable examples, from the late Warring States period

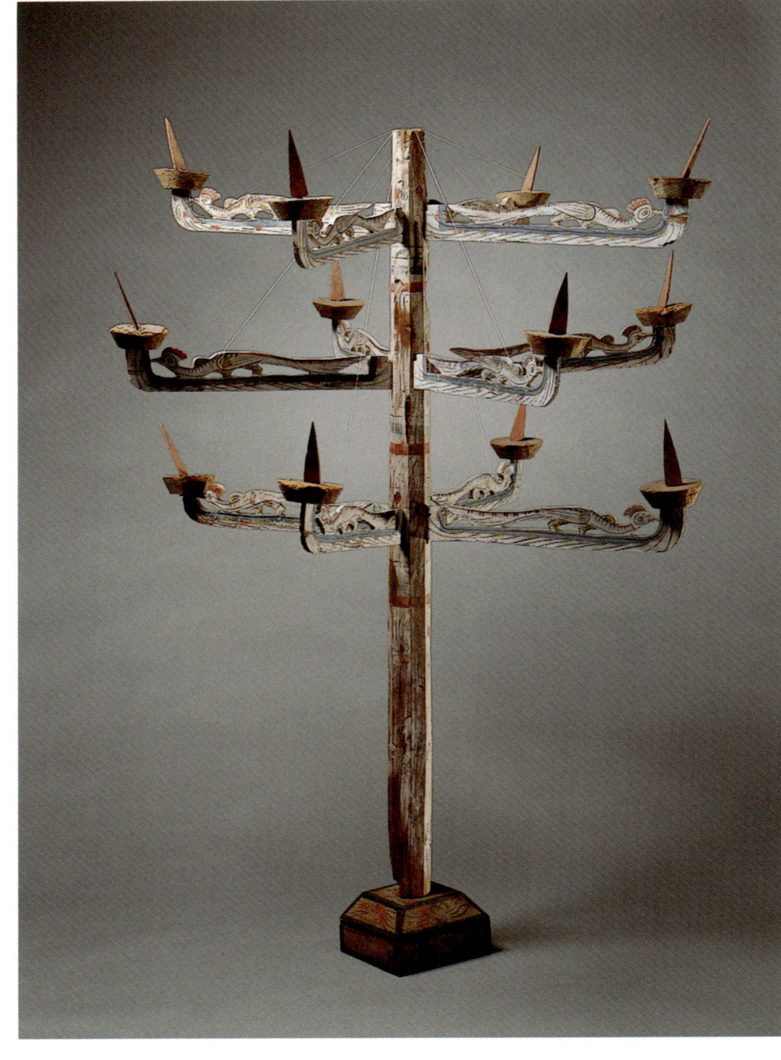

(481–221 B.C.), often demonstrate sophisticated structures, suggesting that their invention may reach even further back in time. Over the following centuries, the manufacture of lamps proliferated and they were made in a variety of materials, including bronze, iron, ceramic, jade, stone, and wood. Different types were developed that incorporated technical innovations such as flues, draft shields, and movable shades, and novel designs were created in the form of human figures, animals, birds, and imaginary creatures.

The lamp with multiple branches was a popular type among this diversity of lighting devices. It was also among the very early types, a well-known example having been recovered from a late fourth-century tomb of the ancient Zhongshan state in Pingshan, Hebei.[1] That masterfully cast bronze lamp has fifteen branches, amid which eight lively monkeys swing and cavort while two servants at the base toss food up to them. The most elaborate is a painted pottery lamp from a late Eastern Han tomb in Henan Province that stands about three feet high.[2] The branches of the lamp fairly teem with animals, human figures, and fantastic creatures in a vivid depiction of the land of the immortals.

To date, the present example is one of the largest among all finds. The twelve branches, arranged in three tiers, extend from a four-foot-high stem supported on a square base. A round wooden disk with a pointed chip in the center to represent a lighted wick in an oil tray is placed on the curved end of each branch. A fabulous bird with a long, extended tail stretches along the length of the branch, facing toward the light. Judging from a similar bronze lamp slightly earlier in date, the abrupt end of the stem must have had a cap at the top, possibly decorated with a bird. The lamp is likely a replica of a bronze original.

ZS

1. Hebei sheng wenwu yanjiusuo 1995: 133–34.
2. Luoyang bowuguan 1975: 116.

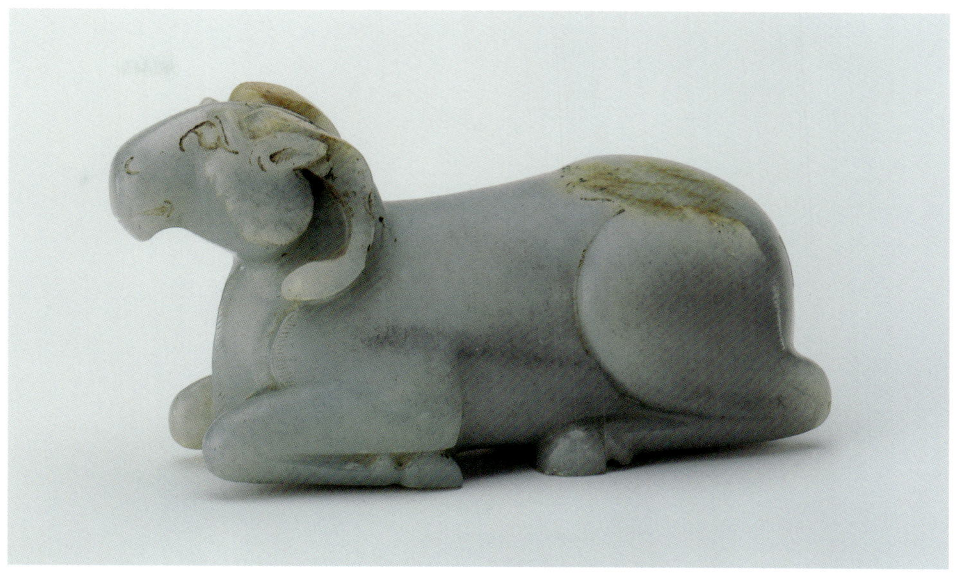

89
Recumbent ram

Eastern Han dynasty, Former Liang dynasty
(25–220) to (314–76)
Jade (nephrite)
Length 5⅞ in. (15 cm)
Excavated at Lingjuntai, Wuwei,
Gansu Province
Gansu Provincial Museum

Reference: Gansu sheng bowuguan 1994

Rams and sheep were common motifs in early Chinese art. They are represented as early as the Shang dynasty (16th–11th century B.C.), when they were depicted on ritual bronzes.[1] Stone and jade examples in the round, however, seem to occur at a much later time. Such sculptures may have been inspired by the art of the steppes, where wild as well as domestic animals were popular subjects for harness and belt ornaments. The recumbent pose, which seems to have been a standard form among Han-dynasty examples, also bears resemblance to images in the nomadic culture.

In this freestanding sculpture, a recumbent ram is presented with its head slightly raised and its four legs folded under its plump body. Deeply incised lines define the mouth, nose, eye sockets, and ears. The horns have rounded tips and form a graceful backward curve reminiscent of those on a ram-shaped bronze lamp from the second-century B.C. tomb of Liu Sheng, prince of Zhongshan state.[2] The staring eyes are raised in hemispheres typical of Han jades. Also indicative of carving techniques of the Han dynasty are the short intaglio lines that describe the hair on the jaws, shoulders, and legs.

Jades dating from the Three Kingdoms (220–80) to the end of the Northern and Southern Dynasties (386–589) are extremely rare, and this figure is one of the very few that have survived. The general characteristics of jades from that period remain unclear. Because major cities, such as Luoyang, were heavily looted and destroyed during constant and widespread wars, the jade-carving industry evidently suffered a devastating blow. In addition, the disintegration of the central government and the interruption of trade over the Silk Road led to the short supply of the raw material—nephrite—which became so rare that Emperor Chengdi (r. 326–42) of the Jin dynasty had to use substitutes for the white jade beads on his crown.[3] The present sculpture was most likely an heirloom passed down from generation to generation, which found its way through a circuitous route to the Sixteen Kingdoms burial.

ZS

1. W. Fong 1980, pl. 20.
2. Zhongguo shehui kexueyuan kaogu yanjiusuo, Hebei sheng wenwu guanlichu 1980, pl. 34.
3. Niu Bingyue 1994: 51; *JS*: 2164.

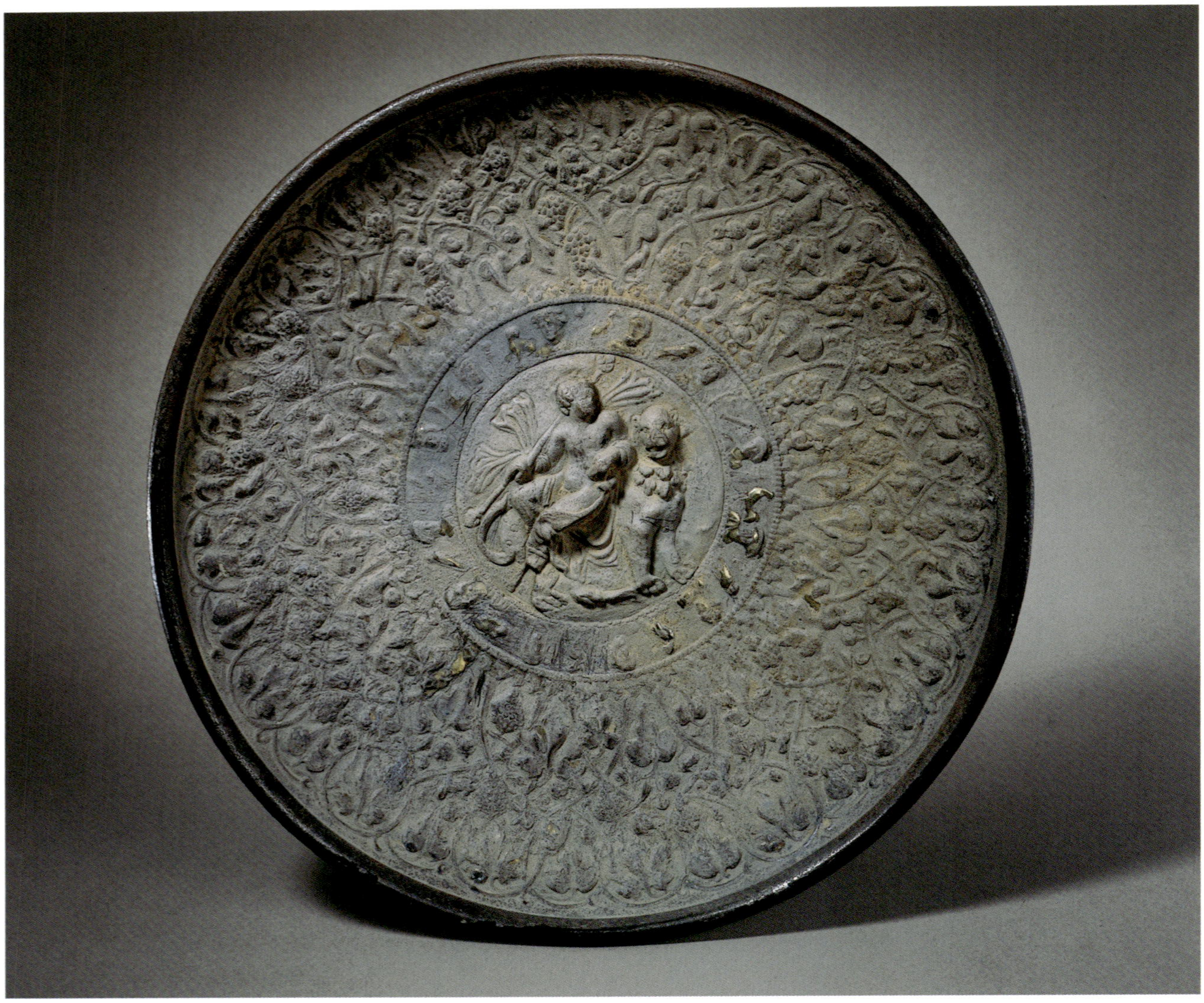

90

Plate with figure of Dionysus

2nd–3rd century
Gilt silver
Diameter 12¼ in. (31 cm)
Found at Beitan, Jingyuan, Gansu Province, 1988
Gansu Provincial Museum

Excav. report in *Wenwu* 1990.5

This plate, which was found in 1988 during construction of a house in Beitan, Gansu,[1] illustrates the complex history of luxury goods that traveled on the Silk Road. Most likely, it was made in an eastern province of the Roman world. The center is decorated with a figure of the god Dionysus on the back of a panther whose neck is decorated with vine leaves and whose mane resembles that of a lion. Busts of twelve Olympian gods, with their identifying symbols, fill the narrow band encircling the central image. Grapevines inhabited by birds, insects, and reptiles decorate the large interior. This imagery may reflect the spread of Neoplatonism in the Late Roman world, which held Dionysus as the most important god.[2]

Two inscriptions, added after the manufacture of the plate, are incised on the bottom. One of them is Sogdian, dating from the fifth to the seventh century. It is the word *šyr*, which is perhaps the name of the owner.[3] The other inscription is written as a dotted line. It translates: "[Weight one] thousand + 20 [drachmas]." Nicholas Sims-Williams has dated the inscription to "not later than the early sixth century." The weight of the plate is 3.108 grams. Thus, one drachma must have been the equivalent of 3.12 grams, since "[one] thousand + 20 [drachmas]" is given as 3.12 grams.[4] Persian, Khorazmian, and Sogdian drachmas, which were approximately equal to each other in weight, were

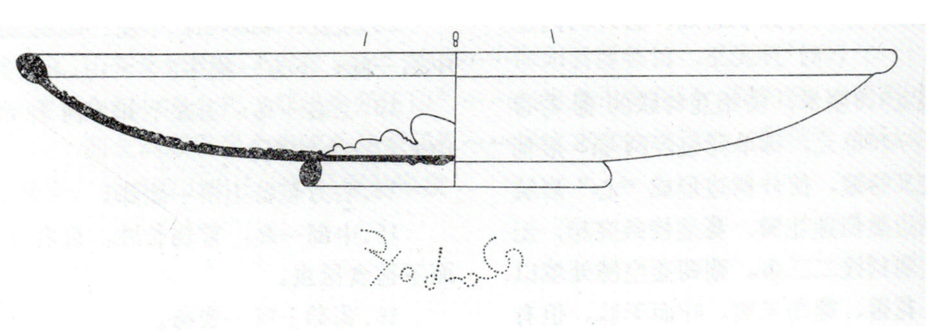

90, section drawing

heavier, more than 4 grams. The Bactrian owner of the vessel could have used caliphate measures in the early eighth century, when the Arabs conquered the Bactrian region, but in this case the inscription might have been deliberately archaistic. Thus, the plate, made in Rome in the second to third century, was owned in the fifth to seventh century by a Sogdian, and later perhaps by someone in the region of Bactria.

BIM

1. Chu Shibin 1990: 1–9.
2. Baratte 1996: 142–47; Carter 1995a.
3. Personal communication from Nicholas Sims-Williams.
4. Sims-Williams 1995: 225. Luo Feng (2000a: 324) published his drawings of the two inscriptions.

91
Bowl with ostriches

5th–6th century
Silver
Diameter 8¼ in. (21 cm)
Found at Qigexing, Yanqi, Xinjiang Uygur Autonomous Region, 1989
Bayingolin Mongolian Autonomous Prefecture Museum

Reference: Sun Ji 1996b

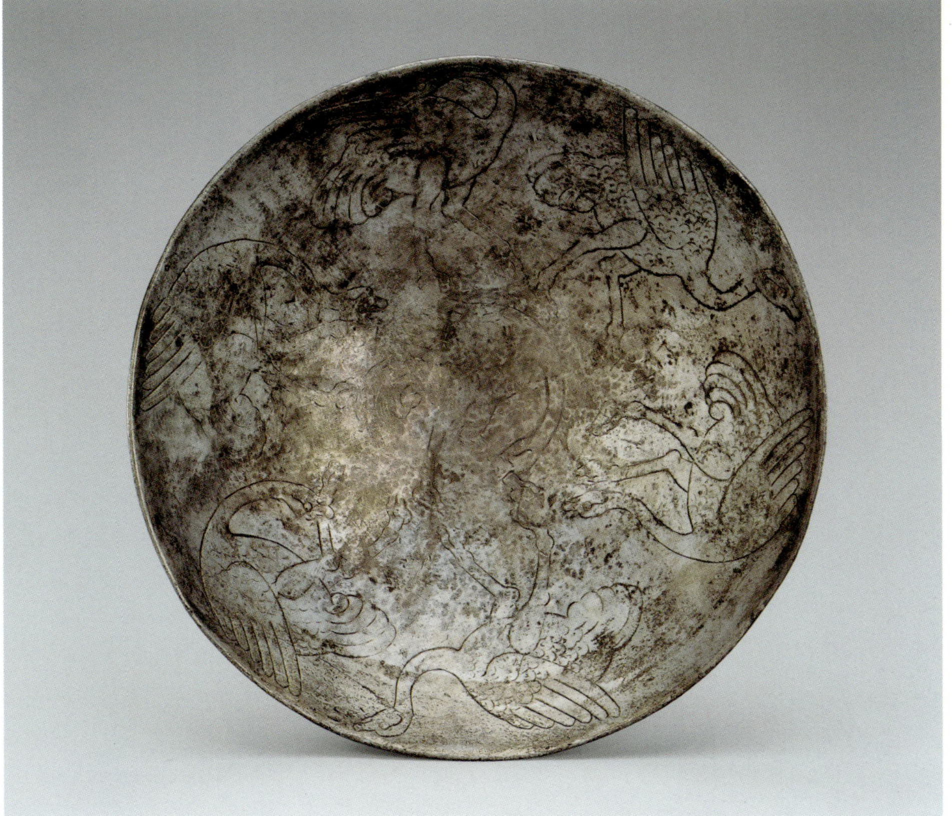

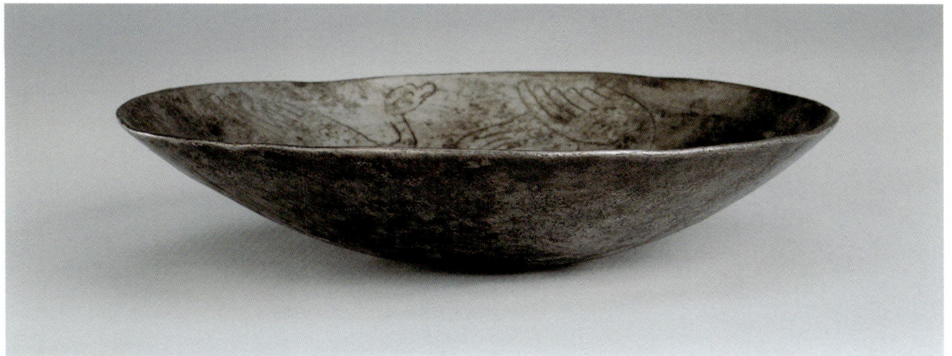

The chased decoration on this shallow silver bowl is on the interior surface and includes five ostriches arranged around the walls of the vessel and one ostrich at the center of the base. Traces of gilding remain.[1] The selection of this exotic creature as the sole motif on a silver vessel is, to my knowledge, without parallel on silver vessels made in Sasanian Iran or in contemporary western Central Asia. The images are simply portrayed in a two-dimensional, linear fashion, a common method of executing designs on late Sasanian silver vessels and on Sogdian metalwork.

The bowl was allegedly found in a hoard with four other silver vessels, two of which are also included in this exhibition (cat. nos. 92, 93), and has parallels in form and decoration to luxury vessels made in mid- and late Sasanian Iran.[2] Another bowl in the group has a central, chased design within a circular frame of a feline striding over a mountainous landscape. The vessel is an open plate having a fluted exterior surface, a type known in the late Sasanian Near East, where many examples in silver and bronze are decorated with simple linear designs of animals and birds usually enclosed within a circular medallion.[3] An excavated example of this vessel type comes from west of Iran in present-day Azerbaijan, a region in antiquity often under Sasanian control.[4] The trees on the bowl decorated with the feline have small oval leaves and grapelike bunches, perhaps a misunderstanding of a grapevine, a motif with accurately rendered leaves and fruit when depicted in Sasanian works of art.

As a motif, ostriches are rarely found in the Sasanian arts of luxury: seals and gems, silver vessels, and textiles. But they were considered an exotic and precious creature in the Near East over the millennia. In the third millennium B.C., ostrich eggshells decorated with colored stones and shell were prized possessions and made into drinking vessels, a fashion that is recorded in the first millennium A.D. in Bukhara and Samarkand.[5] The ostrich also appears in the context of foreign exotica, in hunts, in game parks, and as booty on Assyrian and Iranian works of art of the first millennium B.C. Although this subject is almost entirely absent in the art of Sasanian Iran, Chinese records note that an ostrich was sent by Parthians to China as early as A.D. 101, an indication that the fascination of the Chinese with this bird was known in the West. The source of the birds sent to China is believed to have been western Central Asia. Descriptions explain their appeal: "The head and neck of the adult male were red or pink, the body feathers glossy black, with white plumes in tail and wing."[6] In the first millennium A.D. the ostrich appears in the art of Sogd.

The varied poses of the birds on the present bowl give a somewhat naturalistic appearance to the figures, and in this sense the design is more closely related to works made in western Central Asia, in Bactria, Sogd, and the Kushan region, than to the art of Sasanian Iran, where the designs are more hieratic and formalized.

All three luxury vessels described above, including this bowl decorated with ostriches, share some features with late Sasanian works of art, but none of them is easily attributable to a specific workshop in Iran or Central Asia. They appear to have been made in some minor provincial center open to influences from both Sasanian Iran and Bactria or Sogd. Preserved as valued items by a member of the elite living in western Central Asia, the precious vessels must have eventually passed on to China along the Silk Road in the hands of merchants or diplomats.

POH

1. Sun Ji 1996b: 156–77.
2. Xinjiang Weiwuer zizhiqu wenwu shiye guanliju et al. 1999: 184; Tōkyō kokuritsu hakubutsukan 2002, no. 48.
3. Harper 1993: 101, no. 68.
4. Koshkarly 1985, pl. 13.
5. Schafer 1963: 258.
6. Ibid.: 102.

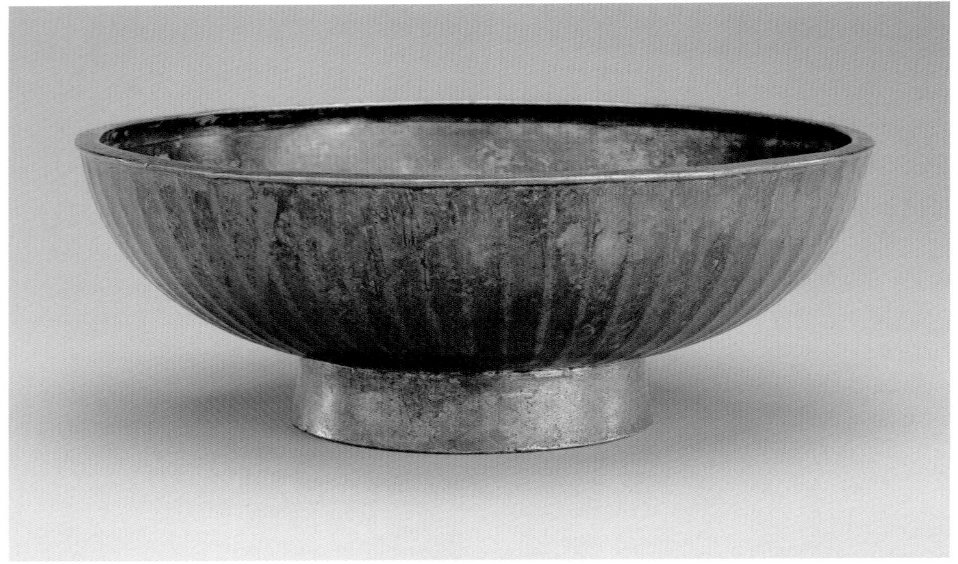

92
Bowl with fluted exterior

5th–6th century
Silver
Diameter 8 in. (20.5 cm)
Found at Qigexing, Yanqi, Xinjiang Uygur Autonomous Region, 1989
Bayingolin Mongolian Autonomous Prefecture Museum

REFERENCE: Sun Ji 1996b

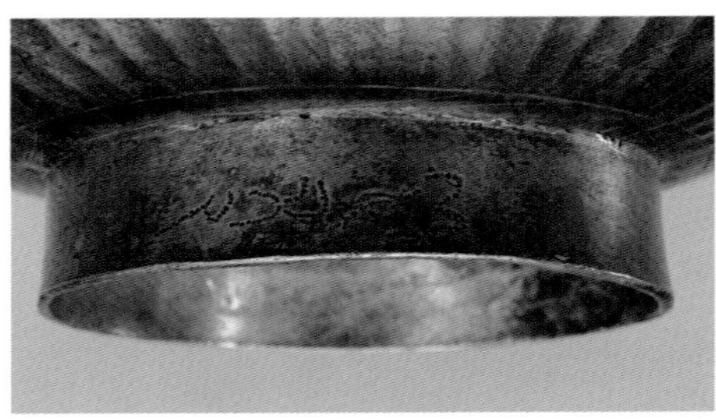

The distinctive shape of the fluted body and the inscriptions dotted onto the low foot ring and the base associate this vessel with the Iranian Sasanian realm (3rd–mid-7th century).[1] A common mid- and late Sasanian form of silver vessel has a fluted bowl of this same size and type, distinctive because of the broad, flattened rim that sharply overhangs the interior. Sasanian examples of this type, however, invariably rest on a thin, high, circular, and slightly flaring foot, the height approximately matching the depth of the bowl.[2] Occasionally decorated on the center of the interior with a chased design of a bird, usually a cock or guinea fowl, the bowls are more often plain and undecorated except for the fluted lines that extend from the foot to the rim on the exterior.

In spite of the relationship to one type of Sasanian luxury vessel, the bowl found in China has a distinctive feature, a low foot ring. Another difference, perhaps due to the presence of the thick foot ring, is the weight of the vessel in this exhibition, 825.5 grams. This weight is greater than that of the general range of Sasanian high-footed bowls, which usually weigh between 300 and 500 grams.

The Middle Persian inscriptions dotted onto the exterior of the foot ring and onto the exterior base of the bowl are numbers preceded, in the reading by Nicholas Sims-Williams, by the letter *D* (for *drachma*). When totaled, the numbers on the foot ring equal 152; the number on the base equals 20. While Middle Persian numerical inscriptions, characteristically dotted, commonly appear on nearly all types of Sasanian silver vessels, they record the weight of the vessel according to the Sasanian standard drachma (coin) weight. Since the weight of the present bowl is known, it is possible to calculate the weight of a drachma following this formula, but the result is a heavier drachma than was in use in either Sasanian Iran or Sogd. Consequently, Lin Meicun has suggested that the numbers refer simply to the vessel's value rather than to its weight, a significant departure from the Sasanian practice.[3]

Because of the shape and fluted decoration of the bowl, it is possible that this part of the vessel was actually made in the Sasanian Near East. However, at some point in its history, the bowl must have passed from the Sasanian heartland to a provincial region, where a low foot ring replaced a lost or damaged high foot and where Middle Persian inscriptions giving the value of the piece rather than its weight were applied. In a catalogue published by the Tokyo National Museum, the vessel is described as worn, which suggests that it was in use for some time.[4] As a luxury object, in its present form it is neither a work made in a Sasanian center nor, unmistakably, is it a Sogdian, Bactrian, or Kushan piece produced in Central Asia. But along with the two other vessels from the same hoard (cat. nos. 91, 93), it does provide some indication of the variety of luxury artifacts produced in an environment where influences from Iran, Rome, India, Bactria, and Sogd predominated to a greater or lesser degree in local workshops.

POH

1. Xinjiang Weiwuer zizhiqu wenwu shiye guanliju et al. 1999: 184.
2. Harper 1993: 101, no. 77.
3. Lin Meicun 1998.
4. Tōkyō kokuritsu hakubutsukan 2002, no. 154.

93
Plate with tiger

5th–6th century
Silver
Diameter 8⅜ in. (21.3 cm)
Found at Qigexing, Yanqi, Xinjiang Uygur Autonomous Region, 1989
Bayingolin Mongolian Autonomous Prefecture Museum

Reference: Xinjiang Weiwuer zizhiqu wenwu shiye guanliju et al. 1999

The long Sogdian inscription on this silver plate, approximately datable to the sixth century, is, characteristically, placed below the rim:

ZNH ZY y'mk ZKwy txs'ycyh γ'δp' nynyh xr'ryh ZKwyh δrsm'tyh xypδ 30 s n'krtk.[1]

A translation reads: "This vessel belongs to Xr'ryh [a female name], responsible for the throne in the temple of Taxsich [a Sogdian deity, the daughter] of δrsm'tyh. Weight 30 s[taters] of silver." The word *γ'δw'nynyh* has been interpreted by Vladimir Livshits as *γ'δp'nynyh*, which he reads as "tableware" instead of "throne."[2] Taxsich temples would have received, on any given day, a number of sacrificial animals. It is possible that the sacrifices were followed by great feasts and that the tableware, in this case, was kept in the temple. A Sogdian bowl, also of silver, was found in Jartepa II, a temple situated between Samarkand and Panjikent.[3]

BIM

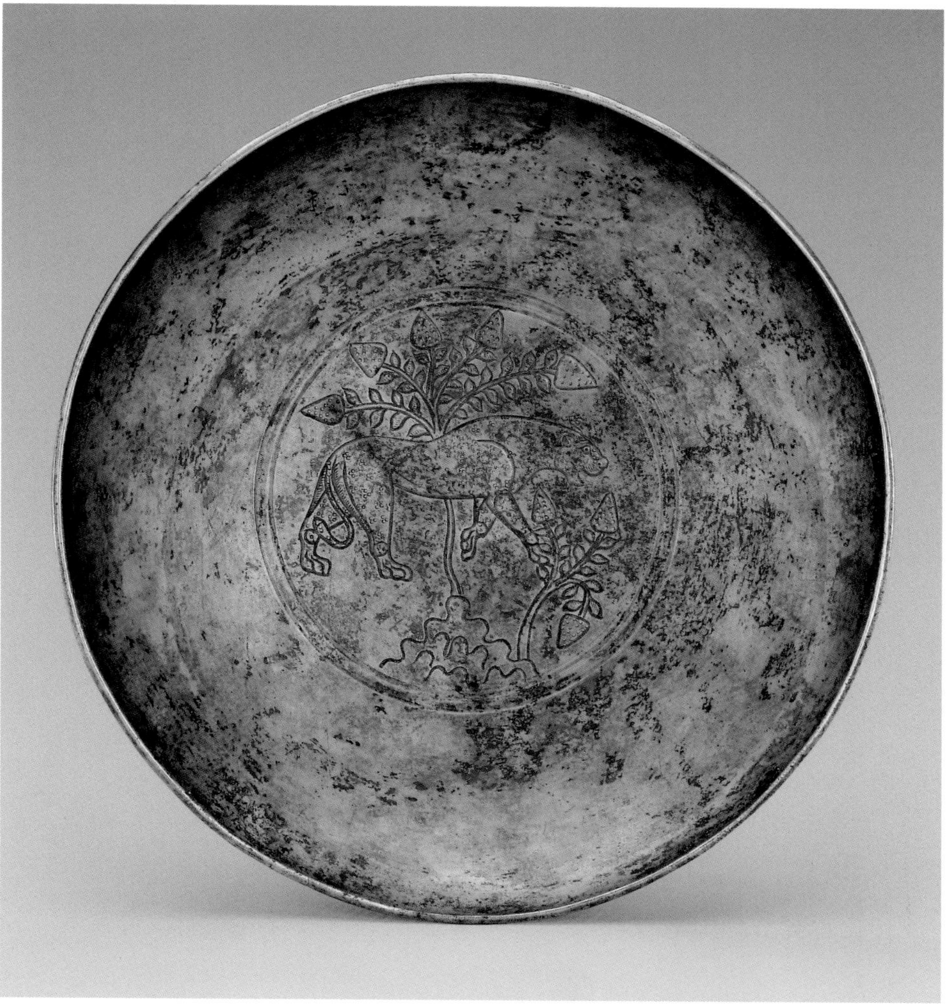

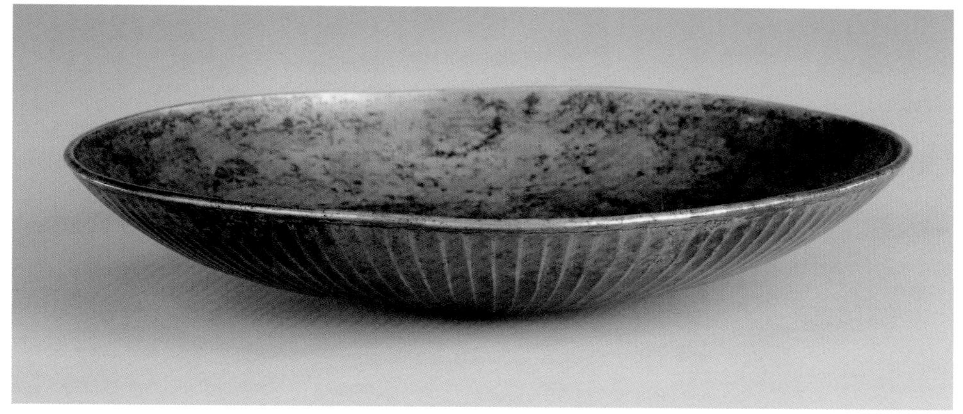

1. Lin Meicun 1998: 160–63; the transcription is by Nicholas Sims-Williams (in ibid.).
2. Personal communication with the author. In his recent article Livshits translates *γ′δty* (plural of γ′δ) as "tableware" in an inscription on a clay jar from Suyab–Ak-Beshim: γ′δyny tγ′r′ <δnn> γ′δty [.]w[..] ′l′n prn(y) p(y)δ′r prβγ-tyt′kw wrnxynty (This vessel along with tableware is presented to His Majesty Alan the prosperous). Livshits 2002: 128–33, 174. See also Lurje and Marshak 2002: 84.3.
3. Berdimuratov and Samibaev 1999, fig. 91.

94
Covered jar

Ca. 5th century
Gold inlaid with rubies
Height 5½ in. (14 cm)
Excavated at Boma, Ili, Xinjiang Uygur Autonomous Region, 1997
Ili Kasak Autonomous Prefecture Museum

Excav. report in *Wenwu* 1999.9

The globular body of this jar stands on a low, separately crafted base and is covered with a hemispheric lid.[1] Four perforations for rivets indicate that the vessel formerly had a square plaque for attaching a ring handle. The edge of the base is decorated with a delicate band of small gold beads. The shoulder is adorned with an ornament that resembles a necklace of thin gold wire strung with pendants consisting of gold sockets inlaid with rubies. One kind of socket is circular, the other is almond-shaped. Each group of the latter forms a trefoil. The shape of the vessel is typically nomadic, but, technically, the jar is more finely crafted than objects in the Hunnish polychrome style.

The lid was perhaps made for a different vessel, as the design seems independent of that on the jar itself. In particular, while the sockets for the precious stones are almond-shaped and circular, the motif on the lid is an acanthus calyx similar to, but more schematic than, that on the foot of the cylindrical cup from Datong (cat. no. 59). Such schematization is typical of late Sasanian architectural decoration in Iran from the fifth to the seventh century.

BIM

1. An Yingxin 1999: 6–7, 15; Xinjiang Weiwuer zizhiqu wenwu shiye guanliju et al. 1999: 382, fig. 1092; Tōkyō kokuritsu hakubutsukan 2002: 29, no. 10; Wang Binghua 2003: 59, fig. 8.

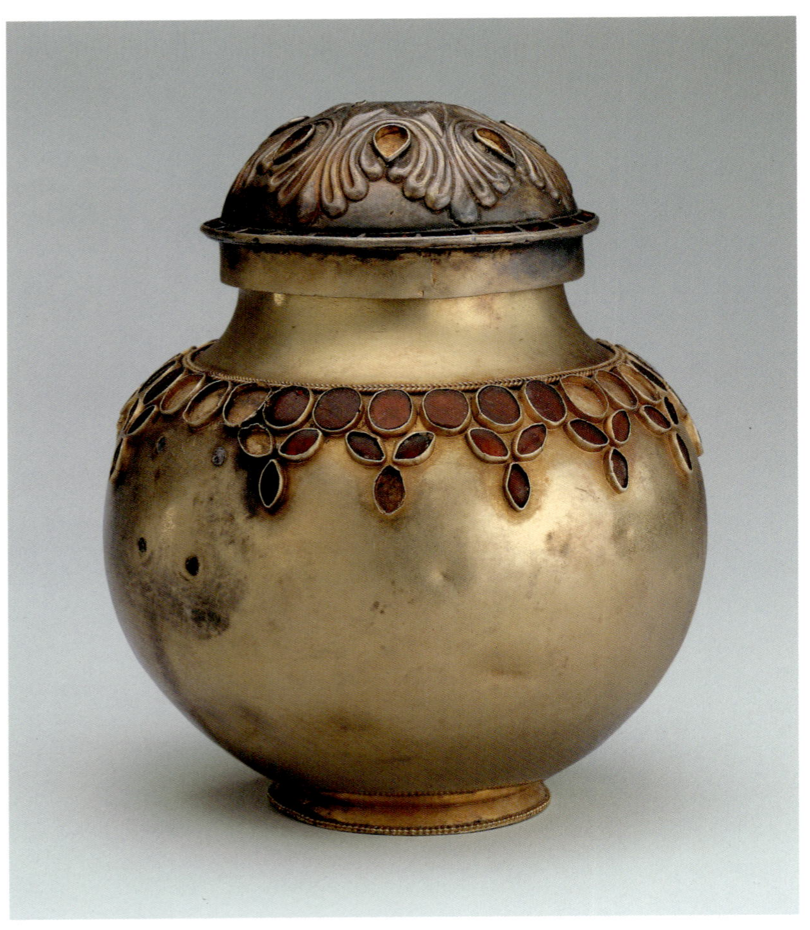

95
Cup with a handle in the shape of a tiger

Ca. 5th century
Gold inlaid with agate
Height 6¼ in. (16 cm)
Excavated at Boma, Ili, Xinjiang Uygur Autonomous Region, 1997
Ili Kasak Autonomous Prefecture Museum

Excav. report in *Wenwu* 1999.9

This vessel was found at Boma together with the inlaid lidded gold jar (cat. no. 94).[1] In form, it resembles many vessels of silver and pottery made for nomadic customers. The regular network composition, however, is not known in the Hunnish style. Nevertheless, in the so-called third group of Hunnish jewelry, oval stones in cabochon are sometimes placed in square compartments, much like the configuration seen here of circular stones in diamond compartments.[2] The handle in the form of a tiger is significant in terms of attribution as it very much resembles the handle of a Sasanian silver mug in The Cleveland Museum of Art.[3] The Boma vessels were certainly made for nomads and reflect nomadic taste, but one cannot rule out the possibility that they were produced by Sasanian master craftsmen. The geographic distribution of the third group is the region of the steppes of Eastern Europe from the Volga to the Danube, excluding Western Europe and the Byzantine dominions in Crimea.[4] Only one object of this group was found in Kazakhstan.[5]

BIM

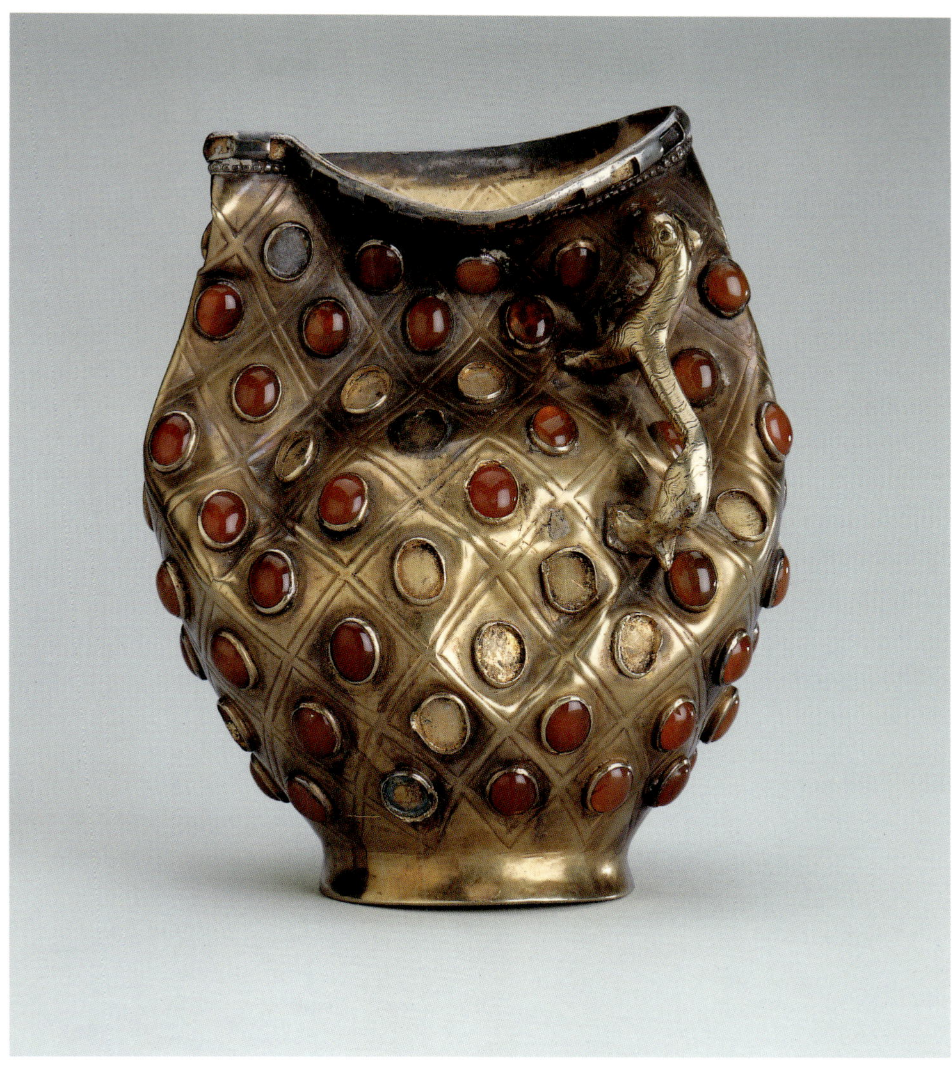

1. An Yingxin 1999: 6–7, 4–19; Xinjiang Weiwuer zizhiqu wenwu shiye guanliju et al. 1999: 382, fig. 1090; Tōkyō kokuritsu hakubutsukan 2002: 28, no. 9; Wang Binghua 2003: 59–60, fig. 9.
2. Zasetskaia 1982, figs. 4, 5, 7.
3. Shepherd 1964: 89–91, figs. 30–32.
4. Zasetskaia 1982: 25.
5. Ibid.: 28–29.

96
Goblet with applied decoration

6th–7th century
Glass
Diameter of mouth rim 4¾ in. (12.1 cm)
Found at Senmusaimu Grottoes, Kucha, Xinjiang Uygur Autonomous Region, 1989
Xinjiang Uygur Autonomous Region Museum

Reference: Tōkyō kokuritsu hakubutsukan 2002, no. 3.

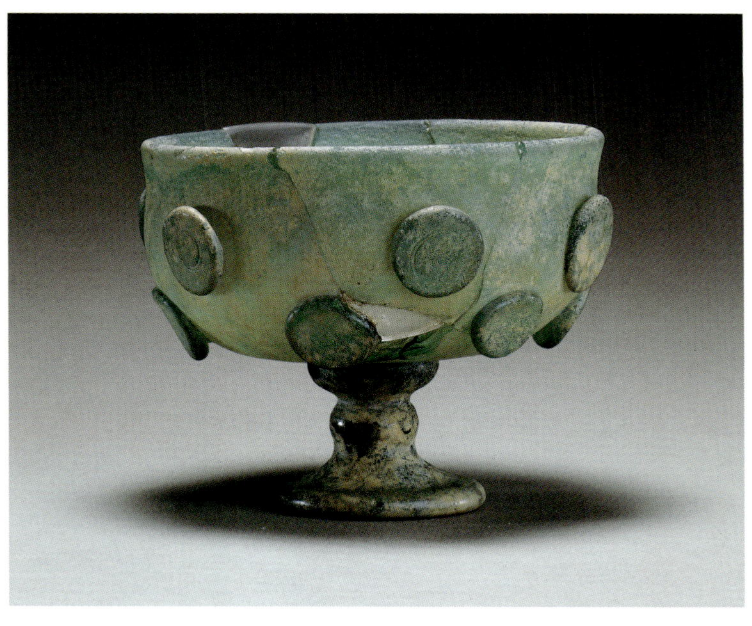

The Senmusaimu (Simsim) Grottoes, where this goblet was found, are located about twenty-five miles northeast of the city of Kucha. There are fifty-two caves, centered around the site of a former Buddhist monastery.

This stemmed glass goblet is light green and transparent. The inner and outer walls are covered with a whitish weathered layer. The straight mouth, curved wall, and tall stem are distinct characteristics of Iranian silverware. The outer wall is decorated with two rows of circular applied ornaments, six in each, recalling the ornaments on the glass bowl excavated from the Northern Zhou tomb of Li Xian (cat. no. 158). Although the ornaments on both works are circular and raised, they are made by different methods, those on the goblet by application, those on the bowl by cutting. High-relief ornamentation made by cutting the thick wall of the vessel is time-consuming and labor-intensive, while applied decoration, as in the present case, may be considered a somewhat facile imitation. In the evolution of glass production on the Plateau of Iran, glassware with circular high-relief ornaments first appeared during the Sasanian Empire (226–651), and those with circular appliqué decorations emerged in the early Islamic period. A glass bottle of the early Islamic period with this embellishment is in the Iran National Museum.[1]

AJ

1. Kordmahini 1994: 69.

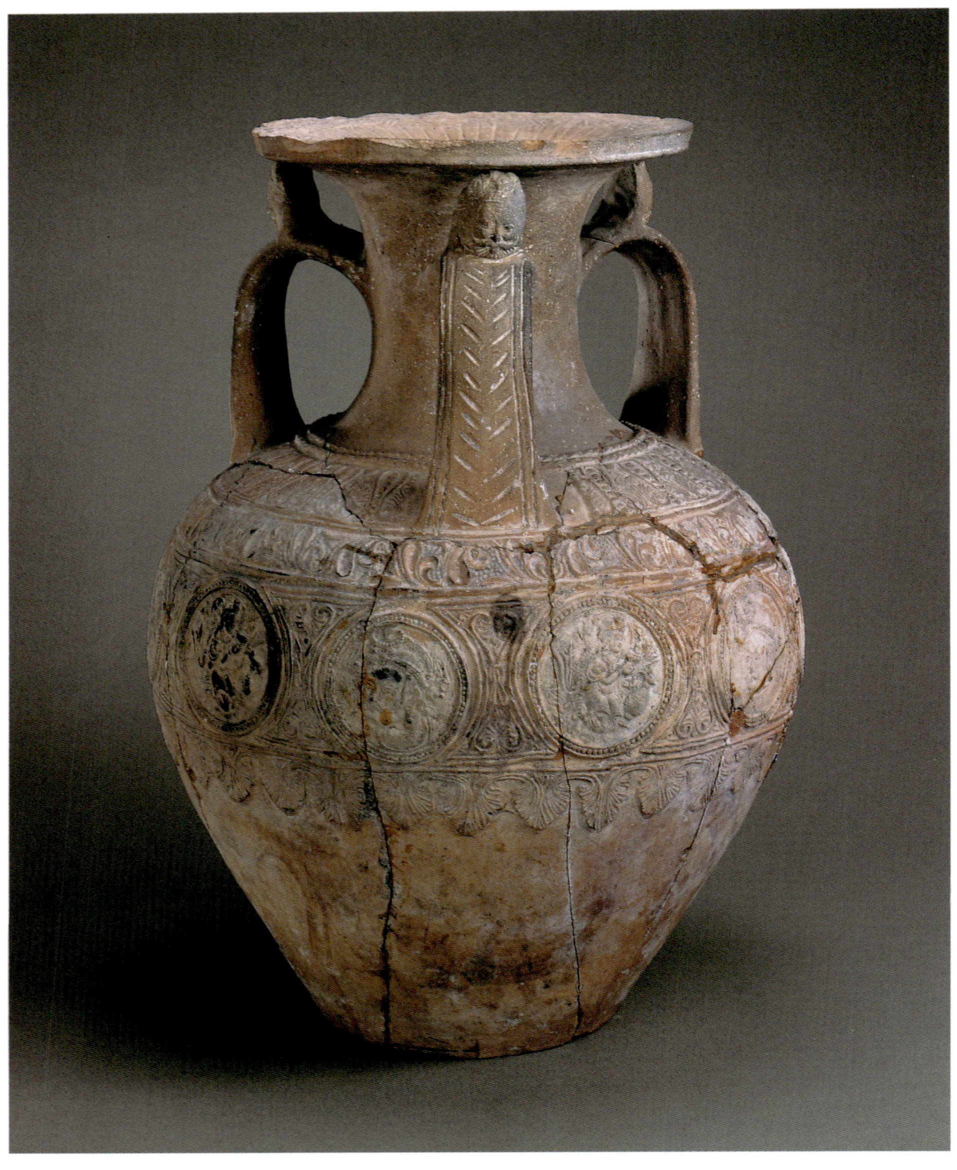

97
Jar with three handles

6th century
Earthenware
Height 22½ in. (57 cm)
Excavated at Yawuluk, Kashi, Xinjiang Uygur Autonomous Region, 1991
Kashi City Museum

Reference: Tōkyō kokuritsu hakubutsukan 2002: 49

Three-handle jars have been found in the areas of Kashgar, Tumshuq, Kucha, and Khotan.[1] A ceramic vessel of another shape but embellished with roundels very similar to those seen here and on the jars from Khotan was recently found in Kirghizia, in the Tianshan Mountains to the north of Kashgar and Tumshuq.[2] The form of these jars derives from Greco-Roman amphoras by way of Parthian and late Bactrian variants. The relief decoration was stamped with compound molds. The floral motifs are basically classical, while the imagery reflects stylistic syncretism in the region of Bactria.

The jovial, smiling heads affixed to the upper part of the handles on this jar, excavated from the site of a Buddhist temple at Yawuluk, appear to imitate

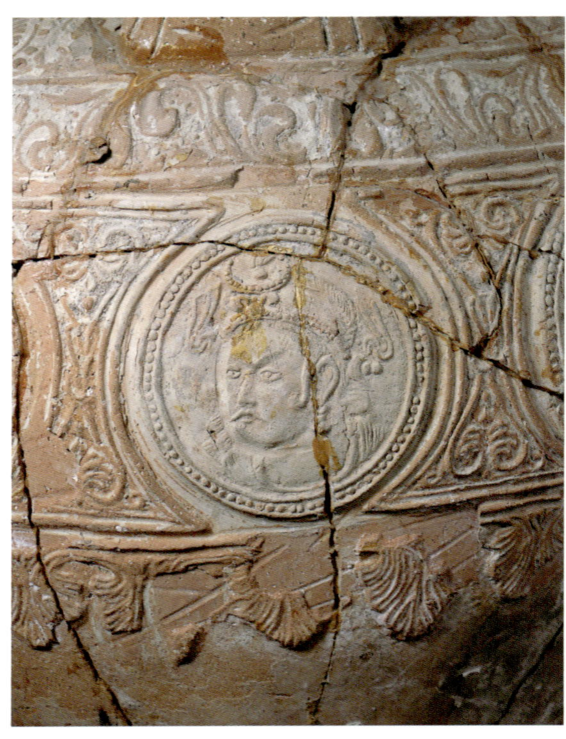

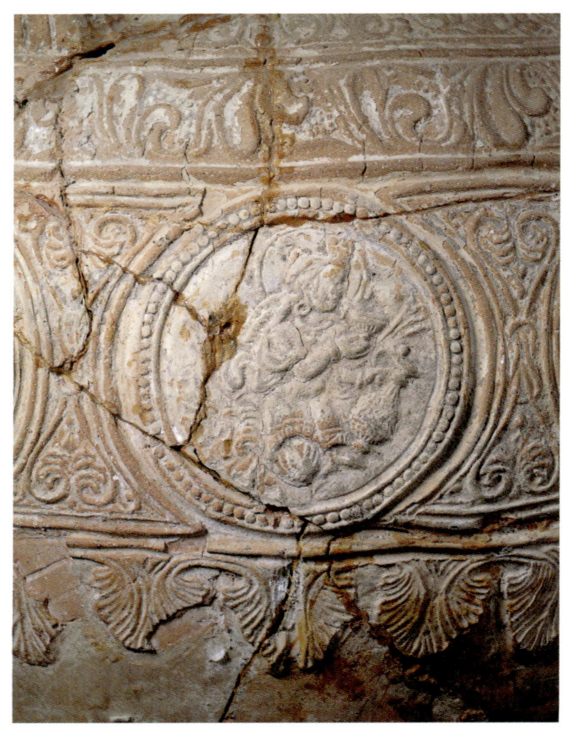

images of the Greek god Pan. However, they wear a three-crescent crown common to Sogdiana, the Hindu Kush area, and Khotan. This crown type is seen in Buddhist art dating to not later than the fifth century; on coins it occurs from the 560s onward.[3] The medallions on the body of the jar encircle, alternately, the bust of a king (opposite, left) and the figure of a female servant offering a bowl of wine (opposite, right). Before the young woman is a bottle of rose water, and she holds a pitcher in her left hand. Thus, each pair of roundels shows the presentation of a royal feast. The scene is not unlike that in the bottom medallion of a silver bowl in the British Museum, London, which shows Kubera, the semidivine ruler of the chthonic Indian yakshas, and his maid.[4] Kubera may be personified as well by the kings depicted on the present jar, as this mythological personage was also the divine protector of Khotan. The Yawuluk jar is a fine example of the interaction between the cultures of western Xinjiang—where the vessel was made—the Bactrian region, and the lands to the south of the Hindu Kush.

BIM

1. Xinjiang Weiwuer zizhiqu wenwu shiye guanliju et al. 1999: 217, fig. 0585, 231, fig. 0625, 267, fig. 0728; Tōkyō kokuritsu hakubutsukan 2002: 49, no. 34. See also Hambis 1961–64, vol. 1, pl. 362, vol. 2: 361; Le Coq 1922: 29, pl. 45.
2. Fedorov 2001: 361–81.
3. Göbl 1963, vol. 1: 113–15, 252–53 (G57) (K35, 46, Em. 147–51), vol. 2: 50, 71–89 passim; Klimburg-Salter 1989: 106–7.
4. Dalton 1964, no. 204.

98

Rhyton in the shape of a human head

3rd–5th century
Earthenware
Length $7\frac{5}{8}$ in. (19.5 cm)
Found at Yotkan, Hotan, Xinjiang Uygur Autonomous Region, 1976
Xinjiang Uygur Autonomous Region Museum

Reference: Wang Bo 1991

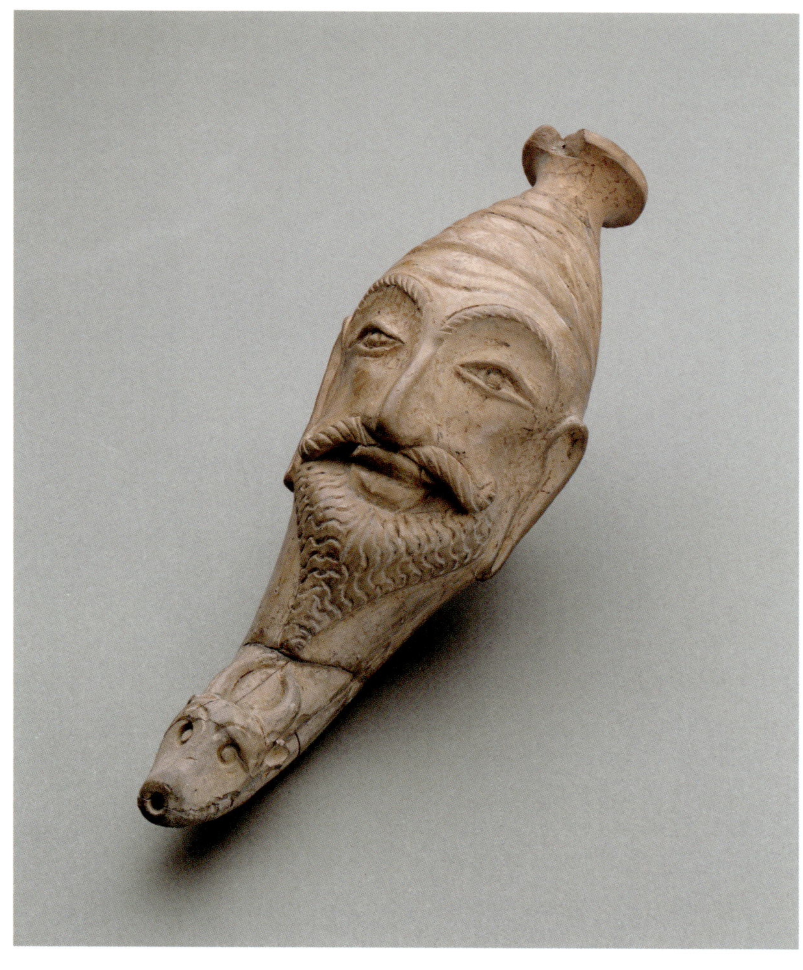

The main part of the body of this rhyton, found at Yotkan, takes the form of a man's head transformed, at the terminal, into a bull's head. While this combination is typical of Sasanian Persian rhyta, the rendering of the man's head is typically Khotanese. Nevertheless, the physical type is not local, and he probably represents a foreign wine seller from Iran or the Near East. Applied details of large vessels also found at Yotkan were formed in similar molds.[1] Another earthenware sculpture of a bearded man was also found, but his ethnic type is different from that of the present example. One of these small sculptures is believed to be a portrait of an Indian Brahman.[2]

The similarity and diversity of such images can be explained if one takes into consideration how the molded terracottas were produced. First, an experienced sculptor would make a figure or a head without a mold. This sculpture was then fired and pressed into wet clay to produce a matrix. A series of nearly identical sculptures made with this mold was then used by an artisan to produce new matrices, and so on. Sometimes in this process a craftsman would alter details of the matrix before firing. It should be noted that after the drying and burning, each generation of matrices and sculptures was somewhat smaller than the previous one. This progression was typical of terracotta production throughout Central Asia.

The date of the Yotkan terracotta is uncertain. The only datable objects found at the site are coins from the first to the third century. Nevertheless, the obvious Sasanian influence makes a date earlier than the third century hardly feasible.[3]

BIM

1. For this piece and a fragment of a very similar rhyton from Yotkan, see Seipel 1996, nos. 182, 183.
2. Ibid.
3. For further discussion, see D'iakonova and Sorokin 1960, no. 951, pl. 20, and N. V. D'iakonova in Tōkyō kokuritsu hakubutsukan 1985, no. 67. See also Sun Ji 1996b: 183–85, fig. 6.

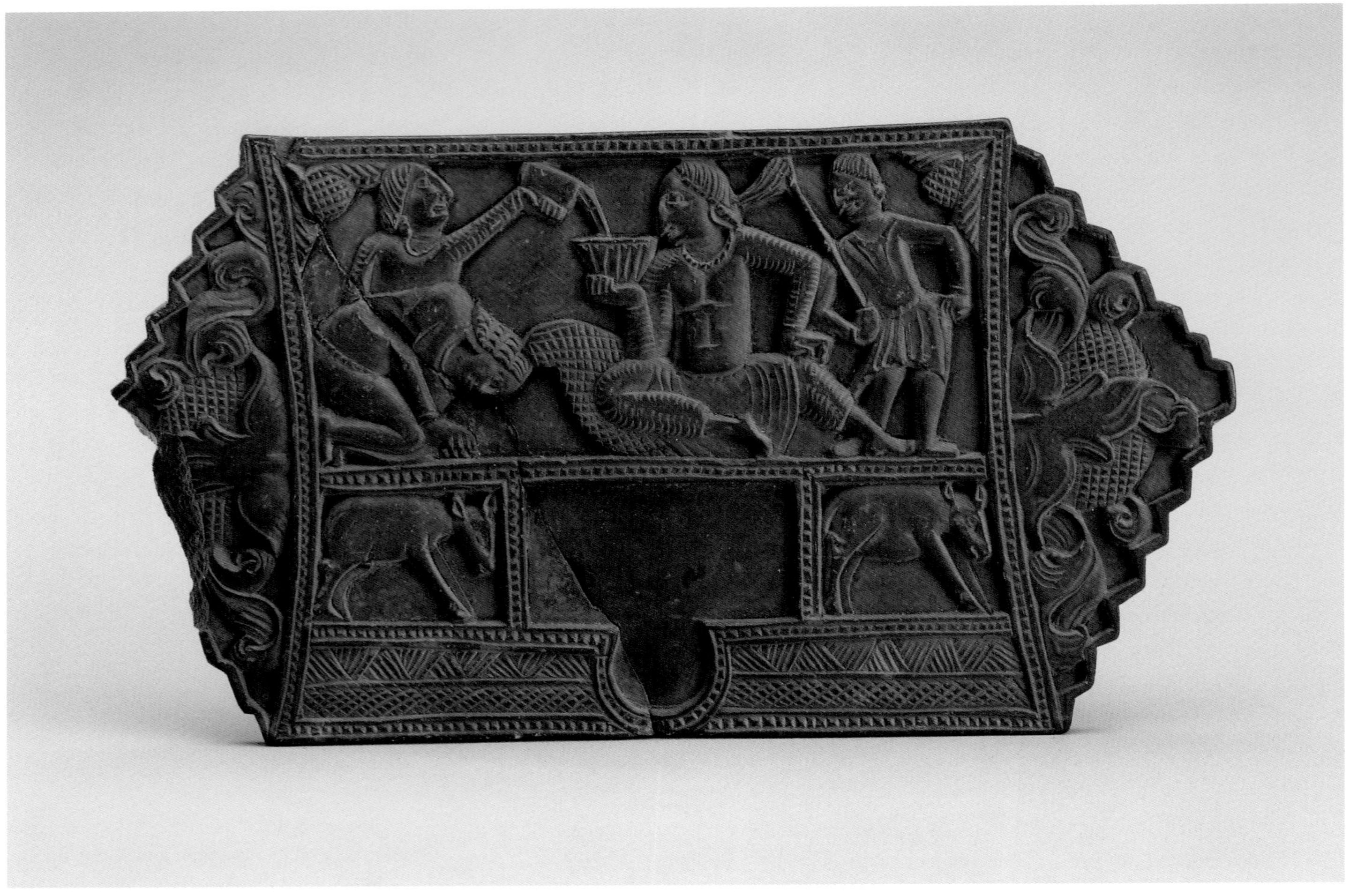

99

Tray with drinking scene

Late 5th–6th century
Gray schist
Length 7¹¹⁄₁₆ in. (19.6 cm)
Reportedly acquired in Kashi, Xinjiang Uygur Autonomous Region
Xinjiang Uygur Autonomous Region Museum

Reference: Tōkyō kokuritsu hakubutsukan 2002, no. 29

Holding a lobed drinking bowl, a man leans against a cushion in the center of this small stone tray reportedly found west of Kashi (Kashgar) in 1972. His right leg is bent, the left extended. One attendant pours liquid into the bowl, another kneels at his feet, and a third stands behind him holding a fly whisk. The figures wear long-sleeved tunics with open necks over trousers, or boots, and have thick, curly hair and aquiline noses. Faces are shown in profile; the torsos are frontal. The central scene is enclosed in a pearl frame that separates the upper and lower parts of the tray and the stepped sides. A quadruped, possibly an allusion to hunting, stands at either side of an undecorated depression in the lower section. Twisted, ribbonlike palmettes encircling large fruit forms decorate the sides.

Often associated with the cult of the heroized dead and linked with images of hunting, the motif of reclining at a banquet has a long history in Greek and related early western Asian imagery. Under the rule of the Sasanians (224–651), the theme also appears in metalwork produced in Iran and neighboring areas. Images dating from the sixth to the eighth century are found in paintings at Panjikent and related sites in Sogdiana (present-day Uzbekistan),[1] among the panels that decorate the ceiling in Cave 1 at Ajanta in India,[2] and on sarcophagi produced in China (see cat. no. 175) for the use of prosperous merchants from Central Asia.[3] The combination of banqueting and hunting may illustrate aspects of a royal funeral or related activities or festivities associated with the Iranian New Year, which had overtones of renewal and regeneration.[4]

Small concave dishes carved in schist from Gandhara (present-day Pakistan and parts of Afghanistan) dating from the second century B.C. to the first century A.D. provide the closest parallels to the structure of the tray found near Kashgar.[5] The function of the dishes, which are often decorated with images of drinking and hunting as well as with themes from Greek mythology, remains enigmatic. Although the dishes have long been identified as containers for cosmetics, it has recently been suggested that they were intended to hold grains or other symbolic offerings in ceremonies associated with royal funerals or, possibly, the New Year.[6] It seems likely that this tray, with a synoptic rendering of the banquet and hunt theme, had a similar cultic function. It was probably used either by a petty dynast in the Kashgar area with ties to Iranian traditions or by a high-ranking member of the Hephthalites (White Huns), who had conquered much of the area in the late fifth century.[7]

DPL

1. Azarpay 1980, ills.
2. See Griffiths 1896–97, vol. 2, pls. 94, 95.
3. Scaglia 1958: 9–28. The piece discussed by Scaglia is the earliest known example of Sogdian imagery in China. For a discussion of more recently discovered works, see the translation of several articles in Chinese on Zoroastrianism in China in *China Archaeology and Art Digest* 4, no. 1 (December 2000): 7–71. The above-mentioned sarcophagus (cat. no. 175) is discussed in these essays.
4. Carter 1974: 171–202.
5. Francfort 1979.
6. Tanabe 2002: 73–100. See also the comments by Steven Kossak in Lerner and Kossak 1991: 60–66.
7. Li Jian 2003, no. 11.

100

Ewer

Ca. 1st century B.C.
Silver
Height 6¼ in. (15.8 cm)
Excavated at Shangsunjiazhai, Datong, Qinghai Province
National Museum of China

Excav. report: Qinghai sheng wenwu kaogu yanjiusuo 1993

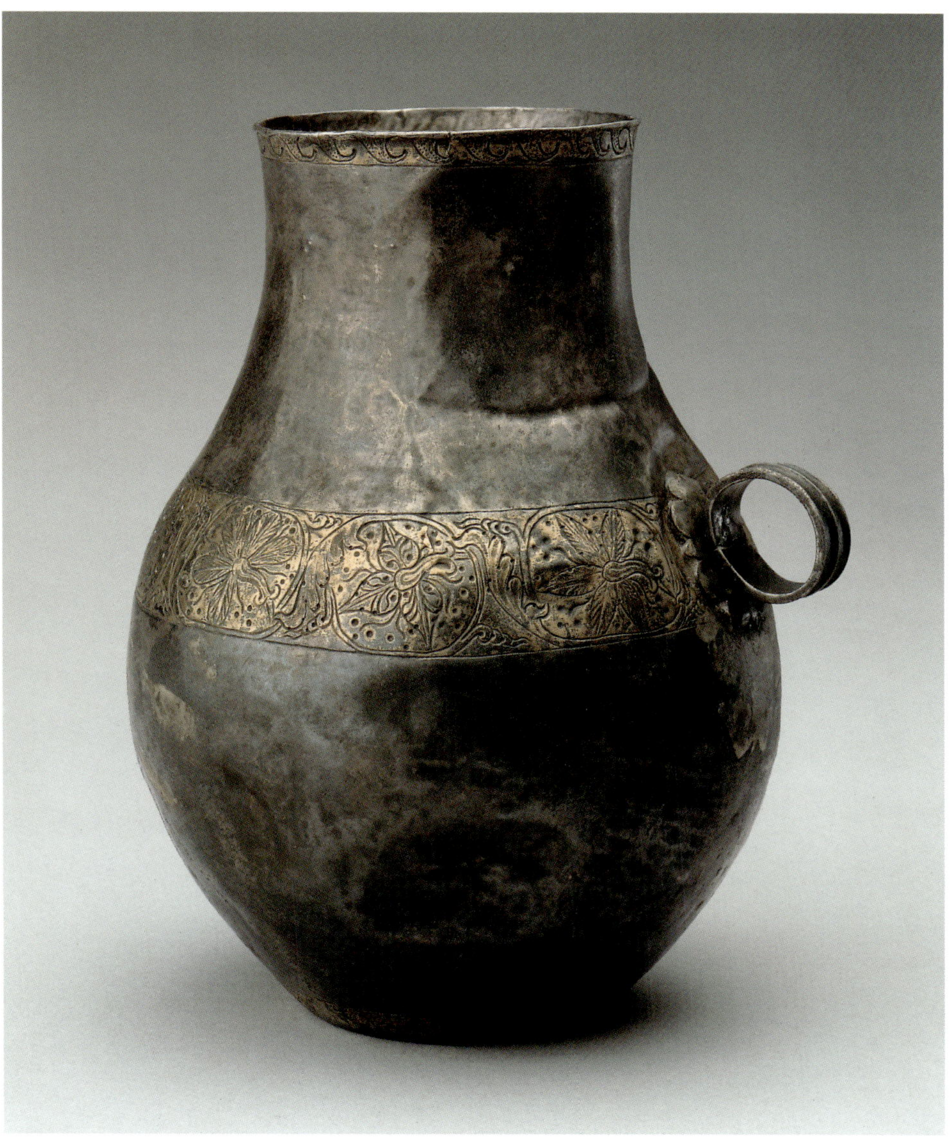

The shape of this vessel is typical of vessels made by the nomadic cultures of Eurasia (for example, ceramic jugs from the famous Issyk tumulus in Kazakhstan of about the fourth century B.C.).[1] The body is beaten from a thin single sheet of silver; the rim is cut. In execution it is very simple, with the exception of the three gilded, ornamented bands. The contrast between the rather pedestrian form of the vessel and the delicately rendered Hellenistic motifs, such as the row of the meandering, wavy pattern and the tendril frieze, shows that the respective traditions of the silversmith and the decorator, as well as their professional skills, were quite different. There are many parallels between the ornaments on the ewer and those on Hellenistic vessels datable not later than the first century B.C.,[2] although the floral frieze is less animated than its Hellenistic prototypes. The band of crenelation, a motif well-known in the Seleucid Empire (323–64 B.C.) but not in the western regions of the Hellenistic world, is of Achaemenid origin.

The ring handle is a later addition, nomadic or Chinese, which provides a clue to the later history of the vessel. It was found in Qinghai, north of the city of Xining, near the frontier between China and the region inhabited by the nomads, in a cemetery datable from the first century B.C. to the third century A.D.[3] This ewer was found in Tomb M3, dated to the third century. Possibly it was made for a steppe aristocrat and decorated by an itinerant craftsman working in the Hellenistic workshop tradition.[4] Its nomadic owners perhaps lost it in the period of Han westward expansion in the first century B.C. or the first century A.D., and it was later found by a Chinese warrior family that had settled in the frontier zone.

BIM

1. Tōkyō kokuritsu hakubutsukan 1985, no. 18.
2. Pfrommer 1993: 21–23, 30, 31, nos. 2–16 (and their profiles on pp. 223–26), pls. 1–3, figs. 16–19, 26. As attested on a silver kylix in the Musée du Louvre, Paris, the three-dot motif on the frieze is already present on early Hellenistic models datable to about 300 B.C. (Bj 2217; ibid., fig. 26, n. 286).
3. Qinghai sheng wenwu kaogu yanjiusuo 1993: 160, pl. 75.
4. A fragment of a similar silver vessel was recently found in the tomb of a Xiongnu prince datable to the first century A.D. See André 2002: 204, fig. 23.

101

Wall hanging with centaur and warrior

2nd century B.C.*–2nd century* A.D.
Tapestry-woven wool
Centaur fragment: Warp 21⅝ in. (55 cm); weft 17 11/16 in. (45 cm)
Warrior fragment: Warp 20½ in. (52 cm); weft 18⅞ in. (48 cm)
Excavated at Sampula cemetery, Lop, Xinjiang Uygur Autonomous Region, 1983–84
Xinjiang Uygur Autonomous Region Museum

Excav. report in *Xinjiang wenwu* 1989.2

From Sampula (Shanpula), Xinjiang (see also cat. no. 102), this wall tapestry was at some time tailored into a pair of wool trousers. As the design of the textile is far more important than the styling of the pants, it was meticulously restored by joining the fragments into one piece. The upper register depicts a centaur playing a horn, while in the lower register is a spear-bearing warrior. The selvedge appears to be to the left of the two figures; the missing right side would have been the main part of the tapestry.

The centaur, a mythical creature with the head of a man and the body of a horse, originated in Greek mythology. It was depicted frequently in classical art, most famously in the marble relief of the Parthenon in Athens. Also found in Central Asia, the image of the centaur was probably brought east by the military conquests of Alexander the Great.[1] Distinctive from centaurs in Western art, he plays a horn and wears a hood and cloak obviously of Central Asian origin. Surrounding the centaur is a diamond-shaped floral wreath, stylized botanical patterns, and part of a wing.

Beneath the centaur stands a gigantic warrior. Only that part of the textile that includes the head and shoulder is included in the exhibition, but another fragment that completes the torso has also survived.[2] The warrior's height, even in the textile's present dilapidated

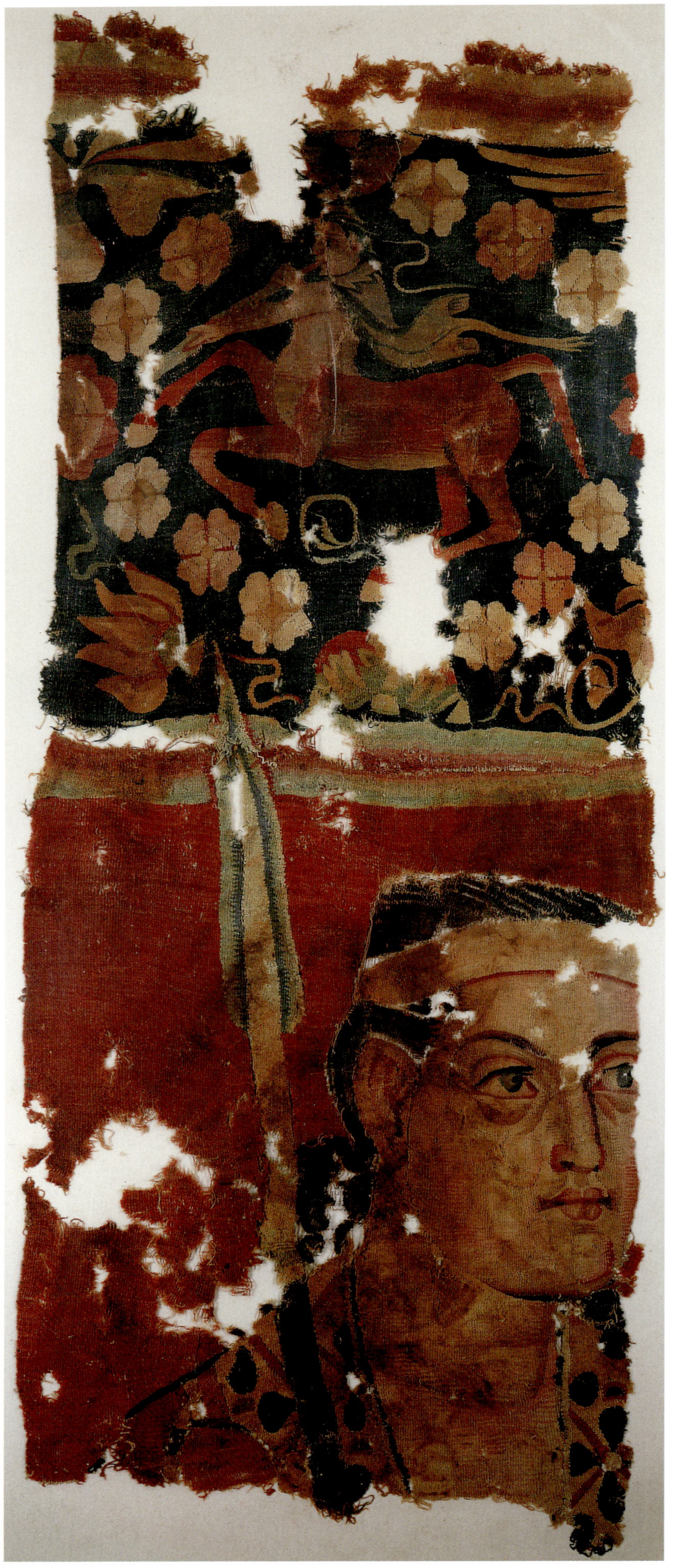

state, is four times that of the centaur. Originally, he would have been about six times as tall. With bare chest and hair pulled back with a band, he wears a robe with a belt around the waist. The lapels are decorated with four-petaled flowers within diamonds, and blue-and-yellow stripes extend along the tight sleeve, forming a cross around the upper arm. The warrior holds a long spear that pierces the boundary of the area devoted to the centaur. The weaving technique allows for a detailed description of the warrior's facial muscles and wrinkles around the eyes. His overall posture, however, looks rather stiff.

Tapestries similar to this one can be found in collections outside China as well as among the finds from Loulan (Lop Nor). All are dated to the same period, that is, roughly between 55 B.C. and A.D. 110. These tapestries evidently did not come from the Mediterranean. The warrior's costume finds no comparable examples in the Mediterranean region, but it is quite close to the fashion in Central Asia and neighboring Xinjiang. The headband, for instance, resembles a cotton band discovered in the same tomb in Sampula.[3] The pattern of tiny flowers within diamonds on the lapel appears on a textile fragment excavated from neighboring Niya.[4] Clothing discovered at the Keriya site features the same design of crossed stripes on the upper arm.[5] This evidence suggests that the present tapestry was probably produced in Central Asia. It would not have been made in Xinjiang, however, because, had it been produced there, it would not have been fashioned into trousers.

ZF

1. Lin Meicun 2003: 2–35.
2. Illustrated in Tokyo Kokuritsu Hakubutsukan 2002: 108.
3. Xinjiang Weiwuer zizhiqu bowuguan and Xinjiang wenwu kaogu yanjiusuo 2001: 232.
4. Xinjiang bowuguan chutu wenwu zhanlan xiaozu 1972.
5. Debaine-Francfort and Idriss 2001: 197.

102

Saddle blanket with leaves

2nd century B.C.–2nd century A.D.
Knotted wool pile (Turkish knot on tabby foundation)
Warp 30 in. (76 cm); weft 29⅞ in. (74 cm)
Excavated at Sampula cemetery, Lop, Xinjiang Uygur Autonomous Region, 1983–84
Xinjiang Uygur Autonomous Region Museum

EXCAV. REPORT in *Xinjiang wenwu* 1989.2

Two burial pits were discovered in Cemetery 1 in Sampula (Shanpula), Xinjiang. Inside each pit was the corpse of a light yellow horse. The skin of the horse in pit K2, which is in a better state of preservation, is basically intact. The pit also contained a complete set of riding gear, including the saddle, felt cushion, breast belt, and wooden and iron clasps. Among the finds was this impressive wool saddle blanket, found on top of the saddle.[1]

The pattern of this piece is formed of yellow, red, brown, white, blue, and green wool Turkish knots on a tabby foundation. The pile measures 1.2 centimeters high. The design comprises a central rectangular section with leaves in diamonds and a surrounding border area decorated with lobed leaves and a crenelated pattern of tendrils. Five leaves are arranged on each side of the border, for a total of sixteen. Red tassels hang from the four corners of the blanket.

Textiles with leaf patterns became quite popular during the Wei, Jin, and Northern dynasties, probably as a result of influences from the West. Sculpture from the Persian period in Taq-e Bustan, Iran, for example, features clothing with similar designs. Silk textiles with leaf patterns were also found in Antinoe, Egypt. Closer to China, numerous examples have been discovered along the Silk Road.[2] *Shuye jin* (*jin* silk with leaf patterns) and *da shuye jin* (*jin* silk with large leaf patterns) are recorded in sixth-century manuscripts excavated from Turfan, attesting to the popularity of leaf-patterned textiles at that time.

ZF

1. Xinjiang weiwuer zizhiqu bowuguan and Xinjiang wenwu kaogu yanjiusuo 2001: 12.
2. Zhao Feng 1999c: 101.

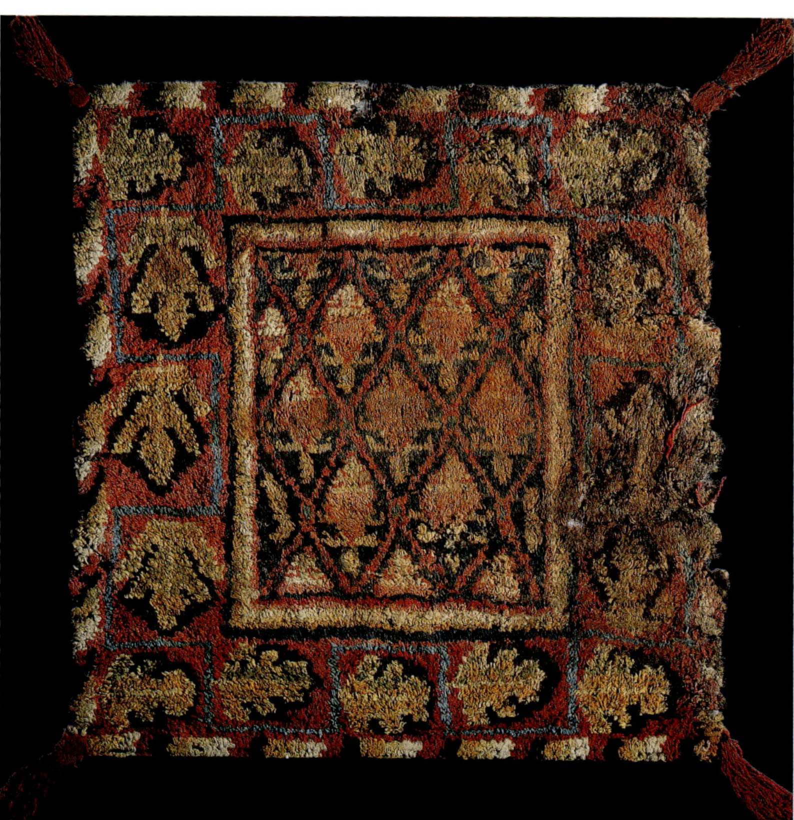

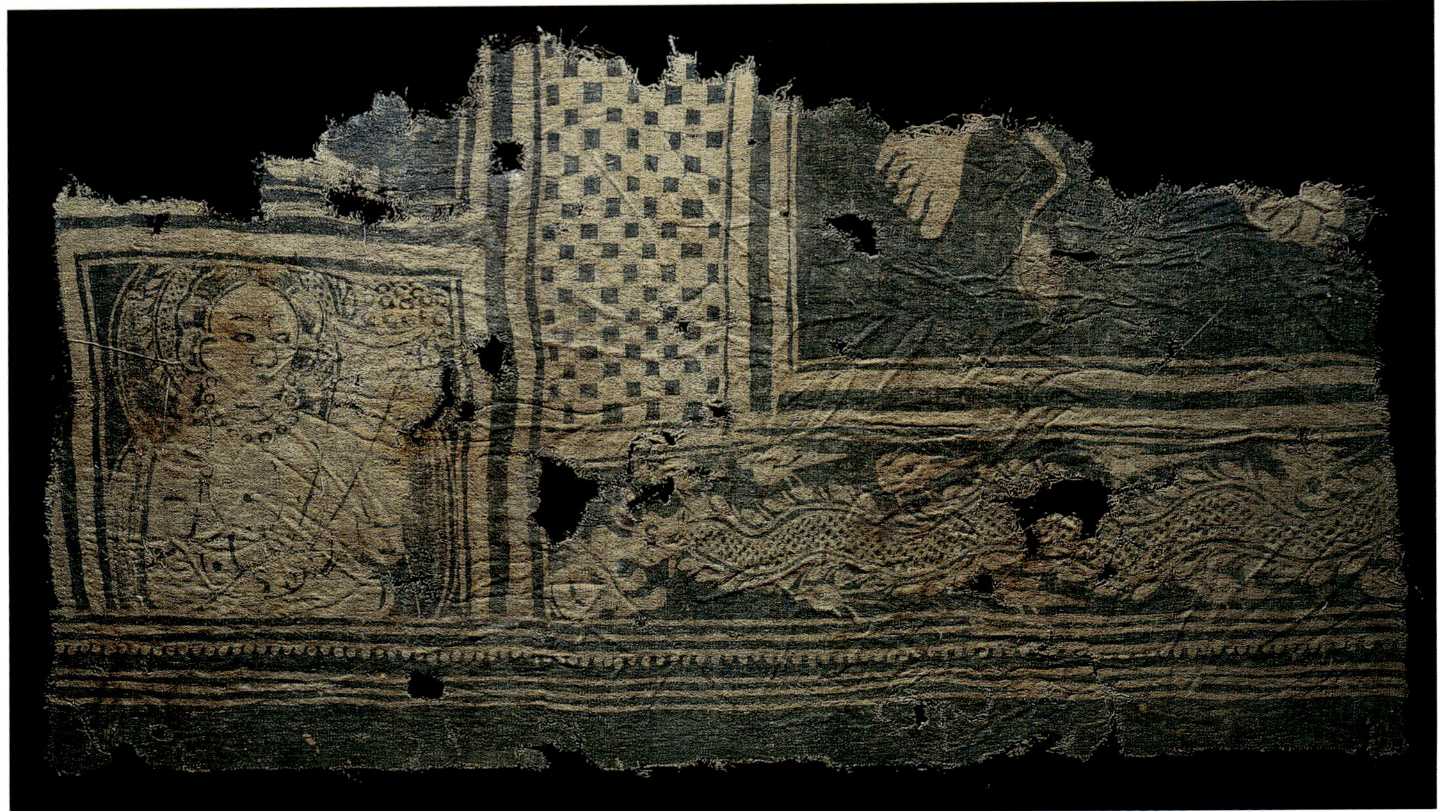

103
Textile with deity

1st–3rd century
Wax-resist dyed cotton
18⅞ x 35⁵⁄₁₆ in. (48 x 89 cm)
Excavated at Niya, Minfeng, Xinjiang Uygur Autonomous Region, 1959
Xinjiang Uygur Autonomous Region Museum

REFERENCE: Tōkyō kokuritsu hakubutsukan 2002, no. 114

The blue background and white pattern of this cotton cloth are typical of wax-resist dyed textiles of the late Eastern Han period (25–220). Excavated in 1959 from Tomb 1 at Niya, Xinjiang, the textile can be joined with other wax-resist dyed cloth from the same tomb.[1] The diagram at right shows the outline of existing fragments within a hypothetical reconstruction of the original piece. Six sections remain of the textile, which probably would have been quite large. Five stripes separated by a zigzag pattern decorate the edge of the cloth.

Section A,[2] in the shape of a vertical rectangle, has an overall pattern of triangles. A substantial portion of this section survives.

Section B, next to section A, is composed of a string of decorative beads.

Section C, a vertical rectangle in shape, is patterned in blue-and-white squares.

Section D depicts a lozenge-patterned creature that could be a fish or a dragon. It is surrounded by seven small birds, and a small animal bites into its tail. Alternatively, the small animal has been identified by Boris Marshak as a makara, a mythical creature that originated in India and was popular in Central Asia. According to this view, the lozenge-patterned fish/dragon would represent a river formed by the water spouting from the mouth of the makara. Birds are seen flying along the river.

Only a boot remains of the design in section E. Presumably, it is worn by a man.

Section F, the best-preserved part of the textile, depicts a goddess with wavy hair, crescent-shaped eyebrows, almond-shaped eyes, a large nose, and full lips. Represented nude and with a nimbus, she

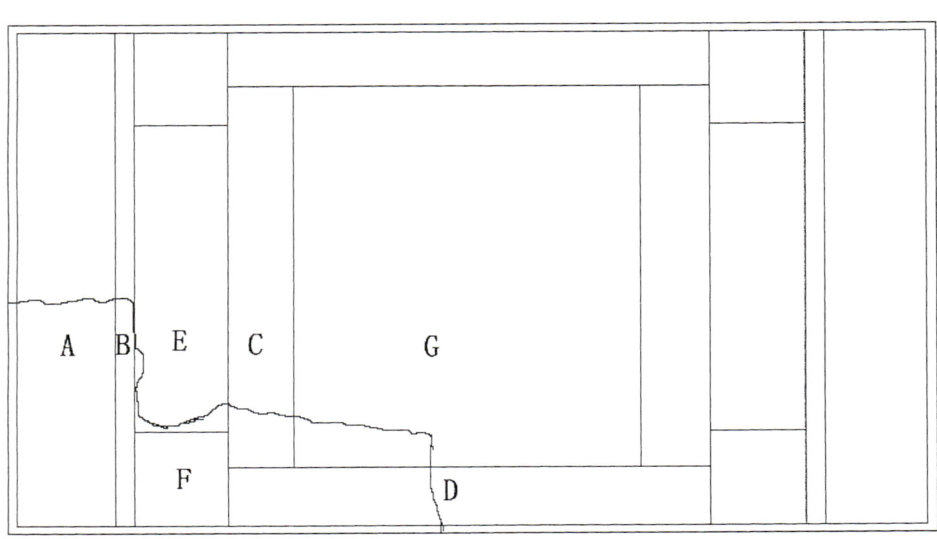

103, diagram of orginal textile

wears earrings and a necklace made of beads and holds a cornucopia in her hands. The goddess has variously been identified as a bodhisattva; Demeter, the Greek goddess of the harvest; the Babylonian goddess Ishtar; Anathita, the Persian goddess of waters and fertility; and Hariti, the Indian deity and Buddhist guardian goddess of children.[3] Tyche, the Greco-Gandharan tutelary goddess has also been suggested.

The most likely identification for the Niya goddess is Ardochsho, the Kushan goddess of wealth. Ardochsho is seen, especially during the reign of Huvishka in the second half of the second century, on Kushan coins, where she appears with a halo and holding a cornucopia with her right hand at the bottom and her left hand at the mouth, perfectly echoing the figure in the textile. Chronologically and geographically, the Huvishka Ardochsho is very close to the Niya goddess.[4]

Section G, the central area of the textile, is badly damaged. Only a man's foot and the paw and tail of a lion are visible. Judging from their positions, the man is probably engaged in a struggle with the lion. Similar designs can be found in Greek and Roman mosaics[5] as well as on textiles produced later in Europe. The human figure probably represents Hercules or Samson.[6]

ZF

1. Xinjiang Weiwuer zizhiqu bowuguan 1960.
2. Illustrated in Sha Biti 1973, PL. 3–1.
3. Laing 1995: 1–18.
4. Sun Ji 1999: 69–80.
5. Dunbabin 1999.
6. Volbach 1969: 107.

V

South China, 3rd–6th Century

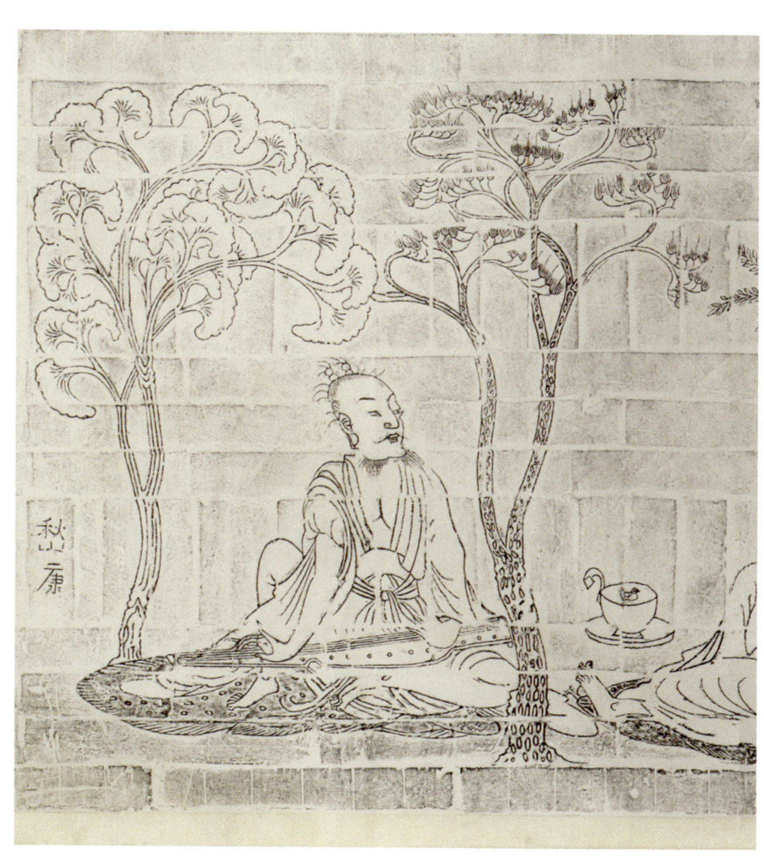

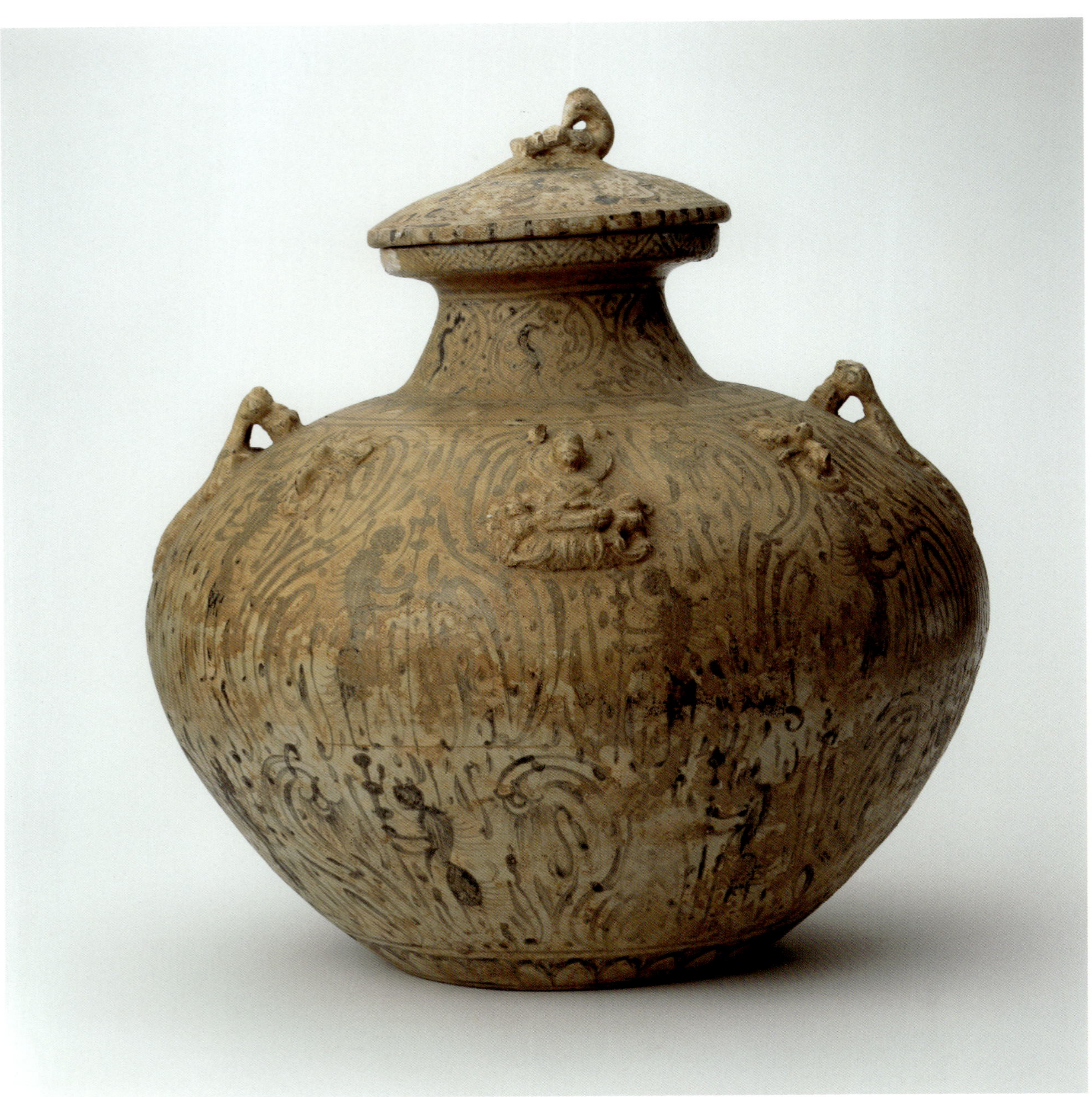

104

Covered jar with winged figures

Three Kingdoms, Wu (222–280), to Western Jin dynasty (265–316)
Porcelain
Height 12⅝ in. (32.1 cm)
Excavated at Yuhuatai, Nanjing, Jiangsu Province, 1983
Nanjing City Museum

Excav. report in *Wenwu* 1988.6

This covered jar has a relatively simple shape that comprises a large bulbous belly, a gently sloping shoulder, a short tapered neck, and a flat bottom. In stark contrast to the form, the surface is densely covered with a multitude of images in a complex scheme. On top of the lid is the molded figure of a bird, around which small birds fly among floral patterns. Seven imaginary animals, each encircled in a roundel with scrolls, grace the neck. The decoration on the body is divided into two registers of fantastic creatures alternating with curling clouds and overhanging floral motifs. With a more intricate design, the upper register is punctuated with twin-headed birds, monster-faced rings, and seated Buddhas. The decorative elements on the jar are painted with a brown-black pigment, except for the rings and Buddhist figures, which are molded and attached onto the surface. The jar is covered with a glossy, gray-green glaze.

A rare example from the early Six Dynasties period (220–589), the jar represents the superior ceramic products of the coastal provinces of Jiangsu and Zhejiang, the leading centers for high-fired stoneware with high-lime glazes. The wheel-thrown body is well balanced and coated with a layer of white slip, a diluted mixture of fine clay that covers the flaws and provides a smooth ground for the painting and glaze. The painted figures and patterns are the earliest known evidence to date of underglazed decoration. Interestingly, this innovative technique remained unexplored for the next few hundred years, until the seventh century, when the development of a more vitreous and translucent glaze made it a favorite decorative approach among ceramic artists.

Apparently, the jar was made for funerary purposes, although its exact function has yet to be determined. The decoration with mythical creatures and animals is generally believed to be a portrayal of the land of the immortals described in Chinese Daoist works.[1] Most notable of all are the seated Buddha figures, which provide a visual record of the changes and developments in religious practice in the area of the Wu kingdom. As Buddhism was beginning to gain a foothold in China, Buddhist images were adopted and came to be viewed, together with native Chinese deity figures, as auspicious signs that would bring happiness and good fortune—to the deceased in his afterlife and to his offspring in the secular world.

ZS

1. Yi Jiasheng 1983: 72–75

105
Man riding an animal

Western Jin dynasty (265–316)
Porcelain
Height 11 in. (28 cm)
The Palace Museum, Beijing

Reference: Gugong bowuyuan 1962, no. 2

This unusual object, of which several are known, may have been made as a stand for a household article, perhaps a lamp or an item of funerary paraphernalia such as a "money tree." What makes it of special interest is that it is the earliest known representation of a Westerner in South China. The figure's features, the style of his attire, the pattern on his coat, composed of medallions within the squares of a lattice and bordered with a line of "pearls"—all suggest an Iranian, possibly a Parthian, connection.

Travelers and immigrants from Central Asia and the Iranian world began to come into China in large numbers during the second century. Unfortunately, there is little mention of them in the official dynastic histories, which are mainly concerned with affairs of state. What record there is of foreigners and their activities is to be found in Buddhist writings, as Westerners played key roles in the spread of Buddhism and in the translation of

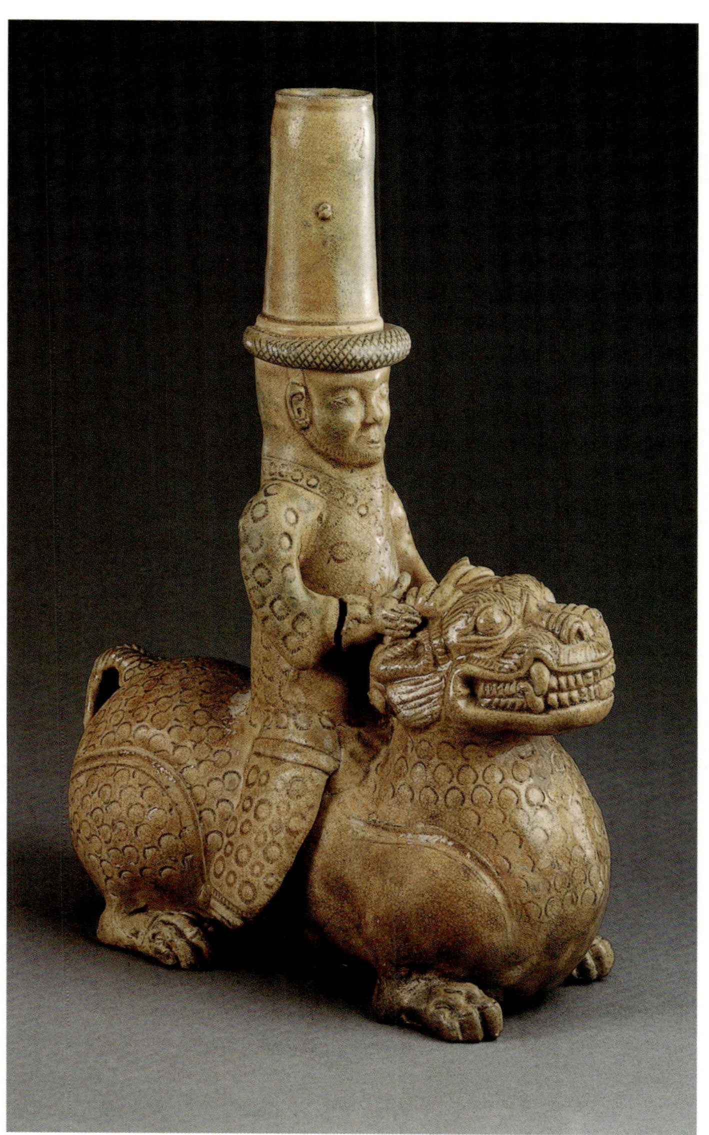

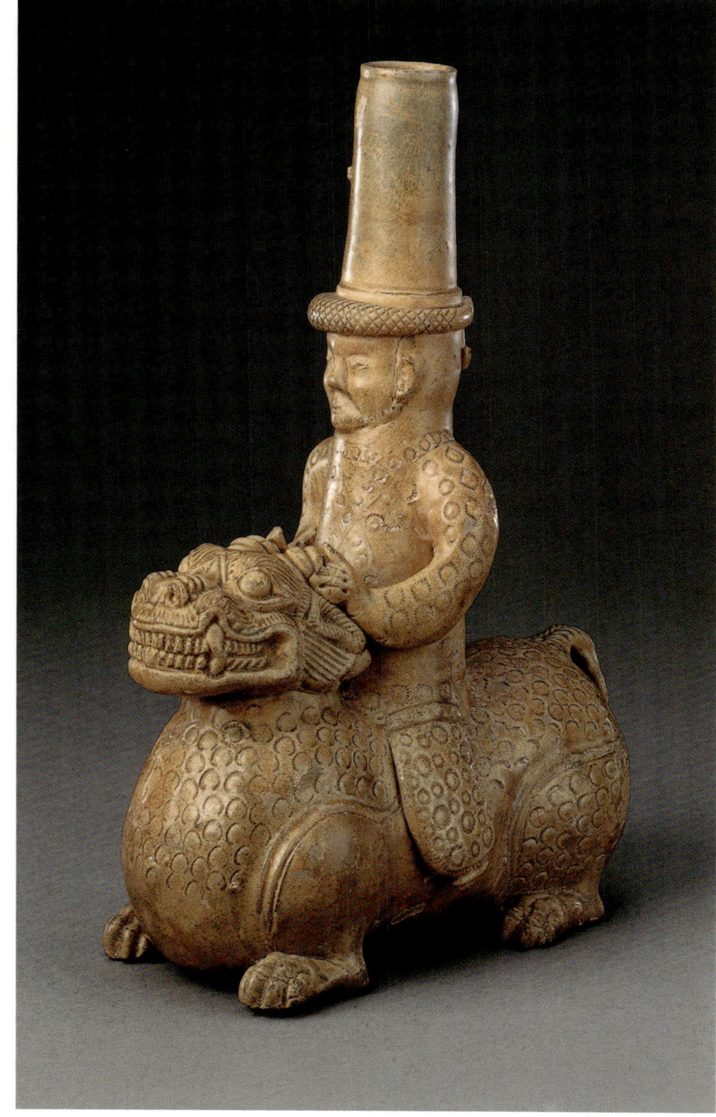

Buddhist scriptures into Chinese. One of the most famous early translators was the Parthian An Qing (An Shigao), who arrived about 147 in Luoyang. He died in the south about 188, having left North China toward the end of the reign of Emperor Lingdi (r. 168–89), when social conditions in the area around the capital cities of Chang'an and Luoyang became highly unstable.[1] Other Westerners resident in Luoyang likely followed suit. Indeed, Iranians and Central Asians must have been a fairly common sight in the cities of South China in the third century.

JCYW

1. See Ma Yong 1990: 46–59. In this important paper, Ma Yong discusses three groups of Central Asians: from Anxi (Parthia), Yuezhi (Bactria, later Kusana, during the Eastern Han period), and Kangju (Sogdiana). He points out that the large communities of Central Asians in China cannot be accounted for by trading and missionary activities alone and that immigration into China was caused also by social and political upheavals in the Kushan empire beginning about 171. Unfortunately for the new immigrants, China itself was about to fall into chaos soon after their arrival.

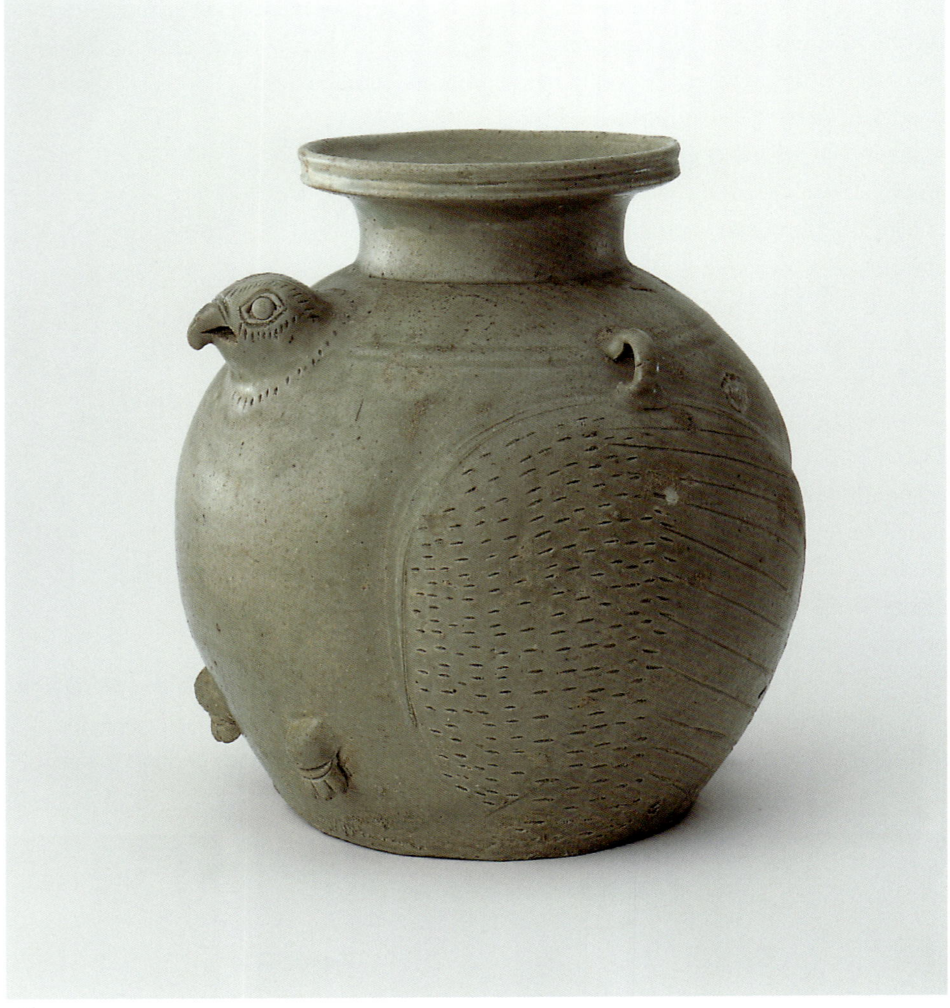

106

106
Vessel in the shape of an owl

Western Jin dynasty (265–316)
Porcelain
Height 4⅝ in. (11.9 cm)
Excavated from the tomb of the governor of Ruyin, Nanjing, Jiangsu Province
Nanjing City Museum

Reference: Nanjing shi wenhuaju 2000: 110

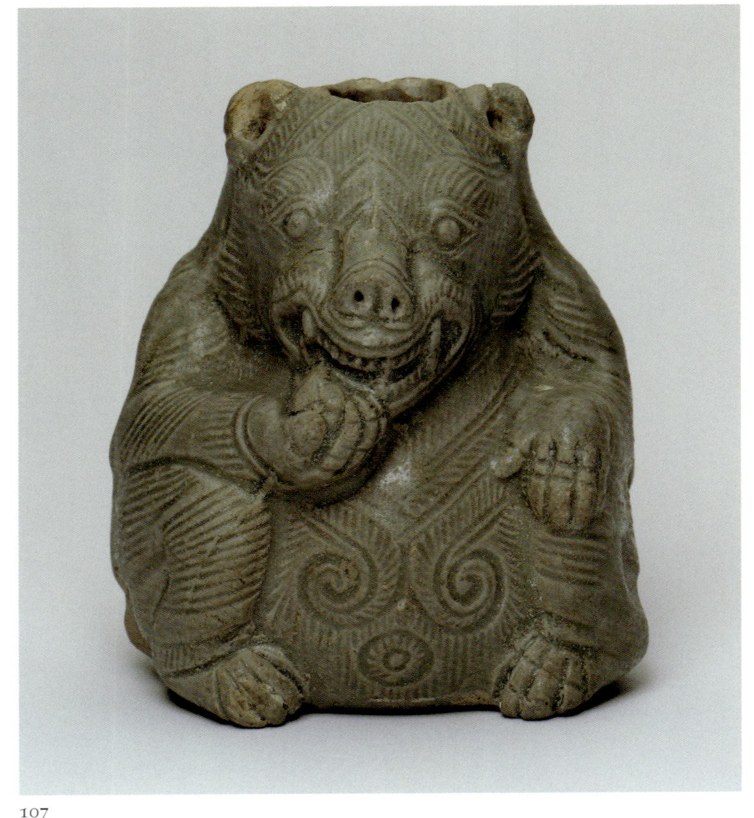

107

107
Water vessel in the shape of a bear

Western Jin dynasty (265–316)
Porcelain
Height 3⅜ in. (8.5 cm)
Excavated at Molingguan, Jiangning, Jiangsu Province, 1966
Nanjing Museum

Reference: Xu Huping 1999: 26

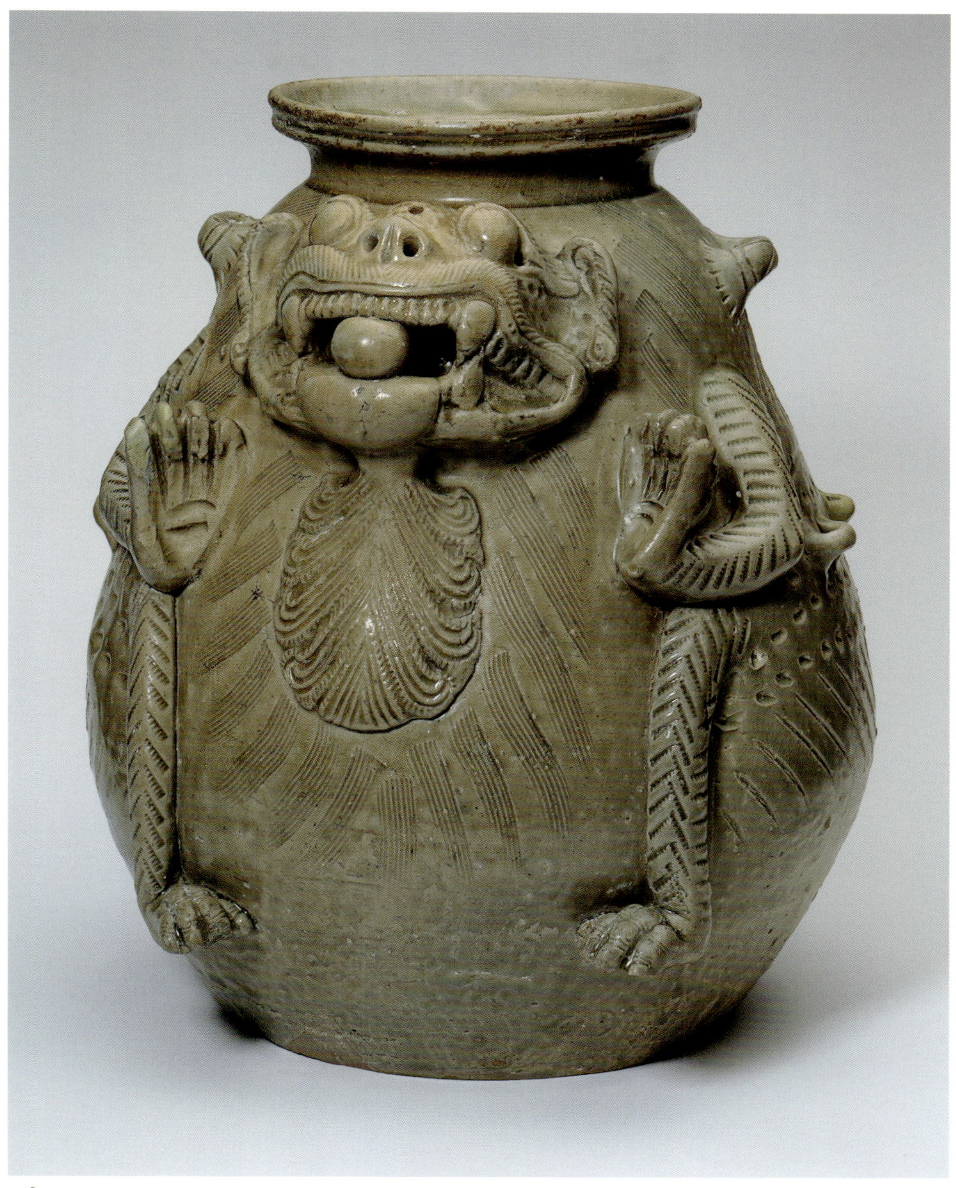

108

109
Water vessel in the shape of a frog

Three Kingdoms, Wu (222–280)
Porcelain
Height 2⅜ in. (5.9 cm)
Excavated from a tomb (dated 273), Guanghuamenwai, Nanjing, Jiangsu Province, 1955
Nanjing Museum

REFERENCE: Xu Huping 1999, pl. 3

These four high-fired pottery vessels (and the object in the previous entry), with a uniform glaze perfectly bonded to the vitrified body, represent an important stage in the development of porcelain in China. This took place in the third century in the regions of Yue (present-day Zhejiang) and Wu (Jiangsu). The forms of these pottery pieces are delightfully playful, with the bird jar (facing page cat. no. 106) displaying possible influence from Iran.

JCYW

108
Water vessel in the shape of a monster

Western Jin dynasty (265–316)
Porcelain
Height 11 in. (27.9 cm)
Excavated at Yixing, Jiangsu Province, 1976
Nanjing Museum

EXCAV. REPORT in *Kaogu* 1977.2

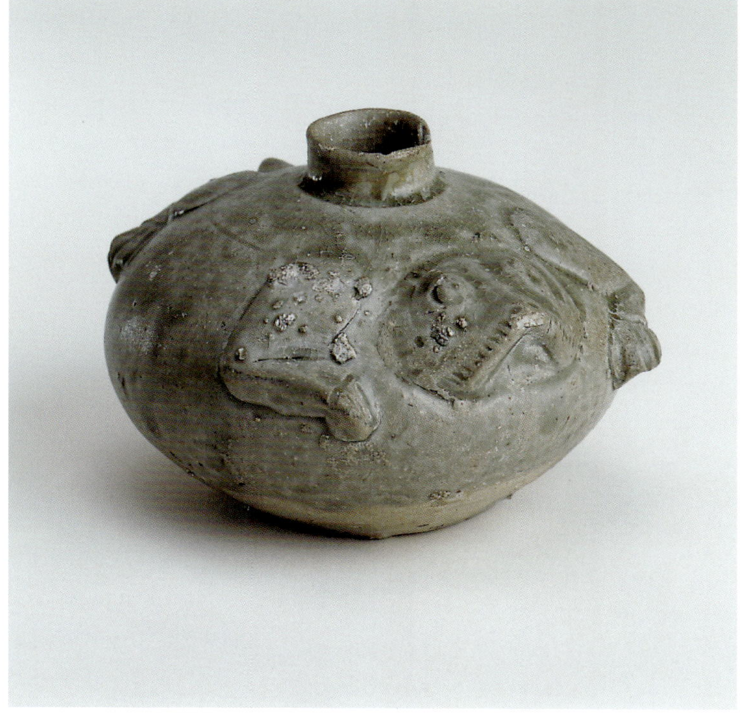

109

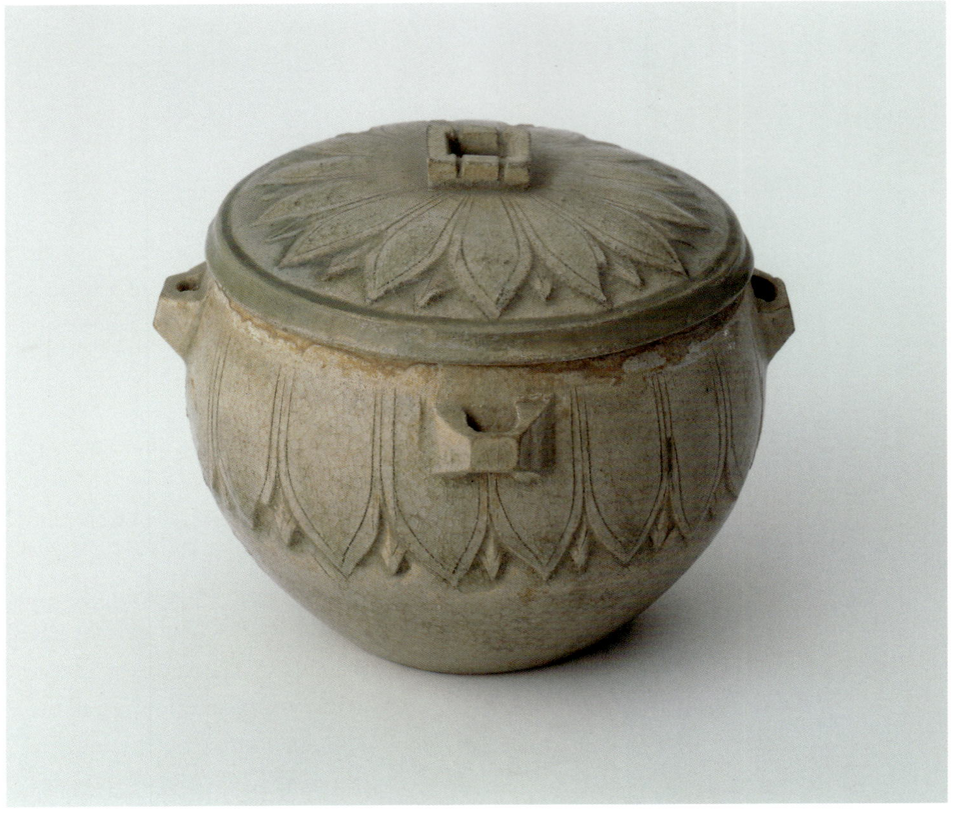

110

Covered jar with design of lotus petals

Southern Dynasties (420–589)
Porcelain
Height 2¾ in. (6.9 cm)
Excavated at Xiangshan, Nanjing, Jiangsu Province, 1960s
Nanjing City Museum

EXCAV. REPORT in *Wenwu* 1965.10

This covered jar, of a later date than the four pieces in the previous entry, represents the next stage in the development of porcelain in China. The glaze is more transparent and lighter in color. In spite of a higher silica content, the glaze still adheres reasonably well to the clay body.

The lotus motif is common in the pottery of the Southern Dynasties (420–589). Its popularity in South China did not necessarily result from the influence of Buddhist art. Frequently, it is referred to in folk songs of the Wu area in southeastern China at this time, where it is used as a pun for "love"—the characters for "lotus" and "love" being homophonic. The lotus was also, of course, an economic plant for this part of China.

JCYW

111

Guardian warrior

Eastern Jin dynasty (317–420), 4th–5th century
Earthenware with slip colors
Height 12⅝ in. (32 cm)
Excavated at Shimenkan, Nanjing, Jiangsu Province, 1955
Nanjing Museum

EXCAV. REPORT in *Kaogu tongxun* 1958.9

Excavated from a modest tomb in the Nanjing area, this sculpture of a guardian warrior was found on the left side of the burial ramp leading into the tomb, prostrate on the ground.[1] The figure is one of a pair found in the tomb, which also included additional pottery figures and traditional jade items, such as a cicada and a *bi* disk.[2]

The guardian holds a puny shield in his right hand and may once have had a lance in the left.[3] He wears a caftanlike garment, with an articulated band in the center, and a raised collar. The helmet appears too small for his head. The physiognomy, including the large eyes and prominent nose, an artistic convention common to guardian figures in the north, suggests that this warrior is a foreigner. Yet he is far from threatening. Indeed, he looks somewhat gloomy. It is possible that the appearance of such figures in tombs constructed during the Eastern Jin (317–420) reflects customs brought south by refugees after the collapse of the Western Jin (265–316). Guardians are also impressed on bricks in entryways, such as those of the slightly later Southern Qi (479–502) tomb at Jinwangchen, Jiangsu,[4] suggesting that as a result of continuing ties with the north, their use had become common in the fifth and sixth centuries.

DPL

1. Li Jianzhao and Tu Sihua 1958: 66–69.
2. The information is courtesy of Hu Chui, who saw (and photographed) the second figure while working on the catalogue.
3. Li Jianzhao and Tu Sihua 1958: 68.
4. Yao Qian and Gu Bing 1981, pl. 203.

112

Female figure

Southern Dynasties (420–589), 5th century
Earthenware
Height 14¾ in. (37.5 cm)
Excavated at Xishanqiao, Nanjing, Jiangsu Province, 1960
Nanjing Museum

EXCAV. REPORT in *Wenwu* 1960.8/9

Funerary sculptures from the southern parts of China are rare, particularly when compared with the profusion of tomb figures produced in the north. The quiet pose and sweet expression of this female figure are typical of works produced in the Nanjing area during the fourth and fifth centuries. It was placed in the front part of the coffin chamber of a tomb noted for its representations of the Seven Sages of the Bamboo Grove (see cat. nos. 113, 114). Five other pottery figures, three of which were male, a small assortment of ceramic animals and implements, and works in jade and other types of stone were also found in the tomb.[1]

The figure stands in a frontal position with her hands clasped at the waist. The

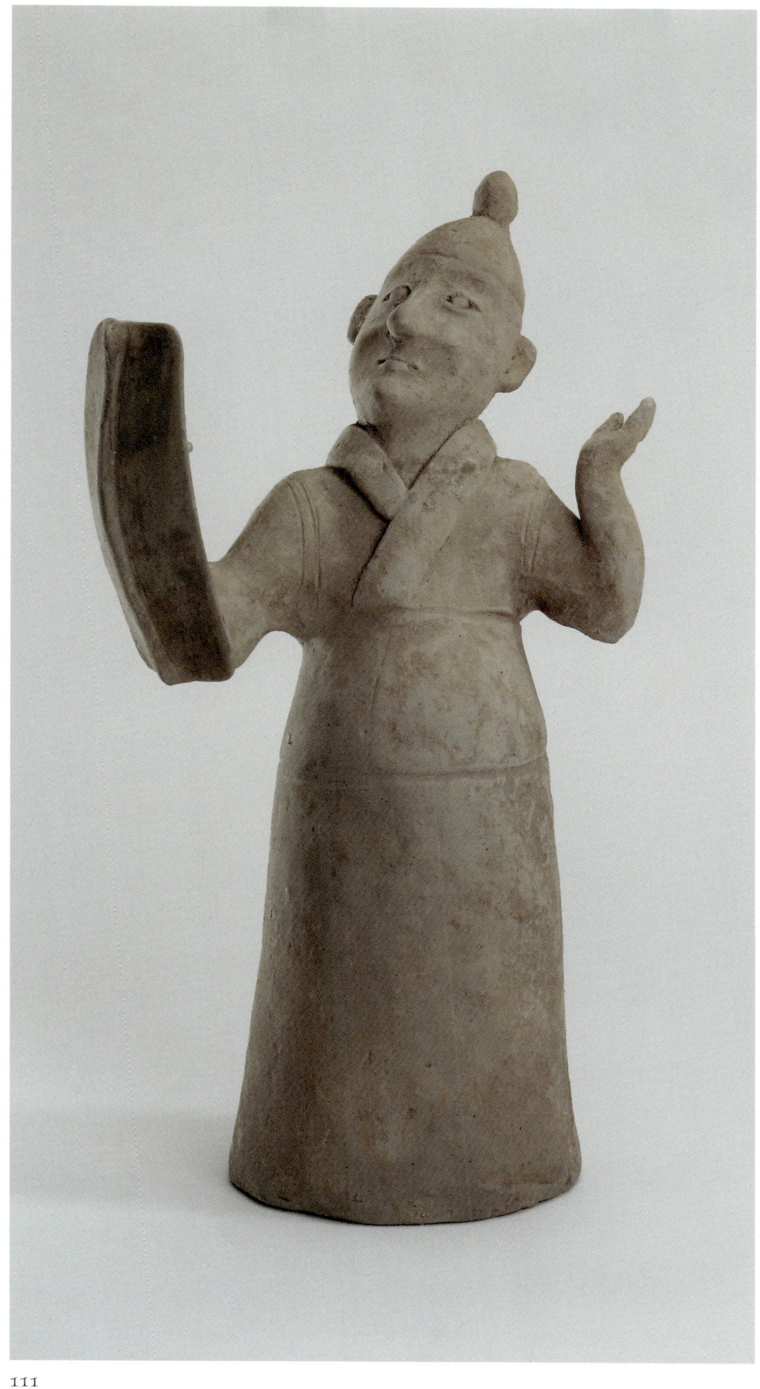

111

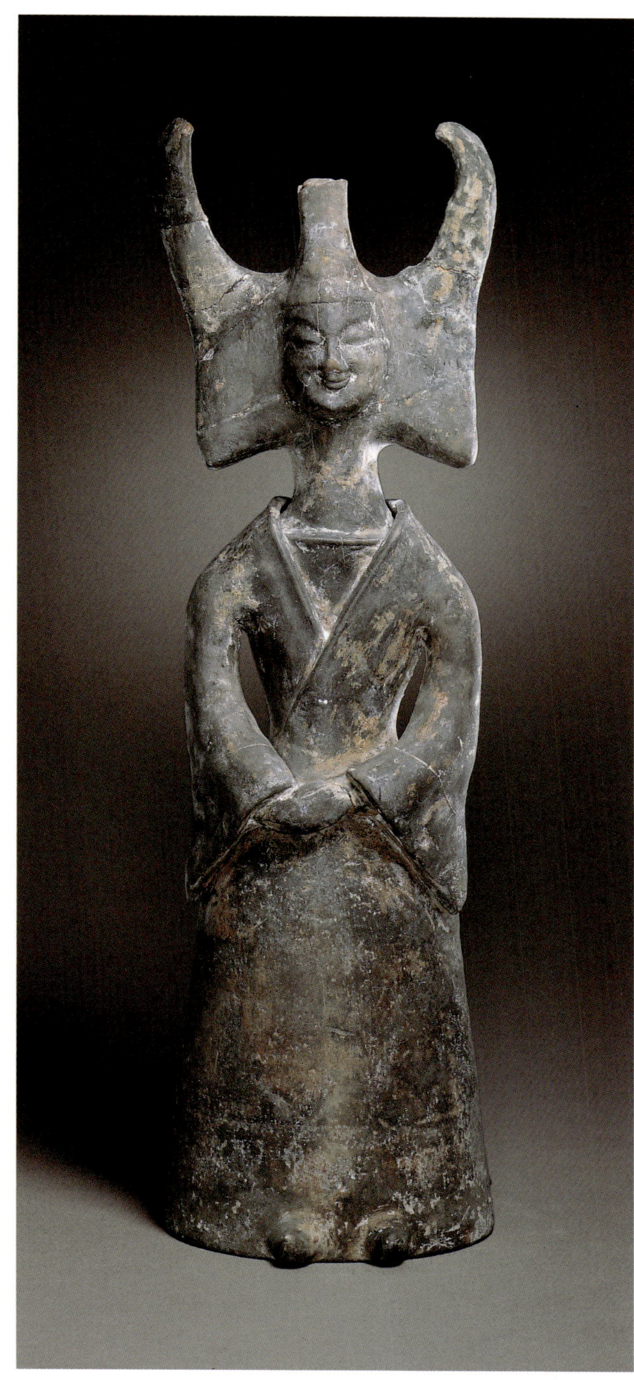

112

astonishing hairdo, in which the hair has somehow been shaped into three distinct forms, has been identified as an example of the *feitianjie*. The identification is based on a citation in the *Songshu* (History of the Song), a record of the Liu Song dynasty (420–479), which controlled parts of South China in the fifth century.[2] The styling of hair into fantastic constructions is associated with the aristocracy in China. The clothing here is more elaborate than that worn by contemporaneous figures in the south. It may also represent courtly attire. The outer garment crosses from left to right and has long sleeves with broad bands at the edges. Another robe is visible at the neckline. It is not clear whether the wide area of fabric at the bottom, which is divided from the rest of the clothing by an incised line, is intended to represent the outer robe or the hem of the undergarment.

DPL

1. Nanjing bowuyuan et al. 1960: 37–42.
2. Bai Ying 1992: 122–23.

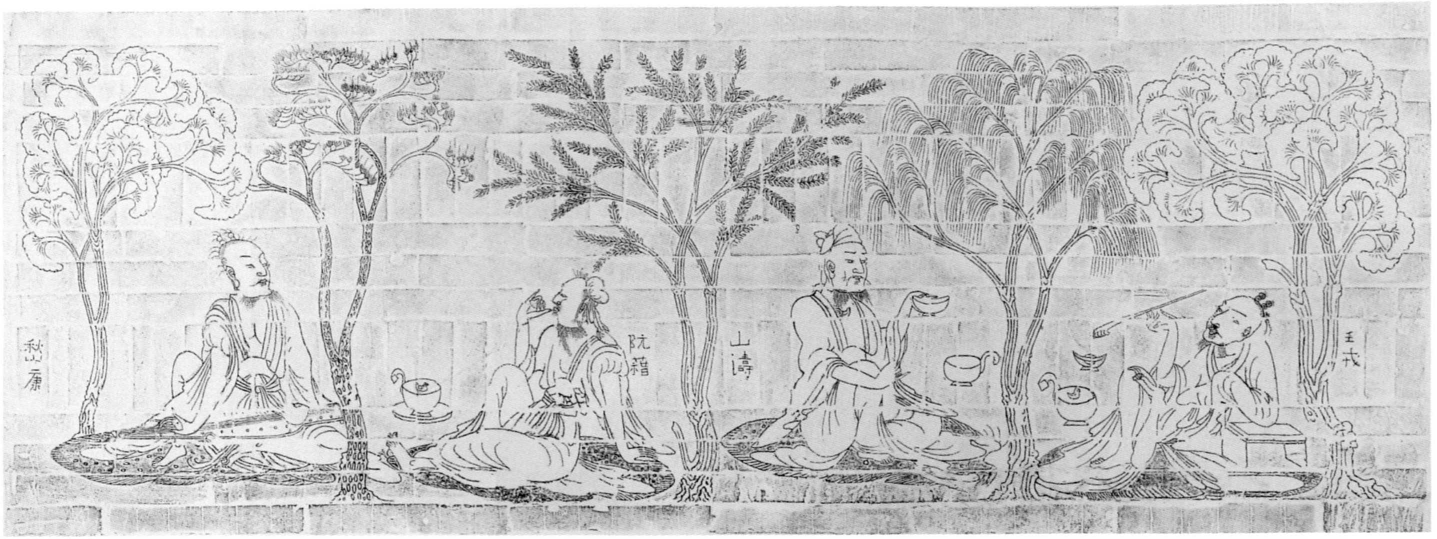

113a

113
Seven Sages of the Bamboo Grove

Southern Dynasties (420–589), second half of the 5th century
Rubbings of a pair of stamped-brick murals, ink on paper
Each: 34⅝ x 94½ in. (88 x 240 cm)
Bricks excavated at Xishanqiao, Nanjing, Jiangsu Province, 1960
Nanjing Museum

EXCAV. REPORT in *Wenwu* 1960.8/9

114
Seven Sages of the Bamboo Grove

Southern Dynasties (420–589), late 5th century
Stamped-brick image of Ji Kang, earthenware
33½ x 98⅜ in. (85 x 250 cm)
Excavated from a tomb at Jinjiacun, Jianshan, Danyang, Jiangsu Province, 1968
Nanjing Museum

REFERENCE: Yao Qian and Gu Bing 1981: 9–10, pls. 199–223

A group of stamped-brick murals excavated from tombs in the capital region of the Southern Dynasties (420–589) is our most direct evidence of the artistic advances that took place in South China during one of the most innovative periods in Chinese figure painting. Close in time and place to Gu Kaizhi (ca. 344–ca. 406) and Lu Tanwei (act. ca. 465–72), patriarchs of Chinese figural art, these murals are also among the most important archaeological discoveries from the Southern Dynasties period.[1]

The finest and most complete pair of these murals, represented here as rubbings, comes from an elite tomb at Xishanqiao on the outskirts of Nanjing.[2] The designs were first incised into clay molds, then stamped onto clay bricks, so that the resulting lines stand out in shallow relief. Every brick was then numbered on the side to facilitate its assembly in the tomb. Each mural consists of more than one hundred bricks arranged in alternating horizontal and vertical courses. Traces of color reveal that such murals were originally brilliantly painted. Indeed, in their scale and placement in the tomb—on opposite walls flanking the coffins—the murals function much as wall paintings would in a palatial residence.[3]

The subject of the murals, the Seven Sages of the Bamboo Grove, reflects a dramatic shift from the Confucian ritual décor of late Han and Jin tombs and funerary shrines—depictions of filial sons, moral paragons, and virtuous rulers—toward a celebration of personal freedom and individualism.[4] Third-century officials, the Seven Sages shared a reputation for unconventional behavior and an attitude of detachment from Confucian decorum that led succeeding generations to canonize them as embodiments of the Neo-Daoist ideal of transcendence in an age of political and social chaos. Their apotheosis as cultural symbols of disengagement and the pursuit of immortality is underscored by their being grouped together with a much earlier legendary figure, Rong Qiqi, a contemporary of Confucius (551–479 B.C.), who was said to have become an immortal.[5] The presence of murals nearly identical in size, composition, and content in two Southern Qi (479–502) imperial mausolea demonstrates the popularity of this subject among the highest echelons of society and indicates that a new set of cultural ideals had taken hold among the intellectual elite in the south.

The Qi tombs are situated near the city of Danyang, at Jinjiacun and Wujiacun.[6] The Jinjiacun murals are closest to those at Xishanqiao. When one compares the figure of Ji Kang in the Jinjiacun mural,

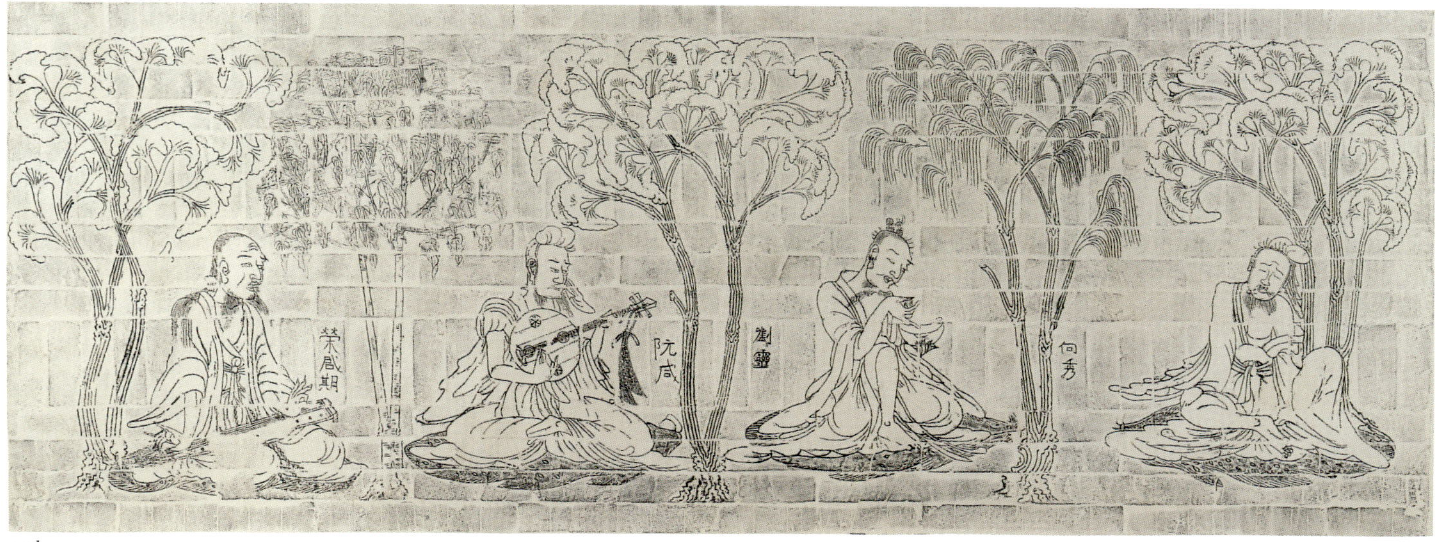

113b

represented here by the original bricks (cat. no. 114, p. 208), with the same figure seen in the rubbing of the Xishanqiao mural, see facing page, far left, it is clear that certain details on the horizontal bricks in both murals—the head and shoulders, the hands and *qin* (zither), and the tree foliage at the top of the composition—are identical, while details on the vertical bricks differ markedly (see below). Even when design elements in the Jinjiacun murals correspond to those from Xishanqiao, however, the Jinjiacun bricks often bear additional elements. The gingko tree to the left of Ji Kang's head in the Jinjiacun mural, for example, has been greatly elaborated in order to match the design on the vertical bricks below. This elaboration indicates that the Jinjiacun artisans may have had some leftover bricks from Xishanqiao, which they impressed

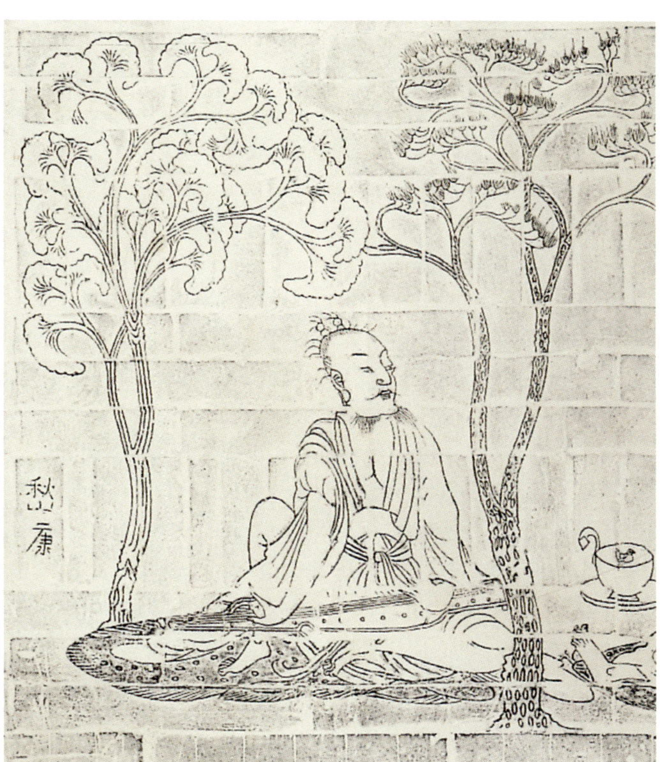

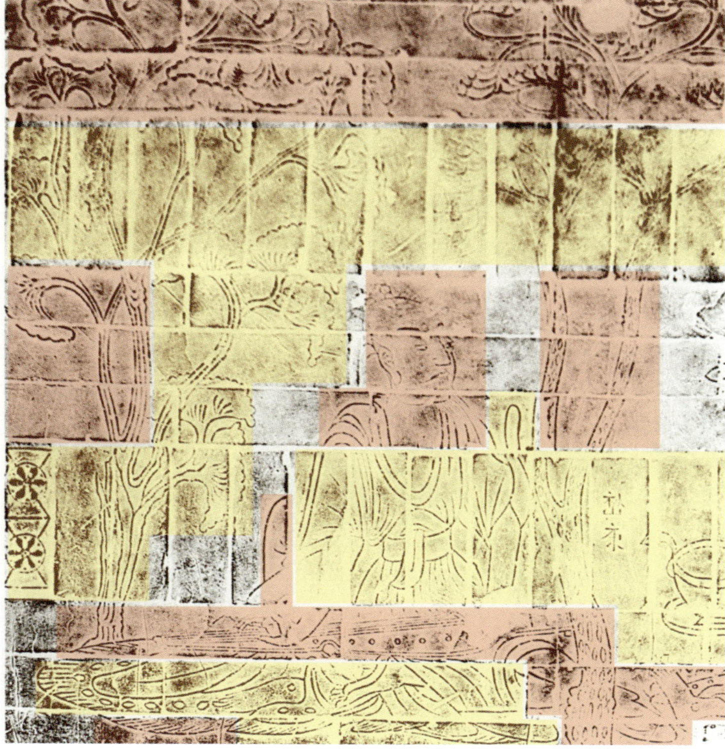

Left: Rubbing of the stamped-brick image of Ji Kang from the tomb at Xishanqiao. *Right:* Rubbing of the stamped-brick image of Ji Kang from the tomb at Jinjiacun. Details of the Jinjiacun design that are identical to those in the Xishanqiao design are highlighted in red.

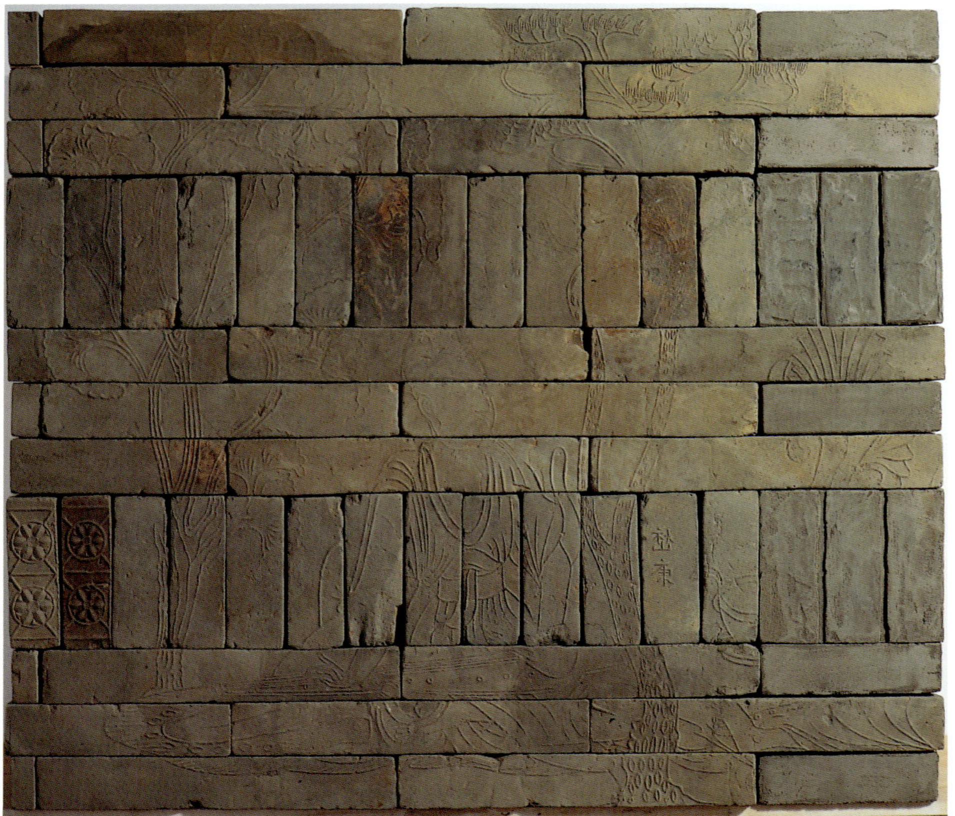

114

into soft clay forms to make new molds. They then incised additional lines into the molds so that the lines would continue the designs on the newly created vertical bricks. The lack of a complete set of templates from Xishanqiao explains why some of the figures were misidentified in the identifying inscriptions and why certain pictorial details were misunderstood.

The murals from the tomb at Wujiacun are, in turn, based on the Jinjiacun murals, but they are from an entirely different set of molds. The drawing is much cruder, with many more errors in content and in the identification of the figures.[7] Thus, while all the murals are clearly based on the same prototype—probably a temple or palace wall painting—the designs used to produce the bricks in the Xishanqiao murals were only imperfectly transmitted to the Danyang area, where the images were increasingly reworked and misinterpreted by artisans who clearly were not familiar with the original. Given the progressive degeneration in the designs, it is clear that the Danyang murals postdate those from Xishanqiao. Nevertheless, the recycling of the Xishanqiao designs in the Jinjiacun and Wujiacun murals indicates that all the murals were made fairly close in time and should be dated to the later fifth century.[8]

The overall consistency of these stamped-brick images indicates that the iconography of the Seven Sages had already become codified by the fifth century. Nevertheless, stylistic variations in the two Xishanqiao murals suggest that they may have been the work of different artists.[9] The mural showing Ji Kang (223–262), Ruan Ji (210–263), Shan Tao (205–283), and Wang Rong (234–305) (see p. 206, cat. no. 113a, left to right) is more advanced. The figures are more varied in their poses, they face one another as if engaged in conversation; their robes overlap with the framing trees to create the illusion of a shallow foreground space; and the drinking cups placed around the figures help define a ground plane. The group on the facing mural, Xiang Xiu (228–281), Liu Ling (ca. 221–ca. 300), Ruan Xian (230–281), and the legendary recluse Rong Qiqi (presumably act. 5th century B.C.)—probably included to make the two groups symmetrical—presents figures that are nearly uniform in height, more compact in their poses, and placed within a less well-defined spatial setting (see p. 207, cat. no. 113b). Evidently, the former group was newly visualized while the latter group was derived from earlier, conventional images.

In spite of the subtle differences between the two Xishanqiao murals, taken together they represent a major advance over Eastern Jin (317–420) figure painting, as exemplified by the more conservative imagery on the roughly contemporaneous lacquer screen (cat. no. 69) from the tomb of Sima Jinlong (d. 484). Instead of being depicted on a blank ground, each figure is set within a shallow but well-defined space framed by trees. More significantly, the figures have broken free of the restrained and ritualized poses dictated by Confucian decorum. Now, facial expressions, poses, and gestures all convey distinct psychological states: aloofness, refinement, playfulness, inebriation, and meditative repose. Anatomical features and garments are well proportioned and rendered with much greater specificity and naturalism. Draperies reflect both the weight of the fabric and the underlying forms of the bodies. Trees are similarly well observed and sufficiently particularized that different species—gingko, pine, willow—can be recognized. Such innovations clearly postdate the work of Gu Kaizhi, whose drapery style of buoyant, billowing forms is still reflected in the Sima Jinlong screen.[10] Instead, the Xishanqiao murals probably reflect the achievements of Lu Tanwei, whom the noted critic Xie He (act. 500–536) considered the single greatest painter of all time, while he placed Gu Kaizhi in the third rank of painters.[11]

While the authorship of the Seven Sages designs may never be known, these brick murals attest to the fact that painting styles were evolving rapidly during the fifth century, most plausibly in response to the new waves of Buddhist art that were entering China from both South and Central Asia. Compared with the Sima Jinlong screen, these murals also suggest that South China led the way in incorporating these influences into traditional Chinese artistic idioms.

MKH

1. For evidence that this pictorial theme existed at the time of Gu Kaizhi, see *LMJ* 5: 70; and Soper 1961: 85.
2. These murals have been treated extensively; see Nanjing bowuyuan et al. 1960: 37–42; Soper 1961: 79–86; Nagahiro 1963: 15–21; Laing 1974: 5–54; Yao Qian and Gu Bing 1981, pls. 162–79; Spiro 1990; and Hsieh Cheng-fa 2001: 1–55.
3. See *NS*, "Basic Annals of Qi: Emperor Fa," 5: 153; see also Lin Shuzhong 1977: 69.
4. On the theme of the Seven Sages, see Holzman 1956 and He Qimin 1966. For a discussion of Han funerary décor, see Wu Hung 1989.
5. Wu Hung makes this point in "The Origins of Chinese Painting" in Yang Xin et al. 1997: 46.
6. See Nanjing bowuyuan 1980a: 1–17. For an English translation of this report, see Till and Swart 1979–80. See also Yao Qian and Gu Bing 1981, pls. 180–223. The Qi mausoleum of Xiao Daosheng (d. 478, reburied ca. 495) also contained depictions of the Seven Sages, but these murals are so badly damaged that they survive only in fragmentary form; see Nanjing bowuyuan 1974: 44–56.
7. For a discussion of the differences in the various murals, see Lin Shuzhong 1977: 68–69; and Nanjing bowuyuan 1980b: 18–23. For comparative illustrations of the three sets of figures, see Machida 1983, figs. 6, 7.
8. Machida Akira (1983: 1099) dates the Xishanqiao tomb to the second half of the Song dynasty (420–479).
9. Wu Hung was the first to make this point; see Yang Xin et al. 1997: 47. Gu Kaizhi also remarked on qualitative differences between figures in an earlier rendering of the Seven Sages; see note 1 above.
10. For Gu Kaizhi, see McCausland 2003.
11. See Hsieh Cheng-fa 2001: 24–28; for Xie He's comments, see Acker 1954: 4–19. See also Su Bai 1998: 134–35.

115
Ox carriage and attendants

Eastern Jin dynasty (317–420), ca. 322
Earthenware
Attendants: max. height 12⅜ in. (31.5 cm)
Excavated at the Wang family cemetery, Xiangshan, Nanjing, Jiangsu Province, 1965–70
Nanjing City Museum

REFERENCE: Nanjing shi bowuguan 1972

Toward the end of the Western Han (140 B.C.–A.D. 8), the ox carriage replaced the horse chariot as a preferred mode of travel for the elite. The selection of the humble ox carriage over the expensive horse chariot was probably the result of a change in fashion rather than economics. Indeed, the slower ox carriage became an emblem of the leisurely literati culture of the south.[1] The Nanjing City Museum discovered this group of figures with an

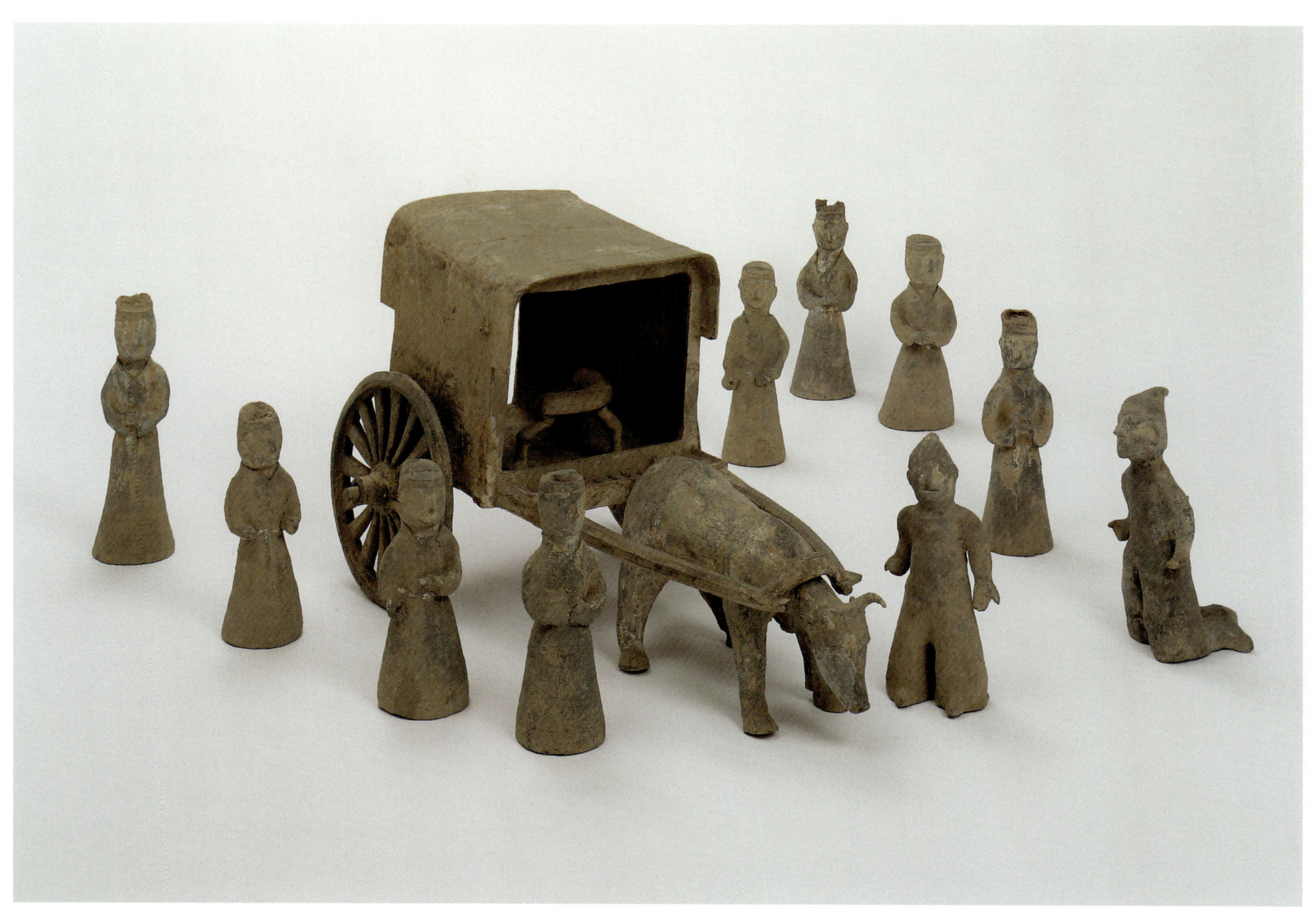

ox carriage in an undisturbed Eastern Jin (317–420) tomb near Nanjing. Placed alongside a red-saddled horse in front of the burial chamber door, both the carriage and the horse presumably served as the means of travel for the dead—two women and one man—interred in the chamber. At the time of excavation, the ox carriage had one ceramic plate and two ear-cups tucked below and a three-legged rest inside.

The ten attendants—eight Chinese and two apparently Iranian—are molded, pared, and fired with white slip. The Chinese figures wear long robes and the *xiaoguan*, a Han flat cloth hat that is raised in the back.[2] They either hold a tablet or have their hands positioned as if grasping a spear. The two Iranian grooms—one leading the ox and the other kneeling—wear the characteristic Iranian-style trousers and pointed felt hat.[3] The kneeling attendant resembles a figure from the Eastern Han (25–220) Wu Liang shrine (dated 151)—a county official also shown kneeling in front of an ox carriage, as he pays his respects to the passenger within, Wu Liang (78–151), the deceased.[4] Thus, in the Eastern Jin, the Chinese bureaucrat is replaced by a foreign groom, indicating the extent of outside influences during this period.

As at Wu Liang shrine, in the Nanjing tomb, the ox carriage forms a pair with a horse chariot. This pairing is illustrated also on Eastern Han pictorial stones, in a tradition that lasted even beyond the Tang dynasty, the horse chariot sometimes replaced by a saddled horse or a camel.

CJL

1. Liu Panxiu 1998: 96–101. See also the brick figures in the Seven Sages of the Bamboo Grove (cat. nos. 113, 114). Images of ox carriages from this period have been found all over China, including Koguryŏ (ca. A.D. 357).
2. Shen Congwen 1992: 178–79.
3. Schloss 1969: fig. 3–4.
4. Wu Hung 1989: 213–14.

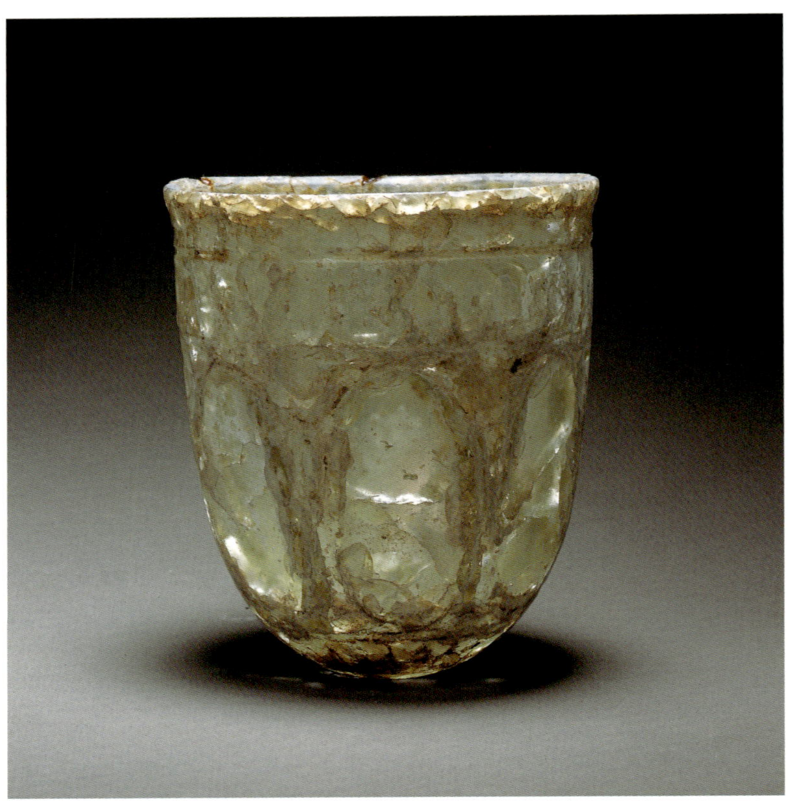

116
Cup

Ca. 4th century
Glass
Height 4⅛ in. (10.4 cm)
Excavated at the Wang family cemetery, Xiangshan, Nanjing, Jiangsu Province, 1965–70
Nanjing City Museum

Excav. report in *Wenwu* 1972.11

This glass cup with ground decoration was excavated from Tomb 7 at Xiangshan, Nanjing, near the front end of a man's coffin. The colorless glass is transparent with a yellowish cast and with relatively few small air bubbles. The outer wall is partially covered with a whitish weathered layer. The cup has a straight mouth, barrel-shaped body, and curved bottom, and the surface below the mouth rim and the body is decorated with ground designs of horizontal lines and petal-like vertical ovals. Seven large vertical ovals are ground on the body, and the bottom has a ground circular pattern. Another similar glass cup of a deeper color, of which only shards remain, was excavated near the front end of the coffin of a woman in the same tomb.

Tomb 7 is located within the cemetery of the Wang family of Langye, Shandong Province, a powerful clan of the Eastern Jin dynasty (317–420). The tomb is believed to be that of Wang Yi, an important member of the clan, who died in the year 322.[1] If this is correct, the two cups can be dated prior to that year. The shape of the cups is not seen in traditional Chinese vessels but often appears in Roman glass of the fourth century. The technique of cut decoration on glass is also Roman, which indicates that the present cup must be imported Roman glass.

The British Museum, London, purchased a glass cup in the 1960s (no. 134885).[2] Similar in shape and with ground decorative ovals on the body, it compares closely with the glass cup found in Tomb 7 at Xiangshan. In 1995, another glass cup of comparable shape and also with cut decoration was excavated by the Xinjiang Institute of Archaeology from Tomb 9 at Yingpan, Yuli.[3] The Yingpan site, situated on the delta of the Tarim River west of Lop Nor, occupied a strategic spot on the Loulan route of the Silk Road. Yingpan cemetery dates to the Han (206 B.C.–A.D. 220) and Jin (265–420) periods. Archaeological finds from this site include objects with elements of both ancient eastern and western cultures. The Yingpan cup sheds light on the route—the Loulan route—by which the cup from Tomb 7 was imported to China.

AJ

1. Nanjing shi bowuguan 1972: 23.
2. British Museum 1993: 128.
3. Li Wenying and Zhou Jinling 1998: 70.

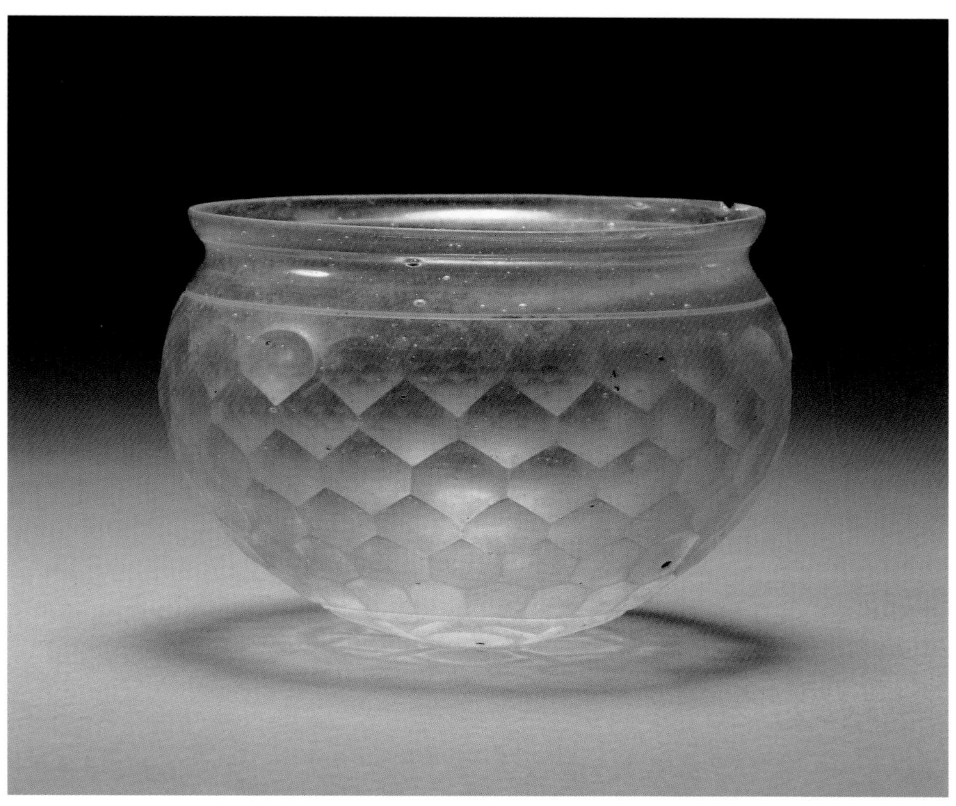

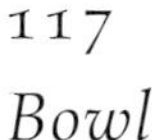

117
Bowl

Ca. 5th century
Glass
Diameter of mouth rim 3⅜ in. (8.5 cm)
Excavated at Chuncheng, Jurong, Jiangsu Province
Jurong Museum

This bowl has a large mouth, compressed neck, spherical body, and curved bottom. The body is decorated with six rows of small hexagonal facets ground on the surface that resemble the hexagonal pattern on the shell of a tortoise. The bottom of the bowl has a pentagonal concavity. The crystal-like transparency of the glass indicates that the raw materials were carefully selected and melted at a relatively high temperature. The wall is thin and the shape regular. The decorations were made by grinding and polishing after the glass had cooled.

The shape of the bowl is identical to that of a vessel excavated from Tomb 121 at Wulidun in Echeng, Hubei,[1] and the tortoiseshell decoration on the body compares closely with that on a white glass bowl in the Shōsō-in in Nara, Japan.[2]

Nearly all glass vessels that have survived in perfect condition in China were excavated from tombs where they were kept in stone coffins or stone coffers. Uncharacteristically, this bowl was found in a wood coffin, and it is fortunate that it survived in one piece. Despite centuries of chemical corrosion, it has only barely darkened and shows no sign of weathering or noticeable iridescence. This state of preservation is probably due to its having been submerged in acid water for fifteen hundred years, the result of the very wet climate. More than a hundred glass vessels similar to this one have been excavated from the Plateau of Iran. Most of them have lost their original luster and beauty and cannot compare with this one from Chuncheng, Jurong. Indeed, it may be considered one of the most beautiful pieces of Sasanian glass to have survived.

AJ

1. An Jiayao 1986a: 173.
2. Yoshimizu 1977, pl. 55.

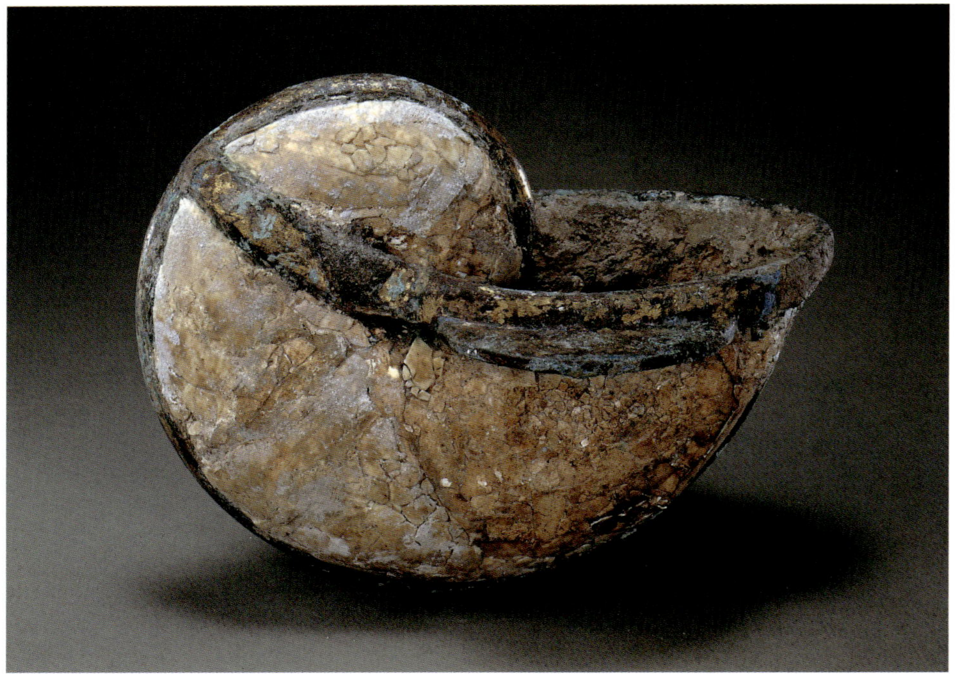

people who formed a branch of a larger group of southern natives known by the general appellation Man. Politically, they were allied with the South and submitted to the administration of the Southern Dynasties. They seem, however, to have retained some distinctive cultural traits of their own, including the manner of dress. Two types of apparel seen on pottery figures found in this area (exemplified here and in the following entry) may be related to those of the Man. This figure also sports a hairstyle—the hair tied up in a pointed bun at the back—that answers the descriptions in the historical literature of people in this region.

JCYW

118
Nautilus cup

4th century
Shell
Length 5¼ in. (13.3 cm)
Excavated from the tomb of Wang Xingzhi (d. 340) and his wife (d. 348), Xiangshan, Nanjing, Jiangsu Province, 1965
Nanjing City Museum

Excav. report in *Wenwu* 1965.6

Nautilus shell is known in China as *yingwu luo* (parrot shell) and the cup which is made from it a *yingwu bei* (parrot cup). The latter is often mentioned in the literature—especially the poetry—of the Sui (581–619) and Tang (618–907), less so in later periods down to the Ming (1368–1644).

This cup is the only early example of a nautilus cup found more or less intact archaeologically (the reconstruction has been possible with the survival of the metal rims), and it predates the earliest known literary references. The shell would have come from Indonesia,[1] providing further evidence for maritime trade between East Asia and island Southeast Asia at this time—already attested by the study of the so-called Indo-Pacific beads.[2]

The parrot cup was, of course, a luxury item, and it is not surprising that it was found in the tomb of Wang Xingzhi (d. 340) and his wife, Song Hezhi (d. 348), both members of prominent families of the Eastern Jin dynasty. Wang Xingzhi was a cousin of Wang Xizhi (ca. 303–ca. 361), the most famous calligrapher in Chinese history.

JCYW

1. Landman 1982.
2. Lee In-sook 1993.

119
Civil official

Western Wei dynasty (535–556)
Earthenware
Height 15¼ in. (38.9 cm)
Excavated at Cuijiaying, Hanzhong, Shaanxi Province, 1977
National Museum of China

Excav. report in *Kaogu* 1981.2

During the time of the Northern and Southern Dynasties, there was an in-between area extending over the drainage of the Han River and its tributaries—in present-day Shaanxi south of the Qinling Mountains, in northern Hubei, and in southeastern Henan—and parts of northern Sichuan. The main inhabitants were a

120
Retainer

Mid-6th century
Earthenware
Height 12¼ in. (31 cm)
Excavated at Changling, Ankang, Shaanxi Province, 1982
Shaanxi History Museum

Excav. report in *Wenbo* 1986.5

Many individuals survived the tumultuous fifth and sixth centuries and escaped conscription and taxation by working as retainers on large estates where they served in various capacities in agriculture and the militia and by providing entertainment. This earthenware figure, possibly the representation of a retainer on such an estate, wears a short tunic with wide sleeves and a sash, flared trousers that are tied at the knees, and an extraordinary hat with a wide brim. Similar garments can be seen on another sculpture excavated in the same region of Shaanxi (cat. no. 119) and on figures depicted on bricks that lined the walls of a tomb at Dengxian, Henan (cat. no. 121).[1]

The head and body of the present sculpture, which is one of fifteen excavated from the site at Changling, Shaanxi,[2] were made separately and then assembled. The decoration on the hat is difficult to read. It

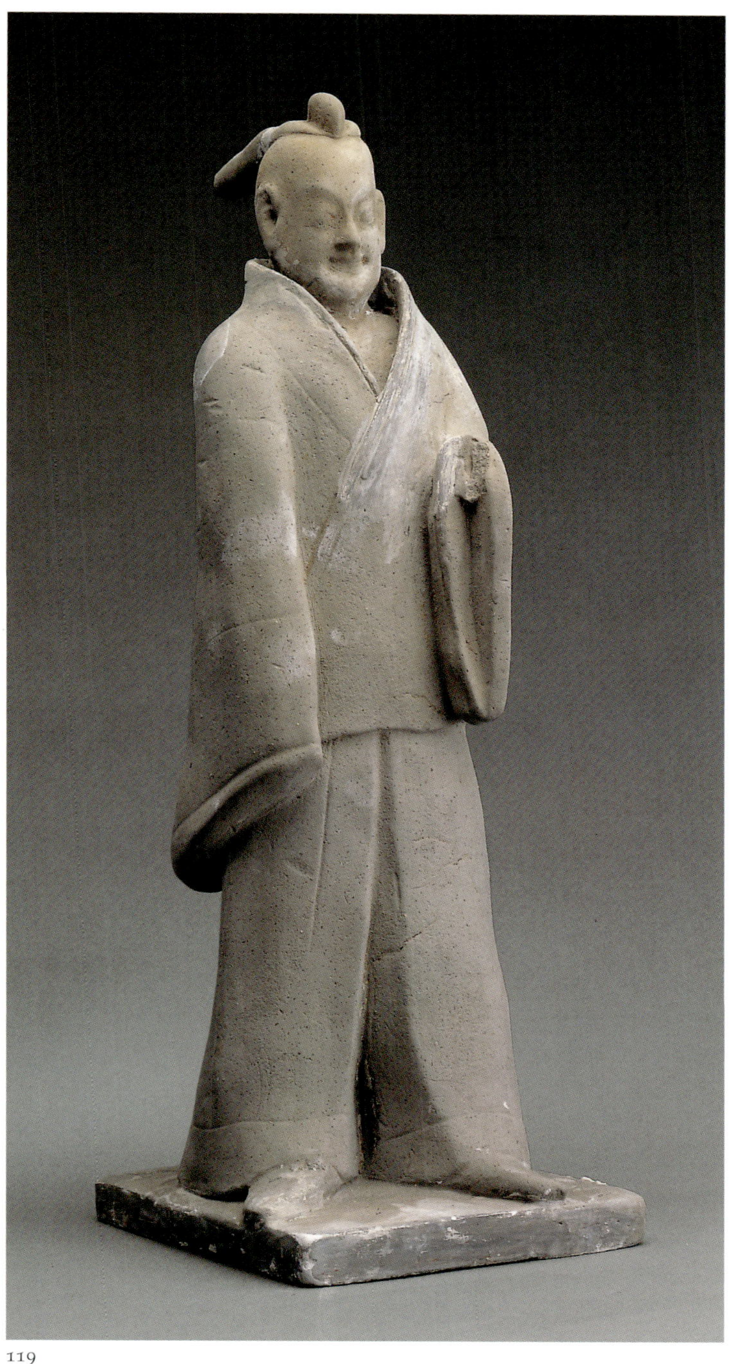

119

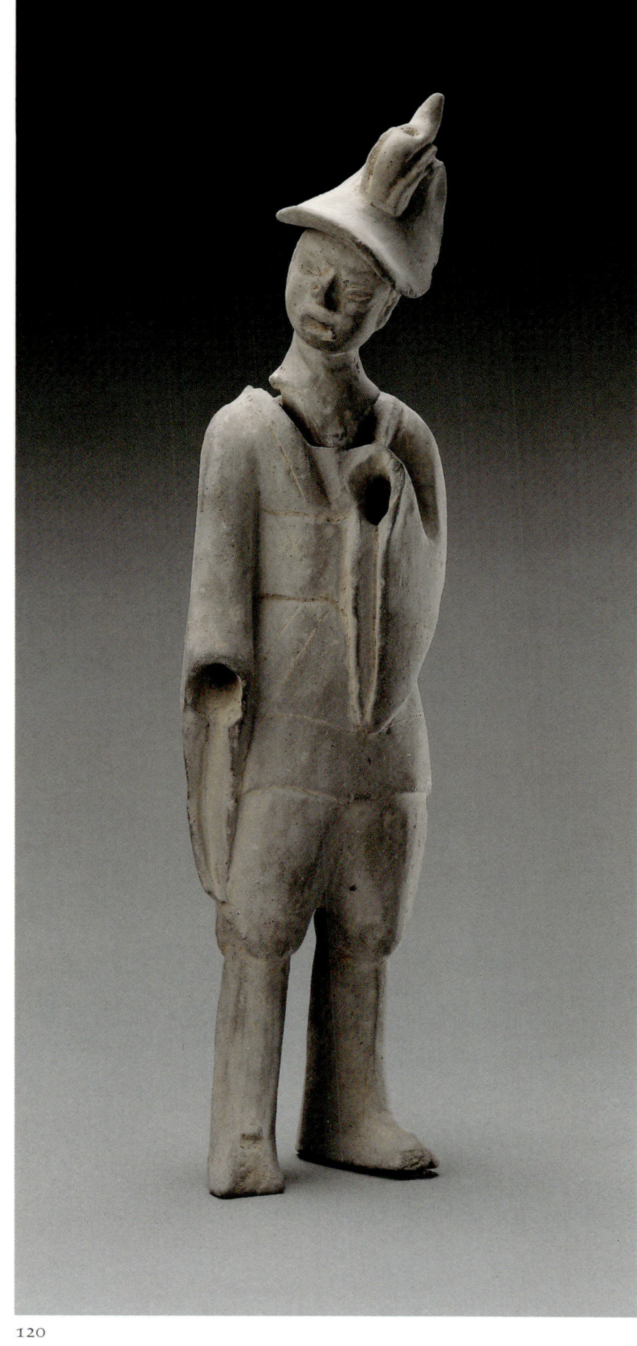

120

may be intended as a plume or some other adornment; however, the curve of the form suggests either a snake or a dragon or some type of bird.[3] Not all figures depicted on the Dengxian bricks wear hats this elaborate, and they are also rare among the pottery figures excavated at that site and elsewhere. It is possible that hairstyles and hats are indicative of function, status, or ethnic origin.[4]

A comparison of the gestures made by this figure, with the right arm lowered and the left arm raised (the hands are missing), with those of the figures on the Dengxian bricks suggests that it may originally have held a banner or musical instrument. A sculpture wearing an identical hat—one of several was found nearby at Ankang, Shaanxi—has been identified as a drummer, possibly one with a military function.[5]

The southern regions of Shaanxi and Henan were separated from northern centers by Qinshan and often maintained close ties with the south. Art from these regions illustrates an interesting blend of northern and southern traditions. Here, the attenuation of the body is reminiscent of styles prevalent in the early fifth century in the area around Luoyang (cat. no. 131). The sweetness of the facial expression, on the other hand, shows parallels to those found on tomb figures excavated from sites in South China (cat. no. 112).

DPL

1. Henan sheng wenhuaju wenwu gongzuodui 1958; Juliano 1980.
2. Berger and Casler 1994: 56.
3. Birds are often found in the helmets of guardian warriors dating to the Tang period. See Sun Hongmei and Deng Xueqing 1999: 79–82; and Zhang Xinyue 2001: 70–77.
4. *Quest for Eternity* 1987: 126.
5. Xu Xinyang 1986: 64, fig. 1.

121

Six bricks with molded decoration

Southern Dynasties (420–589)
Earthenware with pigments
Each: 7½ x 14$^{15}/_{16}$ in. (19 x 38 cm)
Excavated at Dengxian, Henan Province, 1958
Cat. nos. 121a, 121c–f: Henan Museum
Cat. no. 121b: National Museum of China

Excav. report in Henan sheng wenhuaju wenwu gongzuodui 1958

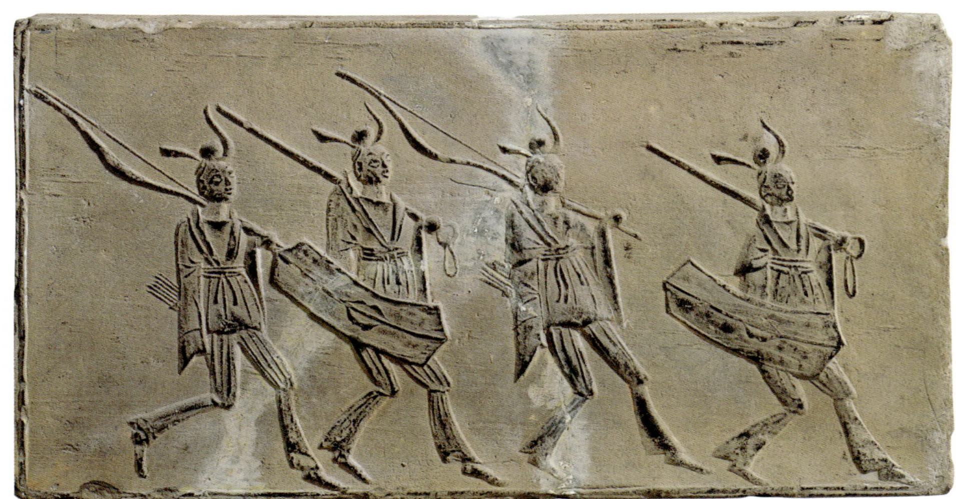

a

These six bricks are selected from a large number of bricks with impress decoration from a tomb in Dengxian, southwestern Henan.[1] Dengxian was in the prefecture of Yongzhou of the Southern Dynasties (420–589), which was the administrative center for the area described in the entry for the civil official (cat. no. 119).

Four of these bricks (a–d) give a vivid picture of the activities of a large class of people in the period of the Northern and Southern Dynasties. Known as *buqu,* they served landowners, leaders of large clans, and military lords in various capacities: as soldiers (a); in military bands (b); as grooms (c); and as bearers on ceremonial occasions (d). They also worked on the land and performed other general duties. The historian Zhou Yiliang has pointed out that the area around Yongzhou was where the administration of the Southern Dynasties recruited a major part of its military forces.[2] As the military of this period consisted mainly of *buqu,* the Dengxian bricks would confirm Zhou's conclusions, drawn from contemporary writings. The *buqu,* of course, were not confined to any part of the country, north or south, but were part of the social structure of the time.

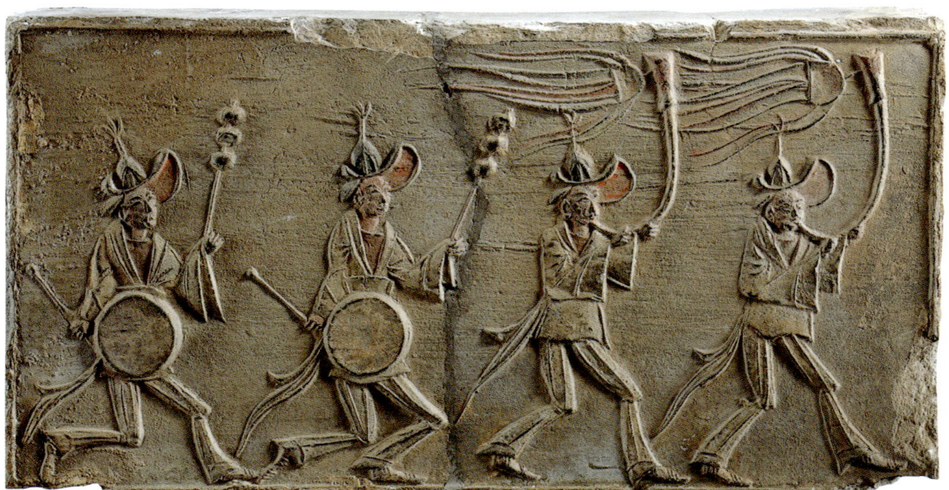

b

Two bricks point to other aspects of the culture of the time. Filial piety, promoted by the authorities of the Eastern Han (25–220) period as a cardinal Confucian virtue, was still obsessively preached all over China for several centuries after the fall of the Han. Brick (e) illustrates

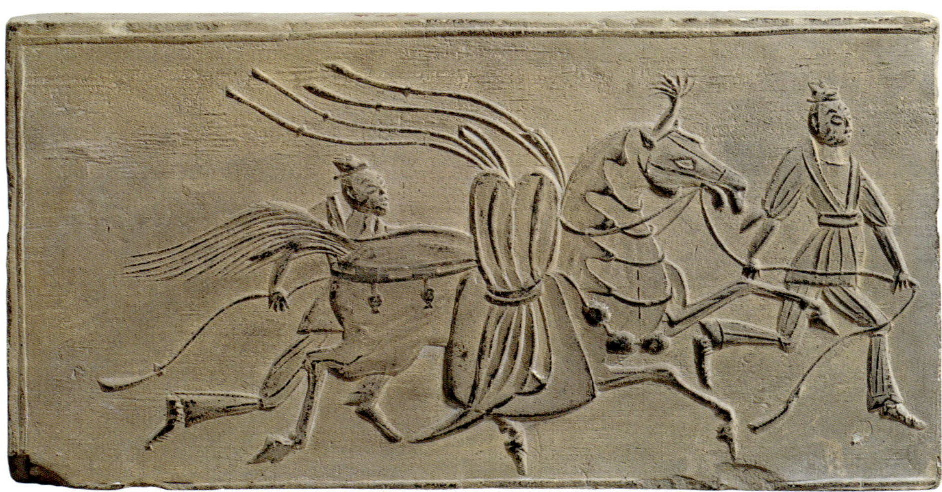

c

an extreme case of the practice of this "virtue." The story, dating back to the first century B.C., tells of a Guo Ju, the son of a very rich man, who gave all his inheritance to his two brothers and undertook to look after his mother. After some time, a son was born to Guo Ju, but he thought that he could not afford to feed another mouth and so resolved to bury the newborn. As he began to dig the burial pit, he discovered a pot of gold together with an iron plaque inscribed "For Guo Ju, the filially pious son." Guo Ju was then able to support the entire family. The brick illustrates the moment that the pot of gold is unearthed; Guo Ju's wife is shown standing by, holding the baby. Brick (f) is a Daoist scene of an immortal calling the phoenix on a mouth organ, the *sheng*.

JCYW

1. For a complete account of the Dengxian site, see Juliano 1980.
2. Zhou Yiliang 1997.

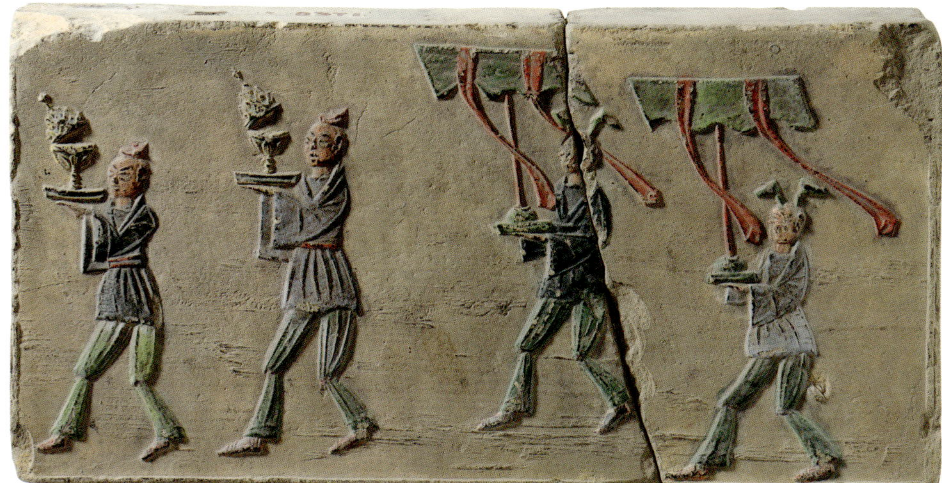

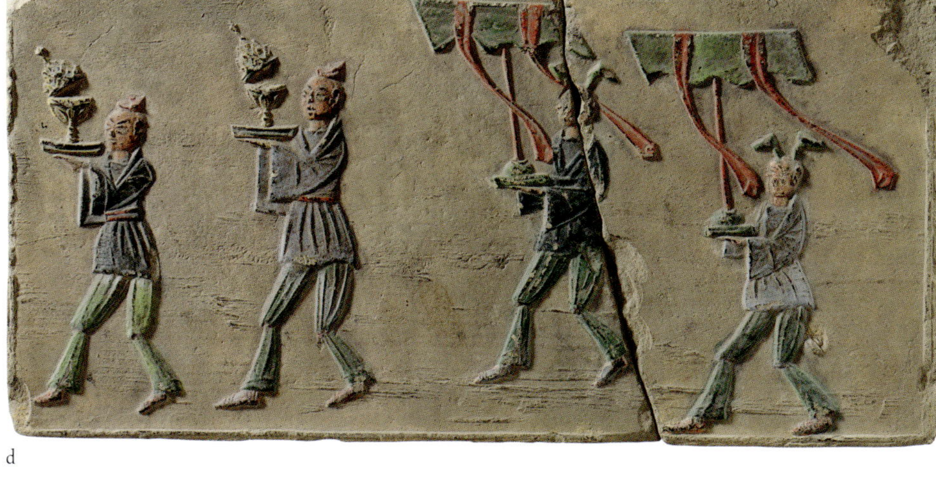

d

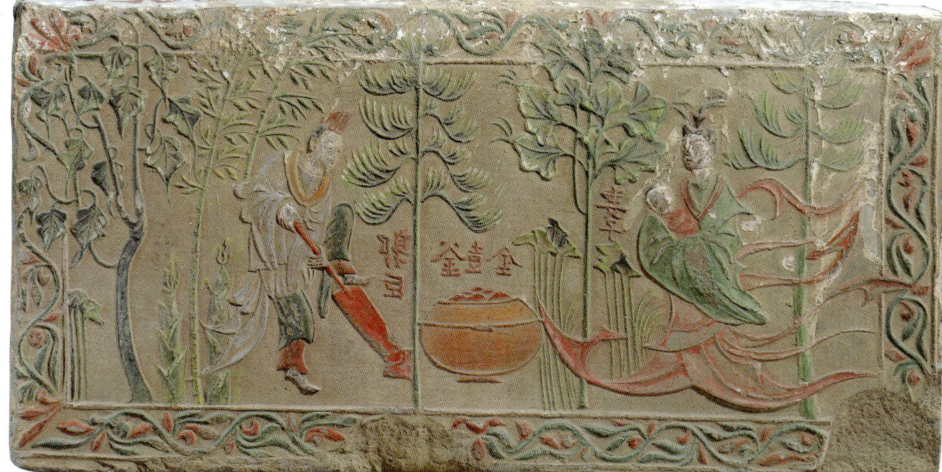

e

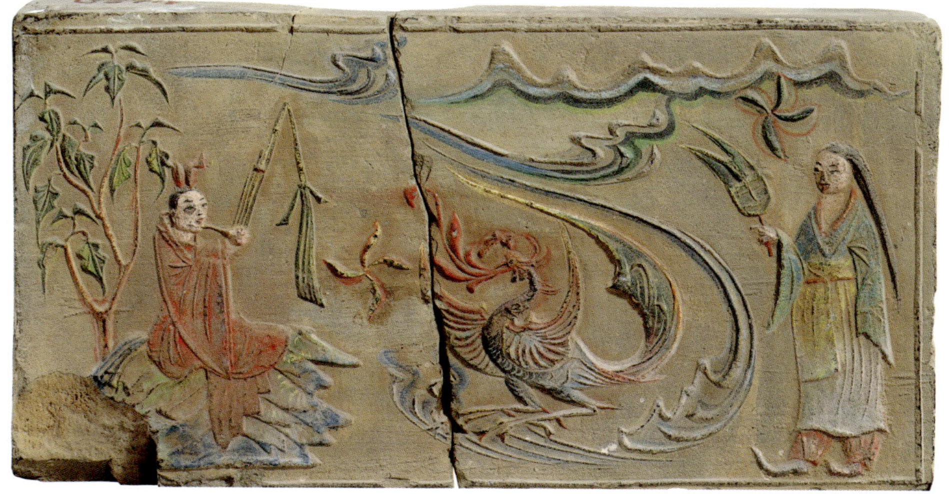

f

122
Maitreya-Amitayus stele

Southern Qi dynasty (479–502),
dated 483
Stone
Height 44½ in. (113 cm)
Found in Maoxian, Sichuan Province
Sichuan Provincial Museum

EXCAV. REPORT in *Wenwu* 1992.2

This stele fragment is notable for a number of reasons, not least its precise dating, with additional information provided regarding donors and the identity of the carved images. The work originally stood more than 67 inches high, considerably taller than it is now. It was discovered about 1920 in Maoxian, northwestern Sichuan. In the 1930s, the two Buddhas carved in low relief, one on each face, attracted the attention of unscrupulous individuals who split the stele into sections, keeping intact only the two images, with the intention of selling them. Although they were apprehended, parts of the stele were never recovered.

In 1992, the Sichuan scholar Yuan Shuguang reconstructed the original work.[1] Several inscriptions were originally carved on the stele but the main one states: "During the [Southern] Qi dynasty, the first year of the Yongming era, cyclical sign *guihai,* the fifteenth day of the seventh lunar month [483], the monk Xuan Song, a prelate of Western Liang [Gansu], reverently commissioned [a sculpture of] the two Buddhas—Wuliangshou [Skt: Amitayus] and Mile [Skt: Maitreya], the Buddha of the Future—for the spiritual benefit of the emperor and his ministers, for many generations of teachers, for his parents and siblings, for seven generations of household members, and for the sake of all sentient beings. He expressed the wish that everyone's mind would open to the wondrous, all-embracing teaching, would clearly place his trust in the Triple Jewels, and practice the Ten Virtues so that one may have the chance to meet with Maitreya at the Three Assemblies under the Nagapushpa tree. . . ."

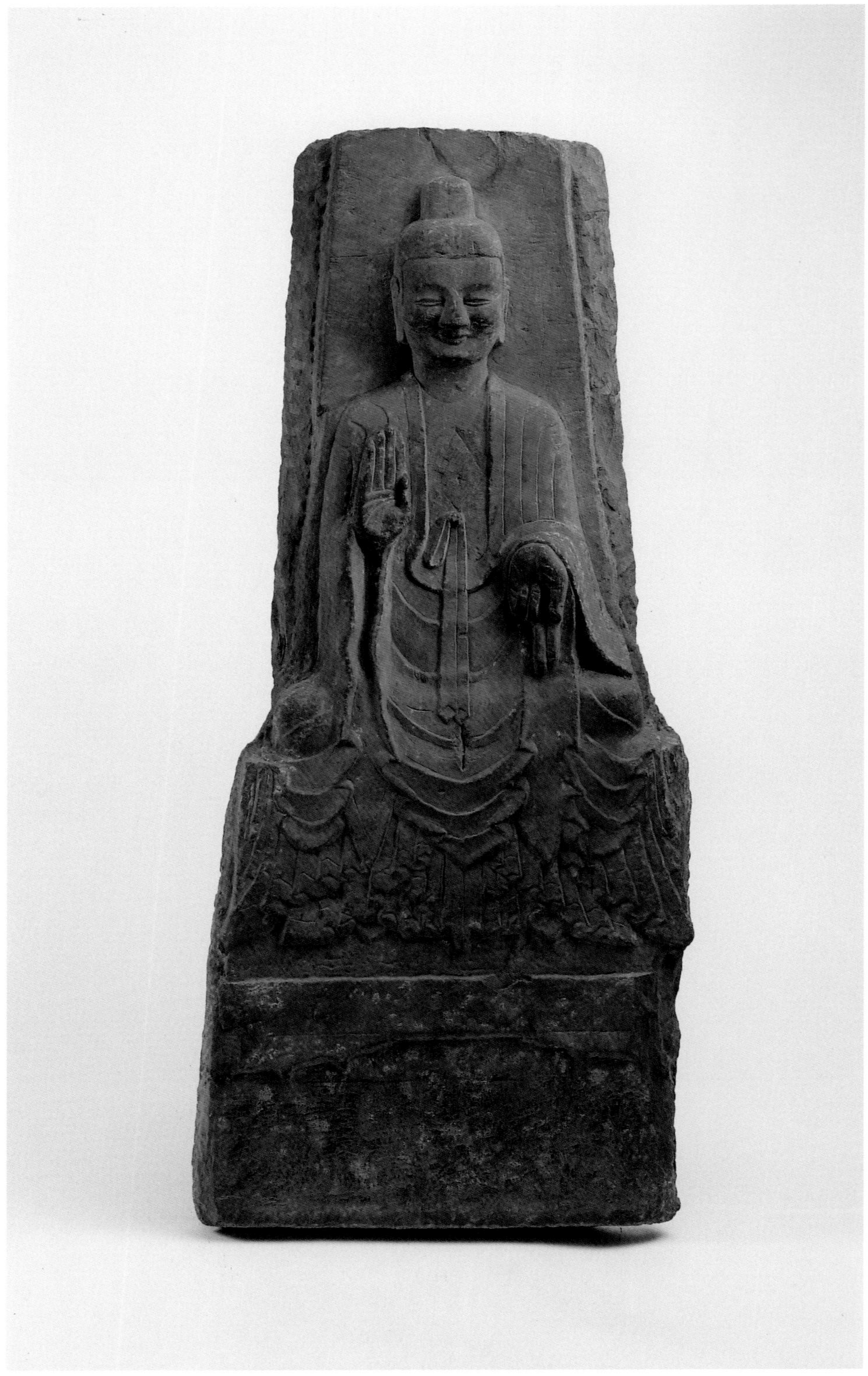

122, front

We have identified Maitreya as the seated Buddha and Amitayus as the incomplete standing figure. Generally, one assumes the front corresponds to Maitreya's panel, as the inscription mentions him several times, whereas Amitayus is mentioned only once.

The stele is the earliest dated work found in Sichuan, and its iconography reveals the veneration in this province of the two Buddhas in tandem. This devotion originated with the teachings of two prelates who lived for some time in the South, Dao An (312–385), a devotee of Maitreya, and Hui Yuan (344–416), a devotee of Amitayus. Both preached the merit of being reborn into the Pure Lands presided over by these two Buddhas. The widespread popularity of the cult is further reflected in two other steles in this exhibition (cat. nos. 124, 126).

The Maitreya exhibits a distinctive

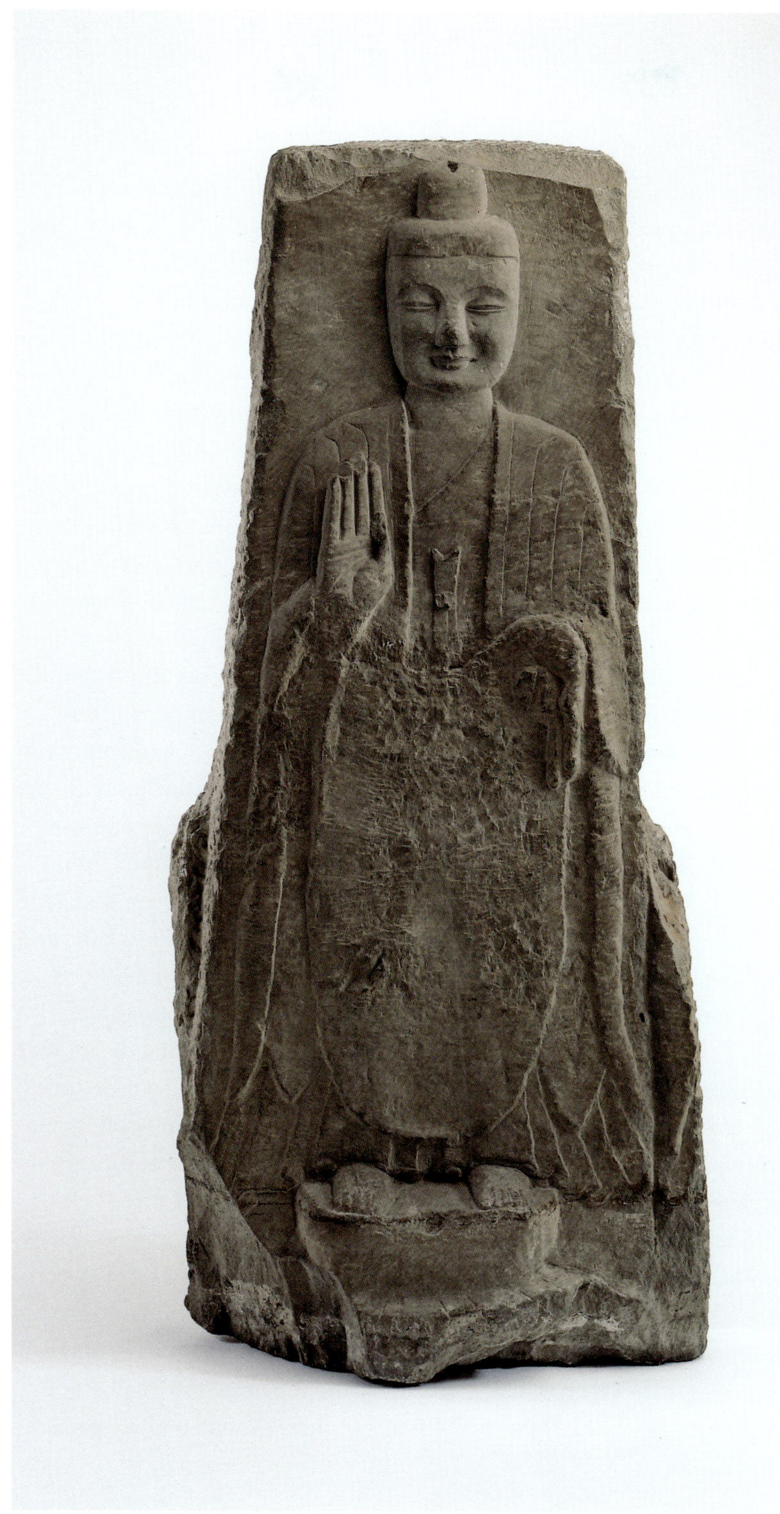

122, back

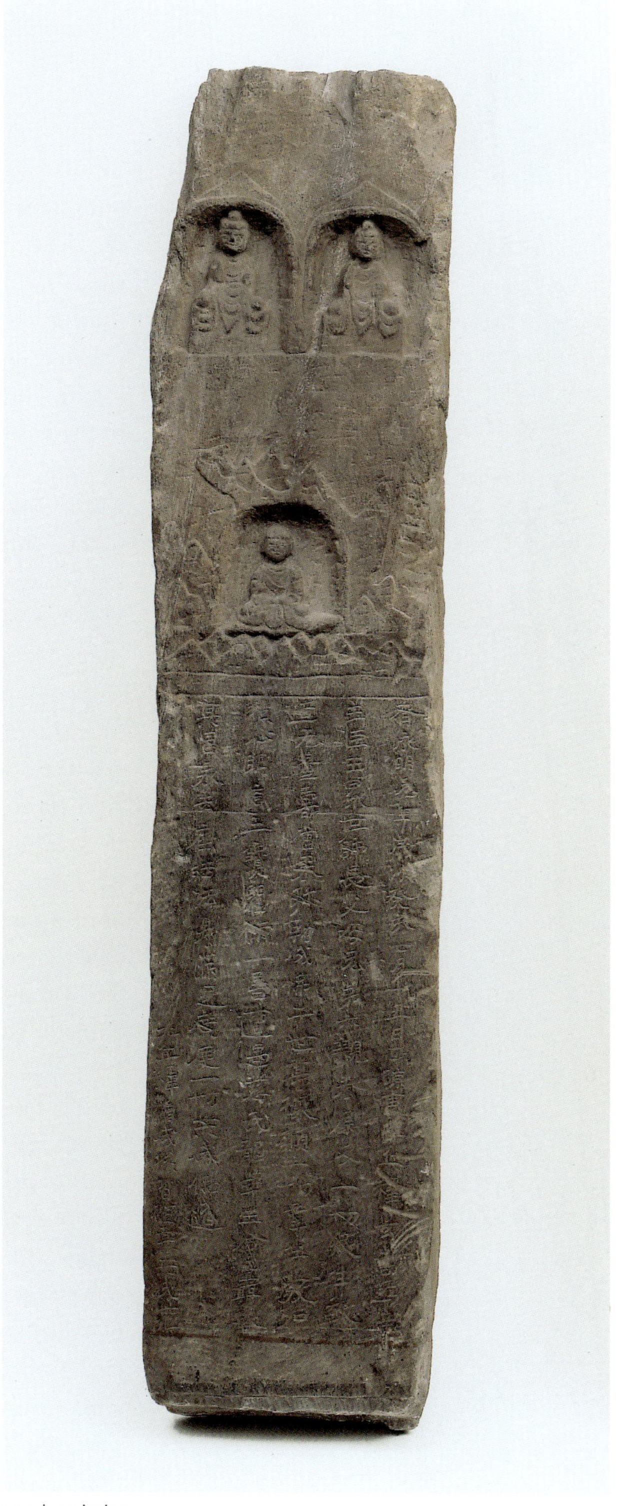

122, inscription

attire and unusual hand gesture. He wears what is possibly a southern mode of dress: a robe that cascades in tiers, forming a linear pattern, and a sash tied above the waist and falling down the front. The *varada* (giving) mudra indicates a variant of the traditional hand gesture, since the Maitreya extends three, rather than five, fingers of the left hand. These two innovations—costume and hand gesture—were adopted forty years later for the Buddhas carved at the Northern Wei site of Longmen, in the imperial Central Binyang Cave, completed in 523. In short, aspects of this southern work became models for the carvers of the north.

AFH

1. Yuan Shuguang 1992: 67–71.

123
Standing Buddha Shakyamuni

Liang dynasty (502–557), dated 529
Sandstone
Height 62¼ in. (158 cm)
Excavated at Wanfosi, Chengdu, Sichuan Province, 1954
Sichuan Provincial Museum

Excav. report in *Wenwu* 2001.10

Sichuan Buddhist sculpture has come to our attention through a series of findings, the richest being those connected with the site of the former Wanfosi (Temple of the Ten Thousand Buddhas) in Chengdu. Discoveries were made at irregular intervals starting in the late 1880s and continuing in the 1930s and 1940s and culminating in 1954. In this exhibition, several other works also represent the Wanfosi site.[1]

This imposing, dark gray stone standing Shakyamuni without head, from Wanfosi, Sichuan, is another example of the Indianized style that influenced the work of sculptors in Shandong and Sichuan during the sixth century. Stylistic innovations from India and Southeast Asia were continually being introduced to Nanjing and would quite naturally have percolated inland (to Sichuan) and northward (to Shandong). The Indianized style derived from Guptan models produced at the artistic centers of Mathura and Sarnath. The Wanfosi Shakyamuni shows a typically Guptan plasticity of form, clearly perceptible beneath the crisply pleated, transparent robe. The prototype is clearly Mathuran, as the pleats form a linear pattern over the entire body. But unlike the Indian prototype, which uses only concentric catenaries on the axis of the body, two distinctive pleat patterns are used here—horizontal U-shaped loops on the left and pronounced verticals on the right. The sculptor followed a variation of the Mathuran mode reminiscent of the South Indian style of Amaravati, notwithstanding the fact that Amaravati Buddhas leave the right shoulder bare, as seen on the Longxingsi Buddha from Qingzhou (cat. no. 165). Because a similar merging of the Mathuran and Amaravati styles is present in Southeast Asian Buddhist statuary of Indonesia and Vietnam, it would seem that the transmission of Indian images to South China occurred through the mediation of Southeast Asian cultures via the maritime route.

The inscription points to a very high patronage linked to the Nanjing court, suggesting that images popular at Nanjing were a model for Sichuan carvers. The two donors of the sculpture were part of the retinue of Fan, the crown prince of Poyang, and a nephew of Emperor Wudi of Liang (r. 502–49). The crown prince was sent to Sichuan as governor of Yizhou (Chengdu). The inscription on the back of the sculpture informs us that in the first year of Zhongdatong (529), Jingguang and Jinghuan, attendants to the crown prince, while stopping at Anpusi (the former name of Wanfosi) on their way west, commissioned this image of Shakyamuni. "With this merit, they hope that seven past generations can be born in the Pure Land and behold the true face of the Buddha and achieve perfection in shining wisdom. They hope that Jingguang and his mother, as well as all their relatives, will live one hundred years and that their good karma will be extended far into the future. That they will be saved from the three obstacles and forever removed from evil. That life after life, generation after generation, mother and son will be reunited to learn the Dharma extensively. And that together with all sentient beings, they will attain the fruits of Buddhahood without fail."

AFH

1. For the most recent report on the Wanfosi findings, see Yuan Shuguang 2001: 19–38; the inscription is on p. 20.

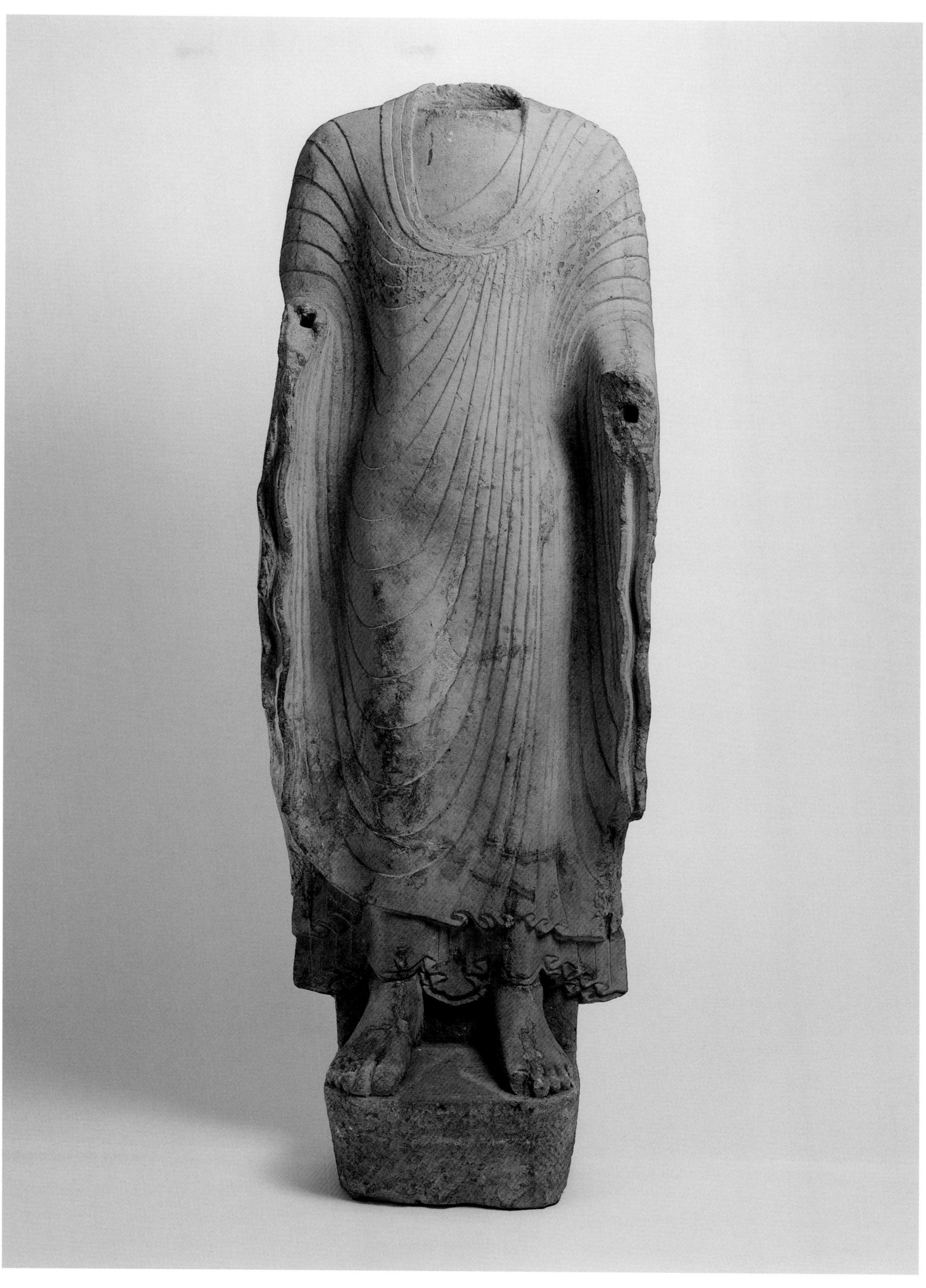

124
Stele with bodhisattvas (front) and landscape scenes (back)

Liang dynasty (502–557), first half of the 6th century
Sandstone
Height 47¼ in. (120 cm)
Excavated at Wanfosi, Chengdu, Sichuan Province, 1953
Sichuan Provincial Museum

Excav. report in *Wenwu* 2001.10

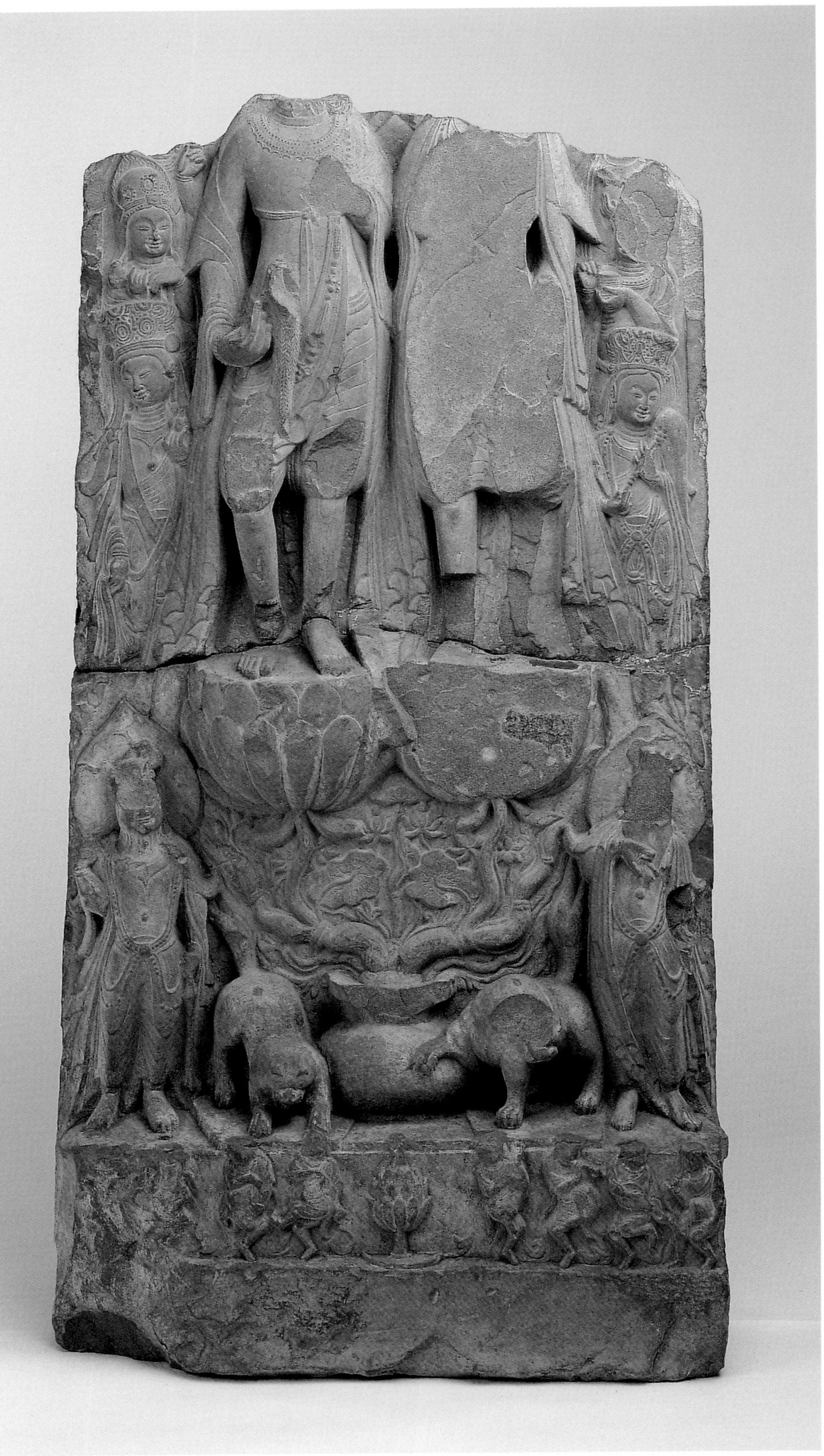

124, front

This tall, sadly fragmentary stele is distinguished by several features from its contemporaries in North China. Form, content, and style reveal purely Sichuanese aesthetic choices and doctrinal content. The rectangular shape has some affinity with steles from Luoyang and Chang'an, but the top, unlike that of northern examples, did not originally terminate with intertwined dragons but may simply have been curved. More important, however, is the well-knit program that visually translates beliefs popular in South China, particularly in Sichuan. The front displays two bodhisattvas standing on lotuses (the heads are now missing) and assisted by superimposed personages, two on each side. At the center is a *purnaghata*, or urn of plenty, filled with water to nourish the luscious lotuses on which the bodhisattvas stand. At either side of the urn are two guardians, while two playful lions cavort below. The bottom section of the stele displays a central incense burner in the form of a lotus that bisects a procession of mirthful dancers.

There is some debate as to the identity of the figures on the back of the stele, but the scene carved in low relief on the upper section is generally accepted as among the earliest renderings of the Pure Land of Amitayus, the Buddha of the West. Amitayus is shown presiding over the pond of rebirth, where the blessed amuse themselves in the water or awaken to full enlightenment inside gradually opening lotuses. Because the Pure Land is depicted on the back, the bodhisattvas on the front can be recognized as the Buddha's two canonical assistants, Guanyin (Skt: Avalokiteshvara) and Dashizhi (Skt: Mahasthamaprapta). Below the Pure Land are numerous vignettes carved in landscape cells, with hills, plants, and flowing waters. These are often interpreted as visualizations of the *paramitas*, or Six Perfections, steps in the path toward enlightenment. The bridge linking the two sections lends support to this interpretation.[1]

It is also possible that the references are, instead, to the cult of the bodhisattva Guanyin, which was at that time thriving in Sichuan.[2] Chapter 25 of the Lotus

the Chinese viewer was likely similar to that on the ninth-century Tang art historian Zhang Yanyuan when he viewed a mural by the contemporary southern artist Zhang Sengyou (act. 500–550): "Novel shapes and strange creatures . . . [an] unending variety of fantastic shapes and strange forms."[1] The adjective "strange" is repeated twice, conveying the sense of curiosity and wonder such works provoked in native (Chinese) viewers, the same reaction shared by onlookers of our own time.

We can only speculate on the function of this circular pedestal. If it served as the base of a seated Buddha, the overhang would have been carved so as not to obstruct the view of the figures. Hence, the Buddha must have been seated on a high throne. The identity of the central figure would surely have shed light on the meaning of these images—on their ethnic origin and the ritual they appear to perform. Represented hieratically, the major personages are haloed, adorned with prominent collar-necklaces, and garbed in simple skirts and capacious stoles. Each carries a special implement—a silken pouch, a lotus, a large bouquet of flowers, musical instruments. And each stands in a slightly contrapposto pose, with the exception of one personage (perhaps the most important), who is shown with a pouch and a rod held between his legs.

The smoothly carved faces and bodies impart a sensuous sweetness reminiscent of Southeast Asian sculpture, though a more precise connection evades us. The secondary figures are not only smaller in size but clothed in plainer attire, as befits their role as assistants or devotees. Notably, they are of different ages. One stands out conspicuously. He is the embodiment of the Hindu elephant god Ganesha, and it is his presence, in particular, that strengthens the argument that the origin of the group is to be found in an Indianized culture of Southeast Asia.

AFH

1. Soper 1959: 80.

126

Stele with Sumeru (front) and Maitreya Paradise (back)

Liang dynasty (502–557), first half of the 6th century
Sandstone
Width 25 ¼ (64 cm)
Excavated at Wanfosi, Chengdu, Sichuan Province, 1954
Sichuan Provincial Museum

Excav. report in *Wenwu* 1998.11

This work is a fragment of a double-faced stele similar in style and composition to the more complete relief of the Pure Land of Amitayus (cat. no. 124), which was excavated at Wanfosi.[1] I would like to suggest that the two steles formed a pair, with images referring, respectively, to the cult of Amitayus, Buddha of the West, and to the cult of Maitreya, Buddha of the Future. In the south, the two deities were worshipped together, by Sichuan Buddhists, as illustrated by the images on the Southern Qi stele dated 483, also from Sichuan (cat. no. 122). This devotional aspect did not have a counterpart in China's contemporary northern provinces.

As in the stele with bodhisattvas and landscape scenes (cat. no. 124), what is represented on the front is intimately linked to the subject matter on the back—the phenomenal world on the one, the realm of Maitreya, Buddha of the Future, on the other. In this case, the incomplete front displays in the upper section the Heaven of the Thirty-three Gods, or Trayastrimsa, which lies on the summit of Mount Sumeru, the world's axis. Sumeru is depicted according to canonical and artistic convention: clusters of unidentified beings walk through a hilly landscape, as if moving from one abode to another. In the scriptures, the Buddhist heavens are described as level lands; here, instead, the carver opted for a mountainscape.

A massive canopy with festooned jeweled ropes enlivened by swooping celestials appears below Sumeru; chimes hooked to dragons are suspended on each side. Similar constructions on contemporaneous Sichuan steles are often seen on the upper portion of aureoles that shelter divine gatherings. I would speculate that originally a sacred group—Maitreya and his attendants—was seated beneath the canopy and that the large dowel protruding from the top of the slab was used to attach an additional section that formed the stele's summit. Thus, the present size would correspond to one-third of the original; what remains is the central section.

On the back, the carver conflated several moments from the last rebirth of the messianic Maitreya and placed them in pockets of rounded hills that are typically Sichuan in flavor. At the top center, Maitreya is shown with attendants in a pavilion marked by prominent spires. He wears a crown and sits with crisscrossed legs, according to his status as a bodhisattva dwelling in Tushita heaven. Immediately below this group, Maitreya is depicted as a Buddha seated in full lotus pose within a smaller pavilion and surrounded by devotees. As a Buddha, he preaches in the mundane land of Ketumati, where he was reincarnated for the last time. We read in the scriptures that in Ketumati, Maitreya preached to the Three Assemblies; thus, two more scenes are carved, one on each side.

In the four corners are terrestrial events that occurred at the same time as these transcendental happenings. In the upper right corner, the cave recalls how Mahakashyapa waited in a similar dwelling for Maitreya's coming, while in the upper left

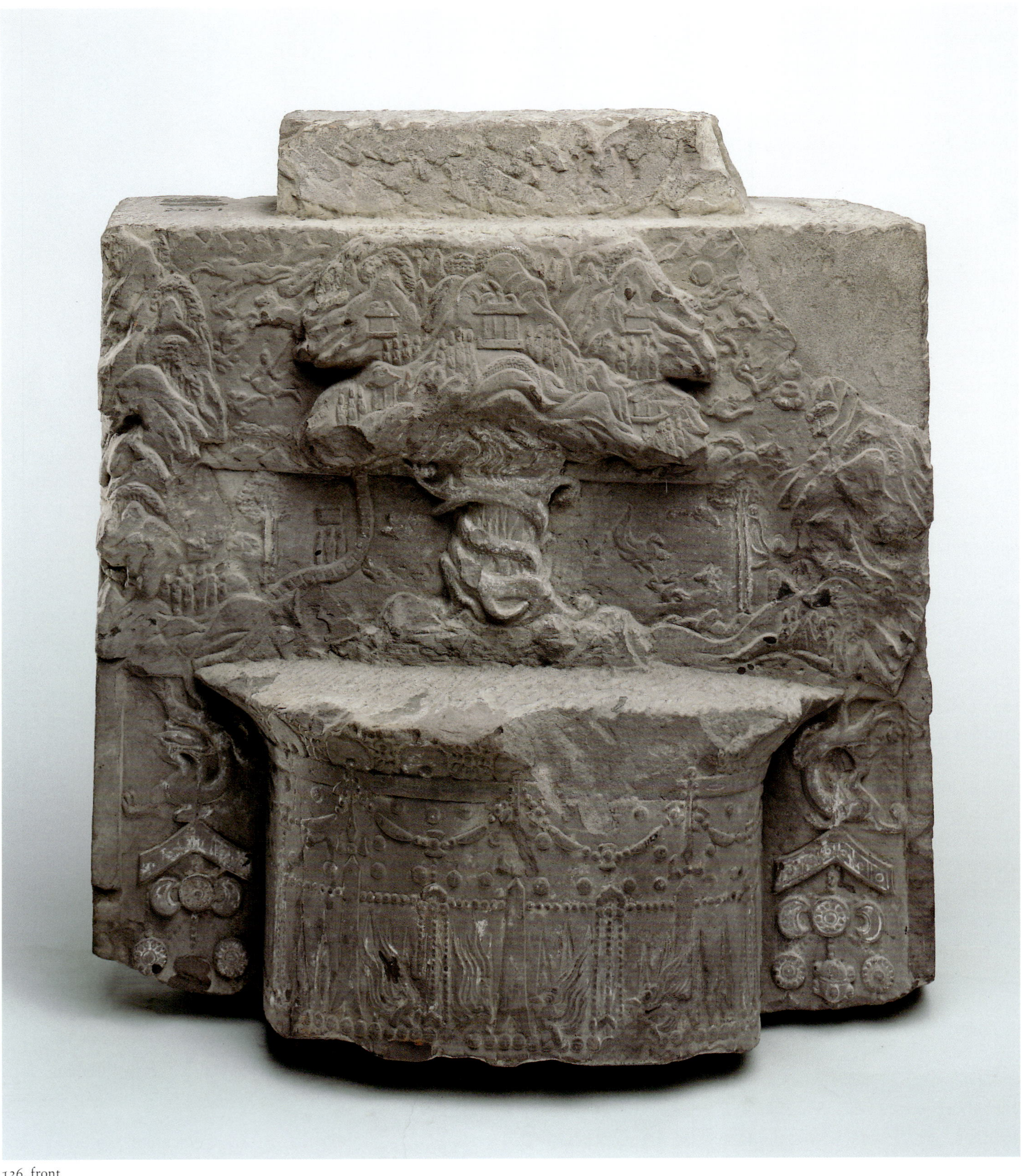

126, front

laborers working in the fields allude to the golden age of plenty, which will mark Maitreya's last rebirth. Along the portion of the frame that remains are small squarish cells filled with stories linked to the Buddha's last life.

As noted earlier, the style of carving is the same as that of the Sichuan stele celebrating Amitayus's Pure Land, also ascribed to the Liang dynasty, and the subject matter of the two steles complement each other. Carved in the first half of the sixth century, Maitreya's Pure Land sets a precedent for an iconography whose popularity in the north, especially at Dunhuang, spread during the Tang dynasty in the late seventh and eighth centuries. Here again is an instance in which Sichuan prelates and carvers were setting a precedent for the north.

AFH

1. See Yuan Shuguang 2001: 19–38; and Zhao Shengliang 2001: 34–42.

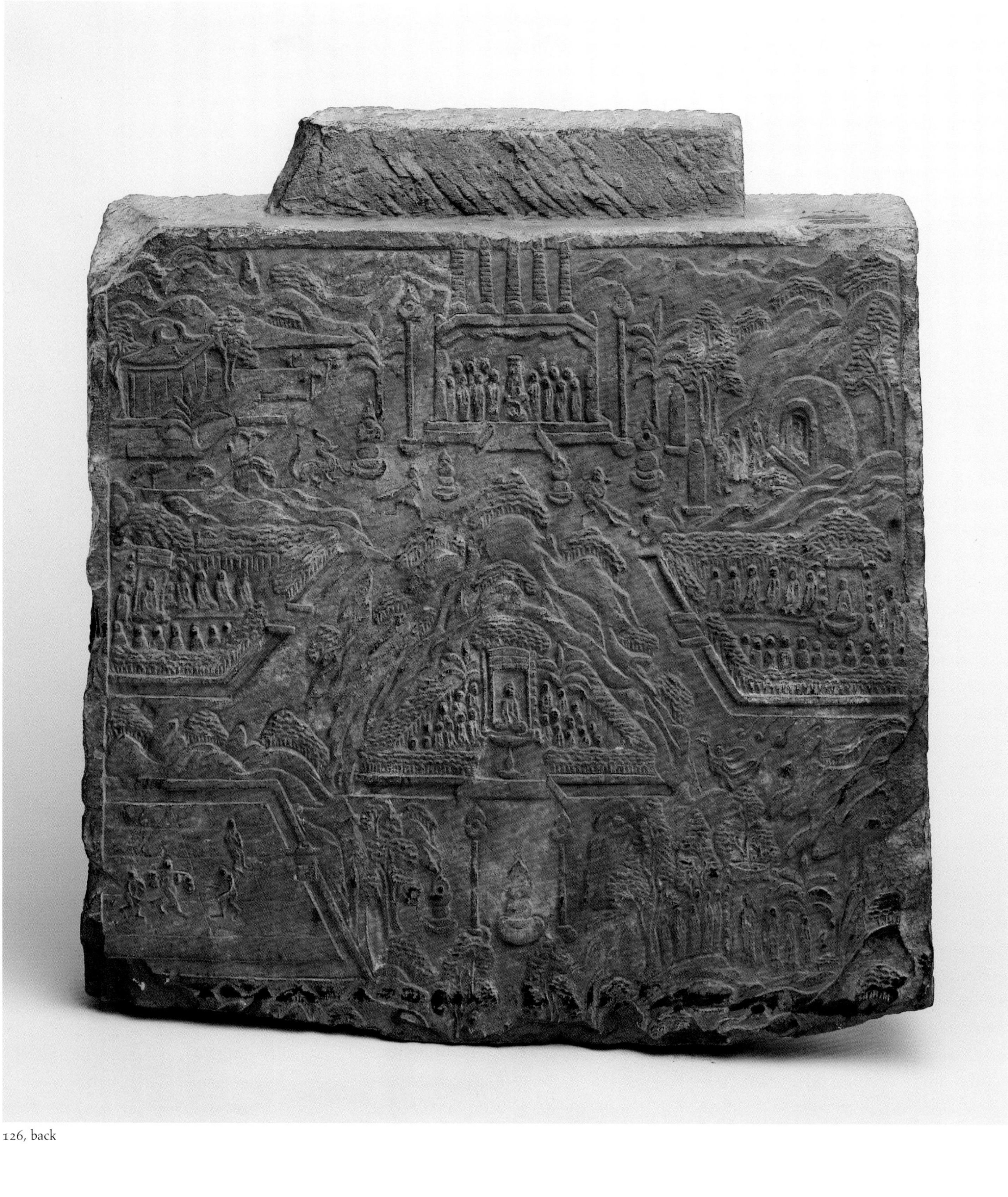

126, back

127
Stele with twin seated Buddhas

Liang dynasty (502–557), dated 545
Sandstone with gilding
Height 16⅞ in. (43 cm)
Excavated in Chengdu, Sichuan Province, 1995
Chengdu City Institute of Archaeology

Excav. report in *Wenwu* 1998.11

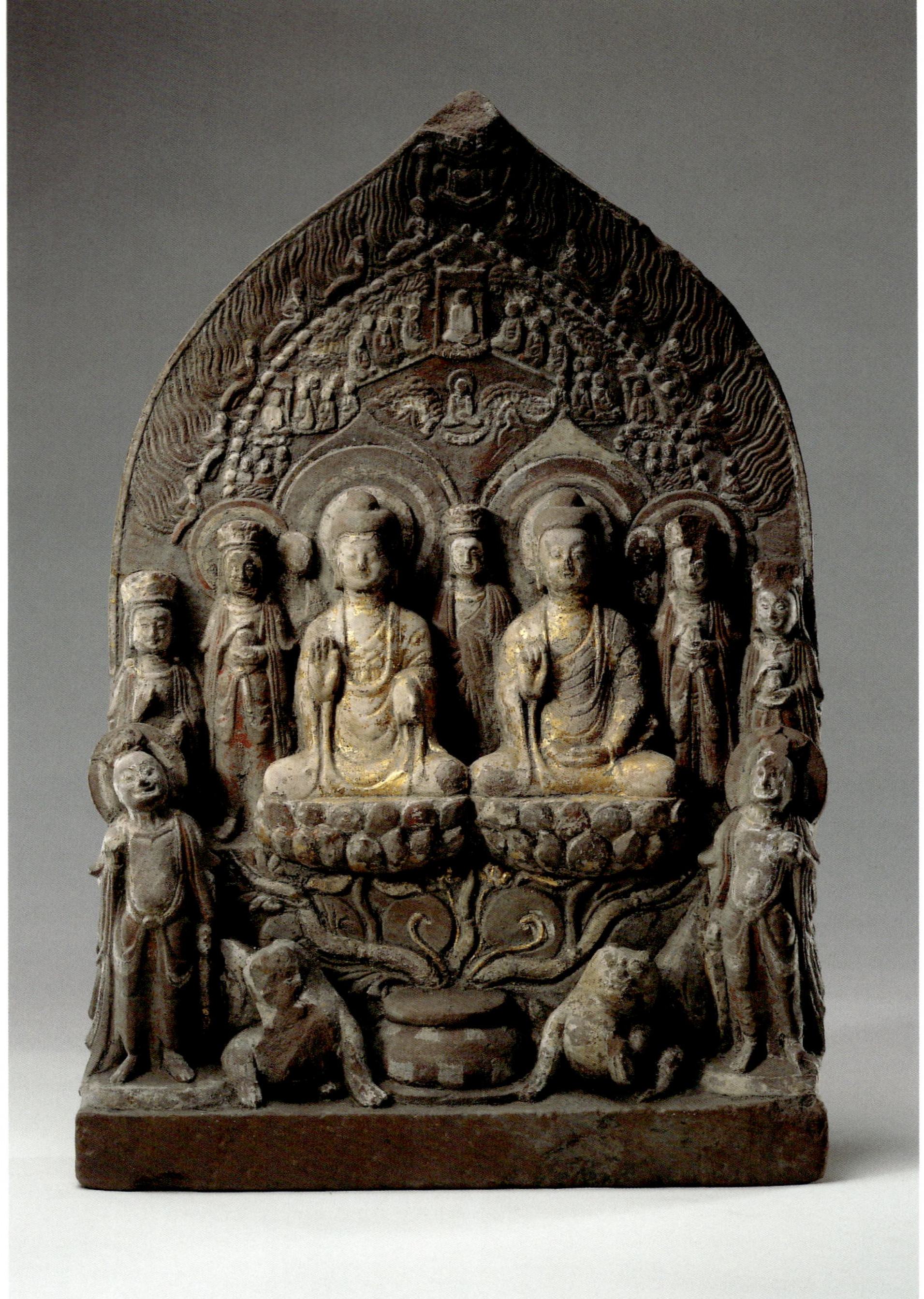

127, front

The shape of this stele is peculiar to southern Buddhist art, in particular that of Sichuan: the base is rectangular and the contour of the grouped figures is rounded within an all-embracing, pointed aureole. Accompanying inscriptions often refer to steles of this kind as *kanxiang*, or images in niches, suggesting that the deities were placed in a receding space similar to a cave.

The surface of this outstanding, well-preserved work retains extensive traces of gilding. The twin Buddhas Prabhutaratna (C: Duobao) and Shakyamuni (C: Shijia), differentiated by hand gestures, are shown assisted by five bodhisattvas with offerings and two smaller monk disciples; they are guarded by two Vajrapanis, or thunderbolt holders. Two minor, secular personages are carved on either side of the stele. The deities' gilded bodies are round and supple, their expressions vibrant but compassionate. The grouping is large, yet rich with minute detailing, some alluding to an Indic source. The Buddhas' lotus thrones sprout from a *purnaghata*, or Indian vase of plenty, which is guarded by two playful lions. Its miraculous properties are reflected in the lusciousness of the flowers.

In the aureole above the Buddhas we see, in ascending order, a seated Buddha and a Buddha presiding over a gathering of monks, perhaps in a Pure Land, with numerous flying celestials. The two topmost angels support an Ashoka stupa-reliquary at the apex of the aureole. The distinctive shape of the reliquary, a square, one-storied structure, distinguishes it from the typical northern Chinese stupa, which has a towerlike form. The Ashoka stupa refers to the legendary origin of the monument in India during the reign of the Mauryan king Ashoka (r. ca. 272–231 B.C.), who converted to Buddhism in the third century B.C. As a demonstration of his devotion, Ashoka erected eighty-four thousand such stupas in a single night. Later on, they miraculously spread throughout the Buddhist countries, ultimately reaching the coastal provinces of Zhejiang and Jiangsu, especially during the rule of the Liang emperor Wudi (r. 502–49). This southern convention was incorporated into Sichuanese iconography, since Sichuan was part of Liang territory, having been annexed by Eastern Jin in 347. The dissemination of special stupas accompanied that of Ashoka-type Buddha images like the one in the exhibition, also from Sichuan, dated 551 (cat. no. 128). Stupas and images such as those seen here thus illustrate the primary role that Indian Buddhism exercised on southern Chinese

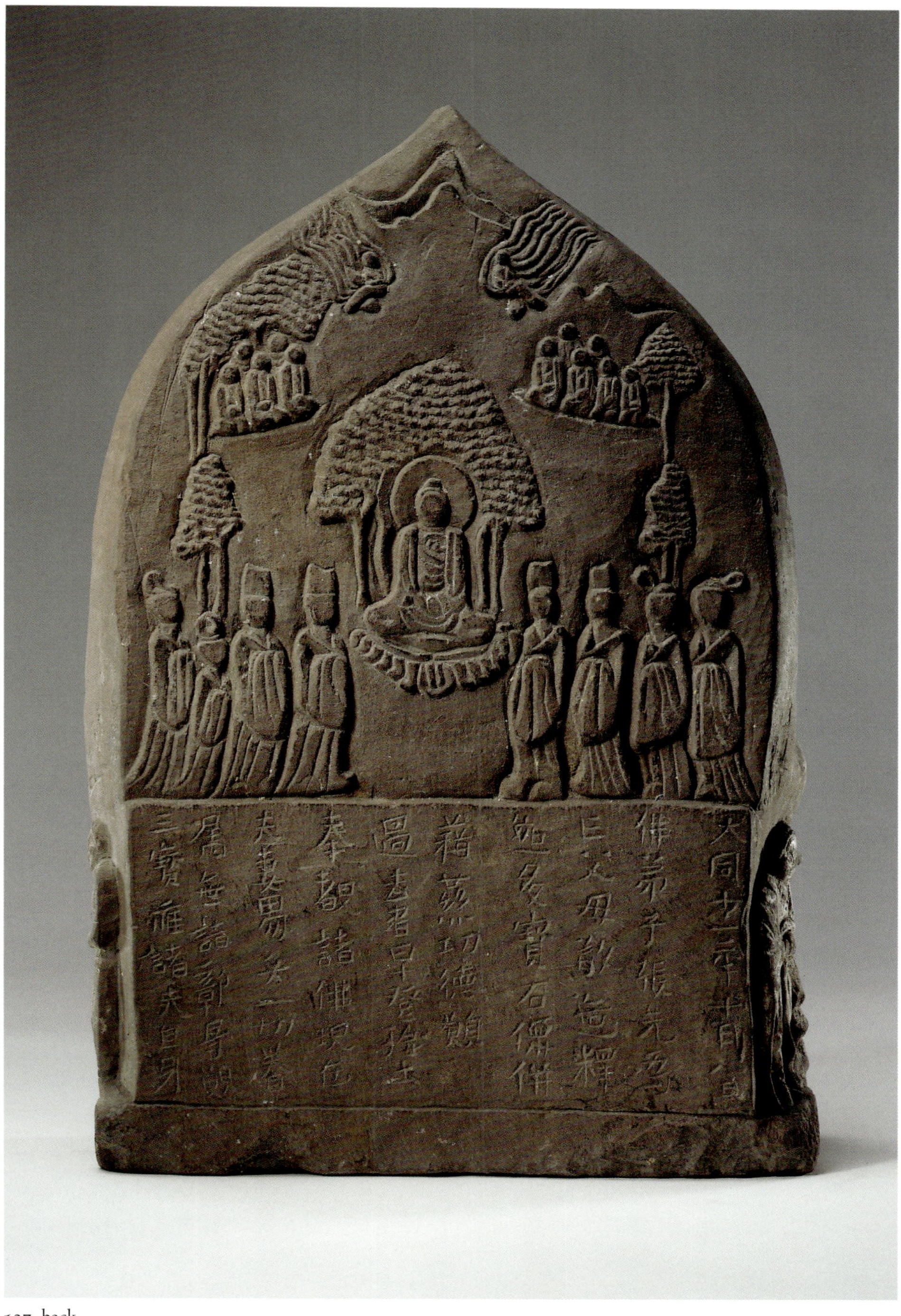

127, back

Buddhist art during the first half of the sixth century.

The inscription carved on the back of the stele states, "In the eleventh year of the Datong era of the Liang dynasty [545], the Buddhist disciple Zhang Yuan respectfully had the images of the Buddhas Duobao and Shijia made as an offering with the wish that all my living and dead relatives will be reborn where they can listen to Buddha preaching the Dharma and that everyone will quickly attain Enlightenment into the true [state] of no rebirth. Similarly, it is hoped that all beings in the six realms of rebirth and those with whom I have had casual connections for the previous seven generations will do the same."[1]

AFH

1. See report on the Xi'an Road finding in Chengdu shi wenwu kaogu gongzuodi et al. 1998: 4–20; the inscription is on p. 9.

128
Standing Ashoka-type Buddha

Liang dynasty (502–557), dated 551
Sandstone with gilding and pigments
Height 18⅞ in. (48 cm)
Excavated at Chengdu, Sichuan Province, 1995
Chengdu City Institute of Archaeology

Excav. report in *Wenwu* 1998.11

This exquisite, partially intact sculpture with a glowing, golden finish embodies a tradition particularly rooted in South China. The inscription, carved atypically on the tablet affixed to the statue's lower back, informs us that in the fifth year of Taiqing (551), the monk Du Sengyi reverently commissioned this Ashoka image (*Ayuwang xiang*) of the Buddha with the hope that all beings will be reborn to hear Buddha's preaching of the Law, will reach early enlightenment, and will avoid the karmic process of rebirth into the Six Destinies. The self-appellation makes reference to the miraculous appearance during the fourth century of images that emerged from the sea along the coastal areas of China, in Jiangsu and Zhejiang. It was believed that the images originated with King Ashoka (reign. ca. 272–231 B.C.), the most celebrated Indian patron of Buddhism (see cat. no. 127). The *Ji shenzhou sanbao gantong lu* (Records of Spiritual Response of the Three Jewels in China), by Daoxuan (596–667), and the *Gao seng zhuan* (Biographies of Eminent Monks), by Shi Huijiao (497–554), carry several records of such occurrences.

In China, Ashoka-type Buddha images, under the patronage of influential members of society and with the backing of distinguished prelates, became widespread during the reign of the Liang emperor Wudi (r. 502–49), who strove in his devotion to emulate his Indian predecessor, the Mauryan emperor Ashoka. Thus, legitimacy was conferred on Chinese Buddhist art by its link to India, the holy land, while the patronage of local elites placed it in a Chinese locale. Very likely, the iconography of Ashoka-type Buddha icons originated in Nanjing, the capital of the Southern Dynasties. Because Sichuan became an integral part of the South politically, we may assume that when Sichuan was annexed by the Eastern Jin in 347, Sichuan Buddhist art to some degree reflected the doctrinal choices and aesthetic taste of the southern capital.

Several aspects of this sculpture—posture, attire, expression, halo, and lotus pedestal—reveal a determined effort to distinguish this image from conventional likenesses of the Buddha. He is shown standing firmly on the ground, with his feet apart; the outlines of the body are clearly visible under his robe; the arms are raised in a gesture of welcome. Originally, the right hand performed the Fear Not mudra, while the left hand held the robe in place. The outer robe, or *sanghati,* is draped to form a V-shaped cowl around the neck and falls to delineate an unusual system of pleats. Wide catenaries mark the body's central axis, contrasting with the rigid vertical folds falling from the arms. The underrobe forms catenaries over the legs and rigid folds in between. The alternation of curved and straight lines becomes the major characteristic of monastic attire, the paradigm of the Ashoka-type Buddha in the sixth century. The back of the sculpture has a much simpler definition of transversal striations over robe and overhang.

The Buddha's face reveals foreign, perhaps Indian, features, especially the mustache and the sharp, high-bridged nose. Unusual, too, is the choice of uncharacteristic curls for the *ushnisha,* or cranial protuberance, and for the cranium. The partially intact halo—not round but indented in the lower section—adheres strictly to Sichuan taste by showing, in the back, a procession of noble ladies in a landscape, while the more conventional representation of the front displays concentric bands filled with seated Buddhas. Finally, the construction of the pedestal is also innovative in that it is made of two rows of superimposed lotus leaves rather than one, the upper embellished with a

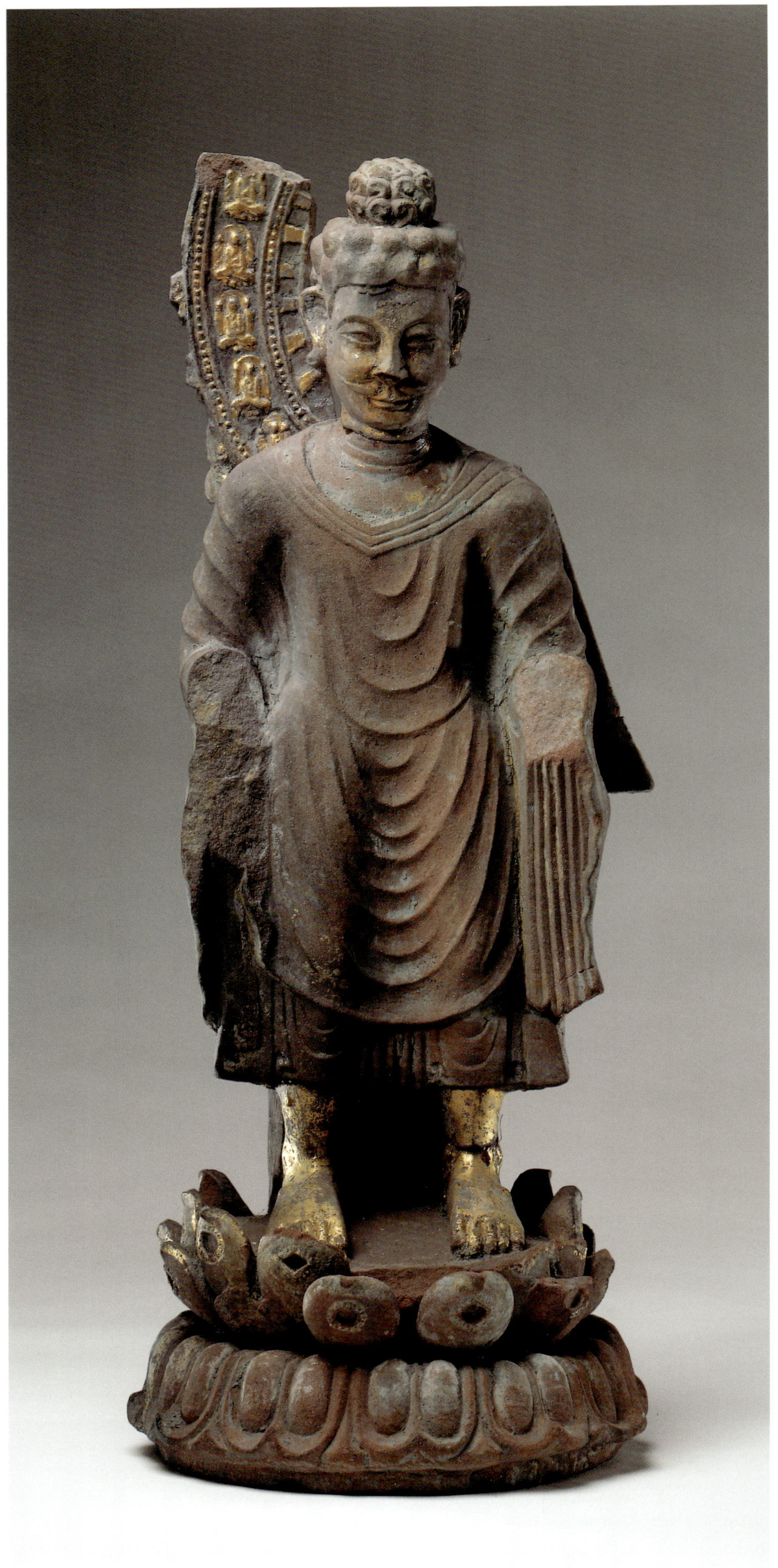

128, front

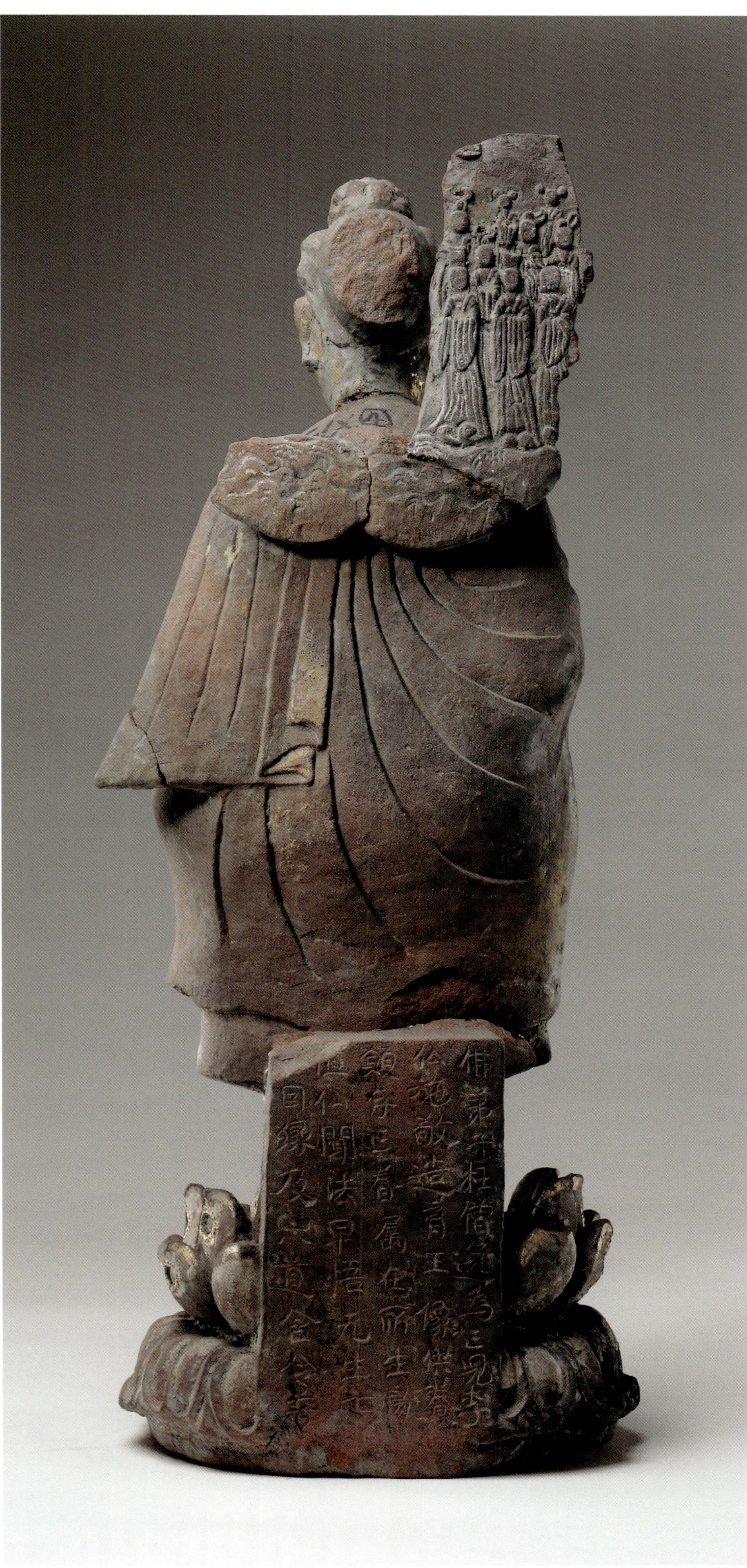

128, back

central rosette, the lower with down-turned double-lobed petals. Most of these traits are also present in all the other extant sculptures of the Ashoka Buddha, suggesting that they apply exclusively to this iconography.[1]

AFH

1. Additional, but much larger (lifesize), Ashoka-type Buddhas from Chengdu, Sichuan, are known; see Yuan Shuguang 2001: 19–38.

VI

Luoyang and After, 6th Century in the North

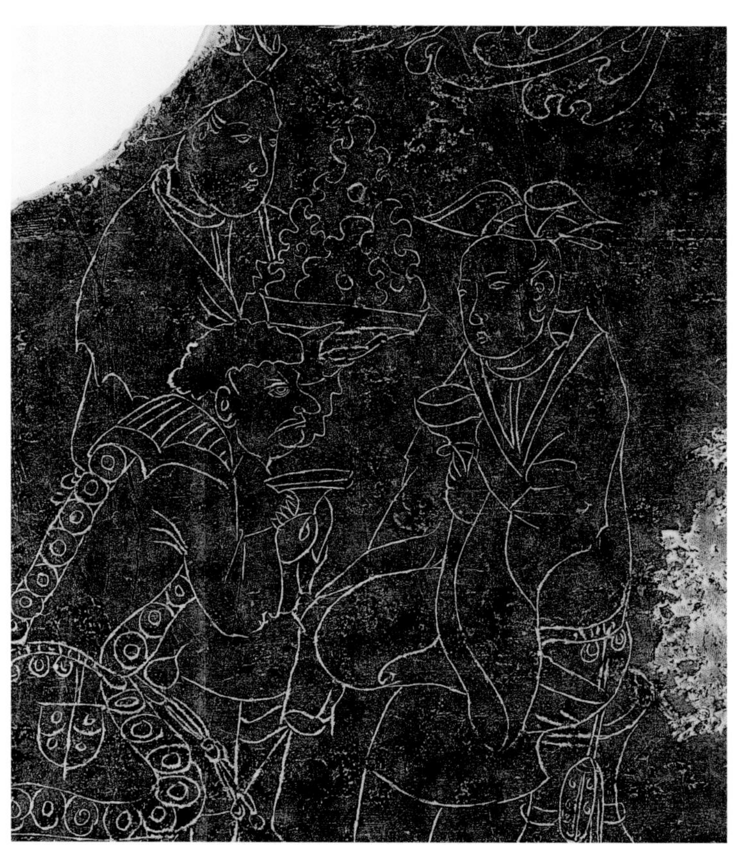

129
Two standing figures

Northern Wei dynasty (386–534), ca. 516
Terracotta with pigments
Height: a. 8 7/8 in. (22.7 cm);
b. 5 3/8 in. (13.8 cm)

130
Six heads

Northern Wei dynasty (386–534), ca. 516
Terracotta with pigments
Max. height 2 7/8 in. (7.3 cm)

Cat. nos. 129 and 130 excavated at Yongningsi, Luoyang, Henan Province, 1979–94
Institute of Archaeology, Chinese Academy of Social Sciences

Excav. report in Zhongguo shehui kexueyuan kaogu yanjiusuo 1996

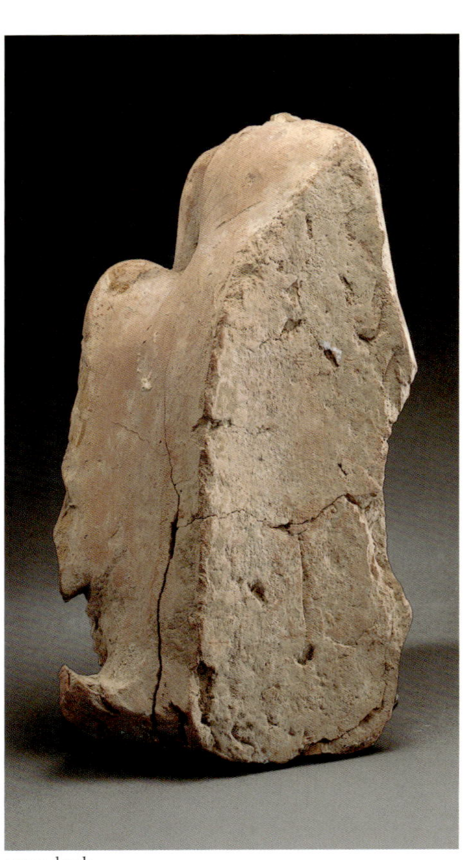

129a, back

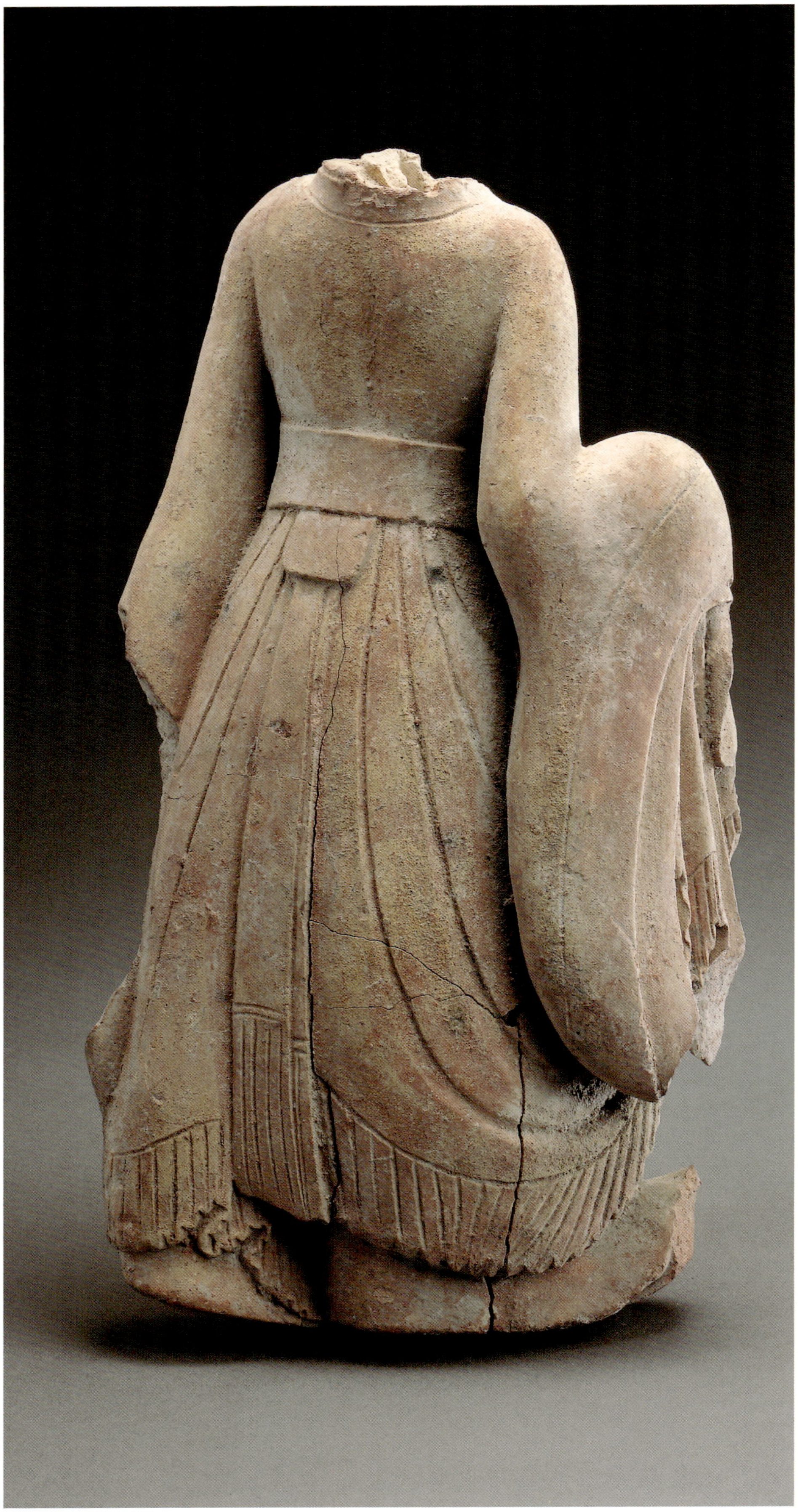

129a

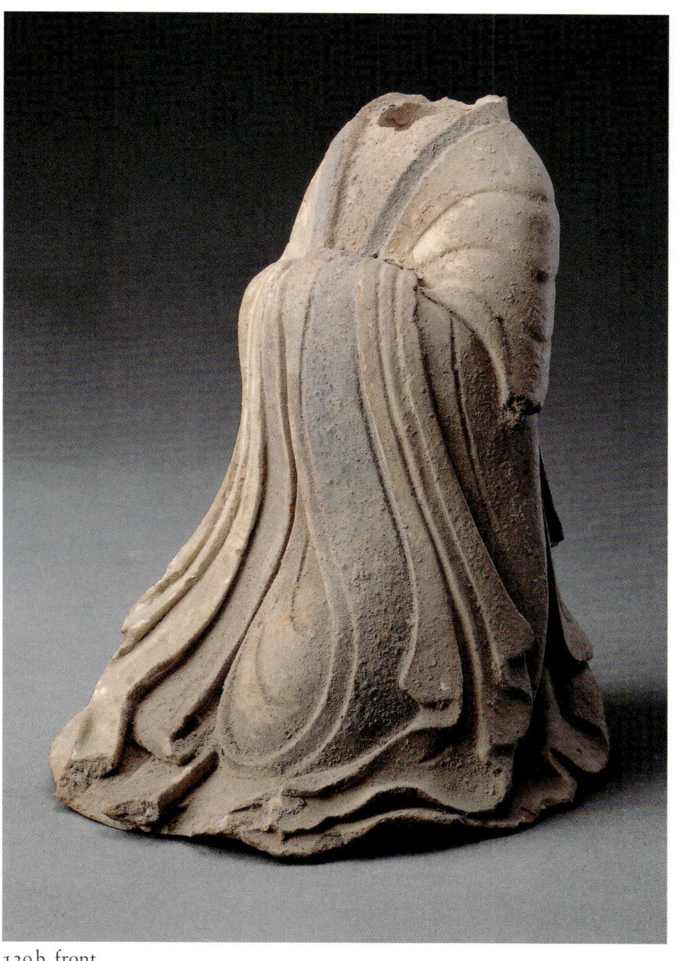

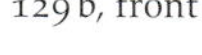
129b, front

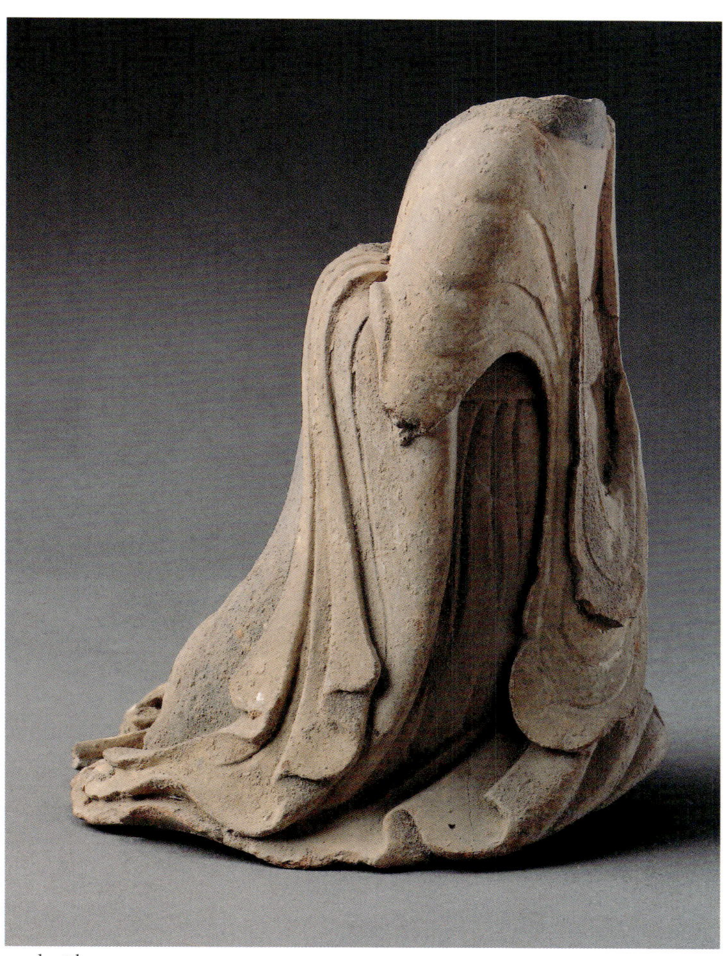

129b, side

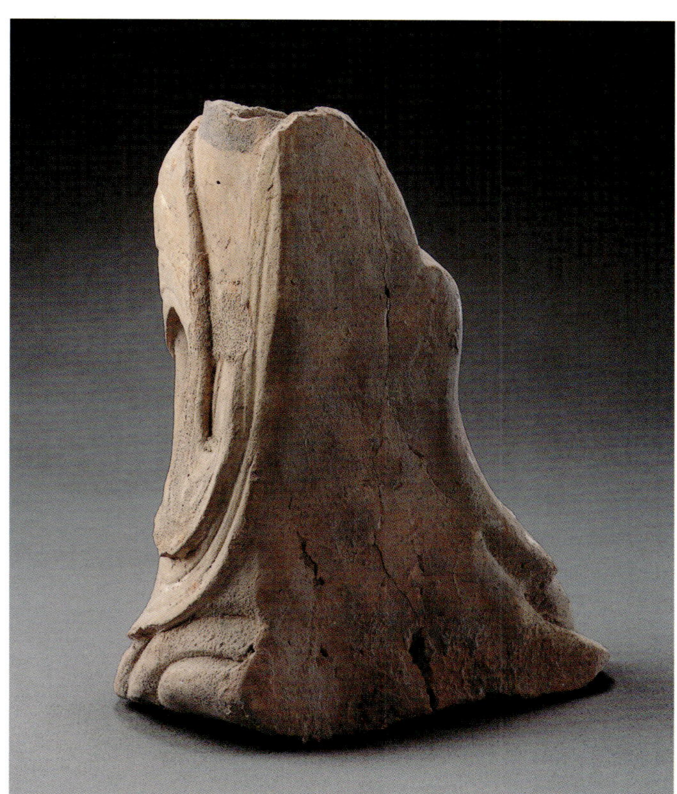

129b, back

These two headless figures and six heads (see overleaf) were found at the site of the great pagoda in the ruins of the imperial temple Yongningi, in Luoyang, capital of the Northern Wei dynasty from 494 to 534. The terracotta heads and bodies were made separately, but none of the complete heads found so far can be matched with the bodies.

The figures, both flat on one side, were presumably attached to the interior walls of the pagoda and originally may have been part of a scene with Buddhist deities and worshippers. It is likely that these religious, or perhaps purely decorative, tableaux were installed by the time the Dowager Empress Hu, patron of the temple, ascended the pagoda on its completion in 419. (The authors of the excavation report think possibly later.)[1] In any case, these terracottas were made less than thirty years after the move of the capital to Luoyang. This means that there was a dramatic change in sculptural style within a relatively short time. The change can be plainly perceived by comparing sculptures of the late Pingcheng period with the terracottas of Yongningsi.

The most remarkable aspect of the Yongningsi sculptures is the radical departure from the traditional Chinese approach to form in the plastic arts, particularly in the representation of humans. Instead of concentrating on intimations of life and movement, with summary treatment of details and an emphasis on the frontal prospect, they are fully three-dimensional, with greater attention to details of facial features, hairstyles, and headdresses. This change is perhaps attributable to the presence of large numbers of western craftsmen in Luoyang at the time. But the new style in sculpture, with the emphasis on volume, also incorporates a component drawn from the ancient artistic tradition of the Central Plain of China: the fluidity of line, which is a striking aspect of the robed terracotta bodies. This happy union makes the Yongningsi sculptures unique in the history of Chinese art.

The six heads give vivid portraits of people of different ethnic and class backgrounds. It is not possible at present to make specific identifications of ethnic groups beyond a broad division into Han and non-Han, but the headdresses provide some indication of class. The "hat" on the head (f) is actually a loosely woven gauze stiffened with lacquer that is placed over a smaller hat which covers the knot of hair (see cat. nos. 131b, 131j). It is secured to the hat by a clasp at the back (see below right). This assemblage can be seen on a wall painting from the tomb of the Tang prince Li Xian (see cat. no. 194). The same type of head covering appears in paintings and sculptures of aristocrats and senior court officials from the sixth to the early eighth century.

Heads (a) and (b) are those of young attendants; (c) and (d) are those of military officers (likely from the northern borders); and (e) is that of a monk. The last is possibly Ananda, one of Buddha's chief disciples. This identification has been suggested by the discovery of another head with features commonly associated with those of Kashyapa, the other chief disciple.[2]

JCYW

1. Zhongguo shehui kexueyuan kaogu yanjiusuo 1996.
2. Ibid., fig. 29.2 on p. 44.

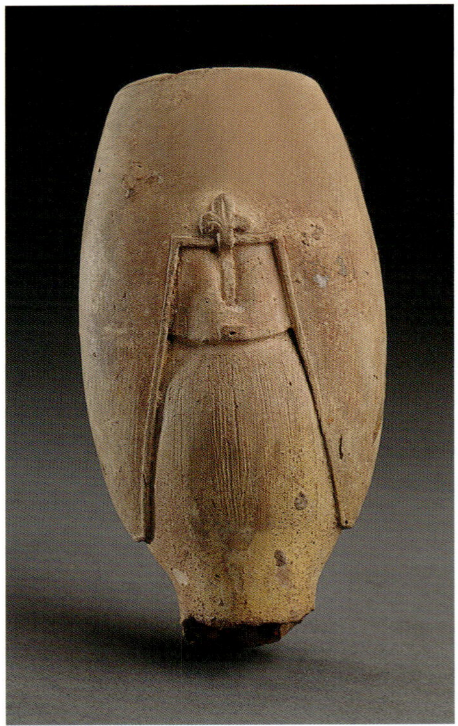

130d, back

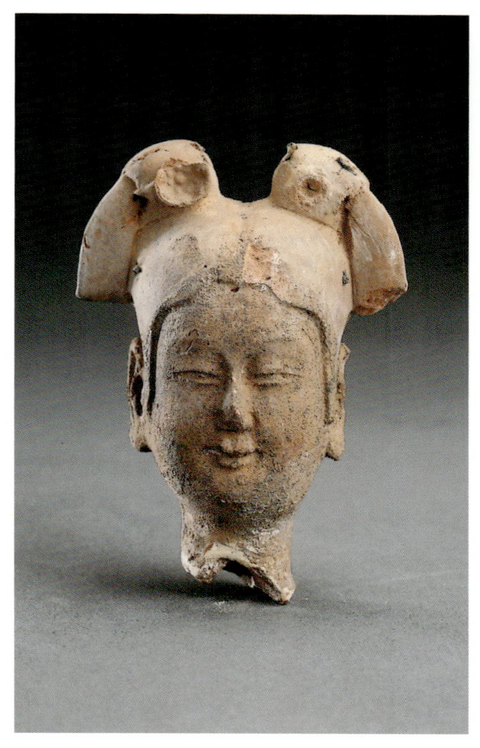
130a

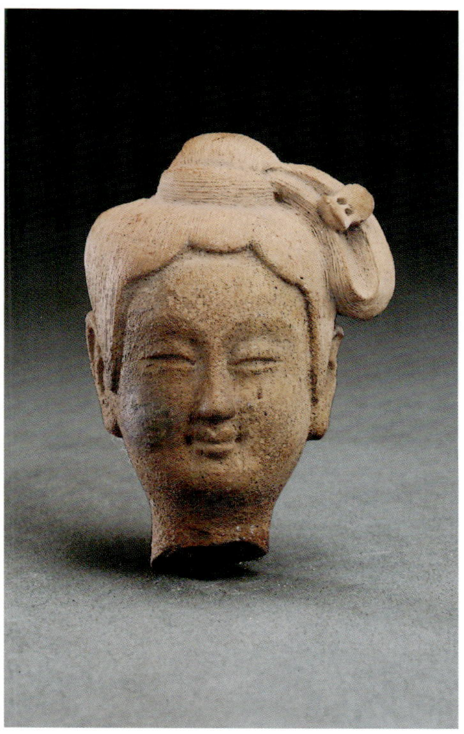
130b

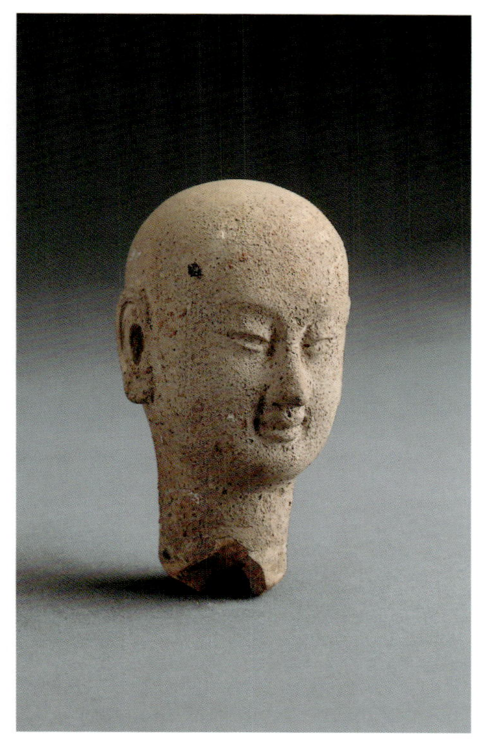
130c

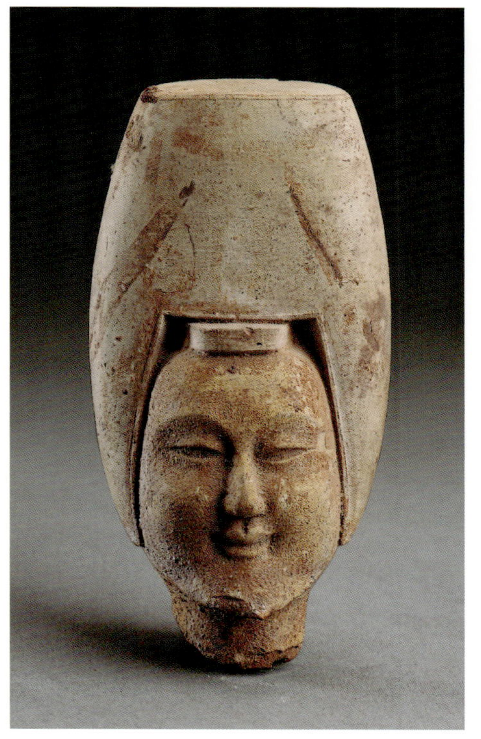
130d

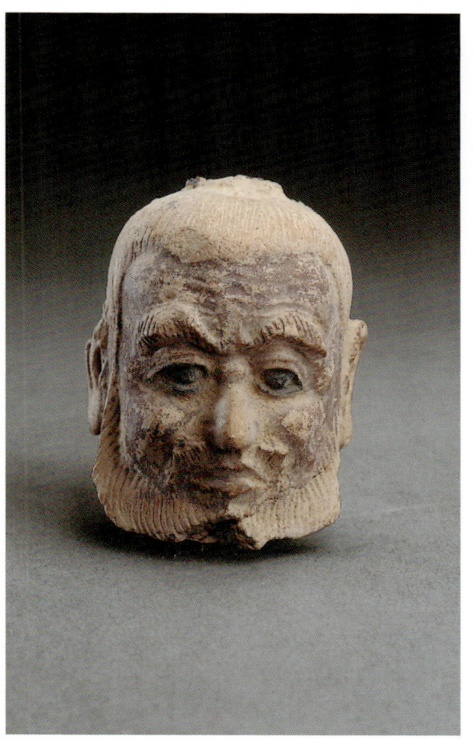
130e

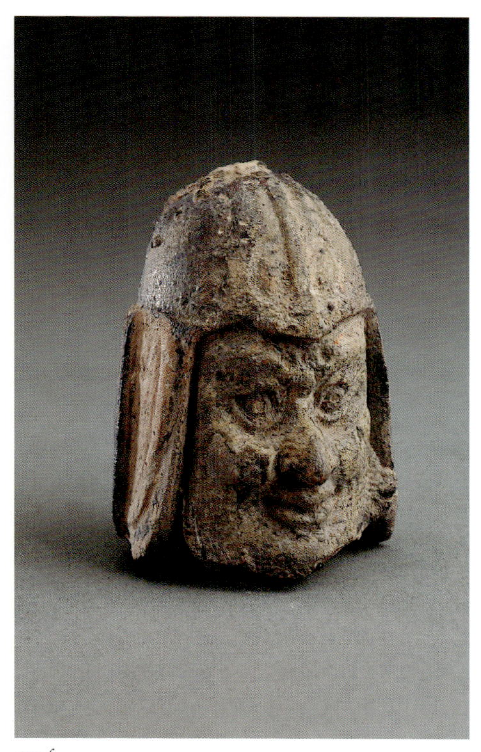
130f

131

Ten figures

Northern Wei dynasty (386–534)
Earthenware with pigments
Max. height 8 5/8 in. (22 cm)
Excavated at Yanshi, Henan Province, 1989
Yanshi City Museum

Reference: Higuchi 1998: 2

These ten pottery figures were found in burials in Yanshi to the east of the old city of Luoyang, capital of the Northern Wei from 494 to 534. They represent social types the deceased would have come across in life, including a fashionably dressed lady (a), civil and military officials (b, c and f, g, h, respectively) and a musician or two (i, j).

The Yanshi figures are stylistically similar to the small sculptures of Yongningsi (see cat. nos. 129, 130) but not as fine. They are sculptures in the round, with naturalistic depiction of drapery, which is rare in Chinese art of any period. This is particularly noticeable in the female figure (a), who wears a high-waisted dress that was likely to have been newly introduced from Central Asia. Both the dress and the sculptural style convey an unmistakable impression of strong western influence.

Another garment worthy of note is the sleeved coat worn by two of the figures (d, e), which provides the earliest clear depiction of this article of clothing in China. The coat with false sleeves, not meant for the arms, originated in the ancient Iranian world and spread throughout the Eurasian steppes.[1] This style of coat must have reached the northern borders of China by the late fifth century and come to Luoyang with the Xianbei from Pingcheng or traveled directly to Luoyang at the beginning of the sixth century. In any case, it was adopted by the Xianbei and is the most common garment seen on pottery figures of the Northern Zhou (557–581), where the ruling classes all came from the northern garrisons of the Northern Wei.[2]

Although the sleeved coat may not have been native to the Xianbei, it was obviously associated with the Xianbei from the north. Wearing this coat would thus have been in defiance of Emperor Xiaowendi's famous edict, pronounced on arrival in Luoyang in 494, forbidding the use of Xianbei language and costumes. Either the edict was not strictly observed or it was ignored after the emperor's death in 499. It would seem that, in spite of Xiaowendi's strenuous efforts to promote sinification, some Xianbei customs still persisted in Luoyang. The culture of Luoyang in the early sixth century was thus a mixture of Han Chinese, Xianbei, and western elements.

JCYW

1. For an account of the sleeved coat from its origins down to modern times in Europe, see Knauer 1978.
2. There are numerous examples illustrated in Yun Anzhi 1992. See, in particular, pl. 192, an image of figures wearing the sleeved coat from the tomb of Dugu Zang (d. 578), a relative of Empress Dugu of the Sui.

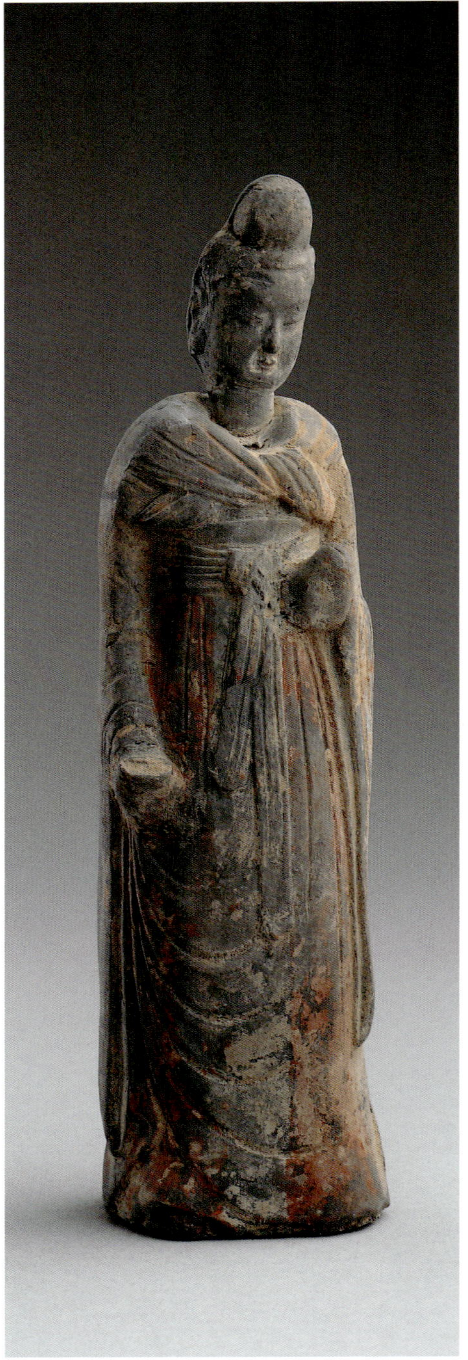

131a

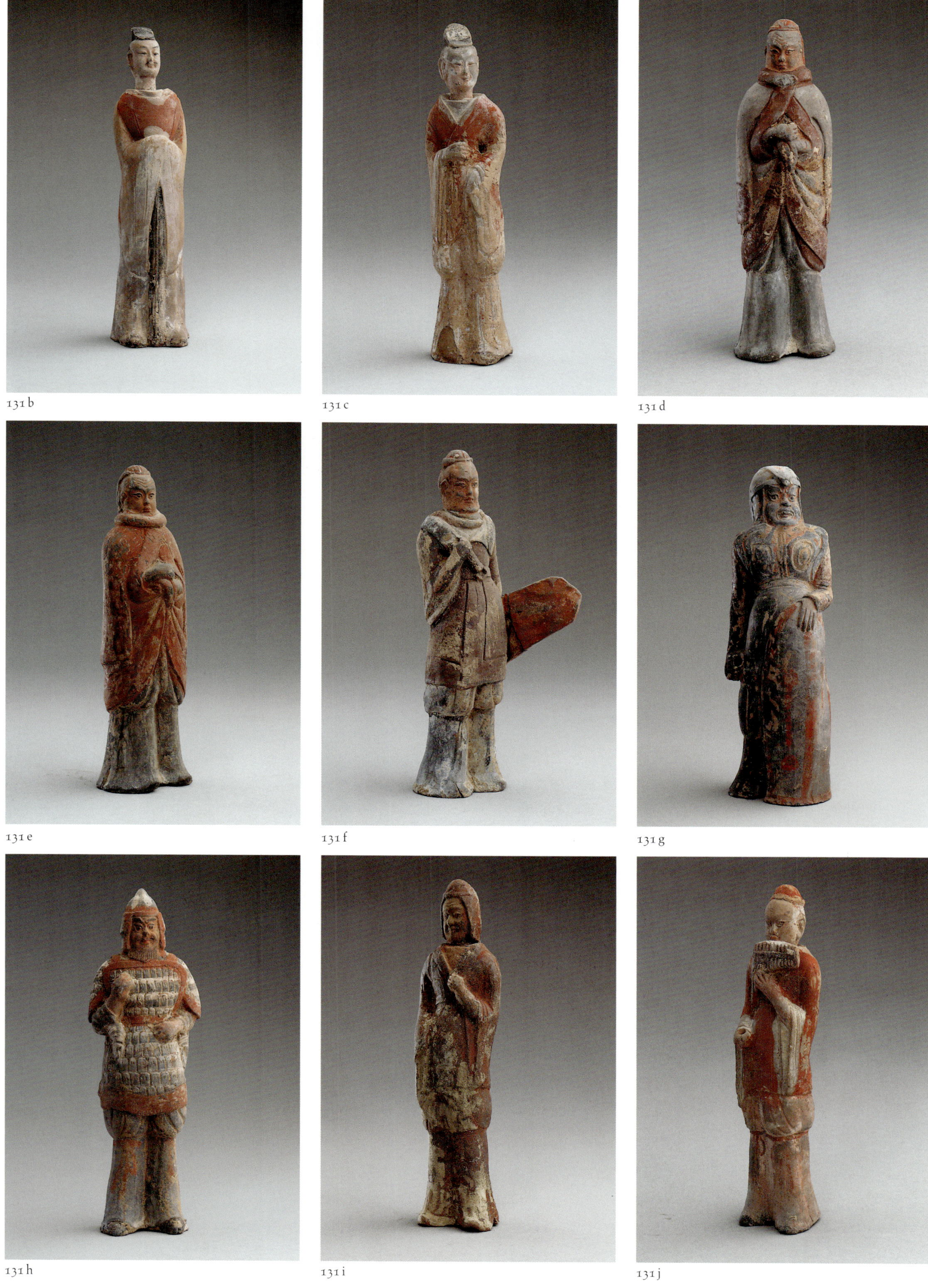

131b

131c

131d

131e

131f

131g

131h

131i

131j

132
Officiant

Eastern Wei dynasty (534–550), ca. 550
Earthenware with pigments
Height 11¾ in. (29.8 cm)
Excavated from the tomb (dated 550) of a Ruru princess, Cixian, Hebei Province, 1979
Cixian Office of Cultural Properties Preservation

Excav. report in *Wenwu* 1984.4

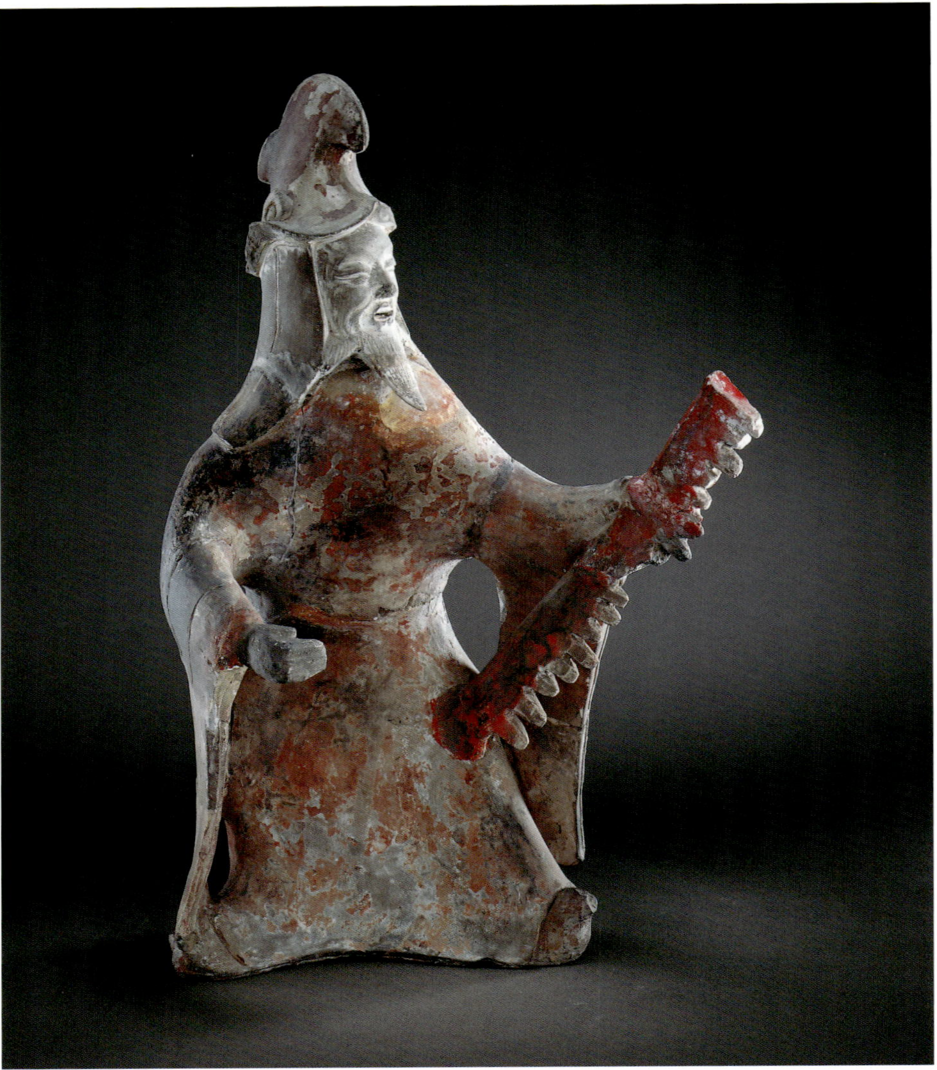

This elderly man, one of the more intriguing sculptures excavated from the tomb of the Ruru princess Linhe (538–550; see also cat. nos. 133, 134),[1] is shown walking with his left leg slightly forward and holding in his left hand an unusual comblike implement.[2] His beard has been carefully styled into three points, and his mouth is open. The figure wears a broad-hemmed long red garment and pointed shoes. The shaped hat, a type made of felt or some other dense material, has long flaps at the sides and back and is adorned with small plaques, probably intended to represent metalwork. Hats with such adornment and tunic-like garments have parallels to clothing worn in the western reaches of Central Asia,[3] and the sculpture presumably represents someone from that region.

Three other figures of this type are known. Two are tomb sculptures. One is in the Nelson-Atkins Museum of Art, Kansas City,[4] and the other was found, with several figures of musicians, in the tomb of Kudi Huiluo (see also cat. no. 147), dated 562.[5] Both wear long open-necked red tunics over trousers, shaped hats, and shoes with pointed toes. A fourth image is depicted on a brick from a tomb excavated in Dengxian, Henan, in 1957.[6] The garments of the figure on the relief from Dengxian are also painted red, and he holds a fan in one hand and in the other an implement—similar to the one seen here—composed of a long, narrow stick from which dangles are suspended by a piece of rope or thread. The figure in the Dengxian relief leads a procession of four additional figures who appear to be dancing.[7]

The conjunction of elderly figures with musicians raises the possibility that the comblike implement is an instrument, perhaps a rattle used to establish the beat for the music. However, no such instruments are known. It may also be understood as a staff or batonlike instrument, used either as part of a dance or to mark time. Because of their association with musicians and their presence in tombs, it has been suggested that such figures represent shamans,[8] although there is no evidence to indicate that they entered trancelike states or communicated with otherworldly forces. It seems more likely that they had a more mundane, albeit ritual, function.

Two of the four figures of this type were found in burials associated with persons of foreign (non-Han Chinese) backgrounds, which raises the possibility that the sculpture from the tomb of the Ruru princess and comparable images illustrate an unrecorded, and as yet unidentified, festal or funerary practice, that involved dancers and musicians. It is also possible that the activity in question represents traditions transmitted to China from one of the many diverse cultures of Central Asia.

DPL

1. Cixian wenwhuaguan 1984: 1–16.
2. It seems likely that this instrument is at least partially reconstructed. There is a break in the center, and the red pigment does not match that found on the garments.
3. Yatsenko 2000: 113.
4. Fontein and Wu 1973, fig. 70.
5. Wang Kelin 1979: 377–402.
6. Henan sheng wenhuaju wenwu gongzuodui, 1958: 26, pl. 30.
7. Zhao Yonghong 1994: 136–43.
8. Fontein and Wu 1973: 146–47.

133
Camel

Eastern Wei dynasty (534–550)
Earthenware with pigments
Height 9⅞ in. (25 cm)
Excavated from the tomb (dated 550) of a Ruru princess, Cixian, Hebei Province, 1979
Cixian Office of Cultural Properties Preservation

EXCAV. REPORT in *Wenwu* 1984.4

By the third century, camels had been added to the ensemble of sculptures placed in tombs, and they are standard in structures dating from the late fifth to the eighth century. The kneeling posture of this camel, one of two excavated from the tomb of Princess Linhe (see also cat. nos. 132, 134),[1] is quite distinctive and first appears in the mid-sixth century. Laden with rolls of cloth, saddleboards, saddlebags, and other accoutrements, the camel rests the left knee on the ground in a fashion that suggests he is either getting up or lowering himself to the ground. As is typical of sculptures produced in the mid-sixth century, the figure is rendered two-dimensionally and lacks the sense of volume found in the few extant sculptures produced in the first decades of the sixth century at the Northern Wei (386–534) court in Luoyang.

A member of the Ruru nationality based in Central Asia, Princess Linhe married into the Gao family, which controlled the Eastern Wei (534–550) and Northern Qi (550–577) dynasties in northeastern China. The marriage was part of a treaty intended both to neutralize Turkic challenges to the Ruru and to bolster the position of the Gao within China. The princess died at the age of twelve and was buried in accordance with her aristocratic rank. Her tomb comprises a long passageway leading to three small antechambers and a large domed coffin chamber. Murals on the walls of the tomb show courtly attendants, mostly female, and mystical creatures such as dragons and phoenixes.[2] The tomb also contained stone lanterns and other objects, metalwork, glazed pottery vessels, and 1,640 funerary sculptures.

DPL

1. Cixian wenhuaguan 1984: 1–16.
2. Tang Chi 1984: 10–15.

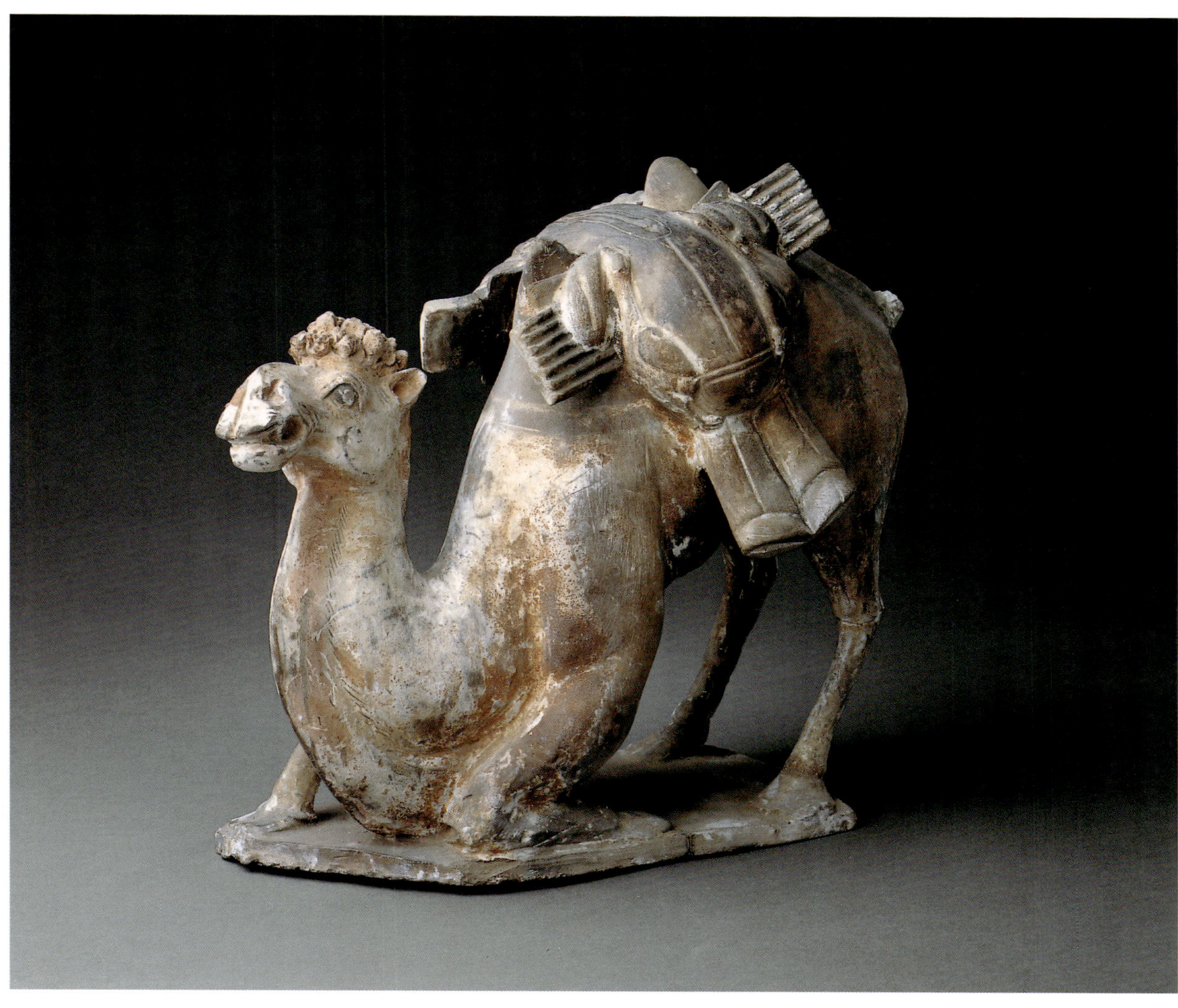

134
Ornamental plaque with figure and apsaras

Eastern Wei dynasty (534–550)
Gold with pearl, amber, and stone inlay
Length 3 in. (10 cm)
Excavated from the tomb (dated 550) of a Ruru princess, Cixian, Hebei Province, 1979
Cixian Office of Cultural Properties Preservation

Excav. report in *Wenwu* 1984.4

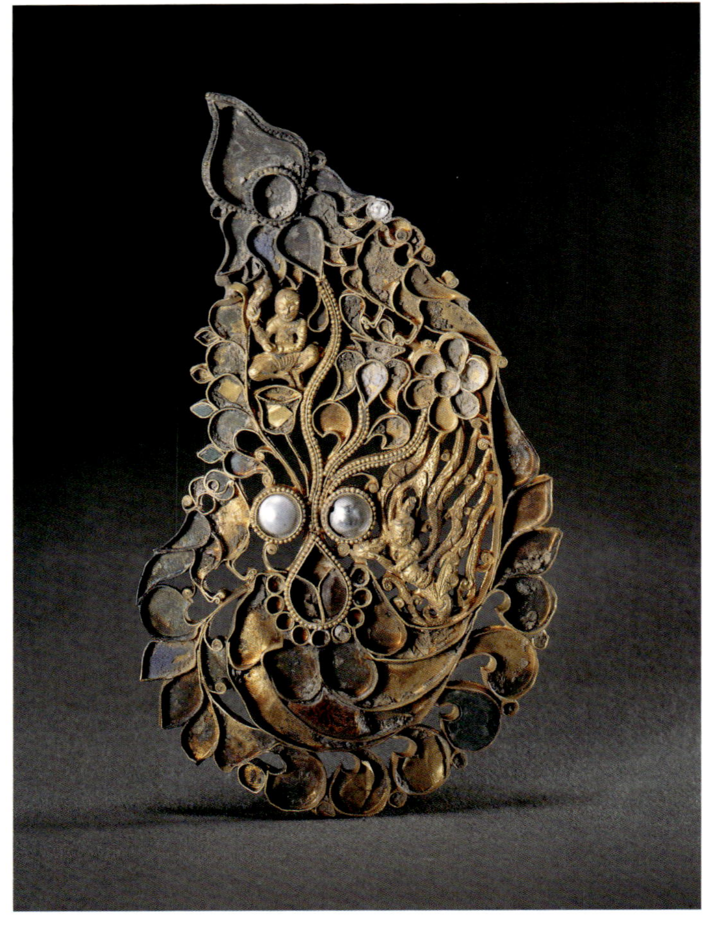

With the exception of a stunning necklace found in the early seventh-century royal tomb of Li Jingxun (cat. no. 187) and a more modest piece from the slightly earlier burial of Kudi Huilo (cat. no. 147), a court official, little information remains concerning the use of personal adornment in China in the fifth and sixth centuries. Few pieces of jewelry are found in tombs, and depictions of such ornaments on funerary sculptures are almost nonexistent. The elaborate necklace that embellishes the late fifth-century figure of a dancer excavated at the site of Yanbei Teachers College in Shaanxi (cat. no. 51) is a notable exception. It would seem that, in light of this dearth of evidence, objects made of precious metals were removed from tombs prior to scientific excavations.

This ornamental plaque is the better preserved of the two found in the tomb of the Ruru princess (Princess Linhe) and is part of a group of fifty-two objects made of gold, including two Byzantine coins.[1] Little information is given in the excavation report regarding the plaque. However, it is possible that it was attached in some fashion to an article of clothing. Formed in the shape of a leaf, the ornament is decorated with sinuous paired lines of granulation, presumably intended to represent the veins. The two large pearls in the center, the green stones (possibly malachite) in some of the cavities, and traces of amber hint at the brilliance of the original decoration, in which semiprecious stones filled the empty enclosures. Two imposing parrotlike birds, shown with their heads twisted backward, perch in the upper left and middle right edges. Although some species of parrot are indigenous to China, other birds were imported from southeastern Asia as early as the third century.[2]

At the upper left, a seated boy holds a flower, possibly a lotus, in his uplifted hand. At the lower right, an *apsaras*, a celestial figure introduced to China as part of Buddhist imagery, wafts beneath two flowers. The thin, elongated form and fluttering scarves of the *apsaras* are comparable to those of celestials that embellish the outer edges of an altarpiece dedicated to the Buddha Maitreya in The Metropolitan Museum of Art (38.158.1). The latter is dated by inscription to 524, and it is possible that the plaque was made a decade or more before it was buried in the tomb of Princess Linhe in 550.

DPL

1. Cixian wenhuaguan 1984: 7.
2. Schafer 1963: 99–102.

135
Civil official

Northern Qi dynasty (550–577)
Earthenware with pigments
Height 56⅛ in. (142.5 cm)

136
Dancing figure

Northern Qi dynasty (550–577)
Earthenware with pigments
Height 11 in. (28 cm)

Cat. nos. 135 and 136 excavated at Wanzhang, Cixian, Hebei Province, 1987
Institute of Archaeology, Chinese Academy of Social Sciences

EXCAV. REPORT in *Kaogu* 1990.7

Although there is no epitaph tablet identifying the deceased, the magnificence of a tomb excavated at Wanzhang, Hebei, and the wealth of grave goods indicate that it was made for a member of the imperial family, possibly Gao Yang, a son of Gao Huan, founder of the Northern Qi dynasty (550–557).[1] Gao Yang, who served as Wenxuandi, the first emperor of the subsequent Northern Qi, ruled from 550 until his death in 559.[2]

More than two thousand goods, including one thousand five hundred pottery sculptures, were excavated from the tomb. With the exception of two large figures placed outside the stone door between the second and third antechambers,[3] the sculptures were found in the coffin chamber itself. They range in height from about eleven to nineteen inches. In addition to housing a large complement of military figures, some mounted and some standing, with variations in armor and clothing indicative of rank, the tomb also contained horses and other animals, including five camels, as well as eighty-three musicians and thirteen dancers.

The two largest figures in the tomb, of which cat. no. 135 is one, represent civil officials. (The location of the second figure

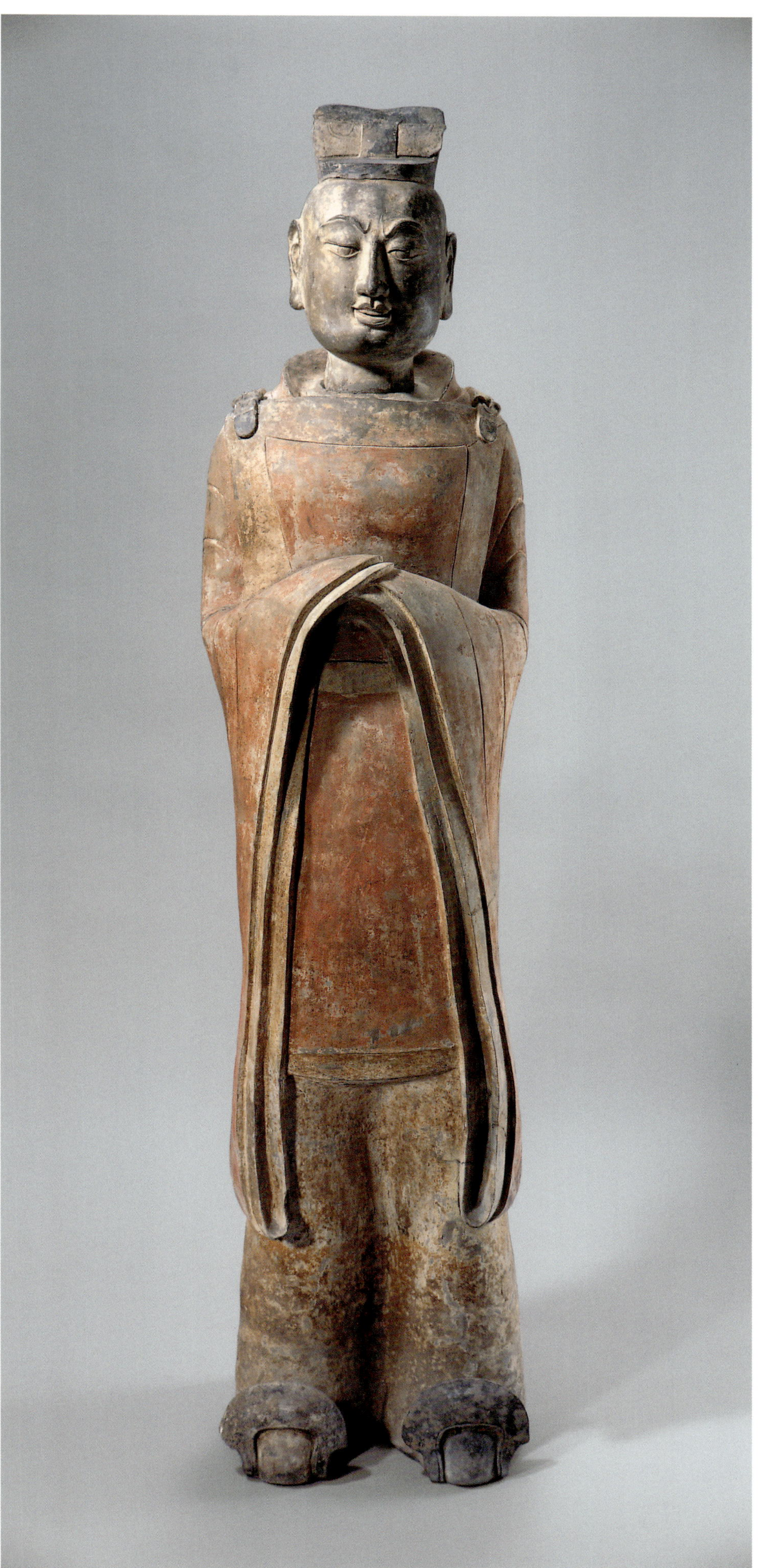

135

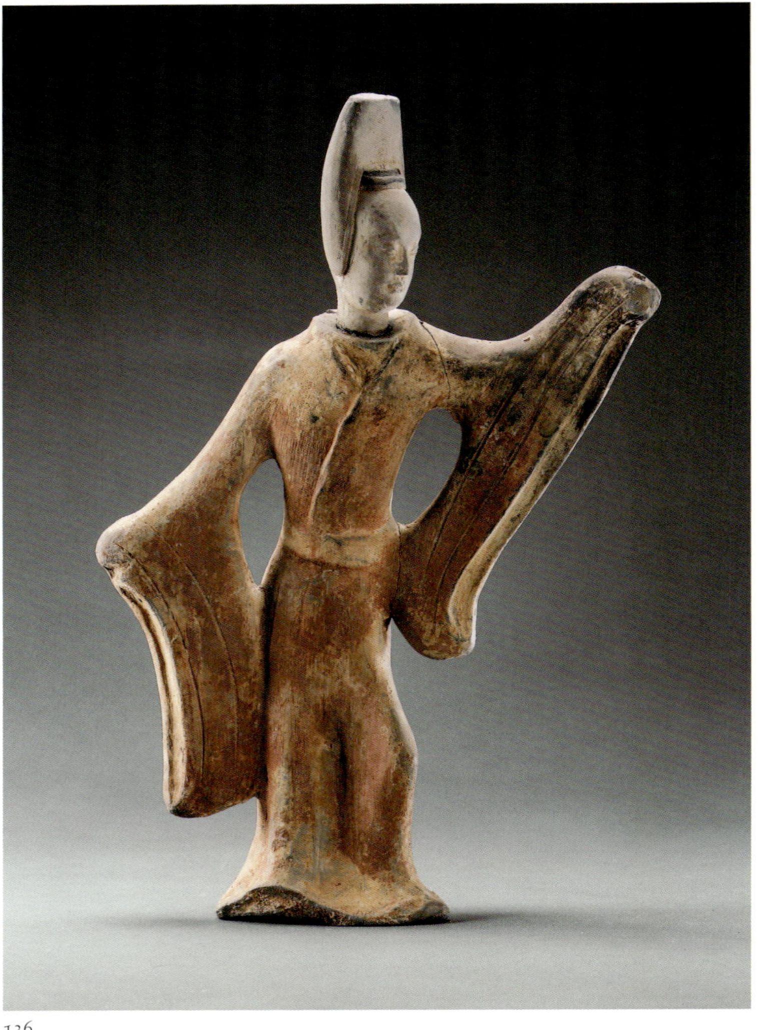

136

is unknown, but the two appear to have been a pair.) Nearly life-size, they measure about fifty-six inches high. Although the excavation report is not explicit, it seems likely that they are the sculptures described as placed outside the stone doors, made of earthenware, and painted in shades of red, with touches of black and white. As is often the case in sixth-century funerary figures, the officials wear a breastplate over the court clothing. They are shown standing frontally, with hands folded together at the waist. It is possible that the hands once rested on the hilt of a large sword or some other weapon. In addition to their administrative responsibilities, civil officials likely served as a type of honor guard for members of the imperial family and the aristocracy. Their prominent position in the tomb most likely reflects the importance of their role at court.

The smaller figure (cat. no. 136) is one of the dancers from the tomb. She wears a flowing outer garment that is belted at the waist and has dramatically flared sleeves. The headdress, which consists of a small hat covered by stiff gauze, indicates Han Chinese ethnicity. Such headdresses are seen in early Chinese paintings and tomb figures and in donor portraits in sixth-century cave temples at Longmen and Gongxian. She stands with arms outstretched and left knee bent, as if captured in a moment of performance. Nonetheless, the figure is conceived as two-dimensional, with an emphasis on front and back views rather than movement in space. DPL

1. Zhongguo shehui kexueyuan kaogu yanjiusuo et al. 1990: 601–7.
2. Xu Guangyi 1996: 71.
3. Such doors, which first appear in high-ranking tombs in the mid-sixth century, become more common in the seventh and eighth centuries. See Fong 1991a: 155.

137
Guardian warrior with shield

Northern Qi dynasty (550–577), ca. 566
Earthenware with pigments
Height 26¾ in. (68 cm)
Excavated from the tomb (dated 566) of Cui Ang, Pingshan, Hebei Province, 1968
Hebei Provincial Museum

Excav. report in *Wenwu* 1973.11

The largest figure from the well-furnished tomb of Cui Ang,[1] this pottery sculpture of a guardian warrior belongs to a subset of tomb guardians popular in northeastern China in the sixth century. Presumably placed at or near the entrance of the tomb, the warrior has glowering eyes, a large nose, and a detailed mustache and beard. The facial hair suggests that he represents one of the many non-Han groups found in North China at the time, possibly someone of Central Asian origin.[2]

The figure wears a helmet, armor, and a heavy belt from which are suspended implements. The armor is presumably made of leather and further strengthened by the addition of breastplates, neck and shoulder guards, and cording. He stands in a frontal position as if at attention in a military setting and holds his right hand in a position that suggests he is lifting a lance. The left hand rests on top of an enormous shield, which is more than half his size.

Four small figures in high relief embellish the shield, which also has a leonine face at the center. The two at the top appear to be dancers, while the two near the base have hooves and wings and seem to be running. At times termed "thunder monsters," hoofed and winged creatures play a decorative and auspicious role in funerary and Buddhist imagery in the sixth century,[3] and it seems likely that they have a similar meaning on the shield. The *Suishu* (History of the Sui) mentions warriors holding shields decorated in gold with lions' heads as accompanying the emperor.[4] It is possible that the warrior excavated from the tomb of Cui Ang and comparable figures represent a type of praetorian guard that served the elite of the northeast.

Unlike most of the guardian warriors found in tombs, figures of this type are placed singly, not in pairs. One of the earliest known examples was excavated from the tomb of Yuan Shao, a grandson of the Northern Wei emperor Xiaowendi (r. 471–99), who was buried in 528.[5] Others have been found in tombs such as that of Lady Zhao Huren[6] and that of Kudi Huiluo,[7] an important official during the Northern Qi dynasty (550–577). After the Sui reunification of the north, the type spread from the northeast to the northwest, where examples continue to be found in elite tombs, such as that of Li Jingxun,[8] the granddaughter of Li Xian (cat. nos. 157, 158), and important officials at the Northern Zhou court.

Cui Ang, a member of a distinguished family from the northeast,[9] was a high-ranking civil official during the Northern Qi dynasty. In addition to containing a large number of pottery sculptures, his tombs, like those of the other individuals mentioned above, also included examples of the glazed ceramics with appliqué and other decoration that were in vogue during the mid- to late sixth century.

DPL

1. Hebei sheng bowuguan wenwu guanli 1973: 27–38.
2. Grousset 1934: 128, fig. 87.
3. Bush 1975a: 24–55; Bush 1975b: 19–34.
4. Dien 1981–82: 32, n. 157.
5. Luoyang bowuguan 1973: 222, pls. 12.1–2.
6. Cixian wenhuaguan 1977, fig. 3.8, pl. 8.3.
7. Wang Kelin 1979: 399–400, pl. 7.1.
8. Zhongguo shehui kexueyuan kaogu yanjiusuo 1980: 10, 25–28, pl. 20.
9. Shandong sheng wenwu kaogu yanjiusuo 1984: 221–44. See also Ebrey 1978.

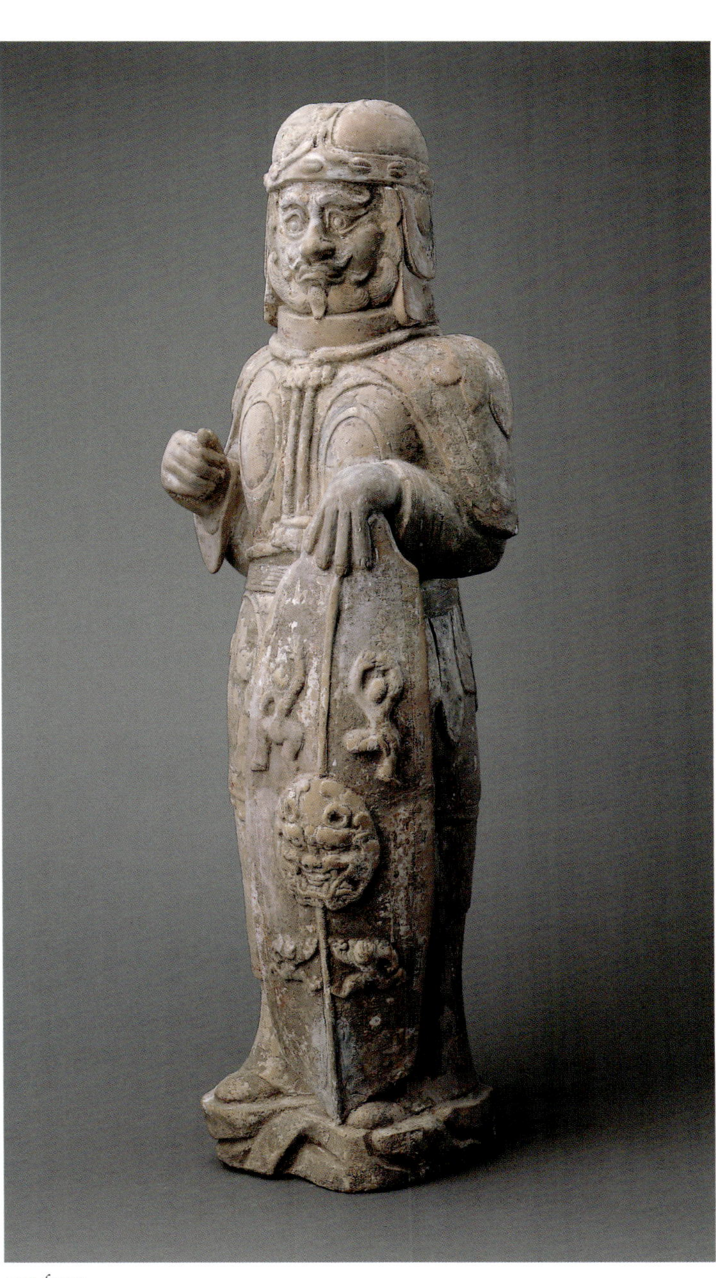

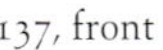

137, front

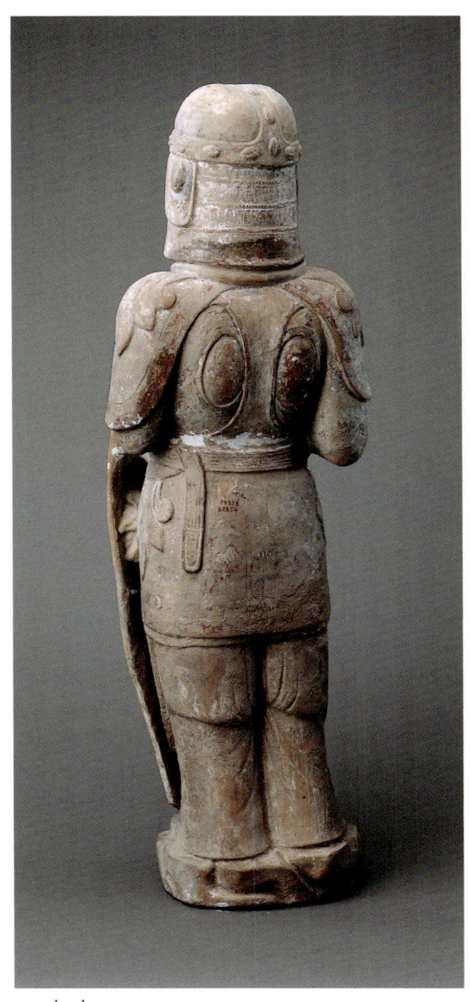

137, back

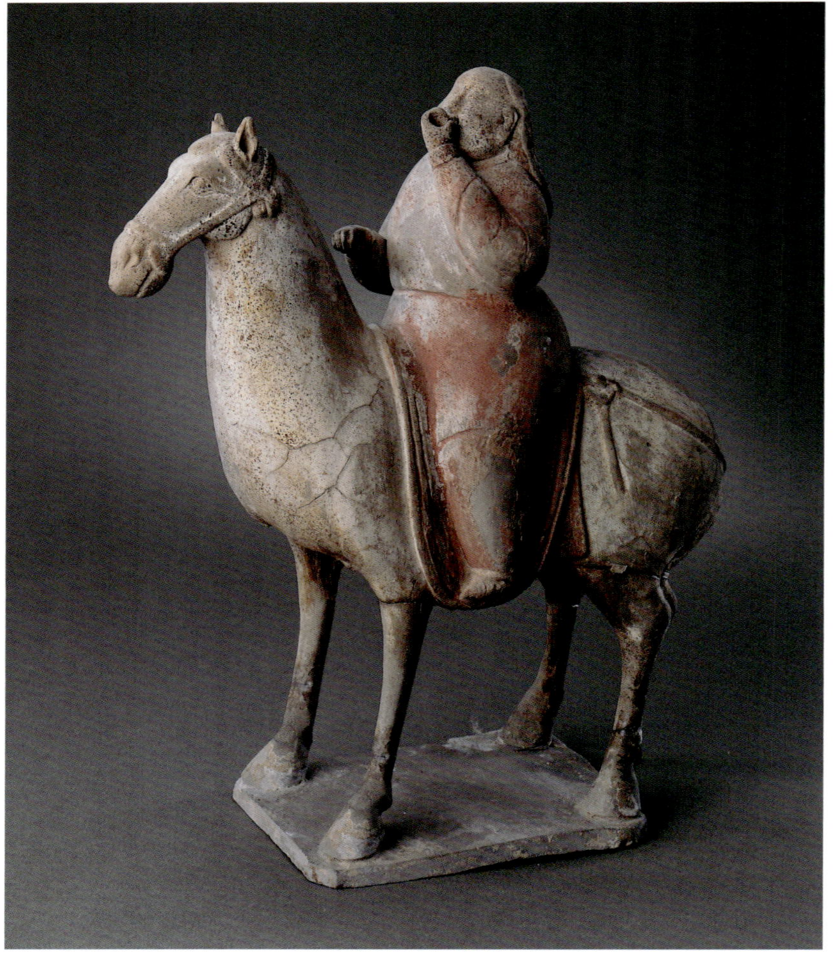

138
Mounted horn player

Northern Qi dynasty (550–577)
Earthenware with pigments
Height 10 in. (25 cm)
Excavated from the tomb of Heba Chang, Taiyuan, Shanxi Province, 1998
Taiyuan City Institute of Archaeology

EXCAV. REPORT in *Wenwu* 2003.3

Horse-mounted military bands beating drums and tooting horns, known in Chinese as *guchui,* were introduced from the steppes in the Han dynasty.[1] The instruments played came to include other winds and percussions, such as flutes and panpipes, and the bands became established complements of the official processions. Not only did they accompany troops on the march but they joined the honor guard of high-ranking officials, signifying their status and prestige.

This handsomely crafted pottery figure of a horn player has a partially shaved forehead and wears his long hair in thirteen neatly braided pigtails tied together with a ribbon to fall just above his waist. The unusual hairstyle is recorded in a seventh-century text as that characteristic of the nomads who lived on the steppes far to the north. The player wears a long red jacket with narrow sleeves and red trousers that are rolled up at the bottom. His horn was apparently made of perishable material and has not survived, but it would likely have been the long, curved type as seen in comparable examples.[2] His left hand raised to his mouth, his puffed cheeks, and animated face indicate that he is engaged in a spirited performance.

The figure was excavated from the tomb of Heba Chang, a general from an eminent nomadic family of the Northern Wei dynasty (386–534). Also found in the tomb were figures of mounted drummers, armored guards, and standard-bearers, which appear to have been part of an official procession. It is difficult to assess the size of the procession, since the tomb was heavily looted and only a fraction of the original contents is extant. But we can assume that the complete set would have been considerable in number, as the epitaph in the tomb records that Heba Chang was prefect of Kuozhou and held the title Commander Unequaled in Honor. These figures were meant not only to accompany him in the afterlife but also to signify the illustrious career that he enjoyed during his lifetime.

ZS

1. Ji Wei and Han Shaojie 2002.
2. Shaanxi sheng wenwu guanli weiyuanhui 1959, pl. 3.

139
Covered jar with appliqué decoration

Northern Qi dynasty (550–577)
Glazed earthenware
Height 15¾ in. (39.8 cm)

140
Ewer with spout in the shape of a chicken head

Northern Qi dynasty (550–577)
Glazed earthenware
Height 19 in. (48.2 cm)

141
Lamp with appliqué decoration

Northern Qi dynasty (550–577)
Glazed earthenware
Height 19¾ in. (50.2 cm)

Cat. nos. 139, 140, and 141 excavated from the tomb (dated 570) of Lou Rui, Taiyuan, Shanxi Province, 1980
Shanxi Institute of Archaeology

EXCAV. REPORT in *Wenwu* 1983.10

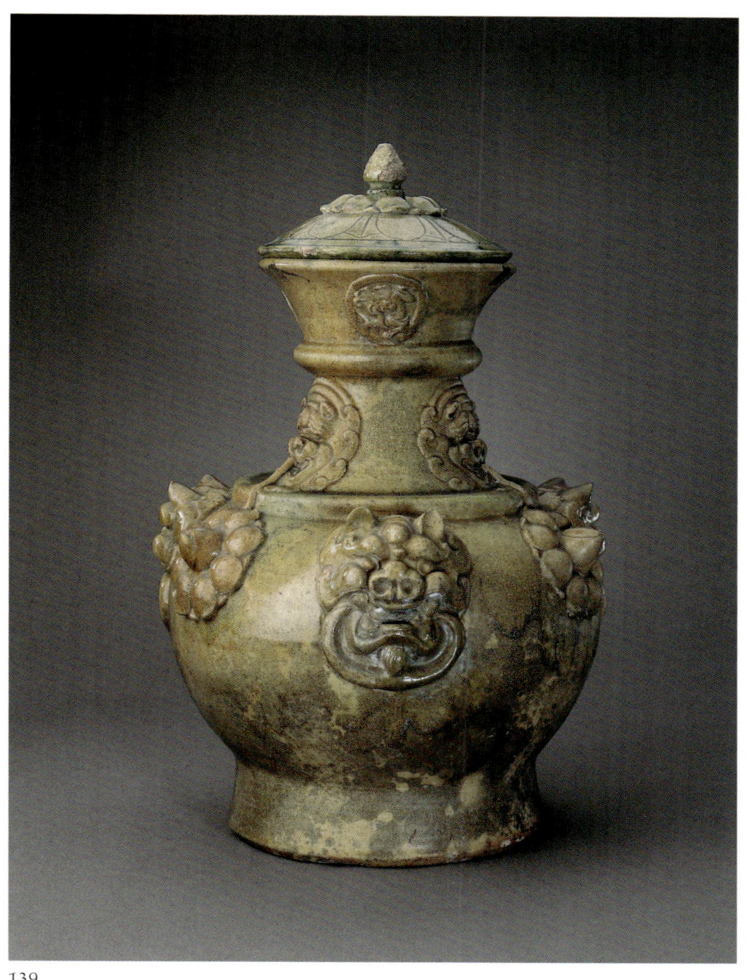
139

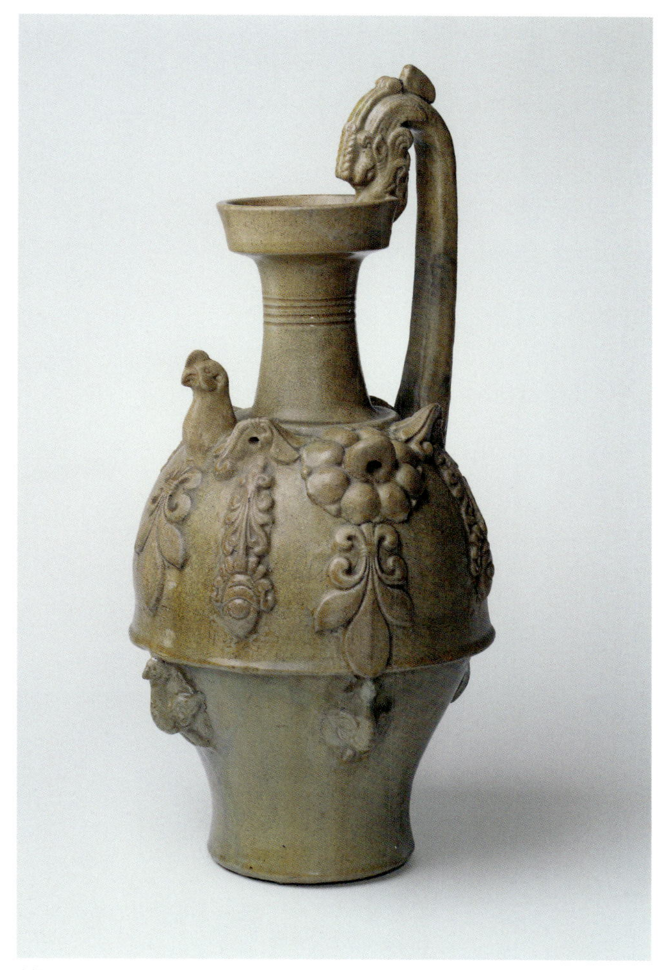
140

These three pottery pieces are from the tomb of Lou Rui (d. 570), one of the grandest Northern Qi tombs in Taiyuan. The immediately noticeable feature of these pots is the appliqué decoration. The common observation is that they were made in imitation of metalware. However, it can also be said that the preference for relief work, whether in stone carving or appliqué on pottery, is generally indicative of western influence. (Traditionally in China, decoration is generally applied on the surface of the object by techniques such as painting, engraving, and inlay.)

Lou Rui was a member of one of the most influential families of the Northern Qi dynasty (550–577). He was brought up by his uncle Lou Zhao, who fought alongside Gao Huan, founder of the dynasty, in all his military campaigns on his path to power. Lou Zhao's sister, Lou Rui's aunt, married Gao Huan and became the dowager empress when her son, Gao Yang, declared himself emperor in 550 and changed the dynasty from (Eastern) Wei to (Northern) Qi. Lou Rui rose to the highest official position at court in spite of his many misdeeds. His wealth and close association with the ruling family ensured that he commanded the services of the best craftsmen in the land for the construction and decoration of his tomb. When the excavation of the tomb was first made public in 1980, it drew a great deal of attention from archaeologists and art historians. Much of the discussion was centered on the wall paintings.[1]

It should be noted that although the city of Ye, in southern Hebei, was the official capital of the Northern Qi (as it was of the Eastern Wei), the emperors spent at least half their time in Taiyuan (Jinyang, as it was then known), the power base of the regime. It can be surmised that, from the time of Gao Huan, the court in its frequent migrations was followed by entertainers from Central Asia and that Central Asian craftsmen worked at building and decorating the palaces at Taiyuan. No structure above

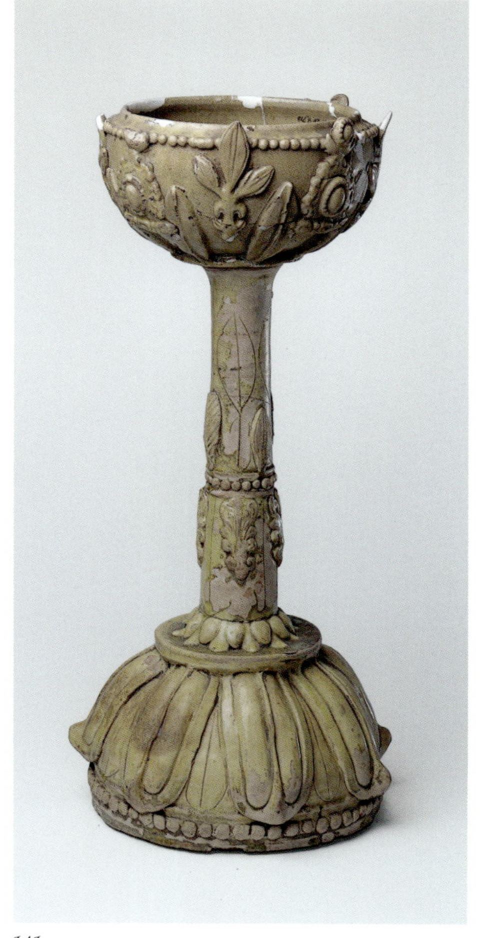
141

ground in Ye and Taiyuan has survived from this period, but the wall paintings in Lou Rui's tomb are in every way comparable to those of a large-scale tomb near Ye, believed to be that of Gao Yang (r. 550–59), the first emperor of the Northern Qi (see cat. nos. 135, 136 for objects from this tomb).

JCYW

1. Comments from a number of scholars are published in Wu Zuoren et al. 1983, following the excavation report.

142
Ox

Northern Qi dynasty (550–577)
Earthenware
Height 13 ¾ in. (35 cm)
Excavated from the tomb (dated 570) of Lou Rui, Taiyuan, Shanxi Province, 1980
Shanxi Institute of Archaeology

Excav. report in *Wenwu* 1983.10

Like the pottery pieces in the previous entry, this figure of an ox comes from the tomb of Lou Rui. The hundreds of pottery figures in standard sets of attendants and guards in this tomb are artistically unexceptional, although some of the sculptures of animals that appear to be individually sculpted and not produced in molds are very fine. This sculpture of an ox is preserved in good condition, except for a small break in the dewlap, and is covered in a perfectly controlled brown glaze, technically the forerunner of the three-color *sancai* glazes of the Tang period.

JCYW

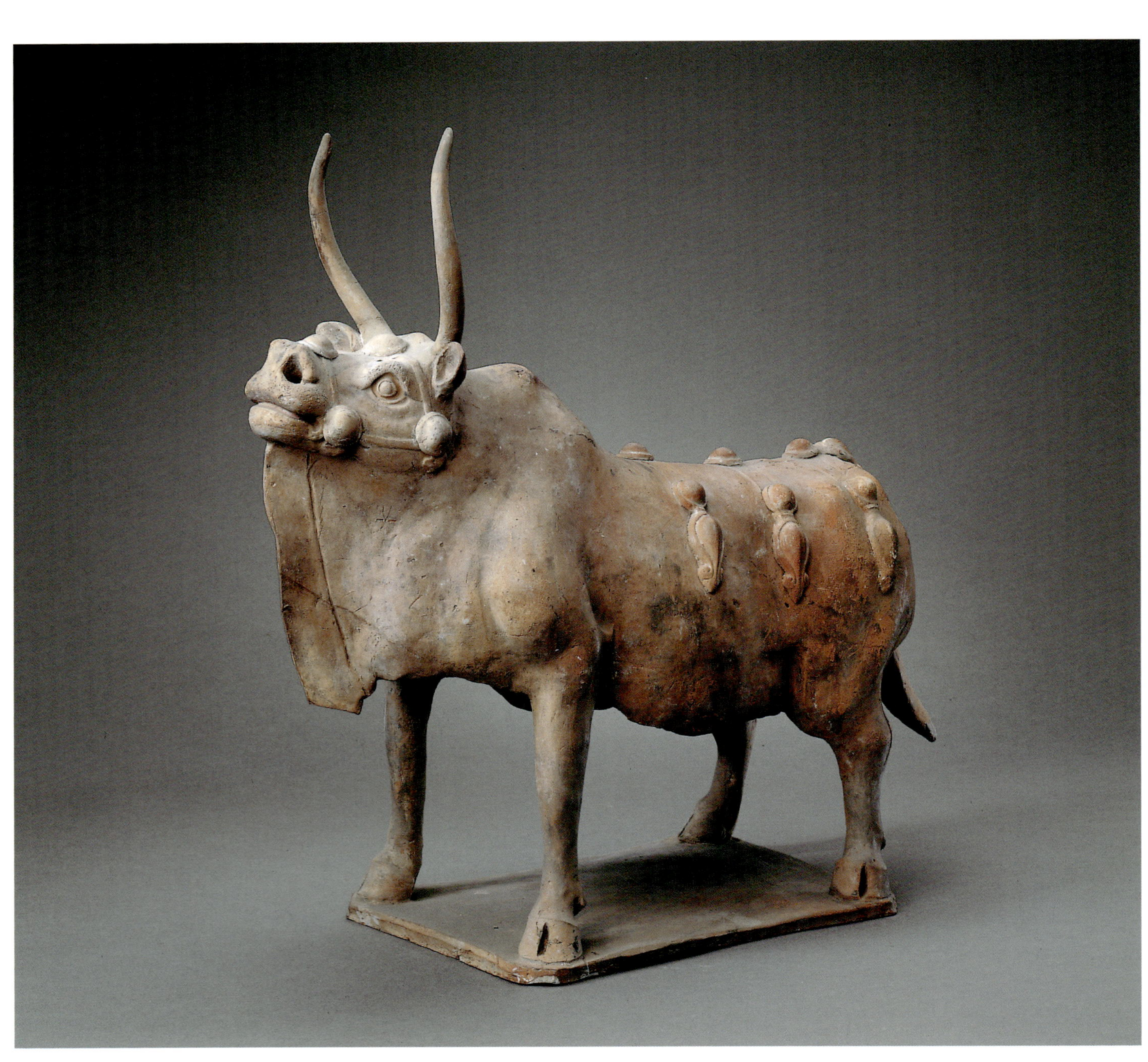

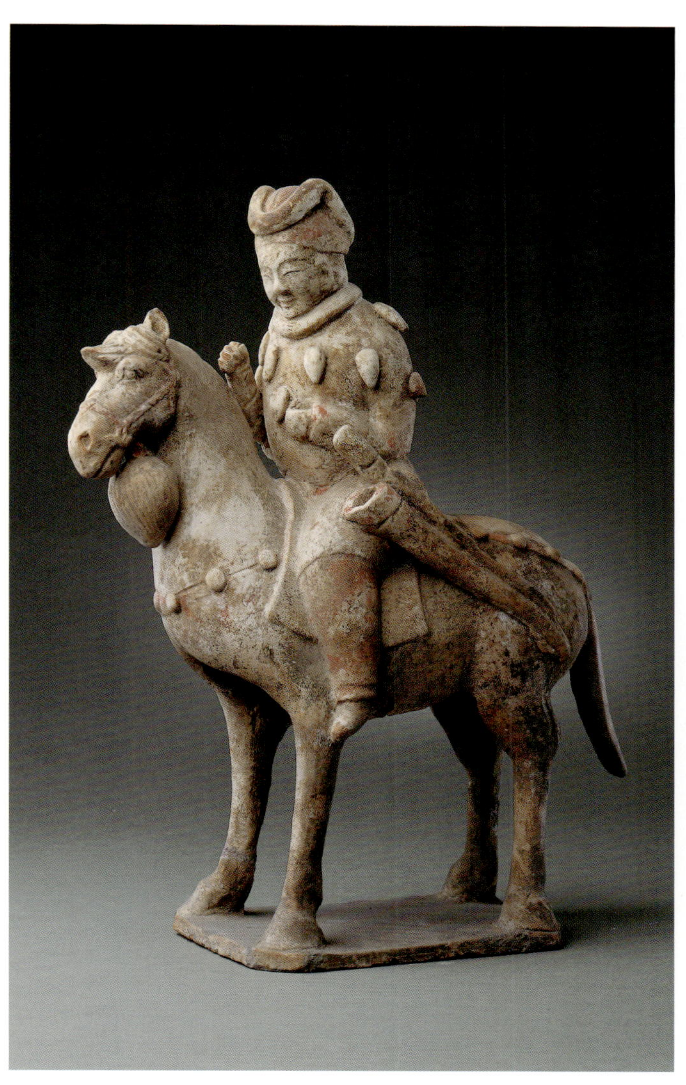

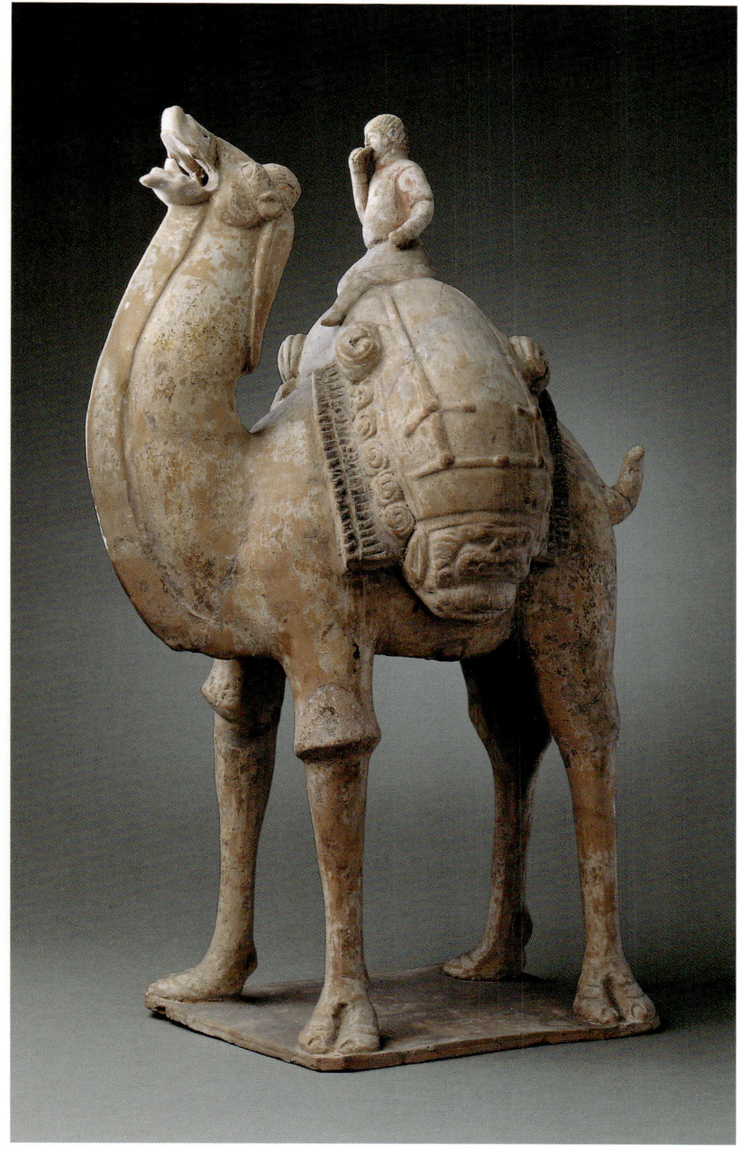

143
Mounted warrior

Sui dynasty (581–619)
Earthenware with pigments
Height 11⅝ in. (29.5 cm)

144
Camel with rider

Sui dynasty (581–619)
Earthenware with pigments
Height 17⅞ in. (45.5 cm)

Cat. nos. 143 and 144 excavated from the tomb (dated 597) of Hulü Che, Taiyuan, Shanxi Province, 1980
Shanxi Institute of Archaeology

Excav. report in *Wenwu* 1992.10

These two pottery sculptures are from the tomb of Hulü Che, who died in 595 in Xi'an, the capital of the Sui dynasty (581–619), and was buried in 597 in Taiyuan, his ancestral home.

The pottery sculptures from this tomb are very similar to those from the tomb of Lou Rui (see cat. no. 142) and other Northern Qi tombs in Taiyuan from thirty years earlier. For example, the mounted warrior, at left, wearing a coat with drop-shaped ornaments (pearls?) is nearly identical to a figure in the earlier tomb.[1] There is also a smaller version from Hulü Che's tomb of the Lou Rui ox sculpture (cat. no. 142). And the camel with the diminutive rider, at right, is stylistically consonant with the Northern Qi horse and rider (cat. no. 138). There are other articles in this tomb that could have been found only in Taiyuan during the Sui period, but on the whole the continuity of material culture in the Taiyuan area dating from the last three decades of the sixth century is remarkable. It is remarkable because the sixth century was a period of rapid change in art forms and styles in North China. The likely explanation for the conservatism in Taiyuan in the late sixth century is that after the conquest of Northern Qi by the Northern Zhou in 577, Taiyuan lost its position as an artistic center and the craftsmen there simply followed models established during the Northern Qi. Innovations would take place at the new capital, Xi'an.

Hulü Che (562–595) was a descendant of the most illustrious family of the Northern Qi. His great-grandfather Hulü Jin was the most famous general under Gao Huan, the founder of the dynasty, and his father, Hulü Guang, repeatedly defeated the armies of the Northern Zhou. In 572, as a result of court intrigue, Hulü Guang was executed together with the entire extended family. (The Northern Zhou declared a general amnesty to celebrate the event.)[2] However, all the Hulü children under the age of fourteen were spared, including Hulü Che. Emperor Wudi of the Northern Zhou had such great respect for Hulü Guang, his mightiest opponent, that he restored all Hulü Guang's descendants to their former estates after his conquest of the Northern Qi in 577 and conferred posthumous titles on Hulü Guang. The Hulü family was similarly honored in the Sui dynasty. JCYW

1. This figure and its dress are discussed in Sun Ji 1996a: 101.
2. *BQS* "The Biography of Hulü Jin" 17: 228.

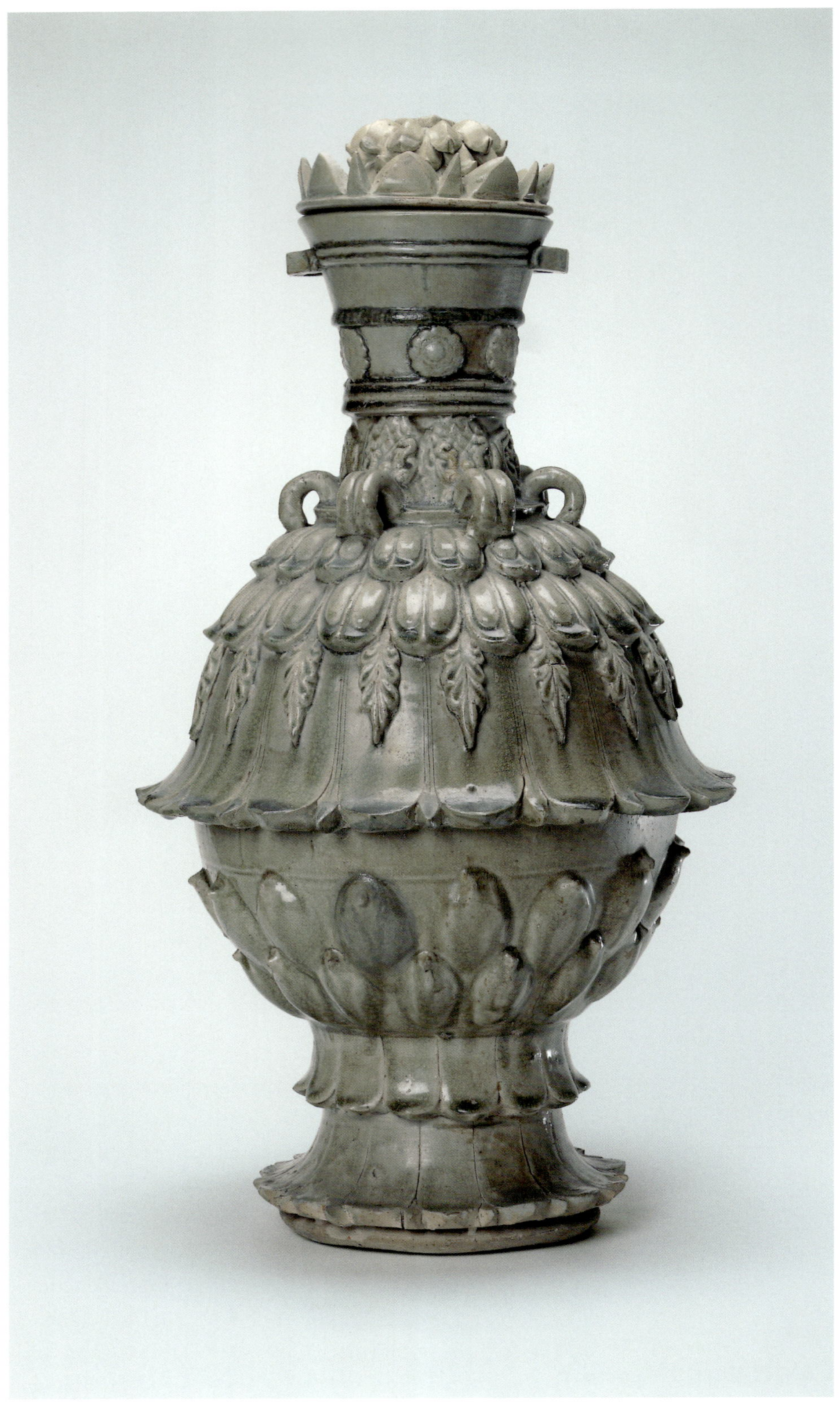

145
Lidded jar with lotus petals

Northern Wei (386–534) to Northern Qi (550–577) dynasty, 6th century
Glazed earthenware
Height 25 ¹⁄₁₆ in. (63.6 cm)
Excavated at the Feng family cemetery, Jingxian, Hebei Province, 1948
National Museum of China

Excav. report in *Kaogu tongxun* 1957.3

This type of high-fired porcelaneous ware with carved and appliqué decoration has been found at sixth-century sites in both North China and the Nanjing area in the south. It is likely that it was produced in Hebei Province, where the majority of the known examples have been found.

This jar comes from the cemetery of the Feng family in Jingxian, Hebei. As the Western Jin dynasty descended into chaos in the early fourth century, most of the grand families in the north moved with the Jin court to south of the Yangzi River. Several families in the Hebei area moved northeast, to what is now Beijing, and farther to western Liaoning. They found service initially with the Yan states of the Murong Xianbei and then with the Northern Wei. From the time when most of North China was under the rule of the Northern Wei, leading members of the Feng family, wherever they served, were returned to their ancestral land in Jingxian to be buried. This practice continued until at least the end of the sixth century.

JCYW

146

Vase with appliqué decoration of lotus petals

Northern Qi dynasty (550–577)
Earthenware with pigments
Height 15 5/8 in. (39.7 cm)

147

Necklace

Northern Qi dynasty (550–577)
Agate and amber
Plaque: height 1 3/4 in. (4.5 cm); beads: max. diameter 3/4 in. (1.9 cm)

Cat. nos. 146 and 147 excavated from the tomb (dated 562) of Kudi Huiluo, Shouyang, Shanxi Province, 1973
Shanxi Institute of Archaeology

EXCAV. REPORT in *Kaogu xuebao* 1979.3

This yellow-glazed pottery jar with appliqué decoration of petals, floral medallions, and what appear to be flaming pearls and the string of beads are from the tomb of Kudi Huiluo and his two (successive) wives, both of whom predeceased him. The beads are mainly of agate of different colors with a few of malachite. The amber plaque was found with the beads, but it is not certain whether originally they were all strung together.

The image of the crouching monster (see below) on the amber plaque was one of the most common motifs in the

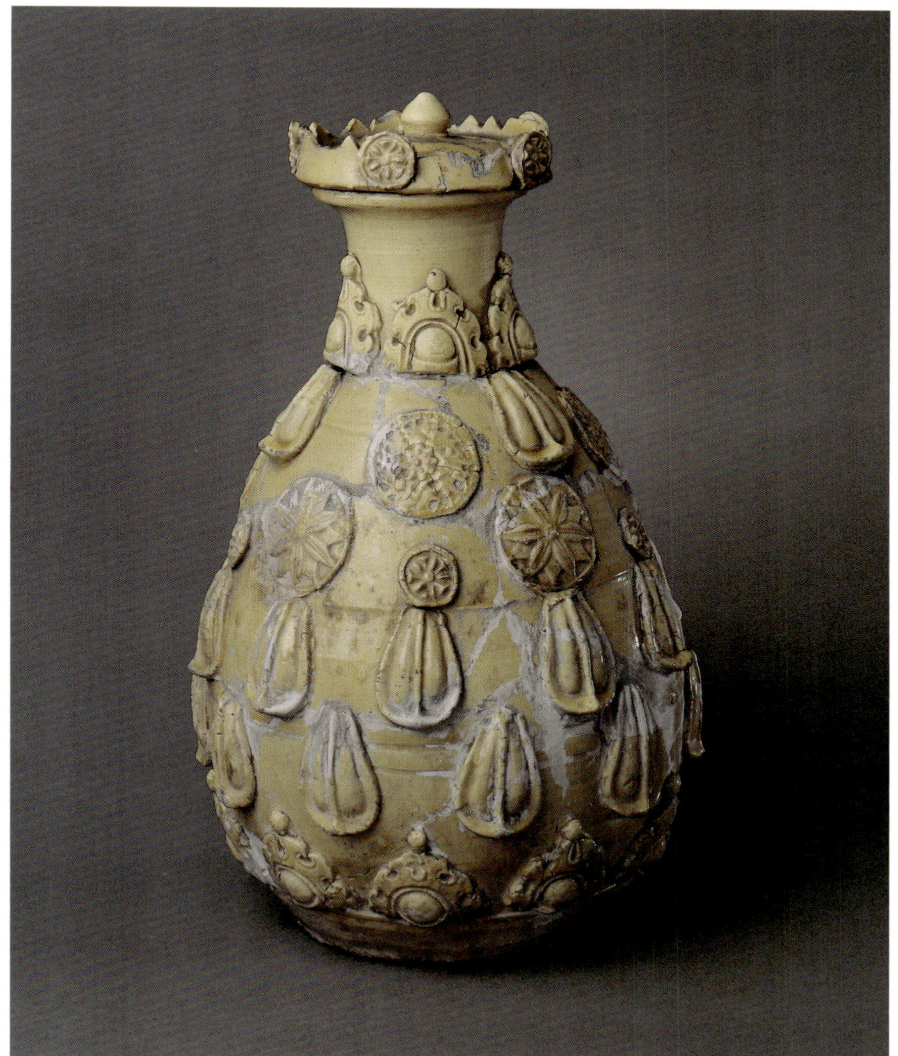

146

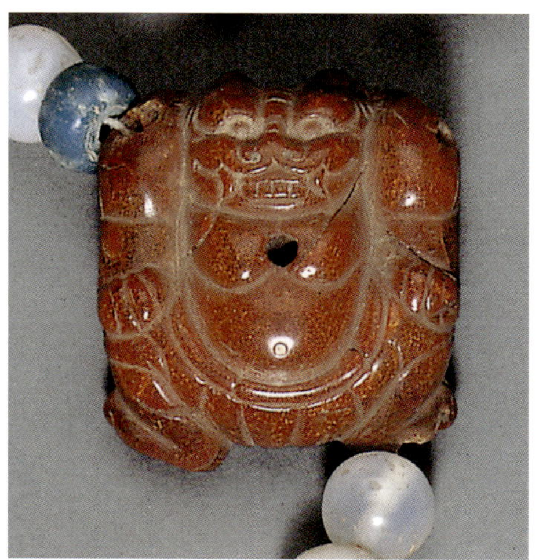

147, detail

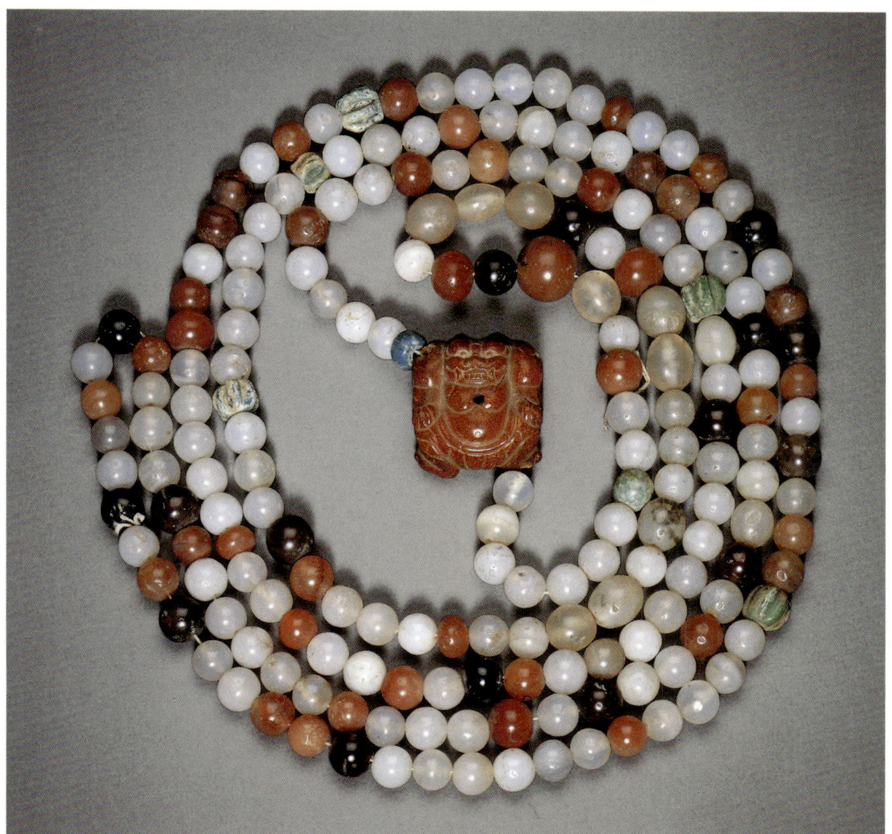

147

architecture and decorative arts of the Northern Qi. The origin of both the motif and the piece of amber is uncertain, but because the sixth century was a period of active long-distance trade, it is not implausible that the amber was imported from the Baltic.

Kudi Huiluo, like Lou Zhao and Hulü Jin (see cat. nos. 143, 144), joined forces with Gao Huan early in his campaign and held the highest official rank in the Northern Qi. The scale and furnishings of his tomb reflect his status.

JCYW

148
Flask with human figure and lions

Northern Qi dynasty (550–577)
Glazed earthenware
Height 10⅞ in. (27.5 cm)
Excavated at Taiyuan, Shanxi Province, 1956
Shanxi Provincial Museum

Reference: Shanxi sheng bowuguan guancang 1999, no. 166

The decoration on this flask illustrates one of the activities of Central Asian entertainers in Taiyuan, the second capital of the Northern Qi: the circus. On either surface of the flask, in relief, stands a lion tamer, holding a whip, between two seated lions. The sides are in the form of elephant heads and trunks. Behind the lions can be seen two people feeding the elephants. The decorative elements, such as the pearl border, were also imported.

JCYW

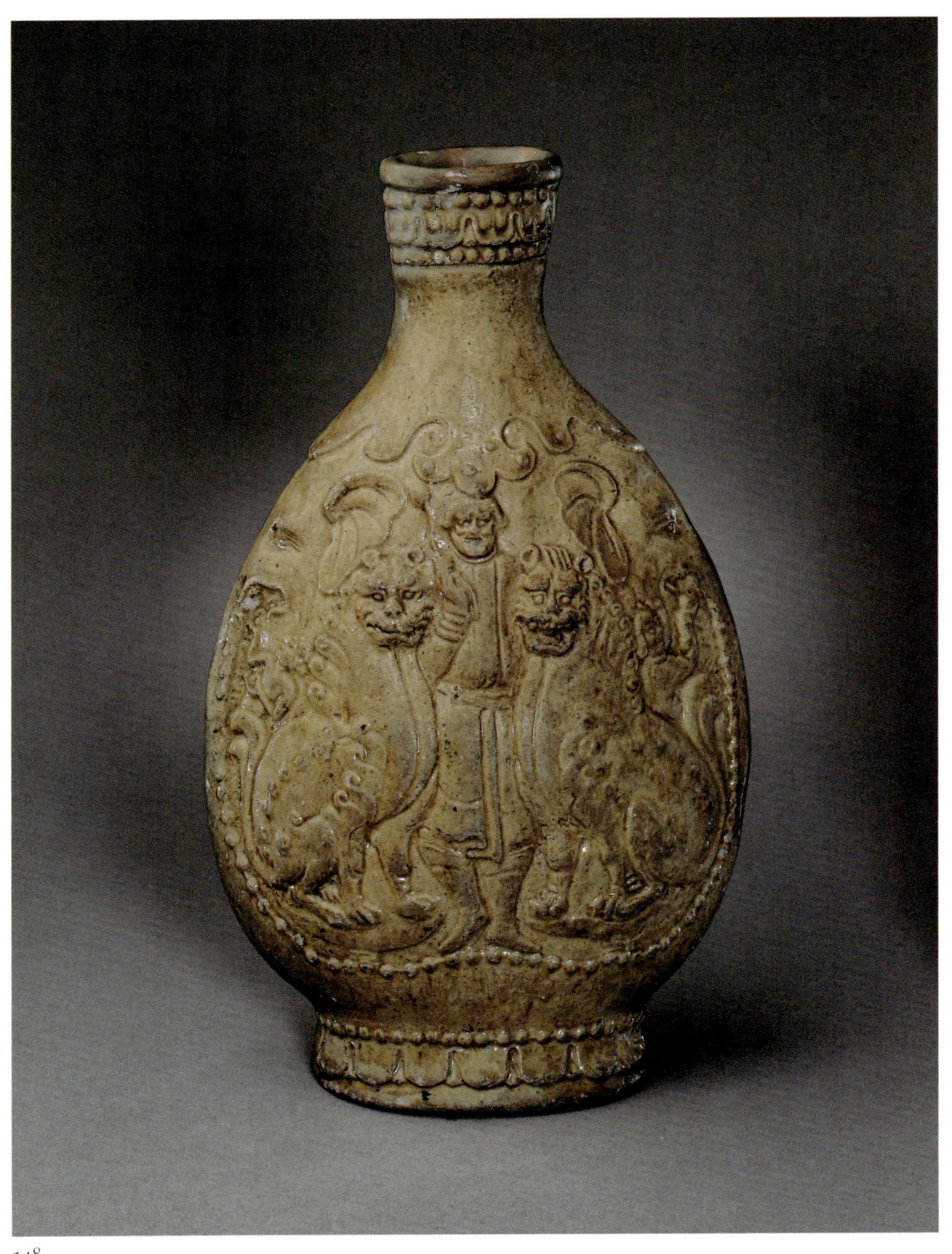

148

149
Flask with dancer and musicians

Northern Qi dynasty (550–577)
Glazed earthenware
Height 7⅞ in. (20 cm)
Excavated from the tomb (dated 576) of Fan Cui, Anyang, Henan Province, 1971
National Museum of China

Excav. report in *Wenwu* 1972.1

The form of this flask derives from the pilgrim's bottle, of West Asian origin. The decoration illustrates the whirling dance, a popular form of entertainment in the sixth and seventh centuries introduced from Central Asia. The dancer swirls and leaps on a small round carpet, here represented as a lotus blossom. The musicians at either side accompany her on the lute, cymbals, and flute, and a man is seen clapping, probably giving the beat.

This is one of four such flasks found in the tomb of Fan Cui, a high official at the Northern Qi court at Ye (near present-day Anyang). This vessel and the flask with a human figure and lions found in Taiyuan (cat. no. 148) demonstrate the presence of Central Asians at the two capitals of the Northern Qi.

JCYW

150

Central Asian dancer, probably Sogdian

Tang dynasty (618–907), 7th–8th century
Bronze with traces of gilding
Height 5⅜ in. (13.7 cm)
Found near Shandan, Gansu Province, 1945–80
Gansu Provincial Museum

Reference: Juliano and Lerner 2001: 254–55

The broad forehead, bulging eyes, and large nose of this small bronze sculpture indicate that it represents a foreigner. He wears a peaked hat and a long-sleeved tunic over leggings, and he carries a double gourd over his left shoulder. Figures of this type are depicted on stone sarcophagi (cat. no. 175) and couches found in the tombs of Sogdians living in China in the late sixth century,[1] as well as on contemporaneous ceramics (cat. no. 149). They are also found on metalwork and tomb doors made in the seventh and eighth centuries.[2] Such figures represent dancers from western Central Asia noted for their performances of whirling, spinning movement accompanied by a wide range of percussion and wind instruments. They are generally shown standing on a rug with one foot on the ground and the other lifted to the side or at the back. Performers from the trading people of Sogdiana, famed for the *huxuan wu,* or Sogdian whirl, were particularly popular in China. Solo itinerant performers and troupes are both mentioned in literature and historical writings.[3]

The presence of similar images in Chinese art from the sixth to the eighth century suggests a comparable date for this rare bronze sculpture. However, questions remain about the piece, which was found in the western province of Gansu, an important area for caravans entering China from the Silk Road. The legs, particularly the right one, are noticeably smaller than those of other images of the same type. It seems likely that both have been repaired. The lotus-bud support may also have been added later. It is unclear whether the sculpture was an independent image or part of an ensemble. In addition, it is unknown if it was intended for use in a tomb or in a temple, presumably one dedicated to West and Central Asian practices such as Zoroastrianism.

DPL

1. Tianshui shi bowuguan 1992, pl. 18.
2. Ningxia Huizu zhiziqu bowuguan 1988, fig. 13. Similar figures are also found on a famous bronze jug in Lhasa, Tibet. See Schroeder 2001, vol. 2, pl. 190.
3. Mair 1994: 486–87.

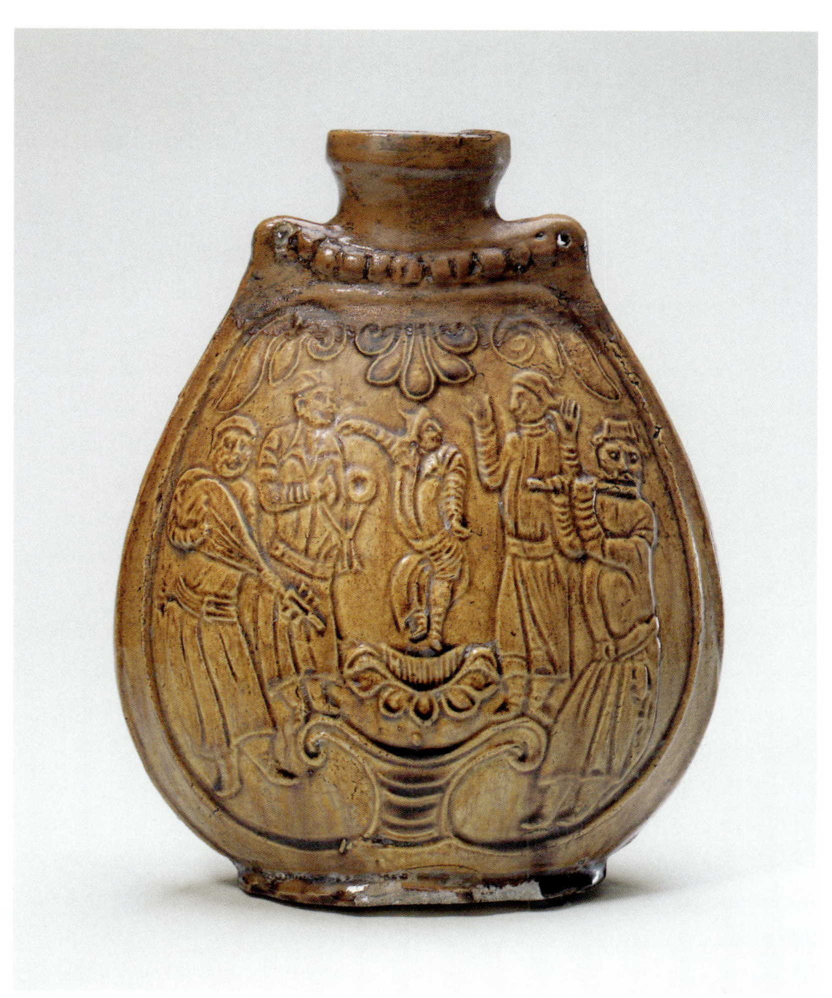

149

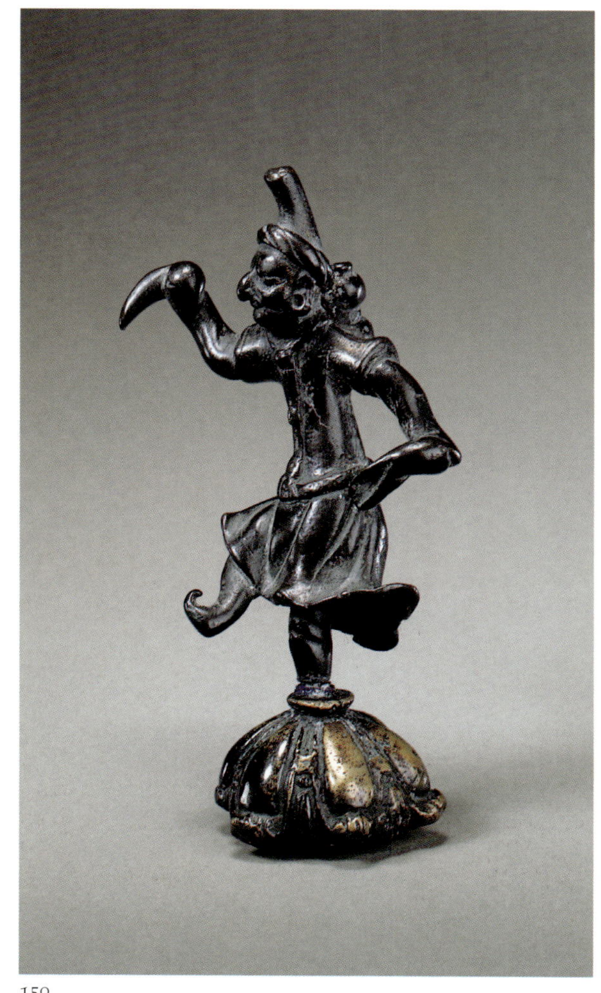

150

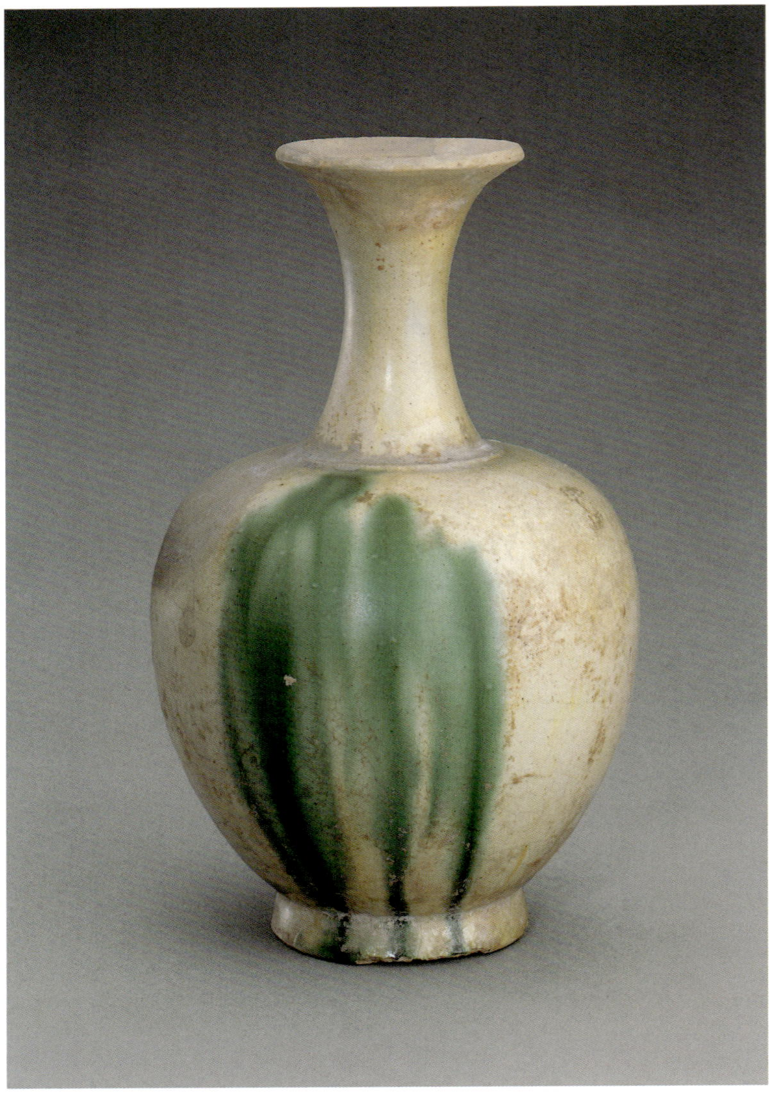

151

Bottle

Northern Qi dynasty (550–577)
Glazed earthenware
Height 8 5/8 in. (22 cm)
Excavated from the tomb (dated 576) of Fan Cui, Anyang, Henan Province, 1971
Henan Museum

Excav. report in *Wenwu* 1972.1

The form of this bottle, with a sharp inflection in the profile, derives from a metal prototype, but the splash glaze decoration is pure ceramic art. The expressive use of color glazes began in the sixth century, about the time the tomb of Fan Cui was built. This may or may not initially have been intentional, but it later became a common decorative element on pottery in the Tang period. The style and technique of splash-color glazing also spread during this time, east to Japan and west to the Middle East.

Three bottles of this shape were found in the tomb of Fan Cui (see cat. no. 149), but only this one has splash-green decoration. The transparent light yellow glaze covering the entire body of the vessel signals the beginning of the development of white porcelain—with a transparent glaze over a white body or slip—in the areas north and south of Anyang. This development would eventually culminate in the famous Xingyao white ware produced in southern Hebei during the eighth and ninth centuries. JCYW

152

Set of wine vessels and a tray

Eastern Wei dynasty (534–550)
Bronze, gilt bronze, silver, and glazed earthenware
Silver bowl: diameter 3 5/8 in. (9.2 cm); bottle: height 5 1/8 in. (13 cm); earthenware bowls: max. diameter 5 in. (12.8 cm); tray: diameter 19 1/4 in. (49 cm)
Excavated from the tomb (dated 544) of Li Xizong and his wife, Zanhuang, Hebei Province, 1975
Zhengding Office of Cultural Properties Preservation

Excav. report in *Kaogu* 1977.6

This set of drinking vessels, composed of a silver cup, a bottle, a wine warmer in gilt bronze, and five pottery bowls all on a bronze tray was found in the tomb of Li Xizong (d. 540, aged thirty-nine) and his wife, Cui Youji (d. 575, aged seventy-one). The date of the tomb can be determined by comparing its contents with those of the tombs of Cui Ang (566) and Fan Cui (576). In all three are found the same types of objects in every medium. For example, the pottery guardian figure from the tomb of Cui Ang (cat. no. 137) is in every respect similar to a figure from the Li–Cui tomb, and the gilt-bronze articles in both tombs are identical. It is likely that the burial furniture of the Li–Cui tomb, including this set of vessels, is that of Cui Youji, who was interred in 576.

Both Li Xizong and Cui Youji came from the most prominent families of Hebei (Shandong in the sixth century). Their ancestral homes were in Zhaojun and Boling, respectively, both not far from Shijiazhuang in present-day Hebei Province; their burial place is near Zhaojun.[1] They were the parents of Li Zu'e, the wife of Gao Yang and later empress when Gao Yang became the first emperor of Northern Qi in 550. Li Xizong never lived to see his daughter become empress, but Cui died less than two years before the demise of the Northern Qi and was aware of the tragic events that happened at the Northern Qi court after the death of Gao Yang in 559.

There are several points to note about the Li–Cui burial. The first is that in spite of the catastrophe that befell the family, the burial furniture for Cui was quite substantial and similar to that of Cui Ang and Fan Cui, both still in good standing at the time of their deaths. The only sign of reduced circumstances is that Cui's epitaph, unlike Li's, is roughly carved and the characters are poorly formed. Another point to note is that the Han Chinese aristocracy also used western-style silver and kept Byzantine coins (see cat. no. 153), one of which was pierced for wearing—like those from the tombs of Sogdiana in Guyuan (cat. nos. 221–223). Thus, whatever their ethnic affiliations, the ruling classes shared the same articles in daily life.

The late sixth century was a time of transition. This is reflected in the material culture. The gilt-bronze wine warmer in this set harks back to an earlier period; the form had been popular since the third century and was soon to disappear. The new form of the bottle became the prototype for metal and pottery bottles during the Tang. The pottery bowls, which do not look precious to the modern viewer, would have been much more highly valued in the sixth century because the high-fired glaze made them impervious to liquid—the next best thing to lacquer or glass. Their simple form is true to the native tradition of the Chinese potter.

JCYW

The silver bowl resembles Sogdian bowls datable to the sixth century.[2] Its fluted side wall, rows of small "beads," embossed center, and overall shape are typically Sogdian, although in Sogdian metalwork the curved flutes are known not earlier than the seventh century.[3] The present bowl, from Nanxingguo, was made by a Chinese craftsman who combined several Sogdian elements with elements not seen in Sogdiana, where the conical foot with embossed upper part was made from a single sheet of silver. The curvature of the center of the bowl itself corresponds to that of the embossed top of the foot. Thus, the bottom becomes a double sheet when the foot is placed in the cavity of the bowl. The artisan who crafted the Li–Cui bowl made, separately, the conical foot, the lotus-shaped roundel, and the bowl with an opening at the bottom. He then placed the foot into the opening and soldered the lotus medallion onto the upper part of the foot. The bottom of the bowl—the medallion—is composed of one sheet of silver. The lotus petals are typical of the lotus bases of Chinese Buddhist sculptures of the sixth century. And last, but not least, the size of the bowl, as well as that of the majority of later Tang replicas of Central Asian silver vessels, is much smaller than that of its models. The Li–Cui bowl is the earliest example of Sogdian influence on Chinese metalwork.

BIM

1. See Ebrey 1978 for an in-depth study of the Cui family of Boling.
2. Marshak 1986: 39–41, 51–53, figs. 35–38; Marshak 1999: 101–10, figs. A, B, 9.
3. Marshak 1986, fig. 80.

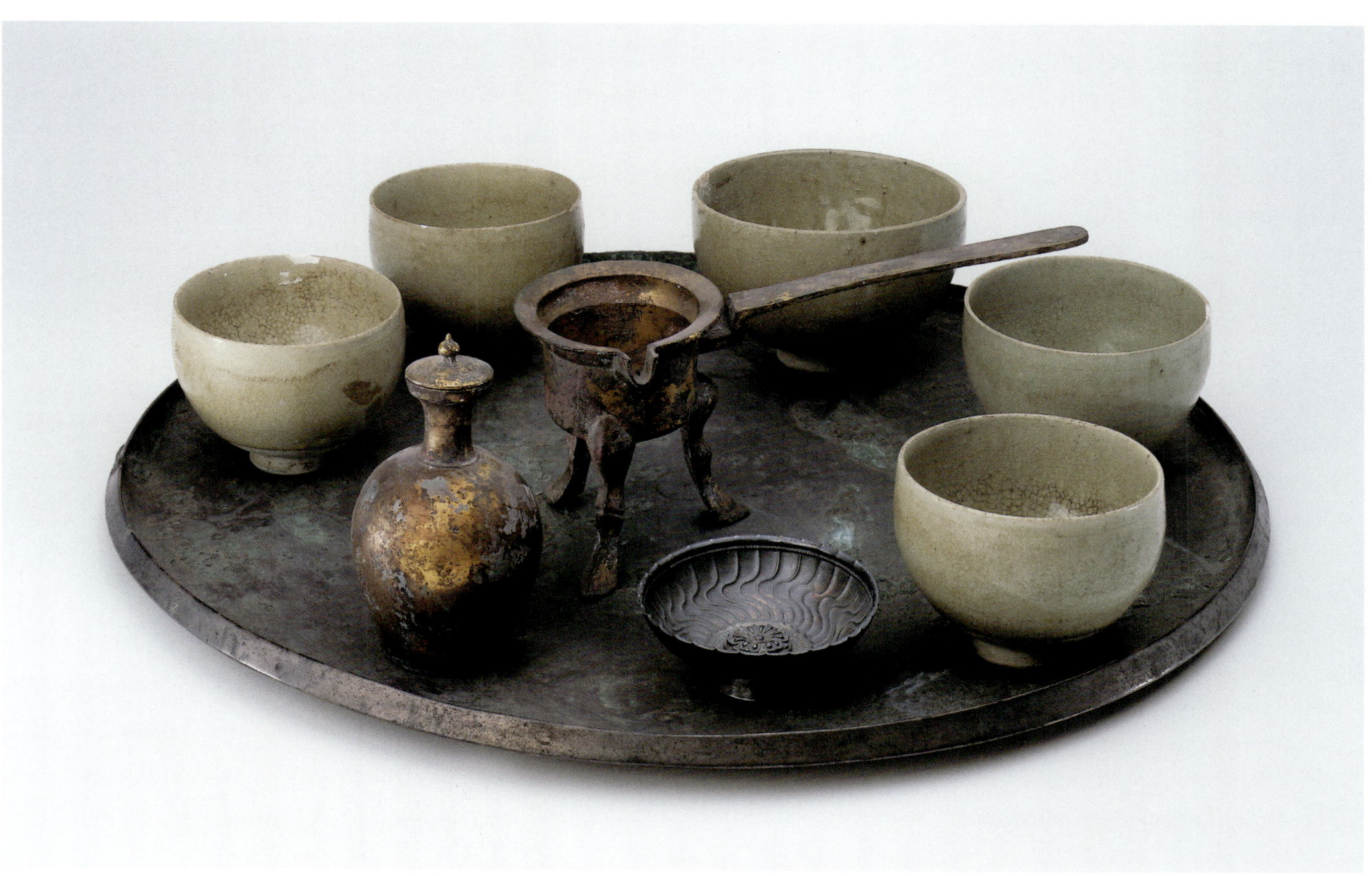

152

153
Three Byzantine coins

Gold
Max. diameter ⅞ in. (2.1 cm)
Excavated from the tomb (dated 544) of Li Xizong and his wife, Zanhuang, Hebei Province, 1975
Zhengding Office of Cultural Properties Preservation

Excav. report in *Kaogu* 1977.6

These three Byzantine solidi were found together with the set of wine vessels and tray (cat. no. 152)[1] in the tomb of Li Xizong, the father-in-law of Emperor Gao Yang, and his wife. Li Xizong died in 540, under the Eastern Wei; his wife died in 575, under the Northern Qi. If the coins belonged to Li Xizong's wife, it seems probable that she would have obtained them when Li Xizong was still alive, not after she became a widow. It is notable that the span of time between the date of Li Xizong's burial and that of two of the three coins, those of Justin I and Justinian I—527—is unusually short.[2]

Coin a is pierced in two places, an indication that it served also as a pendant on a necklace. When the coin was suspended, the bust of the emperor, depicted on the obverse, would have appeared right side up.

a. Theodosius II (r. 408–50) solidus, Constantinople. Obverse: Bust of Theodosius II wearing a diadem and a helmet. The cuirass is possibly of chain mail. He holds a spear in the right hand and a shield in the left. On the shield is a figure of the emperor himself as a rider killing an enemy with a spear. Legend: D[ominus] N[oster] THEODOSIUS P[erpetuus] F[elix] AUG[ustus]. Reverse: Winged Victory holding a cross and a wreath. There is a star between the cross and her head. Legend: VOTXX MULTXXX. Below: CONOB. As is typical of Byzantine coinage, the images that appear on the obverse and reverse, are directionally opposite.

Coins b and c are clipped, making their weight less than that of a normal solidus.

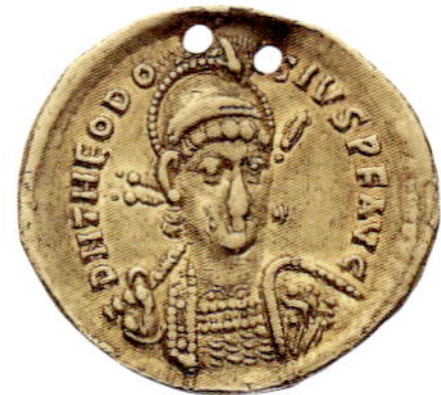
153a, obverse

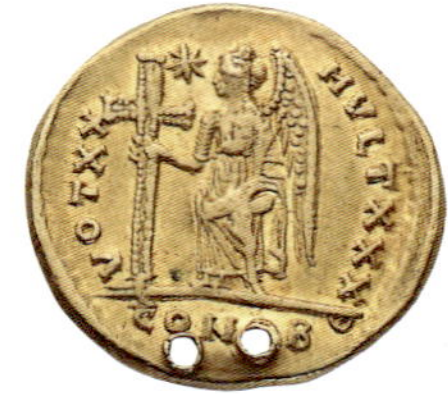
153a, reverse

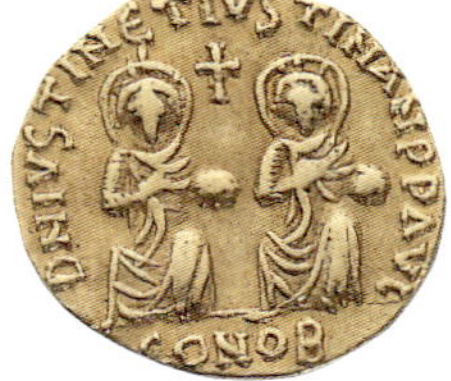
153b, obverse

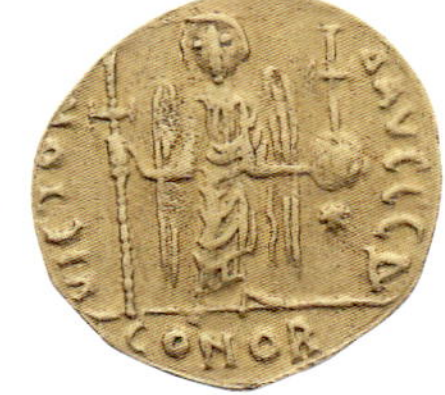
153b, reverse

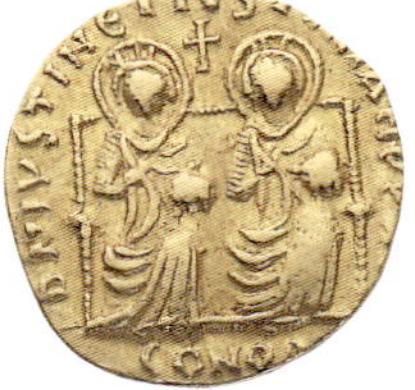
153c, obverse

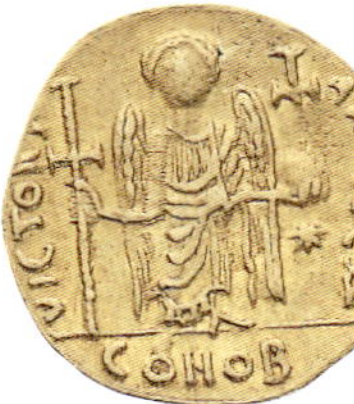
153c, reverse

b. Justin I (r. 518–27) and Justinian I (r. 527–65) solidus, Constantinople, 527, the date at which they reigned together. Obverse: The two emperors are shown seated, although a throne is not in evidence. Each holds a globe. There is a cross between their heads. Legend: D[ominus] N[oster] IUSTIN[us] ET IUSTIN[i]AN[us] P[er]P[etui] AUG[usti]. Below: CONOB. Reverse: Winged Victory standing frontally, holding a cross in the right hand and a globe with a cross mounted on it in the left hand. There is a star below the globe. Legend: VICTOR[i] AAUGGG[ustorum]d(?) (maybe *officina* 4).[3] Below: CONOB.

c. Justin I and Justinian I solidus, Constantinople, 527. Obverse: Same type as coin b. Here, however, there is a throne with a straight back. Legend: D[ominus] N[oster] IUSTIN ET IUSTINIAN PPAUGGG D (*officina* 4). Below: CONOB. Reverse: Same type as coin B. Legend: VICTORI AAUGGGD. Below: CONOB.

Gold coins of Theodosius II were found in Guyuan, Ningxia,[4] and in Panjikent, Sogdiana.[5] Two coins of Justin I and Justinian I were also found in Guyuan, Ningxia, but in another tomb (that of Tian Hong).[6] Alram is of the opinion that coin a could have traveled to China via India, where many Roman and Byzantine coins were made pierced above the bust of the emperor.[7] Coin a is a light solidus of 20 carats. These are rare in Byzantium, but in the sixth and seventh centuries many were found in the "barbario" countries of Europe.[8]

VR

1. Shijiazhuang diqu geweihui wenhuaju wenwu fajuezu 1977: 372, 382–90, pls. 5–7; Xia Nai 1977: 403–6; Thierry and Morrisson 1994: 113 (nos. 24–26), 115.
2. Thierry and Morrisson 1994: 113–15.
3. Ibid.: 113, no. 26.
4. Ibid.: 115, no. 14.
5. Raspopova 1999: 454, figs. 3, 4. The preservation of this coin is very poor, and its attribution to Theodosius II thus remains hypothetical.
6. Yuanzhou lianhe kaogudui 2000, colorpl. 28; Alram 2001: 282–85, nos. 99, 100.
7. Alram 2001: 284–85, n. 3.
8. However, light solidi of 20 carats are recognized only since the reign of Justinian I. Sokolova (1997: 20–25) posits that Byzantine emperors used such light solidi for payments to rulers of the "barbarians." Xia Nai (1977: 404) believes that the light weight of coin A is a result of the gold removed from the two holes; the holes are, however, too small to make the difference in weight anything but negligible.

154
Guardian warriors

Northern Zhou dynasty (557–581), ca. 569
Earthenware with pigments
Height: a. $7\frac{1}{2}$ in. (19.2 cm); b. $7\frac{1}{8}$ in. (18.2 cm)

155
Armored horse and rider

Northern Zhou dynasty (557–581), ca. 569
Earthenware with pigments
Height $6\frac{7}{8}$ in. (17.5 cm)

156
Camel

Northern Zhou dynasty (557–581), ca. 569
Earthenware with pigments
Height $7\frac{1}{4}$ in. (18.4 cm)

Cat. nos. 154, 155, and 156 excavated from the tomb (dated 569) of Li Xian, Guyuan, Ningxia Autonomous Region, 1983
Guyuan Museum

Excav. report in *Wenwu* 1985.11

The two epitaph tablets found in the coffin chamber give biographies of the interred, Li Xian (502–569) and his wife, Wu Hui (d. 547).[1] As is typical of the elite of the period, Li Xian's ancestry is unclear. The family had ties to both the Xiongnu and the Xianbei clans, as well as to members of Turkish families.[2] They are known to have lived in the Guyuan area of Gansu Province for at least three generations, and earlier may have been farther south in the Tianshui region. In addition to serving as a general in the Northern Zhou army, Li Xian was at some point governor of the Dunhuang region.

The awkward rendering of the guardians and the sketchiness of the decoration, which differ noticeably from the refined taste typical of the early sixth century, are characteristic of Northern Zhou funerary sculptures. This may reflect a lack of access to trained artisans in the northwest after the dissolution of the Northern Wei (386–534). On the other hand, the roughness and immediacy in the sculpture may be intentional, serving to illustrate the taste of a ruling elite that defined itself largely by martial prowess. It is also possible that this manner reflects a deliberate rejection of the highly refined imagery

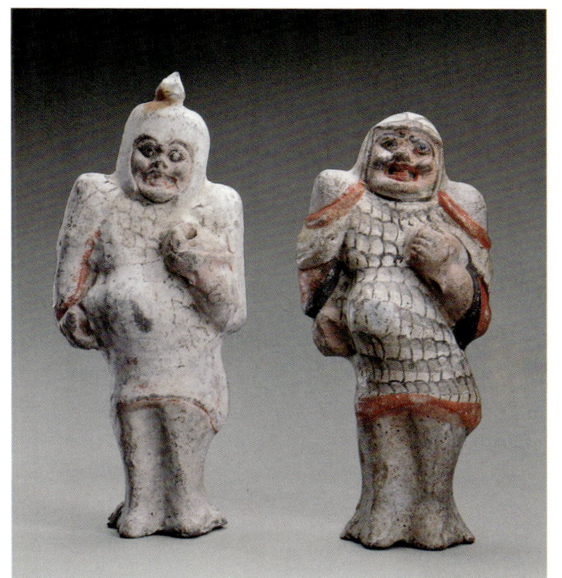

154a, front 154b, front

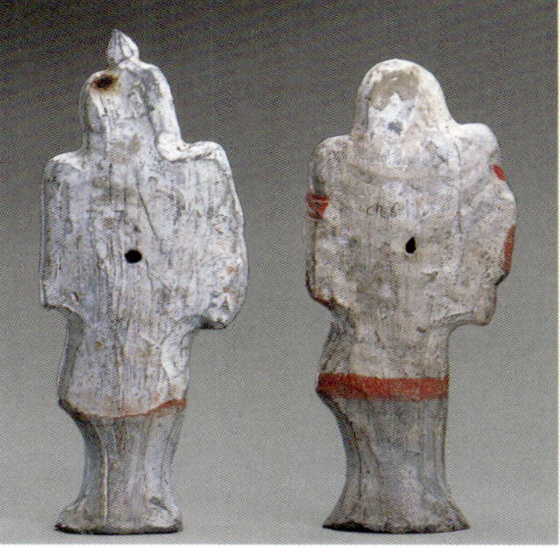
154a, back 154b, back

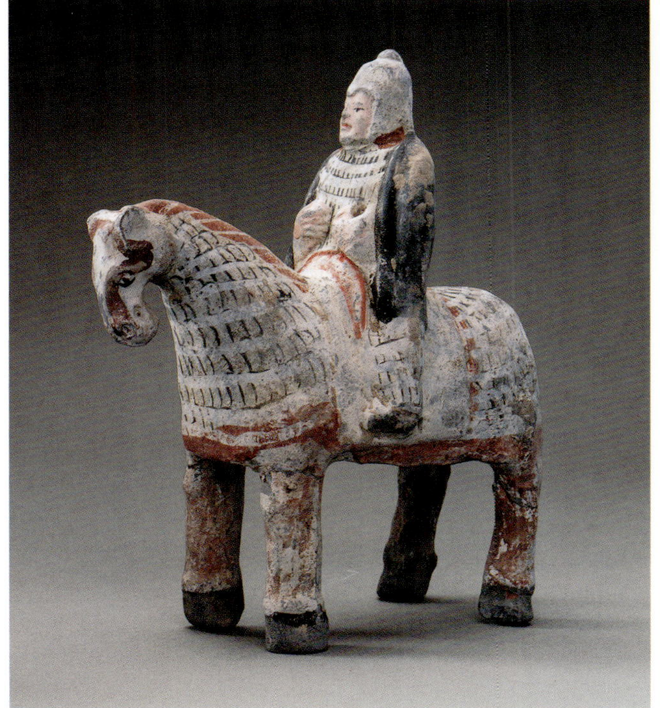
155

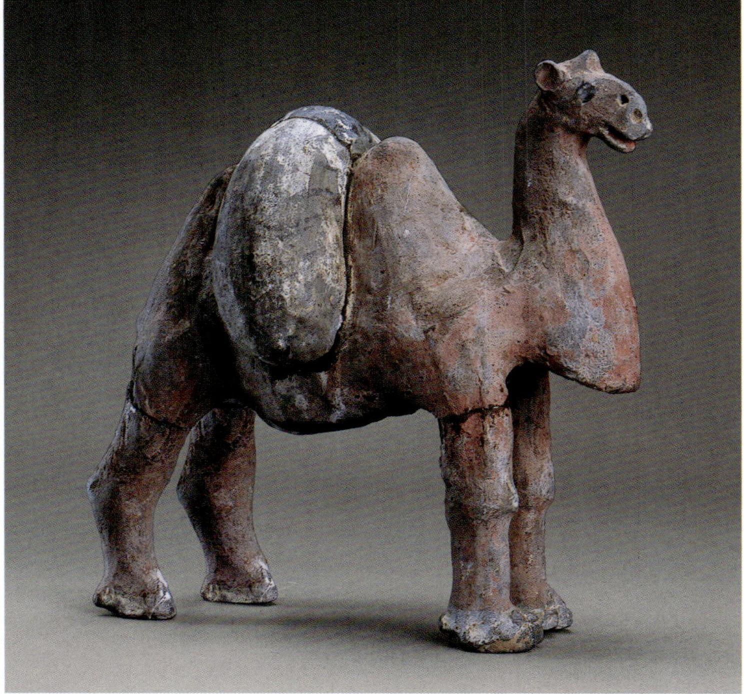
156

favored during the late Northern Wei in the capital city, Luoyang. Conflicts between the cultivated, and somewhat sinicized, taste of the court and the lifestyles of those stationed in remote military garrisons contributed to the rebellions that led to the downfall of the Northern Wei and the subsequent establishment of the Western Wei and Northern Zhou dynasties in the northwest.

The squat, flat form of the armored equestrian, one of six such figures placed behind the standing guardians, exemplifies the representation of men and women in the pottery figures from Li Xian's tomb. The rider holds his hands at the waist and wears a full helmet and a suit of lamellar armor. Draped over his shoulders is a black, sleeved cape, based on Central Asian dress. The horse's short, pudgy legs, unarticulated body, and tiny head are also common in tomb figures of the period. The horse is protected by a head mask, neck, chest, and side armor, and another piece for the rump. Black is used to outline the scales of the armor, while touches of red highlight the edges.

The horse and rider are hollow, as is the camel, one of two excavated from the tomb. Both camels represent the Bactrian, or two-humped, species used for transport and portage in the highlands of Central Asia and also at times in China. Although popular in the later Tang dynasty (618–907) for riding and hunting, Northern Zhou camels were apparently used as pack animals along with horses. Here, the short, thick legs are comparable to those of the horse, as is the small head. The care taken to depict the big soft feet, on the other hand, adds a more naturalistic element, as does the liveliness in the face. Traces of gold remain on the feet and at the top of the pack.

DPL

1. Ningxia Huizu zhizhiqu bowuguan and Ningxia Guyuan bowuguan 1985: 1–20.
2. Albert E. Dien, catalogue entry in Juliano and Lerner 2001: 107–8.

157
Ewer

5th–6th century
Gilt silver
Height 14¾ in. (37.5 cm)
Excavated from the tomb (dated 569) of Li Xian and his wife, Guyuan, Ningxia Autonomous Region, 1983
Guyuan Museum

EXCAV. REPORT in *Wenwu* 1985.11

This ewer was found in the tomb of Li Xian, an important general of the Northern Zhou dynasty (559–581), and his wife.[1] Li died in 569, his wife in 547. At first glance, the ewer is typically Sasanian. A few of its features, however, are not Persian but Central Asian or even Greek. Most likely, it was made in Tokharistan (the area of Bactria now encompassing northern Afghanistan, southern Uzbekistan, and southern Tajikistan), where, from during the fourth to the sixth century, silversmiths often emulated Sasanian and Hellenistic shapes and motifs.

Li Xian's ewer is the most striking example of this stylistic mix, although Sasanian elements are also present in the decoration of so-called Bactrian bowls,[2] which probably date from approximately the same period. Among the Central Asian, non-Sasanian features of the ewer are camel heads that serve as handle terminals and a man's head instead of a ball affixed to the highest point of the handle (see also cat. no. 208). The winged camel was a symbol of good fortune and glory bestowed by one of the gods, most probably Verethragna, god of Victory. It appears also on murals in Sogdiana and on a sixth- to seventh-century Bactrian bowl, the

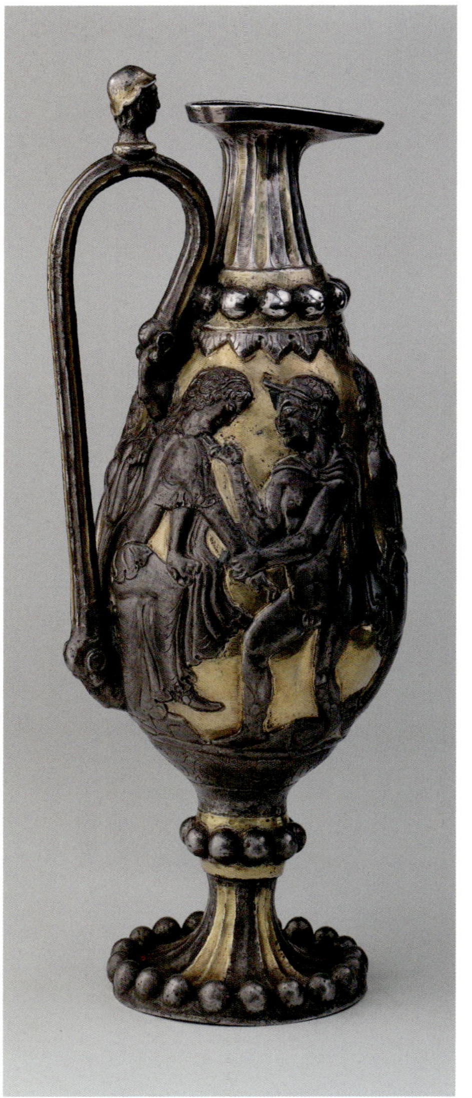

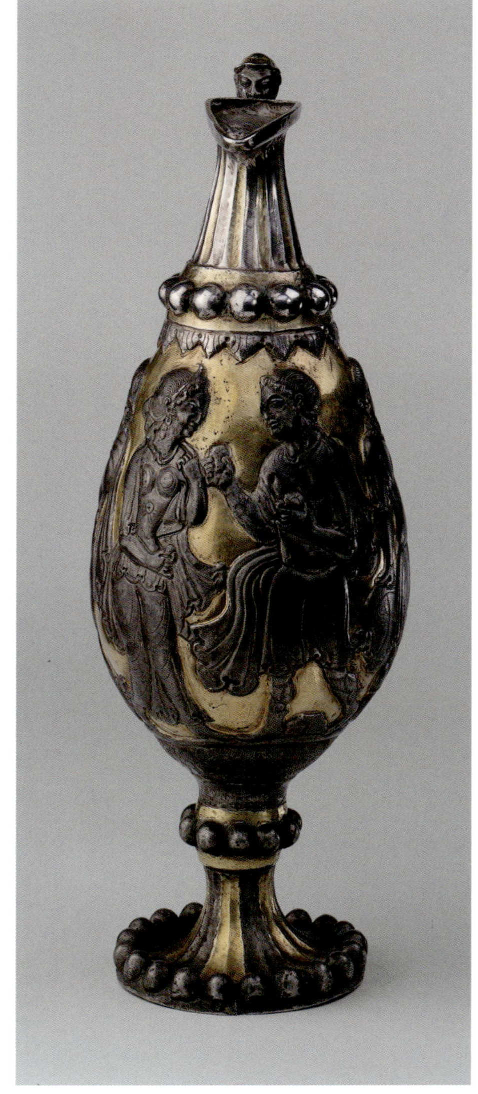

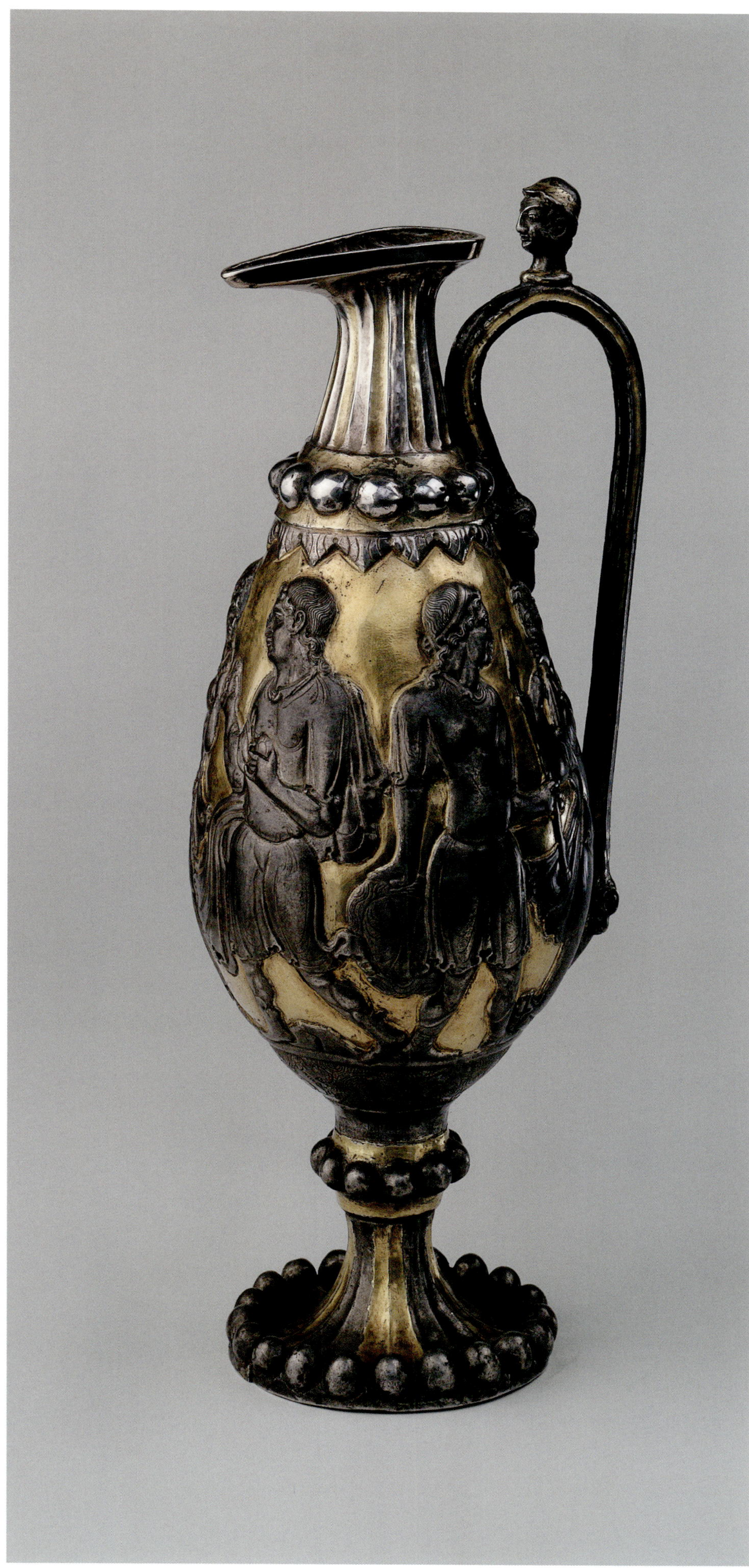

so-called Stroganoff bowl, where it is shown bearing a necklace to a feasting couple.[3] The three episodes depicted on the body of the present ewer possibly belong to the Trojan War cycle,[4] with the middle episode illustrating an excerpt from the Judgment of Paris; the second scene representing the Abduction of Helen from Sparta to Troy (opposite, left); and the third, the reunion of Helen and her husband, Menelaus, after the fall of Troy (opposite, right).

The artist who crafted the ewer made several errors in the interpretation of the story. For example, he gave Paris two apples instead of one. He did not include Paris's ship, which is essential to the narrative. And Menelaus is shown holding his spear in his left hand and a shield in his right hand because the composition had been transposed from left to right. These errors would indicate that the artisan and his patron were perhaps more concerned with emulating a beautiful Greek or Roman composition and a prestigious Sasanian shape than with reproducing the story with precision and accuracy.

BIM

1. Ningxia Huizu Zizhiqu bowuguan and Ningxia Guyuan bowuguan 1985: 1–20; Carpino and James 1989: 71–76; Marshak and Anazawa 1989: 54–57; Wu Zhuo 1989: 61–70; Harper 1991: 67–84; Luo Feng 1998a: 28–33; Ningxia Huizu zizhiqu Guyuan bowuguan and Zhongri Yuanzhou lianhe kaogudui 1999, pl. 78; Luo Feng 2000a: 311–30; Marshak 2001: 99–100.
2. Marshak 1986: 35–39.
3. Weitzmann 1943: 303–7, figs. 9–12; Marshak 1986: 35–36, figs. 15, 16.
4. Marshak and Anazawa 1989, passim.

158
Bowl

Ca. 6th century
Glass
Diameter of mouth rim 3¾ in. (9.5 cm)
Excavated from the tomb (dated 569) of Li Xian and his wife, Guyuan, Ningxia Autonomous Region, 1983
Guyuan Museum

Excav. report in *Wenwu* 1985.11

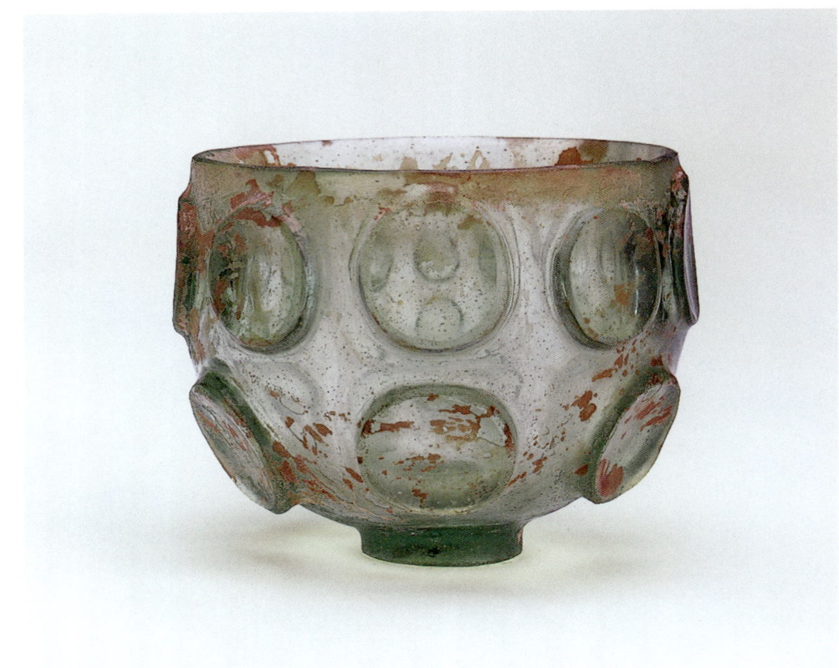

158

This glass bowl has a straight mouth, deep body, curved bottom, and ring foot. It is light yellow with very small, evenly distributed air bubbles. The inner wall is smooth and clean, and the outer wall is partially covered with a beige weathered layer. The mouth rim has horizontal traces of polishing. Two rows of oval ornaments in high relief decorate the outer wall. The ornaments are concave, like sucking disks. The glass is so transparent that through one ornament on the outer wall, one can see three others on the opposite side.

The thickness of the wall is about 4 mm, the thickest part of the raised area, about 7 mm. The raised ornaments are irregular in shape; some are elliptical horizontally or vertically, with a long axis of 27–29 mm and a short axis of 25–26 mm. The disks are more or less in line horizontally and are not evenly spaced. The foot is also a raised disk with a concave surface. The bowl weighs 245.6 grams, with a density of 2.46 gm/cm. X-ray spectroscopy shows that the glass does not contain lead or barium. Judging from the result of the X-ray spectroscopy and the density, this bowl is of soda-lime glass.

The wall is not even in thickness, which suggests that it was made with the blowing technique. The wall was ground thinner on the outside, leaving two rows of circular ornaments and the foot in high relief, the surfaces of which were then ground into concavities. After the grinding process, the entire bowl was polished.

The bowl, an exquisite example of Sasanian glasswork, was excavated in 1983 from the tomb of Li Xian (dated 569) in Guyuan, Ningxia. Glass bowls with shapes and ornaments similar to this one have been excavated on the Plateau of Iran, and glass shards with high-relief ornaments have also been found in Okinoshima, Japan. AJ

159
Plate

Ca. 6th century
Glass
Diameter of mouth rim 4¼ in. (10.8 cm)
Excavated from the tomb (dated 583) of Wang Shiliang and his wife, Xianyang, Shaanxi Province, 1988
Shaanxi Institute of Archaeology

Excav. report in *Yun Anzhi* 1993b: 109–30

This glass dish with cut decoration was excavated from the tomb (dated 583) that

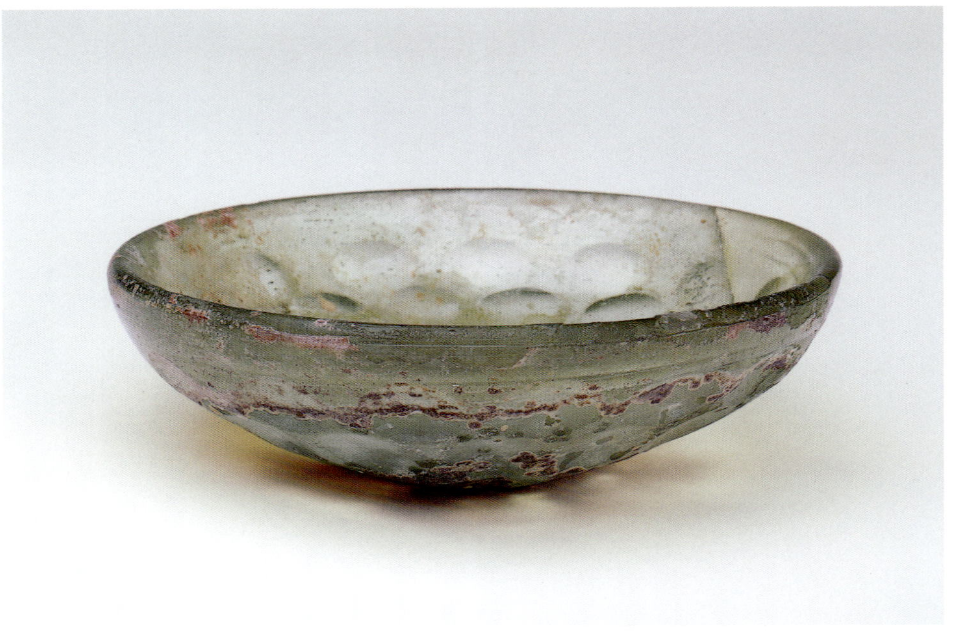

159

contained the bodies of Wang Shiliang, duke of Guang-chang and grand general of the Northern Zhou, two years into the Sui dynasty, and his wife Dong Ronghui (d. 565).[1] Because it was found at the center of the front chamber, the mortuary space of Wang Shiliang, it must have been placed in the tomb in the third year of the Kaihuang era of the Sui dynasty (581–619), the year of Wang's death. The plate has a wide mouth, deep body, and circular bottom. The glass is yellow and very transparent. On the body are two rows of ground horizontal oval facets; a circular concavity decorates the bottom. Although such decoration is typical of Sasanian glass, the shape of the plate is not. The most common form for Sasanian glass is the type represented by a glass bowl in the Shōsō-in in Nara, Japan.[2] A glass plate with shape and decoration similar to the present dish was excavated in Iraq.[3] Both the bowl and the two dishes are vessel types believed to have been inherited by the Sasanians from the Romans.

AJ

1. Yun Anzhi 1993b: 109–30.
2. Yoshimizu 1977: pl. 55.
3. Harden 1934: fig. 4, nos. 6–9.

160

Bowl with pearl design

Northern Wei dynasty (386–534), ca. 6th century
Glazed earthenware
Diameter of mouth rim 3¼ in. (8.2 cm)
Excavated at Luoyang, Henan Province
Institute of Archaeology, Chinese Academy of Social Sciences

Excav. report in *Kaogu* 1991.12

The archaeological excavations (1985–91) at the ancient Northern Wei (386–534) city of Luoyang unearthed more than a dozen shards of glazed earthenware made with unusual techniques and decorated with rarely seen designs.[1] This bowl was restored from some of those shards. It has a straight mouth, deep body, rounded wall, and solid, slightly concave foot that is attached to the bottom. The dark gray earthenware body, fired at a relatively high temperature, is very fine in texture. The surface decoration is composed of two rows that resemble strings of pearls and two rows of raised studs in white slip. Then the entire vessel was covered with dark brown glaze, creating a lustrous, glasslike veneer. Because the body itself is dark gray, the vessel after glazing is nearly black; the raised ornaments are light yellow and somewhat translucent. Other shards found with this bowl are glazed in yellow or green. Technically, the bowl is finely made. In both form and ornament, it is an obvious imitation of imported Sasanian glass bowls, in particular, the kind represented by the example from the tomb of Li Xian (cat. no. 158). This would indicate that Sasanian glass was greatly treasured at the time and that Chinese artisans, unable to reproduce it in glass, resorted to glazed earthenware for imitation.

AJ

1. Zhongguo shehui kexueyuan kaogu yanjiusuo Luoyang gongzuodui 1991:1090–95

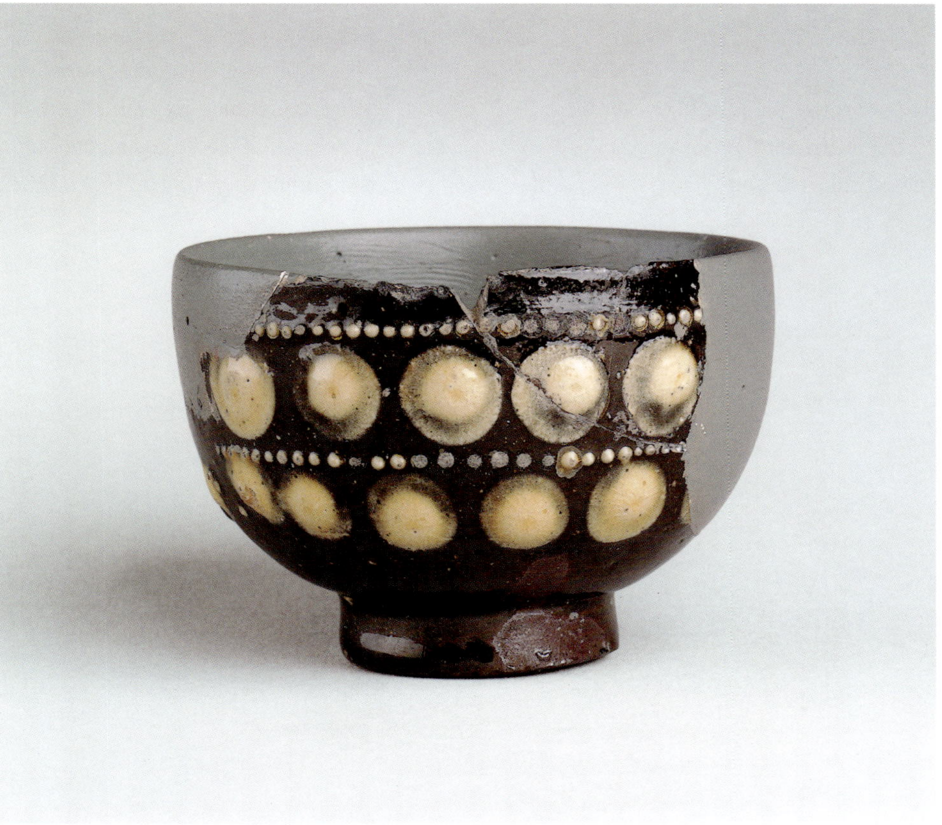

160

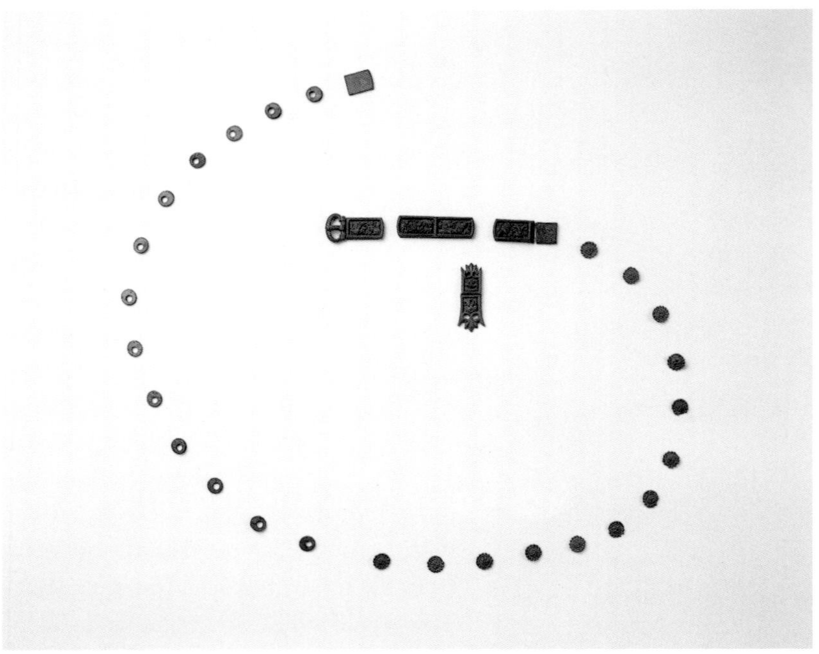

161
Belt buckle and ornamental plaques

Northern Zhou dynasty (557–581)
Bronze
Total length 43 5/16 in. (110 cm)
Excavated from the tomb of Emperor Wudi (r. 561–78), Xianyang, Shaanxi Province, 1994
Shaanxi Institute of Archaeology

Excav. report in *Kaogu yu wenwu* 1997.2

These bronze plaques for a belt were found in the tomb of Emperor Wudi of the Northern Zhou (r. 561–78) and his wife, the Turkic princess Asina, who died in 582, two years into the new dynasty of Sui. Not much was found by archaeologists who undertook the excavation of the tomb in 1993, after it had been looted. The pottery figures recovered are very much like those from Northern Qi tombs (see, for example, cat. nos. 154, 155). The most important objects from this tomb published to date are this set of belt plaques and the gold seal of the empress and her epitaph.

The decoration on the plaques consists of squatting and crouching animals on the large horizontal pieces and an animal mask and another squatting animal on the vertical piece. The circular plaques are in the shape of an animal mask within a pearl roundel. The fantastic animal motif has parallels going back to the early Han period, when the influence of nomadic art was strongly felt; it was revived, with somewhat different treatment, in the sixth century. The pearl roundel is of Iranian origin, and the spiky "palmette" at the two ends of the large vertical plaque may be a version of the acanthus, which was transmitted through Central Asia from the Eastern Roman Empire.

JCYW

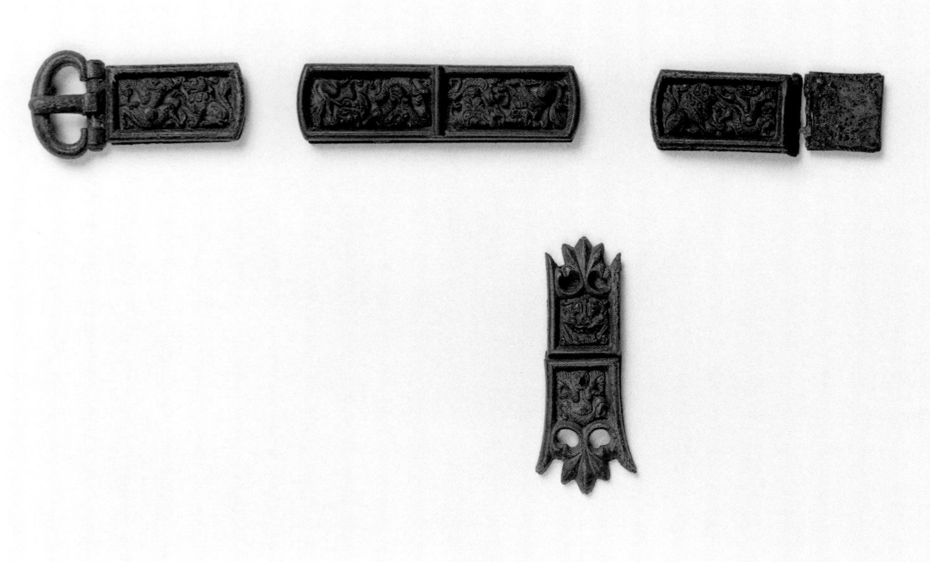

161, detail

162
Two sarcophagus panels

Northern Qi dynasty (550–577), ca. 573
Limestone
Height 53 1/8 in. (135 cm)
Excavated at Yidu, Shandong Province, 1971
Qingzhou City Museum

Excav. report in *Wenwu* 1985.10

These two sarcophagus panels from Shandong are part of a group of nine from a site said to have contained an epitaph tablet bearing the date 573.[1] Some of the panels were relatively intact when they were excavated. Others have been reassembled.[2] Most likely, they once formed the walls of a house-shaped sarcophagus, a type that became common in China in the late fifth and sixth centuries.[3] Such sarcophagi, and related funerary couches, are usually found in the tombs of high-ranking members of the Sogdian community in China. The Sogdians, a trading people from parts of present-day Uzbekistan, settled in China in some number and often rose to positions of prominence during the Northern Qi (550–577) and Sui (581–619) dynasties.

Images of Sogdians and their customs, secular and religious, as well as related motifs are often seen on sarcophagi and related monuments during this period. The palmette scrolls that frame the panels on this example and the birds at the top derive from West and Central Asian imagery. The latter are shown either singly or paired and often have ribbons tied around their necks. Birds with ribbons are sometimes identified as the Sodgian *hvarnah,* or bird of good fortune.

On the panel at left, a dromedary, or one-humped camel (also known as an Arabian camel), is incised together with a horse and groom. Laden with bundles of cloth and other goods, the camel provides an interesting contrast to the horse, whose mane and tail are carefully groomed. Camels and horses, with and without riders, are standard motifs in the decoration of funerary monuments made in China for Sogdians such as the high officials Yu Hong (cat. no. 175) and An Qie.[4] While some of the panels depict scenes of hunting, others illustrate journeys, some taken by the interred in his afterlife, and others representing visits to the deceased.

The groom leading the horse and camel and the more elaborately dressed figure on the panel at right[5] are identified as Sogdian by their clothing and facial features. On the other hand, the headdress worn by the seated figure on the second panel, together with his round face and small features, indicates a different ethnicity, probably Han Chinese. The Sogdian is shown offering an empty tray to the seated figure, while the figure standing behind, probably also Han Chinese, presents a basin filled with coral.

The recipient of these gifts sits on a stool, his left leg resting on the opposite knee and his right leg pendant. The posture illustrates the interaction between funerary and Buddhist imagery in the late sixth century. Known in India and Pakistan, it has traditionally been associated with representations of pensive bodhisattvas in Chinese Buddhist art (see cat. nos. 163, 168). Also found in secular paintings from Sogdiana,[6] the posture is depicted on a funerary couch found at Tianshui, Gansu,[7] and on one of the panels from the sarcophagus of Yu Hong. The former is part of a feasting scene, while the figure in the latter, who has a halo and an elaborate headdress, has been tentatively identified as the Zoroastrian deity Zurvan.[8]

An absence of religious overtones is characteristic of the Shandong panels, which are also distinguished from other, contemporaneous panels in their use of incising rather than relief carving. It is assumed that, based on the features and clothing of the seated figure, the interred was either a Han Chinese or someone of Xianbei ethnicity. It seems likely that he had a close relationship to members of the Sogdian community in China and that these ties influenced the types of imagery

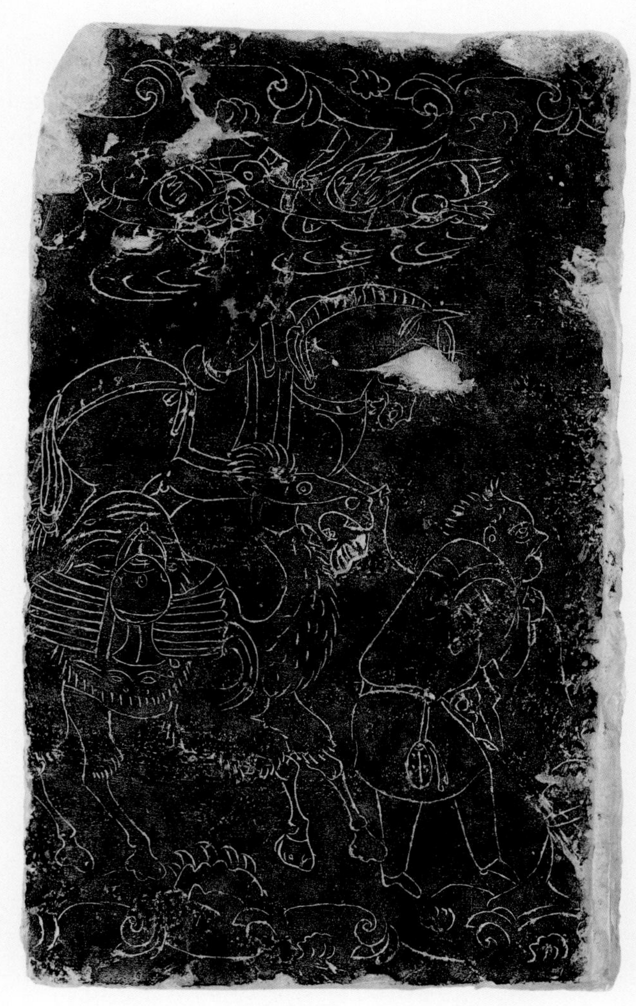

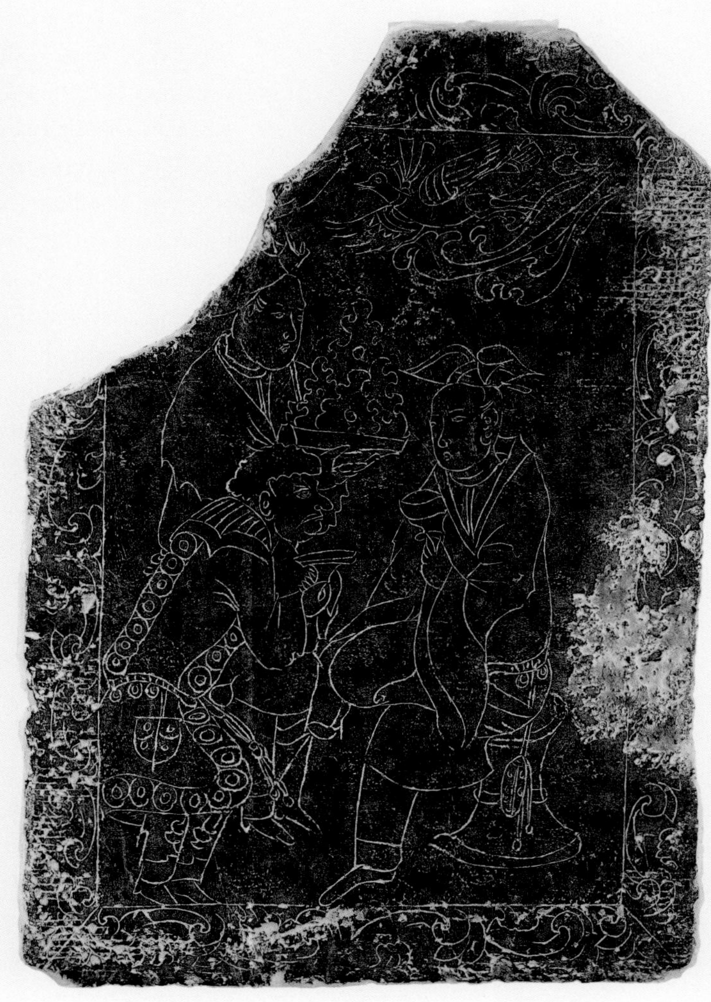

in his tomb. Whether or not this unidentified inhabitant accepted the Zoroastrian practices thought to underlie much of the imagery is unknown, as is his reason for choosing such foreign themes for the decoration of his final resting place.

DPL

1. Xia Mingcai 1985: 49–54; Zheng Yan 2001: 88.
2. Xia Mingcai 2001: 92–93.
3. Wu Hung 2002: 34–41.
4. Tianshui shi bowuguan 1992: 46–68.
5. Azarpay 1980, pl. 21, fig. 43.
6. Zheng Yan 2001, fig. 21.
7. Tianshui shi bowuguan 1992, panel no. 6.
8. Jiang Boqin 2000a: 34.

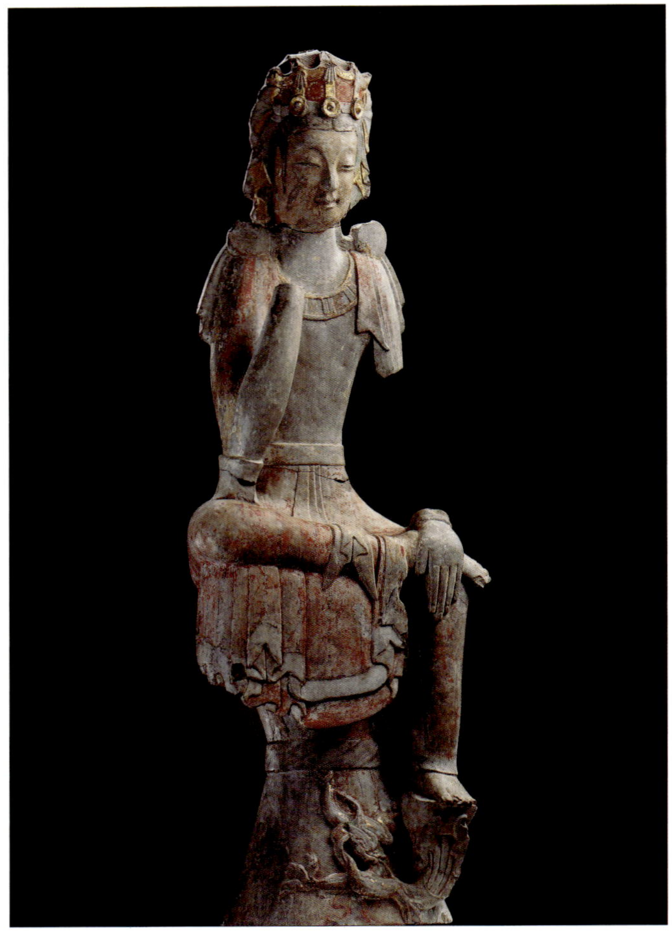

163
Seated Bodhisattva in pensive pose

Northern Qi dynasty (550–577)
Stone with gilding and pigments
Height 31½ in. (80 cm)
Excavated at Longxingsi, Qingzhou, Shandong Province, 1996
Qingzhou City Museum

Excav. report in *Wenwu* 1998.2

The pensive pose depicted in this independent sculpture is the same as that used in the Maitreya altarpiece from Hebei Province dated Northern Qi 562 (cat. no. 168). A youthful, princely figure sits on a tall stool with one leg pendent, the other folded and resting on the seat. The construction of the work is quite ingenious and hardly diminished by the absence of the left arm and the right hand. The interplay of opposites builds the figure: the extended leg corresponds to an extended arm, the folded leg to a similarly bent arm. The left arm once sustained the inclined head, the hand barely touching the cheek (the mark is still visible). To prevent excessive leaning of the torso, a barely noticeable support was inserted between the bent elbow and the folded leg; the image thus maintains both stability and frontality. The interplay of opposites continues in the modeling, where the uncovered torso contrasts with the draped lower body. In this section, artful swags of cloth alternate with smooth passages, especially over the legs. On the pedestal, the contrast is again apparent, as a writhing dragon emerges from the unadorned surface. The supple lotus enveloped in leaves, spouting from the pedestal, serves as the support for the bodhisattva's foot.

Because the sculpture was conceived frontally, the decoration at each side below the waist is not noticed, and yet it is very relevant. Painted (not sculpted) ornamental sashes, comprising ribbons gathered with a conspicuous jade ring, hang from the waist. The ribbons, woven with horizontal stripes and bordered with fringe, are tucked beneath the figure and reemerge to drape over the stool. The Japanese scholar Ōnishi Shūya has recently called attention to this decoration, which is a characteristic of Korean and Japanese pensive-pose images of Miroku (Skt: Maitreya), and has concluded that the iconography originated with this Qingzhou sculpture.[1]

Furthermore, these very special adornments seem to be part of a conventional costume worn by southern Chinese aristocrats for special court functions, as described in the chapter on rituals and regulations in the *Suishu* (History of the Sui). The choice of colors for the crown and attire thus very likely follows a specific code of dress, that of the southern aristocrats. The elegant headpiece studded with rosettes, tassels, and lateral streamers employs cinnabar red, gold, and malachite green. The streamers are painted gold inside and malachite outside, and over the shoulders the wide swags of cloth kept in place by upright disks are cinnabar, to complement the cinnabar skirt.

The image blends an utter simplicity, refined elegance, and a sweet benevolence that transpires from the youthful, dreamy face.

AFH

1. Ōnishi 2003: 55–65.

164

Standing Buddha

Northern Qi dynasty (550–577)
Limestone with gilding
Height 58¼ in. (148 cm)

165

Standing Buddha

Northern Qi dynasty (550–577)
Limestone with gilding
Height 24¾ in. (63 cm)

Cat. nos. 164 and 165 excavated at Longxingsi, Qingzhou, Shandong Province, 1996
Qingzhou City Museum

Excav. report in *Wenwu* 1998.2

These two contemporaneous Buddha images from Longxingsi reveal the familiarity of Qingzhou carvers with a novel source of artistic inspiration—the Indian Gupta style (ca. 300–500), which had inspired the carvers of Sichuan in the first half of the sixth century. In the second half of the century, Guptan models became known to sculptors in Shandong; the Northern Qi style was the immediate result. The sculptors had at their disposal

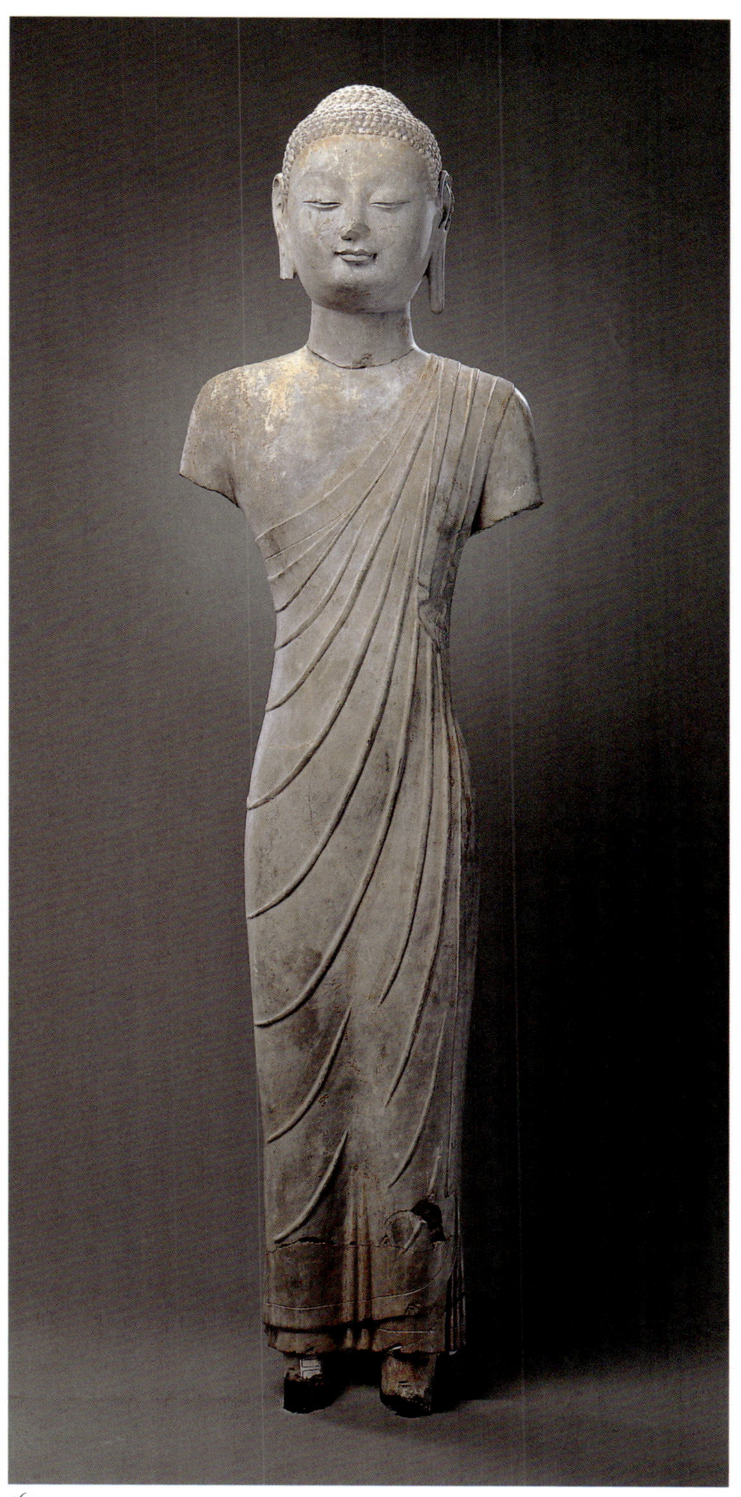

164

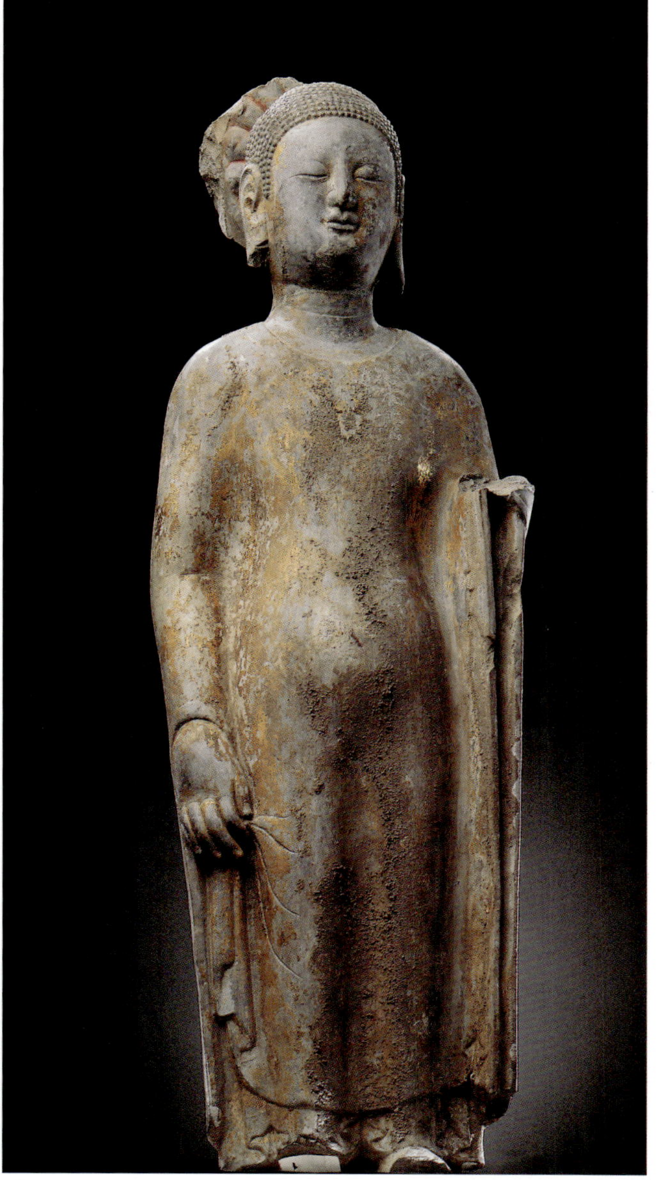

165

two different geographic versions of the Gupta style, Mathura and Sarnath. Both styles extolled the physical beauty of the Buddha's body and the contrasting spirituality of his face. Mathura produced Buddhas barely clad in clinging robes defined by a looped network of stringy pleats; Sarnath pushed the formula even further by eliminating the strings, thereby making the robe indistinguishable from the body beneath. Robe and body became one. Both Mathura and Sarnath present a gently smiling Buddha's face in a state of utter tranquillity and introspection. The spherical head is carved with tightly serrated rows of snail curls, sinuous downcast eyes, and full, sensuous lips.

The two Buddhas from Qingzhou embody these two styles. Following the Indian aesthetic, the perfectly round heads express a deep, trancelike peacefulness. The Buddha at the left (cat. no. 164) wears the pleated robe in the "open" mode, with the right shoulder exposed. Possibly we can trace this interpretation to the mediation of southern India, as the Buddha from Amaravati favored this fashion. Pleats rendered through smoothly rounded grooves descend from the Buddha's left shoulder, forming regular, transversal patterns across the body and revealing rather than concealing the graceful, slender forms beneath. The Buddha at the right (cat. no. 165) translates, instead, the Sarnath mode. A smooth, diaphanous robe covers the body completely and clings to such an extent that the figure's round contours and fleshy anatomy are fully exposed. Only the hem of the robe and its hanging from both hands (the left hand is missing) remind us of a monastic covering cloth. The sculptures are further enhanced by the warm glow of gold applied to both body and robe.

AFH

166
Standing Cosmological Buddha

Northern Qi dynasty (550–577)
Stone with gilding and pigments
Height 17⅜ in. (44 cm)
Excavated at Linqu, Shandong Province
Linqu City Museum

Excav. report in *Wenwu* 2002.9

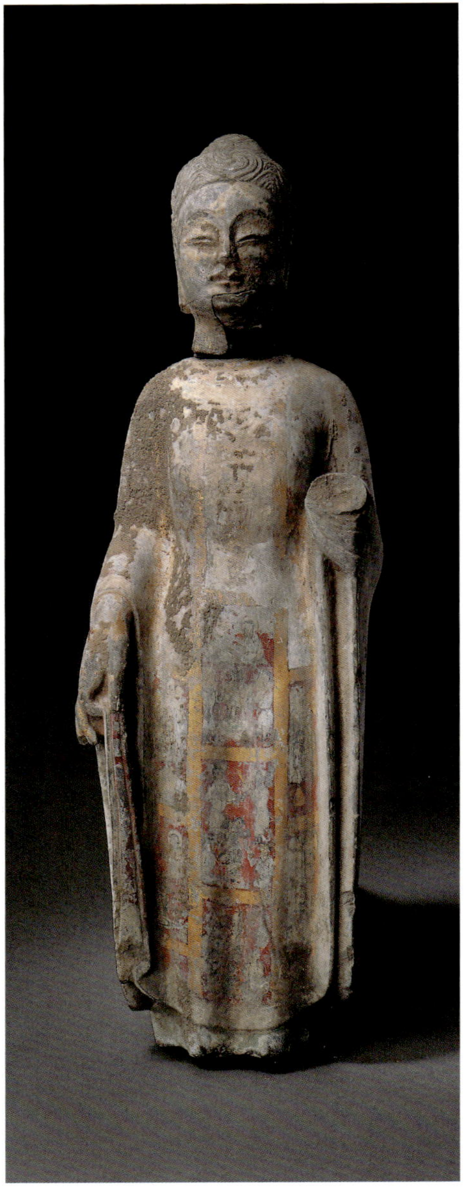

In spite of its modest size, this sculpture embodies many striking features, the rich imagery painted on its surface being the most notable.[1] I begin by describing the Buddha's physical appearance. The hairdo is rendered with whorls and undulating circular patterns; arched eyebrows accented by black paint frame the semiclosed eyes; and a black mustache is painted below the straight nose, while the lips retain a vividly red color. The shoulders are round and the chest and abdomen prominent beneath the monastic robe. The Buddha's face and right hand (the left is broken) and the body's exposed parts were originally painted gold.

The surface covered by the garments is treated almost like a canvas. The inner robe is painted green, while the *kasaya*, or outer robe, is delineated by vermilion patches outlined in gold to form frames for thirty-one vignettes. On the frontal axis, from top to bottom, are an *apsaras*, or flying celestial; the Heaven of the Thirty-three Gods above Mount Sumeru, around which two serpents, or nagas, are coiled; two haloed beings; a horse attended by two grooms (likely foreigners, since they wear long tunics and boots); an entertainment; and two bovine-headed creatures who are shown tormenting human beings. Iconographically, these vignettes refer to the *gathis*, the five (or six) realms of the devas (heavenly beings), man, animal, and hell. Missing is the *preta*, or hungry ghost realm, which is replaced with the entertainment scene.

Most of the side representations are gone, but two *cintamani*, or jewels, are visible on the left upper arm. On the Buddha's right side is a scene of worship and perhaps an ascetic within a flaming aureole. On the back, fragmented paintings suggest flying celestials; a monk seated beneath a tree; two figures, one kneeling; and a threatening personage. While the frontal scenes are quite legible, the remaining references defy precise identification. Perhaps they represent events in the Buddha's former and last lives, as we see in the sculpture in the Freer Gallery of Art, Washington, D.C., which remains the most complete rendering of this deity.[2]

This very special depiction of the Buddha shows him as Lord of the Universe, or the Cosmological Buddha, a form that exalts the deity as the divine receptacle of all that exists, but particularly of the six realms that are integral to the reincarnation process. The iconography originated in the fourth century in the Central Asian kingdom of Kucha (on the northern Silk Road), within the context of the Hinayana (Small Vehicle) doctrine and linked, in particular, to the teachings of the Sarvastivadin school. For the monastic community of Kucha, this deity was Shakyamuni, the historical Buddha in the guise of Lord of the Universe.

Transmitted to China, the image of the Cosmological Buddha became popular after 550 in the frescoes of the caves at Dunhuang, Gansu, and in the sculpture of the northeast. It was, however, reinterpreted and its iconographic scheme enriched. The addition of narrative was an important Chinese innovation, and pictorial cycles were painted or incised on the surface of cave sculpture to complement the narratives that appeared on the cave walls. The identity of the Chinese Cosmological Buddha has been questioned, and some scholars believe him to be Vairocana.[3]

In the province of Shandong, during the Northern Qi (550–577) and Sui (581–619) dynasties, the Cosmological Buddha appears to have become very popular, to the extent that at least ten examples have so far been retrieved. In the execution of this deity, Shandong sculptors and painters joined their respective skills; certain artisans were responsible for the sculpture itself, while others added the painted iconography. Here, regrettably, the loss of pigment has entailed the loss of the imagery—the essential clue to the sculpture's identity. One still recognizes that the representations are associated with the Cosmological Buddha, but the well-knit pictorial program is gone.

AFH

1. The sculpture was first published by Gong Dejie 2002: 84–92.
2. The rise of this iconography in Central Asia and its spread to China and Japan are discussed in Howard 1986. The Shandong examples are not included, as they became known only in the early 1990s.
3. The author is of the opinion that the pre-Tang images represent Shakyamuni, while the Tang examples may represent Vairocana. This change in identity resulted from earlier teachings being incorporated into the Esoteric school. Li Jingjie (1999: 1–52) believes all Cosmological Buddha images without exception represent Vairocana.

167
Altarpiece dedicated to Buddha Maitreya

Northern Wei dynasty (386–534), dated 524
Gilt bronze
Height 30¼ in. (76.9 cm)
The Metropolitan Museum of Art. Rogers Fund, 1938 (38.158a–n)

The attenuated physique and heavy, concealing drapery of the Buddha in the center of this altarpiece typify the art of the early sixth century, particularly sculptures produced in the vicinity of the capital, Luoyang. A badly abraded inscription incised into the back of the base identifies the central figure as the Buddha Maitreya, gives the date, and indicates that a certain Kaizhi commissioned the altarpiece on behalf of his deceased son. The inscription also expresses the hope that the son and other relatives will eventually be united in the presence of the Buddha.

Twelve angel-like beings,[1] known as *apsaras*, many playing musical instruments, encircle the flaming mandorla that surrounds Maitreya and his entourage, and two standing and two seated bodhisattvas attend him. The former stand on top of lotuses that spring from the mouths of coiling dragons, a motif that becomes prominent in the second half of the sixth century. The latter are seated at the Buddha's feet. Four figures wearing Xianbei clothing, who stand behind the seated bodhisattvas, represent donors or devotees.[2] An incense burner is nestled into a burgeoning lotus flower at the front of the altarpiece. Crouching lions and

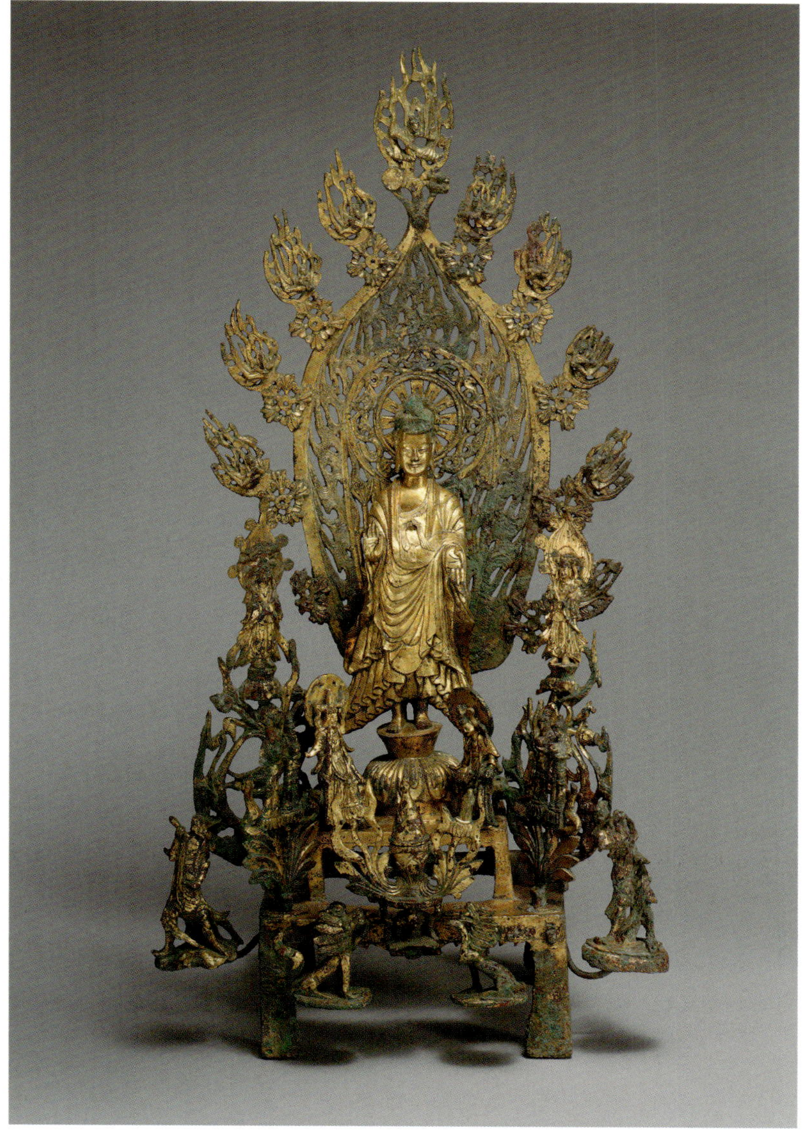

semiclad guardians yielding weapons are placed at the front and sides, respectively.

Maitreya is the only divinity in Buddhism revered as both a bodhisattva and a Buddha. Devotion to Maitreya, and the desire for rebirth in his Pure Land or Buddha Field, known as the Tushita Heaven, was widespread in the late fifth and sixth centuries.[3] Rebirth in the Pure Land offered an escape from the harsh realities of daily life while one awaited another, presumably easier, reincarnation. Elements in the imagery of the altarpiece, which are standard in later paradise imagery, indicate that it represents the descent of the Buddha Maitreya from the Tushita Heaven. The gesture of the raised right and lowered left hand, in which the thumb touches the index finger, is often used to indicate the descent of the Buddha Amitabha from his Pure Land, Sukhavati. It seems likely that the same meaning underlies the use here of such gestures by the primary Buddha.

The pensive pose, the posture of the seated bodhisattvas in which one leg is pendant and the other rests on the opposite knee, is often found in images of the bodhisattva Maitreya. It is also used to represent any bodhisattva who, at a certain stage in his spiritual life, inhabits the Tushita Heaven while awaiting his final reincarnation, during which he will achieve enlightenment.[4] The pensive bodhisattvas refer to the Tushita Heaven, while the standing bodhisattvas are accompanying Maitreya in his descent from that realm. The minuscule figures—one standing, one kneeling—on the lotus pedestals to the right and left of the incense burner represent souls that have been, or will be, reborn into the Pure Land. Such figures are common in later paradise imagery, particularly that of the Buddha Amitabha. Devotion to Amitabha, which becomes dominant in Chinese Buddhism in the late sixth century, is a well-known aspect of the Buddhist belief that each Buddha creates and maintains his own perfected world.[5]

DPL

1. One is missing; only eleven remain on the altarpiece.
2. They have also been identified as the guardians of the four quarters. See Fisher 1995: 17–24.
3. Lee In-sook 1983.
4. Leidy 1990: 21–37.
5. Okazaki 1977.

168
Maitreya altarpiece

Northern Qi dynasty (550–577), dated 562
Marble with gilding and pigments
Height 29½ in. (75 cm)
Excavated at Gaocheng, Hebei Province, 1978
Zhengding Office of Cultural Properties Preservation

Excav. report in *Kaogu yu wenwu* 1980.3

This intricately carved sculpture, miraculously almost intact, is identified in the inscription as a representation of Maitreya, Buddha of the Future: "During the rule of the Northern Qi, in the first year of Heqing [562], a nun of Jianzhongsi, together with other Buddhist followers, respectfully had this white marble image of Maitreya made. The beneficiaries of this pious act are the emperor, teachers, and parents going back seven generations, all beings—living and deceased, ordained clerics, as well as secular believers." The inscription ends by naming Jia Qiande as the patron of the temple.[1]

The inscription specifically addresses the sculpture as a Maitreya, despite the fact that it is the twin Buddhas Prabhutaratna (C: Duobao) and Shakyamuni (C: Shijia) from chapter 11 of the Lotus Sutra who are shown on the front, seated side by side on a jeweled stupa. The allusion to Maitreya is, instead, found on the back of the altarpiece, where two figures are shown in the "pensive" pose (*siwei*). In the fourth and fifth centuries, this iconography was used to represent Prince Siddhartha—later the Buddha Shakyamuni—meditating under the rose apple tree. After 550, however, the same pose was increasingly, if not exclusively, employed in conjunction with Maitreya worship. (In Korea and Japan, such images are in fact recognized as Maitreya.) In the present work, this identification is further supported by the choice of tree under which the pair sits, a dragon flower tree (Skt: Nagapushpa), the canonical tree of the Buddha of the Future. It is puzzling that the two renderings of Maitreya as the central image are portrayed on the back of the altar instead of on the front.

The work is composed of two parts—the altar proper and the unadorned pedestal that carries the incised inscription in the front. Displaying a complex organization overflowing with minute details, it is executed with intricate local (Hebei) technical and stylistic innovations such as the perforated tree canopies that shelter the deities and the smooth, round forms that lack anatomical differentiation. The translucent surface of Hebei marble blends well with the warm tonalities of blue and red and the traces of gold originally used as a surface finish.

On the front, the two symmetrically rendered Buddhas are backed by a mandorla and sheltered by two intertwined gingko trees. Their branches executed by perforation—a Hebei characteristic—form an airy canopy animated by miniature Buddhas, floating celestials, cherubs, and two slithering dragons. The Buddhas are assisted by two monks—or a monk and a nun, perhaps the donatrix herself—and two bodhisattvas standing on lotuses. Two heavenly kings are placed at the base of the altarpiece, sharing the space with two guardian lions, and many children play below the throne.

The back is not as defined as the front. Here, two angels holding a flaming jewel hover over the deities in pensive pose, flanked by a Pratyeka Buddha and bodhisattvas. Beneath the throne are

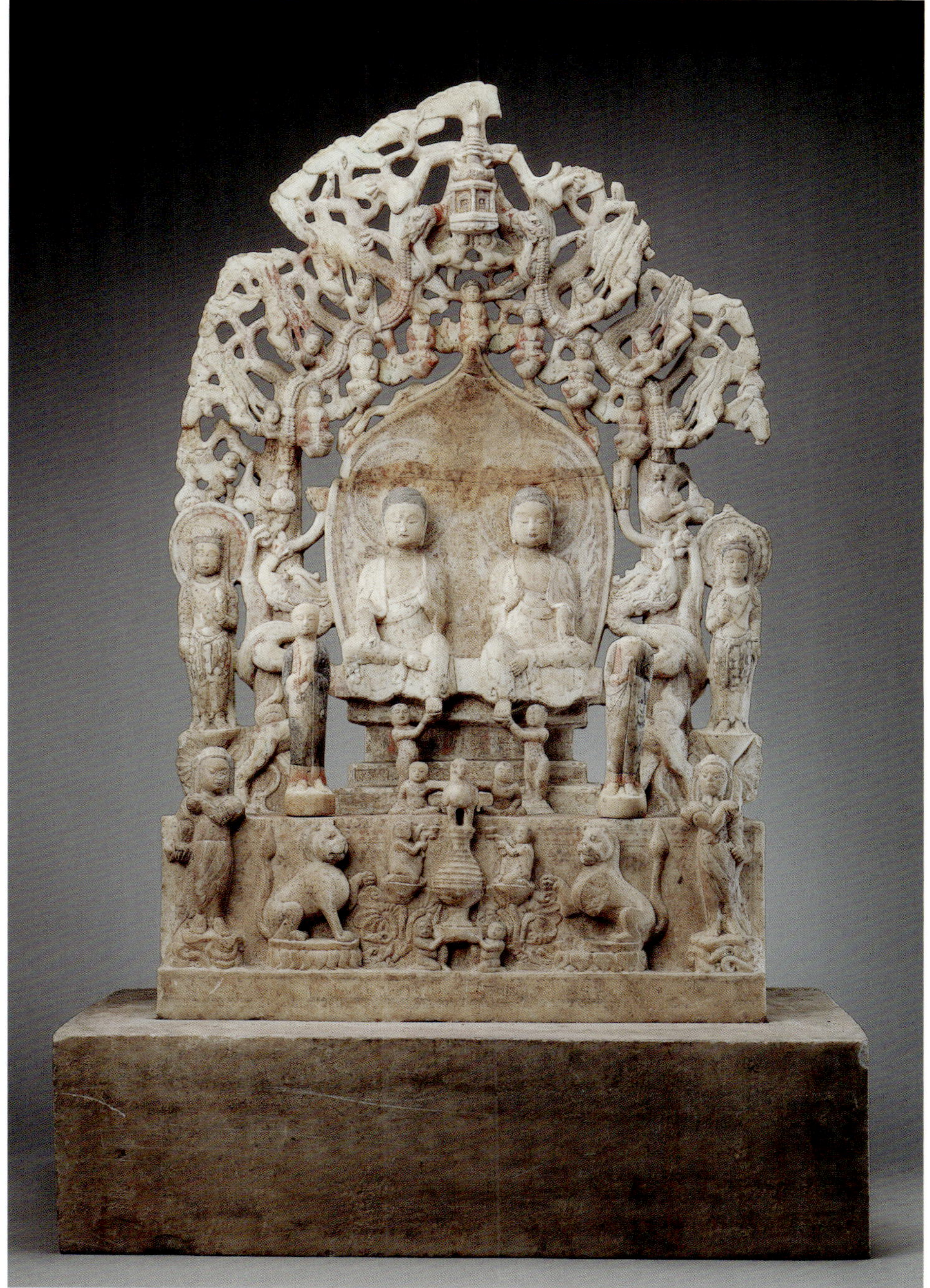

168, front

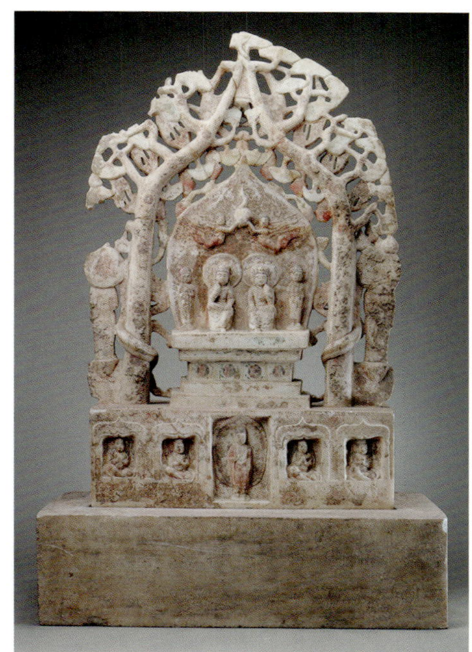

168, back

five niches. The central niche enframes an aureoled image; the other four serve to shelter four personages reminiscent of Spirit Kings. AFH

1. The rubbing of the inscription is in Cheng Jizhong 1980: 242–45.

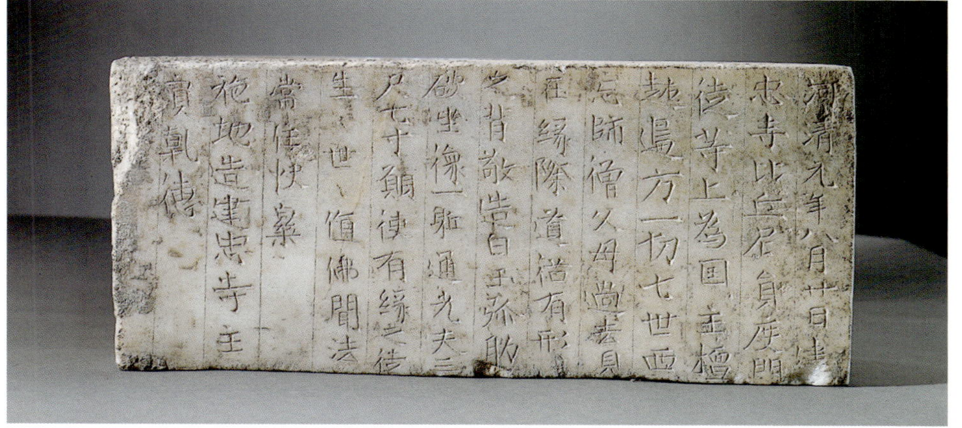

168, inscription

169
Standing Buddha

Northern Zhou dynasty (559–581)
Stone with gilding and pigments
Height 66 ⅞ in. (170 cm)
Excavated at Xi'an, Shaanxi Province, 1978
Xi'an City Institute of Cultural Properties Protection and Archaeology

Reference: Tōkyō kokuritsu hakubutsukan 1998 no.7

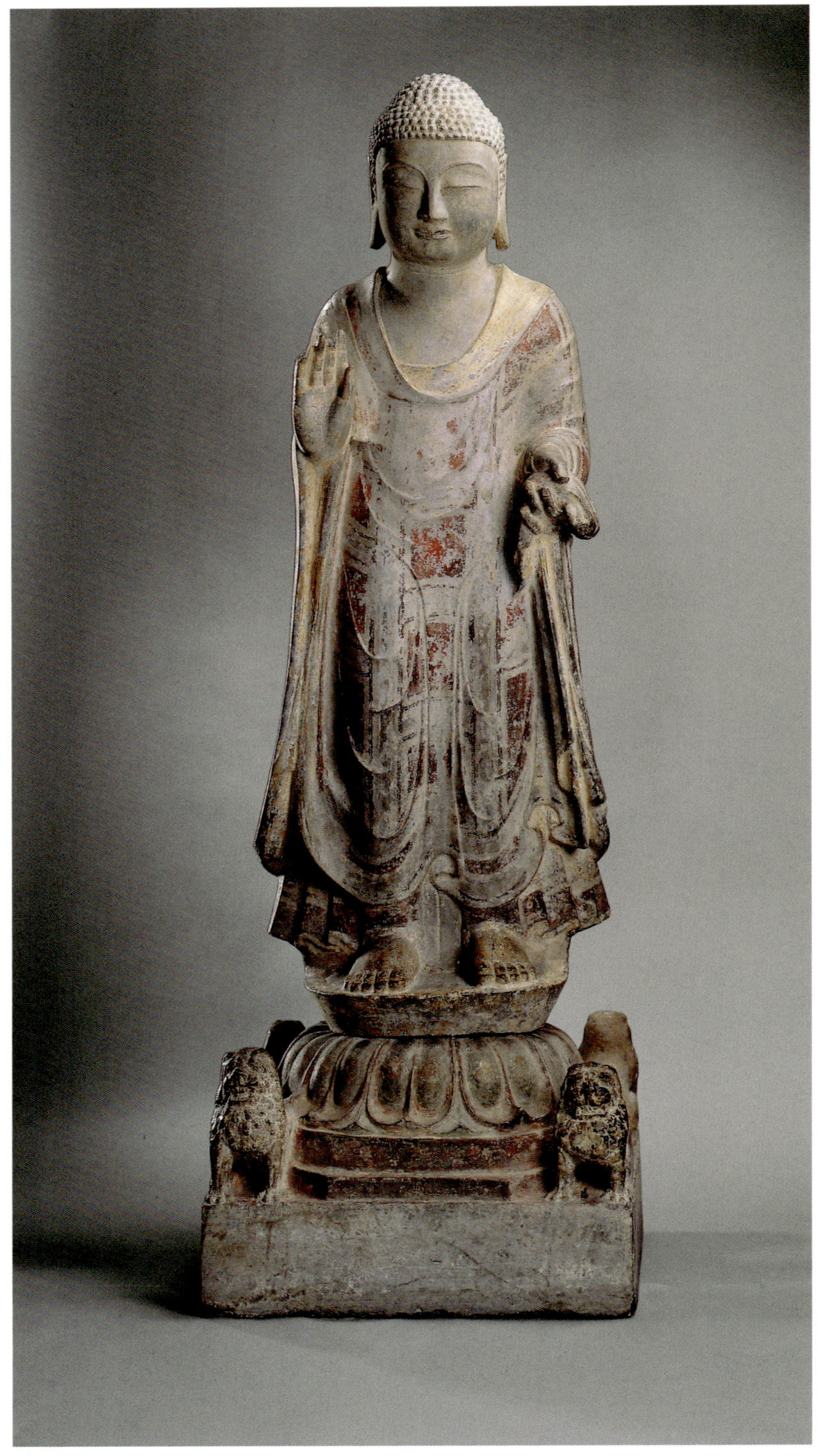

169

The sculpture is a typical example of a Northern Zhou (559–581) Buddha executed at the Xi'an capital, Shaanxi. In contrast with the two contemporaneous bodhisattvas also in this exhibition (cat. no. 170), which display an opulent exterior—a heavily modeled body encumbered with sumptuous jewelry—the Buddha, with stocky physique draped with a weighty pleated robe, projects an austere solemnity. The Buddha's squarish face—defined by a large nose, elongated eyes, and full lips—is its most distinguishing characteristic. The *ushnisha,* or cranial protuberance, is barely visible; the head is embellished with serrated rows of tiny snail curls, once painted a brilliant blue. But the face retains the standard impassive, almost severe, expression, justifying the view that Northern Zhou Buddhas generally lack the introspective serenity of their contemporary Northern Qi counterparts. Features and expression reflect the aesthetic preference of northwestern China (Gansu, Ningxia, and Shaanxi), where they became popular as early as the first decades of the fifth century.

The distinctive hand gestures—one hand raised in the "fear not" mudra, the other lifting the robe—and the interpretation of the monastic garment are reminiscent of the imperially sponsored Northern Wei images in Central Binyangdong Cave, Longmen, carved almost fifty years earlier, in 523. However, the manner in which the outer robe is rendered, by artfully alternating sweeping arches and vertical pleats, is a departure from the previous mode. The painted red and white squares—in imitation of a monastic garment made of patches of cloth—complement the directional contrast.

As it is often the case with Northern Zhou sculpture, the work is composed of two parts, the socle on which the Buddha stands and the square lotus pedestal into which it is inserted. Standard lions sit in the four corners.

AFH

170
Pair of standing bodhisattvas (Guanyin)

Northern Zhou dynasty (559–581)
Marble with gilding and pigments
Max. height 31⅛ in. (79 cm)
Found in Xi'an, Shaanxi Province, 1992
Xi'an City Institute of Cultural Properties Protection and Archaeology

Excav. report in *Wenwu* 1997.2

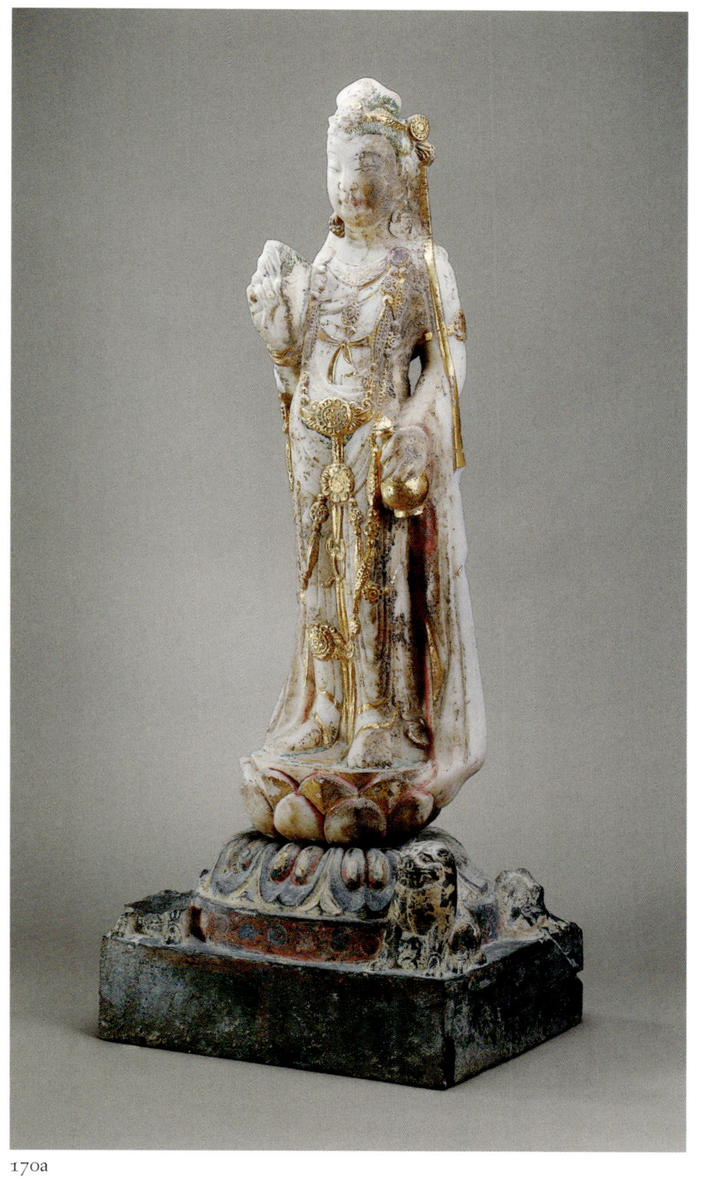

170a

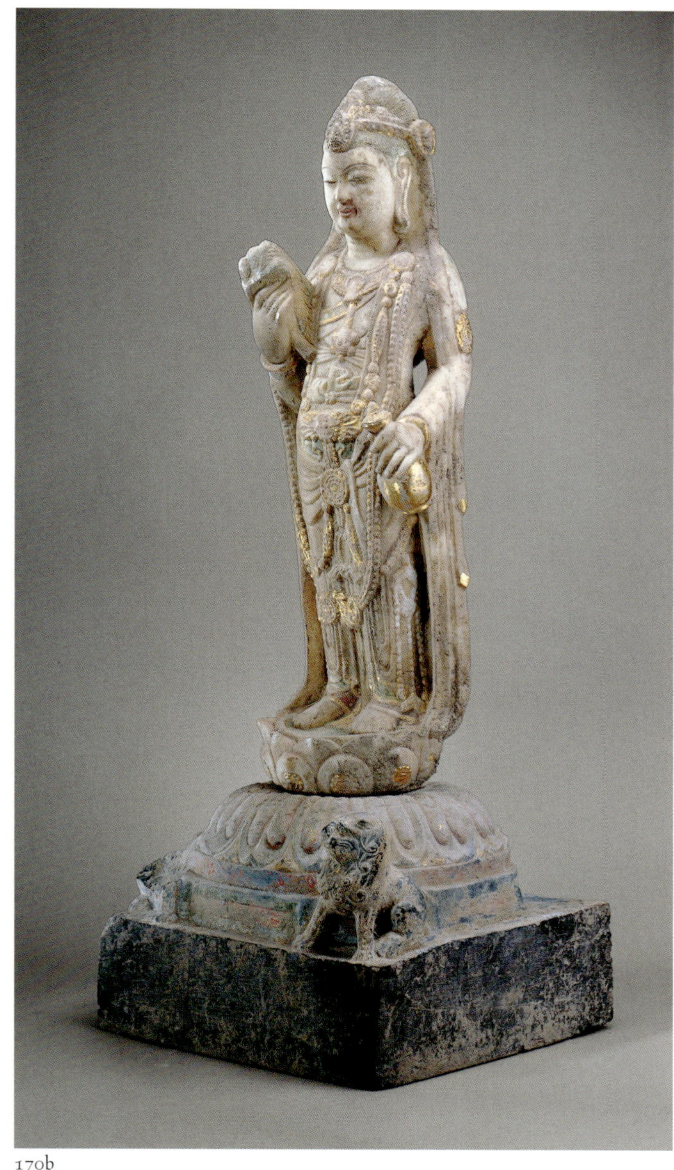

170b

Northern Zhou artisans carved deities with compact, blocklike bodies and stern, passive faces. The two Guanyins from Xi'an, Shaanxi (once part of a trio), possess these qualities and exhibit, in addition, a richness of surface decoration, a typically Northern Zhou characteristic.[1] The two Guanyins differ in that one is slightly taller and chunkier than the other. Their identity is confirmed by the Buddha shown seated in the central medallion of their crowns and also by the implements they carry, a flask and a willow branch. Both stand on sockets inserted in a support formed of an inverted double lotus. The latter, in turn, rests on a square pedestal. Originally, the pedestals carried two and four lions, respectively. While the deities are carved in white marble, the pedestals are made of limestone.

The sculptor disregarded realism of body form. The opulent front is contrasted with the less embellished back. At the front, we are treated to a detailed rendering of a massive and ostentatious necklace, elaborate axial pendants, and three-dimensional beads nestled in the midst of ponderous drapes. The swinging beaded rope creates a visual dissonance by breaking the standard axial verticality: instead of hanging from both shoulders, the chain hangs only from the left shoulder, crosses low in front of the body, and loops over the right arm. The exorbitant amount of embellishment accentuates the sculpture's sense of mass, while the gilding and painting increase its showy effect. This aspect of Buddhist sculpture has, for the most part, been lost through a lack of preservation techniques. In fact, these two images represent standard Northern Zhou bodhisattva traits—a staggering amount of jewelry and a surface covered with colors and gold.

The annexation in 553 of Sichuan by China's northwest (then ruled by the Western Wei dynasty) is essential to understanding the formation of Northern Zhou–style bodhisattva images. Sichuan carvers sculpted bodhisattvas that display plasticity of body and lavish surface décor, a taste transmitted from India that had forged deep roots in Sichuanese Buddhist art. These elements of Northern Zhou style thus appear to have originated in Sichuan. To support the notion of the transmission of stylistic traits between the Sichuan and Shaanxi, I draw attention to the type of pedestal chosen for the taller Guanyin—the double inverted lotus with rosettes carved in the petals. It is nearly identical to that in the 551 Ashoka-type Buddha executed in Sichuan (cat. no. 128).

AFH

1. The set consists of three Guanyin images found together; see the report in Xi'an shi wenwuju 1997: 78–79.

171

Bust of a bodhisattva

Northern Zhou (557–581) or Sui (581–619) dynasty
Stone
Height 36⅝ in. (93 cm)
Excavated at Liquansi, Xi'an, Shaanxi Province, 1986
Xi'an City Institute of Cultural Properties Protection and Archaeology

Excav. report in *Kaogu yu wenwu* 2000.2

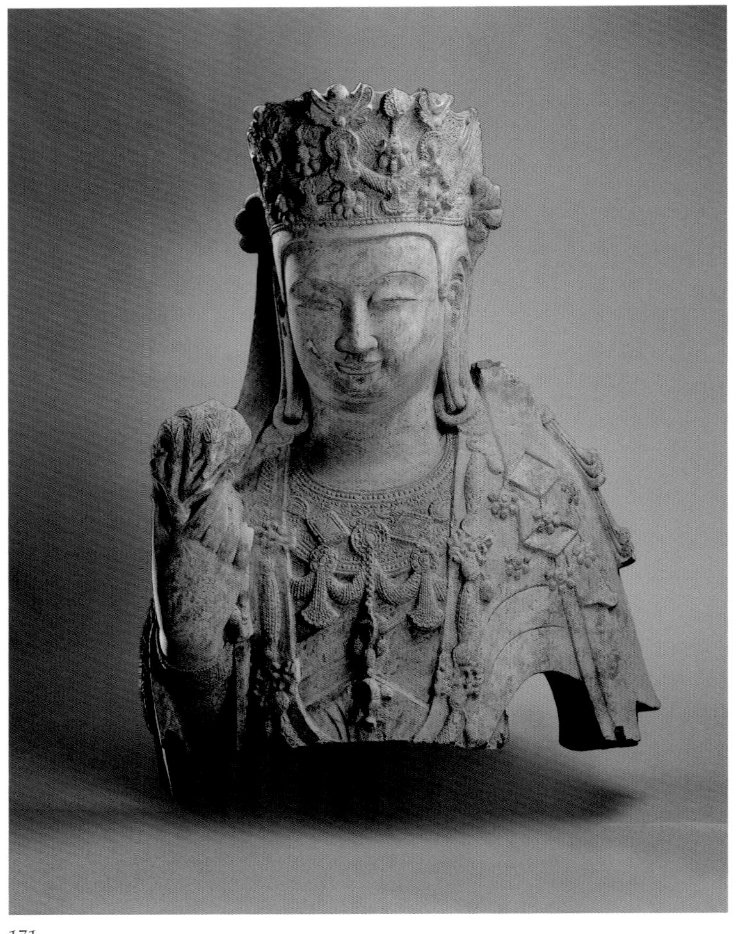

171

This torso fragment originally belonged to a monumental sculpture perhaps more than eight feet high. The bodhisattva's imposing crown and sumptuous costume assert the grandiose conception of the work. Round jewels linked with heavy swags of pearls support tassels and rosettes, while a solar disk embedded in a crescent highlights the center of the headpiece. The textural quality of the crown and its heavy décor contrast sharply with the smoothness of the wide, round face, framed by unnaturally elongated earlobes adorned with striking, multitiered earrings. The figure's thickset neck emerges from a lavishly decorated costume executed in the same style as the crown, with a profusion of jewels in relief against the damasked surface. In the right hand, still intact, the deity holds a willow branch at shoulder level; the left hand is missing. One marvels at the rich ornamentation of the sculpture and the impression of majesty it still generates.

Among the numerous ornaments of the crown, the sun resting on the crescent is the most intriguing and reveals the diffusion in China of motifs originating west of the Silk Road. Traveling westward along the two arteries of the Silk Road, one finds solar symbols such as these in the art of both the northern and the southern oases, in Sorchuk and Khotan. Past the Pamirs, the motifs were used also in the kingdom of Bamiyan (present-day Afghanistan). In ancient Persia, as early as the third century, the sun and crescent embellished the crown of the satrap carved in the Naqsh-I Rustem relief, near Persepolis, clearly a symbol of royal power. The motif was also adopted on Iranian plates and textiles. Ultimately, reaching way back in time and farther west, such emblems are found on Mesopotamian seals and studding the crowns of Egyptian gods.[1]

AFH

1. The origin and diffusion of these motifs are studied by Berthier 1991: 111–21.

172

Laozi and the Jade Emperor

Northern Wei dynasty (386–534), dated 527
Sandstone
Height 11 in. (27.8 cm)
National Museum of China

This is the only work in the exhibition to represent Daoism, China's native religion. The stele shows the deified Laozi, the founder of Daoism, flanked by the Jade Emperor. They are mirror images and hardly distinguishable but for the carved inscription at the upper left, which identifies the figure at the left as Yuhuangshi (Master Jade Emperor). The iconography of the work recalls Buddhist conventions: the placement of the two deities side by side with their assistants behind them in reduced scale; the use of hand gestures; the draping of the costume to overhang the throne; and the presence of a lion at each side. On the other hand, there are also clear differences, namely the figures'

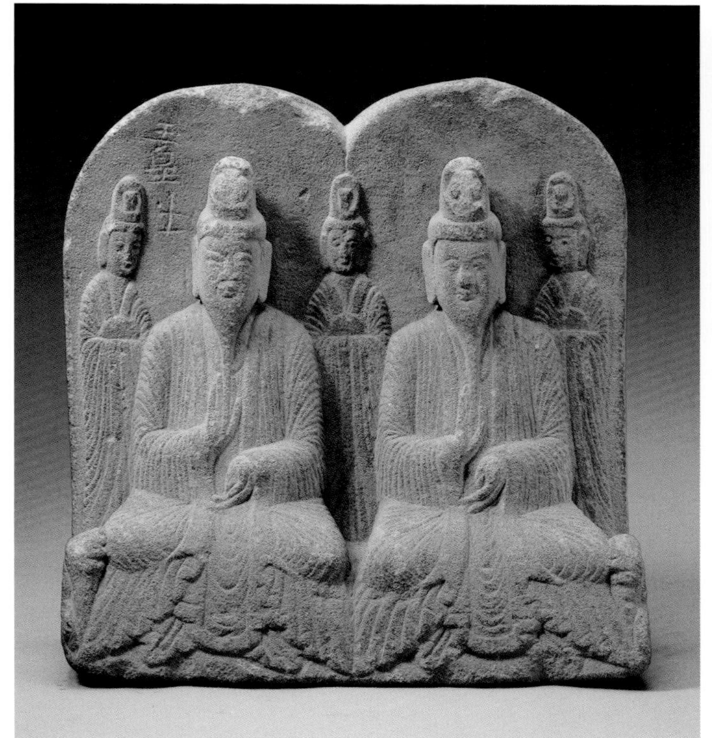
172, front

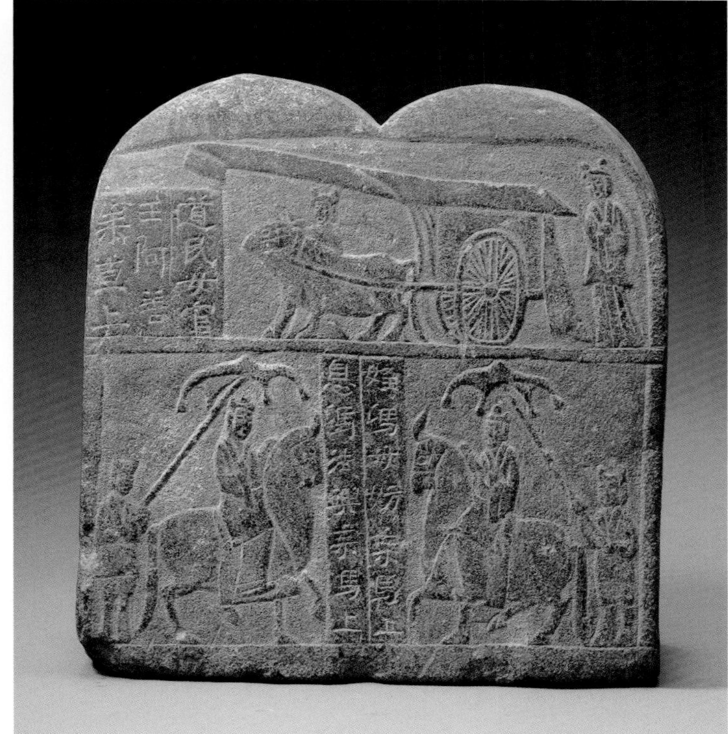
172, back

all-enveloping sleeved garments, their long pointed beards, and their rounded caps, which are prerogatives of Daoist priests.

On the back of the stele, primary and secondary donors are shown riding an oxcart and two horses, respectively. The oxcart, in the upper half, led by a tiny servant, is the conveyance for the principal donatrix, Wang Ashan, a female Daoist practitioner possibly with some official status (*nuguan*). An inscription tells us that Wang Ashan rides the cart, although in fact she is shown standing behind it. At the left, additional writing again identifies the patroness and adds that she commissioned the stele on the twenty-fifth day of the first year of Longxu (527), hoping that her mother and son will always enjoy virtuous households. The two riders on horseback, carved in the lower half of the stele, are relatives of Lady Wang: one is her niece Feng Wufang, the other her son Feng Faxing. Facing each other, they ride under the parasols held by two servants.

The provenance of this stele is not recorded, but the reign name of Longxu gives not only the year but the location of the work, Chang'an. The style of the sculpture is also typical of Shaanxi Province. It is recognizable in the costume of the two gods and three assistants, rendered with serrated drapery folds equally spaced over the surface. Here, the interest in intricate linear patterns prevails over anatomically correct forms. This idiom is also splendidly applied to the four-sided stele dated Northern Wei 501 (cat. no. 78), the product of a Chang'an workshop with higher skills than those of the artisan who carved this work.

AFH

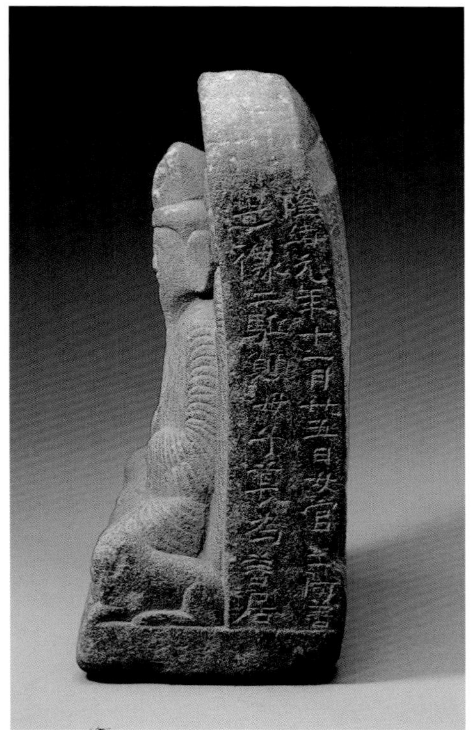
172, side

173
Textile with drinkers in pearl roundel

6th–early 7th century
Woven silk (1:2 warp-faced compound tabby)
Warp 4¾ in. (12 cm); weft 5 in. (12.5 cm)
Excavated from Tomb 507, Astana, Turfan, Xinjiang Uygur Autonomous Region, 1964
Nantong Textile Museum

REFERENCE: Zhao Feng 1999c: 106–7

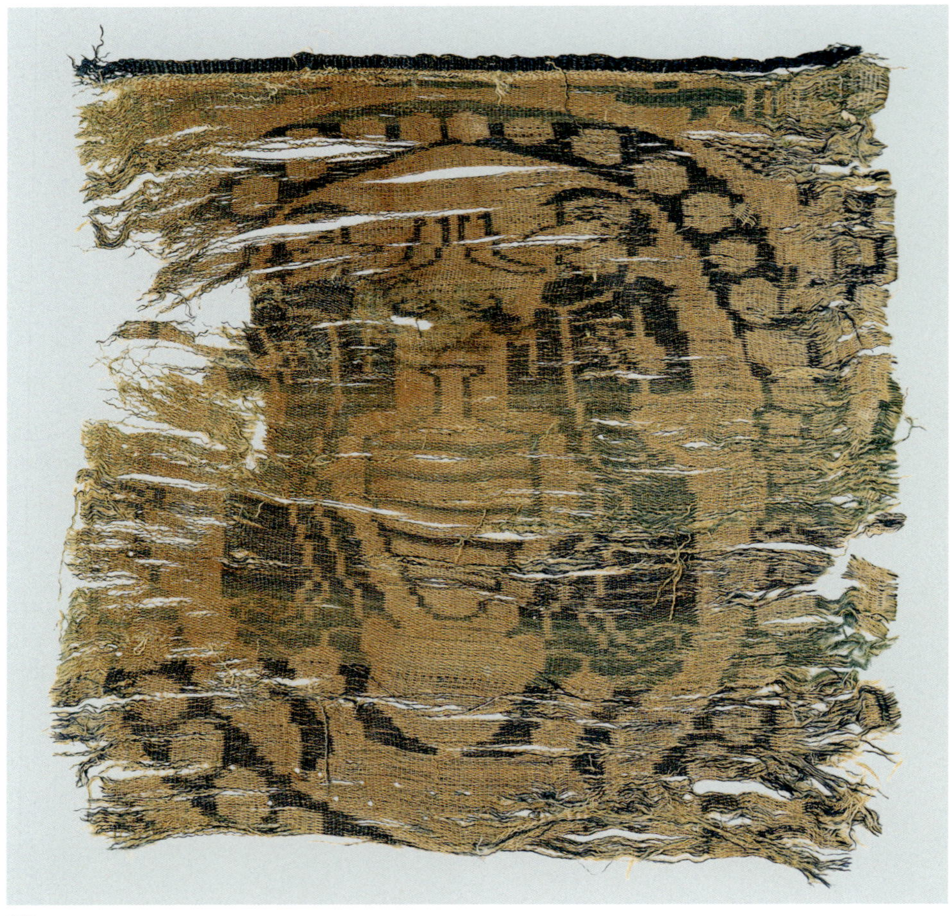

173

Vineyards along the Silk Road catered to traveling merchants who were well known for their drinking and dancing, and images of foreigners entertaining themselves with wine and dance appeared frequently in textiles, cave paintings, and *sancai* (tricolor) pottery.

This textile, structurally a warp-faced compound tabby, was patterned in dark blue, green, and white on a yellow ground. The dark stripe at the top is the selvedge. The roundel, which is decorated with a border of pearls, encloses two figures portrayed in a manner typical of representations of foreigners. They are characterized by their pronounced exotic features of deep-set eyes and large pointed noses and wear long robes with narrow sleeves, belts, and high boots. In their raised hands they hold rhytons. Such vessels have been excavated in areas around the Tang capital, Chang'an (present-day Xi'an). Between the drinkers is a large jar with a pointed base, a type first used by the ancient Greeks that was quite popular in Central Asia.

Similar textiles have been discovered in areas around Turfan and Dulan, attesting to their popularity from the Northern Dynasties (386–581) to the early Tang period (618–907). ZF

174
Textile with hunting scene in roundel

5th–6th century
Woven silk (1:2 warp-faced compound tabby)
Warp 4¾ in. (12 cm); weft 8⅞ in. (22.5 cm)
Excavated from Tomb 101, Astana, Turfan, Xinjiang Uygur Autonomous Region, 1968
Xinjiang Uygur Autonomous Region Museum

Reference: Huang Nengfu 1985

From the Astana cemetery in Turfan, this piece is woven in the technique of 1:2 warp-faced compound tabby. On a yellow ground are two patterns, one with blue and white and the other with green and white. Its design is oriented at right angles to the warp and consists of adjoining roundels connected by rosettes. The double border of the roundel comprises an outer circle with white whorls on a blue or green ground and an inner circle, now difficult to see, with white pearls on a yellow ground. The roundel nearest the selvedge depicts, from top to bottom, patterns of confronted figures: green birds or celestials, running white elephants, blue riders shooting deer, dancing white lions, and green camels. A lotus pedestal is woven between the lions and the floral patterns behind the camels. The second roundel is badly damaged, with only half remaining. Comparison with a similar piece that depicts the Greek sun god Helios on a yellow ground (see below) discovered in Dulan, Qinghai, suggests that the figure in the roundel on the present textile also represents the Greek divinity. He is shown on a lotus seat pulled by four winged horses. What now remains are the crossed blue legs of Helios, a green lotus seat, a blue and green chariot, white wheels, and blue and white horses. Originally, there would have been four horses. White rosettes with twelve petals link the roundels, outside of which, near the

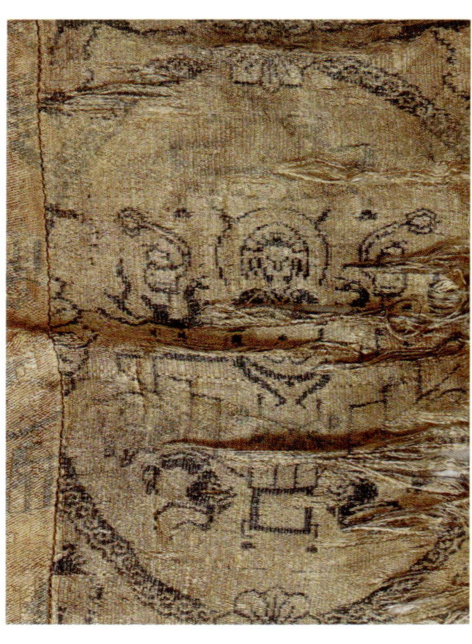

selvedge, are a pair of crouching lions and running horses with floral patterns.

Two *jin* silks with Helios, one, mentioned above, on a yellow ground, and another, also from Dulan, on a red ground,[1] indicate that this piece from Turfan would originally have featured, in the weft direction, three roundels with the Helios in the center and corresponding designs on both sides. The image of the sun god appeared in Europe as early as the Bronze Age. The son of the Titan Hyperion and his sister Theia, Helios was believed to ride a golden chariot drawn by four horses through the sky, bringing light to the earth. His journey would begin in the east and end in the west, after which he would float back through the skies to his eastern palace. Through the military campaign of Alexander the Great, the image of the sun god was brought to Central Asia and northern India. The Hindu sun god Surya, for example, is depicted in a two-wheel horse-drawn chariot on a stone relief dating to about 100 to 70 B.C. in Vihara 19 at Bhaja, Maharashtra.[2] Another similar image can be found on the mural of Cave 155 at Bamiyan, Afghanistan. At Bamiyan, however, the sun god stands on a four-horse chariot and is attired in a distinctly Central Asian fashion.[3] Farther east, images of Helios, usually simplified in design with only two horses, have been discovered in the Kizil caves at Kucha as well as in the Mogao caves in Dunhuang.

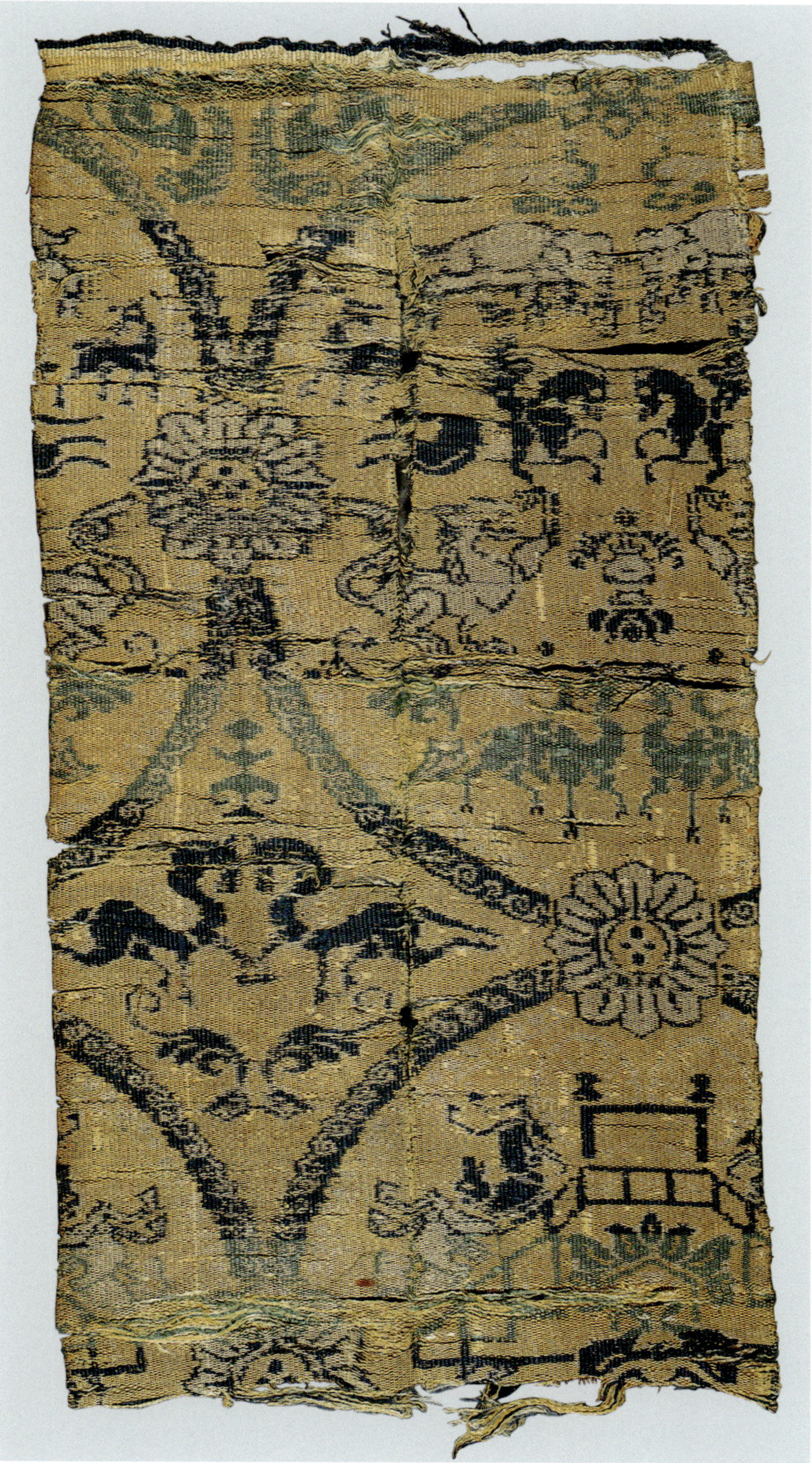

174

The sun god in this textile clearly reflects the diverse artistic traditions along the Silk Road. The image of Helios sitting cross-legged on a lotus pedestal undoubtedly shows the influence of the Buddhist art of India. The winged horses and pearl roundels are probably related to the Sasanian art of Persia. The technique of warp-faced compound tabby, on the other hand, belongs firmly to the Chinese weaving tradition. This is indeed a unique and precious textile that incorporates influences from both east and west.

The images within the side roundels are also closely associated with the cultures of West and Central Asia. Elephants are popular motifs in Indian art; riding and shooting patterns appear frequently in Persian art; and images of lions and camels are motifs commonly seen along the Silk Road.

It has been suggested that textiles woven with the image of Helios correspond to the *tipo jin* (textiles with an image of the god Deva) recorded in manuscripts discovered at Turfan.[4] Deva refers to any god in the Indian religions.

ZF

1. Zhao Feng 2002a: 76–77, no. 27-2.
2. Huntington 1985: 78–80, fig. 5.28.
3. Allchin and Hammond 1978, fig. 5.41.
4. Wu Zhen 2000: 84–103.

VII

Arts of the Sui and Early Tang Dynasties, 581–755

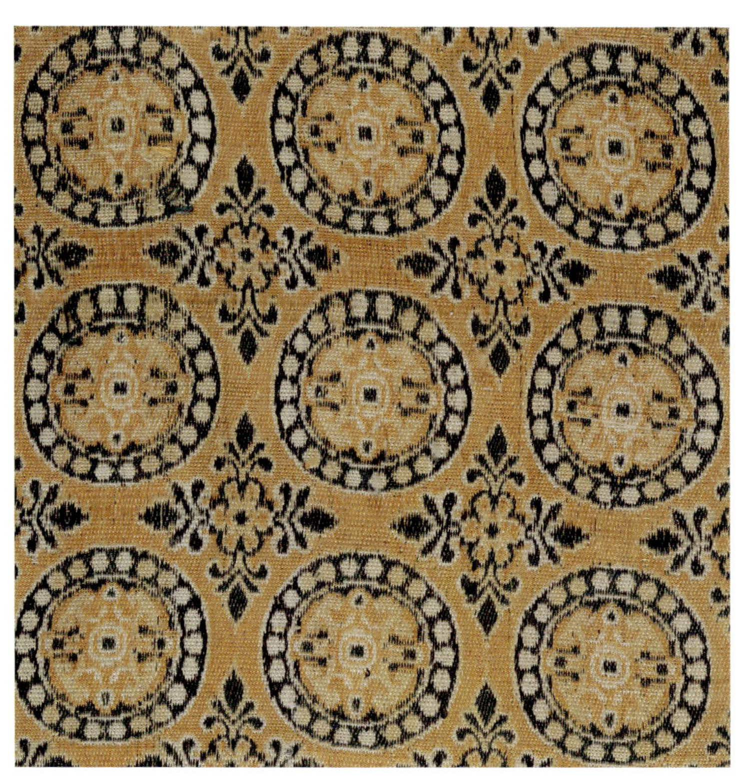

175
Sarcophagus

Sui dynasty (581–619)
Stone with pigments
Side panels: height 37¾ in. (96 cm);
base panels: width 97⅝ in. (248 cm)
Excavated from the tomb (dated 592)
of Yu Hong, Jinyuan, Taiyuan, Shanxi
Province, 1999
Jinyuan Bureau of Cultural Properties
and Tourism

Excav. report in *Wenwu* 2001.1

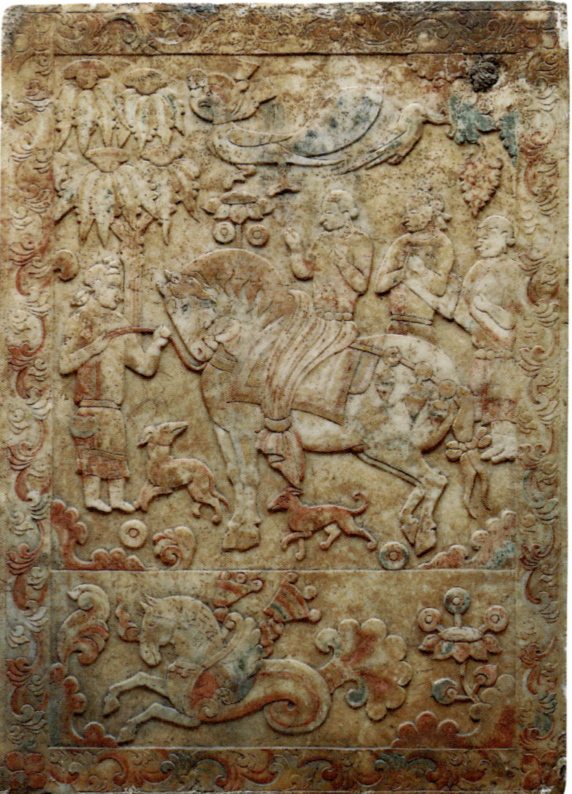

1

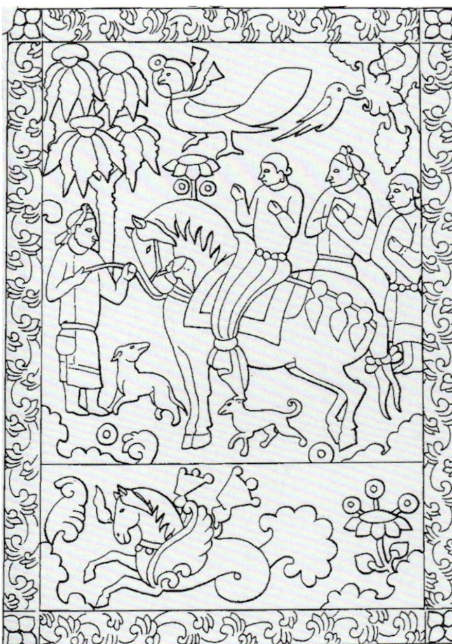

Drawing of panel 1

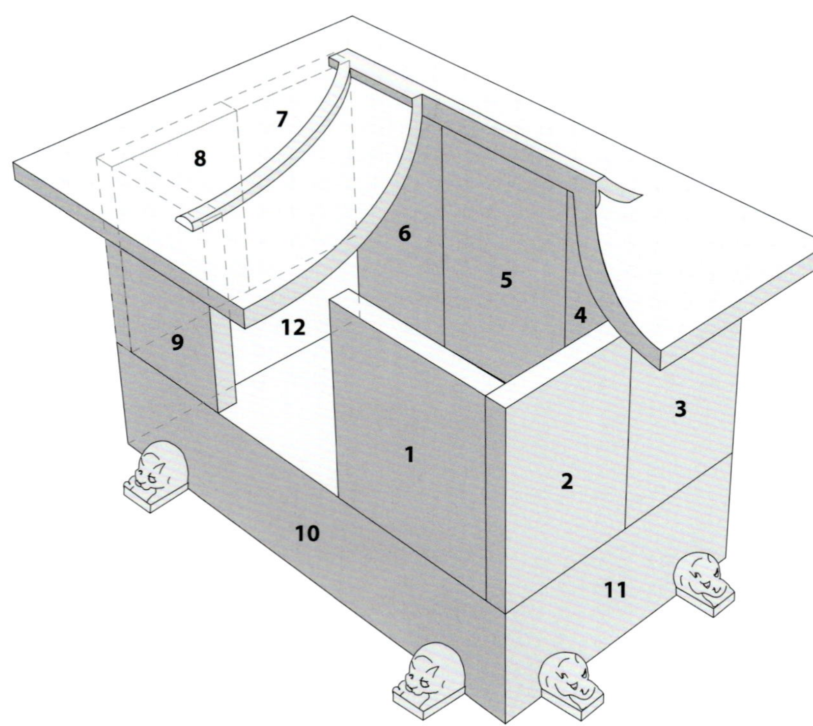

Diagram of sarcophagus

This marble sarcophagus, decorated with relief carving and painting, contained the remains of Yu Hong (interred 592) and his wife (d. 597, interred 598).[1] It was found in 1999, during the construction of a road southwest of Taiyuan (near the site of the old city of Jinyang, the seat of the government of Bingzhou and power base of the imperial house of Northern Qi) and not far from the tomb of Lou Rui (see cat. nos. 139–142). The name Yu and the origin of the people known by this name are something of a mystery. Scholars who have been studying Yu Hong's epitaph have arrived at the conclusion that he came from a community of Turkic-speaking Central Asians who had settled on the northern borders of China beginning in the fourth century.[2] Yu Hong's father, (Yu) Juntuo (and probably his grandfather as well), had the title *lingmin qiuzhang* (people-leading chief), one that was conferred on the leaders of tribes that formed part of the Xianbei confederation.[3] When the Ruru (Rouran) became the most powerful nomadic people of Central Asia and

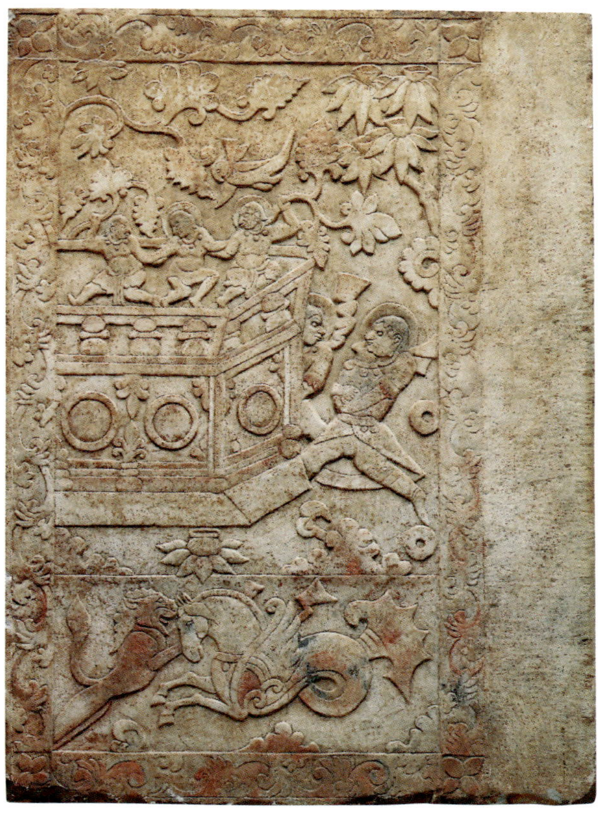

2

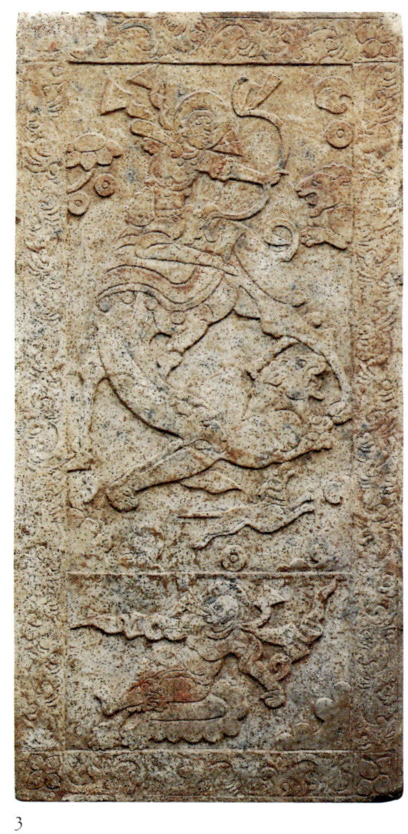

3

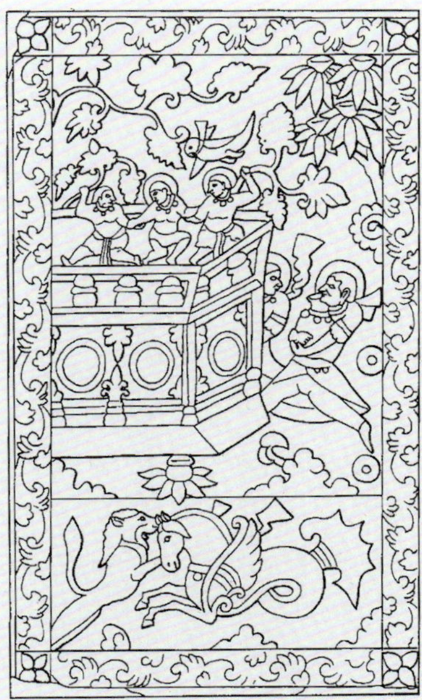

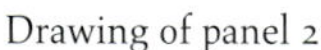

Drawing of panel 2

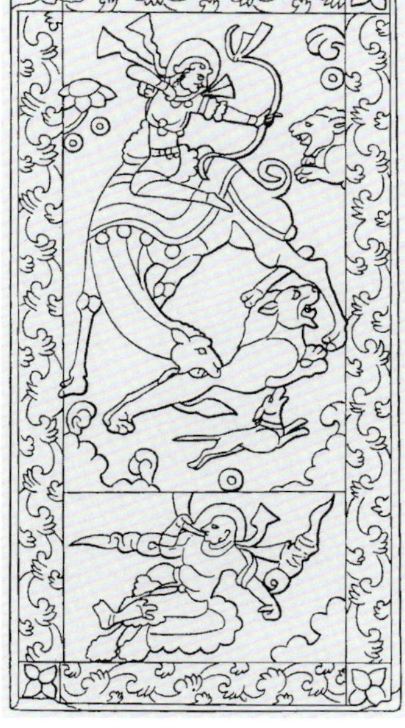

Drawing of panel 3

were a threat on China's northern borders, the Yu tribe defected. Juntuo became a high official for the Ruru and was sent as an emissary to the Eastern Wei. Yu Hong himself began his career in the service of the Ruru when he was barely in his teens and posted as an emissary to countries in Central and West Asia, including Persia and Tuyuhun (in Qinghai). By the time he was sent to the Northern Qi during the reign of Gao Yang (Emperor Wenxuan, r. 550–59), the Ruru were being vanquished by the Turks and he remained in Northern Qi (presumably in Jinyang). After the defeat of the Northern Qi, he served the Northern Zhou as *sabao* and finally in the Sui as *sabao* and governor of Bingzhou, where he died in 592 at the age of fifty-eight.

The form of Yu Hong's sarcophagus is not unlike other known examples from the sixth century. There is a stone sarcophagus, dated 529, of the same form and more or less the same size in the Museum of Fine Arts, Boston, but with pictorial decoration in Chinese style in both subject matter and iconography.[4] There are also smaller versions known from Sui to early Tang burials, such as that of Li Jingxun (608) and Zheng Rentai (664). Objects from these two tombs are included in this exhibition (cat. nos. 183–187). The basic construction of the tomb of Yu Hong and his wife is also similar to Chinese tombs at this time. The unusual feature is the pictorial decoration on the sarcophagus. Similar decoration on a stone sarcophagus in the form of a house and on stone couches in other burials have been found.[5] They are usually in the tombs of Sogdians who held the post of *sabao*.

A detailed study of the iconography of the pictorial decoration on Yu Hong's sarcophagus is beyond the scope of an exhibition entry. Nevertheless, several important themes in the decorative scheme and pictorial representation are discussed below.

The sarcophagus is decorated with both reliefs and paintings. We know that the reliefs were made in 598–99 because one of them—in the interior of the sarcophagus on the back wall (5)—shows Yu Hong and his wife feasting in paradise, surrounded by royal luxury. Both the deceased are crowned, as are the female attendants. Below this composition are two nearly identical scenes in which a man and a lion are shown in combat. This motif is not a variant of the popular theme of the heroic—and always successful—hunt. On the contrary, it is a symbolic scene which illustrates that even the most powerful creatures are not spared in the battle of life.

The other reliefs appear on the interior of the sarcophagus, on the side and back panels, on the facade on either side of the entrance, and on the base. The reliefs in the interior show scenes of daily life in the west. Among them are three scenes of a lion hunt. Two of the hunters ride camels (3, 4), and one rides an elephant (6). It is worth noting that only Arabs—not Iranians or Turks—hunted and fought on camelback. The Persian prince Bahram Gur (r. 420–38), who lived among the Arabs and hunted as an Arab, is depicted as an archer on camelback on silver plates that illustrate episodes from the Arabian period of his life. The other hunting kings and princes of Iran are shown on horseback or on foot.[6] One of the Yu Hong reliefs shows a figure, on a dromedary, who is perhaps Arab, although his clothing would seem to be Iranian (3).

The Yu Hong reliefs appear to depict individuals with characteristics of three different peoples. One shows a long-haired Turk (4). Another represents a crowned hunter riding an elephant, a

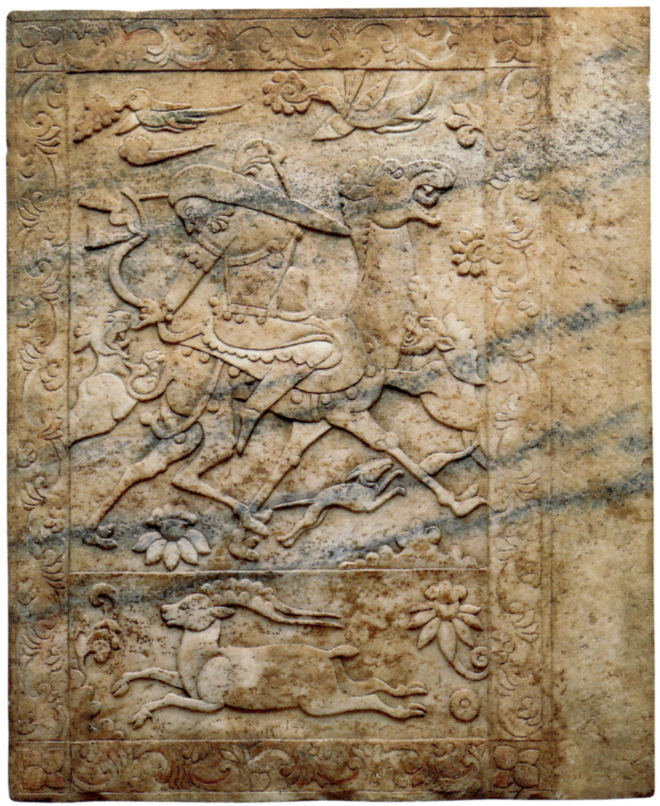

4

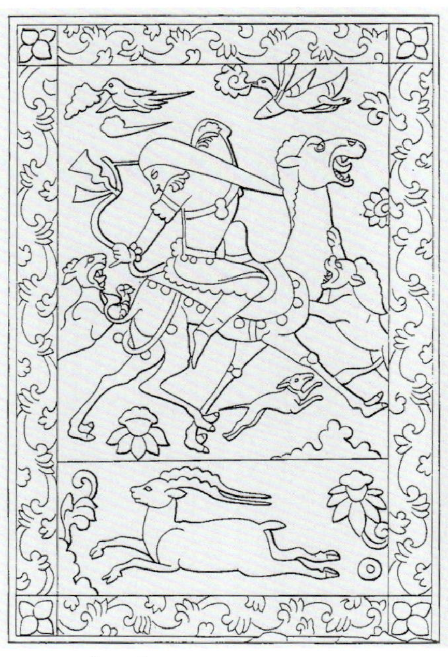

Drawing of panel 4

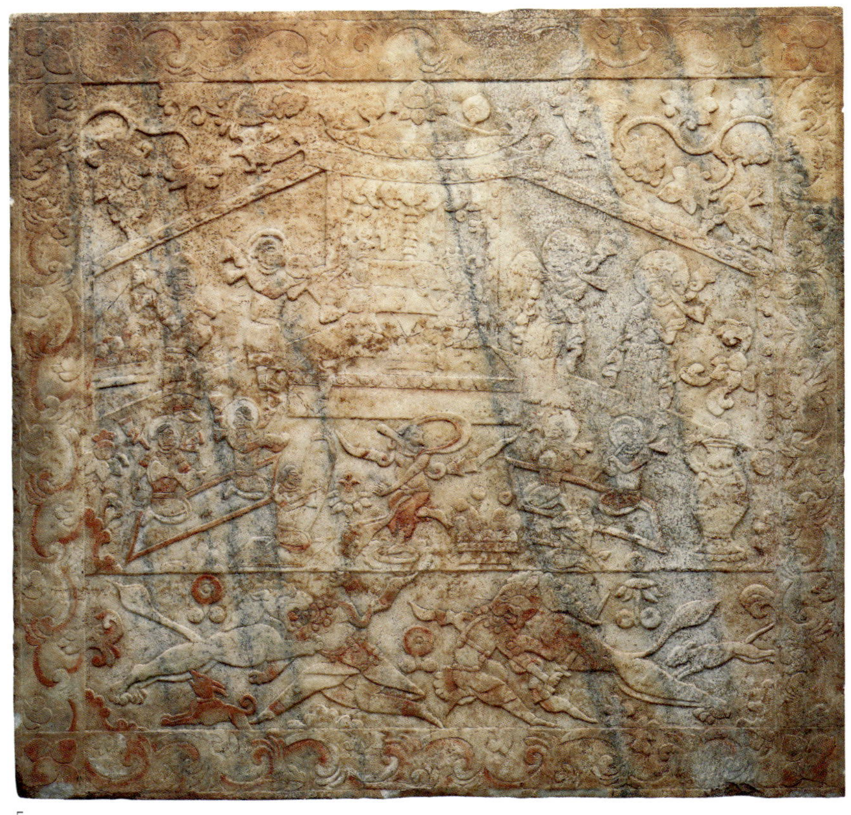
5

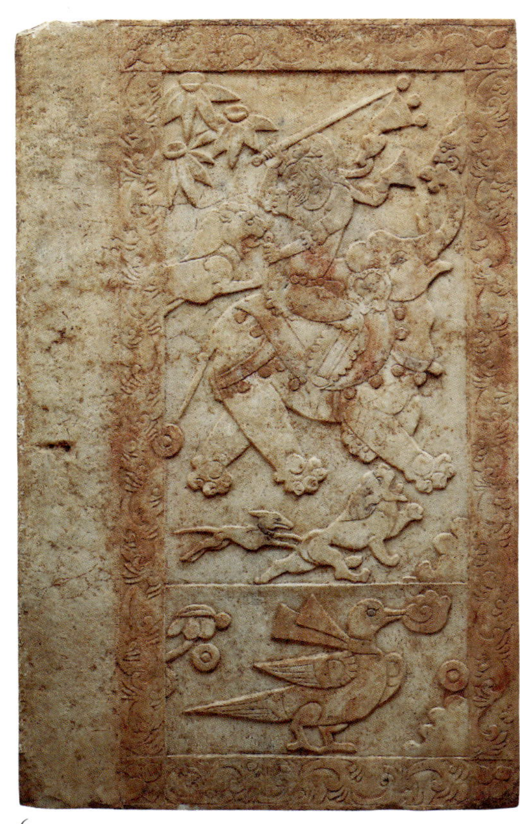
6

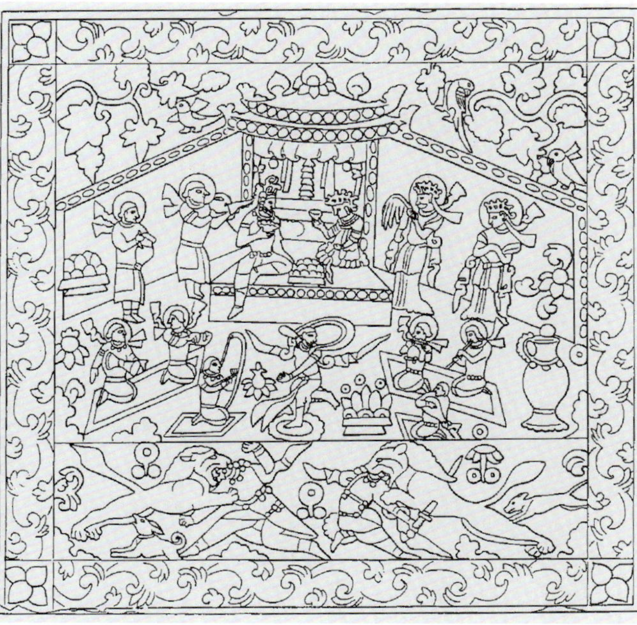
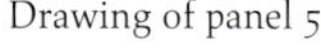
Drawing of panel 5

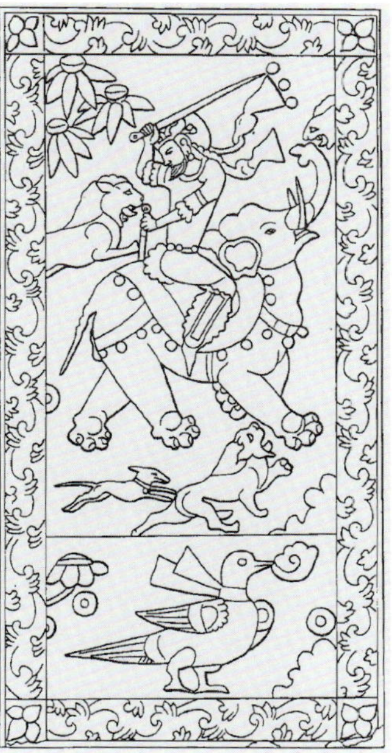
Drawing of panel 6

reference to India (6). Two panels perhaps portray Iranians or Sogdians. These are the scenes of a royal procession (7) and a royal feast (8). Near the king are dogs, animals held in high regard by the Zoroastrians. There does not appear to be any ethnic distinction between the figures in these two scenes. It is possible that both reliefs depict Iranians, although it seems unlikely that the sculptor chose not to represent Sogdians. The last—but not the least important—country represented on the chamber walls is Rome or Byzantium. The putti trampling grapes in the vineyard is a motif common in Late Roman art (2). It is known also in Iran, but is not as widespread in that country. On the same relief are two male figures whose poses betray their state of inebriation. The haloes and fluttering ribbons are purely decorative, pseudo-western motifs.

The facade reliefs situated on the side of the entrance show an equestrian king (9) and a riderless horse, behind which are three standing figures (1). The horse belongs to the deceased, according to the Chinese tradition, or, in Sogdian iconography, is dedicated to a deity. For example, on a Sogdian ossuary from the Kashkadarya valley, dating from the sixth to the seventh century, a horse dedicated to Mithra, a judge of the dead, is placed in a scene of a funerary ceremony.[7] The facade reliefs must be interpreted together. They depict either Yu Hong himself and his horse or Mithra and his horse. The royal rider on the facade opposite the riderless horse would not be merely the king of an earthly country, like the figures that adorn the inner chamber walls. If the patron followed the Sogdian tradition, the royal rider must be Mithra. On the other hand, in paradise Yu Hong could have become a divinity and his wife a heavenly queen, as is demonstrated on the central slab of the back wall (5). In this case, the royal way of life would symbolize the highest level of happiness. The royal insignia that are depicted are those of an Iranian (or Sogdian) king, as all elements on the Yu Hong reliefs are western in character. In this respect, it is worth mentioning that on the base there are equestrian hunters, divine musicians and dancers, and scenes of feasting that symbolize the noble and happy life. On the base of the center facade (10), heavenly Zoroastrian priests—half-men and half-birds—flank a fire altar. This scene is significant because it shows how Yu Hong, whose name is unusual in Sogdian, indicated that he was a co-religionist of the Sogdian merchants who were his subordinates when he served the Northern Zhou as *sabao*.

The winged horse that appears below the riderless horse (1) illustrates that the sculptor was familiar with Sogdian imagery. In Sogdiana, this image is a symbol of *farn* (the glory and good fortune that come to a worthy person and that are borne away from a sinner). In the art of Sogdiana, there are several flying creatures that symbolize different kinds of *farn* relating to various deities. The winged horse with dragon's tail perhaps represents Mithra. However, the sculptor did not understand the iconography of the motif because he placed the horse at the bottom of the composition, whereas in a Sogdian context such "flying dragons" appear only in the upper part.[8] On another slab (2), the divine horse-dragon is shown in combat with a lion, a subject that does not appear in the art of Sogdiana. The other lower compartments of the reliefs are occupied by several images whose original meanings were probably not known by the sculptor. Among them, on the left slab of the facade wall (9), is a typical Iranian motif of a battle between a lion and a bull, perhaps a symbol of the New Year.

Parts of the base are painted and carved (10–12); the side and back exterior walls are only painted. On the latter, instead of a multifigured composition, the entire slab is occupied by only one figure. On the exterior walls, the preservation of the painting is very poor, and it is probable that these were produced earlier than the reliefs, perhaps about 592, the date of Yu Hong's death. On the exterior back wall (not illustrated) are three figures: a seated man between a man and a woman, both standing. These figures are possibly Yu Hong and his relatives. On the side walls, the figures—standing or kneeling men and standing women—face inward toward the main facade. The kneeling man at the right corner holds an object that resembles a portable fire altar.

Certain compositional elements on the sarcophagus reliefs are seen in the art of the native population of North China at the time. For example, the rider with a parasol held above his head (9) often represents a donor figure on Buddhist and Daoist sculptures and monuments in the sixth century (see cat. no. 172). In the latter, however, the attire of the rider is different from that of the attendant, and in the Chinese version the horse's legs are not tied with ribbons. In Iran, the royal horse alone is shown thus adorned. Also in Iran the parasol becomes a royal attribute beginning at least as early as the sixth century B.C. Thus, among the western elements of the Yu Hong reliefs, some were adopted earlier in China and others later.

In spite of the Sogdian/western origin of the iconography and subject matter,

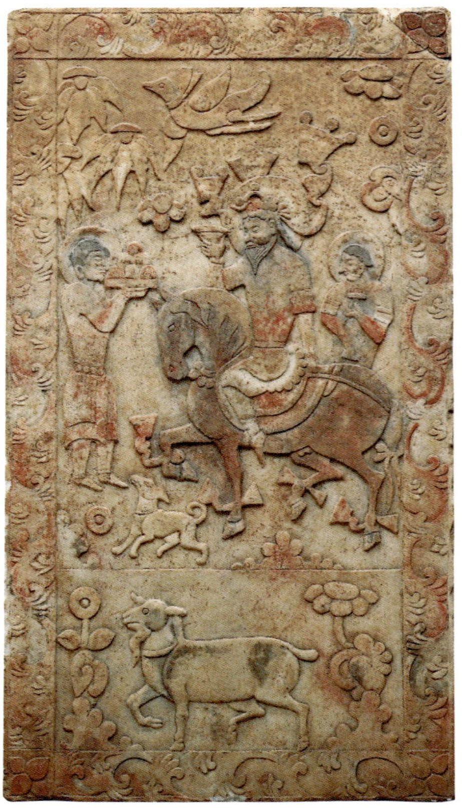

7

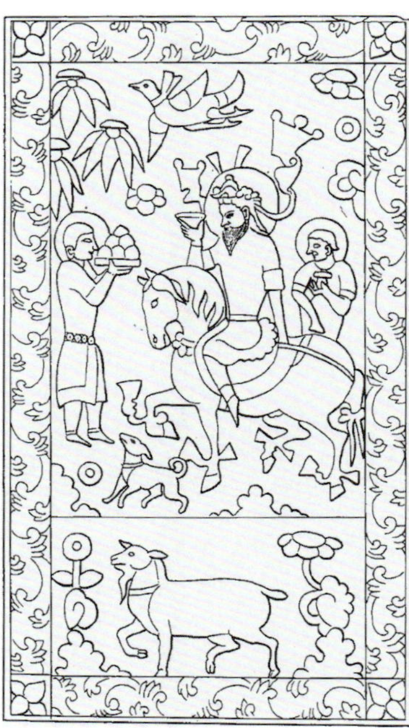

Drawing of panel 7

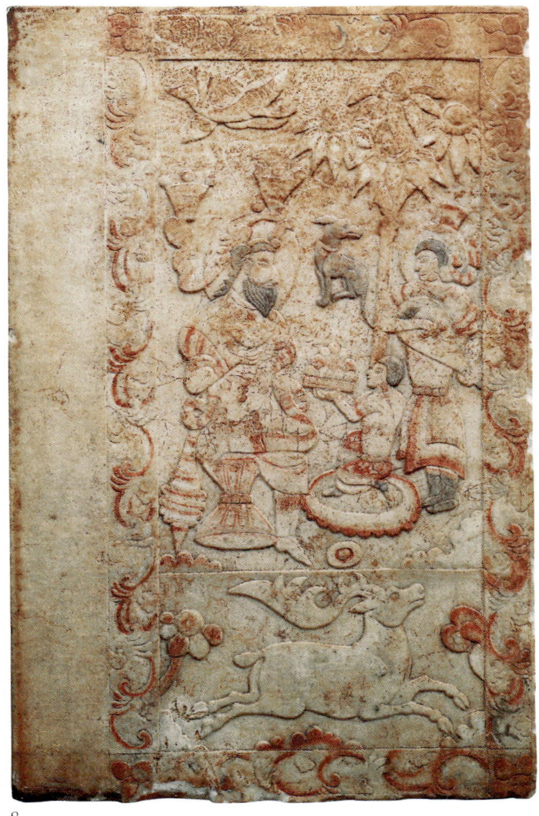
8

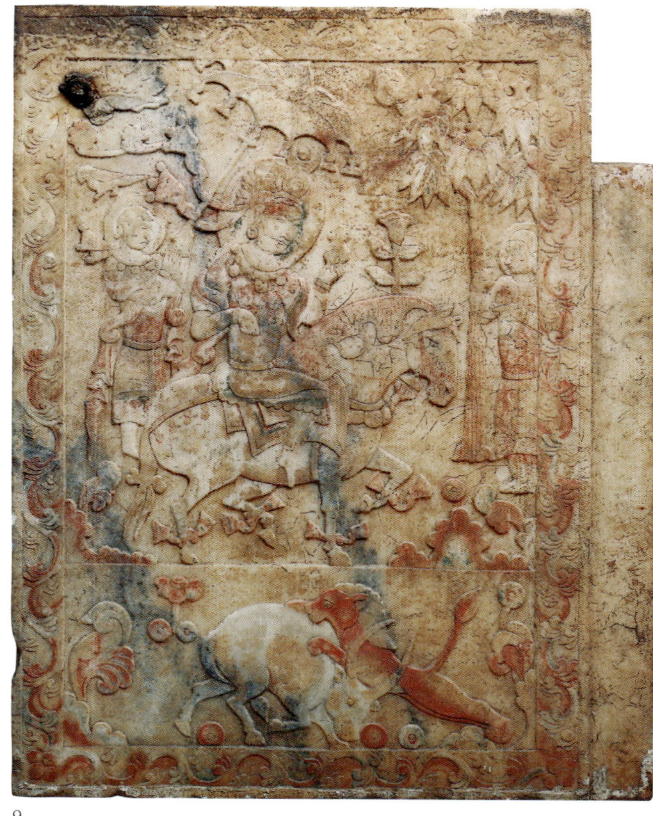
9

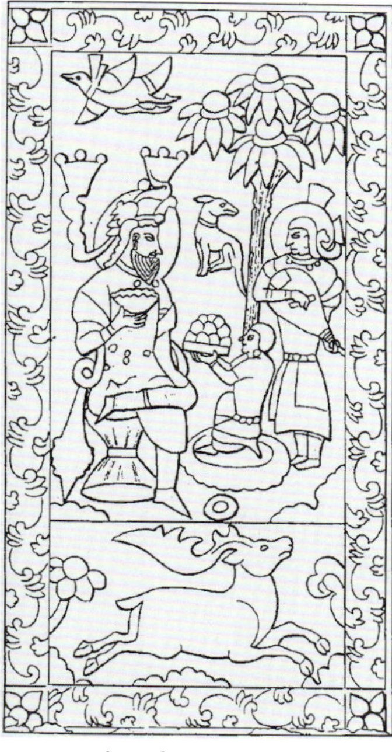
Drawing of panel 8

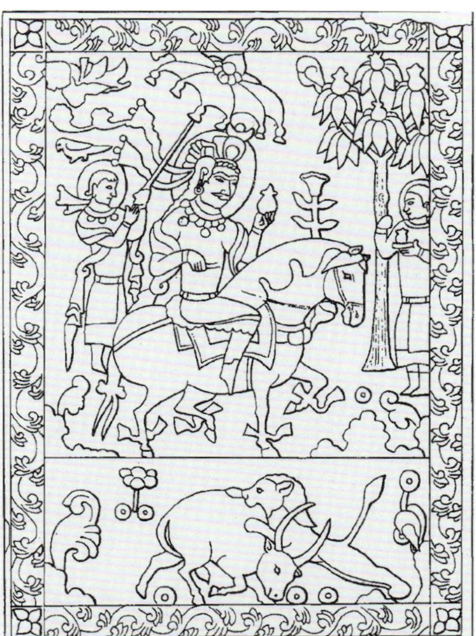
Drawing of panel 9

there is a discernible difference in the pictorial style of the Yu Hong sarcophagus and that of Sogdian art. On the sarcophagus, there is an almost exaggerated dynamism in the rendering of themes introduced from Central Asia, particularly in the depiction of the hunt and animal combat scenes. This vitality may be attributed to the Chinese artist's having brought his own sensibility to the interpretation of these scenes, images that he would have seen in a pattern book.

BIM JCYW

1. There are relief carvings on the exterior walls of panels 1 and 9 (see diagram). On panels 2–8, the carvings are on the interior.
2. Lin Meicun 2002.
3. Zheng Yan 2001.
4. Tomita 1942: 98–110.
5. Shaanxi sheng kaogu yanjiusuo 2001: 4–26; Yang Junkai 2003: 26–29. Yang Junkai 2004; Rong Xinggiang and Zhang Zhiqing (ed): 59–65. For other examples in museums, see Scaglia 1958 and Miho Museum 1997, no. 125.
6. Trever and Lukonin 1987, pls. 27, 28.
7. Gernet 2000: 53–54, pl. v,7.
8. Azarpay 1980: 70, 72; Azarpay 1976: 168–77.

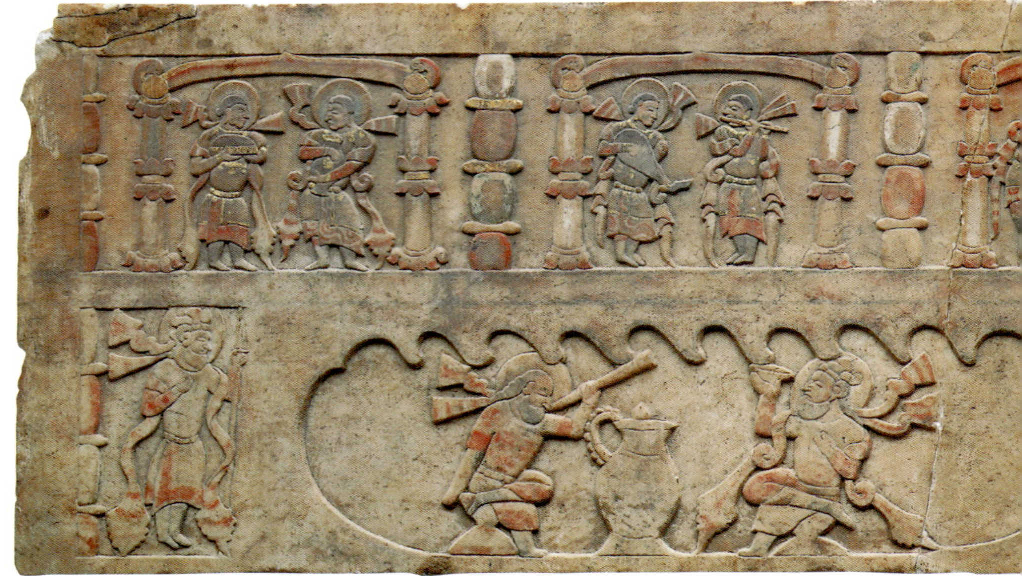

10

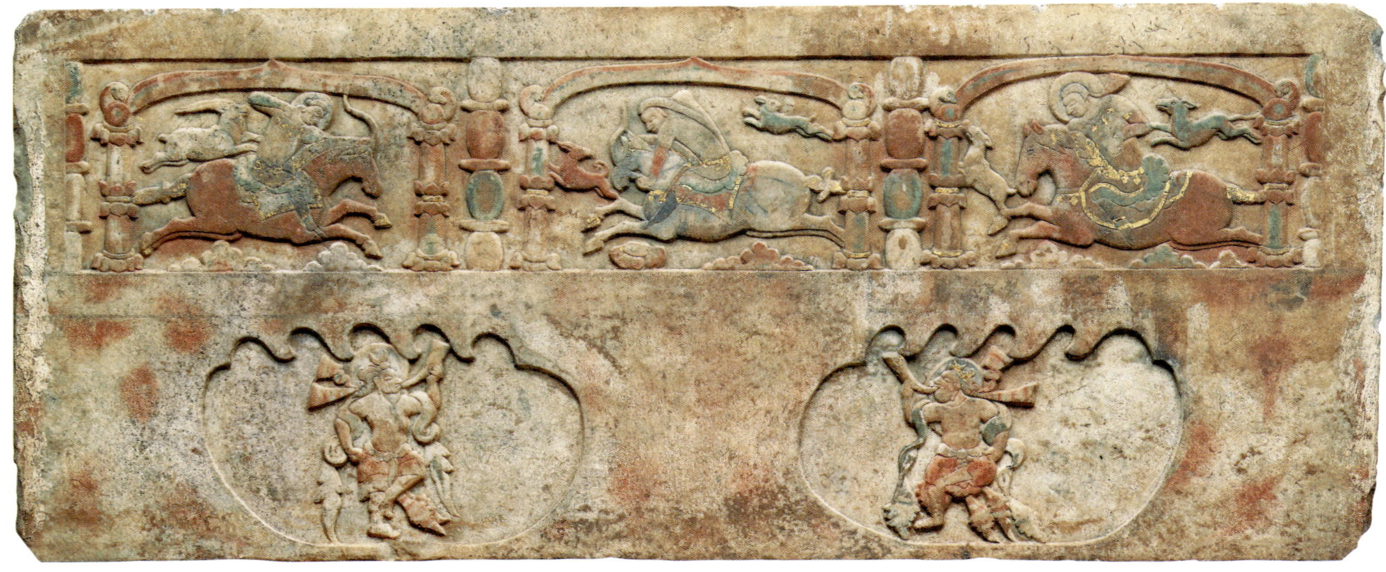

11

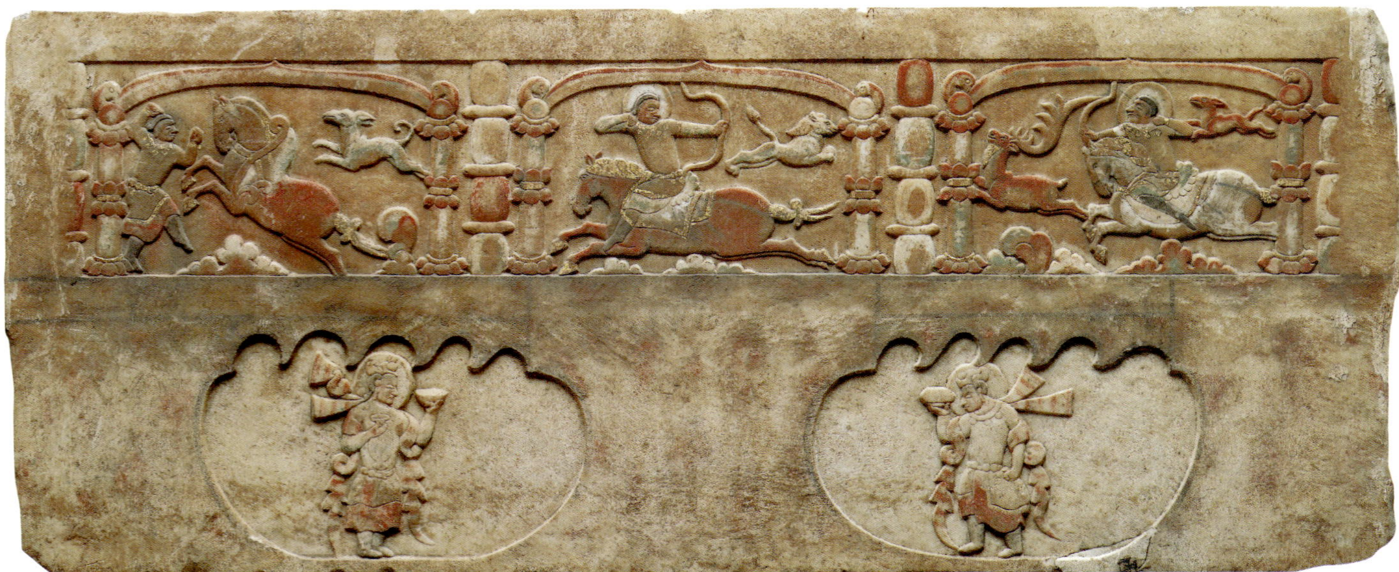

12

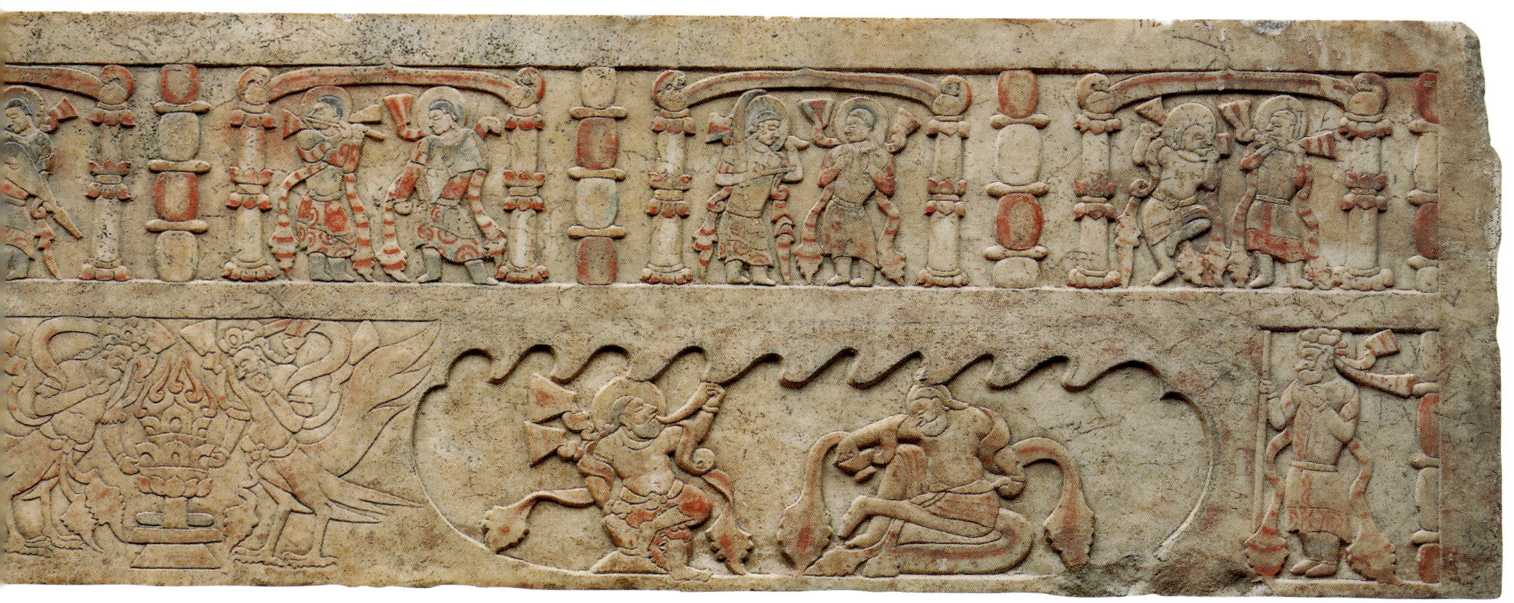

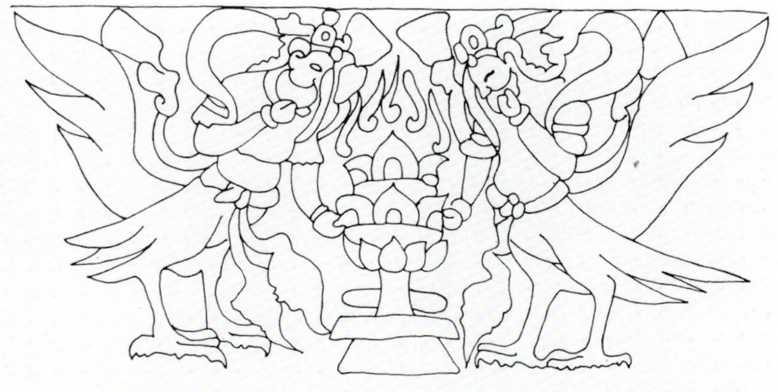

Drawing of detail, panel 10

176
Female musician

Sui dynasty (581–619), ca. 598
Stone with pigments and gilding
Height 19⅝ in. (50 cm)
Excavated from the tomb (dated 592) of Yu Hong, Jinyuan, Taiyuan, Shanxi Province, 1999
Jinyuan Bureau of Cultural Properties and Tourism

Excav. report in *Wenwu* 2001.1

In addition to a spectacular house-shaped sarcophagus (cat. no. 175), approximately eighty objects, including sixteen stone sculptures, were excavated from the late sixth-century tomb of Yu Hong (interred 592). Some of the sculptures were complete; others were in pieces and reassembled. They were placed in various locations around the sarcophagus within the coffin chamber. It is possible that originally they were arranged in a formation of some sort but were disturbed over time.[1]

All the marble sculptures were carved in two pieces and then painted. The figures are separate from the lotus-shaped pedestals into which they are fitted. Such pedestals are common in Buddhist art, where they are understood to reflect the purity of the divinity they support. Pottery figures found in the tomb of Zhang Sheng, a military official who died in 595,[2] also stand on lotus-shaped bases in a funerary context, suggesting that the use of such pedestals was widespread by the Sui dynasty (581–619).

This figure of a female musician wears a long garment with a high waist that is tied in the front with two ribbons and covered by a long jacket. On her head she wears a cloth that has been rolled and knotted in the front and back. Such head-dresses are commonly seen on pottery sculptures of female musicians from the late sixth and early seventh centuries.[3]

The musician plays a Chinese-style lute known as a *pipa,* which she holds with the neck pointing downward. A male *pipa* player was also found in the tomb, as was a woman playing the *paixiao,*

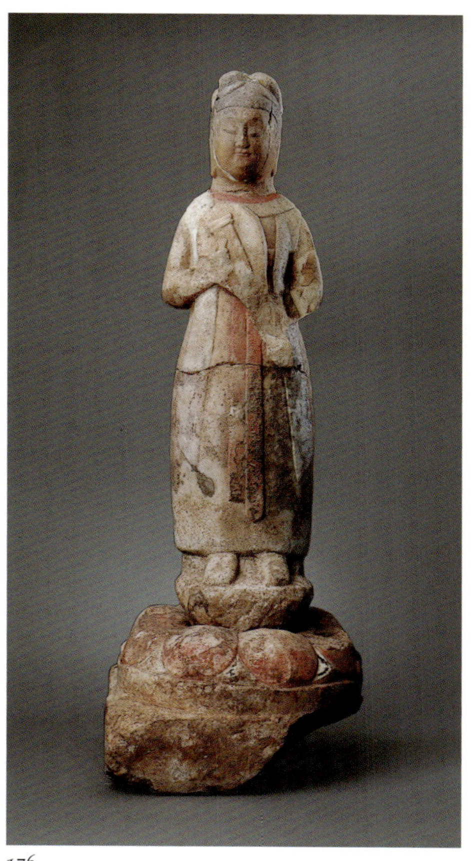

176

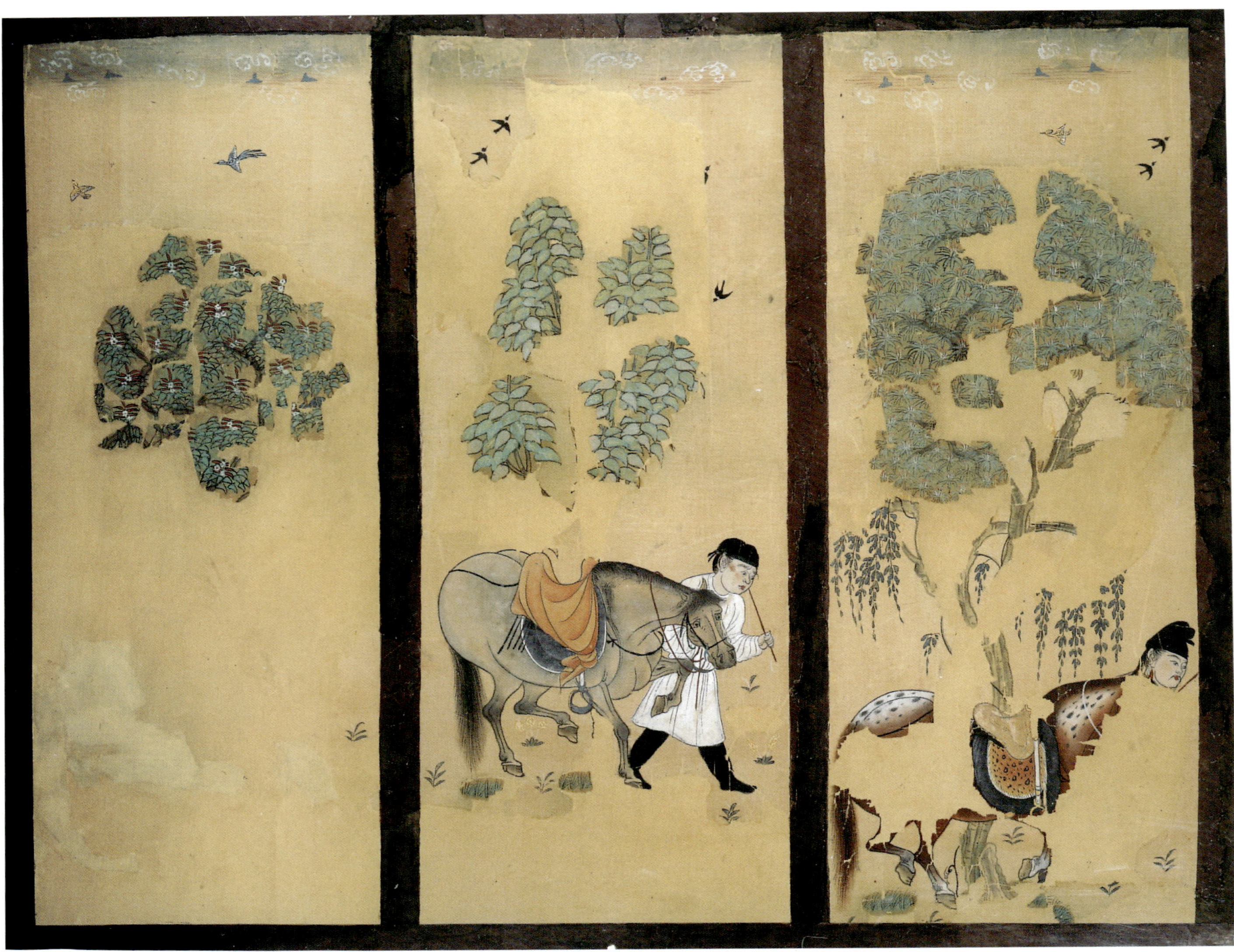

or panpipes. It seems likely that flutes, drums, and other instruments were also included in the ensemble.

DPL

1. Six stone musicians excavated from an early seventh-century tomb were placed at the right and left in front of the stone couch used for the remains of the deceased; see Tianshui shi bowuguan 1992, fig. 2.
2. Kaogu yanjiusuo Anyang dui 1959, pl. 1, nos. 1–3, 6, 7.
3. Ibid., pl. 2, nos. 1–6.

177
Grooms and horses

Tang dynasty (618–907), early 8th century
Six panels from an eight-panel screen, ink and color on silk
Each panel: 21⅛ x 8⅝ in. (53.5 x 22 cm)
Excavated from Tomb 188, Astana, Turfan, Xinjiang Uygur Autonomous Region, 1972
Xinjiang Uygur Autonomous Region Museum

Excav. report in *Wenwu* 1975.10

Paintings on silk or paper dating from the Tang dynasty are exceedingly rare. The majority cannot be securely dated except through stylistic comparison with paintings and murals recovered from datable sites. These six paintings were originally part of an eight-panel screen. Found in an early eighth-century tomb and preserved as a result of the unusually dry climate of Turfan, they are of great importance, not only for elucidating Tang culture but also for authenticating paintings in scroll format traditionally dated to the Tang period.

The subject of these panels, grooms with their horses, was a favorite of Tang painters. Since Han times, sturdy battle chargers had held both strategic and symbolic importance for projecting Chinese power along the Silk Road, where these paintings were found. But by the early eighth century, with China's borders secure, a stable full of finely bred horses became as much a status symbol as a harem of beautiful women and the depiction of horses developed into an independent genre, as did the portrayal of palace ladies.[1]

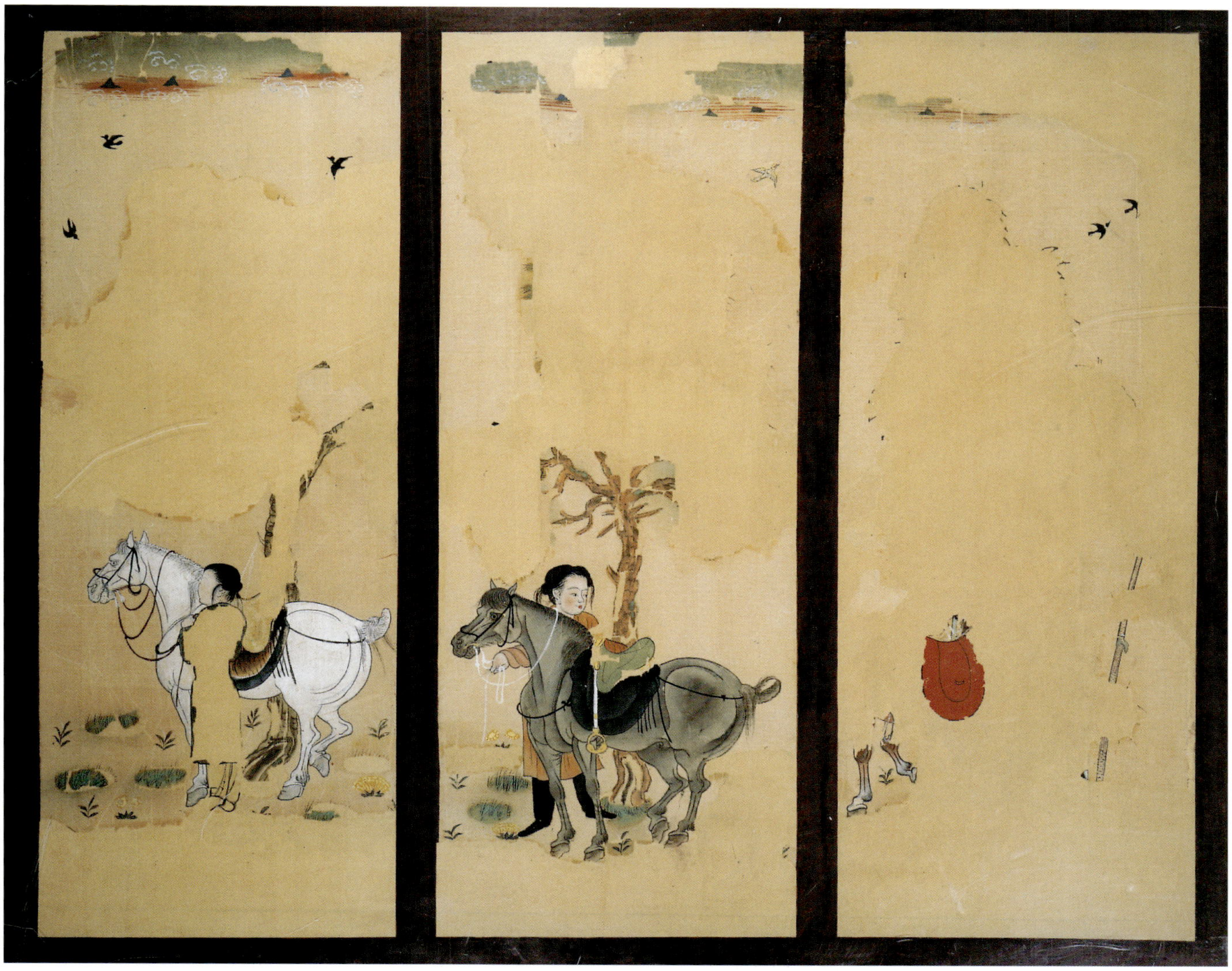

Executed on silk—large portions of which have disintegrated—the six paintings are part of an eight-panel screen from the tomb of Qu Niang (or Qu Xianfei, Divine Concubine Qu), who died in 715, and her husband, a member of the powerful Zhang family, who rose to the rank of commandant (*jiaowei*).[2] Each panel, originally bordered with purple silk and attached to a wooden frame, shows a similar composition, a groom and horse standing beside a tall tree in a shallow foreground space with the ground plane defined by clumps of grass and flowers. Birds dive and soar above, and white clouds—each shaped like an auspicious *lingzhi* fungus—float amid a rose-tinted sky punctuated by distant mountains.[3]

Each panel presents a different breed of horse and a different species of tree, almost like a variation on a theme. Three panels, now restored and mounted as a single unit, show horses facing right. The rightmost panel shows a dappled bay being led in front of a flowering tree with a vine hanging from its lower branches. The horse has been saddled with a leopard-skin blanket, while the groom sports a mustache and a cap. The middle panel shows an older groom walking his charger past a broad-leafed tree. Both groom and horse seem forlorn as they gaze at the ground, perhaps mourning the loss of

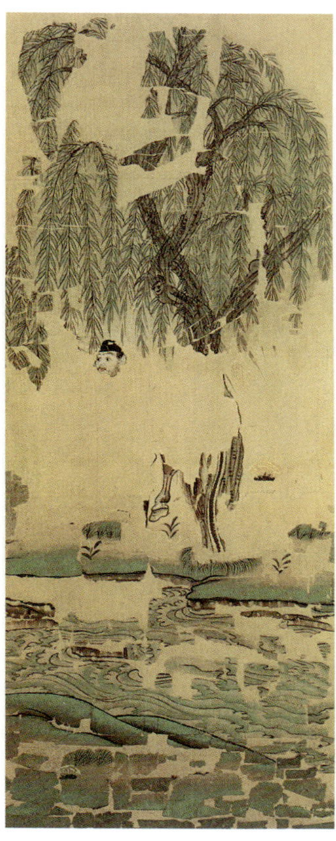

Groom and Horse. Tang dynasty (618–907), early 8th century. Panel from an eight-panel screen, ink and color on silk. Excavated from Tomb 188, Astana, Turfan, Xinjiang Autonomous Region, 1972. Xinjiang Uygur Autonomous Region Museum, Urumqi

their master. The saddle is covered with an orange-yellow cloth, and the horse's tail hangs loose. Only the top of a flowering tree, two birds on the wing, and a distant panorama survive from the left panel.

The second three-panel unit presents horses oriented to the left. The leftmost panel presents a white horse viewed slightly from the rear. The middle panel shows a gray horse standing before a pine tree. Both horses stand with their front legs firmly planted and their heads raised expectantly. They have been saddled (one with a tiger-skin blanket, the other with gilt stirrups and fittings) and have their tails tied up, and both are accompanied by youthful, uncapped grooms. The fragmentary right panel preserves remnants of a chestnut horse with a red saddle blanket and a stalk of bamboo. A seventh panel (not included in the exhibition; see illus. on previous page) shows a leftward-facing horse, accompanied by a foreign groom with a full beard, standing beside a willow and a wide stream.

Multipanel screens with slightly varied elements but following the same basic compositional scheme were highly popular during the Tang dynasty.[4] The antecedents of this formulaic approach to figures in a landscape setting is already recognizable in fifth-century depictions of the Seven Sages of the Bamboo Grove (cat. no. 113). As in the case of the Seven Sages, here the grooms and horses are presented in either profile or three-quarter view and are defined primarily by dynamic outlines filled in with color. Traces of underdrawing are still visible, but the artist has not slavishly followed these preliminary sketches. What has changed, however, is that contours are now occasionally reinforced with shading. The horses are endowed with a graphic energy and an exaggerated rotundity that is typical of the High Tang vision of the finest war steeds.

MKH

1. Wu Hong makes this observation in Yang Xin et al. 1997: 78–79.
2. From 499 until 640, the Qu family ruled Turfan as an independent state. In 640 it was absorbed into the Tang empire and power shifted to the Zhang clan.
3. The same clouds, birds, and mountains appear in a contemporary screen painting of palace ladies from another Zhang family tomb in the same cemetery; see Jin Weinuo and Wei Bian 1975; Li Zheng 1975; and *Zhongguo meishu quanji: Huihua bian 2*, 1984, pl. 9. They also appear in a flower-and-bird mural from a third Tang tomb in Astana; see *Zhongguo meishu quanji: Huihua bian 12*, 1989, pl. 134.
4. A six-panel screen of Tang-style palace ladies in a garden setting is preserved in the Shōsō-in, the imperial repository in Nara, Japan; see *Shōsō-in hōmotsu* 1987–89, vol. 1, pls. 88–99. For a mural representing such a screen, see *Zhongguo meishu quanji: Huihua bian, 12*, 1989, pl. 125.

178
Tomb guardian with human head

Tang dynasty (618–907), 7th century
Baked clay with pigments
Height 33⅞ in. (86 cm)
Excavated from Tomb 224, Astana, Turfan, Xinjiang Uygur Autonomous Region, 1972
Xinjiang Uygur Autonomous Region Museum

Excav. report in *Wenwu* 1975.7

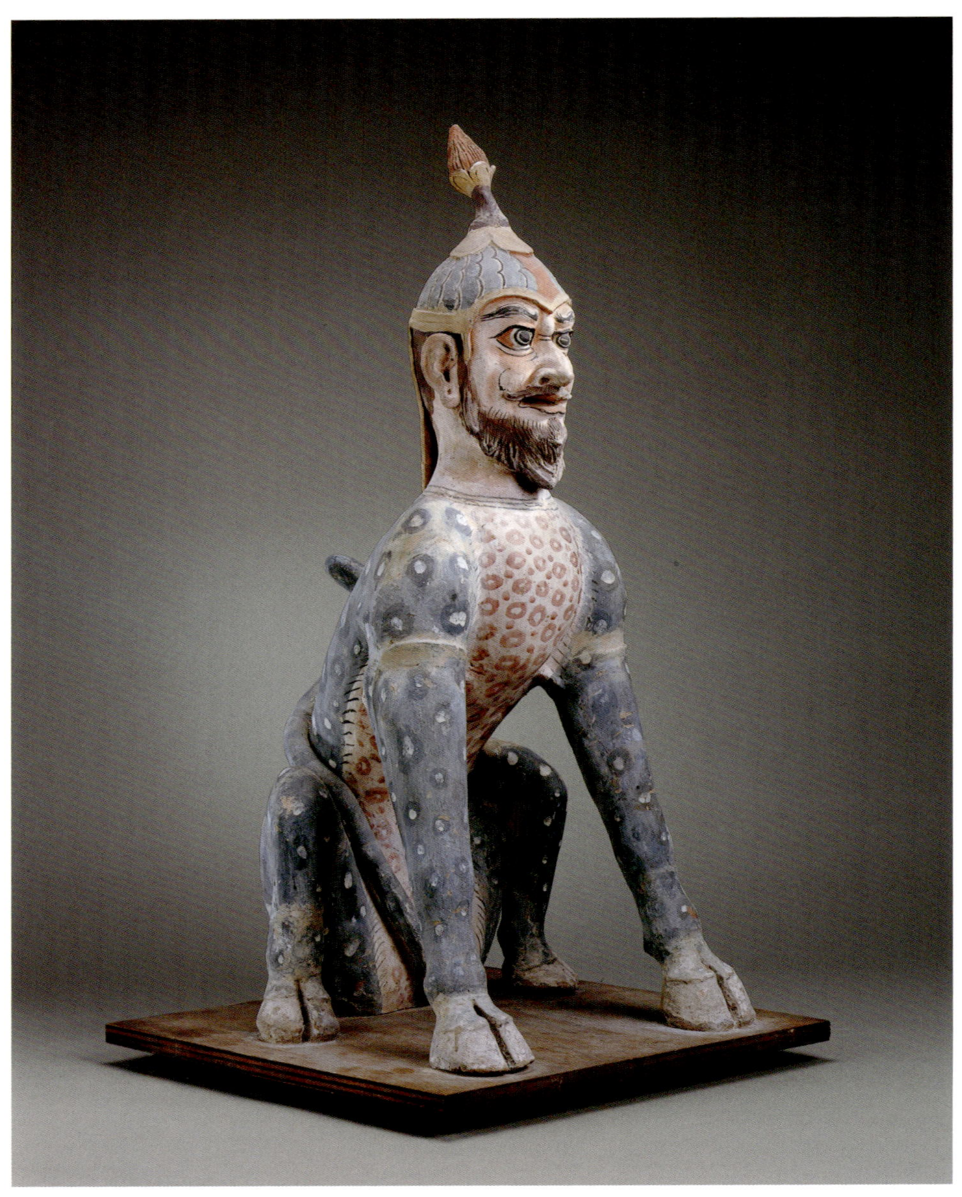

178

179
Tomb guardian with leonine head

Tang dynasty (618–907), 7th century
Baked clay with pigments
Height 29½ in. (75 cm)
Excavated from Tomb 216, Astana, Turfan, Xinjiang Uygur Autonomous Region, 1972
Xinjiang Uygur Autonomous Region Museum

Reference: Xinjiang Weiwuer zizhiqu bowuguan 1991

First excavated by the British archaeologist Sir Aurel Stein (1862–1943) in 1928 as part of his exploration of sites on the Silk Road, the extensive cemetery at Astana in Turfan, Xinjiang, measures about one and one-half miles from east to west and two-thirds of a mile from north to south. The cemetery has long been a major center for the study of the culture of the Turfan area, yielding not only tomb goods but also rare fragments of textiles and manuscripts in several languages.[1]

Found in different tombs at the site, these two figures typify funerary guardian creatures of the seventh and early eighth centuries. Both figures have hooves rather than the claws found on earlier examples. Both are brilliantly painted with speckled patterns covering their bodies that may derive from wax-resist techniques long popular in textile manufacture.

The human-faced guardian wears a tight-fitting helmet crowned by a plume and lamellar flaps covering the back of the head and neck. Although armor is worn by standing human guardian figures beginning in the early seventh century, it is generally not found on guardian beasts. The leonine figure has a tail that curls under the rump and around the front of the body to the left. The mane surrounding the head and the long beard, tufts of hair on the lower legs, and broad tail are painted in vibrant shades of green and red. There is a large spike at the top of the head and in the center of the back and two spikes on each shoulder. Such spikes have their roots in sixth-century depictions of guardian creatures produced in the Central Plain region of China in the early sixth century; they are also found in that region in the seventh and eighth centuries.[2]

It seems likely that such beasts were introduced to the Turfan area after the Tang conquest of the Gaochang (Qoco) kingdom in 640. Chinese control of the region lasted until the mid-eighth century, and there are numerous parallels between art in the urban areas of China and of Turfan. For example, the bold coloring on the figures is comparable to that of the famous three-color glaze, or *sancai*, ceramics produced in Turfan from the fourth quarter of the seventh century to the early decades of the eighth.

Very little information is available to date the tombs at Astana precisely. One tomb, however, number 206, is known to house the remains of Zhang Xiong (584–633) and his wife (607–688), and most of the burial goods are thought to date from the time of the latter's interment. The similarities in the large size and dramatic coloring of these two guardian figures with those of the wooden guardian warrior from Tomb 206 (cat. no. 180) suggest that these ceramic sculptures also date to the late seventh century.

DPL

1. See H. Wang 1999.
2. Fong 1991b: 85–93.

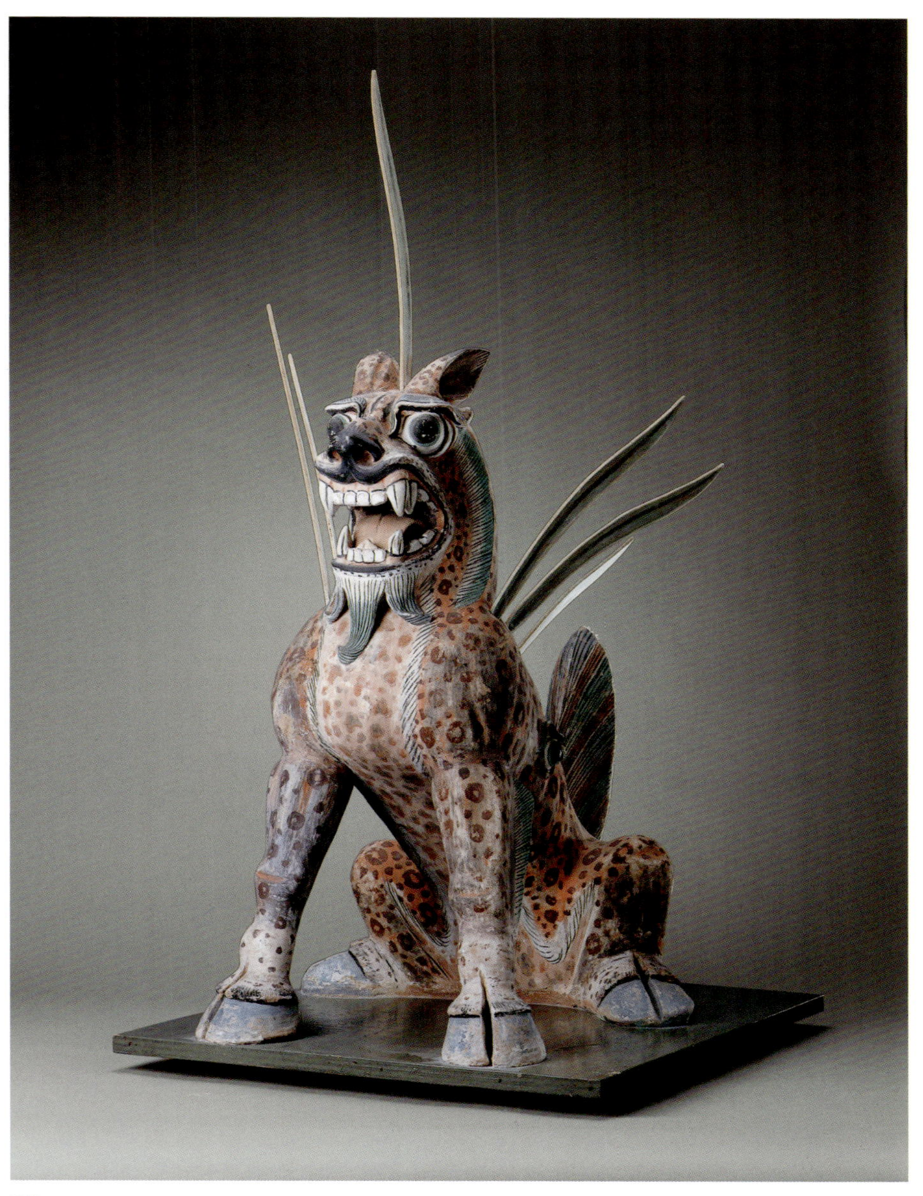

179

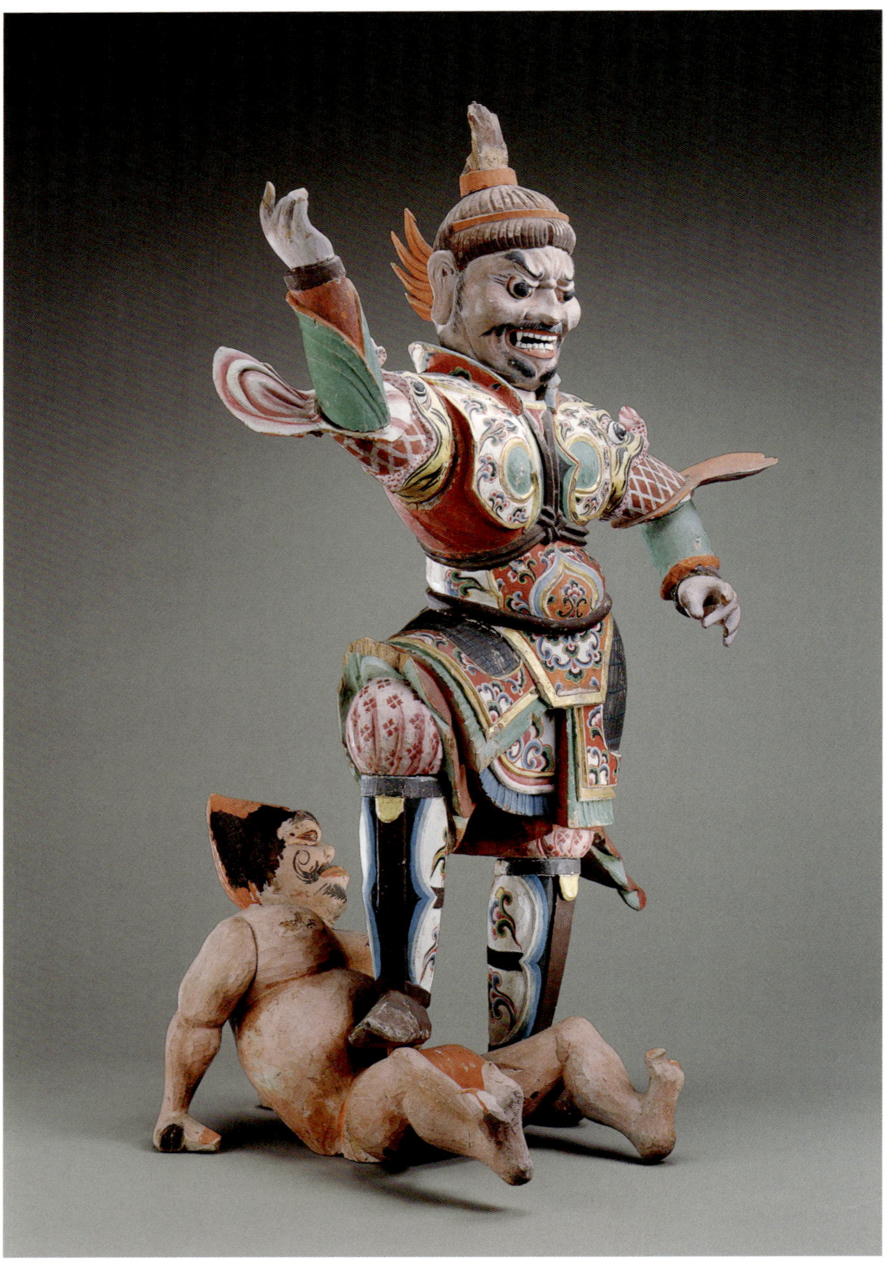

180
Guardian warrior

Tang dynasty (618–907), 7th century
Wood with pigments and gilding
Height 33⅞ in. (86 cm)
Excavated from the tomb (dated 688) of Zhang Xiong and his wife, Astana, Turfan, Xinjiang Uygur Autonomous Region, 1973
Xinjiang Uygur Autonomous Region Museum

Excav. report in *Wenwu* 1975.7

This dramatic guardian warrior, shown stomping on a grimacing demon, was excavated in 1973 from the extensive cemetery at Astana near Turfan (see also cat. nos. 178, 179).[1] An inscription indicates the tomb was that of Zhang Xiong (584–633) and his wife, née Qu (607–688). The Zhang family had longstanding political and marital ties to the Qu, who ruled the Gaochang kingdom (500–640) in the Tarim basin in the sixth and seventh centuries. Zhang was buried in the tomb in 633, and his wife was interred in 688. It has been speculated that the tomb was enlarged during the second burial and that additional goods, such as this guardian, were added in keeping with her rank.

Among the many funerary figures associated with the burial of Qu is this astonishingly well-preserved guardian, carved from more than thirty pieces of wood that were covered with paper, glued at the joints, and then painted and gilded.

Guardians wearing elaborate armor and standing on human figures rather than animals are first found in Buddhist contexts, such as the north wall of the famous Fengxiansi in the Longmen complex in Henan, built between 672 and 676, and become standard in Buddhist environments soon thereafter.[1] In the early eighth century, pairs of such figures also appear as mortuary goods in imperial and aristocratic tombs in the Luoyang and Xi'an areas, where they are generally placed near the opening of the tomb.[2]

DPL

1. Baker 1999: 53–57.
2. Sun Hongmei and Deng Xueqing 1999: 79–82.

181
Female figure

Tang dynasty (618–907)
Wood with pigments, paper, and silk
Height 11⅝ in. (29.5 cm)
Excavated from the tomb (dated 688) of Zhang Xiong and his wife, Astana, Turfan, Xinjiang Uygur Autonomous Region, 1973
Xinjiang Uygur Autonomous Region Museum

Excav. report in *Wenwu* 1975

Among the many spectacular finds from the tomb of Zhang Xiong (d. 633) and his wife, Qu (d. 688), in Turfan are the guardian warrior (cat. no. 180) and this figure of an elegant lady, both associated with the burial of Lady Qu.

The head of the figure is modeled in clay and painted white, with makeup in the latest fashion of the time.[1] The body has a wooden frame with paper padding. The sleeveless jacket is of *jin* silk (see essay by Zhao Feng for a discussion of *jin*), woven to scale with two medallions composed of confronted birds within a

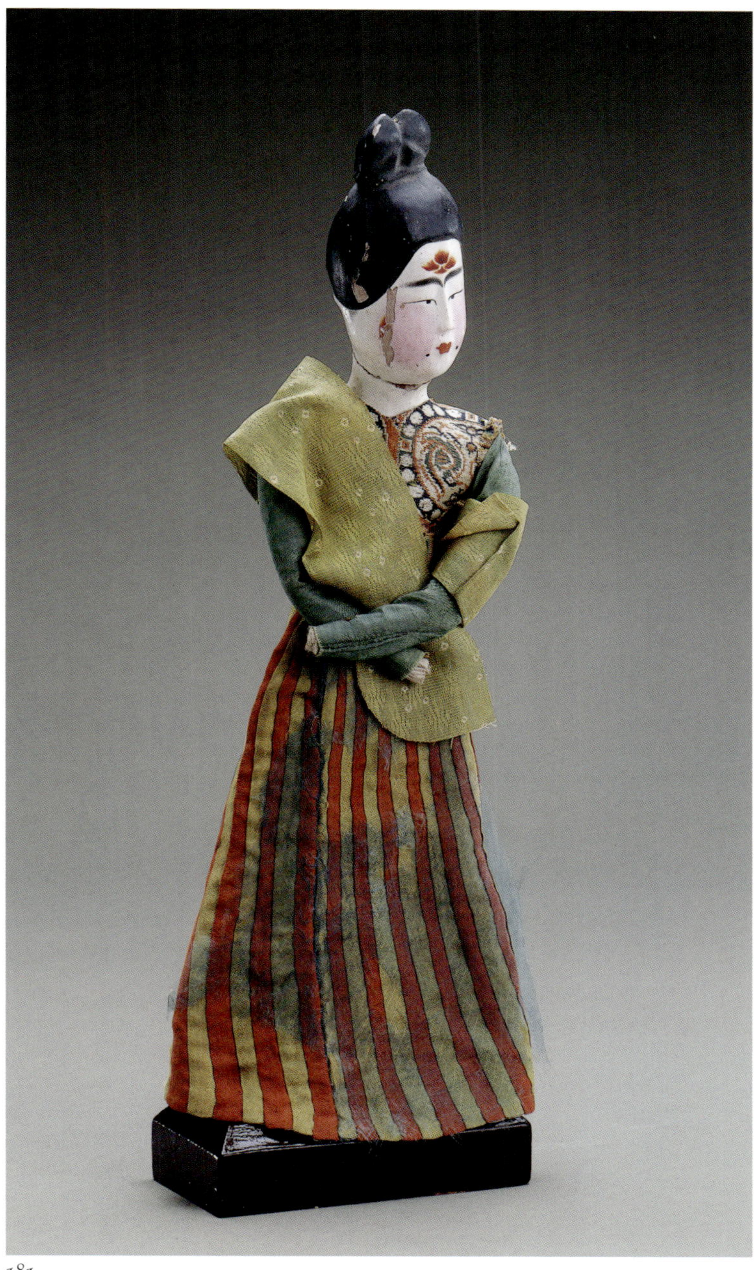

181

pearl roundel. The shawl is of figured silk with resist-dyed patterns of circles. The belt (see detail at right) is silk tapestry, also woven to scale. The skirt is made of alternating strips of patterned silks of two different colors sewn together. There are the remains of a sheer silk cover over the skirt.

The *jin* silk of the jacket, with westernized motifs, was certainly woven locally. This is significant for the history of Chinese silk weaving, as the jacket is datable to before 688. The belt is the earliest known example of silk tapestry in China. Fine gauze weaving has a long history in China going back to at least the third century B.C. The resist-dyeing technique became very popular during the Tang period. The pattern on the textile with hunting scene (cat. no. 241), for example, was produced by a rather elaborate resist-dyeing process.

The immense amount of care and labor that went into making just one of the numerous figures associated with the burial of Lady Qu in this tomb (the full report is not yet published) is indicative of the prosperity of Turfan after its incorporation into the Tang empire in 640.

JCYW

1. This figure provides an excellent illustration of the makeup and hairstyles of fashionable ladies of the Tang period; see Shen Jiawu 1949: 30–35.

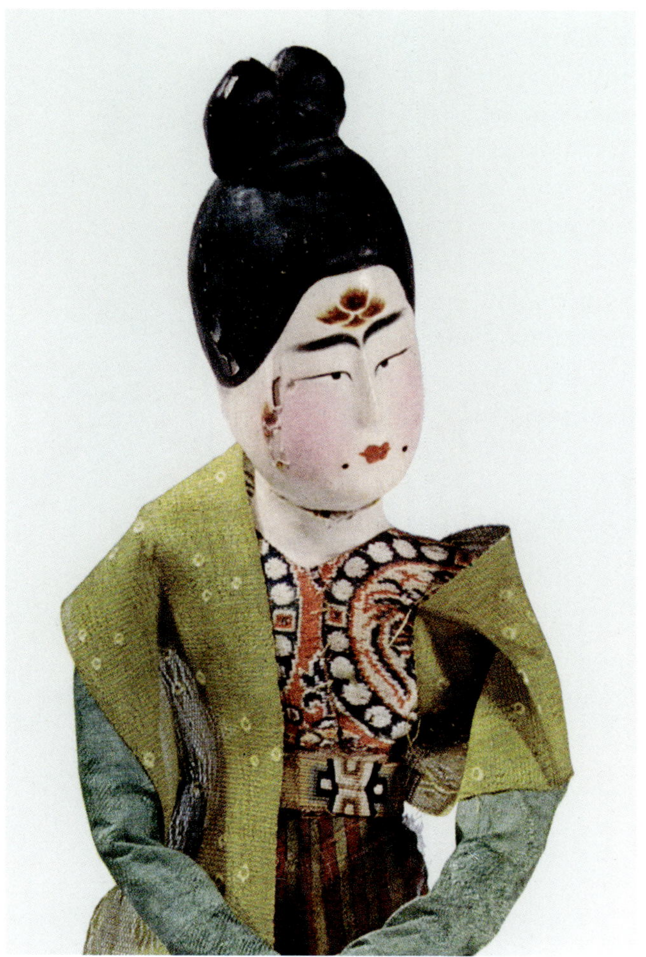

181, detail

182
Horse and female rider

Tang dynasty (618–907), 7th century
Baked clay with pigments, silk, and linen
Height 15 3/8 in. (39 cm)
Excavated from Tomb 187, Astana, Turfan, Xinjiang Uygur Autonomous Region, 1973
Xinjiang Uygur Autonomous Region Museum

Excav. report in *Wenwu* 1975.10

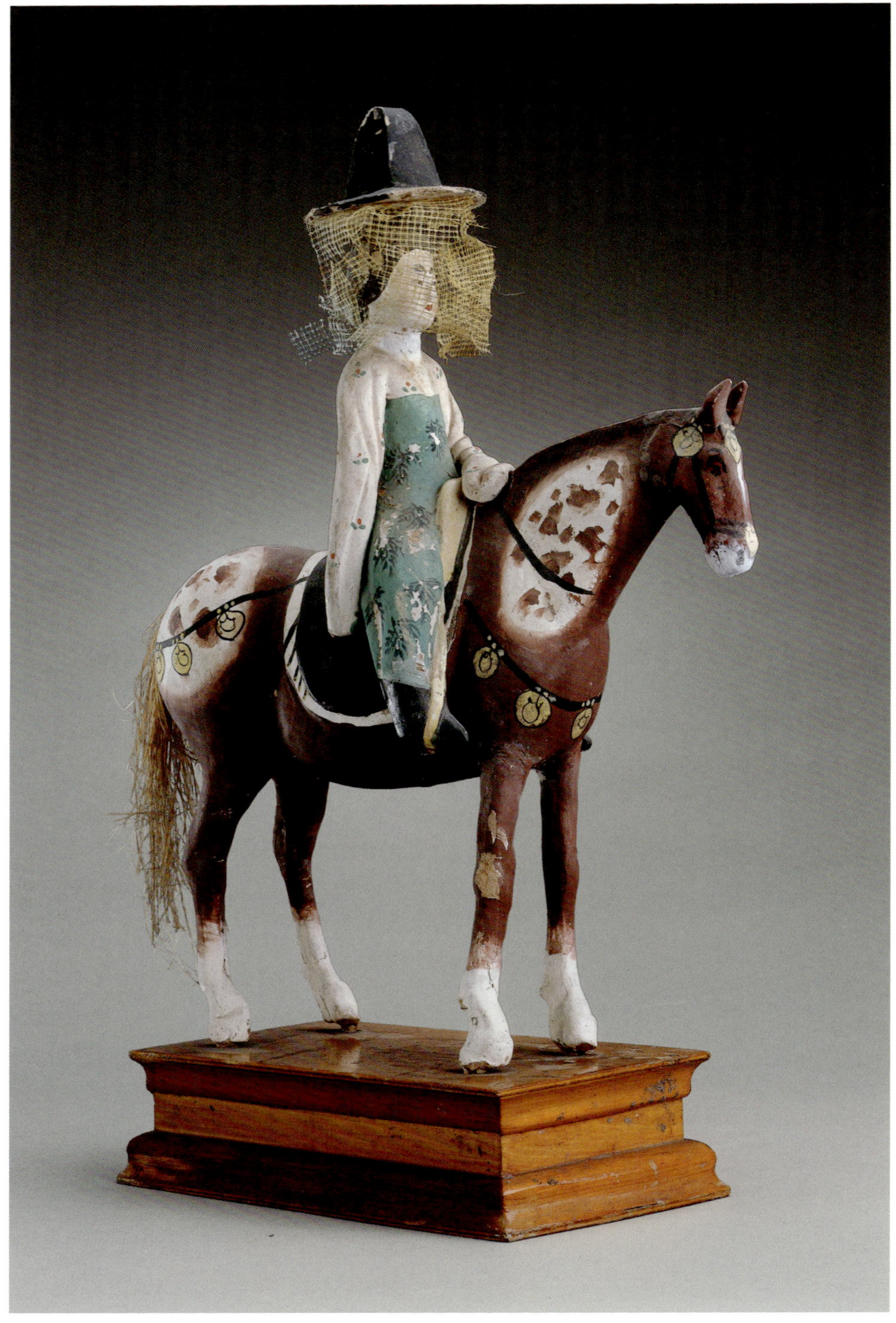

The horse and rider is from the tomb of a member of the Zhang family in Turfan (see cat. nos. 180, 181). It is comparable in style to the pottery figure from Xi'an (cat. no. 183) of several decades earlier. Nevertheless, there is little doubt that the fashion of dress and of riding piebald horses originated in Turfan. In the *Jiutangshu* (Old History of the Tang), it is recorded that at the beginning of the dynasty, court ladies wore a *weimao*, or full-length veil, when they went out and that they would wear a hat with "a skirt going down to the neck" (presumably, a veil like the one worn by the figure shown here).[1] The official historians acknowledged that the custom of wearing veils was "introduced [to the capital] by barbarians," but it was adopted for reasons of modesty. It is, of course, much more likely that it was purely a matter of fashion.

As worn by this figure from Turfan, the veil had a more practical function, that of protecting the wearer against the desert sands.

JCYW

1. *JTS* "Vehicles and Clothing" 45: 1957.

183
Horse and female rider

Tang dynasty (618–907)
Glazed earthenware with pigments
Height 14⅝ in. (37 cm)
Excavated from the tomb (dated 664) of Zheng Rentai, Liquan, Shaanxi Province, 1971
Shaanxi History Museum

Excav. report in *Wenwu* 1972.7

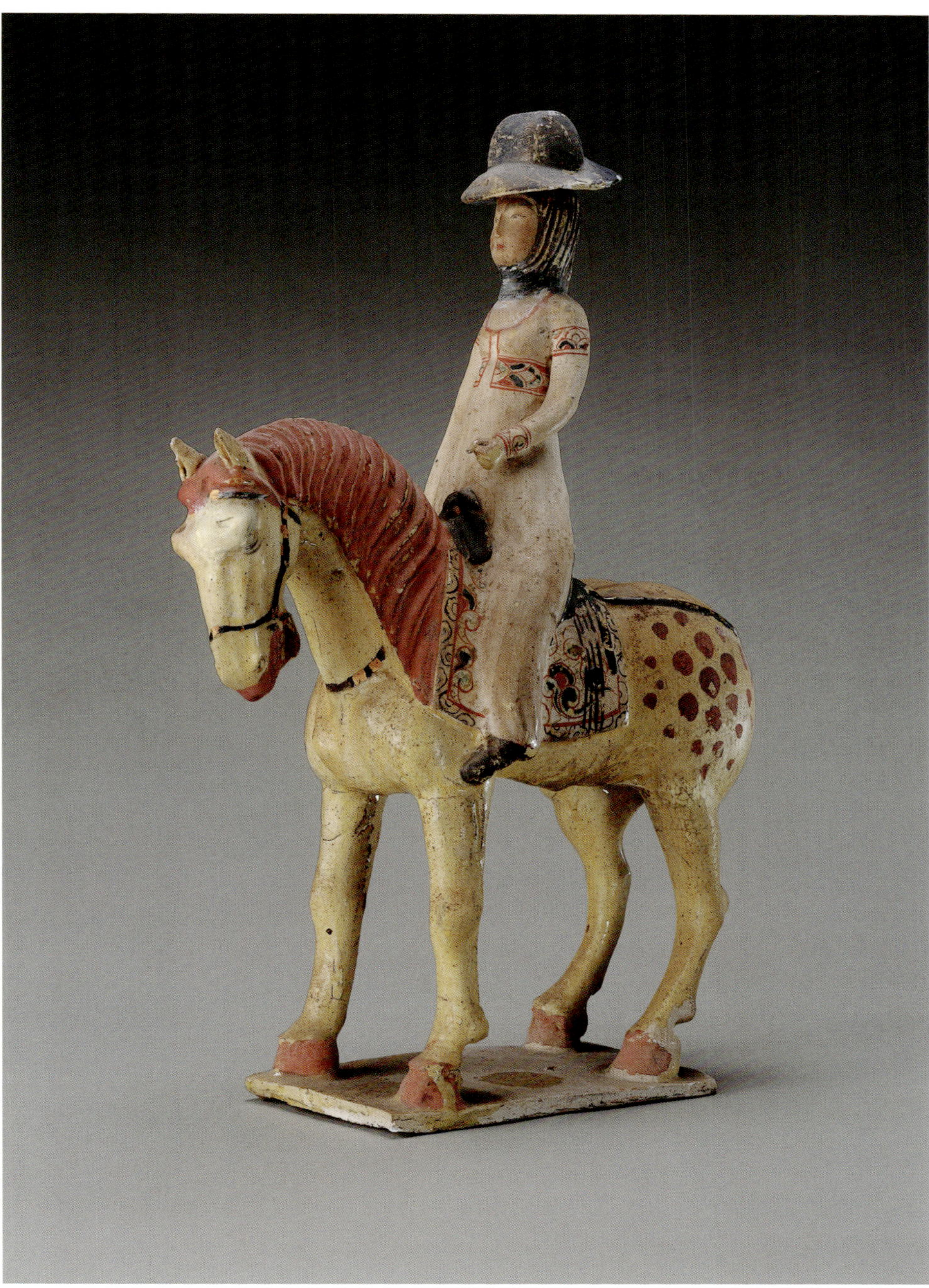

With a pull of her left hand, this elegant horsewoman restrains a spotted horse with a fiery red mane and red hooves to match.[1] The figure, from the tomb of Zheng Rentai (see cat. no. 185),[2] was sculpted and then glazed except for the face, which is painted. She wears either a dress or a shirt tucked into a skirt with vertical yellow and white stripes. The short-sleeved jacket that falls above the waist is embellished with an embroidered border that complements those at the wrist. The figure sports a fashionable black hat that shows to advantage her face below.

During the Sui dynasty (581–619), the *mili,* a body-long veil designed to block the stranger's gaze, became popular for ladies of the imperial and ducal households who rode horses on public roads. Completely covering the body, the *mili,* which was sometimes adorned with jewels, was viewed as an expression of the highest propriety, despite its origins in the foreign Rong and Yi cultures. Toward the end of the Sui, the *mili* had become less conservative in style, as the veil was no longer required to conceal the entire body but only the face. The new wide-brimmed hat with shoulder-length veil was known as a *weimao* (see cat. no. 182). By the 650s, however, the *weimao* had become so popular that edicts—one in the 650s and another in 671—to enforce the wearing of the more modest *mili* were almost completely ignored.[3] The hat worn by the lady rider from the tomb of Zheng Rentai is more radical still. A daring variation of the *weimao,* it is worn without any veil at all and even lacks the holes necessary for attachment. Instead, the rider wears a black balaclava under the hat.

Prior to the Tang dynasty, figures of women riding horses were virtually unknown. Images from the Tang show that women rode horses seated in saddles and wearing full skirts, not sidesaddle as in the European style but with the feet inside stirrups. Sometimes they rode with children propped up in front.[4]

CJL

1. The horse bears an uncanny resemblance to the modern Appaloosa breed, which was popular in China through several dynasties. See Cooke 2000: 140.
2. She was found in the front row of niche 1 on the west side of the tomb. Shaanxi sheng bowuguan et al. 1972: 33–42 (see nos 7.10a, 7.10b, 7.11a, and 7.11b).
3. See *JTS* 45 "Vehicles and Clothing": 1957.
4. This can be seen in the Song copy of the painting by Zhang Xuan (8th century) *The Spring Outing of Madame Haoguo,* in the Liaoning Museum; see *Zhongguo meishu quanji: Hui hua bian* 2, 1984: 41–45, 11 (index).

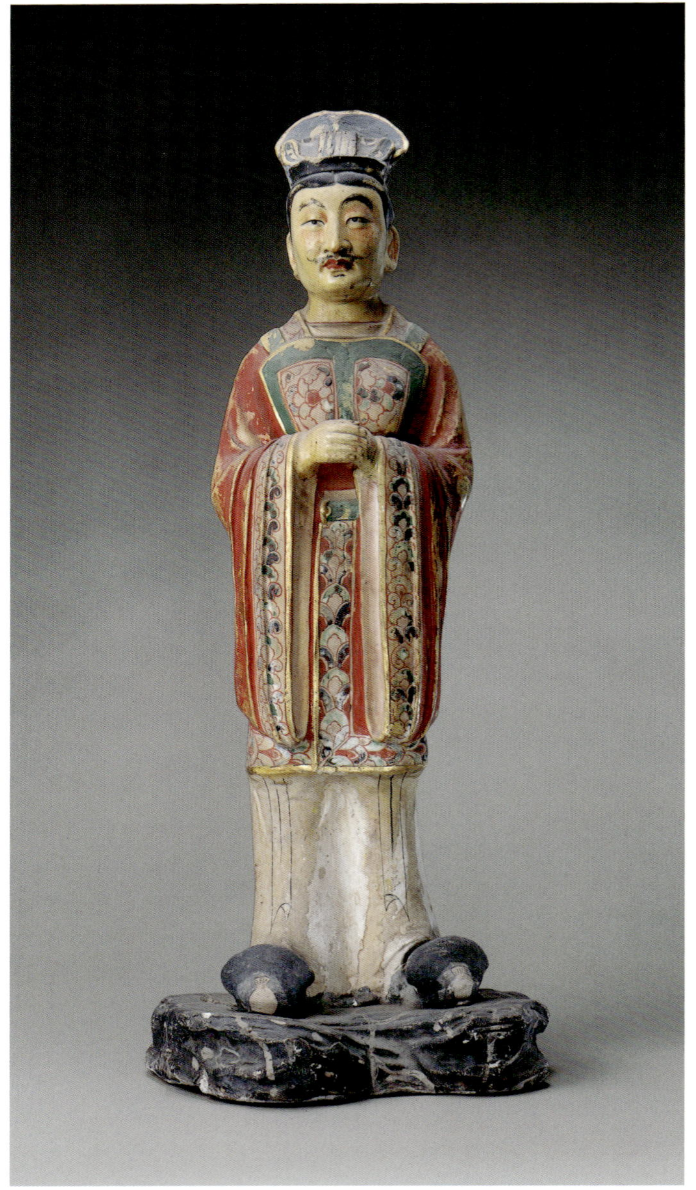

a

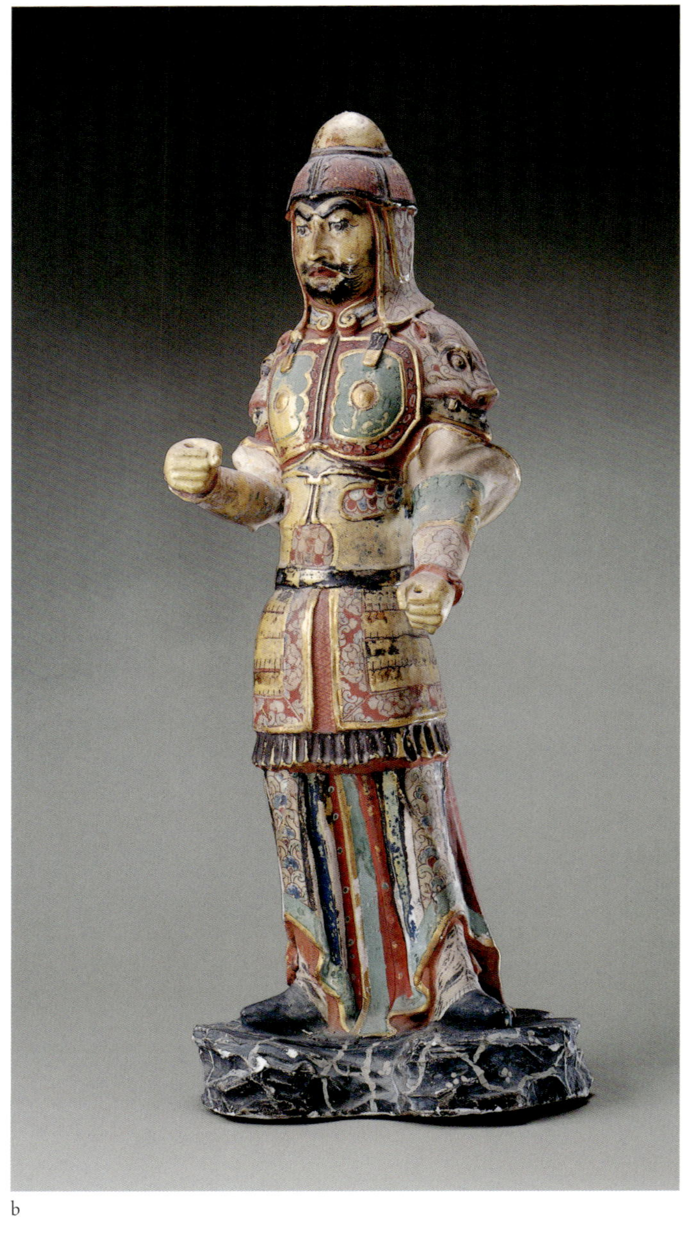

b

184
Civil and military officials

Tang dynasty (618–907)
Glazed earthenware with pigments
Height, a. 27⅛ in. (69 cm);
b. 28⅛ in. (72 cm)
Excavated from the tomb (dated 664) of Zheng Rentai, Liquan, Shaanxi Province, 1971
Shaanxi History Museum

Excav. report in *Wenwu* 1972.7

These colorful figures were found in the tomb of the military commander Zheng Rentai (see also cat. nos. 183 and 185 from the same tomb) and depict a military officer and a civil official from the Tang dynasty. Though not a pair,[1] they are of similar size and both made of hard white clay, the surface fired with yellow and green glaze, and later painted and gilded. They are vibrantly colored, with floral designs on the borders of their gowns and on the breastplates of their armor. Both figures wear a set of cuirasses—a double-piece chest and back armor—but different hats and attire appropriate to their station.

The military man wears a helmet with ear flaps, shoulder guards in the shape of lion heads, a gilded girdle held in place by a black belt, a short skirt that, when in use, would facilitate getting on and off his horse, and another long red, richly decorated skirt. The costume was probably worn for ceremonial purposes. He also wears a light, scaled armor underneath, subtly seen through holes in the girdle. Tiger-striped trousers and black boots complete the set. Each hand has a small hole for grasping an object, perhaps a flag in the right and a weapon in the left. The cuirasses, with round metal plates in the middle, are known in the ancient texts as *mingguangjia* (bright light armor), a description of their reflecting properties.[2]

In contrast, the civil official has a token set of cuirasses with floral designs front and back. Underneath, he wears the long robe with wide sleeves of a court official, here embroidered with roundel-like half flowers. His feet are clad in shoes with a decorative wedge-shaped front, and he wears a bureaucrat's hat called a

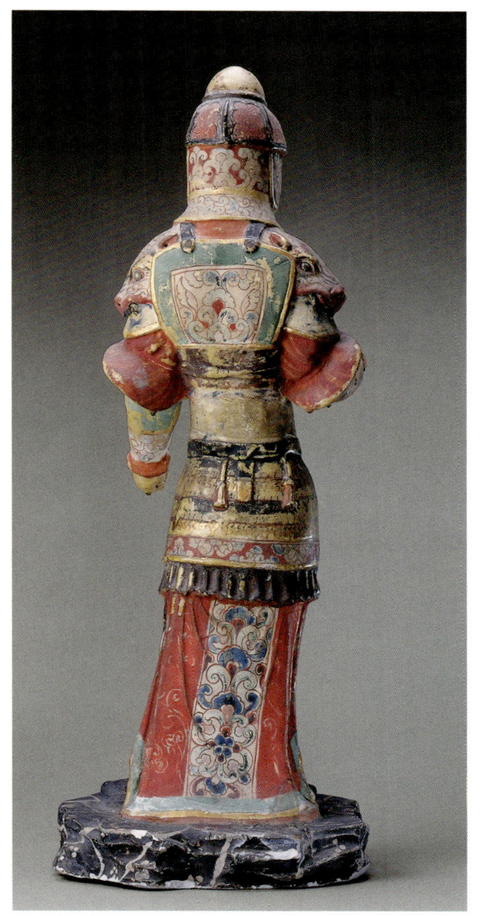

184a, back

jingdeguan (a crown for the imparting of virtue), a reference to the bureaucrat's function as counselor. The official's mustache is fashionably curled, and he folds his hands as if in deference to his lord.

CJL

1. The military official is one of a pair excavated from the tomb and probably functioned much like other pairs of guardians (see cat. nos. 230, 231). The civil official, however, was the only figure of its kind found in the tomb. Shaanxi sheng bowuguan et al. 1972: 33–44.
2. Yang Hong 1980: 46–47.

185
Two female attendants

Tang dynasty (618–907)
Glazed earthenware with pigments
Height, each 12 1/4 in. (31 cm)
Excavated from the tomb (dated 664) of Zheng Rentai, Liquan, Shaanxi Province, 1971
Zhaoling Museum

Excav. report in *Wenwu* 1972.7

Surprisingly, these two servant figures are both female, as one is dressed as a man. They are clad in the popular "western style" and epitomize two Tang ideals of feminine beauty, as eulogized two centuries later by the famous Tang poet Fang Gan (died ca. 888): "The highs and lows of those vermilion lips imitate cherries/ Half covered breasts are snow on a sunny day."[1]

The figure on the left wears a long, striped skirt gathered at the breast by a colorful band with a half-circle border design reminiscent of the Central Asian pearl roundel. A diaphanous blouse with a low neckline and tight sleeves and a short-sleeved jacket complete the upper ensemble. One end of a blue shawl tucks into the band and the other encircles the shoulders, wraps around the two hands folded underneath, and drapes gracefully down the front of the skirt.

The figure on the right is dressed in the fashionable menswear of the day: a blue Persian-style robe, round collared and tight sleeved, with the folds painted in. A band with a Central Asian floral design runs along the front from top to bottom. Just below the waist, a leather belt is slung over the hips, and the hair is swept up into a topknot and wrapped in a black kerchief called a *putou*. In contrast,

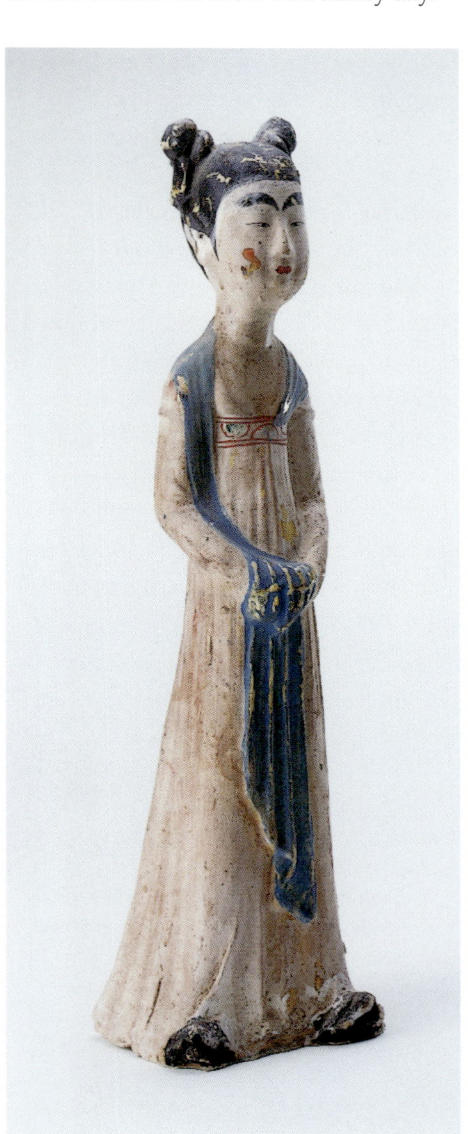

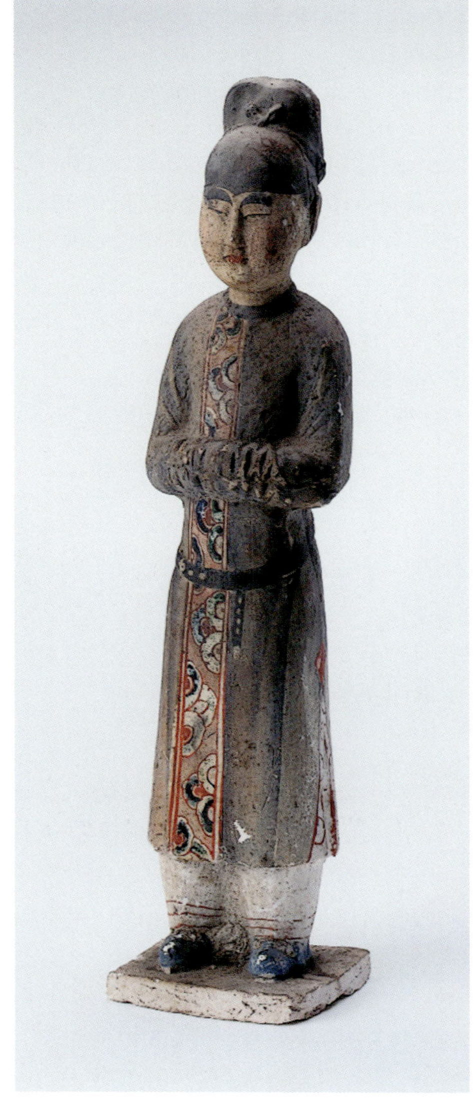

the legs and feet are covered up in feminine red-bordered trousers and sky-blue "thread" shoes.

Many Tang figures of pottery and in painting are shown in men's clothing, though it is still not clear whether women dressed in this manner for pleasure or to fulfill a specific function. Only the shoes peeking out at the bottom or a stray hair escaping from under the *putou* belie the apparent gender. Female figures dressed entirely in men's clothing can also be recognized by their feminine gestures and posture.

The attendants are two of 466 painted and glazed figures recovered from the tomb of Zheng Rentai (601–663).[2] Zheng was an area military commander of strategic towns on the northern Silk Road, along present-day Gansu Province and the southern tip of Xinjiang. When Zheng died in 663 at his post in the northwest, Emperor Gaozong (r. 650–83) decreed that he be buried in Zhaoling, the imperial grounds of his father, Emperor Taizong (r. 627–49), at the expense of the state. Presumably, the tomb was furnished with accoutrements from the imperial workshops. It is thus likely that imperial craftsmen made these figures, as well as other objects from Zheng's tomb (see also cat. nos. 183, 184).

CJL

1. "To a Beauty," by Fang Gan, *QTS*, vol. 19: 7478.
2. Shaanxi sheng bowuguan et al. 1972: 33–42.

186
Goblet

Sui dynasty (581–619)
Gold
Height 2¼ in. (5.7 cm)
Excavated from the tomb (dated 608) of Li Jingxun, Xi'an, Shaanxi Province, 1957
National Museum of China

Excav. report in *Kaogu* 1959.9

This miniature stem cup was found in the tomb of Li Jingxun, a Sui princess who died in 608, when she was nine years old.[1]

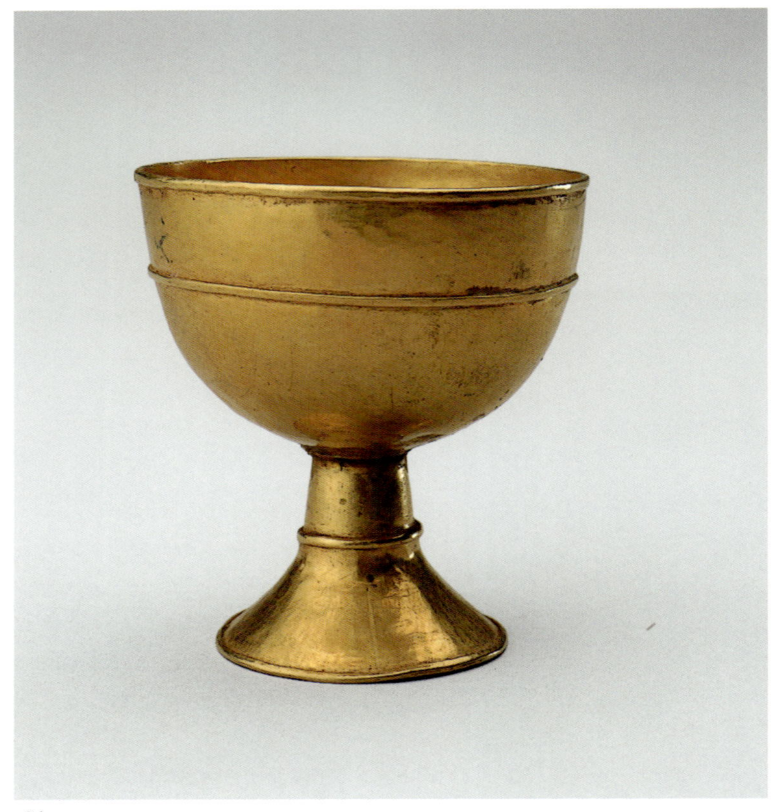

186

Four narrow strips of gold are applied horizontally: around the rim and the foot and bisecting the body and the stem. The upper part of the body is slightly conical, while the lower part is hemispheric. In contrast, the bowls of stem cups produced in Tang China are taller and narrower. The broad bowl and foot and the use of raised bands to divide the vessel into different registers are typical of the nomadic stem cups widespread from China to Hungary.[2]

Li Jingxun's cup is unusually small, either because it belonged to a little girl or because it was executed by a Chinese goldsmith who, like many Chinese metalworkers, had a predeliction for miniature objects. It may also have been made specifically as a burial good for the tomb.

BIM

1. Tang Jinyu 1959: 471–72; Zhongguo shehui kexueyuan Kaogu yanjiusuo 1980: 18, pl. xi.1, 7; Shih Hsio-Yen 1983: 64–65, fig. 14. The necklace (HT164) is from the same tomb.
2. Two such nomadic cups were found in Inner Mongolia together with a Byzantine gold coin, a solidus of Leo I (r. 457–74): Neimenggu wenwu gongzuodui, Neimenggu bowuguan 1975: 182–85; Shih Hsio-Yen 1983: 65, fig. 15.

187
Necklace

Sui dynasty (581–619)
Gold inlaid with pearl and stone
Length 16⅞ in. (43 cm)
Excavated from the tomb (dated 608) of Li Jingxun, Xi'an, Shaanxi Province, 1957
National Museum of China

Excav. report in *Kaogu* 1959.9

Surely one of the finest objects of foreign manufacture recently found in China is this exquisite piece of jewelry fashioned from gold and semiprecious stones.[1] The necklace is a luxurious work of art and skilled craftsmanship that incorporates in its design many of the seven treasures of Buddhism (*saptaratna*) as listed in Buddhist texts of the early centuries A.D. (red stone, blue stone, gold, and pearls). These treasures are described as a "token of valuable decoration, a symbol of wealth, of happiness or of Buddhist paradises."[2] Worn by a young Sui princess, Li Jingxun, when she was laid to rest in her tomb in 608, the jeweled necklet was precious in both a material and a spiritual sense.

All the individual features of the necklace, which is certainly not the work of Chinese craftsmen, can be found in jewelry of the first millennium B.C. and A.D. made in the Hellenistic, Roman, Parthian, and Sasanian west: the loop ends of the necklace, the hooked clasp, the spherical beads decorated with granulation and inlaid with semiprecious materials (in this case pearls), and the large disk beads inlaid with colored stones and arranged in alternating rectangles and pearl-bordered circles.[3] The circular lapis lazuli gem in the clasp has a carved image of a stag and appears to be a reused Sasanian seal stone, but there is nothing to indicate where specifically the necklace was made—in a Roman, Iranian, or western Central Asian workshop.

The conservative nature of jewelry design in antiquity and the widespread exchanges of luxury goods from the Mediterranean to Iran, Central Asia, India, and China following the conquests of Alexander the Great and the settlement of Greeks in the east in the fourth century B.C. resulted in the introduction of Hellenistic forms and styles in West, Southeast and East Asia, where they persisted well into the first millennium A.D. Parallels for nearly all the elements incorporated into the design of the necklace are found at Armazis Khevi (near Mtskheta), the eastern Georgian burial ground of provincial governors and the high nobility in the second to fourth century.[4] In the first millennium A.D. this region, northwest of Iran in the Caucasus, was alternately under the control of Iran and of Rome. Influences from these lands and cultures are evident in the precious luxury items found in the tombs: jewelry, weapons, and vessels. Similarly, east of Iran, in Bactria and Sogd and in the Kushan lands in Afghanistan and India, Hellenistic, Roman, and Iranian fashions were adopted by the elite. The jewelry of the first century A.D. found in the Sirkap mound at Taxila provides illustrations of the taste for works of Greco-Roman origin.[5]

It is not possible to pinpoint the place where the necklace found in the princess's tomb was made, but the mixed Greco-Roman and Iranian background of all the elements in the design suggests a place of manufacture in some region where these two worlds met, in Iran or western Central Asia. Sasanian necklaces (3rd–7th century) depicted on rock reliefs and seals are composed either of spherical beads, with or without a teardrop pendant, or a collar of framed circular and rectangular beads, the latter having concave sides. The necklace found in China combines these two forms and, while it may be a princely Sasanian work, it is also perfectly possible that it was put together in the Buddhist world of western Central Asia and passed from that region to China. Perhaps treasured for its symbolic importance and certainly for its material value, the necklace was a magnificent item of luxury appropriate for adorning the body of the young Chinese princess in her grave.

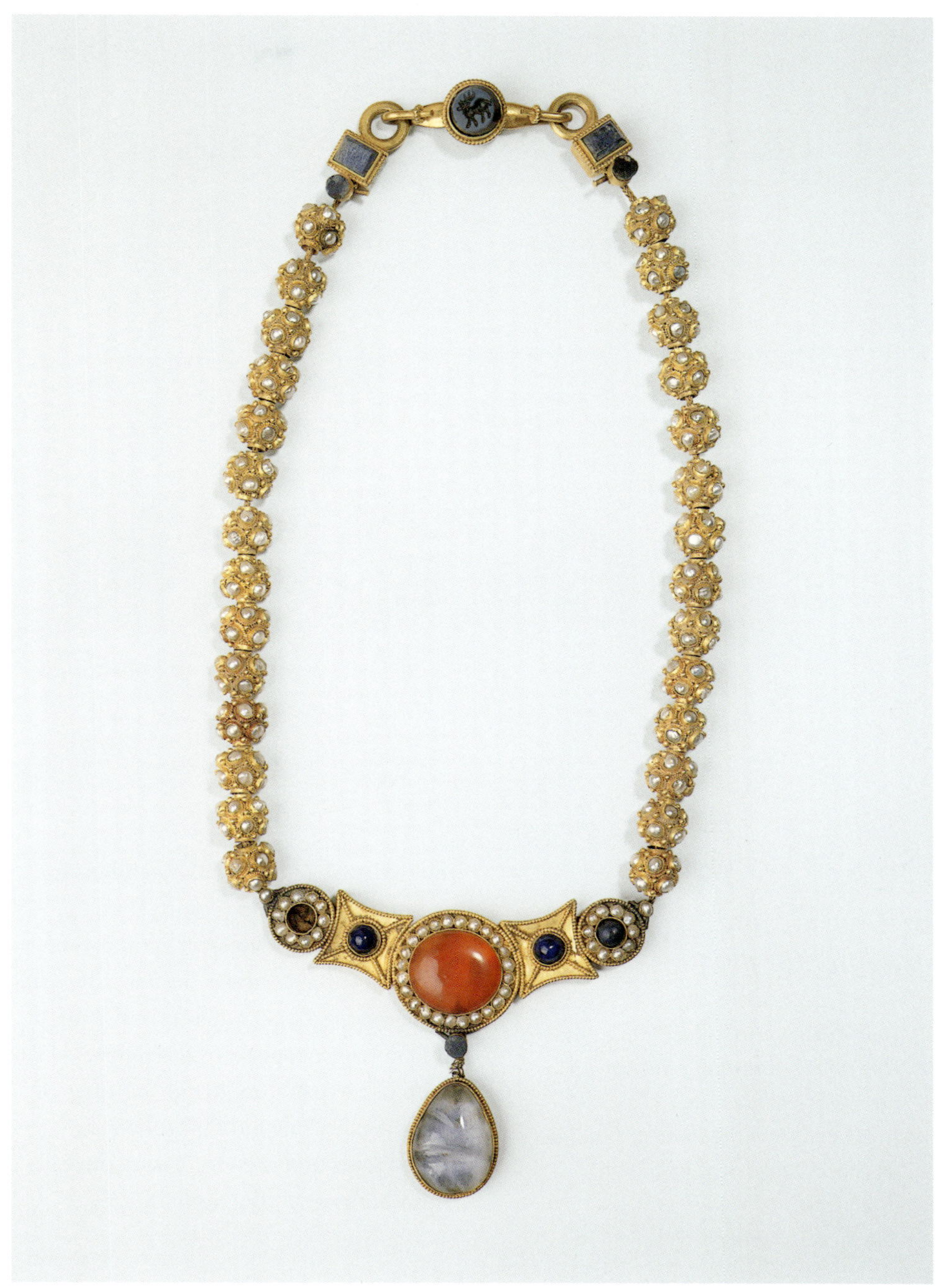

187

POH

1. Tangu Jinyu 1959: 471–72; Zhongguo shehui kexueyuan Kaogu Yanjiusuo 1980: 3–28; Xiong 1987: 77–79; Cen Rui 1990: 103–4; Xiong and Laing 1991: 163–73; Seagraves 2003, no. 114.
2. Liu Xinru 1988: 94.
3. Tait 1976: 86, no. 108, pl. 4.
4. Apakidze et al. 1958: pls. I bis, II, XIII.5, XXXIX.5.
5. Marshall 1951, vol. 2: 627, nos. 56–58; vol. 3: pl. 193.

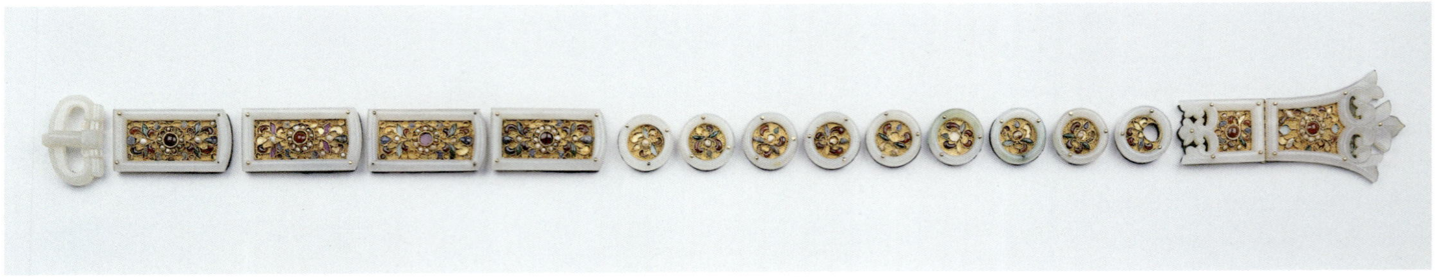

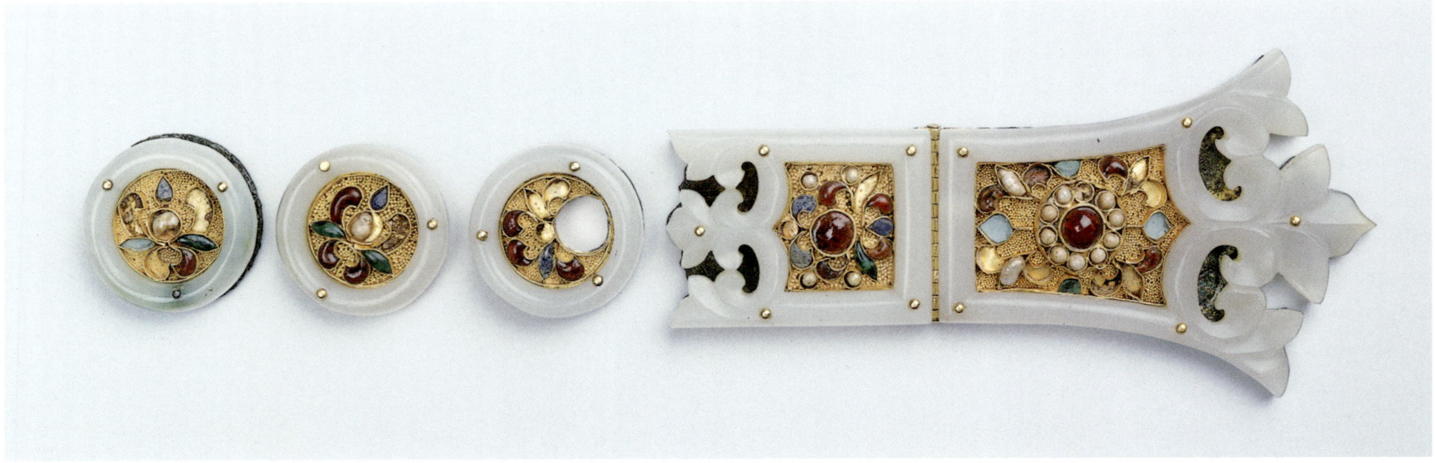

188

Belt buckle and ornamental plaques

Tang dynasty (618–907), 7th century
Jade inlaid with gold, pearl, and glass
Length 59 in. (150 cm)
Excavated from the tomb of Dou Jiao (d. 646), Chang'an xian, Shaanxi Province, 1992
Shaanxi Institute of Archaeology

Reference: Yun Anzhi: 1993

Ornaments in jade are rarely successfully combined with gold and other precious metals. The only time in Chinese history when this was consistently achieved was in the early Tang period. The working of jade and the entire aesthetic associated with carved jade objects—smooth polished surfaces and subtle translucency—go back to prehistoric times in China and are antithetical to bright colors and sparkle. Gold objects inlaid with precious stones, originating in nomadic cultures, were introduced into China and became popular during the Han period (see cat. nos. 9, 10), but this kind of work was not combined with jade. The happy union of the two media in this set of belt buckle and ornaments can be regarded as a reflection of the successful synthesis of different cultures under the Tang dynasty.

The set was excavated from the tomb of Dou Jiao, a nephew of the Empress Dou (wife of Li Yuan, founder of the Tang dynasty). An able military officer, he served with, and then for, his cousin Li Shimin, the great Emperor Taizong (r. 627–49).

JCYW

189

Pair of bracelets

Tang dynasty (618–907), 8th century
Jade (nephrite) and gold
Diameter 3 1/8 in. (8 cm)
Found in Xi'an, Shaanxi Province, 1970
Shaanxi History Museum

Excav. report in Wenwu 1972.1

These two bracelets represent another rare pairing of jade and metal (see cat. no. 188). Each is composed of three pieces of white jade cut into arcs and then polished, with four deep grooves on the exterior and a smooth surface on the interior. The gold fittings, in the form of a lion head, and a three-lobed backing, shaped like the top of a Chinese "cloud," are fastened to the jade by two small rivets that extend from the interior through the exterior of the bracelet. The lion heads, which were not meant to be unfastened, are attached to each other by hinges and a single rivet. Worked in repoussé, they are reminiscent of Northern Wei (386–534) sarcophagus monster masks but have a more natural look. However, the bracelets' ribbed exterior, smooth interior, and locked, mouth-to-mouth lion-head fittings bear a startling resemblance to a Greek bracelet dating to 300 B.C., found in Taranto, Italy, and now in the collection of The Metropolitan Museum of Art.[1]

CJL

1. Fletcher Fund 1924 (24.97.121); illustrated in Williams and Ogden 1994, fig. 152, and Alexander 1928, fig. 82. I wish to thank James C. Y. Watt for bringing this bracelet to my attention.

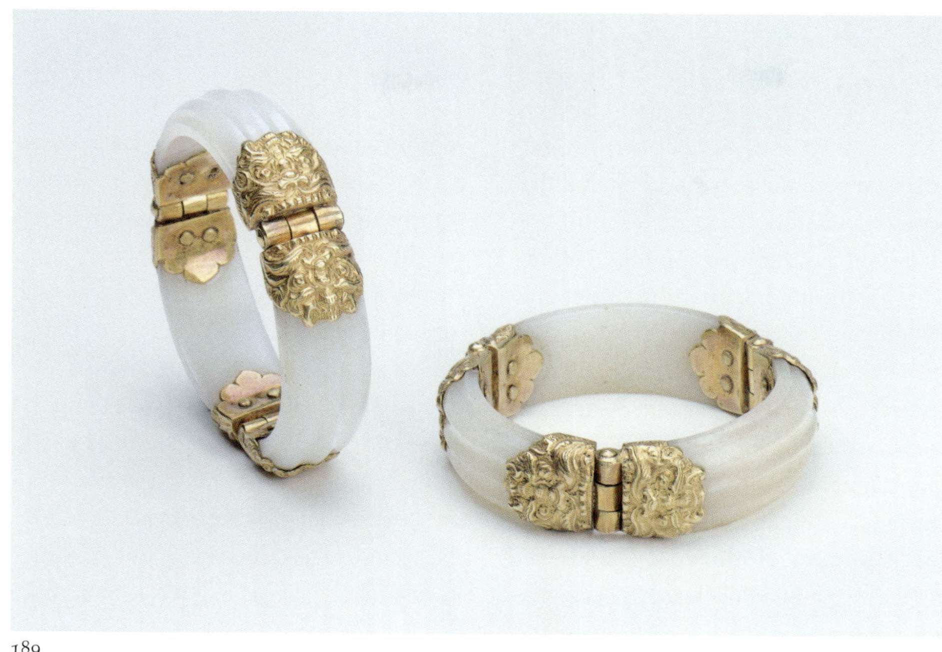

189

1. *THY* 7: 104.
2. *JTS* 78: 2706–7.
3. Ibid. 6: 128.
4. The seventh day of the seventh month is significant as this was the day the Immortal Wang had said that he would return to heaven. Perhaps he was viewed as a messenger to take Empress Wu's message up to the heavens. I would like to thank James C.Y. Watt for improving the translation of the inscription.
5. Zhao was the Empress Wu's first name. It means, literally, "to shine upon." Instead of the usual character, the invented character was used. It was composed of the ideograms for "sun" and "moon" over a "void."
6. For the invented characters of the Zhou dynasty (690–705), see He Han'nan 1987 and Guisso 1979: 305.

190

Tablet inscribed with a prayer

Tang dynasty (618–907), inscription dated 700
Gold
Length 14¼ in. (36.5 cm)
Found at Songshan, Dengfeng, Henan Province, 1982
Henan Museum

Excav. report in *Huaxia Kaogu* 2001.2

This gold tablet was found in 1982 in a crevice on the northern peak of Songshan. The characters are formed of beautifully carved outer lines, possibly by imperial craftsmen. More then twelve hundred years earlier, on May 29, 700, upon the orders of Wu Zetian (r. 690–705), Hu Chao, a minor Daoist official who was part of her entourage, threw this same tablet missive onto the *shanmen*, or central gate, of the middle peak of Songshan. The empress was known to be a devout Buddhist, but this event reflected her increasing interest in Daoist practices. This particular Daoist ritual was called *toujian*, "presenting golden tablets," and it was performed to communicate the wishes of the living to the heavens. In this case, it was intended also to absolve the empress of her sins.

As the empress reached her seventieth year, she became increasingly obsessed with thoughts of death and commemoration, reflected in her offerings to Songshan in 696,[1] her building of the Office for the Control of Cranes in 699,[2] and the writing of the stele on Koushan for the immortal Prince Wang Zijing in 699.[3]

The inscription on the tablet translates:

> Petition: Wu Zhao, monarch of the Country of Zhou, being earnest in [her search for] the True Way and immortality, respectfully approaches the Gates of the Middle [Sacred] Mountain to deliver an epistle on gold. [She] begs the Three Lords and Nine Offices [Daoist gods] to remove her name from the register of [punishable] sinners. Submitted by this humble emissary Hu Chao, with obeisance, on the seventh day of the seventh month in the year Gengzi [700].[4]

Five characters on the inscription deserve some attention. Instead of the traditional characters for the words "country," "Zhao,"[5] "month," "day," and "minister," invented characters authorized by the empress were substituted. Indeed, the presence of such characters on this and other objects provides confirmation that they were made during her reign.[6]

CJL

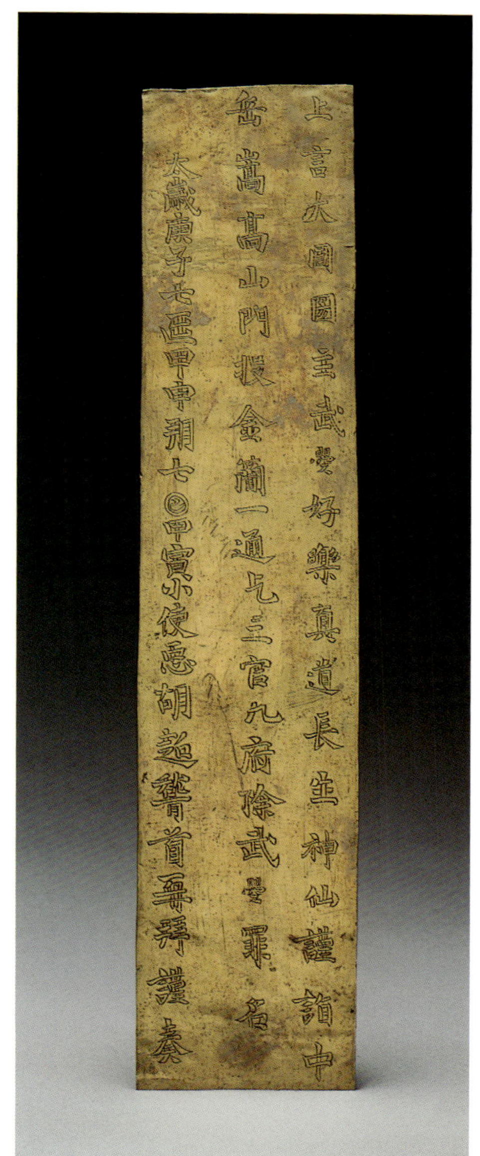

190

191
Set of nested reliquaries

Tang dynasty (618–907), dated 694
Outer chest, stone: 11⅛ x 19⅞ in. (28.3 x 50.5 cm); innermost reliquary, gold: 1¾ x 1⅜ in. (4.6 x 3.5 cm)
Excavated at Dayunsi, Jingchuan, Gansu Province, 1964
Gansu Provincial Museum

Excav. report in *Wenwu* 1966.3

The cult of relics, which begins with the distribution of the remains of Siddhartha Gautama (died ca. 400 B.C.) after his final transcendence (*parinirvana*), represents a long and important tradition in Buddhism. Relics include corporeal remains, objects used by enlightened persons, and other articles that symbolize the immanence of the teachings. Simple stone containers, as well as sets made of precious materials such as sandalwood, gold, silver, and diamonds, are mentioned in the earliest Buddhist texts, as in descriptions of the practice of unearthing and reburying sacred remains.[1]

Sponsored by members of the imperial Yang family, the veneration of relics was particularly important in China in the seventh and eighth centuries. Yang Jian, who ruled as Emperor Wendi (r. 581–604) of the Sui dynasty, distributed relics throughout China in the period from 601 to 604 as an act of devotion intended both to propagate Buddhism and to further unify the nation. Oracles, omens, and the finding and viewing of relics were also important during the reign of Wu Zetian (r. 690–705),[2] who was related to Wendi through her mother, Lady Rongguo, a member of the Yang family.

This set of reliquaries, reburied at Dayunsi (Great Cloud Monastery) in Jingchuan, Gansu, during the Empress Wu's reign, are thought to have contained relics first distributed by Emperor Wendi in the early seventh century.[3] The name of the monastery links it to the eponymous temples established under Wu Zetian in the two capitals and in every prefecture in the country. The name derives from a commentary on the *Dayunjing* (Great Cloud Sutra) presented in 690 to Wu Zetian by a group of monks. The text, which includes a description of a female ruler in southern India who presided over a peaceful and prosperous land, helped to legitimize the empress's usurpation of the throne.

The inscription on the stone chest (opposite, bottom) tells the story of the discovery and reburial of the relics. A monk named Chufa noticed rays of light emanating from the foundation of a ruined pagoda near the monastery. He suspected—though without evidence—that the beams marked the site of one of the 84,000 relics believed to have been buried by the Indian king Ashoka in the third century B.C. Chufa enlisted the help of Meng Shen (ca. 621–ca. 713), vice prefect of the region, and more than sixty workers to excavate beneath the pagoda. They recovered a stone coffer and a glass vase that contained fourteen grains used to symbolize the relics.

The precious grains were set on a piece of sandalwood within a glass bottle that was wrapped, for reburial, in a piece of silk brocade. The bottle was placed in a gold coffin-shaped container with pearls and turquoise stones inlaid to form flower-shaped bevels. The latter was placed in a silver reliquary, which was, in turn, set into a gilt-bronze container. Both the silver and the gilt-bronze boxes are decorated with scrolling flowers. The former has a lock and key. Finally, the set was placed into the incised stone chest and installed, with great ceremony, under the base of the Buddha Hall of the Great Cloud Monastery in 694.[4]

DPL

1. Willis 2000.
2. Chen Jinhua 2002: 33–149.
3. Gansu sheng wenwu gongzuodui 1966: 8–15.
4. It is unusual for relics to be reburied under a Buddha hall rather than a pagoda.

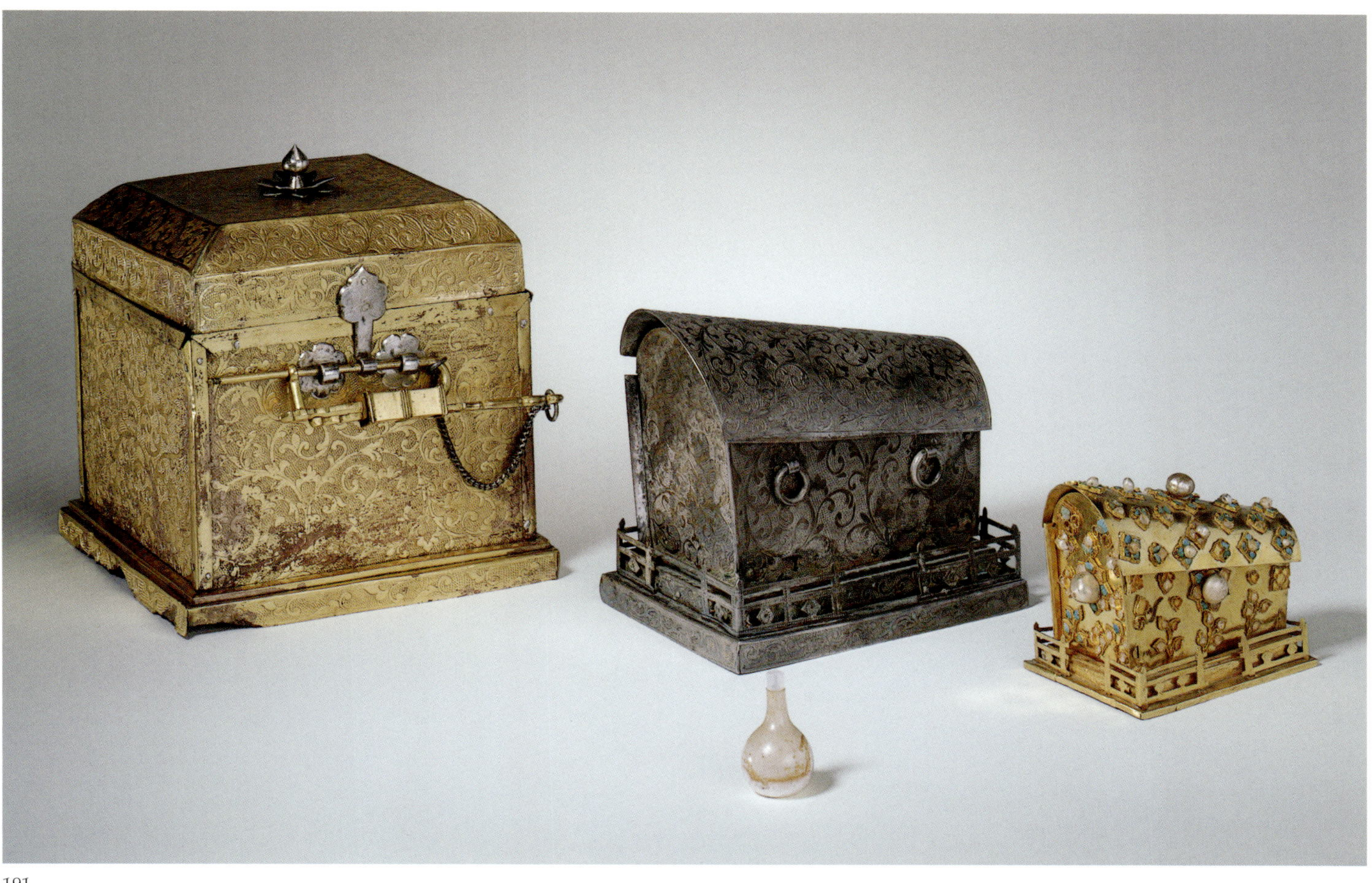

191

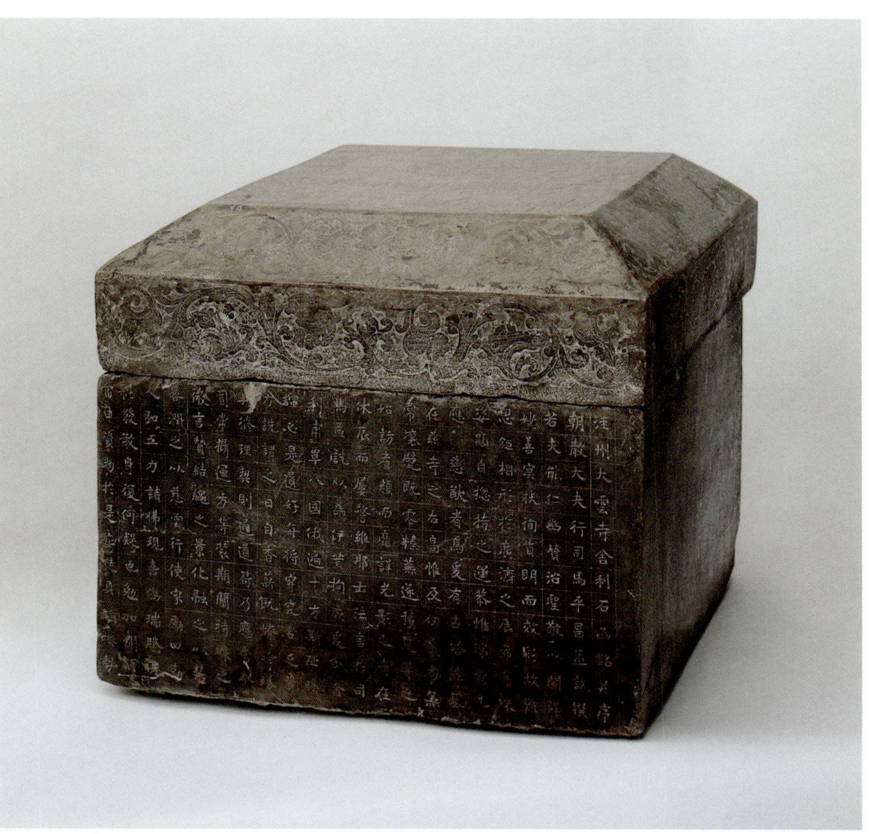

191, stone chest

192
Buddha Vairocana

Tang dynasty (618–907), ca. 700
Limestone
Height 94½ in. (240 cm)
From Southern Leigutai Cave, Longmen, Henan Province
Longmen Caves Research Institute

REFERENCE: Longmen wenwu baoguansuo et al. 1992

The carving of this stately Crowned Buddha is intimately involved with the Empress Wu (r. 690–705), the formidable female ruler of China, who oversaw the building in the Eastern Hill of Longmen of grandiose cave temples enriched with icons that embodied newly formulated doctrinal trends. The two Kanjing Caves served to house processions of patriarchs linked to the emerging Chan, or Contemplative, school of Buddhism, while the Leigutai Caves—where the Crowned Buddha was located—revealed the interest of the empress in the nascent Esoteric school, which came to fruition after her death, during the reign of Emperor Xuanzong (r. 712–56).[1]

The Crowned Buddha was placed in the South Cave of Leigutai against the rear wall of a large sacred space whose surrounding walls were covered with 765 seated bodhisattvas. The deity is shown seated in lotus position on a massive throne (not included in this exhibition). The right hand extends downward in the gesture of "touching the earth." Realism triumphs in the depiction of the powerful body and its latent strength and in the sensitive rendering of the extended right hand. The sculpture is set apart from other images of the Buddha by the elaborate display of jewelry—a tiara-like crown with inset jewels, an embellished collar-necklace, an armlet that resembles a flaming jewel—that ran counter to the monastic vow to reject possessions of any kind.

Similar images of bejeweled Buddhas became associated with painted mandalas, the devotional implements of Esoteric Buddhism that were transmitted to China from India in the first half of the eighth century, following the rule of the empress. The Crowned Buddha reflects the earliest phase of this transmission, which occurred in the mid-seventh century. The jewelry and the hand gesture, which are the primary characteristics of the new icon, perhaps derive from one of the *dharani*, or incantations, described in the *Duolonijijing* (Sutra on the Collection of Dharani), translated from Sanskrit to Chinese in the mid-seventh century by the monk Adigupta.[2]

In the *Duolonijijing*, we read about a manifestation of the Buddha Vairocana called the Buddha Bodhirai. He is presented, seated under the *bodhi* tree, bejeweled and performing the "touching the earth" mudra. At Leigutai, only some of these canonical requirements are respected. Nevertheless, it is clear that the Crowned Buddha seen here represents one manifestation of the Buddha Vairocana.

The text of the sutra offers instruction on the performance of rituals dedicated to specific deities. It is also possible that knowledge of this deity and his likeness were brought back to China by Xuanzang (602–664), the famous pilgrim who journeyed to India to gather Buddhist scriptures.

AFH

1. The original setting of the Crowned Buddha is illustrated in Longmen wenwu baoguansuo et al. 1992, vol. 2, pl. 259.
2. *Taishō*, vol. 18, no. 901.

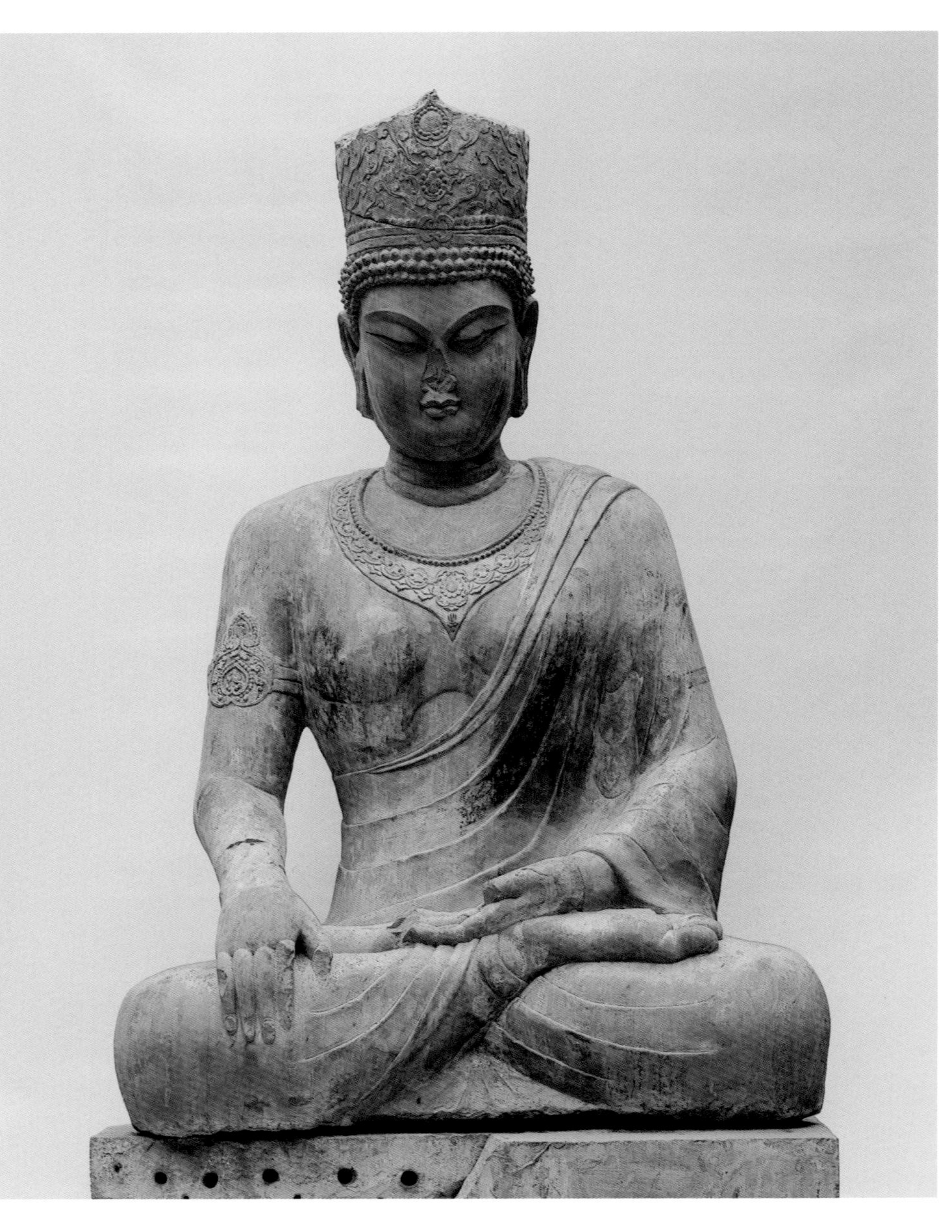

193
Eleven-headed bodhisattva Avalokiteshvara

Tang dynasty (618–907), ca. 703
Sandstone
Height 45 in. (114.3 cm)
From Baoqingsi, Xi'an, Shaanxi Province
Museum of Fine Arts, Boston

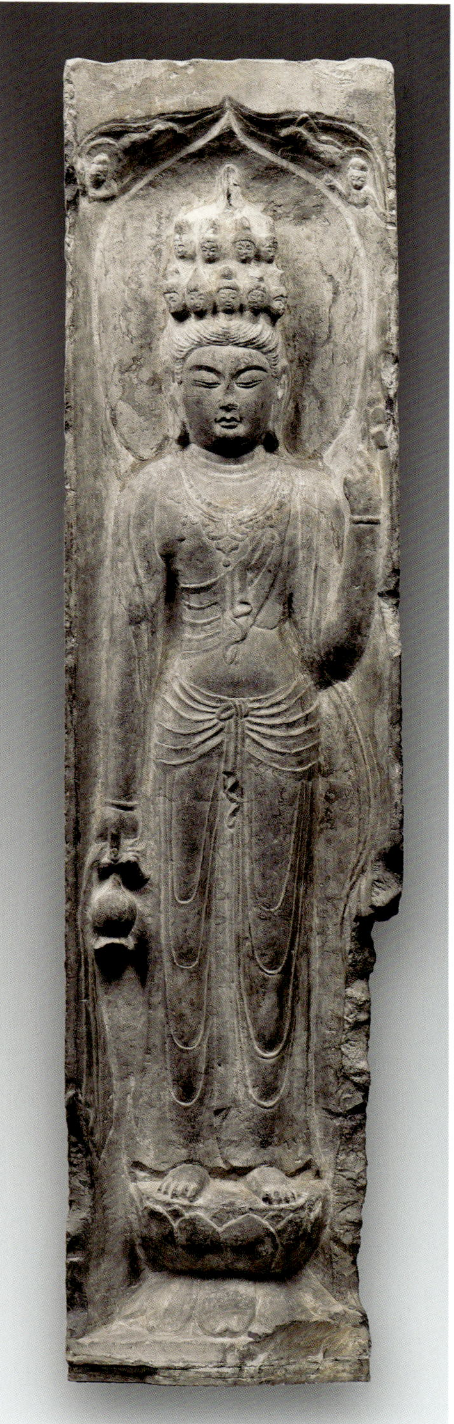

By the sixth century, the bodhisattva Avalokiteshvara (C: Guanyin), who was not prominent in early Indian Buddhism, had come to be revered in multiple manifestations. In his eleven-headed form, he had the power to eliminate disasters and bring blessings.[1] In addition to the central face, the ten additional heads represent vows made by the bodhisattva to save all of humanity. Although texts regarding this form of the bodhisattva were known in China as early as the sixth century, devotion to the deity first gained momentum during the reign of Wu Zetian (r. 690–705).[2] The prominence awarded the bodhisattva at that time may have derived, in part, from the efforts of the monk Fazang (643–712). At the request of the Empress Wu, Fazang established a ritual arena devoted to Avalokiteshvara to invoke his help in the defeat of the Khitan, a group from the northwest who were finally vanquished about 679.[3]

This sculpture of Avalokiteshvara was one of eight placed along the sides of the Qibaotai, or Terrace of Seven Treasures, in the Guangzhaisi compound in the capital, Chang'an (present-day Xi'an). More than thirty sculptures, some depicting a seated Buddha with two bodhisattvas, are thought to have decorated the terrace.[4] The temple was constructed to mark the discovery, in 677, of 10,000 grains (symbolizing relics) in the Guangzhai quarter of Chang'an. The relics were unearthed under the direction Wu Zetian, or possibly her husband, Emperor Gaozong (r. 650–83), after an unnamed soothsayer announced that he had noticed an extraordinary aura in the area. The discovery of these relics, and their distribution throughout the country, is discussed in the commentary on the *Dayunjing* (Great Cloud Sutra), presented to Wu Zetian in 690. The empress used the text, which glorifies her as a female ruler, to help justify her usurpation of the throne. It seems likely that the construction of the Qibaotai, which was begun about 700, was intended both to honor the empress and to create a magnificent edifice to house some of the relics.[5]

Ten small heads are here ranged in three tiers above the primary face of Avalokiteshvara. The thin, clinging drapery is typical of sculptures produced in the later years of the reign of the Empress Wu, as is the plumpness of the cheeks and abdomen. The bodhisattva's broad shoulders and narrow waist and his frontal, somewhat static, stance are also characteristic. Parallels for this style are found in contemporaneous pieces from Kashmir and related centers, which had strong diplomatic ties to China in the early eighth century.[6]

DPL

1. See Huntington 1985, fig. 12.27, for an illustration of the earliest Indian image found in Cave 41 at Kanheri, Maharashtra Province.
2. For a discussion of Chinese and Japanese images of this bodhisattva, see Wood 1985.
3. Yen Chüan-ying 1987: 1–7; Forte 1988.
4. Matsubara 1995, vol. 3, figs. 649–63. At some point, the stones were moved to the nearby Baoqingsi, possibly because of the destruction of the first temple. In the late nineteenth century, several stones were purchased and taken to Japan, and from there traveled to the United States.
5. Chen Jinhua 2002: 80–103.
6. Leidy 1997: 66–70. See also Hinuber 2003: 35–39.

194
Two female attendants

Tang dynasty (618–907)
Ink and color on plaster
66⅛ x 46⅞ in. (168 x 119 cm)
Excavated from the tomb (dated 706) of Prince Zhanghuai, Qianxian, Shaanxi Province, 1971
Shaanxi History Museum

Excav. report in *Wenwu* 1972.7

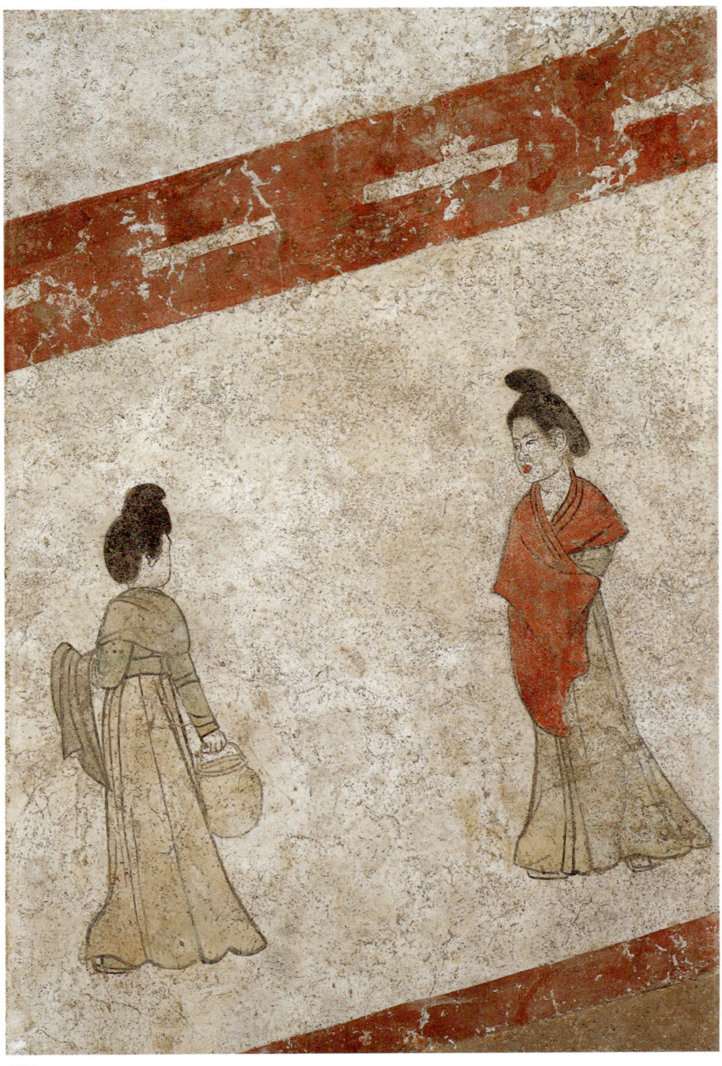

194

Li Xian (655–684) was the sixth son of Emperor Gaozong (r. 650–83) and the second son of Wu Zetian (r. 690–705). He was named heir apparent in 675, but in 680 was accused by his mother of plotting a coup and banished to Sichuan, where he was forced to commit suicide in 684. Following the restoration of Emperor Zhongzong (r. 684, 705–10) and the death of the empress in 705, Li Xian's title of Prince Yong was posthumously reinstated and his remains were reinterred in the Qianling mausoleum complex of his father. In 711, Emperor Ruizong (r. 684–90; 710–12) further restored his status—as heir apparent—with the title Crown Prince Zhanghuai.[1] Later that year, Li Xian's consort, Madame Fang, was buried with him and, although his tomb was not enlarged, the murals were repainted to accord with his more exalted status.[2]

The tomb consists of a walled compound and an earthen pyramid above ground and a tunnel that slopes down about forty-five feet below the surface to a level passageway and two vaulted chambers. Aligned along a north–south axis, the underground complex measures about 230 feet in length. The murals that decorate the walls are organized to suggest a palace set within a landscape.[3] The top of the sloping entrance ramp presents a mounted procession and polo players in rural settings. Farther along the ramp are two scenes of foreign envoys being received by Chinese officials and two contingents of honor guards. As the ramp descends through three gatelike passageways, the scenery changes to suggest a palatial setting with gatekeepers, racks of spears, and eunuchs. A wooden door once marked the point where the entranceway levels off. Beyond this point, the floor is tiled and the murals are given over to images of palace ladies. The antechamber and burial chamber are decorated to suggest garden courtyards.

The two female attendants depicted above are part of a retinue of serving women bearing food or household articles that progresses inward from the base of the entrance ramp to the antechamber. Painted against a blank ground, the figures nonetheless create the illusion of a shallow space through their animated poses. The woman at the right, wrapped in a red shawl, is shown in three-quarter profile, her head turned slightly to the left. The woman at the left, who carries a pail in her right hand, faces away from the viewer but looks over her shoulder as if to meet the gaze of her companion.

The figures are drawn in bold outlines of uniform width, with finer lines delineating facial features. Their hair is shown swept up in a high chignon, with a few cursory hatchmarks to suggest strands that have been brushed back from the face and neck. Color has been uniformly applied within the outlines of the garments with little or no effort to model drapery folds through the use of light and dark shading, as is the case with some of the other figures depicted in the murals. Nonetheless, the ease with which the artist, with just a few deft brushstrokes, has captured form and movement demonstrates the transformation in figural art that occurred in the early eighth century. In contrast to the drawing style of the Seven

Sages of the Bamboo Grove (cat. no. 113) and that of the early Tang master Yan Liben (ca. 600–674), in which concentric drapery lines are arranged in ornamental patterns, figures are now rendered in simple, sketchy brushstrokes that vividly describe their three-dimensionality.[4]

MKH

1. For Li Xian's biography, see *JTS* 86: 2831–32. For his correct date of birth, see Shaanxi sheng bowuguan, Qian xian wenjiaoju tangmu fajuezu 1972a: 19.
2. See Shaanxi sheng bowuguan, Qian xian Qianling wenwu baoguansuo 1973: 67–68, which corrects an earlier interpretation concerning which murals were repainted; see Li Qiushi 1972: 48.
3. See Fu Xinian 1998.
4. For a discussion of Yan Liben's style, see Yang Xin et al. 1997: 60–61.

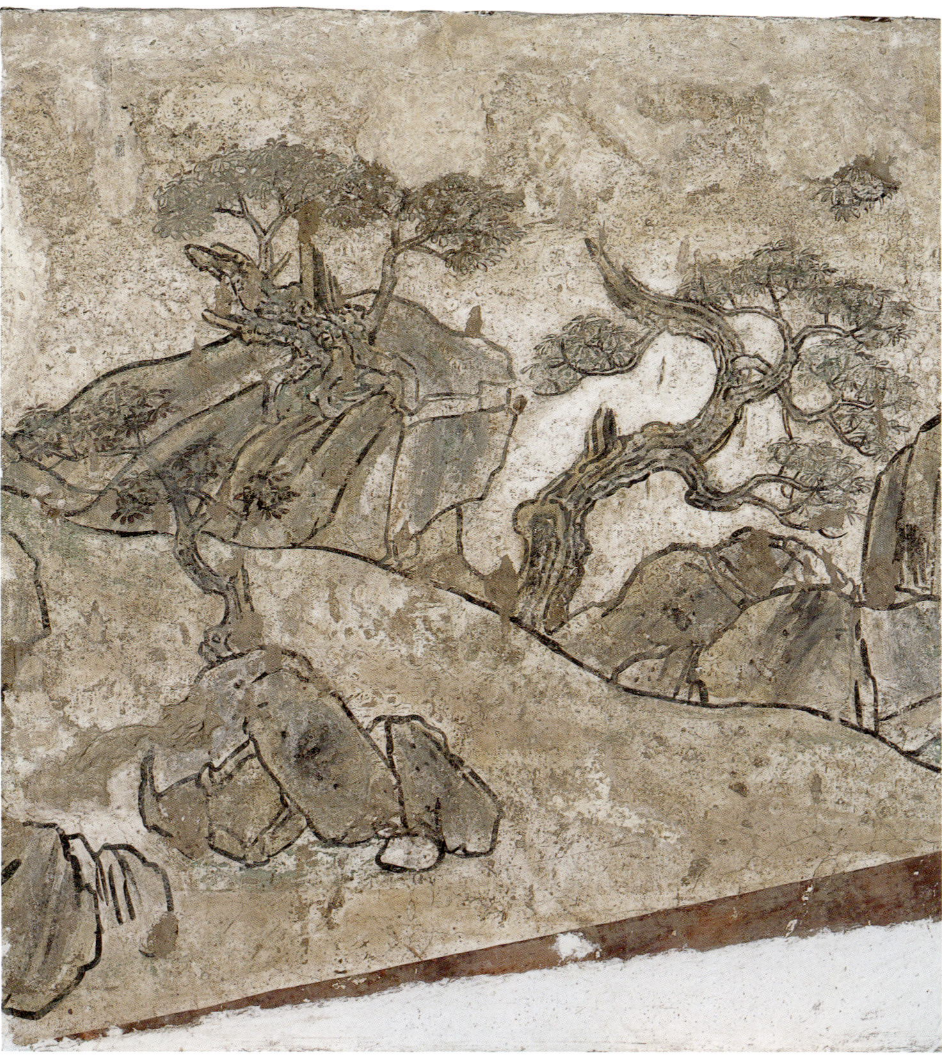

195
Rocks and trees

Tang dynasty (618–907)
Wall painting, ink and color on plaster
44⅞ x 41⅜ in. (114 x 105 cm)
Excavated from the tomb (dated 710) of Prince Jiemin, Fuping, Shaanxi Province, 1997
Shaanxi Institute of Archaeology

Reference: Han Wei and Zhang Jianlin 1998: 101–62

The art of landscape painting first emerged as an independent genre during the Tang dynasty (618–907). This fragmentary scene of rocks and trees comes from the tomb of Li Chongjun, Crown Prince Jiemin (d. 709).[1] Thus, it is contemporary with Li Sixun (651–716), the artist credited with originating the "green and gold" style of landscape painting.[2]

Although smaller in scale than the tomb of Crown Prince Zhanghuai (see cat. no. 194), the murals in this tomb follow a similar organizational schema. The sloping entrance ramp is decorated with depictions of rural scenery outside a palace compound, while the walls of the inner passageway and burial chamber are filled with images of courtiers and ladies within a setting of palatial halls and gardens. This fragment comes from the east wall of the tomb's entryway. Originally, it formed a part of a landscape panorama more than twenty feet long and over six feet high that began at the upper (southern) end of the ramp with a foreground

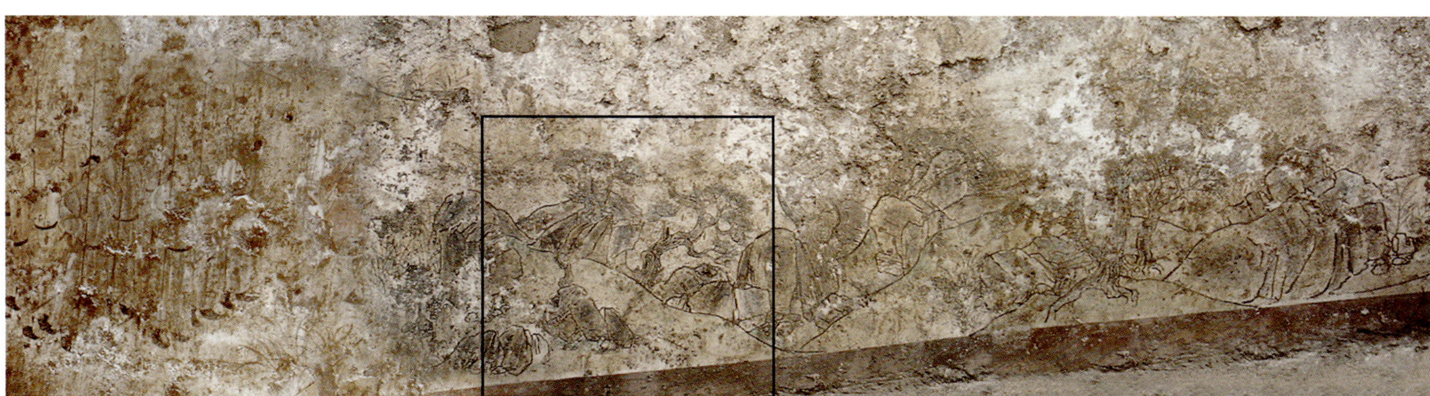

Panorama from the east wall of the tomb's entryway showing the original position of the section included in the exhibition (outlined in black).

depiction of an honor guard of halberd bearers (page 303, bottom).[3] The massive boulders and craggy trees functioned as a foreground repoussoir to set off the panorama from the viewer. Unfortunately, the more distant elements of this scene are now indecipherable. But in a similar panorama from the opposite wall, two groups of polo players, smaller in scale than the halberd bearers, occupy the middle ground.[4] Such large, continuous horizontal compositions represent far more complex and spatially coherent settings for human activity than other, contemporary images of horses and grooms (cat. no. 177).

Here, bold ink lines delineate the contours of rocks and trees, while patches of ink wash—the precursors of texture strokes—serve to model forms and suggest surface features. Finally, color has been applied within some of the outlines: green and red on the foliage, shades of ochre on rock faces and tree trunks, and malachite green highlights along some contours. Although much of this color has been lost, the image is still striking for its specificity of detail. Piles of boulders and faceted rock outcrops vividly convey a sense of volume and mass, while trees are depicted with complex root and branch structures, knotholes, and stippling to suggest roughly textured bark. Forms are still represented primarily as profile silhouettes, but boulders are often set on the diagonal to enhance the sense of three-dimensionality. Spatial recession is created by the overlapping of forms, shifts in scale, and the placement of more distant objects higher up on the picture plane, but there is, as yet, no attempt to delineate a continuously receding ground plane. Nevertheless, the painting vividly evokes a landscape filled with forms that have both shape and mass in which figures may plausibly stand and begin to move.

MKH

1. For Li Chongjun's biography, see *JTS* 86: 2837–38.
2. See Sirén 1956–58, vol. 1: 103–6, and Wu Hung in Yang Xin et al. 1997: 64–70.
3. See Han Wei and Zhang Jianlin 1998, pls. 83-2, 85-1, and 84-1.
4. See ibid., pls. 82, 86–89.

196
Civil officials

Tang dynasty (618–907)
Wall painting, ink and color on plaster
81⅛ x 59in. (206 x 150 cm)
Excavated from the tomb (dated 724) of Prince Huizhuang, Pucheng, Shaanxi Province, 1995
Shaanxi Institute of Archaeology

Excav. report in *Kaogu yu wenwu* 1999.2

Li Hui (ca. 687–725), the second son of Emperor Ruizong (r. 684–90, 710–12), died on February 6, 725. Three days later he was buried as Crown Prince Huizhuang in the Qiaoling mausoleum complex of his father.[1] His speedy burial indicates that the tomb was virtually completed at the time of his death. Nevertheless, last-minute modifications were still possible. The excavation report notes that the murals depicting the ceremonial spears displayed at the entrance to the prince's underground palace initially showed fourteen spears but were repainted to include eighteen—the number granted to the heir apparent—to accord with the prince's honorary status at the time of interment.[2]

The tomb follows the same basic plan as that of Crown Prince Zhanghuai (cat. no. 194) but is more modest in scale, with only one vaulted chamber and a total length of 170 feet. Much of the painting that originally decorated the tomb walls has fallen off, but enough has survived to suggest that the pictorial program followed the typical schema of a palace set within a landscape.

The four officials depicted here come from the west wall of the first "gateway" *(guodong)* that marks the pictorial transition from the landscape setting to the prince's residence. They are similarly dressed, in black official hats and white robes with crimson borders and black pleated hems. The foremost member of this group, at the left, looks forward expectantly and wears the tallest hat, which is ornamented with a sable tail and a plaque decorated with a cicada. In his clasped hands he holds a rectangular tablet, an attribute of high office. His three companions form a knot of tightly overlapping figures. The second official also holds a tablet and wears a cap with a sable tail. He and the fourth official both gaze forward, but the third man has turned his head as if he were about to address the fourth officer. Two lesser officials originally stood behind this group.[3] A parallel cluster of six officials was depicted on the opposite wall.

During the Tang dynasty, the emperor was served by a group of palace officials known as the eight sable dignitaries *(ba diao)*, who wore sable tails in their hats. The senior members of this group, called policy advisers *(sanji changshi)*, were also entitled to wear a gold cicada ornament in their hats. It seems likely that this mural, along with the one on the facing wall, depicts just such a group of officials in attendance to the heir apparent.[4]

In contrast to the depiction of officials receiving foreign dignitaries painted in 706 for the tomb of Li Xian, Crown Prince Zhanghuai (opposite, bottom), these figures appear simpler and more animated. The stylized radiating lines of the drapery folds in the earlier mural, a holdover from the time of Yan Liben (ca. 600–674), have now been greatly simplified.[5] What is most striking is the specificity of the facial expressions, which are drawn with great liveliness. A few casual brushstrokes deftly capture a glance or an expression, anticipating, in their spontaneity, the celebrated brushwork of Wu Daozi (active ca. 710–60).

MKH

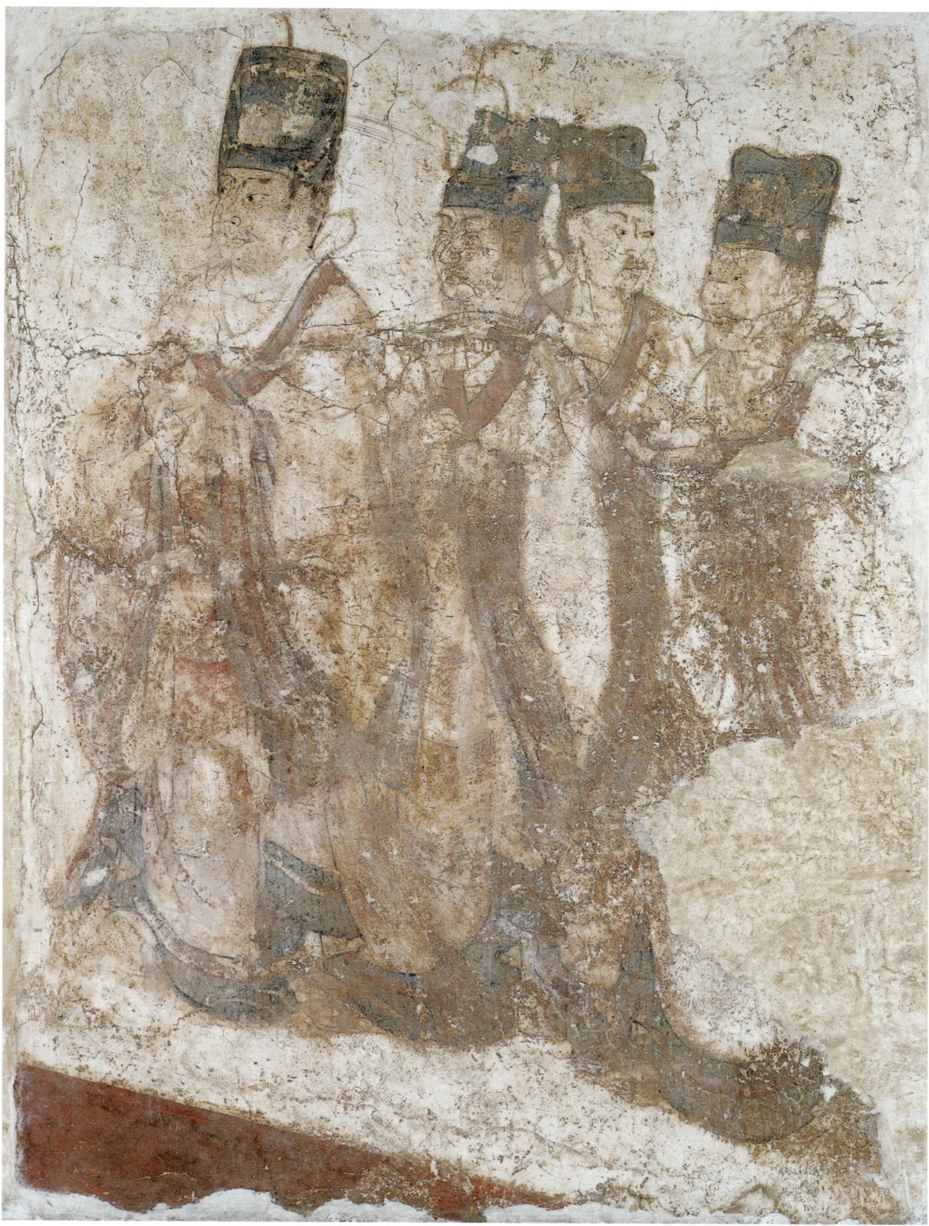

196

1. See Shaanxi sheng kaogu yanjiusuo, Pucheng xian wenti guangdianju 1999: 3; for Li Hui's biography, see *JTS* 95: 3015–16.
2. See Shaanxi sheng kaogu yanjiusuo, Pucheng xian wenti guangdianju 1999: 17, fig. 19.
3. See Han Wei and Zhang Jianlin 1998, pl. 133-1.
4. See *XTS*, Bai guan 2, 47: 1206, and Sun Ji 1993a: 137–39.
5. Compare the anonymous depiction of an emperor and attendants from Cave 220 (dated 642) at Dunhuang with the *Thirteen Emperors* handscroll, attributed to Yan, in the Museum of Fine Arts, Boston; see Yang Xin et al. 1997, pls. 53, 54.

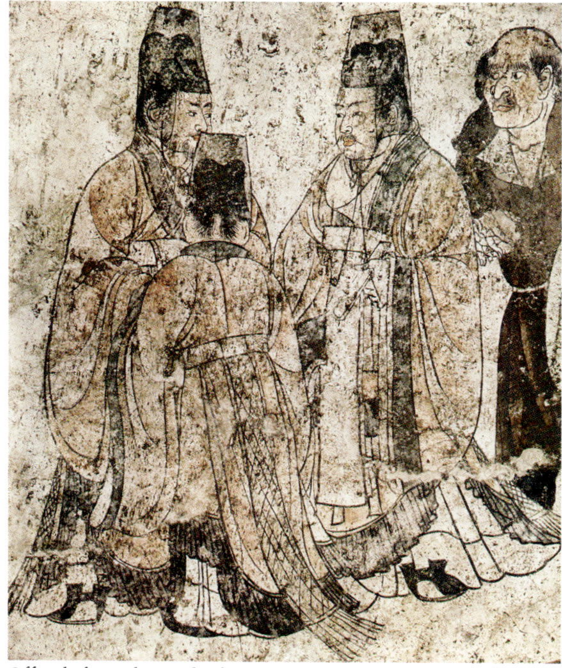

Officials from the tomb of Li Xian (706)

197
Mounted hunter

Tang dynasty (618–907)
Glazed earthenware
Height 14 3/8 in. (36.5 cm)
Excavated from the tomb (dated 706) of Prince Yide, Qianxian, Shaanxi Province, 1972
Shaanxi History Museum

EXCAV. REPORT in *Wenwu* 1972.7

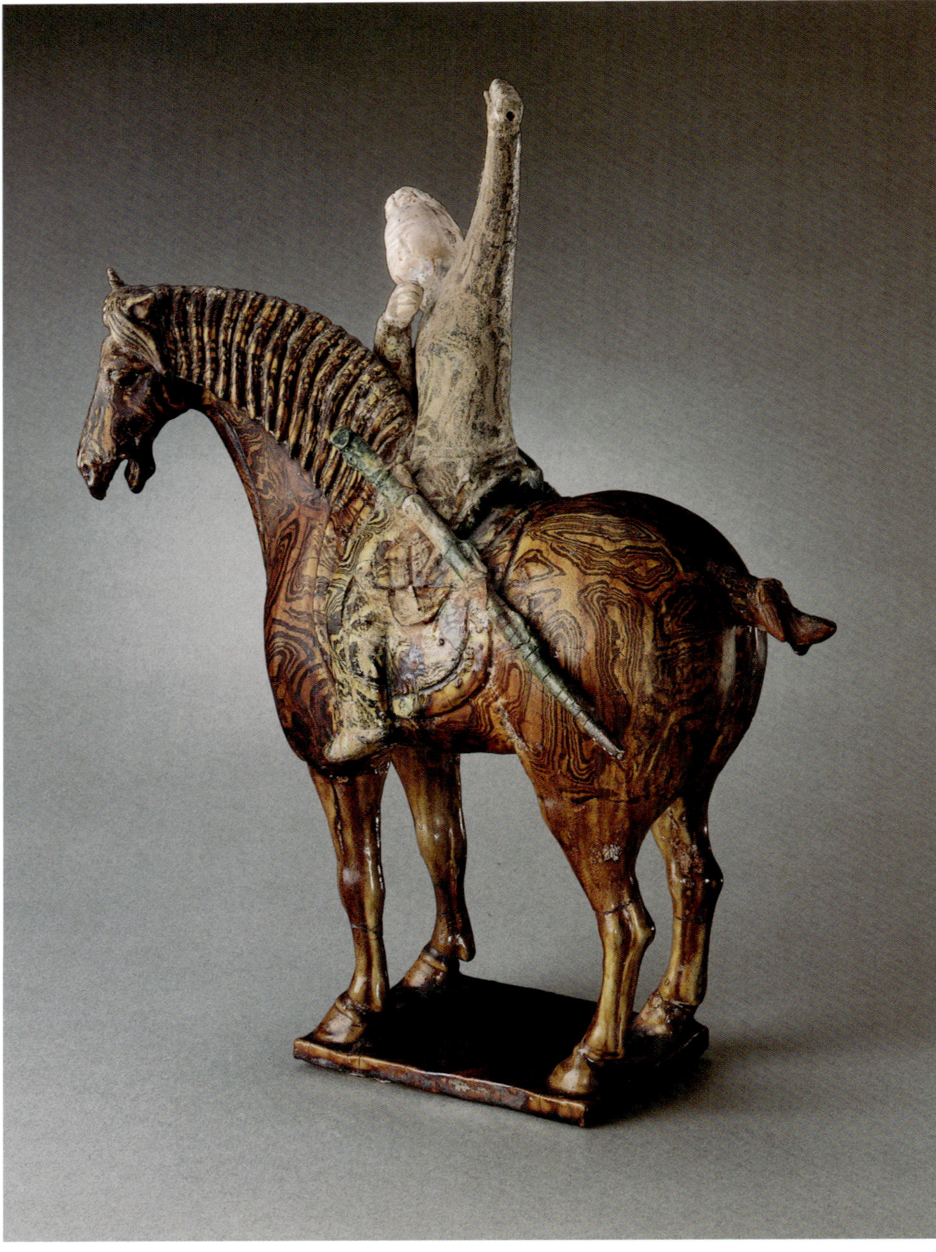

This mounted hunter is a superb example of a rarely seen technique in which two clays of different colors were roughly mixed together to create a marbled effect.[1] It is thought that this type of ceramic was an imitation of western glass vessels.[2]

Here, the marbling covers the smooth areas of the horse and the rider's apparel in a pattern that resembles a swirling wood grain. The pattern extends to raised areas as well—the horse's luxuriant mane and the rider's trousers and shoes. Both horse and figure, with the exception of the hunter's face and hands, are fired with brown glaze.

Images of mounted hunters shooting upward began to appear during the Tang dynasty.[3] The type was so popular that even Emperor Taizong (r. 627–49) was inspired to write "Ode to a Bow":

> As I string my bow, the clear moon is my companion
> I release my arrow and it races the distant shooting star . . .[4]

This figure was found in the tomb of Crown Prince Yide (d. 701), where another marble-textured rider, but in green glaze, was uncovered.[5] Crown Prince Yide, otherwise known as Li Chongrun, was the grandson of Wu Zetian (r. 690–705). In 701, under suspicion of conspiracy, he was put to death along with his sister, Princess Yongtai, and her husband, Wu Yanji.[6] Following the empress's death in 705, they were posthumously rehabilitated and the following year reinterred amid great pomp in the imperial mausoleum of Qiaoling. Presumably this figure, as well as the mounted hunter with cheetah (cat. no. 198), dates from imperial workshops of this period.

CJL

1. This piece has been described as either marbled clay or marbled glaze. Marbled clay employs a technique in which two clays of different color are mixed, resulting in a marbled pattern in the body of the figure. Marbled glaze, on the other hand, is a technique in which a veneer that resembles marbling is applied to the surface, whether with a cross section of marbled clay or a coating of marbled slip, applied to the plain body. Yi Ge (1984), in an iconoclastic view, writes that the design was painted on with a brush and then glazed. Wang Renbo (1979), James C. Y. Watt (1985: 69–78), and Sun Ji (1988) all categorize this piece as marbled clay.
2. Watt 1985: 69–78.
3. Another example of a hunter with bow and arrow is seen on a silver Tang mirror in The Metropolitan Museum of Art (25.20.3); Watt 1990: 67. During the Han dynasty, mounted hunters mostly shot to the front or backward, in what is known as the "Parthian shot." See Rostovtzeff 1943: 174–87, and Lim 1987: 25, 92, 93.
4. "Ode to a Bow by Tang Taizong; translation after Selby 2000: 190
5. Jian 2003: 173.
6. There are several versions of this story. One claims that the three had a quarrel, which resulted in their being discovered by the empress; some sources report that they were caned to death (*JTS:* 2835); others, that they were hanged (ibid.: 2707) or forced to commit suicide (ibid.: 4730, *XTS:* 5838).

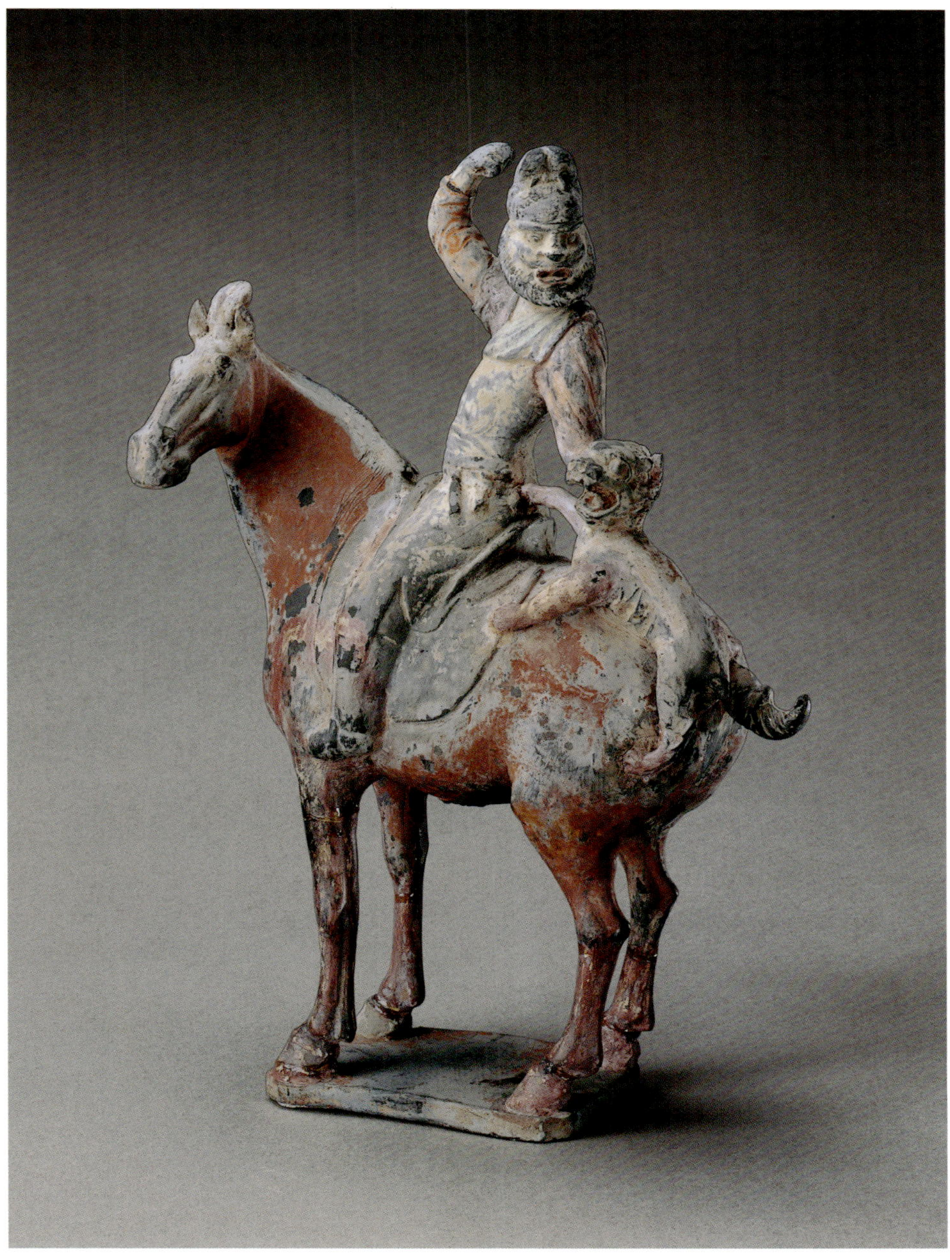

198

Mounted hunter with cheetah

Tang dynasty (618–907)
Earthenware with pigments
Height 12 1/8 in. (30.7 cm)
Excavated from the tomb (dated 706) of Princess Yongtai, Qianxian, Shaanxi Province, 1960–62
Shaanxi History Museum

EXCAV. REPORT in *Wenwu* 1964.1

Imitating practices from the West, Tang hunters of small mammals and fowl trained cheetahs and lynxes to sit alongside them on the horse. Often the animals had their own seats.[1] Cheetahs are often depicted with spots and the distinct black markings that extend from the inner cornea down the nose bridge to the maw; lynxes are shown with upright ears with tufts of black fur. The animal seen here has neither the upright ears of the lynx nor the spots of a cheetah. Nevertheless, it is closer to a cheetah since the rounded ears are characteristic and the body marks may be worn away.[2]

The action here has been interpreted as the cheetah returning to its master.[3] But the hunter twists his body around in anger, his right hand raised as if to strike the snarling feline, which has, in turn, mounted the (oddly placid) horse. The lack of a seat attached to the saddle also throws into question whether the animal belongs to this hunter at all. According to Muhammad Ibn Manglî, act. 1362–76), an Arab trainer, a cheetah that has not caught its prey can sometimes turn on its master. Such so-called spoiled cheetahs would then be given new trainers.[4]

Between 720 and 751, ten envoys from the Western Regions came bearing tribute to the Tang court. Those from Samarkand, Kish, and Maimargh brought cheetahs and dancing girls, both of which were considered of equal value.[5]

CJL

1. One lynx and one cheetah, each sitting on its own seat attached to the back of a saddle, can be seen on horse and hunter figures from the tomb of Princess Jinxiang (653–724). Xi'an shi wenwu guanli weiyuanhui 1997: 52–56.
2. For a picture of a hunting lynx in the tomb of Crown Prince Li Xian (tomb dated 706), Qianxian, Shaanxi, see Shaanxi sheng bowuguan et al. 1974: pl. 9.
3. Zhang Guangda 2001: 178.
4. Ibn Manglî 1984 is quoted extensively in Zhang Guangda 2001: 190.
5. *CFYG*: 3848–50.

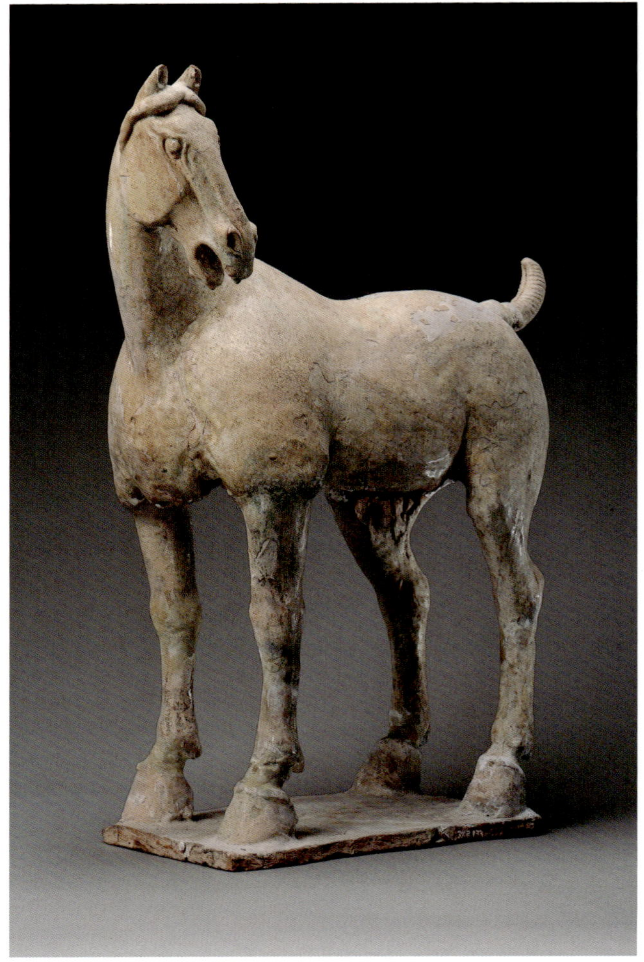

199a

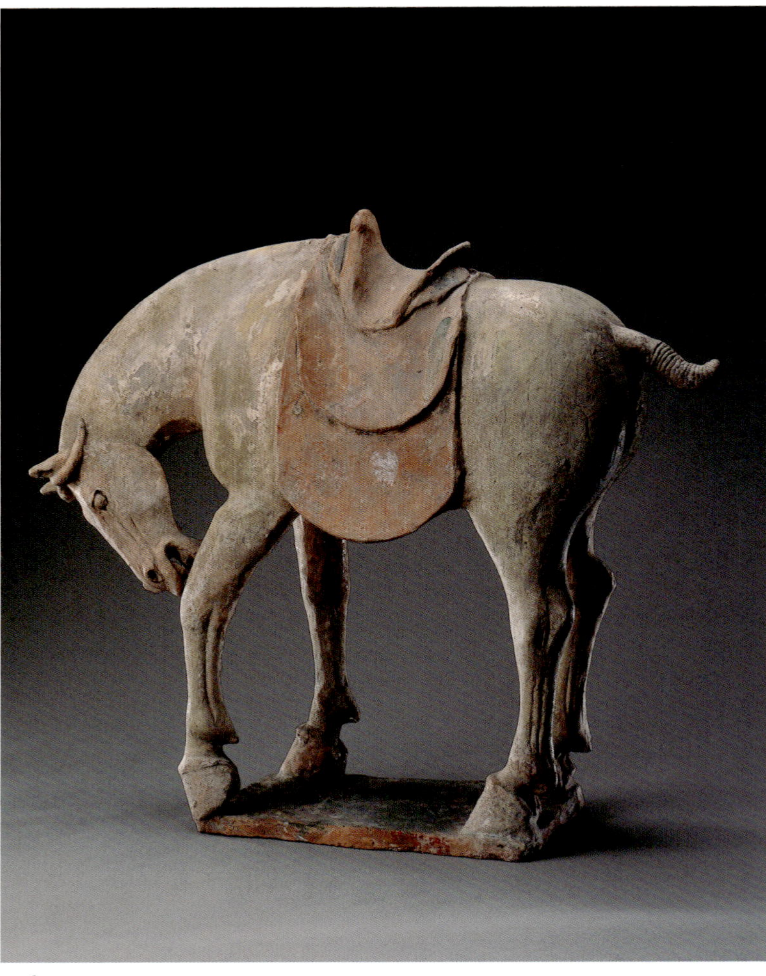

199b

199
Two Horses

Tang dynasty (618–907)
Glazed earthenware
Height: a. 23¼ in. (59.1 cm); b. 19¾ in. (50.3 cm)
Excavated from the tomb (dated 709) of Dugu Sijing and his wife, Xi'an, Shaanxi Province, 1956
National Museum of China

EXCAV. REPORT in Zhongguo shehui kexueyuan kaogu yanjiusuo 1980: 43–51

These two horse figures were discovered in the tomb of the Tang court official Dugu Sijing (d. 709) and his wife. Both have braided tails in the Tang fashion. The larger horse, with perked ears and flaring nostrils, seems to stand at attention, alert to some danger. The smaller horse is saddled and bites at its front left knee, perhaps to ward off flies. The defined faces and natural poses of these horses are characteristic of Tang horse sculpting.

Horses were animals of great prestige during the Tang dynasty, regarded as crucial to the military might of the empire. As stated in the *Xintangshu* (New History of the Tang), "Horses are the military preparedness of the state; if Heaven takes this preparedness away, the state will totter to a fall."[1] Cavalrymen had to provide their own horses and part of their equipment,[2] thus restricting the privilege of owning a horse to the rich. An edict issued in 667 further decreed that only aristocrats could ride horses, a law that seemed to include noble women (see also cat. nos. 182, 183) but that excluded artisans and tradesmen.[3] The Tang emperor Taizong (r. 627–49) so valued his six war steeds that he ordered their portraits to be carved in lifesize bas-relief on large stone panels and placed in Zhaoling, his burial ground.[4]

Dugu Sijing came from a family of distinguished officials. His great-grandfather Dugu Yongye was commander in chief of the Xiang region and was honored with the title Supreme Pillar of the State. Sijing's father was vice director of the Court of Judicial Review, and possibly because of this, Sijing was made Grand Master for Closing Court. More infamously, Sijing was also an administrator in the household of the duke of Ding and his wife, Princess Taiping (d. 713), the willful only daughter of Wu Zetian (r. 690–705).

CJL

1. *XTS* 36: 3718; translation after Schafer 1963: 58.
2. Gernet 1987: 248.
3. *XTS* 3: 66.
4. Two of the carved steeds are now in the collection of the University of Pennsylvania Museum of Archaeology and Anthropology, Philadelphia (acc. nos. C395 and C396), and four are in the collection of the Forest of Steles, Xi'an, Shaanxi.

200

Camel with musicians

Tang dynasty (618–907)
Glazed earthenware
Height 23 in. (58.4 cm)

201

Two entertainers

Tang dynasty (618–907)
Glazed earthenware
Height: a. 18 1/8 in. (46 cm); b. 18 1/8 in. (46 cm)

Cat. nos. 200 and 201 excavated from the tomb (dated 723) of Xianyu Tinghui, Xi'an, Shaanxi Province, 1957
National Museum of China

EXCAV. REPORT: Zhongguo shehui kexueyuan kaogu yanjiusuo 1980: 43–51, 56–65

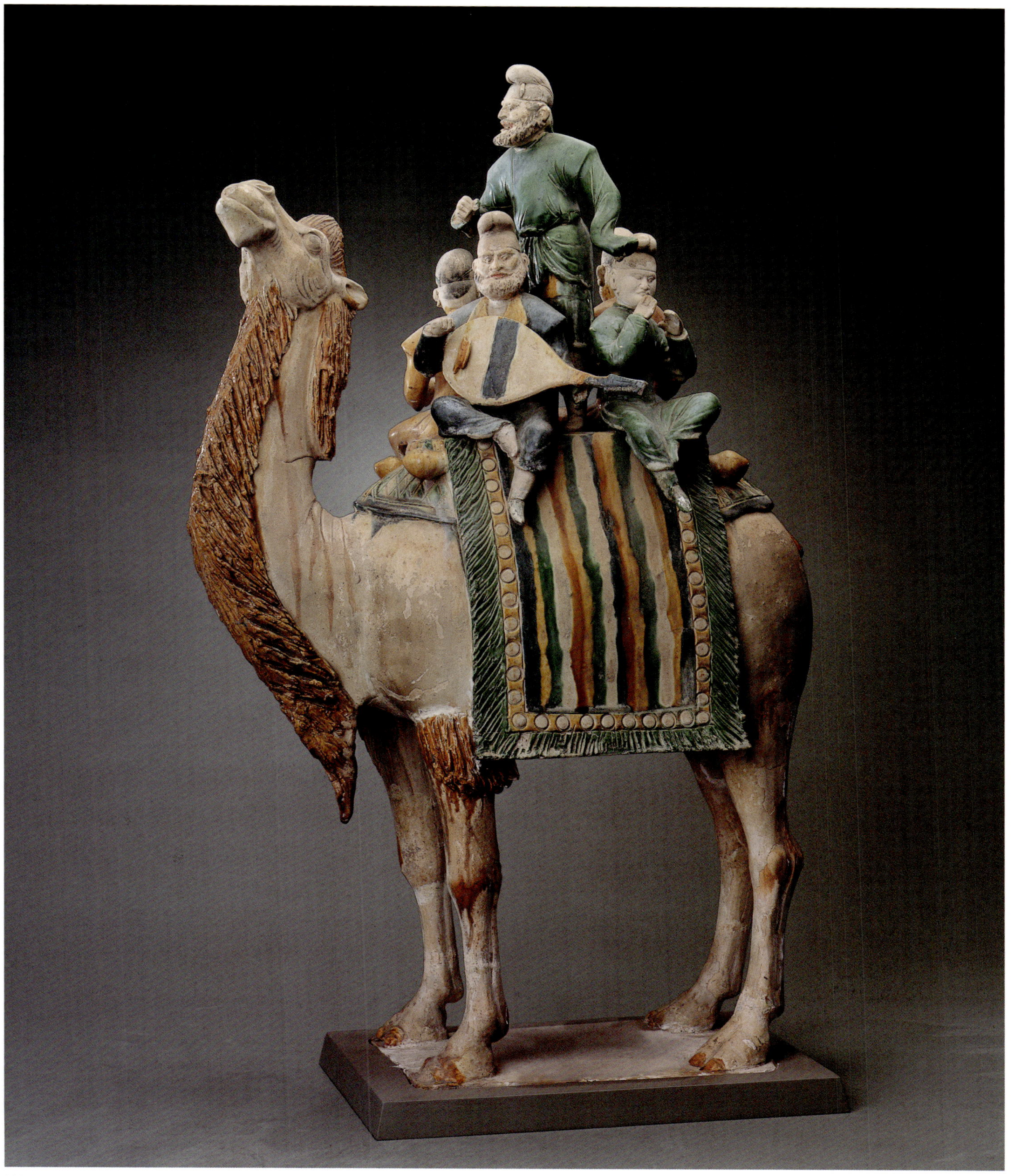

200

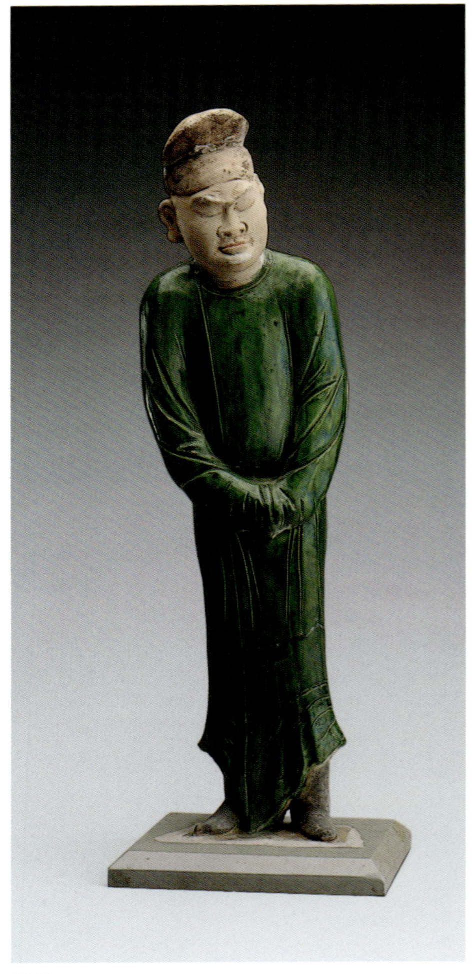

201a

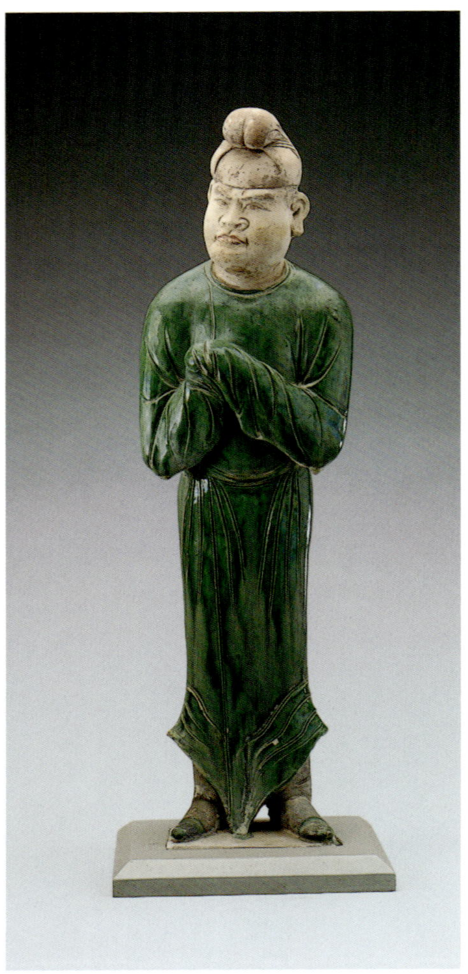
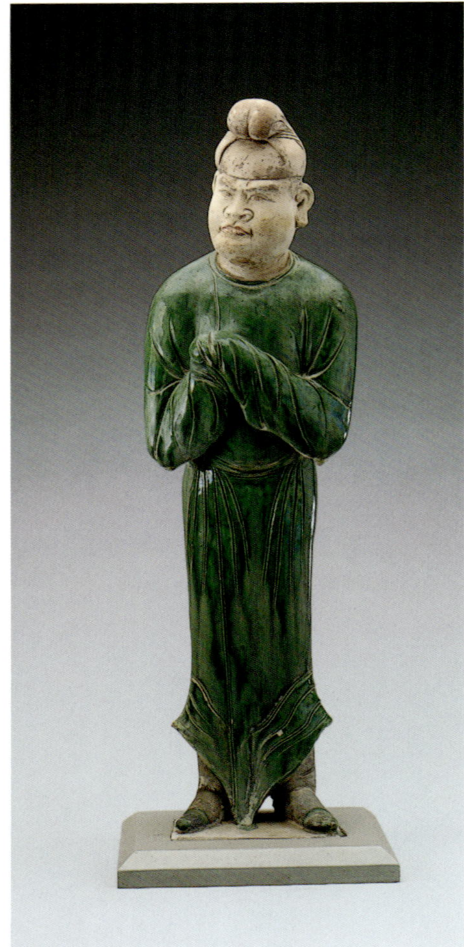

201b

These musicians on a camel and pair of entertainers, like the two court ladies (cat. no. 202), are from the tomb of Xianyu Tinghui (660–723), an official who achieved high military rank during the reign of Xuanzong (712–56). This was a time when music and the performing arts, not to mention poetry, flourished as never before, the emperor himself being the chief patron. The pottery sculptures from Xianyu Tinghui's tomb resonate with the timbre of the time.

Music in the early Tang came from every part of Asia, but the most popular type was from the Western Regions (Sogdiana and Kucha). The western origin of these musicians is signified by the camel on which they ride. This music was first heard in China at the court of Emperor Lingdi (r. 168–89) of the Eastern Han dynasty. Later versions could have come in with Lü Guang in the late fourth century, and the Turkic wife of Emperor Wudi (r. 561–78) of the Northern Zhou is said to have brought Sogdian and Kuchean musicians with her to Chang'an.[1]

The early development of drama in China has not been fully explored. Nonetheless, we do know that during the eighth century, there were no dramatic performances on stage, with actors portraying different characters. These entertainers from Xianyu's tomb bring to life a form of performance popular in the Tang period that involved mainly dialogue, sometimes accompanied by dance and music.[2] Judging by references to this form of theatrical performance in Tang writings, the dialogues were usually comic, sometimes with a satirical edge—perhaps a carryover from the court jester tradition.

JCYW

1. *SS* "Music" 45: 342.
2. Yang Yinliu 1985: 215.

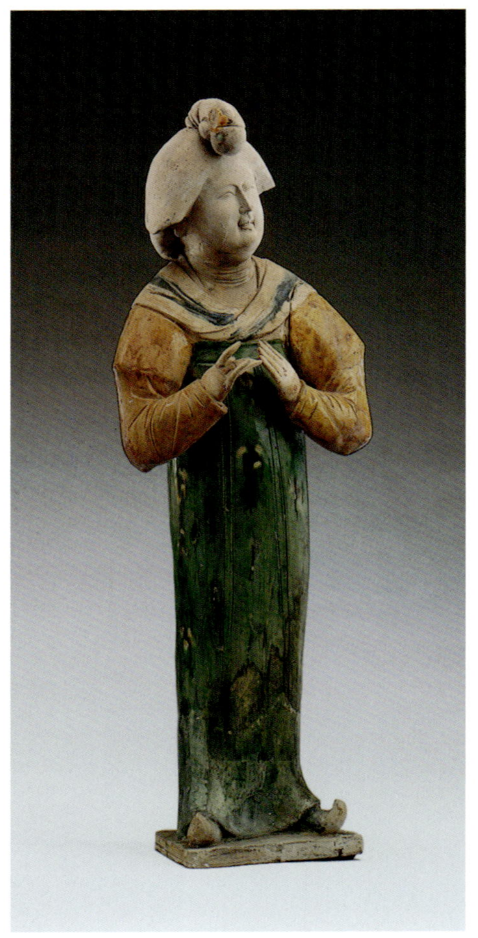

202a

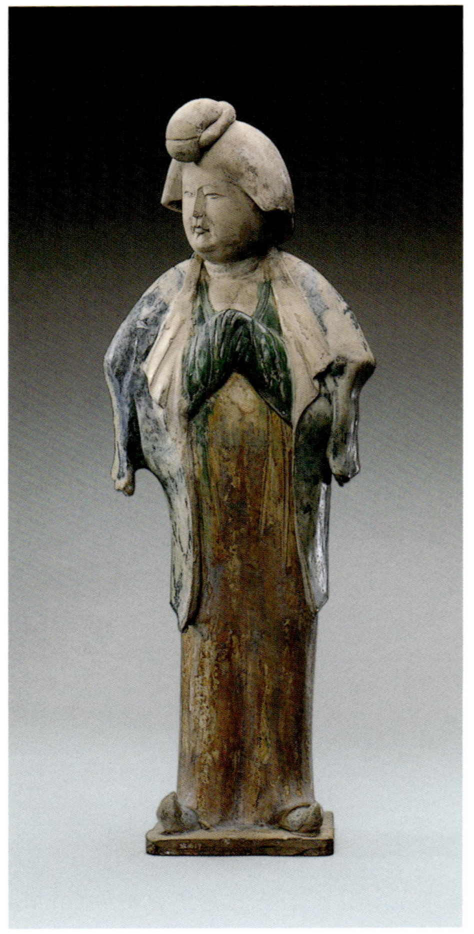

202b

202

Two female attendants

Tang dynasty (618–907)
Glazed earthenware
Height: a.17¾ in. (45.3 cm); b. 17 ⅞ in. (45.5 cm)
Excavated from the tomb (dated 723) of Xianyu Tinghui, Xi'an, Shaanxi Province, 1957
National Museum of China

Excav. report: Zhongguo shehui kexueyuan kaogu yanjiusuo 1980; 43–51

The slender look of the seventh century gave way to a more voluptuous fashion in the eighth century. These two female attendants are, accordingly, more substantial than earlier depictions of ladies-in-waiting (see cat. nos. 183, 185). They wear the basic ensemble of fashionable women's clothing—a blouse, a skirt, and a wrap, here brightly colored with *sancai* glazes of blue, green, and yellow. Variations include the short-sleeved jacket known as a half-arm, evident as the bulge beneath both the yellow long-sleeved blouse of the figure on the left and the blue robe of the figure on the right. The figure on the left wears a long skirt with three-petaled floral patterns that imitate tie-resist dying and a white scarf with blue stripe draped gracefully over her shoulders. A *kuapao,* the tight-sleeved robe with double lapels that came from Central Asia and was usually worn by men, is draped over the shoulders of the figure on the right as a jacket, adding a touch of masculinity. Indeed, histories of the Tang dynasty record that from the beginning of the Kaiyuan period (713–41), women on horses—from palace ladies to commoners—wore "barbarian hats" called *humao* with no veil at all, exposing their faces and hair. Most shocking of all, they wore male clothing and boots (see also cat. no. 183).[1]

The coiffure of these stately, gentle ladies shows the hair gathered in the back, pulled forward over the head, and arranged in a bun over the forehead in a manner called *duomaji,* or "falling horse bun." The name was later changed to *woduoji,* or "short falling bun."[2] The style spread quickly and far from the Tang capital. Indeed, it is worn by a figure in the screen panels *Women under Trees,* dated to 752–56, in the Shōsō-in, Nara, Japan.[3] A variation can be seen as late as the late ninth century, on the Dunhuang scroll *Bodhisattva as a Guide of Souls.*[4]

Descended from a family of military officials from Yuyang, Hebei, the occupant of the tomb in which these figures were found, Xianyu Tinghui, came to prominence in 712, when he allied himself with the nephew of Zhongzong, the future emperor Xuanzong, in quelling a coup by the Wei faction. When Tinghui died, in July 723, Xuanzong commanded the imperial workshops to produce funerary goods for his burial two months later. These two female figures are from a set of four placed in the central eastern niche of the tomb, along with thirteen other *sancai* figurines. Presumably, they are ladies-in-waiting placed in the tomb to serve the general in the afterlife.

CJL

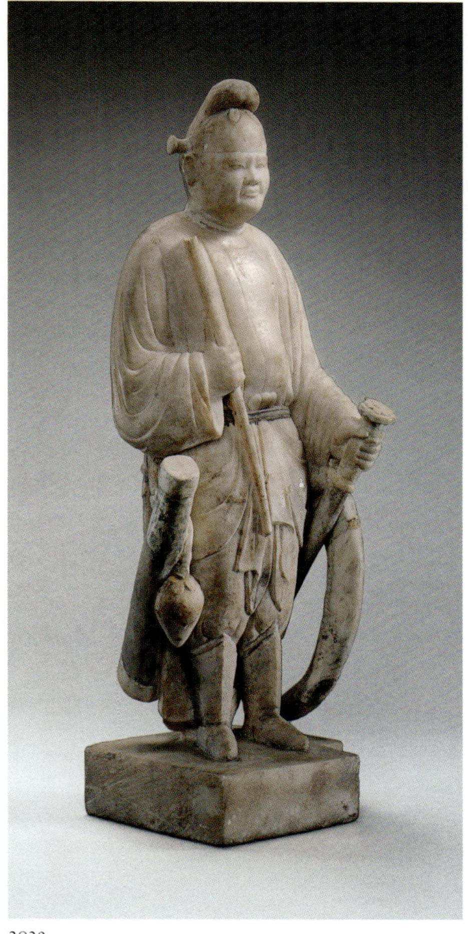
203a

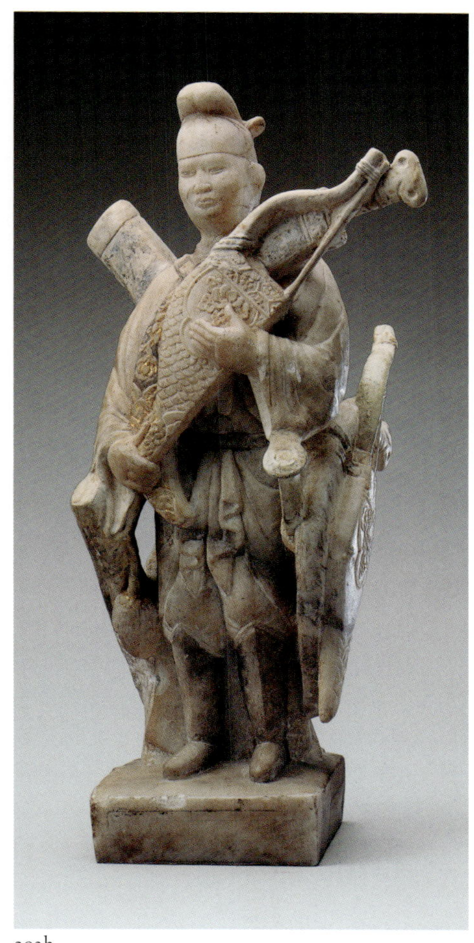
203b

1. *JTS* 45, "Vehicles and Clothing": 1957.
2. Sun Ji 1993: 194–95.
3. Nara kōkuritsu hakubutsukan 1988: 16–23, and 1999: 16–19.
4. Whitfield and Farrer 1990: pl. 41.

203

Two attendants

Tang dynasty (618–907)
Marble with traces of pigments and gilding
Height: a. 15⅞ in. (40.2 cm); b. 15⅞ in. (40.2 cm);
Excavated from the tomb (dated 740) of Yang Sixu, Xi'an, Shaanxi Province, 1957
National Museum of China

Excav. report: Zhongguo shehui kexueyuan kaogu yanjiusuo 1980: 65–86

This handsome set of figures is one of only a handful of excavated Tang sculptures made from Chinese marble (*hanbaiyu*).[1] Found in the burial chamber with the stone sarcophagus,[2] they appear to be soldier attendants of the deceased, the infamous eunuch general Yang Sixu.

Yang Sixu (né Su; 654–740), was a native of Luozhou, a city near the southern seacoast of Guangdong. A eunuch with the surname of Yang adopted him as a child and entered him into the Palace Domestic Service. Yang Sixu gained renown during a palace coup led by Crown Prince Jiemin (d. 707). During the coup, Emperor Zhongzong was forced to flee to the top of Xuanwu Gate with the empress and Princess Anle. When the rebels stormed the gate, Yang Sixu emerged from the emperor's retinue killing the rebel leader, Yu Huli, and turning the tide of the uprising. Having survived bloody wars and received many honors at the service of three successive emperors, Yang died at the age of eighty-seven at his residence in the capital.[3] Yang Sixu's posthumous title was Great General of the Valiant Cavalry, making him one of the only eunuchs in the history of China to have been awarded this honor.

Each of these figures and its base is carved from one piece of marble. Traces of the original gilding and painted color remain on the scabbards. The plump figure on the left holds both a sword and a bow-and-arrow set and grasps in his right hand a mysterious rod.[4] The figure on the right has similar trappings but is outfitted with two bows instead of one.[5] He also holds another two-bow set for his master, more elaborate in décor, with peony, fish-scale, and plum patterns carved in relief and gilded. The *Xintangshu* (New History of the Tang) records that soldiers should be outfitted with "one bow, thirty arrows, one arrow container, one sword, one whetstone, one horn awl, a felt hat, a felt outfit, and leggings."[6]

To date, this pair remains the finest extant marble sculptures ever excavated from a Tang tomb.

CJL

1. Few marble figurines were made for graves during the Tang period. The few that have survived are thought to be representations of the grave occupants.
2. The figure on the right was found at the southern end of the sarcophagus bed; the one on the left was found among smashed pottery figurines.
3. Zhongguo shehui kexueyuan kaogu yanjiusuo 1980: 85.
4. The rod is perhaps a horn awl used for untying rope knots.
5. One bow has taut strings, the other, loose strings. Parts of the statue were restored, perhaps incorrectly, when first excavated. The weapon in question is the arched, tiger-striped object worn at the side by the attendants. Restorers believed that this object was a saber and restored the handle as such. This interpretation has recently been challenged by studies which assert that the striped tiger casing is a case for a bow with slack string. This is therefore an interesting combination of two bows—one strung and one not strung. See Zhong Shaoyi and Wang Yuanchao 1995: 473–81.
6. *XTS:* 1325.

204
Two foreign attendants

Tang dynasty (618–907)
Earthenware with pigments
Height: a. 5¾ in. (14.5 cm);
b. 5¾ in. (14.5 cm)
Excavated from the tomb of Pei Tai, Xi'an, Shaanxi Province, 1954
Shaanxi History Museum

Reference: Du Baoren 1979

Representations of dark-skinned attendants are frequently found among Tang pottery figurines. Known in the Chinese texts as *kurung,* these attendants in fact include two distinct peoples: aborigines from South and Southeast Asia and blacks from Africa. These two figurines are identified as African by their broad nose, sensuous lips, and prominent eyes.

Black Africans were more precisely called *zangi* by Tang Chinese.[1] The name derives from Zanguibar (now Zanzibar), a large region in equatorial East Africa, to which trading ships sailed by way of the Persian Gulf, aided by the northeast monsoon. Africa, a continent many thousands of miles from China, is recorded in many Tang sources. (*Youyang zazu;* Miscellaneous Notes of Youyang), for

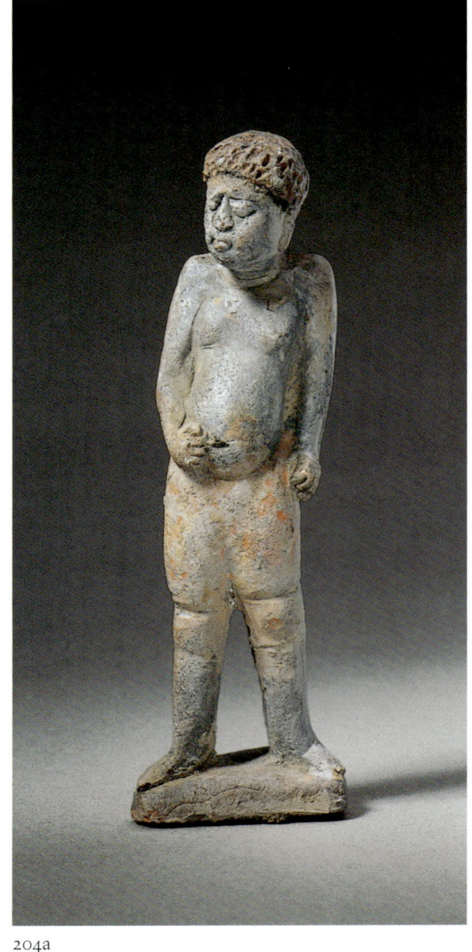

204a

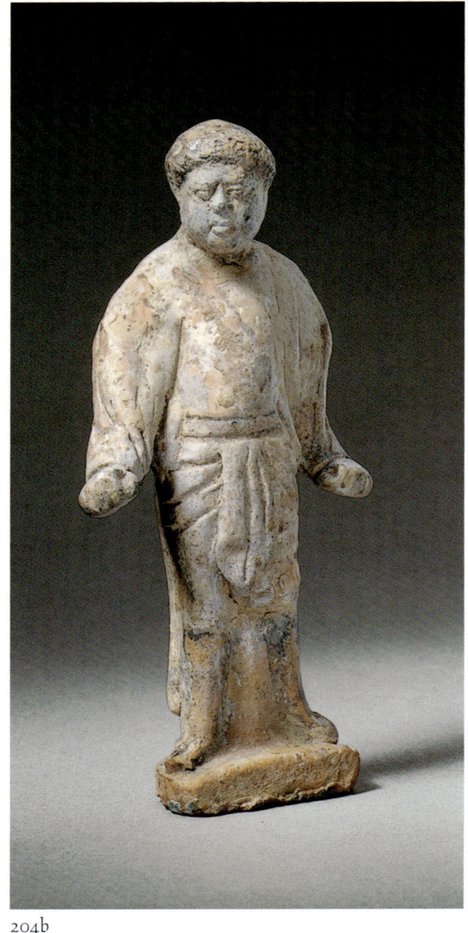

204b

example, describes the state of Bobali "in the southwestern sea," which scholars have identified as Berbera, on the coast of Somalia.[2] Official documents of the Tang court also recorded a number of occasions when foreign states in Sumatra and Java presented *zangi* attendants to the Tang court.[3] Indeed, Chinese trade ships may have traveled to Africa, as Tang coins found on the coast of Zanzibar and Somalia and pottery shards found near Fustat in Egypt would suggest.[4]

Most black Africans did not arrive on the Chinese shore voluntarily. Many were brought by dealers in the slave trade to West or Southeast Asia, where they were subsequently sold. Their owners may themselves have taken them to China or sold them to the Chinese. In many cases, Africans were presented as "gifts" to Chinese envoys or to the Chinese court.

These two figures were excavated from the tomb of a young girl named Pei Tai in the southern suburb of Xi'an. Pei Tai was a descendant of the renowned statesman Pei Xingjian (619–682) who, as Ambassador of Appeasing Dashi (Arabia), escorted the Persian prince Fīrūz to his homeland in 677.[5] It is likely that these figures are representations of the African attendants her family had acquired.

ZS

1. Sun Ji 1996b: 255–57.
2. Du Baoren 1979: 89. See also Duan Chengshi 1983: 46.
3. *XTS:* 6302, 6305.
4. Du Baoren 1979: 89.
5. Ibid.: 88.

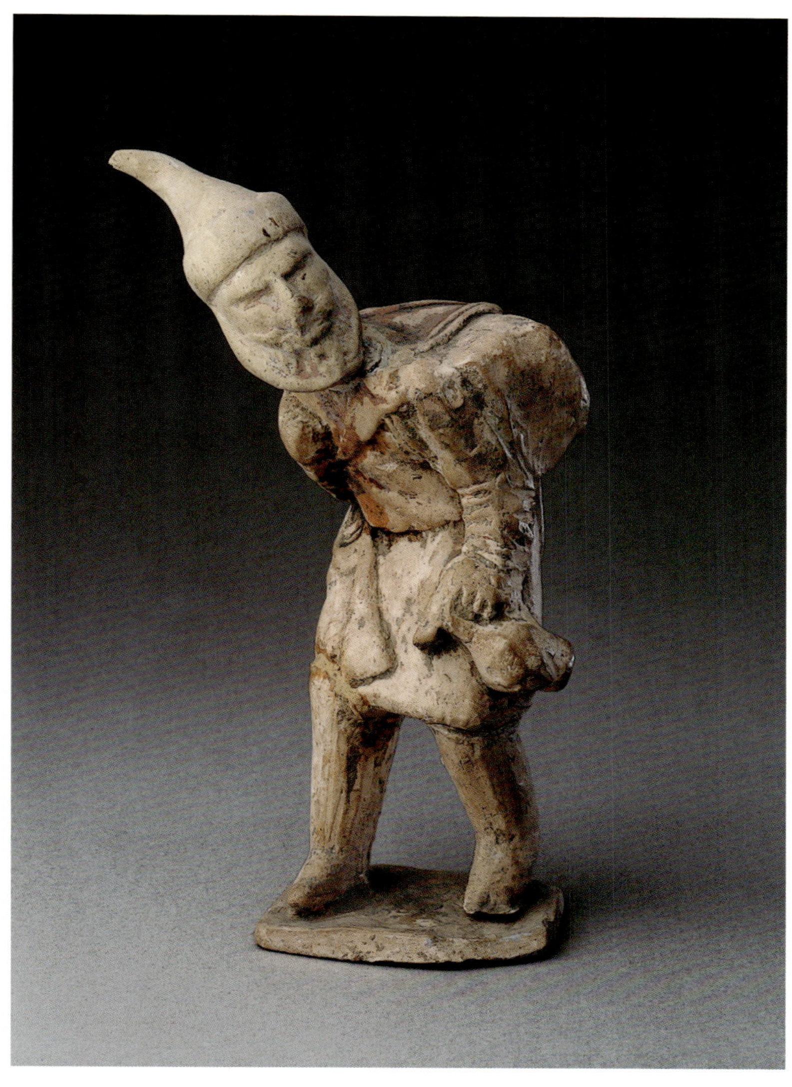

205
Merchant from West Asia

Tang dynasty (618–907), 7th–early 8th century
Glazed earthenware
Height 9¼ in. (23.5 cm)
Excavated at Luoyang, Henan Province
Luoyang Museum

Merchants from other lands, either individual peddlers or members of caravans, were common in the capital, Chang'an, and other centers during the Tang dynasty. Some traveled along maritime routes, others came overland. They brought exotic goods—medicines, wines, and spices—and luxuries such as metalwork and jewelry, which contributed to the cosmopolitan culture of the period. In addition to merchants, foreign entertainers and attendants, such as grooms for horses and camels, arrived in large numbers, as is attested by their frequent appearance in Tang funerary sculpture.

This packman wears a tall pointed hat, probably made of felt or some other soft material, a short tunic with wide lapels, a wide sash, and tall boots. A rectangular sack, presumably containing trade goods, is strapped to his back; his stooped posture is an indication of its weight. The style of clothing and the luxuriant beard and mustache identify the sculpture as a representation of any one of a number of ethnic groups—Arab, Persian, or Semitic—from centers in western Asia and the western parts of Central Asia. At least two identical sculptures are known,[1] however, which suggests that this figure represents a very specific group, or perhaps mercantile type, well known in China at the time. It has been postulated that this and other examples depict either Semitic merchants or traders from the Kashgar region of Central Asia,[2] although neither possibility can be verified.

The merchant holds a bird-headed ewer in his left hand. Possibly used for pouring wine, it is one of the more popular vessel

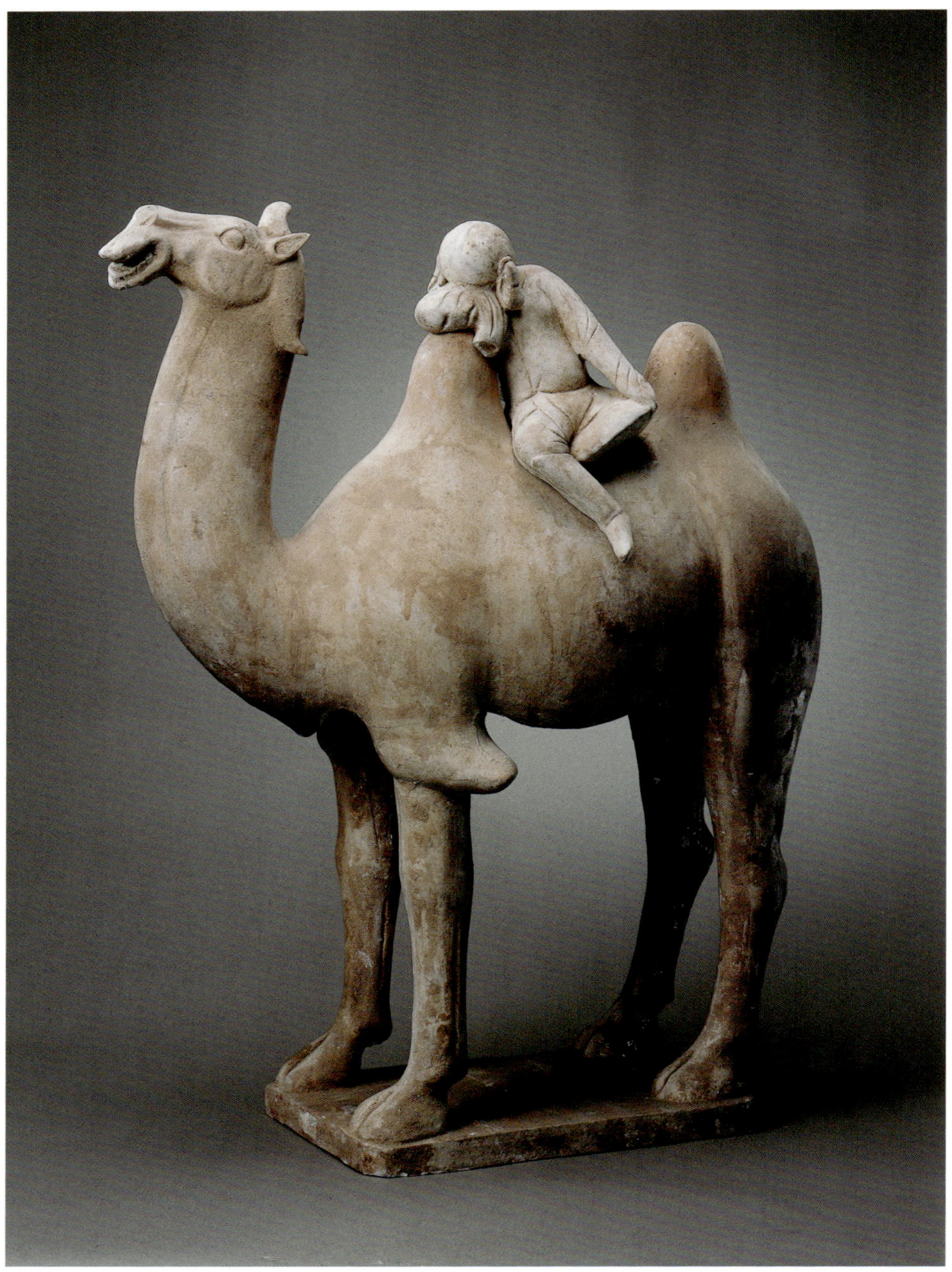

forms in Tang China. Examples were produced in both metalwork and ceramics (see cat. no. 218). Here, the bulbous body, splayed foot, elongated neck, and oval rim reflect the influence of glass and metal vessels from Sasanian Persia (224–651) and related centers such as Sogdiana, in parts of present-day Uzbekistan.

DPL

1. Mahler 1959: pl. 17b, and Thorp and Bower 1982: fig. 51.
2. Mahler 1959: figs. 2d, 17b.

206
Girl resting on a camel

Tang dynasty (618–907), 7th–early 8th century
Earthenware with pigments
Height 28¾ in. (73 cm)
Excavated at Hansenzhai, Xi'an, Shaanxi Province, 1988
Xi'an City Institute of Cultural Properties Protection and Archaeology

Reference: Zhang Wenbin 1999

This appealing young girl rests with her head on her right arm on the back of a towering Bactrian camel. The uplifted head and perked ears of her mount provide a poignant contrast to her exhausted pose. The roundness and softness of the figures and the static pose of the camel date the figures to the seventh or early eighth century. They are known to have been unearthed from a tomb in the Xi'an area; however, no additional information is available. Nonetheless, the large size and elegance of the sculpture suggest a burial of high rank.

The girl's costume, a long-sleeved tunic over trousers and high boots, reflects the continuing influence of Central Asia on the lifestyle of Tang China. Such influence is also found in metalwork, textiles, and other objects from the period. Women enjoyed a great deal of freedom during this time, and scenes of females hunting and traveling on horse and camel are found in both tomb painting and funerary sculpture. It seems likely that this charming duo was once part of a larger grouping, one that may have included only women or both women and men.

DPL

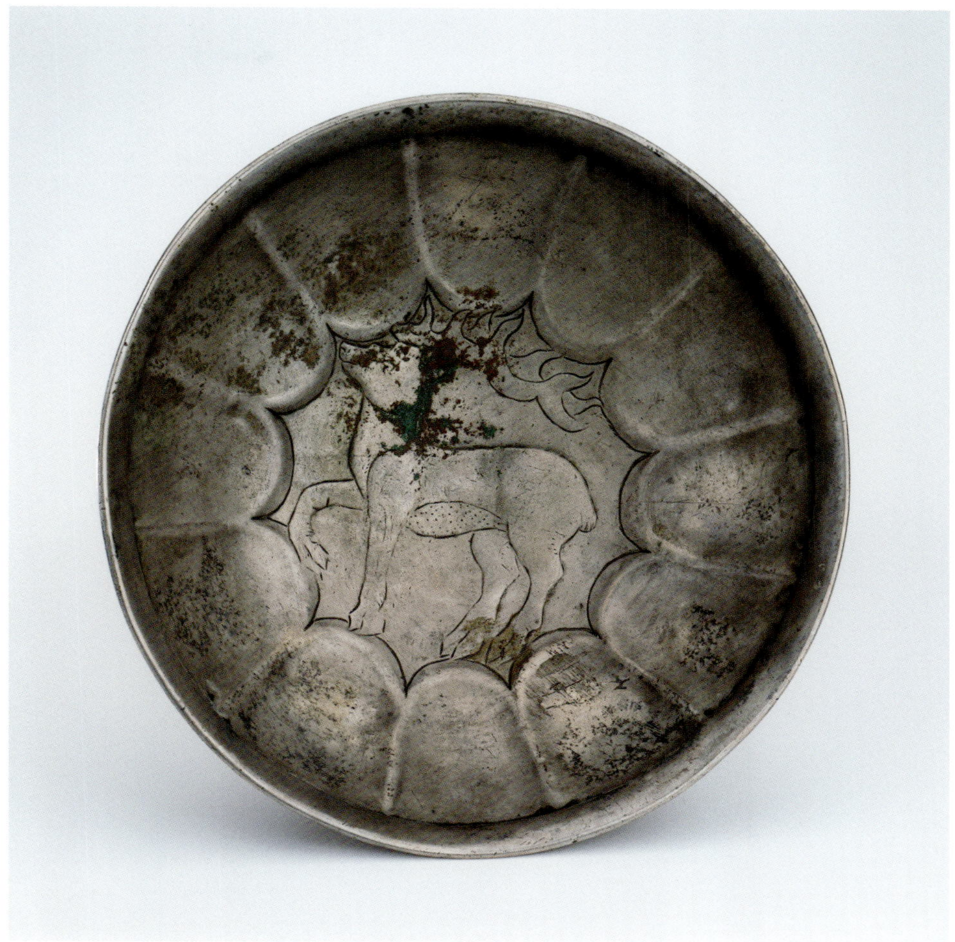

207

Bowl with a stag

Sogdiana, 6th–7th century
Silver
Diameter 5¾ in. (14.7 cm)
Excavated at Xi'an, Shaanxi Province, 1963
National Museum of China

Excav. report in *Wenwu* 1964.6

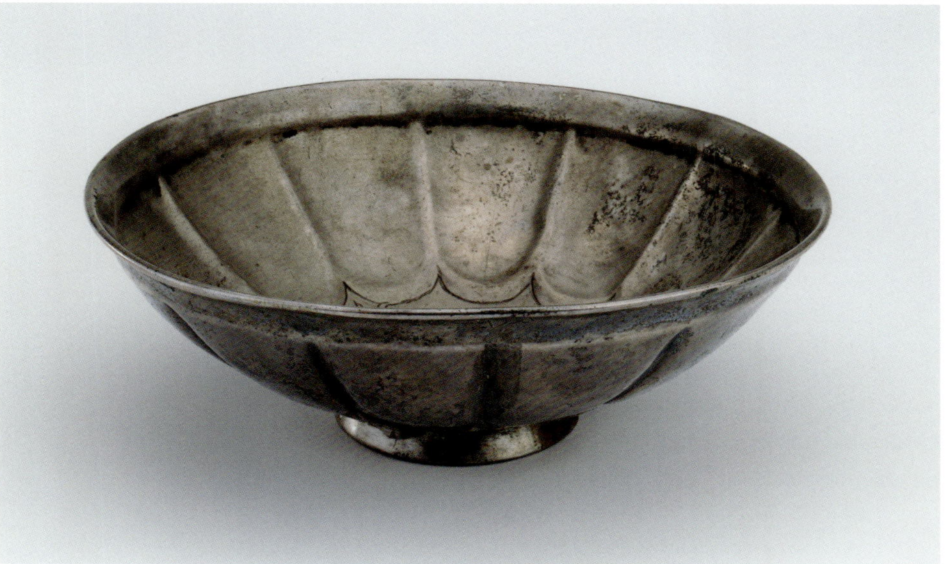

The bowl was found in a hoard with fourteen other Tang silver vessels in present-day Shapo village, near Xi'an, inside the city walls of the Tang capital. The shape of the bowl, with a low base, twelve-lobed body, and plain border, is typically Sogdian, datable to the late sixth or the early seventh century.[1] The motif of a stag, on the interior medallion, confirms this early date. Animals were not depicted on Sogdian silver vessels until the seventh century, when they were generally accompanied by plants.[2] As the symbol of a goddess analogous to Artemis, the Greek goddess of the hunt, the stag probably

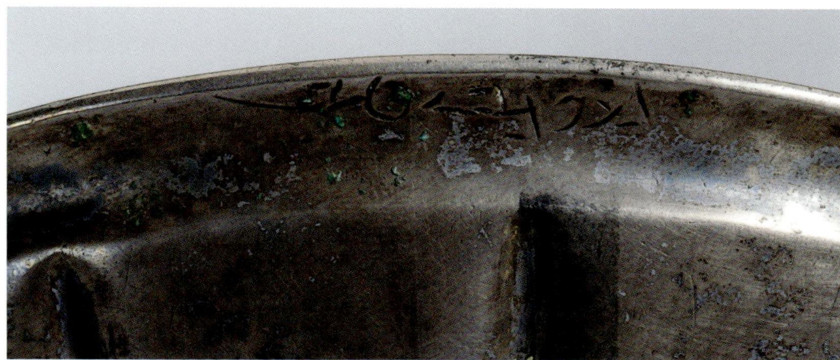

207, inscription

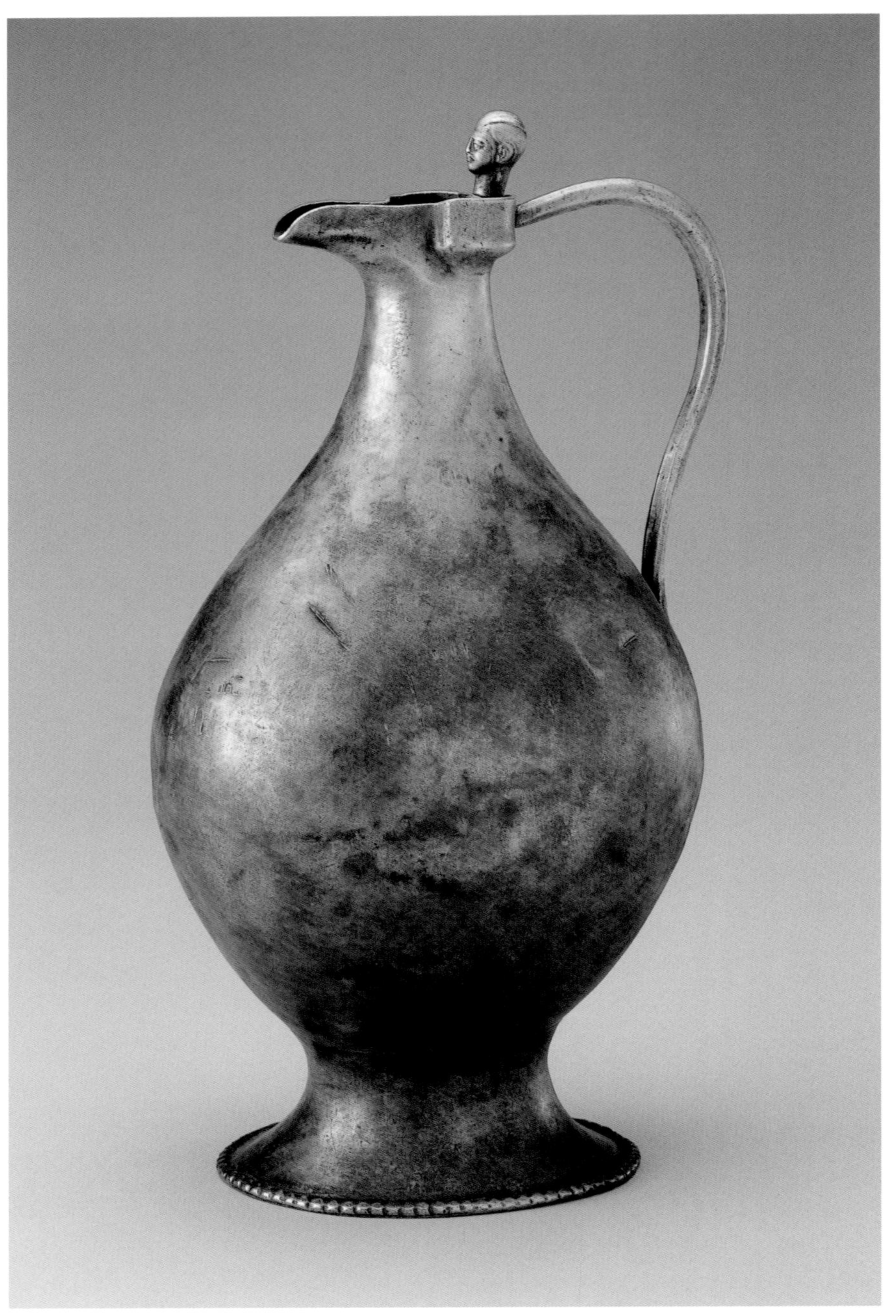

had a religious significance. On the outer border, the owner's name is inscribed in Sogdian: "Servant of [god], Zurvan."[3]

BIM

1. Xi'an shi wenwu guanli weiyuanhui 1964: 30–32; Shih Hsio-Yen 1983: 67, 72, 74, fig. 38 and figs. 18–25, 39–41, 57 (the other vessels from Shapo); Lu Jiugao and Han Wei 1985: 2, 168, pls. 11, 12; Qi Dongfang 1999a: 15–20; Qi Dongfang 1996b: 45–50; Qi Dongfang 1999b: 333–34, figs. 3–26, 3–27.
2. Marshak 1986, figs. 35–41, 67, 69; Marshak 1999, figs. 1–5, 9.
3. Lin Meicun 1997a: 50–54; Lin Meicun 1998: 158–60, figs. 11, 12, quoting a letter he received from Nicholas Sims-Williams.

208
Ewer

Sogdiana, 7th century
Silver with parcel gilding
Height 11 in. (28 cm)
Excavated at Aohan Banner, Chifeng, Inner Mongolia Autonomous Region, 1975
Inner Mongolia Autonomous Region Museum

Excav. report in *Kaogu* 1978.2

This silver ewer was found in a tenth-century Liao-dynasty tomb, but in fact it was made three centuries earlier.[1] In form, it is typically Sogdian, more organic and fluid than comparable Sasanian examples. The terminals of the handle—which in profile resembles a question mark—are attached at the rim and shoulder. Early ewers of this type made of gold and silver[2] were imitated by potters in both Sogdiana[3] and Tang China.[4] A Sogdian silver ewer in the Kasteyev State Museum of Arts of the Republic of Kazakhstan, Almaty, has five crosslike stamps on the bottom,[5] a quotation from stamped silverware from Constantinople of the first half of the seventh century. The master craftsman who fashioned the present ewer perhaps thought he could pass it off as Byzantine.

Today, of course, the distinction is easily recognizable, but Byzantine or earlier classical inspiration is undeniable. The top of the handle bears the image of a human head. Such heads are well known in the Bactrian region and China as well as in Sogdiana. Here, the young man's features—his mustache, sparse beard, and hairdo with shaven temples—are unmistakably Sogdian.[6] The beaded edge of the base of the ewer finds parallels in Sogdian and Tang metalwork.[7] Silver wine ewers from Sogdiana and its colonies were in use in the nomadic regions of Central Asia in the late seventh to the ninth century. A similar vessel was found in Tuva together with two silver cups with handles.[8]

BIM

1. Aohanqi wenhuaguan 1978: 117–18. A high cup with handle found there is datable to the tenth century; Shih Hsio-Yen 1983, fig. 8. A dish with a lynx design from the same tomb is not Sogdian.
2. Hsia Nai's Sasanian attribution (1980: 157–58, pls. 2, 3) was corrected by Qi Dongfang (1999b: 306, 307, 322, pl. 111). The ewer in ibid., fig. 3.1,3, is not Sogdian. The neck is too high and narrow; the mouth is unquestionably not Sogdian.
3. See Belenitskii 1968, pl. 79, pottery strewed with mica powder from Kafyr-kala near Samarkand, ca. 700.
4. Marshak 1971, fig. T24.
5. Ibid., fig. T11.
6. Marshak 2002a, pl. 14, figs. 85, 86.
7. Qi Dongfang 1999b, colorpls. 6–8, 10, 24.
8. Pletneva 1981, fig. 33.14.

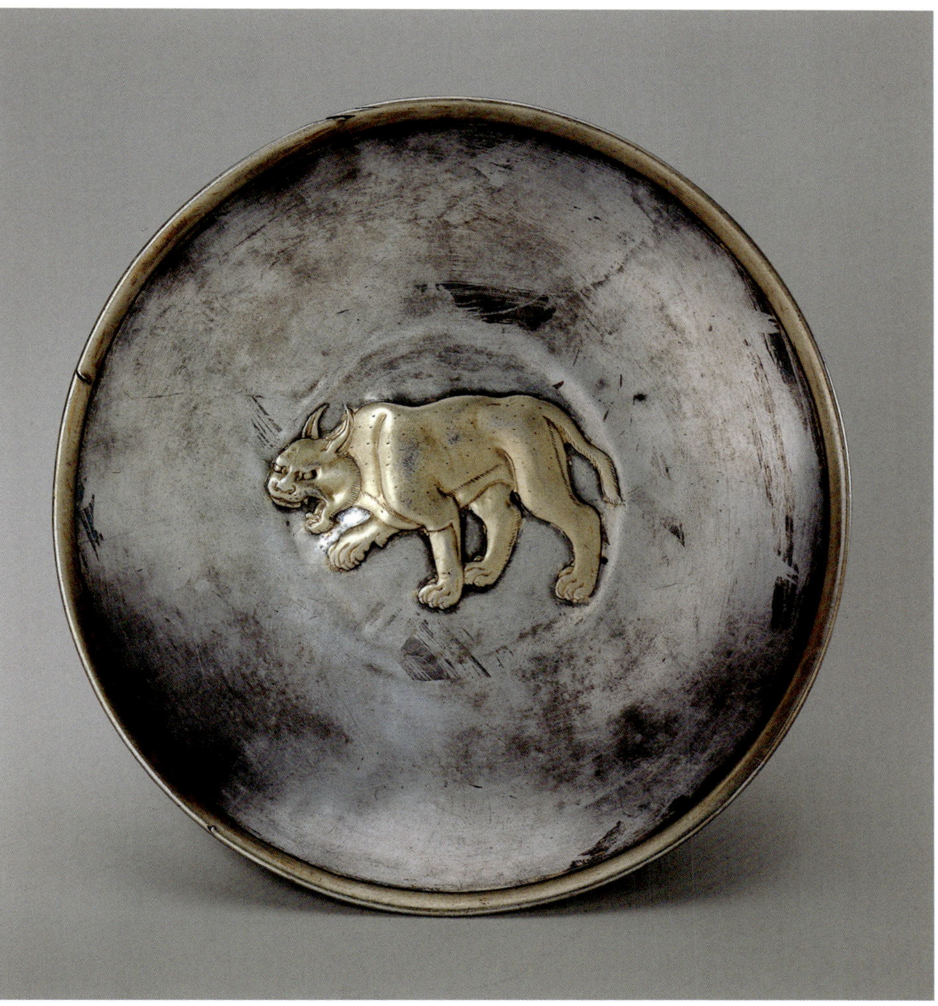

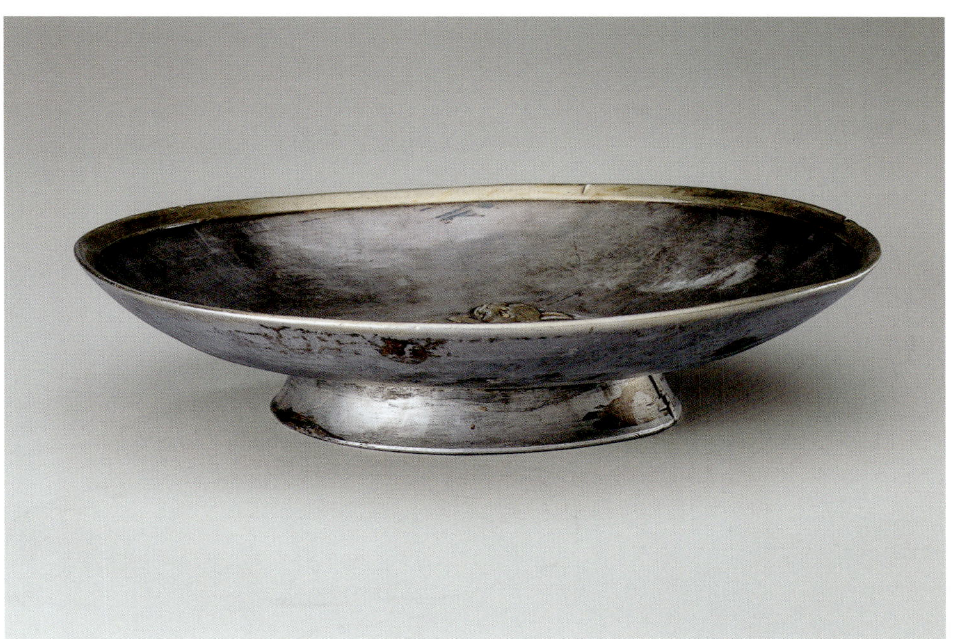

209

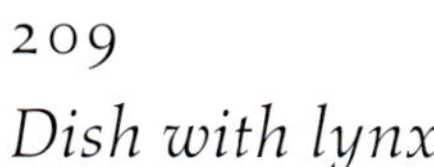

Dish with lynx

Ca. 7th century
Silver with parcel gilding
Diameter 7 1/8 in. (18 cm)
Excavated at Aohan banner, Chifeng, Inner Mongolia Autonomous Region, 1975
Inner Mongolia Autonomous Region Museum

Excav. report in *Kaogu* 1978.2

This silver dish was found at the same site as the Sogdian ewer (cat. no. 208), in Chifeng, Inner Mongolia, an area where a community of Sogdians may well have lived in the seventh century. It is likely to be of local manufacture, copying the form and style of Sogdian silver. JCYW

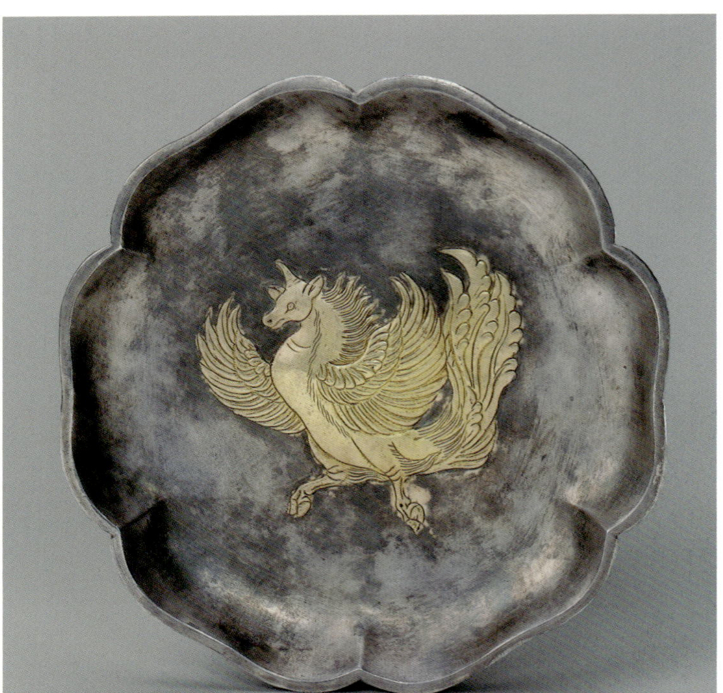
210

210
Six-lobed dish with mythical animal

Tang dynasty (618–907), 8th century
Silver with parcel gilding
Diameter 6 ¼ in. (15.8 cm)
Excavated at Hejiacun, Xi'an, Shaanxi Province, 1970
Shaanxi History Museum

Excav report in *Wenwu* 1972.1

This dish from the famous hoard of Hejiacun was, like cat. no. 209, made after the style of Sogdian silver, but it is more Chinese in expression. The animal in the center is perhaps inspired by the senmurv on Sogdian silver vessels, but the formal details are close to the fabulous animal on the wall painting in the great tomb at Wanzhang (see fig. 28). A similar animal is depicted in the tomb of Lou Rui (see cat. nos. 139–42).

JCYW

211
Bowl with grapevine

Tang dynasty (618–907), 8th century
Silver with parcel gilding
Diameter of mouth rim 5 in. (12.7 cm)

212
Cup with eight musicians

Tang dynasty (618–907), 8th century
Silver with parcel gilding
Diameter of mouth rim 2 ¾ in. (7 cm)

213
Eight-lobed cup with dancing and hunting scenes

Tang dynasty (618–907), 8th century
Silver with parcel gilding
Diameter of mouth rim 3 ½ in. (8.9 cm)

214
Bowl

Tang dynasty (618–907), 8th century
Gold
Diameter of mouth rim 5 ⅜ in. (13.7 cm)

Cat. nos. 211–213 and 214 excavated at Hejiacun, Xi'an, Shaanxi Province, 1970
Shaanxi History Museum

Excav. report in *Wenwu* 1972.1

These well-published cups and bowls, all from the hoard at Hejiacun, Xi'an, represent the different ways and the degrees to which the Chinese silversmith adopted the style and decorative language of Sogdian silver.

The bowl with grapevine pattern, with a dragon on the base within the foot ring (cat. no. 211), is perhaps the most Chinese, as the pattern is executed by chasing on a ground of ring-matting, which is to say that the decoration is entirely on the surface as opposed to the raised decoration seen on other examples of Tang silver in this exhibition. The two cups with ring handles display much stronger Sogdian influence, in both form and decorative technique. The pictorial images—chased or in relief—whether the subject matter is Central Asian musicians or court scenes, are all to be seen in paintings and in decorative arts of the first half of the eighth century. The one innovation of the Chinese silversmith is to line the interior of cups with a plain sheet of silver, creating a double wall (cat. nos. 212, 213). The purpose was probably to hide the reverse of the repoussé work on the exterior wall. Where the raised areas on the walls are parts of the form of the bowl, as seen on the lotus-shaped bowl (cat. no. 214), there is no interior lining.

JCYW

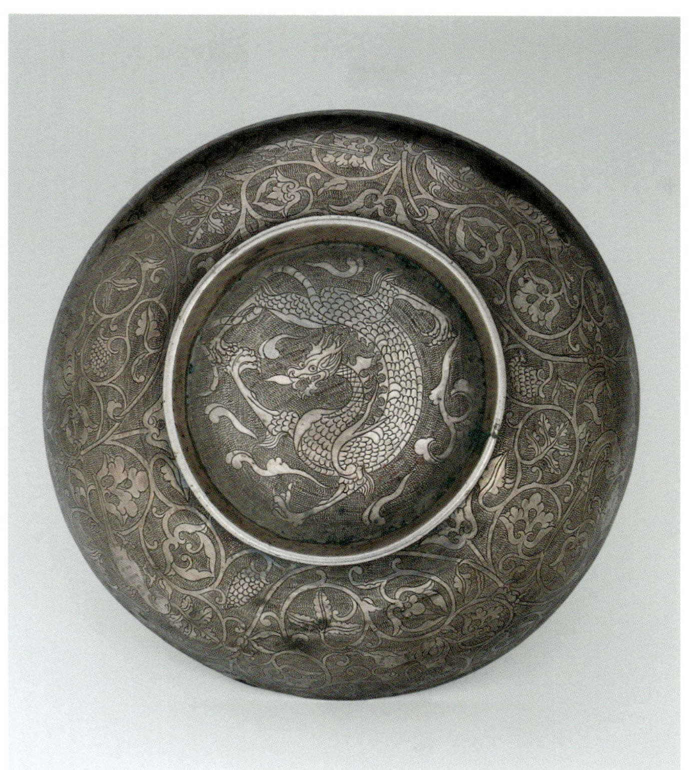

211, bottom

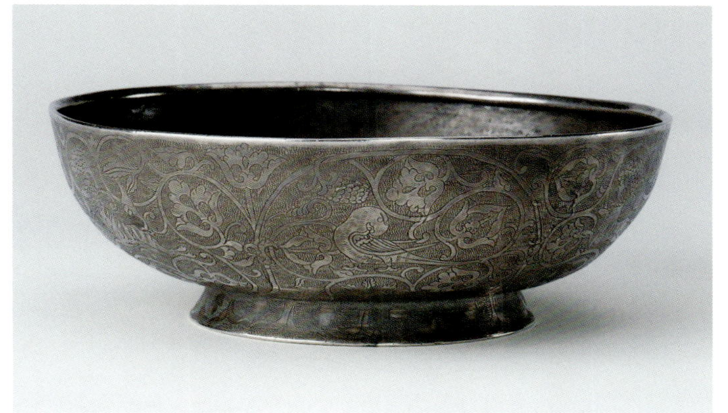

211, side

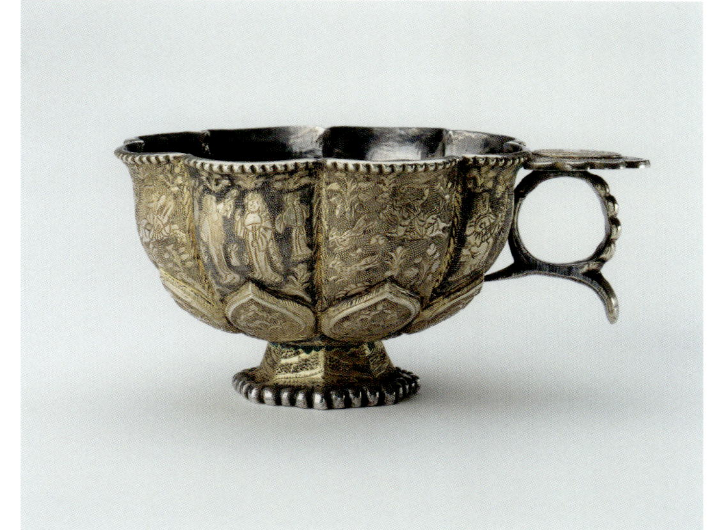

213, side

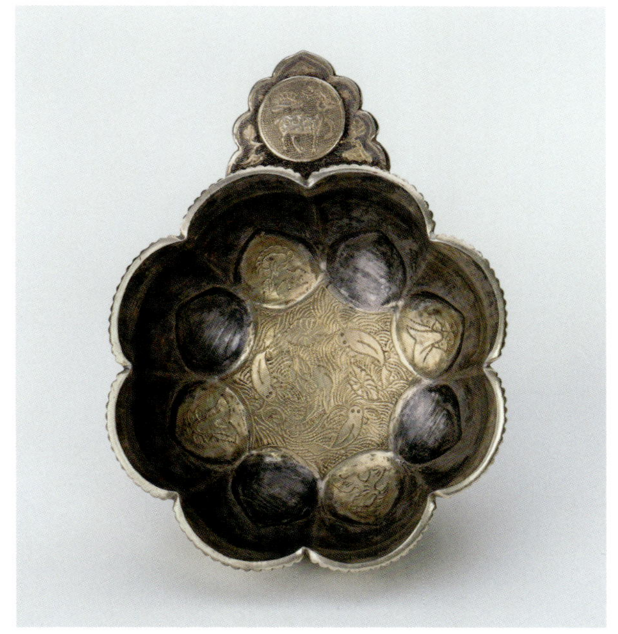

213, interior

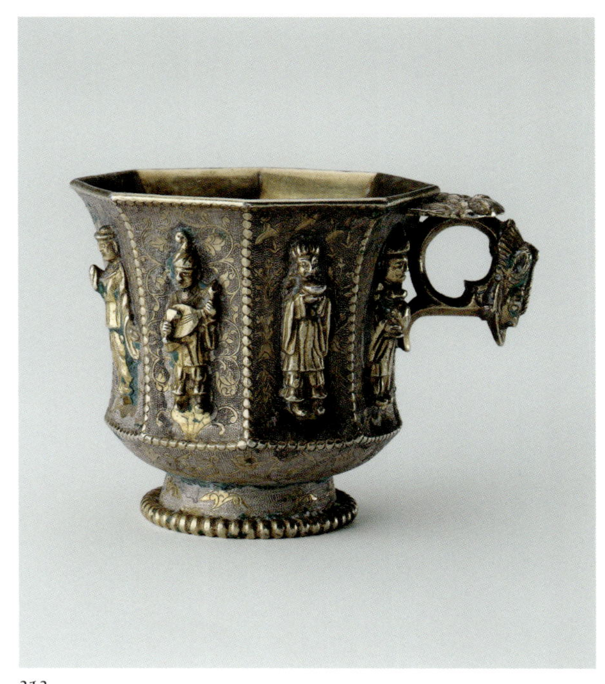

212

214

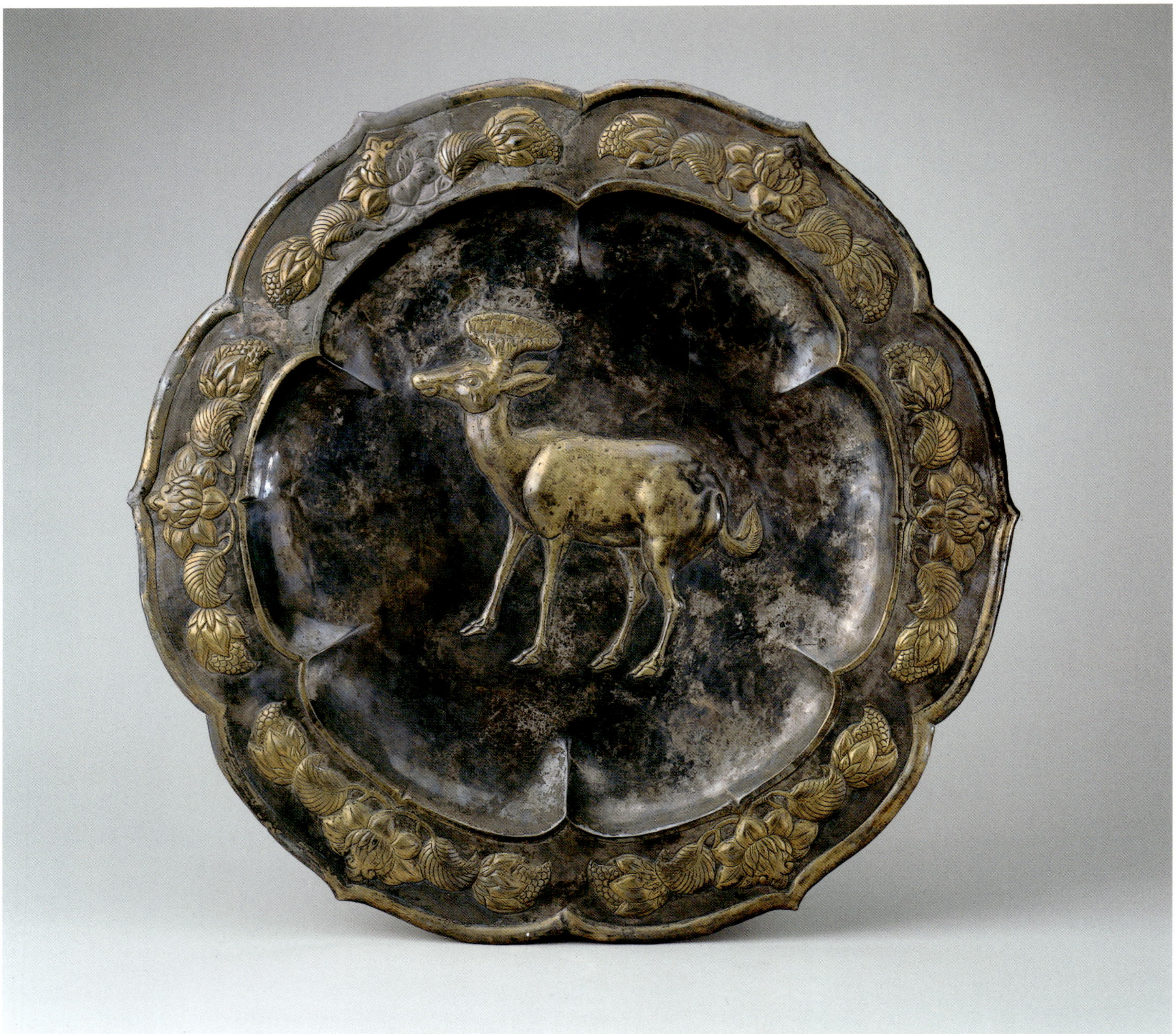

215
Platter with deer

Tang dynasty (618–907)
Silver with parcel gilding
Diameter 19¾ in. (50.2 cm)
Excavated at Dayejiyu, Kuancheng, Hebei Province, 1984
Hebei Provincial Museum

Reference: Liu Xingwen et al. 1985

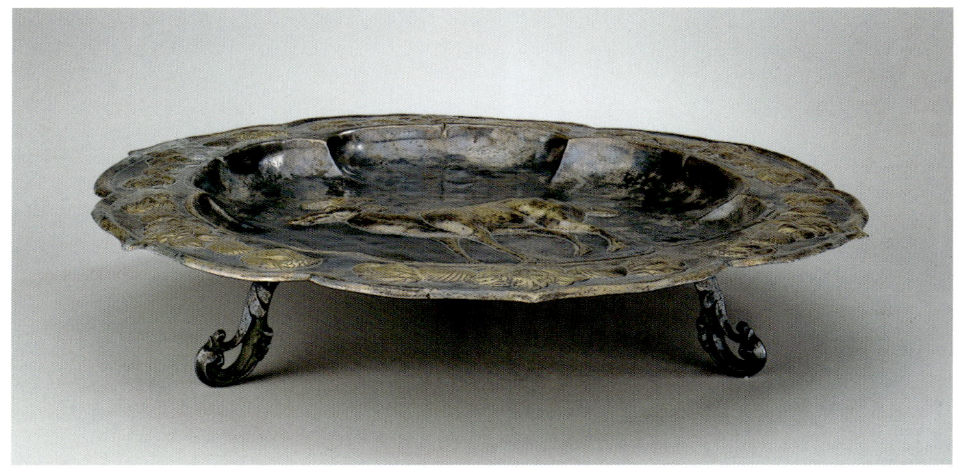

This platter, found in Kuancheng, Hebei,[1] represents the mature style of Tang silver, which emerged toward the end of the reign of Xuanzong (r. 712–56). By the mid-eighth century, motifs ultimately of foreign origin, such as the deer with the crown-shaped horn and leaf-shaped legs seen here, had been "naturalized" so that their foreign sources became irrelevant. Unlike the two cups from Hejiacun (cat. nos. 212, 213), where Sogdian influence is still in evidence, this tripod platter is expressive of a unique Tang style, in which all decorative elements are subjugated to a native sensibility.

Beginning in the second half of the eighth century, after the An Lushan rebellion, production of silver would be concentrated in the Jiangnan area in the south, where workmanship would rapidly deteriorate and Central Asian forms and designs would slowly disappear. One motif, that of the deer with the unusual-looking horn, would somehow survive in Chinese decorative arts for the rest of the Tang period and remain popular into the tenth century.

JCYW

1. Liu Xingwen 1985: 857–58.

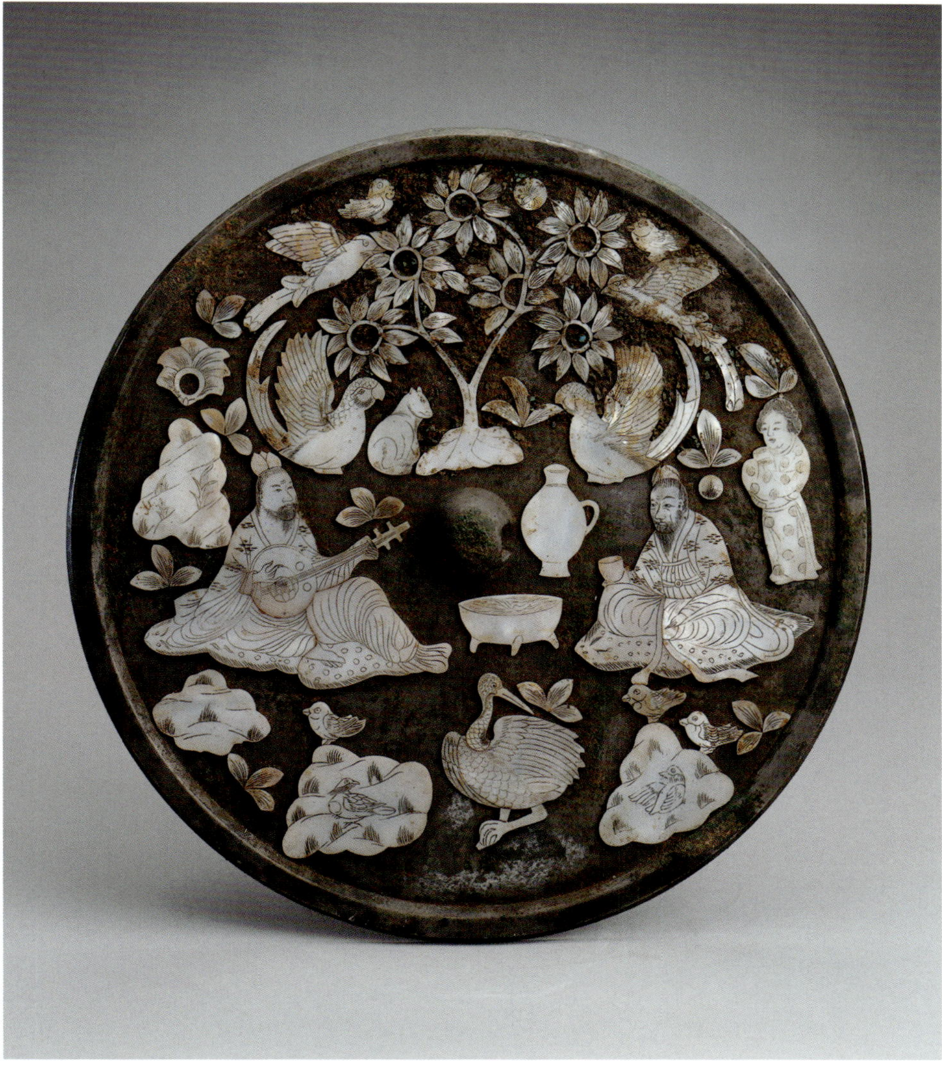

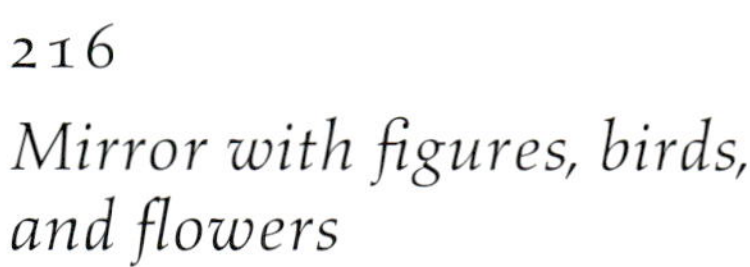

216
Mirror with figures, birds, and flowers

Tang dynasty (618–907)
Bronze with mother-of-pearl inlay
Diameter 9⅞ in. (25 cm)
Excavated at Luoyang, Henan Province, 1955
National Museum of China

Excav. report in *Wenwu* 1956.5

A fine lacquerware with elaborate decoration was made during the Han dynasty in Sichuan in southwestern China.[1] Some production continued into the third century, when Sichuan was under the administration of the Shu kingdom (221–263), after which the craft was abruptly terminated as a result of years of civil war in the region. During the Tang period, lacquer was used in the decorative arts mainly as an adhesive and as background for inlay work, as in the case of the two mirrors in this exhibition (see also cat. no. 217).

This mirror is one of the very few relatively well-preserved examples with mother-of-pearl inlay on lacquer as decoration. The scene depicts two men and an attendant in a garden setting, with a tree, garden rocks, birds, and what looks like a cat. One man is drinking and the other plays the *ruanxian*—a four-string instrument that takes its name from the person famously associated with it. Ruan Xian (230–281) is seen playing this instrument in the pictorial bricks from Nanjing (the third figure from the right in cat. no. 113b). The lacquer ground on the mirror is nearly all lost. There are small fragments of stone inlay in the center of the blossoms on the tree and on either side of the bird's wings to the right of the tree.

The epitaphs in the tomb where the mirror was found record the death dates of a man (759) and his wife (779).[2] It is likely that the mirror dates from about 750.

JCYW

1. For an account of the manufacture of luxury lacquerware in the imperial wokshops of the Han dynasty, see Willetts 1958: 188–206.
2. See *Wenwu* 1956.5.

217
Mirror with phoenixes and floral sprays

Tang dynasty (618–907)
Bronze with silver and gold inlaid lacquer
Diameter 7½ in. (19.2 cm)
Leonard C. Hanna Jr. Fund, 1973.74
The Cleveland Museum of Art

Decoration inspired by luxury goods from western and Central Asia that were brought to China by travelers and traders on the Silk Road is often found on mirrors produced in the seventh and early eighth centuries. New technologies, such as the use of silver and gold and extremely thin metal sheets also appear during this period. A rare surviving example of a fragile type, this mirror is one of the best-preserved in Western collections.[1] Executed in silver and gold, the delicate patterns were set in lacquer. The phoenixes and large floral sprays are executed in chased silver sheets, while the smaller blossoms, birds, and butterflies are rendered in gold. Traces of silver foil are also visible along the raised edges. The structured organization of the floral arabesque that encircles the central knobs reflects traditions from West Asia, as do the small branches held in the mouth of the phoenixes and birds. It seems likely that a lady of the court once used this elegant mirror, which was presumably stored in a delicately decorated lacquer box.

DPL

1. Cunningham et al. 1998: 42–43. Another example is found in the Mr. and Mrs. John D. Rockefeller 3rd collection in The Asia Society, New York (1979.119).

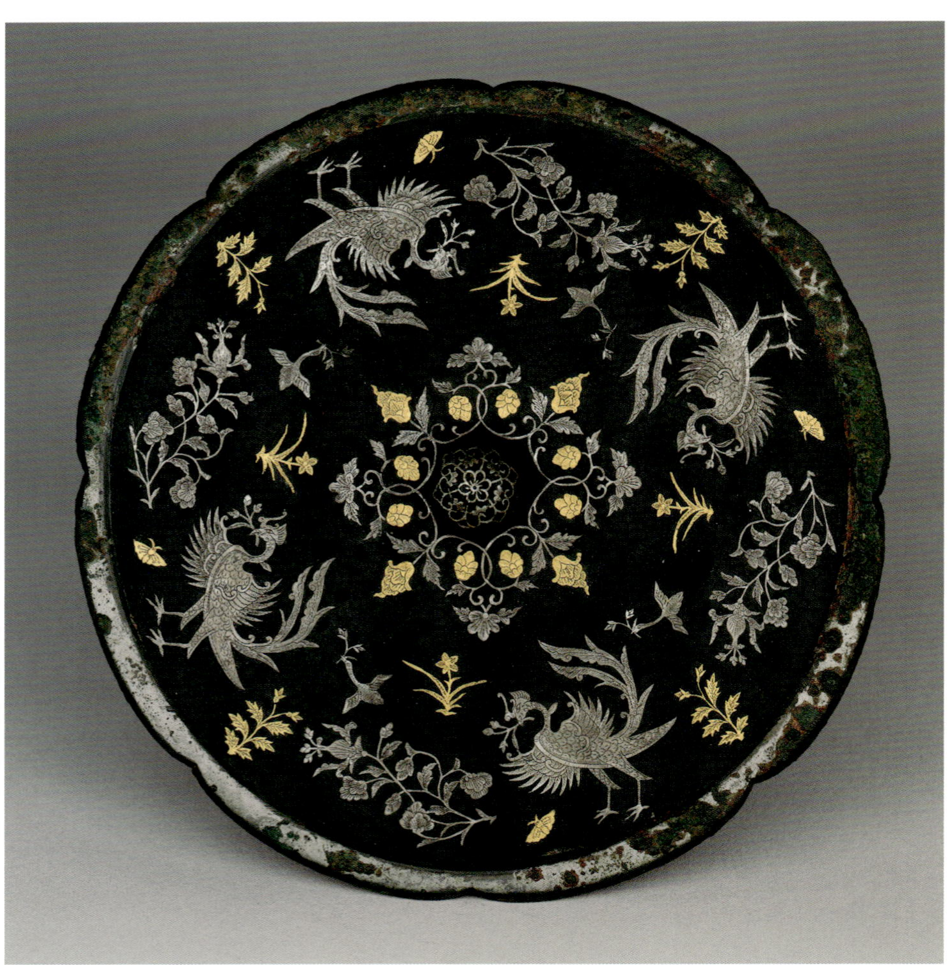

218
Bird-headed ewer with molded decoration

Tang dynasty (618–907)
Porcelain
Height 16½ in. (41.9 cm)
The Palace Museum, Beijing

Reference: Gugong bowuyuan 1962, no. 8

This ewer is a supreme embodiment of the spirit of Tang art and the sources of its inspiration. The bird-headed vessel is of Iranian origin. Also Iranian are the encircling pearl borders and the roundel that encloses the unsteady-looking naked figure with (wine?) vessels at his feet. This figure may well be a version of the Indic god Kubera. The scattered palmettes and the complicated vegetal motif in the lower part of the body may be traced ultimately to the Mediterranean world. Finally, the animal handle would have come into China with metal vessels from Central Asia, like the cup with a tiger handle (cat. no. 95), a distant reflection of nomadic art from the steppes.

The ewer was reportedly found in Jixian, northern Henan, in the general area in which early white porcelain was developed, beginning in the second half of the sixth century.[1] As a work of ceramic art, it is a masterpiece. The potter has brought a number of disparate elements into one complex but coherent whole; it could have been accomplished only with total technical confidence.

JCYW

1. Gugong bowuyuan 1962, pl. 8, caption.

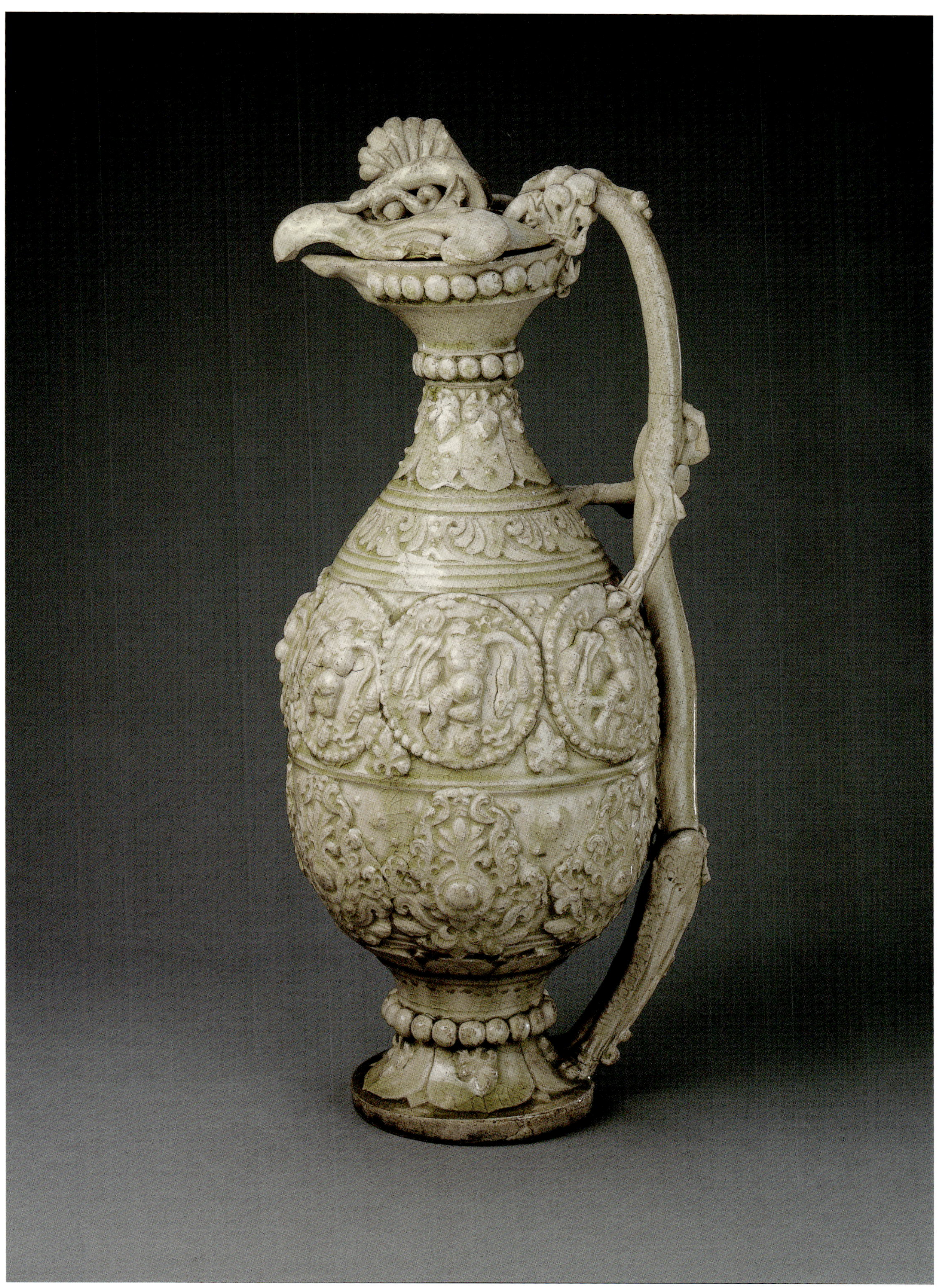

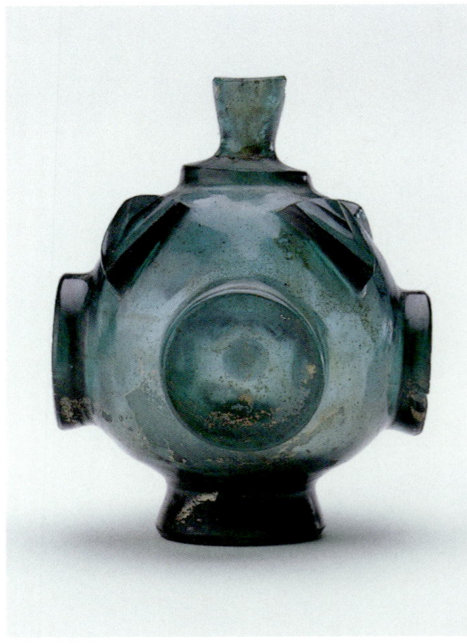

219
Bottle

Sui dynasty (581–619), ca. 6th century
Glass
Height 2¾ in. (7 cm)
Excavated at Xi'an, Shaanxi Province
Shaanxi History Museum

Excav. report in *Kaogu yu wenwu* 1988.1

This glass bottle is green and very transparent. It has a thin neck, spherical body, and ringed foot. On the body are four circular relief ornaments with concave surfaces. The ornaments are 2.5 cm in diameter and less than 3–5 mm thick. The ringed foot is formed with another such circular relief ornament with a concave surface but is slightly larger than those on the body. It is 3 cm in diameter and 1 cm thick. On the shoulder are four triangular relief ornaments that are less than 3–5 mm thick. The surface of each is marked with two oval grooves. The decorative technique used for this bottle is the same as that for the glass bowl from the Northern Zhou (559–581) tomb of Li Xian in Guyuan, Ningxia (cat. no. 158). The decoration of both was ground on the surface after the glass had cooled. The wall of the bottle was originally very thick, over 1 cm. After the grinding process, the wall became thinner, leaving the ornaments raised above the surface in high relief. A glass bottle in the Corning Museum of Glass, Corning, New York (59.1.435), compares very closely with this bottle.[1] It, too, is green, but a lighter shade, and it is 7 cm high. The shape and decoration of the two works, however, are identical.

The epitaph on the tomb in the eastern suburb of Xi'an, Shaanxi, where this bottle was found, indicates that the interred was a Buddhist monk from Qingchan Monastery at Xingningfang, whose name began with the character for *de* (virtue). He died in the ninth year (589) of the Kaihuang era of Emperor Wendi (r. 581–604) of the Sui dynasty.[2] Not many objects were buried with him, but in addition to this glass bottle, there were some glass beads and glass chessmen. It would appear that during the Sui–Tang period (581–907) foreign glass works were a treasured commodity, even among members of the Buddhist community.

AJ

1. Jenkins 1986, no. 23.
2. Zheng Hongchun 1988.

220
Bottle

Ca. 7th century
Glass
Height 4⅜ in. (11 cm)
Excavated at Guanlin, Luoyang, Henan Province
Luoyang Museum

This glass bottle has a small mouth, slender neck, spherical belly, and slightly concave bottom. The glass is green and transparent, covered on the outer surface with a thick weathered layer of bright yellow color. It is without decoration. The form is relatively simple, made by the blowing technique without the use of molds. This type of bottle was commonly used as a container for perfume on the Syrian coast during the Late Roman and early Islamic periods. It is also seen in Sasanian glass made from the third to the seventh century in Gilan Province on the Plateau of Iran. A published piece of Iranian glass from this area is nearly identical to the present one.[1] Chemical analysis of the shards from the present bottle indicates that the material is soda-lime glass and, judging from the relatively high amount of magnesium and potassium, it is likely to be Sasanian.

A glass vessel of the same shape and now in the Royal Ontario Museum,

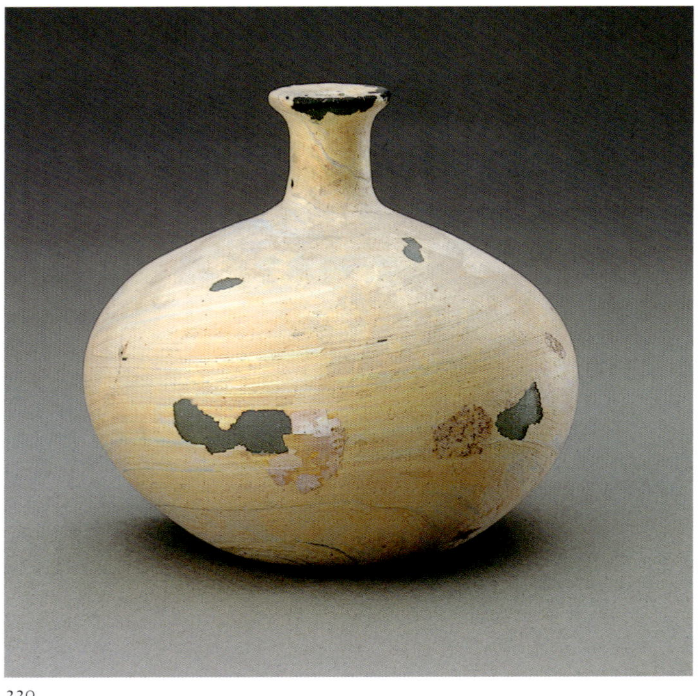

220

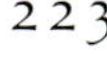

Toronto, was excavated, prior to 1949, from a tomb near Luoyang and later taken out of China.[2] Like the present bottle, it too may have come from the Plateau of Iran and date to the seventh century.

AJ

1. Fukai 1977, pl. 34.
2. Yoshimizu 1992, pl. 48.

221

Bracteate

Ca. 6th century
Gold
Diameter ¾ in. (1.9 cm)
Excavated from the tomb (dated 664) of Shi Suoyan and his wife, Guyuan, Ningxia Autonomous Region, 1985
Guyuan Museum

Excav. report in Luo Feng 1996: 31–54

This bracteate was found in the tomb of Shi Suoyan, a Chinese official whose ancestors had emigrated from southern Sogdiana, and his wife.[1] He was buried in 664.

Obverse: Bust of an emperor, helmeted, cuirassed, and holding a spear and shield. The legend is illegible. The coin is thinner than cat. no. 222, and of the two it is closer to Byzantine prototypes—the solidi of the fifth century or the first half of the sixth. The wide, plain border is typical of Sasanian coins,[2] but it is also seen on a Sogdian silver medallion from Panjikent that portrays a Hellenistic monarch.[3] The face is executed in higher relief than those on Byzantine coins.

VR

1. Thierry and Morrisson 1994, no. 17; Luo Feng 1996: 37, 151, pl. 48, colorpl. 17; Ningxia Huizu zizhiqu Guyuan bowuguan and Zhongri Yuanzhou lianhe Kaogudui 1999: 113; Alram 2001: 287, no. 102.
2. Alram 2001: 288.
3. Marshak and Raspopova 1998, fig. 4.2.

222

Bracteate

Ca. 6th century
Gold
Diameter ⅞ in. (2.3 cm)
Excavated from the tomb (dated 671) of Shi Hedan, Guyuan, Ningxia Autonomous Region, 1986
Guyuan Museum

Excav. report in Luo Feng 1996: 55–77

The present bracteate was found in the tomb of Shi Hedan, a Chinese official whose ancestors hailed from southern Sogdiana.[1] Almost certainly it was produced in Sogdiana or some adjacent region. The coin is similar to the gold bracteate found in the tomb of Shi Suoyan, also in Guyuan county (cat. no. 221).

Obverse: Bust of an emperor facing right in three-quarter profile. Like the Byzantine emperors on fifth- and sixth-century solidi, he holds a spear and a shield. This bracteate is similar to one found in Panjikent, in Sogdiana, in a house dating to the seventh or eighth century.[2] On both bracteates there are still-recognizable letters of the name Anastasius, the Byzantine emperor who reigned from 491 to 518. Rather than being imitations of Byzantine coins themselves, they imitate Central Asian replicas of Byzantine coins. Two small holes are pierced through the metal, one above and the other below the bust of the emperor.

VR

1. Luo Feng 1996: 57, 151–52, pl. 48, colorpl. 17; Alram 2001: 287, no. 102 (mistakenly attributed to Shi Suoyan's tomb).
2. Raspopova 1999, fig. 5.

223

Bracteate

Ca. 7th century
Gold
Diameter 1 in. (2.5 cm)
Excavated from the tomb (dated 670) of Shi Tiebang, Guyuan, Ningxia Autonomous Region, 1986
Guyuan Museum

Excav. report in Luo Feng 1996: 78–86

This bracteate was found in a coffin in the tomb of Shi Tiebang, a Tang official of southern Sogdian origin who died in 666.[1] It was worn as a pendant and has a hole above the head of the king portrayed on the obverse. As with all bracteates, the reverse is blank. The obverse was struck with a die identical to those of the silver drachmas of Ardashir III, one of the last Sasanian rulers of Iran, who reigned from 628 to 630. The face on the bracteate, without mustache or beard, is unique on Sasanian coins. Notably, Ardashir III was only a boy during his short reign (he ascended the throne when he was seven). The bracteate was perhaps struck with a genuine Sasanian die, albeit one that originated in Iran. Following the Arab conquest of Iran in 651, many Persians, including Peroz, the heir to the throne, fled to Tang China. It is plausible that a Sasanian die was taken to Central Asia or China, where it was used to produce this expensive and exceptionally heavy coin, a remnant of the recently devastated Sasanian empire. Silver coins of the last Sasanians (though not of Ardashir III) have been found in Xinjiang and China proper.[2]

VR

1. Luo Feng 1996: 156–58, colorpl. 19; Ningxia Huiza zizhiqu Guyuan bowuguan and Zhongri Yuanzhou lianhe kaogudui 1999: pl. 29; Alram 2001: 281, no. 96.
2. Thierry 1993: 7–139.

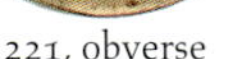

221, obverse

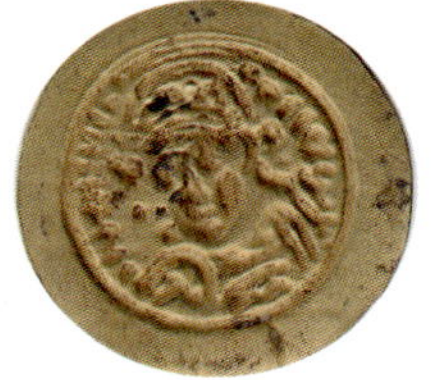

221, reverse

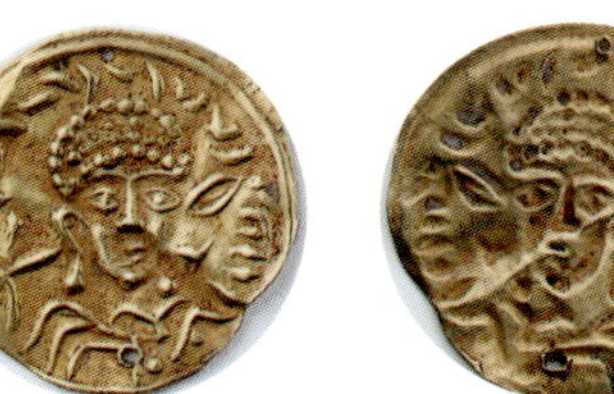

222, obverse

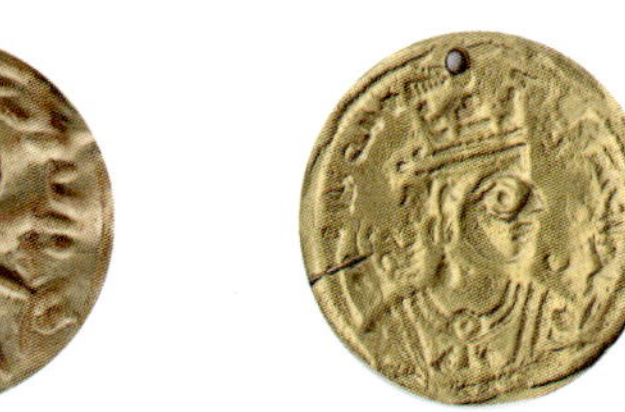

222, reverse

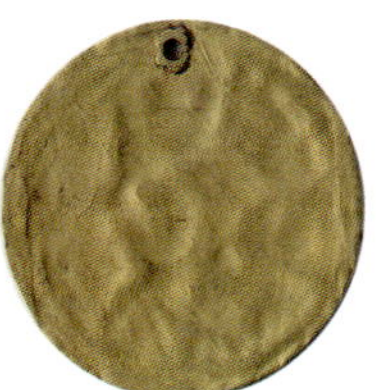

223, obverse

223, reverse

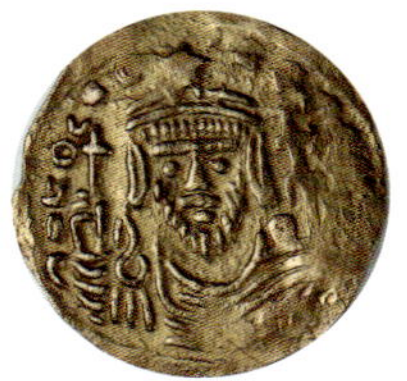
224, obverse

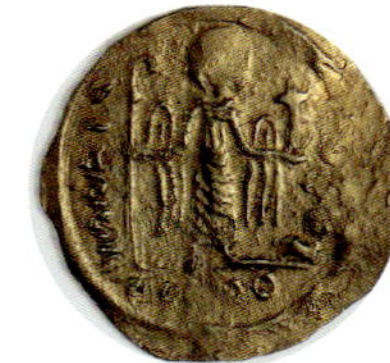
224, reverse

224
Byzantine coin

Gold
Diameter ⅞ in. (2.2 cm)
Excavated from the tomb (dated 709) of An Pu and his wife, Luoyang, Henan Province, 1981
Luoyang Museum

Excav. report in *Zhongyan wenwu* 1982.3

225
Two Sasanian coins

5th–7th century
Silver
Diameter, a. 1 in. (2.6 cm); b. 1 in. (2.6 cm)
Excavated at Mangshan, Luoyang, Henan Province, 1955
Luoyang Museum

The Byzantine gold coin (cat. no. 224) was found in the tomb of General An Pu, a man whose ancestors probably came to China from Bukhara, and his wife.[1] An Pu died in 709. His wife's ancestors were from He in Sogdiana. This coin from his tomb is similar to the solidi of the Eastern Roman emperor Phocas (r. 602–10).[2] It is not clipped.

Obverse: Frontal bust of the emperor. He has a long beard and mustache. The crown, which bears at the top a cross mounted on a circlet, is adorned with pendilia. The emperor's cloak is fastened with a fibula decorated with three pendants. He holds a cross in the right hand. Legend: O(?) N(?) FOCAS almost illegible; the second part of the legend is even more distorted.

Reverse: Winged Victory stands frontally. She holds in the right hand a cross finial in the shape of a P and in the left hand a globe crowned with a cross. In the legend, only a few letters of the word for "Victory" are decipherable. It is probable that the coin is a "barbarian" imitation of the Phocas solidi. Found near the body of the deceased, it was possibly held in his (or her) hand. In the same tomb were two Chinese *kaiyuan tongbao* coins.

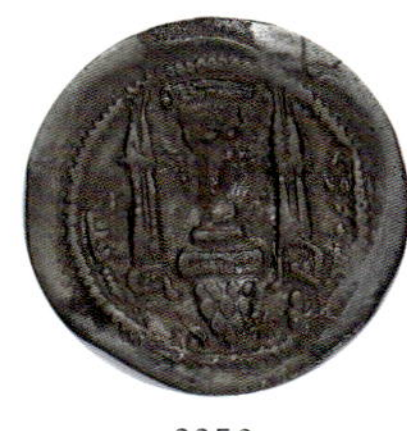
225a

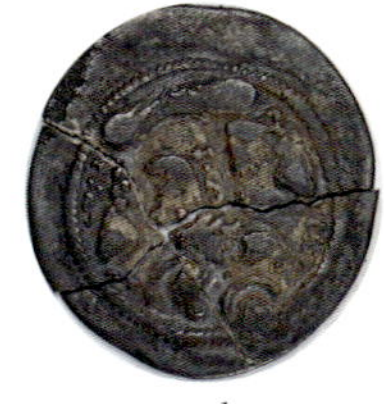
225b

Coins of precious metals such as the rare silver *kaiyuan tongbao* from Luoyang (cat. no. 226; see below) and these two Sasanian silver drachmas (cat. no. 225) were issued as imperial gifts. The drachmas are those of Emperor Peroz I (457/59–84) and his son Kavad I (484; 488; 497–531). They were excavated from Tomb 30, Mangshan, Luoyang, in 1955. Both coins bear the mint mark AY. Peroz's crown is his type III.[3]

VRSC

1. Luoyang shi wenwu gongzuodui 1982.3: 21–26, 41.
2. See, for example, Grierson 1968, pl. I: 1a.1, 2; 5a.1; 5b.2; 5f.1; 5i; 10a.1; 10c.7; 10j.7; 11b.1; 11c.3; 13b; 14; and Grierson 1982, pl. 2.25, 26.
3. Zhao Guobi 1960: 94; Thierry and Morrisson 1994: 91, 100, no. 9.

226
Kaiyuan coin

Tang dynasty (618–907), early 8th century
Silver
Diameter 1 in. (2.5 cm)
Found in Luoyang, Henan Province, 1956
Luoyang Museum

This Tang-dynasty silver coin has exactly the same shape and dimensions as the copper coins of the same period. Even the inscription on the face, *kaiyuan tongbao* (circulating treasure of Kaiyuan), matches that on the copper examples. A surface

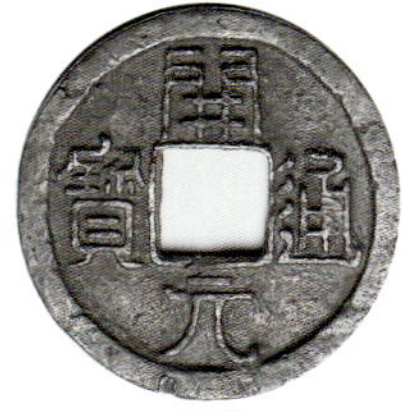

226

find, the coin provides little archaeological context for dating, but a comparison with Tang copper coins, especially the calligraphic style of the inscription, suggests that it was probably cast during the reigns of Wu Zetian (r. 690–705) and Emperor Xuanzong (r. 712–56), in the early eighth century.

Tang coins of gold and silver were likely inspired by Persian and Byzantine coins, which were brought into China by foreign merchants in considerable quantity. They do not, however, seem to have been in circulation, but were used instead as expensive gifts in the Tang court at the celebration of royal weddings and births. The *Jintangshu* (Old History of the Tang), for example, records that "when holding a banquet on [the terrace of] Chengtian Gate, Emperor Xuanzong ordered his attendants to toss gold and silver coins [to the officials gathered below] and allowed those above rank five in the Secretariat and Chancellery and those above rank three in all other offices to collect them."[1]

Gold and silver coins account for only a small percentage of the Tang coins that have been found to date. Except for the large number recovered from a hoard from what is believed to be the residence of the prince of Bin at Hejiacun, in the southern suburb of Xi'an, few finds have been reported.[2] This scarcity corroborates the historical records, which indicate that such coins were made to mark special occasions among royal and aristocratic families. And, indeed, the present coin, discovered in Luoyang, is likely to have been from an elite tomb.

It is notable that the word *kaiyuan* in the inscription does not refer to the Kaiyuan reign (713–41) of Emperor Xuanzong but bears the alternative meaning of "establishing the new era." In contrast to coins of silver and gold, Kaiyuan coins of copper were made for general circulation. An exception to the convention of introducing a new currency during a new reign, these coins were first manufactured in the beginning years of the Tang dynasty—the new era—almost a hundred years before the named reign. Cast in the largest quantity during the Tang, they remained in circulation for several centuries after the dynasty's demise, with the longest period of use of all Chinese coins.[3]

ZS

1. *JTS:* 71.
2. Shaanxi sheng bowuguan 1972: 30.
3. Peng Xinwei 1965: 296.

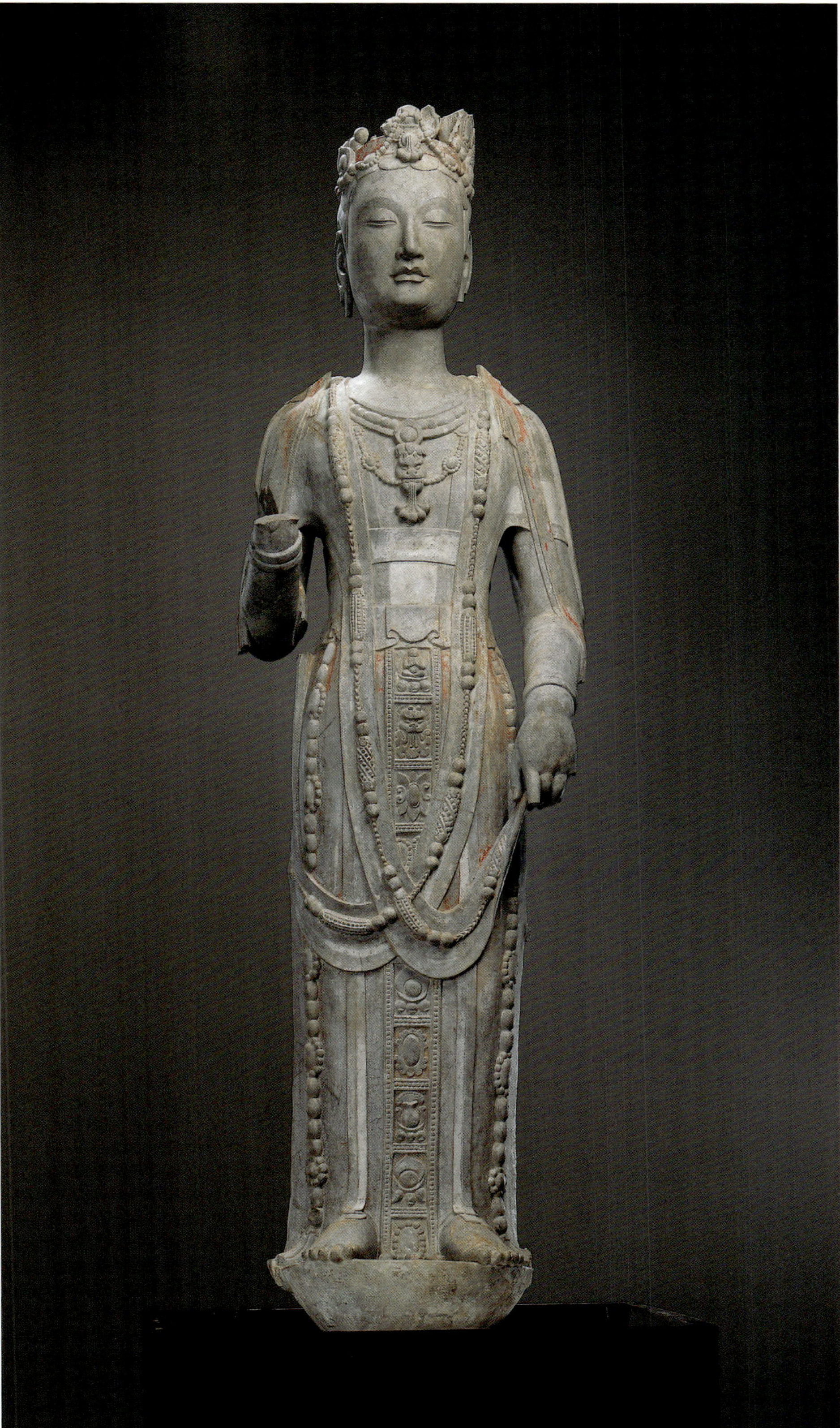

227
Standing bodhisattva

Sui dynasty (581–619)
Limestone with gilding and pigments
Height 53½ in. (136 cm)
Excavated at Longxingsi, Qingzhou, Shandong Province, 1996
Qingzhou City Museum

Excav. report in *Wenwu* 1998.2

Excavated in 1996 from a pit adjacent to the former Longxingsi (Temple of the Rising Dragon) of Qingzhou, this standing bodhisattva is exceptional for its beauty among the many notable sculptures of this find. The images from the temple had been ceremonially interred in the twelth century and were no longer in use.[1] What is remarkable is that this image has come to light almost intact.

The carver executed the image in the round, achieving beautifully harmonious body proportions and a perfect interaction of opulent jewelry and intricate costume. Here, stylization and naturalism merge. The fleshy hand that grasps the cloth is convincingly real, but the ovoid face, defined by arched eyebrows, downcast eyes, a high-bridged nose, and sensuous lips, is closer to an ideal type. The emphatic stylization, seen in the unnaturally flat back, is apparent in the side view.

The costume consists of three garments: a bodice that tightly adheres to the bust, a gauzy capelet decorated with gold stripes and painted red circles whose ends crisscross in front, and a *dhoti* or skirt kept in place by two heavy sashes. The skirt is particularly ornate, with nine superimposed panels filled with carved auspicious symbols. The back, in contrast, is plain, with the exception of the dainty knot on the sash, on which there is an inscription. On the surface of the knot, the characters are inscribed with a brush, indicating an incomplete date—the twenty-fifth day of the ninth month, but without a specific era designation.

Profuse and extremely inventive, the jewelry includes an openwork tiara, partly damaged, formed at the sides by clusters of oval gems contoured with pearls and *mani* jewels and by a most unusual central decoration with a kneeling being (not a Buddha) holding a strand of pearls that drapes along the tiara's base. A long, roped chain hangs from the shoulders, forming an X pattern in the back as it passes through a jade disk above the waist and intersects low at the knees in the front. An intriguing ornament, representing a fantastic horned creature spouting pearls and crowned by a lotus and a *cintamani,* is suspended from a massive necklace. Possibly it is an adaptation of a makara, or aquatic monster, used as a propitious symbol in Buddhist cultures of Southeast Asia.[2]

This extraordinary example of Sui statuary combines two distinct traits. The interpretation of the face and body is still defined by geometric reduction, but the dazzling array of jewels that animates the surface with both three-dimensionality and glittering colors is highly realistic. The blending of the spiritual, so evident in the aloof serenity of the face, with the secular, transpiring from the opulent decoration and elegance of attire, is perfect.

AFH

1. Nickel 2002a: 5–23.

228
Standing headless bodhisattva

Tang dynasty (618–907), early 8th century
Marble
Height 62¼ in. (158 cm)
Excavated at Xiudesi, Quyang, Hebei Province, 1954
Hebei Provincial Museum

Reference: Hebei sheng bowuguan 1999: 215, no. 113

229
Standing bodhisattva Guanyin

Tang dynasty (618–907), early 8th century
Sandstone
Height 63 in. (160 cm)
Exavated at Longxingsi, Pengzhou, Sichuan Province, 1994
Pengzhou City Museum

Excav. report in *Sichuan wenwu* 2003.9

These two contemporaneous bodhisattvas, from northern Hebei and southwestern Sichuan, exemplify different regional interpretations of the same theme. The headless and armless marble statue from Hebei is executed to technical perfection. The verticality of the torso and the long slender legs, as comely as two fluted columns, convey a refined and stately grace. The scarves looped across the body and the multiple pleats draped over the legs, all cut with confident precision, soften the bodhisattva's powerful stance. While the subtly yielding and swelling flesh is easily perceived, the carver has avoided full realism of forms. Indeed, the style of this sculpture moves in the direction of the more expansive forms and languid effects of Tianlongshan statuary in nearby Shanxi, which expresses the aesthetic taste of the Xuanzong court during the Kaiyuan era (713–41).

The Sichuanese sculpture of Guanyin (Skt: Avalokiteshvara) was excavated only recently, at the site of Longxingsi in Pengzhou, south of Chengdu, as part of a sizable cache of works spanning more than two hundred years, from the Southern Liang (397–414) through the Sui (581–619) to the Tang dynasty. The steles and statues were found beneath the pagoda of the temple, interred perhaps for safekeeping, as was the case with the Longxingsi statues of Qingzhou (cat. nos. 163–165, 227). This Guanyin is one of a large group of Tang standing and seated images (at least eighteen had been retrieved by the time of my visit in 2001), all exceptionally well preserved and uniform in style. Some of them have inscriptions with dates corresponding to the last years of the reign of Wu Zetian (r. 690–705) or immediately after. In short, the sculpture was executed at the same time as its Hebei counterpart.

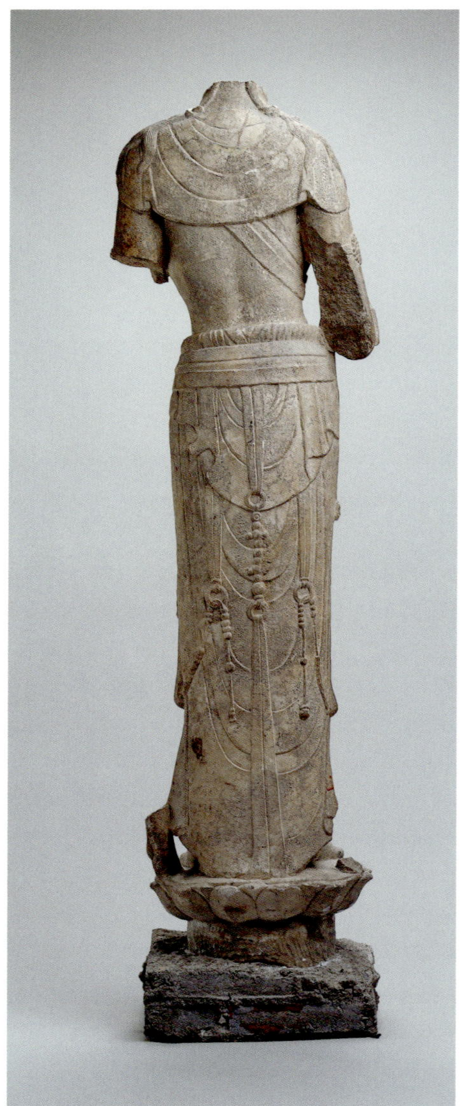
228, back

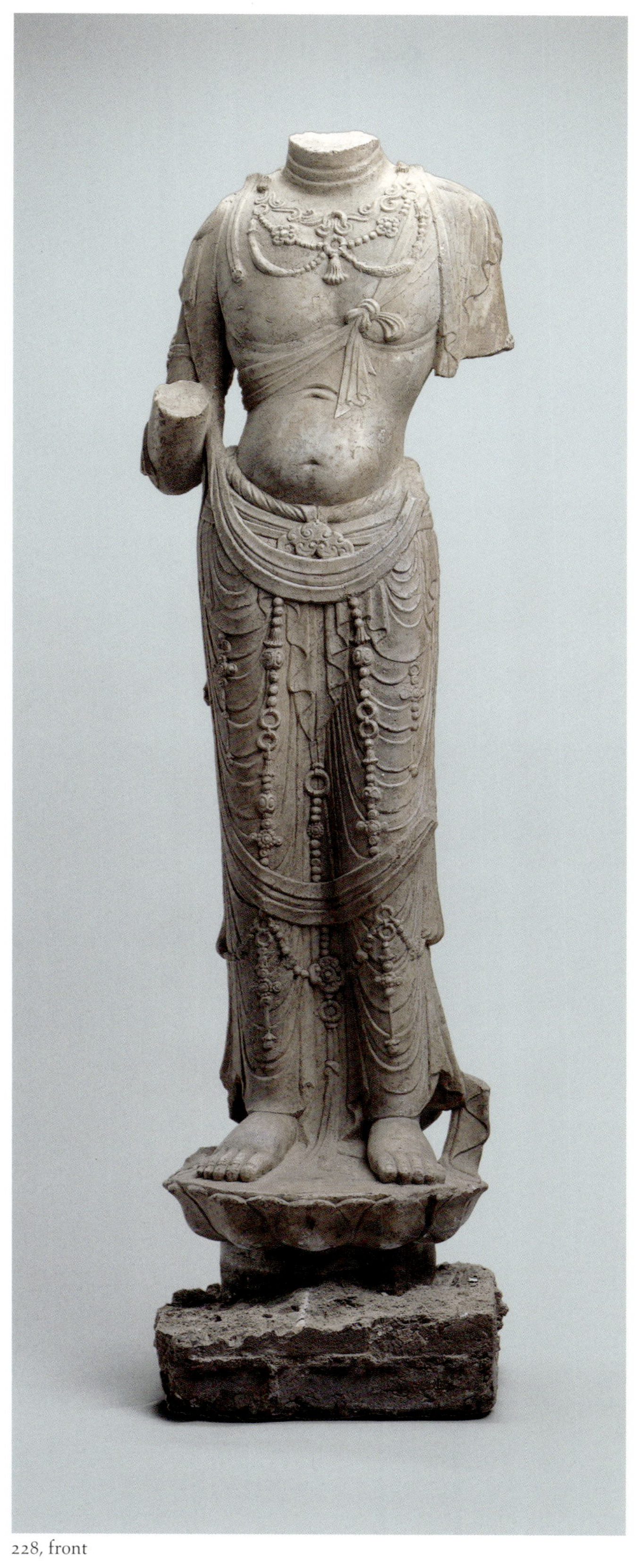

228, front

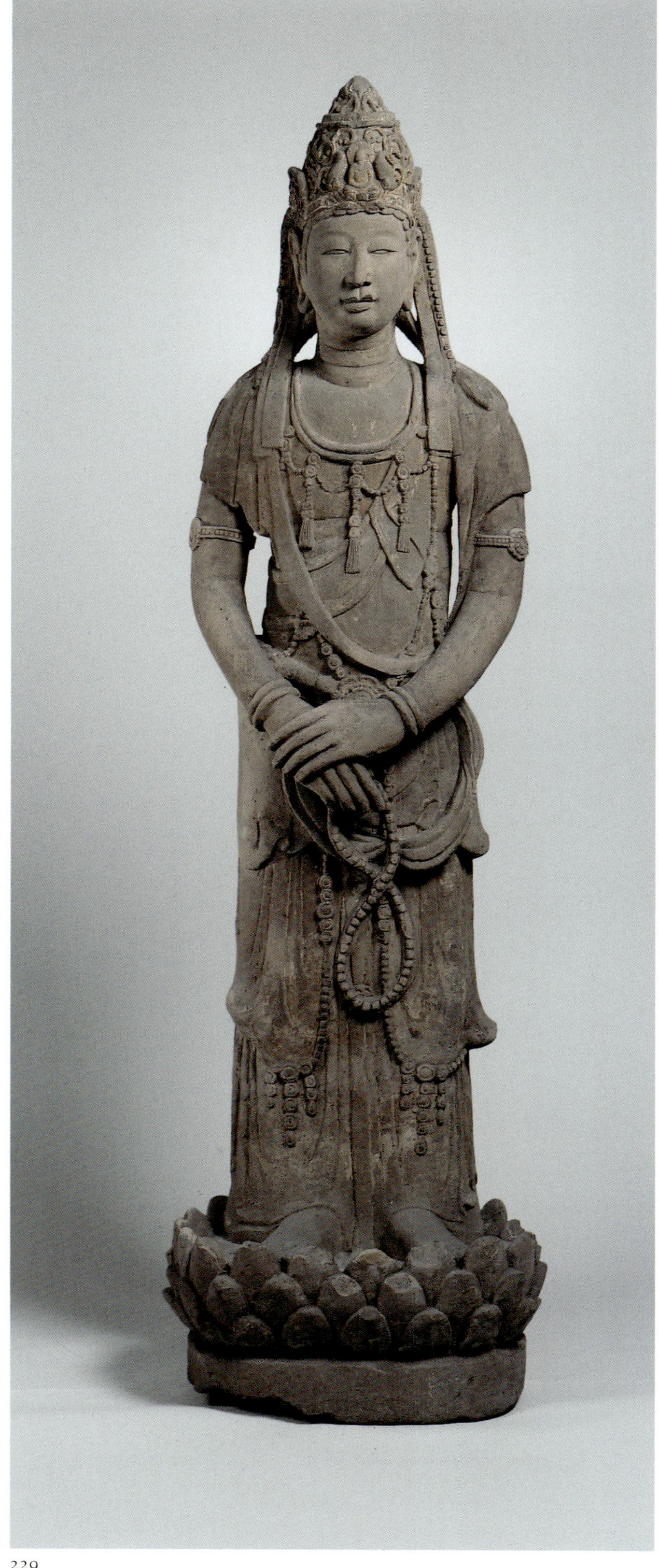

229

Exquisite carving skills, matching those of Hebei carvers, define the sumptuous attire and jewelry and the detailed rendering of the crown, which bears the seated Buddha, emblem of the deity. Diverse artistic concerns are, however, at work in the Pengzhou bodhisattva. The demure pose—underlined by the hands clasping a rosary (a convention developed in Sichuan)—and the rather static, compact modeling, while contrasting with the flamboyance and strong physical presence of the Hebei sculpture, propose a different, but nonetheless highly satisfying, artistic choice. The compassionate expression of the face is Guanyin's most striking trait, balancing dignity and kindness in equal measure. This face has shed the sacred in favor of a human dimension.

AFH

230
Pair of guardian warriors

Tang dynasty (618–907), 8th century
Gilt bronze
Height: a. 26¾ in. (68 cm);
b. 25⅝ in. (65 cm)
Found at Baoji, Shaanxi Province
a. Shaanxi History Museum
b. National Museum of China

References: a. Tōkyō kokuritsu hakubutsukan 1998, no. 25; b. Guggenheim Museum 1998, no. 169

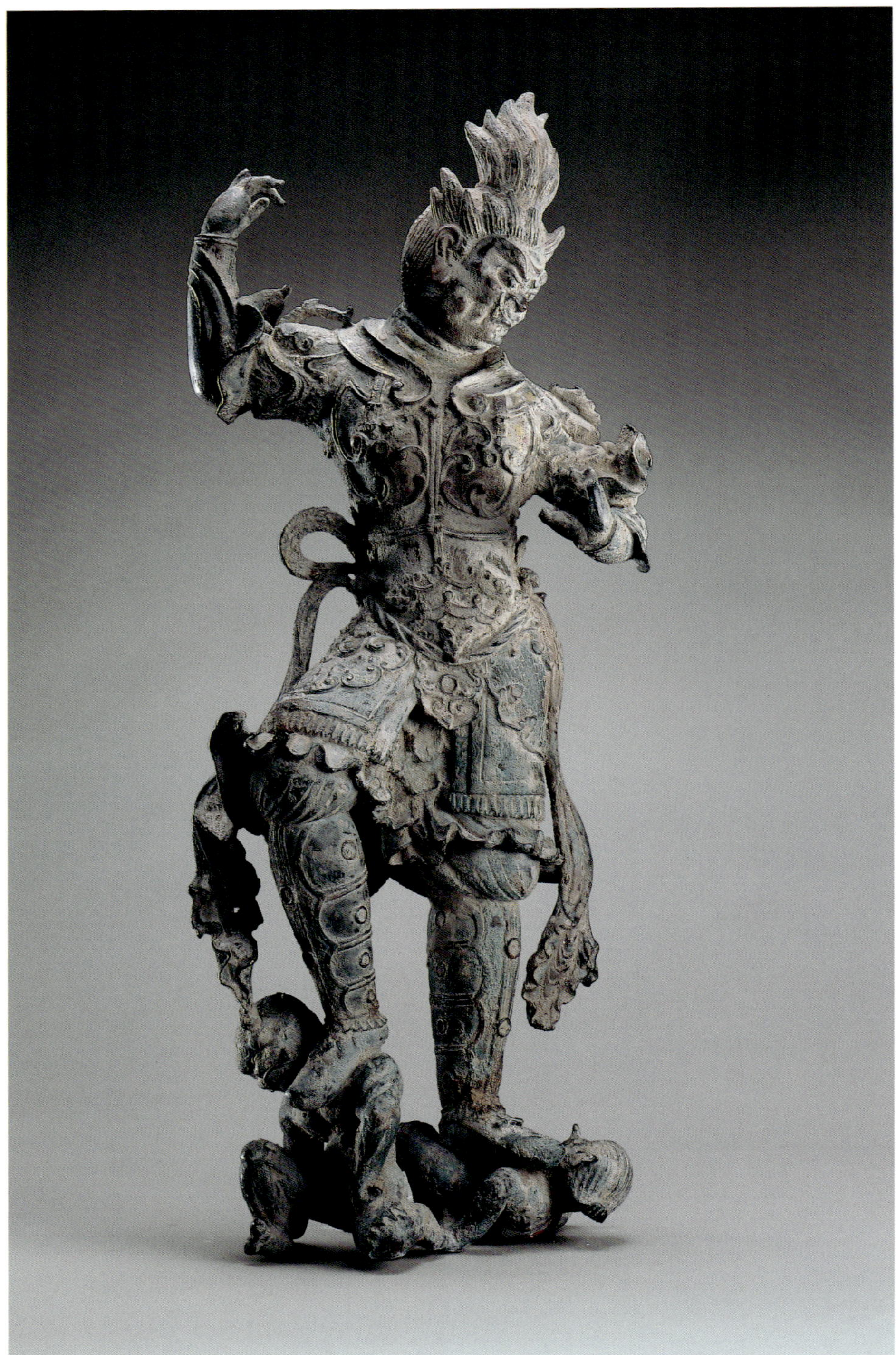
230a

By the third quarter of the sixth century, armored guardians standing on the backs of animals or demons are seen in both Buddhist temples and tombs. The temple sculptures are generally made of stone or wood; the funerary works are earthenware. Guardian figures of gilt bronze, such as this striking pair, are extremely rare. These two were found together near a pit housing a sculpture of the Bodhisattva of Compassion, Avalokiteshvara (C: Guanyin).[1] It is unusual for guardian warriors to accompany a bodhisattva, and it is likely that the three figures were part of a larger group of images once housed in a temple in the area.

The baroque detailing of the overgarments, the fluttering edges of the scarves and tunics, and the flaming hair help date the pieces to the eighth century. The guardians are mirror images. One stands with his right leg and arm lifted, the other raises the left. The hands of the guardian with the uplifted right arm suggest that he once held a spear, while the other guardian may have held a staff.

Guardians of this type are often identified as the *lokapala* (C: *tianwang*), or Heavenly Kings, of the Buddhist tradition, who guard the four directions of the universe. Individual *lokapala* are found in the first century B.C. at Indian sites such as Bharhut, in Madhya Pradesh.[2] A distinct group of four protectors, on the other hand, was not codified until the fifth or sixth century. A version of the *Suvarnaprabhasa sutra* (Sutra of Golden Light) redacted in the Khotan region is often cited for the imagery of the four kings and for the definition of their role as protectors of the state. The earliest Chinese examples are four small guardians painted on the east and west walls of Cave 285 at Dunhuang, which is dated 538.[3]

Unlike *lokapala,* however, Chinese guardian warriors are usually shown in pairs, rather than as a group of four, bringing into question the accuracy of the identification of these protective beings with the directional guardians. Indian tradition provides several other prototypes for the Chinese sculptures, including paired *dvarapala,* or entryway guardians, and a host of wrathful protective deities known generically as *kordha-vighnantaka.*[4] Unlike guardian warriors, however, both types are shown barely clad. Nonetheless, their grimacing expressions and flaming hair provide a possible prototype for the Sinitic images, as does the presence of demons beneath their feet. It seems likely that in the late seventh century the

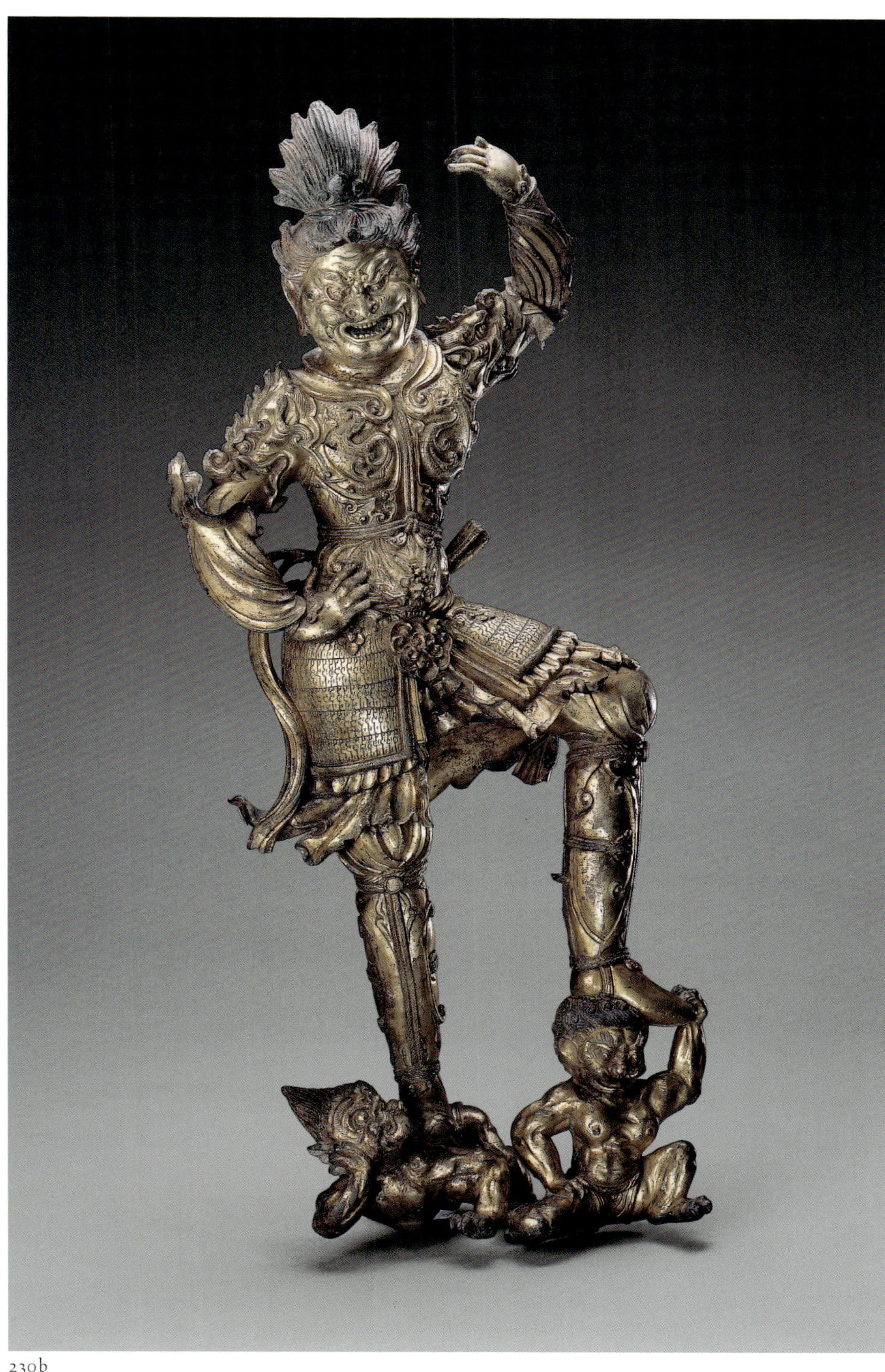

230b

Chinese development of armored warriors with exaggerated facial features, who are shown trampling on demons, reflects a growing awareness of Indian Esoteric traditions, which would become prominent in many Asian centers in the eighth and ninth centuries.

DPL

1. Li Jian 2003, no. 79.
2. Fisher 1995: 17–24.
3. *Tonkō Bakukōkutsu* 1980–82, vol. 1, pl. 114.
4. Linrothe 1999.

231

Pair of standing Lokapalas, or Heavenly Kings

Tang dynasty (618–907), ca. 725
Marble
Height, a. 43⅜ in. (110 cm);
b. 42⅛ in. (107 cm)
Excavated at Xi'an, Shaanxi Province, 1983
Xi'an City Institute of Cultural Properties Protection and Archaeology

Reference: Tōkyō kokuritsu hakubutsukan 1998, no. 24

These two personages were originally part of a quartet. They are protectors of the four directions, thus their Sanskrit name, *lokapala,* an appellation the Chinese rendered as *tianwang,* or Heavenly King. They are commonly referred to as Heavenly Guardians. In Buddhist cosmology, they reside on the four slopes of Mount Sumeru, the legendary axis of the world, but their effigies are placed in temples—specifically, at the four corners of the altar—to protect the main deity, the sacred space, and ultimately the Buddhist faith itself from any challenge. As defenders of individuals, temples, and the nation, it is thus fitting that they should be represented as formidable warriors who can rouse fear in their adversaries. Their demeanor further embodies the international stature of the Tang dynasty as the most powerful nation of Asia. In general, they are depicted with several fixed conventions: they are attired in military garb, assume a threatening pose, and carry specific implements—some martial, such as a sword, others symbolic, such as a stupa.

The highly realistic modeling of the figures is a style that first appeared in 675 at Fengxiansi, Longmen, part of the grand program of Emperor Gaozong (r. 650–83) and his consort, the future Empress Wu Zetian (r. 690–705). It was also adopted for the three-color glazed (*sancai*) guardians of contemporaneous elite tombs (see cat. no. 180).

The height of this pair of Heavenly Kings is approximately lifesize. They are

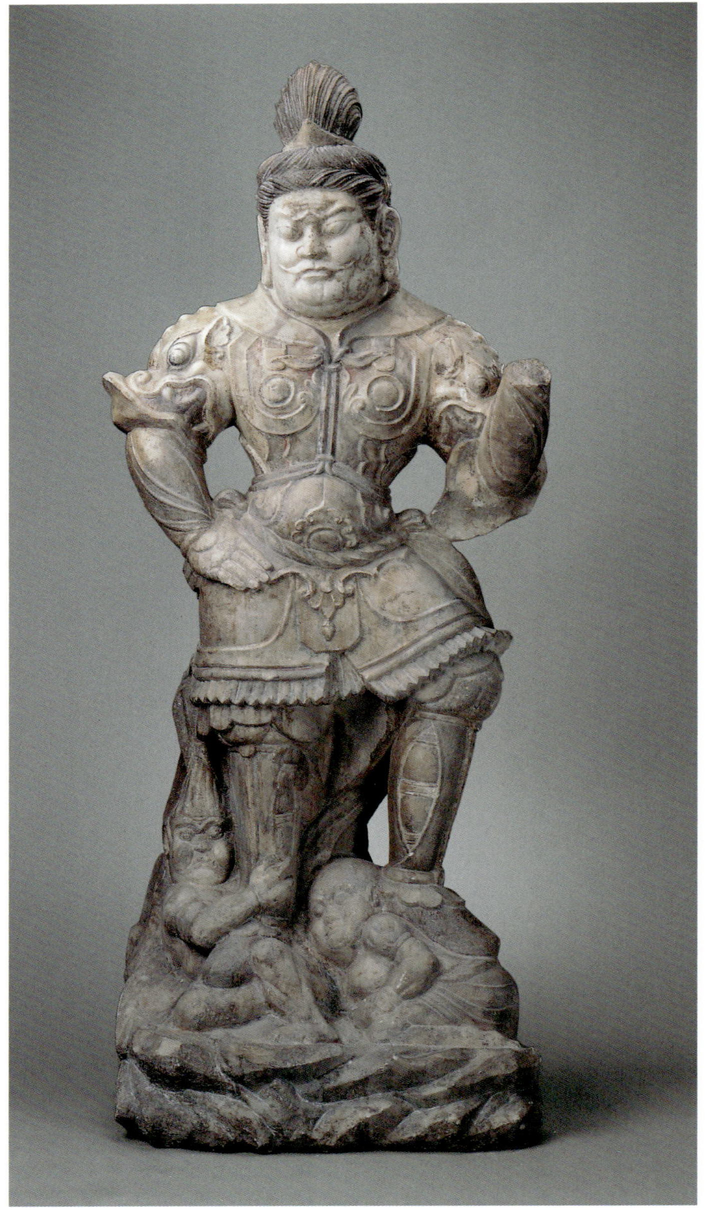

231a

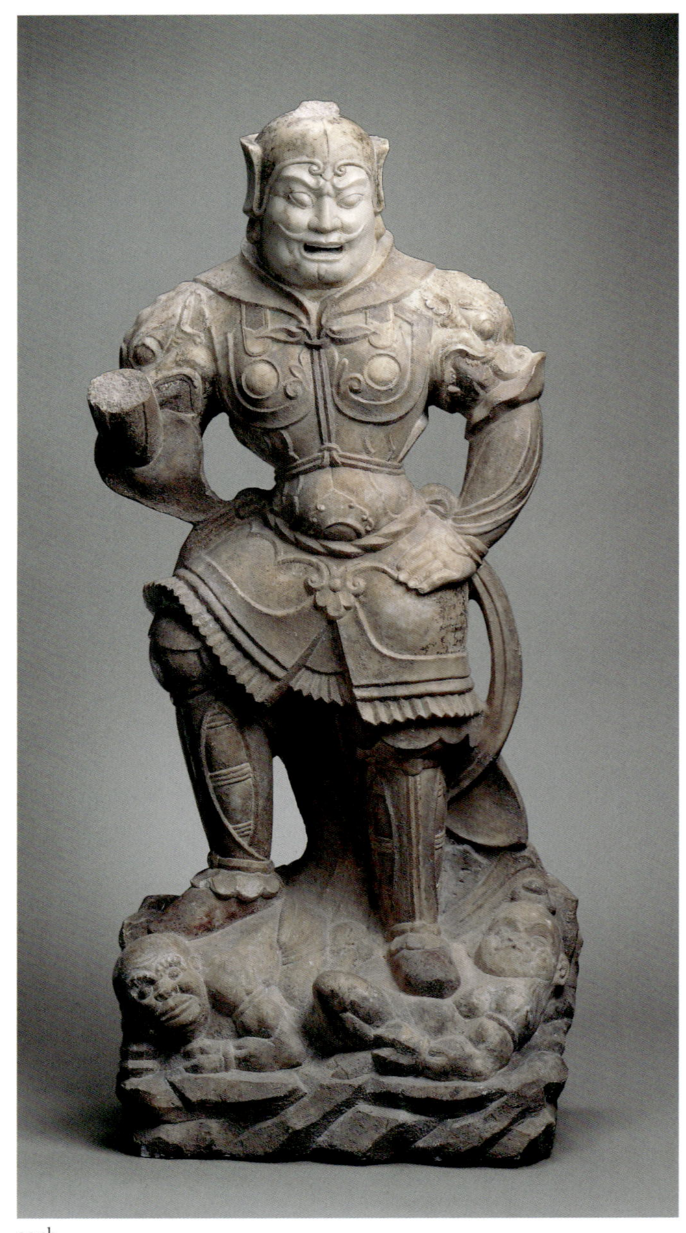

231b

conceived symmetrically, with reversed contrapposto postures. Each sculpture is missing a hand; the other hand is placed over the hip. The lost hand may have held a weapon. These stout protectors tower defiantly over brutish, chubby, dwarflike creatures in contorted poses. A rocky ledge supports them all. The guardians are suitably garbed in armor, pleated skirts, and boots. Most of the armor embellishment is stylized pattern, except for the masks at shoulder level, ferocious beasts that bite into the upper arm of the deity. The figures are distinguished from one another by the different interpretations of the heads. One deity wears a helmet and is open-mouthed as if he were shouting; the other wears his hair swept up into a knot and projects an air of inner concentration.

AFH

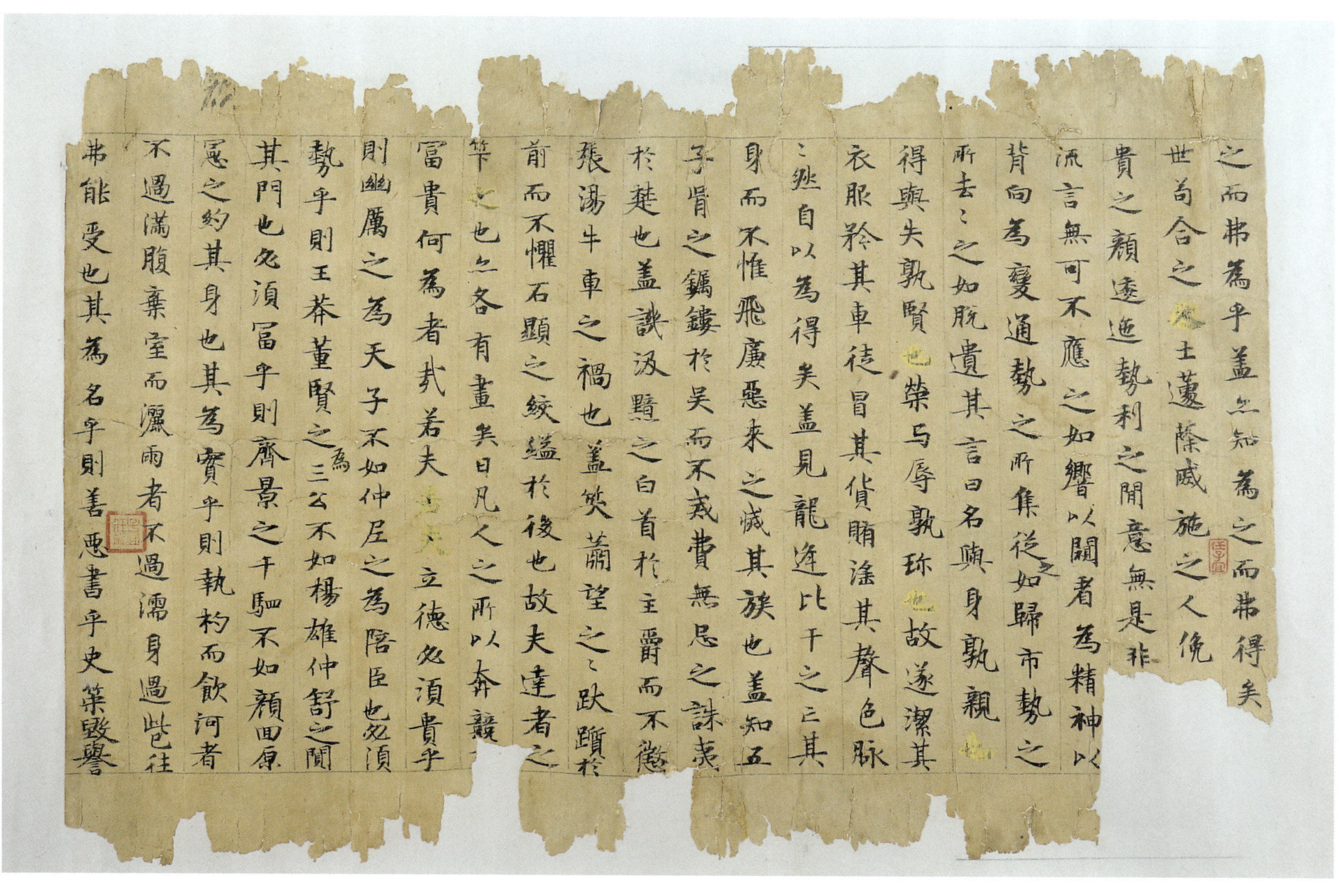

232

Excerpt from "Literary Selections"

Sui dynasty (581–619)
Fragment of a handscroll, ink on paper
11⅛ x 16¾ in. (28.3 x 42.5 cm)
Recovered from Cave 17, Dunhuang, Gansu Province, 1900
Dunhuang Research Institute

Reference: Xu Zufan, Qin Mingzhi, and Rong Sigi 1985

This fragment preserves a passage from China's earliest surviving literary anthology, *Wen xuan* (Literary Selections), compiled by Xiao Tong, Prince Zhaoming (501–531), the eldest son of the founder of the Liang dynasty (502–557). The surviving passage is a portion of chapter 53, "Treatise on Fate" (*Yunming lun*), by Li Kang (act. early 6th century).[1] Two modern seals impressed at either end of the fragment indicate that, after its recovery from Cave 17, the Library Cave at Dunhuang, this piece passed through the hands of a local collector, Ren Ziyi, before being acquired by Dunhuang Research Institute.[2]

Unlike the thousands of religious texts found in the Library Cave, this manuscript stands out as a work of secular literature that, notably, originated in South China, not in the north. Its presence in this remote oasis bespeaks a new cosmopolitanism along the Silk Road. More significantly, unlike the religious texts found at Dunhuang, which were usually copied by professional scribes, the calligraphy of this manuscript, one of the most elegant examples of standard script to survive from this period, is evidently by a member of the cultural elite. The refined brush movements, dynamic forms, and spontaneity of execution suggest a highly cultivated hand. At the same time, there is a distinctly casual quality to the writing. Mistranscribed characters have been obscured, characters have been written in variant forms, omitted characters have been added in the margins, and the spacing between ideographs varies considerably, so that characters are often squeezed into the bottom of a column. All of these characteristics would suggest that, rather than being the product of a scriptorium, the manuscript was a highly personal and informal creation.

Some Chinese scholars have dated this writing to the Sui dynasty (581–619) on the basis of its resemblance to Sui sutras and because the writer did not observe the Tang taboo against writing the characters of the emperors' personal names.[3] However, the Tang emperor Taizong (r. 627–49) did not require the observation of taboo characters until 627, and even the early Tang edition of this text, edited by Li Shan (630–689) in 658, is inconsistent in its substitution of variant forms for tabooed characters. More important, the calligraphy shows no trace of clerical-script manner-

233, epitaph tablet

isms found in Sui sutras, nor does it resemble the regimented and conventionalized "sutra style" of that time (see cat. no. 87). The elongated horizontals and taut diagonals in the character *bu* 不, for example, are quite distinct from the fuller, heavier forms in Sui sutras. The stylistic similarities between this calligraphy and that of such early Tang masters as Ouyang Xun (557–641) and Chu Suiliang (596–658) make it more likely that the fragment dates to the first half of the seventh century.

MKH

1. For an annotated version of the text, see *WX* (53: 13b–15b) 1983, vol. 3:733–34. For a general introduction to *Literary Selections*, see Knechtges 1982–.
2. Another fragment of this handscroll is in the Pelliot archives of the Bibliothèque Nationale, Paris; see *Dunhuang yishu zongmu suoyin* 1983: 269, no. 2645.
3. See Li Yongning 1983: 164–65; see also Xu Zufan, Qin Mingzhi, and Rong Sigi 1985, introduction (unpaginated) and pp. 73–74.

233
Epitaph of Yan Ren
after Zhang Xu (act. mid-8th century)

Tang dynasty (618–907), dated 742
Stone
Cover: 21 5/8 x 20 7/8 in. (55 x 53 cm); tablet: 20 5/8 x 20 5/8 in. (52.5 x 52.5 cm)
Excavated at Yanshi, Henan Province, 1992
Yanshi City Museum

Excav. report in *Wenwu* 1992.12

The tradition of erecting monumental stone steles to eulogize or celebrate the achievements of meritorious individuals (see cat. no. 22) was complemented by a parallel tradition of creating smaller memorial tablets engraved with an epitaph and placing them in tombs. The epitaph tablet recovered from the tomb of Yan Ren (689–742), district defender (*xianwei*) of Longmen district (near Luoyang, Henan), is a modest example of this kind of mortuary monument.[1] The square stone slab is incised with a grid that enframes each character.[2] The stone was originally covered with a stone lid inscribed in large seal script: "Epitaph of former master Yan of the Great Tang [dynasty]." The beveled sides are decorated with floral patterns. Thus, the entire ensemble resembles a box or reliquary.[3] The modest size of Yan Ren's epitaph stone is in keeping with both his relatively low official position and the simple tomb in which he was buried.

Given Yan's modest rank and means, it is striking that his epitaph bears the signature of Zhang Xu, one of the best-known calligraphers of the High Tang era.[4] Zhang often executed his wild cursive calligraphy while drunk, as described by Du Fu (712–770), who immortalized Zhang as one of the Eight Immortals of the Wine Cup: "Give calligrapher Zhang Xu three cupfuls and, even in front of dignitaries, he will throw off his cap and draw forth clouds on the paper with his brush."[5] But Zhang Xu's standard script was also praised. The late Tang critic Zhang Yanyuan (act. ca. 847) would later write: "Madman Zhang became famous for his mastery of cursive script, so that his standard and clerical scripts were not so prized, yet I once saw his small standard script [transcription of] *Essay on General Yue Yi*. It was comparable to [the writings of the early Tang masters] Yu [Shinan (558–638)] and Chu [Suiliang (596–658)]."[6]

When one compares the calligraphy of the epitaph with that of Zhang Xu's *Lang guan shi ji* (Stone Record of the Court Gentleman) of 741, written just one year earlier than the epitaph, it is clear that the two are by different hands, even taking into account the poor carving of Yan Ren's stone.[7] While the basic character structures of the two works are similar, the brushwork of each is quite distinct. The brushstrokes of the epitaph are generally fleshier and show greater variation in width. Most notable are the diagonal strokes, which have a pronounced wavelike curve. In the *Stone Record*, these strokes are thinner and straighter. The fuller, more modulated forms of the epitaph anticipate the style of Yan Zhenqing (708–784), demonstrating that the period style was already beginning to shift away from the early-Tang model established by Ouyang Xun (557–641) and Chu Suiliang, whose writing style the *Stone Record* still resembles. Clearly, the identity of the calligrapher of this epitaph needs further investigation.

MKH

1. I would like to acknowledge Zhixin Sun for recommending this piece for inclusion in the exhibition and for offering suggestions about its attribution. For a description of the tomb and its contents, see Fan Yousheng and Li Xianqi 1992. According to his epitaph, Yan Ren was from Yuhang Commandary (near present-day Hangzhou, Zhejiang Province), the third son of Yan Tong, who rose to the post of district magistrate of Jinhua (present-day Zhejiang Province).
2. The text, inscribed in a grid of twenty-one units on a side, was authored by a certain Zhang Wanqing from Wu Commandary (present-day Suzhou, Jiangsu Province). Zhang Xu was also from Wu.
3. For a rubbing of the epitaph cover, see Fan Yousheng and Li Xianqi 1992: 35, fig. 4.
4. For a biography of Zhang Xu, see *XTS* 202: 5764.
5. Translation after Hung 1952: 52.
6. Translation after Acker 1954: 201. Zhang Yanyuan also stated that Zhang's calligraphy inspired the brush methods of the painting master Wu Daoxuan (active ca. 710–60); see ibid.: 179.
7. See Toyama 1974: 180–81, pls. 101–3. See also Fushimi 1971: 33–52, 103–5.

234
Textile with figures and camels

6th century
Woven silk (1:2 warp-faced compound tabby)
Warp 7⅝ in (19.4 cm); weft 5⅞ in. (15 cm)
Excavated from Tomb 18 (dated 589), Astana, Turfan, Xinjiang Uygur Autonomous Region, 1964
Xinjiang Uygur Autonomous Region Museum

EXCAV. REPORT in *Wenwu* 1973.10

The design of this *jin* silk, structurally a warp-faced compound tabby, is organized like that of the *jin* silk with Helios (cat. no. 174). It consists of several roundels framed with twisted ropes, the interstices filled with four-directional palmettes. The pattern within the roundel is woven in green with red outlines on a yellow ground. Inside the roundel are depicted two images of a merchant leading a camel, one upright and the other upside down, as if they are looking at their own reflections in clear water. Two characters, *hu wang* (barbarian king), are woven between the merchants and the camels. Along the Silk Road, which traverses the Gobi Desert, the vista is filled with endless sand. With little water and few oases, camels, known as the ships of the desert, became the major means of transport between east and west. Images of camels also appear in contemporary cave paintings, brick carvings, and *sancai* (three-color glazed) ceramic wares.

In the Sui dynasty (581–619), *jin* silk with roundels generally measured 40 to 50 cm wide, with four to six roundels in one loom width. The adjacent fragmentary roundel on this textile features an incomplete lion in orange pattern with a blue outline on a cream ground. Comparable *jin* silks from Turfan suggest that the missing roundels probably included images of elephants, animal trainers, Buddhas, or bodhisattvas.[1] Similar motifs, such as merchants leading camels,

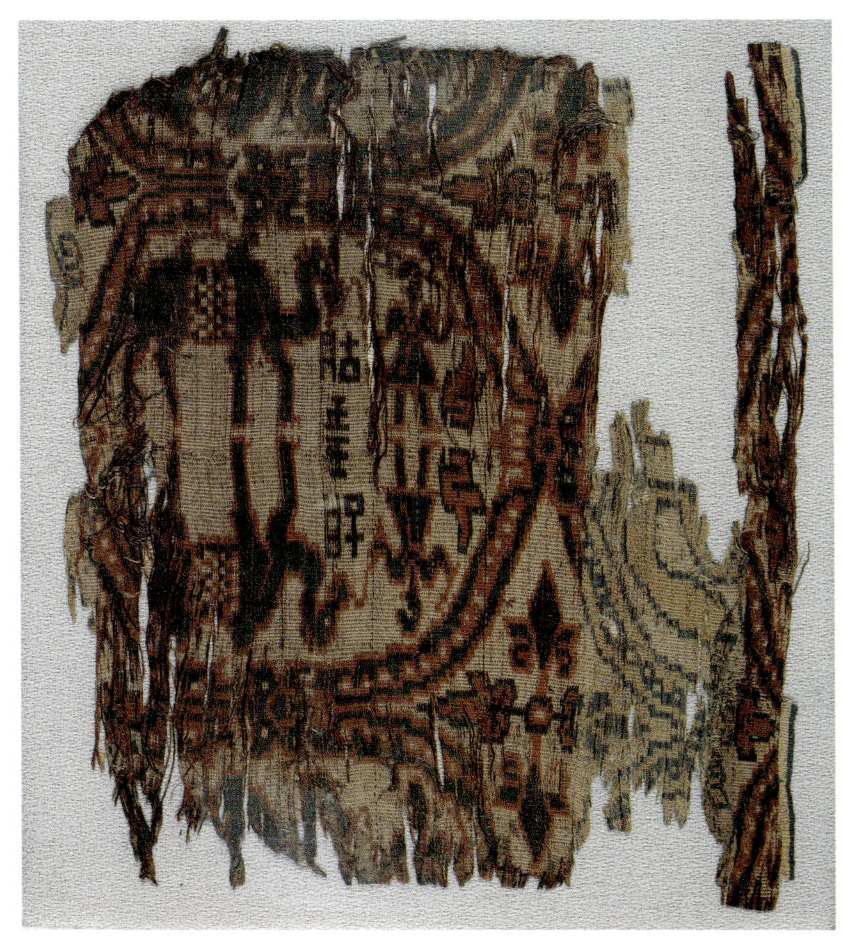

elephants walking, and seated lions arranged in a wave pattern, have also appeared in a textile from Dulan, Qinghai.[2]

Distinctive from the innovative pattern method of the *jin* silk with Helios (cat. no. 174) and the *jin* silk with drinkers (cat. no. 173), in which the design is oriented at right angles to the warp, the pattern on this piece is oriented in the warp direction. This is a traditional pattern method, one that has been employed since the Han dynasty.

ZF

1. Wu Min 1984: 70–80, esp. illus. 1 on p. 71.
2. Zhao Feng 1999c: 104.

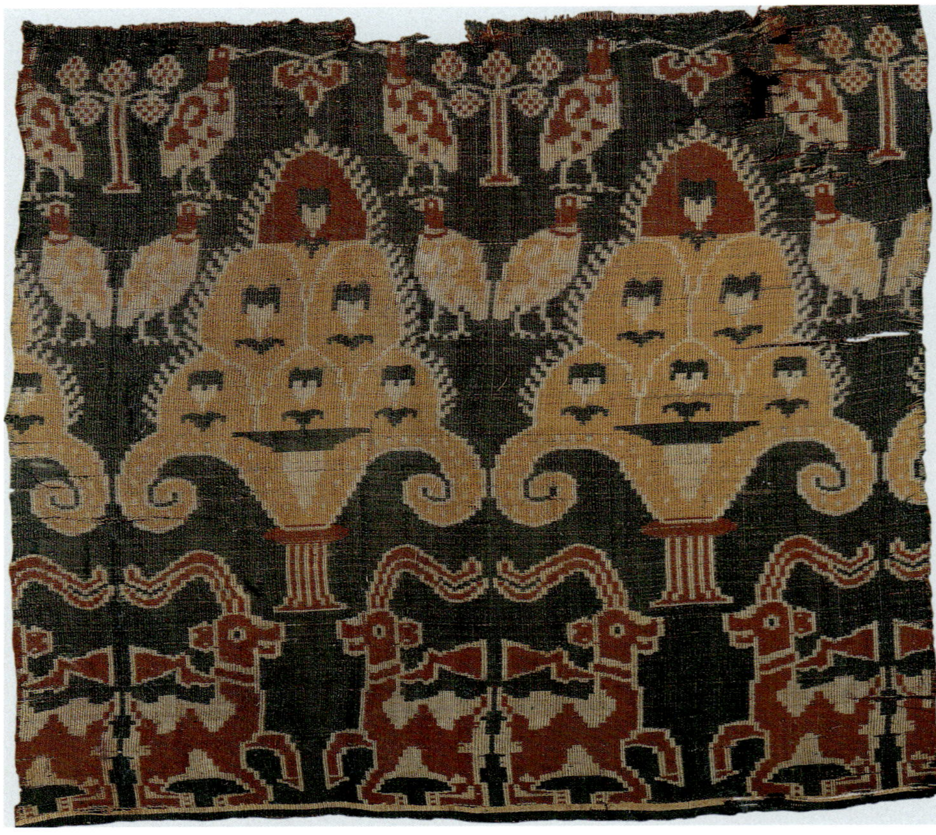

235
Textile with trees, birds, and mountain goats

Late 6th–early 7th century
Woven silk (1:2 warp-faced compound tabby)
Warp 9½ in. (24.1 cm); weft 8¼ in. (21 cm)
Excavated from Tomb 186, Astana, Turfan, Xinjiang Uygur Autonomous Region, 1972
Xinjiang Uygur Autonomous Region Museum

Reference: Xinjiang Weiwuer zizhiqu bowuguan 1991: pl. 46

This *jin* silk with a green ground dating to the late Northern Dynasties (386–581) to early Tang (618–907) was discovered in Astana, Turfan, where additional textiles with similar patterns, all warp-faced compound tabbies, have also been found. The design is strictly symmetrical in one complete loom width. Closest to the selvedge (the stripe at the lower edge) are red mountain goats kneeling and facing each other, with long curved horns and a red ribbon around the neck. Above the goats stands a sizable tree with a trunk shaped like a column. Called a lamp tree, it bears branches with leaf-shaped lamps. Four confronted birds, one above the other, are depicted on both sides of the tree. The two on top hold a bud in their beaks. Behind this pair, a small tree displays lamps in the shape of grapes. On a similar textile from the same tomb the Chinese character *ji* (auspicious) is inserted between the patterns.[1]

The term *yang shu* (sun tree) *jin* was recorded in manuscripts from Turfan dated to Zhanghe eighteenth year of the Gaochang kingdom (548). According to Wu Zhen, the word *yang* meaning "sun" is interchangeable with the word *yang* meaning "goat" in the Turfan manuscripts. *Yang shu jin* therefore refers to *jin* silk with designs of goats and trees.[2] This motif was quite popular at the time, as demonstrated by a silver plate of similar design from Central Asia.[3]

The present *jin* silk, structurally a 1:2 warp-faced compound tabby, is woven in the traditional coloring method. The fabric employs blue or green for the ground and white for outlines and alternates red, gray green, and orange yellow for the pattern. As seen in another piece from the same textile, the rigorously symmetrical pattern, its most distinctive feature, repeats not only in the warp direction but in the weft direction as well.[4] This textile is one of the earliest warp-faced compound tabbies with pattern repeats in both warp and weft directions.

ZF

1. Zhongguo Xinjiang Weiwuer zizhiqu bowuguan and Riben Nailiang sichou zhi lu xue yanjiu zhongxin 2000, pl. 99.
2. Wu Zhen 2000: 84–103.
3. Gunter and Jett 1992: 128.
4. See note 1 above, pl. 101.

236
Textile with hexagons and character

7th century
Woven silk (1:1 weft-faced compound tabby, taquete)
Warp 12⅜ in. (31.4 cm); weft 12 in. (30.5 cm)
Excavated from Tomb 44 (dated 655), Astana, Turfan, Xinjiang Uygur Autonomous Region, 1966
Xinjiang Uygur Autonomous Region Museum

Reference: Xinjiang Weiwu'er zizhiqu bowuguan 1973: pl. 31

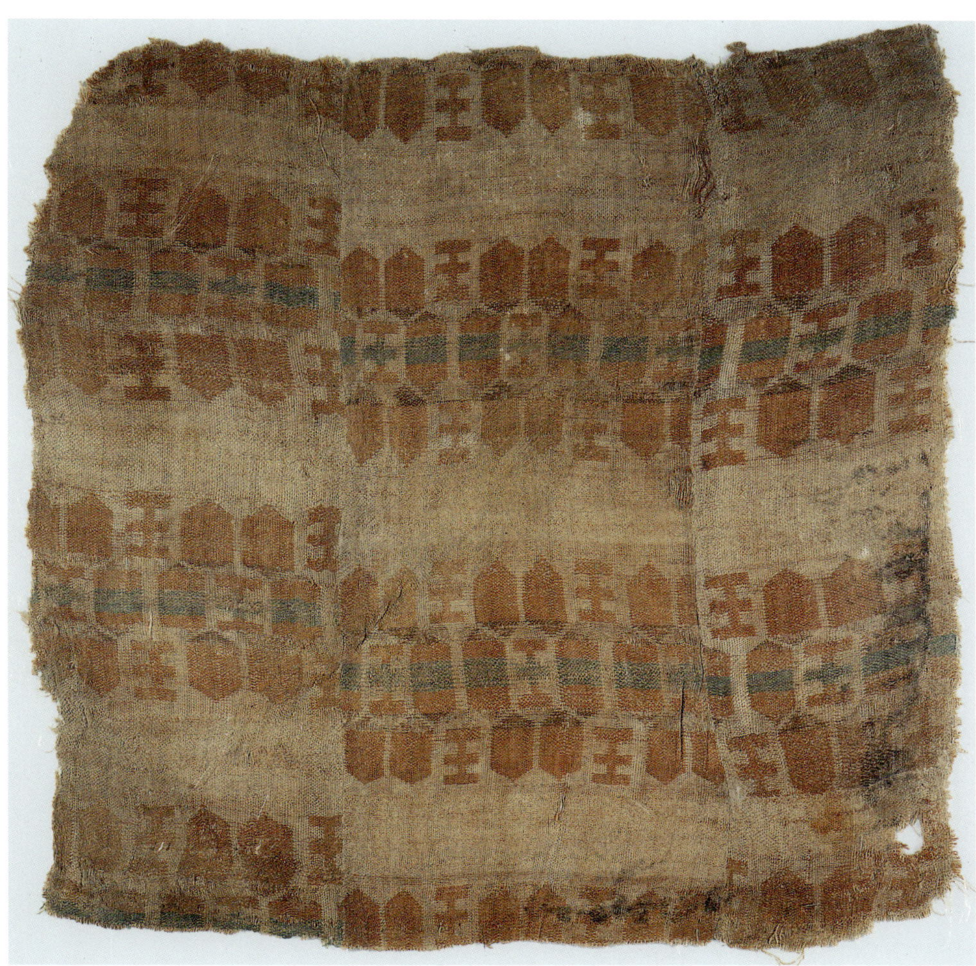

This piece was reconstructed from three fragments. It has a simple pattern of rows of repeating units, each consisting of six hexagons and three instances of the character *wang* (king). The pattern unit, made up of interlocking hexagons and characters, resembles a rosette with six hexagons forming the petals and one character in the center. Woven on a white ground, the pattern is red except near the center of each row, where a band of blue wefts flanked by narrow bands of dark red wefts is substituted.

This taquete, structurally a weft-faced compound tabby, is woven in an unusual technique in which z-twisted red silk was employed for the warp but wide and flat silk for the weft. A similar piece from Turfan, also with a red design on a white ground, has a pattern of three rows: the character *ji* (auspicious) interspersed with three interlacing ovals, a group of five stripes, and a hexagonal design (see fig. 69). These two pieces were probably examples of the *baidi jin* (*jin* silk with white ground) recorded in Turfan texts. The term *baidi jin* was referred to in a contract from Tomb 99, in Karakhoja, Turfan, dated to Yixi fifth year of the Gaochang kingdom (514) and again in an inventory of burial items, dated to Zhanghe eighteenth year (548), in Tomb 313 in Astana, Turfan. The contract reported that "the Daoist priest Hong Du borrowed from Zhai Shaoyuan half a *zhang* of *baidi jin* [four feet long and four feet wide]." The inventory listed one hundred *zhang* of *baidi jin* among the burial objects. *Zhang* was the unit used for textiles made in weft-faced compound weave, which were generally produced in Xinjiang and areas farther west. The presence of the Chinese characters *ji* and *wang* suggests that these two textiles were probably woven in locales such as Gaochang, where populations of Han Chinese were concentrated.

ZF

237
Face cover with boar's head in pearl roundel

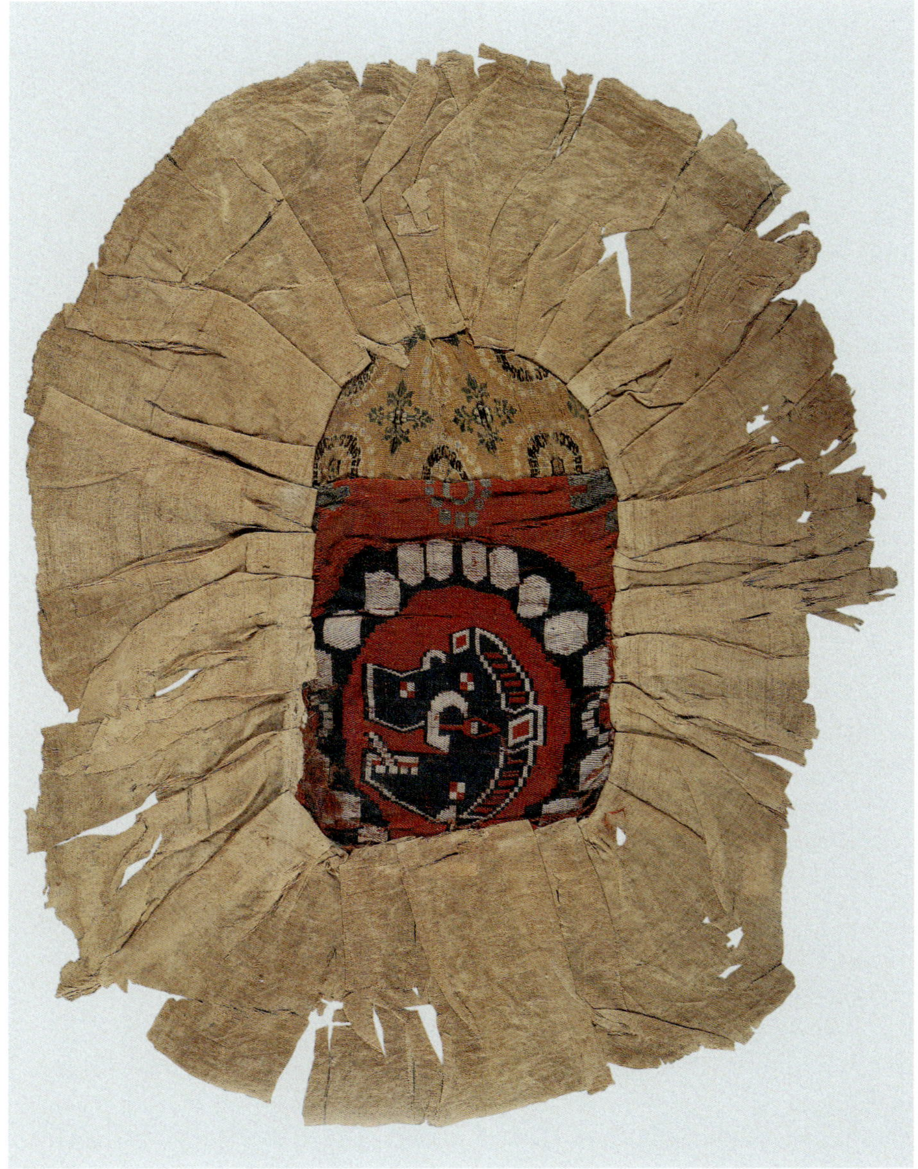

7th century
Boar's head textile: woven silk (1:2 weft-faced compound twill, samite)
Rosette textile: woven silk (1:2 warp-faced compound twill)
Surrounding textile: woven silk (tabby)
Warp 18½ (47 cm); weft 15¾ in. (40 cm)
Excavated from Tomb 138, Astana, Turfan, Xinjiang Uygur Autonomous Region, 1969
Xinjiang Uygur Autonomous Region Museum

REFERENCE: Zhu Min 1972

Used to cover the face of the dead, this textile from Astana, Turfan, includes a fragment of samite depicting a boar's head on a red ground.[1] Technically, it is a weft-faced compound twill, the same weave structure as silks with ibexes or ribbon-holding birds found in Turfan. This group of textiles is characterized by z-twisted warps, a flat surface, and animal motifs in pearl roundels.

The textile attached to the samite with boar's head is a twill *jin* silk with rosettes and quatrefoils, a pattern that was very popular in the early Tang dynasty. Many examples have been found in Astana, Turfan, and the pattern was imitated in various media, such as murals and clay objects for burial. The piece surrounding the two polychrome textiles is silk tabby.

The boar's head, an image thought to have come from Persia, represents the deity Verethragna of Zoroastrianism.[2] Boars' heads in pearl roundels rendered in stone, cave paintings, and textiles have been discovered in sites along the Silk Road, such as Bamiyan. In Xinjiang, two more samites with a boar's-head pattern have been unearthed. The earliest find was removed from Turfan by the archaeologist Sir Aurel Stein (1862–1943) and is preserved in the National Museum, New Delhi. The other find, now in the Uygur Museum, Xinjiang, and also from Turfan, is larger and woven with blue, yellow, and white silk. Compared with the two other pieces with a boar's-head pattern, the head in the present textile is quite appealing and was mistaken for that of a bear.[3] All three pieces are dated to the early Tang dynasty.

The term *Bosi jin* (Persian textiles) was recorded in several texts from Turfan. The earliest document, excavated from Tomb 173 and dated Zhanghe thirteenth year of the Gaochang kingdom (543), listed "ten pieces *[zhang]* of *Bosi jin*" among the burial items. A "Persian face cover" is mentioned in two later burial inventories, one that of an individual named Yuan Er, dated Yanshou tenth year (633), and the other for a certain Tang Chonghai (ca. 641) excavated from Tomb 15, Astana. It would appear that face covers were often made from Persian "textiles," which probably referred to samites with animals in pearl roundels.

ZF

1. Xinjiang bowuguan 1960.
2. Lukonin 1967: 177.
3. Xinjiang bowuguan chutu wenwu zhanlan xiaozu 1972.

238

Textile with confronted birds in pearl roundels

7th century
Woven silk (1:2 weft-faced compound twill, samite)
Warp 10¼ in. (26 cm); weft 6¾ in. (17 cm)
Excavated from Tomb 134 (dated 662), Astana, Turfan, Xinjiang Uygur Autonomous Region, 1969
Xinjiang Uygur Autonomous Region Museum

Excav. report in *Wenwu* 1972.1

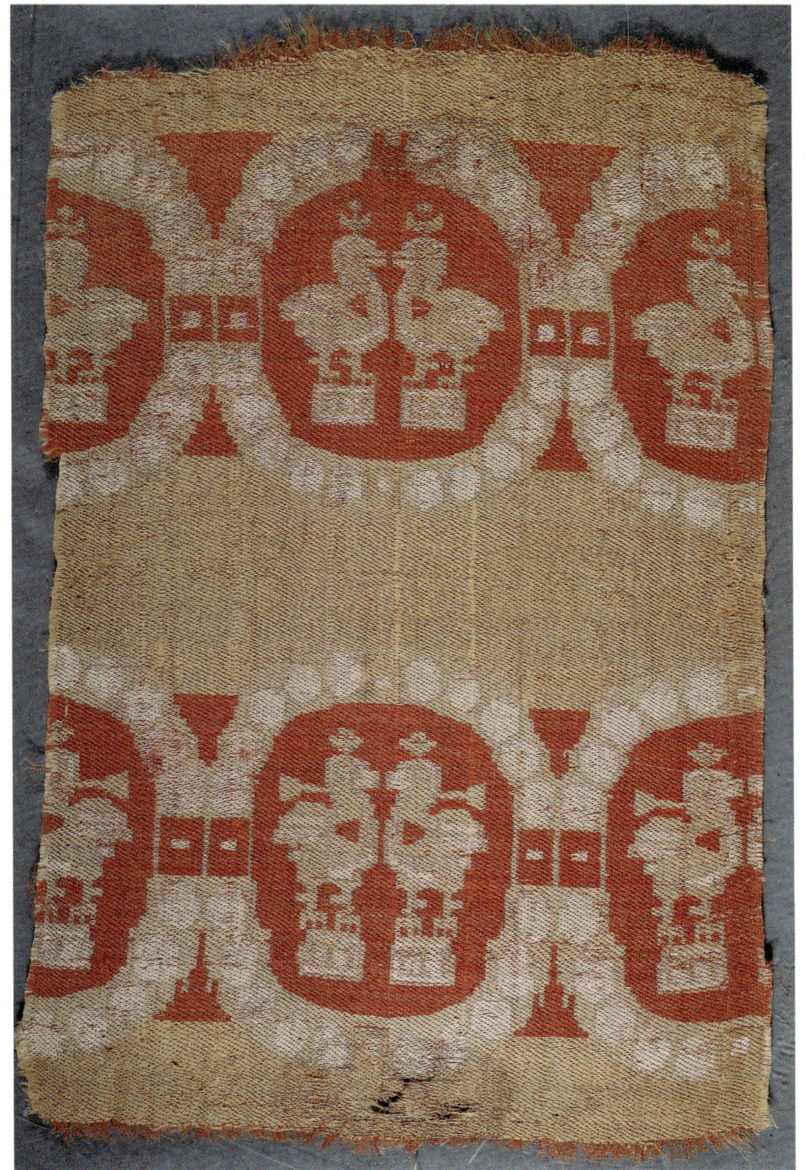

This samite from Turfan was originally used as a face cover. The surviving design shows two rows of roundels. Each roundel consists of a border of white pearls on a yellow ground and confronted yellow birds with details in white on a red ground. Distinctive from other avian motifs such as falcons or ribbon-holding birds, the fledgling cocks are depicted with simplicity and naïveté. They are crowned with crescents and stars and stand on a pearl platform. The patterns of the two rows are rendered differently. Most strikingly, the cocks in the lower row are decorated with ribbons around the neck, which are absent in the upper row. This difference in pattern demonstrates the special weaving method, which was popular in Central Asia.

The weaving technique, including z-twisted warps and samite weave (weft-faced compound twill), is unique to the Persian and Central Asian system. As in many textiles from West and Central Asia, the pattern repeats only in the weft direction but not in the warp direction. Although it is difficult to identify the repeat unit in most western samite textiles because they usually have large patterns and were cut into small pieces, the two rows of small roundels in this example provide a rare opportunity to judge the weaving system. The design of this samite shows that Persian textiles were woven from a patterning loom that could control the repeat only in the weft direction but not in the warp direction. This technique continued until about the tenth century in Central Asia and Europe.[1]

ZF

1. Zhao Feng 1999c: 94–99.

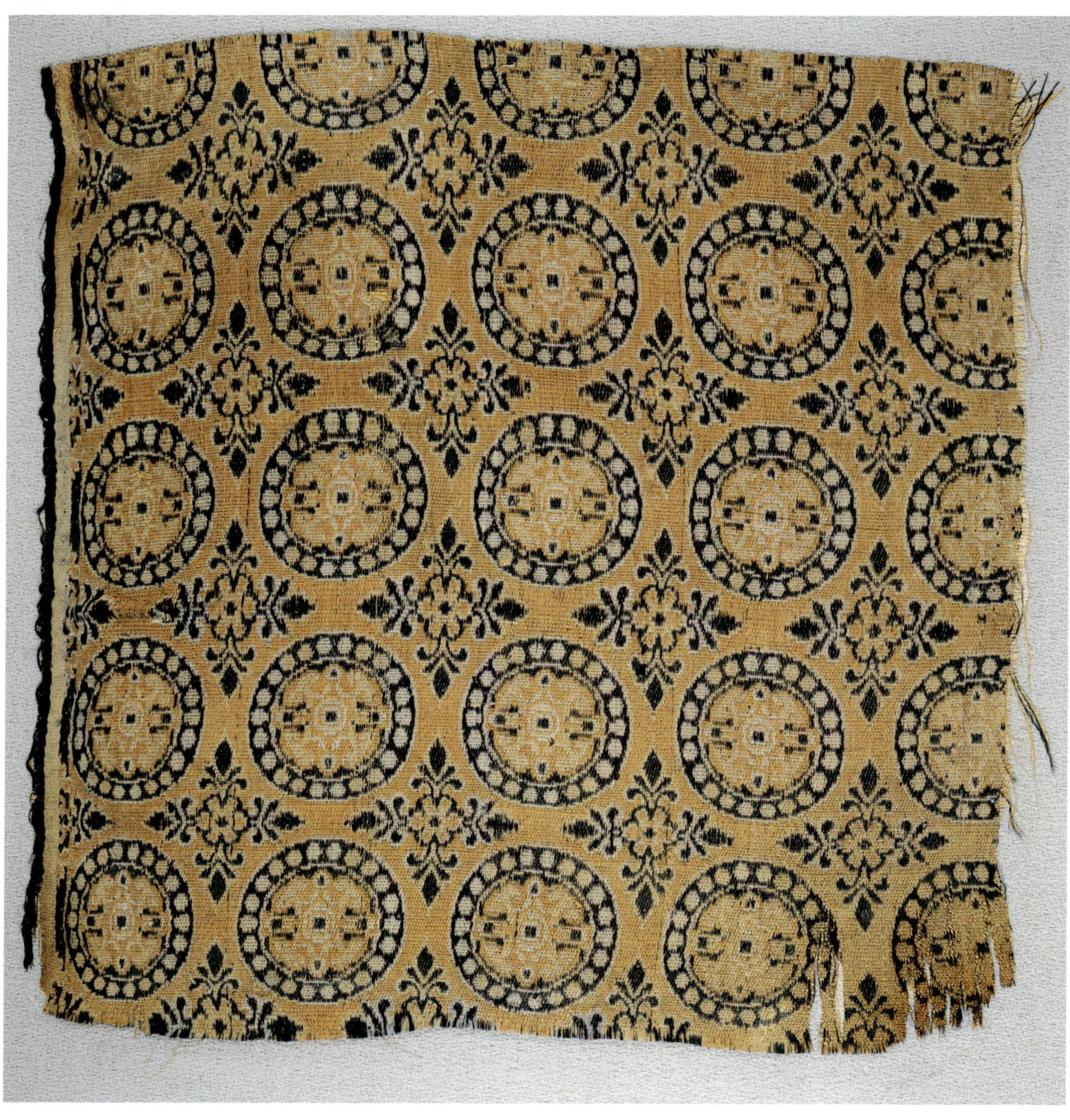

239

Textile with pearl roundels and palmettes

7th century
Woven silk (1:2 weft-faced compound twill)
Warp 7½ in. (19 cm); weft 7½ in. (19 cm)
Excavated from Tomb 211 (dated 653), Astana, Turfan, Xinjiang Uygur Autonomous Region, 1973
Xinjiang Uygur Autonomous Region Museum

REFERENCE: Wu Min 1984

Around the time of the Northern Dynasties, from the fifth to the sixth century, the pattern of the pearl roundel was introduced into central China. The original large pearl roundels with animal motifs, however, appeared only in regions with considerable foreign populations. It was the sinicized patterns, such as the small pearl roundels with rosettes, that became popular in China. Textiles with similar designs were found not only along the Silk Road but also in Chang'an (present-day Xi'an), the capital of the Sui (581–619) and the Tang (618–907) dynasties.

This piece employs the structure of warp-faced compound twill, a new technique developed during the early Tang that was based on warp-faced compound tabby. Yellow is used for the ground, blue for the ground of the pearls, and white for the pearls and for the inner borders of the rosettes. Blue four-directional palmettes outlined in white are woven outside the roundels. The pattern unit is rather small, allowing for eight repeats in one loom width. Significantly, the rosette is repeated in both the warp and weft directions, making this textile one of the earliest known with pattern repeats in both directions. The pattern repeats signaled the development of a real drawloom, a patterning loom that can control the pattern repeat in both the warp and the weft directions.

ZF

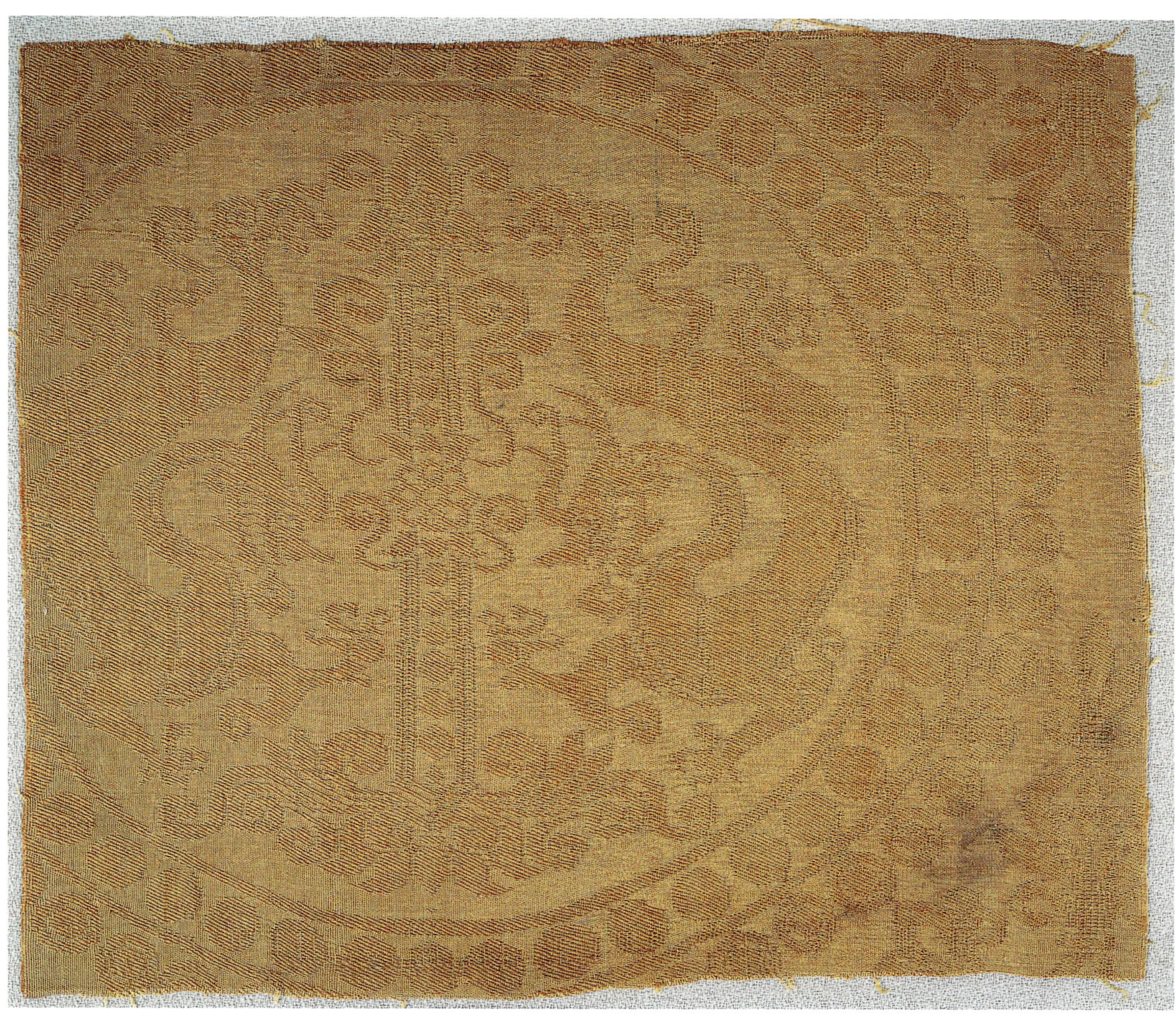

240

Textile with confronted dragons in pearl roundel

Early 8th century
Woven silk (damask of twill and tabby)
Warp 8¼ in. (21 cm); weft 9⅞ in. (25.1 cm)
Excavated from Tomb 221, Astana, Turfan, Xinjiang Uygur Autonomous Region, 1973
Xinjiang Uygur Autonomous Region Museum

Reference: Zhou Xuejun and Song Wenmin 1998, no. 53

The pattern of confronted dragons in a double-pearl roundel illustrates another development through which the western design of the pearl roundel became sinicized. This textile, from Turfan, Xinjiang, depicts a pair of dragons enclosed in a roundel bordered with double rings of pearls. Palmettes indicating the four directions embellish the areas outside the roundels. The dragons' powerful bodies are exaggeratedly contorted, with galloping front legs and upturned hind legs. The dragons are separated by a column of pearls decorated with a rosette in the middle and lotuses at the top and bottom. The pattern is oriented at right angles to the warp.

This design was usually woven in a damask twill pattern on a tabby ground. Another fragment from Turfan is inscribed on the back, "one bolt [*pi*] of silk damask [*ling*] for taxation from Shuangliu county, in the first year of the Jingyun reign [710]." The fragment, which is identified through the inscription as from Shuangliu, Sichuan, and dated to the year 710,[1] is consistent in style, date, and provenance with the Lingyang school of textiles, as recorded in contemporary documents.

Numerous textiles with similar designs have been discovered along the Silk Road, from Turfan in Xinjiang, Dulan in Qinghai, and sites in Russia. One is also preserved in the Shōsō-in, the eighth-century imperial repository in Nara, Japan.

A textile in The Metropolitan Museum of Art (1998.147) has a similar design but is woven in the structure of 4-end twill damask with pattern and ground differing in the direction of the twill. It is interesting to note that in this piece the dragons in the roundels are missing their heads, which suggests that the textile was produced in an area where the motif was not well understood. In other words, the characteristically Chinese motif was adopted in areas removed from central China and unfamiliar with the image of the dragon.[2]

ZF

1. Wu Min 1992: 134.
2. Zhao Feng 1999c: 140.

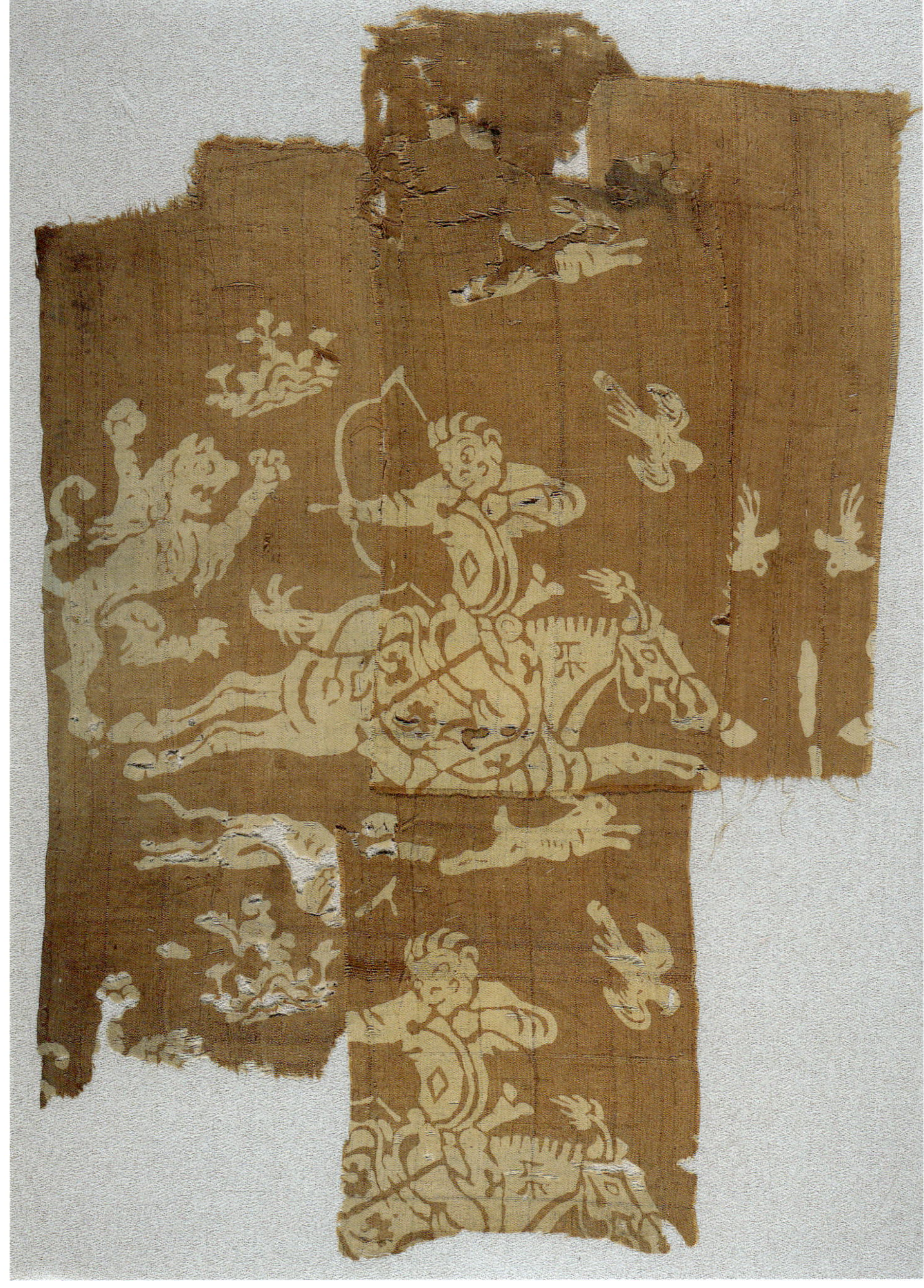

241
Textile with hunting scene

Late 7th–early 8th century
Resist-dyed silk tabby
Warp 16½ in. (41.9 cm); weft 11 ½ in. (29.2 cm)
Excavated from Tomb 191, Astana, Turfan, Xinjiang Uygur Autonomous Region, 1973
Xinjiang Uygur Autonomous Region Museum

Reference: Xinjiang Weiwu'er zizhiqu bowuguan 1991: 185, no. 61

In addition to weaving and embroidery, the dyeing of silk textiles developed rapidly during the Tang dynasty. Advanced dyeing techniques, the famous "four dyeings" of the Tang, encompass tie-dyeing, wax-resist dyeing, clamp-resist dyeing, and ash-resist dyeing. Many resist-dyed textiles have been found in Turfan, Xinjiang, including this resist-dyed silk fragment with a hunting scene.

This item was made from a silk tabby of light yellow color. It was folded in half in the warp direction and then clamped between two wooden blocks carved with the design. The blocks had holes for the application of a resist agent. After the resist agent was applied, the textile was removed from the blocks and put into a vat of red dye, resulting in a piece with the original light yellow color for the pattern and the dyed light red color as the background. The identity of the resist agent is yet to be determined. In the past, wax as well as some combination of ash and paste has been proposed as the resist agent, but, judging from the condition of the yellow resisted area, it is probably an alkaline-based material such as ash or lime.[1]

The design depicts a vibrant hunting scene. The rider, in a western-style robe with narrow sleeves and a wide collar, is shown shooting an arrow toward the lion at his back. Falcons and other birds are seen swooping in the sky; on the ground dogs chase rabbits; and a symbolic mountain with forest floats in the distance. On the horse's back is the Chinese character *fei* (flying), indicating an imperial breed. The hunting motif, which originated in Persia, appears on a large number of textiles discovered in northwestern China. A silk with lion hunters riding horses branded with the character *shan* (mountain) is preserved in the Shōsō-in imperial repository in Nara, Japan.[2]

ZF

1. Wu Min 1973.
2. Matsumoto, no. 38.

242

Textile with flowers and birds

Second half of 8th century
Woven silk (1:4 weft-faced compound twill, samite)
Warp 14⅜ in. (36.5cm), weft 9⅝ in. (24.4 cm)
Excavated from Tomb 48 (dated 778), Astana, Turfan, Xinjiang Uygur Autonomous Region, 1968
Xinjiang Uygur Autonomous Region Museum

Reference: Xinjiang Weiwu'er zizhiqu bowuguan 1991

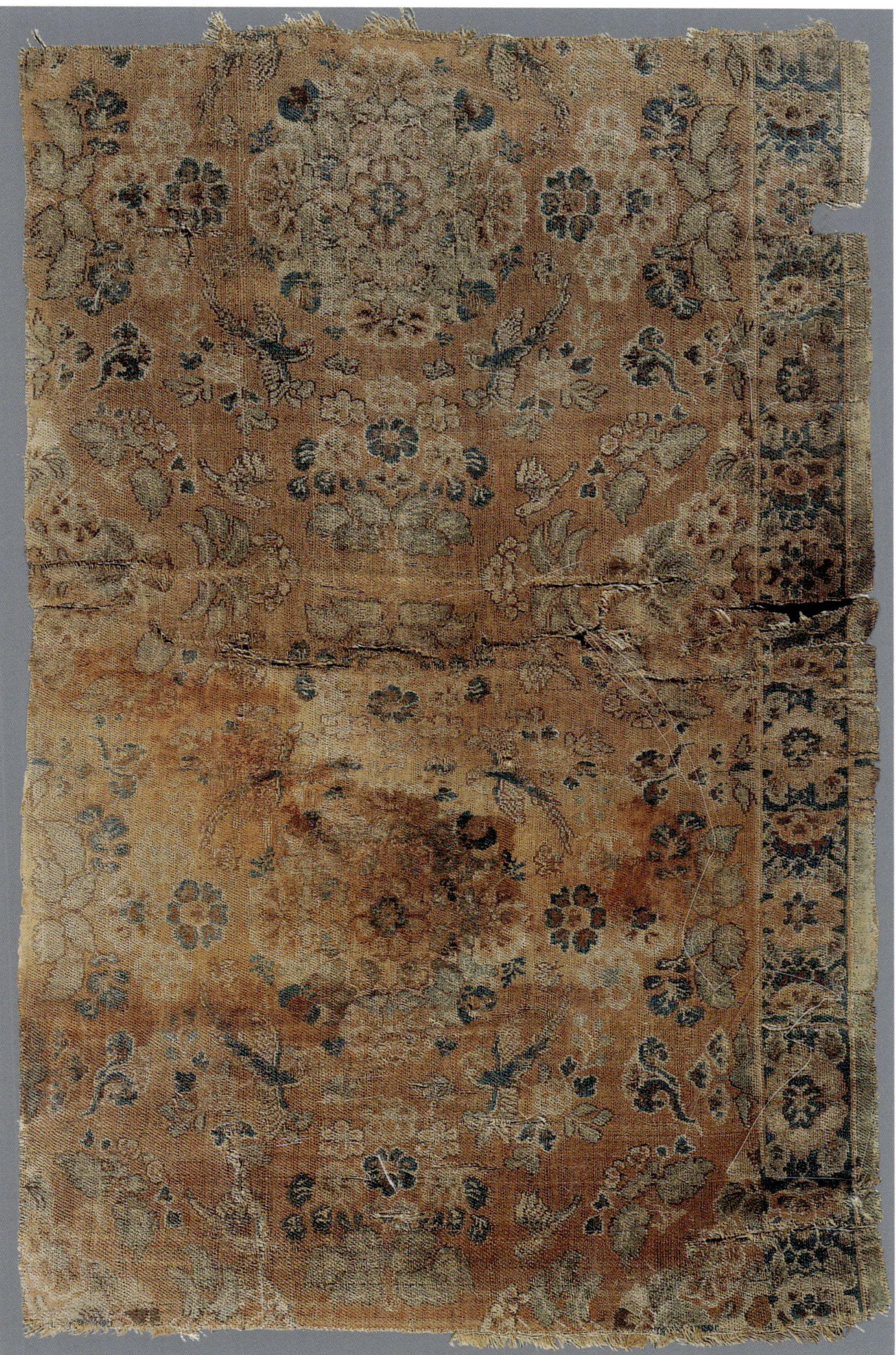

This samite silk was excavated from a mid-Tang tomb dated 778 in Turfan, Xinjiang. The red, pink, apple green, brown, and sea blue colors were very well preserved when first unearthed.[1] The floral medallion, composed of an eight-petaled rosette enclosed by eight small flowers alternating blue and red, is surrounded by four naturalistic flower sprays and four birds holding ribbons in their beaks. Eight butterflies among the birds and flowers complete a bustling spring scene.

The floral sprays popular during the mid- and late Tang dynasty reflect a change in taste toward naturalistic representation. The arrangement of birds and floral medallions in this piece is similar to that in a damask with running deer and floral medallions from Dulan, Qinghai, from the same period.[2] Another textile with a similar arrangement is preserved in the Shōsō-in imperial repository in Nara, Japan.[3]

In its fragmentary state, the present textile's pattern is incomplete. Nevertheless, information suggested by the pattern itself coupled with our knowledge of the width of woven silks of the Tang period provides a rationale for a reconstruction of the pattern. The roundels are symmetrical, but the vertical border stripe is not. This suggests that both the border stripe and the roundel are part of the same pattern and that the border occurs again in mirror image on the opposite side of the roundel. One group of roundel and borders adds up to a width of approximately 28 cm, about half the usual width of Tang textiles. Thus, in its original state, the textile probably consisted of four stripes and two roundels in one width.

Textiles with border stripes were unusual in China, but regularly produced in Central Asia, where the center and border sections were controlled by different patterning devices on the loom.[4] The design on the border stripes of this example, on the other hand, was not strictly symmetrical, indicating that only one set of patterning devices was used. While this samite obviously of Tang origin imitates the pattern arrangement of Central Asian textiles, its patterning technique belongs firmly to the Chinese weaving tradition.

ZF

1. Wu Min 1984: 70–80.
2. In the collection of the Qinghai Institute of Archeology, not yet published.
3. Matsumoto 1984: 41, fig. 30.
4. Otavsky 1998: 13–41. See, for example, a bordered textile in Liège Cathedral; ibid.: 207, fig. 107.

243
Embroidered sock

7th–8th century
Ankle: Woven silk (1:1 warp-faced compound twill)
Instep: Embroidered silk (split stitch on damask of twill and tabby)
Sole: Embroidered silk
Height 8⅞ in. (22.5 cm)
Length 10¾ in. (27.3 cm)
Excavated at Reshui, Dulan, Qinghai Province, 1983
Qinghai Institute of Archaeology

Reference: *Zhongguo wenwu jinghua 1997: 338*

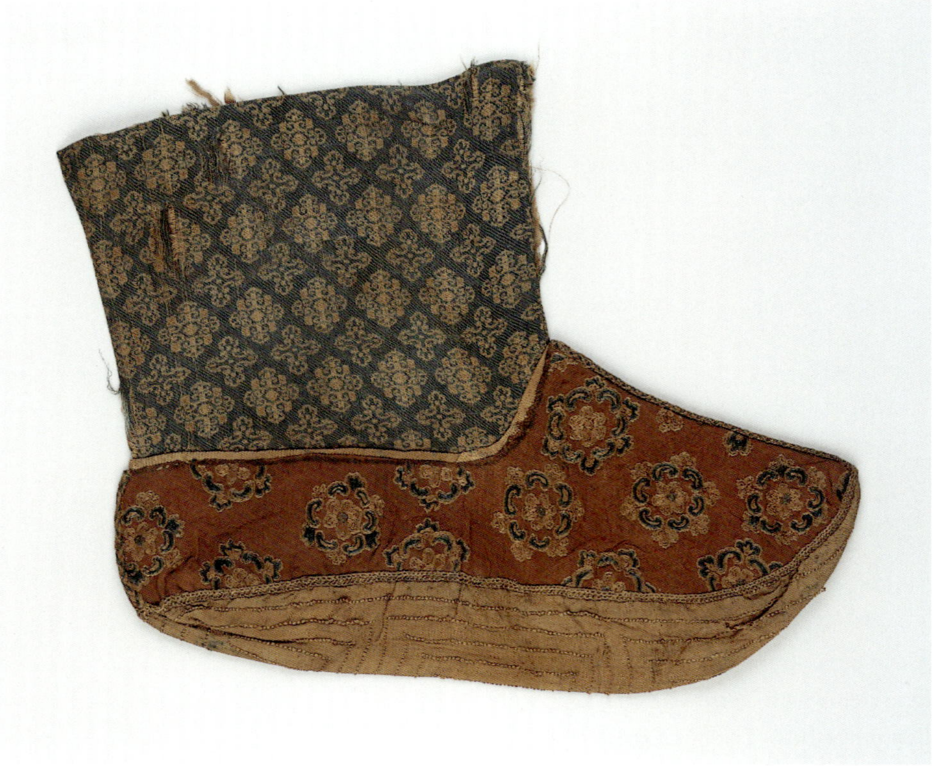

This well-preserved silk sock was excavated at the Reshui site in Dulan, Qinghai. It is made of three separate textiles with different designs. The only known sock of its kind dating to the Tang dynasty, it may have been worn indoors by the ethnic groups living in northwestern China. Twill *jin* silk (warp-faced compound twill) is used for the ankle. On the blue ground woven yellow floral patterns and four-directional palmettes are arranged in staggered rows, a popular design at that time. Similar *jin* silks with more elaborate color schemes have been found in Turfan, as well as in Dunhuang. For the instep, small floral medallions in blue, yellow, and green are embroidered in split stitch on a red damask with a pattern of checks. The floral medallions are hexagonal, with a six-petaled rosette in the center, a ring of six lobes in the middle, and an outer edge of six leaves. Each of the somewhat freely arranged floral units has a slightly different design. The sole is made of yellow damask, with a geometric pattern and lines of stitches that form embroidered rectangles. The three pieces—ankle, instep, and sole—are sewn together with yellow thread in a rarely used complex stitch that is related to needle looping.

ZF

244
Textile with woven Pahlavi inscription

8th century
Woven silk (1:4 weft-faced compound twill, samite)
Warp 3⅛ in. (8 cm); weft 11¼ in. (28.5 cm)
Excavated at Reshui, Dulan, Qinghai Province, 1983
Qinghai Institute of Archaeology

Reference: Xu Xinguo 1996

This textile, like the emboidered sock (cat. no. 243), was unearthed at Reshui, in Dulan, Qinghai. It was sewn into a flattened tubular shape with two sides. The pattern on the front is a stripe woven in red, yellow, blue, white, and green and patterned in heart shapes decorated with strings of pearls on both edges. On the back are woven characters in yellow against a red ground. The inscription—translated as "King of kings, the great and glorious"—has been identified as written in medieval

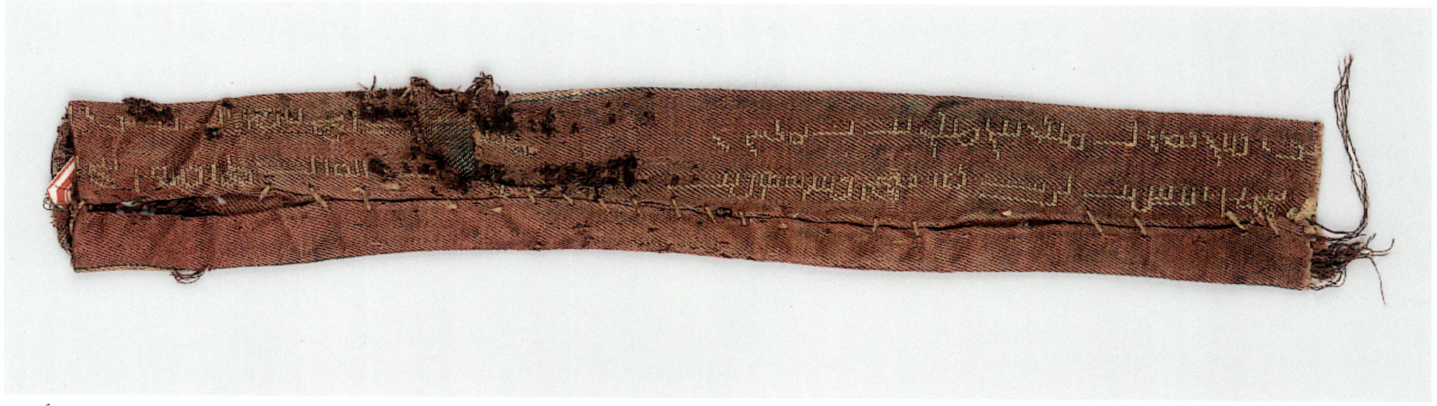

244, front

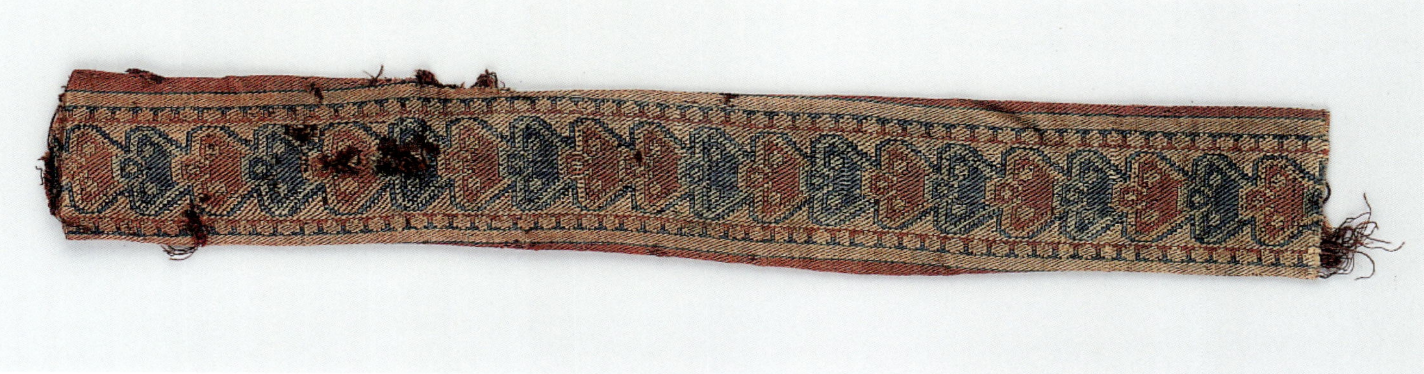

244, back

Persian Pahlavi, a script widely used during the Sasanian period (214–641). This piece can therefore be securely associated with the Persians.[1]

Stripes with decorative heart patterns and inscriptions usually functioned as the beginning or end of a weaving. A similar strip from Egypt, with heart motifs in the center flanked by strings of pearls, is instead inscribed in Arabic.[2] In general, one would expect the heart motif to correspond to the border design of the roundels in the main body of the textile. However, textiles with heart roundels have not been discovered among the Dulan finds. This fragment was therefore most likely joined to a samite with a pattern of birds holding ribbons, a great number of which were found in the same tomb (see illus. at right). Only fragments of those samites have survived.

A reconstruction of the pattern shows a bird in the center enclosed in an oval with a border of eight petals.[3] The bird has upward-curving wings, a brushlike tail, and feathers shaped like fish scales. The wings and tail are composed of horizontal and diagonal stripes. Standing on a platform decorated with linked pearls, the bird is adorned with a ribbon with linked pearls, and knotted streamers flutter from the back of its head. In its beak is a ribbon embellished with pearls, from which dangle three linked beads. Floral motifs frame the central design at the four corners of the textile, and buds grow in toward the center.[4]

Such textiles, with designs of birds holding ribbons in their beaks, are probably the *wucai niao* (five-colored silk with birds) referred to in the Dunhuang manuscripts. Presumably, they were produced by Persian-speaking Central Asian weavers.

ZF

1. Xu Xinguo 1996: 3–26.
2. Illustrated in *Senshoku no bi* (Textile Art) 29 (1984): 35. The textile is in the collection of the Victoria and Albert Museum, London.
3. Zhao Feng 1999c: 114.
4. Ibid.: 112–17.

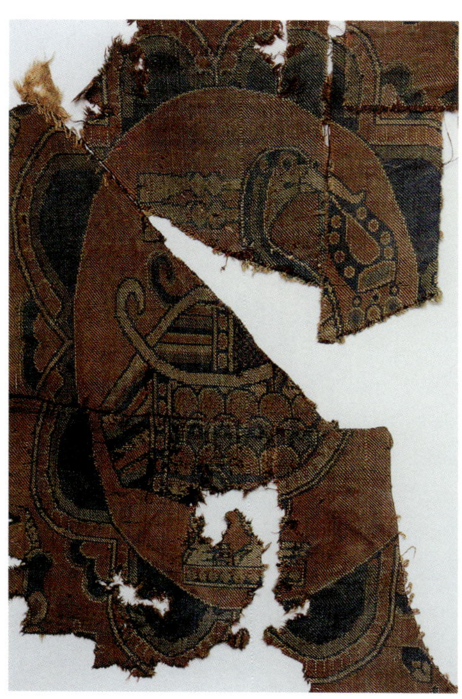

245
Textile with floral pattern

8th century
Tapestry-woven silk
Warp 10 in. (25.5 cm); weft 2¼ in. (5.5 cm)
Excavated at Reshui, Dulan, Qinghai Province, 1983
Qinghai Institute of Archaeology

Reference: Zhao feng 1999c: 132

Kesi, silk tapestry, is woven with one set of warps and discontinuous wefts of different colors. Instead of passing from selvedge to selvedge, the wefts are carried back and forth within one given color area, allowing for greater freedom in the use of colors in a simple tabby weave structure. Examples of *kesi* from the Tang dynasty have been discovered in Turfan, Xinjiang, as well as in Dulan, Qinghai. A piece from Turfan, which is long and narrow, was found in Dulan in the tomb of a man and his wife. The tomb tablet commemorates their deaths, which date to 633 and 688, respectively. The present blue-ground *kesi*, is from Dulan. The warp is undyed silk of 2-s ply, and the weft is polychrome z-twisted silks that are primarily green, yellow, and white. Eighteen warps and 40 to 60 wefts are woven per centimeter, with a rosette pattern unit of 4 cm in the warp and 2.8 cm in the weft direction. Slits in the weaving are used not only where the color changes but also within a single color area. The technique, which enhances the texture of the textile, derives from wool tapestry. It is characteristic of early *kesi* and clearly reveals the origin of this fragment.

ZF

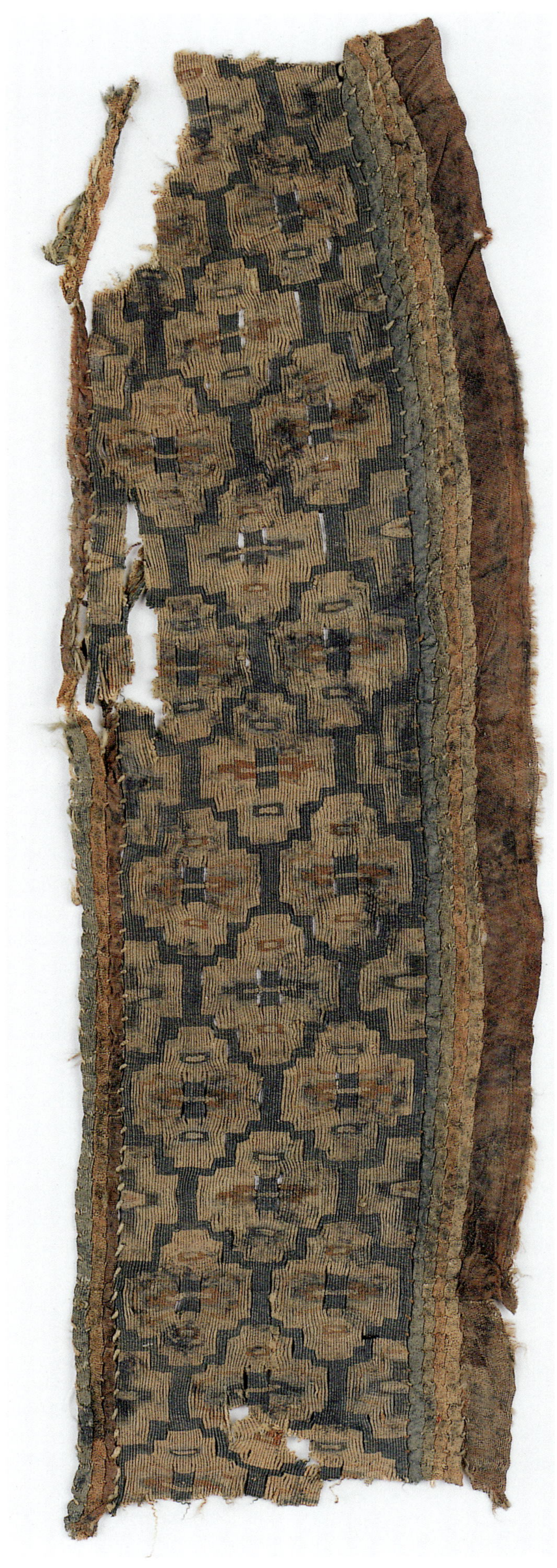

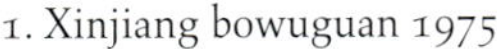

1. Xinjiang bowuguan 1975.

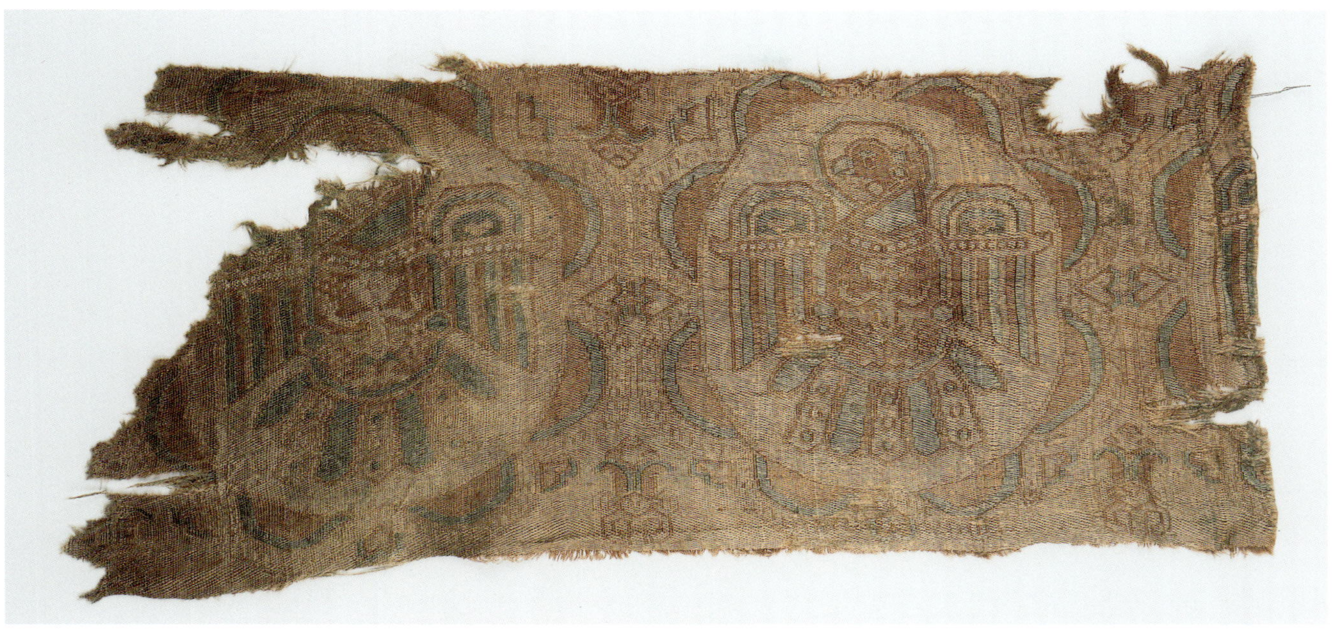

246
Textile with raptor in roundel

8th century
Woven silk (1:2 weft-faced compound twill, samite)
Warp 7 in. (18.1 cm); weft 19¼ in. (48.9 cm)
Excavated at Reshui, Dulan, Qinghai Province, 1983
Qinghai Institute of Archaeology

Reference: *Zhongguo wenwu jinghua* 1997: 338

The falcon is a popular motif in Central Asian art. Patterns with falcons and snakes are seen, for example, on wool textiles excavated in Yingpan, Xinjiang. Until the Tang dynasty (618–907), however, a large proportion of avian motifs on textiles are domesticated species such as birds holding ribbons, peacocks, and phoenixes. At present, there are only two known textiles from the Tang dynasty patterned with fierce birds. One is this piece, a samite with a *lingjiu*, or raptor, found at Reshui, in Dulan, Qinghai. The other is a samite with confronted raptors in medium-sized roundels excavated at Lusi, in Xiariha, Dulan.[1]

The raptor on the present example, depicted frontally, with wings outstretched and head turned to the left, is enclosed in a roundel with eight petals. The figural motif on its breast, seen in the pattern reconstruction (see illus. at right), is unusual. It may be related to a pattern found on a Sasanian plate in the State Hermitage Museum, Saint Petersburg, as well as on a later textile.[2] The weaving technique is different from that of the Sogdian group of Central Asia (cat. no. 237) but similar to that of textiles from farther west.[3] The distinction is related to the "weft order."[4] However, further research is needed before broad generalizations can be made about categorizing this textile and others.

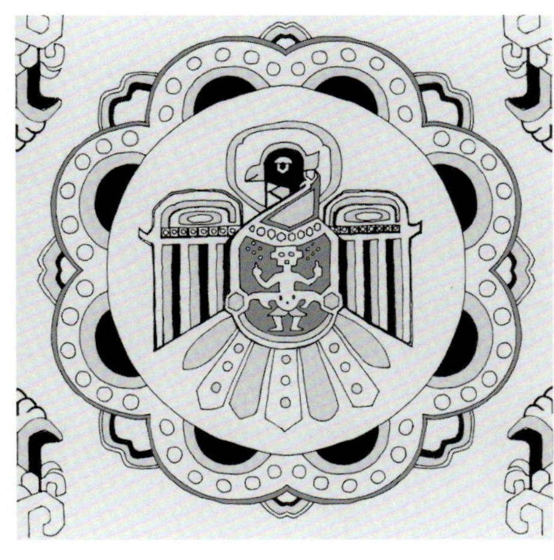

ZF

1. Zhao Feng 1999c: 118–19.
2. The pattern of the plate appears as a drawing in Pope and Ackerman 1964–65, vol. 2: 882, fig. 306; a photograph of the plate can be found in Trever and Lukonin 1987, no. 22. The pattern of the textile appears as a drawing in Pope and Ackerman 1964–65, vol. 5: 2014, fig. 649.
3. The textiles from farther west are often referred to as Byzantine. An example of the type can be found in Weibel 1952, no. 63.
3. The weft order of the present piece is 123321'

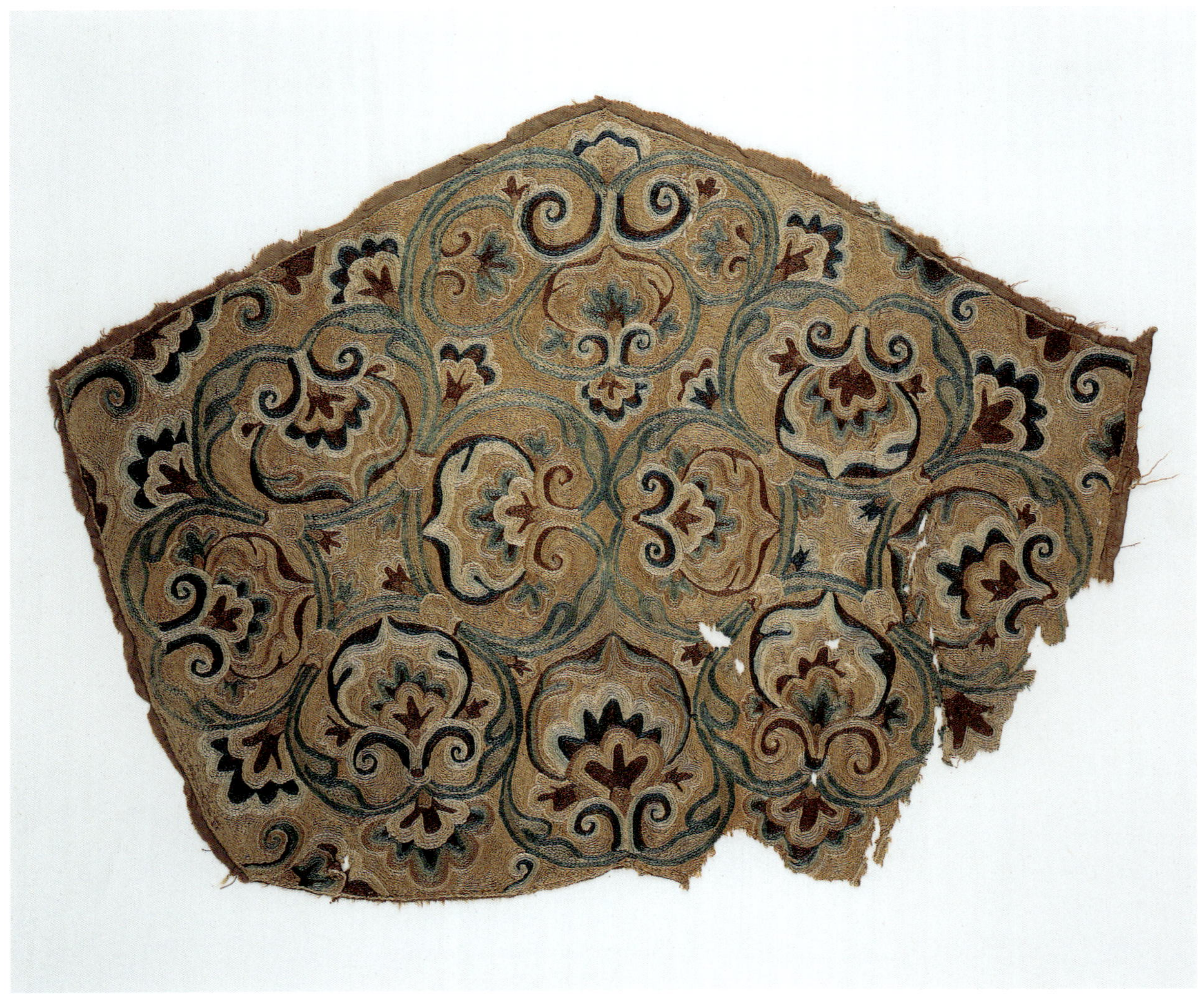

247
Saddle blanket with floral pattern

8th century
Embroided silk (split stitch on tabby)
13¾ x 19⅝ in. (34.9 x 49.8 cm)
Excavated at Reshui, Dulan, Qinghai Province, 1983
Qinghai Institute of Archaeology

Reference: Heller 1998

This fragmentary embroidery from the Reshui tomb in Dulan, Qinghai, was originally part of a saddle blanket, the cloth placed under the saddle to protect the body of the horse. White, brown, blue, and green 2-z ply silk threads, about 0.3 to 0.4 mm in diameter, are used to embroider the Tang-style floral scrolls in split stitch on yellow silk tabby. The floral motif is composed of four heart-shaped petals, each enclosing a bud and interconnected with one another to form a sumptuous design.

The Tang-style scroll has its origin in the vinelike motif of the Northern Dynasties (386–581). It can be found in many cave paintings and other art forms dating to the Tang dynasty and became extremely popular during the High Tang. While the present embroidery is the only known textile with a Tang-style scroll, similar designs can be seen on a lady's jacket in a Tang silk painting from Turfan,[1] as well as on a dyed box cover in the Shōsō-in, in Nara, Japan.[2]

ZF

1. Ma Chengyuan and Yue Feng 1998, no. 88.
2. Matsumoto 1984: 143.

BIBLIOGRAPHY OF WORKS CITED

INDEX

PHOTOGRAPH CREDITS

Bibliography of Works Cited

Compiled by Jean Wagner, with Chao-Hui Jenny Liu

Primary Sources

BQS *BeiQishu* 北齊書 (History of the Northern Qi). Li Baiyao 李百藥 (Tang) et al. Beijing: Zhonghua shuju, 1972.

BS *Beishi* 北史 (History of the Northern Dynasties). Li Yanshou 李延壽 (Tang) et al. Beijing: Zhonghua shuju, 1974.

CFYG *Cefu Yuangui* 冊府元龜 (Outstanding models from the storehouse of literature.) Compiled by Wang Qinruo 王欽若 (1005–13) et al. Beijing: Zhonghua shuju, 1989.

CS *Chenshu* 陳書 (History of the Chen; appended with concordance). Compiled by Yao Chai 姚察 (Sui) and Yao Silian 姚思廉 (Tang) et al. Beijing: Zhonghua shuju, 1972 ed., reprint, 1982.

DTLD *Datang liudian* 大唐六典 (The six administrative divisions and institutions of the great Tang). 30 chapters. By Li Longji 李隆基 (Tang) et al. Xi'an: Santai, 1991.

DTX *Da Tang xiyuji* 大唐西域記 (Record of travels in the western regions during the Great Tang dynasty). Xuan Zhuang 玄奘 (602–664), vol. 12. Xi'an: Shaanxi People's Publishing House, 1985.

GSZ *Gao seng zhuan* 高僧傳 (Lives of eminent monks). Compiled by Shi Huijiao 釋慧皎 (497–554) et al. Beijing: Zhonghua shuju, 1992 ed., reprint, 1997.

HHS *Hou Hanshu* 後漢書 (History of the Later Han). By Fan Ye 范曄 (398–445) et al. Beijing: Zhonghua shuju, 1979.

HNZ *Huai Nanzi* 淮南子. In *Zhuzi ji cheng* 諸子集成. Shijiazhuang Shi : Hebei renmin chubanshe chuban faxing, 1935 ed., reprint, 1992.

HS *Hanshu* 漢書 (History of the Former Han). Ban Gu 班固 (32–92 A.D.); punctuated by Yan Shigu 顏師古 (Tang). Beijing: Zhonghua shuju, 1962 ed., reprint, 1983.

JS *Jinshu* 晉書 (History of the Jin; 644 A.D.). Compiled by Fang Xuanling 房玄齡. Beijing: Zhonghua shuju, 1974.

JSC *Jinshi cuibian* 金石萃編 (Essential collection of bronze and stone inscriptions). Compiled by Wang Chang 王昶 (1725–1806) et al. In Guojia tushuguan shanben jinshi zu, eds., *Lidai shike shiliao huibian* 歷代石刻史料匯編. Beijing: Beijing tushuguan chubanshe, 2000.

JTS *JiuTangshu* 舊唐書 (Former Book of the Tang). Compiled by Liu Xu 劉昫 (945) et al. Beijing: Zhonghua shuju, 1975 edition, 1986 reprint.

LH *Lun heng* 論衡 (The Balanced Inquiries). Wang Chong 王充 (A.D. 27–c. 100). Reprinted. Shanghai: Shanghai Renmin Chubanshe, 1974.

LMJ *Lidai minghua ji* 歷代名畫記 (Record of Famous Paintings in Successive Dynasties). Zhang Yanyuan 張彥遠 (Tang). Beijing: Renmin chubanshe, 1983. Also *Huashi Congshu*, 1963.

LNZ *Lie nü zhuan yi zhu* 列女傳譯注 (The annotated Biographies of virtuous women). Compiled by Liu Xiang 劉向 (77–6 B.C.) et al. Ji'nan: Shandong Daxue chubanshe, 1990.

LQJ *Luoyang qielan ji jiaozhu* 洛陽伽藍記校注 (Record of the monasteries of Luoyang). Yang Yuanzhi 楊衒之 (active 5th century). Annotated by Fan Xiangyong 范祥雍 et al. Shanghai: Shanghai guji chubanshe, 1978.

LS *Liangshu* 梁書 (History of the Liang). Yao Silian 姚思廉. Beijing: Zhonghua shuju. 1973 ed., reprint, 1984.

LXZ *Lie xian zhuan jiao jian* 列仙傳 (Biographies of various immortals). Liu Xiang 劉向 (ca. 77–6 B.C.) et al. Taipei: Zhongyang yanjiuyuan Zhongguo wenzhe yanjiusuo choubeichu, 1995.

NQS *NanQishu* 南齊書 (History of the Southern Qi). Xiao Zixian 蕭子顯 (489–537) et al. Beijing: Zhonghua shuju, 1972.

NS *Nanshi* 南史 (History of the Southern Dynasties). 80 chapters. Compiled by Li Yanshou 李延壽 (Tang) et al. Beijing: Zhonghua shuju, 1995.

QTS *Quan Tangshi* 全唐詩 (The complete poetry of the Tang dynasty). Compiled by Wang Quan 王全 et al. Beijing: Zhonghua shuju, 1960.

QTW *Quan Tangwen* 全唐文 (The complete prose of the Tang dynasty). Edited by Dong Gao 董誥 et al. Beijing: Zhonghua shuju, 1982.

SS *Songshu* 宋書 (History of the Song). Shen Yue 沈約 (Liang) et al. Beijing: Zhonghua shuju, 1974 ed., reprint, 1983.

SSXY *Shishuo xinyu* 世說新語 (A new account of Tales of the World). Liu Yiqin 劉義慶 (403–444). 2 vols. Reprint of 1891 ed. Shanghai: Shanghai guji chubanshe, 1982.

SuS *Suishu* 隋書 (History of the Sui). Wei Zhen 魏徵 et al. (Tang). Beijing: Zhonghua shuju, 1973.

TD *Tong dian* 通典 (A compendium of institutions). Du You 杜佑 (Tang) et al. Beijing: Zhonghua shuju, 1988.

TDZJ *Tang da zhaoling ji* 唐大詔令集 (Imperial edicts of the great Tang). 130 chapters. Song Minqiu 宋敏求 (1019–1079) et al. Beijing: Shangwu yinshuguan, 1959.

THY *Tang huiyao* 唐會要 (Tang compendium of the essential statutes). Compiled by Wang Pu 王溥 (Song) et al. Beijing: Zhonghua shuju, 1998.

TJS *Tuhua jian wen zhi* 圖畫見聞誌 (Experiences in painting). Compiled by Guo Ruoxu 郭若虛. Congshu jicheng chu bian (1648). Beijing: Zhonghua shuju, 1985.

TPYL *Taiping yulan* 太平御覽 (Imperial digest of the Taiping reign period). Compiled by Li Fang 李昉 (925–996) et al. Shanghai: Shangwu yinshuguan, 1935; reprint, Beijing: Zhonghua shuju, 1960.

WS *WeiShu* 魏書 (History of the Wei). Wei Shou 魏收 (505–572) et al. Beijing: Zhonghua shuju, 1974.

WX *Wen xuan* 文選 (Literary selections). Compiled by Xiao Tong 蕭統 (501–531). Beijing: Zhonghua shuju, 1983.

XTS *Xin Tangshu* 新唐書 (New history of the Tang; 1043–60). Compiled by Ouyang Xiu 歐陽修 et al. Beijing: Zhonghua shuju, 1975 ed., reprint, 1986.

YWLJ *Yiwen leiju* 藝文類聚 (A categorized collection of literary writing). Compiled by Ouyang Xun 歐陽詢 et al. Beijing: Xinhua shudian Shanghai faxing suo, 1965.

YYZZ *Youyang zazu* 酉陽雜俎 (Miscellaneous Notes of Youyang). Duan Chengshi 段成式 Beijing: Zhonghua shuju, 1955; reprint, ed., Taipei: Taiwan shangwu yinshuguan, 1983.

YZJ *Ye zhongji Jinji jiben* 鄴中記 晉紀輯本 (Records of Ye city; Jin edition). Lu Hui 劉翽 (4th century). Shanghai: Shangwu Yinshuguan, 1937.

ZS *Zhoushu* 周書 (History of the Zhou). By Linhu Defen 令狐德棻 (Tang) et al. Beijing, Zhonghua shuju, 1971 ed., reprint, 1983.

ZZTJ *Zizhi tongjian* 資治通鑑 (Comprehensive mirror for aid in government). By Sima Guang 司馬光 (1019–1086) et al. Beijing: Guji chubanshe, 1956.

SECONDARY SOURCES

Abe, Stanley K.
2002 *Ordinary Images*. Chicago: University of Chicago Press.

Acker, William R. B., trans. and ed.
1954 *Some T'ang and pre-T'ang Texts on Chinese Painting*. Vol. 1. Sinica Leidensia, vol. 8. Leiden: E. J. Brill.

Alexander, Christine
1928 *Jewelry: The Art of the Goldsmith in Classical Times as Illustrated in the Museum Collection*. New York: The Metropolitan Museum of Art.

Allchin, F. Raymond, and Norman Hammond, eds.
1978 *The Archaeology of Afghanistan from Earliest Times to the Timurid Period*. London: Academic Press.

Alram, Michael
2001 "Coins and the Silk Road." In *Monks and Merchants: Silk Road Treasures from Northwest China, Gansu, and Ningxia Provinces, 4th–7th Century*, edited by Annette L. Juliano and Judith A. Lerner: 282–85. New York: Harry N. Abrams with the Asia Society.

Ambroz, Anatolii K.
1981 "Vostoznoevropeiskie i sredneaziatskie stepi V-pervoi poloviny VIII v." (East European and Middle Asian Steppe in the 5th to the first half of the 8th centuries). In *Stepi Evrazii v epokhu srednevekov'ia* (Eurasian Steppes during the Middle Ages), edited by Svetlana A. Pletneva: 10–23. Moscow.

An Jiayao 安家瑤
1983 "莫高窟壁畫上的玻璃器皿" (Images of glassware in the mural paintings of the Mogao Grottoes). In *Dunhuang Tulufan wenxian yanjiu lunji* 敦煌吐魯番文獻研究論集 (Anthology of studies of Dunhuang and Tulufan): 425–64. Beijing: Beijing Daxue chubanshe.

1986a "北周李賢墓出土的玻璃碗–薩珊玻璃器的發現與研究" (The glass bowl excavated from the tomb of Li Xian of the Northern Zhou period: The discovery and study of a Sassanian glass). *Kaogu* 考古, no. 2: 173–81.

1986b "我國古代玻璃研究中的幾個問題" (Some issues in studies of ancient Chinese glassware). In *Zhongguo kaoguxue yanjiu* 中國考古學研究 (Chinese archaeology studies): 337–45. Beijing: Wenwu chubanshe.

1986c 《鎮江文物精華》筆談 – 玻璃器 (Remarks on essential cultural relics of Zhenjiang: Glassware). *Zhongguo lishi bowuguan guankan*, no. 9: 28–29.

1987 *Early Chinese Glassware*. Translated by Mathew Henderson. Oriental Ceramic Society Translations, no. 12. Hong Kong: Millennia.

1990 "試探中國近年出土的伊斯蘭早期玻璃器" (On early Islamic glassware recently unearthed in China). *Kaogu*, no. 12: 1116–26.

1991 "Dated Islamic Glass in China." *Bulletin of the Asia Institute*, n.s., 5: 123–37.

1993a "中國古代玻璃與日本吉野的玻璃管飾" (Glass eye-bead decoration of ancient China and Yoshinoga ri of Japan). In *Zhongguo kaogu xueluncong* 中國考古學論叢 (Anthology of Chinese archaeology studies): 415–21. Beijing: Kexue chubanshe.

1993b "陳國公主與駙馬合葬墓出土的玻璃器皿及其問題" (Issues related to the glassware found in the tomb of Princess Chen and her husband). In *Liao Chen Guo gongzhu mu* 遼陳國公主墓 (Princess Chen's tomb of the Liao): 179–86. Beijing: Wenwu chubanshe.

1996 "環嵌玻璃珠的傳入及發展" (Glass eye beads in China). In *Shi shiji qian de sichou zhi lu he dong xi wenhua jiaoliu* 十世紀前的絲綢之路和東西文化交流 (Land routes of the Silk Road and cultural exchanges between the East and West before the 10th century): 351–68. Beijing: New World Press.

An Yingxin 安英新
1999 "新疆伊犁昭蘇縣古墓葬出土金銀器等珍貴文物" (Gold and silver vessels and other precious relics excavated from ancient tombs in Zhaosu County, Yili, Xinjiang Province). *Wenwu*, no. 9: 4–15.

André, Guilhem
2002 "Une tombe princière Xion Gnu à Gol Mod, Mongolie (campaignes des fouilles, 2000–2001)." *Arts asiatiques* 57: 194–205.

Anonymous
1972 "大同南郊北魏遺址" (The Northern Wei site in the southern suburbs of Datong). *Wenwu*, no. 1: 83–87.

Antichnye gosudarstva Severnogo Prichernomor'ia
1984 *Antichnye gosudarstva Severnogo Prichernomor'ia* (Archaeology of the U.S.S.R.: Ancient states along the north shore of the Black Sea). Edited by Gennadii Andreevich Koshelenko, Irina Timofeevna Kruglikova, and V. S. Dolgorukov; contributions by Ekaterina Mikhailovna Alekseeva et al. Arkheologiia SSSR. Moscow: Nauka.

Anwei sheng wenwu kaogu yanjiusuo 安徽省文物考古研究所 (Anwei Institute of Archaeology)
1986 "安徽馬鞍山東吳朱然墓發掘簡報" (Bulletin on the excavation of the Zhu Ran tomb of the Eastern Wu in Ma'an Mountain, Anwei Province). *Wenwu*, no. 3: 1–15.

Aohanqi wenhuaguan 敖漢旗文化館 (Aohan Banner Cultural Center, Liaoning Province)
1978 "敖漢旗李家營子出土的金銀器" (Gold and silver vessels discovered at Lijia yingzi in Ao-han Banner, Liaoning Province). *Kaogu*, no. 2: 117–18.

Apakidze, A. M., et al.
1958 *Mtskheta: Itogi arkheologicheskikh issledovanii.* Vol. 1, *Arkheologicheskie pamiatniki Armazis-Khevi po raskopkam, 1937–1946 gg.* Tbilisi: Izd-vo Akademii Nauk Gruzinskoi SSR.

Arbore-Popescu, Grigore, Chiara Silvi Antonini, and Karl Baipakov, eds.
1998 *L'uomo d'oro: La cultura delle steppe del Kazakhstan dall'età del bronzo alle grandi migrazioni.* Exh. cat. Mantua: Palazzo Te; Milan: Electa.

Aruz, Joan, et al.
2003 *Art of the First Cities: The Third Millennium B.C. from the Mediterranean to the Indus.* Exh. cat. New York: The Metropolitan Museum of Art.

Azarpay, Guitty
1969 "Nine Inscribed Choresmian Bowls." *Artibus Asiae* 31: 185–203.

1976 "Some Iranian Iconographic Formulae in Sogdian Painting." *Iranica antiqua* 9: 168–77.

1980 *Sogdian Painting: The Pictorial Epic in Oriental Art.* Contributions by A. M. Belenitskii, Boris I. Marshak, and Mark J. Dresden. Berkeley and Los Angeles: University of California Press.

Bader, O. N., and A. P. Smirnov
1954 *"Serebro Zakamskoe" pervykh vekov nashei ery: Bartymskoe mestonakhozhdenie"* (Silver from the lands beyond the Kama River of the first centuries C.E.: The Bartym site). Moscow.

Bagley, Robert, ed.
2001 *Ancient Sichuan: Treasures from a Lost Civilization.* Seattle: Seattle Art Museum; Princeton: Princeton University Press.

Bai Ying 白英
1992 "南朝劉宋時期的陶女俑" (A pottery figure of a woman from the Liu Song era of the Southern Dynasties). In *Nanjing Bowuyuan cang baolu* 南京博物院藏寶錄 (Treasures from the Nanjing Museum) 122–23. Hong Kong: Sanlian Publishing.

Baker, Janet
1999 "Sui and Early Tang Period Images of the Heavenly King in Tombs and Temples." *Orientations* 30, no. 4 (April): 53–57.

Baratte, François
1996 "Dionysus en Chine: Remarques à propos de la coupe en argent de Beitan." *Arts asiatiques* 51: 142–47.

Belenitskii, Aleksandr
1968 *Central Asia.* Translated by James Hogarth. Archaeologia mundi. Cleveland: World Publishing Co.

1980 *Mittelasien: Kunst der Sogden.* Translated by Lisa Schirmer. Leipzig: Seemann.

Belting, Hans
1994 *Likeness and Presence: A History of the Image before the Era of Art.* Translated by Edmund Jephcott. Chicago: University of Chicago Press.

Berdimuratov, A. E., and M. K. Samibaev
1999 *The Temple of Jartepa-II (the Problems of the Cultural Life of Sogdiana in the 4th–8th c. A. D.).* Tashkent.

Berger, Patricia, and Jennifer Randolph Casler
1994 *Tomb Treasures from China: The Buried Art of Ancient Xi'an.* Exh. cat. San Francisco: Asian Art Museum of San Francisco; Fort Worth: Kimbell Art Museum.

Berthier, François
1991 "Le voyage des motifs, II. La lune, le soleil et le feu." *Arts asiatiques* 46: 111–21.

Bingham, Woodbridge
1941 *The Founding of the T'ang Dynasty: The Fall of Sui and Rise of T'ang. A Preliminary Survey.* Baltimore: Waverly Press.

Blair, Dorothy
1973 *A History of Glass in Japan.* Tokyo: Kodansha International; Corning, N.Y.: Corning Museum of Glass.

Blum, Dilys E.
1997 *The Fine Art of Textiles: The Collections of the Philadelphia Museum of Art.* Philadelphia: Philadelphia Museum of Art.

Bo Xiaoying 薄小瑩
1992 "吐魯番地區發現的聯珠紋織品" (Textile of roundel designs found in the Tulufan area). In *Tulufan gu muzang chutu yishupin* 吐魯番古墓葬出土藝術品 (Art works found in the ancient tombs in Tulufan): 147–76. Urumchi: Xinjiang meishu sheying chubanshe.

Boardman, John
1994 *The Diffusion of Classic Art in Antiquity.* Bollingen Series, XXXV, 42. Princeton: Princeton University Press.

Bobrinskoi, A.A.
1914 "Pereshchepinskii klad" (The Pereshchepino treasure). *Materialy po arkheologii Rossii* (Petrograd) 34: 111–20.

Bol'shakov, Oleg G.
2001 *Srednevekovyi gorod Blizhnego Vostoka, VII–seredina XIII v.* (Medieval cities of the Near East, 7th–mid-13th centuries). Moscow: Vostochnaia Literatura.

Borisov, Andrei Ia., and Vladimir G. Lukonin
1963 *Sasanidskie gemmy* (Sasanian gems). Leningrad: Hermitage.

von Bothmer, Dietrich, ed.
1990 *Glories of the Past: Ancient Art from the Shelby White and Leon Levy Collection.* Exh. cat. New York: The Metropolitan Museum of Art.

British Museum
1993 "Review of Acquisitions 1963–70 of Western Asiatic Antiquities (2)." *British Museum Quarterly* 37.

Brunner, Christopher J.
1978 *Sasanian Stamp Seals in the Metropolitan Museum of Art.* New York: The Metropolitan Museum of Art.

Bunker, Emma C.
2002 *Nomadic Art of the Eastern Eurasian Steppes: The Eugene V. Thaw and Other New York Collections.* Contributions by James C. Y. Watt and Zhixin Sun. Exh. cat. New York: The Metropolitan Museum of Art.

Bunker, Emma C., with Trudy S. Kawami, Katheryn M. Linduff, and Wu En
1997 *Ancient Bronzes of the Eastern Eurasian Steppes from the Arthur M. Sackler Collections.* New York: The Arthur M. Sackler Foundation.

Burnham, Dorothy K.
1980 *Warp and Weft: A Textile Terminology.* Toronto: Royal Ontario Museum.

Burnham, Harold B.
1965 "Technical Aspects of the Warp-Faced Compound Tabbies of the Han Dynasty." *Bulletin de Liaison du Centre International d'Étude des Textiles Anciens,* no. 22 (July): 25–45.

Bush, Susan

1975a "Thunder Monsters and Wind Spirits in Early Sixth Century China and the Epitaph Tablet of Lady Yuan." *Boston Museum Bulletin* 72, no. 367: 24–55.

1975b "Thunder Monsters, Auspicious Animals and Floral Imagery in Early Sixth-Century China." *Ars Orientalis* 10: 19–34.

1976 "Floral Motifs and Vine Scrolls in Chinese Art of the Late Fifth to Early Sixth Centuries, A.D." *Artibus Asiae* 38, no. 1: 40–83.

Cadonna, Alfredo, and Lionello Lanciotti

1996 *Cina e Iran: Da Alessandro Magno alla dinastia Tang.* Orientalia venetiana, 5. Florence: Olschki.

Callieri, Pierfrancesco

1997 *Seals and Sealing from the North-West of the Indian Subcontinent and Afghanistan (4th century B.C.–11th century A.D.): Local, Indian, Sasanian, Greco-Persian, Sogdian Roman.* With contributions by Elizabeth Errington, Ricardo Garbini, Philippe Gignoux, Nicholas Sims-Williams, Wladimir Zwalf. Naples.

2002 "The Bactrian Seal of Khingula." *Silk Road Art and Archaeology* 8: 121–41.

Cammann, Schuyler.

1953 "The Lion and Grape Patterns on Chinese Bronze Mirrors." *Artibus Asiae* 16, no. 3: 265–91.

Cao Guicen 曹桂岑

1983 "郾城縣彼岸寺石幢" (The Stone Tower in Bi'an Temple of Yancheng County). *Zhongyuan wenwu,* no. 4: 25–28.

Carpino, Alexandra, and Jean M. James

1989 "Commentary on the Li Xian Silver Ewer." *Bulletin of the Asia Institute,* n.s., 3: 71–76.

Carter, Martha L.

1974 "Royal Festal Themes in Sasanian Metalwork." *Acta Iranica* 1: 171–202.

1990 *The Mystery of the Udayana Buddha.* Naples: Istituto Universitario Orientale.

1995a "The Ancient Orient Museum." *Bulletin of the Asia Institute* 9: 229–38.

1995b "A Note on Metalwork from the Hellenistic East." *Bulletin of the Asia Institute,* n.s., 9: 257–66.

2002 "Notes on Two Chinese Stone Funerary Bed Bases with Zoroastrian Symbolism." In *Iran: Questions et connaissances; actes du IVe Congrès européen des études iraniennes, 6–10 septembre 1999,* vol. 1, *La période ancienne,* edited by Philip Huyse: 263–87. Paris.

Caswell, James O.

1988 *Written and Unwritten: A New History of the Buddhist Caves at Yungang.* Vancouver: University of British Columbia Press.

Cen Jiawu 岑家梧

1949 *Zhongguo yishu lunji* 中國藝術論集 (Collected essays on Chinese art). Beijing: Qinghua Printing House.

Cen Rui 岑蕊

1990 "試論東漢魏晉墓葬中的多面金珠用途及其源流" (On the use and origin of multi-faceted gold beads found in tombs of the Eastern Han and Wei-Jin dynasties). *Kaogu yu wenwu,* no. 3: 85–87.

Chang Yimin 常一民

2003 "彩繪的排場" (The extravagance of color). *Wenwu tian di,* no. 1: 1–5.

Chen Dawei 陳大為

1960 "遼寧房身村晉墓發掘簡報" (Excavation bulletin on the Jin tombs of Fangshen village, Beipiao, Liaoning). *Kaogu,* no. 1: 24–26.

Chen, Jinhua

2002 "*Sarira* and Scepter: Empress Wu's Political Use of Buddhist Relics." *Journal of the International Association of Buddhist Studies* 25, no. 102: 33–149.

Chen Liangwei 陳良偉

1988 "試論西域冶鑄文明的起源" (A preliminary study of the origin of smelting and casting in western regions). *Xinjiang wenwu,* no. 1: 58–67.

1989 "試論西域石刻人像的起源及其相關問題" (On the origin of stone figures in western regions and some related issues). *Xinjiang wenwu,* no. 4: 64–72.

Chen Mengjia 陳夢家, Zhongguo kexueyuan kaogu yanjiusuo 中國科學院考古研究所 (Institute of Archaeology), and Gansu sheng bowuguan 甘肅省博物館 (Gansu Provincial Museum)

1964 *Wuwei Han jian* 武威漢簡 (Han dynasty bamboo slips from Wuwei). Beijing: Wenwu chubanshe.

Chen Shan 陳山

2003 "北票新發現的三燕馬具" (Newly discovered Three Yan kingdom's horse equipment from Beipiao). *Wenwu,* no. 3: 52–58.

Chen Yinke 陳寅恪

1974 *Sui Tang zhidu yuanyuan lue lun gao* 隋唐制度淵源略論稿 (Essays on the origins of institutions from the Sui and Tang dynasties). Based on the Shanghai Shangwu Yinshuguan 1946 ed. Hongkong: Zhonghua shuju.

Chen Zhi 陳值

1961 "對於南京西善橋南朝墓磚刻竹林七賢圖的管見" (An opinion on the molded brick depiction of the Seven Sages of the Bamboo Grove in the Southern Dynasties tomb at Xishanqiao, Nanjing). *Wenwu,* no. 10: 47–48.

Cheng Jizhong 程紀中

1980 "河北　城縣發現一批北齊石造像" (Stone Buddha statues of the Northern Qi dynasty found at Gaocheng in Hebei). *Kaogu,* no. 3: 242–45.

Cheng Yongkui 程永魁

1994 "托克托縣鎏金銅釋迦佛像淺釋" (An explanation for the Togeton County gilded bronze Buddhist image). *Neimenggu wenwu kaogu,* no. 2: 67–69.

Cheng, Yue

1996 "A Summary of Sogdian Studies in China." *China Archaeology and Art Digest* 1, no. 1 (January–March): 21–30.

Chengdu shi wenwu kaogu gongzuodui et al. 成都市文物考古工作隊 (Archaeological Team of Chengdu Municipality)

1998 "成都市西安路南朝石刻造像清理簡報" (Stone carvings of the Southern Dynasties in Chengdu, Sichuan). *Wenwu,* no. 11: 4–20.

Chu Shibin 初師賓

1990 "甘肅靖遠新出土東羅馬鎏金銀盤略考" (Brief discussion on a newly excavated gilt silver dish in Jingyuan, Gansu). *Wenwu,* no. 5: 1–9.

Chu Shibin 初師賓 and Zhang Pengchuan 張朋川

1982 "雷台東漢墓的車馬組合和墓主人初探" (The assemblage of chariots and cavalry of Leitai tomb of the Eastern Han). *Kaogu yu wenwu,* no. 2: 76–80.

Chutu wenwu zhanlan gongzuozu 出土文物展覽工作組, ed.

1973 *Wenhua dageming qijian chutu wenwu, I.* 文化大革命期間出土文物 (Cultural relics unearthed during the period of the Great Cultural Revolution, vol. 1). Beijing: Wenwu chubanshe.

Cixian wenhuaguan 磁縣文化館 (Ci County Cultural Center)
1977 "河北磁縣東陳村東魏墓" (Excavation of an Eastern Wei tomb at Dongchen village in Cixian, Hebei Province). *Kaogu*, no. 6: 391–400.

1984 "河北磁縣東魏茹茹公主墓發掘簡報" (Excavation of the Eastern Wei tomb of the princess of the Ruru at Ci county in Hebei). *Wenwu*, no. 4: 1–16.

Clairmont, Charles
[1959] *Das Parisurteil in der antiken Kunst.* Zürich: The author.

Classical Chinese Literature
2000 *Classical Chinese Literature: An Anthology of Translations, Volume 1: From Antiquity to the Tang Dynasty.* Edited by John Minford and Joseph S. M. Lau. New York: Columbia University Press; Hong Kong: Chinese University Press of Hong Kong.

Cooke, Bill
2000 *Imperial China: The Art of the Horse in Chinese History*. Prospect, Kentucky: Kentucky Horse Park and Harmony House Publishers.

Creel, Herrlee G.
1965 "The Role of the Horse in Chinese History." *American Historical Review* 70, no. 3: 647–72.

Cribb, Joe
1979 "An Historical Survey of the Precious Metal Currencies of China." *Numismatic Chronicle*: 185–209.

Cunningham, Michael R., et al.
1998 *Masterworks of Asian Art.* Cleveland: Cleveland Museum of Art in association with Thames and Hudson.

Daim, Falko, Karl Kaus, and Péter Tomka
1996 *Hunnen und Awaren: Reitervölker aus dem Osten.* Exh. cat. Bad Vöslau: Druckhaus Grasl.

Dalton, O. M.
1964 *The Treasure of the Oxus, with Other Examples of Early Oriental Metal-Work.* 3d ed. London: British Museum.

Darkevich, Vladislav Pertrovich
1976 *Khudozhestvennyi metall Vostoka vos'mogo-trinadtsatogo vv.: proizvedeniia vost torevtiki na territorii Evrop. Chasti SSSR i Zauralia* (Artistic metalwork of the East, eighth to thirteenth centuries A.D.: Production of Eastern metalwork in the territory of the European part of the USSR and Ural Mountains). Moscow: Nauka.

Davis-Kimball, Jeannine
2000 "Enarees and Women of High Status: Evidence of Ritual at Tillya Tepe (Northern Afghanistan)." In *Kurgans, Ritual Sites, and Settlements: Eurasian Bronze and Iron Age*, edited by Jeannine Davis-Kimball et al.: 223–39. BAR International Series 890. Oxford: Archaeopress.

Debaine-Francfort, Corinne, and Abduressul Idriss
2001 *Keriya: Mémoires d'un fleuve: Archéologie et civilisation des oasis de Taklamakan.* Exh. cat. Paris: Fondation Electricité de France; Suilly-la-Tour: Findakly.

Delacour, Catherine
2001 *De bronze, d'or et d'argent: Arts somptuaires de la Chine.* Trésors du Musée Guimet. Paris: Réunion des musées nationaux.

Delbrück, Richard
1932 *Antike Porphyrwerke.* Studien zur spätantiken Kunstgeschichte im Auftrage des Deutschen Archäologischen Instituts, vol. 16. Berlin and Leipzig: W. de Gruyter.

Deng Hongli 鄧宏里 and Cai Quanfa 蔡全法
1983 "沁陽縣西向發現北朝墓及畫像石棺床" (A Northern Dynasty tomb and stone coffin bed with carved figures at Xixiang, Qinyang County). *Zhongyuan wenwu*, no. 1: 4–12.

Dengxian caise huaxiangjuan mu
1958 *See* Henan sheng wenhuaju wenwu gongzuodui 1958.

Denwood, Philip
1973 "A Greek Bowl from Tibet." *Iran* 9: 121–27.

Desroches, Jean-Paul, ed.
2000 *L'Asie des steppes: D'Alexandre le Grand à Gengis Khan.* Exh. cat. Paris: Réunion des Musées Nationaux; Barcelona: Fundació la Caixa.

D'iakonova, Natal'ia Vasil'evna, and Sergei Sergeevich Sorokin
1960 *Khotanskie drevnosti: Katalog khotanskikh drevnostei, khraniashchikhsia v Otdele Vostoka Gosudarstvennogo Ermitazha. Terrakota i shtuk* (The antiquities of Khotan). Leningrad: State Hermitage Museum.

Di Cosmo, Nicola
1994 "Ancient Inner Asian Nomads: Their Economic Basis and Its Significance in Chinese History." *Journal of Asian Studies* 53, no. 4 (November): 1092–1126.

Dien, Albert E.
1962 "The *'sa-pao'* Problem Re-examined." *Journal of the American Oriental Society* 82: 335–46.

1981–82 "A Study of Early Chinese Armor." *Artibus Asiae* 43, no. 1–2: 5–66.

1986 "The Stirrup and Its Effect on Chinese Military History." *Ars Orientalis* 16: 33–56.

1990 "The Role of the Military in the Western Wei/Northern Zhou State." In *State and Society in Early Medieval China*, edited by Albert E. Dien, 331–67. Stanford: Stanford University Press.

1991 "A New Look at the Xianbei and Their Impact on Chinese Culture." In *Ancient Mortuary Traditions of China: Papers on Chinese Ceramic Funerary Sculptures*, edited by George Kuwayama: 40–59. Los Angeles and Honolulu: Far Eastern Art Council and Los Angeles County Museum of Art.

Ding Mingyi 丁明夷
1986 "從強獨樂建周文王佛道造像碑看北朝道教造像" (Northern Dynasty Dao images from the perspective of the Buddhist Daoist stele from the 'Qiangdu Le' 557 stele). *Wenwu*, no. 3: 52–62.

Dingxian bowuguan 定縣博物館 (Dingxian Museum)
1973 "河北定縣43號漢墓發掘報告" (Report on the excavation of Tomb 43 at Dingxian, Hebei). *Wenwu*, no. 11: 8–20.

Dong Li 董理
2001 "關於武則天金簡的幾個問題" (A few questions regarding Wu Zetian's gold tablet). *Huaxia kaogu*, no. 2: 79–85.

Du Baoren 杜葆仁
1979 "從西安唐墓出土的非洲黑人陶俑談起" (Pottery figures of African Blacks unearthed from Tang tombs in Xi'an). *Wenwu*, no. 6: 88–90.

Duan Chengshi 段成式
1983 *See YYZZ.*

Dunbabin, Katherine

1999 *Mosaics of the Greek and Roman World.* Cambridge: Cambridge University Press.

Dunhuang Research Institute, comp.

2000 *Dunhuang: A Centennial Commemoration of the Discovery of the Cave Library*. Beijing: Morning Glory Publishers.

Dunhuang wenwu yanjiusuo 敦煌文物研究所 (Dunhuang Research Institute)

1972 "新發現的北魏刺繡" (Recently discovered embroidery from the Northern Wei). *Wenwu*, no. 2: 54–60.

Dunhuang yanjiuyuan 敦煌研究院 (Dunhuang Research Institute)

1986 *Dunhuang yishu xiao congshu* 敦煌藝術小叢書 (The murals of Mogao caves). Vol. 3, *Mogaoku bihua yishu* 莫高窟壁畫藝術. Lanzhou: Gansu renmin meishu chubanshe.

Dunhuang yishu zongmu suoyin

1983 *Dunhuang yishu zongmu suoyin* 敦煌遺書總目索引 (Comprehensive catalogue index to the surviving manuscripts from Dunhuang). Edited by Shangwu yinshuguan. Beijing: Zhonghua shuju.

Ebrey, Patricia Buckley

1978 *The Aristocratic Families of Early Imperial China: A Case Study of the Po-ling Ts'ui Family*. New York: Cambridge University Press.

Echeng Liuchao mu 鄂城六朝墓

n.d. Echeng Museum and the Department of History of Nanjing University. *Echang Liuchao mu* (The Six-Dynasties Tomb at Echeng). Forthcoming.

Effenberger, Arne, et al.

1978 *Spätantike und früh-byzantinische Silbergefässe aus der Staatlichen Ermitage Leningrad. Ausstellung der Staatlichen Ermitage Leningrad.* Exh. cat. Berlin: Frühchristlich-Byzantinische Sammlung, Staatliche Museen zu Berlin.

Elsner, Jas

1998 *Imperial Rome and Christian Triumph: The Art of the Roman Empire, AD 100–450*. Oxford: Oxford University Press.

Emmerick, Ronald E.

1983 "The Iranian Settlements to the East of the Pamirs." In *The Cambridge History of Iran*, edited by Ehsan Yarshater, vol. 3, part 1: 263–75. Cambridge.

Fajans, Salomea

1957 "Recent Russian Literature on Newly Found Middle Eastern Metal Vessels." *Ars Orientalis* 2: 55–76.

Fan Wenlan 范文瀾

1994 *Zhongguo tong shi* 中國通史 *(Chinese history)*. Vols. 1–4. Beijing: Renmin chubanshe.

Fan Xiangyong 范祥雍

1978 *See LQJ.*

Fan Yousheng 樊有升 and Li Xianqi 李獻奇

1992 "河南偃師唐嚴仁墓" (The tomb of Yan Ren of the Tang dynasty, Yanshi, Henan). *Wenwu*, no. 12: 34–36.

Fedorov, Mikhail

2001 "A Sogdian Incense-Burner of the Late VII–Early VIII C. AD from Koshoi Korgon Hillfort." *Iranica antiqua* 36: 361–81.

Fisher, Robert E.

1995 "Noble Guardians: The Emergence of the Lokapalas in Buddhist Art." *Oriental Art* 41, no. 2 (summer): 17–24.

Fong, Mary H.

1991a "Antecedents of Sui–Tang Burial Practices in Shaanxi." *Artibus Asiae* 51: 159–87.

1991b "Tomb Guardian Figurines: Their Evolution and Iconography." In *Ancient Mortuary Traditions of China: Papers on Chinese Ceramic Funerary Sculptures*, edited by George Kuwayama, 84–105. Los Angeles and Honolulu: Far Eastern Council and Los Angeles County Museum of Art.

Fong, Wen, ed.

1980 *The Great Bronze Age of China: An Exhibition from the People's Republic of China.* Exh. cat. New York: The Metropolitan Museum of Art.

Fontein, Jan, and Tung Wu

1973 *Unearthing China's Past.* Exh. cat. Boston: Museum of Fine Arts.

1976 *Han and T'ang Murals: Discovered in Tombs in the People's Republic of China and Copied by Contemporary Chinese Painters.* Exh. cat. Boston: Museum of Fine Arts.

Forte, Antonino

1988 *Mingtang and Buddhist Utopias in the History of the Astronomical Clock: The Tower, Statue and Armillary Sphere Constructed by Empress Wu.* Serie Orientale Roma, vol. 59. Rome: Istituto Italiano per il Medio ed Estremo Oriente; Paris: École Française d'Extrême-Orient.

Francfort, Henri-Paul

1979 *Les palettes du Gandhāra.* Mémoires de la délégation archéologique française en Afghanistan, vol. 23. Paris: Diffusion de Boccard.

Frye, Richard N.

1992 "Sasanian–Central Asian Connections." In *Contacts between Cultures*, vol. 1, *West Asia and North Africa; Selected Papers from the 33rd International Congress of Asian and North African Studies, Toronto, August 15–25, 1990*, edited by Amir Harrak. Louiston, N.Y.: Edwin Mellen Press.

1993 "Sasanian-Central Asian Trade Relations." *Bulletin of the Asia Institute*, n.s., 7: 73–77.

Fu Qifeng

1985 *Chinese Acrobatics through the Ages.* Translated by Ouyang Caiwei and Rhoda Stockwell. Beijing: Foreign Languages Press.

Fu Xinian 傅熹年

1998 "唐代隧道型墓的形制構造和所反映出的地上宮室" (The construction and form of Tang era tunnel tombs and their reflection of above-ground palaces). In *Fu Xinian jianzhu shilun wenji* 傅熹年建築史論文集 (Collected essays by Fu Xinian on architectural history): 245–63. Beijing: Wenwu chubanshe.

Fukai Shinji

1973 *Perushia no garasu* (Persian Glass). Kyōto: Tankosha.

1977 *Persian Glass.* Translated by Edna B. Crawford. New York: John Weatherhill.

Fushimi Chūkei 伏見冲敬

1971 Tō Chō Kyoku: Koshi shijō, rōkan sekki, totsūjō 唐張旭 古詩四帖，郎官石記， 肚痛帖. *Shoseki meihin sōkan* 書跡名品叢刊 (Series of masterpieces of calligraphy), vol. 168. Tokyo: Nigensha.

Gansu sheng bowuguan 甘肅省博物館 (Gansu Provincial Museum)

1972 "武威磨咀子三座漢墓發掘簡報" (Report of three Han tombs of Mojuzi in Wuwei). *Wenwu*, no. 12: 9–25.

1994 *Sichou zhilu: Gansu wenwu jinghua*

絲綢之路：甘肅文物精華 (The Silk Road: Cultural relics of Gansu). N.p.

Gansu sheng bowuguan甘肅省博物館 (Gansu Provincial Museum) and Gansu sheng Wuwei Xian wenhuaguan甘肅省武威縣文化館 (Cultural Center of Wuwei County, Gansu Province)

1973 "武威旱灘坡漢墓發掘簡報" (Bulletin on the Han tombs at Hantanpo, Wuwei). *Wenwu*, no. 12: 18–22.

Gansu sheng wenwu gongzuodui 甘肅省文物工作隊 (Cultural Relics Team of Gansu Province)

1966 "甘肅省涇川縣出土的唐代舍利石函" (A Tang period stone reliquary discovered in Jingchuan county in Gansu). *Wenwu*, no. 3: 8–15.

Gansu sheng wenwu gongzuodui 甘肅省文物工作隊 (Cultural Relics Team of Gansu Province) and Binglingsi wenwu baoguansuo 炳靈寺文物保管所 (Bureau of Cultural Relics Preservation of Binglingsi)

1989 *Yongjing Binglingsi* 永靖炳靈寺 (The Binglingsi grottoes). Zhongguo shiku series. Beijing: Wenwu chubanshe.

Gansu sheng wenwu guanli weiyuanhui 甘肅省文物管理委員會 (Gansu Cultural Properties Management Committee)

1959 "酒泉下河清第1號墓和第18號墓發掘簡報" (Report on the discovery of tomb 1 and tomb 18 at Xiaheqing, Jiuquan). *Wenwu*, no. 10: 71–77.

Geary, Patrick J.

2002 *The Myth of Nations: The Medieval Origins of Europe*. Princeton, N.J.: Princeton University Press.

Gernet, Jacques

1987 *A History of Chinese Civilization*. Cambridge: Cambridge University Press.

1995 *Buddhism in Chinese Society: An Economic History from the Fifth to the Tenth Centuries*. Translated by Franciscus Verellen. New York: Columbia University Press

Giles, Herbert A.

1898 *A Chinese Biographical Dictionary*. London: Bernard Quaritch; Shanghai: Kelly and Walsh.

Göbl, Robert

1963 *Dokumente zur Geschichte der iranischen Hunnen in Baktrien und Indien*. 2 vols. Wiesbaden.

Gombrich, E. H.

1961 *Art and Illusion: A Study in the Psychology of Pictorial Representation*. The A.W. Mellon Lectures in the Fine Arts, 1956. 2d. ed. New York: Bollingen Foundation.

1984 *The Sense of Order: A Study in the Psychology of Decorative Art*. The Wrightsman lectures series 9. Oxford: Phaidon. First published 1979.

Gong Dejie 宮德杰

2002 "臨朐縣博物館收藏的一批北朝造像" (Some Northern Wei Buddhist sculptures recently acquired by the Linqu Museum). *Wenwu*, no. 9: 84–92.

Gregory, Peter N., and Patricia B. Ebrey

1993 "The Religious and Historical Landscape." In *Religion and Society in T'ang and Sung China*, edited by Patricia B. Ebrey and Peter N. Gregory: 1–44. Honolulu: University of Hawaii Press.

Grenet, Frantz

2000 "Troi documents sogdiens d'Afrasiab." In *Sredniaia Aziia: Arkheologiia, istoriia, kul'tura. Materialy mezhdunarodnoi konferentsii, posviashchennoi 50-letiiu nauchnoi deiatel'nosti G. V. Shishkinoi: Gosudarstvennyi Muzei Vostoka, 14–16 dekabria 2000 g.*, edited by T. G. Alpatkina: 196–202. Moscow: Gosudarstvennyi Muzei Vostoka.

Griaznov, Mikhail Petrovich

1969 *The Ancient Civilization of Southern Siberia*. Translated by James Hogarth. New York: Cowles Book Co.

Grierson, Philip

1968 *Catalogue of the Byzantine Coins in the Dumbarton Oaks Collection and in the Whittemore Collection*. Vol. 2, part 1, *Phocas and Heraclius (602–641)*. Washington, D.C.

1982 *Byzantine Coins*. Berkeley and Los Angeles: University of California Press.

Griffiths, John

1896–97 *The Paintings in the Buddhist Cave-Temples of Ajantâ, Khandesh, India*. 2 vols. London: Printed by W. Griggs.

Grose, David F.

1977 "Early Blown Glass." *Journal of Glass Studies* 19: 9–29.

1984 "Glass Forming Methods in Classical Antiquity: Some Considerations." *Journal of Glass Studies* 26: 25–34.

Grousset, René

1934 *The Civilizations of the East*. Vol. 3, *China*. Translated by Catherine Alison Phillips. New York: Knopf.

Gu Tiefu 顧鐵符

1982 "奔馬・襲鳥・馬式 – 試論武威奔馬的科學價值" (Galloping horse, "bird-capturing," and horse model – On the scientific value of the galloping horse of Wuwei). *Kaogu yu wenwu*, no. 2: 81–87.

Guangzhou shi wenwu guanli weiyuanhui 廣州市文物管理委員會 (Cultural Relics Management Committee of Guangzhou), Zhongguo shehui kexueyuan kaogu yanjiusuo 中國社會科學院考古研究所 (Institute of Archaeology, Chinese Academy of Social Sciences [CASS]), and Guangdong sheng bowuguan 廣東省博物館 (Guangdong Province Museum)

1991 *Xi Han Nanyue wang mu* 西漢南越王墓 *(Tomb of the king of Nanyue of Western Han)* Beijing: Wenwu chubanshe.

Guangzhou wenwu weiyuanhui 廣州市文物管理委員會 (Committee on Cultural Relics of Guangzhou)

1955 "廣州市東北郊西漢木槨墓發掘簡報" (Excavation report of a western Han tomb with a wooden coffin in the northeastern suburb of Guangzhou). *Kaogu tongxun*, no. 4: 40–45.

Gugong bowuyuan 故宮博物院 (Palace Museum)

1962 *Gugong bowuyuan cang ci xuanji* 故宮博物院藏瓷選集 (A selection of porcelains from the Palace Museum). Beijing: Wenwu chubanshe.

Guisso, Richard W. L.

1979 "The Reigns of the Empress Wu, Chung-tsung, and Jui-tsung (684–712)." In *The Cambridge History of China*, vol. 3, part 1, *Sui and T'ang China, 589–906*, edited by Denis Twitchett: 290–332. Cambridge: Cambridge University Press.

Gulik, Robert H. van

1941 *Hsi K'ang and His Poetical Essay on the Lute*. Tokyo: Sophia University. Rev. ed., Tokyo, 1969.

Gunter, Ann Clyburn, and Paul Jett

1992 *Ancient Iranian Metalwork in the Arthur M. Sackler Gallery and the Freer Gallery of Art*. Washington, D.C.: Arthur M. Sackler Gallery; Freer Gallery of Art, Smithsonian Institution.

Guo Suxin 郭素新

1977 "內蒙古呼和浩特北魏墓" (A Northern Wei tomb from Hohhot in Inner Mongolia). *Wenwu*, no. 5: 38–41, 77.

Guojia wenwuju 國家文物局主編 (Cultural Relics Bureau), ed.

1996 *Zhongguo wenwu jinghua da cidian: Jinyin yushi juan* 中國文物精華大辭典: 金銀玉石卷 (The essential dictionary of China's cultural properties: Gold, silver, jade, and stone). Shanghai: Shanghai cishu chubanshe.

2000 "山西大同雁北師院北魏墓群" (A group of Northern Wei tombs excavated at Yanbei Teachers College, Datong, Shanxi). In *2000 Zhongguo zhong yao kaogu faxian* 2000 中國重要考古發現 (Major archaeological discoveries in China in 2000): 88–94. Beijing: Wenwu chubanshe.

Guoli lishi bowuguan 國立歷史博物館 (National Museum of History)

1998 *Zhongguo gudai taoyong yanjiu tezhan taoyong lunwenji* 中國古代陶俑研究特展：陶俑論文集 (Special exhibition of ancient Chinese figurines from the National Museum of History). Edited by Chen Yongyuan. Taibei: Guoli lishi bowuguan.

Gyllensvärd, Bo

1957 *T'ang Gold and Silver*. Göteborg: Elanders. Reprinted from Östasiatiska samlingarna (Stockholm), *Bulletin*, no. 29.

1971 *Chinese Gold, Silver, and Porcelain: The Kempe Collection*. Exh. cat., circulated by the International Exhibitions Foundation. New York: Asia Society.

Hackin, Joseph, with J.-R. Hackin, J. Carl Hamelin, and P. Hamelin

1954 *Nouvelles recherches archéologiques à Begram, ancienne Kâpicî, 1939–1940; rencontre de trois civilisations, Inde, Grèce, Chine*. Mémoires de la Délégation Archéologique Française en Afghanistan, vol. 2. Paris: Impr. Nationale.

Hambis, Louis, ed.

1961–64 *Toumchouq*. 2 vols. Mission Paul Pelliot, Documents archéologiques, 1–2. Paris.

Han Baoquan 韓保全

1998 "長安出土的佉盧文銘鎏金銅造像" (A gilt bronze seated Buddha with Qulu inscription excavated at Chang'an). *Shoucangjia*, no. 3: 21.

Han Tang bihua

1974 *Han Tang bihua* 漢唐壁畫 (Murals of the Han and Tang). Beijing: Wenwu chubanshe.

Han Wei 韓偉

1991 "唐代金銀器拾零" (Miscellaneous notes on gold and silver of the Tang). *Wenbo*, no. 6: 25–32.

1996 "唐代長安之女性世界 – 為日本兵庫縣大唐王朝之花 – '長安婦女展'" (The Feminine world in Tang dynasty Chang'an). *Wenbo*, no. 1: 26–30.

Han Wei 韓偉 and Zhang Jianlin 張建林

1998 *Shaanxi xin chutu Tang mu bihua* 陝西新出土唐墓壁畫 (Newly excavated Tang tomb murals from Shaanxi). Chongqing: Chongqing chubanshe.

Han Zhigang 韓志剛

1994 "寧夏鹽池唐墓石刻所反映的胡旋舞" (Images of Huxuan dance from Tang tomb stone carvings at Yanchi county, Ningxia). *Wenbo*, no. 3: 64–66.

Haraprasad, Ray

1995 "從中國至印度的南方絲綢之路 – 一篇來印度的探討" (The southern Silk Road from China to India—an approach from India). In Jiang Yuxiang 江玉祥, *Gudai xinan sichouzhilu yanjiu* 古代西南絲綢之路研究 (Studies of the ancient Silk Road in southwestern China). Chengdu: Sichuan daxue chubanshe.

Harden, Donald B.

1934 "Glass from Kish." In "Excavations at Kish and Barghuthiat, 1933." *Iraq* 1: 131–36.

Harmatta, János

1979 "Sogdian Sources for the History of Pre-Islamic Central Asia." In *Prolegomena to the Sources on the History of pre-Islamic Central Asia*: 153–65. Budapest: Akadémiai Kiadó.

Harper, Prudence O.

1978 *The Royal Hunter: Art of the Sasanian Empire*. Contributions by Jens Kröger, Carol Manson Bier, and Martha L. Carter. Exh. cat. New York: Asia Society in association with John Weatherhill.

1990a "An Iranian Silver Vessel from the Tomb of Feng Hetu." *Bulletin of the Asia Institute*, no. 4: 51–59.

1990b "Silver-Gilt Plate." In *Glories of the Past: Ancient Art from the Shelby White and Leon Levy Collection*, edited by Dietrich von Bothmer: 58–59. Exh. cat. New York: The Metropolitan Museum of Art.

1991 "Luxury Vessels as Symbolic Images in Parthian and Sasanian Iran and Central Asia." In *Histoire et cultes de l'Asie centrale préislamique: Sources écrites et documents archéologiques; Actes*, edited by Paul Bernard and Frantz Grenet: 67–84. Paris.

1993 "La vaiselle en métal." In *Splendeur des Sassanides*. Brussels: Musées Royaux d'Art et d'Histoire.

1998 "Sassian and Early Islamic Silver and Bronze Vessels." In "Entlang der Seidenstrasse: Frühmittelalterliche Kunst zwischen Persien und China in der Abegg-Stifftung." *Riggisberger Berichte* 6: 215–38.

2002 "Iranian Luxury Vessels in China from the Late First Millennium B.C.E. to the Second Half of the First Millennium C.E." In *Silk Road Studies VII: Nomads, Traders and Holy Men along China's Silk Road. Papers Presented at a Symposium Held at the Asia Society in New York, November 9–10, 2000*, edited by Annette L. Juliano and Judith A. Lerner: 97–100. Turnhout: Brepols.

Harper, Prudence O., and Pieter Meyers

1981 *Silver Vessels of the Sasanian Period*. Technical study by Pieter Meyers. New York: The Metropolitan Museum of Art.

Harrist, Robert E., Jr.

1997 *Power and Virtue: The Horse in Chinese Art*. Exh. cat. New York: China Institute Gallery.

1999 "Reading Chinese Calligraphy." In Robert E. Harrist and Wen C. Fong, *The Embodied Image: Chinese Calligraphy from the John B. Elliott Collection*: 3–27. Princeton: The Art Museum, Princeton University.

Hayashi Ryōichi

1975 *The Silk Road and the Shōsō-in*. Translated by Robert Ricketts. Heibonsha Survey of Japanese Art, 6. New York: Weatherhill/Heibonsha.

He Han'nan 何漢南

1987 "武則天改制新字考" (A study of the new characters created by Wu Zetian). *Wenbo*, no. 4: 63–67.

He Qimin (Ho Ch'i-min) 何啟民

1966 *Zhulin qixian yanjiu* 竹林七賢研究 (Research on the Seven Sages of the Bamboo Grove). Taipei: Commercial Press.

Hearn, Maxwell K.

2003 "The Evolving Significance of Gu Kaizhi and the *Admonitions of the Court Instructress*." In *Gu Kaizhi and the Admonitions Scroll*, edited by Shane McCausland: 183–89. London: British Museum.

Hebei sheng bowuguan 河北省博物館 (Hebei Provincial Museum)
1999 *Hebei sheng bowuguan wenwu jingpin ji* 河北省博物館文物精品集 (Treasures from Hebei Provincial Museum). Beijing: Wenwu chubanshe.

Hebei sheng bowuguan wenwu guanli 河北省博物館文物管理 (Hebei Province Museum Cultural Properties Management Office)
1973 "河北平山北齊崔昂墓調查報告" (Investigation of the tomb of Cui Ang of the Northern Qi dynasty at Pingshan, Hebei). *Wenwu*, no. 11: 27–38.

Hebei sheng wenhuaju wenwu gongzuodui 河北省文化局文物工作隊, (Hebei Provincial Cultural Center and Cultural Properties Team)
1964 "河北定縣北莊漢墓發掘報告" (Report on the excavation of Han tombs at Beizhuang, Dingxian, Hebei). *Kaogu xuebao*, no. 2: 127–75.

1966 "河北定縣出土北魏石函" (The Northern Wei stone coffer excavated from Ding county, Hebei). *Kaogu*, no. 5: 252–59.

Hebei sheng wenhua ju wenwu gongzuo dui 河北省文化局文物工作隊 (Work Team of the Culture Bureau, Hebei Province)
1964 "定縣北庄漢墓出土文物簡報" (Bulletin on relics from the Han tomb at Beizhuang, Ding county). *Kaogu*, no. 12: 26–32.

Hebei sheng wenwu yanjiusuo 河北省文物研究所 (Hebei Institute of Cultural Properties Research)
1990 "河北阜城桑莊東漢墓發掘報告" (Bulletin on the eastern Han tomb of Zhuocheng, Hebei). *Wenwu*, no. 1: 19–30.

1995 *Cuo Mu: Zhanguo Zhongshan guo guowang zhimu* 嚳墓：戰國中山國國王之墓 (The tomb of Cuo, the king of the Zhongshan State in the Warring States period). Beijing: Wenwu chubanshe.

Heireiji sekkutsu
1986 *Heireiji sekkutsu* 炳靈寺石窟 (The Binglingsi Grottoes). Chūgoku sekkutsu (The grotto art of China). Tokyo: Heibonsha.

Heller, Amy
1998 "Some Preliminary Remarks on the Excavations at Dulan." *Orientations* 29 (October): 84–92.

2003 "The Silver Jug of Lhasa Jokhang." *Asian Arts*, May 3, 2002.

Hemudu yizhi kaogudui 河姆渡遺址考古隊 (Hemudu Archaeological Team)
1980 "浙江河姆渡遺址第二期發掘主要收獲" (The second season of the excavation at Hemudu, Zhejiang). *Wenwu*, no. 5: 1–15.

Henan sheng wenhuaju wenwu gongzuodui 河南省文化局文物工作隊 (Henan Province Bureau of Culture and Cultural Properties Team)
1958 *Deng xian caise huaxiangjuan mu* 鄧縣彩色畫象磚墓 (Tomb with colored moulded bricks in Deng district [Henan]). Beijing: Wenwu chubanshe.

Henan sheng wenwu yanjiusuo 河南省文物研究所 (Henan Province Institute of Cultural Properties Research)
1989 *Zhongguo shiku: Gongxian shikusi* 中國石窟：鞏縣石窟寺 (China's grottoes: The Gongxian grotto temple). Beijing: Wenwu chubanshe.

Higuchi Takayasu 樋口隆康
1998 "60 武侍樂俑"(Entry 60: Set of pottery figurines). In *Dai Kōga bunmei ten: Chūgoku Kanan-shō hassennen no shihō* 大黄河文明展：中國河南省八千年の至寶: 92. Tokyo: Nihonkeizaishinbunsha.

Hinuber, Oskar von
2003 "The Magnificent Bronze of Nandikramadityananda: A Delight for the Beholder, a Worry for the Epigraphist." *Orientations* 34, no. 4 (April): 35–39.

Hinz, Walther
1955 *Islamische Masse und Gewichte: Umgerechnet ins metrische System.* Leiden: E. J. Brill.

Hirth, Friedrich
1885 *China and the Roman Orient: Researches into Their Ancient and Mediaeval Relations as Represented in Old Chinese Records*. Leipzig: Georg Hirth.

Holzman, Donald
1956 "Les Sept Sages de la Forêt des Bambous et la société de leur temps." *Toung Pao* 44: 317–46.

Howard, Angela F.
1986 *The Imagery of the Cosmological Buddha*. Studies in South Asian Culture, vol. 13. Leiden: E. J. Brill.

1996 "Buddhist Cave Sculpture of the Northern Qi Dynasty: Shaping a New Style, Formulating New Iconographies." *Archives of Asian Art* 49: 6–25.

2000 "Liang Patronage of Buddhist Art in the Gansu Corridor during the Fourth Century and the Transformation of a Central Asian Style." In *Han Tang zhi jian de zongjiao yishu yu kaogu* 漢唐之間的宗教藝術與考古 (Between Han and Tang: Religious art and archaeology in a transformative period), edited by Wu Hung: 235–75. Beijing: Wenwu chubanshe.

Hsia Nai (Xia Nai)夏鼐
1980 "Sassanian Objects Recently Found in China." *Social Science in China*, no. 2: 156–58. Translated from *Kaogu* 1978.2: 111–16.

Hsieh Cheng-fa 謝振發
2001 "北魏司馬金龍墓的漆畫屏風試析" (Analysis of the screen lacquer painting of the Northern Wei tomb of Sima Jinlong). *Meishushi yanjiu jikan*, no. 11: 1–55.

Huang Nengfu 黄能馥
1985 *Zhongguo meishu quanji: Yin ran zhi xiu* 中國美術全集・印染織繡（上）(The Complete Collection of Chinese Art: Textiles). Vol. 1. Beijing: Wenwu chubanshe.

Hubei sheng Jingzhou diqu bowuguan 湖北省荆州地区博物馆 (Jingzhou District Museum, Hubei Province)
1985 *Jiangling Mashan yi hao Chu mu* 江陵马山一号楚墓 (Chu dynasty tomb no. 1, Jiangling, Mashan). Beijing: Wenwu chubanshe.

Hubei sheng wenhuaju wenwu gongzuodui 湖北省文化局文物工作隊 (Hubei Province Bureau of Culture and Cultural Properties Team)
1966 "湖北江陵三座楚墓出土大批重要文物" (Important artifacts excavated from three Chu tombs at Jiangling, Hubei). *Wenwu*, no. 5: 33–55.

Hucker, Charles
1985 *A Dictionary of Official Titles in Imperial China*. Stanford: Stanford University Press.

Hung, William
1952 *Tu Fu, China's Greatest Poet*. Cambridge, Mass.: Harvard University Press.

Huntington, Susan
1985 *The Art of Ancient India*. Contributions by John Huntington. New York and Tokyo: Weatherhill.

Huo Xuchu 霍旭初
1993 "克孜爾石窟的分期問題" (Dating of periods of the Kizil Grottoes). *Xiyu Studies*, no. 2: 58–70.

Ibn Manjli, Muhammad

1984 *De la chasse: Commerce des grands de ce monde avec les bêtes sauvages des déserts sans onde.* Translated by François Viré. Bibliothèque arabe; collection des classiques. Paris: Sindbad.

Ierusalimskaia, Anna A.

1972 "K slozheniyu shkoly khudozhestvennogo shelkotkachestva v Sogde" (Formation of the Sogdian school of artistic silk weaving). *In Sredniaia Azaii i Iran (sbornik statei)*: 5–46. Leningrad. Gosudarstvennyi Ordena Lenina Ermitazh.

Isings, Clasina

1957 *Roman Glass from Dated Finds.* Archaeologica Traiectina, 2. Groningen: J. B. Wolters.

Ivanov, A. A., V. G. Lukonin, and L. S. Smesova

1984 *Iuvelirnye izdeliia Vostoka. Kollektsiia Osoboi kladovoi otdela Vostoka Gosudarstvennogo Ermitazha* (Oriental jewelry; collection of the Near East Department, State Hermitage Museum). Moscow: "Isskustvo."

Jao Tsung-i 饒宗頤

1993 "蜀布與 Cinpatta— 論早期中，印，緬之交通." (*Shubu* and Cinpatta: early China, India, and Burmese transports). In *Fanxueji* 梵學集: 223–60. Shanghai: Shanghai guji chubanshe. Originally published in *Zhongyang yanjiuyuan shiyusuo jikan* 45, no. 4 (1974).

Jenkins, Marilyn

1986 "Islamic Glass: A Brief History." *The Metropolitan Museum of Art Bulletin* 44, no. 2 (fall).

Ji Wei 李偉 and Han Shaojie 韓紹杰

2002 "漢代的鼓吹樂" (The fife and drum band in the Han dynasty). *Nandu xuetan*, no. 7.

Jiang Boqin 姜伯勤

1994 *Dunhuang Tulufan wenshu yu sichou zhi lu* 敦煌吐魯番文書與絲綢之路 (Dunhuang and Turfan documents concerning the Silk Road). Beijing: Wenwu chubanshe.

1999 "山西介休祆教古建築裝飾的圖像學考察" (A Study of the decorative iconography in old buildings in Jiexiu, Shanxi). *Wenwu*, no. 1: 56–66.

2000a "The Pictorial Program of the Reliefs on the Stone Sarcophagus of Yu Hong." *Chinese Archeology and Art Digest* 4, no. 1 (December): 34.

2000b "The Zoroastrian Art of the Sogdians in China." Translated by Bruce Doar. *China Archaeology and Art Digest* 4, no. 1 (December): 35–71.

Jiang Qixiang 蔣其祥

1990 "新疆古代錢幣的發現與研究" (Discoveries and studies of ancient coins in Xinjiang). In *Xinjiang gudai minzu wenhua lunwen ji* 新疆古代民族文化論集 (An anthology of treatises on the cultures of the ancient nationalities in Xinjiang), edited by Xu Haisheng 許海生: 183–215. Urumqi: Xinjiang daxue chubanshe.

Jiang Wenguang 蔣文光

1989 "孤本《北涼沮渠安周造佛寺碑》研究" (A study on the rare copy of Stone tablet inscription of buddhist temple built by Juqu Anzhou in the northern Liang). *Xinjiang wenwu*, no. 2: 55–74.

Jiang Yuxiang 江玉祥

1995 *Gudai xinan sichou zhi lu yanjiu* 古代西南絲綢之路研究 (Studies of the ancient Silk Road in southwestern China). Chengdu: Sichuan daxue chubanshe.

Jilin sheng wenwu gongzuodui 吉林省文物工作隊 (Jilin Province Cultural Properties Team)

1984 "吉林集安五盔墳四號墓" (Tomb no. 4 of Wukuifen in Ji'an, Jilin). *Kaogu xuebao*, no. 1: 121–36.

Jin Weinuo 金維諾 and Wei Bian 衛邊

1975 "唐代西州墓中的絹畫" (Silk paintings in Tang dynasty Xizhou tombs). *Wenwu*, no. 10: 36–43.

Ji'nan shi bowuguan 濟南市博物館 (Ji'nan City Museum)

1985 "濟南市馬家莊北齊墓" (The Northern Qi tomb of Majiazhuang, Ji'nan). *Wenwu*, no. 10: 42–48, 66.

Jing Zengli 井增利 and Wang Xiaomeng 王小蒙

1997 "富平縣新發現的唐墓壁畫" (Newly discovered frescos from a Tang tomb in Fuping county, Shaanxi Province). *Kaogu yu wenwu*, no. 4: 8–11.

Juliano, Annette L.

1980 *Teng-hsien: An Important Six Dynasties Tomb.* Artibus Asiae, Supplementum 37. Ascona, Switzerland: Artibus Asiae.

Juliano, Annette L., and Judith A. Lerner

1997 "Cultural Crossroads: Central Asian and Chinese Entertainers on the Miho Funerary Couch." *Orientations* 28, no. 9: 72–78.

2001 as editors. *Monks and Merchants: Silk Road Treasures from Northwest China, Gansu, and Ningxia Provinces, 4th–7th Century.* Essays by Michael Alram et al. New York: Harry N. Abrams with the Asia Society.

Kahil, Lilly

1955 *Les enlèvements et le retour d'Hélène dans les textes et les documents figurés.* 2 vols. Paris: E. de Boccard.

Kaogu yanjiusuo Anyang dui 考古研究所安陽隊 (Anyang Archaeological Team, IOA)

1959 "安陽隋張盛墓發掘記" (Excavation of the Sui dynasty tomb of Zhang Sheng at Anyang). *Kaogu*, no. 10: 541–45.

Kashihara kokogaku kenkyujo fuzoku hakubutsukan (Nara Kenritsu) 奈良 縣立橿原考古研究所附屬博物館 (Museum of the Archaeological Institute of Kashihara, Nara Prefecture)

1992 *Niizawa senzuka no iho to sono genryu: Sengohyakunenmae no shirukurodotokubetsuten*年前のシルク-ド新沢千塚遺寶とその遠流 (Art from the Silk Road region 1500 years ago: Archaeological treasures of Niizawa-Senzuka burial mounds cluster, 1500). Kashihara: Museum of the Archaeological Institute of Kashihara, Nara Prefecture.

Klimburg-Salter, Deborah E.

1989 *The Kingdom of Bamiyan: Buddhist Art and Culture of the Hindu Kush.* Series maior, 5. Naples: Istituto Universitario Orientale; Rome: Istituto Italiano per il Medio ed Estremo Oriente.

1995 *Buddha in Indien: Die Frühindische Skulptur von König Aśoka bis zur Guptazeit.* Contributions by Maurizio Taddei, Eva Allinger, Françoise Härtl, and Christian Luczanits; edited by Wilfried Seipel. Exh. cat. Vienna: Kunsthistorisches Museum Wien; Milan: Skira.

Knauer, Elfriede R.

1978 "Toward a History of the Sleeved Coat." *Expedition* 21, no. 1 (fall): 18–39.

Knechtges, David R.

1982– Xiao Tong. *Wen xuan, or, Selections of Refined Literature.* Translated, with annotations and introduction by David R. Knechtges. 3 vols. Princeton, N.J.: Princeton University Press, ca. 1982–96.

1997 "Gradually Entering the Realm of Delight: Food and Drink in Early Medieval China." *Journal of the American Oriental Society* 117, no. 2 (April–June): 229–39.

Koizumi Akio 顯夫小泉
1927 "慶州瑞鳳塚の発掘" (The Excavataion at the Site of Zuifu in Keishu). *Shigaku zasshi* 38, no. 1.

Kong Xiangxing 孔祥星
1979 "隋唐銅鏡的類型與分期" (The typology and periodization of Sui and Tang bronze mirrors). In *Di yi ci nianhui lunwenji* 第一次年會論文集, edited by Zhongguo kaogu xuehui. Beijing: Wenwu chubanshe.

Kordmahini, Helen A.
1994 *Glass from the Bazargan Collection.* Tehran: Iran National Museum.

Koshkarly, Koshkar Orudzhogly
1985 *Antichnaia i rannesrednevekovaia torevtika iz Azerbaidzhana.* Baku: "Elm."

Kungnip Chungang Pangmulgwan
1975 *Han'guk Kungnip Chungang Pangmulgwan myongp'um togam / Selected Treasures of the National Museum of Korea.* Seoul: Samhwa Ch'ulp'ansa.

Kuwayama, George, ed.
1991 *Ancient Mortuary Traditions of China: Papers on Chinese Ceramic Funerary Sculptures.* Los Angeles and Honolulu: Far Eastern Council and Los Angeles County Museum of Art.

Kuwayama, George, et al.
1987 *See Quest for Eternity* 1987.

Laing, Ellen Johnston
1974 "Neo-Taoism and the Seven Sages of the Bamboo Grove in Chinese Painting." *Artibus Asiae* 36, no. 1–2: 5–54.

1991 "A Report on Western Asian Glassware in the Far East." *Bulletin of the Asia Institute* (Detroit), n.s., 5: 109–21.

1995 "Recents Finds of Western-Related Glassware, Textiles, and Metalwork in Central Asia and China." *Bulletin of the Asia Institute*, n.s., 9: 1–18.

Landman, Neil H.
1982 "In Pursuit of the Pearly Nautilus" and "Aristotle, Alexander and the Pearly Nautilus." *Discovery* 16, no. 1: 11–19, 21–23.

Laufer, Berthold
1919 *Sino-Iranica, Chinese Contributions to the History of Civilization in Ancient Iran with Special Reference to the History of Cultivated Plants and Products.* Chicago: Field Museum of Natural History.

Le Coq, Albert von
1922 *Die buddhistische Spätantike in Mittelasien.* Vol. 1, *Die Plastik.* Berlin: Dietrich Reimer.

Ledderose, Lothar
2001 "Aesthetic Appropriation of Ancient Calligraphy in Modern China." In *Chinese Art: Modern Expressions. An International Symposium Held in Conjunction with the Exhibition Nineteenth- and Twentieth-Century Chinese Paintings from the Robert H. Ellsworth Collection in The Metropolitan Museum of Art,* edited by Maxwell K. Hearn and Judith K. Smith: 212–45. New York: The Metropolitan Museum of Art.

Lee, In-sook
1993 "The Silk Road and Ancient Korean Glass." *Korean Culture* 14, no. 4: 4–13.

2001 "Silk Road Trade and Roman Glass from Korea." *Central Asian Studies* 5: 327–37.

2002 "Comparison of Prehistoric Glass Beads from Korea and Thailand." *Man and Environment* 7, no. 1: 161–63.

Lee, Yu-min
1983 "The Maitreya Cult and Its Art in Early China." Ph.D. dissertation, Ohio State University, Columbus.

Leidy, Denise Patry
1990 "The Ssu-wei Figure in Sixth-Century A.D. Chinese Buddhist Sculpture." *Archives of Asian Art* 43: 21–37.

1997 "Kashmir and China: A Note about Styles and Dates." *Orientations* 28, no. 2 (February): 66–70.

Lerner, Judith
1995 "Central Asians in Sixth-Century China: A Zoroastrian Funerary Rite." *Iranica Antiqua* 30: 179–90.

Lerner, Martin, and Steven Kossak
1991 *The Lotus Transcendent: Indian and Southeast Asian Art from the Samuel Eilenberg Collection.* Exh. cat. New York: The Metropolitan Museum of Art.

Li Jian, ed.
2003 *The Glory of the Silk Road: Art from Ancient China.* Essays by Valerie Hansen et al. Exh. cat. Dayton: Dayton Art Institute.

Li Jianzhao 李鑑昭 and Tu Sihua 屠思華
1958 "南京石門坎鄉六朝墓清理記" (Excavation report of a Six Dynasties tomb in Shimenkan village, Nanjing). *Kaogu tongxun,* no. 9: 66–69.

Li Jingjie
1999 "盧舍那法界圖像研究 " *Fojiao wenhua*: 1–52.

Li Junming 李均明 and He Shuangquan 何双全, eds.
1990 "甘肃武威旱滩坡19号晋墓木牍" (Inscribed wooden tablets from tomb 19, Hantanpo, Wuwei, Gansu). In *Sanjian jiandu heji* 散见简牍合辑 (Compendium of wooden slips from various sources): 26–29. Beijing: Wenwu chubanshe.

Li Lin 李琳
1991 "從青海出土木龍馬看漢代馬神崇拜" (The horse cult of the Han dynasty reflected in a wood dragon horse excavated in Qinghai). *Wenbo,* no. 1: 56–59.

Li Ling 李零
2001 "論中國的有翼神獸" (On the winged mythological animals in China). *Zhongguo xueshu,* no. 1: 62–133.

Li Mingwei 李明偉 et al.
1997 *Sichou zhilu maoyi shi* 絲綢之路貿易史 (History of the Trade along the Silk Road). Gansu: Gansu renmin chubanshe.

Li Ping 李憑
2000 *Bei Wei Pingcheng shidai* 北魏平城時代 (The Pingcheng period of the Northern Wei dynasty). Beijing: Shehui kexue wenxian chubanshe.

Li Qiushi 李求是
1972 "談章懷，懿德兩墓的形制等問題" (Discussion of the structures and other questions concerning the two tombs of the [Crown Princes] Zhanghuai and Yide). *Wenwu,* no. 7: 45–50, 58.

Li Ruoqing 李若晴
2003 "'竹林七賢與榮啟期' 畫像磚淵源考" (Research on the origins of the pictorial bricks of the Seven Sages of the Bamboo Grove and Rong Qiqi). In *Guangzhou meishu xueyuan wenji* 廣州美術學院文集 (Collected writing by the Guangzhou Institute of Art): 328–37. Nanchang: Jiangxi meishu chubanshe.

Li Wenying 李文瑛 and Zhou Jinling 周金玲
1998 "营盘考古收獲及相關問題" (Finds of the archaeological excavation of the tombs at Yingpan and related questions). In *Xinjiang Weiwuer zizhiqu silu*

kaogu zhenpin 新疆維吾爾自治區絲路考古珍品 (Archaeological treasures from the Silk Road in the Uygur Autonomous Region in Xinjiang): 63–74. Shanghai: Shanghai yiwen chubanshe.

Li Xijing 李錫經
1955 "河北曲陽縣修德寺遺址發掘記" (Excavation of the Xiude temple site in Quyang county, Hebei). *Kaogu tongxun*, no. 3: 38–44.

Li Yaobo 黎瑤渤
1973 "遼寧北票縣西官營子北燕馮素弗墓" (The tomb of Feng Sufu of the Northern Yan at Xiguanyingzi in Beipiao county, Liaoning Province). *Wenwu*, no. 3: 2–28.

Li Yongliang 李永良
1998 *Helong wenhua: Lianjie gudai Zhongguo yu shijie de zoulang* 河隴文化：連接古代中國與世界的走廊 (The culture of Helong: Linking ancient China to the Passageway to the World). Hong Kong: Shangwu yinshuguan.

Li Yongning 李永寧
1983 "本所藏《文選。運命論》殘卷介紹" (Introduction to a fragmentary handscroll of the "Treatise on Fate" chapter of *Literary Selections* in the Institute's collection). *Dunhuang yanjiu*: 164–72.

Li Zheng 李徵
1975 "新疆阿斯塔那三座唐墓出土珍貴絹畫及文書等文物" (Excavation of silk paintings, texts, and other artifacts from three Tang tombs in Astana, Xinjiang). *Wenwu*, no. 10: 89–90.

Liaoning sheng wenwu kaogu yanjiusuo 遼寧省文物考古研究所 (Liaoning Institute of Archaeology)
2002 *San Yan wenwu jingcui* 三燕文物精粹 (The best of the Three Yan kingdoms relics). Shengyang: Liaoning renmin chubanshe.

Lim, Lucy
1987 *Stories from China's Past: Han Dynasty Pictorial Tomb Reliefs and Archaeological Objects from Sichuan Province, People's Republic of China*. Exh. cat. San Francisco: Chinese Cultural Foundation of San Francisco.

Lin Meicun 林梅村
1988 "漢佉二體錢佉盧文解詁" (Interpretation of the Kharosthi inscription on a Han dynasty Kharosthi coin). *Kaogu yu wenwu*, no. 2: 85–87.

1991 "A *Karosthi* Inscription from Chang'an." In *Ji Xianlin jiaoshou bashi huadan jinian lunwenji* 季羨林教授八十華誕紀念論文集 (Papers in honour of Prof. Dr. Ji Xianlin on the occasion of his 80th birthday), edited by Li Zheng 李諍 and Jiang Zhongxin 蔣忠新. 2 vols. Beijing: Beijing waiwen yinshan he Jiangxi renmin chubanshe.

1997a "固原粟特墓所出中古波斯文印章及其相關問題" (On the seal with Middle Persian characters excavated from a Sogdian tomb in Guyuan, Ningxia and some related problems). *Kaogu yu wenwu*, no. 1: 50–54.

1997b "On the Seal Bearing Persian Characters from a Sogdian Tomb in Guyuan and Related Issues." Summary in *China Archaeology and Art Digest*. 2, no. 1: 170–71. Originally published in *Kaogu yu wenwu*, no. 1: 50–54.

1998 *Han Tang xiyu yu Zhongguo wen ming* 漢唐西域與中國文明 (The western regions of the Han–Tang dynasties and Chinese civilization). Beijing: Wenwu chubanshe.

2002 "稽胡史跡考－太原新出隋代虞弘墓誌的幾個問題" (An inquiry into the historical evidence for the Qihu—A few problems concerning the Sui dynasty Yu Hong tomb epitaph recently discovered in Taiyuan). *Zhongguo shi yanjiu* 1: 71–84.

2003 "漢代西域藝術中的希腊文化因素" (Elements of the Xila culture in the Xiyu art of the Han dynasty). *Jiuzhou xuelin*, (winter): 2–35.

Lin Shuzhong 林樹中
1977 "江蘇丹陽南齊陵墓磚印壁畫探討" (An inquiry concerning the stamped brick murals in the Southern Qi mausoleum at Danyang, Jiangsu). *Wenwu*, no. 1: 64–73.

Lingtong xian bowuguan 臨潼縣博物館 (Lingtong County Museum)
1985 "臨潼唐慶山寺舍利塔基精室清理記" (Excavation of the room of Buddhist relics in the pagoda foundation of Qingshan temple in Lintong). *Wenbo*, no. 5: 12–37.

Linrothe, Rob
1999 *Ruthless Compassion: Wrathful Deities in Early Indo-Tibetan Esoteric Buddhist Art*. London: Serindia Publications.

Litvinsky, Boris A., R. Shabani Samghabadi, and Zhang Guangda, eds.
1996 *History of Civilizations of Central Asia*. Vol. 3, *The Crossroads of Civilizations*, A.D. *250 to 750*. Paris: Unesco Publishing.

Liu Jianhua 劉建華
1999 "北齊趙郡王高睿造像及相關文物遺存" (The Northern Qi Buddhist figures and related objects dedicated by Gao Rui, count of Zhao). *Wenwu*, no. 8: 66–77.

2002 "北魏泰常五年彌勒銅佛及相關問題的探討" (Discussion of issues relating to a bronze Milefo Buddhist statue from the 5th year of the reign of Taichang of the Northern Wei dynasty). In *Su Bai xiansheng bazhi huadan jinian wen ji* 宿白先生八秩華誕紀念文集 (Papers in honor of Su Bai on his 80th birthday), vol. 2: 371–98. Beijing: Wenwu chubanshe.

Liu Junxi 劉俊喜
2001 "平城考古再現輝煌" (Pingcheng archaeology reveals another splendid find). *Wenwu shijie*, no. 1: 3–8.

Liu Liangyou 劉良佑
1999 "華光流彩如霞虹：中國玻璃工藝的形成與發展" (The origin and development of the craft of Chinese glassware). *Lishi wenwu*, no. 1: 6–17.

Liu Panxiu 劉磐修
1998 "魏晉南北朝社會上層乘坐牛車風俗述論" (A discussion of the fashion for riding in ox-drawn carriages among the upper classes in the Wei–Jin and Southern and Northern Dynasties period). *Zhongguo dianji yu wenhua*, no. 4: 96–101. English summary in *China Archaeology and Art Digest* 3, no. 4 (2000): 274–78.

Liu, Shi-yee
2003 "An Actor in Real Life: Chen Hongshou's *Scenes from the Life of Tao Yuanming*." Ph.D. diss., Yale University, New Haven.

Liu, Ts'un-yan
1976 "Traces of Zoroastrian and Manichaean Activities in Pre-T'ang China." In Liu Ts'un-yan, *Selected Papers from the Hall of Harmonious Wind*: 3–24. Leiden: E. J. Brill.

Liu Xingwen 劉興文, and Kuancheng xian wenwu Baohu Guanli suo 寬城縣文物保護管理所 (CPAM of Kuancheng County)
1985 "河北寬城出土兩件唐代銀器" (Two Tang silver vessels excavated at Kuancheng, Hebei). *Kaogu*, no. 9: 857–58.

Liu Xinru
1988 *Ancient India and Ancient China: Trade and Religious Exchanges, A.D. 1–600.* Delhi: Oxford University Press.

Liu Yang
2001 "Images for the Temple: Imperial Patronage in the Development of Tang Daoist Art." *Artibus Asiae* 61, no. 2: 189–261.

Liu Yiqing 劉義慶
1982 *See SSXY.*

Liu Yunhui 劉雲輝
1999 "北周若干雲與其玉帶考查" (Ruo Ganyun of Northern Zhou and his jade belt). *Lishi wenwu,* no. 72, (July): 52–56.

Liu Zhiyuan 劉志遠 and Liu Tingbi 劉廷壁, eds.
1958 *Chengdu Wanfosi shike yishu* 成都萬佛寺石刻藝術 (The art of stone sculpture of Wanfo Temple, Chengdu). Beijing: Zhongguo gudian yishu chubanshe.

Livshits, Vladimir A.
2002 "Sogdiiskaia nadpic' na khume iz Ak–Beshima" (A Sogdian inscription on a *khum* [a large jar] from Ak-Besim). In *Suyab – Ak-Beshim*: 128–33, 174. St. Petersburg: State Hermitage Museum.

Longmen wenwu baoguansuo 龍門文物保管所 (Longmen Office of Cultural Properties Preservation) and Beijing daxue kaoguxi 北京大學考古系 (Beijing University, Department of Archaeology), eds.
1992 *Longmen shiku* 龍門石窟 (Longmen caves). 2 vols. Zhongguo shiku series. Beijing: Wenwu chubanshe.

Lu Ji 陸機 (261–303)
1951 *The Art of Letters: Lu Chi's "Wen fu," A.D. 302; a Translation and Comparative Study.* Translation and notes by E. R. Hughes. Bollingen Series, vol. 29. New York: Pantheon Books.

Lu Jiugao 陸九臯 and Han Wei 韓偉
1985 *Tang dai jin yin qi* 唐代金銀器 (Research on Tang gold and silver). Beijing: Wenwu chubanshe.

Lu Kinko 魯金科 (S. L. Rydenko)
1957 "論中國與阿爾泰部落的古代關係" (Relations between Ancient Altai tribes and China). *Kaogu xuebao,* no. 2: 37–48.

Lu Liancheng
1993 "Chariot and Horse Burials in Ancient China." *Antiquity* 67: 824–41.

Lu Sixian 陸思賢 and Chen Tangdong 陳棠棟
1984 "達茂旗出土的古代北方民族飾件" (Ornaments of the ancient northern people excavated from Damaoqi). *Wenwu,* no. 1: 81–83, 29.

Lu Zhaoying 盧兆蔭
1993 *Zhongguo yuqi quanji.* Vol. 4, *Qin Han-Nan beichao* 中國玉器全集四：秦漢－南北朝 (The complete collection of Chinese jades. Vol. 4, From Qin-Han to the Northern and Southern Dynasties). Hebei: Hebei meishu chubanshe.

Lukonin, Vladimir G.
1967 *Persia II.* Translated by James Hogarth. Geneva: Nagel Publishers; Cleveland: World Publishers.

Luo Feng 羅豐
1988 *See* Ningxia Guyuan bowuguan 1988.

1990 "Lacquer Painting on a Northern Wei Coffin." *Orientations* 21, no. 7 (July): 18–29.

1996 *Guyuan nanjiao Sui Tang mudi. See* Ningxia Huizu Zizhiqu Guyuan Bowuguan and Luo Feng.

1998a "A Central Asian-Style Gilt-Silver Ewer." *Orientations* 29, no. 7: 28–33.

1998b "薩寶: 一個唐朝唯一外來官職的再考察" (Re-examining the Sabao: A unique foreign official position in the Tang dynasty). In *Tang Studies* 4: 215–49.

2000a "北周李賢墓出土的中亞風格鎏金銀瓶 – 以巴克特里亞金屬制品為中心" (A gilded silver vase in the Central Asian style from the tomb of Li Xian's of the Northern Zhou period). *Acta Archaeologica Sinica (Kaogu xuebao)*: 311–30.

2000b "*Sabao*: Further Consideration of the Only Post for Foreigners in the Tang Dynasty Bureaucracy." Translated by Bruce Doar. *China Archaeology and Art Digest* 4, no. 1 (December): 165–91.

Luo Zongzhen 羅宗真
1994 *Liuchao kaogu* 六朝考古 (Archaeology of the Six Dynasties). Nanjing: Nanjing daxue chubanshe.

Luoyang bowuguan 洛陽博物館 (Luoyang Museum)
1973 "洛陽北魏元邵墓" (The Northern Wei tomb of Yuan Shao in Luoyang). *Kaogu,* no. 4: 218–24.

1975 "洛陽澗西七里河東漢墓發掘報告" (Report on the excavation of an Eastern Han tomb at Qilihe, Jianxi, Luoyang). *Kaogu,* no. 2: 116–23.

Luoyang shi di er wenwu gongzuodui 洛陽第二文物工作隊 (The 2nd Archaeological Team of Luoyang City)
2000 "洛陽春都路西晉墓發掘簡報" (Excavation of a Jin dynasty tomb in Luoyang). *Wenwu,* no. 10: 26–34.

Luoyang shi wenwu gongzuodui 洛陽市文物工作隊 (Luoyang Cultural Relics Work Team)
1982 "洛陽龍門唐安菩夫婦墓" (The tomb of An Pu and his wife in Longmen, Luoyang). *Zhongyuan wenwu,* no. 3: 21–26, 41.

1990 *Luoyang chutu wenwu jicui* 洛陽出土文物集粹 (Ancient treasures of Luoyang). Beijing: Zhaohua chubanshe.

Lurje, P. B., and Boris I. Marshak
2002 "Sogdian Inscription from Panjikent—2001 Excavations." In *Otchet o raskopkakh drevnego Pendzhikenta v 2001 g.* (Excavations in Panjikent in 2001. A yearly report): 84–86. Saint Petersburg.

Ma Changshou 馬長壽
1985 *Beiming suo jian qian Qin zhi Sui chu de guangzhong buzu* 碑銘所見前秦至隋初的關中部族 (The clans of Guangzhong mentioned in steles and inscriptions from the Former Qin to the early Sui dynasties). Beijing: Zhonghua shuju.

Ma Chengyuan 馬承源 and Yue Feng 岳峰, eds.
1998 *Xinjiang Weiwu'er zizhiqu silu kaogu zhenpin* 新疆維吾尔自治區絲路考古珍品 (Archaeological treasures of the Silk Road in Xinjiang Uygur Autonomous Region). Exh. cat. Shanghai: Shanghai Museum; Shanghai yiwen chubanshe.

Ma Yong 馬雍
1983 "北魏封和突墓及其出土的波斯銀盤" (Notes on the Northern Wei dynasty tomb of Feng Hetu and the Persian silver plate unearthed). *Wenwu,* no. 8: 8–12.

1990 *Xiyu shidi wenwu cong kao* 西域史地文物叢考 (History and cultural relics of the Western Regions). Beijing: Wenwu chubanshe.

Ma Yuji 馬玉基
1983 "大同市小站村花圪塔台北魏墓清理簡報" (Excavation of the Northern Wei tomb at Huagedatai in Xiaozhancun, Datong). *Wenwu,* no. 8: 1–4.

MacCallum, Donald
1996 "The Saidaiji Lineage of the Seiryoji Shaka Tradition." *Archives of Asian Art* 49: 51–67.

Machida Akira 町田章
1983 "南齊帝陵考" (A reexamination of the chronology of the imperial tombs of the Southern Qi dynasty). In *Bunkazai ronsō* 文化財論叢 (Studies in cultural properties): 1071–1104. Kyōto: Dōhōsha.

Mahler, Jane Gaston
1959 *The Westerners among the Figurines of the T'ang Dynasty of China.* Serie Orientale Roma, 20. Rome: Istituto Italiano per il Medio ed Estremo Oriente.

Mair, Victor, ed.
1994 *The Columbia Anthology of Traditional Chinese Literature.* New York: Columbia University Press.

Mango, Marlia Mundell
1990 "Der Seuso-Schatzfund." *Antike Welt* 2: 70–88.

Mao Ming 毛民
2003 *Tu shuo silu shang de huaguo* 圖說絲路上的花果 (Flowers and fruits in images and writing on the Silk Road). Beijing: Renmin meishu chubanshe.

Marshak, Boris Il'ich
1971 *Sogdiiskoe serebro: Ocherki po vostochnoi torevtike* (Sogdian silver). Kultura narodov Vostoka: Materialy i issledovaniia / (Culture of the Peoples of the East: Materials and research). Moscow: Nauka.

1978 "Baktriiskie chashi" (Bactrian Bowls). In *Antichnost'i antichnye traditsii v kul'ture i iskusstve narodov Sovetskogo Vostoka* (Classical Traditions in the Art of the Peoples of the Soviet East): 258–68. Moscow: Nauka.

1986 *Silberschätze des Orients: Metallkunst des 3.–13. Jahrhunderts und ihre Kontinuität.* Leipzig: E. A. Seemann.

1994 "Le programme iconographique des peintures de la 'Salle des ambassadeurs' à Afrasiab (Samarkand)." *Arts asiatiques* 49: 5–10.

1999 "A Sogdian Silver Bowl in the Freer Gallery of Art." *Ars Orientalis* 29: 101–10.

2001 "Ewer Showing Greek Mythological Scenes." In Annette L. Juliano and Judith A. Lerner, *Monks and Merchants: Silk Road Treasures from Northwest China, Gansu, and Ningxia, 4th–7th Century:* 99–100, no. 31. New York: H. Abrams and the Asia Society.

2002a *Legends, Tales, and Fables in the Art of Sogdiana.* Appendix by Vladimir A. Livshits. Biennial Ehsan Yarshater Lecture Series, no. 1. New York: Bibliotheca Persica Press

2002b "Pre-Islamic Painting of the Iranian Peoples and Its Sources in Sculpture and the Decorative Arts." In Eleanor Sims, Boris I. Marshak, and Ernst J. Grube, *Peerless Images: Persian Painting and Its Sources:* 7–19, 92, 100, 105–7, 114, 121, 127–28, 130, 142, 210, 218–19, 220–23, 235, 240–41, 250, 268–69, 288, 293–94, 305–6, 321–23. New Haven: Yale University Press.

Marshak, Boris I., and Wakou Anazawa
1989 "Some Notes on the Tomb of Li Xian and His Wife under the Northern Zhou Dynasty at Guyuan, Ningxia and Its Gold-Gilt Silver Ewer with Greek Mythological Scenes Unearthed There." *Cultura Antiqua* 41, no. 4: 54–57.

Marshak, Boris I., and N. N. Negmatov
1996 "Sogdiana." In *History of Civilizations of Central Asia,* vol. 3, *The Crossroads of Civilizations:* A.D. *250 to 750,* edited by B. A. Litvinsky. Paris: Unesco Publishing.

Marshak, Boris I., and Valentina I. Raspopova
1990a "A Hunting Scene from Panjikent." *Bulletin of the Asia Institute* 4: 77–94.

1990b "Wall Paintings from a House with a Granary, Panjikent, 1st Quarter of the Eighth Century A.D." *Silk Road Art and Archaeology* 1: 123–76.

1998 "Les trouvailles dans la chapelle nord-ouest du Temple II de Pendjikent: À propos de l'héritage classique dans l'art sogdien." *Bulletin of the Asia Institute* 12: 161–69.

Marshall, Sir John Hubert
1951 *Taxila: An Illustrated Account of Archaeological Excavations Carried out at Taxila under the Order of the Government of India between the Years 1913 and 1934.* Cambridge: University Press.

Martiniani-Reber, Marielle
1986 *Lyon, Musée Historique des Tissus: Soieries sassanides, coptes et byzantines, Ve–XIe siècles.* Inventaire des collections publiques françaises, 30. Paris: Éditions de la Réunion des Musées Nationaux.

Mather, Richard B., trans. and ann.
1976 *Shih-shuo Hsin-yü: A New Account of Tales of the World by Liu I-ch'ing.* Commentary by Liu Chün. Minneapolis: University of Minnesota Press.

Matsubara Saburō
1995 *Chūgoku bukkyō chōkoku shiron* (History of Chinese Buddhist sculpture). 4 vols. Tokyo: Yoshikawa Kōbunkan.

Matsui Joryū 松井如流
1959 *Kan Sozen no hi* 漢曹全碑 (The Han dynasty stele for Cao Quan). *Shoseki meihin sôkan* 書跡名品叢刊 (Series of masterpieces of calligraphy), vol. 5. Tokyo: Nigensha.

Matsumoto Kaneo 松本包夫
1984 *Shōsōin-gire to Asuka Tenpyōno senshoku / Jōdai Gire: 7th and 8th Century Textiles in Japan from the Shōsō-in and Hōryū-ji* 仓院裂と飞鸟天平の染织. Kyōto: Shikōsha.

McCausland, Shane, ed.
2003 *Gu Kaizhi and the Admonitions Scroll.* Colloquies on Art and Archaeology in Asia, no. 21, Percival David Foundation of Chinese Art. London: British Museum Press.

McNair, Amy
1995 "Engraved Calligraphy in China: Recension and Reception." *Art Bulletin* 77, no. 1 (March): 106–14.

Melikian-Chirvani, Assadullah Souren
1970 "Iranian Silver and Its Influence in T'ang China." In *Pottery and Metalwork in T'ang China: Their Chronology and External Relations—A Colloquy Held 29 June to 2 July 1970,* edited by William Watson. Colloquies on Art and Archaeology in Asia, no. 1. London: University of London.

1995 "The Wine Birds of Iran from Pre-Achaemenid to Islamic Times." *Bulletin of the Asia Institute,* no. 9: 41–97.

Mi Shijie 米士誡 and Su Jie 蘇捷
1987 "洛陽藏鏡述論" (The bronze mirrors in Luoyang). *Kaogu yu wenwu,* no. 4: 45–53.

Miho Museum
1997 *Miho Museum: South Wing.* [Shigaraki, Shiga Pref.]: Miho Museum.

2001 *Ryūmon sekkutsu* 龍門石窟 *Longmen Caves.* Exh. cat. [Shigaraki, Shiga Pref.]: Miho Museum.

Miki Fumio 三木文雄, ed.
1964 *Nihon Genshi Bijutsu* 日本原始美術

(Japanese prehistoric arts). Vol. 6. Tokyo: Kodansha.

Minyaev, Sergey
2000 "The Origins of the 'Geometric Style' in Hsiungnu Art." In *Kurgans, Ritual Sites, and Settlements: Eurasian Bronze and Iron Age,* edited by Jeannine Davis-Kimball et al.: 293–303. BAR International Series, 890. Oxford: Archaeopress.

Mu Shunying 穆舜英
1987 "從考古材料看唐朝統治下的西域經濟" (Economy in the western regions under the Tang dynasty as reflected in archaeological materials). *Xinjiang wenwu,* no. 3: 49–60.

Mu Shunying 穆舜英 et al., eds.
1994 *Zhongguo Xinjiang gudai yishu* 中國新疆古代藝術 (Ancient art in Xinjiang, China). Urumqi: Xinjiang meishu sheying chubanshe.

Müller, Shing
2002 "The Nomads of the Fifth Century: The Tuoba Xianbei." In *Nomads, Traders and Holy Men along China's Silk Road: Papers Presented at a Symposium Held at the Asia Society in New York, November 9–10, 2001,* edited by Annette L. Juliano and Judith A. Lerner: 33–44. Silk Road Studies, 7. Turnhout, Belgium: Brepols.

Murck, Alfreda
2003 "The Convergence of Gu Kaizhi and Admonitions in the Literary Record." In *Gu Kaizhi and the Admonitions Scroll,* edited by Shane McCausland. London: British Museum.

Museum of Fine Arts, Boston
1982 *Asiatic Art in the Museum of Fine Arts, Boston.* Boston: Museum of Fine Arts.

Nagahiro Toshio 長廣敏雄
1963 "晉宋の竹林七賢と榮啟期の畫圖" (On the wall paintings of 'The Seven Sages of the Bamboo Grove' and Yung Ch'i-ch'i, dated between the Chin and Sung dynasties of China). *Kokka,* no. 857 (August): 15–21.

1969 *Rikuchō jidai bijutsu no kenkyū* 六朝時代美術の研究 (The representational art of the Six Dynasties period). Tokyo: Bijutsu shuppansha.

Nagoyashi hakubutsukan 名古屋市博物館 (Nagoya City Museum) and Chūnichi Shinbunsha 中日新聞社 (Chūnichi Press)
1989 *Chuka jinmin kyowakoku Nankin hakubutsuin meihoten* 中華人民共和國南京博物院名宝圖 (An exhibition of art treasures from the Nanjing Museum collection). Nagoya: Nagoyashi Hakubutsukan and Chūnichi Shinbunsha.

Nakata Yūjirō, ed.
1983 *Chinese Calligraphy.* Translated and adapted by Jeffrey Hunter. Tokyo: Weatherhill/Tankosha. Originally published in Japanese as *Chūgoku no bijutsu: Shoseki* (The arts of China: Calligraphy). Kyōto: Tanokosha, 1982.

Nanjing bowuyuan 南京博物院 (Nanjing Museum)
1974 "江蘇丹陽南朝大墓及磚刻壁畫" (The large Southern Dynasties tomb with stamped-brick murals at Huqiao, Danyang, Jiangsu). *Wenwu,* no. 2: 44–56.

1980a "江蘇丹陽縣胡橋，建山兩座南朝墓葬" (Two tombs of the Southern Dynasties at Huqiao and Jianshan, Danyang, Jiangsu). *Wenwu,* no. 2: 1–17.

1980b "試談'竹林七賢及榮啟期'磚印壁畫問題" (An analysis of the problem of the impressed bricks of "The Seven Sages of the Bamboo Grove"). *Wenwu,* no. 2: 18–23, 36.

1981 "江蘇邗江甘泉二號漢墓" (Tomb 2 at Ganquan, Hanjiang, Jiangsu). *Wenwu,* no. 11: 1–10.

2003 *See* Zhuang Tianming 2003.

Nanjing bowuyuan 南京博物院 (Nanjing Museum) and Nanjing shi wenwu baoguan weiyuanhui 南京市文物保管委員會 (Nanjing City Cultural Relics Preservation Committee)
1960 "南京西善橋南朝墓及其磚刻壁畫" (The Southern Dynasties tomb at Xishanqiao, Nanjing, and its impressed-brick images). *Wenwu,* no. 8/9: 37–42.

Nanjing daxue lishixi kaoguzu 南京大學歷史系考古組 (Nanjing University, the Archaeology Unit of the Department of History)
1973 "南京大學北園東晉墓" (The Eastern Jin tomb in the North Park of Nanjing University). *Wenwu,* no. 4: 36–50.

Nanjing shi bowuguan 南京市博物館 (Nanjing City Museum)
1972 "南京象山5號6號7號墓清理簡報" (Bulletin on the excavation of Tombs 5, 6, and 7 at Xiangshan, Nanjing). *Wenwu,* no. 11: 23–41.

1983 "南京北郊東晉墓發掘簡報" (Excavation report of the Eastern Jin tomb in the northern suburb of Nanjing). *Kaogu,* no. 4: 315–322.

2001 "江蘇南京仙鶴觀東晉墓" (The Eastern Jin tomb at Xianheguan, Nanjing, Jiangsu). *Wenwu,* no. 3: 4–40, 91.

Nanjing shi wenhuaju 南京市文化局 (Nanjing City Cultural Bureau) and Nanjingshi wenwuju 南京市文物局 (Nanjing City Cultural Properties Bureau), eds.
2000 "青釉鷹形瓷器口壺" (Eagle-shaped celadon pot). In *Nanjing wenwu jinghua: qiwu bian* 南京文物精華：器物編 (Highlights of Nanjing's Cultural Properties: Objects): 110. Shanghai: Shanghai renmin meishu chubanshe.

Nara kokuritsu hakubutsukan 奈良国立博物館 (Nara National Museum)
1988 *Shirukurōdo bukkyō bijutsu denrai no michi* シルクロード仏教美術伝来の道 (The path of Buddhist art). Shirukurōdo dai bunmei ten (The grand exhibition of Silk Road civilizations). Exh. cat. Nara: Nara National Museum.

1999 *Shōsōin ten* 正倉院展 (Exhibition from the Collection of Shōsōin Depository). Nara: Nara Kokuritsu Hakubutsukan.

Narain, A. K.
1994 "Indo-Europeans in Inner Asia." In *The Cambridge History of Early Inner Asia,* edited by Denis Sinor. Cambridge: Cambridge University Press.

Needham, Joseph
1974 *Science and Civilisation in China.* Vol. 5, *Chemistry and Chemical Technology,* part 2, *Spagyrical Discovery and Invention: Magisteries of Gold and Immortality.* Cambridge and New York: Cambridge University Press.

Neimenggu wenwu gongzuodui, Neimenggu bowuguan 內蒙古文物工作隊，內蒙古博物館 (Inner Mongolia Archaeological Team and the Inner Mongolia Museum)
1975 "呼和浩特市附近出土的外國金銀幣" (Some Foreign Gold and Silver Coins Unearthed in the Vicinity of Huhehot). *Kaogu,* no. 3: 182–85.

Neimenggu wenwu kaogu wenji 內蒙古文物考古文集
1994 *Neimenggu wenwu kaogu wenji* 內蒙古文物考古文集 (Compedium of cultural relics from Inner Mongolia). Edited by Li Yiyou and Wei Jian. 2 vols. Beijing: Zhongguo dabaike quanshu chubanshe.

Neimenggu zizhiqu bowuguan 內蒙古博物館 (Inner-Mongolia Autonomous Museum)
1987 *Neimenggu lishi wenwu: Neimenggu bowuguan jianguan sanshi zhou nian*

jinian. 內蒙古歷史文物：內蒙古博物館建館三十周年紀念 (Relics of Inner-Mongolia: The thirtieth anniversary of the Inner-Mongolia Museum). 2d ed. Hohhot: Neimenggu zizhiqu bowuguan.

Nickel, Lukas

2002a "Ein Fund erregt Aufsehen: Die Skulpturen aus Qingzhou und der urbane Buddhismus des 6. Jahrhunderts." *Ostasiatische Zeitschrift,* no. 3 (Frühyahr): 5–23.

2002b as editor. *Return of the Buddha: The Qingzhou Discoveries.* Eng. ed. Exh. cat. Zürich: Museum Rietberg; London: Royal Academy of Arts.

Ningxia Guyuan bowuguan 寧夏固原博物館 (Guyuan Museum of Ningxia)

1988 *Guyuan Beiwei muqi guanhua* 固原北魏墓漆棺畫 (An introduction to the lacquer coffin paintings and other objects unearthed in a northern Wei tomb in Guyuan, Ningxia). Ningxia: Ningxia renmin chubanshe.

Ningxia Huizu zizhiqu bowuguan 寧夏回族自治區博物館 (Museum of Ningxia Hui Autonomous Region)

1988 "寧夏鹽池唐墓發掘簡報" (Excavation of the Tang tombs at Yanchi, Ningxia). *Wenwu,* no. 9: 43–56.

Ningxia Huizu zizhiqu bowuguan 寧夏回族自治區博物館 (Museum of Ningxia Hui Autonomous Region) and Ningxia Guyuan bowuguan 寧夏固原博物館 (Guyuan Museum of Ningxia)

1985 "寧夏固原北周李賢夫婦墓發掘簡報" (Excavation of the Northern Zhou dynasty tomb of Li Xian and his wife at Guyuan, Ningxia). *Wenwu,* no. 11: 1–20.

Ningxia Huizu zizhiqu Guyuan bowuguan 寧夏回族自治區固原博物館 (Museum of Ningxia Hui Autonomous Region) and Luo Feng 羅豐

1996 *Guyuan nanjiao Sui Tang mudi* 固原南郊隋唐墓地 (A graveyard of the Sui and Tang dynasties in the southern suburbs of Guyuan). Beijing: Wenwu chubanshe.

Ningxia Huizu zizhiqu Guyuan bowuguan 寧夏回族自治區固原博物館 (Museum of Ningxia Hui Autonomous Region) and Zhongri Yuanzhou lianhe kaogudui 中日原州聯合考古隊 (Sino-Japanese Yuanzhou joint archaeological team)

1999 *Yuanzhou gu mu jicheng* 原州古墓集成 (Collection of the ancient tombs in Yuanzhou). Beijing: Wenwu chubanshe.

Ningxia wenwu kaogu yanjiusuo 寧夏文物考古研究所 (Ningxia Institute of Archaeology) and Ningxia Guyuan bowuguan 寧夏固原博物館 (Guyuan Museum of Ningxia)

1992 "寧夏固原隋史射勿墓發掘簡報" (Excavation of the Sui tomb of Shi Shewu in Guyuan county, Ningxia). *Wenwu,* no. 10: 15–22.

Niu Bingyue 牛秉鉞

1994 *Feicui shihua* 翡翠史話 (A popular history of jadeite), Beijing: Zijincheng chubanshe.

Oakeshott, Walter F.

1967 *The Mosaics of Rome, from the Third to the Fourteenth Centuries.* Greenwich, Conn.: New York Graphic Society.

1968 *Die Mosaiken von Rom.* Leipzig.

Okazaki, Joji

1977 *Pure Land Buddhist Painting.* Translated and adapted by Elizabeth ten Grotenhuis. New York and Tokyo: Kodansha.

Ōnishi Shūya

2003 "The Monastery Kōryūji's 'Crowned Maitreya' and the Stone Pensive Bodhisattva Excavated at Longxingsi." In Washizuka Hiromitsu, Park Youngbok, and Kang Woobang, *Transmitting the Forms of Divinity: Early Buddhist Art from Korea and Japan,* edited by Naomi Noble Richard: 55–65. Exh. cat. New York: Japan Society.

Otavsky, Karel

1998 *Entlang der Seidenstrasse: Frühmittelalterliche Kunst zwischen Persien und China in der Abegg-Stiftung.* Contributions by Sheila Blair et al. Riggisberger Berichte, 6. Riggisberg: Abegg-Stiftung.

Oxus

1993 *Oxus: Tesori dell'Asia centrale.* Essays by Evgenii Vladislavovich Zejmal et al. Exh. cat. Rome: Palazzo Venezia; Rome: Edizioni De Luca.

Pandey, C. B.

1982 *Mauryan Art.* Delhi: Varanasi.

Parlasca, Klaus

1980 "Griechisches und Römisches im alten China." *Allgemeine und vergleichende Archäologie* (Bonn) 2: 297–304.

Pavchinskaia, L. V.

1994 "Sogdian Ossuaries." *Bulletin of the Asia Institute,* n.s., 8: 209–25.

Peng Xinwei 彭信威

1965 *Zhongguo huobi shi* 中國貨幣史 (A history of Chinese currency). Shanghai: Shanghai renmin chubanshe.

Pengzhou shi bowuguan 彭州市博物館 (Pengzhou City Museum) and Chengdu shi wenwu kaogu yanjiusuo 成都市文物考古研究所 (Chengdu City Institute of Archaeology), eds.

2003 "四川彭州龍興寺出土石造像" (Stone Buddhist statues found in Longxingsi, Pengshou, Sichuan). *Wenwu* 9: 74–86.

Pfister, R.

1934 *Textiles de Palmyre découverts par le Service des Antiquités du Haut-commissariat de la République française dans la nécropole de Palmyre, III.* Paris: Les Éditions d'Art et d'Histoire.

Pfister, R., and Louisa Bellinger

1945 *The Excavations at Dura-Europos. Final Report.* Vol. 4, part 2, *The Textiles.* New Haven: Yale University Press.

Pfrommer, Michael

1993 *Metalwork from the Hellenized East: Catalogue of the Collections.* Malibu: J. Paul Getty Museum.

Pletneva, Svetlana A., ed.

1981 *Stepi Evrazii v epokhu srednevekov'ia* (The Eurasian Steppes during the Middle Ages). Arkheologiia SSSR. Moscow: Nauka.

Pohl, Walter and Helmut Reimitz, eds.

1998 *Strategies of Distinction: The Construction of Ethnic Communities, 300–800.* Leiden: E. J. Brill.

Pope, Arthur Upham, and Phyllis Ackerman, eds.

1964–65 *A Survey of Persian Art, from Prehistoric Times to the Present.* 15 vols. Reissue, with corrigenda and addenda, of the 6 vol. 1938–39 ed. Tokyo: Meiji-shobo; London and New York: Oxford University Press.

Popova, Irina F.

1999 *Politicheskaia praktika i idealogiia rannetanskogo Kitaia* (Political practice and ideology during early Tang China). Saint Petersburg: Rossiiskaia Akademiia Nauk, Institut Vostokovedeniia; Moscow: Izdatel'skaia firma "Vostochnaia Literatura."

Pugachenkova, Galina A.

1994 "The Form and Style of Sogdian Ossuaries." *Bulletin of the Asia Institute,* n.s., 8: 227–43.

Qi Dongfang 齊東方

1996a "A Silver Bowl with a Deer Design

Unearthed at Shapo Village in Xi'an." *China Archaeology and Art Digest* 1, no. 1 (January–March): 15–20.

1996b "西安沙坡村出土的粟特鹿紋銀碗考" (Study of the silver bowl with Sogdian deer design excavated in Shapo village of Xi'an). *Wenwu*, no. 2: 45–50.

1999a "略論中國新出土的羅馬,薩珊玻璃器" (Sassanian and Roman glassware excavated in China). *Lishi wenwu*, no. 1: 23–29.

1999b *Tangdai jinyinqi yanjiu* 唐代金銀器研究 (Research on Tang gold and silver). Beijing: Zhongguo shehui kexue chubanshe.

1999c "玉潤瑩淨話玻璃" (*Yu run ying jing*: On glassware). *Lishi wenwu*, no. 1: 18–22.

Qi Dongfang 齊東方 and Zhang Jing 張靜
1998 "薩珊式金銀多曲長杯在中國的流傳與演變" (Evolution of the Sasanian type of multilobed oval gold and silver dish in China). *Kaogu*, no. 6: 63–73.

Qi Gong 啟功, ed.
1987 *Zhongguo meishu quanji: Shufa zhuanke bian 1: Shang Zhou zhi Qin Hanshufa* 中國美術全集：書法篆刻編一，商周至秦漢書法 (Complete collection of Chinese arts: Calligraphy and seal carving series 1: From the Shang–Zhou to the Qin–Han era). Beijing: Renmin meishu chubanshe.

Qi Jixiang 齊吉祥
2001 *Zhongguo lishi bowuguan* 中國歷史博物館 (Chinese History Museum). Chengdu: Sichuan shao nian er tong chubanshe.

Qian Boquan 錢伯泉
1995 "從新疆發現的有翼人像看希臘、羅馬文化的東傳" (The eastern transmission of Xila and Roman culture through the discovery of winged figure images in Xinjiang). *Sichou zhi lu*, no. 5: 32–34.

Qin Liexin 秦烈新
1972 "前涼金錯泥筒" (Former Liang vessel for [seal] clay with gold inlay). *Wenwu*, no. 6: 36–37.

Qinghai sheng wenwu kaogu yanjiusuo 青海省文物考古研究所 (Qinghai Provincial Institute of Archaeology)
1993 *Shangsunjiazhai Han Jin mu* 上孫家寨漢晉墓 (The Han–Jin cemetery at Shangsunjiazhai). Beijing: Wenwu chubanshe.

Qiu Ling 邱陵
1994 "米蘭佛寺'有翼天使'壁畫新探" (A new study of the images of angels with wings in the mural paintings of Buddhist temples in Miran). *Xinjiang wenwu*, no. 1: 42–47.

Quest for Eternity
1987 *The Quest for Eternity: Chinese Ceramic Sculptures from the People's Republic of China*. Exh. cat. Los Angeles: Los Angeles County Museum of Art; San Francisco: Chronicle Books.

Raspopova, Valentina
1999 "Gold Coins and Bracteates from Pendjikent." In *Coins, Art, and Chronology: Essays on pre-Islamic History of the Indo-Iranian Borderlands*, edited by Michael Alram and Deborah E. Klimburg-Salter: 453–60. Beiträge zur Kultur- und Geistesgeschichte Asiens, no. 31. Vienna: Österreichischen Akademie der Wissenschaften.

Rawson, Jessica
1977 "Chinese Silver and Its Western Origins." *Connoisseur* 196: 36–43.

1982 *The Ornament on Chinese Silver of the Tang Dynasty (AD 618–906)*. Occasional Paper, no. 40. London: British Museum.

1984 *Chinese Ornament: The Lotus and the Dragon*. London: British Museum Publications.

1991 "Central Asian Silver and Its Influence on Chinese Ceramics." *Bulletin of the Asia Institute*, n.s., 5: 139–51.

1995 *Chinese Jade from the Neolithic to the Qing*. London: British Museum.

Read, Herbert
1965 *The Origins of Form in Art*. New York: Horizon Press.

Ren Rixin 任日新
1981 "山東諸城漢墓畫像石" (Pictorial stone reliefs from a Han tomb in Zhucheng, Shandong). *Wenwu*, no. 10: 14–21.

Rhie, Marilyn Martin
1982 "Late Sui Buddhist Sculpture: A Chronology and Regional Analysis." *Archives of Asian Art* 35: 27–54.

1988 "Interrelationships between the Buddhist Art of China and the Art of India and Central Asia from 618–755 A.D." *Annali* (supplement) 48, no. 54, fasc. 1: 1–44.

1995 "The Earliest Chinese Bronze Bodhisattva Sculptures." *Arts of Asia* 25, no. 2: 86–98.

1999 *Early Buddhist Art of China and Central Asia*. Vol. 1, *Later Han, Three Kingdoms and Western Chin in China and Bactria to Shan-shan in Central Asia*. Handbuch der Orientalistik, ser. 4, vol. 12. Leiden: Brill.

2002 *Early Buddhist Art of China and Central Asia*. Vol. 2, *The Eastern Chin and Sixteen Kingdoms Period in China, Tumshuk, Kucha and Karashar in Central Asia*. Handbuch der Orientalistik, ser. 4, vol. 12. Leiden: Brill.

Riboud, Krishna
1977 "Some Remarks on Face Covers (Fu-mien) Discovered in the Tombs of Astana." *Oriental Art* 23: 438–54.

Riboud, Krishna, and Gabriel Vial
1970 *Tissus de Touen-Houang conservés au Musée Guimet et à la Bibliothèque nationale*. Mission Paul Pelliot, Documents archéologiques, 13. Paris.

Riegl, Alois
1992 *Problems of Style: Foundations for a History of Ornament*. Translated from German by Evelyn Kain; annotations, glossary, and introduction by David Castriota. Princeton: Princeton University Press.

Rong Xinjiang 榮新江
1993 "古代塔里木盆地週邊的粟特移民" (Ancient Sogdian immigrants along the border of the Taklimakan Basin). *Xiyu Studies*, no. 2: 8–15.

2000a "The Juqu Anzhou Stele and the Daliang in Qoco." *China Archaeology and Art Digest* 3, no. 4 (June): 318–21.

2000b "Research on Zoroastrianism in China, 1923–2000." Translated by Bruce Doar. *China Archaeology and Art Digest* 4, no. 1 (December): 7–13.

Rong Xinjiang 榮新江 and Zhang Zhiqing 張志清
2004 *Cong sama'ergan dao Chang'an* 從撒馬爾干到長安 (From Samarkand to Chang'an: Cultural traces of the Sogdians in China). Beijing: Beijing tushuguan chubanshe.

Rosenfield, John M.
1967 *The Dynastic Arts of the Kushans*. Berkeley and Los Angeles: University of California.

Rostovtzeff, M.
1943 "The Parthian Shot." *American Journal of Archaeology* 47, no. 2: 174–87.

Ruan Qiurong 阮秋榮
1998 "茱萸回紋錦覆面" (Brocade face cover with dogwood and square spiral design). In *Xinjiang Weiwuer zizhiqu silu kaogu zhenpin* 新疆維吾爾自治區絲路考古珍品 (Archaeological treasures of the Silk Road in Xinjiang Uygur Autonomous Region): 261–62. Shanghai: Shanghai yiwen chubanshe.

Sarianidi, Viktor Ivanovich
1985 Institute of Archaeology of the USSR Academy of Sciences, Moscow, and National Museum of Afghanistan, Kabul. *Bactrian Gold from the Excavations of the Tillya-tepe Necropolis in Northern Afghanistan.* Translated by Arthur Shkarovsky-Raffé. Leningrad: Aurora, New York: Harry N. Abrams.

Sāsān-cho Perusiano koin
2003 *Sāsān-cho Perusiano koin: Ō no shōzō ga kataru to bunka Sāsān-Cho Perusiano koin* ササン朝ペルシャのコイン:王の肖像画語る文化とササン朝のコイン (Coins of Sasanian Persia: History and culture as seen in portraits of kings). Tokyo: Center of Near Eastern Culture.

Scaglia, Gustina
1958 "Central Asians on a Northern Ch'i Gate Shrine." *Artibus Asiae* 21, no. 1: 9–28.

Schafer, Edward H.
1963 *The Golden Peaches of Samarkand: A Study of T'ang Exotics.* Berkeley: University of California Press.

Schloss, Ezekiel
1969 *Foreigners in Ancient Chinese Art from Private and Museum Collections.* Exh. cat. New York: China House Gallery, China Institute in America.

Schmidt, J. Heinrich
1932 "Sasanian Silverwork." *Apollo* 15: 20–26, 124–26.

Schmidt-Colinet, Andreas
1995 *Palmyra: Kulturbegegnung im Grenzbereich.* Zaberns Bildbände zur Archäologie, vol. 27. Mainz am Rhein: Verlag Philipp von Zabern.

Schroeder, Ulrich von
2001 *Buddhist Sculptures in Tibet.* Vol. 2, *Tibet and China.* Hong Kong: Visual Dharma.

Seagraves, Julie
2003 "Necklace." In *The Glory of the Silk Road: Art from Ancient China,* edited by Li Jian, no. 114. Exh. cat. Dayton: Dayton Art Institute.

Seipel, Wilfried
1996 *Weihrauch und Seide: Alte Kulturen an der Seidenstrasse.* Exh. cat. Vienna: Kunsthistorisches Museum Wien in collaboration with the State Hermitage Museum, St Petersburg.

Sekai bijutsu daizenshū
1997 *Sekai bijutsu daizenshū: Tōyōhen* 世界美術大全集 (New history of world art: East Asian series). Vol. 4: *Zui-Tō* 隋唐 (Sui-Tang). Donohashi Akio 百橋明穂 and Nakano Tōru 中野徹. Tokyo: Shōgakkan.

Selby, Stephen
2000 *Chinese Archery.* Hongkong: Hongkong University Press.

Serruys, Henry
1969 "A Note on China's Northern Frontier." *Monumenta Serica* 28: 442–61.

Sha Biti 沙比提
1973 "從考古發掘資料看新疆古代的棉花種植和紡織" (Cotton planting and weaving in ancient Xinjiang in the light of archaeological data). *Wenwu,* no. 10: 48–51.

Shaanxi kaogu yanjiusuo 陝西考古研究所 (Shaanxi Institute of Archaeology) et al.
1997 "北周武帝孝陵發掘簡報" (Bulletin on the excavation of Xiaoling mausoleum of Emperor Wudi of Northern Zhou). *Kaogu yu wenwu* 2: 8–28.

Shaanxi sheng bowuguan 陝西省博物館 (Shaanxi Provincial Museum)
1990 *Shaanxi sheng bowuguan* 陝西省博物館. Zhongguo bowuguan congshu series, vol. 1. Beijing: Wenwu chubanshe.

Shaanxi sheng bowuguan 陝西省博物館 (Shaanxi Provincial Museum) et al.
1972 "唐鄭仁泰發掘簡報" (Excavation of the tomb of Zheng Rentai of the Tang dynasty). *Wenwu,* no. 7: 33–42.

1974 as editors. *Tang Li Xian mubihua* 唐李賢墓壁畫 (Mural paintings from the tomb of Prince Li Xian of the Tang dynasty). Beijing: Wenwu chubanshe.

1983 as editors, with Li Yuzheng 李域錚, Zhao Minsheng 赵敏生, and Lei Bing 雷冰. *Xi'an Beilin shufa yishu* 西安碑林書法藝術 (Calligraphic art in the Forest of Steles, Xi'an). Xi'an: Shaanxi renmin meishu chubanshe.

1988 as editors, with Li Yuzheng 李域錚, Zhao Minsheng 赵敏生, and Lei Bing 雷冰. *Xi'an Beilin shufa yishu* 西安碑林書法藝術 (Calligraphic art in the Forest of Steles, Xi'an). Rev. ed. Xi'an: Renmin meishu chubanshe.

Shaanxi sheng bowuguan 陝西省博物館 (Shaanxi Provincial Museum), Qian xian Qianling wenwu baoguansuo 乾縣乾陵文物保管所 (Bureau of Cultural Properties Preservation Qianling, Qian Province)
1973 "對《談章懷，懿德兩墓的形制等問題》一文的幾點意見" (Some observations on the "Discussion of the structures and other questions concerning the two tombs of the [Crown Princes] Zhanghuai and Yide"). *Wenwu,* no. 12: 67–68.

Shaanxi sheng bowuguan geiweihui xiezuo xiaozu 陝西省博物館革委會寫作小組 (Writing Group of Shaanxi Provincial Museum Revolutionary Committee)
1972 "西安南郊何家村發現唐代窖藏文物" (Relics of the Tang dynasty hoard found at Hejiacun in the southern suburbs of Xi'an). *Wenwu,* no. 1: 30–42.

Shaanxi sheng bowuguan, Qian xian wenjiaoju Tangmu fajue zu 陝西省博物館和乾縣文教局唐墓發掘組 (Shaanxi Provincial Museum, Tang Tombs Excavation Group, Qian County Bureau of Culture and Education)
1972a "唐章懷太子墓發掘簡報" (Excavation of the tomb of Prince Zhanghuai of the Tang dynasty). *Wenwu,* no. 7: 13–25.

1972b "唐懿德太子墓發掘簡報" (Excavation of the tomb of Prince Yide of the Tang dynasty). *Wenwu,* no. 7: 26–31.

Shaanxi sheng kaogu yanjiusuo 陝西省考古研究所 (Shaanxi Institute of Archaeology)
2001 "北周安伽墓圍屏石榻之相關問題淺見" (Some observations on questions on the Northern Zhou An Jia tomb excavated in Xi'an). *Wenwu,* no. 1: 4–26.

Shaanxi sheng kaogu yanjiusuo 陝西省考古研究所 (Shaanxi Institute of Archaeology), Pucheng xian wenti guangdianju 蒲城縣文體廣電局 (Pucheng County Cultural Broadcast Bureau)
1999 "唐惠庄太子墓發掘簡報" (Excavation bulletin on the Tomb of Prince Huizhuang of the Tang Dynasty). *Kaogu yu wenwu,* no. 2: 3–21.

Shaanxi sheng kaogu yanjiusuo 陝西省考古研究所 (Shaanxi Institute of Archaeology), Shaanxi lishi bowuguan 陝西歷史博物館 (Shaanxi History Museum), and Zhaoling bowuguan 昭陵博物館 (Zhaoling Museum)
1997 "唐昭陵新城公主墓發掘簡報"

(Excavation report of the tomb of Princess Xincheng in Zhaoling Mausoleum). *Kaogu yu wenwu*, no. 3: 3–38.

Shaanxi sheng wenwu gongzuo weiyuanhui 陕西省文物工作委員會, Zhaoling wenguanhui 昭陵文管會 (Shaanxi Provincial Cultural Relics Administrative Committee and Zhaoling Cultural Relics Administrative Committee)
1978 "陕西禮泉唐張士貴墓" (Excavation of the tomb of Zhang Shigui in Liquan County of Shanxi). *Wenwu*, no. 3: 168–78.

Shaanxi sheng wenwu guanli weiyuanhui 陕西省文物管理委員會 (Shaanxi Province Cultural Properties Management Committee)
1959 "西安南郊草場坡村北朝墓的發掘" (Excavation of a tomb of the Northern Dynasties at Caochangpo village in the southern suburb of Xi'an). *Kaogu*, no. 6: 285–87.

Shandong sheng Qingzhou shi bowuguan 山東省青州市博物館 (Qingzhou city Museum, Shandong Province)
1998 "山東省青州市龍興寺佛教造像藏清理簡報" (Bulletin on the excavation of a storage pit of Buddhist icons in the Longxing Temple at Qingzhou, Shandong). *Wenwu*, no. 2: 4–15.

Shandong sheng wenwu kaogu yanjiusuo 山東省文物考古研究所 (Shandong Institute of Archaeology)
1984 "臨淄北朝崔氏墓" (The Cui Clan graveyard of the Northern Dynasties at Linzi in Shandong Province). *Kaogu xuebao*, no. 2: 221–44.

Shandong sheng wenwu kaogu yanjiusuo 山東省文物考古研究所 (Shandong Institute of Archaeology) et al.
1989 "濟南市東八巴里洼北朝壁畫墓" (The Northern dynasty tomb murals at Dongbaliwa, Jinan). *Wenwu*, no. 4: 67–78.

Shanghai bowuguan 上海博物館 (Shanghai museum)
2000 *Cao yuan guibao: Neimenggu wenwu kaogu jingpin* 草原瑰寶：內蒙古文物考古精品 (Treasures of the Grassland: Archaeological Finds from the Inner Mongolia Autonomous Region). Shanghai: Shanghai shuhua chubanshe.

Shanghai shi fangzhi kexue yanjiuyuan et al. 上海市紡織科學研究院等 (Shanghai City Textile Sciences Research Institute)
1980 *Changsha Mawangdui yihao Hanmu chutu fangzhipin di yanjiu* 長沙馬王堆一號漢墓出土紡織品的研究 (A study of the textiles unearthed from Han tomb no. 1 at Mawangdui in Changsha). Beijing: Wenwu chubanshe.

Shangwu Yinshuguan
1998 *See* Li Yongliang 1998.

Shanxi sheng Datong shi bowuguan 山西省大同市博物館 (Datong City Museum, Shanxi Province) and Shanxi sheng wenwu gongzuo wei yuan hui 山西省文物工作委員會 (Shanxi Province Committee for the Cultural Properties Work Team)
1972 "山西大同石家寨北魏司馬金龍墓" (The Northern Wei tomb of Sima Jinlong in Shijiazhai, Datong, Shanxi). *Wenwu*, no. 3: 20–33, 64.

Shanxi sheng kaogu yanjiusuo 山西省考古研究所 (Shanxi Institute of Archaeology)
1992 "大同南郊北魏墓群發掘簡報" (Excavation of the Northern Wei Tombs in the southern suburbs of Datong city). *Wenwu*, no. 8: 1–11.

2001 "太原隋代虞弘墓清理簡報" (Bulletin on the excavation of the Sui tomb of Yu Hong in Taiyuan). *Wenwu*, no. 1: 27–51.

Shanxi sheng kaogu yanjiusuo 山西省考古研究所 (Shanxi Institute of Archaeology) and Datong shi kaogu yanjiusuo 大同市考古研究所 (Datong City Institute of Archaeology)
2001 "大同市北魏宋紹祖墓發掘簡報" (Excavation of Song Shaozu's tomb of the Northern Wei dynasty in Datong). *Wenwu*, no. 7: 19–39.

Shanxi sheng kaogu yanjiusuo 山西省考古研究所 (Shanxi Institute of Archaeology) and Taiyuan shi wenwu guanli weiyuanhui 太原市文物管理委員會 (Taiyuan City Cultural Properties Management Committee)
1992 "太原隋斛律徹墓清理簡報" (Excavation of the Sui tomb of Hulu Che in Taiyuan county). *Wenwu*, no. 10: 1–14.

She Taishan 佘太山
1995 *Xiyu wenhua shi* 西域文化史 (A cultural history of the western regions). Beijing: Zhongguo youyi chubanshe.

Shen Congwen 沈從文
1992 *Zhongguo gudai fushi yanjiu* 中國古代服飾研究 (Research on ancient Chinese clothing). Hong Kong: Shangwu yinshuguan.

Sheng, Angela.
1999 "Woven Motifs in Turfan Silks: Chinese or Iranian?" *Orientations* 30, no. 4 (April): 45–52.

Shepherd, Dorothy G.
1964 "Sasanian Art in Cleveland." *Bulletin of the Cleveland Museum of Art* 41, no. 4: 66–92.

1966 "Two Silver Rhyta." *Bulletin of the Cleveland Museum of Art* 53, no. 8 (October): 289–311.

1981 "Zandaniji Revisited." In *Documenta Textilia: Festschrift für Sigrid Müller-Christensen*, edited by Mechthild Flury-Lemberg and Karen Stolleis: 105–22. Munich: Deutscher Kunstverlag.

Shepherd, Dorothy G., and W. B. Henning
1959 "Zandaniji Identified?" In *Aus der Welt der islamischen Kunst: Festschrift für Ernst Kühnel zum 75. Geburtstag am 26. 10. 1957*: 15–40. Berlin: Gebr. Mann.

Shih Hsio-Yen
1983 "Gold and Silver Vessels Excavated in North China: Problems of Origin." *New Asia Academic Bulletin* 4: 63–82, figs. 1–64.

Shijiazhuang diqu geweihui wenhuaju wenwu fajuezu 石家庄地區革委會文化局文物發掘 (Cultural Properties Excavation Group, Bureau of Culture, Shijiazhuang Region Revolutionary Committee)
1977 "河北贊皇東魏李希宗墓" (The Eastern Wei tomb of Li Xizong at Zanhuang, Hebei). *Kaogu*, no. 6: 372, 382–90.

Shiruku rōdo-gaku kenkyū sentā シルクロード学研究センター (Research Center for Silk Roadology)
2000 *Torufan chiiki to shutsudo kinuorimono* トルファン地域と出土絹織物 (Tulufan basin and Paleo silk textiles). Nara-shi: Shiruku rōdo-gaku kenkyū sentā.

Shodō zenshū
1954–68 *Shodō zenshū* 書道全書 (Compilation of calligraphic works). New series. 26 vols. Tokyo: Heibonsha.

Shoseki meihin sōkan
1958–79 *Shoseki meihin sōkan* 書跡名品叢刊 (Series of masterpieces of calligraphy). 203 vols. Tokyo: Nigensha.

Shōsō-in hōmotsu 正倉院
1987–89 *Shōsō-in hōmotsu: Hokusō* 正倉院宝物：北倉 (Treasures of the Shōsō-in: North Depository). Tokyo: Asahi Shinbunsha.

Shumei Family Collection
1996 *Ancient Art from the Shumei Family Collection*. Texts by Dorothea Arnold et al. Exh. cat. New York: The Metropolitan Museum of Art.

Sichuan sheng wenwu guanli weiyuanhui 四川省文物管理委員會 (Sichuan Provincial Relics

Management Committee)

1985 “四川省忠縣涂井蜀漢崖墓” (A Shu-Han cliff tomb at Chujing, Zhong County, Sichuan). *Wenwu* no. 7: 49–86.

Sims-Williams, Nicholas

1989 *Sogdian and Other Iranian Inscriptions of the Upper Indus.* 2 vols. Corpus inscriptionum iranicarum, part 2, Inscriptions of the Seleucid and Parthian Periods and of Eastern Iran and Central Asia, vol. 3, Sogdian. London: School of Oriental and African Studies.

1995 “A Bactrian Inscription on a Silver Vessel from China.” *Bulletin of the Asia Institute,* n.s., 9: 225.

1996 “The Sogdian Merchants in China and India.” In *Cina e Iran: Da Alessandro Magno alla dinastia Tang,* edited by Alfredo Cadonna and Lionello Lanciotti: 45–67. Florence: Olschki.

2002 “The Bactrian Inscription on the Seal of Khingila.” *Silk Road Art and Archaeology* 8: 143–48.

Sirén, Osvald

1956–58 *Chinese Painting: Leading Masters and Principles.* 7 vols. New York: Ronald Press.

Skaff, Jonathan K.

1998 “Sasanian and Arab–Sasanian Silver Coins from Turfan: Their Relationship to International Trade and Local Economy.” *Asia Major* 11, no. 2: 67–115.

Smilenko, Alla T.

1965 *Hlodos'ki skarby* (The Glodosy treasure). Kiev: Vyd-vo “Naukova Dumka.”

Smirnov, Iakov Ivanovich

1909 *Vostochnoe serebro.* Saint Petersburg: N.p.

Smith, Anthony D.

1988 *The Ethnic Origins of Nations.* Oxford: Basil Blackwell.

Sofukawa Hiroshi 曾布川寛

1991 “南朝帝陵の石獣と磚畫” (Stone guardian animals and brick murals of the royal tombs of the Southern Dynasties). *Tohō gakuhō,* no. 3: 115–263.

Sokolova, Irina V.

1997 “Monety Pereshchepinskogo klada” (Coins of the Pereshchepino Hoard). In Vera N. Zalesskaia et al., *Kubrat Khan khazinalare / Sokrovishcha khana Kubrata: Pereshchepinskii klad* (The treasures of Khan Kubrat: The Pereshchepino hoard): 17–41. Exh. cat. Saint Petersburg: State Hermitage Museum.

Song Boyin 宋伯胤

1992 “竹林七賢磚畫散考” (A study of the Seven Sages of the Bamboo Grove). In *Nanjing bowuyuancang baolu* 南京博物院藏寶錄 (Record of the treasures of the Nanjing Museum): 264–69. Shanghai: Shanghai wenyi chubanshe.

Soper, Alexander Coburn

1958 “Northern Liang and Northern Wei in Kansu.” *Artibus Asiae* 21, no. 2: 131–64.

1959 *Literary Evidence for Early Buddhist Art in China.* Artibus Asiae, Supplementum, 19. Ascona, Switzerland: Artibus Asiae.

1960 “South Chinese Influence on the Buddhist Art of the Six Dynasties Period.” *Bulletin of the Museum of Far Eastern Antiquities* 32: 47–112.

1961 “A New Chinese Tomb Discovery: The Earliest Representation of a Famous Literary Theme.” *Artibus Asiae* 24, no. 2: 79–86.

1966 “Imperial Cave-Chapels of the Northern Dynasties: Donors, Beneficiaries, Dates.” *Artibus Asiae* 28, no. 4: 241–70.

1990 “Whose Body? (With apologies to Dorothy L. Sayers).” *Asiatische Studien* 44: 205–16.

Spiro, Audrey

1990 *Contemplating the Ancients: Aesthetic and Social Issues in Early Chinese Portraiture.* Berkeley and Los Angeles: University of California Press.

Splendeur des Sassanides

1993 *Splendeur des Sassanides: L'empire perse entre Rome et la Chine (224–642).* Exh. cat. Brussels: Musées Royaux d'Art et d'Histoire.

Stavisky, Boris

1989 “Zoomorphic Capitals in Central Asia and Transcaucasia: Origins and Development.” *Bulletin of the Asia Institute,* n.s., 3: 53–60.

1997 “Bactria and Gandhara: The Old Problem Reconsidered in the Light of Archaeological Data from Old Termez.” In *Gandharan Art in Context: East-West Exchanges at the Crossroads of Asia,* edited by F. Raymond Allchin et al., 29–53. New Delhi: Regency Publications.

Su Bai 宿白

1978 “北魏洛陽城和北邙陵墓，鮮卑遺跡輯錄之三” (Northern Wei Luoyang City and Beimang tombs—A compilation of excavation reports of Xianbei sites, part 3). *Wenwu,* no. 7: 42–52.

1996 *Zhongguo shikusi yanjiu* 中國石窟寺研究 (Studies on the cave temples of China). Beijing: Wenwu chubanshe.

1998 “Origins and Trends in the Depiction of Human Figures in China of the Fifth and Sixth Centuries.” In *China 5,000 Years: Innovation and Transformation in the Arts,* selected by Sherman Lee: 132–43. Exh. cat. New York: Solomon R. Guggenheim Museum.

1999a “青州城考略－青州城與龍興寺之一” (Textual research on the city of Qingzhou: Qingzhou city and Longxing temple, part 1). *Wenwu,* no. 8: 47–56.

1999b “龍興寺沿革－青州城與龍興寺之二” (Historical evolution of Longxing Temple: Qingzhou City and Longxing Temple, part 2). *Wenwu,* no. 9: 37–42.

1999c “青州龍興寺窖藏所出佛像的幾個問題-青州城與龍興寺之三” (Issues of Buddhist sculptures found in Qinglong temple: Qingzhou City and Longxing temple, part 3). *Wenwu,* no. 10: 44–59.

2002 *Su Bai xiansheng bazhi huadan jinian wenji.* 宿白先生八秩華誕紀念文集 (Papers in honor of Su Bai on the occasion of his 80th birthday). 2 vols. Beijing: Wenwu chubanshe.

Su Beihai 蘇北海

1989 “蘇北海哈薩克草原塞種人的文化” (The culture of the Saka in the Kazakh prairie). *Xinjiang wenwu,* no. 4: 94–105.

Su Jian 蘇建

1995 “洛陽新獲石辟邪的造型藝術與漢代石辟邪的分期” (The art and dating of the Han stone chimera recently recovered in Luoyang). *Zhongyuan wenwu,* no. 2: 66–71.

Suixi xian bowuguan 遂溪縣博物館 (Suixi County Museum)

1982 “廣西遂溪縣發現南朝窖藏金銀” (The Southern Dynasties silver and gold vessel hoard found at Suixi County, Guangdong). *Kaogu,* no. 3: 243–46.

Sun Hongmei 孫紅梅 and Deng Xueqing 鄧學清
1999 "唐代天王俑藝術形象賞析" (An appreciation of the art of Tang-dynasty Heavenly Kings). *Zhongyuan wenwu,* no. 4: 79–82.

Sun Ji 孫機
1988 "絞胎器與癭器" (Jiaotai marbled clay vessels and Ying vessels). *Wenwu,* no. 12: 66–68.

1989 "固原北魏漆棺畫研究" (Study of Northern Wei painted coffin pictures in Guyuan). *Wenwu,* no. 9: 38–44.

1993 *Zhongguo guyufu lunji* 中國古輿服論集 (Essays on ancient Chinese vehicles and garments). Beijing: Wenwu chubanshe.

1996a "建國以來西方古器物在我國的發現與研究" (Discovery and study of Western antiquities found in China since 1949). *Wenwu jikan,* no.10: 69–80.

1996b *Zhongguo shenghuo: Zhongguo gu wenwu yu dong xi wenhua jiaoliu zhong de ruogan wenti* 中國聖火：中國古文物與東西文化交流中的若干問題 (China's sacred fire: Problems regarding Chinese antiquities and East–West cultural contacts). Shenyang shi: Liaoning jiao yu chubanshe.

1999 "建國以來西方古器物在我國的發現與研究" (Discovery and study of Western antiquities found in China since 1949). *Wenwu,* no. 10: 69–79.

Sun Peiliang 孫培良
1977 "略談大同市南郊出土的幾件銀器和銅器" (Discussion on the silver and bronze vessels excavated from the southern suburbs of Datong). *Wenwu,* no. 9: 63, 68–75.

Tait, Hugh, ed.
1976 *Jewellery through 7000 Years.* London: British Museum.

Tan Dahai 覃大海
1990 "焉耆古代銀器" (Ancient silverware from Yanqi County). *Zhongguo kaogu xuenian jian* 中國考古學年鑒 (Chinese archaeology yearbook): 331.

Tanabe, Katsumi
2002 "Greek, Roman and Parthian Influence on the Pre-Kushana 'Toilet Trays' and Forerunners of Buddhist Paradise." *Silk Road Art and Archaeology* 8: 73–100.

Tang Chi 湯池
1984 "東魏茹茹公主墓壁畫試探" (Discussion of the murals in the Eastern Wei Ruru Princess tomb). *Wenwu,* no. 4: 10–15.

Tang Jinyu 唐金裕
1959 "西安西郊隋李靜訓墓發掘簡報" (Excavation report of Li Jingxun's tomb in western suburb of Xi'an). *Kaogu,* no. 9: 471–72.

Tang Li Xian mu bihua
1974 *Tang Li Xian mu bihua* 唐李賢墓壁畫 (Wall paintings from the tomb of Li Xian of the Tang dynasty). Edited by Shaanxi sheng bowuguan and Shaanxi sheng wenwu guanli weiyuanhui. Beijing: Wenwu chubanshe.

Tang Yongtong 湯用彤
1991 *Han Wei Liang Jin Beichao fojiao shi* 漢魏兩晉北朝佛教史 (History of Buddhism in the Han, Wei, Chin, Northern-and-Southern Dynasty periods). Lithograph of the 1938 Shangwu yinshuguan ed. Shanghai: Shanghai shudian.

Tang Zhangru (Changru) 唐長孺
1978 *Wei Jin Nanbei chao shi luncong* 魏晉南北朝史論叢 (Collection of Writings on the history of Wei-Jin Northern and Southern Dynasties). Vol. 1. Reprint of 1955 original. Beijing: Sanlian.

Tatsumura
1993 *Tatsumura Heizō no sekai: Karei naru ori no bi* (The sophisticated beauty of the work of Tatsumura Heizō, a retrospective). [Kyōto]: Tatsumura Institute of Textile Art and Tatsumura Textile Co., Ltd.

Thierry, François
1993 "Circulation des monnaies, des marchandies et des biens." *Res orientales* 5: 7–139.

Thierry, François, and Cécile Morrisson
1994 "Sur les monnaies byzantines trouvées en Chine." *Revue numismatique,* ser. 6, 36: 109–45.

Thorp, Robert L., and Virginia Bower
1982 *Spirit and Ritual: The Morse Collection of Ancient Chinese Art.* Exh. cat. New York: The Metropolitan Museum of Art.

Tian Guangjin 田廣金 and Guo Suxin 郭素新
1986 *Eerduosi shi qingtongqi* 鄂爾多斯式青銅器 (Ordos bronzes). Beijing: Wenwu chubanshe.

Tian Jian 田建
1990 "甘肅武威旱灘坡出土前涼文物" (Some Qian Liang antiques unearthed from Hantanpo in Wuwei, Gansu). *Wenbo,* no. 3: 49–53.

Tian Jin 田進 [pseud. of Xu Pingfang 徐蘋芳]
1959 "唐戲弄俑"(Tang jesters). *Wenwu,* no. 8: 43–46.

Tian Likun 田立坤 and Zhang Keju 張克舉
1997 "前燕的甲騎具裝" (Horse armor of Qian Yan). *Wenwu,* no. 11: 72–75.

Tian Yuqing 田餘慶
1998 "北魏後宮子貴母死之制的形成和演變" (The practice of killing the mother of the Crown Prince in the Northern Wei Dynasty). *Guoxue yanjiu,* no. 5: 359–405.

Tianshui Maijishan shiku yishu yanjiusuo 天水麥積山石窟藝術研究所 (Maijishan Caves Art Research Institute, Tianshui), ed.
1998 *Tianshui Maijishan* 天水麥積山 (Maijishan grottoes). Beijing: Wenwu chubanshe.

Tianshui shi bowuguan 天水市博物館 (Tianshui City Museum)
1992 "天水市發現隋唐屏風石棺床墓" (A Sui–Tang tomb with a stone coffin bed and a "screen" discovered in Tianshui city). *Kaogu,* no. 1: 46–68.

Till, Barry
1980 "Some Observations on Stone Winged Chimeras at Ancient Chinese Tomb Sites." *Artibus Asiae* 4: 261–81.

Till, Barry, and Paula Swart, trans.
1979–80 "Two Tombs of the Southern Dynasties at Huqiao and Jianshan in Danyang County, Jiangsu Province." *Chinese Studies in Archaeology* 1, no. 3: 74–124.

Tōkyō kokuritsu hakubutsukan 東京國立博物館 (Tokyo National Museum)
1985 *Shirukurōdo no ihō: Kodai chūsei no tōzai bunka kōryū* シルクロードの遺寶: 古代の東西文化交流 (Cultural contacts between East and West in antiquity and the Middle Ages from USSR). Exh. cat. Tokyo: Tōkyō kokuritsu hakubutsukan; Osaka: Ōsaka shiritsu Bijutsukan.

1987 *Tokubetsuten kondōbutsu: Chūgoku, Chōsen, Nihon/ Special Exhibition of Gilt Bronze Buddhist Statues.* Exh. cat. Tokyo: Tokyo National Museum.

1998 *Tōno jotei Sokuten Bukō to sono jidaiten: Kyūtei no eiga* 唐の女帝則天武后とその時代展 (Empress Wu of the Tang dynasty and her times: The glory of the court). Exh. cat. Tokyo: Tōkyō kokuritsu hakubutsukan.

2002 *Shirukurōdo kinu to ōgon no michi: Nitchū kokkō seijōka 30 shūnen kinen, tokubetsuten* シルクロード絹と黄金の道：日中国交正常化周年記念 (Brocade and gold along the Silk Road). Exh. cat. Tokyo: Tōkyō kokuritsu hakubutsukan; Osaka: Ōsaka shiritsu bijutsukan.

Tomita, Kojiro
1942 "A Chinese Sacrificial Stone House of the Sixth Century A.D." *Bulletin of the Museum of Fine Arts* 40, no. 242: 98–110.

Tonkō Bakukōkutsu 敦煌莫高窟
1980–82 *Tonkō Bakukōkutsu* 敦煌莫高窟 (The Mogao Grottoes at Dunhuang). 5 vols. Chūgoku sekkutsu (The grotto art of China). Tokyo: Heibonsha.

Toyama Gunchi 外山軍治
1974 "張旭について" (On Zhang Xu). In *Shodō zenshū*, n.s., vol. 8: 28–32, 180–81. Tokyo: Heibonsha.

Trever, K. V.
1940 *Pamiatniki greko-baktriiskogo iskusstva* (Monuments of Greco-Bactrian art). Moscow and Leningrad: Izdatel'stvo Akademii nauk SSSR.

Trever, K. V., and V. G. Lukonin
1987 *Sasanidskoe serebro: Sobranie Gosudarstvennogo Ermitazha. Khudozhestvennaia kul'tura Irana III–VIII vekov* (Sasanian silver: Collection of the State Hermitage. Artistic culture of Iran in the 3rd through 8th century). Moscow: Iskusstvo.

Tsukamoto Zenryū
1979 *Chūgoku Bukkyō tsūshi*. Tokyo: Shunjūsha. 1985 Eng. ed.: *A History of Early Chinese Buddhism from Its Introduction to the Death of Hui-yüan*. 2 vols. Translated from Japanese by Leon Hurvitz. Tokyo and New York: Kodansha International.

Twitchett, Denis, ed.
1979 *The Cambridge History of China*. Vol. 3, *Sui and T'ang China, 589–906, Part I*. Cambridge: Cambridge University Press.

Uldry, Pierre
1994 *Chinesisches Gold und Silber: Die Sammlung Pierre Uldry*. Zürich: Museum Rietberg Zürich.

Unkō sekkutsu 雲岡石窟
1989–90 *Unkō sekkutsu* 雲岡石窟 (Yungang grottoes). 2 vols. Chūgoku sekkutsu (The grotto art of China). Tokyo: Heibonsha.

Valenstein, Suzanne G.
1997–98 "Preliminary Findings on a 6th-Century Earthenware Jar." *Oriental Art* 43, no. 4: 2–13.

1999 "Dish." *The Metropolitan Museum of Art Bulletin* 57 (fall): 75.

Vogel, Jean Philippe
1930 *La sculpture de Mathurâ*. Paris and Brussels: Les Éditions G. van Oest.

Volbach, W. Fritz
1969 *Early Decorative Textiles*. Translated from Italian by Yuri Gabriel. London: Paul Hamlyn.

Wan Shengnan 萬繩楠, ed.
1995 *Chen Yinke Wei Jin Nanbei chao shi jiangyanlu* 陳寅恪魏晉南北朝史講演錄 (Lectures by Chen Yinke on the history of the Wei, Jin, and Northern and Southern Dynasties). Chinese history study series 2. Taipei: Yunlong chubanshe.

Wang Binghua 王炳華
1985 "天山東部的石雕人像" (Stone figures from the eastern Tianshan) *Xinjiang wenwu*, no. 1: 12–16.

1991 "絲路考古新收獲" (New results borne from archaeological discoveries along the Silk Road). *Xinjiang wenwu*, no. 2: 21–41.

2003 "Gold and Silver Discovered in Boma, Xinjiang." In *The Glory of the Silk Road: Art from Ancient China*, edited by Li Jian: 57–63. Dayton: Dayton Art Institute.

Wang Bo 王博
1991 "人首牛頭形陶飲器" (Rhyton in the shape of a human head and ox head). *Xinjiang Weiwuer zizhiqu bowuguan* 新疆維吾爾自治區博物館 (Xinjiang Uygur Autonomous Region Museum): 166, no. 19.

Wang Changqi 王長啟 and Gao Man 高曼
1991 "西安新發現的東羅馬金幣" (The newly discovered gold coins of the Eastern Romans in Xi'an). *Wenbo*, no. 1: 38–39.

Wang, Helen, ed.
1999 *Handbook to the Stein Collections in the UK*. Occasional paper, no. 129. London: British Museum.

Wang Jinyu 王进玉
2001 *Dunhuang Kexue jishu huajuan* 敦煌科學技術畫卷 (Dunhuang technologies—Paintings). Hong Kong: Shangwu yingshuguan.

Wang Kelin 王克林
1979 "北齊庫狄迴洛墓" (The northern Wei tomb of Kudi Huiluo). *Kaogu xuebao*, no. 3: 377–401.

Wang Qufei 王去非
1979 ""千秋萬歲" 及其他" (Images of *Qianqiu wansui* [long life] from Sui tombs and others). *Kaogu*, no. 3: 275–76.

Wang Renbo 王仁波
1979 "唐三彩騎馬狩獵俑" (The Tang Sancai mounted hunter). *Wenwu*, no. 1: 67.

Wang Xin 王欣
1993 "吐魯番出土文書所見 唐語 '譯語人'" (A Tang term "*yiyu ren*" from writings unearthed in Turpan). *Xinjiang wenwu*, no. 1: 150–54.

Wang Yintian 王銀田 et al.
2000 "大同南郊北魏墓群 M107 發掘報告" (Excavation report of tomb 107 in the northern Wei cemetery in the southern suburb of Datong). In *Beichao yanjiu* 北朝研究 (Studies on the Northern Dynasties): 143–62. Beijing: Yanshan chubanshe.

Wang Yi-t'ung
1984 *A Record of Buddhist Monasteries in Lo-yang*. Princeton: Princeton University Press.

Wang Zhangqi 王長啟
2000 "禮泉寺遺址出土佛教造像" (The excavation of Buddhist sculptures from the ruins of Liquan temple). *Kaogu yu wenwu*, no. 2: 3–16.

Wang Zhongluo 王仲犖
1994 *Wei Jin Nanbeichao shi* 魏晉南北朝史 (History of the Wei–Jin Northern and Southern Dynasties). 7th ed. Shanghai: Shanghai renmin chubanshe.

Wang Zhuanghong 王壯弘
1981 *Zeng bu "Jiao bei sui bi"* 增補校碑隨筆 (Additions and amendments to "Random jottings on the comparison of stele texts" [by Fang Ruo 方若]). Shanghai: Shanghai shuhua chubanshe.

Wang Zili 王自立 and Zhang Quanmin 張全民
1992 "西安西郊出土的唐代玉帶" (Jade belts unearthed from the western suburb of Xi'an). *Kaogu yu wenwu*, no. 5: 46–51.

Watt, James C. Y.
1985 "Marbled Ware of the Tang and Song Periods." In *Mikami Tsugio Hakushi kiju kinen ronbunshū/ Mikami Tsugio Hakushi Kiju Kinen*

Ronbunshū 三上次男博士喜壽記念論文集 (Essays in Honor of Prof. Dr. Tsugio Mikami on his 77th birthday), vol. 2: 69–78. Tokyo: Heibonsha.

1990 "The Arts of Ancient China." *The Metropolitan Museum of Art Bulletin* 48, no. 1 (summer).

2002 "The Legacy of Nomadic Art in China and Eastern Central Asia." In *Nomadic Art of the Eastern Eurasian Steppes*, edited by Emma C. Bunker, with contributions by James C.Y. Watt and Zhixin Sun: 199–209. New York: The Metropolitan Museum of Art.

Wei Zheng 韋正

1999 *Jinyinqi: Nanjing Bowuyuan Zhencang xilie* 金銀器：南京博物院珍藏系列 (Gold and silver wares: Gems in the collection of the Nanjing Museum). Edited by Xu Huping. Shanghai: Shanghai Guji Chubanshe.

Weibel, Adèle Coulin

1952 *Two Thousand Years of Textiles: The Figured Textiles of Europe and the Near East*. New York: Published for the Detroit Institute of Arts by Pantheon Books.

Weitzmann, Kurt

1943 "Three 'Bactrian' Silver Vessels with Illustrations from Euripides." *Art Bulletin* 24: 289–324.

Weixian bowuguan 蔚縣博物館 (Weixian Museum)

1989 "河北蔚縣北魏太平真君五年朱亞微石造" (On the sculpture of the Northern Wei Taiping Zhenjun at Wei county, Hebei). *Kaogu*, no. 9: 807–10.

Wenwu chubanshe bianjibu 文物出版社編輯部 (Editorial Department of the Cultural Relics Publishing House), comp.

1987 *Wenwu yu kaogu lunji: Wenwu chubanshe chengli sanshi zhounian jinian* 文物與考古論集：文物出版社成立三十周年紀念 (Treatises on archaeology and culture: The thirtieth anniversary of the Cultural Relics Publishing House). Beijing: Wenwu chubanshe.

Whitfield, Roderick

1982 *The Art of Central Asia: The Stein Collection in the British Museum*. 3 vols. Tokyo: Kodansha International in cooperation with the Trustees of the British Museum.

Whitfield, Roderick, and Anne Farrer

1990 *Caves of the Thousand Buddhas: Chinese Art from the Silk Route*. Exh. cat. of a special exhibition of the Stein collection. London: British Museum Publications.

Willetts, William Y.

1958 *Chinese Art*. Vol. 2. Harmondsworth, Middlesex: Penguin Books.

Williams, Dyfri, and Jack Ogden

1994 *Greek Gold: Jewelry of the Classical World*. Exh. cat. New York: The Metropolitan Museum of Art.

Willis, Michael

2000 *Buddhist Reliquaries from Ancient India*. With contributions by Joe Cribb and Julia Shaw. London: British Museum Press.

Wolters, O. W.

1967 *Early Indonesian Commerce: A Study of the Origins of Srīvijaya*. Ithaca, N.Y.: Cornell University Press.

Wong, Dorothy C.

1998–99 "Four Sichuan Buddhist Steles and the Beginning of Pure Land Imagery in China." *Archives of Asian Art* 51: 56–79.

2000 "Women as Buddhist Art Patrons during the Northern and Southern Dynasties." In *Han Tang zhi jian de zongjiao yishu yu kaogu* 漢唐之間的宗教藝術與考古 (Between Han and Tang: Religious art and archaeology in a transformative period), edited by Wu Hung: 535–66. Beijing: Wenwu chubanshe.

Wood, Donald A.

1985 "Eleven Faces of the Bodhisattva." Ph.D. dissertation, University of Kansas, Lawrence.

Woven Treasures

1959 *Woven Treasures of Persian Art: Persian Textiles from the 6th to the 19th Century*. Exh. cat. Los Angeles: Los Angeles County Museum.

Wu En 烏恩

1984 "論我國北方古代動物紋飾的淵源" (On the origin of ancient animal patterns in northern China). *Kaogu yu wenwu*, no. 4: 46–58, 104.

Wu Hung

1989 *The Wu Liang Shrine: The Ideology of Early Chinese Pictorial Art*. Stanford: Stanford University Press.

2002 "A Case of Cultural Interaction: House-Shaped Sarcophagi of the Northern Dynasties." *Orientations* 33 (May): 34–41.

Wu Min 武敏

1973 "吐魯番出土絲織品中的唐代印染" (The printing and dying techniques of the Tang dynasty as indicated by the silk fabrics unearthed at Turfan, Xinjiang). *Wenwu*, no. 10: 37–47.

1984 "吐魯番出土蜀錦的研究" (A study on the Sichuan silk unearthed in Turfan). *Wenwu*, no. 6: 70–80.

1992 *Zhi Xiu* 織繡 (Weaving and embroidery). Taibei: Youshi wenhua shi ye youxian gongsi.

1999 "吐魯番古墓出土絲織品新探" (A new look at textiles excavated from Astana graves at Turfan). In *Dunhuang Tulufan yanjiu* 敦煌吐魯番研究 (Anthology of studies of Dunhuang and Turfan), vol. 4: 299–322. Beijing: Beijing daxue chubanshe.

Wu Tung

1997 *Tales from the Land of Dragons: 1,000 Years of Chinese Painting*. Exh. cat. Boston: Museum of Fine Arts.

Wu Yiru 吳怡如

1988 "北周王令猥造像碑" (The Northern Zhou pictorial stele of Wang Lingwei). *Wenwu*, no. 2: 69–71.

Wu Zhen 吳震

1987 "阿斯塔那336號墓所出戲弄俑五例" (Pottery figurines of comedians unearthed from Tomb 336 at Astana). *Wenwu*, no. 5: 77–82.

2000 "吐魯番地域與出土絹織物" (The excavated silk textiles from the Tulufan area). In *Tulufan chutu wenshu zhong de sizhipin kaobian* 吐魯番出土文書中的絲織品考辨 (An examination of silk textiles from documents excavated in Turfan), edited by Zhongguo Xinjiang Weiwuer zizhiqu bowuguan et al.: 84–103. Nara: Riben Nailiang sichou zhi lu xue yanjiu zhongxin.

Wu Zhuo 吳焯

1989 "Notes on the Silver Ewer from the Tomb of Li Xian." *Bulletin of the Asia Institute* 3: 61–75.

1992 "四川早期佛教遺物及其年代與傳播途徑的考察" (A study of the early Buddhist relics in Sichuan and their dates and dissemination). *Wenwu*, no. 11: 40–50, 67.

Wu Zuoren 吳作人 et al.

1983 "筆談太原北齊婁叡墓" (A collection of essays on the tomb of Lou Rui of the Northern Qi in Taiyuan). *Wenwu*, no. 10: 24–39.

Xia Mingcai 夏明采

1985 "益都北齊石室墓線刻畫像" (The Northern Qi line-engraved stone in a tomb chamber in Yidu). *Wenwu*, no. 10: 49–54.

2001 "青州傅家北齊線刻畫像補遺" (Additional remarks on the line engraved stones of the Northern Qi dynasty in Fujia, Qingzhou). *Wenwu*, no. 5: 92–93.

Xia Nai 夏鼐

1962 "和闐馬錢" (Coins from Hetian). *Wenwu*, no. 7: 60–63.

1977 "贊皇李希宗墓出土的拜占廷金幣" (The Byzantine gold coin excavated in the tomb of Li Xizong at Zanhuang). *Kaogu*, no. 6: 403–6.

1983 "北魏封和突墓出土薩珊銀盤考" (A Sasanian silver plate from the tomb of Feng Hetu in the Northern Wei dynasty). *Wenwu*, no. 8: 5–7.

Xi'an shi wenwu guanli weiyuanhui 西安市文物管理委員會 (Xi'an City Cultural Properties Management Committee)

1964 "西安市東南郊沙坡村出土一批唐代銀器" (The Tang silvers excavated from the Shapocun in the southeastern suburb of Xi'an city). *Wenwu*, no. 6: 30–32.

1997 *Tang Jinxiang xianzhu mu caihui taoyong* 唐金鄉縣主墓彩繪陶俑 (Tang painted pottery figures from the tomb of Princess Jinxiang). Shaanxi: Shaanxi lüyu chubanshe.

Xi'an shi wenwuju 西安市文物局 (Xi'an Municipal Cultural Relics Bureau)

1997 "西安北郊出土北周白石觀音造像 (White stone Guanyin sculptures excavated in the northern suburb of Xi'an). *Wenwu*, no. 11: 78–79.

Xiang Da 向達

1933 *Tangdai Chang'an yu xiyu wenming* 唐代長安與西域文明 (Tang dynasty Chang'an and the civilization of the Western Regions). Beijing: Hafo Yanjing she.

Xianyang wenwuguan 咸陽文物館 (Xianyang Relics Bureau) and Xianyang bowuguan 咸陽博物館 (Xianyang Museum)

1987 "咸陽市胡家溝西魏侯義墓清理簡報" (Bulletin of the excavation of the western Wei tomb of Houyi at Hujiagou, Xianyang). *Wenwu*, no. 12: 57–58.

Xiao Tong

1983 *See WX.*

Xie Guihua 謝桂華

2001 "中國出土魏晉以後漢文簡紙文書概述" (A brief report on wooden and paper Chinese documents of the post Wei-Jin period discovered in China). In *Jianbo yanjiu erlinglingyi* 簡帛研究二〇〇一 (2001 research on ancient silk documents), edited by Li Xueqin 李學勤 and Xie Guihua 謝桂華: 546–59. Guilin City: Guangxi shifan daxue chubanshe.

Xie Zhenfa 謝振發

2001 "北魏司馬金龍墓的漆畫屏風試析" (Analysis of the screen lacquer painting in the Northern Wei tomb of Sima Jinlong). *Meishushi yanjiu jikan*, no. 11: 1–55.

Xing Jun 邢軍

1990 "廣元千佛崖初唐密教造像析" (Analysis of early Tang Esoteric sculpture at the Thousand Buddhas cave, Guangyuan). *Wenwu*, no. 6: 37–40.

Xinjiang bowuguan 新疆博物館 (Xinjiang Museum)

1960 "新彊吐魯番阿斯塔那北區墓葬發掘簡報" (Bulletin on the excavation of the Xinjiang Turfan northern Astana burials). *Wenwu*, no. 6: 13–21.

1975 "吐魯番阿斯塔那古墓群發掘簡報" (Bulletin on the excavation of ancient tombs at Astana in Turfan, Xinjiang, in 1973). *Wenwu*, no. 7: 8–26.

1989 "洛甫縣山普拉古墓發掘報告" (Excavation of ancient tombs at Shanpula village, Luofu). *Xinjiang wenwu*, no. 2: 1–48.

Xinjiang bowuguan chutu wenwu zhanlan xiaozu 新疆博物館出土文物展覽小組 (Xinjiang Museum Exhibition Committee on Excavated Relics)

1972 *Sichou zhi lu—Han Tang zhiwu* 絲綢之路 - 漢唐織物 (The Silk Road: Han–Tang textiles). Beijing: Wenwu chubanshe.

Xinjiang Loulan kaogudui 新疆樓蘭考古隊 (Xinjiang Loulan archeology team)

1988 "樓蘭城郊古墓群發掘簡報" (Bulletin on a group of ancient tombs on the outskirts of Loulancheng, Xinjiang). *Wenwu*, no. 7: 23–39.

Xinjiang Weiwuer zizhiqu bowuguan 新疆維吾爾自治區博物館 (Xinjiang Uygur Autonomous Region Museum)

1960 "新疆民豐縣北大沙漠中古遺址墓葬區東漢合葬墓清理簡報" (Excavation report of an ancient cemetery with an eastern Han tomb of a couple). *Wenwu*, no. 6: 9–12.

1972 "吐魯番阿斯塔那363號墓發掘簡報" (Bulletin on the excavation of Tomb 363 in Astana, Turfan). *Wenwu*, no. 2: 7–9.

1973 "吐魯番縣阿斯塔那 - 哈拉和卓古墓群發掘簡報" (Report on the excavation of the ancient tomb of Halahezhuo in Astana cemetery in Turfan county). *Wenwu*, no. 10: 7–21.

1991 *Xinjiang Weiwuer zizhiqu bowuguan* 新疆維吾爾自治區博物館 (Xinjiang Uygur Autonomous Region Museum). Zhongguo bowuguan congshu 中國博物館叢書 (Museums of China series), vol. 9. Beijing: Wenwu chubanshe and Kodansha.

Xinjiang Weiwuer zizhiqu bowuguan 新疆維吾爾自治區博物館 (Xinjiang Uygur Autonomous Region Museum) and Chutu wenwu zhanlan gongzuozu 出土文物展覽工作組 (Exhibition Committee on Excavated Relics)

1975 *Xinjiang chutu wenwu* 新疆出土文物 (Excavated relics from Xinjiang). Beijing: Wenwu chubanshe and Kodansha.

Xinjiang Weiwuer zizhiqu bowuguan 新疆維吾爾自治區博物館 (Xinjiang Uygur Autonomous Region Museum) and Xinjiang wenwu kaogu yanjiusuo 新疆文物考古研究所 (Xinjiang Institute of Archaeology)

2001 *Zhongguo Xinjiang shanpula: Gudai Yutian wenming de tishi yu yanjiu.* 中國新疆山普拉：古代于闐文明的提示與研究 (Sampula in Xinjiang of China: A revelatory example and study of ancient Khotan civilization). Xinjiang: Xinjiang renmin chubanshe.

Xinjiang Weiwuer zizhiqu wenwu shiye guanliju 新疆維吾爾自治區文物事業管理局 (Xinjiang Weiwuer Autonomous Region corporate management bureau) et al.

1999 *Xinjiang wenwu guji daguan* 新疆文物古跡大觀 *(A Grand View of Xinjiang's Cultural Relics and Historic Sites, China)*. Xinjiang: Xinjiang meishu sheying chubanshe.

Xinjiang Weiwuer zizhiqu wenwuguanli weiyuanhui 新疆維吾爾文物管理委員會 (Xinjiang Autonomous Region Cultural Relics Committee), Baichengxian Kezi'er Qianfodong wenwu baoguansuo 拜城縣克孜尒千佛洞文物保管所 (Baichengxian, Kezier, Qianfodong Cultural Relics Bureau), and Beijing daxue kaoguxi 北京大學考古系 (Beijing University, Department of Archaeology)

1989–97 *Zhongguo Shiku Kezi'er shiku* 中國石窟 克孜尒石窟 (Kizil caves). 3 vols. Beijing: Wenwu chubanshe.

Xinjiang wenwu kaogu yanjiusuo 新疆文物考古研究所 (Xinjiang Institute of Archaeology)

1999 “新疆尉犁縣營盤墓地15號墓發掘簡報” (Bulletin on the excavation of Tomb 15 at the Yingpan site, Yuli, Xinjiang). *Wenwu*, no. 1: 4–16.

2000 “Tulufan Astana di shi ci fajue jianbao (1972–1973)”吐魯番阿斯塔那第十次發掘簡報 (Bulletin on the tenth excavation in Astana, Turfan, 1972–1973). *Xinjiang wenwu*, no. 3–4: 84–167.

Xiong, Victor Cunrui 熊存瑞
1987 “隋李静訓墓出土金項鏈，金手鐲的產地問題” (The origin of the gold necklace and bracelet from the Sui tomb of Li Jingxun). *Wenwu*, no. 10: 77–79.

Xiong, Victor Cunrui, and Ellen Johnson Laing
1991 “Foreign Jewelry in Ancient China.” *Bulletin of the Asia Institute*, n.s., 5: 163–73.

Xu Bingkun 徐秉琨
1996 *Xianbei, sanguo, gumu* 鮮卑，三國，古墓 (Xianbei, Three Kingdoms, and ancient tombs). Shenyang: Liaoning guji chubanshe.

Xu Guangyi 徐光冀
1996 “河北磁縣灣漳北朝大型壁畫墓的發掘與研究” (Excavation and research of large-scale mural paintings in a Northern Dynasty tomb, Cixian). *Wenwu* no. 9: 69–71.

Xu Huping 徐湖平
1999 *See* Wei Zheng 韋正 1999.

Xu Xinguo 許新國
1994 “都蘭吐番墓中鍍金銀器屬粟特系統的推定” (On gilt silver found in Tibetan tombs of Dulan and their possible Sogdian origin). *Zhongguo zangxue*, no. 4: 31–45.

1996 “都蘭吐番墓出土含綬鳥織錦研究” (A study of textiles with bird designs excavated in Tibetan tombs of Turufan). *Zhongguo zangxue*, no. 1: 3–25.

Xu Xinguo 徐新國 and Zhao Feng 趙豐
1993 “都蘭出土絲織品初探” (On textiles discovered in Dulan). *Zhongguo lishi bowuguan guankan*, no. 15–16: 63–81.

Xu Xinyang 徐信仰
1986 “安康長嶺出土的南朝演奏歌舞俑” (Figurines of musical players of the Southern Dynasties unearthed from Changling, Ankang). *Wenbo*, no. 5: 64–65.

Xu Xinyin 徐信仰
1986 “安康長嶺出土的南朝演奏歌舞俑” (Figurines of musicians and dancers of the Southern Dynasties unearthed from Changling Village of Ankang). *Wenbo*, no. 5: 64–65.

Xu Zhen'e 徐震堮 [Liu Yiqing]
1984 *See SSXY.*

Xu Zufan 徐祖蕃, Qin Mingzhi 秦明智, and Rong Siqi 荣思奇
1985 “敦煌遺書的字體演變及書法藝術” (The stylistic change of characters and the art of calligraphy in Dunhuang manuscripts). In *Dunhuang yishushu faxuan* 敦煌遺書書法選 (Calligraphy of Dunhuang Buddhist manuscripts): 73–74. Lanzhou: Gansu renmin chubanshe.

Xue Zongzheng 薛宗正
1996 “魏晉南北朝時期塔里木綠洲城邦諸國的社會生活” (Social life in the states of Tarim Oases in Wei-Jin, Southern and Northern Dynasties). *Xinjiang wenwu*, no. 2: 58–75.

Xuzhou bowuguan 徐州博物館 (Xuzhou Museum)
1974 “江蘇徐州西漢墓” (A Western Han tomb at Quishan, Xuzhou, Jiangsu). *Kaogu*, no. 2: 121–22.

Xuzhou bowuguan 徐州博物館 (Xuzhou Museum) et al.
1988 “徐州北洞山西漢墓發掘簡報” (Excavation report of the Western Han tomb on Mount Beidong in Xuzhou). *Wenwu*, no. 2: 2–18.

Yan Xinzhi 晏新志
1989 “試論唐代舞蹈的分期” (On the development of dance in the Tang dynasty). *Wenbo*, no. 4: 40–44.

Yang Boda 楊伯達, ed.
1986 *Zhongguo meishu quanji: Gongyi meishubian, 9: Yuqi* 中國美術全集：工藝美術編：玉器. (Chinese art—crafts: jades). Beijing: Wenwu chubanshe.

Yang Hong 楊泓
1980 as editor. *Zhongguo gu bingqi luncong* 中國古兵器論叢 (Weapons in ancient China). Beijing: Wenwu chubanshe.

1986 “三國考古的新發現讀朱然墓簡報雜記” (New archaeological finds of the Three Kingdoms). *Wenwu*, no. 3: 16–24.

1991 “山東北朝墓人物屏風壁畫的新啟示” (New revelations on the Shandong Northern Dynasty murals of figures and screens). *Wenwu tiandi* 3: 6-8.

1993 “南北朝墓的壁畫和拚鑲磚畫” (Wall paintings and impressed brick murals of the Southern and Northern Dynasties). *Zhongguo kaoguxue luncong*: 429–37.

Yang Hsüan-chih
1984 *A Record of Buddhist Monasteries in Lo-yang*. Translated by Yi-t'ung Wang. Princeton: Princeton University Press.

Yang Junkai 楊軍凱
2003 “關於祆教的第三次重大發現－西安北周薩保史君墓” (The third major discovery regarding Zoroastrianism— the Northern Zhou Buddhist tomb of Shi Jun). *Wenwu tiandi*, no. 11: 26–29.

2004 “入華粟特聚落首領墓葬的新發現 –北周涼州薩保史君墓石槨圖像初釋” (Newly discovered burials of Sogdian Community Leaders in China: A preliminary decoding of the illustrations on the stone sarcophagus of the Sabao Shi of Liangzhou dating from the Northern Zhou dynasty). In *Cong sama'ergan dao Chang'an* 從撒馬爾干到長安 (From Samarkand to Chang'an: Cultural traces of the Sogdians in China), edited by Rong Xinjiang and Zhang Zhiqing: 17–26. Beijing: Beijing tushuguan chubanshe.

Yang Xin, Richard M. Barnhart, et al.
1997 *Three Thousand Years of Chinese Painting*. New Haven: Yale University Press, and Beijing: Foreign Languages Press.

Yang Yinliu 楊蔭瀏
1985 *Zhongguogudaiyinyueshigao* 中國古代音樂史稿 (A history of ancient Chinese music). Vols. 1, 2. Beijing: Renmin yinyue chubanshe. First published 1981.

Yangzhou bowuguan 揚州博物館 (Yangzhou Museum)
1991 “江蘇邗江縣甘泉老虎墩漢墓” (A Han dynasty tomb at Laohudun, Ganquan, Hanjiang, Jiangsu). *Wenwu*, no. 10: 62–70.

Yao Qianju 姚遷居 and Gu Bing 古兵, eds.
1981 *Liuchao yishu* 六朝藝術 (The art of the Six Dynasties). Beijing: Wenwu chubanshe.

Yatsenko, Sergei A.
2000 “The Costume of the Yueh-Chihsī: Kushans and Its Analogies to the East and West.” *Silk Road Art and Archaeology* 7: 113.

Yen Chüan-ying
1986 “The Sculpture from the Tower of Seven Jewels: The Style, Patronage and Iconography of the Monument.”

Ph.D. dissertation, Harvard University, Cambridge, Mass.

1987 "The Tower of the Seven Jewels and Empress Wu," *National Palace Museum Bulletin, Taipei* 32, no. 1 (March/April): 1–7.

Yi Ge 弋戈
1984 "李重潤墓 '絞胎馬'有誤" (The mistaken identification of a 'Jiaotai' [marbled clay] horse from the tomb of Li Chongrun). *Wenbo,* no. 3: 57–58.

Yi Jiasheng 易家勝
1983 "南京出土的六朝早期青瓷釉下彩盤口壺" (An early Six Dynasties celadon jar with a flared rim and underglaze decoration excavated in Nanjing). *Wenwu,* no. 6: 72–75.

Yi Shui 易水
1981 "漢魏六朝的軍樂 - 鼓吹和橫吹" ("Fifes and drums" vs. "horns": The military musical band of the Han, Wei, and Six Dynasties). *Wenwu,* no. 7: 85–89.

Yin Guangming 殷光明
2000 *Beiliang shita yanjiu* 北梁石塔研究 (The stone stupas of the Northern Liang dynasty). Xinzhu: Juefeng fojiao yishu wenhua jijinhui.

Yin Qing 殷晴
1987 "唐代塔里木盆地南緣的社會經濟生活 - 試論和田出土的一張帳簿殘頁" (Social and economic life on the southern border of Taklimakan — A preliminary study of pages of an account book discovered in Hetian). *Xinjiang wenwu,* no. 3: 60–73.

1989 "古代新疆商業的發展及商人的活動" (Commercial development and merchants' activities in ancient Xinjiang). *Xinjiang wenwu,* no. 3: 32–47.

Yin Shenping, Li Ming, and Xing Fulai
2000 "Notes on the Excavation of the Tomb of An Jie." *China Archaeology and Art Digest* 4, no. 1 (December): 15–29.

Yoshida, Yutaka
1996 "Additional Notes on 'Sims-Williams' Article on the Sogdian Merchants in China and India." In *Cina e Iran: Da Alessandro Magno alla dinastia Tang,* edited by Alfredo Cadonna and Lionello Lanciotti: 69–78. Florence.

Yoshimizu Tsuneo 由水常熊
1977 *Tōyō no garasu: Chūgoku, Chōsen, Nihon* 東洋のガラス：中国、朝鮮、日本 (Oriental glass: China, Korea, Japan). Tokyo: Sansaisha.

1992 *Sekaigarasubijutsu*zenshū世界ガラス美術全集 (A survey of world glass). 6 vols. Tokyo: Kyūryūdō.

Yoshimura Rei
1985 "南朝の法華経普門品変相" (Chapter of the Universal Gateway of the Bodhisattva from the Lotus Sutra in the Southern Dynasties). *Bukkyo geijutsu,* no. 162: 11–28.

You Zhenyao
1989 "An Everlasting Record of Craftsmanship: Treasures from Han Period Royal Tombs." *Orientations* 20 (May): 52–62.

Yu Anlan 于安瀾
1963 *Huashi congshu* 畫史叢書 (Compendium of painting histories). Vol. 1. Shanghai: Shanghai renmin meishu chubanshe.

Yu Weichao 俞偉超
1980 "東漢佛教圖像考" (Notes on the Eastern Han dynasty images of the Buddha). *Wenwu,* no. 5: 68–77.

Yuan Shuguang 袁曙光
1992 "四川茂汶南永明造像碑及有關問題" (The figure steles of the Yongming period of the southern Qi dynasty at Maowen in Sichuan and related issues). *Wenwu,* no. 2: 67–71.

2001 "四川省博物館藏萬佛寺石刻造像整理簡報" (Bulletin on Wangfosi stone sculptures from the Sichuan Museum). *Wenwu,* no. 10: 19–38.

Yuanzhou lianhe kaogudui 原州聯合考古隊 (Joint Team of Archaeologists of Yuanzhou)
1999 *To Shi Doraku bo / Tang shi Daoluo – Yuanzhou lianhe kaogudui fajue diaocha baogao 1*唐史道洛墓 (Shi Daoluo of the Tang dynasty: Excavation report of the Joint Archaeological Team of Yuanzhou, part 1). In Japanese and Chinese. Tokyo: Bensei Shuppan.

2000 Yuanzhou Archaeological Joint Excavation in 1996. *Tomb of Tian Hong of the Northern Zhou Dynasty. The Yuanzhou Archaeological Joint Excavation in 1996* (in Chinese and Japanese). Tokyo.

Yun Anzhi 員安志
1993a "北周甲士俑與甲馬甲士騎俑綜述" (A summary of figurines of armored soldiers and armored horses and riders of the Northern Zhou). *Wenbo,* no. 2: 9–18.

1993b as compiler. *Zhongguo Beizhou zhengui wenwu: Beizhou muzang fajue baogao* 中國北周珍貴文物：北周墓葬發掘報告 (The northern Zhou's precious historical relics [China]: northern Zhou graves. Excavation report). Xi'an: Shaanxi renmin meishu chubanshe.

Yungang shiku wenwu baoguansuo 雲岡石窟文物保管所 (Cultural Relics Preservation Bureau of Yungang Caves)
1991–94 *Yungang shiku* 雲岡石窟 (Yungang Caves). 2 vols. Zhongguo shiku series. Beijing: Wenwu chubanshe.

Yunnan sheng bBowuguan 雲南省博物館 (Yunnan Provincial Museum)
1959 *Yunnan Jinning Shizhaishan gumu qun fajuebao gao* 雲南晉寧石寨山古墓群發掘報告 (Excavation report of the ancient tomb group from Shizhaishan at Jinning, Yunnan). Beijing: Wenwu chubanshe.

Zalesskaia, Vera N., et al.
1997 *Kubrat Khan Khazinalare / Sokrovishcha Khana kubrata: Pereshchepinskii klad* (The treasures of Khan Kubrat: The Pereshchepino Hoard). Exh. cat. Saint Petersburg: State Hermitage Museum.

Zasetskaia, Irina Petrovna
1975 *Zolotye ukrasheniia gunnskoi epokhi: Po materialam osoboi Kladovoi Gos. Ermitazha* (Gold ornaments of the Hunnish period). Leningrad: Avrora.

1982 "Klassifikatsiia polichromnykh izdelii gunnskoi epokhi po stilisticheskim dannym" (The classification of the polychrome objects of the Hunnish period based on their stylistic features). In *Drevnosti epokhi velikogo pereseleniia narodov V–VIII vekov* (Antiquities of the great migration period, 5th–8th centuries), edited by Anatolii K. Ambroz and István F. Erdélyi: 14–20, 246–48. Moscow: Nauka.

Zeimal, Evgeniy
1994 "The Circulation of Coins in Central Asia during the Early Medieval Period (Fifth–Eighth Centuries A.D.)." *Bulletin of the Asia Institute* 8: 245–67.

Zerwick, Chloe
1990 *A Short History of Glass.* New York: Harry N. Abrams in association with Corning Museum of Glass.

Zhang Baizhong 張柏忠
1989 "內蒙古科左中旗六家子鮮卑墓群" (Xianbei tomb groups in

Kezuozhongqi, Inner Mongolia). *Kaogu*, no. 5: 430–43.

Zhang Guangda 張廣達
1995 *Xiyu shidi cong chubian* 西域史地叢初編 (Essays on the history and geography of the Western regions). Shanghai: Shanghai guji chubanshe.

1998 "評介 '古代和中世紀早期的西域'" (Comment on *Ancient and Early Mediaeval Eastern Turkestan*). In *Dunhuang Tulufan yanjiu* 《敦煌吐魯番研究》 (Anthology of studies of Dunhuang and Turfan), vol. 3: 339–70. Beijing: Beijing daxue chubanshe.

2001 "唐代的豹獵 - 文化傳播的一個實例" (An example of cultural exchange: The hunting cheetahs of the Tang dynasty). *Tang yanjiu* 7: 177–204.

Zhang Ji 張季
1957 "河北景縣封氏墓群調查記" (Examination of the Feng family tomb groups at Jin county, Hebei). *Kaogu tongxun*, no. 3: 28–37.

Zhang Jiatai 張家泰
1981 "元代匠師劉庭秀及其建築考察" (A study of the Yuan dynasty craftsman Liu Tingxiu and his architecture). *Zhongyuan wenwu*, no. 2: 43–46.

Zhang Jingming 張景明
2002 "內蒙古涼城縣小子灘金銀器窖藏" (The gold and silver vessel hoard at Liangcheng County, Inner Mongolia). *Wenwu*, no. 8: 50–52, 69.

Zhang Jingming 張景明 et al.
1995 *Life on the Saddle: History of Nomadic Culture in Northern China* / 鞍馬文化：中國古代北方遊牧民族. Hong Kong: Hong Kong Regional Council and the Inner Mongolia Autonomous Region Museum.

Zhang Keju 張克舉
1996 "剽悍獨特的草原文化 - 遼寧北票鮮卑（三燕）墓地" (A unique and vigorous steppe culture—the Xianbei cemetery at Beipiao, Liaoning). *Zhonghua wenhua huabao*, no. 2: 3–9.

Zhang Pengchuan 張朋川 and Wu Yiru 吳怡如, eds.
1984 *Wuwei Han dai mudiao* 武威漢代木雕 (Han dynasty wood carving from Wuwei). Beijing: Remin meishu chubanshe.

Zhang Qingjie
2002 "New Archaeological and Art Discoveries from the Han to the Tang Period in Shanxi Province." *Orientations* 34, no. 5: 54–60.

Zhang Tao 張濤
1990 *Lie nu zhuan yi zhu* 列女傳譯注 (The annotated Biographies of virtuous women). Ji'nan: Shandong Daxue chubanshe.

Zhang Wenbin 張文彬
1999 *Guo zhi guibao: Zhongguo wenwu shiye wushi* 國之瑰寶：中國文物事業五十年 (The treasures of a nation: China's cultural heritage, 1949–1999): 207–209. Beijing: Chaohua chubanshe.

Zhang Xinyue 張新月
2001 "河南鞏義市文館所藏鎮墓獸" (Tomb guardians in the collection of the Gongyi Municipal Institute, Henan Province). *Kaogu yu wenwu*, no. 4: 70–77.

Zhang Yingqun 張英群
1983 "安陽隋代張盛墓出土的舞樂俑試探" (A preliminary study of music and dance figurines of the Sui tomb of Zhang Sheng of Anyang). *Zhongyuan wenwu*, no. 4: 21, 78–81.

Zhang Yuzhong 張玉忠
1996 "從考古資料看西漢以前新疆與東南沿海地區的聯係" (Relations between Xinjiang and the southeastern coastal region in pre-Western Han times as reflected in some archaeological materials). *Xinjiang wenwu*, no. 3: 27–31, 48.

Zhao Chengze 赵承泽 et al.
1979 "關於西周絲織品（岐子和朝阳出土的）初步探讨" (About Western Zhou silk excavated from Qizi and Chaoyang). *Beijing fang zhi* 2.

Zhao Feng 趙豐
1992 *Sichou yishu shi* 絲綢藝術史 (A history of silk art). Hangzhou: Zhejiang meishu xueyuan chubanshe.

1999a "漢代的云气動物紋錦" (Cloud-and-animal patterns in Han-dynasty textiles). *Zhejiang gongyi meishu*, no. 2: 1–2.

1999b "Satin Samite: A Bridge from Samite to Satin." *Bulletin de CIETA* (Centre International d'Étude des Textiles Anciens, Lyon), no. 76: 46–63.

1999c *Zhixiu zhenpin: Tu shuo Zhongguo sichou yishu shi / Treasures in Silk: An Illustrated History of Chinese Textiles*. Hongkong: ISAT/Costume.

2002a *Fangzhipin kaogu xin faxian* 紡織品考古新發現 Recent excavations of textiles in China. Zhongguc sSichou bowuguan (China National Silk Museum). Hangzhou: Yi sha tan / Fu shi gong zuo dui.

2002b *See* 2003.

2003 "Three Textiles from Turfan." Orientations 34, no. 2 (February): 25–31.

Zhao Feng 趙豐 and Yu Zhiyong 于志勇
2000 *Shamo wangzi yibao: Sichou zhi lu Niya yizhi chutu wenwu* 沙漠王子遺寶：絲綢之路尼雅遺址出土文物 / *Legacy of the Desert King: Textiles and Treasures Excavated at Niya on the Silk Road*. Exh. cat. Hangzhou: Zhongguo si chou bowuguan; Hong Kong: ISAT/Costume.

Zhao Guobi 趙國壁
1960 "洛陽發現的波斯薩珊王朝銀幣" (A discovery of Persian Sasanian coins in Luoyang). *Wenwu*, no. 8–9: 94.

Zhao Hua 趙華
1992 "吐魯番出土絲織品圖案及其源流初探" (A preliminary study on the textile designs unearthed in Turfan and their original sources). In *Tulufan gu mu zang chu tu yi shu pin* 吐魯番古墓葬出土藝術品 (Works of art from ancient Turefan tombs): 131–46. Urumchi: Xinjiang meishu sheyin chubanshe.

Zhao Shengliang 趙聲良
2001 "成都南朝浮雕彌勒經變與法華經變考論" (An illustration of Maitreya and Saddharma-pundarika in the Southern Dynasties in Chengdu). *Dunhuang yanjiu*, no. 1: 34–42.

Zhao Wanli 趙萬里
1956 *Han Wei Nanbeichao muzhi jishi* 漢魏南北朝墓誌集釋 (Epitaphs from the Han, Wei, and Northern and Southern Dynasties). 6 vols. Beijing: Kexue chubanshe.

Zhao Yonghong 趙永紅
1994 "南北朝胡叟舞蹈俑考" (Funeral figurines of elderly male dancers in the northern tribes of the Southern and Northern Dynasties). In *Han Tang yu bianjiang kaogu yanjiu* 漢唐與邊疆考古研究 (Archaeological researches on the Han–Tang period and border areas of ancient China): 136–43. Beijing: Kexue chubanshe.

Zhao Zhenhua 趙振華 and Zhu Liang 朱良
1982 "安菩墓誌初探" (A preliminary study of the epitaph of Anpu). *Zhongyuan wenwu*, no. 3: 37–40.

Zhaoling bowuguan 昭陵博物館 (Zhaoling Museum)

1988 "唐昭陵長樂公主墓" (The tomb of Princess Changle in Zhaoling mausoleum of Tang). *Wenbo*, no. 3: 10–13.

1989 "唐昭陵段簡壁墓清理報告" (Excavation of the tomb of Duan Jianbi of the Tang dynasty). *Wenbo*, no. 6: 3–13.

Zheng Hongchun 鄭洪春

1988 "西安東郊隋舍利墓清理簡報" (Excavation report of the Sheli tomb of the Sui dynasty in the eastern suburb of Xi'an). *Kaogu yu wenwu*, no. 1: 61–65.

Zheng Minzhong 鄭珉中

1986 "對南京西善橋六朝墓畫像的看法" (Concerning the viewpoints expressed regarding the pictures from the Six Dynasties tomb at Xishanqiao, Nanjing). *Gugong bowuyuan yuankan*, no. 3: 49–54.

Zheng Yan 鄭岩

2001 "青州北齊畫像石與入華粟特人美術－虞弘墓等考古新發現的啟示" (Northern Qi pictorial carvings from Qingzhou and sinicized Sogdian art: An observation inspired by the Yu Hong sarcophagus and other new archaeological finds). In *Han Tang zhi jian wenhua yishu de hudong yu jiaorong* 漢唐之間文化藝術的互動與交融 (Between Han and Tang: Religious art and archaeology in a transformative period), edited by Wu Hung: 73–109. Beijing: Wenwu chubanshe.

2002 "南昌東晉漆盤的啟示－論南北朝墓葬藝術中高士圖像的含義" (An inspiration from the Eastern Jin lacquer plate of Nanchang). *Kaogu*, no. 2: 77–86.

Zhi Gong 志工

1972 "略談北魏的屏風漆畫" (Notes on a Northern Wei lacquer screen painting). *Wenwu*, no. 8: 55–60.

Zhong Shaoyi 鐘少異 and Wang Yuanchao 王援朝

1995 "唐楊思勖墓石刻俑復原商確" (A re-examination of the restored stone sculptures from Tang Yang Sixun tomb). *Tang yanjiu*, no. 1: 473–81.

Zhong Xiaoqing 鍾曉青

2000 "北魏洛陽永寧寺復原探討" (On the reconstruction of the Northern Wei pagoda of Yongning in the city of Luoyang). In *Han Wei Luoyang gucheng yanjiu* 漢魏洛陽故城研究 (Studies on the ancient city of Luoyang during the Han and Wei): 559–77. Beijing: Kexue chubanshe.

Zhongguo guojia tushuguan 中國國家圖書館 (National Library of China)

2001 *Zhongguo guojia tushuguan beitie jinghua* 中國國家圖書館碑帖精華 (Masterpieces of stele and letter writings from the National Library of China). 8 vols. Beijing: Beijing tushuguan chubanshe.

Zhongguo huihua quanji 1

1997 *Zhongguo huihua quanji 1: Zhan guo–Tang* 中國繪畫全集一：戰國至唐 (Complete collection of Chinese painting, 1: Warring States to Tang). Edited by Zhongguo gudai shuhua jianding zu 中國古代書畫鑑定組 (Organization for the authentication of ancient Chinese calligraphy and painting). Beijing: Wenwu chubanshe.

Zhongguo kaogu xue yanjiu

1986 *Zhongguo kaogu xue yanjiu: Xia nai xiansheng kaogu wushi nian jinian lunwen ji* 中國考古學研究：夏鼐先生考古五十年紀念論文集 (Archaeological researches in China: A collection of papers in commemoration of the fiftieth year of Prof. Xia Nai's work in archaeology). Compiled by the Editorial Committee of Archaeological Researches in China. Beijing: Wenwu chubanshe.

Zhongguo kexueyuan kaogu yanjiusuo Neimenggu gongzuodui 中國科學院考古研究所內蒙古工作隊 (Inner Mongolian Archaeological Team, IOA, Academia Sinica)

1964 "內蒙古巴林左旗富河溝門遺址發掘簡報" (Excavation of a neolithic site at Fuhegoumen, Balin Left Banner, Inner Mongolia). *Kaogu*, no. 1: 1-5.

Zhongguo Meishu Fenlei Quanji

1993 *Zhongguo yuqi Quanji*. Vol. 4, *Qin Han Nanbeichao* 中國玉器全集四：秦漢至南北朝 (Compendium of Chinese jade objects: From Qin Han to Nanbei chao). Zhongguo Meishu Fenlei Quanji 中國美術分類全集. Shijiazhuang shi: Hebei meishu chubanshe.

Zhongguo meishu quanji: Diaosu bian 10

1988 *Zhongguo meishu quanji: Diaosu bian, 10: Yungang shiku diaoke* 中國美術全集：雕塑編十，雲岡石窟雕刻 (Complete collection of Chinese arts: Sculpture series, vol. 10, Sculpture of the Yüngang Cave Temple). Beijing: Wenwu chubanshe.

Zhongguo meishu quanji: Huihua bian 1

1986 *Zhongguo meishu quanji: Huihua bian 1, Yuanshishehui zhi Nanbeichao huihua* 中國美術全集：繪畫編一，原始社會至南北朝繪畫(Complete collection of Chinese arts: Painting series, vol. 1, Neolithic to the Northern and Southern Dynasties painting). Edited by Zhang Anzhi and Xue Yongnian. Beijing: Renmin meishu chubanshe.

Zhongguo meishu quanji: Huihua bian 2

1984 *Zhongguo meishu quanji: Huihua bian 2, Sui, Tang, Wudai huihua* 中國美術全集：繪畫編二，隋、唐、五代繪畫 (Complete collection of Chinese arts: Painting series, vol. 6, Sui, Tang, and Five Dynasties painting). Edited by Jin Weinuo et al. Beijing: Renmin meishu chubanshe.

Zhongguo meishu quanji: Huihua bian 12, Mushi bihua

1989 *Zhongguo meishu quanji: Huihua bian, 12, Mushi bihua* 中國美術全集：繪畫編十二，墓室壁畫(Complete collection of Chinese arts: Painting series, vol. 6, Tomb murals). Edited by Su Bai et al. Beijing: Renmin meishu chubanshe, 1989.

Zhongguo meishu quanji: Shufa zhuanke bian

1986–89*Zhongguo meishu quanji: Shufa zhuanke bian* 中國美術全集：書法篆刻編(Complete collection of Chinese arts: Calligraphy and seal carving series). 7 vols. Beijing: Renmin meishu chubanshe.

Zhongguo shehui kexueyuan kaogu yanjiusuo 中國社會科學院考古研究所 (Institute of Archaeology, Chinese Academy of Social Sciences [CASS])

1980 *Tang Chang'an cheng jiao Sui Tang mu* 唐長安城郊隋唐墓 (Excavation of the Sui and Tang tombs at Xi'an). Beijing: Wenwu chubanshe.

1984 *Xin Zhongguo de kaogu faxian he yanjiu* 新中國的考古發現和研究 (Archaeological excavation and researches in New China). Beijing: Wenwu chubanshe.

1985 "河南偃師杏圓村的兩座魏晉墓" (Two tombs of the Wei-Jin period from Xiangyuan Village, Yanshi, Henan). *Kaogu*, no. 8: 721–35.

1996 *Bei Wei Luoyang Yongning si: 1979–1994 nian kaogu fajue baogao* 北魏洛陽永寧寺1979至1994年考古發掘報告 (Yongning Temple in Northern Wei Luoyang, excavations in 1979–1994). Beijing: Zhongguo da baike quanshu chubanshe.

Zhongguo shehui kexueyuan kaogu yanjiusuo Anyang gongzuodui 中國社會科學院考古研究所安陽工作隊 (Anyang Team, Institute of Archaeology, Chinese Academy of Social Sciences [CASS])

1981 "安陽隋墓發掘報告" (Excavations of the Sui Tombs at Anyang). *Kaogu xuebao*, no. 3: 369–406.

1983 "安陽孝民屯晉墓發掘報告" (Bulletin on the excavation of some Jin tombs at Xiaomintun, Anyang). *Kaogu*, no. 6: 501–11.

Zhongguo shehui kexueyuan kaogu yanjiusuo, Hebei sheng wenwu guanlichu 中國社會科學院；河北省文物管理處 (Institute of Archaeology, CASS, Hebei Cultural Properties Management Office)

1980 *Mancheng Han mu fajue baogao* 滿城漢墓發掘報告 (Report on the excavation of Han tombs at Mancheng). Beijing: Wenwu chubanshe.

Zhongguo shehui kexueyuan kaogu yanjiusuo Luoyang gongzuodui 中國社會科學院考古研究所洛陽工作隊 (Luoyang Team, Institute of Archaeology, CASS)

1991 "北魏洛陽城內出土的瓷器與釉器" (The porcelain and glazed earthenware excavated from the Luoyang city of the Northern Wei dynasty). *Kaogu*, no. 12: 1090–95.

Zhongguo shehui kexueyuan kaogu yanjiusuo 中國社會科學院考古研究所, Yecheng kaogu gongzuidui 鄴城考古工作隊, Hebei wenwu yanjiusuo 河北文物研究所 (Yecheng Archaeological Team, Hebei Institute of Cultural Properties Research, Institute of Archaeology, CASS),

1990 "河北磁縣灣漳北朝墓" (Excavation of a Northern dynasties tomb in Wanzhang, Cixian, Hebei). *Kaogu*, no. 7: 601–7.

Zhongguo shiku: Gongxian shikusi 中國石窟

1989 See Henan sheng wenwu yanjiusuo 1989.

Zhongguo shufa jianshang da cidian

1989 *Zhongguo shufa jianshang da cidian* 中國書法鑒賞大辭典 (Dictionary for the authentication and appreciation of Chinese calligraphy). 2 vols. Beijing: Dadi chubanshe.

Zhongguo wenwu jinghua

1997 *Zhongguo wenwu jinghua* 中國文物精華 (Gems of China's cultural relics). "Zhongguo wewu jinghua" bian ji wei yuan hui 中國文物精華編輯委員會 (Editorial committee of the Zhogguo wewu jinghua), eds. Beijing: Wenwu chubanshe.

Zhongguo Xinjiang Weiwuer zizhiqu bowuguan 中國新疆維吾爾自治區博物館 and Riben Nailiang sichou zhi lu xue yanjiu zhongxin 日本奈良絲綢之路學研究中心

2000 *See* Shiruka rodo-gaku kenkyu senta 2000.

Zhou Jingbao 周菁葆

1988 "新疆石窟壁畫中的樂器考辯（上，下）" (A research study of musical instruments in the grotto mural paintings in Xinjiang [part 1]). *Xinjiang wenwu*, no. 1: 68–75. Part 2 published in *Wenwu*, no. 4: 92–105.

1992 "西域摩尼教文明" (The civilization of Manichaeism in western regions). *Xinjiang wenwu*, no. 1: 69–88.

Zhou Ming 周明

1994 "陝西關中唐十八陵靈寢建築型制初探" (A preliminary study of architectural designs in eighteen imperial Tang tombs in Xi'an). *Wenbo*, no. 1: 64–67.

Zhou Ti 周倜, ed.

1998 "敦煌石室藏經選" (A selection of Buddhist scriptures from Dunhuang cave). In *Zhongguo moji jingdian daquan* 中國墨跡經典大全 (A complete compendium of Chinese calligraphy), vol. 1: 376–77. Beijing: Jinghua chubanshe.

Zhou Weizhou 周偉州

1980 "從鄭仁泰出土的樂舞俑談唐代音樂和禮儀制度" (Tang music and ritual systems reflected in music and dancing figurines from the tombs of Zheng Rentai). *Wenwu*, no. 7: 42–46.

Zhou Xuejun 周學軍 and Song Weimin 宋偉民

1998 "黃色龍紋綺" (Yellow qi silk with a dragon design). In *Xinjiang wenwu zizhiqu silu kaogu zhenpin* 新疆維吾自治區絲路考古珍品: (Archaeological treasures of the Silk Road from the Uygur Autonomous Region of Xinjiang): 140, 268–69. Shanghai: Shanghai yiwen chubanshe.

Zhou Yiliang 周一良

1985 *Wei Jin Nanbei chao shi zha ji* 魏晉南北朝史札記 (Essays on the Wei, Jin, and Northern and Southern Dynasties). Beijing: Zhonghua shuju.

1991 *Wei Jin Nanbei chao shi lunji xubian* 魏晉南北朝史論集續編 (Supplement to the Essays on the Wei, Jin, Northern and Southern Dynasties). Beijing: Beijing daxue chubanshe.

1997 "南朝境內各種人及政府對待之政策" (Governmental policies on the various peoples within the borders of the Southern Dynasty). In *Wei Jin nanbei chao shi lunji* 魏晉南北朝史論集 (Essays on the Wei, Jin, Northern and Southern Dynasties): 33–101. Beijing: Beijing daxue chubanshe. Originally published in *Lishi yuyan yanjiusuo jikan* 歷史語言研究所集刊 7, no. 4 (1939).

Zhu Min 竺敏

1972 "吐魯番新發現的古代絲綢" (Recent discoveries of ancient silks in Turfan). *Wenwu*, no. 2: 28–31.

Zhu Xinyu 朱新予

1992 *Zhongguo sichou shi (tonglun)* 中國絲綢史（通論） (The Chinese silk industry). Beijing: Fangzhi gongye chubanshe.

Zhu Yanshi 朱岩石

1994 "'千秋萬歲' 圖像源流淺識" (A preliminary study of the origins of images of *Qianqiu Wansui*). In *Han-Tang yu bianjiang kaogu yanjiu* 《漢唐與邊疆考古研究》 (Archaeological research on the Han–Tang period and border areas of ancient China), edited by Zhongguo shehui Kexueyuan kaogu yanjiusuo, vol. 1: 131–35. Beijing: Kexue chubanshe.

Zhu Yingrong 朱英榮

1985 "密教與克孜爾千佛洞密教畫" (Esotericism and esoteric paintings in Kizil Caves). *Xinjiang wenwu*, no. 1: 46–51.

Zhuang Tianming 莊天明 and Wu Weishan 吳為山

2003 *Sishui wangling chutu Xi Han mudiao* 泗水王陵出土西漢木雕 (Wood carvings from the excavation of the Western Han imperial tomb of Sishui Wang). Tianjing shi: Tianjin renmin meishu chubanshe.

Zin, Monika

1999 *Guide to the Ajanta Paintings*. Vol. 2, *Devotional and Ornamental Paintings*. New Delhi: Munshiram Manoharlol Publishers.

Zou Houben 鄒厚本, ed.

2000 *Jiangsu kaogu wushi nian* 江蘇考古五十年 (Fifty years of archaeology in Jiangsu). Nanjing: Nanjing chubanshe.

Zürcher, Erik

1959 *The Buddhist Conquest of China: The Spread and Adaptation of Buddhism in Early Medieval China*. 2 vols. Sinica Leidensia, vol. 11. Leiden: E. J. Brill.

1972 *The Buddhist Conquest of China: The Spread and Adaptation of Buddhism in Early Medieval China*. Reprint, with additions and corrections. 2 vols. Sinica Leidensia, vol. 11. Leiden: E. J. Brill.

Zwalf, Wladimir

1996 *A Catalogue of the Gandhāra Sculpture in the British Museum*. 2 vols. London: British Museum Press.

Selected Index

Compiled by Cathy Dorsey

Photograph Credits

Figures and comparative illustrations are reproduced courtesty of the institutions and collections cited in the captions and the sources listed below.

Fig. 1: Hebei sheng bowuguan 1999, pl. 86
Fig. 2: Bunker 2002: 205, fig. 63
Fig. 4: Hu Chui, The Palace Museum, Beijing
Fig. 5: Ibid.
Fig. 6: Bunker 2002, no. 71
Fig. 7: Sarianidi 1985a, fig. 45
Fig. 8: F. C. Maisey, *Sanchi and Its Remains* (London, 1892), pl. 5
Fig. 9: Liaoningsheng wenwu kaogu yanjiusuo 2002, fig. 7
Fig. 10: Sarianidi 1985a, fig. 15
Fig. 11: Kulturstiftung Ruhr Essen, *Korea: Die Alten Königreiche* (Munich, 1999): 163
Fig. 12: *Kaogu* 1985.8, pl. 3
Fig. 13: *Wenwu* 1972.3: 25, fig. 5
Fig. 14: James C. Y. Watt
Fig. 15: Ningxia Guyuan bowuguan 1988
Fig. 16: Oi-Cheong Lee, The Photograph Studio, The Metropolitan Museum of Art
Fig. 17: Chutu wenwu zhanlan gongzuozu 1973: 145
Fig. 18: Ningxia Guyuan bowuguan 1988
Fig. 19: Roderick Whitfield, ed., *Treasures from Korea: Art through 5000 Years* (London, 1984): 94, no. 85
Fig. 20: Guangdong Provincial Museum and the Art Gallery, Chinese University of Hong Kong, *Guangdong chutu Jin zhi Tang wenwu / Archaeological Finds from the Jin to the Tang Periods in Guangdong* (Hong Kong, 1985): 100, no. 37 (20a); 148, fig. 15 (20b)
Fig. 21: *Zhongguo lishi bowuguan: Huaxia wenming shi tujian* (Beijing, 2002): 108, no. 6-6-9
Fig. 22: Oi-Cheong Lee, The Photograph Studio, The Metropolitan Museum of Art
Fig. 23: Yao Qianju and Gu Bing 1981, pl. 10
Fig. 24: Oi-Cheong Lee, The Photograph Studio, The Metropolitan Museum of Art
Fig. 25: *Kaogu xuebao* 1984.1: 128, fig. 7.2
Figs. 26 and 27: Oi-Cheong Lee, The Photograph Studio, The Metropolitan Museum of Art
Fig. 28: *Hebei sheng wenwu yanjiusuo, Hebei Gudai muzang bihua* (Beijing, 2000), pl. 62
Fig. 30: Zhongguo shehui kexueyuan kaogu yanjiusuo 1980, pl. 22.4 (30a), pl. 23.2 (30b)
Fig. 31: *Zhongguo meishu quanji: Diaosu bian 11, Longmen shiku diaoke* (Beijing, 1988): 151
Fig. 32: *Shoseki meihin sōkan*, vol. 89 (1962): 8
Fig. 35: Fajans 1957
Fig. 36: Desroches 2000: 63, pl. 29
Fig. 37: Gunter and Jett 1992: 40
Fig. 38: Dalton 1964, pl. XXXV
Fig. 39: *Indian and Southeast Asian Art*, sale cat. (New York: Christie's, March 27, 2003): 79, lot 78
Fig. 42: Shepherd 1964, fig. 30
Fig. 43: *Kaogu* 1986.3: 243
Fig. 44: Marshak 1999: 102
Fig. 60: Zhao Feng 1999c: 59
Fig. 61: Ma Chengyuan and Yue Feng 1998: 115, pl. 34
Fig. 62: Xinjiang Weiwuer zizhiqu bowuguan 1973, pl. 24
Fig. 63: Zhao Feng 2003, fig. 1
Fig. 64: Pfister and Bellinger 1945, pl. 1, no. 263
Fig. 65: Jacqueline Simcox Ltd.
Fig. 66: Zhao Feng 2002a: 50, no. 15
Fig. 67: Blum 1997: 109, pl. 195
Fig. 68: Zhao Feng 2002a: 59, no. 19-1
Fig. 69: *Xinjiang wenwu* 2000.3-4: 4, fig. 1
Fig. 70: Huang Nengfu 1986: 158, no. 150
Fig. 71: Shiriku rodo-gaku kenkyu senta 2000, pl. 88a, no. 18
Fig. 72: Martiniani-Reber 1986, no. 11
Fig. 73: Chang Yimin 2003: 4
Fig. 74: Zhao Feng 1999c: 143, no. 04.07
Fig. 75: Whitfield 1982, vol. 3, no. 6
Fig. 77: Su Bai 2002, vol. 2, 373
Fig. 78: Tōkyō kokuritsu hakubutsukan 1987, colorpl. 7
Fig. 79: Zhongguo Fojiao diaoke shi lun tuban-pian, vol. 1 (1995): 20
Fig. 80: Gansu sheng wenwu gongzuodui and Binglingsi wenwu baoguansuo 1989, pl. 12
Fig. 81: *Kaogu* 1989.9: 807
Fig. 82: *Yungang shiku wenwu baoguansuo* 1991-94, vol. 2, pl. 184
Fig. 83: *Zhongguo meishu quanji: Diaosu bian 10*, 1988, pl. 47
Fig. 84: *Yungang shiku wenwu baoguansuo* 1991-94, vol. 2, pl. 171
Fig. 85: Ibid., pl. 10
Fig. 86: Ibid., pl. 199
Fig. 87: Ibid., pl. 42
Fig. 88: Tianshui Maijishan shiku yishu yan-jiusuo 1989, pl. 217
Fig. 89: *Wenwu* 1999.8: 72
Fig. 92: *Wenwu* 1998.11: colorpl. 2
Fig. 93: Xinjiang Weiwuer zizhiqu wenwuguan-li weiyuanhui 1989-97, pl. 26
Fig. 94: Ibid., pl. 103
Fig. 95: Longmen wenwu baoguansuo, eds., *Longmen shiku* (Beijing, 1996): 29
Fig. 96: Hu Chui, The Palace Museum, Beijing
Fig. 97: Angela F. Howard
Fig. 98: *Ryūmon sekkutsu*, vol. 1. *Chūgoku sekkutsu* (Tokyo, 1987), fig. 8
Fig. 101: Angela F. Howard
Fig. 104: Ibid.
Fig. 105: Vidya Dehejia, *Indian Art* (London, 1997): 99, pl. 70
Fig. 106: Tokiwa Daijō and Takahi Sekino, *Shina Bukkyō shiseki*, 6 vols. (Tokyo, 1925–38), vol. 5: 104, fig. 5
Fig. 107: *Ryūmon sekkutsu*, vol. 2. *Chūgoku sekkutsu* (Tokyo, 1987): pl. 209

p. 160: *Orientations* 6 (June 2001): 25, fig. 4
p. 184: *Wenwu* 1990.5: 2, fig. 1
p. 196: *Wenwu* 1973.10, fig. 1
p. 207: Yao Qianju and Gu Bing 1981, fig. 206
p. 272: Zhao Feng 2002a: 80, no. 28
p. 289: Xinjiang Weiwuer zizhiqu bowuguan 1975: 82, pl. 121
p. 303: Han Wei and Zhang Jianlin 1998, pls. 83-2, 85-1, 84-1
p. 345: Shaanxi sheng bowuguan et al. 1974, pl. 26
p. 345: Zhao Feng 1999c: 15
p. 347: Zhao Feng 2002a: 93